Revised Second Edition

Masterplots

1,801 Plot Stories and Critical Evaluations
of the World's Finest Literature

Revised Second Edition

Volume 9
Pet – Ric
4979 – 5610

Edited by
FRANK N. MAGILL

Story Editor, Revised Edition
DAYTON KOHLER

Consulting Editor, Revised Second Edition
LAURENCE W. MAZZENO

SALEM PRESS

Pasadena, California   Englewood Cliffs, New Jersey

96- 282

Editor in Chief: Dawn P. Dawson
Consulting Editor: Laurence W. Mazzeno   *Managing Editor:* Christina J. Moose
Project Editors: Eric Howard   *Research Supervisor:* Jeffry Jensen
Juliane Brand   *Research:* Irene McDermott
Acquisitions Editor: Mark Rehn   *Proofreading Supervisor:* Yasmine A. Cordoba
Production Editor: Cynthia Breslin Beres   *Layout:* William Zimmerman

Library of Congress Cataloging-in-Publication Data
Masterplots / edited by Frank N. Magill; consulting editor, Laurence W. Mazzeno. — Rev. 2nd ed.
    p.   cm.
Expanded and updated version of the 1976 rev. ed.
Includes bibliographical references and indexes.
1. Literature—Stories, plots, etc. 2. Literature—History and criticism. I. Magill, Frank Northen, 1907-   . II. Mazzeno, Laurence W.
PN44.M33   1996
809—dc20   96-23382
ISBN 0-89356-084-7 (set)   CIP
ISBN 0-89356-095-2 (volume 11)

Revised Second Edition
First Printing

LIST OF TITLES IN VOLUME 9

PETER IBBETSON

Type of work: Novel
Author: George du Maurier (Louis Palmella Busson, 1834-1896)
Type of plot: Historical
Time of plot: Mid-nineteenth century
Locale: France and England
First published: 1891

Principal characters:
PETER IBBETSON
COLONEL IBBETSON, his guardian
MIMSY SERASKIER, his dearest friend and later the duchess of Towers
MR. LINTOT, his employer
MRS. DEANE, a widow

The Story:

Peter Pasquier moved from England to Paris, where he was called Pierre, when he was five years old. His father was a dreamy-eyed inventor, his mother a soft-spoken woman devoted to her family. During his childhood, Peter had many friends, but the dearest were Mimsy Seraskier and her beautiful mother, who lived nearby. Mimsy was a delicate, shy child. She and Peter were inseparable friends, making up their own code language so that no one could intrude on their secret talks.

When Peter was twelve years old, his father was killed in an explosion, and less than one week later his mother died giving birth to a stillborn child. His mother's cousin, Colonel Ibbetson, came from England to take Peter home with him. Peter wept when he was forced to leave his friends, and Mimsy was so ill from her grief that she could not even tell him good-bye. Colonel Ibbetson gave Peter his name, and he became Peter Ibbetson. The colonel sent him to school, where he spent six years. Events at the school touched him very little, and he spent most of his time dreaming of his old life in Paris.

When he left school, Peter spent some time with Colonel Ibbetson. The colonel's only request was that Peter become a gentleman, but Peter began to doubt that the colonel himself fitted the description, for he had a very poor reputation among his acquaintances. His most recent victim was Mrs. Deane, a woman he had ruined with malicious lies. The colonel seemed to derive great pleasure from telling scandalous tales about everyone he knew, and Peter grew to hate him for this habit. After a time, he ran away to London and joined the cavalry for a year. Following his term in the army, he was apprenticed to Mr. Lintot, an architect whom he had met through Colonel Ibbetson. He took rooms in Pentonville and began a new chapter in his life there.

He worked industriously for Mr. Lintot and achieved some success, but his outer life was lonely and dull. The only real joy he found was in music, which moved him deeply. He saved carefully in order to attend a concert occasionally. His nightly dreams were still of his childhood in Paris and of Mimsy, but these dreams were becoming blurred.

Peter viewed the belief in a creator and life after death with skepticism, believing instead that humans would have to work back to the very beginning of time before they could understand anything about a deity. He believed it was possible to go back, if only he knew the way. His ideas on sin were unorthodox; to Peter, the only real sin was cruelty to the mind or body of any living thing. During this period of his life, his only acquaintances were the friends of Mr. and Mrs. Lintot, for Peter was a shy young man, too much concerned with his speculations and dreams for social gaiety. At one party, however, he saw a great lady who was to be his guiding star for the rest of his life. He was told she was the duchess of Towers, and although he was not introduced to her, he noticed her look at him in a strange manner, almost as if she found his face to be familiar.

Sometime after his first sight of the duchess of Towers, Peter revisited Paris, where he found his old home and those of his friends replaced with modern bungalows. The only news he had of his old friends was that Madame Seraskier had died and that Mimsy and her father had left Paris many years ago. He returned to his hotel that night, emotionally exhausted from the disappointments of the day.

That night, his real and true inner life began, for he learned how to dream true. When he fell asleep, the events of the day passed before him in distorted fashion. He found himself surrounded by demon dwarfs. As he tried to escape them, he looked up and saw the duchess of Towers standing before him. She took his hand and told him he was not dreaming true, and then he was transported back to the happy days of his childhood and saw himself as he was then. At the same time, he retained his adult identity. He was two people at the same time, his adult self looking at his child self. The duchess told him he could always transport himself into any scene he had experienced if he would only dream true. To do this, he must lie on his back with his arms over his head, and as he went to sleep, he must think ceaselessly of the place he wanted to be in his dreams. He must, however, never forget in his dream who and where he was when awake; in this way, his dream would be tied to reality. She had learned the trick from her father and could revisit any place she chose. When he awoke, he knew that at last one of his greatest desires had come true; he had looked into the mind of the duchess. Nevertheless, the matter puzzled him, for he had always thought such a fusion was possible only between two people who knew and loved each other. The duchess was a stranger to him.

Peter returned to Pentonville and outwardly resumed his normal life. His inner self, however, became his real life, and he mastered the art of dreaming true and reliving any experience he wished. He visited with his mother and Mimsy frequently in his dreams, and his life was no longer bleak and lonely. One day, he again met the duchess of Towers in his outer life. Then he discovered why she had been in his true dream. She was Mimsy, grown now and married to a famous duke. She had had the same dream as he when she had rescued him from the dwarfs, and she too had been unable to understand why a stranger had invaded her dreams.

Although he did not meet again the grown Mimsy in his dreams, Peter saw the child Mimsy almost every night. His life went along without interruption until he met Mrs. Gregory, formerly Mrs. Deane, whom Colonel Ibbetson had tried to ruin with slander. She told him that Colonel Ibbetson had told her and many others that he was Peter's real father. The recorded marriage and birthdates proved he was lying; the story was another product of the colonel's cruel mind. Peter was so enraged that he went to the colonel's house to force an apology. The two men fought; in his fury, Peter struck blindly at Colonel Ibbetson and killed him.

Peter was tried and sentenced to be hanged for the murder of his uncle. While he was in prison, the grown Mimsy came into his dream again and told him his sentence had been changed to life imprisonment because of the circumstances under which the murder had been committed. She promised Peter that she would continue to come to him in his dreams and thus they would spend the rest of their lives together.

In his prison cell, Peter was the happiest man in England. Attendants were kind to him during the day, and he was with Mimsy at night. At last, they learned that they were distant cousins, and then they discovered that they could project themselves into the past through the character of any of their direct ancestors. Either of them, not both at once, could become any ancestor he or she chose, and thus they relived scenes in history that had occurred hundreds of years before. They went back to the days when monsters roamed the earth and might have gone back to the beginning of time, but Mimsy died.

She came back to Peter seven times after she had died, urging him to continue his search for the beginning of time. She could come to him now only because he was the other half of her soul. She asked him to write down his method and to urge others to follow him, and she gave him some books in their secret code, telling him of things she had learned. Before he could begin to write the secrets she told him, he died in his cell. His cousin, Madge Plunket, who later arranged for the publication of the manuscript, felt that she would remember until her own death the look of happiness and peace upon his face.

Critical Evaluation:

After a long and successful career as an artist and illustrator, George du Maurier, at the age of fifty-five and with the urging of his friend Henry James, began to write his first novel, *Peter Ibbetson*. In this work, he wrote about subjects and themes that obsessed him—his childhood in Passy, France; the fantasies of youth; the power of dreams; and the transcendent nature of romantic love. The work is structured in two parts. In part 1, du Maurier gives a loving autobiographical account of his childhood in Passy, which he tells with precise detail. He describes that time as one of remote innocence. He then abandons the illusion of reality established there and in part 2 develops the theme of psychic phenomenon, or "dreaming true," as he calls it.

The duality of the plot is consistent with other dualities in the novel. Peter embodies the two cultures of his parents. His emotional life is centered in Passy. As he matures, however, he exhibits the traits of a cultivated Englishman, admires the British aristocracy, enters into manly sports such as boxing and swimming, adopts a snobbish persona, and proclaims a conventional morality.

The duality extends to Peter's name as well. Born Pierre Pasquier de la Mariere, he is reborn, so to speak, in England as Master Peter Ibbetson. Colonel Ibbetson, who gives Peter his new name, becomes his surrogate father. Although dead, Peter's actual father, "le beau Pasqsuier," continues to live in Peter's dreamworld. Colonel Ibbetson, on the other hand, plays no part in Peter's inner life but determines his external existence. The colonel's villainous role leads to Peter's imprisonment, where all of his dreaming begins. The splitting of the father figure into two distinct roles—one hated, the other admired—is an attractive fantasy. The ambiguous attitude that a child may have toward his father is dealt with by a screening process that simplifies the ambiguity by dividing the parent into two personalities, one threatening and the other loving.

The theme of duality also involves the central women of the novel, Madame Seraskier, Madame Pasquier, and the duchess of Towers. Both the descriptions and illustrations (done by du Maurier himself) reveal them to be nearly identical in beauty and stature. Madame Seraskier is presented with an idealized beauty that is associated with Peter's mother. Like his mother, she possesses warmth, kindness, simplicity, grace, naturalness, courtesy, sympathy, and joy. It is not surprising, therefore, that they both die about the same time. What appears to be involved here is the Oedipal wish to possess the mother without guilt by splitting he mother figure into the virginal and the sexual object. With the deaths of the idealized mother and the "divine" Madame Seraskier, Peter is free to fall in love with the duchess of Towers. The duchess is thus a composite figure: She is an allowable sexual object because she is sufficiently distanced from the mother, and yet her character includes all of the desirable traits of Peter's mother.

Finally, the most important duality is that of Peter's mind itself, as he conducts his life for about thirty years on two levels, that of everyday consciousness and that of dreams. As the novel moves toward its conclusion, du Maurier goes beyond the theme of reality versus dreaming to imply that dreaming may actually be the most compelling reality. The duality is more an aesthetic than a moral one. Associated with Peter's dreams are childhood, unspoiled nature, songs, beautiful people, works of art and literature, freedom, and timelessness. In his waking life, on the other hand, there are ugly people (Colonel Ibbetson, Pentonville schoolmates, and prison inmates), ugly scenes (in Pentonville), spoiled nature (the stump of his childhood apple tree and the general destruction wrought by "progress" on Passy), and imprisonment.

There is a progression of styles in *Peter Ibbetson* that reinforces that theme of lost innocence and joy. In the last chapter of the novel the spirit of the duchess of Towers returns to Peter to inform him what life is like beyond death. No matter how intensely or for how long she proclaims the joys of the afterlife (an amazing twenty pages), her style betrays her and her language reflects the loss of the childhood life. As the novel moves Peter further and further from his childhood, the language and tone reflect his loss. It is starkly philosophical in the Pentonville section, fragmented and anxious in the prison scenes, and lyrical but abstract and hollow toward his death. The powerful imagery, the charming simplicity, and the quickened joyful tone of the early chapters stand for the reader and for the hero as a potent memory of a lost paradise.

The most notable feature of *Peter Ibbetson* that marks it as romantic fiction is that it is filled with the author's own personality made larger than life. His personal dreams and conflicts are visible on every page. Yet although it is an intensely personal novel, it embodies a universal theme. In the words of Deems Taylor, who turned the novel into an opera in 1931, du Maurier's tale is "the Freudian wish expressed in terms of romance, our rebellious human hope of a world more enjoyable than the one we live in, our flight into dreams, wherein we can find sanctuary from a waking life that is, on the whole, a disappointment."

Du Maurier had the unusual advantage of being able to illustrate his own novels. *Peter Ibbetson* includes eighty-four drawings with depictions of all the major characters, the dreamy scenes of Passy, and the dark and threatening world of Pentonville and, later, of prison. The female characters all bear a striking resemblance to one another in their tall, elegant, genteel figures. The theme of lost innocence and youth is visually reinforced in the last few illustrations. Peter is drawn as a gaunt, wrinkled figure in a shabby, wrinkled suit, but the duchess of Towers retains her elegance, though her hair has become white.

"Critical Evaluation" by Richard Kelly

Bibliography:
James, Henry. "George du Maurier." *Harper's Weekly Magazine* 38 (April 14, 1894): 341-342. A short but perceptive discussion of *Peter Ibbetson* and *Trilby*. As a personal friend of du Maurier and as a great novelist himself, James's commentary on du Maurier's fiction is highly instructive.
Kelly, Richard Michael. *The Art of George du Maurier.* Hants, England: Scolar Press, 1995. Examines the relationship between du Maurier's art and his fiction.
_____. *George du Maurier.* Boston, Twayne, 1983. A comprehensive discussion and analysis of du Maurier's life, art, and novels. Contains a lengthy analysis of *Peter Ibbetson* that explores the psychodynamics of the work.

Ormond, Leonee. *George du Maurier*. Pittsburgh, Pa.: University of Pittsburgh Press, 1969. The definitive biography of du Maurier, profusely illustrated. Ormond relates many elements of du Maurier's life directly to the subjects and themes of *Peter Ibbetson*.

Stevenson, Lionel. "George du Maurier and the Romantic Novel." In *Essays by Divers Hands*, edited by N. Wallis Wallis. London: Oxford University Press, 1960. Argues persuasively that du Maurier's three novels are "masterpieces of romantic fiction."

Wood, T. Martin. *George du Maurier, the Satirist of the Victorians: A Review of His Art and Personality*. London: Chatto & Windus, 1913. Contains an appreciative commentary on *Peter Ibbetson*, concluding, "It is by this book I like to think du Maurier will be remembered as a writer."

PETER PAN
Or, The Boy Who Wouldn't Grow Up

Type of work: Drama
Author: Sir James M. Barrie (1860-1937)
Type of plot: Fairy tale
Time of plot: Late nineteenth century
Locale: London and Never Land
First performed: 1904; first published, 1928; first published as novel, *Peter and Wendy,* 1911

>   *Principal characters:*
>   PETER PAN, the boy who would not grow up
>   WENDY, his friend
>   TINKER BELL, Peter's fairy
>   CAPTAIN JAMES HOOK, a pirate captain
>   NURSE NANA, a dog

The Story:

In the nursery of the Darling home, a dog was the Nana. Perhaps that was one reason there was so much joy there. Nana bathed the three children and gave them their suppers and in all ways watched over them. One night Mrs. Darling, on Nana's night off, sat with the children as they slept. Drowsing, she was awakened by a slight draft from the window, and looking around she saw a strange boy in the room. As she screamed, Nana returned home and made a lunge for the intruder, but the boy leaped out of the window, leaving only his shadow behind. He had been accompanied also by a ball of light, but it too escaped. Mrs. Darling rolled up the shadow and put it in a drawer. She thought that the boy would come back for it one night soon and thus could be caught.

Mr. Darling considered the affair a little silly, his thoughts being more concerned with getting a different nurse for the children. Believing that the dog, Nana, was getting too much authority in the house, Mr. Darling dragged her out of the house and locked her up.

When the Darlings went out that night, they left only a maid to look in on the children occasionally. After the lights were out and the children asleep, the intruder returned. The boy was Peter Pan. With him was the fairy, Tinker Bell, the ball of light. Peter found his shadow after searching in all the drawers, but in his excitement he shut Tinker Bell in one of the dressers. Peter could not get his shadow to stick to him again, and the noise he made in trying awakened Wendy, the daughter of the household. Peter told Wendy that he had run away the day he was born because he heard his parents talking about all the things he would do when he was a man, and he went to live with the fairies so that he would never have to grow up. Suddenly he remembered Tinker Bell, whom he looked for until he found her in the dresser. Tinker Bell, a ball of light no bigger than a fist, was so small that Wendy could hardly see her. She was not a very polite fairy; she called Wendy horrible names.

Peter told Wendy, the only girl of the three children and instantly his favorite, that he and Tinker Bell lived in Never Land with the lost boys, children who fell out of their perambulators and were never found again. He had come to Wendy's house to listen to her mother tell stories to the others. Peter, begging Wendy and her brothers to go back to Never Land with him, promised to teach them to fly. The idea was too much for the children to resist. After a little practice they all flew out the window, barely escaping the Darlings and Nana, who had broken her chain to warn them of the danger to the children.

In Never Land the lost boys were guarded against the mean pirates, led by Captain Hook, by the Indians and their chief and princess. It was Hook's greatest desire to capture Peter Pan, for Peter had torn Hook's arm off and fed it to a crocodile. The crocodile had so liked the taste of the arm that he followed Hook everywhere, waiting for the rest of him. The crocodile had, unhappily, also swallowed a clock, and its ticking warned Hook of his approach.

To this queer land Wendy and her brothers flew with Peter Pan. The lost boys, seeing Wendy first, thought her a giant bird and shot her with a bow and arrow. Jealous Tinker Bell had suggested the deed. Peter arrived and saw that Wendy was only stunned, and after banishing Tinker Bell for a week, he told the others that he had brought Wendy to them. They promptly built her a house and asked her to be their mother. Wendy thought so many children a great responsibility, but she quickly assumed her duties by telling them stories and putting them to bed.

Jealous, the pirates planned to steal Wendy and make her their mother; the other children they would force to walk the plank. Peter overheard their plan and saved the children and Wendy. He himself escaped by sailing out to sea in a bird's nest.

Wendy and her brothers, beginning to worry about their parents, thought that they should return home. The lost boys, delighted at the thought of a real grown-up mother, eagerly accepted Wendy's invitation to come live with her and her brothers and parents. Peter refused to go, because he wanted always to be a little boy and have fun. He let the others go, however, and sent Tinker Bell to show them the way. The Pirates had learned of the proposed journey, and as the children ascended from Never Land, Hook and his men seized them and bound them fast, all but Peter. When Peter found that Hook had all his friends, he vowed to get revenge on the pirate, once and for all.

On the pirate ship the children prepared to walk the plank. They were all taken on the deck and paraded before Wendy, who was tied to the mast. Unknown to the pirates, however, Peter was also on board, and by tricks and false voices he led first one pirate and then another to his death. These strange happenings were too much for Hook. When he knocked the seat from under Peter and then saw the boy calmly sitting on air, the pirate threw himself overboard, into the waiting jaws of the patient crocodile.

Meanwhile, in the nursery of the Darling home, Mrs. Darling and Nana waited hopelessly for the children. They had left the window open so that their loved ones might get back easily should they ever return. Peter and Tinker Bell flew ahead of the other children and closed the window so that Wendy and the others would think they were not wanted. Peter, however, did not know how to get out of a door, and thus he was forced to fly out the window again, leaving it open behind him. Wendy and her brothers flew in and slipped into their beds. Mrs. Darling and Nana were overcome with joy when they found their darlings safe again.

The lost boys, adopted by Wendy's family, had great fun romping with her father. Peter returned and tried to get Wendy to fly away with him, but she refused to leave her parents again. She did go once each year to clean his house for him, but each time she saw him a little less clearly. Once or twice she tried to get him to see her as something more than a mother, but Peter did not know what she meant. Then came the day when Wendy could no longer fly without a broomstick to help her. Peter, watching her, sadly wished he could understand all she said. He picked up his pipes and played softly, perhaps too softly to awaken humans in a grown-up world.

Critical Evaluation:

Loved by adults as much as by children, *Peter Pan* portrays the joys of perpetual childhood. Even in a realistic age few can resist the mischievous Peter and his followers, for in him adults can live again those carefree days filled with dreams and play. The special magic of James Barrie was his ability to make dreams real, and for that reason his charming, whimsical play marks the high point of pure fantasy in the modern theater. The play has had a successful stage history, with many famous names listed in its cast.

Barrie insisted that he did not recall having written *Peter Pan*, his most famous work and probably the greatest of all children's plays. In fact, the final stage version grew over a number of years in a haphazard fashion. It began as a six-chapter segment in an adult novel, *The White Bird* (1902), then became, in turn, a three-act stage play (1904), a novel based on the earlier prose version (1906), a longer novel, *Peter and Wendy* (1911), taken from the play with an extra chapter "When Wendy Grew Up," and finally emerged as the well-known drama in 1928. In spite of all these versions and revisions, Barrie may have been right in saying that he was not the primary author of *Peter Pan*. As he explains in his dedication, the real genesis of *Peter Pan* was a series of stories he made up and told to five young brothers, the sons of close friends, in the late 1890's and the summer of 1901: "I made Peter by rubbing the five of you violently together, as savages with two sticks produce a fire. That is all he is, the spark I got from you."

One of the primary reasons for the popularity of *Peter Pan* has been that Barrie, one of the shrewdest judges of public taste ever to write, takes the two most basic elements of popular children's literature—the fairy tale and the adventure tale—and synthesizes them into a single work. Utilizing an extraordinary theatrical sense, he compresses an enormous amount of vivid detail into the temporal and spatial limitations of the stage. Nearly as much happens in the play as in *Peter and Wendy*, a full-length novel. Almost every fantasy adventure imaginable is presented in *Peter Pan*—encounters with Indians and pirates, wild beasts (wolves, a crocodile)—and each scene climaxes with a cliff-hanger. Wendy is accidentally shot by an arrow, Peter is abandoned on a rock surrounded by rising water, the children are captured by pirates, Tinker Bell is poisoned and near death (to be rescued by the audience), and Captain Hook threatens the boys with walking the plank.

At the same time, the play offers the safety of an ideal children's dream. The beasts look ferocious but are easily tamed (the boys foiled the wild animals by looking between their legs at them). Benevolent magic pervades the atmosphere and is always available when needed (to save Wendy from the arrow, Peter from the rock), and for all of his demoniac appearance, Captain Hook is no match for Peter who, in fact, toys with the pirate leader in their final clash.

In addition to providing excitement on the level of plot, *Peter Pan* also evokes basic emotional and psychological responses. The primary struggle in the play is over possession of Wendy—as a mother. Thus, the play explores the ambivalent attitudes of children toward parents, and, by extension, the human conflict between a desire for freedom versus the need to be part of a family and a society. The authoritarian father figure, Captain Hook, is villainous (traditionally the same actor plays Hook and Mr. Darling), but the "mother," Wendy, is idealized. While the children are having adventures, they play at being siblings in a family, and, when offered adoption into a real one, they desert Never Land to join the Darling household.

Only Peter refuses to grow up, and even his rejection is based on disappointment at having been abandoned. (Once, in his absence from home, his mother had forgotten about him, and when he returned, there was another boy sleeping in his bed.) So only Peter remains in Never Land. At the end of the play, he has forgotten most of the adventures he had had with Wendy and the others. For Peter there can be neither past nor future, only the joyous immediate moment. It is a state of being that all, children and adults alike, can enjoy for a few delightful hours in the theater—before returning to the real world where children grow up and parents grow older.

Bibliography:

Birkin, Andrew. *J. M. Barrie and the Lost Boys: The Love Story That Gave Birth to Peter Pan.* New York: Clarkson N. Potter, 1979. Collective biography of Barrie and the Davies family, told primarily through documentary evidence. Explores in considerable detail the significance of Barrie's love for the boys and their mother for the writing of *Peter Pan.*

Frey, Charles H., and John W. Griffith. *The Literary Heritage of Childhood.* Westport, Conn.: Greenwood Press, 1987. Treats play as a fantasy that, against tradition, emphasizes its own distance from reality. Focuses on Never Land as a psychic map, simultaneously revealing unconscious desires (specifically, mother fixation) and attempting to deny those desires by shutting them out of the fantasy world.

Geduld, Harry M. *Sir James Barrie.* Boston: Twayne, 1971. Clear account of the development of the Peter Pan story from Peter's first appearance. Freudian interpretation of womb imagery and of Mr. Darling and Wendy.

Hanson, Bruce K. *The Peter Pan Chronicles: The Nearly One Hundred Year History of "The Boy Who Wouldn't Grow Up."* Secacaus, N.J.: Carol Publishing Group, 1993. Performance history of the play, with detailed discussions of the most famous productions. Organized around the performer playing Peter in various productions.

Rose, Jacqueline. *The Case of Peter Pan: Or, The Impossibility of Children's Fiction.* Philadelphia: University of Pennsylvania Press, 1993. Heavily theoretical analysis questions how the play constructs a child audience for the benefit of adult illusions about childhood.

PHAEDRA

Type of work: Drama
Author: Jean Baptiste Racine (1639-1699)
Type of plot: Tragedy
Time of plot: Antiquity
Locale: Troezen, in ancient Greece
First performed: Phèdre, 1677 (English translation, 1701)

Principal characters:
THÉSÉE, king of Athens
PHÈDRE, his wife
HIPPOLYTE, Thésée's son
ARICIE, an Athenian princess
OENONE, Phèdre's nurse

The Story:

After the death of his Amazon queen, Thésée, slayer of the Minotaur, married Phèdre, the young daughter of the king of Crete. Phèdre, seeing in her stepson, Hippolyte, all the bravery and virtue of his heroic father, but in more youthful guise, fell in love with him. In an attempt to conceal her passion for the son of Thésée, she treated him in an aloof and spiteful manner until at last Hippolyte decided to leave Troezen and go in search of his father who was absent from the kingdom. To his tutor, Théramène, he confided his desire to avoid both his stepmother and Aricie, an Athenian princess who was the daughter of a family which had opposed Thésée. Phèdre confessed to Oenone, her nurse, her guilty passion for Hippolyte, saying that she merely pretended unkindness to him in order to hide her real feelings.

Word came to Troezen that Thésée was dead. Oenone talked to Phèdre in an attempt to convince the queen that her own son, not Hippolyte, should be chosen as the new king of Athens. Aricie hoped that she would be chosen to rule. Hippolyte, a fair-minded young man, told Aricie that he would support her for the rule of Athens. He felt that Phèdre's son should inherit Crete and that he himself should remain master of Troezen. He also admitted his love for Aricie, but said that he feared the gods would never allow it to be brought to completion. When he tried to explain his intentions to his stepmother, she in turn dropped her pretense of hatred and distrust and ended by betraying her love for Hippolyte. Shocked, he repulsed her, and she threatened to take her own life.

The people of Athens, however, chose Phèdre's son to rule over them, to the disappointment of Aricie. There were also rumors that Thésée still lived. Hippolyte gave orders that a search be made for his father. Phèdre, embarrassed by all she had told Hippolyte, brooded over the injury she now felt, and wished that she had never revealed her love. Phèdre was proud, and now her pride was hurt beyond recovery. Unable to overcome her passion, however, she decided to offer the kingdom to Hippolyte so that she might keep him near her. Then news came that Thésée was returning to his home. Oenone warned Phèdre that now she must hide her true feeling for Hippolyte. She even suggested to the queen that Thésée be made to believe that Hippolyte had tempted Phèdre to adultery.

When Thésée returned, Phèdre greeted him with reluctance, saying that she was no longer fit to be his wife. Hippolyte made the situation no better by requesting permission to leave Troezen at once. Thésée was greatly chagrined at his homecoming. When scheming Oenone told the king that Hippolyte had attempted to dishonor his stepmother, Thésée flew into a terrific rage. Hippolyte, knowing nothing of the plot, was at first astonished by his father's anger and threats. When accused, he denied the charges, but Thésée refused to listen to him and banished his son from the kingdom forever. When Hippolyte claimed he was really in love with Aricie, Thésée, more incensed than ever, invoked the vengeance of Neptune upon his son.

Aricie tried to convince Hippolyte that he must prove his innocence, but Hippolyte refused because he knew that the revelation of Phèdre's passion would be too painful for his father to bear. The two agreed to escape together. Before Aricie could leave the palace, however, Thésée questioned her. Becoming suspicious, he sent for Oenone to demand the truth. Fearing that her plot had been uncovered, Oenone committed suicide.

Meanwhile, as Hippolyte drove his chariot near the seashore, Neptune sent a horrible monster, part bull and part dragon, which destroyed the son of Thésée. When news of his death reached the palace, Phèdre confessed her guilt and drank poison. Thésée, glad to see his guilty queen die, wished that the memory of her life might perish with her. Sorrowfully, he sought the grief-stricken Aricie to comfort her.

Critical Evaluation:

The issue of free will, predestination, and grace that interested Jean Baptiste Racine in the seventeenth century was a restatement, in theological terms, of a problem of universal concern. To what extent is one free to create one's own existence and to be responsible for one's actions? Are the terms of human existence within the arena of human control or are they established by some external force? Can human suffering be justified as the result of one's actions or is it the imposition of a capricious deity?

The specific manner in which these questions are answered depends upon one's view of human nature and human potential. When one chooses between predestination and free will, one is either asserting or denying a belief in one's ability to make wise and ethically sound decisions. Emphasis on the dignity of humanity and on the potential for choice often coincides with an optimism regarding human behavior. Conversely, a belief in humanity as depraved and irresponsible will be found in conjunction with a distrust of humanity's ability to act in a positive and meaningful way. This view of the human condition is presented in *Phaedra* by Racine and presents humankind as predetermined or predestined.

Racine was reared by the Jansenists at Port-Royal, and he returned to Port-Royal after completing *Phaedra*. The Jansenists held ideas on the problem of free will and predestination in opposition to the dominant position of the Catholic church as set forth by the Jesuits. The Jesuits attempted to bring salvation within the grasp of all humanity, whereas the Jansenists emphasized a rigid determinism. They rejected the Jesuit doctrine that people could attain salvation through good works and insisted that humans were predestined to salvation or damnation. This denial of free will was based on the conviction that humankind was left completely corrupt and devoid of rational control after the fall from God's grace suffered by Adam and Eve. Humanity was incapable of participating in the process of regeneration because original sin had deprived it of its will. The passions had gained control, and they could only lead to evil. Human passion was seen as capable of leading to falsehood, crime, suicide, and general destruction. It is inevitable that the Jansenists would regard with alarm any doctrine that allowed for the activity of human free will. Only God's gift of mercy could save humanity, and that mercy was reserved for those who had been elected to salvation.

The basic ideas in *Phaedra* present a similar distrust of the passions, a similar curtailment of free will, and a consequent emphasis upon humanity's lack of control. Human passion is depicted as controlling reason. The area of human choice and responsibility is severely limited. Phèdre is pursued by an overwhelming sense of fatality.

In the preface to *Phaedra*, however, Racine suggests the possibility of free will. He states that Phèdre is "neither completely guilty nor completely innocent. She is involved, by her destiny and by the anger of the gods, in an illicit passion of which she is the first to be horrified. She makes every effort to overcome it." Does Phèdre actually make the effort Racine attributes to her? To what extent is she free to make a choice? To what extent is this merely the illusion of free will? For Racine continues to state in the preface that "her crime is more a punishment of the gods than an act of her will."

Phèdre's genealogy would seem to support the argument of fatality. She is initially referred to, not by name, but as the "daughter of Minos and Pasiphae." Throughout the play, she gives the appearance of being overwhelmed by a cruel destiny that is linked to her past. She exhibits perfect lucidity regarding the full implications of her situation, yet she seems incapable of resolving her dilemma. All of her actions are performed "in spite of myself."

Phèdre's fall precedes the opening of the play and is the result of passion overwhelming reason. One learns that Phèdre made numerous but ineffective attempts to overcome her love for Hippolyte. She built a temple to Venus, sacrificed innumerable victims, and attempted to surmount her passion through prayer.

As the play opens, Phèdre resorts to her final effort—suicide. Ironically, her attempted suicide will only serve to add physical weakness to her already weakened emotional condition and prevent her from overcoming the temptations with which she will be confronted.

The first temptation is offered by her nurse, Oenone. By implying that her suicide would constitute betrayal of the gods, her husband, and her children, Oenone attempts to persuade Phèdre to turn back on death and reveal her love for Hippolyte. The news of Thésée's apparent death further tempts Phèdre by removing the crime of potential adultery. In addition, Phèdre is tempted to offer the crown to Hippolyte in order to protect her children and to appeal to his political aspirations.

Her interview with Hippolyte, however, turns into a confession of love which unfolds without any semblance of rational control. Although she expresses shame at her declaration, her passion is presented as part of the destiny of her entire race. At the moment following the confession to Hippolyte, Phèdre prays to Venus, not as in the past to free her from passion, but to enflame Hippolyte with a comparable passion. Whereas Phèdre had previously implored Oenone to aid her in overcoming her love, she now beseeches her assistance in furthering it.

Thésée's return presents Phèdre with a choice of either revealing or denying her love for Hippolyte. She, however, allows Oenone to deceive Thésée by accusing Hippolyte of fostering the illicit passion. Yet is this actually a moment of choice, assuming that choice involves a rational action? On the contrary, Phèdre's statement to her nurse at the end of Act III, scene iii, implies complete lack of control.

The final temptation to which Phèdre succumbs is her refusal to reverse the course of events by confessing her lies to Thésée. Once again Phèdre is prevented from acting in a rational manner, for upon learning of Hippolyte's love for Aricie, she is overwhelmed by a blinding jealousy and even goes so far as to wish for the destruction of Aricie.

Despite Racine's enigmatic remarks in the preface, the pattern of temptation and defeat developed in the play eliminates entirely the possibility of free will. Although Phèdre wishes to overcome her passion, all of her efforts are in vain. The series of temptations presented to Phèdre serves to emphasize her lack of control and conspires to bring about her ruin. From the possibility of an early death with honor, Phèdre is led, through a series of defeats, to a guilty and dishonorable death. The play concludes on a note of pessimism. There is no possibility of salvation for those afflicted with passion. Racine presents humanity's fate as predestined and not subject to human control.

"Critical Evaluation" by Phyllis Mael

Bibliography:

Abraham, Claude. *"Phèdre."* In *Jean Racine*. Boston: Twayne, 1977. This chapter in Abraham's book focuses on Racine's radical alterations of the characterizations from his sources, Euripides and Seneca. He also emphasizes the musicality of Racine's language and his emphasis on the importance of eyes.

Clark, A. F. B. *"Phèdre."* In *Jean Racine*. New York: Octagon Books, 1969. An overview of Racine's work that includes chapters on the age of Racine, classical tragedy before Racine, Racine's life, and each of his plays. Clark demonstrates that *Phaedra* marks Racine's transition from secular to sacred plays as the protagonist is a "Greek woman with a Jansenist conscience," full of the consciousness of her sin.

Mourgues, Odette de. *Racine: Or, The Triumph of Relevance*. London: Cambridge University Press, 1967. This study focuses on the patterns created by the interdependence and function of Racine's tragic components. Mourgues praises Racine's poetic depth and asserts that, in his tragedies, language reigns supreme.

Weinberg, Bernard. *"Phèdre."* In *The Art of Jean Racine*. Chicago: University of Chicago Press, 1963. Weinberg's book contains one chapter for each of Racine's plays. He declares *Phaedra* to be the author's most completely achieved drama because of its originality, unity, and characterization.

Yarrow, Philip John. "From *Mithridate* to *Phèdre*." In *Racine*. Totowa, N.J.: Rowman & Littlefield, 1978. In this chapter of his exhaustive study of Racine's oeuvre, Yarrow examines Racine's motivations for writing *Phaedra*, explores Racine's debt to Euripides and Seneca, and proclaims that the play is the culmination of Racine's work.

PHARSALIA

Type of work: Poetry
Author: Lucan (Marcus Annaeus Lucanus, 39-65 C.E.)
Type of plot: Epic
Time of plot: 70-47 B.C.E.
Locale: Rome, Spain, Northern Africa, Greece, and Asia Minor
First transcribed: Bellum civile, 60-65 C.E. (English translation, 1614)

> *Principal characters:*
> CAESAR, emperor of Rome
> CRASSUS, a triumvir
> JULIA, daughter of Pompey, wife of Caeser
> POMPEY, an enemy of Caesar, eventually decapitated
> GAIUS TREBONNIUS, one of Caesar's generals
> KING JUBA, Libyan ruler
> SCAEVA, a hero in Caesar's army
> CATO, another enemy of Caesar
> BRUTUS, another enemy of Caesar

The Story:

The First Triumvirate dissolved after the deaths of Crassus and Julia, who was Caesar's wife and the daughter of Pompey. After his conquest of Gaul, Caesar advanced to the Rubicon, then stopped to consider his next move. Public morality in Rome had been corrupted by the wealth acquired from plundering its conquests, and public officials were dishonest. When Caesar decided to march on Rome, news of his decision terrified the Romans. The senate fled, and Pompey hurried to the Adriatic port of Brindisi. Realizing he had lost the allegiance of Rome, and that crossing the Alps to reach his allies in Spain was impractical, Pompey sent for help from Oriental cities. Although Rome was ready to fall, Caesar decided to seize the area under Pompey and block the seaport controlling the Adriatic, but Pompey abandoned Brindisi to Caesar.

Pompey decided to seek help from Sicily and Sardinia, while Caesar marched on Rome. In Rome, Caesar was greeted with silence except from a defiant Metellus, and he looted the treasury. Meanwhile, Pompey found support from Greece and Asia Minor, so Caesar hurried back to Gaul. There he found Marseilles pleading neutrality and prepared an assault against it. Leaving Gaius Trebonius in charge, Caesar moved on to Spain, where he attacked the Pompeians. At first they successfully resisted him, but finally surrendered.

Caesar met with less success elsewhere. At Curicta, the Pompeians strung underwater cables across the straits and wrecked Caesar's ships. Curio, Caesar's lieutenant in Sicily, sailed to Libya, where in a battle with King Juba, he and his men were massacred. There was now a stalemate. The Roman senators, in exile, met in Epirus and appointed Pompey dictator.

Caesar hurried to Rome to declare himself dictator before joining his fleet at Brindisi and sailing across the Adriatic to Illyria, where Pompey was encamped. The two armies faced each other. Pompey tried to breach Caesar's defenses under cover of a wood. Pompey would have won a victory had not one of Caesar's men, Scaeva, rallied his comrades and slaughtered the Pompeians. Scaeva was killed, and Pompey trapped Caesar, but Pompey restrained his troops, having scruples against killing his son-in-law.

Caesar now quit this region and led his army into Thessaly. Pompey was urged by councillors to reoccupy Rome, but decided he should pursue Caesar until he had a peace and could disband his army. Despite a witch's predictions of disaster and ominous portents, Pompey's men were eager for battle, and Pompey reluctantly assented. The armies clashed at Pharsalus with great enthusiasm: one to establish tyranny, the other to resist it. The slaughter was great, and Pompey was defeated.

Caesar surveyed the scene and gloated. Pompey rode off without waiting for the final scene. He rode from city to city, greeted by weeping citizens, his fame undimmed by the defeat. He now looked to his former allies among the Eastern princes, focusing on Parthia. His associates insisted that he approach Ptolemy, the boy king of Egypt, and Libya instead, so Pompey sailed to Egypt. Ptolemy was persuaded by his councillors to murder Pompey and keep the Romans out of their country. Pompey was decoyed ashore, stabbed to death, and decapitated. His trunk was rescued from the ocean by one of his servants, cremated on a pyre, and buried in a mound.

Pompey's ghost now swooped down for vengeance, first in Cato's heart and then in noble Brutus'. Cato assumed the role of protector of Rome, rearming the partisans of liberty and rescuing the survivors of Pharsalia. The dead Pompey sent his son Sextus back to Egypt to take orders from Cato. Gnaeus, his other son, in Libya, set out to rescue his father's body and ravage Egypt's sacred pyramids, but was dissuaded by Cato. The Pompeians were inspired again by Cato to fight tyranny and renew the war. They crossed the desert sands of Africa and reached the Oracle of Jupiter Ammon. There they met emissaries from the Eastern powers who wanted to consult the Oracle, but Cato proceeded.

In the meantime, Caesar pursued the Pompeian survivors of Pharsalia as far as the Hellespont, where he stopped to identify himself as a descendant of Aeneas. He then proceeded to Alexandria and took Ptolemy hostage. Ptolemy's sister, Cleopatra, proceeded to seduce Caesar. Pothinus, who had engineered the assassination of Pompey, now conspired the death of Caesar but postponed the deed so as not to endanger Ptolemy. The attack on Caesar failed, and Caesar set fire to the ships and the city and seized the Pharos, capturing Pothinus and putting him to death. Cleopatra's younger sister now took command of the Egyptian army. She ordered the execution of Ptolemy as a sacrifice and the assassination of Caesar, but Caesar successfully beat off the attack.

Critical Evaluation:

In *Pharsalia*, Lucan is more rhetorical than poetic, often epigrammatic, and often invective, although there are passages of real brilliance. Lucan, who completed his education in Athens, was a Stoic—influenced partly by his uncle, Seneca, and partly by his studies under the Stoic philosopher Cornutius in Athens—and a republican, and this poem reflects his philosophical views. It was written over the last five years of his life; the first three books were completed only before the last year, and the poem was broken off at the tenth book when he was executed for conspiring against Nero. Evidence within the poem indicates Lucan intended two more books in which Caesar would return to Rome and defeat Scipio and Cato, leaders of the Pompeians; Pompey's ghost would reappear; and Caesar would be assassinated. Lucan's views, which included a hatred of the Caesarean dynasty, were affected by the events in those years: his estrangement from Nero, involvement in a plot to assassinate Nero, and final trial.

As Lucan indicates in his opening lines, the theme of the poem is the civil war between Pompey and Caesar. This involved not only fellow citizens but also fratricide between relatives (Caesar and his father-in-law, Pompey) and affected not only Rome but also the Western world. *Pharsalia*'s title in the early manuscripts was *Bellum civile* (concerning the civil war). Throughout the epic, Lucan introduces passages that reinforce this theme: In book 1, as Caesar approaches Rome, Lucan points out that there is panic similar to that in Thebes when two powerful brothers turned on each other. In book 2, the feud between Sulla and Marius, with its brutal slaughter, is recalled. As the poem progresses, it is clear that Lucan is also lamenting the tragic destruction of the Roman Republic and the demise of liberty.

The theme enables Lucan to indulge his predilection for violent realism and his taste for the macabre to present the horror of civil war. He depicts bizarre incidents in the sea battle off Marseilles, where a body is torn in half, the top half falling into the sea to vainly struggle against drowning, and two fathers fight over a headless body, each claiming it is his son. In the bloody battle of Pharsalia, brother despoils brother, son mutilates father, and a victorious Caesar is served breakfast where he can survey the mounds of corpses settling into corruption and the streams running red. Packs of wild animals and huge flocks of birds feast on the corpses, dropping fragments of gore and flesh as they take flight after gorging themselves.

Although the poem is a lament for the losses of the civil war, the greatest casualty, from Lucan's point of view, was the destruction of the Republic, and with it, republican liberty, at the hands of the Caesarian dynasty. Liberty is the key image, and republican Cato, the third and last of the major characters, is the nearest to being the hero of the poem. Lucan set out to offset or undercut Vergil's glorification of the founders of Rome, the reputed ancestors of the Caesars. In so doing, he embarks upon innovations in epic poetry, the most obvious being discarding the role of gods and goddesses, setting a precedent for a new fusion of history and poetry, mingling both pleasing and revolting details.

There is a progression of events in which first Pompey, then Caesar, and finally Cato dominate. Caesar is depicted as a ferocious and treacherous ogre, tireless and ruthless, the antihero who destroyed the republic. One cannot help but relate Lucan's hatred of Caesar to his feud with Nero, Caesar's descendant and successor. Pompey is identified with the republican cause, but his motives and intentions are suspect, and he is unable, sometimes reluctant, to defend himself or his cause against an energetic and ruthless Caesar. He is an eminently respectable person, but not an engaging one. He is neither a successful general nor a leader of men, and he has outlived his reputation, although he continues to have a large following. Cato is the moral hero, a superhuman figure near to the Stoic ideal of a perfect man. He is the only one of the protagonists to emerge from the catastrophic civil war with his luster undimmed, the embodiment of liberty. Although the unfinished epic ends with a victorious Caesar in Alexandria, allied to Cleopatra, his life is still in danger because of a plot for his assassination. Hints within the poem indicate that Cato will emerge at the end as the hero, with his suicide on behalf of the republican cause, and that Caesar will be assassinated in the senate.

Lucan has been described as the classic exponent of the Stoicism of the Age of Nero, showing confrontations between the forces of destiny and fortunes and individuals with strong moral virtues. When omens appear, as when Caesar crosses the Rubicon, and before the battle at Pharsalia; when allies want to consult the Delphic Oracle about the future of Rome; when Sextus Pompey disgraces his father by insisting on consulting the witch Erichtho—the noble characters defy that future.

Lucan's treatment of some women characters—the vignettes of Marcia, Cato's wife, and Cornelia, wife of Pompey—may reflect the strong affection between Lucan and his wife, Polla Argentaria. After Lucan's death, his widow celebrated his birthday every year until her death with a gathering of his friends. According to tradition, she also assisted him in the writing of *Pharsalia*.

The poet Robert Graves has labeled Lucan the father of the costume film. *Pharsalia*, he said, "consists of carefully chosen, cunningly varied, brutally sensational scenes, linked by . . . historical probability and alternated with soft interludes in which deathless courage, supreme self-sacrifice, memorable piety, Stoic virtue, and wifely devotion" appeal to popular taste.

Thomas Amherst Perry

Bibliography:
Clark, John. "The Later Roman Epic." In *A History of Epic Poetry: Post-Virgilian.* New York: Haskell House, 1964. Summarizes the epic, book by book, and finds its strength in its exalted style and earnest dedication. Labels Lucan the foremost writer of Latin literature of decadence.
Dilke, O. A. W. "Lucan's Political Views and the Caesars." In *Neronians and Flavians. Silver Latin I,* edited by D. R. Dudley. London: Routledge & Kegan Paul, 1972. A study of Lucan's developing antagonism to Nero, as reflected in this epic.
Graves, Robert. Introduction to *Lucan, "Pharsalia": Dramatic Episodes of the Civil Wars.* London: Cassell, 1961. Argues that this epic is a historical phenomenon anticipating many twentieth century literary genres.
Sullivan, J. P. "The Stoic Opposition? Seneca and Lucan." In *Literature and Politics in the Age of Nero.* Ithaca, N.Y.: Cornell University Press, 1985. Argues that this epic is written from the standpoint of an emotional republican who believes that Julius Caesar and the later heads of the Roman state held power illegally and that power must be restored to the senate.
Tillyard, E. M. W. "Lucan." In *The English Epic and Its Background.* New York: Oxford University Press, 1954. Finds that Lucan is important because he departed from the precedent of Vergil and is a writer of genuine feelings and brilliant intellect.

PHENOMENOLOGY OF SPIRIT

Type of work: Philosophy
Author: Georg Wilhelm Friedrich Hegel (1770-1831)
First published: Phänomenologie des Geistes, 1807 (English translation, 1931)

Phenomenology of Spirit is perhaps the most important philosophical treatise of the nineteenth century. It laid the foundation for the many philosophical and psychological investigations and controversies of that century and continues to be an important, if not essential, text. Though it is often critiqued, qualified, and even violently rejected, no serious thinker has ever been able to ignore *Phenomenology of Spirit*'s central claim of the dialectical progress of consciousness toward an absolute understanding of the world. A challenging but rewarding text, Hegel's landmark study of the history and progress of human consciousness toward what he calls spirit developed and brought into common usage essential notions such as phenomenology, the dialectic, and the master/slave relation.

Phenomenology is not the study of an object or of the world but the study of the mind's ability to perceive and bring meaning to an object or the world. To quote Hegel, phenomenology "is the science of knowing in the sphere of appearance." Like his immediate predecessor, Immanuel Kant, Hegel was an idealist who believed that the mind creates the vast system of meanings and relationships that constitute the human world. Yet what sets *Phenomenology of Spirit* apart from Kant and the work of other idealists is that they did not discuss the lessons of history, while Hegel argued that the circular progress of history brings humanity to a full realization of its knowledge of the world. Where Kant asserted that there are nonchanging and nonhistorical rules and categories, called apriori, which help guide individuals to give meaning to the world, Hegel taught that the progressive unfolding of history develops what constitutes human understanding of the world. He refers to this hard-won and progressively created gallery of images, past customs, cultural laws, and feelings as spirit.

In Hegel's study of the human ability to see the world, the human spirit has mutated and developed through time in a dialectical process. For Hegel, there is no such thing as progress without an opposition between two parties, peoples, or ideas. He writes that there must always be a thesis, or dominant force, and an antithesis, an opposing and subordinate force to the thesis. These two opposites, far from simply ignoring or destroying each other, engage in a conversation, or dialogue (hence the word "dialectic") that results in what Hegel calls a synthesis. This synthesis is often a combination of the two previously opposing ideas, but it can also be an entirely new notion created by the dialogue between the two. *Phenomenology of Spirit* does not simply show that any concept or knowledge is developed out of two opposing ideas. No one synthesis is ever the culmination or the end in Hegel. *Phenomenology of Spirit* teaches that with the passage of time, any new synthesis becomes itself a thesis, which through time inevitably becomes opposed to an antithesis, resulting in another dialectic that in turn creates another new synthesis. Hegel defined this continuing process, the "long process of culture toward genuine philosophy," as the progress of human history.

Phenomenology of Spirit has three major divisions: the preface, the introduction, and the body of the text. The preface, essential reading for anyone who wishes to understand Hegel's phenomenological system, is one of the most quoted passages of Hegel's philosophy. It contains a synopsis of Hegel's notion of the dialectic, his study of the progress of consciousness to absolute spirit, and a discussion of the importance of the study of consciousness, or phenomenology. Hegel wrote this preface in 1807 after he had finished writing the rest of the book, and it provides a lucid and useful alembic of *Phenomenology of Spirit.*

Hegel's introduction is useful for providing fairly clear definitions of many of the terms used in the rest of the book. The bulk of the text consists of eight chapters, which Hegel organized into six major discussions respectively entitled "Consciousness," "Self-Consciousness," "Reason," "Spirit," "Religion," and finally "Absolute Knowing." Each of the six division titles represents major shifts and mutations in the shape of human consciousness, or spirit, toward the goal of absolute knowing.

The first discussion describes early forms of consciousness that provide only a realization of the world as an object (sense-certainty), of a set of chaotic particulars (perception), and finally of a crude unity where the conscious mind is nevertheless still unaware of itself in its surroundings (appearance). The subsequent step, self-consciousness, occurs when the mind becomes aware that it in large part helps create the world, and that the very ability to perceive is also an object in the world. This self-awareness can become self-indulgent. The next dialectical mutation of spirit, which Hegel calls reason, turns away from self-indulgence but still keeps the positive elements of self-awareness. Reason then begins to posit laws that focus consciousness on the structure of the world and thereby end the possibly fatal fascination with the self. Eventually, reason becomes so sure of its ability to understand the world, that this mode of perception appears, to the person who is watching the world, as actual truth.

This leap or transformation of spirit (which Hegel rather confusingly calls spirit, whereby he does not mean the same spirit as the complete spirit that develops through the dialectic of history) is of great importance, for it is the first time that humanity "is conscious of itself as its own world, and of the world as itself." In other words, humanity is beginning to understand its relation with itself and with all of the facts, images, and objects that have come to constitute the human perception of the world through time. The next step, religion, is taken when spirit takes a new shape in seeking for something that transcends human spirituality. This shape tends to see the world as an expression of a supreme God, which Hegel believes is actually humanity's spirit become externalized. For Hegel, religion is largely humanity's temporary need for a reality larger than itself. He believed that God is a dialectically created form of consciousness that fulfills this need.

The final mutation—which Hegel insists is not an ending but another starting point where "Spirit starts afresh and apparently from its own resources to bring itself to maturity"—is absolute knowing. This is where a person or whole society can attain "the goal, Absolute Knowing, or Spirit . . . as they are in themselves and as they accomplish the organization of their realm." The perceiving self is able to see the world in a new way and also able to become aware of its own relationship with itself and thus embark on another journey of phenomenological self-discovery: "In the immediacy of this new existence, the spirit has to start afresh to bring itself to maturity as if, for it, all that preceded were lost and it had learned nothing from the experience of the earlier spirits."

Hegel takes great pains specifically to discuss the shapes of consciousness created by the dialectic of history. He provides these different states in order to show how our understanding of the world is historically developed or mediated rather than being simply the result of whimsical ideas, God's laws, or some abstract eternal forces such as Kant's apriori. Below is a summary of the more important modes. It is important to understand that these specific modes of consciousness further develop the previous categories.

In chapters 1-3 (the "Consciousness" section), Hegel describes sensory, perceptual, and understanding consciousness. These describe the movement from simple object-perception to a mode of impulsive categorization of everything and from then to the first steps toward an overall unifying mode of consciousness. Chapter 4 discusses how, during the struggles of different cultures and individuals, master and slave consciousnesses develop. The master is ruler of his own realm, but as ruler the master is not interested in progress and only maintains the boundaries of his domain. Progress depends upon the slave consciousness, which develops new forms of consciousness in order to provide for the master. These are, respectively, the stoic (which teaches self-denial), the skeptical (where happiness is found in a cynical rejection of authority), the unhappy (resulting in a strong will), and the idealistic consciousness (which can help to change mere ideas into reality).

Chapter 5 catalogs the rational, empirical, and ethical shapes of reason. These are to show that reason exists solely within the subject, then solely in the perceived object. Finally, reason creates the ethical consciousness, which tries to reconcile these two opposing perspectives. The result of these dialectical developments is that the "real world" becomes known as an extension of both the individual mind and the ever-developing spirit. This means that spirit expresses itself within the human mind and then within the world, but also that material objects and cultural institutions begin to express the same spirit. Chapter 6 further catalogs how spirit exists and develops within physical and cultural objects and laws by its discussion of the legal and spiritual consciousness, culminating in the tragic and alienation consciousness. This unhappy collection of states of mind lead, however, to what Hegel calls the beautiful soul, which forgives and comes to terms with its alienation.

Chapter 7 includes discussions of the natural religious consciousness, where what was once a mental idea of spirit becomes externalized and worshiped in the forms of animals or celestial objects. One of the more fascinating and important forms of consciousness Hegel discusses is the artistic consciousness, which describes how art can itself express the shape of the spirit of the age in which the object was created. This passage alone has inspired volumes of art and literary criticism. This shape of consciousness leads to what Hegel calls the revealed religion (consciousness), which he feels is one of the ultimate expressions of spirit in the world. Of the New Testament of the Bible, Hegel writes that it captures some of the best revelations of spirit to be found.

The final chapter discusses the absolute consciousness. This is what enables the writing of *Phenomenology of Spirit* itself, and it is a moment where spirit is able to go beyond the subject/object dichotomy and become both the subject and object of individual perception. The idea that subject and object can be thus intermingled may seem confusing, but this is part of the beauty—and frustration—of *Phenomenology of Spirit*. While it may seem that Hegel runs in circles, his definition of the truly absolute way of seeing the world is to be able to become part of "a circle that returns into itself, that presupposes its beginning, and reaches its beginning only in its end."

"Critical Evaluation" by James Aaron Stanger

Bibliography:
Abrams, M. H. *Natural Supernaturalism.* New York: Norton, 1971. Though predominantly a discussion of British and German Romantic poetry, the book contains a valuable discussion of *The Phenomenology of Spirit.* Abrams' book is also an instructive application of Hegel's conclusion that art expresses spirit, particularly in chapters 3 and 4.
Hegel, George Wilhelm Friedrich. *Phenomenology of Spirit.* Translated by A. V. Miller. New York: Oxford University Press, 1977. The authoritative translation. Contains a helpful intro-duction and an insightful summary of the work.

Hyppolite, Jean. *Genesis and Structure of Hegel's "Phenomenology of Spirit."* Evanston, Ill.: Northwestern University Press, 1974. Discusses the directions Hegel's thought took after the publication of *Phenomenology of Spirit.* Also has key insights about the work's structure.

Kaufmann, Walter Arnold. *Hegel: Reinterpretation, Texts, and Commentary.* Garden City, N.Y.: Doubleday, 1965. Contains a useful translation of Hegel's seminal preface to *Phenomenology of Spirit*, as well as Kaufmann's scholarly yet clearly written insights.

THE PHENOMENON OF MAN

Type of work: Philosophy
Author: Pierre Teilhard de Chardin (1881-1955)
First published: Le Phénomène humain, 1955 (English translation, 1959)

When *The Phenomenon of Man* appeared in France in December, 1955, it was hailed as a major publishing event. The English translation, which appeared in 1959, appeared to be an event of equal interest and importance among English-speaking readers. Pierre Teilhard de Chardin, born in Auvergne, France, in 1881, was an ordained member of the Society of Jesus. Early in his student days at a Jesuit college, he became interested in geology and mineralogy. He then began to study philosophy, followed by an interval of teaching physics and chemistry, and then began the study of theology. During his teaching years and theological studies, he acquired a competence in paleontology, and it was as a paleontologist that he was to become best known to the world. His interests gradually centered on the general facts and theories of the evolutionary process and finally were pinpointed on what was to become his life's work: the evolution of the human race. Professionally, he was a geologist and paleontologist; as a thinker, he felt impelled to formulate a philosophy of evolution that would take into account human history, human personality, and the future possibilities for humanity on the earth. It is this for-mulation of concepts that constitutes Teilhard de Chardin's *The Phenomenon of Man.* Sir Julian Huxley, in an illuminating introduction, remarks that Teilhard de Chardin was a visualizer of power who saw the whole sweep of the natural history of the world, from the alpha of the origins of things to the omega of collective reflection and the fulfillment of personality. Teilhard de Chardin saw these matters with the eyes of the poet and mystic, but always with an imagination and faith supported by rational inquiry and scientific knowledge. His thoughts and conclusions are bold and visionary, but the vision is always disciplined by the demands of reality.

The Phenomenon of Man admittedly presents many difficulties for the lay reader, and pos-sibly for the professional, but Teilhard de Chardin tells the story of the evolutionary process in a style at once so finished and so engaging that the reader will find it well worth the time and concentration it will require. Much of the pleasure is a result of the excellence of the translation by Bernard Wall, who is quick to say that the writer's style is completely and indisputedly his own.

Teilhard de Chardin's basic hypothesis of the interiority of all created things may be presented in his own interpretation: Teilhard de Chardin believes that things possess both an exterior and an interior aspect that are coextensively related. A person who looked closely would find an interior even in his or her own depths. Once this fact has been realized, it may also be ascertained, in one manner or another, that the interior is present everywhere in nature since the beginning of time. When speaking of the "within" of the earth, for example, Teilhard de Chardin means not its depth in matter but the "psychic" part of the stuff of the universe that has been enclosed since the first appearance of earth. In every portion of sidereal matter, throughout the cosmos, the interior world lines all points of the exterior one.

From this hypothesis, Teilhard de Chardin develops a law of complexity and consciousness, according to which a consciousness becomes more perfected as it forms the interior lining of a more complicated structure, so that the more developed the consciousness, the fuller and more organized the structure. Spiritual perfection and material complexity are only dual aspects of the same phenomenon. *The Phenomenon of Man* is the story of the application of this law, which is dealt with on three levels of the evolutionary spiral: prelife, life, and thought.

In physical perspective, life presupposes and supports the theory of a prelife. In the beginning, apparently through some fantastic accident, a fragment of particularly stable atoms detached itself from the sun, took its place in the cosmos, folded in on itself, and assumed the spherical shape that Teilhard de Chardin regards as of utmost importance in the evolution of matter and the emergence of consciousness. The fundamental composition of this earth seems to have established itself from the beginning in a series of complex substances arranged in layers that form what are known as the barysphere, lithosphere, hydrosphere, atmosphere, and stratosphere, and demonstrating the powers of synthesis inherent in the universe. On the small, spherical surface of the new planet, the powers of synthesis had ideal conditions under which to operate. Teilhard de Chardin explicates the process of cosmogenesis in the life-before-life of the early earth—the genesis of ever more elaborate structures and organizations shown in the passage from subatomic units to atoms, from atoms to inorganic molecules, and later to organic molecules.

Prelife, dormant because of its diffusion in outer space, had no sooner entered the nascent sphere of the new earth than its activities were awakened and set in motion, along with the awakening of the powers of synthesis enclosed in matter. Throughout the millions of years of prelife, the "complexification" of matter, the energies of synthesis were causing ever greater tensions within the earth. Something tremendous was about to happen: the advent of life in the world and the formation of another envelope over the planet, the biosphere.

Teilhard de Chardin regards the appearance of life on the globe as a point of coming to maturity in the process of terrestrial evolution, a forward step of magnitude, the start of a new order in the evolutionary process. The fact that life had a beginning at one point in the natural history of the earth in no way denies the basic condition of our knowledge that each thing has its roots in the cosmos, but to accept the theory that every being has had a cosmic embryogenesis does not contradict or disprove its beginning at some definite moment in history, a change in aspect or nature. Teilhard de Chardin describes a time before the threshold of life was passed—a terrestrial era of megamolecules out of which there originated the cell, the natural granule of life with its increase in consciousness in accordance with the law of complexification. Life had no sooner started than it swarmed over the face of the earth, ramifying as it expanded. To illustrate this process of expansion and ramification, Teilhard de Chardin uses the picture of the Tree of Life, with its roots lost in the unknowable world of primordial matter and its trunk branching out into an unbelievable multitude of types. In the course of the millions of years of its growth, the Tree of Life pushed through the fish, the amphibia, the reptiles, the birds, the mammals, the placentals, and on to the primates. These last had reached such a degree of complexification—of cephalization and cerebralization—that they became the leading shoot of the tree. Psychic tension was increasing on the earth, presaging a new order of things for the world; the active lines of descent become warm with consciousness as they achieved their most complex structure. In the mammals—the most highly developed of creatures in structure and consciousness—after millennia, the brain began to function and thought was born at some localized point of development.

When humans first come into the reader's view, they are already a crowd spread all over the Old World, from the Cape of Good Hope to Peking. Their infancy or "hominization" lasted thousands of years. As to what the nature of this leap from primate to human is, Teilhard de Chardin believes that hominization was more than simply the rise of a new species. Hominization brought a new quality into the world and has added a new (and final) envelope to the earth. That which makes humans different from all other species and places them at the summit of the evolutionary process is the phenomenon of reflection, the power acquired by consciousness to turn in upon itself, to regard and know itself, to know and to know it knows. This power of reflection makes humans not only different but also quite "other," separating humanity from the rest of creation by an abyss that no other species can cross.

Has evolution stopped after its long process leading to humankind, which apparently has undergone no significant physical change since its first appearance on the planet? In answer to this question, Teilhard de Chardin launches out on bold speculations that are not easy to follow. He asserts that humanity spread over an earth whose sphericity has caused it to turn in on itself rather than to become diffuse and separated as it would have done on an unlimited surface. Through migration and intermarriage, humankind has formed an almost solid mass of hominized substance, and the process still continues. As a result of recent inventions, humans are found over earth and sea, in every part of the world. From the first spark of conscious reflection, there came a glow that, in ever-widening circles, has covered the earth with a new layer that has spread over and above the biosphere. This is the "thinking" layer that Teilhard de Chardin has called the noosphere.

It would appear that evolution is an ascent to consciousness. Therefore, the further complexification of the noosphere should be expected to culminate in a supreme consciousness, which Teilhard de Chardin calls the Omega point, where the noosphere will be intensely unified and will have achieved a hyperpersonal organization. The Omega point may well be reached outside of time and space, but since, for Teilhard de Chardin, the supreme importance of the human personality is a matter of faith, Omega must be in some way loving and lovable at this very moment. To satisfy the requirements of humanity's reflective activity, Omega must be independent of the collapse of the forces with which evolution is interwoven. Its four attributes are autonomy, actuality, irreversibility, and transcendence. Teilhard de Chardin suggests that it is humanity's task to organize this global layer of thought (the noosphere) more adequately so that humans might better understand the process of evolution on the earth and direct it more fully toward the fulfillment of human personality.

It is possible that the reader will find it extremely difficult—perhaps impossible—to follow Teilhard de Chardin's theories in their line of development to the point of convergence and realization he visualizes. There are, however, paths along which the reader can follow with the immense pleasure and profit attendant on being in the presence of a unique mind and a rare spirit. Teilhard de Chardin has the gifts to bring into full play humanity's matchless endowment, its power of reflection.

Bibliography:
Birx, H. James. *Pierre Teilhard de Chardin's Philosophy of Evolution.* Springfield, Ill. Charles C Thomas, 1972. Presents, from a philosophical perspective, an overview of Teilhard de Chardin's attempt to synthesize science and religion. Addresses his emphasis on evolutionary theory addressed primarily in *The Phenomenon of Man.*
Faricy, Robert L. *Teilhard de Chardin's Theology of the Christian in the World.* New York: Sheed & Ward, 1967. Synthesizes the central theme in Teilhard de Chardin's writings, that of the relationship between human endeavor and Christian revelation, including his attempt to address topics such as evolution, anxiety, death, and the finite nature of humanity, while dealing with areas such as supernatural revelation and the Second Coming.
Grau, Joseph A. *Morality and the Human Future in the Thought of Teilhard de Chardin.* Cranbury, N.J.: Associated University Presses, 1976. Discusses ethical considerations in the philosophy of Christian humanism presented in *The Phenomenon of Man* and other works, including thoughts on love, education, politics, and freedom.

Lubac, Henri de. *Teilhard de Chardin: The Man and His Meaning*. Translated by René Hague. New York: Hawthorn Books, 1966. A theological perspective on Teilhard de Chardin's writings interspersed with his personal letters and notes. Divided into two periods: his spiritual development and his defense of Christianity.

Speaight, Robert, et al. *Teilhard de Chardin: Re-Mythologization*. Waco, Tex.: Word Books, 1970. Three symposium papers presented at Seabury Western Theological Seminary that offer the three facets of Teilhard de Chardin: the man, the theologian, and the philosopher. Presents an intriguing comparison between Teilhard de Chardin and Paul Tillich.

96-282

PHILASTER
Or, Love Lies A-Bleeding

Type of work: Drama
Author: Francis Beaumont (c. 1584-1616) and John Fletcher (1579-1625)
Type of plot: Tragicomedy
Time of plot: The past
Locale: Sicily
First performed: c. 1609; first published, 1620

> *Principal characters:*
> PHILASTER, the heir to the crown of Sicily
> THE KING OF SICILY, a usurper
> ARETHUSA, his daughter
> PHARAMOND, a pompous Spanish prince
> DION, a Sicilian lord
> EUPHRASIA, his daughter, disguised as Bellario the page

The Story:

The king of Calabria had usurped the crown of Sicily from Prince Philaster's father, now dead. Because the Sicilian people loved their young prince, however, the king did not dare imprison him or harm him in any way, but he did plan to marry his daughter Arethusa to Pharamond, a Spanish prince, who would thereby become heir to both thrones. Pharamond proved to be a pompous, conceited man. When Philaster, who was quite free and outspoken in his manners, told Pharamond that only over his dead body could he marry Arethusa, the king admonished Philaster to restrain himself. Philaster declared that he would restrain himself only when he was better treated; he believed that he was suddenly possessed by the spirit of his late father. Philaster was promised aid by the loyal Lord Dion and by the two noble gentlemen Cleremont and Thrasilene.

At an audience with the Princess Arethusa, Philaster was taken aback when he heard Arethusa tell him that she loved him deeply, and he declared his love for her in return. To avoid detection under the suspicious eyes of the court, he promised to send his servant to Arethusa as their messenger. When Pharamond entered Arethusa's apartment, Philaster departed with words of scorn for the boastful Spanish prince. Later he had difficulty in persuading his servant Bellario—who was actually Lord Dion's daughter Euphrasia in disguise—to enter Arethusa's service.

At court, meanwhile, Pharamond attempted the virtue of Galathea, a court lady who led him on but refused all his base suggestions. Later he made an assignation with Megra, a court lady of easy virtue. Galathea, having overheard the conversation between Pharamond and Megra, reported the prince's dissolute ways to Arethusa.

That night the king discovered Megra in the prince's apartment. Pharamond was in disgrace. Megra, however, managed to extricate herself to some extent by insinuating that Arethusa was as wicked as she and that Bellario was more than a mere servant to Arethusa. The princess had made much of Bellario because the page was a gift from Philaster. The king, who had not even heard of Bellario's existence, was confounded by Megra's suggestions.

Megra's story convinced even Philaster's friends that Arethusa was unfaithful to the prince, but when they told Philaster what had happened he refused to believe them. Nevertheless, his trust in Arethusa was shaken. When Bellario delivered a letter from Arethusa to Philaster, who was still in doubt, the disguised girl innocently damned herself by speaking in praise of Arethusa and by describing Arethusa's virtuous affection for the page. Philaster accused Bellario of perfidy and, overcome with the passion of jealousy, threatened to take the page's life. Only because of Bellario's sincere protestations of innocence did Philaster, although still not convinced, spare his servant.

The king had ordered Arethusa to discharge her young page. When Philaster found Arethusa depressed over Bellario's dismissal, he revealed his suspicions and declared that he would give up his claim to the throne and become a hermit. The wretched Arethusa, knowing that she was guiltless, could do nothing to prevent Philaster's departure.

Philaster went to a nearby forest and wandered about disconsolately. At the same time the king and the court entered the forest to hunt. During the chase Arethusa disappeared. The hunters found her riderless horse but no trace of the princess. Bellario, having been banished from court, had also gone into the forest. When he encountered Philaster, the page was brusquely ordered away. In another part of the forest, Arethusa, stunned by recent events and without direction in her wandering, sat down to rest and suddenly fainted. Bellario appeared in time to revive her, only to be told by Arethusa that efforts to help her in her distress were wasted; the princess was prepared to die.

Philaster came upon the pair. Thinking that their meeting had been planned, and that Bellario and Arethusa were lovers, he told the page to take his wretched life. When Bellario disregarded his order, Philaster angrily dismissed the page and then, assuming the role of an agent of justice, attempted to kill Arethusa. He only wounded her, however. A peasant came upon the scene of violence. In the fight that followed, Philaster was seriously wounded, but he fled when he heard horsemen approaching.

When Pharamond, Lord Dion, and others of the hunting party arrived to find Arethusa wounded, they immediately went in search of her attacker. In his flight Philaster, hurt and bleeding, came upon Bellario asleep. Distractedly, Philaster wounded the page before collapsing from loss of blood. Faithful Bellario administered gently to Philaster and convinced the prince that he had made a mistake in his belief that Arethusa had been unfaithful to him. Hearing Philaster's pursuers, they fled. Bellario was captured, but not before the page had led them away from the prince. In order further to protect the fugitive, Bellario confessed to the attack on Arethusa. When Philaster overheard this confession, he came out of hiding to defend Bellario. The king ordered that both be imprisoned, but Arethusa, somewhat recovered from her hurt, prevailed upon her father to give her the custody over the prince and the page.

In prison, Philaster, about to be executed, and Arethusa, his guard, pledged their troth. The king disavowed his daughter when he learned of the marriage. The people of Sicily, aroused by Philaster's imprisonment and impending execution, seized Pharamond and threatened total revolt. The king, fearful for his safety and at last repentant for his usurpation of the throne, promised to restore the crown of Sicily and to approve Arethusa's marriage to Philaster, if the prince would only calm the enraged citizens. The people returned quietly to their homes when Philaster assured them that he was now quite free and that he was their new ruler.

The king, still not satisfied with the relationship between Arethusa and Bellario, commanded that Bellario be tortured in order that he might learn the truth. Philaster protested vehemently against the order. As the king's servants prepared to strip Bellario for the ordeal, the page revealed that she was, in reality, Euphrasia, daughter of Lord Dion. Having loved Philaster from childhood and despairing, because of a difference in rank, of ever marrying him, she had allowed everyone to think that she had gone overseas on a pilgrimage. Instead, she had disguised herself as a boy and had taken service with Philaster in order to be near him. Philaster and Arethusa, moved by Euphrasia's devotion, made her a lady in waiting to the queen.

Critical Evaluation:

Philaster: Or, Love Lies A-Bleeding is the first tragicomedy on which Francis Beaumont and John Fletcher collaborated for London's King's Men company between approximately 1608 and 1613. Beaumont probably wrote most of it, but it was likely Fletcher who made it a tragicomedy, following the pattern he had introduced in his first play, *The Faithful Shepherdess* (c. 1608). In that play's preface, Fletcher explains, "A tragi-comedy is not so called in respect of mirth and killing, but in respect it wants deaths, which is enough to make it no tragedy, yet brings some near it, which is enough to make it no comedy, which must be a representation of familiar people, with such kind of trouble as no life be questioned. . . ." Closely related to the sixteenth century Italian pastoral romance, *Philaster* and other tragicomedies also are distinguished by distant and exotic settings, plots that move quickly and often unrealistically, shallow and stereotypical characters, sudden character reversals for which an audience is unprepared, and contrasts between love and lust, honor and deceit. Whereas uncertainty about the fate of the heroes assures some degree of tension in tragicomedy, happy conclusions are the norm, although they usually follow from surprises or sudden revelations.

Philaster shares traits with comedies and tragedies by William Shakespeare. In *As You Like It* (1599-1600), for example, a usurper rules, young women don male disguises, and there is a pastoral element. In *Twelfth Night* (1600-1602), whose also has an exotic setting, a young woman disguises herself as a male and becomes part of a love triangle. *Hamlet* (1600-1601), like *Philaster*, opens with a young prince suffering the indignities of disenfranchisement in his usurper's court; in *Othello* (1604), a father denounces his daughter for marrying without his advice and consent.

Despite its improbable plot and its rapid succession of short scenes, *Philaster* has dramatic integrity, which is largely attributable to the unifying presence of its title character, whose fate is the focal point. Widely admired and loved, Philaster initially is portrayed as honorable, loyal, and stoic, an icon of perfection. Later, however, his easy embrace of the false story of Arethusa and Bellario's deception and his inexplicable wounding of Arethusa somewhat diminish him while also making him more human—a good man, although flawed. From the beginning, the playwrights develop a clear contrast between Philaster and Pharamond, a prince of Spain who comes to Sicily as official suitor to claim a bride and thus eventually gain control of the kingdom. He is a boorish and sexually promiscuous young man who is marrying Arethusa solely for dynastic reasons. The courtier Dion says that Pharamond is prince only by accident of birth and just as easily could have been born a slave. In other words, there is nothing inherently princely about him. His quick liaison with the lascivious Megra not only heightens the contrast between him and the regal Philaster, setting the stage for inevitable conflict, but also ironically victimizes the unlawful king. At the end, however, the monarch benevolently pardons Pharamond and Megra and blesses the forthcoming marriage of his daughter to Philaster, who will inherit the throne.

The king is a peripheral figure in the play despite his office, an ineffectual villain with only minor bouts of conscience. His failure to gain the citizenry's acceptance of his usurpation, his impotence during the uprising crisis, and his inability to orchestrate a political marriage for Arethusa dramatize the public and private consequences of the man's earlier illegal actions. These details may be oblique allusions by Beaumont and Fletcher to intemperate behavior in the court of King James I. Indeed, the prominence of the three courtiers, led by Dion, keeps politics in the forefront. Functioning as chorus, they are superficially loyal to the present monarch while retaining a reservoir of affection and respect for Philaster. Dion hopes to encourage Philaster to lead an insurrection, but one erupts without Philaster's leadership and ironically he ends it.

The king's acceptance of the marriage between Arethusa and Philaster initially seems incredible because his daughter, in an affront to traditional parental responsibility, not only has wed secretly but also has made a match with her father's blood rival. In fact, the king has no choice, for he is informed only after the marriage has taken place, and his preferred suitor proved to be totally unacceptable. Most important, Philaster, the putative rival, saves the king's crown by putting down the rebellion, thus demonstrating not only loyalty and usefulness but also worthiness as a future ruler.

Although Beaumont and Fletcher do not develop Arethusa in any depth, the princess is an important figure in the action and comes across as strong-willed and independent, in the tradition of such Shakespearean comic heroines as Beatrice, Rosalind, and Viola; in her willful disregard in the conflict with her father she outdoes Desdemona. Arethusa also has other forebears. When in trouble, she flees to the country, like the heroines of Sir Philip Sidney's *Arcadia* (c. 1580) and other sixteenth century pastoral romances. The page who serves her, supposedly the male Bellario but actually Dion's daughter Euphrasia, is also a stock character of the pastoral.

Emerging from both the love and political plots, the play's primary theme is a Renaissance commonplace: Virtue is rewarded. Beaumont and Fletcher use their characters to dramatize various manifestations of love: Philaster and Arethusa exemplify romantic love that culminates in marriage; the behavior of Pharamond and Megra illustrates lust and base sexuality; and Bellario (Euphrasia) represents the ideal of platonic love and selfless, disinterested friendship.

Successful when it was initially performed at the public (Globe) and private (Blackfriars) theaters, *Philaster* continued to be popular both on stage and in print throughout the seventeenth century. Its lasting appeal can be attributed in part to the fact that it is a forerunner of Restoration heroic drama, tragic epic plays in which love and honor were presented in an exaggerated and improbable manner, usually in the context of political or military conflict. In 1695, Elkanah Settle wrote an opera based on the play, and an adaptation (attributed to the duke of Buckingham) was presented in 1714: *The Restauration: Or, Right Will Take Place.*

"Critical Evaluation" by Gerald H. Strauss

Bibliography:
Appleton, William W. *Beaumont and Fletcher: A Critical Study.* London: George Allen & Unwin, 1956. This standard critical study of the playwrights' collaborative work favorably compares *Philaster* to their earlier and later tragicomedies, discusses Shakespearean influences (tragic and comic), and shows how Beaumont and Fletcher modified traditional pastoralism.
Ashe, Dora Jean. Introduction to *Philaster.* Lincoln: University of Nebraska Press, 1974. The introduction to this authoritative text, edited by Ashe, analyzes the play, dealing with such matters as genre, plot, characterization, the pastoral tradition, and political satire.
Davison, Peter. "The Serious Concerns of *Philaster.*" *Journal of English Literary History* 30 (1963): 1-15. Notes similarities between play dialogue and a speech by King James I, and between ideas in the play and writings of the king. Concludes that the playwrights were dramatizing contemporary political problems to influence public opinion.

Finkelpearl, Philip J. *Court and Country Politics in the Plays of Beaumont and Fletcher.* Princeton, N.J.: Princeton University Press, 1990. Claims that the playwrights dramatized the amorality of their age through political criticism of the monarch and court. Groups *Philaster* with *The Maid's Tragedy* (1608-1611) and *A King and No King* (1611) as a trilogy about the consequences of a ruler's intemperance.

Leech, Clifford. *The John Fletcher Plays.* London: Chatto & Windus, 1962. Wide-ranging study asserting that *Philaster* is notable for its variety, for how the playwrights deal with pretense, and for the importance of comedy in a largely serious play. Points out that Fletcher places stereotypical characters in atypical situations that provide novelty for audiences.

THE PHILIPPICS

Type of work: Essays
Author: Demosthenes (384-322 B.C.E.)
First transcribed: Philippicae, fourth century B.C.E. (English translation, 1852)

Occasionally in history, genius and a crisis in human affairs unite to produce one whose name rings down through the ages long after the particular events that produced the person have faded into the dimness of antiquity. Such a man was Demosthenes. Almost every educated person has heard of him and knows that he was a famous Greek orator. The events and the crisis in ancient Greece that helped make him famous, however, are unknown except to students of ancient history.

As an Athenian lawyer and orator, Demosthenes might have won little fame had it not been for Philip of Macedon, whose ambition was to conquer and rule as much of the world as he could. When the danger to Athens became great, Demosthenes did all he could to arouse his fellow Athenians to the defense of their city-state. The crisis was one that has recurred in various forms throughout history. On the one hand was Philip of Macedon, a tyrant who sought control of many lands and peoples; on the other, Demosthenes, a believer in democracy and local sovereignty who did all that one person could to arouse his contemporaries to fight against Philip and, later, his son, Alexander the Great. In this conflict between democracy and tyranny there is no doubt of Demosthenes' sincerity; it rings out from his orations almost as clearly today as it must have more than twenty-three centuries ago.

By common consent of his contemporaries and later generations, Demosthenes was the greatest of the Greek orators, in a culture that produced a great many with ability in rhetoric and oratory. Scholars of all periods have praised his speeches, and the number of manuscripts found in Egypt containing fragments of his speeches has been second only to papyri containing fragments of the Homeric epics. In modern times it is difficult to appreciate the greatness of the speeches from the standpoint of formal rhetoric as the ancient Greeks knew and used it. What Cicero praised in the orations is now to be found only by the serious student of Greek language and culture.

On the other hand, modern readers may find in the speeches what Demosthenes' admirers in the ancient world seem to have overlooked or ignored. Readers can see that Demosthenes was an able and sincere statesman laboring for democratic ideals at a time when his fellow citizens in Athens were inclined to do little to oppose the forces of tyranny led by Philip of Macedon. Demosthenes knew human nature as he knew his art, and he employed his knowledge of both to speak out forcefully for what he believed in. He spoke out not for the sake of his rhetoric but for the sake of Athens; he spoke not to a select group, to no aristocracy, but to all Athenians. He wished to persuade them to rise to the defense of their city and the way of life and government that it represented. In the orations there is, at least as they are translated, little flamboyance. Demosthenes spoke plainly and sincerely; his art was like all great art, hiding, beneath the cloak of apparent simplicity, great care and preparation. Demosthenes' tone is serious, befitting his topic.

As in the case of so many ancient authors, the authenticity of work supposedly done by Demosthenes is open to question. More than sixty orations, as well as some letters and poems, have been attributed to him. Scholars currently accept only about forty of the speeches as authentic. Many of the orations accepted as his are nonpolitical, having been composed for delivery in cases at law. These orations furnish much material about Greek culture. Demosthenes' true fame rests on the speeches called *The Philippics*. These were not the only orations on political subjects that he made, nor were they the only speeches he gave which had to do with the threat of Philip to Athens. Quite a number of other orations, like the *Olynthiacs*, deal with Philip's depredations in the Greek peninsula and other portions of the eastern Mediterranean world.

The first *Philippic* was delivered in 351 B.C.E. At that time Philip, stopped at Thermopylae, had sent his armies into Thrace, dispatched a fleet to attack the islands of Lemnos and Imbrus, and interfered with the commerce of Athens by attacking shipping. Demosthenes spoke that the Athenians might be made aware of the danger and take steps to defend themselves. The orator obviously felt that Athens in 351 B.C.E. had more to fear from the Macedonian king than its traditional enemy, Thebes, or from a combination of other unfriendly city-states. It was not as an alarmist that Demosthenes spoke; he spoke, rather, to awaken his fellow Athenians to an awareness of the need for watchfulness and preparedness. In this first *Philippic* he encouraged his city to meet the danger, pointing out its advantages and strengths. In practical fashion, he suggested ways in which the city could economically take steps to meet the danger, which at that time was not as great as it would become in passing years. It was not enough, as Demosthenes knew, merely to hope that Philip had died, as rumor had it. Demosthenes realized that failure to provide for defense through inaction sets up circumstances which are an invitation to strong-armed tyranny. Later history has shown that leaders have often failed to realize this truism of politics. Demosthenes realized, as leaders sometimes have failed to do, that free people do not have a choice between action and inaction. To oppose Philip, to warn him that Athens was prepared to defend itself, the orator suggested a military force of moderate size, with good officers to lead it. He recommended that at least twenty-five percent of the personnel be Athenians, the rest mercenaries. Knowing that to equip, pay, and keep in the field a large force was beyond the economic power of the city, he urged a small, but efficient military force. The answer to the problem, he said, lay in making the best use of what could be afforded, not in hitting blindly only at places where Philip had already struck.

Nothing was done by the Athenians. In 344 B.C.E., seven years later, he again spoke pointedly in the second *Philippic*. By that time Philip, allied with the Messenians, had become a more powerful threat to Athens. Demosthenes himself had headed an embassy to Messene and Argos to warn those cities against the oppressor, to no avail. Philip, in turn, had sent an emissary to Athens to complain about Demosthenes' charges and to vindicate his conduct. Demosthenes spoke to explain carefully what Philip was doing and what the pro-Macedonian group in Athens was doing to endanger the city. He ended by pointing out that Philip's conduct now made the Athenians' problem one of defending their city and homes, not merely of looking after claims and interests abroad. Philip's benevolence was shown to be double-edged.

In the third of the *Philippics*, delivered in 341 B.C.E., Demosthenes cried out that Athenians had to learn that a state of war existed, even though Philip talked of peace. Philip aimed at the Chersonese, which controlled the route of grain ships between Athens and the Euxine. Demosthenes urged that the Chersonese be protected as a means of protecting Athens. He was right in his predictions: Philip attacked the Propontine cities in the following year. The Athenians, to their credit and Demosthenes', played their part in resisting the tyrant. The fourth and last of the *Philippics* was also delivered in 341 B.C.E., just before Philip laid siege to the Propontine cities. In this oration, as he had in the third *Philippic*, Demosthenes urged resistance, even advocating an alliance with Persia. Although the fourth *Philippic* is generally accepted as authentic, some scholars have viewed it with suspicion, claiming for several reasons that it is spurious and not really a product of Demosthenes' own hand.

Bibliography:

Bury, J. B., and Russell Meiggs. "Rise of Macedonia." In *A History of Greece to the Death of Alexander the Great*. 4th ed. New York: St. Martin's Press, 1975. Includes discussion of *The Philippics* within an account of the conflict between Athens and Philip of Macedon. Favorable to Philip at Demosthenes' expense, but a good historical introduction.

Jaeger, Werner. "Demosthenes." In *Paideia: The Ideals of Greek Culture*. Translated by Gilbert Highet. New York: Oxford University Press, 1943. An excellent short introduction to Demosthenes' political orations, including *The Philippics*, within the context of a cultural history of Greece. A provocative challenge to the orator's detractors.

_____. *Demosthenes: The Origin and Growth of His Policy*. Translated by Edward S. Robinson. Berkeley: University of California Press, 1938. An investigation of Demosthenes' orations for the purpose of understanding his political thought. Ample treatment of the speeches opposing Philip. Interesting reading for beginner or specialist.

Pickard-Cambridge, A. W. *Demosthenes and the Last Days of Greek Freedom: 384-322 B.C.* New York: G. P. Putnam's Sons, 1914. Clear and concise summaries, with translation of key passages, of speeches against Philip are worked into a detailed history of Demosthenes' times. Favorable to Demosthenes.

Wooten, Cecil W. "Style and Argumentation in the Speeches of Demosthenes." In *Cicero's "Philippics" and Their Demosthenic Model*. Chapel Hill: University of North Carolina Press, 1983. A good description of the basic feature of Demosthenes' oratorical style. Includes illustrations. Suitable for the novice.

PHILOCTETES

Type of work: Drama
Author: Sophocles (c. 495-406/405 B.C.E.)
Type of plot: Tragedy
Time of plot: Antiquity
Locale: The island of Lemnos
First performed: Philoktētēs, 409 B.C.E.

Principal characters:
　PHILOCTETES, an abandoned Greek warrior
　NEOPTOLEMUS, Achilles' son
　ODYSSEUS, the king of Ithaca
　A SAILOR, disguised as a trader
　HERAKLES, a Greek immortal
　CHORUS OF SAILORS, under the command of Neoptolemus

The Story:
　Odysseus had abandoned Philoctetes on the barren island of Lemnos after the warrior had been bitten on the foot by a snake while preparing to make a sacrifice at the shrine on the island of Chrysa. The wound never healed, and the smell that came from it and the groans of suffering of Philoctetes were the reasons Odysseus gave for making him an outcast. Philoctetes, however, with his invincible bow, once the property of Herakles, had become indispensable to the Greeks in their war against Troy. Landing for the second time on Lemnos, Odysseus described the cave in which Philoctetes lived. Neoptolemus identified it by the stained bandages drying in the sun, the leaf-stuffed mattress, and the crude wooden cup he found.

　Instructed by Odysseus, Neoptolemus was to lure Philoctetes on board with his bow by declaring that he too hated Odysseus because the king had deprived him of the weapons of his father Achilles. Neoptolemus was disgusted by this deception, but wily Odysseus pleaded necessity and promised him honor and glory. When Neoptolemus had agreed to obey, Odysseus left him.

　The chorus of sailors reported that they heard the painful approach of Philoctetes. He asked who they were and whether they too were Greeks. Imploring their pity, he told them not to fear him, although he had become a savage through solitude and great suffering. Neoptolemus answered Philoctetes, who asked Neoptolemus who he was and why he had come. The young warrior said that he was the son of Achilles and that he did not know Philoctetes, who replied that he must indeed be vile if no word of him had reached the Greeks. His wound had grown worse and because he was alone on the island he had to use all his energy to remain alive. He shot birds with his great bow, and, in order that he might drink in winter, he was forced to build a fire to melt the ice. He cursed the Atreidae and Odysseus, who had abandoned him, and wished that they might suffer his agony. Neoptolemus, answering as he had been instructed, said that he too had cursed Odysseus, who had deprived him of his rights and robbed him of his father's arms. He asserted that he intended to sail for home.

　Philoctetes, declaring that their grief was equal, wondered also why Ajax had allowed these injustices. He was told that Ajax was also dead. Philoctetes was certain that Odysseus was alive, and this fact Neoptolemus confirmed. After hearing of the death of other friends, Philoctetes agreed with Neoptolemus that war inevitably killed the good men but only occasionally and by chance killed the bad. Neoptolemus stressed his determination never to return to Troy. He then said good-bye to Philoctetes, who implored them not to abandon him and to suffer for one day the inconvenience of having him on board the ship on which Neoptolemus was sailing. When he begged on his knees not to be left alone again, the chorus expressed their willingness to take him with them. After Neoptolemus agreed, Philoctetes praised the day that had brought them together and declared himself bound in friendship to the young warrior for all time.

As Odysseus had planned, a sailor disguised as a trader came to help Neoptolemus in tricking Philoctetes. He said, hoping to persuade Philoctetes to go quickly on board, that Odysseus was pursuing him in order to compel him to rejoin the Greek army, for Helenus, Priam's son, had prophesied that Philoctetes was the one man who would defeat Troy. Philoctetes swore that he would never go with his most hated enemy, and the disguised trader returned to his ship.

Neoptolemus asked permission to hold the mighty bow while Philoctetes prepared to leave the island. Suddenly the wound in Philoctetes' foot began to pain him beyond endurance. He handed the bow to Neoptolemus and writhed on the ground until the abscess burst and the blood flowed. The sailors advised Neoptolemus to leave with the bow while the exhausted man slept. Neoptolemus refused, for the bow was useless without Philoctetes.

When Philoctetes awoke, Neoptolemus revealed to him that he had come to take the warrior to fight against Troy. Philoctetes refused to go. When Neoptolemus insisted on keeping the bow, Philoctetes, enraged and despairing, cursed such treachery and declared that he would starve without his weapon. Neoptolemus' loyalties were divided between duty and compassion, but before he had decided on the course to pursue, Odysseus arrived and demanded that Philoctetes should accompany them. When he remained adamant, Odysseus and Neoptolemus left, taking with them the bow.

The chorus of sailors assured Philoctetes that it would be best to fight on the side of the Greeks, but, out of pride, he was determined not to fight alongside the men who had made him an outcast. He begged for a sword to kill himself. Then Neoptolemus returned, followed by Odysseus; he had decided to redress the wrong he had done Philoctetes and to return the bow. Odysseus, unable to change the young warrior's decision, went to tell the other Greeks of this act of treachery. Meanwhile, Neoptolemus again tried to persuade Philoctetes to join them. When Philoctetes again refused, Neoptolemus, in spite of the return of Odysseus, gave back the bow. He was then forced to keep Philoctetes from killing Odysseus.

When Odysseus had again left them, Neoptolemus revealed the whole of Helenus' prophecy, which foretold that the wound would be cured when Philoctetes returned and that, together with Neoptolemus, he would conquer Troy. Philoctetes, declaring Odysseus had been faithless once and would be so again, implored Neoptolemus to take him home, as he had first promised. Neoptolemus, however, was afraid that the Greeks would attack his country in retaliation. Philoctetes swore that he would defend the country with his bow.

Before they could leave, Herakles, from whom Philoctetes had inherited the bow, appeared on the rocks above the cave. He informed Philoctetes that Zeus had made a decision. Philoctetes should return to the Greek army where he would be healed. Also, with Neoptolemus, he would kill Paris and take Troy. Philoctetes, heeding the voice of the immortal, willingly left Lemnos to fulfill his destiny.

Critical Evaluation:

Scholars consider Sophocles in many ways the greatest and most modern of the Greek tragedians. Sophocles' innovations include increasing the number of actors from two to three and diminishing the role of the chorus, thus making room for greater character depth, psychological complexity, and intricate plots. Greek myth still provides the background, yet each of Sophocles' plays focuses on unique moral dilemmas in human terms.

One of Sophocles' main themes, seen in *Oedipus Tyrannus* (c. 429) and *Antigone* (441) as well as in *Philoctetes*, is the suffering of the individual caused when a strong-willed person contradicts the will of the gods or the rational solution to a problem. Sophocles does not reveal the will of the gods until the end of *Philoctetes*, when the Greek sailor disguised as a trader explains that Helenus, a prophet and son of the Trojan king Priam, had been captured by Odysseus. Helenus prophesied before the warriors that the Greeks would never take Troy until they persuaded Philoctetes to leave his island and come with them. This put the burden of responsibility upon Odysseus, since it had been his idea to maroon Philoctetes, and now Philoctetes was needed to win the war.

In Homer's epic the *Iliad* (c. 800 B.C.E.), the poet reviews the Greek troops gathering to begin the assault upon Troy to retrieve Helen, wife of commander Menelaus. Homer says that seven ships were led by Philoctetes, the master archer "superbly skilled with bow in lethal combat." Homer explains that after the battle, Philoctetes lay in agony upon the shores of the island of Lemnos. From this threadbare legend, Sophocles develops his three primary characters—Philoctetes, Odysseus, and Neoptolemus—in a profound statement about the meaning of suffering and personal integrity.

Sophocles' drama explores the idea that people learn the meaning of life only through suffering. Often in Greek stories, misery and torment are caused by the arbitrary workings of the universe. Knowledge and virtue are attained through coping with difficult circumstances such as the ten years of Philoctetes' abandonment or the twelve "impossible" labors of Herakles.

Philoctetes and Herakles, the most famous of Greek heroes, share similar stories. Herakles suffered because of the wrath of Hera, queen of the universe; Philoctetes suffered because of the help he had given to Herakles. According to some Greek authorities, Hera had sent the snake to injure Philoctetes. When the dying Herakles lay upon a funeral pyre on Mount Oeta, none of his followers would light the fire. Herakles offered Philoctetes his bow in exchange for lighting the fire, thus helping Herakles to be transposed to Olympus. Both Herakles and Philoctetes experience restoration. Herakles becomes an immortal after his labors; physicians heal Philoctetes' incurable wound after his bow brings about the fall of Troy.

Philoctetes' identity is linked to enduring pain. According to one myth, Philoctetes was wounded accidentally while in the act of sacrificing to Apollo on the island of Chrysa. The snake that bit him may either have been the guardian of an unmarked shrine or a punishment sent by Hera for helping Herakles. Philoctetes' pain is so great that he cries out, uttering oaths and curses, becoming a nuisance to Odysseus and his men. Odysseus regards the festering wound as a bad omen that terrifies the warriors. Philoctetes tells Odysseus that "You have joy to be alive, and I have sorrow/ because my very life is linked to this pain."

Yet while isolated on Lemnos, Philoctetes builds his skills and attempts to restore his confidence. His arrows never miss the birds and wild animals that are his food during his isolation. When Herakles rescues him at the end of the play, Philoctetes' restoration is complete.

In *Philoctetes*, Sophocles compares a multidimensional hero (Odysseus) to a static, one-dimensional sufferer (Philoctetes). Philoctetes' unhealed wound is a symbolic blemish upon his psyche, a sign that he has not yet been initiated into complete understanding of himself and the gods. Odysseus was himself wounded in a boar hunt according to Homer's *Odyssey*. Odysseus was also nearly killed by a host of other monsters like the Cyclopes, Circe, and Skylla, but he always overcame the physical challenge with knowledge and craft. Odysseus' and Philoctetes' wounds are important signs of contact with the transcendent, divine world. Odysseus overcame his wounds, earning his glory through craft and cunning, and Philoctetes must also rise to the occasion.

Odysseus' advice to Neoptolemus to lie to Philoctetes when they go to Lemnos shows his willingness to abandon absolutes. However, Odysseus is in error by telling Neoptolemus that only Philoctetes' bow is needed for the Greeks to have victory. In fact, the prophet Helenus had specifically stated that both Philoctetes and his weapon needed to be transported to Troy. Philoctetes needs to rise above the limitations and challenges imposed upon him in order to obey the command of the gods and salvage his place in history. However, Philoctetes waits until he sees the *deus ex machina* appearance of Herakles in order to make his decision to leave the island.

Neoptolemus' name means "young warrior," and he is just that—pure and strong but gullible and naive. When Odysseus brings Neoptolemus with him to Lemnos, Sophocles presents the problem of two very different people with the same desire: to win the Trojan war. Neoptolemus is Achilles' son, who may feel sublimated hatred against Odysseus because of the fact that Odysseus had received his father's armor after his death. Neoptolemus feels ashamed of his part in tricking the innocent Philoctetes, and he gives him his word that he will take Philoctetes back to Greece—directly countering Odysseus' desire to get the bow.

A sympathetic brotherhood emerges between Neoptolemus and Philoctetes as the full extent of his pain and suffering becomes apparent. Neoptolemus is too honest to fully comply with Odysseus' trickery, changing his mind once he gets to know Philoctetes' story. Sophocles raises the question of whether the greater end (winning the Trojan War) justifies the smaller means (telling lies to Neoptolemus and Philoctetes). Sophocles shows the value of personal integrity and honesty over scheming and conniving to achieve a desired result. Neoptolemus willingly goes with Odysseus to retrieve Philoctetes, but then he feels sympathetic toward the abandoned man and guilty that he used trickery to get the bow. In the end, the honor goes to the one who endured suffering with grace, Philoctetes.

"Critical Evaluation" by Jonathan L. Thorndike

Bibliography:

Gardiner, Cynthia P. *The Sophoclean Chorus: A Study of Character and Function.* Iowa City: University of Iowa Press, 1987. Uses *Philoctetes* to reexamine the undervalued role of the chorus in Greek drama and how Sophocles skillfully uses choral odes for dramatic irony. Discusses the extent to which the chorus participates in the plot of deception.

Harsh, Philip Whaley. *A Handbook of Classical Drama.* Stanford, Calif.: Stanford University Press, 1944. A classic survey of the range of Greek and Roman drama, arguing for the greatness of the achievement and for its influence on modern literature. Skillful thematic reading of *Philoctetes* and the Sophoclean plays leading up to it.

Kitto, H. D. F. *Greek Tragedy: A Literary Study.* London: Methuen, 1939. An excellent study of Sophocles' innovations such as his emphasis on character development, especially of Neoptolemus in *Philoctetes*, which Kitto claims has a wider range than any other character in Greek tragedy.

Segal, Charles. *Tragedy and Civilization: An Interpretation of Sophocles.* Cambridge, Mass.: Harvard University Press, 1982. Develops the idea of the civilizing power of tragedy and the importance of society, language, and friendship. Discusses the difference between heroic and civilized values and how Sophocles juxtaposes them.

Whitman, Cedric H. *Sophocles: A Study of Heroic Humanism*. Cambridge, Mass.: Harvard University Press, 1951. The chapter "The Paradox of Will: *Philoctetes*" explores tragedy defined by the division between the gods and humans. Presents heroism as that which allows the mortal to transcend environment and assimilate the will of the gods. Explores how Sophocles changed his concept of heroism from those found in his simple sketches to those in his more complex artistic renderings.

PHILOSOPHER OR DOG?

Type of work: Novel
Author: Joaquim Maria Machado de Assis (1839-1908)
Type of plot: Psychological
Time of plot: 1869-1872
Locale: Rio de Janiero and Barbacena, Brazil
First published: Quincas Borba, 1891 (English translation, 1954)

> *Principal characters:*
> RUBIÃO (PEDRO RUBIÃO DE ALVARENGA), the protagonist
> CHRISTIANO DE ALMEIDA E PALHA, an entrepreneur
> SOPHIA, Christiano's wife
> MARIA BENEDICTA, her cousin
> CARLOS MARIA, an arrogant young man
> DR. JOÃO DE SOUZA CAMACHO, a lawyer and publisher
> MAJOR SIQUEIRA, a talkative retired officer
> DOÑA TONICA, his unmarried, middle-aged daughter
> QUINCAS BORBA, a dog named after his late owner
> DOÑA FERNANDA, a kind woman

The Story:

Quincas Borba (Joaquim Borba dos Santos), a wealthy man and a self-proclaimed philosopher, died and left his large estate to his friend Rubião, a teacher. The only condition of the bequest was that Rubião care for Quincas Borba's dog, also named Quincas Borba, as if the dog were human. Rubião went from the provincial town of Barbacena to the city of Rio de Janiero to establish himself with his newly inherited wealth. On the train, he met Christiano Palha and Palha's wife, Sophia. Rubião soon became infatuated with Sophia.

In Rio, Palha borrowed money from Rubião to invest in business, and the two men became partners. Rubião also met Carlos Maria, an arrogant young man, and Freitas, an unsuccessful middle-aged man, who exploited Rubião for his wealth and innocence. Major Siqueira and his thirty-nine-year-old daughter, Doña Tonica, attached themselves to Rubião, hoping that Rubião would marry Doña Tonica, who meanwhile became jealous of Sophia.

Rubião misinterpreted as a love offering a box of strawberries Sophia had sent him. At the Palhas' house in Santa Thereza, he clutched her hand and made his affection for her clear to her. Distressed by Rubião's advances, Sophia suggested to her husband that they end their relationship with Rubião. Having borrowed money from Rubião, however, Palha was reluctant to break with him.

Guilt-ridden about his infatuation with Sophia, Rubião began to worry that the deceased human Quincas Borba had somehow transmigrated into the dog's body. This anxiety was one of the first signs of Rubaio's impending madness.

Rubião became friends with Dr. Camacho, a lawyer and editor of a politically oriented newspaper called *Atalaia.* On his way to meet Dr. Camacho, Rubião rescued a small child, Deolindo, in danger of being run over by a carriage and horses. Rubião then went on to Dr. Camacho's office, where he subscribed generously to the capital fund for *Atalaia.* Dr. Camacho flattered Rubião by publishing an account of Rubião's heroism in saving Deolindo. Although

Rubião was at first modest and dismissive about his heroism, as he read Camacho's account he became increasingly self-important.

Maria Benedicta, Sophia's young cousin, was another potential wife for Rubião, but Rubião was too infatuated with Sophia to be interested in Maria Benedicta. After the incident at Santa Thereza, Rubião appeared to become more cosmopolitan and confident. He spent his inherited money freely, often in support of others in addition to Palha and Dr. Camacho. When his impoverished friend, Freitas, fell ill, Rubião generously gave Freitas' mother a substantial sum of money. Later he paid Freitas' funeral expenses.

Rubião tried to stay away from Sophia, but he found an envelope addressed in Sophia's handwriting to Carlos Maria. When he confronted her with the envelope, she told him to open it. He refused and left. Although Carlos Maria had flirted with Sophia, inside the envelope was only a circular about a charitable committee on which Sophia served.

Palha's business flourished as Rubião's wealth began to dwindle. Rubião became subject to fits of madness, believing that he was Napoleon III of France. When Rubião got into a carriage alone with Sophia, she thought he was still attracted to her. She panicked and ordered him to get out. Thinking he was Napoleon III, Rubião treated Sophia as if she were the emperor's mistress, but eventually he left the carriage.

After Carlos Maria's flirtation with Sophia, Doña Fernanda acted as a matchmaker and brought Carlos Maria and Maria Benedicta together. Although Maria Benedicta was not beautiful, Carlos Maria married her because she adored him. Following their marriage, they traveled to Europe, returning to Rio de Janiero after Maria Benedicta became pregnant.

For a time, Rubião's friends accepted his madness as he continued to provide meals and entertainment for them. Eventually, however, Rubião's house fell into disrepair as his belief in himself as the emperor became constant. Doña Tonica became engaged to a man who died before the wedding. Children on the street, including Deolindo, whose life Rubião had saved, made fun of him as a madman. Prodded by Doña Fernanda, a woman who barely new Rubião, Sophia convinced Palha to set Rubião up in a little rented house on Principe Street. No one visited Rubião in his new humble residence. His former "friends" missed the luxury of Rubião's wealthy surroundings in the house in Botafogo.

Rubião continued to believe he was Napoleon III, but Doña Fernanda thought he could be cured. She managed to get him to enter an asylum. She also rescued Quincas Borba and sent the dog to the sanatorium to be with Rubião. After a short time, appearing to be regaining his sanity, Rubião escaped the asylum and returned to Barbacena with the dog, Quincas Borba, his only friend. There he died. Three days later, Quincas Borba died too.

Critical Evaluation:

Considered by many to be Brazil's greatest novelist, Joaquim Maria Machado de Assis was the son of a mulatto house painter and a Portuguese woman. Little is known of his early life, but, by the time he was seventeen, he was working as an apprentice printer and had already published his first poems. *Philosopher or Dog?*, which serves as a sequel to *Epitaph of a Small Winner* (1880), is one of the masterpieces with which his long career culminated.

Philosopher or Dog? does not pretend to be realistic. Rather, it presents a world rich in metaphor and illusion, a world like the one we live in but also more orderly and more harrowing. One of the novel's themes is summed up in the philosopher Quincas Borba's apparently comical moral to an eccentric story he tells Rubião, "To the victor the potatoes." Though Quincas Borba thinks the story is about the triumph of humanity, it in fact describes the amorality of the human struggle for survival.

The main subject of the novel is self-love, whose antidote is love. Self-deception and self-justification support the self-love of almost all the characters. Palha and Sophia both love themselves and care about Rubião only for what they can get from him. Carlos Maria is a blatant narcissist. Dr. Camacho is a self-involved manipulator who appeals to Rubião's vanity by printing in his newspaper the story of Rubião's rescue of Deolindo. Doña Tonica and Maria Benedicta blindly seek husbands to assure them of their own identities and worth. Only Doña Fernanda and Quincas Borba, the dog, love selflessly and faithfully. Although he begins as a naïve innocent, Rubião gradually succumbs to the conflicting egos of those around him and escapes into a madness in which he imagines himself to be a powerful emperor. Machado de Assis does not offer stereotypical heroes and villains. Rather, he portrays his characters with insight and compassion.

Early in the novel, Rubião withholds the fact that the human Quincas Borba has sent him a letter which suggests his own insanity. Rubião is afraid that, on the basis of the philosopher's madness, Quincas Borba's will might be nullified. Rubião would therefore receive no inheritance. Rubião, however, is not a bad man. The good are beguiled by selfish and vain thoughts, and the selfish and vain are capable of acts of kindness and charity. One may expect Palha to cheat Rubião, but the results both reward and frustrate that expectation. Palha appears to be a conniving spendthrift more interested in Rubião's money than in Rubião himself.

Palha nevertheless proves to be a successful businessman, and, in the end he assumes at least minimal responsibility for Rubião's care by renting the little house for him. He also visits Rubião in the asylum and unhesitatingly gives him a small amount of money, enabling Rubião to escape. It is clear, however, that Palha's generosity is not proportional to the generosity Rubião had shown him. In his portrayal of Palha, Machado de Assis is mocking the illusions that self-interest may create. He is also showing that if self-interest were the only criterion for villainy, all people could be considered villains.

Philosopher or Dog? is carefully built out of metaphorical details that can help one understand the author's intentions. "Palha" means "straw" in Portuguese and "Rubião" refers to an ear of a particular type of red corn. Thus, by his name, Rubião is identified as a product of the country. Palha, the character, represents a sophisticated city man in contrast with the country bumpkin Rubião. He is also a man of straw rather than a man of real substance. "Sophia" is the Greek word for "wisdom." Rubião is infatuated with Sophia, the woman, but cannot possess her. He is also attracted to the idea of wisdom and, even before his madness, cannot possess it either. Sophia herself is only ironically "wise." A self-centered social climber, she exhibits little wisdom.

The stars in the constellation called the Southern Cross also provide Machado de Assis with a metaphor that frames the action of the story. Viewing things from the stars' point of view is a way of gaining perspective on human foibles. The author's understanding of the stars' perspective is also ironic. Early in the novel, the remote stars "seemed to be laughing at the inextricable situation" of Rubião's infatuation with Sophia. The reader also sees their relationship as gently comical. Rubião tells Sophia her eyes are more beautiful than the stars, because the closer one gets to the stars the less beautiful they seem, while the reverse is true of Sophia's eyes. Knowing of Rubião's infatuation, however, one suspects that a careful examination of Sophia's eyes would reveal her shallow vanity.

Rubião also asks Sophia to look at the Southern Cross every night, wherever she is. He too, wherever he is, will stare at the stars, "and their thoughts would join them in intimacy between God and men." The very last words of the novel tell us: "The Southern Cross, which the beautiful Sophia would not gaze upon as Rubião begged her to do, is too high in the heavens to distinguish between man's laughter and tears." The humor in *Philosopher or Dog?* similarly evokes laughter and tears. Though often comical, Rubião is as good a man as exists in the world of the novel. Nevertheless, he suffers a sad fate because of causes and effects beyond his control. God, like the stars, is too far away to see details clearly, and selfish humans are left to make the best they can of their lives. Though undeniably pessimistic, *Philosopher or Dog?* reminds us that selfless love, such as is exhibited by the dog Quincas Borba and the kindly Doña Fernanda, is our only hope of salvaging human decency in an indifferent universe.

Thomas Lisk

Bibliography:
Caldwell, Helen. *Machado de Assis: The Brazilian Master and His Novels.* Berkeley: University of California Press, 1970. Caldwell was one of the first to translate Machado de Assis' work into English. Her chapter on *Philosopher or Dog?* provides a succinct and helpful overview of the major themes and unities of the novel, which she calls "a subtle web of allusion and symbol."

Fitz, Earl. *Machado de Assis.* Boston: Twayne, 1989. A good introduction to Machado de Assis' work. Contains chapters on the major themes, analysis of style and technique in Machado de Assis' work, including *Philosopher or Dog?*, and an annotated bibliography.

Gledson, John. *The Descriptive Realism of Machado de Assis: A Dissenting Interpretation of Dom Casmurro.* Liverpool: Francis Cairns, 1984. One of the few critical studies of Machado de Assis' work in English. Much of the social background Gledson gives for *Dom Casmurro* applies to *Philosopher or Dog?*

Machado, José Bettencourt. *Machado of Brazil: The Life and Times of Machado de Assis, Brazil's Greatest Novelist.* New York: Charles Frank, 1962. An English translation, this Brazilian study of Machado de Assis' life and work is interesting though not always completely reliable.

Nuñes, Maria Luisa. *The Craft of an Absolute Winner: Characterization and Narratology in the Novels of Machado de Assis.* Westport, Conn.: Greenwood Press, 1983. Gives a detailed analysis of Machado de Assis' handling of characterization and narrative technique in his novels, including *Philosopher or Dog?*

PHILOSOPHIAE NATURALIS PRINCIPIA MATHEMATICA

Type of work: Science
Author: Sir Isaac Newton (1642-1727)
First published: 1687 (English translation, 1729 as *Mathematical Principles of Natural Philosophy*)

One of the most influential books in history is Sir Isaac Newton's *Philosophiae Naturalis Principia Mathematica*. Published in 1687, the book immediately led to intellectual controversy among the scientists and philosophers of the day. Men as distinguished as Gottfried Wilhelm Leibniz, Dr. Robert Hooke, and John Flamsteed, the British Astronomer-Royal, felt it necessary to argue with many of the propositions and conclusions Newton advanced. These arguments gave at least as much testimony to the importance of *Philosophiae Naturalis Principia Mathematica* as they undermined its theories. Newton's book remained the principal document in the field of physics for two hundred years.

Newton's work in physics has never been supplanted or debunked; relativity and other discoveries of the twentieth century are more modifications and additions to his scientific discoveries than they are replacements. The philosophical implications of relativity and other discoveries of the twentieth century, however, are radically different from the philosophical implications of Newton's discoveries. During the eighteenth century and after, Newton's masterpiece was also a highly revered work of philosophy. Newton became one of the most honored figures in Western culture, one of the first formulators of scientific method and the man whose work formed the basis for scientific study and application of principles. Physics, as a field of theory and knowledge, did not exist before Newton's work.

Newton's preface to the *Philosophiae Naturalis Principia Mathematica* announces that he was interested in the laws of mathematics as a means of discovering nature, or getting at philosophical truth. He thought that mathematics was not a pure, abstract system, but rather a human and rational means for discovering the principles of the universe, for making a kind of universal order out of the disparate experience of the senses. In fact, he believed in this function of mathematics so strongly that, in the body of the *Philosophiae Naturalis Principia Mathematica*, every experiment or demonstration is concluded with a scholium. Each scholium is a short essay giving the philosophical implications or the speculative use of the mathematical or physical principle just demonstrated. Thus Newton's book is a philosophical as well as a scientific work.

After the preface, Newton supplies a series of definitions for such terms as motion, force, and quantity, terms necessary for even an elementary understanding of his work. These definitions are still standard among students of physics. Newton thereupon states his famous three axioms or laws of motion. These axioms are still relevant in any account of physical forces in the everyday world; relativity comes into play to a significant extent at the level of the atom and at speeds at or near the speed of light. Newton stated these laws as axioms on which his whole account of the universe rested. The first axiom states that a body remains in its existing state of motion or rest unless acted upon by an outside force. This is also known as the law of inertia. The second axiom states that the change in motion of a body is proportional, in precise mathematical terms, to the force applied to it. This is known as the law of acceleration. The third axiom states that for every action there is an equal and opposite reaction. Newton could not prove these axioms universally; rather, these principles are what best explain the various facts and data that people found in physical phenomena around them. The axioms, like the definitions, were necessary beginnings, points that must be accepted in order that all physical data could make rational sense. The axioms have six corollaries, propositions that could be established from the axioms and that could be used in turn to establish other propositions.

In the first book of the *Philosophiae Naturalis Principia Mathematica*, Newton deals with the motion of bodies. In order to simplify and explain his theories, in the first book he confines his observations and proofs to bodies moving in a vacuum. He begins with the more purely mathematical: establishing ratios (demonstrating the logic of the number system), determining the vectors of forces, tracing and proving how bodies move in various arcs, parabolas, and ellipses. For all these geometric demonstrations he gives mathematical proof by inventing and proving his equations and by making frequent reference to his many diagrammatic figures. He also develops and proves equations dealing with the ascent and descent of bodies, again confining his work to bodies in a vacuum. He also devises a mathematical explanation for the oscillations of a pendulum. Finally, at the end of the first book, Newton deals with the attractions of bodies for one another, setting up equations to demonstrate this necessary and universal principle of attraction and repulsion. In addition to defining the terms of physics, the basic laws of physics, and the mathematics to describe the laws of motion, Newton "discovered" gravity.

In the second book, he deals with the motion of bodies in resisting mediums. The nature of resisting mediums, such as water or air, make his proofs become more intricate and complicated. Newton usually attempts to simplify his demonstrations by assuming that the medium is constant. These experiments allow Newton to calculate and, more important, to explain the resistance of substances such as water and air to the motion of bodies passing through them. He gives further demonstrations of motion, analyzing some of the problems dealt with in his first book. He brings up, for example, the oscillations of the pendulum and charts the equations for the motion of a pendulum through air. His consideration of the resistance to bodies allows Newton to present and demonstrate the solution to other problems in the physical universe. In this section, dealing with means of determining the density and compression of fluids, he develops equations to explain the behavior of fluids: the density they offer as resistance and the force they exert when compressed. This work on fluids permitted Newton to establish his equations to determine the velocity of waves.

Newton called his third book the "System of the World," his specific intention in this book being to develop the philosophical principles that he believed followed directly from his mathematical proofs and his experimentation. He begins the book by stating his rules for accurate reasoning, based on his belief that there are no superfluous causes in nature. Each cause that one can talk of sensibly has direct effects, which one is able to observe and subdue to order with mathematical and rational equipment. In other words, Newton thought that the simplicity of the design of the universe is a basic rule; causes are never extraneous. Causes are the basis for observable and frequently calculable phenomena. Another significant rule is Newton's belief that all conclusions are based on induction. One reasons from the observable facts and always needs to refer one's conclusions or theories to observable facts. In this complete devotion to scientific method, there is the necessity of constant application of all of the data to the theory. Newton fully realized, therefore, that theories might well have to be altered to provide explanations for data that challenge the theory. Post-Newtonian physics would not have surprised Newton, for he always acknowledged that scientific theories could be no more than the best conclusions available from the data at hand at the moment the conclusion was made. Thus Newton made his significant contribution to the scientific method, which is a basis for the many discoveries made since his time.

The third book sets forth Newton's mathematical demonstrations of the periodic times and movements of the planets. Again, he derives many new equations to demonstrate, with accuracy, the movements of the planets and to correlate this knowledge with the system of time on earth. He also proves that gravity applies to all bodies and calculates the ratio of gravity. Much of the third section is devoted to lunar motion, establishing equations and calculating, in terms of time, the various changing relationships between the moon and the earth. These matters lead Newton into consideration of the effect of the sun and the moon on the waters of the earth, and he devises means of measuring the tides. He also computes the times and ranges of recurrent comets. Newton thereby provides practical applications for his theories and mathematics.

In a long, final "Scholium" designed to tie the extensive parts of the *Philosophiae Naturalis Principia Mathematica* together, Newton develops the basis for his belief in God. He asserts that such a perfect, and perfectly simple, system must have, as its ultimate or final cause, a perfect, and perfectly simple, Being. This Being must embody all the intelligence, the rationality, the perfection, of the system itself. Newton views God as this ultimate principle, not as a personal God or a larger edition of a human being. Firm in his devotion to his principle, he answered, in later editions of the *Philosophiae Naturalis Principia Mathematica*, charges of atheism brought against his system. This principle, the final cause, is the originator of the whole Newtonian universe, the perfectly rational origin of all the laws, mathematics, and reason that people can use in order to develop and describe the meaningful pattern in his universe. God, the perfect Being, having set this vast plan in constant motion, is constantly at hand to make sure the universe does not run down.

This concept of God became, during the eighteenth century, one of the principal concepts held by intellectuals. The religion of Deism, of viewing God as the perpetrator and final cause of a complete, perfect, mechanistic universe, was derived from Newton's thorough and systematic explanation.

As science and as philosophy, the *Philosophiae Naturalis Principia Mathematica* is one of humanity's great achievements. The book vastly increased the store of human knowledge and derived a sound and rational basis for making conclusions about the physical universe. In addition, Newton, in his *Philosophiae Naturalis Principia Mathematica*, illustrates and defines the method by which people may continue to test his observations, develops a whole new and important area for the human intellect, and establishes a metaphysical system that governed the thought and scientific investigation of the world's leading intellects for more than a century.

Bibliography:

Cohen, I. Bernard. *Introduction to Newton's "Principia."* Cambridge, Mass.: Harvard University Press, 1971. A massive work of scholarship. Presents the background to the publishing of the variorum edition of Newton's influential book. Itemizes revisions and corrections in the various editions and translations. Surveys the early reviews. Comprehensive bibliography.

Fauvel, John, et al., eds. *Let Newton Be!* New York: Oxford University Press, 1988. Twelve articles explicate the modern and historical contexts of Newton's work. John Roche's accessible overview is an excellent starting point for students new to Newton's difficult work.

Gjertsen, Derek. *The Newton Handbook.* London: Routledge & Kegan Paul, 1986. Provides a wealth of information, including a chronology and discussion of the origin and production of the work, and an assessment of the difficulty of the work. The contents and central arguments of the *Philosophiae Naturalis Principia Mathematica* usefully summarized.

Herivel, John. *The Background to Newton's "Principia": A Study of Newton's Dynamical Researches in the Years 1664-84*. Oxford, England: Clarendon Press, 1965. A frequently-cited analysis of the intellectual and scientific basis of *Philosophiae Naturalis Principia Mathematica*.

Stayer, Marcia Sweet. *Newton's Dream*. Kingston, Ontario: McGill-Queens University Press, 1988. Marks the tercentenary of Newton's seminal work. Examines the work's enduring impact. The title essay by physics Nobel laureate Steven Weinberg is especially lucid.

PHILOSOPHICAL INVESTIGATIONS

Type of work: Philosophy
Author: Ludwig Wittgenstein (1889-1951)
First published: 1953

Philosophical Investigations is the work of one of the most creative and controversial philosophers of the twentieth century. In it, Ludwig Wittgenstein presents his ideas concerning the nature of mind and language, often focusing on the relation between language and states of consciousness. The book is composed of numbered sections of various length that were compiled from notes that the author kept but never published. Unlike Wittgenstein's earlier work the *Tractatus Logico-Philosophicus* (1921; English-German bilingual edition, 1922), composed of meticulously numbered aphorisms in the form of a mathematical proof, the *Philosophical Investigations* gives the impression of an informal discussion, covering a wide range of the author's concerns.

Born in Vienna in 1899 to a wealthy Austrian family, Wittgenstein studied engineering but soon shifted his interest to the more theoretical areas of mathematics and philosophy. Wittgenstein studied at Cambridge with philosophers Bertrand Russell and G. E. Moore. At Cambridge, Wittgenstein's unusual capacity for philosophical enquiry first came to the attention of the academic world. It was also at Cambridge that Wittgenstein began to develop the philosophy that was to make him famous in the following years.

Continuing a lifelong interest in language and mind, the *Philosophical Investigations* introduces the concept of the "language-game," which Wittgenstein uses to explain the functioning of language in a variety of contexts. It has been pointed out that while many of the arguments in the *Philosophical Investigations* can be viewed as attempts to correct errors in philosophy as a whole, a number of Wittgenstein's discussions are seemingly attempts at correcting or refuting positions that he set out in the earlier *Tractatus Logico-Philosophicus*. A large portion of the *Philosophical Investigations* is concerned with setting out a philosophy that is at considerable variance with the work he had done in the early years of the twentieth century.

The construction of the *Philosophical Investigations* is such that the reader is called upon to unify the various themes treated by Wittgenstein. While Wittgenstein might have objected that the work was not properly finished, and so cannot be assumed to have the coherence of a well-polished treatise, there are nevertheless a number of issues, in particular those of language-games, and the possibility of private languages, that the philosopher returns to repeatedly. Wittgenstein begins with a passage from Saint Augustine's *Confessions* (397-400) meant to illustrate a common but, according to Wittgenstein, limited view of how language works. Wittgenstein admits that Augustine's conception of how he learned the proper names and significance of objects by ostensive definition (uttering an object's name and pointing to it) has some relevance. Wittgenstein argues that though Augustine describes a system of communication, "not everything that we call language is this system." Language, for Wittgenstein, is much richer and more complex than the simple naming and recognition described by Augustine.

Wittgenstein argues for a much more expansive and flexible view of language as an intricate yet integrated system in which each part acquires meaning by virtue of its relationship to other elements in the system. Language allows words to perform a wide variety of functions, even though, as he points out, they all look alike (they are all words in a language). While the earlier *Tractatus Logico-Philosophicus* is exceptionally difficult to understand because of its compactness and abstract language, Wittgenstein's expression in the *Philosophical Investigations* tends toward concrete examples to illustrate particular points. He frequently draws from mechanics and relies heavily upon metaphor to help the reader grasp his arguments.

In section 11, Wittgenstein suggests that just as tools in a toolbox have many diverse functions, so do words, though people are often at pains to recognize this. In one of Wittgenstein's most powerful metaphors, in section 12 he compares language to looking into the cabin of a locomotive. There, one sees handles all more or less alike. One should not think they are all simply handles (though they are indeed handles); Wittgenstein tells us that each performs a singularly different function such as opening a valve, starting a pump, or braking. Just as turning the wrong handle in the cabin of a locomotive might have dire consequences, so the misuse of language (confusing the uniform appearance of words with their diverse functions), for Wittgenstein, is the main cause of error and nonsense in philosophy.

Wittgenstein calls the many processes and activities of language learning and use language-games. He calls the whole, "consisting of language and the actions into which it is woven" the language game, and it is the operation of this game, its rules as it were, that he wishes to explain. Wittgenstein is not concerned with showing how to play the language-game. Most people are already capable and experienced at playing the language game in a vast array of situations, although, oddly enough, few can do much to explain the rules of the game. Most people, Wittgenstein implies, express themselves without knowing how or why they make themselves understood. In a pivotal passage of the *Philosophical Investigations*, section 23, Wittgenstein insists that the term "language-game" itself is meant "to bring into prominence the fact that the *speaking* of a language is part of an activity, or a form of life." Giving orders, and obeying them, giving a description, play-acting, guessing riddles, telling a joke, solving an arithmetic problem, as well as other activities are all typical of the many ways language can be used.

Just as words, phrases, and sentences are part of the web of language-games, each obtaining meaning through relationship to the other parts of the system, so too, according to Wittgenstein, there is no one aspect common to all that we call language. Instead, all language is made up of language-games that are related to one another in multiple, diverse ways. Sections 65 to 67 deal explicitly with the concept of "family resemblances," a metaphor Wittgenstein uses to illustrate how the many activities of language are linked to one another. Wittgenstein concedes that it might be objected that he has not provided the "essence" of a language-game, and thus the core of language. He argues that upon careful examination, no such essence may be found to exist. There is no atom of language. In section 66, Wittgenstein provides the example of games ("board games, card-games, Olympic Games, and so on"), insisting that people "*look and see,*" not think, but simply look carefully at how such games function. The result is that "we see a complicated network of similarities overlapping and crisscrossing: sometimes overall similarities, sometimes similarities of detail," but no one thing common to all. Such similarities are like the various resemblances between members of a family: build, feature, color of eyes, gait, temperament, and others, that interlace and overlap.

Wittgenstein's aim in the *Philosophical Investigations* is to end, once and for all, the notion that there can be one and only one fundamental aspect of language that governs meaning. It is in this assertion, in particular, that the reader reads the philosopher arguing against the efforts of himself, Russell, and others to locate and describe the basic, or atomic, components of language. The result of misconceptions about the way language functions, according to Wittgenstein, has been a confusing and mostly fruitless approach to solving philosophical problems. Rather than break phrases or sentences down into their "atomic" components in order to see what they mean, people must instead carefully investigate their context. It is through context and relationship that meaning is revealed. The activity of philosophy thus is one of untying knots, dissolving confusion, or as Wittgenstein puts it in section 109, "a battle against the bewitchment of our intelligence by means of language." Thus, philosophy in the *Philosophical Investigations* takes on a therapeutic aspect, as the focus shifts from solving problems to uncovering pieces of nonsense and confusion that have cropped up in human understanding.

Concerned about the misuse of philosophy, Wittgenstein sees the shifting of its aims as clearly beneficial to its conduct. From an admission of human ignorance of the nature of a philosophical problem, Wittgenstein envisions working, through understanding the connections between the parts of language, to lay everything out in front of oneself in a clear fashion. Philosophy, he stresses, "neither explains nor deduces anything," since "everything lies open to view." Philosophy, then, consists in the revealing of the hidden aspects of things whose importance is veiled because of their simplicity and familiarity. One might say, it is like putting on a pair of glasses when one's vision is blurred, or discovering that a hammer one has been searching for has been in one's hand all along.

Wittgenstein's belief in the communal nature of language and experience is seen also in his arguments against the possibility of private language, a language whose words refer exclusively to the private sensations of an individual, and which can only be known by that person. Wittgenstein wishes to refute certain empiricist philosophers who assert that knowledge of language and even of our own experiences depends upon a private inner slate on which words are affixed to particular experiences. Wittgenstein does not deny the possible existence of private experiences, he argues that any reference to them is meaningless since such private experience is unverifiable. Wittgenstein's focus is on correcting errors that have caused philosophy to go awry as well as avoiding a skepticism that would undermine the fundamentally shared experience of language and meaning.

The remainder of section 1 and the entirety of section 2 deal with a number of issues, including Wittgenstein's further thoughts on the nature of language and mind, problems in philosophy, the foundations of mathematics, intentionality, verification, understanding, anticipation, perception, and meaning. In addition, some of Wittgenstein's concerns in the *Philosophical Investigations*, especially those having to do with the connection between perception and knowing, look forward to what would be his final philosophical exercises on the nature of certainty in the year and a half before his death. The *Philosophical Investigations*, as Wittgenstein notes in the preface to his work, is a journey over a wide range of "landscapes," involving many and varied approaches to a number of philosophical concerns. Its modest purpose, he stresses, is only to stimulate others to think, not to present a single or even fully consistent vision of the world. In this, most agree he succeeded.

Howard Giskin

Bibliography:
Bartley, William Warren, III. *Wittgenstein.* 2d rev. ed. La Salle, Ill.: Open Court, 1985. A lively intellectual biography, focusing on some of the more controversial aspects of Wittgenstein's philosophy and life. Chapter 4 deals specifically with the concept of the language-game.
Grayling, A. C. *Wittgenstein.* New York: Oxford University Press, 1988. An introduction to Wittgenstein's philosophy, outlining the main tenets of Wittgenstein's thought. Also discusses the place of Wittgenstein's work in twentieth century analytical philosophy.
Janik, Allan, and Stephen Toulmin. *Wittgenstein's Vienna.* New York: Simon & Schuster, 1973. An account of Habsburg Vienna in the early years of the century. Janik and Toulmin discuss

Wittgenstein the man and his philosophy in the context of other important thinkers and artists of this era.

Kenny, Anthony. *The Legacy of Wittgenstein*. New York: Basil Blackwell, 1984. Ten essays that stress the continuity of Wittgenstein's work. Four essays investigate Wittgenstein's own ideas, while six apply Wittgenstein's thought to the works of other philosophers.

_____. *Wittgenstein*. Cambridge, Mass.: Harvard University Press, 1973. A readable introductory account of the range of Wittgenstein's thought, focusing on his philosophy of language and mind. Chapters 9 and 10 deal with language-games and private languages, respectively.

PHILOSOPHY OF ART

Type of work: Aesthetics
Author: Hippolyte-Adolphe Taine (1828-1893)
First published: Philosophie de l'art: Leçons professées à l'École des Beaux-Arts, 1865
  (English translation, 1865)

Hippolyte Taine, author of *The History of English Literature* (1863-1869) and of *The Origins of Contemporary France* (1875-1894), combined a historical interest in his subjects with a philosophical one. He was able to do this because he regarded history and philosophy as sciences; he believed that a study of the nature of art and of art production could proceed, in the manner of any scientific study, by attention to the observable facts and by the framing of inductive generalizations. Consequently his *Philosophy of Art* is to some extent a description of some predominant art periods and to some extent an attempt to generalize philosophically from the data of his historical inquiries. Other Taine studies were of the art of Greece, The Netherlands, and Italy.

Taine's working assumption is that no work of art is isolated and that the only way to understand a particular work of art or the nature of art in general is by attending to the conditions out of which works of art come. According to this theory the character of a work of art is determined by the artist, but that artist is shaped by a number of inescapable cultural influences. Taine believed that works of art present, in perceptible form, the essential character of the time and place in which the artist works. In his words, "The work of art is determined by an aggregate which is the general state of the mind and surrounding manners." Taine points out that the nude statues of Greek art reflect the Grecian preoccupation with war and athletics and with the development of the healthy human animal; that the art of the Middle Ages reflects the moral crisis resulting from feudal oppression; that the art of the seventeenth century reflects the values of courtly life; and that the art of industrial democracy expresses the restless aspirations of human beings in an age of science.

The work of art itself is conditioned by the wholes of which it is a part and a product. In the first place, according to Taine, the work of art exhibits the artist's style, that prevailing mode of aesthetic treatment that runs through all the works of an artist, giving them an underlying resemblance to one another. Second, the work of art reflects the prevailing manner of the school of artists to which the individual artist belongs. Finally, it expresses the times and the social milieu of taste, conviction, and manners within which the artist is working and by which he must be affected. Taine summarized his belief when he wrote that "in order to comprehend a work of art, an artist or a group of artists, we must clearly comprehend the general social and intellectual condition of the times to which they belong."

In addition to the influence of taste and style, Taine also believed in considering "moral temperature," the spiritual milieu, whether mystic or pagan or something foreign to both, that infects the artist and, consequently, his work. The philosophy of art, as Taine understood it, is the attempt to study the art of various countries and ages in order to discover the conditions under which the art of a particular place and time was created, and, finally, the conditions in general for any art whatsoever. A report of those general conditions would be a philosophy of art.

In examining individual works of art, the first step in aesthetics, Taine found that imitation was an important feature in most of them, particularly in works of poetry, sculpture, and painting. Taine was interested in arriving by inductive means at a theory of the nature of art. He speculated whether exact imitation was perhaps the ultimate goal of art, but he concluded that it is not because exact imitation does not produce the finest works of art. Photography, for example, is useful as a means of making accurate reproductions of scenes, but he did not believe that it can be ranked with such fine arts as painting and sculpture. Another reason for concluding that works of art are not essentially concerned with exact imitation is that many works of art are intentionally inexact.

There is a kind of imitation, however, that is essential to art, according to Taine, and that is the imitation of what he calls "the relationships and mutual dependence of parts." Just as a painter, even when reproducing a human figure, does not represent every feature of the body, its exact size, color, and weight, but rather what might be called the logic of the body, so artists in general, in creating works of art, do not aim at deception through exact representation but, rather, at presenting the essential character of an object. Because the essential character of an object is simply the predominant feature of the object as affected by the place and time of its existence, the artist's objective, according to Taine's analysis, is to put that principal feature of the object into perceptible form. In painting a lion, for example, the important thing is to represent him as carnivorous; in painting the Low Countries the artist must imitate its alluvial character.

Taine was aware that the artist is often doing something quite different from making the dominant feature of nature the predominant feature of the work of art, but he believed that all art can be explained as the imitation of essential quality. What the artist presents may be not the essential character of some physical scene or object; it may be the prevailing temper of his times. This view is made clear in part 2 of *The Philosophy of Art*, in which Taine considers artistic production. The first part, on the nature of art, concludes with the summary statement that "The end of a work of art is to manifest some essential or salient character, consequently some important idea, clearer and more completely than is attainable from real objects. Art accomplishes this end by employing a group of connected parts, the relationships of which it systematically modifies."

The law of art production—that a work of art is determined by the general state of mind and surrounding circumstances—Taine defends in two ways. He refers to experience to argue that the law of production applies to all works of art; he then analyzes the effects of "a general state of mind and surrounding circumstances" to claim that the law reveals a necessary connection.

As an example, Taine considers the effect of melancholy as a state of mind, together with the circumstances that made melancholy characteristic of an age. He argues that in a melancholy age the artist is inevitably melancholy. As a result, the artist portrays all objects as being predominantly melancholy, painting "things in much darker colors." During a renaissance, when there is "a general condition of cheerfulness," the works of art will express a joyful condition. Whatever the combination of moods in an age, the art of that age will reflect the combination. It could not be otherwise, Taine argues, because artists cannot isolate themselves from their age. As historical examples, he refers to the Greek period, the feudal age, the seventeenth century, and the nineteenth century.

A "general situation" resulting from a condition of wealth or poverty, or of servitude or liberty, or from a prevailing religious faith, or from some other feature of the society, has an effect on individual artists, affecting their aptitudes and emotions.

In Greece we see physical perfection and a balance of faculties which no manual or cerebral excess of life deranges; in the Middle Ages, the intemperance of overexcited imaginations and the delicacy of feminine sensibility; in the seventeenth century, the polish and good breeding of society and the dignity of aristocratic salons; and in modern times, the grandeur of unchained ambitions and the morbidity of unsatisfied yearnings.

According to Taine, the four terms of a causal series by reference to which the production of art can be explained are the general situation, the tendencies and special faculties provoked by that situation, the individual who represents and embodies the tendencies and faculties, and the material—such as sounds, forms, colors, or language—by the use of which the character is given sensuous form. Taine argues that artists imitate the prevailing quality of their age because they cannot escape being a part of his age, because nothing else would be accepted, and because they work for acceptance and applause.

Taine's *Philosophy of Art* is a clear and sensible defense of the idea that art reflects the spirit of the times. Opposing his position are those theories that emphasize the role of the extraordinary individual, those eccentrics who by their genius transcend the perspectives and sentiments of their age. The attempt to reconcile these two basic philosophical perspectives only hides the truth that resides in each. The moral seems to be to read Taine for an appreciation of the influence of the social milieu, and someone else, say Friedrich Nietzsche, for an aesthetics in which the artist is shown as an individual rebel who falsifies nature.

Bibliography:

Eustis, Alvin. *Hippolyte Taine and the Classical Genius.* Berkeley: University of California Press, 1951. Focuses on Taine's assessment of classical society and its artists, noting the importance the critic places on social conditions and on the production of high-quality art.

Goetz, Thomas H. *Taine and the Fine Arts.* Madrid: Playor, 1973. Extensive analysis of Taine's writings on the fine arts, focusing particularly on those about sculpture and painting. One chapter is devoted to explicating the critic's theory of the fine arts.

Gullace, Giovanni. "The Concept of Art in Taine and Brunetière." In *Taine and Brunetière on Criticism.* Lawrence, Kans.: Coronado Press, 1982. Excellent analysis of Taine's ideas about art in his *Philosophy of Art*; extracts salient comments from the work and provides a summary of the critic's principal beliefs about the objective qualities of all great art.

Kahn, S. J. *Science and Aesthetic Judgment: A Study in Taine's Critical Method.* London: Methuen, 1953. Extended scholarly examination of Taine's writings on art, exploring ways he is able to balance the need for objective analysis with the more elusive art of judgment, especially value judgment. Emphasizes the importance of the historical dimensions of art criticism.

Weinstein, Leo. *Hippolyte Taine.* New York: Twayne, 1972. General study of the writer. Discusses Taine's analysis of the nature of art and the conditions necessary for its production. Examines his judgments on the art of Europe, his notion of the ideal, and the emphasis he places on personal and national "character" in creating great art.

PHINEAS FINN
The Irish Member

Type of work: Novel
Author: Anthony Trollope (1815-1882)
Type of plot: Political realism
Time of plot: Mid-nineteenth century
Locale: British Isles
First published: serial, 1867-1869; book, 1869

Principal characters:
PHINEAS FINN, a personable young Irishman
LORD BRENTFORD, an important Whig
LORD CHILTERN, his profligate son
LADY LAURA STANDISH, Brentford's beautiful daughter
MR. KENNEDY, a very wealthy member of Parliament
VIOLET EFFINGHAM, a charming girl with a large fortune
MADAME MARIE MAX GOESLER, a pretty, wealthy young widow
MARY FLOOD JONES, a pretty young Irish woman

The Story:

Young Phineas Finn, just admitted to the bar, was tempted to postpone his career as a barrister by an offer to run for election as a member of Parliament from the Irish borough of Loughshane. Phineas' father, a hardworking Irish doctor, reluctantly agreed to support Phineas, as a member of Parliament received no salary and could only hope that once his party was in power he would be rewarded with a lucrative office.

Phineas was elected. Among those to whom he said good-bye before leaving for London was pretty Mary Flood Jones, a girl devoted to Phineas but no richer than he. Phineas' well-wishers in London included Lady Laura Standish, the daughter of Lord Brentford, an influential Whig. Phineas began to fall in love with Laura and saw a rival in the aloof and unprepossessing but rich Mr. Kennedy, who was also a Whig and a member of Parliament. Laura tried to encourage a friendship between Phineas and her brother, Lord Chiltern, a violent young man who had quarreled with their father. Lord Brentford would have reconciled with his son if Chiltern were to marry rich, lovely, and witty Violet Effingham, a friend from childhood. Chiltern loved her deeply and had proposed repeatedly, but Violet was levelheaded and, although she was fond of Chiltern, did not intend to ruin herself deliberately.

At Laura's recommendation, Phineas accepted an invitation to visit Loughlinter, the Kennedy estate in Scotland. Phineas made friends there with several Whig leaders and became the special disciple of Mr. Monk, a cabinet minister with independent views. Phineas proposed to Laura, who told him she was engaged to marry Kennedy. She explained that against her father's wishes she had exhausted her personal fortune by paying her brother's debts; she was consequently obliged to marry someone with money.

Last-minute fright prevented Phineas from carrying out his elaborate plans for his first speech in Parliament. Laura had been married for several months when she began to find life with her strict, demanding husband oppressive. Chiltern, having once again unsuccessfully proposed to Violet, invited Phineas to hunt with him. After suffering a hunting injury, Chiltern was cared for by Phineas, and they became intimate friends. Although he had no hopes for being successful with Violet, the young nobleman confided that he would fight any other aspirant for her hand.

In the voting on the Reform Bill, the question of the ballot divided Parliament, and the government was dissolved. The capriciousness of Lord Tulla, who had insured Phineas' original success, prevented his running again for Loughshane. Lord Brentford, however, who had the English borough of Loughton "in his pocket," offered it to Phineas, who was easily elected.

Phineas, who had rescued Kennedy from two attackers late one night, visited at Loughlinter again. Gradually, he had transferred his affections from Laura to Violet, but his plan to confide in Laura was prevented by her confession to him that life with her husband had grown intolerable. Phineas, despairing of an opportunity to see Violet, found his excuse in a letter from Chiltern that contained a conciliatory message for his father. Phineas took the letter to Lord Brentford, at whose house Violet was staying. Lord Brentford agreed to forgive his son if Chiltern resumed his courtship of Violet. Phineas sent this message to Chiltern; to avoid duplicity, he added that he himself hoped to win Violet's hand. He later found the opportunity to propose to Violet. Although she rejected him, he felt that her negative answer was not conclusive.

Because Phineas refused to give up his courtship of Violet, Chiltern challenged him to a duel. They fought secretly in Belgium, but the news leaked out, partly because of Phineas' injury; he had been wounded before he could fire. At last, Phineas confided in Laura, who was angry—as much because of her own affection for him as because of her brother's claims on Violet.

Phineas met the beautiful and charming widow Madame Goesler, who became interested in him. Phineas had been left a legacy of three thousand pounds and soon received an even more substantial income upon being appointed to an office that paid one thousand pounds annually. Laura felt that she had wronged Phineas and took it upon herself to urge his suit with Violet. Violet, however, knew that Phineas had originally courted Laura, and she disliked being in second place. She refused when Phineas proposed to her again.

The English Reform Bill was passed, which redistributed parliamentary representation to conform to actual population. The borough of Loughton was among those voted out of existence. Because Phineas had proven an able and loyal Whig, he had been promoted to a higher office that paid two thousand pounds a year. Having no borough to run for, he despaired of keeping the office after the next election. Loughshane, however, was made available again by the caprice of Lord Tulla, and Phineas was assured success.

Chiltern proposed to Violet once more and was finally accepted, and he and his father were at last reconciled. Miserable over Violet's engagement, Phineas confided in Madame Goesler. He also told Laura of his heartbreak, but she chided him, saying he would soon forget Violet just as he had forgotten her.

Lord Brentford finally learned of the duel between his son and Phineas, whom he accused of treachery. Phineas discovered the real cause of Lord Brentford's anger: Chiltern and Violet, quarreling over Chiltern's unwillingness to work, had broken their engagement.

Madame Goesler had made a conquest of the elderly and all-respected Duke of Omnium. Although tempted to accept, she finally refused his proposal of marriage. Not the least of her motives was her attachment to Phineas. When her husband accused her of having Phineas as a lover, Laura decided to leave her husband. Phineas again asked Violet to marry him. She answered that, although she and Chiltern had quarreled, she could not love anyone else.

Phineas caused a great sensation at home by bringing Mr. Monk to Ireland with him. Caught up with Mr. Monk in political fervor, Phineas pledged himself to support Irish tenant rights in Parliament. Mr. Monk had warned him against such promises; he predicted that Phineas would be forced to resign his office if he voted in opposition to his party. Without means of support, he then would have to give up his promising career. Phineas confided in Mary Flood Jones about this danger and about his unsuccessful love for Violet. Phineas and Mary became engaged.

After Laura had taken up residence with her father, Kennedy sought legal aid to force her to return to him. To escape persecution, she decided to live abroad. She confessed to Phineas that she had always loved him and worked for him, although she had been heartbroken when he told her of his love for Violet. Laura urged him to assure his career by marrying Madame Goesler for her money. Phineas did not mention his engagement to Mary. When Madame Goesler offered her hand and money to Phineas, he could only refuse. His first feeling was one of bitter disappointment.

Chiltern and Violet were reconciled. The Irish Reform Bill was passed, abolishing Phineas' borough of Loughshane. Phineas' career in Parliament was over. The intervention of governmental friends, however, gave Phineas a permanent appointment: a poor-law inspector in Ireland. It paid a yearly salary of a thousand pounds, enabling Phineas and Mary to plan an immediate wedding.

Critical Evaluation:

Anthony Trollope's *Phineas Finn*, an example of literature of political reform, has been grouped with George Eliot's *Felix Holt* (1866), Walter Bagehot's *The English Constitution* (1867), Thomas Carlyle's *Shooting Niagara* (1867), and Matthew Arnold's *Culture and Anarchy* (1869). A portrait of the British parliament in the early nineteenth century, *Phineas Finn* has a straightforward plot, in which the protagonist during his six years in Parliament eventually acquires the wisdom and courage to act upon his convictions. His own character and the particular conflict contribute to his development, in the course of which Trollope is able to make the point that the government is far more dedicated to status quo than to significant reform.

By novel's end, the change Phineas has undergone is revealed when he supports legislation proposed by his friend Joshua Monk that will help his native Ireland but simultaneously threatens the political establishment. By doing so, Finn learns that those who act on their convictions and attempt to initiate social change endanger their political careers. Thus, after voting for Monk's Irish bill, which grants tenants in Ireland specific rights, Phineas resigns from office.

Finn's acquisition of wisdom may be seen as a partial response to those among his acquaintances who seem to hold few personal political beliefs. Barrington Earle, for instance, is opposed to change and despises conviction. It is Earle who encourages Phineas to enter politics in the first place, but when Phineas reveals that he plans to use his vote to serve Ireland and not necessarily the Liberal party, Earle feels only disgust for him, for he realizes that Finn cannot be immediately useful to him. Earle's sentiments are echoed by Finn's countryman and fellow politician Lawrence Fitzgibbon: "I never knew a government yet that wanted to do anything." For doing nothing, Fitzgibbon is eventually awarded with a secretaryship.

The character who most influences Phineas is Joshua Monk, a member of the Cabinet. Monk maintains that individuals should enter politics only as a means of implementing personal conviction. Toward the end of the novel, Monk tells Finn, whose job as an undersecretary has shifted his attention away from Ireland toward North America, that "most probably you know nothing of the modes of thought of the man who lives next door to you." Monk criticizes his peers for their insensitivity to their constituents. He himself, before proposing before the British Parliament his Irish reform legislation, accompanies Finn to Ireland and acquaints himself with the conditions of that country.

Other minor characters also serve as Phineas' mentors. Phineas' London landlord Jacob Bunce reminds Finn that Parliament has never yet improved the lot of the common people, and this notion justifies Bunce's taking his views to the streets and finding himself arrested and jailed for standing too near Minister Turnbull's carriage. Mr. Low, Phineas' legal mentor, believes that Finn entered politics for the wrong reasons and that he should have first established himself in the legal profession, as Low had done before he ran for office. According to Low, Finn does not have a sufficient grasp of the laws of the land to serve his country. Somewhat like Monk, Mr. Low asserts that Phineas is out of touch with elements vital to true political effectiveness. Indeed, Trollope's characterization of Finn as a pleasant young man who knows how to make himself useful in Parliament and who seeks reelection twice because he loves the social life of a politician confirms Mr. Low's observations.

The wisdom that Phineas gradually acquires is also born out of his own conflict between expediency and conscience, between doing what is useful for his party and acting upon what is right. Trollope uses several other characters to illustrate the poles of Phineas' conflict. Lawrence Fitzgibbon and Barrington Earle clearly stand in opposition to Joshua Monk, who, in contrast to Earle and Fitzgibbon, is a man of conviction. The conflict is also represented by Sir Robert Kennedy and Lord Chiltern. Kennedy, who is married to Laura Standish, is a middle-aged member of Parliament whose reticence reveals not the wisdom acquired through years of political involvement but the total absence of any personal convictions that would endanger his career or party. By contrast, Laura's brother, Lord Chiltern, a social outcast, is ruled almost entirely by passion and conviction. A "wild" man who has reputedly killed a man with his bare hands, Chiltern refuses to obey his father on almost every issue. He stays out of politics and refuses to give up the blood sports that associate him with the old English nobility, which Trollope seems to consider more representative of true masculinity than the politicians with whom Phineas associates. Phineas develops a lasting contempt for Robert Kennedy, but he respects and befriends Lord Chiltern. This friendship is significant in the development of Phineas' character, especially considering that Phineas and Chiltern at one point duel over Violet Effingham, but Trollope implies that this act demonstrates conviction, courage, and manhood in both of them.

Trollope also suggests the intensity of Phineas' conflict through his female characters. Laura Standish, for example, makes a marriage of convenience to Robert Kennedy, who proves to be a tyrant and whom she eventually leaves. Violet Effingham, on the other hand, follows her heart in finally agreeing to marry Lord Chiltern, whom she has loved since childhood. Drawn to the dangerous though masculine side of Chiltern, she refuses a marriage of convenience and seems headed toward a happy life with him. Trollope also contrasts Madame Max Goesler and Mary Flood. Marriage to Madame Max, as she is called, would ensure Phineas access to the most prestigious political circles in London. Eventually, however, Finn follows his heart, rejects Madame Max, and marries his first love, Mary Flood, the most sincere and steadfast female of the novel.

Phineas Finn is a satirical, somewhat cynical novel about British politics. In his analysis, Trollope shows that those who wish to maintain their political office must vote with their party, thus often presumably against the heart or conviction. Those who wish to advance socially and politically had best choose a marriage of convenience. Finally, those who wish to maintain the unsullied reputation necessary for staying in office might be wise to follow in Robert Kennedy's footsteps by holding few convictions and saying nothing.

"Critical Evaluation" by Richard Logsdon

Bibliography:

Halperin, John. *Trollope and Politics: A Study of the Pallisers and Others*. London: Macmillan, 1977. Views Trollope's political novels as a direct reflection of political activities of the day.

McMaster, Juliet. *Trollope's Palliser Novels: Theme and Pattern*. London: Macmillan, 1978. A consideration of Trollope's political novels from an aesthetic, nonpolitical point of view.

Pollard, Arthur. *Trollope's Political Novels*. Hull, England: University of Hull, 1968. Argues that the effectiveness of Trollope's political novels derives from the author's own engagement in politics.

Sadleir, Michael. *Trollope: A Commentary*. 3d ed. London: Oxford University Press, 1961. A helpful biography on Trollope that focuses on the events of the author's life and political career as reflected in his novels.

Trollope, Anthony. *Phineas Finn: The Irish Member*. Edited with an introduction by Jacques Berthoud. New York: Oxford University Press, 1982. Includes a good introduction to *Phineas Finn*, which elucidates the novel's political and cultural background.

PHINEAS REDUX

Type of work: Novel
Author: Anthony Trollope (1815-1882)
Type of plot: Political
Time of plot: Mid-nineteenth century
Locale: England
First published: serial, 1873-1874; book, 1874

Principal characters:
PHINEAS FINN, an Irish politician and a widower
MADAME MARIE MAX GOESLER, a wealthy and pretty widow
LADY LAURA KENNEDY, Phineas' beloved
MR. KENNEDY, her estranged husband
LORD CHILTERN, Laura's brother
VIOLET CHILTERN, his wife
MR. BONTEEN, a conniving politician

The Story:

The conservatives had been in control of the government for more than a year. In planning their return to power, the liberals wanted to get every good man they could muster. Thirty years of age, Phineas Finn had retired from politics two years earlier to marry his childhood sweetheart and settle down in a modest but permanent position in Ireland. He was invited back to resume his political career. His wife had died in the interval, and he had saved enough to permit him to live two or three years without being given an office. The urging of his friends seemed to imply that he would not have to wait long for an office, so he agreed to give up his security for the more exciting life of a member of Parliament. He was to run for the borough of Tankerville, which was held by a corrupt conservative named Browborough.

While awaiting the election, Phineas visited Chiltern and Violet, who were happily married. Chiltern had at last found the occupation perfectly suited to his temperament and enthusiasm for hunting—Master of the Brake Hounds. Also visiting the Chilterns were Adelaid Palliser and Mr. Maule, a gloomy and idle but rather pleasing young man, who was devoted to and loved by Adelaid.

In the Tankerville election, Phineas campaigned for separation of church and state. Although Browborough won by seven votes, the seat was to be contested on evidence that Browborough had bought votes. In a desperate effort to keep his party in power, the conservative leader also advocated separation of church and state.

On his way to visit Lady Laura Kennedy and her father in Dresden, Phineas was summoned by her estranged husband to his estate. Kennedy's mind had become deranged; his one purpose in life was to get his wife back. He forbade Phineas to visit her and accused him of adultery. Although he knew himself to be guiltless, Phineas could not reason with Kennedy. Later, in Dresden, Laura confided that her love for Phineas had been the real reason behind the failure of her marriage; Phineas, however, had long felt nothing but friendship for Laura.

On his next visit to the Chilterns, Phineas saw Madame Goesler. The first meeting was awkward because of their earlier relationship, but soon they were old friends again. She told Phineas that she had been acting as unofficial companion and nurse to the old Duke of Omnium, now on his deathbed. Lady Glencora, the duke's niece, had become her intimate friend.

Adelaid's good breeding attracted the uncouth squire and fox hunter Spooner. Unaware of the subtleties of social behavior, Spooner felt himself to be more eligible than Maule, whose income was small. Spooner's proposal of marriage was refused with horror, and Maule's proposal was accepted. Maule and Adelaid felt that they could marry if his father would let them live in the abandoned Maule Abbey. Mr. Maule, Sr., however, was opposed to his son's marriage to a fortuneless woman. Angry at the implied reminder that the property would be his son's after his death, he refused the request.

Quintus Slide, representative of all that is bad in journalism, gave Phineas a letter written to his newspaper by Kennedy. The letter was a madman's accusation, implying that Phineas and Laura were guilty of adultery. Slide intended to print the letter and enjoyed the feeling of power its possession gave him; believing that he was interested only in upholding the institution of marriage, he offered to give Phineas a day to persuade Laura to return to Kennedy. Instead, Phineas went to Kennedy's hotel to urge him to retract the letter. Kennedy shot at Phineas but missed. Despite efforts to keep the affair hushed up, the news leaked out later. When Phineas obtained an injunction against Slide that forbade him to print the letter, the journalist became enraged and wrote an editorial in which he referred to the letter, although he could not quote it. He made the story seem even worse than it was, and the whole affair was damaging to Phineas' career.

Long disliked by and jealous of Phineas, Mr. Bonteen had achieved advancement through party loyalty. After the death of the old Duke of Omnium, the new duke had given up his former office of chancellor of the exchequer, a post that Bonteen was now expected to fill as soon as the liberals returned to power. Bonteen was using his influence against Phineas, who despaired of getting an office, so Madame Goesler and her friend Lady Glencora, now Duchess of Omnium, resolved on a counterintrigue. Although the duchess was able to prevent Bonteen from acquiring the position of chancellor, she was unable to secure an office for Phineas.

Normally, the liberal party supported separation of church and state, but they decided officially to oppose it, knowing that the conservatives used the issue only to keep control of the government. Although with some misgivings at first, Phineas went along with his party. The conservatives were defeated.

Bonteen and his wife had befriended a woman victimized by a fortune-hunter turned preacher and named, variously, Emilius or Mealyus. Mealyus hoped to get half of his wife's fortune as a settlement, but Bonteen was working to prove a rumor that Mealyus was a bigamist. One night, after Phineas had been publicly insulted by Bonteen in their club, Bonteen was murdered. Phineas and Mealyus were both arrested, but the latter was released when he proved he could not have left his rooming house that night. Circumstances looked dark for Phineas. Laura, Madame Goesler, the Duchess of Omnium, Phineas' landlady, and the Chilterns were the only ones convinced of his innocence.

Kennedy died and left everything to Laura; she dreamed that she might be happy with Phineas at last, although she sensed at the same time that her hope was impossible. On the trail of evidence to help Phineas by destroying Mealyus' alibi, Madame Goesler went to Prague; she suspected Mealyus of having another rooming house key made there during a recent trip. Then Mealyus' first wife was discovered, and he was arrested for bigamy. At Phineas' trial, the circumstantial evidence against him broke down when Madame Goesler wired from Prague that she had found proof of Mealyus' duplicate key. Laura realized that Madame Goesler had saved Phineas and hated her as a rival.

The late Duke of Omnium had willed a handsome fortune to Madame Goesler. She did not need the money and was afraid of suspicion that she had been the duke's mistress, so she refused to accept it. The duchess took up the cause of Maule and Adelaid; they were too poor to marry, and it was out of the question to expect Maule to work. Adelaid had been a niece of the old duke, and the duchess persuaded Madame Goesler to let Adelaid have the fortune she herself would not accept. Adelaid and Maule were able to marry, and Mr. Maule, Sr., was so pleased with her fortune that he turned Maule Abbey over to them after all. Spooner, who had clung to his hope of marrying Adelaid, was so miserable that he gave up fox hunting for a time. Quintus Slide, who had consistently denounced Phineas and Laura in his newspaper, was sued for libel by Chiltern. Chiltern won the suit, and Slide was forced to leave the paper.

Phineas was the hero of the day—overwhelmingly reelected in Tankerville, sought by the ladies, acclaimed everywhere—but the knowledge that he had been suspected by friends as well as by strangers made him miserable and bitter. Gradually, as his spirits improved, he was able to meet people and to resume his seat in the House. He also was offered the same office he had filled so well in his earlier parliamentary career. Although he was almost at the end of his funds and needed the position, the knowledge that the offer was made simply because he had not committed murder prompted him to refuse.

While visiting Laura at her request, he felt it only honorable to tell her that he planned to propose to Madame Goesler. At first, Laura was violent in her denunciation of Madame Goesler, but she was at last calmed. Hers was the unhappiness of knowing that she had brought all of her misery on herself by marrying one man while loving another. Now deeply in love with Madame Goesler, Phineas proposed marriage and was joyfully accepted. No longer a poor man, Phineas would be able to continue his career in Parliament without being the slave of his party.

Critical Evaluation:

The fourth novel of Anthony Trollope's famous Palliser series, *Phineas Redux* extends the story of one of the author's favorite heroes while offering a sobering portrait of political life in the nineteenth century. Inspired in part by Trollope's own unsuccessful bid for political office, the novel exposes the backroom dealings that brought men to power and led to alliances more often aimed at keeping incumbents in office than doing what was right for the country.

At the center of the novel is the young Irish politician whose name graces two titles in the Palliser series. In the first, *Phineas Finn* (1869), the hero is introduced to political life when he becomes the darling of high-ranking members of the Liberal party, including one destined to be prime minister, Plantagenet Palliser. At the end of that novel, Phineas leaves London for his homeland to marry his childhood sweetheart. When the action of *Phineas Redux* opens, he is back in London, a widower and political aspirant once more. Through him, Trollope gives readers a look at the machinations involved in bringing political issues before Parliament and the British people; he also gives a realistic look at campaigning techniques and the efforts of the press to influence political decisions.

Throughout the novel, the author's focus is on character as well as action. In the course of running for a seat in Parliament, debating key issues such as church disestablishment, and defending himself against a murder charge, Phineas Finn emerges as a man of high moral fiber, willing to stand up for unpopular ideas even at the expense of losing favor with his own party. Trollope also portrays the human side of his hero, as he agonizes over his feelings for Laura Kennedy, once his beloved but now married to a man whose extreme jealousy leads to near catastrophe for the hero. Phineas engages in social situations with a number of other figures, notably Lady Glencora Palliser, Plantagenet's wife; Madame Marie Max Goesler, a rich widow who assists in a number of ways to further his career; and the Chilterns, a family whose domestic bliss offers readers a portrait of the idyllic life prized by Trollope and many of his contemporaries.

A number of memorable villains also populate the novel, several of whom rise above the stereotypes normally associated with the popular fiction of the period. Phineas' political nemesis, Mr. Bonteen, is filled with a hatred brought on by the snubs and jostlings that occur in the world of elective and appointive officeholding; after readers have come to despise him, however, he is murdered, and Phineas accused of the crime. The twist permits Trollope to humanize both villain and hero, as readers' sympathies go out to the man slain unjustly and to the accused, who cannot be guilty. Similarly, Trollope manages to evoke both contempt and pity for Kennedy. A recluse whose dabblings into politics have brought him nothing but trouble, Kennedy becomes fixated on his hatred for Phineas; Trollope is careful to paint him as a character whose actions stem from a dementia that makes him deserving of treatment rather than incarceration.

The journalist Quintus Slide does not fare so well, however; through him, Trollope strikes out at the muckraking press, that insidious creation of the nineteenth century that preyed on people like Phineas. Slide makes his living by appealing to the prurient interests of readers more interested in salacious gossip than the truth. His pursuit of the lurid details of Phineas' relationship to Laura Kennedy—many of them invented—is the spur for much of the hero's misfortune, and Trollope offers no excuse to compensate for Slide's despicable behavior.

Perhaps the greatest triumph in the novel, however, is Trollope's depiction of his female characters. Three women dominate the novel: Laura Kennedy, Lady Glencora Palliser, and Madame Goesler. Each plays a significant role in Phineas' growth toward mature self-awareness. Laura's sad tale, a life married to the wrong man, is presented sensitively, without undue sentiment; readers feel genuine sympathy for her when Phineas finally recognizes that he cannot rekindle his old passion after Kennedy is out of the way. Although he has no amorous interest in Lady Glencora, nor she in him, their genuine friendship is the source of her patronage of him; her insistent pursuit of appointments for Phineas permits him to rise—and fall—in the political arena, getting a taste of the sordidness of the profession as well as its rewards. Similarly, the patronage of Madame Goesler plays a key role in the hero's rise to prominence in his party; however, the two become more than friends, and in Madame Goesler, Phineas finds a fit partner for life. Through Phineas' relationships with these women, Trollope demonstrates his strong belief in the role of women as men's equals in society. Whereas Laura Kennedy is treated as an object to be possessed by her husband, both Lady Glencora and Madame Goesler are seen as partners with the men they love, helping them achieve greatness in their fields without becoming mere helpmates in the more traditional sense. It is not surprising that Trollope's novels have become a favorite among twentieth century feminist critics for studying the question of male-female relationships in the nineteenth century.

Establishing the place of *Phineas Redux* in the Trollope canon is not easy. Just as he uses the Barsetshire series of novels to depict country life with all its joys and all its faults, Trollope intends *Phineas Redux* and the other novels in the Palliser series as a means of exploring London life and national politics. Each of the novels in the series contributes in some way to filling in that portrait. Although *Phineas Redux* has cut connections to other novels in the series, and to others by Trollope, it can stand alone as a complex, sensitive, and, at times, chilling portrait of Victorian society.

"Critical Evaluation" by Laurence W. Mazzeno

Bibliography:
Hall, N. John. *Trollope: A Biography*. Oxford, England: Clarendon Press, 1991. The standard

critical biography of the novelist. Reviews the publication history of *Phineas Redux* and analyzes its political background; points out ways in which Trollope allows his characters to grow as the story progresses.

Morse, Deborah Denenholz. *Women in Trollope's Palliser Novels*. Ann Arbor: UMI Research Press, 1987. Examines Trollope's ambivalent attitude toward women in the Palliser series. A chapter on *Phineas Finn* and *Phineas Redux* analyzes portraits of the three Englishwomen whom Phineas loves, all of whom are strong and articulate.

Pollard, Arthur. *Trollope's Political Novels*. Hull, England: University of Hull, 1968. Analyzes the influence of Trollope's life on the Palliser novels, in which he dramatizes political issues in Great Britain. Describes ways in which *Phineas Redux* reveals the novelist's disillusionment with the political system of his country.

Super, R. H. *The Chronicler of Barsetshire: A Life of Anthony Trollope*. Ann Arbor: University of Michigan Press, 1988. Critical biography by a distinguished scholar; praises *Phineas Redux* as being the novel most "firmly embedded in contemporary British politics" of all those Trollope wrote. Notes the confusion caused by the author's introduction of the murder and trial, which distract readers from political issues.

Walton, Priscilla L. *Patriarchal Desire and Victorian Discourse: A Lacanian Reading of Anthony Trollope's Palliser Novels*. Toronto: University of Toronto Press, 1995. Although somewhat specialized in its approach, a chapter on *Phineas Redux* illuminates Trollope's attitudes toward feminist issues.

THE PHOENICIAN WOMEN

Type of work: Drama
Author: Euripides (c. 485-406 B.C.E.)
Type of plot: Tragedy
Time of plot: Antiquity
Locale: Thebes
First performed: Phoninissai, 409 B.C.E. (English translation, 1781)

Principal characters:
JOCASTA, Oedipus' wife
ANTIGONE, Oedipus' daughter
POLYNICES, Oedipus' exiled son
ETEOCLES, Polynices' brother and the king of Thebes
CREON, Jocasta's brother
MENOECEUS, Creon's son
TIRESIAS, the blind prophet
OEDIPUS, the deposed king of Thebes
CHORUS OF PHOENICIAN MAIDENS

The Story:

Before the royal palace of Thebes, Jocasta, the mother of King Eteocles, prayed to the sun god for aid in reconciling her two sons and avoiding fratricidal war over the kingdom of Thebes. In her supplication she recalled that her family had already suffered unbearable horrors when her husband Oedipus plucked out his eyes upon discovering that in marrying her he had married his own mother and had conceived two sons and two daughters by her. At first the sons had confined their father in the palace in order to hide the family shame and had decided to rule the kingdom between them in alternate years. However, Eteocles had refused to yield the throne to Polynices, who, after marrying the daughter of Adrastus, King of Argos, had raised a host from seven city-states and was already at the gates of Thebes to win his rightful place by force of arms.

Antigone, viewing the besieging armies from the palace tower, recognized the justice of Polynices' claim but prayed that Thebes would never fall. In desperate fear, Jocasta cut off her hair and dressed in mourning. Then in the hope that the war could be averted, she arranged a meeting under a truce between her two sons. Eteocles was willing to receive Polynices back in Thebes, but not as an equal to share the throne; Polynices, on the other hand, unable to endure exile and equally unable to accept such ignoble terms, remained bent on war.

Eteocles then sent for his uncle Creon to work out battle strategy. The two, agreeing that the situation was grave, finally decided not to attempt any counterattack with their vastly outnumbered troops but to post men at the seven gates of the city in a defensive action. Creon also sent his son Menoeceus to summon the prophet Tiresias for further advice. The blind prophet, after warning Creon that the means for saving Thebes would be one he would be unwilling to accept, announced that Menoeceus must be sacrificed. Horror-stricken, Creon refused and urged his son to flee at once. Menoeceus pretended to agree, but shortly after his departure a messenger hurried to Creon with the news that his son had plunged a sword into his own throat at the very moment that the Argive hosts launched their first fruitless assault against the gates of the city.

Jocasta, upon hearing that her two sons had decided to determine the fate of Thebes by a single combat apart from their armies, rushed off with Antigone to the battlefield to stop them if she could. As she departed, Creon entered carrying the corpse of his dead son and seeking Jocasta's aid in the funeral preparations. A second messenger brought him word that Jocasta had gone outside the walls of Thebes and had found her two sons dying, each the other's victim. Eteocles, unable to speak, bade his mother farewell with his eyes, and Polynices with his dying breath begged his mother to bury him in Theban soil. Then the grief-stricken Jocasta seized a sword and thrust it through her throat. Upon that stroke the Theban warriors fell upon the surprised Argives and drove them from the field. Menoeceus' sacrifice had not been in vain.

Antigone, returning with servants bearing the bodies of her mother and her two brothers, was met by blind King Oedipus, who had emerged from his confinement in the palace and who began to express his grief in groans and lamentations. Creon, resolutely taking over the rule bequeathed to him by Eteocles, commanded him to cease and to prepare for exile. Determined to restore order in the tragic city, Creon was compelled to put aside personal feelings in submitting to the prophecies of Tiresias. Antigone, the new king insisted, must prepare to marry his son Haemon; furthermore, while the body of Eteocles was to be given burial fit for a king, Polynices' corpse must be left to rot, a prey to birds, as a warning to all who might contemplate taking up arms against the city. Oedipus, refusing to beg from Creon, prepared to leave at once, but Antigone flouted his commands. Rather than marry Haemon, she was determined to accompany her father into exile and to bury the body of Polynices with proper religious rites. As father and daughter set out from Thebes, Oedipus lamented the sad history of his life but courageously submitted to the fate that the gods had decreed for him.

Critical Evaluation:

Euripides was the youngest of the three great dramatic playwrights of Greek antiquity. An outspoken social critic and artistic innovator, his plays were considerably less popular with Athenian audiences of the fifth century B.C.E. than those of Aeschylus and Sophocles, his older theatrical peers. His disenchantment with official Athenian policy led him to forsake his native city late in life, and he spent his last years as a voluntary exile in the court of King Archelaus of Macedonia. Succeeding generations, however, found his unique blend of intense emotion, psychological realism, and lush poetic dialogue more congenial than the relatively austere dramas of his rivals, and his plays were frequently revived and produced in late Hellenic and Hellenistic times. The fact that nineteen complete plays by Euripides exist, while only seven each by Sophocles and Aeschylus survive, attests to Euripides' preeminence as dramatic poet in later antiquity.

Written late in his career, *The Phoenician Women* is remarkable in several respects. It is the longest of Euripides' surviving plays, and boasts the largest cast of characters in any Greek drama. Moreover, it is the most innovative and original retelling of the story of the royal house of Thebes, a tale that had already served as the basis for some of the earlier dramas of Euripides' peers. The broad mythic resonance, exceptional range of emotional and melodramatic material, and linguistic richness of *The Phoenician Women* made it a favorite with actors, audiences, and scholars, and it became one of the most widely read, performed, and studied of the great Greek dramas for nearly one thousand years after its first performance. Knowledge of Greek language and literature, however, died out in Western Europe in the years following the collapse of the Roman Empire, and when it was revived during the Renaissance the prevailing taste for more tightly constructed dramas, such as Sophocles' *Antigone* (441 B.C.E.), caused *The Phoenician Women* to suffer a loss of reputation and popularity from which it has not yet fully emerged.

Verbally ornate, artistically ambitious, simultaneously intellectual and emotional, and bitingly ironic, *The Phoenician Women* is a brilliant product of Euripides' late style. Despite the absence of a main character to provide dramatic focus, the logic of its thematic development and the powerful coherence of its imagery transcend these limitations to create a superbly crafted poetic drama.

The ostensible theme of the play is war; however, the treatment of this theme is so complex that in the end warfare becomes a metaphor for the tragic vicissitudes of the human condition. No single character dominates the play's action, but as the members of the Theban royal family—Jocasta, Antigone, Creon, Polynices, Eteocles, Creon, and Oedipus—interact with one another in various ways, each encounter brings a different facet of family life, politics, and statecraft into conjunction with the problem of war. Interlinked images of blood and bloodshed permeate the language of the text, providing a constant reminder that the blood-ties that bind the family (and the state) together cannot prevent—indeed all to frequently cause—the shedding of blood. Brooding over the entire action of the play is the changeable, and finally inimical, presence of the gods. This presence makes itself felt—not through the actual presence or appearance of a divine character, but rather through a complex pattern of shifting references to the gods, which takes on life in the language of the play. In the play's closing moments the remorseless operation of divine compulsion in human affairs is recapitulated in Oedipus' final speech. He recalls that his victory over the Sphinx was divinely ordained, and that it has led him not to glory, but to incest, dishonor, and exile. Euripides' pessimistic view of the human condition echoes in the defeated resignation of the last words Oedipus speaks: "The constraint the gods lay on us we mortals must bear."

This complex theme is developed through an equally complex structure. Intricate patterns of linked opposites are integrated into an edifice of balanced paradox. For example Dionysus, ordinarily regarded as a beneficial deity, is called "gentle and terrible," and the dancing of his maenads is compared to the "dance of death"; the salvation of the city of Thebes requires that all surviving branches of the royal house of Thebes must be destroyed. The dramatic structure reflects the same principle of balance: Jocasta's prologue speech matches Oedipus' entering speech later in the play; her monody matches Antigone's; the entrance of blind Teiresias led by his daughter as he returns to Thebes from Athens at the end of the play. Within this carefully balanced structure Euripides plays out his pessimistic theme: Neither human intellect, attempted negotiation, nor noble self-sacrifice can prevent the divinely ordained destruction of the Theban royal family.

The high order of artistry with which Euripides develops his tragic theme allows it to transcend his own time and speak across the centuries. For the original Athenian audience there was one final interlocking piece to his design: Thebes unmistakably parallels Athens, and the war between Argos and Thebes thus mirrors the great war between Sparta and Athens which was drawing to a close outside the city walls. As Thebes is besieged in the play, so was Athens besieged at the time of the plays's first production. The city's resources drastically depleted, no salvation was possible for Athens, which faced an inevitable defeat at the hands of its bitterest enemy, Sparta. Feeling, like Oedipus, the "constraint" of the gods, that first Athenian audience heard the Chorus close the play with a deeply ironic and finally hopeless response to his last speech: "Great Victory, continually crown my life."

"Critical Evaluation" by R. A. Martin

Bibliography:
Collard, Christopher. *Euripides.* Oxford, England: Clarendon Press, 1981. A short overview of

textual and critical scholarship of Euripides' work, with the emphasis on directing attention to bibliographical resources in each area; written for high school students.

Euripides. *The Phoenician Women.* Edited with translation and commentary by Elizabeth Craik. Warminster, Wiltshire, England: Aris & Phillips, 1988. The most recent edition of Euripides' play contains the Greek text, a literal English translation on facing pages, more than one hundred pages of detailed textual commentary, and an excellent, up-to-date introductory essay.

Melchinger, Siegfried. *Euripides.* Translated by Samuel R. Rosebaum. New York: Frederick Ungar, 1973. A clearly written introduction to Euripides' work. Includes brief summaries and interpretations of all the extant plays.

Vellacott, Philip. *Ironic Drama: A Study of Euripides' Method and Meaning.* Cambridge, England: Cambridge University Press, 1975. This important study of Euripidean drama as veiled social criticism deals with all the extant plays and offers interpretations of them in the context of Athenian civic and military history from approximately 438 B.C.E. to the posthumous production of *The Bacchae* in 405 B.C.E.

Webster, T. B. L. *The Tragedies of Euripides.* New York: Methuen, 1967. A study of the development of Euripides' career as an artist through a detailed study of the complete plays and of the existing fragments. The most complete work of its kind. Summaries and interpretations of every piece of Euripidean text that has survived.

PHORMIO

Type of work: Drama
Author: Terence (Publius Terentius Afer, c. 190-159 B.C.E.)
Type of plot: Comedy
Time of plot: Second century B.C.E.
Locale: Athens
First performed: 161 B.C.E. (English translation, 1598)

> *Principal characters:*
> CHREMES, a rich gentleman of Athens
> DEMIPHO, Chremes' rather miserly brother
> ANTIPHO, Demipho's son
> PHAEDRIA, Chremes' son
> GETA, a slave
> PHORMIO, a parasite
> NAUSISTRATA, Chremes' wife

The Story:

Demipho and Chremes, two wealthy Athenian brothers, left the city on journeys and entrusted the welfare of their two sons to Geta, a slave belonging to Demipho. For a time, the two young men, Antipho and Phaedria, who were both of exemplary habits, gave the slave little trouble. When both fell in love, however, before their fathers returned, Geta's troubles began. His sympathy for Antipho and Phaedria caused him to help both of them, but he realized only too well that both fathers would be angry when they learned what had happened.

Phaedria, the son of Chremes, had fallen in love with a lovely young harp player owned by a trader named Dorio, who refused to part with the girl for less than thirty minae. Unable to raise the money, Phaedria was at his wits' end. His cousin Antipho had fallen in love with a young Athenian girl of a good but penniless family.

Antipho had already married the girl, even though he knew that his father, who was something of a miser, would be furious to learn that his son had married a girl who brought no dower. Geta, in an effort to smooth out the problem, had contacted a parasitical lawyer named Phormio, who had brought suit against Antipho under an Athenian law that made it mandatory for an unprovided-for girl to be married to her nearest relative. Antipho did not contest the suit, and so he had the excuse that he had been forced by the court to marry the young woman.

Shortly after the wedding, the two older men returned. As soon as he learned what had happened, Demipho ordered his son to give up his wife, whereupon Antipho and Geta again called on Phormio for assistance. Phormio warned the old man that he would be unable to avoid keeping the girl, even though Demipho claimed that the girl was not actually a relative. Phormio contended that the girl was a relative, the daughter of Demipho's kinsman Stilpo, who had lived in Lemnos. Demipho declared he never had a relative by that name.

During this time, Phaedria was trying desperately to raise the thirty minae to purchase his beloved harpist from Dorio, who had given him three days to find the money. Then Phaedria learned from a slave that a sea captain, about to sail, wanted to purchase the girl and that Dorio, anxious to make a sale, had promised to sell the girl to him. Phaedria appealed to Dorio, but he would promise only to hold off the sale of the slave girl until the following morning.

After seeing Phormio, Demipho went to his brother Chremes and talked over the situation with him. They finally agreed that the only answer to the problem of Antipho's wife was to send her away with a sum of money. Chremes agreed to have his wife, Nausistrata, tell the girl that she was to be separated from her husband. While they were planning, Geta went to Phormio once again.

Phormio hatched a plan to satisfy everyone and make some money for himself. He offered to marry Antipho's cast-off wife if he were given a large sum of money. With part of that money he expected to have a good time, and with the rest, which he was to turn over to Phaedria, that young man was to purchase his beloved harpist. Geta presented the first part of Phormio's plan to the brothers, who readily acquiesced, even though Demipho hated to see Phormio receive payment for marrying the girl.

After the arrangements had been made, Chremes was horrified to learn that the girl he was advising his brother to cast off was his own daughter by a second wife whom he had married in Lemnos. Even worse was the fact that his Athenian wife, Nausistrata, did not know of the other marriage. Chremes took his brother into his confidence and told him what had happened. They both agreed to let the marriage stand, and Chremes offered to add a dower to the girl.

The only difficulty, as the old men saw it, was how to redeem their money from Phormio, who no longer needed to marry the girl. Phormio, having given part of the money to Phaedria, was unwilling to return that part of the money that was to have been his for his trouble.

While the old men were hunting for Phormio, he was in conversation with Antipho. Geta went to them with the news that Antipho's uncle was also his father-in-law and that Antipho's troubles were at an end. Asked where he had learned this fact, Geta replied that he had overheard a conversation between Chremes and a servant. The information made both Antipho and Phormio happy, Antipho because he would be able to keep his wife, Phormio because he had information to use in keeping the money he had received from Chremes and Demipho.

When Chremes and Demipho confronted Phormio, he refused to give back the money, and in answer to their threats he replied that if they tried to bring a suit against him he would tell Nausistrata about Chremes' affair in Lemnos and the true identity of Antipho's wife. During the argument the brothers laid hands on the lawyer. Phormio, infuriated by their treatment of him, called out to Nausistrata. When she came out of the house, Phormio told her about Chremes' other wife. She was somewhat mollified, however, when she realized that the other woman was dead and that she would have something to hold over her husband's head.

Seeing that Nausistrata had been converted to his side, Phormio told them also that he had given thirty minae to Phaedria so that he might purchase the harpist from Dorio. Chremes began to protest, but Nausistrata silenced him with the statement that it was no worse for the son to have such a mistress than for the father to have two wives. Nausistrata, pleased at the turn events had taken—for her son had his beloved and her rival was dead—asked Phormio if there were anything she could do for him. Fun-loving Phormio said that he would be vastly pleased, and her husband much exasperated, if she would ask the lawyer to dinner. Nausistrata, proud of her newly found power over her husband, agreed.

Critical Evaluation:

Unlike much of Terence's other work, *Phormio* is highly amusing. In addition to presenting one of the most engaging rascals in the history of the theater, the play is fast-paced, brilliantly constructed, suspenseful, and rich in irony. Terence's ability in characterization is evident, but *Phormio* tends to be more farcical than his other comedies, though it is also more vigorous. This may be because the playwright did not adapt it from Menander, as was usually the case in Terence, but from Apollodorus of Carystus, a contemporary of Menander. Because the original source has not survived, it is difficult to judge how much of *Phormio* is derived from its source.

Certain features are distinctly Terentian, such as the dual romance, the excellent use of plot, the smooth colloquial dialogue, and the polished maxims. Others are attributable to the Greek New Comedy, among them the stock character types, the concentration on domestic problems, and the prominence of a love story. The most likely estimate is that Terence took his material from Apollodorus in this play and reworked it according to his own formula, in the same way that Molière borrowed from *Phormio* in writing *The Cheats of Scapin* (1671).

When *Phormio* was first performed at the Roman games in 161 B.C.E., Terence was about twenty-six and had established a reputation as a successful dramatist. Of low birth and originally a slave, he had enjoyed a meteoric rise in his fortunes, becoming a member of the Scipionic coterie, a group of Roman aristocrats interested in the importation of Greek culture. His success as a dramatist can be indirectly gauged from his prologues, in which he self-confidently answers the attacks of the elderly playwright Luscius Lanuvinus. One year after *Phormio* was presented, however, Terence took a trip to Greece from which he never returned. It is thought that his ship sank as he was returning to Rome in 159 B.C.E.

In *Phormio*, Terence shows an unusual detachment from the plight of the two adolescent young men, Antipho and Phaedria, presenting them as rather silly, impulsive, and feckless youths who are helpless before their fathers. Instead of differentiating them, which is his normal practice, Terence emphasizes their similarity. Moreover, he pokes fun at their superficiality and self-absorption. It seems clear that Terence was growing beyond the stage of taking youthful romances seriously. He does not even present the young women whom Antipho and Phaedria love: They are incidental to the plot except as prizes.

What does interest Terence is the character of Phormio: self-possessed where the two youths are cowardly, roguish where the two youths wish to appear respectable, clever where the two youths are witless, and determined where the two youths are fickle. Phormio is mature and confident of his powers, the ideal hero of many young men. It is he alone who outwits the two formidable fathers to award Phaedria his harp player; and it is he who enabled Antipho to marry in the first place through a ruse that, surprisingly enough, turns out to be true. Terence, having outgrown his interest in adolescent lovers, apparently needed a more vital character to command the stage, and he found one in the adventurer Phormio.

Instead of giving Antipho and Phaedria contrasting qualities, Terence chooses to give them different problems. Antipho's difficulty is to keep the wife he already has in the face of his father's opposition. Phaedria's trouble is that he cannot raise the money to purchase the mistress he loves from her pimp, who is presented as a practical businessman. Phormio undertakes to solve both problems, not so much for his own gain but to demonstrate his gift for intrigue. He wants to show off his virtuosity before the admiring slave Geta and the two young men. He is shown thinking on his feet, as it were, outfacing Demipho and his three toady lawyers, discarding a useless alibi, obtaining a large sum from Chremes under false pretenses, and adapting quickly to a dangerous situation in which Demipho is intent on regaining the money. In all of this, through chance and his quick wit, he is master of the situation.

Demipho and Chremes after all deserve to be swindled, as tightfisted and authoritarian old men, and their sons, being the shallow, erotic boys they are, deserve a hard time before their problems are settled. The complex but clearly developed plot provides opportunities to witness the chagrin of all four in an amusing light. The most amusing scenes however are the climactic ones in which Chremes tries his hardest to keep the secret of his bigamous marriage from his wife, while Demipho's concern over money forces Phormio to reveal it, thereby ensuring that Chremes will be henpecked for the rest of his life.

In the end, once the plot has been unraveled and the characters have received their proper rewards and punishments, the Terentian comedy seems rather trivial and commonplace, requiring no great effort of thought. If it is amiable and technically skilled, the assumptions behind it are those of middle-class audiences everywhere: that young love should be fulfilled, that the old should make allowances for the fancies of youth, and that parental authority should be respected by youth. These premises make Terence, along with Plautus, the forerunner of bourgeois comedy from William Shakespeare to Neil Simon.

"Critical Evaluation" by James Weigel, Jr.

Bibliography:

Barsby, John. "The Stage Action of Terence, *Phormio*." *Classical Quarterly* 43, no. 1 (1993): 329-335. Discusses how a production of *Phormio* was set up. Helpful for those concerned with dramatic technique.

Duff, J. Wight. *A Literary History of Rome: From the Origins to the Close of the Golden Age.* 3d ed. New York: Barnes & Noble Books, 1960. Gives a plot line and places *Phormio* in the context of Terence's other plays. Discusses other playwrights' influence on *Phormio* and examines the chronology of Terence's plays in relation to the prologues. Claims that discrepancies exist in play presentation that could confuse interpretation of prologues.

Flickinger, R. C. "A Study of Terence's Prologues." *Philological Quarterly* 9 (1940): 81-93. Examines the prologues and explains that Terence used them as a defense of his works; in *Phormio*, for example, Terence refers to himself as "the old playwright" and says his aim in writing this play is "to answer, not provoke." Flickinger claims the study of prologues is important in understanding Terence.

Norwood, Gilbert. *The Art of Terence.* Oxford, England: Basil Blackwell, 1923. Discusses *Phormio* critically and gives the plot line of the play. Compares *Phormio* with other works by Terence. Discusses the influences of other playwrights on *Phormio* and how the playwright's life influenced his writing of this work.

Rose, H. J. *A Handbook of Latin Literature from the Earliest Times to the Death of St. Augustine.* 3d ed. London: Methuen, 1967. Covers Terence's major works in chronological order. Summarizes play, then discusses literary criticism of it. Claims that *Phormio* is one of Terence's better plays.

PICKWICK PAPERS

Type of work: Novel
Author: Charles Dickens (1812-1870)
Type of plot: Social realism
Time of plot: 1827-1828
Locale: England
First published: serial, 1836-1837; book, 1837

Principal characters:
MR. PICKWICK, the founder of the Pickwick Club
MR. AUGUSTUS SNODGRASS,
MR. TRACY TUPMAN, and
MR. NATHANIEL WINKLE, other members of the club
MR. WARDLE, the owner of Manor Farm
RACHAEL WARDLE, his sister
EMILY WARDLE, his daughter
MRS. BARDELL, Mr. Pickwick's housekeeper
MR. PERKER, a lawyer
SAM WELLER, Mr. Pickwick's servant
ARABELLA ALLEN, Mr. Winkle's beloved
MR. ALFRED JINGLE, a rascal

The Story:

Samuel Pickwick, Esquire, was the founder and perpetual president of the justly famous Pickwick Club. To extend his own researches into the quaint and curious phenomena of life, he suggested that he and three other Pickwickians should make journeys to places remote from London and report on their findings to the stay-at-home members of the club. The first destination decided upon was Rochester. As Mr. Pickwick, Mr. Tupman, Mr. Winkle, and Mr. Snodgrass went to their coach, they were waylaid by a rough gang of cab drivers. Fortunately, the men were rescued by a stranger who was poorly dressed but of the friendliest nature. The stranger, who introduced himself as Alfred Jingle, also appeared to be going to Rochester, and the party mounted the coach together.

After they had arrived at their destination, Mr. Jingle aroused Mr. Tupman's curiosity by telling him that there was to be a ball at the inn that evening and that many lovely young ladies would be present. Because, said Mr. Jingle, his luggage had gone astray, he had no evening clothes and so it would be impossible for him to attend the affair. This was a regrettable circumstance because he had hoped to introduce Mr. Tupman to the many young ladies of wealth and fashion who would be present. Eager to meet these young ladies, Mr. Tupman borrowed Mr. Winkle's suit for the stranger. At the ball, Mr. Jingle, observing a middle-aged lady being assiduously attended by a doctor, went up to her and started dancing with her, much to the doctor's anger. Introducing himself as Dr. Slammer, the angry gentleman challenged Mr. Jingle to a duel, but Mr. Jingle refused to give his name.

The next morning, a servant identified Mr. Winkle as the gentleman wearing the suit as described by the doctor and told Mr. Winkle that Dr. Slammer was awaiting his appearance to fight a duel. Mr. Winkle had been drunk the night before, and he decided he was being called out because he had conducted himself in an unseemly manner that he could no longer remember. With Mr. Snodgrass as his second, Mr. Winkle tremblingly approached the battle-field. Much to his relief, Dr. Slammer roared that he was the wrong man. After much misunderstanding, the situation was satisfactorily explained, and no blood was shed.

During the afternoon, the travelers attended a parade, where they met Mr. Wardle in a coach with his two daughters and his sister, Miss Rachael Wardle. Mr. Tupman was impressed by the elder Miss Wardle and accepted for his friends and himself Mr. Wardle's invitation to visit his estate, Manor Farm. The next day, the four Pickwickians departed for the farm, which was a distance of about ten miles from the inn where they were staying. They encountered difficulties with their horses and arrived at Manor Farm in a disheveled state, but they were soon washed and mended under the kind assistance of Mr. Wardle's daughters. In the evening, they played a hearty game of whist, and Mr. Tupman squeezed Miss Wardle's hand under the table.

The next day, Mr. Wardle took his guests rook hunting. Mr. Winkle, who would not admit himself unable to cope with any situation, was given the gun to try his skill. He proved it by accidentally shooting Mr. Tupman in the arm. Miss Wardle offered her aid to the stricken man. Observing that their friend was in good hands, the others went off to a neighboring town to watch the cricket matches. There Mr. Pickwick unexpectedly encountered Mr. Jingle, and Mr. Wardle invited him to return to Manor Farm with his party.

Convinced that Miss Wardle had a great deal of money, Mr. Jingle misrepresented Mr. Tupman's intentions to Miss Wardle and persuaded her to elope with him. Mr. Wardle and Mr. Pickwick pursued the couple to London. There, with the help of Mr. Wardle's lawyer, Mr. Perker, they went from one inn to another in an attempt to find the elopers. Finally, through a sharp-featured young man cleaning boots in the yard of the White Hart Inn, they were able to identify Mr. Jingle. They indignantly confronted him as he was displaying a marriage license. After a heated argument, Mr. Jingle resigned his matrimonial plans for the sum of one hundred and twenty pounds. Miss Wardle tearfully went back to Manor Farm. The Pickwickians returned to London, where Mr. Pickwick engaged as his servant Sam Weller, the sharp, shrewd young bootblack of the White Hart Inn.

When Mrs. Leo Hunter invited Mr. Pickwick and his friends to a party, they spied Mr. Jingle. He, seeing his former acquaintance, disappeared into the crowd. Mrs. Hunter told Mr. Pickwick that Mr. Jingle lived at Bury St. Edmonds. Mr. Pickwick set out in pursuit in company with his servant, Sam Weller, for the old gentleman was determined to deter the scoundrel from any fresh deceptions he might be planning. At the inn where Mr. Jingle was reported to be staying, Mr. Pickwick learned that the rascal was planning to elope with a rich young lady who stayed at a boarding school nearby. Mr. Pickwick agreed with the suggestion that in order to rescue the young lady he should hide in the garden from which Mr. Jingle was planning to steal her. When Mr. Pickwick sneaked into the garden, he found nothing of a suspicious nature; he had been deceived, and the blackguard had escaped.

Mr. Pickwick's housekeeper was Mrs. Bardell, a widow. When he was trying to tell her about having hired Sam Weller, Mr. Pickwick had beaten about the bush in such a manner that she had mistaken his words for a proposal of marriage. One day, Mr. Pickwick was resting in his room when he received notice from the legal firm of Dodgson and Fogg that Mrs. Bardell was suing him for breach of promise. The summons was distressing; but first, Mr. Pickwick had more important business to occupy his time. After securing the services of Mr. Perker to defend him, he went to Ipswich, having learned that Mr. Jingle had been seen in that vicinity. The trip to Ipswich was successful. The Pickwickians were able to catch Mr. Jingle in his latest scheme of deception and to expose him before he had carried out his plot.

At the trial for the breach of promise suit brought by Mrs. Bardell, lawyers Dodgson and

Fogg argued so eloquently against Mr. Pickwick that the jury fined him seven hundred and fifty pounds. When the trial was over, Mr. Pickwick told Dodgson and Fogg that even if they put him in prison he would never pay one cent of the damages, since he knew as well as they that there had been no grounds for suit.

Shortly afterward, the Pickwickians went to Bath, where fresh adventures awaited Mr. Pickwick and his friends. On that occasion, Mr. Winkle's weakness for the fair sex involved them in difficulties. In Bath, the Pickwickians met two young medical students, Mr. Allen and Mr. Bob Sawyer. Mr. Allen hoped to marry his sister, Arabella, to his friend, Mr. Sawyer, but Miss Allen professed extreme dislike for her brother's choice. When Mr. Winkle learned that Arabella had refused Mr. Sawyer because another man had won her heart, he felt that he must be the fortunate man, because she had displayed an interest in him when they had met earlier at Manor Farm. Mr. Pickwick kindly arranged to have Mr. Winkle meet Arabella in a garden, where the distraught lover could plead his suit.

Mr. Pickwick's plans to further his friend's romance were interrupted, however, by a subpoena delivered because he had refused to pay Mrs. Bardell. Mr. Pickwick found himself returned to London and lodged in Fleet Street prison. With the help of Sam Weller, Mr. Pickwick arranged his prison quarters as comfortably as possible and remained deaf to the entreaties of Sam Weller or Mr. Perker, who thought that he should pay his debt and regain his freedom. Dodgson and Fogg proved to be of lower caliber than even Mr. Pickwick had suspected. They had taken Mrs. Bardell's case without fee, gambling on Mr. Pickwick's payment to cover the costs of the case. When they saw no payment forthcoming, they had Mrs. Bardell arrested as well and sent to the Fleet Street prison.

While Mr. Pickwick was trying to decide what to do, Mr. Winkle with his new wife, Arabella, came to the prison and asked Mr. Pickwick to pay his debts so that he could visit Mr. Allen with the news of Mr. Winkle's marriage to Arabella. Arabella felt that Mr. Pickwick was the only person who could arrange a proper reconciliation between her brother and her new husband. Kindness prevailed; Mr. Pickwick paid the damages to Mrs. Bardell so that he would be free to help his friends in distress.

Winning Mr. Allen's approval of the match was not difficult for Mr. Pickwick, but when he approached the elder Mr. Winkle, the bridegroom's father objected to the marriage and threatened to cut off his son without a cent. To add to Mr. Pickwick's problems, Mr. Wardle came to London to tell him that his daughter Emily was in love with Mr. Snodgrass and to ask Mr. Pickwick's advice. Mr. Wardle had brought Emily to London with him.

The entire party came together in Arabella's apartment. All misunderstandings happily ended for the two lovers, and a jolly party followed. The elder Mr. Winkle paid a call on his new daughter-in-law. Upon seeing what a charming and lovely girl she was, he relented, and the family was reconciled.

After Mr. Snodgrass had married Emily Wardle, Mr. Pickwick dissolved the Pickwick Club and retired to a home in the country with his faithful servant, Sam Weller. Several times, Mr. Pickwick was called upon to be a godfather to little Winkles and Snodgrasses; for the most part, however, he led a quiet life, respected by his neighbors and loved by all of his friends.

Critical Evaluation:

Mr. Pickwick, the lovable, generous old gentleman of one of Charles Dickens' most popular novels, is one of the best-known characters of fiction. Mr. Pickwick benignly reigns over all activities of the Pickwick Club; under every circumstance, he is satisfied that he has helped his fellow creatures by his well-meaning efforts. The height of this Dickensian comedy is reached, however, with the creation of Sam Weller and his father. Sam's imperturbable presence of mind and his ready wit are indispensable to the Pickwickians.

Pickwick Papers has importance beyond its humorous incidents and characterization. It is the first novel of a literary movement to present the life and manners of lower- and middle-class life.

At the time a publisher in 1836 proposed that Dickens write the text for a series of pictures by the sporting artist Robert Seymour, Dickens was experiencing the first thrill of fame as the author of *Sketches by Boz*. He was twenty-four years old and had been for some years a court reporter and freelance journalist; *Sketches by Boz* was his first literary effort of any length. The work the publisher proposed was of a similar kind: short, primarily humorous descriptions of cosmopolitan life, sometimes illustrated, and to be published monthly. Although Dickens already had the plan of a novel in mind, he was in need of cash and accepted the offer as a stopgap. He made one stipulation: that he and not Seymour have the choice of scenes to be treated. He did this because he himself was no sportsman and had little knowledge of country life beyond what his journalistic travels had shown him. It is evident from the digressive character of the first few chapters that he viewed the enterprise as an expedient.

Dickens was able to disguise his ignorance of country life by a canny selection of scenes and topics. Actual sporting scenes are kept to a minimum and treated with broad humor and slight detail. On the other hand, he knew country elections, magistrates, and newspapers well, and the chapters describing the Eatanswill election and those dealing with Mr. Nupkins, the mayor of Ipswich, and Mr. Pott, the editor of the Eatanswill *Gazette*, abound in atmosphere and choice observation. Most useful of all was his intimate knowledge of stagecoach travel, of life on the road, and of the inhabitants and manners of inns great and small. The device of a journey by coach unifies the first part of the novel, and a large portion of the action, including several key scenes, takes place in inns and public houses: Mr. Pickwick meets Sam Weller at the White Hart Inn, Mrs. Bardell is apprehended at the Spaniards, Sam is reunited with his father at the Marquis of Granby, and the Wellers plot Stiggins' discomfiture at the Blue Boar.

A theme that Dickens developed in later works appears in embryo here: the quicksand quality of litigation. Readers note that every figure connected with the law is portrayed as venal if not downright criminal, except Mr. Perker who is merely a remarkably cold fish. Another feature of later works is the awkward treatment of women. The author's attitude toward women is extremely ambiguous. Two of the women in the novel are unqualifiedly good. Sam's Mary is described perennially as "the pretty housemaid," and the fact that Sam loves her appears to complete the list of her virtues in Dickens' view. As a character, she has neither depth nor ethical range; no more has Arabella Allen, the dark-eyed girl with the "very nice little pair of boots." She is distinguished at first by flirtatious archness and later by a rather servile docility. The daughters of old Wardle first come to the reader's attention in the act of spiting their unmarried aunt and never redeem this impression. Other female characters are rather poorly developed. None has, as do some of the male figures such as Jingle and Trotter, a human dimension.

The author's sentiments about the institution of marriage are also curious. Mr. Winkle makes a runaway match, Mr. Snodgrass is only forestalled from doing so by a lack of parental opposition, and Mr. Tupman escapes after a ludicrously close call. Mr. Pickwick, the great advocate of heart over head, however, is not and never has been married, and in fact, he shows his greatest strength as a character in his struggle for justice in a breach-of-promise suit; Mr. Weller, the other beneficent father-figure of the work, makes no bones about his aversion to the connubial state: "'vether it's worth while goin' through so much, to learn so little . . . is a matter o' taste. I rayther think it isn't.'"

Angus Wilson, among others, contends that *Pickwick Papers*, like most first novels, is autobiographical. There is evidence for this position in the fact that Dickens' estimation of the women in his life also tended to extremes of adulation and contempt. More pertinent to the main thrust of the novel, which is the development of Mr. Pickwick from buffoon to "angel in tights," and the concurrent development of Sam, is the author's relationship to his father, whom he adored. The elder Dickens' imprisonment for debt in 1824 was the great trauma of the author's childhood; it was made the more galling by the fact that he, the eldest son, was put to work at a blacking factory and able to join the family circle in the prison only on Sundays. Scarcely more than a child, he felt unable either to aid or to comfort his father in his distress; at the same time, he felt that his father had abandoned him to a harsh world.

As a young man, Dickens wrote into his first novel an account of those times as he would have wished them to be. Mr. Pickwick is the epitome of those qualities of Dickens senior that so endeared him to his son, which included unsinkable good spirits and kindness that did not count the cost. To these, Pickwick adds financial sense, ethical sense, and most important, a sensitivity to the best feelings of his spiritual son, Sam Weller. Sam, in turn, bends all of his cockney keenness of eye and wit, courage, and steadfastness, to the service not only of this ideal father unjustly imprisoned but also of his immensely endearing shadow-father Tony Weller. Clearly, this material has its roots in Dickens' life, but it is just as clear that his genius tapped a universal longing of sons to see their fathers as heroes and themselves as heroic helpers.

"Critical Evaluation" by Jan Kennedy Foster

Bibliography:

Dexter, Walter. *Pickwick's Pilgrimages*. New York: Haskell House Publishers, 1992. A study of the actual places Mr. Pickwick visited in Dickens' novel. The actual conditions he and his companions would have encountered illuminate the story. Particularly good descriptions of Rochester, Ipswich, Bath, Bristol, and Tewkesbury.

Dexter, Walter, and J. W. T. Ley. *The Origin of Pickwick*. Folcroft, Pa.: Folcroft Library Editions, 1974. A study of some of Dickens' early sketches that were used, *Pickwick Papers*. Examines the publishing history of the early numbers of *Pickwick Papers* and Dickens' early illustrators.

Fitzgerald, Percy. *Bozland: Dickens' Places and People*. Ann Arbor, Mich.: Gryphon Books, 1971. A consideration of people and places in Dickens, with emphasis on Pickwickian inns and actual towns and locales depicted in *Pickwick Papers*. Examines Mr. Pickwick's relationship to lawyers in the light of actual legal practice during Dickens' time.

Lockwood, Frank. *The Law and Lawyers of Pickwick*. New York: Haskell House, 1972. A late Victorian study of the legal mores depicted in *Pickwick Papers*. Mr. Pickwick's trial took place in 1827, a time before the legal reforms of 1843, which the author examines in relationship to the novel.

Noyes, Alfred, et al. *A Pickwick Portrait Gallery*. Port Washington, N.Y.: Kennikat Press, 1970. A series of insightful character analyses of various members of the Pickwick Club by outstanding writers and critics of the first half of the twentieth century. Particularly good for Samuel Pickwick, Samuel Waller, and Mrs. Bardell.

THE PICTURE OF DORIAN GRAY

Type of work: Novel
Author: Oscar Wilde (1854-1900)
Type of plot: Fantasy
Time of plot: Late nineteenth century
Locale: England
First published: serial, 1890; book, 1891

Principal characters:
DORIAN GRAY, a Faustian young man
LORD HENRY WOTTON, his tempter
BASIL HALLWARD, an artist
SIBYL VANE, an actress
JAMES VANE, her brother

The Story:

One day in his London studio, Basil Hallward was putting a few finishing touches on a portrait of his handsome young friend, Dorian Gray. Lord Henry Wotton, a caller, indolently watched the painter at work. When his friend admired the subject of the painting, the artist explained that Dorian was his ideal of youth and that he hoped Lord Henry would never meet him because the older man's influence would be absolute and evil.

While they were talking, Dorian Gray himself came to the studio and Hallward, much against his will, was forced to introduce the young man to Lord Henry. Hallward signed the portrait and announced that it was finished. When Lord Henry offered to buy the picture, the painter said it was not his property and that it belonged to Dorian, to whom he was presenting it. After listening to Lord Henry's witty conversation, Dorian looked at his portrait and grew sad. He would become old and wrinkled, he said, while the picture would remain the same. Instead, he wished that the portrait might grow old while he remained forever young. He said he would give his soul to keep his youth.

Dorian and Lord Henry became close friends. One of the gifts Lord Henry gave the boy was a book about a young man who attempted to realize in his brief lifetime all the passions of man's history. Dorian made the book a pattern for his own life. In a third-rate theater, he saw a young actress named Sibyl Vane playing the role of Juliet with such sincerity and charm that he fell in love with her on the spot. After he had met her in person, Dorian dreamed of taking her away from the cheap theatrical troupe and making her a great actress who would thrill the world. One night, he took Lord Henry to watch her performance. That night, Sibyl was listless and wooden; she was so uninspired in her acting that the audience hissed her. When Dorian went to her dressing room after the final curtain, she explained that before meeting him she had thought acting her only reality. Now, she said, Dorian's love had taught her what reality actually was, and she could no longer act. Dorian coldly told her she had killed his love and that he never intended to see her again.

When the young man returned to his home that night, he noticed something in his portrait that he had never seen before, a faint line of cruelty about the mouth. Looking at his own features in a mirror, he found no such line on his own lips. Dorian Gray was disturbed, and he resolved to reform, to see no more of Lord Henry, and to ask Sibyl Vane to forgive and marry him. That night, he wrote her a passionate letter, but before he could post the letter, Lord Henry visited him the next morning and brought the news that Sibyl had killed herself in her dressing room the night before.

After his friend had gone, Dorian decided there was no point to his good resolutions. The portrait would have to bear the burden of his shame. That night he attended the opera with Lord Henry. The next day, when Basil Hallward attempted to reason with him over scandalous reports that were beginning to circulate about his behavior, Dorian expressed no emotion over Sibyl's suicide. His part in her tragic story would never be revealed, for she had known him only as Prince Charming. When Hallward asked to see his painting, Dorian refused and in a sudden rage shouted that he never wished to see the painter again. Later, he hung the portrait in an old schoolroom upstairs, locked the door, and hid the key where only he could find it.

Rumors about Dorian Gray continued, and the young man became suspected of strange vices. Gentlemen walked out of their club rooms when he entered them, he was invited to fewer balls and parties at country houses, and many of his former friends refused to acknowledge him when they met. It was reported that he had been seen in low dives with drunken sailors and thieves. Dorian's looks did not change, however; only the portrait reflected his life of crime and debauchery. Like the hero of the book Lord Henry had given him, Dorian Gray spent his life pursuing fresh experiences and new sensations. One interest succeeded the next, and he immersed himself in turn in the study of religious rituals, perfumes, music, and jewels. He frequented opium dens and had sordid affairs with women.

On the eve of Dorian's thirty-eighth birthday, Basil Hallward visited him again. Although the two had been estranged for years, Hallward came in a last attempt to persuade Dorian to change his dissolute ways. He was still unable to believe many of the stories he had heard about Dorian. With a bitter laugh, Dorian said that Hallward should see what he had truly become. He took Hallward to the schoolroom and unveiled the portrait. The artist was horrified, for only by the signature could he identify his own handiwork. In anger that he had betrayed his true self to his former friend, Dorian seized a knife that lay nearby and stabbed Hallward in the neck and back.

Dorian relocked the door and went down to the drawing room. Because Hallward had intended to leave for Paris that night, Dorian knew the painter would not be missed for some time. He decided that removal of the body was not enough. He wanted it completely destroyed. Suddenly, he thought of Alan Campbell, a young chemist who had once been his close friend. By threatening the young scientist with exposure of a crime only he knew about, Dorian forced Campbell to destroy Hallward's body with fire and chemicals. After that night, the hands of the portrait showed smears of blood.

Late one night, commonly dressed, Dorian was leaving an opium den when a drunken woman addressed him as Prince Charming. A sailor who overheard followed him out. The sailor was James Vane, Sibyl's brother, who had sworn revenge on the man who had betrayed his sister. He would have killed Dorian Gray then and there if Dorian had not looked so unspoiled and young. Sibyl had committed suicide eighteen years before, yet the man before James Vane seemed no more than twenty years old. When Vane returned to the opium den, the woman told him that Dorian Gray had also ruined her many years before and that he had not changed in appearance since then.

Some time later, at his country home, Dorian saw James Vane watching him outside a window, but during a hunt on the estate, Vane was accidentally shot and killed. Alan Campbell had committed suicide some time earlier under strange circumstances, and Basil Hallward's disappearance was being investigated.

Back in London, Dorian decided to destroy the picture that stood as the awful record of his guilt; he went to the old schoolroom. The portrait now also had an appearance of cunning and triumph. Using the knife with which he had murdered Basil Hallward, Dorian stabbed the frightful portrait. The servants in the house heard a horrible cry of agony. When they forced open the locked door of the room, they found, hanging on the wall, a fine portrait of their master as they had last seen him. On the floor was a dead body, withered, wrinkled, in evening dress, with a knife in its breast. Only by his jewelry did they recognize Dorian Gray, who had killed himself in the desperate attempt to kill his conscience.

Critical Evaluation:

Oscar Wilde wrote a number of great comedic plays, two volumes of children's stories, and a range of critical studies and reviews. *The Picture of Dorian Gray* was his only full-length novel. The idea for the story probably goes back to his acquaintance with a painter named Basil Ward. Once, visiting him in his studio and finding him painting the portrait of a handsome young man, Wilde expressed a wish that the man remain young while the portrait aged in his stead.

On the most basic and literal level, *The Picture of Dorian Gray* is a horror story with the common plot device of a man who sells his soul to the devil in exchange for eternal youth. There are, however, other levels to consider for a more complete understanding of this novel.

There are no direct references to homosexuality in the story, though there is a suggestion of love underlying the relationship with Lord Henry, who serves as Dorian's tempter, as there definitely is love in the feelings of Hallward for Dorian. There may even be some jealousy between the two older men in regard to their standing with Dorian. At a deeper level, however, this is a story about narcissism. Dorian Gray is in love with himself, particularly with his physical self, and he does not wish to change.

It is worth noting that Dorian generally takes appearances more seriously than reality. When he rejects Sybil Vane, it is not Sybil the person whom he rejects but Sybil the actress.

Closely allied to the theme of narcissism is the idea of pride, in the biblical sense of the term. Dorian Gray is unwilling to accept the reality of his own aging and of the loss of his youthful beauty. He even kills Hallward, the creater of the portrait, as a symbolic act of defiance; in effect, he is rejecting God, for he destroys the creator of what he considers to be reality.

The Picture of Dorian Gray was met with critical disapproval, which Wilde apparently enjoyed immensely until his own defenses backfired a few years later when he was convicted of sodomy and spent two years in prison. In the preface to his novel, he had written: "There is no such thing as a moral or an immoral book. Books are well written or badly written. That is all." The prosecutors in the case against the author seized upon this statement gleefully and used it to "prove" that Wilde was immoral.

It is difficult to ascertain how much of Oscar Wilde himself went into the character of Dorian Gray. The author did not live long enough to grow old, and there is no evidence that he was attracted to the kind of depravity and violence that his fictional character practiced. In the late twentieth century, some critics suggested that the portrait itself served as a sort of "closet" in which Dorian Gray could hide his true nature by allowing the portrait to show the depths to which his soul had sunk, while to all outward appearances the man remained pure and innocent.

As a horror story, *The Picture of Dorian Gray* continue to appeal to readers. The theme of eternal youth is as universally interesting as the fear of death that ultimately inspires it. Writers as diverse as George Bernard Shaw and Robert Heinlein have written on this subject. The real question posed by the work is the nature of Dorian's crimes and sins. Certainly, he committed murder, but this was less important ultimately than the sin of blasphemy. He sold his soul to the devil by allowing his crimes to be shown in the features of his portrait while his own appearance remained youthful and even beautiful. This sin set his feet on the path to hell. When, along the way, he destroyed his portrait's creator, he symbolically crucified God in the process. When he destroyed the portrait, he destroyed himself, since he had allowed his own soul to enter the portrait.

"Critical Evaluation" by Marc Goldstein

Bibliography:
Ellmann, Richard, ed. *Oscar Wilde: A Collection of Critical Essays*. Englewood Cliffs, N.J.: Prentice-Hall, 1969. An anthology of essays on the works of Oscar Wilde, by a series of well-known authors. Includes two essays on *The Picture of Dorian Gray*, a contemporary (1891) review of the book by Walter Pater, "A Novel by Mr. Oscar Wilde," and a 1947 treatment by Edouard Roditis, "Fiction as Allegory: *The Picture of Dorian Gray*."
Nunokawa, Jeff. *Oscar Wilde*. New York: Chelsea House, 1995. Part of a series entitled "Lives of Notable Gay Men and Lesbians." Includes an extensive discussion of *The Picture of Dorian Gray* as a love story, emphasizing the relationships between Gray and the two other major male characters in the book, Lord Henry Wotton and Basil Hallward.
San Juan, Epifanio, Jr. *The Art of Oscar Wilde*. Westport, Conn.: Greenwood Press, 1967. An analysis of Wilde's major works. Includes a long chapter dealing with *The Picture of Dorian Gray*, which emphasizes Wilde's treatment of psychology. Also includes a discussion of the work's influence on later writers.
Sedgwick, Eve Kosofky. *Epistemology of the Closet*. Berkeley: University of California Press, 1990. A discussion of homosexuality in literature. In her treatment of *The Picture of Dorian Gray*, the author emphasizes sentimental love rather than sex. Also includes a discussion of the narcissistic qualities of the title character.
Weintraub, Stanley. *Literary Criticism of Oscar Wilde*. Lincoln: University of Nebraska Press, 1968. A collection of the critical works of Wilde. Of particular interest is the series of letters Wilde wrote to various newspapers in response to the negative criticism the book received when first published.

PIERRE
Or, The Ambiguities

Type of work: Novel
Author: Herman Melville (1819-1891)
Type of plot: Philosophical
Time of plot: Early nineteenth century
Locale: New York
First published: 1852

Principal characters:
> PIERRE GLENDINNING, a wealthy, cultivated young man
> MRS. GLENDINNING, his mother
> LUCY TARTAN, his fiancée
> ISABEL, his illegitimate half sister
> GLEN STANLY, his cousin
> DELLY ULVER, a farm woman

The Story:

Pierre Glendinning was a young man who lived amid luxury and ease, the heir to vast estates that formed the larger portion of two counties in New York state. His time was taken up with outdoor recreation, reading, and the courting of beautiful and well-to-do Lucy Tartan, a woman of whom Pierre's mother approved completely. Mrs. Glendinning, who was jealous of her influence over her son, saw nothing to fear in quiet, unaggressive Lucy Tartan.

One evening, however, a strange incident occurred when Mrs. Glendinning and Pierre visited a sewing bee in a nearby home. One of the women who was there shrieked and fainted when she saw Pierre. The incident bothered the young man, but he was totally unprepared for a note which he received from the young woman a short time later. In the note, she requested that Pierre visit her in the evening at the farm where she was employed. Pierre, disturbed by the mystery involved, went to the farm and discovered that the woman, Isabel, was his half sister, the illegitimate child of his father and a Frenchwoman. Pierre resolved immediately to acknowledge Isabel as his sister, but the question of how to accomplish the acknowledgment was a weighty one.

At first, Pierre intended to tell his mother of his discovery, but his mother's attitude toward Delly Ulver, a farm woman who had been born an illegitimate child, warned Pierre that he could expect no sympathetic understanding from Mrs. Glendinning. He next thought of approaching his minister for help with his problem, but the minister followed his mother's opinion, which caused Pierre to fall back on his own thinking. He also realized that his mother could not bear to have her husband proven to be an adulterer, nor could he bring himself to dishonor his father's name. The only road that seemed open to Pierre was to acknowledge Isabel by making her his wife rather than his sister.

When Pierre told his mother that he had been married secretly, she ordered him to leave the house immediately. Disowned and cast forth from his mother's affections, he also told Lucy Tartan that he had married another woman. His story threw Lucy into an almost fatal illness.

Having been disowned by his family, Pierre took Isabel from her home at the farm and went to New York City. They were accompanied by Delly Ulver, whom Pierre had decided to help. Although he had announced that he and Isabel had been married, Pierre and his half sister had entered into no such union; the announcement was only a means to permit them to live together.

In New York City, they found life barren and difficult, for Pierre had only a small supply of money. He had hoped to find a haven for himself and the two women with his wealthy cousin, Glen Stanly, but the cousin refused to recognize Pierre and had him thrown out of Stanly's home.

Forced to rely upon his own resources, Pierre resolved to become an author. He had, he thought, acquired quite a reputation by publishing some short poems and some essays in various periodicals. He also thought he had great talent, sufficient, at least, to enable him to write a philosophical work. After much difficulty, he managed to find a publisher who agreed to take his unwritten novel and to advance him enough money to live. For months Pierre, struggling to write his great work, lived in three miserable, unheated rooms in a vast tenement, along with Isabel and Delly Ulver, who acted in the capacity of servant to them both.

One day, word came to Pierre that his mother had died just a few weeks after he had left for New York City; her heir was Pierre's cousin, Glen Stanly. The news made Pierre very bitter, particularly when he discovered that his cousin was a suitor for the hand of Lucy Tartan, whom Pierre still loved dearly. Despite the feeling of utter helplessness that the news created in his mind, Pierre kept at work upon his book. Pierre was unable to keep Isabel from realizing that she was not alone in his affections, and the woman became jealous and disliked the fact that another woman could claim his attentions and love. Her attachment for Pierre went much deeper than ordinary love for a brother by a sister.

Sometime later, Pierre received a letter from Lucy. She had rebuffed Glen Stanly's suit, and she wrote to tell Pierre that he alone had her affections. She told Pierre that, even though he was married, she wished to travel to New York City to live near him. Pierre could not prevent her from joining his household, although he lied to Isabel and told her that Lucy was his cousin. Lucy arrived the next day. As she entered the tenement where Pierre lived, her brother and Glen Stanly tried to take her away by force. Pierre interfered on her behalf, and the two men had to leave without her.

Lucy, listening only to the prompting of her heart, refused to leave Pierre, even though he told her that Isabel was his wife. Having brought along her painting materials, she intended to support herself as a painter of portraits. Isabel disliked the idea of a third woman in the home, but she was powerless to turn Lucy out. The two women lived in a state of distrustful and watchful truce.

Glen Stanly and Lucy's brother, not wishing to see Lucy remain near Pierre, sent him a letter of premeditated insults in hopes of provoking him. Angered by their message, Pierre found two pistols in the apartment of a friend and set out to find Stanly and Lucy's brother. He encountered them on a crowded street. When they met, Stanly lashed at Pierre with a whip, whereupon Pierre drew his pistols and killed his cousin. The police immediately seized Pierre and took him to prison.

In prison, Pierre had no hope of life. Nor did he care to live, for he felt that fate had been too cruel to him. One evening, Isabel and Lucy were allowed to visit him for a few hours. When Isabel revealed that she was Pierre's sister, the shock of her announcement killed Lucy immediately. Pierre, driven mad by her death, seized a vial of poison which he knew Isabel carried in her bosom. He drank a portion of the poison, and Isabel emptied the vial of the remainder.

A short time later, Lucy's brother came looking for her, still hoping to rescue her from Pierre's influence. When the turnkey opened the cell door, Pierre was already dead, lying close to Lucy. Isabel still had sufficient life to say that no one had known the real Pierre. Then she too died, completing the tragedy of their ambiguous relationship.

Critical Evaluation:

Pierre is the most controversial of Herman Melville's novels. When it was published, it was condemned by contemporary reviewers, and readers since then have had difficulty in understanding the book and in determining Melville's intent. Critics still differ widely, with some regarding *Pierre* as a failure and others praising it as Melville's masterpiece.

Travel books about a world which was still being explored and discovered fascinated mid-nineteenth century readers, and Melville pleased this audience with his first two books about travels in the South Seas, *Typee* (1846) and *Omoo* (1847). The erudite and brilliant Melville could not restrain his intellect and imagination, however, and his third novel, *Mardi* (1849), was, in the guise of a travel book, really a philosophical satire. This effort confused readers and reviewers, and the book was a failure. Melville returned to relatively simple accounts of sea voyages in his next two books, *Redburn* (1849) and *White-Jacket* (1850), but in *Moby Dick* (1851), his interest in psychological and philosophical issues burst forth again, and this novel received a mixed critical and commercial response.

Pierre was Melville's next work, and in it he initially appears to give his audience what they wanted. Melville's account of the idyllic life lived by Pierre Glendinning and his mother on their country estate is similar in tone and style to the sentimental romances which were then popular, particularly among female readers. Although the first third of the novel is filled with purple passages, and a reader might suspect a legpull, Melville's style and story are no different from many nineteenth century novels which presented such scenes without irony. Nevertheless, there are some unsettling touches, such as Pierre and his mother calling each other brother and sister. This rhetorical attempt to increase the closeness between mother and son is a foreshadowing of the darker forces that destroy the lives of both.

The fact that Melville does intend the book as a satire becomes clear when Pierre meets his "sister," Isabel. It is never established without doubt that Isabel is, indeed, Pierre's sister—some critics have maintained that Pierre's interest in Isabel is primarily sexual and therefore incestuous, and that he accepts the "sister" hypothesis in order to be near her, but also because this arrangement prevents him from acting on a physical urge which frightens and confuses him. Readers of romances expected complications before the obligatory happy ending, but plot changes with such sordid overtones were not welcome.

The middle portion of the novel switches the satire to the gothic novel, another type of fiction popular in the nineteenth century. The mystery surrounding Isabel's parentage, the dark forest in which she lives, Pierre's internal struggle when faced with the evidence of his father's portrait, and his taunting stay under the balanced rock are elements and scenes which suggest the standard plot devices of the gothic novel with its delight in weird plot twists and touches of the supernatural. Before Melville shifts the direction of *Pierre* again, he has toyed with the excesses of this literary form.

Pierre's acceptance of Isabel as his sister, which he considers a noble gesture, has disastrous effects for him and everyone else he knows. His fiancée, Lucy Tartan, who has also been like a sister, since she and Pierre have grown up together, is momentarily cast aside for a stranger. The idea that two people who have known each other since childhood and are as close as brother and sister are the best candidates for marriage is another plot device familiar in nineteenth century novels, and, like Pierre's relationship with Isabel, again raises the issue of incest. Instead of explaining what he takes to be the truth about Isabel's parentage to his mother, Pierre chooses to spare his father's reputation (which, if he is correct, he no longer has any reason to respect) by concocting the fiction that Isabel is his wife, a lie which eventually kills his mother, grievously wounds Lucy, and causes the loss of his inheritance. Here the satire of the first part of the novel bears fruit; Melville may be suggesting that people nurtured in sentimental fantasies are so ill-equipped to deal with reality that when they must do so, the result is yet another sentimental fantasy. Incestuous wishes, familiar in literature since the Greeks, are symbolic of human self-absorption.

The last part of the novel has still another orientation occasioned by the philosophical theories of Plotinus, which appear in a pamphlet Pierre finds. Plotinus asserts that there are two measures of time, the "chronometrical" or celestial measure, which does not change with changing circumstances (like a clock set to Greenwich time), and the "horological," which is a measure set to a specific locality. Plinlimmon argues that although the chronometrical time may be more correct in an absolute sense, to attempt to live one's life according to it at all times (to go to bed at noon in China, for example, because it is nighttime by Greenwich time) is to invite difficulties which would make life impossible. We live in a horological world, flawed by all sorts of local customs, and to attempt to live chronometrically is to invite disaster. Pierre fails to understand the meaning of this warning, and in the last part of the novel he is trying and failing to write a chronometrical book. He becomes enraged when Glen Stanly receives what he takes to be his inheritance, and he shoots his cousin. Then Pierre and Isabel commit suicide, in another attempt to live up to a code of honor which only they understand.

In Pierre, Melville gives readers a main character with whom they at first identify, then whose motives and actions they suspect, and finally, from whom they recoil. Although Pierre tries to base his actions (such as his relationship with Isabel) on what he thinks are firm moral principles, his shooting of Stanly and his suicide demonstrate that he is, in fact, thrown by the winds of emotion. The entire novel is riddled with contradictions and puzzles, so it is well to remember its alternate title, which might well have been its only designation: *The Ambiguities*.

"Critical Evaluation" by Jim Baird

Bibliography:

Dillingham, William B. "The Wonderful Work on Physiognomy: *Pierre*" and "Convenient Lies and Duty-Subterfuges: *Pierre*; or the Deceptions," in *Melville's Later Novels*. Athens: University of Georgia Press, 1986. Discusses Melville's satirical treatment of Pierre as a victim of several strange nineteenth century theories, including physiognomy (reading character through facial expression).

Dimock, Wai-Chee. "*Pierre:* Domestic Confidence Game and the Drama of Knowledge." *Studies in the Novel* 16, no. 4 (Winter, 1984): 396-409. Sees *Pierre* as a battleground for Melville's investigations of theories of epistemology and psychology, with no clear conclusions being reached about either field in the novel.

Duban, James. "Subjective Transcendentalism: Pierre." In *Melville's Major Fiction: Politics, Theology, and Imagination*. DeKalb: Northern Illinois University Press, 1983. Regards *Pierre* as Melville's comment on the disastrous consequences of what the Transcendentalists proposed, using intuition as a guide to action. The notes contain an excellent review of criticism.

Higgins, Brian, and Hershel Parker, comps. Critical Essays on Herman Melville's "Pierre: Or, The Ambiguities." Boston: G. K. Hall, 1983. A collection of critical essays. Contains a bibliography of other works on Pierre.

Wilson, James C. "The Sentimental Education of Pierre Glendinning: An Explanation of the Causes and Implications of Violence in Melville's *Pierre*." *American Transcendental Quarterly*, n.s. 1, no. 3 (September, 1987): 167-177. Indicates that Pierre is a flawed product of a society that gave its young a false view of reality.

PIERS PLOWMAN

Type of work: Poetry
Author: William Langland (c. 1332-c. 1400)
Type of plot: Religious
Time of plot: Fourteenth century
Locale: England
First published: The Vision of William, Concerning Piers the Plowman, A Text, c. 1362; B
  Text, c. 1377; C Text, c. 1393

> *Principal characters:*
> THE POET
> PIERS THE PLOWMAN, an English plowman who becomes an allegorical
>   figure of Christ incarnate
> LADY MEDE, an allegorical figure representing both just reward and
>   bribery
> CONSCIENCE,
> REASON,
> THOUGHT,
> WIT,
> STUDY,
> CLERGY,
> SCRIPTURE,
> FAITH,
> HOPE,
> CHARITY, and other allegorical figures

The Story:

The narrator, generally referred to as "Will" and presented as the author of the poem, wandered the world dressed as a hermit, until one May morning, near Malvern Hills, he fell asleep and had a dream. In the vision, he saw a field full of folk of all social classes, including beggars, members of religious orders, knights, kings, and plowmen, going about the various activities of life, with a tower at one end and a dungeon located in a hollow beneath. At this point, a group of mice and rats assembled to determine what action to take against a cat at court who had been terrorizing them for some time. They agreed that the best plan would be to put a bell around the cat's neck but realized that they did not have the courage to attempt it. One sensible mouse suggested that they were better off with the cat than with a different cat or on their own.

A woman named Holy Church explained to him that the castle was the home of Truth, or God, and that the dungeon was the home of Wrong, or Satan. She advised Will that in order to save his soul he needed to follow Truth. The poet then witnessed the making of arrangements to marry Lady Mede (Reward) to False; dispute over the marriage was eventually brought to London to be adjudicated before the king. The king proposed instead that she marry Conscience, who refused the marriage, precipitating a series of debates on the nature of meed. The vision ended hopefully, with the king resolved to rule with the help of Reason and Conscience.

In a second dream vision, the poet heard a sermon calling for the repentance of society delivered to the field of folk by Reason, followed by the public confessions of representatives of each of the seven deadly sins. Society decided to search for St. Truth, and the farmer Piers Plowman, a long time follower of Truth, offered to show the people the way if they would help him plow his half-acre field. The attempt at plowing together eventually failed, despite the efforts of Hunger to help Piers motivate the workers. Before they left to seek Truth, Piers was offered a pardon by Truth, which told him only to "Do-Well." Piers then tore the pardon to pieces, vowing to seek Truth himself. After waking, the dreamer spent a long time pondering the meaning of this vision and became a wanderer again.

The poet continued to seek Do-Well, and, after a waking dispute with two Franciscan friars on the nature of Do-Well and Do-Evil, fell into a third dream. In this vision Thought advised him to progressively explore key stages called Do-Well, Do-Better, and Do-Best. In his exploration he met such characters as Wit and his wife Dame Study, who directs him to her cousin Clergy and his wife Scripture. Failing to understand their explanations of Do-Well, Do-Better, and Do-Best, the frustrated dreamer fell asleep in his dream, and was snatched up in this dream-within-a-dream by Fortune, accompanied by such followers as Lust and Recklessness, whom the poet in turn follows throughout his life. Scripture and the Emperor Trajan, who had been a virtuous man although a pagan, showed him the error of his ways before he had a vision of the natural universe as guided by Reason before waking back into the "outer" dream. Then he met Imaginative, with whom he engaged in a series of discussions about the nature of learning and religion.

After spending several years as a wandering beggar, Will fell into a fourth vision, in which he continued his investigation of religious ideas at a dinner at the house of Conscience with such characters as Clergy, Patience, and Scripture. After hearing some dubious advice from a Doctor of Divinity, Conscience and Will went traveling with Patience and met Hawkin the Active Man, who wore a badly soiled coat of Christendom. Hawkin underwent a religious conversion himself, recognizing his sinfulness and his dependence upon grace as a result of their discussions.

During the fifth vision, Will listened to Anima's discourse on the ideals of spiritual development and the nature of charity. In an inner dream within this dream, he met Piers Plowman again, who showed him the Tree of Charity that grows in people's bodies. The narrator then met the characters of Faith (Abraham), Hope (Moses), and the Good Samaritan (Charity and Christ). The Samaritan explained the nature of the Trinity and the need for repentance.

After another long period of travel, the poet slept again and, in a sixth vision, witnessed the Crucifixion, a debate by Mercy, Truth, Righteousness, and Peace on the ethical issues of the Redemption, and the Harrowing of Hell.

In another waking section, Will wrote down the dreams to this point and then attended Easter Mass with his family before falling into the seventh dream, in which he saw Piers, now identified with Jesus Christ, beginning the building of the Christian church, a house called Unity. The church community was attacked by Pride and his host of vices, and took refuge in Unity with Conscience leading the resistance.

In the next waking section, the poet met Need, then fell asleep and, in the eighth dream vision, saw the Antichrist and the massed powers of sin attack Unity. After the dreamer was smitten by Old Age, he entered Unity to find it under attack by Hypocrisy. After some discussion, in which Conscience argued that only Piers Plowman was needed to help them, Good Manners persuaded Peace to let Friar Flatterer into Unity to see to the sick, but once in, he weakened Contrition and opened the way for the entry of Sloth and Pride. Conscience called for Clergy to help defend Unity, but he had been put into a daze by the Friar. The dream ended with Conscience resolved to set off on a pilgrimage in search of Piers Plowman, at which point the dreamer awoke.

"The Story" by William Nelles

Critical Evaluation:

Like Geoffrey Chaucer's *Canterbury Tales* (1387-1400), William Langland's *The Vision of William, Concerning Piers the Plowman* (often called simply *Piers Plowman*) is one of the great vernacular works of the fourteenth century. Unlike Chaucer's poetry, however, Langland's work is apparently of and for the people, rather than the court. That the poem was popular can be seen in the meter in which it was written and by the fact that more than fifty manuscripts of the poem are still extant. Within the manuscripts are three different texts, the second and third being revisions containing additions to the first and earliest. The three versions have been dated respectively by scholars at about 1362, 1377, and 1393.

Langland's poem is in part a work of social protest, written from the viewpoint of the common person. The last half of the fourteenth century was a period of disaster and social unrest, the time of severe visitations of the plague (with accompanying moral, social, and economic upheavals), of the Peasant Revolt of 1381, and of John Wycliffe's Lollard movement. Langland often inserted, on behalf of the common folk, protests against unfair dealings by the crown, the courts, the clergy, and even the tradesmen. Being of the common folk himself, the poet recognized the trouble visited upon them, and he cried out bitterly against the cheating of the poor by the butcher, the baker, the miller, and others.

Most authorities now grant that the poem was probably written by one man, although some doubt has been expressed in the past on this point. Internal evidence indicates the author to be William Langland, a recipient of minor orders in the Church and a married man living in London. Despite allusions and references to himself and to happenings of the times, however, the author has retained the anonymity typical of the medieval author. The alliterative verse, much like the metrical structure used in *Beowulf* (c. 1000) and other Anglo-Saxon poems, was the native style of versification lost when the conventions of our present metrical system were popularized by court poetry. In the hands of medieval writers, including Langland, the Old English alliterative verse had not the subtlety and power it had once had in the ninth and tenth centuries. As used by Langland the measure consisted of lines of any number of syllables, divided into half-lines. Each half-line was given two heavy beats in important words, with the heavy beats accentuated by alliteration, as in such a line as "And wo in winter-tyme—with wakynge a nyghtes."

To emphasize the social or metrical aspects of *Piers Plowman* seems totally unfair to the poem, for it is essentially a religious work, filled with the religious doctrines, dogma, views, and sentiments of medieval Catholicism. In the poem, the poet has a series of visions which he relates to the reader, each vision concerned with humanity's relationships to God, relationships which concerned every aspect of life, according to medieval thought. In the first vision, which is probably the best known, the poet dreams of a vast field of people going about all the tasks and activities of the poet's world. The vision was explained to him by a lady named Holy Church, who informed him that the castle at one end of the field was the home of Truth, or God, and that in the dungeon in the valley dwelt the Father of Falsehood, or Satan. When asked by the poet how he might save his soul, the lady replied that he should learn to accept Truth, along with love and pity for his fellow humans. The poet then envisioned a long, involved sequence in which appeared Lady Mede, representing just reward and bribery simultaneously. A king proposed to marry Lady Mede to Conscience, after her rescue from False, but Conscience proclaimed against her and refused. Bribery, it is implied, cannot be reconciled with conscience. Reason, sent for by the king, promised to serve him, too, if Conscience would be another counselor. One interesting part of this sequence of the poem is Conscience's explanation of Latin grammar, with its declensions and agreement of noun and adjective, as a symbolic representation of the relationship between humanity and God. The king in the vision demanded a full explanation because, as he pointed out, English, the only language he knew, had no such grammatical relationships.

In another vision, the poet viewed the seven deadly sins. After a sermon by Conscience, Piers Plowman offered to show the company the way to Holy Truth, but only after he had plowed a half-acre field. Mentioned in this section are Piers' wife and children: Dame Work-while-I-am-Able, Daughter Do-this-or-thy-Dame-shall-beat-thee, and Son Suffer-thy-Sovereigns-to-have-their-Wishes-Dare-not-Judge-them-for-if-thou-Dost-thou-shalt-Dearly-Abide-it. At the end of this vision Piers Plowman was granted a pardon for himself and his heirs forever.

In the next sequence the poet took up Piers Plowman's quest for Truth. This quest is divided somewhat ambiguously into three parts, searches for Do-Well, Do-Better, and Do-Best. To achieve the state of Do-Well, the poet learned, one must fear God, be honest, be obedient, and love one's fellow man; this seems to be the task of the ordinary man. Do-Better, apparently the lot of the priest, represents the teaching of the gospel and helping everyone. Do-Best, the seeming lot of the bishop, involves everything in the first two categories, as well as the wise administration of the Church to save all souls.

Piers Plowman appears again and again in the poem, each time being more clearly an incarnation of the Christ. Seen at first as a hardworking, sincere, and honest plowman, Piers later shows up in the poem as the figure who can explain to the poet the Tree of Charity and the nature of the Trinity of God. He appears also as the Good Samaritan and, later, as the builder of the Church and the one who will joust in God's armor against Satan. These appearances serve to hold the poem together; without them the work would be a too loosely coupled series of episodes and digressions.

Much biblical lore is presented, from both the Old and New Testaments. The events in Eden, Job's trials, the perfidy of Judas, Jesus' suffering and crucifixion, along with many other familiar and traditional Christian elements are recorded in the poem. There are digressions on sin and virtue, on the nature and value of learning, and on the activities of laity and clergy, some good and some bad. These individual portions of the poem are beautifully executed and deeply moving. They are probably of more worth when considered by themselves insofar as a present day reader is concerned. To read *Piers Plowman* in its entirety is tedious, largely because of its rambling qualities, and few general readers will have the patience to do so nowadays, even with the help of a translation into modern English.

Bibliography:

Alford, John A., ed. *A Companion to "Piers Plowman."* Berkeley: University of California Press, 1988. A collection of eleven original essays, each followed by a selective bibliography, designed to furnish both beginning and advanced students with the essential information on every major aspect of the work. Includes an introduction surveying the six hundred years of the poem's critical history.

Blanch, Robert J., ed. *Style and Symbolism in "Piers Plowman": A Modern Critical Anthology.* Knoxville: University of Tennessee Press, 1969. The thirteen essays are gathered from a number of scholarly journals in the field, many of them unavailable in smaller libraries. Designed to orient the beginning student to the major issues in *Piers Plowman* studies.

Hussey, S. S., ed. *"Piers Plowman": Critical Approaches*. London: Methuen, 1969. Twelve essays, all of which were written especially for this collection. Hussey's introduction to the collection surveys the basic information about Langland and his poem for the beginning student.

Salter, Elizabeth. *"Piers Plowman": An Introduction*. Cambridge, Mass.: Harvard University Press, 1962. A short and readable, though somewhat dated, introductory survey of the structure and meaning of the poem, treating it as an alliterative poem, sermon, vision, and allegory.

Simpson, James. *"Piers Plowman": An Introduction to the B Text*. New York: Longman, 1990. A detailed overview of the B version, which is the most frequently encountered form of the poem. Summarizes the range of critical opinion on key issues and includes comparisons to similar material found in the contemporary *Canterbury Tales*, by Geoffrey Chaucer.

THE PILGRIM HAWK
A Love Story

Type of work: Novel
Author: Glenway Wescott (1901-1987)
Type of plot: Psychological realism
Time of plot: An afternoon in May, 1929
Locale: Chancellet, a town in France
First published: 1940

>   *Principal characters:*
>   ALWYN TOWER, a young American novelist
>   MADELEINE CULLEN, a wealthy, middle-aged, and attractive Irishwoman
>   LARRY CULLEN, her husband and an Irish aristocrat
>   ALEXANDRA HENRY, Tower's friend, a wealthy young American
>   RICKETTS, the Cullens' young Cockney chauffeur

The Story:

In the late 1920's, when Americans lived in romantic self-exile in Europe, Alwyn Tower's friend Alexandra Henry had renovated a stable in Chancellet. The interior was ultramodern, with a gigantic picture window looking out on a wild English-type garden in the back. Unexpectedly, Madeleine Cullen, en route to Budapest in a sleek, dark Daimler, stopped off to see her friend Alexandra. A handsome woman with Irish eyes and a London voice, she emerged from the car in fine French clothes and on spectacularly high heels. On her wrist, encased in a blood-stained gauntlet, perched a leashed hawk wearing a plumed Dutch hood. Ricketts, a dapper young Cockney chauffeur, and the stout, slightly inebriated Mr. Cullen helped her over the cobblestones. Lucy, the hawk, was an exemplary bird, a symbol of love and lust.

Tower, Alexandra, and the two guests gathered in the living room, where Mr. Cullen talked volubly about falcons and falconry. Later, the four took a walk in the formal garden of a nearby chateau. The Cullens had, after leaving their two wild boys at Cullen Hall in Ireland, traveled constantly; they had become involved with Irish revolutionaries and gone on pig-sticking hunts in Tangier and lion hunts in the jungle. In these activities, Mrs. Cullen was the initiator; Mr. Cullen merely followed where she led.

After the ritual feeding of Lucy in the living room, the bird was placed on a bench in the wild garden, while Mrs. Cullen and Alexandra rested before dinner. At the chromium bar on the balcony, the drunken Cullen talked to Tower as he would have to a bartender. He told Tower that he had almost killed an Irish poet out of jealousy (not really justified, as his wife allowed him his own infidelities). Comparing himself with his superlative wife, he mentioned that he was a bad horseman, marksman, and sportsman, loathed travel, and above all, despised Lucy because the bird was constantly perched on Madeleine's wrist, preventing him from getting close to his wife. As Cullen continued to talk, Tower's malice (the scorn of a captive hawk by a potentially captive hawk) increased.

Finally, the very drunken Cullen crept up on Lucy, removed her hood, and cut her leash. Madeleine Cullen thereupon kicked off her high heels and recaptured the bird. Then, just as the Cullens were about to resume their journey to Budapest, Cullen himself tried to get free by pulling a gun. It was unclear whether he intended to shoot the chauffeur (whom he suspected of coveting his wife), Madeleine herself, Lucy, or himself, but Madeleine, with the bird on her wrist flapping madly in the attempt to hold on, rushed back into the house and out to the garden to throw the revolver into the pond.

Critical Evaluation:

Glenway Wescott's *The Pilgrim Hawk* is a tapestry woven of five layers: the hawk's intrinsic or obvious resemblance to the characters; the extrinsic significance imposed by Alwyn Tower as a young man observing the relationship between the Cullens and the hawk; Tower's interpretations ten years later as the middle-aged narrator; the actual intentions of the author (who is very close to Tower); and the reader's opportunities to see symbolic meaning in the hawk. With complete control, Wescott conducts the reader in and out of this labyrinth of symbols.

Wescott differentiates his characters partly by the degree of awareness with which each plucks the bird of its symbolic resemblances to human nature. Tower and Alexandra (who is normally not curious) are eager to see such correspondences. Sitting erect in a straight kitchen chair, Mrs. Cullen makes swift transitions from hawk to human until she sees that her husband, sunk into a soft easy chair, senses certain comparisons to himself.

Tower and his ambiguous responses are almost as interesting and crucial to the story as the exotic characters whose behavior he witnesses. One of the experiences Wescott creates is the reader's puzzled effort to sift and separate the narrator's reflections and judgments in 1929 from those he makes in 1940 as he reflects. Wescott cunningly keeps Tower's voice out of the dialogue until the end, when he converses with Alexandra; the effect is that readers hear his mature voice at some distance, contemplating, musing, shifting back and forth in time and attitude. His tone fluctuates between intense curiosity, intellectual excitement, emotional reserve, repulsion, fascination, sadness, amusement, wit, and irony. Tower constantly sees symbols, and he seizes any pretext to express insights on love, marriage, drunkenness, the aristocracy, animals as compared with people, sports, and numerous other subjects. Out of all this, his character is distilled.

Tower's interest in the Cullens is an extension of his interest in himself. Outdoors people, the Cullens are self-centered, nonintrospective, self-indulgent, strenuous, and emotionally idle. Tower feels a cool affinity first with Mrs. Cullen (who signals her desire for his understanding), because, like an artist, she is in control of an artificial but satisfying situation that may at any moment revert to the chaos of nature. Then, reluctantly, Tower's sympathy shifts to Cullen, for Tower too is a lover, and he understands the predicament of a drunken, weak, vain, jealous, dull, mediocre, irritable, boring, conceited, childish fool who is in love with his wife.

Tower sees that Madeleine Cullen tries to create situations that will give full rein to her husband's masculinity while at the same time she restrains his wildness. He is a passionate man with streaks of animal ferocity and a desire for the liberty of the wilderness; like the falconer in Yeats's "The Second Coming," Mrs. Cullen strives to control his gyrings, but she is wild herself. She has always wanted to possess and herself train a real haggard, or trained falcon; now she has two. She needs to feel on her pulse an avatar of wildness: Controlling the falcon, she controls herself. When she persuades Tower to take Lucy on his wrist, Mrs. Cullen becomes electric with restlessness.

Like most falcons, Lucy makes frequent, though hopeless escape attempts. As a species, birds are free; only individuals are captive. All human beings are captives, however, and all must attempt to free themselves individually. Exceptional is the bird that loves captivity; exceptional is the human being who truly loves freedom. In captivity, both birds and people require a falconer. The human paradox is seen in the Cullens' relationship: He needs freedom, but she needs a captive; at the same time, he fears freedom, and she is loath to be a captor. Thus Lucy both humiliates and sublimates Cullen: He frees Lucy both to be rid of her and to make a symbolic gesture of escape; he attempts his own actual release when he pulls the gun.

Wescott shows Mrs. Cullen's falconry to be expert when she recaptures first the hawk, then the husband. Drink, food, and philandering are to Cullen what a hood, a pigeon, and Mrs. Cullen's stroking fingers are to Lucy: a tranquilization of the instinct to wildness. Blind to what she is doing to her husband, Mrs. Cullen, too, is hooded. Both the gun and the hawk are new in the Cullens' life, because in middle age they have exhausted love and become dependent on such semblances of love as distractions, deceptions, and disguises.

Tower predicts that, having been given the Cullens as examples, Alexandra will never marry. Alexandra returns to the United States, however, where she meets and marries Tower's brother; it is Tower who does not marry. Married or not, every man becomes a haggard and must spend most of his life on some perch. Having surrendered to domestication, hawks become scornful of each other; they never breed in captivity. Even wild hawks rarely die of disease, but death by starvation is common. Madeleine has seen people in the Dublin insane asylum whose eyes had an expression similar to that of a starving hawk. Like the lover and the artist, hawks that lose their technique enter a hopeless spiral of deterioration. The hawk in the sky looks down on his prey; Tower the writer looks down from his tower on human behavior, as when he devours Cullen's story, with the conscious intention of remembering every word and image of that afternoon. Although he occasionally turns his scrutinizing eye upon himself, Tower employs diversionary tactics to avoid the truth. Told the details of the aging hawk's life, he has an intuition of growing old as an artist and a lover; he was failing in 1929; in 1940, he is bitter, nervous, apathetic, full of false pride, bereft of inspiration, and bored.

The concept of vision is one of Wescott's most effective motifs. He describes the hawk's eyes, their function in the hunt, the purpose of the hood; then in various ways, he compares the hawk's eyes with those of the other characters. Tower mentions his long-sightedness, expresses fear of going blind, and his immediate fear (which he shares with Cullen) that the hawk may attack his eyes. Tower's testimony, with its ambiguous tone and compulsive philosophizing, is a failed artist's and lover's means of trying to see while remaining purblind to the meaning of that bizarre afternoon. At the same time, however, the reader's vision comes into focus. Wescott's use here of the Jamesian point of view is one of the most successful in American literature.

Bibliography:

Johnson, Ira. *Glenway Wescott: The Paradox of Voice*. Port Washington, N.Y.: Kennikat Press, 1971. A chapter on *The Pilgrim Hawk* provides a comprehensive analysis of the novel that focuses on its composition, characterization, use of symbols, treatment of the theme of love, and Wescott's integration of autobiographical elements.

Phelps, Robert, and Jerry Rosco, eds. *Continual Lessons: The Journals of Glenway Wescott*. New York: Farrar, Straus, Giroux, 1990. Excellent source for determining Wescott's ideas about the value of *The Pilgrim Hawk*. Includes comments on the novel's composition and publication history, as well as brief remarks by the novelist about thematic issues.

Rueckert, William H. *Glenway Wescott*. New York: Twayne, 1965. General study of the writer's literary achievements. Places *The Pilgrim Hawk* in the context of Wescott's career, seeing it as part of a trilogy that includes *The Grandmother* (1927) and *The Apple of the Eye* (1924); together these form a "symbolic autobiography" of the novelist.

Schorer, C. E. "The Maturing of Glenway Wescott." In *Twentieth-Century American Literature*, edited by Harold Bloom. New York: Chelsea House, 1988. Discusses *The Pilgrim Hawk* as an international novel and links Wescott with other American authors of the 1920's and 1930's. Reviews the novel's organization and comments on Wescott's style.

Zaubel, Morton Dauwen. *Craft and Character in Modern Fiction*. New York: Viking Press, 1957. In the chapter entitled "The Whisper of the Devil," Zaubel provides extensive commentary on *The Pilgrim Hawk* and discusses techniques Wescott employs in his fiction.

PILGRIMAGE

Type of work: Novels
Author: Dorothy Richardson (1873-1957)
Type of plot: Bildungsroman
Time of plot: Late nineteenth and early twentieth centuries
Locale: England
First published: 1938: *Pointed Roofs*, 1915; *Backwater*, 1916; *Honeycomb*, 1917; *The*
    Tunnel, 1919; *Interim*, 1919; *Deadlock*, 1921; *Revolving Lights*, 1923; *The Trap*, 1925;
    Oberland, 1927; *Dawn's Left Hand*, 1931; *Clear Horizon*, 1935; *Dimple Hill*, 1938;
    March Moonlight, 1967

> *Principal characters:*
> MIRIAM HENDERSON, an Englishwoman
> MICHAEL SHATOV, a Russian émigré
> HYPO WILSON, an admirer of Miriam
> AMABEL, a female admirer

The Story:

Miriam climbed the staircase. She looked down from the bedroom of the second floor to the garden below, aware of the sense that she was leaving behind everything familiar to her. She thought back over her days of quiet, sun-filled mornings. She remembered the afternoons she had spent reading books, and the moments when she had played duets on the piano with her sister, Harriet. Her packed trunk stood in the hallway downstairs, ready for the trip to Hanover, Germany the next morning. A governess position at a girls' boarding school awaited Miriam.

Miriam crossed the English Channel and took a train to Germany. She already regretted her decision to become a governess. As night fell, the train rushed her across the countryside toward Germany, and Miriam doubted her ability to teach English to young girls. She was leaving the house of her family because her father was bankrupt. There was no looking back. Miriam knew that she had to take her place in the world. Nervous but expectant, she felt freedom might await her.

After several months at her position in the boarding school, Miriam was confronted by Fräulein Pfaff, headmistress of the school. They stood in the central room of the school, along with the other teaching staff. While Fräulein Pfaff chastised the teachers for talking about men in front of the schoolgirls, Miriam grew angry. She realized that the Fräulein was talking about her. She vowed not to bow to Fräulein Pfaff's spiteful attitude, but saw that she might be asked to resign her teaching post with the girls. Meanwhile, back in England, one of Miriam's sisters became engaged to be married. Miriam announced to Fräulein Pfaff that she would go home to England. Once again, she boarded a train. This time, when it pulled out from the bright platform in the night, it was to return to England. Miriam disembarked at the English station with her first year of work behind her.

Upon her return to England, Miriam was asked by her mother to assume a teaching position with young children. At her eighteenth birthday, Miriam put up her hair and went to work as a resident governess in a school for the daughters of gentlemen. By the end of the teaching year, she went on a seaside holiday in Brighton and visited the Crystal Palace.

Dispirited by her year of teaching at the boarding school, Miriam accepted another position as governess. She traveled to the home of a wealthy English family. She watched the Corrie family, occupants of a large house, with their evening gowns and decorum. Miriam puzzled over her own position as worker in the home. She recalled that her own father was bankrupt and that she could not give up the necessary income from her governess work, regardless of her feelings about her position. In addition, she quizzed the father of the family on the fact that she, Miriam, must instruct the children in religion. How could she do this, she wanted to know, while she herself was a nonbeliever?

Lacking other occupational options, despite her wide reading and knowledge of music, the young Miriam continued to chafe at her position as governess. She left to take a job as a dental assistant, and she took up residence in the London boarding house of Mrs. Bailey.

It was while she boarded at Mrs. Bailey's that Miriam met Michael Shatov, a Russian Jew. She tutored him in English and became engaged to him. The two discussed philosophy, Zionism, and feminism. Through their conversations, Miriam realized that she was caught. Their differences were too much. Miriam grew frustrated. She knew that she did not want to marry Michael. When Michael approached her physically, Miriam could not respond. Unable to respond to Michael's physical advances, and at odds with him on other points, Miriam knew that she would leave England and Michael.

Troubled, Miriam embarked on a long tour of Switzerland. She returned to England only to return to Michael. After a long conversation, Michael again asked Miriam to accept his proposal of marriage. Miriam tried to impress upon him the value that she assigned to friendship. She was pursued, also, by Hypo Wilson, a persistent lover. In addition, a female friend named Amabel grew increasingly attached to Miriam. Startled, Miriam realized that Amabel wanted to consume Miriam's life in the same way her other attachments did. Miriam realized that she had the temperament of both the male and the female. Yet increasingly, she wanted close contact with neither.

Ensconced in Mrs. Bailey's boarding house, Miriam decided to break free of all of her attachments except one. She left her lover, Hypo Wilson. In a further effort to free herself from attachments, she introduced Michael to Amabel with the hopes that they would become interested in each other. They did. Quietly, Miriam rejoiced. Not long afterward, Michael and Amabel were married. Miriam left again for Switzerland after a sojourn on a Quaker farm.

Amabel and Michael, married and settled in London, were unhappy. Miriam spent a weekend with them when she returned to London, and she claimed little responsibility for their unhappiness in life. Alone in a different room in London, Miriam looked out the window and surveyed her life. After the long years of her journey, Miriam claimed that writing would be the central act of her life.

Critical Evaluation:

Considered by many critics to be an innovator in form, Dorothy Miller Richardson completed the nine volumes of *Pilgrimage* during a lifetime of clerical jobs and a writing career that included book reviews, columns, and the extended novel form. Richardson's formal education was brief, but she read widely in the literature and science of her day. Upon settling in London in 1895, to work as a dental assistant, she met the writer H. G. Wells; through her extended liaison with Wells, Richardson was introduced to the world of writers, feminism, and social criticism. This environment was the foundation of her adult life as well as of her most important work, *Pilgrimage*. *Pilgrimage* consists of a series of novels: *Painted Roofs* (1915), *Backwater* (1916), *Honeycomb* (1917), *The Tunnel* (1919), *Interim* (1919), *Deadlock* (1921), *Revolving Lights* (1923), *The Trap* (1925), *Oberland* (1927), *Dawn's Left Hand* (1931), *Clear Horizon* (1935), *Dimple Hill* (1938), and *March Moonlight* (1967).

In *Pilgrimage*, Richardson located herself as an innovator in the novel form and as a social critic. *Pilgrimage* marks an attempt to create a new language for writing, a language modernism reveled in. Richardson's deliberate record of details, conversations, actions, and thoughts reflected her idea that all phenomena were important.

More particularly, her experiments in sentence structure supported her view of a female writing style. As she once wrote, "Feminine prose, as Charles Dickens and James Joyce have delightfully shown themselves to be aware, should properly be unpunctuated, moving from point to point without formal obstructions." Richardson's complicated and innovative experiments with syntax also mirrored the effect that life had on Miriam Henderson, the protagonist of Richardson's work. In Miriam's quest for a life both examined and independent, she could not move, free and unobstructed as Richardson's sentences do. One might say that Miriam's life experience is the very opposite of Richardson's stylistic effects. The "feminine sentence" runs unfettered and free, but the feminine life, as seen by Richardson, runs into obstacles and problems from young adulthood onward. Miriam, as she embarks on her pilgrimage out of her family home and into the world, demonstrates the complexity of a woman's existence.

The theme of *Pilgrimage* may be broadly stated as the coming-into-being of a woman writer after a long journey. Miriam states in the last volume of *Pilgrimage*, "While I write, everything vanishes but what I contemplate." *Pilgrimage* holds at its center the duality of internal and external life. Richardson validates each moment of her heroine's life by laying claim to it in print; even so, her heroine proclaims the joy of obliterating all experience but one: the act of writing. In this sense, one could argue that the narrator and author are fused, which is a demonstration of the theme of *Pilgrimage*.

The novel begins with Miriam leaving the family home for Germany, and the entire nine volumes are told through Miriam's point of view. Seen originally as a novel without a plot, the work has since been understood as a *Bildungsroman*. In an interesting twist on the novel of education, Richardson begins with her subject as an adult, rather than with the more usual story of a child approaching the end of youth. In each advancing section, a new dimension to Miriam's journey unfolds in a haphazard fashion. As Miriam moves from youth to womanhood, issues of female identity, romance, and work are raised. Richardson asks the reader to share in the examination of these issues. Upon receiving Michael Shatov's proposal of marriage, Miriam meditates on marriage as a prison in which a woman has no place for herself. Since there is no narrator adding comments or analysis, the reader must go along with Miriam on her quest, finding answers as the journey proceeds.

Richardson achieves her highest artistic success in her fusion of protagonist and narrator; as Miriam proceeds through her pilgrimage, no particular outcome is assured. The reader becomes as much a participant in the journey as the protagonist. Miriam critiques the nature of male and female existence as she reaches for a way of being that will encompass reality in all of its forms. The form of *Pilgrimage*, in its fractured passages, reminiscences, and dialogue, makes ample room for all these forms.

R. C. S.

Bibliography:
Fromm, Gloria G. *Dorothy Richardson: A Biography.* Champaign: University of Illinois Press, 1977. An excellent starting point for an examination of Dorothy Richardson's life and work. Interesting analysis of *Pilgrimage*, highlighting the relationship between Richardson's life and her art.

Gregory, Horace. *Dorothy Richardson: An Adventure in Self-Discovery*. New York: Holt, Rinehart and Winston, 1967. A compelling study of the events of Richardson's life. Important work for the reader interested in the autobiographical nature of *Pilgrimage*.

Hanscombe, Gillian E. *The Art of Life: Dorothy Richardson and the Development of Feminist Consciousness*. London: Peter Owen, 1982. Offers textual examination of *Pilgrimage*. Includes interesting assessment of Richardson's attempt to develop a feminine writing style. Comprehensive index provides access to important sections.

Radford, Jean. *Dorothy Richardson*. Bloomington: Indiana University Press, 1991. Analyzes structure, characters, and themes. Contains a useful section on reading and readership in Richardson's novel. An excellent resource for current scholarship on *Pilgrimage*.

Staley, Thomas F. *Dorothy Richardson*. Boston: Twayne, 1976. A lucid examination of Dorothy Richardson's life. A place to start in Richardson study.

THE PILGRIMAGE OF CHARLEMAGNE

Type of work: Poetry
Author: Unknown
Type of plot: Folklore
Time of plot: c. 800
Locale: Paris, Jerusalem, and Constantinople
First transcribed: Voyage de Charlemagne à Jérusalem et à Constantinople, c. 1100
  (English translation, 1927)

> *Principal characters:*
> CHARLEMAGNE, the Frankish king and emperor of the West
> HUGO, the emperor of Greece and of Constantinople
> ROLAND,
> OLIVER,
> WILLIAM OF ORANGE,
> NAIMES,
> OGIER OF DENMARK,
> GERIN,
> BERENGER,
> TURPIN THE ARCHBISHOP,
> ERNAUT,
> AYMER,
> BERNARD OF BRUSBAN, and
> BERTRAM, Charlemagne's twelve peers

The Story:

One day Emperor Charlemagne, accompanied by his queen, the twelve peers, and many others, went to the Abbey of St. Denis. Charlemagne was elegantly garbed and wore his fine sword as well as his splendid crown. Proud of his prepossessing mien, he boasted of his power and majestic appearance, confidently asking the queen if she had ever seen another as impressive as he. Impatient with this vanity, the queen chided Charlemagne for his inordinately high opinion of himself and suggested that there was a king handsomer than he. The emperor, angry over this public humiliation, commanded the queen to name the rival king so that their respective courts could meet and decide which of the two was handsomer, threatening the queen with decapitation if it were determined that she had spoken falsely about the other king's superior appearance. Frightened, the queen tearfully pleaded for mercy, pretended forgetfulness, and then amended her claim to say that, although richer, the other king was not nearly so brave as Charlemagne. Still unsatisfied, Charlemagne demanded to know the identity of the other king, again threatening to cut off the queen's head immediately if she did not acquiesce. The queen then admitted that it was Hugo, the emperor of Greece and Constantinople and ruler of vast lands in Persia.

When Charlemagne and his entourage returned to the palace in Paris, the emperor declared to the assembled peers and knights of France that, attended by his imperial retinue, he would go on a pilgrimage to the Holy Land to pray in Jerusalem at the Holy Sepulchre, to make the Stations of the Cross, and then to continue on to Constantinople to visit Emperor Hugo. For the journey, with the blessings of Archbishop Turpin, all twelve peers—Roland, Oliver, William of Orange, Naimes, Ogier of Denmark, Gerin, Berenger, Ernaut, Aymer, Bernard of Brusban, Bertram the Strong, as well as Turpin—the rest of the imperial retainers, and Charlemagne himself, were outfitted as pilgrims. Equipped with pilgrims' scrip, they carried no weapons, only sharp oaken staves, but they were accompanied by many beasts of burden, laden with riches. With blessings from the Abbey of St. Denis, the imperial troupe, including Turpin, set off. Along the way, Charlemagne drew Bertram aside to call his attention to the 80,000-man pilgrimage and to boast once more of the power and the might of the leader of such a group.

Arriving in Jerusalem, the emperor and his fellows visited the shrine of the Last Supper, where the bearded Charlemagne and his twelve peers audaciously sat in the chairs allegedly once occupied by Christ and his twelve disciples. A passing Jew observed this charade and forthwith informed the patriarch of Jerusalem, who instantly collected a procession of priests and acolytes to investigate the phenomenon.

The patriarch of Jerusalem respectfully greeted Charlemagne, who identified himself as Charles of France, mighty conqueror of twelve kings in search of a thirteenth conquest, and as a devout Christian pilgrim. The patriarch declared that he who occupied Christ's seat must be Charles the Great—Charles Magnus or Charlemagne—above all other crowned heads. The patriarch generously acceded to Charlemagne's request for sacred relics, giving him St. Simon's armlet; Lazarus' shroud; a vial of St. Stephen's blood; a piece of the Holy Shroud; one of the nails from the Cross; the crown of thorns; the chalice, the silver bowl, and Christ's own dinner knife from the Last Supper; clippings from the whiskers and the hair of St. Peter; a vial of the Virgin's milk; and a piece of the Virgin's robe. As Charlemagne accepted these relics, a lame person was cured of his afflictions, attesting the divine power of the relics. A magnificent gold and silver chest was made for transporting these holy treasures, and the collection was consigned to the keeping of Archbishop Turpin.

Charlemagne and his men stayed four months in Jerusalem. Then, with pledges of Christian fealty and defense of the faith, they left for Constantinople, where Charlemagne's thoughts had lately turned again to Emperor Hugo. Arriving a few miracles later, the travelers were stunned by the beauty and opulence of Constantinople. Emperor Hugo, however, was not there to greet them. Inquiry disclosed that he was plowing, under a silken-canopied chariot with a gold plow and golden-yoked oxen, making furrows as straight as a taut bowstring. When Charlemagne sought out Hugo, the two emperors greeted each other cordially, each noting the other's comely physique. Hugo, having earlier been apprised of Charlemagne's noble bearing, welcomed the French peers and knights graciously, promising lavish gifts and warm hospitality if they would remain for an extended visit. Remembering the queen's words, Charlemagne and his company were astonished by the richness of Hugo's palace and courtiers. Suddenly, however, the palace was struck by a strong wind. The entire building seemed to spin, and the Frenchmen became dizzy and could not stand up. Just as suddenly the wind died down, and the Frenchmen regained their balance. Then dinner was served, a fine feast in which no gustatory request or desire was not met. Spiced claret flowed freely. Oliver was smitten with love for Hugo's beautiful blonde daughter. Minstrels sang to musical accompaniment, and a great entertainment was mounted.

After the feast was over, Hugo led Charlemagne and his twelve peers to a luxuriously appointed apartment where they were to spend the night. More wine was brought, and the Frenchmen began to make themselves comfortable. The wily Hugo, however, unbeknownst to his guests, posted a spy in a nearby stairwell to report on the visitors' postprandial conversation. Filled with wine and unaware that they were being overheard, Charlemagne and his twelve companions waxed jolly and daring. They began to brag, as was their late-evening custom following much wine. At first, they merely noted the vulnerability of Hugo's rich estates to their superior military power, but then each one, in turn, began making a derogatory boast about individually overpowering Hugo's might. In this way, *les gabs* (a typical epic-formula device) were played out—the bragging, boasting, half-serious and half-joking vaunts of Charlemagne and his twelve peers.

As was fitting, Charlemagne began the boasts. He scoffed that, were Hugo to array his best knight in two suits of armor, he, Charlemagne, would wield Hugo's own sword to penetrate that armor and pin the knight into the earth to a long spear's depth. Charlemagne's nephew Roland, who was next, boasted that he would take Hugo's ivory horn and, with a single blast, level Constantinople as well as singe Hugo's very beard. At Roland's urging, Oliver spoke: If Hugo would but loan him his daughter for a night, Oliver would demonstrate his sexual prowess by possessing her one hundred times before the morrow. Archbishop Turpin was invited to make the next contribution. Befitting his calling, Turpin proposed a harmless physical feat involving the juggling of apples while vaulting two galloping horses to mount a third. William of Orange thereupon proposed to use a large, decorative gold-and-silver ball in that very room to demolish more than 160 cubits of wall around Hugo's palace, and Ogier of Denmark jeered that he would play Samson and dislodge a palace pillar to bring the entire structure down. Then the aged Naimes boasted that, clad in Hugo's own chain-mail tunic, he would jump from the battlements of the palace and back so quickly that Hugo would not even notice and then destroy the hauberk with a mere quiver. Berenger bragged that he would jump from the highest tower in the palace onto the upturned blades of the swords of all of Hugo's knights without suffering a scratch. Bernard then claimed he would divert a river, cause a flood, and force Hugo to beg from a high tower for surcease. Ernaut boasted that he would sit in a vat of molten lead until it hardened and then shake himself loose from it. In like manner, Aymer boasted that he would banquet at Hugo's table, then don a cap to make himself invisible and deliver Hugo a beard-shattering blow. Bertram offered to beat two shields together so loudly that the sound would deafen or disperse all wildlife in the area. Finally, Gerin bragged that he would stack two coins upon a post, stand at a league's distance, and, with his spear, topple one coin without disturbing the other, then run the league's distance to catch the falling coin before it hit the ground.

Hugo's spy promptly reported these mocking, derisive taunts to Hugo, which both spy and emperor construed literally. Hugo, outraged at such an affront to his hospitality, gathered his knights and confronted Charlemagne the next morning. Somewhat taken aback, Charlemagne tried to soothe Hugo's ire by explaining the influence of the claret and the French custom of *les gabs*, but Hugo would have none of it. Hugo demanded that the boasts be fulfilled or he would order Charlemagne and his twelve peers beheaded. In desperation, Charlemagne prayed over his trove of relics. Then an angel appeared to him, reassuring him that no peer would fail to execute his boast—yet another miracle to rescue the French—but warning him to foreswear such mockery and bragging in the future.

Charlemagne called together his peers and offered Hugo the choice as to which boast should be attempted first. William of Orange was given the initial challenge. With divine assistance, he heaved the gold-and-silver ball through more than 160 cubits of wall and the palace as well, causing massive destruction. Next, Bernard, with God's aid, created a mighty flood, which God abated in his own good time. So impressed was Hugo that he required no further demonstrations of Frankish power and immediately became Charlemagne's vassal.

The occasion was celebrated with great feasting, and the two emperors displayed themselves regally before their assembled knights and attendants. The combined courts judged Charlemagne the fairest of the two kings. Then the French departed for their journey back to Paris.

Buoyed by this bloodless conquest, Charlemagne was in such a good mood that he forgave the queen and did not behead her.

Critical Evaluation:

Some twentieth century scholars have claimed that medieval writers were deficient in imagination and thus unable to create plots, depending instead on historical events to provide their stories. Charlemagne's journey to Jerusalem, a complete fabrication, is a literary work that clearly demonstrates that heroic legends when embodied in medieval romances did not, and did not need to, rely on historical events. Charlemagne never went to Jerusalem. In fact, the closest he came to Jerusalem was when the patriarch of Jerusalem sent him the keys to the city and to the Holy Sepulchre as a reward for his generous support of Christian churches in the Holy Land. In Charlemagne's fictional pilgrimage to Jerusalem, medieval writers combined real persons with fantasized events to create original literature of a kind that would later be compared to a historical novel.

The source of this tale is alleged to have been the Abbey of St. Denis, which claimed to possess a number of holy relics brought back by Charlemagne from the Holy Land. The best known of these putative relics was the crown of thorns. However, skeptical twentieth century scholarship also credits missionary zeal, possibly venality, with the creation of this tale of Charlemagne's pilgrimage.

As for the vanity, arrogance, and braggadocio of Charlemagne's spurious exploits, such actions undoubtedly create a reasonable counterbalance for the more respectful histories and legends that depict Charlemagne as a pious, noble, and high-minded leader. When Charlemagne is described as feeling threatened by the possibility that Emperor Hugo might be more handsome than he is, Charlemagne becomes less imperial and more human. Although such impertinent questions were certainly never raised in Charlemagne's authoritarian times, the freer atmosphere of the High Middle Ages—sometimes characterized as "The Renaissance of the Twelfth Century," during which time this poem appears to have been written—must have tolerated such irreverence. Thus the earthy tale of Charlemagne's imagined trip to Jerusalem suggests but another facet of Charlemagne's undoubtedly multifaceted personality, however fanciful the depiction may be.

Bibliography:

Cobby, Anne Elizabeth. Introduction to "The Pilgrimage of Charlemagne" and "Aucassin and Nicollette," translated by Glyn S. Burgess, and edited by Glyn S. Burgess and Anne Elizabeth Cobby. New York: Garland, 1988. Discusses the aesthetic qualities of the work, provides information on textual matters, and comments on possible sources.

Grigsby, John L. "A Note on the Genre of The Voyage of Charlemagne." In *Essays in Early French Literature Presented to Barbara M. Craig,* edited by Norris J. Lang and Jerry C. Nash. York, S.C.: French Literature Publishing, 1982. Comments on the implications of different titles used by medieval and twentieth century editors. Claims that the author creates a new genre by altering traditional elements of medieval romances.

Holmes, U. T. *A History of Old French Literature, from the Origins to 1300.* New York: F. S. Crofts, 1938. Describes ways in which the French version of the tale was linked to the legend of St. Denis and the city of Paris, where it was used as part of an annual ceremony honoring the patron saint of the city.

Muir, Lynette. *Literature and Society in Medieval France: The Mirror and the Image, 1100-1500.* New York: St. Martin's, 1985. Traces the composition history of the poem; notes how the work differs from other *chansons de geste* in its extensive use of humor and fantastic detail.

Polak, Lucie. "Charlemagne and the Marvels of Constantinople." In *The Medieval Alexander Legend and Romance Epic*, edited by Peter Noble et al. Millwood, N.Y.: Kraus International Publication, 1982. Examines the technological marvels described as part of the hero's visit to Constantinople; suggests possible historical inspirations for them.

THE PILGRIM'S PROGRESS

Type of work: Novel
Author: John Bunyan (1628-1688)
Type of plot: Allegory
Time of plot: Any time since Christ
Locale: Indeterminate
First published: part 1, 1678; part 2, 1684

Principal characters:
>CHRISTIAN
>FAITHFUL
>HOPEFUL
>MR. WORLDLY WISEMAN
>EVANGELIST
>DESPAIR
>IGNORANCE
>APOLLYON, a giant devil

The Story:

One day, according to John Bunyan, he lay down in a den to sleep; in his sleep, he dreamed that he saw a man standing in a field and crying out in pain and sorrow because he and his whole family, as well as the town in which they lived, were to be destroyed. Christian, for that was his name, knew of this catastrophe because he had read about it in the book he held in his hands, the Bible. Evangelist, the preacher of Christianity, soon came up to Christian and presented him with a roll of paper on which it was written that he should flee from the wrath of God and make his way from the City of Destruction to the City of Zion. Running home with this hope of salvation, Christian tried to get his neighbors and family to go away with him, but they would not listen and thought he was either sick or mad. Finally, he shut his ears to his family's entreaties to stay with them and ran off toward the light in the distance. Under the light, he knew he would find the wicket gate that opened into Heaven.

On his way, he met Pliant and Obstinate; Christian was so distracted by them that he fell in a bog called the Slough of Despond. He could not get out because of the bundle of sins on his back. Finally, Help came along and aided Christian out of the sticky mire. Going on his way, he soon fell in with Mr. Worldly Wiseman, who tried to convince Christian that he would lead a happier life if he gave up his trip toward the light and settled down to the comforts of a burdenless town life. Fearing that Christian was about to be led astray, Evangelist came up to the two men and quickly showed the errors in Mr. Worldly Wiseman's arguments.

Soon Christian arrived at a closed gate where he met Good-Will, who told him that if he knocked, the gate would be opened to him. Christian did so. He was invited into the gate-keeper's house by the Interpreter and learned from him the meaning of many of the Christian mysteries. He was shown pictures of Christ and Passion and Patience; Despair in a cage of iron bars; and a vision of the Day of Judgment, when evil people will be sent to the bottomless pit and good people will be carried up to Heaven. Christian was filled with both hope and fear after having seen these things. Continuing on his journey, he came to the Holy Cross and the Sepulchre of Christ. There his burden of sins fell off, and he was able to take to the road with renewed vigor.

Soon he met Sloth, Simple, Presumption, Formalism, and Hypocrisy, but he kept to his way and they kept to theirs. Later, Christian lay down to sleep for a while. When he went on again, he forgot to pick up the roll of paper Evangelist had given him. Remembering it later, he ran back to find it. Running to make up the time lost, he suddenly found himself confronted by two lions. He was afraid to pass by them until the porter of the house by the side of the road told him that the lions were chained and that he had nothing to fear. The porter then asked Christian to come into the house. There he was well treated and shown some of the relics of biblical antiquity by four virgins, Discretion, Prudence, Piety, and Charity. They gave him good advice and sent him on his journey, armed with the sword and shield of Christian faith.

In the Valley of Humiliation, Christian was forced to fight the giant devil, Apollyon, whose body was covered with the shiny scales of pride. Christian was wounded in this battle, but after he had chased away the devil, he healed his wounds with leaves from the Tree of Life that grew nearby. After the Valley of Humiliation came the Valley of the Shadow of Death, in which Christian had to pass one of the gates to Hell. In order to save himself from the devils who issued out of the terrible hole, he recited some of the verses from the Psalms.

After passing through this danger, he had to go by the caves of the old giants, Pope and Pagan; when he had done so, he caught up with a fellow traveler, Faithful. As the two companions went along, they met Evangelist, who warned them of the dangers in the town of Vanity Fair.

Vanity Fair was a town of ancient foundation that, since the beginning of time, had tried to lure travelers away from the path to Heaven. Here all the vanities of the world were sold, and the people who dwelt there were cruel and stupid and had no love for travelers such as Christian and Faithful. After having learned these things, the two companions promised to be careful and went on down into the town. There they were arrested and tried because they would buy none of the town's goods. Faithful was sentenced to be burned alive, and Christian was put in prison. When Faithful died in the fire, a chariot came down from Heaven and took him up to God. Christian escaped from the prison. Accompanied by a young man named Hopeful, who had been impressed by Faithful's reward, he set off once more.

They passed through the Valley of Ease, where they were tempted to dig in a silver mine free to all. As they left the valley, they saw the pillar of salt that had once been Lot's wife. They became lost and were captured by a giant, Despair, who lived in Doubting Castle; there they were locked in the vaults beneath the castle walls and lay there until Christian remembered he had a key called Promise in his pocket; with this, they escaped from the prison.

They met the four shepherds, Knowledge, Experience, Watchful, and Sincere, who showed them the Celestial Gate and warned them of the paths to Hell. Then the two pilgrims passed by the Valley of Conceit, where they were met by Ignorance and others who had not kept to the straight and narrow path. They passed on to the country of Beulah. Far off, they saw the gates of the city of Heaven glistening with pearls and precious stones. Thinking that all their troubles were behind them, they lay down to rest.

When they went on toward the city, they came to the River of Death. They entered the river and began to wade through the water. Soon Christian became afraid, and the more afraid he became, the deeper the waters rolled. Hopeful shouted to him to have hope and faith. Cheered by these words, Christian became less afraid, the water became less deep, and finally they both got across safely. They ran up the hill toward Heaven. Shining angels led them through the gates.

Critical Evaluation:

The seventeenth century's literary greatness began with such dramatic works as William

Shakespeare's *Hamlet* (c. 1600-1601) and *The Tempest* (c. 1611-1612). To the seventeenth century belongs the height of Jacobean drama, the flowering of the sonnet, and the achievements of Renaissance lyric poetry. Such works may all be considered literary products of a Humanistic century—they are the high-water mark of Humanistic philosophy with its belief in the importance of humanity and of human interests. In the middle of Humanism's great artistic accomplishment appeared John Bunyan's *The Pilgrim's Progress*. The full title of the work published in 1678 is *The Pilgrim's Progress from This World to That Which Is Come*. In 1684, Bunyan published *The Pilgrim's Progress from This World to That Which Is Come the Second Part*.

The Pilgrim's Progress reaches back to medieval literature for its dream-vision form; Bunyan's narrator goes to sleep and dreams his fable of the Christian religion. Bunyan's "novel" is a classic example of the multifaceted nature of a literary century, reflecting as it does the popularity of the conversion story during the time. What is more significant, it shows with much skill one of the most attractive qualities of the age, for Bunyan draws on his Humanist contemporaries and their techniques to make his tale of the salvation of a soul one of the unique masterpieces of English literature.

The Pilgrim's Progress is usually classified as a novel, but according to traditional definitions of the novel genre, *The Pilgrim's Progress* is decidedly too predestined in the outcome of its plot to make it engaging, as a novel should be. The work is also so allegorical that one may decide that it is not a novel, since novels generally are realistic at least to an extent. It is Bunyan's literary genius that endowed the book with classic appeal. The success of *The Pilgrim's Progress*, as distinguished from the countless other stories of personal salvation that were written at about the same time, is its ability to show the Christian experience through the character Christian's eyes. By making all the pitfalls, the specters of doubt and fear, and the religious terror that Christian experiences real to this believable, impressionable narrator, Bunyan makes them just as real to his reader. Therefore, the reader of the book is really not any more sure than Christian that his salvation is assured. Bunyan has struck a true and profound element of Christianity through his use of the Humanistic technique of viewing events through the eyes of his narrator.

Christian is a gullible, hence believable, character. He understands, perhaps too well for his own soul's well-being, the doubts and terrors that plague the would-be good Christian. Christian understands how one may lose faith under dire and trying conditions. Christian himself suffers through his commitment to his faith. His journey is a test of endurance; the straight-and-narrow path is not necessarily filled with rejoicing, as Bunyan shows.

For example, Christian and his companion traveler, Hopeful, find a meadow paralleling their way and an inviting stile to help them cross the fence. So they choose the easier path. After a while, it becomes pitch dark, and they lose their way. To make matters worse, a traveler ahead of them falls into a pit and is "dashed in pieces with his fall." Christian and Hopeful rush to the pit and hear only groans. The two of them repent and muster courage to return to the river. By now, the waters have risen greatly, adding to their dangers. "Yet they adventured to go back, but it was so dark, and the flood was so high, that in their going back they had like to have been drowned nine or ten times." These are the perils and dangers of trying to be a Christian in the world. With a stroke of genius, Bunyan turns what could be a dry, pessimistic sermon into high adventure.

Bunyan seemed most productive in his own life when under duress. *The Pilgrim's Progress* was begun and largely written during prison terms that Bunyan served for preaching without a license. A Baptist minister, he was a religious outlaw after the Restoration restored the Church of England, but he refused to stop preaching. Originally arrested in 1660 and sentenced to three months, he eventually served twelve years because he continued to preach. During these years, he wrote his autobiography, *Grace Abounding to the Chief of Sinners* (1666).

In *Grace Abounding to the Chief of Sinners*, Bunyan reveals that he considers himself to be a chief sinner, and he relates the experiences of his dissolute youth and of his reckless membership in the parliamentary army for three years beginning when he was sixteen years old. Therefore, readers assume that Christian's trials in *The Pilgrim's Progress* originated in real life with a man who knew temptation.

The Pilgrim's Progress has been translated into more than one hundred languages over the centuries, and the simple story's appeal continues. It combines biblical language and the subject of simple folk in a combination that has brought it popularity. Bunyan's ability to draw pictures with words has no doubt aided the novel's classic success. One critic has noted that Bunyan seems to have thought in pictures. Bunyan heightens the dramatic effect of his story, for example, with the picture of Christian opening the book at the beginning of the dream, reading, weeping, and asking, "What shall I do?"

Bunyan was apparently a simple man, or at any rate, he had a keen sense of priorities about his life. In his autobiography, for example, he does not name his father or mother, and he hardly mentions such ordinary points in time as his birthplace or home. Such lack of particular detail indicates a literary intention: Bunyan aims, in his autobiography, to universalize his experience. *Grace Abounding to the Chief of Sinners* tends to emphasize Bunyan's own personal conflicts, while playing down other people in his life. Bunyan understood well what was real to him, and it is this sense of realism that has made *The Pilgrim's Progress* a classic. *The Pilgrim's Progress* is thoroughly convincing in describing the momentousness of Christian's experiences. Bunyan's ability to convey with a sense of realism this significance endows the novel with the enduring quality of being able to strike a note of universality among the millions who read the book.

"Critical Evaluation" by Jean G. Marlowe

Bibliography:

Furlong, Monica. *Puritan's Progress*. New York: Coward, McCann & Geoghegan, 1975. Although dated, this is an excellent starting point for research. A good summarized discussion of both parts 1 and 2 of *Pilgrim's Progress*. Includes a solid introduction to John Bunyan and the life of the Puritans. Excellent bibliography.

Hill, Christopher. *A Tinker and a Poor Man: John Bunyan and His Church, 1628-1688*. New York: Alfred A. Knopf, 1988. Examines John Bunyan, his writings, his life, and the turbulent times in which he lived. Gives an extensive list of publication dates of all of Bunyan's work.

Luxon, Thomas, H. *Literal Figures: Puritan Allegory and the Reformation Crisis in Representation*. Chicago: University of Chicago Press, 1995. Good discussion of allegory, specifically in relation to Puritanism, and a solid starting point for study. A modern interpretation of Bunyan, his work, and its relation to allegory.

Newey, Vincent, ed. *"The Pilgrim's Progress": Critical and Historical Views*. New York: Barnes & Noble Books, 1980. A wonderful collection of concise essays. Essays cover Bunyan, symbolism, and theology in relation to *Pilgrim's Progress*.

Sadler, Lynn Veach. *John Bunyan*. Boston: Twayne, 1979. Good summation of Bunyan's life with excellent explanations of *Pilgrim's Progress*. Includes an extensive bibliography and chronology of Bunyan's life.

THE PILLARS OF SOCIETY

Type of work: Drama
Author: Henrik Ibsen (1828-1906)
Type of plot: Psychological realism
Time of plot: Nineteenth century
Locale: Norwegian seaport
First performed: 1877; first published, 1880 as *Samfundets støtter* (English translation, 1880)

Principal characters:
> CONSUL BERNICK, the leader of the town
> MRS. BERNICK, his wife
> OLAF, their son
> MARTHA, the consul's sister
> JOHAN TONNESEN, Mrs. Bernick's brother
> LONA HESSEL, her half sister
> DOCTOR RORLUND, a schoolmaster
> DINA DORF, Bernick's charge
> AUNE, a foreman shipbuilder

The Story:

Consul Bernick was the unquestioned leader of the town, with his wealth and influence extending into every enterprise. He owned the large shipyard which was the source of most of the townspeople's income, and he had successfully fought the project of building a seacoast railway. He had introduced machines into the yards, and Aune, his foreman, was stirring up the workers because the machines meant the loss of jobs. Bernick, not wishing to have his authority questioned, threatened Aune with loss of his job if he did not stop his speaking and writing against the machines.

There was only one breath of scandal about Consul Bernick, and that concerned his wife's family. Many years before, Johan Tonnesen, Mrs. Bernick's brother, had been seen leaving the rear window of the house of Mrs. Dorf, a married woman. Later, Johan left town and went to America. It was said that before he left he stole the strongbox containing Bernick's mother's fortune. What made the matter worse was that Mrs. Bernick's half sister, Lona Hessel, had followed her younger half brother to America and had been like a mother to him. Only Bernick's standing in the town prevented his ruin, and he had made it clear to his wife that her family was a disgrace to him.

Mrs. Dorf's husband deserted her and their daughter. When Mrs. Dorf died soon afterward, Bernick's sister Martha took the child into their home. The girl, Dina, was a constant annoyance to Bernick. Not only did she have a disgraceful background, but she talked constantly about exercising her own free will and acting independently of his desires. Dr. Rorlund, the schoolmaster, loved Dina, but he would not marry her or let anyone know of his attachment because he was afraid of the town's feelings about her. His beautiful words about goodness and kindness concealed his moral cowardice. He promised that they would be married when he could improve her position.

In the meantime, Bernick had changed his mind about allowing a railroad to come to the community. Formerly the proposed road would have competed with his shipping. Now he realized that a spur line through the town would bring timber and minerals to his shipyard. The railroad would be a good thing for the town because it was a good thing for Bernick. He was aiding the town, a pillar of society.

There was constant trouble at the shipyard. The American owners of a ship he was repairing had sent a cable to Bernick, instructing him to get the ship under way immediately, although it was so rotted that it would require several weeks to make it safe. Bernick was torn between the profits to be gained by getting the ship afloat at once and the conscience that kept him from sending her crew to certain death.

He grew even more disturbed because Lona and Johan had returned from America and the town had revived the old gossip. Many tried to ignore the pair, but Lona refused to be ignored. She felt no disgrace, nor did Johan. Johan and Dina were at once drawn to each other, and she begged him to take her back to America so that she could be free and independent. Bernick and his wife would not hear of this plan, but for quite different reasons. Mrs. Bernick still felt her brother's disgrace. Bernick, however, knew that Johan was blameless. It had been Bernick, not Johan, who had been forced to flee the married woman's house. Johan had taken the blame because he had no great reputation to save and he was anxious to leave the town and strike out for himself. What he did not know was that Bernick had spread the story about the theft of his mother's money.

Johan, thinking that the town would soon have forgotten a boyish escapade with another man's wife, renewed his promise not to tell that it was Bernick who had been involved. He told Bernick that Lona knew the true story but that she would not reveal the secret. Johan was grateful to Martha, Bernick's sister, for caring for Dina. Martha had refused several offers of marriage in order to care for the younger girl who had been so disgracefully orphaned.

Johan learned also that Martha had not married because she had always loved him and had waited for him to return. Martha told Johan that her brother's strict moral principles had made him condemn Johan and try to turn her against him. Johan was puzzled, for he thought Bernick had been grateful to him for assuming Bernick's own guilt. Johan could not understand his brother-in-law's attitude.

Lona, too, forgave Bernick for his past acts, even his jilting of her in favor of her rich half sister. Bernick told her why he had acted as he did. His mother's business had been in great danger, and he had needed money to avoid bankruptcy. For that reason he had renounced Lona, whom he loved, for her wealthier relative. For the same reason, he had spread the story that Johan had taken old Mrs. Bernick's money. In reality, there had been no money at all; had the town learned the truth, it would have meant ruin for Bernick. Bernick completely justified himself by saying that as the pillar of the town, he had been forced to act deceitfully and maliciously.

Lona begged him to tell the truth at last, to keep his life from being built on a lie. Bernick said that the cost was too great; he could not lose his money and his position. In addition, the railway project would fail if a whisper of scandal were heard. The railway was to make Bernick a millionaire. While he struggled with his conscience over this problem, repair of the American ship still confronted him. He forced Aune to get it ready to sail in two days, even though its unseaworthiness meant death for its crew. At the same time, he laid plans to pretend that it was Aune who had failed to take proper time and precautions to make the vessel safe. Then he would stop the sailing and take credit for losing his profit rather than risk the lives of the sailors. He needed public acclaim, for soon the town would learn that he had bought up all the land through which the railroad would run. It would be hard to convince the townspeople that they would benefit from his wealth.

To make matters worse, Johan became difficult. He had not known about the story of the theft, but he would forgive the lie if Bernick would now tell the truth. Johan wanted to marry Dina, but his name must first be cleared. Bernick refused the pleas of both Johan and Lona, lest he be ruined. He would not release Johan from his promise of secrecy. Lona would not tell the true story because she still loved Bernick. Besides, she thought he himself should tell the truth so that he would be whole again. When Johan, planning to leave on the American ship, vowed to return in two months and to tell the truth at that time, Bernick decided to allow the ship to sail. If it sank, he would be free of Johan forever.

On the night of the sailing Bernick arranged for a celebration in his honor for the purpose of getting the citizens into the proper frame of mind before they learned that he had bought property along the railroad route. Shortly before the celebration, he learned that his son Olaf had stowed away on the unseaworthy ship. He tried to call it back, but it was already out to sea. Then he was told that Johan had taken Dina with him to America, but that they had sailed on a different ship. He would lose his son and gain nothing.

He was overjoyed when he learned that his wife had found the boy on board and brought him home before the ship sailed. Word came also that Aune stopped the sailing of the ship and brought her back to the harbor. Bernick, saved from the evil of his deeds, stood up before the townspeople and confessed that he and not Johan had been the guilty man. He promised also that he would share the profits from the railroad. Lona was happy. She told Bernick that at last he had found the real pillars of society—truth and freedom. Only on them could society build a firm foundation.

Critical Evaluation:

Measured against such Ibsen masterpieces of social realism as *A Doll's House* (1879), *Ghosts* (1881), and *The Wild Duck* (1884), *The Pillars of Society* is obviously an inferior work. It was, however, the drama in which he first committed himself to the realistic form and is, therefore, crucial to an understanding and appreciation of Ibsen's theater. *The Pillars of Society* contains in embryo most of the major subjects, themes, and character types that were to dominate Ibsen's plays over the succeeding dozen years. There are three obvious concerns in *The Pillars of Society* that became central to his realistic dramas: the nature and powers of "society," the relationship between exceptional individuals and that society, and the manner in which suppressed corruption in the past inevitably surfaces to destroy present success.

Nineteenth century middle-class Norwegian society was, to Ibsen, hypocritical, materialistic, stifling, and essentially corrupt. The alliance between narrow religious moralism, with its emphasis on sin, guilt, and rigidly controlled behavior, and selfish business interests, with their respectable façade that concealed the greedy exploitation of the many by the few, had resulted in a society that corrupted or stifled all evidence of creativity or imagination.

The exceptional individual has one of two choices: involvement or rejection. If the exceptional person accepts the community's mores and practices, the person will inevitably be corrupted; if the person rejects them, social ostracism and condemnation are the necessary consequences. Karsten Bernick accepted the values and exploited them in his drive for money, power, and respectability. For the nonconformist, social isolation is the only option—if the individual is strong enough to make the break. Lona Hessel has the requisite determination and imparts enough of it to Johan Tonnesen to enable them both to flee the country. However, the price of such a divorce from their roots is great, and the impulse to return and find some sort of "compromise," with all its dangers of contamination, is very strong.

In addition to presenting the pervasive atmosphere of inhibition and hypocrisy, Ibsen usually structures his realistic social plays on specific examples of concealed corruption. Karsten

Bernick has based his public image, his business success, and his marriage on a lie when, as a young man, he enticed his fiancée's brother, Johan Tonnesen, into taking the blame for his illicit love affair, then later blamed him for the "theft" of the "Bernick family fortune." In Ibsen's view, however, nothing can be successfully founded on a lie. Bernick's affair with Mrs. Dorf and the subsequent voluntary disgrace of Johan necessarily tempt Bernick to expand the lie to cover his company's financial insolvency, to abandon the woman he really loves in favor of a financially advantageous match, to commit conscious fraud, and, finally, to attempt murder. In *The Pillars of Society*, as in other plays, it is a figure out of the past, Lona Hessel, who crystalizes these pressures and forces the revelation of the truth.

In spite of the complexities and ambiguities that Ibsen explores in *The Pillars of Society*, he supplies a conventional "happy ending." This final victory of optimism over dramatic logic is one of the signs that this play stands at the beginning of Ibsen's mature career. If the story is more contrived, the characters more manipulated, and the themes more boldly stated than in Ibsen's subsequent masterpieces, all of the ingredients are present in *The Pillars of Society* to make it the essential play in Ibsen's transition from an impressive, but traditional, nineteenth century playwright to his historical role as "the father of modern drama."

Bibliography:
Haugen, Einar. *Ibsen's Drama: Author to Audience.* Minneapolis: University of Minnesota Press, 1979. Written by a superb teacher and scholar, this volume is a masterful introduction to Ibsen's works and their place in European cultural history. Comments on *The Pillars of Society* are found throughout the book.
Johnston, Brian. *The Ibsen Cycle: The Design of the Plays from "Pillars of Society" to "When We Dead Awaken."* Boston: Twayne, 1975. With emphasis on the philosophical content of Ibsen's later plays, this volume discusses *The Pillars of Society* in the context of nineteenth century capitalist society.
McFarlane, James. *Ibsen and Meaning: Studies, Essays, and Prefaces, 1953-87.* Norwich, England: Norvik Press, 1989. In a major contribution to Ibsen criticism, McFarlane discusses *The Pillars of Society* in the context of *A Doll's House* and *Ghosts*, concluding that Ibsen's portrait of Bernick, the male protagonist, is marked by a great deal of irony.
Meyer, Michael. *Ibsen: A Biography.* Garden City, N.Y.: Doubleday, 1971. A standard biography of Ibsen, it contains a good discussion both of the play itself and of its place in Ibsen's oeuvre. Meyer regards it primarily as an indictment of the universal pettiness of small town life but also gives a helpful summary of its historical background.
Weigand, Herman J. *The Modern Ibsen: A Reconsideration.* New York: Holt, 1925. An excellent introduction to Ibsen's later plays, this volume contains a good essay on *The Pillars of Society*. Weigand finds the play interesting although it is not representative of Ibsen's best work.

THE PILOT
A Tale of the Sea

Type of work: Novel
Author: James Fenimore Cooper (1789-1851)
Type of plot: Historical
Time of plot: Late eighteenth century
Locale: Northeastern coast of England
First published: 1823

> *Principal characters:*
> LIEUTENANT RICHARD BARNSTABLE, the commander of the *Ariel*
> MR. EDWARD GRIFFITH, an officer aboard an American frigate
> LONG TOM COFFIN, the coxswain of the *Ariel*
> MR. MERRY, a midshipman
> MR. GRAY, the pilot, in reality John Paul Jones
> COLONEL HOWARD, a Tory
> KATHERINE PLOWDEN, his niece
> CECILIA HOWARD, another niece of Colonel Howard
> CAPTAIN MANUAL, an officer of the Marine Corps
> CAPTAIN BORROUGHCLIFFE, a British officer
> CHRISTOPHER DILLON, a kinsman of Colonel Howard
> ALICE DUNSCOMBE, a friend of Katherine and Cecilia

The Story:

Toward the close of a bleak wintry day during the American Revolution, a small schooner and a frigate sailed through shoal waters off the northeastern coast of England and anchored in a small bay beneath some towering cliffs. As darkness settled, a whaleboat was put ashore from the schooner *Ariel*. The boat was in the charge of the *Ariel*'s commander, Lieutenant Richard Barnstable, who had been ordered to make a landing near the cliffs and bring off a pilot known only as Mr. Gray.

With the aid of a weather-beaten old Nantucket whaler, Long Tom Coffin, Barnstable climbed the cliff and there met his mysterious passenger, a man of middle height and sparing speech. Before he had completed his mission, however, he also encountered Katherine Plowden, his fiancée, who gave him a letter and a signal book. The woman was staying temporarily at the St. Ruth's Abbey manor house, the home of her uncle, Colonel Howard, a wealthy South Carolina Tory who had fled from America at the outbreak of the war. From her, Barnstable learned that another niece, Cecilia Howard, and her friend, Alice Dunscombe, were also guests at the abbey. Cecilia was in love with Lieutenant Edward Griffith, first officer aboard the frigate. Alice Dunscombe was reported to be in love with the mysterious pilot, but she refused to marry him because she was completely Loyalist in her sympathies.

Darkness had fallen by the time the pilot had been put aboard the deck of the frigate, and a storm was rising. Only Captain Munson of the frigate knew the pilot's identity, a secret concealed from everyone else aboard the ship and its escort, the *Ariel*. Captain Munson, seeing the pilot by the light of the battle lanterns on deck, thought him greatly changed in appearance since their last meeting.

As the storm rose, the pilot guided the frigate safely through dangerous, wind-lashed shoal waters and out to open sea. At sunrise, the frigate signaled the *Ariel* and ordered Barnstable to go aboard the larger ship for a council of war. There plans were made to harass the English by sending landing parties ashore to raid the mansions and estates of the gentry in the neighborhood.

Barnstable wanted these expeditions to serve another purpose, for he hoped to rescue Katherine Plowden and Cecilia Howard from the abbey, where they lived unhappily with Colonel Howard, their uncle and guardian.

Meanwhile, at the abbey, Colonel Howard was holding a conference with Christopher Dillon, a kinsman, and Captain Borroughcliffe, a British officer in charge of a small detachment of troops stationed at the abbey. Dillon, an impoverished gentleman, hoped to marry, with the Colonel's approval, one of his wealthy cousins. The three men discussed the progress of the American Revolution, other political questions, and the piracies of John Paul Jones. They agreed that extra precautions should be taken, for there were rumors that Jones himself had been seen in the neighborhood.

That night, Griffith and the pilot, accompanied by a Marine Corps captain named Manual, went ashore on a scouting expedition. As a result of Griffith's imprudent conduct, they were seen and seized. When a sentry reported the arrest of strange seamen lurking in the neighborhood, Captain Borroughcliffe ordered them brought to the abbey for examination.

On their arrival at the abbey, the prisoners would say only that they were seamen out of employment, a suspicious circumstance in itself. When the seamen offered no further information of any consequence, they were imprisoned to await Borroughcliffe's pleasure. Katherine and Cecilia bribed the sentry on duty and obtained permission to visit the prisoners. They recognized Griffith in disguise. Alice Dunscombe also went to visit the pilot, whom she recognized. After drinking too much wine at dinner, Borroughcliffe began to interview the men and, in his intoxicated condition, unwittingly helped them to escape.

Believing that the men had come from a ship lying offshore, Dillon mounted a horse and rode to a neighboring bay, where the war cutter *Alacrity* lay at anchor. Alarmed at the possible presence of an American ship in the area, the cutter put out to sea, with Dillon among its volunteer crew. Barnstable and Long Tom Coffin, waiting in the *Ariel*'s whaleboat, engaged the cutter in a furious battle that ended when Coffin pinned the captain of the cutter to the mast with his whaler's harpoon. Dillon was among the prisoners taken. Frightened, he offered to return to the abbey and, in return for his own freedom, secure the release of the Americans held there.

After their escape, the pilot left Griffith and Manual, who rejoined a party of marines who had remained in hiding while their captain went with Griffith and the pilot to reconnoiter the abbey. Attacked by Borroughcliffe and his troops, the marines were surrounded. Griffith was recaptured, and Manual was forced to surrender.

Trusting Dillon's word of honor, Barnstable had sent Long Tom Coffin with Dillon to the abbey to arrange for the transfer of prisoners. Dillon, however, dishonoring his parole, had Coffin held prisoner while he and Borroughcliffe planned to trap Barnstable and his men. When Borroughcliffe boasted of his intentions, Coffin made a surprise attack upon him and seized and bound the British officer. He then followed Dillon to the apartments of Katherine and Cecilia and there took Dillon prisoner. He succeeded in getting Dillon aboard the *Ariel*, as a British battery on the shore opened fire on the schooner. A lucky shot wrecked her mainmast as the schooner put out to sea, where a heavy storm completed the *Ariel*'s destruction.

Before the schooner sank, Barnstable, a true captain, decided to go down with his ship, and he ordered Mr. Merry, a midshipman, to take charge of the crew and lower the boats. Coffin threw Barnstable overboard and in this manner saved his commander's life. The ship went down with Coffin and Dillon aboard. When Dillon's body was later washed up by the sea,

Barnstable ordered his burial. Shortly afterward, Mr. Merry appeared at the abbey in the disguise of a peddler. Barnstable signaled by means of flags to Katherine, using signals from the code book which she had given him. Later, they met secretly and laid plans for surprising the abbey and the soldiers who guarded it. Borroughcliffe heard of the plot, however, and Barnstable walked into Borroughcliffe's ambush. At this juncture, however, the pilot arrived with a party of marines from the frigate and made prisoners of the Tories and the British.

Later, Griffith released Borroughcliffe and his soldiers because Borroughcliffe had behaved in an honorable manner toward his prisoners. There was a final interview between Alice Dunscombe and the pilot. During their talk, she addressed him as John and said that if she should speak his real name, the whole countryside would ring with it. The pilot insisted that he would continue his activities for the cause of patriotism, regardless of the unsavory reputation it might gain for him in England. Colonel Howard and his two nieces were taken aboard the frigate for the return voyage to America.

The American ship was not yet out of danger. The next morning, a man-of-war broke through the morning mists, her decks cleared for action. There was tremendous activity aboard the frigate in preparation for the battle, and the women were taken below for safety as the English ship of the line blazed a three-tiered broadside at the American vessel. One shot struck Captain Munson and cut him down. Griffith, who now knew the pilot's identity, begged for permission to reveal it to the crew, to encourage them in the fight, but the pilot refused. Meanwhile, the British ship had been reinforced by two others, but the Americans were lucky enough to disable the smallest of their attackers. Then, as the other ships closed in upon the battered American ship, the pilot took the wheel and daringly guided her through the shoal waters that only he knew well. Outmaneuvered, the pursuing British ships dropped behind.

Colonel Howard, wounded during the engagement, lived long enough to see his nieces married by the ship's chaplain to their lovers. He died insisting that he was too old to change his politics and blessing the king.

The frigate sailed to Holland, where the pilot was put ashore. To all but Griffith, among those who watched his small boat dwindling to a speck against the horizon, his identity remained a mystery.

Critical Evaluation:

The Pilot is a novel that combines military adventure, a certain romantic interest, and a political analysis within the confines of a particular historical era. The mixture is not always successful, but aspects of *The Pilot* remain interesting as both literature and political argument.

James Fenimore Cooper said that *The Pilot* was originally conceived as a sea novel, one which would be accurate in its details of naval life and strategy. One way that Cooper demonstrated his expertise was in the multitude and variety of the technical terms he used. This terminology is so pervasive in *The Pilot* that much of the action, especially during sea battles, is nearly incomprehensible. On the other hand, this mystification (resembling the "wood lore" of the Leatherstocking series) does work to make the pilot himself, the hero of the novel, appear superhuman. The reader, to whom much of the terminology remains inaccessible, can only marvel at the skill and knowledge of Cooper's hero, who not only defeats the enemy in several battles but stands above the other officers (such as Griffith) in seafaring skill.

In *The Pilot*, Cooper claims to have drawn his characters according to "palpable nature," without reference to unknown or metaphysical qualities. This intention, though undoubtedly sincere (and a reaction against the excesses of romantic fiction), is not carried out in practice in regard to the pilot himself who, the reader is meant to understand, embodies the ideal qualities of a leader. For example, the pilot is calm even under the most severe stress. Cooper opens the novel with Mr. Gray extricating the ship from a severe storm. Everyone else is terrified, and with good reason, it appears, but the pilot is completely steady and absolutely unafraid.

Furthermore, when the pilot gives an order, the crew obeys as if he were the commander. Cooper describes this obedience in almost mystical terms. The pilot is able to impose discipline when no one else can. So Cooper's intention to describe his characters only according to "palpable nature" is subordinated to the need he felt for portraying an authentic leader, hero, and warrior. This need flows from the political intent of the work. *The Pilot* raises a political question that was important in Cooper's own life and, more significantly, was critical during the Revolutionary War. The issue was one of loyalty.

The Pilot is a novel centered on characters torn between conflicting loyalties. When the American War for Independence began, men and women in the Colonies were faced with a clear choice. Those Americans who remained loyal to England were disloyal to the emerging nation. Those who fought on the side of the Revolution were accused of treason. This accusation is, for example, repeated frequently by Colonel Howard and his supporters against the rebels.

To answer this charge, it was necessary for Cooper to show both that a noble conception of loyalty was maintained by the Americans and that there were leaders among the rebels—wise, cool-headed, and selfless—who could inspire genuine loyalty. It was to fill this requirement that Gray is described by Cooper as an authentic leader and hero and, most of all, is defended against the charge of treason. (John Paul Jones, born in Scotland, served in the English merchant marine before emigrating to America.) Treason and loyalty, then, cease being absolute terms, as Colonel Howard argues, and become politically relative.

It is in the romantic threads of the novel that Cooper attempts to show the divisions of loyalty, and the relative nature of the term, in its sharpest and most dramatic form. Alice Dunscombe is an old friend and sweetheart of Gray, but she was born in England and, unlike Gray, has remained passionately loyal to the land of her birth.

The two are united in the friendship of the past and, indeed, in their current feelings for each other. At the same time, they are divided by conflicting political loyalties. Thus, the reader is asked to judge the political beliefs and feelings of characters, not in absolute terms but in historical terms. Cooper wants these characters understood as they understand themselves; so, although readers may tend to sympathize with the views of one rather than the other, they are still able to feel sympathy for each as a person.

The villain in *The Pilot* is Christopher Dillon; Dillon's villainy lies not in his loyalty to England and to Colonel Howard, but in his cowardice and opportunism. Mr. Gray, or John Paul Jones, has not committed treason, precisely because he is loyal to his own beliefs; he is not dishonest or cowardly—because he openly defends what he believes. The content of these beliefs is another matter. As characters such as Alice and Colonel Howard debate with the Americans, two distinct political positions emerge. On the one hand, the colonel supports a notion of loyalty based on birth and on the established social and political order. Disruption of that order, he argues, leads to nothing but misery and bloodshed. The Americans answer that loyalty can only be freely and consciously given. Theirs is a romantic view, derived from the theory of social contract, a theory which states that political society is based only upon the agreement of each of its members to participate. Hence the Americans argue that they are loyal only to liberty and, furthermore, that liberty is a necessary condition for genuine loyalty. Cooper does capture the political arguments raging during the Revolutionary War. He not only expresses these arguments in terms of conflicting loyalties, but he also penetrates the political assumptions behind the labels.

The Pilot, however, also suffers from a weakness common to many novels that attempt to explore the political reality within a historical conflict. This weakness is especially evident in Cooper's big scenes (those scenes, for example, between Alice Dunscombe and John Paul Jones), in which there is a tendency for characters to make speeches to the reader rather than to talk with one another. In other words, the ideas are expressed verbally rather than through dramatic action.

In *The Pilot*, Cooper faced the double necessity of creating a hero—which he could accomplish through action at sea—and, at the same time, of exploring the historical and political motives of that hero. The shape of *The Pilot*, and its strengths and weaknesses as a novel, flow from Cooper's attempt to resolve this difficulty.

Howard Lee Hertz

Bibliography:

Darnell, Donald. "Manners in a Revolution: *The Spy, The Pilot*, and *Lionel Lincoln*." In *James Fenimore Cooper: Novelists of Manners*. Newark: University of Delaware Press, 1993. Discusses Cooper's ambivalence toward his hero, John Paul Jones, a strong leader of questionable ethics. Darnell believes Cooper's criticism of Jones stems from Jones's humble birth, which makes him unfit for true heroism.

House, Kay Seymour. "The Unstable Element." In *James Fenimore Cooper: A Collection of Critical Essays*, edited by Wayne Fields. Englewood Cliffs, N.J.: Prentice-Hall, 1979. Describes how the sea functions for Cooper's seamen much as the forest does for his frontiersmen. Tom Coffin shares many traits with Natty Bumppo, and both show what can happen to the common man when he is challenged by the elements.

Philbrick, Thomas. *James Fenimore Cooper and the Development of American Sea Fiction*. Cambridge, Mass.: Harvard University Press, 1961. Claims for Cooper the title of creator of the genre of the American sea novel. Shows how Cooper drew from history and from British writers to write *The Pilot*.

Ringe, Donald A. *James Fenimore Cooper*. New York: Twayne, 1962. The best book-length introduction to Cooper. The brief section on *The Pilot* describes themes and influences, and shows the importance of physical environment to this novel.

Walker, Warren S. "The Gull's Way." In *James Fenimore Cooper: An Introduction and Interpretation*. New York: Holt, Rinehart and Winston, 1962. Describes how *The Pilot* established the genre of the sea novel in America, and traces the influences of earlier British sea novels. Includes a chronology and a bibliography.

PINCHER MARTIN

Type of work: Novel
Author: William Golding (1911-1993)
Type of plot: Psychological realism
Time of plot: World War II
Locale: Mid-Atlantic Ocean
First published: 1956

Principal characters:
CHRISTOPHER MARTIN
NATHANIEL, his shipmate and friend
MARY, eventually Nat's fiancée
MR. CAMPBELL and
MR. DAVIDSON, searchers in the rescue

The Story:

Christopher Martin was a crew member of the English destroyer *The Wildebeest*, which was sunk by a German torpedo in the Mid-Atlantic during World War II. Martin did not make it into the safety boats that other survivors managed to get aboard. Christopher Martin had his lifebelt on, however, and, after the ship sank, he worked to inflate the belt. He succeeded in this, and then, in his own imagination, he managed to kick off his seaboots. Christopher Martin's struggle to survive in the Mid-Atlantic began.

Christopher Martin found himself struggling to keep mind and body together. At times, he transcended his physical situation and saw himself as pure mind. He had an enormous will to survive, and it is that struggle of will that readers encounter throughout the novel; Martin insists, "I will not die!"

After believing himself to have successfully removed his seaboots, Martin began the impossible task of orienting himself in a reality in which the horizon was the same, no matter which way he looked. The first order of business was to get through the night. Without the aid of a compass, Martin had to wait until dawn to get a sense of where he was. He found himself focusing on a "bright patch" against the sky; he decided that he was not far from the coast of North Africa.

The physical suffering that Martin endured is detailed in the opening seventy-five pages of the novel. Not only did Martin have to survive the blistering rays of the sun glinting off the ocean, but he also had to fight fatigue and the harsh effects of the saltwater. During this time, Martin's mind flashed back to his memories of his friend and shipmate, Nathaniel. Nathaniel had seemed the least likely to survive, but, in Martin's imagination, Nathaniel had made it into a lifeboat. Martin, who had been in the crow's nest when the destroyer was hit, had called for Nathaniel's help but had received no immediate response. Martin spent much of his psychic energy worrying that he had not given the correct call regarding the ship's position and the position of the destroyer that had launched the fatal torpedo. He finally decided that he had made the right call, and those thoughts no longer tormented him.

Miraculously, Martin was washed up on a large cluster of rocks that surfaced seemingly out of nowhere. On this rocky surface, Martin clung to life, fighting off not only despair and fatigue, but also the life-threatening presence of the limpets that fed off the waters surrounding the rock.

For some time Martin fought his way through the limpets; he finally gained supremacy—tentatively—of the rocky surface.

As Martin became more desperate, he realized that he must fight not only the elements, but the threat of madness as well. Physical survival was difficult, but Martin found fresh rainwater in small pools across the rock, and he protected himself from the tempests and the scorch of the sun by wedging himself into a crevice. Crablike, he retreated to this crevice when danger became intolerable.

At one point, Martin questioned his sanity when he saw a red lobster feeding from the rock just below the water's surface. He questioned his sanity at this point because lobsters are not red when they are alive; they only turn that color as they are being boiled to death.

Martin began to see pictures, and as Martin's chances for survival became less and less, the pictures became brighter and more real. These pictures included scenes in which he tried to seduce Mary, the woman that Nat had intended to marry. Martin recalled Mary struggling to remove herself from his presence. She fought him off by pushing down her skirt and telling him that she wanted nothing to do with him. Martin recalled the shock and the sense of betrayal that he felt when Nathaniel told him that he intended to wed Mary.

Many times during his ordeal, Martin wished that he had saved his seaboots because the cold and the harshness of the ocean were causing him great pain. At the same time, he found it increasingly difficult to concentrate on his survival and do what he could to aid in a rescue. At one point, Martin imagined that he had managed to affix a piece of tinfoil to the highest part of the rock. This piece of foil would, supposedly, give off reflections that rescue ships in the area would pick up.

Throughout his ordeal on the rock, Martin's mind wandered to memories of his friends and of women he had tried to love. The pictures of these memories alternately caused him anguish and hope. He continually repeated to himself that his mind and his body had not yet completely separated, and his ability to recall the pictures was proof that he was still alive. Finally, however, the elements were too much for Martin to withstand. At this point, the novel shifted to the perspective of Mr. Campbell and Mr. Davidson, who were searchers in the rescue effort. As they pulled Martin's lifeless body out of the water, Mr. Davidson cursed the lifebelt, for it gave men hope in hopeless circumstances. Mr. Campbell wondered if Martin had suffered a great deal. Mr. Davidson told him not to worry; after all, Martin was still wearing his seaboots—he had not even had time to kick them off.

Critical Evaluation:

Published in 1956, William Golding's *Pincher Martin* is one of the strongest literary links between the age of British high modernism and the post-modern novel. The novel has been overlooked for many years, but it has begun to receive the attention that it deserves. In many ways, *Pincher Martin* is a literary achievement on the scale of James Joyce's *Ulysses* (1922) and Virginia Woolf's *Mrs. Dalloway* (1925). Although *Pincher Martin* lacks the symbolic scope of these earlier novels, it is, just as they were, concerned with the mental processes of a main character observed over a relatively short span of time. In *Pincher Martin*'s case, this time span is the life that can be lived and fought for in the very brief minutes before death. James Joyce and Virginia Woolf focused on the extension of the modern novel and used both realism and symbolism, but Golding was much more concerned with the allegorical relationship between seen reality and hidden reality. The medieval allegorist took as the starting point of meaning the intersection between the physical and spiritual worlds, but Golding worked his allegory in the intersection between the physical world and the world of the subconscious.

As the American title, *The Two Deaths of Christopher Martin*, implies, the story concerns Christopher Martin's struggle to survive both physical and metaphysical death. The novel is one of psychological realism, but the main focus of the work is on one man's ontology, or being, in the world.

The first focus of Christopher Martin's ontological status after the shipwreck is his determination to lighten himself, thus increasing his chances for survival, by removing his seaboots. He believes that he has accomplished this feat, and he begins to hope for survival. His lifebelt, an allegorical symbol for the reality of hope, becomes his next focus. He relies on his lifebelt to hold him above the waters, but as the novel demonstrates, he still takes in enormous amounts of water—amounts that will drown him, though his will to live survives.

It is the focus on this will to live that forms the major drama of the first half of the novel. Christopher Martin continues to insist, long after the physical point of death, that he will not die. At first, this will to live engages readers in a sympathetic struggle for survival along with Martin. Readers are enthralled by the drama and can hope, along with Martin, that this will to live will, indeed, save him.

Rescue remains a virtual impossibility through Martin's psychological survival on the rock. It becomes clear that Martin is a man obsessed with a fear of death, rather than a man being saved by a will to live. This will to live parallels the "will to power" that has influenced questions of the role will plays in the determination of not only life and death, but also people's everyday negotiations with the world.

As important as this struggle of will is for Martin, Golding also makes the point that in order for the "will to survive" to have any meaning, there must be a point of reference for people to refer to in order to center their being. This point of reference is at first completely lacking in Martin's struggle. Shipwrecked at night, with no reference point by which to orient himself, Martin is allegorically cast from and into an amniotic life where external references are lacking. In this opening section of the book, Martin struggles by focusing completely on himself. Martin becomes his own center to his own universe. His lifebelt—a symbol, as Davidson says at the end of the novel, of false hope—along with his struggle to remove his seaboots, become the reference points on which Martin must focus.

This struggle to find reference points for hope and a meaning in life is allegorized by Golding in the references to the Christian faith. First, Martin's own first name, Christopher, recalls the legend of the man who bore the Christ child across dangerous waters and who was then given his name, meaning "Christ-bearer." Christopher Martin's failure causes readers to question the simplicity of an understanding of life that merely floats along the surface of experience. The rock that Martin imagines himself as having reached is symbolic of the "rock," or St. Peter, upon which Christ founded his church. Again, the rock, as readers learn at the end of the novel, is a figment of Martin's imagination and permits the questioning of the foundations of faith. Finally, Martin's recollections of his seemingly inferior partner, Nathaniel, reinforce the Christian symbolism of the novel. Nathaniel, it is to be remembered, was a disciple of Christ and was, in fact, that disciple in which Christ found no guile. In the novel, the Nathaniel of Martin's imagination is also a figure of guilelessness, his innocence underscored by his pledge to marry Mary, a woman whose name extends the symbolism of the Christian story allegorized in Martin's struggle for survival.

Finally, Golding's novel displays the many ways in which psychology has come to figure in people's lives. There is much imagery of the subconscious, with perhaps the lobster, a scuttling creature whose presence invokes a reference to T. S. Eliot's Prufrock. The lobster represents the unnatural circumstance of Martin's "two deaths"—the death of the body and the death of consciousness. The novel lends itself to interpretations along psychological, symbolic, allegorical, and archetypal lines.

Susan M. Rochette-Crawley

Bibliography:
Babb, Howard S. *The Novels of William Golding*. Athens: Ohio State University Press, 1970. In his chapter on *Pincher Martin*, Babb sees the novel as Golding's most "problematic." Babb focuses on the difficulty of reading the novel and Martin's extreme rationality.
Dick, Bernard F. *William Golding*. Boston: Twayne, 1987. In the Twayne series tradition, this book serves as an excellent starting point. Contains a chronology and, in the section on *Pincher Martin*, Dick focuses upon the existential aspects of the novel.
Kinkead-Weekes, Mark, and Ian Gregor. *William Golding: A Critical Study*. Winchester, Mass.: Faber & Faber, 1967. One of the earliest studies of Golding's novels. In their section on *Pincher Martin*, Kinkead-Weekes and Gregor struggle with the question of realism that the novel poses.

THE PIONEERS
Or, The Sources of the Susquehanna

Type of work: Novel
Author: James Fenimore Cooper (1789-1851)
Type of plot: Historical
Time of plot: 1793
Locale: New York state
First published: 1823

Principal characters:
JUDGE TEMPLE, a frontier landowner
ELIZABETH TEMPLE, his daughter
NATTY BUMPPO, an old hunter, sometimes called Leatherstocking
OLIVER EDWARDS, in reality, Edward Oliver Effingham, Natty's young
 friend
INDIAN JOHN, Natty's Indian companion
HIRAM DOOLITTLE, a local magistrate

The Story:

On a cold December day in 1793, Judge Temple and his daughter Elizabeth were traveling by sleigh through a snow-covered tract of wilderness near the settlement of Templeton. Elizabeth, who had been away from her home attending a female seminary, was now returning to preside over her father's household in the community in which he had been a pioneer settler after the Revolutionary War. Hearing the baying of hounds, the Judge decided that Leatherstocking, an old hunter, had startled game in the hills, and he ordered his coachman to stop the sleigh so he could have a shot at the deer if it came in his direction. A few minutes later, as a great buck leaped onto the road, the Judge fired both barrels of his fowling piece at the animal, apparently without effect. Then a third report and a fourth were heard, and the buck dropped dead in a snowbank.

At the same time, Natty Bumppo, the old hunter, and a young companion appeared from the woodland. The Judge insisted that he had shot the buck, but Leatherstocking, by accounting for all the shots fired, proved that the Judge could not have killed the animal. The argument ended when the young stranger revealed that he had been wounded by one of the shots fired by the Judge. Elizabeth and her father then insisted that he accompany them into the village in their sleigh, so he could have his wound dressed as soon as possible.

The young man got into the sleigh with obvious reluctance and said little during the drive. In a short time, the party arrived at the Temple mansion, where his wound was treated. In answer to the Judge's questions, he gave his name as Oliver Edwards. His manner remained distant and reserved. After he had departed, a servant in the Temple home reported that Edwards had appeared three weeks before in the company of old Leatherstocking and that he lived in a nearby cabin with the hunter and an Indian known as Indian John.

Judge Temple, wishing to make amends for having accidentally wounded Edwards, offered him a position as his secretary. When Elizabeth added her own entreaties to those of her father, Edwards finally accepted the Judge's offer, with the understanding that he would be free to terminate his employment at any time. For a while, he attended faithfully and earnestly to his duties in Judge Temple's mansion during the day, but his nights were spent in Leatherstocking's cabin. So much secrecy surrounded his comings and goings, and the reserve of Leatherstocking and his Indian friend, that Richard Jones, the sheriff and a kinsman of the Judge, became suspicious. Among other things, he wondered why Natty always kept his cabin closed and never allowed anyone except the Indian and Edwards to enter it. Jones and some others decided that Natty had discovered a mine and was working it. Jones also suspected that Edwards was an Indian half-breed, his father a Delaware chief.

Hiram Doolittle, the local magistrate, prowled around the shack and set the dogs guarding it free. In the meantime, Elizabeth and Louisa Grant, the minister's daughter, went walking in the woods. There they were attacked by a savage panther and were saved only by the timely arrival of Leatherstocking, who shot the animal. Natty, however, had also shot a deer, in defiance of Judge Temple's strict game laws. With the charge that the old hunter had killed a deer out of season as his pretext, Doolittle persuaded Judge Temple to sign a warrant so that the magistrate could gain entrance into the cabin and search it. Jones was more convinced than ever that Leatherstocking was secretly smelting ore he had mined.

When Doolittle went to the cabin, Leatherstocking, rifle in hand, refused him entrance. Then the magistrate attempted to force his way over the threshold, but the old hunter seized him and threw him twenty feet down an embankment. As the result of his treatment of an officer, Leatherstocking was arrested. Found guilty, he was given a month's jail sentence, a fine, and was placed in the stocks for a few hours. When Elizabeth went to see what assistance she could give the humiliated old woodsman, she learned that he was planning to escape. Edwards, who had given up his position with the Judge, was planning to flee with his aged friend; he had provided a cart in which to carry the old hunter to safety. Elizabeth promised to meet Leatherstocking the following day on the top of a nearby mountain and to bring with her a can of gunpowder he needed.

The next day, Elizabeth and her friend Louisa started out on their expedition to meet Leatherstocking. On the way, Louisa changed her mind and turned back, declaring that she dared not walk unprotected through the woods where they had lately been menaced by a panther. Elizabeth went on alone until she came to a clearing in which she found old Indian John, now dressed in the war costume and feathers of a great Mohican chief. When she stopped to speak to the Indian, she suddenly became aware of dense clouds of smoke drifting across the clearing and discovered that the whole mountainside was ablaze. At that moment, Edwards appeared, followed by Leatherstocking, who led them to a cave in the side of the mountain. There the old Indian died of exhaustion, and Elizabeth learned that he had been in earlier days Chingachgook, a great and noble warrior of the Mohican tribe. When danger of the fire had passed, Edwards conducted Elizabeth down the mountainside until she was within hearing of a party of men who were looking for her. Before they parted, Edwards promised he would soon reveal his true identity.

The next day, the sheriff led a posse up the mountain in search of Leatherstocking and those who had aided him in his escape from jail. Leatherstocking was again prepared to defend the cave to which he had taken Elizabeth the day before with his rifle, but Edwards declared that the time had now come to let the truth be known. He and Natty brought from the depths of the cave an old man seated in a chair. The stranger's face was grave and dignified, but his vacant eyes showed that his mind was gone. Edwards announced that the old man was really the owner of the property on which they stood. Judge Temple interrupted with a shout of surprise and greeted the old man as Major Effingham.

The young man told his story. His name, he said, was Edward Oliver Effingham, and he was the grandson of the old man who sat before them. His own father had been, before the revolutionary war, a close friend of Judge Temple. They had gone into business together, but the outbreak of the war found them on opposite sides during the struggle. Judge Temple had some money entrusted to him by his friend, money that actually belonged to his friend's father, but when he received no reply to letters he wrote to the Effinghams, he at last decided that all the family had been lost in a shipwreck off Nova Scotia. He had invested the money in his own enterprises.

The Judge had never met Major Effingham; he would not have recognized him if he had seen the helpless old man who had for years been hidden in the cabin on the outskirts of Templeton. During those years, he was nursed faithfully by Leatherstocking and his Indian friend; by Leatherstocking because he had served with the Major on the frontier years before, by Indian John because the Major was an adopted member of the Mohican tribe.

Judge Temple ordered that the old man be carried to the Temple mansion at once, where he would receive the best of care. Old Major Effingham thought himself back home once more, and his eyes gleamed with joy. He died, happy and well cared for, soon afterward.

Edward Effingham also explained his belief that Judge Temple had stolen his father's property and the money left in trust years before. In his resentment, he had come to Templeton to assist his grandfather and to regain in some manner the property that he believed Judge Temple had unrightfully possessed. Now the Judge was happy to return that part of the property which belonged to the Effinghams, and there was a reconciliation between the two men. As it turned out, however, the property stayed in the family, for Elizabeth and Edward Effingham were married within a short time.

Elizabeth and Edward wanted to build a new cabin for Leatherstocking, but the old hunter refused their offer. He intended to go off into the woods to hunt and trap in the free wilderness until he died. Settlements and towns were not for him. He would not listen to their pleas but set out soon afterward on his long journey, pausing only long enough to view the stone tablet on Indian John's grave, a monument Edward Effingham had erected. Then he trudged off toward the woods, his long rifle over his shoulder. Elizabeth and her husband watched him go. Tears were in their eyes as they waved a last farewell to the old hunter just before he disappeared into the forest.

Critical Evaluation:

At the time that *The Pioneers: Or, The Sources of the Susquehanna* was written, authors in the United States were working on establishing a definitive American fiction, one that drew from the rich literary tradition of Europe but still reflected the newly emerging character of the young country. Hailed as the American Sir Walter Scott, James Fenimoore Cooper appeared to be the writer that would spearhead the development of a characteristically American literature. Cooper's novels had the stirring adventure, moral concerns, elevated sentiment, and sense of historical significance that Scott's works possessed. The Leatherstocking tales also portrayed a distinctively American scene, focusing on characters and issues unique to the American experience. Like the other Leatherstocking novels, *The Pioneers* deals with many issues important to the new America: the vanishing frontier, the making of law, property rights, the role of class in a new democracy, and the treatment of Native Americans.

Although skinny old Natty Bumppo hardly seems a nineteenth century romantic hero (his handsome young friend Oliver Edwards was intended to fulfill that type), his popularity led Cooper to write four more novels tracing the hunter's adventures as a youth to his death as an aged man: *The Last of the Mohicans* (1826), *The Prairie* (1827), *The Pathfinder* (1840), and *The Deerslayer* (1841). Cooper's series first established the frontier hero as an American legend who would continue to grace novels, film, and television. Leatherstocking is a mythic figure, possessing almost superhuman abilities even as an old man. He has the skill to shoot through a turkey's head from one hundred yards away and the strength to save the character Benjamin from drowning by lifting him out of the water with a fishing spear. He seems to run through walls of fire when he saves Elizabeth, Judge Temple's daughter, on the burning mountain. Natty represents the natural man, akin to French philosopher Jean-Jacques Rousseau's "noble savage," an uncompromising individualist living outside social and institutional boundaries.

The novel's opening scene, in which Natty and Judge Marmaduke Temple both lay claim to the slain deer, embodies the novel's central theme. In the conflict between Natty and Temple, the interest in preserving the wilderness encounters civilization's desire to domesticate it. Natty witnesses the rapid encroachment of civilization on his beloved wilderness. Living peacefully in nature, altering it only slightly to fulfill his limited needs, Natty laments the changes wrought by the growing town of Templeton. He abhors the "wasty ways" of the townspeople, who shoot hundred of pigeons at one time using cannons, trap thousands of fish in their large nets, and chop down huge numbers of trees for their fireplaces. Temple, with an Anglo-European education and a middle-class background, represents the civilized man. He values the environment not for its own sake, like Natty, but for its usefulness to society. But he also represents an American ideal. Like Cooper's father (founder of Cooperstown, New York), Temple is a loyal American; having supported the revolutionary cause, he is now helping to build the country by establishing a small town in the midst of the wilderness.

Law and land are pervasive themes. Temple believes in written law, while Natty follows the natural law. Natty had been living upon the land years before it became the town of Templeton. The game laws and property rights established by the newly emerging institutions seem ridiculous to him. A man should be allowed to shoot a deer whenever and wherever he wants, Natty believes. He hunts responsibly and sparingly in contrast to the wasteful methods of the townspeople; he clearly adheres to the spirit of the law. Ironically, however, he is caught by the letter of it. Charged with violating the game laws and assaulting Hiram Doolittle, a deceitful and blundering fool, Natty stands trial. The trial and his imprisonment are a cruelly pathetic display. This harmless frontiersman is painfully out of place in the institutional arena of written law. Cooper complicates the notion of law, showing that it is rarely black and white and often administered inequitably. Natty is thrown in prison for shooting a deer, but Judge Temple suffers no consequences for wounding Oliver. Temple is faced with passing judgment on a man who has saved his daughter's life, a man he knows does not deserve punishment. For the sake of preserving the image of the law, Temple tries to have it both ways, convicting Natty but offering to pay his fine. Cooper asks the reader to consider the fine distinctions between law and justice, to consider carefully how the law should be designed and administered.

The notion of property also leads to complicated conflicts in the novel. Temple believes in property rights. Natty, like his Indian friend Chincachgook (Indian John), is suspicious of anyone's right to own what should be shared by everyone. The novel seems to emphasize the concept of property by tracing a complex trail of land ownership; the land in question first belonged to the Mohican tribe, then to Major Effingham, then to Judge Temple, who wills it to his daughter Elizabeth, and then finally to Effingham's grandson Oliver. The source of animosity among Natty and Oliver and Temple is their belief that Temple stole the land from Effingham. The concepts of land ownership and property rights are obscured by the presence of Chincachgook, a constant reminder that the new country is being established on the backs and with the blood of Native Americans. On two occasions, at the turkey shoot and on Mount Vision, Chincachgook speaks of the demise of his people and of the lies of white people. By defending Effingham's property rights, Natty and Chincachgook take part in their own demise. The interests of property, the foundation of the new civilization, isolate and eventually ruin the natural man.

Neither Natty nor Temple is completely sainted or vilified for Cooper understands the complex issues facing the country. Cooper seems to cherish the frontiersman as an American icon, but recognizes that he must be sacrificed for the sake of the emerging America. Natty Bumppo is a symbol of the country's lost innocence.

"Critical Evaluation" by Heidi Kelchner

Bibliography:
Clark, Robert, ed. *James Fenimore Cooper: New Critical Essays.* London: Vision, 1985. Three essays on *The Pioneers*, addressing Cooper's representation of Native American languages as elements of the "frontier," the importance of game laws in defining American democracy, and issues of ownership and property. Somewhat dense, but illuminating.

Darnell, Donald. "Manners on a Frontier: *The Pioneers, The Pathfinder*, and *The Deerslayer.*" In *James Fenimore Cooper: Novelist of Manners.* Newark: University of Delaware Press, 1993. Describes the variety of social classes presented in the novel and how the classes coexist without overt conflict. Against this backdrop, it is natural that the gentleman Oliver Edwards should emerge as leader.

Franklin, Wayne. *The New World of James Fenimore Cooper.* Chicago: University of Chicago Press, 1982. Proposes Cooper as a major and undervalued artist who used striking imaginative energy to address important issues. Examines Cooper's comment that *The Pioneers* was written to show as false the idea that American society was unpolished.

Philbrick, Thomas. "Cooper's *The Pioneers*: Origins and Structure." In *James Fenimore Cooper: A Collection of Critical Essays*, edited by Wayne Fields. Englewood Cliffs, N.J.: Prentice-Hall, 1979. Demonstrates how Cooper was inspired by descriptive poetry, specifically by James Thomson's *The Seasons* (1730). This influence leads to Cooper's images of natural change and to the corresponding themes of social change.

Rans, Geoffrey. *Cooper's Leather-Stocking Novels: A Secular Reading.* Chapel Hill: University of North Carolina Press, 1991. Somewhat difficult. The introduction explains why interest in Cooper has lasted so long. The chapter "Interrupted Prelude" explores the ideologized landscape and characterization important to an understanding of all the Leatherstocking tales.

THE PIRATES OF PENZANCE
Or, The Slave of Duty

Type of work: Drama
Author: W. S. Gilbert (1836-1911)
Type of plot: Operetta
Time of plot: Nineteenth century
Locale: England
First performed: 1879; first published, 1880

> *Principal characters:*
> MAJOR GENERAL STANLEY, of the British Army
> RICHARD, the pirate king
> FREDERIC, the pirate apprentice
> MABEL,
> EDITH,
> KATE, and
> ISABEL, General Stanley's daughters
> RUTH, a pirate maid of all work

The Story:

Frederic, the pirate apprentice, had reached his twenty-first birthday, and at midnight he would be free of his indenture. The pirate king announced that Frederic would then become a full-fledged member of the band. Frederic said that he had served them only because he was a slave to duty; now he was going to leave the pirates. Astounded, the king asked for reasons. Frederic would not tell, but Ruth, the pirate maid of all work, confessed that she had been Frederic's nurse when he was a baby. She had been told to apprentice him to a pilot, but being hard of hearing, she had thought the word was "pirate." Afraid to reveal her mistake, she too had joined the pirates to look after her charge.

Frederic also announced that when he left the pirates he was going to do his best to exterminate the whole band. Individually, he loved them all, but as a crew of pirates they must be done away with. The pirates agreed that they were such unsuccessful pirates that they could not blame him for leaving. Frederic told them he knew why they were such poor pirates. When they reminded him that he would still be one of them until midnight, he felt that it was his duty to give them the benefit of his knowledge. The trouble was that they were too kindly. They would never attack a weaker party and were always beaten by a stronger one. Then, too, if any captive said he was an orphan, he was set free; the pirates themselves had all been orphans. Word about the soft-hearted pirates had spread, and now everyone who was captured declared himself an orphan. The pirates knew that Frederic was right, but they hated to be grim and merciless.

Asked what Ruth would do when he left their band, Frederic said he would take her with him. He wondered if she was attractive. Ruth declared that she was, but since he had had no opportunity to see another female face, Frederic could not be sure. The king assured him that she was still a fine-appearing woman, but when Frederic tried to give her to the king, he would not have her.

Ruth had him almost convinced that she was a fair woman when Frederic saw a bevy of beautiful maidens approaching. Ruth, realizing that her cause was lost, admitted that she had deceived him; she was forty-seven years of age. Frederic cast her aside.

Frederic hid himself as the girls approached, but he felt that he ought to reveal himself again as the women, believing themselves alone, prepared for a swim. When they heard his story, they were filled with pity for his plight and admiration for his handsome figure. From a sense of duty, one of the sisters, Mabel, accepted his affection. Her sisters, Kate, Edith, and Isabel, wondered whether her sense of duty would have been so strong had Frederic been less handsome.

Frederic warned the women about the pirates. Before they could escape, however, the band, led by their king, appeared and seized them. At the same time, their father, Major General Stanley, appeared in search of his daughters. He bragged of his great knowledge—he knew about everything but military skill. As soon as he learned something of military tactics, he would be the greatest general ever. When the pirates told him they were going to marry his daughters, the general, much to their sorrow, begged them not to take his lovely daughters from him because he was an orphan. Unhappily, the pirates gave up their prizes; they could not harm an orphan.

Later, at his home, a ruin that he had purchased complete with ancestors, the general grieved because he had lied to the pirates. He knew that his falsehood about being an orphan would haunt him and his newly purchased ancestors. Frederic consoled him by telling him that the lie was justified to save his daughters from the pirates. At midnight Frederic would lead the police, who would capture the outlaw band. He must wait until then, because he was still one of them.

When the police entered, the women praised them for going so nobly to their deaths. The police, not cheered by the praise, agreed that theirs would be a noble death. At midnight, Frederic prepared to lead them to the pirate hideout. At that moment, the pirate king and Ruth appeared, laughing at a joke they had just discovered. Frederic had been born on February 29 in a leap year. Thus he was not twenty-one years old, but only five years old. His apprenticeship would not be up until 1940. Frederic, thinking that he looked more than five, also laughed at that paradox.

Because Frederic was again one of the pirate band, he felt it his duty to tell the pirates that Major General Stanley was not an orphan, that he had lied. The pirates went at once to capture the villain and to torture him for his falsehood. A struggle took place between the pirates and the police. The pirates won, but when the police challenged them to surrender in the name of Queen Victoria, the pirates yielded, for they loved their queen. Before the police could take them away, Ruth entered and told all assembled that the pirates were really noblemen gone wrong. Then the general forgave them their youthful fling and sent them back to their ranks, giving them his daughters for their brides.

Critical Evaluation:

W. S. Gilbert collaborated with the composer Arthur Seymour Sullivan on eleven highly successful comic operettas between 1875 and 1889, of which *The Pirates of Penzance* is the fourth major work. Like the others, *The Pirates of Penzance* combines topical satire and parody with essentially conservative themes. Penzance, in the rugged coastal area of Cornwall (traditionally known for smuggling) provides a picturesque backdrop for a work that has remained a favorite because of its whimsical plot devices; good-humored satire of the army, the police, and the institution of marriage; and sparkling songs and dialogue.

In his libretto, Gilbert shapes the timeless tale of cruel pirates falling upon innocent maidens into a mock-heroic romp, in which virtue ultimately triumphs, but not before extremes of duty have led to absurdly funny situations. In the world of Victorian England, duty reigned as a supreme virtue, but by 1879, even the most earnest Victorians were ready to laugh at themselves as long as their basic values were ultimately affirmed. Gilbert bases his work on the premise that anything, even commitment to doing one's duty, can become silly if carried beyond reasonable limits. Frederic, the hero, desires nothing more than to be an honest man, but he takes the notion of duty so seriously that he regards breaking the terms of his apprenticeship to the pirates as worse than actually being a pirate. He accepts, in all seriousness, the extension of his commitment to the pirates because of a paradox in reckoning dates. Major General Stanley, having lied to the pirates to save himself and his adopted daughters, feels overwhelming guilt for this betrayal of his duty to be honest. Ruth, whose incredible mistake in apprenticing Frederic to a pirate instead of a pilot sets the entire plot into motion, has joined the pirate band herself rather than abandon her duty to her charge. The pirates are so softhearted that they never actually hurt anyone, and they finally give up without a struggle when reminded of their duty to Queen Victoria.

While the absurd extensions of duty provide a universal satiric theme, Gilbert also satirizes specific Victorian institutions. Gilbert deftly exploits the humorous possibilities in the ways that newly professionalized policemen and military officers changed during the nineteenth century. The first modern urban police forces had been introduced in London in 1829, and the police jokes in *The Pirates of Penzance* show some ambivalence about the place of the police in society. Like many citizens, Gilbert demonstrates a good-natured affection for policemen, whose "lot is not a happy one" because they are torn between their duty to arrest wrongdoers and their natural sympathies with criminals' "capacity for innocent enjoyment." At the same time, the police are ridiculed both for their false bravado before the confrontation with the pirates and for their bumbling inability to overcome and arrest the pirates.

The Victorian era saw not only the novelty of professionalized law enforcement, but also pressure for changes in the tradition-bound military forces. Three laws reforming the army were passed in the early 1870's, but officers at the time of *The Pirates of Penzance* were still more likely to be gentlemen whose military knowledge, like that of "The Very Model of A Modern Major General" Stanley, had "only been brought down to the beginning of the century." Officers usually purchased their commissions and had been educated in British public schools (privately run, all-male, boarding academies) at which they learned much more about classical languages and playing sports than about modern science, technology, or warfare. Gilbert satirizes the Major General from the middle-class perspective, portraying him as a pompous product of moneyed, behind-the-times aristocracy and over-education in the totally useless knowledge required on the entrance examinations for the two service academies.

The women in the operetta personify the stereotypical Victorian maiden, whose goal it is to hold out for the best marriage possible, and the stereotypical Victorian spinster, whose goal it is to marry anyone at all. The pirates desire to marry the maidens "with impunity," circumventing the women's calculations and avoiding the tedious negotiations with fathers that were common at the time. The young women refuse until the finale, when the pirates' true identities as noblemen are revealed. This patently silly turn of events parodies the harsh reality that, in an age of limited opportunities for women to be independent and of nearly impossible divorce, a young woman's husband was her destiny. One of the maidens, Mabel, seems to have the best of all possible situations when she and Frederic fall in love, because she is both doing her duty by redeeming him from a life of crime and winning a handsome husband. When Frederic and Mabel promise, in their duet, to be faithful to each other "till we are wed, and even after," Gilbert makes even these starry-eyed lovers express the typical Victorian combination of romantic idealism and hardheaded realism about marriage. Ruth's hopeless love for Frederic even more poignantly demonstrates the woman's position: Devoid of youth, beauty, and wealth, she can only watch sadly as the young, beautiful, rich Mabel wins his heart in an instant.

Even as the curtain falls at the end of the operetta, she is alone, with no sympathy from the other characters.

Despite the subversive possibilities in satirizing the concept of duty, the uniformed authorities, and the institution of marriage, *The Pirates of Penzance* concludes with the accepted Victorian order of things restored. The outlaws give up when the police invoke the queen's name; Major General Stanley not only gives his daughters in betrothal to the formerly pirate noblemen, but also orders them to "resume [their] ranks and legislative duties," thus bringing full circle the theme of duty. By scrupulously doing one's duty, the finale asserts, one brings about the best possible results for the greatest number of people. These good results include, for the males, assuming their rightfully high places in the social structure, and for the females, marrying well.

"Critical Evaluation" by Julia Whitsitt

Bibliography:

Ansen, David. "Linda's Lot Is a Happy One." *Newsweek*, August 11, 1980, 80. Review of the revival of *The Pirates of Penzance* in Central Park. Contains photographs; helps the reader to understanding the relationship between the play and acting styles.

Benford, Harry. *The Gilbert and Sullivan Lexicon in Which Is Gilded the Philosophic Pill.* New York: Richard Rosen Press, 1978. Explains jokes, allusions, institutions, and slang terms used by Gilbert and Sullivan.

Geis, Darlene. *The Gilbert and Sullivan Operas.* New York: Harry N. Abrams, 1983. Supplies a history and synopsis of *The Pirates of Penzance*. Contains photographs from a television series of Gilbert and Sullivan operas.

Mander, Raymond, and Joe Mitchenson. *A Picture History of Gilbert and Sullivan.* London: Vista Books, 1962. Contains a foreword by Bridgette D'Oyly Carte, whose family is famous for its production of the original versions of Gilbert and Sullivan operas. Photos of historic performances and notes give the reader special insight into the style of production.

Williamson, Audrey. *Gilbert and Sullivan Opera.* London: Marion Boyars, 1953. Contains a chapter on *The Pirates of Penzance*. Explains the development of some ideas and the relation of *The Pirates of Penzance* to other Gilbert and Sullivan operas.

THE PIT
A Story of Chicago

Type of work: Novel
Author: Frank Norris (1870-1902)
Type of plot: Naturalism
Time of plot: 1890's
Locale: Chicago
First published: 1903

> *Principal characters:*
> CURTIS JADWIN, a speculator in wheat
> LAURA DEARBORN, later his wife
> SHELDON CORTHELL, an artist in love with Laura
> MR. and MRS. CRESSLER, friends of the Jadwins
> GRETRY, Jadwin's broker

The Story:

From the first evening that Laura Dearborn met Curtis Jadwin, she knew that she interested him. She had attended the opera with her sister, Page, and her Aunt Wess, as the guests of their longtime friends, the Cresslers. Jadwin had also been a guest that evening, and the marked attention he paid her was so flattering to her that she listened only absently to avowals of love from her old and devoted suitor, Sheldon Corthell. Corthell was an artist. The life of the capitalist who made and broke fortunes and human lives from the floor of the Board of Trade seemed to Laura more romantic than painting.

The next day, Mrs. Cressler told Laura part of Jadwin's story. He had been born into a poor family and had worked to educate himself. When he gained possession of some land in Chicago in default of a loan, he sold it, bought more real estate, and by shrewd dealings eventually owned a portion of one of the wealthiest sections of real estate in Chicago. He also speculated in the wheat market, and he was a familiar figure on the floor of the Board of Trade.

Stopping by the Board of Trade one morning in answer to the summons of Gretry, his broker, Jadwin paused in the Pit—the huge room downstairs in which all the bidding took place—to watch the frenzied excitement of bidders and sellers. Gretry had received advance information that in a few days the French government would introduce a bill placing heavy import duties on all foreign goods. When this news became more widely known, the price of wheat would drop considerably. Gretry urged Jadwin to sell his shares at once, and Jadwin agreed.

The deal was a tremendous success. Jadwin pocketed a large profit. The Cresslers tried to persuade Jadwin to stop his speculating. Mr. Cressler had almost ruined himself at one time through his gambling with wheat, and he feared that the same might eventually happen to his friend. Jadwin, however, was too much interested in Laura to pay attention to the warning or even to hear the words of his friends. One evening at the Cresslers, he asked Laura to marry him. Laura, in a capricious mood, said that, although she loved no one as yet, she might some day come to love him. She had given Sheldon Corthell the same encouragement. That night, ashamed of her coquetry, she wrote to both men to tell them that she did not love them and that they must never speak of love to her again if they were to continue as friends. Corthell accepted her refusal and left for Europe. Jadwin came to call on Laura while she was out and refused to leave until he had spoken to her. He was eloquent in pleading his suit, and they were married in July.

The early years of their marriage were completely happy. Their home was a mansion, exquisitely furnished and with beautiful grounds. At first, Laura found it difficult to adjust to her luxurious surroundings, but as time passed, she found great pleasure in satisfying her interests in art, decorating her home, and entertaining her friends.

Jadwin, caught up in the excitement of the Pit, invested all his money in successful speculative enterprises. For some time, he aligned himself with the bears in the wheat market. As he saw that the country was becoming more prosperous and the wheat crops were increasing, he decided to change to the side of the bulls. He resolved to buy as much wheat as he could and, if possible, to corner the market. Luck was with him. One year, when European crops were very poor, Jadwin bought a tremendous amount of wheat at a low price, determined to hold it until he could ask his own price. Laura was worried by his constant attendance at the Board of Trade, and he promised to give up speculating as soon as he concluded an important deal.

One evening, Laura had dinner with Sheldon Corthell, who had returned from Europe. Late that night, Jadwin came home with the announcement that the deal had been concluded and that he had cleared five hundred thousand dollars. He kept his promise to give up speculating in the Pit, but within a short time, he grew restless. He began again to try his luck in the wheat market.

Because he kept his activities hidden from the public, he was spoken of as the unknown bull. After he had purchased as much wheat as he could, it suddenly became evident that he was in a position to corner the world's wheat and name his own price. Cressler, meantime, had been drawn into speculation by the group of bears who were certain that they could break the unknown bull. He had no idea that the bull was his own friend, Jadwin.

Weeks went by while Laura saw her husband only at breakfast. He spent his days and many of his nights at the board. Laura, lonely and unhappy, began to see more and more of Corthell. Corthell was still in love with Laura and finally declared his feelings for her. Laura, who still loved her husband, was kind in her dismissal.

In cornering the market, Jadwin had risen on a wave of power and prosperity, but he began to have strange, irritating headaches. He attempted to ignore them, just as he disregarded his moods of loneliness and depression.

Mrs. Cressler confided that her own husband was not well. She invited Laura to call on her one afternoon. When Laura arrived, Mrs. Cressler was not yet home. She wandered into the library and saw Mr. Cressler seated in a chair. He had shot himself through the temple.

Jadwin was horrified when he realized that Cressler had lost all of his money in speculation with the bears, and he felt that he was responsible for his friend's death. Jadwin himself was in a tight spot, for now that he had forced the price of wheat to a new high, he needed to corner a bumper crop in addition to the millions of bushels he already owned. His enemies were waiting for the time when the unknown bull could buy no more wheat. At that moment, the price would drop considerably. Jadwin put every penny he owned into his attempt to keep wheat cornered, but he was defeated by the wheat itself. The grain flowed in, millions of bushels at a time. Almost out of his mind, he bought and bought, and still the wheat harvest continued. He no longer controlled the market. He was ruined.

He walked into his home one night a broken man. Laura nursed him through days and nights of illness. When he was well enough, the two set out for the West to begin life again. Although they had lost their money, the Jadwins were much happier than they had been for many years.

Critical Evaluation:

Scientific theories and economic realities have often influenced a writer's assumptions and style. The biological and economic determinism popular in the late nineteenth century shaped the literary theory of naturalism that Émile Zola popularized in Europe. Stephen Crane, the first American proponent of this genre, introduced readers to the forms of naturalism during the early 1890's and was soon followed by Jack London, Theodore Dreiser, Frank Norris, and others. Authors who drew on naturalism dealt with four implicitly antagonistic elements—frankness, objectivity, determinism, and fatalism. As with a scientific theory in the hands and heads of subjective human observers, naturalism often succumbed to a not-so-subtle moralism.

Frank Norris, one of the most promising American followers of Zola, died a young man. His fame as a novelist had been secured by the publication of *McTeague* in 1899, and the brilliance of his career grew more intense with the appearance of *The Octopus* in 1901. The latter title was the first volume of Norris' intended Epic of the Wheat trilogy. *The Octopus* dealt with the production of wheat, while *The Pit* described the marketing of the grain; the final, unwritten volume, *The Wolf*, was to have covered the consumption of wheat.

Like his mentor Zola, Norris depicts large, dramatic scenes, such as the vast expanses of the San Joaquin Valley in California or the tumult on the floor of the Chicago grain exchange. These vivid scenes testify to the nation's fertile soil, a hard-working populace, the technological imagination of inventors, and the organizational flair of entrepreneurs. Considering the menacing determinism in the titles of Norris' books, it becomes evident that the human and social potential of the growing nation is countered by the fatalism of the life-cycle analogy, and the realities of the victors and the vanquished syndrome.

James and Howells were abandoned; Norris and his colleagues became the literary spokesmen of the populists, and the vanguard of the muckrakers. Norris sensed the passing of the old America of warmth, community, and lasting personal relationships. He was eager to humanize the new emerging society that was altered by the impersonal forces of urbanization and controlled by unsavory business tactics. To others, the decline of the genteel tradition signaled the passing of the great race and the entrance of mass culture. To Norris, both the individual and the masses were at the mercy of society and its fixed patterns. Norris' voice was the voice of a generation, like many before, bewildered and adrift. He opposed the basic premise of a society without a core, a society in which the acquisition of money had become a sanctified goal. The ideal of objectivity would have been difficult to achieve.

Zola bequeathed objectivity to naturalism, and Norris wrestled with its thin edge. *The Pit*, like its predecessor *The Octopus*, was a propaganda novel but by no means a cheap diatribe. Norris, an ethical person, could not detach himself from the unethical values and practices of his society, but he could condemn them. He was candid in his descriptions of the undesirable changes that had taken place. A deterministic universe worked out its inexorable process through the activities that took place on the floor of the Chicago grain exchange. As if the occupants of that great building were a nationwide audience viewing a play in its bowels, the pit, the Jadwins of the world rise and fall, just as they had throughout recorded history. Norris' characters were the microcosm of larger society.

To be sure, there was some destruction of character in the principal personages of *The Pit*, but their demise represents something much larger than the individual. The acquisition of fortunes had its shortcomings. The new leisure class, the Curtis and Laura Jadwins of America, often discovered too late that wealth did not always improve the quality of life.

Chicago was an ideal location for the story. There one could find almost everything that money could buy. Chicago had become the clearinghouse for western America, a mecca for would-be financiers, meat-packing tycoons, and grain gamblers. This was the raw yet dynamic city that would later inspire poet Carl Sandburg. At one time, Jadwin gave up his speculating, but the addiction was too strong; eventually it nearly killed him. Such was the charisma of the city, of its seemingly infinite potential for success. Many had perished before Jadwin; tragedy was timeless and inevitable.

In the opening pages, the reader is presented with the inside story about the "pit." Anxiously waiting for the opening act of an opera, and the prestigious patrons, Laura hears of a man's failure to dominate the corn market. Even before being introduced to Curtis Jadwin, Laura becomes acquainted with disaster and with the cruelties of the market. Yet she is drawn to the men who speculate. She admires their social position and envies their luxury-filled lives. Laura looks to the future as if nothing inopportune could possibly happen. She would not always face life with such naïveté.

When Jadwin's friend Cressler was lured back into wheat speculation, he lost everything. Jadwin's efforts to corner the market could have been successful, but fate stepped in and, through nature, destroyed his plans. He had tested luck once too often and overnight was ruined financially and broken in health and spirit. In nursing her husband back to health, Laura asserted her own strength and demonstrated her love for Curtis.

While the novel's conclusion is to some extent tragic, it is not without an optimistic note. The Jadwins lost everything they thought life had to offer, but they regained their future. They had each other's love for the first time in years. In possession of one of life's most simple sources of strength and happiness, marriage, Curtis and Laura left Chicago and moved to the West, probably to California. Norris himself lived in California, and there naturalism had most productively taken root. There, as he had proclaimed in *The Octopus*, the endless struggle of the individual against economic forces was well under way.

"Critical Evaluation" by Eric H. Christianson

Bibliography:

Graham, Don, comp. *Critical Essays on Frank Norris*. Boston: G. K. Hall, 1980. Includes the anonymous contemporary review "*The Pit*: A Dispassionate Examination of Frank Norris' Posthumous Novel," Warren French's "It's When You Are Quiet That You Are at Your Best," and Joseph Katz's "Eroticism in *The Pit*."

_____. *The Fiction of Frank Norris: The Aesthetic Context*. Columbia: University of Missouri Press, 1978. The chapter on *The Pit* discusses differences between this novel and Norris' other fiction. It is, for example, set in Chicago rather than California, it contains many musical and literary allusions, and, most significant, it reflects Norris's preoccupation with drama. Like a drama, the novel has few main characters and is staged in confined settings. In addition, *The Pit* includes a professional opera, an amateur play, and other plays.

Hochman, Barbara. *The Art of Frank Norris, Storyteller*. Columbia: University of Missouri Press, 1988. This study of recurrent motifs shows Norris as a more complex writer than do traditional assessments of his work. The chapter "Coming of Age in *The Pit*" uses the symbolic wheat pit to discuss the novel.

McElrath, Joseph R., Jr. *Frank Norris Revisited*. New York: Twayne, 1992. This critical biography offers a thorough discussion of *The Pit*, which McElrath calls "a novel of complications" because of its "sustained alternating portraits of [Laura and Jadwin's] worsening psychological condition."

Pizer, Donald. *The Novels of Frank Norris*. Bloomington: Indiana University Press, 1966. Discusses Norris' rationale and creation process in writing *The Octopus* and *The Pit*, as well as the influence of French naturalists Joseph LeConte and Émile Zola.

THE PLAGUE

Type of work: Novel
Author: Albert Camus (1913-1960)
Type of plot: Impressionistic realism
Time of plot: 1940's
Locale: Oran, Algeria
First published: La Peste, 1947 (English translation, 1948)

> *Principal characters:*
> DR. BERNARD R. RIEUX, a young physician
> JEAN TARROU, a traveler
> COTTARD, a fugitive
> JOSEPH GRAND, a clerk
> RAYMOND RAMBERT, a journalist
> FATHER PANELOUX, a priest

The Story:

At first, Dr. Bernard Rieux gave little thought to the strange behavior of the rats in Oran. One morning, he found three on his landing, each animal lying inert with a rosette of fresh blood spreading from the nostrils. The concierge grumbled at having to clean up the rats, but Rieux was a busy doctor and just then he had personal cares. Madame Rieux was leaving Oran. She suffered from a lingering illness, and Rieux thought that a sanatorium in a different town might do her good. His mother was to keep house for him while his wife was absent. The doctor was also being bothered by Rambert, a persistent journalist, who wanted to do a story for his metropolitan paper on living conditions among the workers in Oran. Rieux refused to help him, for he knew that an honest report would be censored.

Day by day the number of dead rats increased in the city. After a time, trucks came by each morning to carry them away. People stepped on the furry dead bodies when they walked in the dark. Rieux's first case of fever involved his concierge, who had a high temperature and painful swellings. Rieux was apprehensive. By making telephone inquiries, he learned that his colleagues were getting similar cases.

The prefect was averse to taking any action because he did not want to alarm the population. Only one doctor was convinced that the sickness was bubonic plague; the others reserved judgment. When the deaths rose to thirty a day, however, even the town officials became worried. When a telegram came instructing the prefect to take drastic measures, the news spread like wild fire: Oran was in the grip of the plague.

Rieux was called to the apartment of someone named Cottard, who had tried to hang himself. Grand, a clerk and Rieux's former patient, had cut the man down just in time to save him, but he could give no satisfactory reason for his attempt to kill himself. Rieux was interested in Cottard, who seemed rather an eccentric person.

Grand, too, was a strange man. For many years, he had been a temporary clerk, overlooked in his minor post, whom a succession of bureaucrats kept on without investigating his status. Grand had been too timid to call attention to the injustice of his position. In the evenings he worked hard on a novel he was writing, from which he seemed to derive much solace. Rieux was surprised when he saw the work. In all of those years, Grand had only the first sentence of his novel finished, and he was still revising it. He had once been married to Jeanne, but she had left him.

Tarrou was an engaging fellow, a political agitator concerned with governmental upheavals over the whole continent. He kept a meticulous diary of the ravages and sorrows of the plague. One of his neighbors was an old man who each morning called the neighborhood cats to him and shredded paper for them to play with. Once all the cats were around him, he would spit on them with great accuracy. After the plague grew worse, the city authorities killed all cats and dogs to check possible agents of infection. The old man, deprived of his targets, stayed indoors, disconsolate.

As the blazing summer sun dried the town, a film of dust settled over everything. The papers were meticulous in reporting the weekly total of deaths, but once the number passed the nine hundred mark, the press reported only daily tolls. Armed sentinels were posted to permit no one to enter or leave the town. Letters were forbidden. Since the telephone lines could not accommodate the increased traffic, the only communication with the outside was by telegraph. Occasionally, Rieux received an unsatisfactory wire from his wife.

The disposal of the dead bodies presented a problem. The little cemetery was soon filled, but the authorities made more room by cremating the remains in the older graves. At last two pits were dug in an adjoining field, one for men and one for women. When those pits were filled, a greater pit was dug, and no further effort was made to separate the sexes. The corpses were simply dropped in and covered with quicklime and a thin layer of earth. Discarded streetcars were used to transport the dead to the cemetery.

Rieux was in charge of one of the new wards at the infirmary. There was little he could do, however, for the serum from Paris was not effective. He observed what precautions he could, and to ease pain he lanced the distended buboes. Most of the patients died. Castel, an older physician, was working on a new serum.

Father Paneloux preached a sermon on the plague in which he called Oran's pestilence a retribution. Monsieur Othon, the judge, had a son under Rieux's care by the time Castel's new serum was ready. The serum did the boy little good; although he did show unexpected resistance to the disease, he died a painful death. Father Paneloux, who had been watching as a lay helper, knew the boy was not evil; he could no longer think of the plague as a retribution. His next sermon was confused. He seemed to be saying that human beings must submit to God's will in all things. For the priest, this view meant rejecting medical aid. When he himself caught the fever, he submitted to Rieux's treatment only when forced to do so. Father Paneloux died a bewildered man.

Rambert, who was not a citizen of Oran, tried his best to escape. Convinced that there was no legal means of leaving the city, he planned to leave with some illicit smugglers. Then the spirit of the town affected him, and he chose to stay to help Rieux and the sanitation teams. He had realized that only in fighting a common evil could he find spiritual comfort.

Tarrou had left home at an early age because he disliked his father's profession as prosecutor; the thought of the wretched criminals condemned to death because of his father's zeal horrified him. After having been an agitator for years, he finally realized that the workings of politics often resulted in similar executions. He had fled to Oran just before the plague started. There he found an answer to his problem in organizing and directing sanitary workers.

Cottard seemed content with plague conditions. Wanted for an old crime, he felt safe from pursuit during the quarantine. When the plague eased a little, two officers came for him, but he escaped. He was recaptured in a street gunfight.

Grand caught the fever but miraculously recovered to work again on his manuscript. Tarrou, also infected, died in Rieux's house. As the colder weather of January came, the plague ended. Rieux heard by telegram that his wife had died.

The streets became crowded again as lovers, husbands, and wives were reunited. Rieux dispassionately observed the masses of humanity. He had learned that human contact is important for everyone. For himself, he was content to help fight disease and pain.

Critical Evaluation:

In the decade and a half after the end of World War II, as the West strove to repair the physical, psychic, and spiritual damage, the voice of Albert Camus was one of the major artistic, philosophical, and moral sources of strength and direction. Camus offered reasoned yet passionate affirmation of human dignity in the face of an "absurd" universe, an absurdity that had been made evident to all by the Nazi horrors.

The Plague is the most thorough fictional presentation of Camus' mature thinking. In earlier works—notably the play *Caligula* (1938), the novel *The Stranger* (1942), and the essay *The Myth of Sisyphus* (1942)—Camus articulated his concept of the "absurd." Human beings are absurd because they have neither metaphysical justification nor essential connection to the universe. They are not part of any divine scheme and, being mortal, all of their actions, individual and collective, eventually come to nothing. The only question, then, is how to deal with their absurdity.

Camus' answer lies in his concept of "revolt." Human beings revolt against their condition first by understanding it and then, in the face of their cosmic meaninglessness, creating their own human meanings. In his earlier works, Camus explored that problem in terms of the individual; in *The Plague*, Camus extends his moral and philosophical analysis to the question of human beings as social creatures. What, Camus asks, in the face of an absurd universe, is one person's relationship to, and responsibility for, another?

The paradox that lies at the center of Camus' revolt concept is that of heroic futility. People struggle in spite of—even because of—the fact that, ultimately, they must lose. While the idea of the absurd denies a cosmic meaning to human beings, it does affirm their common bond. Since all people must die, all are brothers and sisters. Mutual cooperation, not self-indulgence, is the logical ethic that Camus derives from his perspective of the absurd. Camus chooses a plague as an appropriate metaphor for the human condition, since it intensifies this awareness of human mortality and makes the common bond especially clear.

Camus carefully divides the novel into five parts that correspond to the progression of the pestilence. Parts 1 and 5 show life before the plague's onslaught and after its subsidence. Parts 2 and 4 concentrate on the details of communal and personal suffering and, in particular, on the activities and reactions of the main characters as they battle the disease. Part 3, the climax of the book, shows the epidemic at its height and the community reduced to a single collective entity, where time has stopped, personal distinctions are lost, and suffering and despair have become routine.

The story is narrated by Dr. Bernard Rieux, who waits until almost the end of the novel to identify himself, in a factual, impersonal, almost documentary style. His account is occasionally supplemented by extracts from the journal of Jean Tarrou, but these intrusions, while more subjective and colorful, are characterized by an irony that also keeps the reader at a distance. Both narratives are juxtaposed against vivid, emotionally charged scenes. This continual alternation between narrative austerity and dramatic immediacy, and from lucid analysis to emotional conflict, gives *The Plague* much of its depth and impact.

Three of the principal characters—Rieux, Tarrou, and the clerk Joseph Grand—accept their obligation to battle the epidemic as soon as it is identified. Rieux is probably the character who comes closest to speaking for Camus. Since Rieux is a medical doctor who has devoted his life to the losing battle with disease and death, the plague is simply an intensification of his normal life. From the outset, he accepts the plague as a fact and fights against it with all the skill, endurance, and energy he can muster. He finds his only "certitude" in his daily round. There is no heroism involved, only the logic of the situation. Even after the plague has retreated, Rieux has no conviction that his actions had anything to do with its defeat. Yet Rieux learns much from his experience and, as the narrator, his is Camus' final word on the meaning of the ordeal.

Unlike Rieux, whose ideas are the practical consequence of his professional experience, Jean Tarrou first experiences the philosophical revelation, then shapes his life to it. Seeing his father, a prosecuting attorney, condemn a man to death, Tarrou becomes enraged with the inhumanity of his society and turns to revolutionary politics. That, too, he comes to realize, inevitably involves him in condemning others to death. Thus, long before coming to Oran, he has felt infected with the "plague"—defined as whatever destroys human life—which has reduced him to a purposeless life colored only by the ironical observations he jots down in his journal. When the plague arrives, he quickly and eagerly organizes the sanitation squads; the crisis gives him the opportunity to side with the victims of life's absurdity without fearing that his actions will inadvertently add to their misery. Such obvious, total commitments, however, are not available under normal conditions, and so Tarrou appropriately dies as one of the plague's last victims.

Both Rieux and Tarrou are too personally inhuman—Rieux with his abstract view of humanity, Tarrou with his desire for secular sainthood—to qualify as heroic; the most admirable person in the book is the clerk Joseph Grand, who accepts his role in the plague automatically, needing neither professional nor philosophical justifications, simply because "people must help each other." His greater humanity is further demonstrated by the fact that, while carrying out his commitment to the victims of the plague, he continues to show active grief over the loss of his wife and tenaciously revolts in his artistic attempt to write the perfect novel (even though he cannot manage the perfect first sentence).

Among the other principal characters, the journalist Raymond Rambert opts for "personal happiness"; Father Paneloux presents the Christian reaction to the pestilence; and Cottard acts out the role of the criminal. Caught in Oran by accident when the plague breaks out, Rambert turns his energies to escape, exhausting every means, legal and otherwise, to rejoin his wife. It is in him that the issue of exile or separation from loved ones is most vividly presented. For most of the novel he rejects the view that the plague imposes a social obligation on all, insisting that individual survival and personal happiness are primary. Although Rieux is the book's principal advocate of collective responsibility, he admits to Rambert that happiness is as valid an option as service. Even when Rambert finally decides to remain voluntarily and continue the fight, the issue remains ambiguous. At the end, as Rambert embraces his wife, he still wonders if he made the right moral choice.

If Rieux accepts Rambert's happiness as a decent option, he does not extend that tolerance to Father Paneloux's Christian view of the epidemic. *The Plague* has been called the most anti-Christian of Camus' books and that is probably correct, although it could be argued that the ethical values advocated are essentially Christian ones. As a system of beliefs, however, it is clear that Christianity—at least as understood by Paneloux—is tested by the pestilence and found wanting. If the priest's beliefs are inadequate, however, his actions are heroic, and it is this incongruity between his theological convictions and his existential behavior that gives his character and fate a special poignancy.

Near the beginning of the epidemic, he preaches a sermon in which he proclaims that the plague is a manifestation of divine justice. Later in the book, after he has become one of the most active fighters against the plague and a witness to the suffering and death of many innocent people, Paneloux's simple vision of sin and punishment is shaken. He preaches a second sermon in which he advocates a blind, total acceptance of a God who seems, from the human vantage point, to be indifferent, arbitrary, even, perhaps, evil. Driven to this extreme, Paneloux finally dies of the plague. Significantly, he is the only victim whose body is unmarked by the disease; he has been destroyed emotionally and spiritually because his religious vision is inadequate to the challenge and because he cannot live without that theological justification.

The most ambiguous character of all is Cottard. A criminal, he has lived in a constant state of fear and exile. Unable to endure such separation, he attempts to commit suicide near the beginning of the book. Once the plague sets in and all are subjected to that same sense of fear and solitude, Cottard rejoins humanity and flourishes; the plague is his natural element. Once it dissipates and he is again faced with isolation, Cottard goes berserk.

Thus, Camus describes the various human reactions to the plague—acceptance, defiance, detachment, solitary rejection, social commitment, criminality. The only value of the epidemic, Rieux admits, is educational, but the price paid for the knowledge is high. Nevertheless, even in the midst of the ordeal, there are moments of supreme pleasure and meaningful human connection. Shortly before the plague's last onslaught that takes Tarrou's life, he and Rieux defy regulations and go for a short swim. For a few brief moments, they are at one with the elements and in natural instinctive harmony with each other. The interlude is brief, of course, and both men return to the struggle—Tarrou to die, Rieux to chronicle its passing. He finally concludes that the only victory won from the plague amounts to "knowledge and memories" and the conviction that human beings are, on the whole, admirable.

"Critical Evaluation" by Keith Neilson

Bibliography:

Amoia, Alba. *Albert Camus.* New York: Continuum, 1989. An introduction to Camus as an important "Mediterranean" literary figure. In a chapter on *The Plague* entitled "A Holograph," the author is particularly attentive to the novel's coordinates in North Africa.

Fitch, Brian T. *The Narcissistic Text: A Reading of Camus' Fiction.* Toronto: University of Toronto Press, 1982. A sophisticated study of Camus as a metafictionalist. The chapter on *The Plague* examines how, through the use of several writer figures and by calling attention to its own narrative design, the novel makes its own artifice overt.

Kellman, Steven G., ed. *Approaches to Teaching Camus's "The Plague."* New York: Modern Language Association, 1985. A collection of essays primarily concerned with pedagogical strategies for the college-level study of Camus' novel. Provides a bibliographical survey and thirteen individual essays that situate the novel within the contexts of French literature, philosophy, medicine, and history.

_____. *"The Plague": Fiction and Resistance.* New York: Twayne, 1993. A general overview, including chronology and bibliography, of Camus' novel. Discusses the historical, philosophical, and biographical contexts of the work, and provides analyses of its style, structure, characters, and themes.

Tarrow, Susan. *Exile from the Kingdom: A Political Rereading of Albert Camus.* Tuscaloosa: University of Alabama Press, 1985. A rereading, in chronological order, of Camus' journalism and fiction as works that are linked to historical events and as embodiments of his ambivalences about political issues. Includes one chapter on *The Plague*, entitled "A Totalitarian Universe."

THE PLAIN-DEALER

Type of work: Drama
Author: William Wycherley (1641?-1715)
Type of plot: Comedy of manners
Time of plot: Seventeenth century
Locale: London
First performed: 1676; first published, 1677

> *Principal characters:*
> CAPTAIN MANLY, a misanthropic gentleman in the king's service
> FREEMAN, Manly's lieutenant
> OLIVIA, Manly's mistress
> VERNISH, Manly's only trusted friend
> WIDOW BLACKACRE, a rich widow gulled by Freeman
> FIDELIA, Manly's page, an heiress in disguise

The Story:

The Plain-Dealer, Captain Manly, returned to London after his ship had been sunk in a battle with the Dutch. He sought another ship because he disliked the hypocrisy of the age and wished to be away from the sycophancy of court and social life. Among the acquaintances who called at his quarters in London was Lord Plausible, who attempted to persuade the captain to seek his ship through influential people instead of waiting for an assignment. Manly demonstrated his love of plain dealing by showing Lord Plausible the door.

After Lord Plausible's departure, Manly instructed the two sailors who served him not to admit anyone to his lodgings except his ship's lieutenant, Freeman. When Freeman came, he and Manly discussed the relative merits of plain dealing and hypocrisy. Freeman held that no one could have a successful career without being hypocritical, but he could not convince Manly that such a policy was better than telling the truth at all costs.

While they talked, Widow Blackacre forced her way past the sailors and entered Manly's rooms. Manly made her welcome because she was a cousin of his fianceé, Olivia. The widow, who was extremely litigious, wanted Manly to appear on her behalf at a court hearing the following day. She threatened to have him subpoenaed if he did not appear. Freeman, well aware that the widow had a great deal of money, started to court her. The widow, who had a son, Jerry, who was almost as old as Freeman, ridiculed the idea because she wanted to manage her own affairs and would not be able to do so if she were married.

Manly went to seek information about Olivia, whom he had entrusted with most of his fortune while he was at sea. Olivia had heard of Manly's arrival in London, but she was none too anxious to see him because she had used his fortune as her own and had married Vernish, the only man Manly trusted and called his friend. Olivia pretended to be a Plain-Dealer like Manly. When visited by her cousin Eliza, Lord Plausible, and others, she belabored them for their hypocrisy, saying they spoke only ill of people in their absence but praised them to their faces. Her cousin reminded her that her comments about people were much worse and that she was not invited out enough in company to have an opportunity to say anything good about people to their faces.

Olivia, going on to speak plainly about Captain Manly, revealed that she did not love him and wished to be rid of his attentions. No one present knew as yet of her secret marriage to

Vernish. Manly had entered her apartment unnoticed, and after the others left, he and Olivia had words. Freeman and Manly's page reminded him to recover his money and jewels from Olivia, so Manly went back to request them. Olivia announced to all three that she was married, though she did not say to whom, and that she could not return the money because her husband had it.

Olivia, noticing Manly's page, became infatuated and told Manly to send the young page as messenger if they were to have any further dealings. As Manly left, Widow Blackacre, accompanied by her son, entered, and Freeman once more began his suit for her hand. When she repulsed him, he decided to use law instead of ordinary courtship to gain his ends.

The following morning, Manly, Freeman, and the page appeared at Westminster Hall as witnesses in Widow Blackacre's lawsuit. While away from Freeman for a time, Manly instructed his page to go to Olivia and arrange an assignation for him, for Manly had decided to get revenge by making her unknown husband a cuckold. That was a bitter errand for the page, who was actually a young woman in disguise. She had some time before fallen in love with Manly and had disguised herself as a boy in order to be near him.

At the court session, Freeman found Widow Blackacre's son and befriended him by giving him some money. The boy told Freeman that his mother refused to let him have any money until he came of age. Learning that the boy had not yet appointed a guardian for himself, Freeman persuaded the boy to name him as guardian, an act that transferred Widow Blackacre's money from her hands into his. Freeman also had the boy turn over to him all the widow's legal documents.

When Manly returned to his lodgings, his page informed him that she had succeeded in setting up an assignation with Olivia; Manly could substitute himself for the page in the darkness. When Manly heard the comments Olivia had made about him, he became even more furious and eager to have revenge. A little later, Widow Blackacre arrived, hoping to find Freeman and her son. When she confronted them, they told her that she was helpless, since they had her documents and Freeman had been appointed the boy's guardian. The widow threatened to prove that her son was illegitimate and so could not inherit her husband's estate.

That evening, the page went to Olivia's home. When Vernish appeared, the page escaped without being discovered, only to return later with Manly after Olivia had sent her husband away. Manly refused to seduce Olivia and left. The page was trapped when Vernish returned unexpectedly, but she escaped by disclosing herself to Vernish as a woman, incapable of cuckolding him. Vernish's attempt to ravish her was foiled by the entrance of his wife.

The page escaped through a window and returned to Manly. Later, Manly and Vernish met. Manly was not yet aware that Vernish was Olivia's husband, and Vernish was unaware that Manly was trying to seduce Olivia. Because they still trusted each other as the best of friends, Manly told Vernish he had been intimate with Olivia before her marriage, a fact that made Vernish all the more certain she had cuckolded him after marriage. The page, entering during the conversation, took Manly aside and told him another assignation with Olivia had been set for that evening. When they parted, Vernish told himself that he would pretend to leave town and thus trap the unknown man who was seducing Olivia.

In the meantime, Freeman and several bailiffs overheard Widow Blackacre plan to use court hangers-on to prove that her son was born out of wedlock. Rather than marry Freeman and lose control of her estate, the widow finally granted an allowance to the boy and an annuity to Freeman. The lieutenant was satisfied, as the money was all he wanted.

That evening, Manly and the page went to Olivia's apartment. There Manly overcame Vernish in a duel. Olivia, in shame, tried to escape with the jewels and money, but Manly took them from her. In the scuffle the page's wig came off, disclosing her as a woman. Manly, impressed by her faithfulness and beauty, immediately asked her to marry him. She told Manly she was Fidelia, heiress to a large fortune. They planned to begin a new life in the West Indies.

Critical Evaluation:

William Wycherley's final play, *The Plain-Dealer*, signaled a change in late-Restoration comedy. Unlike the sophisticated, witty comedies of Sir George Etherege and his own early mannered plays, *The Plain-Dealer* is a sharp, mordant satire upon false wit. Wycherley's railing, bitter, misanthropic tone greatly influenced the exaggerated style of such writers as John Crowne, Nathaniel Lee, Thomas Otway, and others. Nineteenth century critics, most notably Thomas Macaulay, considered Wycherley a libertine playwright whose indecent morality, as represented by Manly's conduct, rendered his drama repugnant for serious investigation. Among early twentieth century critics of Restoration comedy, Montague Summers regarded *The Plain-Dealer* as a moral satire and Manly as Wycherley's representative, and he noted how the hero's invective is directed at the prime evils of the age: hypocrisy, materialism, vice. The judgment of later scholars, who carefully studied seventeenth century social conventions, tended to reject Summers' view of the comedy as a moral satire, just as it rejected the stuffy Victorian prejudices concerning the play's supposed immorality.

For Wycherley, as for his contemporaries, the touchstone of wit was not mere cleverness, although spontaneity, freshness, and pungency were, to be sure, important signs of wit; rather, sound judgment was the practical test that separated a would-be wit from a true one, a coxcomb from a gallant. To this convention, Wycherley insists on adding the virtue of naturalness—truth to reality—as a necessary part of wit. In *The Plain-Dealer* Manly, the protagonist, is the major test for the author's theory of wit, but he is not, as some critics have asserted, either the mouthpiece for the author or the perfect model for his type of wit. Until the conclusion of the play, Manly is deficient in judgment. He has mistaken the pretense of loving for real love, the affectation of friendship for truth. Olivia, his faithless lover, is quite correct in her cynical view of him: "He that distrusts most the world, trusts most to himself, and is but the more easily deceived, because he thinks he can't be deceived." Olivia puts her finger on the chief flaw in Manly—his vanity. Because he rebukes so heartily the evils of the world, he cannot believe that he himself can be guilty of the same evils. Yet Olivia is right when she says, "I knew he loved his own singular moroseness so well, as to dote upon any copy of it." By imitating the image of moroseness in Manly, Olivia and Vernish easily deceive him.

Yet in his satire on false wit, Wycherley makes the point that at least some people in the world possess integrity, despite the fact that they neglect to rail, as Manly does, against society. Fidelia is true to Manly, even though he mistreats her when she is disguised as a man. To be sure, she is a stock theatrical figure, quite wooden and lacking in human responses, except when Vernish threatens to rape her. A more convincing character is Freeman, a "complier with the age," who is nevertheless a friend to Manly, outspoken but not candid to the extent of injuring his own fortunes or humiliating fools. Although he cheats the Widow Blackacre out of three hundred pounds a year, he shows her some slight generosity when he has power over her in settling for money instead of marriage. For a widow with property, as she says, "Matrimony . . . is worse than excommunication, in depriving her of the benefit of the laws." Freeman is not perfect, as Manly wishes to be, and prefers to live with people, despite their faults, rather than condemn them as rascals. The chief model for tempered wit in the play is Eliza, a minor character so far as the action is concerned yet always an example of good judgment. Eliza is cozened neither by Olivia's fine speeches nor by her actions: She judges clearly, with wit, honesty, and amused detachment. A good test of her mettle is her conversation with Olivia concerning *The Country*

Wife (1675), a cuckolding comedy and Wycherley's third and most vigorous play. To Olivia, the play is a "hideous obscenity," although she remembers perfectly its ribald scenes. To Eliza, however, the play is not obscene but amusing; with admirable tact, she says that she can "think of a goat, a bull, or satyr, without any hurt." In another scene of the play, she expresses her contempt for the ill-tempered conventions of the age: "railing now is so common, that 'tis no more malice, but the fashion"; Eliza's integrity is secure, so she responds to life naturally and rejects the artificial fashions that mark the failure of wit.

Some characters of the play lack wit and are satirized as fools, coxcombs, and mean-spirited materialists. The "petulant" Widow Blackacre belongs to the last group. She is by no means a fool, but because her energy is expended in litigation she is an object of censure. The subplot involving the widow, Freeman, and Major Oldfox, an old fop who imagines himself a poet, is coarse but not offensive. With sharp realism, Wycherley satirizes the creatures of the law courts, schemers, and cheats. Yet his satire cuts more at the form than the substance of their corruption. Similarly, the author reduces to a single facile dimension the coxcombs who surround Olivia. Novel, as his name suggests, pretends to be a wit by copying the latest fashions of decorum, but he lacks originality. Lord Plausible, a "ceremonious," flattering coxcomb, employs the old-fashioned courtesies of the previous age; he too is unoriginal. As for Jerry, the widow's son, together with the sailors from Manly's ship and assorted minor characters, they are all block-heads too simple even to imitate the manners of their betters or to understand the spirit of wit.

Manly, to be sure, understands most of the conventions governing true wit, although he exaggerates railing as necessary for plain dealing. Yet the coxcomb Novel disproves the need for railing when he says: "railing is satire, you know; and roaring and making a noise, humor." Novel is wrong; so is Manly, whose misanthropy drives him to excess. Unlike Novel, Manly is, however, capable of reformation, and Wycherley's point is precisely that the imperfect hero may improve himself by learning the truth about his nature. From Fidelia, Manly learns that not all women are treacherous; from Freeman, he learns to be tolerant of the imperfections of others; from his own experiences, he learns the most valuable lessons—that revenge is mean-spirited and that true wit must come from true judgment. By the end of the play, having learned both wit and judgment, Manly is able to satirize his previous folly: "I will believe there are now in the world/ Good-natured friends, who are not prostitutes,/ And handsome women worth to be friends."

"Critical Evaluation" by Leslie B. Mittleman

Bibliography:
Holland, Norman. *The First Modern Comedies*. Bloomington: Indiana University Press, 1959. The chapter on *The Plain-Dealer* focuses on the play as the dramatization of the question: Can an idealist live in the real world? Discusses the play's focus on the conflict between appearance and nature, and suggests that the title character is both innately good and a deviant from his society.

Hughes, Leo. Introduction to *The Plain Dealer*, edited by Leo Hughes. Lincoln: University of Nebraska Press, 1967. A very useful general introduction to Wycherley's play. Includes information on definitive texts and variants, stage history, and social and theatrical contexts. Compares Wycherley's drama with that of Ben Jonson and John Dryden; briefly discusses the play's origins in Molière's *Le Misanthrope*.

Rogers, Katharine M. *William Wycherley*. New York: Twayne, 1972. A good basic introduction to Wycherley's dramatic work. The chapter on *The Plain-Dealer* discusses Wycherley's adaptation of Molière's *Le Misanthrope* to the English stage and suggests that in this play, Wycherley's moral zeal nearly overbalances the comedy, resulting in a main character who is almost tragic. Points out that the play has two incompatible moral viewpoints and two conflicting levels of reality.

Thompson, James. *Language in Wycherley's Plays*. Tuscaloosa: University of Alabama Press, 1984. Focuses on the role of language in exposing characters' inner psychological realities. Suggests that the sense of extremes in *The Plain-Dealer* is created by linguistic contrasts and describes the play as Wycherley's most chaotic and discordant work.

Zimbardo, Rose A. *Wycherley's Drama*. New Haven, Conn.: Yale University Press, 1965. Discusses Wycherley's plays as Restoration revisions of formal classical satire and views the major characters in *The Plain-Dealer* as English manifestations of the classical satirist and adversarius. Treats the play as both satire and a satiric questioning of satire itself.

PLANTATION BOY

Type of work: Novel
Author: José Lins do Rêgo (1901-1957)
Type of plot: Regional
Time of plot: Early twentieth century
Locale: Northeastern coast of Brazil
First published: 1966: *Menino de Engenho*, 1932; *Doidinho*, 1933; *Bangüê*, 1934 (English
translation, 1966)

Principal characters:
CARLOS DE MELLO, the narrator
COLONEL JOSÉ PAULINHO CAZUZA, his grandfather and the owner of
Santa Rosa plantation
UNCLE JUCA, Colonel José Paulinho's son
AUNT MARIA, Colonel José Paulinho's daughter
MR. MACIEL, a schoolmaster
COELHO, Carlos' schoolmate
MARIA ALICE, a married cousin of Carlos
COUSIN JORGE, the owner of the Gameleira plantation
MARREIRA, a tenant farmer on the Santa Rosa plantation

The Story:
Menino de Engenho. At the age of four, Carlos de Mello saw the bloody body of his dead
mother shortly after his father killed her in an insane rage. The boy was taken from his city
home in Recife to live with his maternal grandfather and aunts and uncles at the family sugar
plantation, Santa Rosa. His father was interned in an asylum for the insane where he died,
completely paralyzed, ten years later; Carlos never saw him again.

At Santa Rosa, Carlos began a new life, the life of a plantation boy. His Aunt Maria became
his mother. His first morning he was initiated into country life by learning to drink milk warm
from the cow's udder and to bathe in a pool by the waterfall. A few day later his cousins arrived:
two boys and a girl. The boys taught him wild country ways—how to ride bareback, go on secret
swims, dive for stones. His cousin Lili, who was quiet, fair, and fragile, soon died of a childhood
illness.

One day, the famous bandit, Antonio Silvino, came to Santa Rosa. Everyone feared what he
would do, but he only came to visit the colonel and pay his respects. Another time, the family
had to abandon the plantation mansion and move to higher ground because the annual rains had
turned into a flood, threatening the sugar mill and the house itself but leaving behind rich soil
that would mean a superior crop of sugar cane the next year. When a fire threatened the cane,
all the plantation workers and neighboring owners came to cut the swath between the fire and
the rest of the fields to prevent the fire from spreading yet further.

Carlos always went with his grandfather on his inspection tours of the plantation. Colonel
José Paulino had expanded the original Santa Rosa plantation by buying neighboring proper-
ties. Now the plantation measured nine miles from end to end. The colonel had more than four
thousand people under his protection, including the former slaves, who had stayed on after the
abolition of slavery in 1888 and still did the same work they had before. There were also tenant
farmers who worked the plantation in exchange for living on and farming their patch of land.

On his inspection tours the Colonel would threaten shirkers, reward the trustworthy, gather news, offer food to the hungry and medicine to the ill, "the lord of the manor " visiting his lands and his "serf." The colonel was judge and jury for his workers. Carlos saw him put a man in stocks for "compromising" a young girl, but the man continued to deny his guilt. Finally, the girl confessed that Uncle Juca had made her pregnant.

Carlos' country education included the alphabet and reading lessons, but he learned much beyond his years from the plantation workers. As Zé Guedes walked him to his lessons, he taught him the lessons of life, introducing him to the prostitute Zefa Cajá, who provided his first experience with sex—and syphilis—at the precocious age of twelve. He learned country tales and superstitions as well. For him, there was a werewolf in the forest and *zumbis* and *caiporas* (the spirits of dead cattle and dead goats) on the plantation.

When Aunt Maria got married, Carlos felt abandoned. It was the second time he had lost a mother. Soon after, however, at the age of twelve, he was sent away to a secondary school. On the train to the city with his Uncle Juca he watched the beloved fields and forests of Santa Rosa plantation recede in the distance.

Doidinho. An anxious Carlos arrived with his Uncle Juca at the Institute of Our Lady of Mount Carmel, a boy's school dominated by a rigid Jewish master, Mr. Maciel, who relied on discipline and was completely lacking in knowledge of child psychology. Although Carlos made painful academic progress, his social adjustment was impossible from the onset. His extreme sensitivity set him apart from his peers and led him into flights of imagination that manifested themselves in exaggerated stories that he told his schoolmates. Withdrawn, restless, and unable to endure his failure in military exercises, he ran away from school. As he approached the plantation, he felt as alone and frightened as he had felt upon leaving it.

Bangüê. Nine years after his flight from the institute, Carlos, at the age of twenty-four, was graduated from law school and returned to Santa Rosa. He described himself as a neurotic young man, unsure of his place and purpose in life. He had become an ambivalent daydreamer, one moment on top of the world with imagined plans for Santa Rosa and for himself as the powerful lord, the next moment in the depths of disillusionment and despair. For one entire year, Carlos did nothing but lie in his room reading newspapers and swatting flies.

A beautiful married cousin, Maria Alice, brought warm love into Carlos' life. When she arrived at Santa Rosa, he was at last aroused from his indolence, and for a time he seemed to live through her, believing that she would help him to become the great lord of his dreams. During their affair, he became a new person, riding over the plantation, shouting orders, settling quarrels, and taking an interest in the work of the plantation for the first time since childhood. Eventually, Maria Alice returned to her husband. For the third time, Carlos lost a woman he had idolized, and his despair became greater than ever. He returned to his room, his newspaper, and his flies. Alternately filled with hate and desolate self-pity, he wished Maria dead one day and dreamt of marrying her the next.

When old José Paulinho died, it was found that Carlos had inherited the Santa Rosa Plantation. Once again he became energetic, full of plans and dreams of restoring the estate to its former glory. The situation at Santa Rosa became increasingly hopeless, however. Crops failed and workers deserted in search of higher wages. Worst of all, Carlos became convinced that Uncle Juca, bitter at not having inherited the plantation, was conspiring with a black tenant named Marreira to kill him and take over the plantation. Instead of caring for the declining land, Carlos became preoccupied with fearfully watching Marreira, whose success was representative of the rise of the working class in Brazil. Carlos finally gathered enough courage to ask Marreira to leave, but when he turned from his imagined enemy it was to find that his real enemy had defeated him. The factory that ground the plantation's cane and refined the sugar refused to extend credit any longer. Faced with the prospect of disposing of the Santa Rosa at public auction, Carlos instead sold it to Uncle Juca and left the plantation without having learned anything of value from his experience. As the train sped away with him, Carlos glimpsed Marreira's prosperous mansion, symbol of the new social environment in which he had been unable to compete.

Critical Evaluation:

José Lins do Rêgo's *Plantation Boy* is the title given in English translation to three of the six novels known as the Sugar Cane Cycle. The trilogy *Menino de Engenho*, *Doidinho* (literally, "daffy boy"), and *Bangüê* (old plantation) was followed by *O Moleque Ricardo* (1935; black boy Richard), *Usina* (1936; the sugar refinery), and *Fogo Morto* (1943; dead fires), none of which has been translated. *Menino de Engenho* views the plantation through the eyes of Carlos from the age of four to twelve; *Doidinho* describes Carlos' early schooling under the tough discipline of a parochial school; *Bangüê* picks up after a lapse of time in which Carlos has finished law school, and traces his inability to follow in his grandfather's footsteps. Lins do Rêgo wrote thirteen novels and published several collections of essays, but he remains best known for the Sugar Cane Cycle.

Meninho de Engenho is somewhat autobiographical, for the author's mother died a few months after his birth, and he was raised by his aunts and grandfather on his father's plantation. The novel is divided into forty chapters that are more like vignettes, or related tales, than chapters of a sustained narrative. Indeed, the narrative seems modeled after a collection of personal observations or memories. Characters are developed by accretion, their appearance in various vignettes gradually producing more rounded images. Uncle Juca, for example, who at first appears merely as the man responsible for bringing the four-year-old boy from Recife to Santa Rosa, gradually emerges as a hard-working and competent plantation boss, who satisfies his sexual urges with whatever worker's daughter, sister, or even wife is at hand and unattended. The grandfather's character is similarly sketched in brief, seemingly unconnected observations that coalesce work to create the gruff but actually beneficent plantation owner whom all admire.

No less important than the characters is the setting, which also emerges gradually and provides the historical backdrop of a Brazilian plantation early in the twentieth century. The setting is what one critic has called "the debris of a vanishing order." Evidence of the previous order is visible everywhere, particularly in the relationship between Carlos' grandfather and his workers. Once slaves and now free, their lives go on much as they had before the abolition of slavery. The colonel is shown to be a kind, just patriarch who rules over them, but they depend on him for everything—their land, their food, their livelihood, and the settling of their disputes.

Carlos' observations re-create the world of plantation life and the local customs, religious festivals, superstitions, and folklore. Carlos describes bandits, storytellers, mystics, and idiosyncratic characters like his curmudgeonly Aunt Sinhàzinha, who terrifies everyone, young or old. The content and structure of the chapter-tales are reminiscent of the popular folktales of northeastern Brazil known as *literatura de cordel*, or stories on a string, so called because the crudely published pamphlets were literally strung along a string to catch the eye of prospective buyers.

An important influence on the novels is Gilberto Freyre's sociohistorical work. Freyre's most famous work, *Masters and Slaves* (1933) is recalled in the narrator's admittedly precocious comments on "the Big House and the slave quarters," a literal translation of Freyre's original-language title, *Casa Grande e Sanzala*. Lins do Rêgo was involved in the Region-Tradition movement founded by Freyre, who is considered his most profound intellectual influence. The result in *Plantation Boy* is a regionalism that fuses a lively view of local life and history with a submerged critique of the patriarchal plantation system. Carlos loves and admires his grandfather, but he also notices the poverty in which the workers live. He observes the shacks in which the families live and the many children clothed in tatters or even naked, some with the big bellies of constant hunger. He notes the difference between his childhood and that of the little plantation boys with whom he plays. Woven among all these reminiscences is Carlos' longing for maternal love, his morbid fear of death and disease, and his ever-present pessimism.

Lins do Rêgo's creation of a decadent post-slavery Brazilian Northeast has been compared to William Faulkner's decadent rural American South. Certainly both writers are regionalists who describe crumbling plantation societies based on a single-crop economy that is ruled by a formerly slave-holding aristocracy. *Plantation Boy* is enjoyable reading, but its major strength lies in its vivid documentation of a time and place long since gone.

Linda Ledford-Miller

Bibliography:
Chamberlin, Bobby J. "José Lins do Rêgo." In *Latin American Writers*, edited by Carlos A. Solé and Maria Isabel Abreu. New York: Charles Scribner's Sons, 1989. A fine introduction for the beginning reader of Lins do Rêgo. Notes the autobiographical elements of his work along with its regional and folkloric influences.
Ellison, Fred. P. *Brazil's New Novel: Four Northeastern Masters*. Berkeley: University of California Press, 1954. Provides an excellent introduction to the new Brazilian regionalism of the 1930's and 1940's. One chapter is devoted to an examination of Lins do Rêgo's works. A classic in the field.
Hulet, Claude L. "José Lins do Rêgo." In *Brazilian Literature 3, 1920-1960: Modernism.* Washington, D.C.: Georgetown University Press, 1975. An anthology of Brazilian literature in Portuguese with introductions in English. Short biography of Lins do Rêgo followed by critical commentary. Discussion of Lins do Rêgo's style and techniques.
"José Lins do Rêgo (Calvalcânti)." In *World Authors, 1950-1970*, edited by John Wakeman. New York: H. W. Wilson, 1975. Gives an overview of Lins do Rêgo's life and summarizes each of the novels of the Sugar Cane Cycle. Includes a brief discussion of Lins do Rêgo's detailed naturalism and simple, direct style.
Vincent, Jon. "José Lins do Rêgo." In *Dictionary of Brazilian Literature*, edited by Irwin Stein. New York: Greenwood Press, 1988. Provides an overview of Lins do Rêgo's life and work and discusses his involvement in the Region-Tradition school of thought and writing founded by the great Brazilian sociologist, Gilberto Freyre.

PLATERO AND I
An Andalusian Elegy

Type of work: Poetry
Author: Juan Ramón Jiménez (1881-1958)
First published: Platero y yo, 1914; complete edition, 1917 (English translation, 1956)

Juan Ramón Jiménez was awarded the Nobel Prize in Literature in 1956. Though most famous for his poetry, his contributions to the development of Spanish prose are considered equally important. He began writing poetry at the age of fourteen, and he began experimenting with prose poetry at seventeen. His first prose poem, "Andén" ("The Railway Platform"), shows a strong influence of Spanish Romanticism in its imagery, structure, and vocabulary. It tells of a woman afflicted with a mental disorder that causes her to wait forever on the platform for a train to bring her the child that she had never had. The Spanish romantic poet Gustavo Adolfo Bécquer and the Nicaraguan modernist Rubén Darío, along with the Germans Johann Wolfgang von Goethe and Heinrich Heine and the French Charles Baudelaire and Stéphane Mallarmé, were clearly influential in his early prose poems. Jiménez went on from there to set new standards for prose poetry in a series of highly original works that started in 1917 with *Platero and I*, one of the best examples of prose poetry in Spanish literature.

Platero and I, written between 1907 and 1912, is based on material Jiménez gathered in his hometown of Moguer (in the province of Andalusia) while recuperating from the severe depression caused by his father's sudden death in 1900. At a time when many of his contemporaries—the writers of the literary Generation of 1898—were focusing on Castile, a province long dominant in the history of Spain, Jiménez turned for inspiration to his native Andalusia. *Platero and I* draws on many of the area's resources and characteristics, including the country towns, the ringing bells, the sounds of children, the animals, the small houses, and the golden moon. He also drew on the traditionally impressionistic style of the region. The elegiac tone of *Platero and I*, however, is markedly different from Jiménez's other poetry of that time. The tone here expresses grief and real suffering.

The first publication of *Platero and I*, in 1914, was an abbreviated version of the poem, written for a collection of children's literature, that contained only 73 of the 135 prose poems that were composed over a number of years and make up the complete edition of 1917. During his lifetime, Jiménez wrote 250 prose poems that he ultimately hoped to publish in a collection titled *Versos para ciegos* (verses for the blind). This title reveals that Jiménez thought poetry to be distinguished from prose based only on the presence in poetry of assonant or consonant rhyme. Once an author eliminates rhyme, the verses become like poetry read to a blind person. Unable to see the physical disposition of the text on the printed page and unguided by the familiar presence of rhyme, the blind person would not be able to distinguish between poetry and prose. The poetic element of *Platero and I* is Jiménez's masterful use of the natural rhythm of the Spanish language to generate melodic sentences that are flexible in syntax and in the use of clause structures—sentences that produce the almost cinematographic effects of slow motion and close-up and wide-angle views. He frequently suppresses cause-and-effect relationships and logical connections in an impressionistic style of writing that values the poetic image above all else.

"Platero" (*plata* is silver in Spanish) is the name generally given to a type of silver-colored donkey. In these prose poems, the donkey is Jiménez's companion, the one to whom the author makes his observations and in whom he confides. Although it may be tempting to look for parallels between Platero and Juan Ramón and Miguel de Cervantes' Sancho Panza and Don

Quixote, Platero, unlike Sancho, neither speaks nor participates actively in the work. On the contrary, Platero is the ideal listener and, though not "blind," perhaps also the ideal reader.

The events in *Platero and I* take place in one year, starting in one spring and ending in the next. Platero is actually a synthesis of the many silver donkeys the author knew during the years of his recuperation in Moguer. The symbolism in Platero's year of life is important for Jiménez, for it represents the natural cycle of birth to rebirth. As if to underline the importance of rebirth, Jiménez associates a second, traditional symbol with Platero's death: the butterfly, whose evolution from larva to winged creature has for centuries symbolized the transformation and renewal of life. In the last chapter of *Platero and I*, Jiménez, accompanied by children from the area, visits Platero's grave. As if responding to the poet's question, "Do you still remember me?" a butterfly appears and flies "like a soul" from lily to lily. These symbols anticipate a new beginning for Jiménez who, only a few years before, was so fearful of death that he had to have a doctor with him at all times.

Jiménez uses the first person and third person to alternate between subjective and objective narrative perspectives. The perspectives also vary between a child's view and that of an adult. What the views have in common, though, is a firm grounding in reality; in this work, Jiménez first introduces death, violence, abuse, cruelty, deformity, racism, the ugly side of social reality, human suffering, and human abuse of other human beings. Jiménez's descriptions of nature and its beauty, of the joy of being a child, of being with children, counterbalance the work's sometimes overwhelming accumulation of harsh realism.

Death has many manifestations in *Platero and I*. It is part of a larger process of growth and transformation such as that of Platero. It is sad and lonely like that of Pinito (poem 94), the loner whom the townspeople had dehumanized to being the epitome of stupidity, and it can be tender and sorrowful like that of the young girl who died of tuberculosis (poem 46) or that of the little girl who so loved to play with Platero (poem 81).

Violence, abuse, and cruelty to animals appear frequently in the poems. In "The Mangy Dog" (poem 27), the vineyard guard kills a dog with his shotgun for no other reason than for being physically unattractive. "The Old Donkey" (poem 113) shows what can happen to animals that grow old and are of no further use to their human owners. The dog saves itself once from death in the boneyard only to have its life ended by the winter's cold wind. The animal in "The White Mare" (poem 108) must cope not only with old age, like the old donkey, but also with its master beating it with a stick and a sickle. As the mare lies dying, people gather to curse it and poke fun at it, and the children throw stones at it. Jiménez tells Platero that in the darkness of the street, the mare's cadaver attains a cloudlike whiteness and light that the cold evening sky complements with small pink clouds. In Jiménez's works, whiteness, like that of the lilies at Platero's grave, consistently symbolizes purity and transcendence.

Deformity appears in "The Half-Wit Child" (poem 17), which describes a mute who, while not worthy of the attention of others, was all that his mother had in life. Jiménez looks back, remembering him and, after his death, he looks ahead to envision him enjoying his eternal reward.

The poem "Sarito" (no. 74) presents the problem of racism. A former black servant of a friend in Seville is now a traveling bullfighter who has stopped to visit. Most people eye him with suspicion, and one resident starts a fight with him. Jiménez receives him openly and affectionately. Nevertheless, the black Sarito knows to keep his distance, as he must, even from a friend.

Poem 95, "The River," chronicles the decline that pollution from the copper mines upstream has brought to an area. In retrospect, Jiménez looks back on the lively hustle and bustle of the fishermen, wine merchants, and others who had once sailed the waters; when he looks at the lifeless stream, the color of rust, he compares it to the trickle of blood from a cadaver.

Nature has many manifestations in *Platero and I*. In "The Eclipse" (poem 4), nature is a source of humor as the gradual darkening of the sun fools the hens into returning to their roost early, as if it were night. An unexpected warm spell, a rather cruel joke, tricks the swallows (poem 13) into returning, only to have them suffer when it turns cold again. Thunderstorms pound the area, keeping all in fear and suspense (poem 71) and sometimes killing people (poem 18).

Jiménez is at his impressionist best when describing nature. A sunset becomes a "Scarlet Landscape" (poem 19), wounded by its own crystals and dressed in a bleeding purple. Its light turns small plants and flowers transparent. Employing a synesthesia that combines the senses of touch, sight, and smell, Jiménez describes the light as embalming the moment with a moist, luminous, and pungent perfume. This technique frequently appears elsewhere in *Platero and I*, as in "The Pomegranate" (poem 96), where the poet describes the bitter, dry taste of the outer skin, then the first taste of sweetness—a "dawn made briefly into a ruby"—and finally the center of the fruit, "edible amethysts." He extends this poetic image to the limits of language: silence. The poet confesses that he can no longer talk, caught up as he is in a taste as sweet as what the eye sees when lost in the multiple colors of a kaleidoscope.

Children come and go constantly through the poems of *Platero and I*. Jiménez had a special place in his heart for children, whether rich or poor, whether from Moguer or from Argentina, where he visited in 1948, or from Puerto Rico, where he lived and finally died. "The Magi" (poem 122) is typical. Jiménez's description of this day in January when Spanish children normally receive their Christmas gifts combines the excitement of a child with an adult's love of children. Once the children have finally gone to bed, the poet plans with Platero how they and other adults will dress up in sheets, quilts, and old hats and parade at midnight beneath the window of the children's room, leaving the children astonished, trembling and marveling at the magi who have come to leave them gifts.

Joseph A. Feustle, Jr.

Bibliography:
Cardwell, Richard A. "'The Universal Andalusian,' 'The Zealous Andalusian,' and the 'Andalusian Elegy.'" *Studies in Twentieth Century Literature* 7, no. 2 (Spring, 1983): 201-224. Explores the influence that Francisco Giner de los Ríos and the philosophy of Krausism had on Jiménez. Also discusses how the intellectual atmosphere of the time influenced Jiménez's contemporaries, including those well-known members of the literary Generation of 1898 Antonio Machado, José Ortega y Gassett, and Miguel de Unamuno.
Fogelquist, Donald. *Juan Ramón Jiménez.* Boston: Twayne, 1976. An excellent starting place. Offers a solid overview of the poet's life and works.
Jiménez, Juan Ramón. *Platero and I.* Translated by Antonio T. de Nicolás. Boulder, Colo.: Shambhala, 1978. A complete, excellent translation, though the translator's claim to having kept the lyricism, rhythm, and beauty of the original text intact is a linguistic impossibility.
Olson, Paul R. *Circle of Paradox: Time and Essence in the Poetry of Juan Ramón Jiménez.* Baltimore: The Johns Hopkins University Press, 1967. An important and essential study of the major symbols in Jiménez's poetry.
Wilcox, John C. *Self and Image in Juan Ramón Jiménez: Modern and Post-Modern Readings.* Champaign: University of Illinois Press, 1987. By concentrating on the relationship between the author and the reader, this study reveals the art of Jiménez's early poetry. Many of the poems that Wilcox studies have parallels in *Platero and I*.

THE PLAYBOY OF THE WESTERN WORLD

Type of work: Drama
Author: John Millington Synge (1871-1909)
Type of plot: Comic realism
Time of plot: Early twentieth century
Locale: County Mayo, Ireland
First performed: 1907; first published, 1907

Principal characters:
CHRISTOPHER "CHRISTY" MAHON, a braggart
OLD MAHON, his father
MARGARET "PEGEEN" FLAHERTY, his sweetheart
WIDOW QUIN, a villager
SHAWN KEOGH, a young farmer in love with Pegeen

The Story:

One evening a young man arrived at a small inn on the wild Mayo coast of Ireland and announced that he had run away from home. He said that his name was Christopher Mahon and that he was running away because he had killed his father during a fight. The farmers who were passing the time in the inn were very much pleased by his exhibition of courage. Christopher was especially admired by Pegeen, the pretty young daughter of Michael Flaherty, the inn-keeper. She, along with the others, pressed the young man to tell his story again and again.

At home Christopher had been a meek and obedient son, controlled by his domineering father. He accepted the insults of his parent until the latter tried to force him into marrying a rich old woman. At last, in desperation, he hit his father over the head. Seeing the old man fall, Christopher presumed that he was dead.

The experience at the inn was something new for Christopher, who for the first time in his life was regarded as a hero. When the news of his story spread among the villagers, they flocked to look at this paragon of bravery. The young women were particularly interested in him—and the not so young as well. Dame Quin, a thirty-year-old widow, was much taken with the young taproom hero. Christopher, however, was attracted to pretty Pegeen. He was flattered by her admiration, and, in an attempt to live up to her opinion of him, he began to adopt an attitude of bravado. Before long, he himself believed that he had done a courageous deed.

Each year the village held a festival in which the men competed with each other in various sports. Christopher was naturally expected to take part. His early timidity having long since disappeared, he made every effort to appear a hero in the eyes of Pegeen, to whom he was now openly betrothed. She had broken her engagement with a young farmer, Shawn Keogh, soon after Christopher arrived on the scene.

While her Playboy, as Pegeen called him, was taking part in the sports, an old man came to the inn. He was looking for a young man whose description fitted Christopher's appearance. Dame Quin, who still had designs on the boy, deliberately misdirected the stranger. When the man returned from his wild goose chase, he arrived in time to see Christopher hailed as a hero because he had just won the mule race. Old Mahon, not dead from Christopher's blow, recognized his son and flew into a rage. He insisted that Christopher go home with him, and, through his angry tirade, he humiliated his son in front of the spectators.

The Playboy, however, had enjoyed too long the thrill of being a hero. He did not give in timidly as he would have done at an earlier time. Much to his father's astonishment, he again struck the old man over the head. Once again it appeared that old Mahon was dead. The reaction of the people, however, was not at all what Christopher might have expected. Killing one's father some miles away was one thing. Killing him in front of a number of spectators who might be involved in the affair was another. The people muttered angrily among themselves, and even Pegeen joined with them in denouncing the murderer.

Deciding at last that the only thing to do was to hang Christopher for his crime, they tied up the struggling young man and prepared to lead him away. Old Mahon, however, had proved himself a tough fellow once before, and he did so again. The first blow that Christopher had given him had only stunned him, so that, soon after the boy had run away, his father was able to follow him to the village. This second blow had merely knocked him unconscious for a short time. As Christopher struggled and the noose was slipped over his head, Mahon crawled through the door on his hands and knees.

While the villagers stood around dumbfounded, he walked over to his son and quickly untied him. Far from being angry with Christopher for hitting him, he was pleased to discover that his son was not the timid weakling he had thought him to be. The two left the inn, arm in arm, deaf to the pleas of Pegeen, both of them jeering at the foolishness of the people on the Mayo coast.

Critical Evaluation:

The Playboy of the Western World, John Millington Synge's last completed work, is the author's greatest play, and in many ways his most difficult to interpret. The play may be viewed as a satire of Western myths and conventions, beginning with the age-old habit in the West of cheerfully, even eagerly, extending a welcome to criminals and fugitives seeking shelter. In the romantic sphere, the play uses a comic reversal of the traditional situation of man as the sexual aggressor, instead having Christopher hotly pursued and competed for by Pegeen and her rivals. Greek myths are also satirized, beginning with the obvious parallel between Christopher and Oedipus as having committed patricide. In the same vein, Christopher becomes a mock-heroic counterpart to Odysseus as he wanders into the Mayo village seeking refuge, and eventually crowns his conquests there by winning a mule race.

On another level, *The Playboy of the Western World* is a deeply symbolic play; its meaning revolves around the emotional and moral growth of the hero through a series of three ritual "murders" of his father. The first "murder" is a spontaneous, unconscious, almost accidental act; Christopher's blow is a reflex reaction to his father's incessant taunting and ridiculing of the young man's physical and sexual abilities. It is crucial to examine the reactions of the Irish peasants to Christopher's deed. Steeped in mythical, preintellectual concepts, they view the patricide as a necessary and admirable act. Because the violence occurred far away and reaches them only by the report of an intriguing visitor, it exists for them only as a fantasy, not as a down-to-earth, bloody deed; the murder is like another folktale in which the hero gloriously kills all obstacles in his path. Thus they lionize Christopher, who as a result blossoms from a sniveling, terrified boy to a confident braggart and ladies' man.

Unfortunately, Christopher's new stature is based on a lie, as becomes known when Old Mahon appears in the village and humiliates his son, thus necessitating the second "murder." This second act of violence, however, is essentially different from the first; faced with a threat to his self-image, reputation, and independence, Christopher now makes a conscious—and therefore moral—decision to kill his father. The qualitative difference in the two acts is immediately reflected in the villagers' reaction to this second "murder." They are horrified and drag the hero off to hang him; he has grown, through this rational and very real action, past the comprehension of their primitive unconsciousness and must be punished.

Christopher's growth is completed and his triumph as hero complete, however, only with the third "murder." This time the act is purely verbal and symbolic, and consists of Christopher's discovery that he can order his father to do his will. Thus Christopher at the end of the play has transcended the primitive stage of physical murder; he has asserted his power by throwing off the domination of a tyrannical father, thus reaching the full status of hero.

Bibliography:
Bloom, Harold, ed. *Modern Critical Interpretations: John Millington Synge's "The Playboy of the Western World."* New York: Chelsea House, 1988. Eight representative essays consider Christopher's self-transformation and parallels with Christ, the realistic and fantastic aspects of the play, its complexity and ambiguity, and its irony, wit, and poetry.
Greene, David, and Edward M. Stephens. *J. M. Synge: 1871-1909.* Rev. ed. New York: Macmillan, 1989. The standard, authorized biography based on Synge's diaries, letters, and manuscripts. Provides the basic accounts of the composition of *The Playboy of the Western World* and of its riotous reception in 1907.
Kopper, Edward A., Jr., ed. *A. J. M. Synge Literary Companion.* Westport, Conn.: Greenwood Press, 1988. A valuable collection of sixteen chapters by leading scholars, covering all aspects of Synge's life and work. Excellent introduction to the critical literature. Good bibliographies.
Owens, Cóilín, and Joan Radner, eds. *Irish Drama: 1900-1980.* Washington, D.C.: Catholic University of America Press, 1990. Places the play in the general context of the Irish dramatic movement. Concise introduction, map, and the best detailed annotations to the text of the play.
Whitaker, Thomas R., ed. *Twentieth Century Interpretations of "The Playboy of the Western World": A Collection of Critical Essays.* Englewood Cliffs, N.J.: Prentice-Hall, 1969. Thirteen judicious selections on the composition of the play, its milieu, early audience reaction, and production values. Interpretive essays consider the paradoxes of Christopher's characterization, Synge's ironic language, and the play's surrealistic qualities.

THE PLOUGH AND THE STARS

Type of work: Drama
Author: Sean O'Casey (John Casey, 1880-1964)
Type of plot: Social realism
Time of plot: 1916
Locale: Dublin, Ireland
First performed: 1926; first published, 1926

> *Principal characters:*
> FLUTHER GOOD,
> PETER FLYNN,
> MRS. GOGAN,
> MOLLSER GOGAN,
> BESSIE BURGESS,
> THE COVEY,
> NORA CLITHEROE and
> JACK CLITHEROE, neighbors in a Dublin tenement house
> CAPTAIN BRENNAN, of the Irish Citizen Army
> CORPORAL STODDART and
> SERGEANT TINLEY, of the Wiltshires

The Story:

Fluther Good had put a new lock on the Clitheroes' door when Mrs. Gogan brought in a hatbox, just delivered for Nora Clitheroe. Mrs. Gogan was convinced that Nora was putting on airs and buying too many new clothes in order to hold on to her husband. Nora's Uncle Peter Flynn drifted in and out, readying his uniform of the Irish National Foresters. Peter had a chip on his shoulder which all the tenement dwellers took turns knocking off. He was an ineffectual man and he knew it.

When the Covey, Nora's cousin, came in, telling them that he had been laid off from work because the boys had mobilized for a demonstration for independence, he aroused both Peter and Fluther. The Covey was less inclined to follow the flag of the Plough and the Stars than to go ahead with his work. Peter and the Covey were arguing away when Nora came home and quieted them, declaring that there was small hope of ever making them respectable. She was pleased with the way Fluther had put on the lock, but Bessie Burgess, a vigorous but rather coarse woman, scornfully berated Nora for treating her neighbors shamefully, not trusting them. As Fluther broke up the women's wrangling, Jack Clitheroe came home and sent Bessie away. He told Nora that he would speak to Bessie when she was sober again.

Jack was despondent because the Citizen Army was to meet that night. He had lost the rank of captain to Ned Brennan and, sulking, had refused to attend meetings. Wanting to be a leader, he did not have strength of leadership. Nora tried to get his mind off the meeting by making love to him. They were interrupted by the new Captain Brennan with a dispatch from the general telling Jack where to report. Jack did not understand why he was to report until Brennan told him that the boys had given him the title of Commandant, word of which had been in a letter Nora had never delivered. Disturbed because Nora had withheld the letter, Jack went off to the meeting with Brennan.

Mollser Gogan, a child in the last stages of tuberculosis, asked Nora if she might stay with her, since everyone else had gone to the demonstration. Fluther and Peter, overwhelmed by the oratory of the speakers at the demonstration, repaired to a bar to pour in more courage. Even in the public house, the voice of the speaker followed them, urging bloodshed and war. Bessie and Mrs. Gogan were engaged in a verbal battle when they entered. Bessie, drunk, was ready for a hair-pulling, but the barman sent both women away. Peter was left holding Mrs. Gogan's baby, for she had forgotten the child when she was piloted out of the bar. He hurried out to find her.

Fluther, though he had intended to give up drinking before the meeting, decided the time had come for all the liquor he could hold, and he was generous enough to stand treat, even to the Covey and Rosie, a prostitute. Fluther and the Covey got into an argument on the labor movement and the barman had to separate them. Rosie and Fluther left when Jack, Brennan, and other officers, their eyes shining with excitement, came in for a drink before moving off with the Citizen Army.

The next day Mollser was so much weaker that Mrs. Gogan put her out in the sun in front of the house; they could hear shooting in the distance. Looking for Jack, Nora and Fluther had spent the night going to all the barricades without finding him. When they came back to the house, Nora was leaning heavily on Fluther. Bessie shouted down curses from her window. The Covey sighed that the fight would do the poor people no good.

Bessie brought Mollser a mug of milk when she came downstairs. The men began to gamble to keep their minds off the shooting, but they stopped when Bessie reappeared, laden down with booty, to say that looting had begun in the shops. Fluther and the Covey went off immediately. The guns scared Mollser so much that Bessie took her into the house. Even timid Peter started to follow Bessie and Mrs. Gogan when they set out with a baby carriage to hold their loot, but the sound of the big guns again stopped him. He was envious, however, when he saw the Covey, then Bessie and Mrs. Gogan, return with piles of loot.

Brennan and Jack stopped at the steps to let a wounded comrade rest. It was with difficulty that Jack got away from Nora, who had run down to him when she heard his voice. When the two officers finally took their man away, Nora was ready to faint.

Fluther came back with a jug of whiskey. Roaring drunk, he was too fuddled to go out for a doctor for Mollser, who was suddenly very sick. Bessie, praying when she heard the guns, went off toward the shooting to find a doctor.

A few days later the rebellion was still going on. Mollser had died, and Nora had had a stillborn baby. Both bodies were in the same coffin in Bessie's room, the only room in the tenement that seemed safe from the shooting. Fluther, the Covey, and Peter, having taken refuge there, played cards to while away the time.

Nora was on the verge of insanity. Bessie had stayed up with her for three nights and was herself almost dead for sleep. Each time Bessie sat in the chair in front of the fireplace for a nap, Nora would wake up. Once, when Nora got up, Brennan, in civilian clothes, was in the room telling the men how Jack had died. Nora did not recognize him. Brennan wanted to stay with the others; he said there was nowhere to go any more. Corporal Stoddart, an English soldier, came in to escort the coffin out of the house. Mrs. Gogan was the only one allowed to go with it. As she was thanking Fluther for making the funeral arrangements, the soldier heard a sniper nearby shoot another English soldier. The English, trying to find the sniper, were rounding up all the men in the district, and so Fluther, the Covey, Peter, and Brennan were forced to go with the corporal to spend the night in the Protestant church.

Bessie had again fallen asleep. Nora got up to prepare tea for Jack. As she stood at the window looking for him, the soldiers below shouted for her to go away. Bessie, awakened, tried to pull her back, but Nora struggled so hard that Bessie fell back against the window frame as she pushed Nora. Two shots, fired quickly, struck Bessie. She was dead before Mrs. Gogan came home.

Two English soldiers, investigating the room for snipers, found the mistake they had made in killing Bessie. They calmly poured themselves cups of tea while Mrs. Gogan took Nora downstairs to put her into Mollser's bed.

Critical Evaluation:

Sean O'Casey's bitter childhood and early manhood help account for his adherence to the Marxist idea of class war. He believed that the Irish would have to reckon with the problem of Irish poverty before they could ever hope to win independence. It is with this problem of some poor people caught in the midst of the famous Easter Rebellion of 1916 that O'Casey deals in *The Plough and the Stars*. In the play, the desperate situation of a group of tenement dwellers overshadows the dream of national independence. The Covey seems always to give O'Casey's own views on humanity versus nationality. The play was the cause of a patriotic riot when it was first produced by the Abbey Theatre in Dublin.

The Plough and the Stars is the last of Sean O'Casey's realistic plays about the Irish Civil War and, along with *Juno and the Paycock* (1924), represents the high point of his artistic achievement. Although it may lack the depth of characterization present in *Juno and the Paycock*, it probably has a greater theatrical impact. Juxtaposing scenes of the most intense pain and violence against moments of earthy, vital humor, O'Casey succeeds in capturing and dramatizing both the folly and the heroism of this Irish national tragedy.

The play is set during the Easter Uprising of 1916, when extremists proclaimed an Irish Republic and seized the Dublin General Post Office. A short, bloody struggle ensued and ravaged most of the city for several days before the nationalists surrendered. *The Plough and the Stars* describes the impact of these events on the inhabitants of a single tenement dwelling, which, because of O'Casey's careful selection of characters and conflicts, becomes a microcosm of Dublin at war.

The play's title points to many of its themes. On one level the title refers to the flag of the Citizen Army, a leftist labor movement that was one of the two groups sponsoring the uprising. Thus, O'Casey specifically identifies himself with the radical workers rather than with the ardent nationalists. On a more symbolic level, however, the flag suggests a conflict—the "plough" versus "the stars"; that is, the practical realities of poverty and human relationships versus the abstract ideal of pure nationalism. While O'Casey admired the courage and dedication of the rebels, he felt that their fanatical actions at best attacked only superficial evils and at worst were suicidal, unleashing forces that destroyed not only the insurrectionists but also large numbers of innocent people caught up in the resulting violence. The ways in which impersonal, abstract ideals can destroy human relationships, a major theme in O'Casey's previous plays, reaches its fullest statement in *The Plough and the Stars*.

This theme is illustrated in the play's first act in the dispute between newlyweds Jack and Nora Clitheroe. In spite of her social and cultural pretensions, Nora is the embodiment of domesticity, valuing only her husband, her home, and her family to be. She can understand neither Jack's devotion to a political cause nor his apparent taste for the military style; she fears only his injury or death and is willing to deceive him to keep him out of combat. For his part, Jack seems deeply, if sentimentally, in love with Nora, and at times he is tempted to accede to her desires, but his commitment is too strong. He and his comrades are caught up in the fervor of the times.

O'Casey makes the audience wonder, however, how much of that commitment is dedication, how much is ego, and, when the fighting becomes intense, how much is fear of being thought a coward. The outcome of the domestic conflict is predictable: Jack is killed in combat and Nora, too delicate to stand the pressure, goes insane. Others are not so weak. If O'Casey's vision does not spare those who bring havoc on themselves and their loved ones, he also pays homage to those victims who are forced by circumstance to assume the burdens. Frequently, those who seem the least promising become, under pressure, the most heroic.

Fluther Good behaves like an amiable drunk during most of the play and is quick to loot liquor stores when given the opportunity. When Mollser Gogan dies and Nora has her breakdown, however, he braves bullets and arrest to bring aid and comfort. Bessie Burgess, the lone English partisan in the tenement, seems ill-tempered and bigoted in the early parts of the play, deriding Nora and fighting constantly with Mrs. Gogan, another querulous lady. Yet, in the last act, it is Bessie who ministers to the dying Mollser and the mad Nora, finally sacrificing her life trying to shield the girl from sniper fire. Her rival, Mrs. Gogan, assumes the burdens after Bessie dies.

Bessie and Mrs. Gogan, like Juno in the earlier play, represent the strength of an Ireland torn to pieces by civil war. They do what they can—and must—to keep the continuity of life intact while the men, with their abstract notions of nationalism, heroism, and manhood, destroy. While the fighting rages, young Mollser dies of tuberculosis because there is no one available to help her. Mollser is O'Casey's symbol for the real Irish situation: poverty and neglect are the real evils, and until they are dealt with, the question of nationalism is largely irrelevant. As long as the Jack Clitheroes and the Brennans can be stirred up to violence by the demagogic appeals of the "Voice," these problems will continue to be ignored. However, as long as Ireland is capable of producing people like Bessie Burgess, Mrs. Gogan, and Fluther Good, O'Casey suggests that there is hope.

Bibliography:
Ayling, Ronald. *Sean O'Casey: Modern Judgments.* Nashville, Tenn.: Aurora Press, 1970. Includes valuable comments on *The Plough and the Stars.* Considerations of O'Casey's poetic gifts, his use of symbols, his socialism, and his place in the Irish Dramatic Movement.
Hogan, Robert. *The Experiments of Sean O'Casey.* New York: St. Martin's Press, 1960. A refreshing synthesis of dramatic theory and theatrical practice. Argues that in his Dublin trilogy O'Casey is expanding his technical capacities, and that *The Plough* is a stage in his continuing experimentation.
Kilroy, Thomas, ed. *Sean O'Casey: A Collection of Essays.* Englewood Cliffs, N.J.: Prentice-Hall, 1975. An excellent selection from leading Irish, British, and American O'Casey critics, discussing his politics, dramatic technique, and development. Represents disagreements about O'Casey's achievement as a political dramatist.
Krause, David. *Sean O'Casey: The Man and His Work.* New York: Macmillan, 1975. The best study of O'Casey's dramatic work. Describes the economic, political, and religious tensions in the Dublin of his time.
Sean O'Casey Review 3 (Spring, 1976). Special issue on *The Plough and the Stars.* Valuable essays on the first production, O'Casey's realism and pacifism, socialism, the historical background, the O'Casey-Pearse relationship, and Bessie Burgess as Cathleen Ni Houlihan.

THE PLUMED SERPENT

Type of work: Novel
Author: D. H. Lawrence (1885-1930)
Type of plot: Psychological realism
Time of plot: Twentieth century
Locale: Mexico
First published: 1926

Principal characters:
 KATE LESLIE, an Irishwoman
 DON RAMÓN CARRASCO, a Spanish-Indian scholar and the reincarnated
  Quetzalcoatl
 GENERAL CIPRIANO VIEDMA, the reincarnated Huitzilopochtli, god of war
 DOÑA CARLOTA, Don Ramón's first wife
 TERESA, his second wife
 OWEN RHYS, Kate Leslie's cousin

The Story:
 Kate Leslie was the widow of an Irish patriot. Restless after her husband's death, she had gone to Mexico with Owen Rhys, her American cousin. Mexico, however, oppressed her. Dark and secretive, the arid land weighed upon her spirit like a sense of doom. She saw it as a country of poverty, brutality, and bloodshed.
 Owen and one of his friends took her to a bullfight. It was a distressing experience, for to her the ritual of death was like modern Mexico, vulgar and cruel, without muster or passion. She was unable to endure the spectacle and the reek of warm blood and announced that she was returning alone to the hotel. A downpour of rain began as she was leaving the arena, and she was forced to wait in the exit tunnel with a crowd whose speech and gestures filled her with alarm. She was rescued from her predicament by a small, authoritative man in uniform who introduced himself as General Cipriano Viedma. A full-blooded Indian, he was impassive and withdrawn yet vitally alert. They talked while waiting for the automobile he had summoned to take Kate to her hotel, and she felt unaccountably drawn to him.
 Mrs. Norris, the widow of a former English ambassador, invited Kate and Owen to her house for tea the next day. The general and his friend, Don Ramón Carrasco, were among the guests. Don Ramón was a landowner and a distinguished scholar. There were reports of a strange happening near his estate at Sayula. A naked man was supposed to have risen from the Lake of Sayula and told the villagers that Quetzalcoatl and the old gods of Mexico were soon to return to earth. Don Ramón had promised an investigation. The story appealed to Kate's Celtic imagination; she wanted to go to Sayula to see the lake from which the Aztec gods were to be reborn.
 Kate and Owen dined with Ramón before his return to Sayula. The guests talked about Mexican politics and the happening at the lake. One impassioned young man declared that only a great miracle, like the return of Quetzalcoatl, could save Mexico. Cipriano seldom spoke but sat, his eyes black and unfathomable, looking from Kate to his host. After dinner, he and Kate walked in the garden. In the darkness, she felt that he was a man of strange, almost primitive potency and impulses.

5135

When Owen returned to the United States, Kate decided to go to Sayula for a time. There she found an old Spanish house that pleased her. With the house went a servant, Juana, and her two sons and two daughters. Kate liked the house and its surroundings, and she rented it for an indefinite stay.

The people of Sayula were restless and filled with a spirit Kate had not seen elsewhere in Mexico. One night, she heard drums beating in the village plaza. Men naked to the waist were distributing leaflets printed with a hymn to Quetzalcoatl. Later, the peons began to dance to the savage, insistent rhythms of the drums. In the torchlight, the dance looked like a ritual out of old, almost forgotten times, a ritual men remembered in their blood rather than in their minds. Some people said that Don Ramón was behind the new cult of Quetzalcoatl that was springing up.

Several weeks after Kate arrived in Sayula, Don Ramón and his wife, Doña Carlota, came to call. Doña Carlota was devoutly pious and eager to be friendly. When Kate visited Jamiltepec, Don Ramón's hacienda, she found soldiers guarding the gates. A drum was beating in the patio. Doña Carlota hated the sound and told Kate that she was afraid because her husband was involved in the business of Quetzalcoatl. She confided that he wished to become a god, the reincarnation of the Plumed Serpent that the Aztecs had worshiped. Cipriano arrived at the hacienda for supper. That night there was a dance in the patio. Don Ramón promised that the reborn gods would bring new life to the country. The rains began, ending the hot, dry season.

Refusing to witness her husband's heresies, as she called them, Doña Carlota returned to Mexico City. Meanwhile, the work of the men of Quetzalcoatl continued. During one of his visits, Cipriano asked Kate to marry him, but she put him off. Don Ramón continued to write and publish his hymns to Quetzalcoatl. Cipriano's soldiers distributed them. After he had been denounced by the clergy, Don Ramón had the holy images removed from the church at Sayula and burned.

One day a group of his political and religious enemies, disguised as bandits, attacked Jamiltepec and tried to assassinate Don Ramón. Kate happened to be at the hacienda when the raiders appeared; she killed one of the attackers and saved Don Ramón's life after he had been seriously wounded. Afterward, she stayed much to herself, afraid of her own disturbed emotions; but she was being drawn slowly toward the dark, powerful forces of primitive awareness and power that she found in Don Ramón and Cipriano. The general had come to believe himself to be the living Huitzilopochtli, god of war. Fascinated and repelled, Kate yielded at last to his masculine dominance. Don Ramón married them with pagan rites, and she became Malintzi, bride of the red-knifed god of battles.

When Don Ramón reopened the church, which he had converted into a sanctuary of the old Aztec gods, Doña Carlota protested against his blasphemy. Overcome by hysteria and fear of his implacable will, she suffered a stroke and died a short time later. Meanwhile, Cipriano had been spreading the new doctrines among his soldiers. On an appointed night, he was declared the living Huitzilopochtli, god of the knife. In the rites of his assumption, he sacrificed three of the prisoners captured after the attack on Don Ramón some weeks before.

Don Ramón married again. His bride was Teresa, daughter of a dead landowner of Jalisco. Watching Teresa's passive, female submission to her husband, Kate began to fear the dark potency, the upsurge of blood with which Don Ramón and Cipriano were arousing all Mexico. Men wearing the white and blue serapes of Quetzalcoatl and the red and black serapes of Huitzilopochtli were seen everywhere. When the Church excommunicated the leaders, revolt broke out. The President of Mexico declared the Church outlawed, and the faith of Quetzalcoatl became the official religion of the republic. Kate viewed these happenings with a sense of horror. The pride and strength of the old gods seemed to menace her spirit and her womanhood. She decided to return to Ireland.

In the end, however, she could not go. Cipriano's attraction was stronger than her European sensibility and her woman's will. Afraid of his violence but awed by the strength of a spirit stronger than her own, she felt wanted but not needed. The need, she realized, was her own, not Cipriano's. He had revealed to her the deep, dark, hot life of the senses and the blood, and she was trapped in his primitive world. She could never escape.

Critical Evaluation:

The Plumed Serpent provides a stage for the talents of the modernist period's least understood novelist. In this tale of revolution and romance, D. H. Lawrence combines many of the striking aspects of his better-known works of fiction. The novel is set in Mexico, a country that represents a frightening and intriguing exoticism to Lawrence's English-speaking characters. Lawrence chose Mexico not only because of his personal fascination for the country but also because of the turbulent political climate he describes with hope and fear. *The Plumed Serpent* is a never quite successful attempt by Lawrence to work out the conflict within himself concerning issues of social class and political power. Bound up in the interweaving of fear and hope, Lawrence's political philosophies found a topical context in a fictional Mexico. For contemporary readers, the novel may be read as a discussion on the relationship between the individual and his society.

In the consciousness of an individual, Kate Leslie, *The Plumed Serpent*'s heroine, the novel does its finest work. The narrative displays Lawrence's unique ability to construct characters whose physical, spiritual, and psychological characteristics impress readers as the kind of truth about the human condition that only good fiction can tell. The relationship between Irish Kate and the Mexico and Mexicans she encounters engenders the thematic and artistic accomplishments that should give readers of Lawrence good reason to reappraise *The Plumed Serpent*.

Mexico's role in the novel serves many artistic purposes for Lawrence, and must be understood by *The Plumed Serpent*'s readers as a complex entity that is setting and symbol. Lawrence was drawn to and made a study of Mexico and New Mexico. *The Plumed Serpent* can be compared to E. M. Forster's *A Passage to India* (1924); the non-English settings of both works are wrought with painstaking authenticity. The literary critic F. R. Leavis was of the opinion that the long passages of the novel describing native rituals and costume must have entertained Lawrence but were likely to bore readers. This sentiment was not shared by the novelist Katherine Anne Porter, who praised Lawrence's evocation of the spirit and detail of Lawrence's portrayal of Mexico in an early review of *The Plumed Serpent*. Of course, Lawrence's Mexico represents more than the country itself.

As a politically unstable nation, and as a society that is characterized by a profound gulf between its classes, Mexico functions as an analogy for any climate in which revolution might be fomented. This logic is most clear in Kate's initial attempts to understand the Mexican condition in terms of her own national identity. The Irish, like the Mexicans, bear the psychic scars of oppression and grapple with the impulse to revolt. Mexico, Kate is warned early in the novel, is another Ireland. Mexico in the novel represents any modern nation in which political institutions, be they fascist, democratic, or socialist, fail those who subscribe to them. Furthermore, both Mexico and Ireland are nations in which the Catholic church exerts great influence. Lawrence's disillusionment with both politics and Christianity as modes of social order yields another role for Mexico to fulfill in *The Plumed Serpent*. It is Mexico's ancient rhythms, its gone but not forgotten pantheon of pagan deities that become, for Lawrence, metaphors for the kind of reinvention that one might submit to in pursuit of new power and perspective.

Although the cult of Quetzalcoatl is a part of Mexico's history and therefore a return to old ways for its native practitioners, for Kate, the central figure of the novel, the mystical religion represents a new language, new customs, and new beliefs. Lawrence seems to hope that the resurgent religion might serve the expansion of human consciousness. Kate, after all, has come to Mexico with an expatriate's desire to escape the problems of her native land. Although contemporary Mexico, much to Kate's dismay, shares Ireland's sense of turmoil, it also proposes, at least in Lawrence's fiction, solutions.

The shock of Quetzalcoatl, with its visceral imagery and violent rituals, jars Kate into a self-examination that makes the novel as much of a psychic examination as it is a physical adventure. Don Ramón and Cipriano exploit the frustrations of downtrodden peasants, and Kate is forced to question her own assumption that she is born to a ruling class, that she is separate from the rabble that initially frightens her. She must question too the importance of the individual in relation to the masses and the structure that governs them. Lawrence refuses to offer his reader the kind of simple solution to the problem of social inequity that he has, in the form of contemporary politics and religion, already derided. Critics have complained that Kate's submission to Cipriano and the new order represent a subjugation of the individual will to the elite few who are strong enough to hold culture's reigns. Kate's submission, one may argue, underscores the importance of the individual as the receiver of political as well as artistic information. Kate is not brainwashed into marrying Cipriano and staying in Mexico; she searches her own soul for clues to the proper course of action. By making Kate responsible for authorizing the ascension of Quetzalcoatl, Lawrence reminds his readers of their ultimate responsibility for the meaning of the novel he offers them. This is a role new readers of Lawrence may relish.

"Critical Evaluation" by Nick David Smart

Bibliography:

Clark, L. D. *Dark Night of the Body: D. H. Lawrence's "The Plumed Serpent."* Austin: University of Texas Press, 1964. Includes biographical and bibliographic materials. Noteworthy for the strong focus on Kate.

Draper, R. P., ed. *D. H. Lawrence: The Critical Heritage*. London: Routledge & Kegan Paul, 1970. Reflects the mixture of criticism and praise with which Lawrence's contemporaries reacted to his work. Responses by W. B. Yeats, Virginia Woolf, and T. S. Eliot (on *The Plumed Serpent*) are included.

Leavis, F. R. *D. H. Lawrence: Novelist*. New York: Alfred A. Knopf, 1956. Leavis' appraisal of the artist is a must-read, although the critic does not care for *The Plumed Serpent*.

Parmenter, Ross. *Lawrence in Oaxaca: A Quest for the Novelist in Mexico*. Salt Lake City, Utah: Peregrine Smith Books, 1984. Reveals the depth of the novelist's fascination with Mexico. An extensive chapter on how Lawrence's time in Oaxaca affected the composition of *The Plumed Serpent*.

Scheckner, Peter. *Class, Politics, and the Individual: A Study of the Major Works of D. H. Lawrence*. London: Associated University Presses, 1985. Focuses on the impact of Lawrence's sensitivity to the English class system.

PLUTUS

Type of work: Drama
Author: Aristophanes (c. 450-c. 385 B.C.E.)
Type of plot: Satire
Time of plot: Fifth century B.C.E.
Locale: Athens
First performed: Ploutos, 388 B.C.E. (English translation, 1651)

> *Principal characters:*
> CHREMYLUS, a poor but honest farmer
> CARIO, his servant
> BLEPSIDEMUS, his friend
> PLUTUS, the god of wealth

The Story:

Chremylus, a Greek farmer, went to the temple of Apollo in Athens. There he asked the oracle how his son might attain affluence without having to resort to knavery. The oracle directed him to follow the first man he encountered on his emerging from the temple and to take the stranger home with him. The first man Chremylus saw was a blind beggar, whom he followed impatiently. At first the beggar refused to reveal his identity to Chremylus, but when Cario, Chremylus' servant, threatened to push the blind man over a cliff, he fearfully revealed that he was Plutus, the god of riches, blinded by Zeus when he told the god that he would favor only good men. Zeus did not want Plutus to discriminate among men. The unhappy Plutus declared to Chremylus that had he his sight back again he would favor only the good and shun the wicked.

When Chremylus offered to restore his sight to him, Plutus expressed fear of the wrath of Zeus. Chremylus declared that if Plutus had his sight back, even for a moment, Zeus would be superseded, because the dispensation of all wealth, upon which Zeus was dependent for his authority, would be in the power of Plutus; money, after all, even paid for sacrifices offered up to Zeus. It would then be Plutus, according to Chremylus, not Zeus, who would be all things to all men. Plutus was delighted to hear these words.

Chremylus, after sending Cario to summon the neighboring farmers, ushered Plutus into his house. When Cario told the farmers that Plutus was at Chremylus' house and that he would lift them out of their poverty, they were delirious with joy. Chremylus, welcoming them, noticed that his friend Blepsidemus was skeptical of Cario's report; he suspected that Chremylus had stolen a treasure. Chremylus declared that Plutus was truly in his house and that all good and deserving people would soon be rich. Even Blepsidemus was convinced, and he agreed that it was essential to restore to Plutus his eyesight.

As Chremylus prepared to take Plutus to the Temple of Asclepius, there to have his sight restored, the goddess of poverty, a hideous old woman, appeared and objected to the prospect of being cast out of Chremylus' house after having lived with him for many years. Blepsidemus and Chremylus were terrified at the sight of her. Chremylus quickly regained his composure and engaged the goddess in a debate over which deity, the god of riches or of poverty, was more beneficial to humanity. Chremylus declared that with Plutus once again able to see, those who deserved it would receive money. Thus society would be benefited. The goddess of poverty answered that progress would come to a halt because Plutus would distribute money equally.

5139

The pair then argued the difference between beggary and poverty; the goddess maintained that men who entertained her were brave, alert, and strong, while those who entertained Plutus were soft, fat, and cowardly. She declared that men were virtuous when she was their guest, but were corrupted when Plutus was their guest. Chremylus was not convinced by her arguments.

The goddess, having been defeated, departed in sorrow and anger. Chremylus now took Plutus to the temple of Asclepius, the god of healing. He observed every detail of the ritual and laid Plutus on a couch. A priest told them to sleep. Plutus' eyes were wiped with a cloth; then a purple mantle was placed over his head. At a signal from Asclepius, two serpents came forth from the sanctuary and slithered under the mantle. In a short time, Plutus, his sight restored, arose from the couch.

Now, those people who had got their wealth by unfair means looked with fear upon Plutus, but the poor rejoiced at their new good fortune. Plutus was happy; he vowed to correct all of the mistakes he had made when he was blind. Chremylus was rewarded with great wealth for his service to the god. While Plutus was a guest in the house of Chremylus, a just man came to petition the god. He had helped his friends when they were in need, but they had not responded in kind when he himself had become indigent. The man became wealthy again through the power of Plutus. He offered an old cloak and a worn-out pair of sandals as tribute to the god.

Soon afterward an informer came to the house and complained that he had been ruined by the change wrought in Plutus. Cario stripped the informer of his fine coat and bedecked him in the just man's threadbare cloak. An old woman, presuming to be a young one, came to see the god. She was distressed because her young lover, who had flattered her in order to get money from her, had deserted her now that Plutus had made him independent. The youth appeared with a wreath to give to Plutus in appreciation.

Hermes, the messenger of the gods, appeared and reported that Zeus and the other gods were furious because men no longer made oblations to them. He declared that he himself was actually starving since there were no more offerings in the form of cakes or figs or honey, and he urged Cario to succor him. Cario condescended to retain Hermes to preside at the games that Plutus surely would sponsor.

A priest of Zeus came and complained of hunger; when everyone was rich, there were no more offerings to the gods. Chremylus, calling attention to the fact that Plutus had now taken the place of Zeus in human fortunes, hinted that the priest of Zeus would do well to become the priest of Plutus. Zeus having been deposed, Plutus was installed as the supreme god.

Critical Evaluation:

If *Plutus* had not survived, a vital link in the history of Greek comedy would have been lost. So different is this play from the other surviving works of Aristophanes, one might suppose it to be an aberration or to have been written by a different author. In fact, evidence suggests that Aristophanes wrote other works similar to *Plutus*, which was presented in 388 B.C.E. The unusual features of this play are also not explained away by noting that the work was written when Aristophanes was approximately sixty. The poet went on to write two more plays, now lost. *Plutus* may be regarded as the sole surviving example of a new comic genre, called Middle Comedy. The term distinguishes this play from the other surviving plays of Aristophanes, all of which are representative of the style and concerns of Old Attic Comedy. On the other hand, *Plutus* is not to be classed with New Comedy, which is best represented by Menander (342-291 B.C.E.).

What distinguishes *Plutus*—and thus the genre of Middle Comedy—from other plays of Aristophanes is a general retreat from direct political or personal satire, an absence of crude obscenity, and a curtailing or complete omission of some of the traditional elements of Old Comedy, such as choral lyrics. The beginnings of some of these changes are apparent in *Ecclesiazuae*. There are other features of *Plutus* that are not so common in Aristophanes' earlier work, such as the use of moral allegory with personified abstractions (the Greek word *ploutos* means "wealth"), the focus on social interaction that suggests the comedy of manners, which would develop later, and passionate, unapologetic idealism. Also different from Aristophanes' earlier plays is *Plutus'* lack of topical controversy: Virtually no person could object to the central concept of *Plutus*, that Wealth is a blind god and therefore may favor scoundrels and abandon good men to the misery of poverty.

Plutus is not devoid of humor. Although verbal jesting is reduced in comparison to earlier plays, the play contains some of the irrelevancy and situational humor of the earlier plays. For example, the antics that Cario reports from the Temple of Asclepius, where Plutus' sight is restored, are mildly amusing as a parody of ancient techniques of healing. Cario's wife is interesting as a comic character who happens to be female. Her reception of her husband's news adds significantly to the humor of the scene. When the god Hermes comes seeking employment, there is some amusement in the fact that despite his varied skills a suitable position is discovered only with considerable difficulty: Finally it is decided that he is to take charge of games that Plutus will soon celebrate.

The reader will detect some of the typical structure of Aristophanic comedy in *Plutus*, especially observable in the contest between Plutus and Penia (poverty) and in the series of episodes that follow the restoration of Plutus' sight. The various individuals who appear before him serve to underscore the consequences of restoring his sight. In form, at least, this design is paralleled in earlier plays of Aristophanes in which the protagonist realizes a plan and then contemplates the positive and negative results. A diminished role for the chorus is the most outstanding characteristic of *Plutus*. Despite some traces of lost choral lyrics, in most of the text the presence of the chorus is indicated merely by the Greek word *chorou*. It is doubtful that the chorus sang a composition relevant to the action of the play. More likely, the notation indicates some kind of interlude during which the chorus danced and played music before the next scene took place.

Many of the characteristics of *Plutus* prefigure developments in later Greek and Roman comedy. The reduction of the role of the chorus, for example, has an effect of placing more emphasis on the episodes that were originally seen as insertions between choral songs. The consequent development of a play in five acts, which is typical of New Comedy and becomes the established pattern for all later drama, is already seen in this play. The move away from topicality, that is, specific references to actual individuals and events, naturally results in a preference for types who exemplify common human traits. Cario, for example, is a prototype for the wily slave who will have a role to play in nearly every subsequent Greco-Roman comedy. Misers, shrewish wives, young men in love, and other types common to European drama may have their origin in the works of Greek Middle Comedy, of which *Plutus* is the one surviving example. The play's turning away from politics and toward larger aspects of the human condition must have acted to release comedy from the close link to the city of Athens and to the worship of Dionysus, the god of drama. The gradual freeing of drama from the context of Athenian political life and the specific sacred festivals gave birth to a wide range of new dramatic plots and characters.

Some political satire at the expense of specific individuals is still to be found in *Plutus*, and the reduced economic circumstances of Athens in the fourth century leave a direct mark on the play because economic conditions may no longer have permitted the provision and training of an expensive chorus. The play is much more concerned, however, with the moral metaphysical aspects of wealth and poverty than with specific economic, social, or political conditions that created the distribution of wealth. Some of the features of Old Comedy that *Plutus* lacks worked to ensure its survival in later times. The play is virtually free from topical references that need explanation to all but ancient Athenians and offers an edifying moral message, so *Plutus* became the most popular work of Aristophanes in later centuries, especially during the Byzantine period.

"Critical Evaluation" by John M. Lawless

Bibliography:
Dover, K. J. *Aristophanic Comedy*. Berkeley: University of California Press, 1972. Useful and authoritative study of the plays of Aristophanes. Chapter 16 gives a synopsis of the play, discusses the role of slaves in this new genre of comedy, and comments on the connection between wealth and morality that is made in the play. An essential starting point for study of the plays.
Harriott, Rosemary M. *Aristophanes: Poet and Dramatist*. Baltimore: The Johns Hopkins University Press, 1986. A study of Aristophanes. The plays are discussed not in individual chapters but as each illustrates the central themes and techniques of Aristophanes' work.
McLeish, Kenneth. *The Theatre of Aristophanes*. New York: Taplinger, 1980. An overview of the dramatic technique of Aristophanes. Useful for understanding the magnitude of the changes from Old to Middle Comedy.
Murray, Gilbert. *Aristophanes: A Study*. Oxford, England: Oxford University Press, 1933. Contains valuable insights into all the plays of Aristophanes. Chapter 10 offers an excellent discussion of *Plutus*.
Spatz, Lois. *Aristophanes*. Boston: Twayne, 1978. A reliable introduction to the comedy of Aristophanes for the general reader. Chapter 9 discusses the themes of the play and emphasizes its differences from earlier Aristophanic comedy.

POEM OF THE CID

Type of work: Poetry
Author: Unknown
Type of plot: Epic
Time of plot: c. 1075
Locale: Fief of Bivar, to the north of Burgos, Spain
First published: Cantar de mío Cid, early thirteenth century (English translation, 1808)

Principal characters:
RUY DÍAZ, called My Cid, Lord of Bivar
ALFONSO, the king of León, by whom the Cid was exiled
DOÑA XIMENA, the Cid's wife
MARTÍN ANTOLINEZ, one of the Cid's chief lieutenants
DOÑA ELVIRA and
DOÑA SOL, the Cid's daughters
MINAYA ALVAR FÁÑEZ, the Cid's chief lieutenant and companion
FÉLIX MUÑOZ, the Cid's nephew and rescuer of his daughters
GARCÍA ORDOÑEZ, lord of Grañón, the Cid's enemy
DIEGO and
FERNANDO GONZÁLEZ, the princes of Carrión, suitors and husbands to
the Cid's daughters, two villains
GONZALO ANSÚREZ, the count of Carrión, father of Diego and Fernando
González

The Story:
By royal edict, the Cid was banished from Christian Spain by King Alfonso VI of Castile. The royal edict allowed him nine days in which to leave the kingdom but forbade him from taking with him any of his wealth and goods. Anyone in the kingdom who offered aid to the Cid would forfeit his estate. Nevertheless, the Cid enlisted the aid of Martín Antolinez in swindling two money-lenders, Raquel and Vidas, in exchange for two large sealed coffers, supposedly loaded with the Cid's riches but containing only sand. The Cid and a small force of vassals then rode away and made a secret camp. On the morning of his actual departure from the country, with a fair-sized group of loyal vassals, Mass for all was said at the abbey where Doña Ximena, the Cid's wife, and his two infant daughters, Doña Elvira and Doña Sol, had been ordered to remain.

Becoming a soldier of fortune, the knight led his host in conquest of one Moorish territory after another, each time with a generous sharing of spoils and booty among his knights and vassals, even the lowliest. Thus he built up a larger and stronger force with every foray, and after each victory Mass was said in thanksgiving. The Cid fought his way to the eastern side of the peninsula, where he fought his most crucial battle and won his greatest victory when he took as his prisoner Count Ramón of Barcelona. After Count Ramón had been humbled and forced to give up all his property, he was granted his liberty.

Although Minaya Alvar Fáñez returned to King Alfonso with gifts and a glowing report of the Cid's successes, the king did not revoke his decree of banishment. Minaya's estates were restored, however, and he was granted freedom to come and go without fear of attack. The Cid continued his campaigns against the Moorish territories in order to increase his favor with King

Alfonso. After he had conquered the provinces of Valencia and Seville, his men grew tired of fighting and many wished to return to Castile. The Cid, although still generous and understanding, proved himself master by threatening all deserters with death.

Again the Cid sent Minaya to King Alfonso with a gift of one hundred horses and a request that Doña Ximena and her daughters be permitted to join him in Valencia. Visibly softened by the Cid's growing power, King Alfonso granted this request. In addition, he returned to the Cid's men their former estates.

Shortly after a triumphant reunion with his family in Valencia, the Cid overcame the King of Morocco. As a gesture of victory he sent the Moroccan's tent to King Alfonso. This dramatic gift earned the Cid's pardon and the request that he give his daughters in marriage to Diego and Fernando, the princes of Carrión. At the victory feast, many marveled at the great length and abundance of the Cid's beard, for he had sworn at the time of his banishment that his beard would never again be cut and that it would grow very long. A mystical significance of power and success was now attached to the fullness of his beard.

The Cid had reservations about giving his daughters to the princes of Carrión. They were, he thought, too young for marriage. Also, he distrusted the two men. However, with a great show of humbleness and subservience, he returned Doña Elvira and Doña Sol to the king with word that Alfonso would honor the Cid by disposing of his daughters' future as the monarch saw fit.

After the weddings, the elaborate wedding feast, to which all the Cid's vassals as well as those of the territory of Carrión had been invited, lasted for more than two weeks. The Cid expressed some satisfaction in having his family united with noblemen as rich as Prince Diego and his brother Fernando. Two years of happiness followed.

One day one of the Cid's pet lions escaped. Far from showing valor in the emergency, Diego hid from the lion under the bench on which the Cid was asleep, while Fernando fled into the garden and hid behind a wine press. After the Cid's vassals had easily subdued the lion, the favored princes became the butt of much crude humor and scorn, but the Cid, choosing to ignore the evident cowardice of his daughters' husbands, made excuses for them.

Once again the Cid was forced to war with the Moroccans, this time against mighty King Bucar. After a great battle, Bucar was killed and his vassals were subdued. The Cid was jubilant. As the spoils were divided, he rejoiced that at last his sons-in-law had become seasoned warriors. His vassals were half-amused, half-disgusted, because it was common knowledge among them that neither Diego nor Fernando had shown the slightest bravery in the conflict, and at one time the Cid's standard-bearer had been forced to risk his life in order to cover for Fernando's shocking cowardice.

Diego and Fernando were richly rewarded for their supposed valor, but their greed was not satisfied. Resentful and injured by the insults and scorn heaped on them by the Cid's vassals, they began a scheme for revenge by telling the Cid that, proud of their wives and their wealth, they would like to make a journey to Carrión in order to show off their wives and to sing the Cid's praises. In secret, they planned not to return. The noble and generous Cid, always ready to think the best of anyone, granted their request without question.

The Cid added further to the princes' treasure and sent them off with a suitable company of his own vassals as an escort of honor. Then, belatedly concerned for the safety of his daughters, he also sent with them his nephew, Félix Muñoz, after charging the young nobleman with the care of Doña Elvira and Doña Sol.

When they were safely away from Valencia, the princes sent the company on ahead and took their wives into the woods. There, with viciousness, they stripped the women of their rich garments and their jewels, whipped them, and left them, bleeding and wounded, to die. His suspicion aroused by the desire of the princes to separate their wives from the rest of the party, Félix Muñoz followed the princes' tracks and found the women. He nursed them back to consciousness and returned them to the Cid.

The princes' scheme of revenge rebounded to their further disgrace. Word of their wicked and dishonest acts spread quickly, and King Alfonso, in his great displeasure with the Carrións, swore to try them in Toledo. The Cid swore that he, to avenge the treatment his daughters had received, would marry them to the richest in the land.

At the trial, the princes were first ordered to return the Cid's valued swords, which he had given them as tokens of his high regard. Then they were ordered to return his gold. Having squandered it all, they were forced to give him equal value in horses and property. In the meantime ambassadors from Aragón and Navarre had arrived to ask for the Cid's daughters as queens for their kings. The Cid was jubilant, but still he demanded that the princes of Carrión pay in full measure for their brutality: trial by combat with two of the Cid's chosen knights. King Alfonso charged the princes that if they injured their opponents in the least, they would forfeit their lives. Proved craven in the fight, the princes were stripped of all honor and wealth. The Cid rejoiced that, once banished, he could now count two kings of Spain among his kinsmen. He died, Lord of Valencia, on the Day of Pentecost.

Critical Evaluation:

In this national epic of eleventh century Spain, there are 3,735 lines of uneven length in three cantos that relate the major events in the Cid's life. The poem is based on historical fact. Such a man lived, and died in 1099. His character and exploits have been, as one might expect, embroidered, amplified, and distorted to suit the purpose of making him a heroic figure in Spanish history and legend. Of all the epics of the Cid, *Poem of the Cid* is unique in its qualities of realism, verity, and poetic excellence. The Cid is drawn as a typical Spanish warrior, proud, ruthless, realistic, and calculating. At the same time he shrewdly doles out praise and favors to his vassals and is generous to a fault. In victory, he is quick to do honor—even to overdo it—to his loyal lieutenants. Although exiled by King Alfonso VI, he continued to hold the position of the king, if not the man himself, in high regard.

Poem of the Cid, while partly based upon historical characters and actual events, has its origin as literature in ancient folklore and in early European epic. The traditional plot of *Poem of the Cid* may first be found in *The Story of Si-Nuhe*, an ancient Egyptian legend that dates to the Twelfth Dynasty (c. 1950 B.C.E.) and recounts events remarkably similar to those of the later Spanish poem. In the Egyptian legend, Si-Nuhe, a governmental official under Amenemhet I, is forced to flee Egypt when the pharaoh dies and his son, Sesotris I, comes to the throne. Si-Nuhe's wanderings take him as far as Retenu (Syria and Israel), where he marries the king's eldest daughter and rules over a pastoral paradise known as Yaa. Despite all these achievements, however, Si-Nuhe wishes only to return home. Word of Si-Nuhe's victories repeatedly reaches Sesotris, who forgives Si-Nuhe, permitting him to reenter Egypt. Si-Nuhe leaves Yaa in the care of his son and arrives in Egypt, where he finds himself greeted as a great hero.

This story pattern, that of the nobleman who accomplishes great deeds in exile until he is restored to his lands by a monarch, is common throughout world literature. What the author of *Poem of the Cid* has done is to associate this traditional tale with a specific historical figure, Ruy Díaz of Bivar (or Vivar), who was also known as the Cid Campeador. "Cid" is a Spanish corruption of the Arabic title "Seid," which means "Lord," and "Campeador" is a term of uncertain origin that appears to mean "victor." (This is a common title for epic heroes. The

German word for "victor," *Siegfried*, is the name of the hero in the *Nibelungenlied*.)

The poem's author has also adopted an ancient literary style that may be traced to the early European epics, the *Iliad* and *Odyssey* (c. 800 B.C.E.). This style uses formulaic phrases, stylized battle scenes, and frequently repeated epithets. Such a style is commonly associated with oral poetry. For this reason, it is believed that *Poem of the Cid* either existed as an oral poem before it was written down or was intentionally written in an archaic style so that it would appear to have been an oral poem.

Most scholars believe that the origins of *Poem of the Cid* may be found among the *juglares*, wandering storytellers who preserved and embellished traditional tales. It has been argued, however, that *Poem of the Cid* was a specific literary creation, the work of an individual unknown author. Complete agreement on this issue is unlikely to occur. Nevertheless, whether the product of a single author or a long-standing oral tradition, *Poem of the Cid* contains themes and elements of plot that may be observed elsewhere in European folklore.

One central motif that appears throughout *Poem of the Cid* is the importance of loyalty. The ill treatment that the Cid receives from King Alfonso might have caused the Cid to resent the king, but the hero continues to remain loyal, and he is ultimately rewarded for his allegiance. In turn, the Cid demonstrates that he is the sort of figure who is owed loyalty by others. He is generous and forgiving, ready to honor the deeds of his followers. He is also ready to demand loyalty from vacillating vassals. Through these qualities, the Cid is contrasted sharply to the worthless characters of the poem, Diego and Fernando, who take advantage of the Cid's generosity. Genuine nobility, the poem suggests, is not found in aristocratic birth as much as it is in a person who has learned compassion and refinement. While a true gentleman may be proud, he is never haughty; while he may take pride in his possessions, he is never greedy. Many of the same values that are later described by Baldassare Castiglione in *The Book of the Courtier* (1528) trace their origin to medieval epics such as *Poem of the Cid*.

Somewhat incongruous with the Cid's character as straightforward, guileless, and trusting is that he occasionally takes on the aspect of a folkloric trickster. The Cid is capable of outright deceit if this proves necessary to remove himself from difficulty. The Cid himself thinks of the plan that will cheat Raquel and Vidas, the two moneylenders, out of six hundred marks in return for two coffers of sand. The Cid makes it clear, however, that he does this only "because I must and have no other choice."

Side by side with all that is mythic in *Poem of the Cid* is a keen attention to the details of Spanish history and of the countryside. The poem is filled with the names of towns, rivers, and historical figures. Far more realistic than other medieval Spanish epics, *Poem of the Cid* includes recognizable settings rather than idealized and magical kingdoms. In its description of actual places and realistic events, *Poem of the Cid* stands at the beginning of a tradition that would lead to gritty novels such as *Lazarillo de Tormes* (1554), *Guzmán de Alfarache* (1599), *The Life of the Swindler* (1626), and even *Don Quixote de la Mancha* (1605).

Poem of the Cid should be viewed, therefore, as a combination of a folkloric plot, courtly values, and realistic geographic and historical details. Its influence extended to the later Spanish novel.

"Critical Evaluation" by Jeffrey L. Buller

Bibliography:
Chasca, Edmund de. *The Poem of the Cid*. Boston: Twayne, 1976. The best place to begin for a general literary and historical account of the poem. Includes a discussion of medieval epic

poetry, the historicity of *Poem of the Cid*, use of humor, epic formulas, and speculation on authorship.

Fletcher, Richard A. *The Quest for the Cid.* New York: Random House, 1990. A historical account of the period 711-1516, providing a valuable discussion of the cultural background to *El Cid*. Also contains an extensive bibliography.

Matulka, Barbara. *The Cid as a Courtly Hero.* New York: Columbia University, Institute of French Studies, 1928. Explores the figure of the Cid from his appearance in medieval epic through Corneille's treatment in *The Cid* (1636). Short, useful account of such literary motifs as the love-test, voluntary death, and the Cid's sword.

Menéndez Pidal, Ramón. *The Cid and His Spain.* Translated by Harold Sunderland. London: John Murray, 1934. A detailed discussion of *El Cid* and its background by the author of the poem's most influential critical edition. Includes attention to the struggle for Valencia, the invasion (and subsequent repulsion) of the Almoravides, the court of the Cid, and the process by which the historical figure of the Cid was transformed into a legend.

Smith, Colin. The Making of the *"Poema de mío Cid."* Cambridge, England: Cambridge University Press, 1983. Claims that *Poem of the Cid* was an experimental work, the first epic to be composed in Castilian, and that Per Abad, the figure who is usually regarded as the poem's copyist, was actually its author.

POEMS

Author: Sidney Lanier (1842-1881)
First published: 1877 and 1884

The poetic fame of Sidney Lanier, after Edgar Allan Poe the most important nineteenth century poet of the Southern United States, rests upon a small body of poetry found in the posthumous volume *Poems.* This contains the verse Lanier included in his earlier *Poems,* along with a number of pieces that had received only magazine publication before the poet's death in 1881, plus a group of unrevised early poems that his wife felt were worthy of publication.

Lanier was a poet of both theory and practice. His theory of technique was influenced by his great love for music. Precociously musical, he became a brilliant flutist who played with symphony orchestras in Dallas and Baltimore. His moralistic theory of poetic content was possibly influenced by his early training in a devoutly Christian family as well as by his own, fundamentally religious nature. This shows itself in some of his nature poems as a passionate love for God's plants and creatures, which approaches that of St. Francis of Assisi.

Lanier's theory of prosody is expounded principally in *The Science of English Verse* (1880), which develops in extensive detail and with copious illustration the thesis that the same laws govern both versification and music. Three brief quotations will illustrate this thesis:

> . . . when we hear verse, we *hear* a set of relations between sounds; when we silently read verse, we *see* that which brings to us a set of relations between sounds; when we imagine verse, we *imagine* a set of relations between sounds.

> When those exact coordinations which the ear perceives as rhythm, tune, and tone-color are suggested to the ear by a series of *musical sounds,* the result is . . . MUSIC.
> When those exact coordinations which the ear perceives as rhythm, tune, and tone-color, are suggested to the ear by a series of *spoken words,* the result is . . . VERSE.

> . . . there is absolutely no difference between the sound-relations used in music and those used in verse.

Lanier's application of his prosodic theory may be studied in many of his poems, but it may be easily seen in such poems as "The Symphony," "The Marshes of Glynn," and "Song of the Chattahoochee."

In "The Symphony," Lanier attempted the difficult task of composing a poem somewhat as a musician would. Such instruments as violins, flute, clarinet, horn, and hautboy (oboe) are personified and used to develop the theme of love, the enemy of trade (materialism), which pervades the poem. Nowhere is Lanier's belief in the essential identity of sound relations in music and in verse better illustrated than in the four lines that introduce the horn passage in the poem:

> There thrust the bold straightforward horn
> To battle for that lady lorn.
> With hearthsome voice of mellow scorn,
> Like any knight in knighthood's morn.

It has been objected that Lanier tried the impossible in "The Symphony" and that his achievement, though notable, is successful only in part. Perhaps his theory is better illustrated in "Sunrise" and "The Marshes of Glynn." In "Sunrise," the sibilance of the forest can be heard:

Ye lispers, whisperers, singers in storms,
Ye consciences murmuring faiths under forms,
Ye ministers meet for each passion that grieves,
Friendly, sisterly, sweetheart leaves.

In "The Marshes of Glynn," the sounds and even the silence of the great marshes near Brunswick, Georgia, may be heard and felt by the reader. A passage near the close of the poem describes in this fashion the coming of the high tide of evening:

The creeks overflow: a thousand rivulets run
'Twixt the roots of the sod; the blades of the marsh-grass stir;
Passeth a hurrying sound of wings that westward whirr;
Passeth, and all is still; and the currents cease to run;
And the sea and the marsh are one.

In these lines the sounds of the moving waters and grasses and of the whirring wings are followed by a silence that is palpable.

Because of Lanier's repeated use of onomatopoeia in his verse he has often been compared with Poe, but Lanier's theory of poetic content is quite different. Poe, in "The Philosophy of Composition," concedes that "passion, or even truth, may . . . be introduced, and even profitably introduced, into a poem"; but, he asserts that "Beauty is the sole legitimate province of the poem." In another essay, "The Poetic Principle," Poe attacks what he calls "the heresy of *The Didactic*." "Every poem, it is said, should inculcate a moral," he declares, "and by this moral is the poetical merit of the work to be adjudged." He continues:

would we but permit ourselves to look into our own souls, we should immediately there discover that under the sun there neither exists nor *can* exist any work more thoroughly dignified—more supremely noble than this very poem—this poem *per se*—this poem which is a poem and nothing more—this poem written solely for the poem's sake.

Lanier loved art as much as Poe did, but Lanier was on the side of the moralists. In the series of lectures posthumously published as *The English Novel and the Principle of Its Development* (1883), he leaves no doubt as to his position when he states:

We may say that he who has not yet perceived how artistic beauty and moral beauty are convergent lines which run back into a common ideal origin, and who therefore is not afire with moral beauty just as with artistic beauty—that he, in short, who has not come to that stage of quiet and eternal frenzy in which the beauty of holiness and the holiness of beauty mean one thing, burn as one fire, shine as one light within him; he is not yet the great artist.

Although Lanier wrote occasional poems such as his verse narrative "The Revenge of Hamish," in which the moral element is not a major one, most of his poetry is charged with moral purpose or shines with "the beauty of holiness." "The Symphony" bitterly indicts the cruel, greedy practices of trade and sings the gospel of brotherly love. In "The Marshes of Glynn," he writes, "As the marsh-hen secretly builds on the watery sod,/ Behold I will build me a nest on the greatness of God." Even a dialect poem such as "Thar's More in the Man than Thar Is in the Land" contains a moral lesson, as the title itself suggests. Occasionally his moral earnestness dims Lanier's artistic sight, however, as in "Song of the Chattahoochee," in which the river is made to say, ". . . I am fain for to water the plain./ Downward the voices of Duty call—." This is a flagrant example of what John Ruskin called the "pathetic fallacy." People may act with moral purpose; when the Chattahoochee River flows downward, however, it is not because it knows that, "The dry fields burn, and the mills are to turn,/ And a myriad flowers mortally yearn," but because, as Lanier himself very well knew, the law of gravity is a part of the earthly scheme of things.

Though Lanier is not primarily a regional poet, many of his lines sing eloquently of his Southern origin. He is in love with the beautiful Marshes of Glynn, with their "moss-bearded live-oaks." He mourns that "Bright drops of tune, from oceans infinite/ Of Melody" were ended when a pet mockingbird "died of a cat, May, 1878." He grieves in "Corn" that the rich soil of his native state is being washed away because of the greed of cotton farmers who lay the surface bare and then leave their erosion-ruined areas and head for Texas to repeat their folly. In "A Florida Sunday," he holds "in my being" rich-scented orange trees, pea green parakeets, "pranked woodpeckers that ne'er gossip out," palmettos, pines, and mangroves. In such poems, Lanier is as clearly a Southern poet as Robert Frost is a New England one when he describes his New Hampshire countryside.

A fault that many readers have found with Lanier is that, as a poet, he too often lets his heart overflow and his whole being "quiver with the passionate thrill"; at times a noble emotion may descend into sentimentality and at others the poet's feeling may blur the expression of "the great thought."

The lush music of Lanier's lines may also create the lulling mental effect that one finds in Algernon Charles Swinburne. Part of Lanier's trouble seems to be that he is striving too hard to attain the right combination of "rhythm, tune, and tone-color." He sometimes forces his comparisons so that they become too-obvious poetic conceits, as in "Marsh Song—at Sunset," with its metaphors drawn from William Shakespeare's *Tempest* (1611). Some of his sentences, such as the thirty-six-line one that opens "The Marshes of Glynn," lack clarity because of their great length and intricate structure.

In spite of the undisciplined emotionalism, hazy thought, and strained effects of his lesser poems, Lanier seems well assured of a permanent place in American literature. The melody of his best lines; the love of God, human beings, and nature found in poems such as "The Marshes of Glynn" and "The Symphony"; the simple beauty of "A Ballad of Trees and the Master"; and the stoic acceptance of "The Stirrup-Cup," in which the consumptive poet says uncomplainingly to Death, "Hand me the cup whene'er thou wilt"—for these Lanier will continue to be loved.

Bibliography:
De Bellis, Jack. *Sidney Lanier*. New York: Twayne, 1972. Perhaps the best critical overview of Lanier's life and works. Includes careful readings of the major poems, a discussion of Lanier's fiction, a biographical chronology, and a brief, selected bibliography.
_____. *Sidney Lanier: Poet of the Marshes*. Atlanta: Georgia Humanities Council, 1988. A brief but fine introduction to Lanier's major works. Includes careful readings of selected poems and focuses on the poetry's relationship to nature and music.
Gabin, Jane S. *A Living Minstrelsy: The Poetry and Music of Sidney Lanier*. Macon, Ga.: Mercer University Press, 1985. A fine account of Lanier's life and artistic career. Includes sensitive readings of the poems and is particularly enlightening on the subject of the relationship of the poetry to music.
Parks, Edd Winfield. *Sidney Lanier: The Man, the Poet, the Critic*. Athens: University of Georgia Press, 1968. Discusses Lanier's complete artistic life. Focuses on the poet's own writings as well as his commentary on and concern with the works of others. Considers why

Lanier never became a major poet as it traces his development as an artist and a thinker.

Starke, Aubrey Harrison. *Sidney Lanier: A Biographical and Critical Study*. New York: Russell & Russell, 1964. Contains a full, critical exploration of Lanier's poetry and creative nature. Includes a useful bibliography.

POEMS

Author: Sir Walter Ralegh (c. 1552-1618)
First published: Poems of Sir Walter Raleigh, with Biographical and Critical Introduction, 1813

Sir Walter Ralegh, like so many other Renaissance courtiers, considered the writing of poetry one of the polite arts, to be practiced in one's leisure moments for the pleasure of friends. In his busy political, military, and adventuring career, his poetic efforts apparently carried little weight, and he never seems to have encouraged their publication, although he was much interested in presenting to the public his *History of the World* (1614) and his treatises on his expeditions to the new world. As a result of this carelessness, on his part and on the part of publishers who did publish his work and who sometimes published work that was not his under his name, over the years countless verses have been attributed to him, and no one can be sure how many of them he actually wrote. The small body of work that is unquestionably his, however, shows him to be a poet of high ability.

Ralegh was perhaps second only to Edmund Spenser and Sir Philip Sidney as poets in the court of Elizabeth I. He shunned the opulence of the typical poetry of his time for a sparse, dignified style that has many echoes of his predecessors, Sir Thomas Wyatt and Henry Howard, Earl of Surrey. The melancholy quality that pervades much of Ralegh's work is close to that of almost all of Wyatt's poems and to the last lyrics of Surrey, written while he was in the Tower awaiting trial and execution. Ralegh himself spent more than ten years in the Tower, hoping against hope for release, and a sense of the constant closeness of death runs through his later work. Life is precarious, "beauty, fleeting," and death near at hand for all. Ralegh's answer to Christopher Marlowe's famous pastoral lyric "Come Live with Me and Be My Love" (1600) is filled with this sense of the transience of all things:

> Time drives the flocks from field to fold,
> When rivers rage and rocks grow cold,
> And Philomel becometh dumb;
> The rest complains of cares to come.
> The flowers do fade, and wanton fields
> To wayward winter reckoning yields;
> A honey tongue, a heart of gall,
> Is fancy's spring, but sorrow's fall.

Ralegh protests against the actions of time in another lyric, "Nature that washt her hands in milke," in which he describes the creation of the perfect woman by Nature, at the request of Love. This paragon no sooner exists than Time, "being made of steel and rust,/ Turns snow, and silk and milk to dust." The final stanza is the eternal human lament:

> Oh, cruel time! Which takes in trust
> Our youth, our joys and all we have,
> And pays us but with age and dust,
> Who in the dark and silent grave
> When we have wandered all our ways
> Shuts up the story of our days.

While Wyatt's laments are most often those of the Petrarchan lover, scorned by the lady to whom he offers devotion, Ralegh's melancholy seems to derive from a more general vision of the human condition. Even in those sonnets in which he takes the conventional stance of the rejected lover, he seems conscious of a larger world. One of these concludes, "And at my gate despair shall linger still,/ To let in death when love and fortune will."

Ralegh's sense of the destructive powers of time has particular force in his elegy on Sir Philip Sidney, an excellent poem in which the writer pays tribute to a fellow courtier-soldier-poet. There is in the "Epitaph" a touch of envy of Sidney, who died with an unblemished reputation and was freed from the threats of time and evil men:

> What hath he lost, that such great grace hath won?
> Young years for endless years, and hope unsure,
> Of fortune's gifts, for wealth that still shall dure,
> Oh, happy race, with so great praises run!

Like many other writers of his century, Ralegh uses his poetry to chastise the court for its hypocrisy, its vice, and its folly. Few men, indeed, suffered more from the false appearances of monarchs and their ministers. The brief stanzas of "The Lie" move over the whole spectrum of society:

> Say to the court it glows,
> And shines like rotten wood;
> Say to the church, it shows
> What's good, and doth no good:
> If church and court reply,
> Then give them both the lie.

The tone of Ralegh's poetry is not unmitigated gloom; few men were more vibrantly alive than this courtier-adventurer, and he could compose sprightly, witty lyrics with the best of his contemporaries, following out a pseudo-logical argument in the manner of John Donne, singing lyrically about the beauty of the moon, or defining love in the ordinary vocabulary of his day:

> Yet what is love? I pray thee sain.
> It is a sunshine mixed with rain;
> It is a tooth-ache, or like pain;
> It is a game where none doth gain;
> The lass saith no, and would full fain:
> And this is Love, as I hear sain.

There is much of the medieval heritage in Ralegh's work. Folk wisdom, proverbs, and the haunting quality of many of the early ballads lurk under the surface of several of his poems, notably one addressed to his son. The poem begins quietly and continues in a matter-of-fact way that reinforces its horror. Three things, "the wood, the weed, and the wag," prosper separately, but, together they bring destruction:

> The wood is that, that makes the gallows tree,
> The weed is that, that strings the hangman's bag;
> The wag, my pretty knave betokens thee.
> Now mark, dear boy: while these assemble not,
> Green springs the tree, hemp grows, the wag is wild;
> But when they meet, it makes the timber rot,
> It frets the halter, and it chokes the child.

Medieval in a different sense is one of Ralegh's last and best poems, "The Passionate Man's Pilgrimage." Its Christian allegory is that of a traveler's journey to salvation:

> Give me my scallop-shell of quiet,
> My staff of faith to walk upon,
> My scrip of joy, immortal diet,
> My bottle of salvation,
> My gown of glory, hope's true gage,
> And thus I'll take my pilgrimage.

Ralegh's irregular metrical pattern is admirably suited to his subject; the simplicity of his acceptance of redemption in the second section is mirrored in the short rhymed lines, the clarity of the language, and the images of silver, nectar, milk, and crystal. The fourth section, with its theme of judgment, is harsher in both rhythm and vocabulary, as Ralegh speaks of Christ as the advocate, pleading the cause of sinful man in a court where bribery and forgery have no place, a compelling allusion to the trial in which Sir Edward Coke, not Christ, was the King's Counsel, and the verdict was, in the minds of most, a travesty of justice. The concluding stanza has a macabre quality. Ralegh is said to have written these last lines on the night before his execution:

> Just at the stroke when my veins start and spread
> Set on my soul an everlasting head.
> Then am I ready like a palmer fit,
> To tread those blest paths which before I writ.

Ralegh's longest extant poem is a fragment of a still more extensive work called "Ocean's Love to Cynthia." The original version, so far as scholars have been able to deduce, was addressed to Queen Elizabeth about 1587, when Robert Devereux, Earl of Essex, seemed to be replacing Ralegh in her esteem. In its first form the poem evidently served its purpose, for Ralegh was reinstated in Her Majesty's favor until his indiscreet affair and hasty marriage with one of her maids of honor in 1592. It has been suggested that the surviving fragment of the poem was written from the Tower, where Ralegh had been imprisoned with his bride, in an attempt to mollify Elizabeth's resentment.

The quatrains of the extant text are presented as the outpourings of a disillusioned lover of the queen. There is no real narrative link; the whole poem is essentially the exposition of a state of mind. It is written in four-line stanzas with alternate rhymes, a compact form that lends itself to the development of a slightly different point in each quatrain. The extant manuscript is evidently an unfinished version of the poem, for occasionally Ralegh left two, three, or five lines as a separate unit to be revised later. However, even if the poem as it exists is unfinished, it demonstrates forcefully Ralegh's power to convey his deep and intense disillusionment. Toward the end of the fragment the poet, speaking as a shepherd, ponders the paradox of his state of mind. His mistress may treat him well or ill, but she is with him forever: "She is gone, she is lost, she is found, she is ever fair." He can only take life as it comes, let his flocks wander at will, and live with his despair:

> Thus home I draw, as death's long night draws on;
> Yet every foot, old thoughts turn back mine eyes;
> Constraint me guides as old age draws a stone
> Against the hill, which over-weighty lies

He must, in the last analysis, trust in the mercies of God.

Ralegh never entirely fulfilled his promise as a poet. His intense interest in colonizing projects, his career at court, and his later political misfortunes probably combined to prevent his devoting his energies to poetry, and his gigantic project, the history of the world, left far from complete at his death, occupied his last years in the Tower. Yet the works he did leave are among the best of the Elizabethan age. The virtues of his poems are their quiet strength and the melancholy tone which was the almost inevitable result of his skeptical, inquiring mind.

Bibliography:

Hammond, Gerald, ed. Introduction to *Selected Writings*, by Sir Walter Ralegh. Manchester, England: Carcanet, 1984. Hammond's introduction to this collection gives substantial attention to Ralegh's poetry, addressing its themes and styles as well as the influence of others on Ralegh's work.

Latham, Agnes M. Introduction to *The Poems of Sir Walter Ralegh*, by Sir Walter Ralegh. Cambridge, Mass.: Harvard University Press, 1951. Latham's introduction to this collection is a forty-page essay about Ralegh's life and work. Examines his sources, the relationship between his position as courtier and his writing, his prosody, and the printing history of the poems.

May, Steven W. *The Elizabethan Courtier Poets: The Poems and Their Contexts*. Columbia: University of Missouri Press, 1991. Includes a discussion of Ralegh's career. Examines Ralegh's genres and looks closely at the relationship between Ralegh's poetry and his position as courtier to Elizabeth I.

_____. *Sir Walter Ralegh*. Boston: Twayne, 1989. Provides a solid general introduction to the life and major works of the writer.

Ure, Peter. "The Poetry of Sir Walter Ralegh." In *Elizabethan and Jacobean Drama: Critical Essays*. Edited by J. C. Maxwell. Liverpool, England: Liverpool University Press, 1974. Ure examines Ralegh's friendship with Spenser and its effects on Ralegh's poetry. Notes particularly the dark quality of Ralegh's writing from the Jacobean period.

POEMS AND BALLADS

Author: Algernon Charles Swinburne (1837-1909)
First published: First Series, 1866; *Second Series,* 1878; *Third Series,* 1889

Poems and Ballads, published in three series, contains the major part of Algernon Charles Swinburne's great lyric poetry. Whether the first series of these remarkable poems brought him fame or notoriety is a debatable question. One critic has called him the most immoral of all English poets and has pointed to *Poems and Ballads: First Series* as the most obscene book of poetry in the English language. Other critics, like George Meredith and John Ruskin, were fascinated by Swinburne's rich melodies and technical virtuosity. These two opinions of Swinburne reflect the most striking qualities of *Poems and Ballads*: The poems are an open revolt against Victorian prudery, and they are among the most technically perfect poems in English. To the reader of 1866, they were unlike anything hitherto published in England; while the critics loudly and indignantly denounced the volume, the public avidly bought it.

Swinburne's major themes in the 1866 volume are sex, freedom, sadism, masochism, and the beauty of evil and of things corrupt or decaying. Influenced by the growing interest in the Marquis de Sade and Charles Baudelaire, Swinburne presents his themes without equivocation. Few poems before 1866 celebrated the pleasures of physical love with the straightforwardness of "Les Noyades," in which the sexual act is public and intensified by impending death, or "Fragoletta," in which the act is given overtones of psychological maladjustment. Such sexual deviations are used by Swinburne for their ability to shock the prudish reader. In the 1866 volume, sexual deviations include homosexuality, in the group of poems called "Hermaphroditus" and in "Sappho"; incest, in "Phaedra"; and sexual flagellation, in such poems as "A Match." The reasons for this focus, however, may be far greater than merely the desire to shock. Swinburne was celebrating the human body itself, the sexual pleasure that alone remained after the soul was eliminated. In this sense, his use of the shocking was both a way to jar the apathetic public and to point toward a new religion.

This paganism is especially evident in "Laus Veneris," Swinburne's rehandling of the Tannhäuser legend. In this poem, the tragedy is that the knight who has renounced Christ believes in him and the lover who has embraced Venus does not believe in her. Another poem that glorifies this pagan outlook is "Hymn to Proserpine," in which the speaker, a pagan of 313 C.E., when Christianity was proclaimed to be the state religion, bitterly laments the passing of pagan sensuality and predicts an eventual collapse of Christianity.

The glorification of sensuality, however, leads Swinburne into another characteristic theme: If sexual ecstasy is truly to be the height of human existence, humans must be free from all restraints. In the bitter "St. Dorothy," the chaste virgin and her lover die horrible deaths because they are trapped by the restraints of Christianity; in "The Masque of Queen Barsabe" (a "miracle play" about David, Bathsheba, and Nathan), the prophet is forced to admit that the adulterous queen is right. Related to this desire for sexual freedom is Swinburne's adoration of the prostitute. In "Dolores," the peak of Swinburne's masochistic eroticism, the prostitute is "Our Lady of Pain," a semigoddess who gives the worshiper an excessive pleasure of suffering. "Faustine," addressed to another prostitute, revels in the pleasure of damnation, a pleasure that only a masochist could enjoy. Sadistic love is the theme of "Satia Te Sanguine" ("Satiate thyself with blood"), and "The Leper," in which the lover has the sadistic pleasure of coldly watching his beloved while she is slowly consumed by a fatal disease.

Sensuality, however, would lack much of its charm to Swinburne if it were a permanent state;

thus, he places it within a world that is characterized above all by the passing of time. "Ilicet" ("Let us go") is a lament for this passing of time, and "The Triumph of Time," as its title implies, laments the mutability of human existence and the inevitable ending to love. "Before Parting" and "Before Dawn" are further laments for the ending of love. Related to these poems are the two eulogies, "In Memory of Walter Savage Landor" and "To Victor Hugo," both of which rather sentimentally note the transience of human life. In contrast to the sentimentality of these eulogies are the two grotesque ballads "After Death" and "The Bloody Son," which present realistic pictures of death. This view is the exception in Swinburne's poetry; the number of poems that have a yearning to die far outnumber the realistic ones. In "The Garden of Proserpine," the weariness of life is contrasted with the peaceful rest of death, and in "Hendecasyllabics" the speaker seeks rest from "the long decline of roses."

Poems and Ballads: Second Series marks a change in Swinburne's thought. No longer is he the outspoken rebel against Victorian conventionality. His tone has changed from nervous ranting and naughty excitement to a calm, sad strain, almost of lamentation. During the twelve years between the two series, Swinburne's friends—Dante Gabriel Rossetti, George Meredith, and Benjamin Jowett—had brought his attention to Elizabethan drama, and in the 1878 volume, he published the lyrics that this study had produced.

Instead of the eroticism of 1866, the second series is obsessed with death, so much so that more than half the fifty-five poems are either eulogies or laments. The theme of death can, in fact, be divided into three parts, each of which Swinburne describes: the death of famous men, the death of youth, and the death of nature. Some of the most remarkable poems in this volume are on the deaths of famous men: Barry Cornwall, Charles Baudelaire, Théophile Gautier (one of Swinburne's favorite contemporaries), and Victor Hugo (the leading exponent of French Romanticism). In these poems, Swinburne's concern is twofold: In each, he laments the passing of a great poet, to him the crown of existence, and the defeat of a struggling, vivacious man by a force over which he has no control. This last concern partly relates him to the then-growing movement of Naturalism, especially as interpreted by Émile Zola, as well as to his own sense of futility, which had already appeared in the 1866 volume. A second aspect of the theme of death deals with the death of nature. This is the theme of the poem that many consider to be the best in the volume—"A Forsaken Garden." Here Swinburne laments the mutability of life and the decay that characterizes nature. Other poems related to this theme are "At a Month's End," "The Year of the Rose," and "Four Songs of Four Seasons"; in each, the poet observes the decay and death that are part of the world of nature. Finally, there is a group of lyrics in which Swinburne laments the death or the passing of youth and, with youth, the passing of love. "A Wasted Vigil" and "Age and Song," for example, show the inevitable decay of youth itself which, being caught up in the world of nature, must die even as nature dies.

The second series also reveals Swinburne's increased dependence upon and appreciation for Continental poetry, especially the mature poetry of Baudelaire and Gautier. More and more, Swinburne concentrates on the sharply defined image or symbol as developed by these poets and takes his emphasis from the melodious line.

It is in *Poems and Ballads: Third Series*, published in 1889, that Swinburne most shows the fruits of this influence. During 1879, he was so near death that his friends thought there was no hope for him, but Theodore Watts-Dunton rescued him and, by caring for him with almost parental control, nursed him back to health. The third series reflects this encounter with death and the reconciliation of the rebel to the middle class.

By far the least remarkable of the three volumes, the 1889 *Poems and Ballads* introduced a thread of patriotism that was hardly noticeable in Swinburne's work before this time. "The

Commonweal," for example, extols the jubilee of Queen Victoria, an attitude that would have been inconceivable in the young Swinburne, and "The Armada" is an almost Tennysonian exaltation of English sea power. In this volume, there is a more obvious attempt to rely on literary experiences rather than his own experiences for the source of his poetry. Especially striking are the echoes of Robert Browning's "Caliban upon Setebos" (1864) in "Caliban on Ariel," for example.

The most interesting poems in this otherwise mediocre volume are those lyrics capturing, through fleeting but precise symbols, moments that are as ephemeral but profound as those captured in words by Paul Verlaine and Stéphane Mallarmé. In poems such as "In Time of Mourning," "The Interpreters," "The Recall," and "By Twilight," Swinburne grasped the poetic vision that was fundamental to the French Symbolists and would be of utmost importance in twentieth century lyrical poetry.

In the three series of *Poems and Ballads*, Swinburne shows a profundity of thought expressed in a depth of emotion, a combination that easily accounts for his widespread influence on the poets who followed him. There are few forms of versification, however difficult, that do not appear in these pages. In his translations of François Villon and in his re-creations of the early English ballad, Swinburne shows that translation and the meager ballad could be the vehicles of great art. In the sestinas and sonnets, he shows that he has mastered the most difficult rhyme patterns. In fact, he shows a mastery in technical matters that is perhaps unmatched in English poetry. All in all, Swinburne's *Poems and Ballads* is one of the most unusual and most outstanding works of nineteenth century poetry, a publication that mocked its contemporaries with such art that it became a seminal work in the formation of the poetic theory of the following age.

Bibliography:
Henderson, Philip. "Atlanta: *Poems and Ballads:* Notes on Poems and Reviews." In *Swinburne: The Portrait of a Poet*. London: Routledge & Kegan Paul, 1974. A review of criticism of *Poems and Ballads* by Swinburne's contemporaries, which helps to illuminate the thematic notions of morality, religion, mythmaking, and decadence evidenced in his work. Arranged by date, with full index and annotated photographs.

Louis, Margot K. *Swinburne and His Gods: The Roots and Growth of an Agnostic Poetry*. Buffalo, N.Y.: McGill-Queen's University Press, 1990. Divided into two sections, "Sacred Elements" and "The New Gods," this ambitious work explores the mythological overtones of demons and angels, violence and harmony, and the individual and god in Swinburne's poems.

McGann, Jerome J. *Swinburne: An Experiment in Criticism*. Chicago: The University of Chicago Press, 1972. Emphasizes new criticism, which looks beyond the actual text to the author's life and environment for interpretation. The discussions of Swinburne's use of language, the social context of *Poems and Ballads*, and the autobiographical ambiguity of *Poems and Ballads* are provocative. Comprehensive and well-organized.

Riede, David G. *Swinburne: A Study of Romantic Mythmaking*. Charlottesville: University Press of Virginia, 1978. Primarily concerned with distinguishing between mythmaking and mythologizing. Discusses how Swinburne's poetry progresses from the central unifying thought of alienation through romanticism and beyond, into the creation of new myths. The discussion of Swinburne's basic religious underpinnings—despite his proclaimed agnosticism—illuminates the role religion plays in his poetry.

Stoddart, Judith. "The Morality of *Poems and Ballads*: Swinburne and Ruskin." In *The Whole*

Music of Passion: New Essays on Swinburne, edited by Rikky Rooksby and Nicholas Shrimpton. Brookfield, Vt.: Ashgate, 1993. John Ruskin's social criticism is used to explore Swinburne's poetry as an expression of a fallen age, devoid of family values, discipline, and order. Concise writing and illuminating endnotes.

POEMS, CHIEFLY IN THE SCOTTISH DIALECT

Author: Robert Burns (1759-1796)
First published: 1786

Since the first publication of Robert Burns's verse in the famous Kilmarnock edition entitled *Poems, Chiefly in the Scottish Dialect,* the poet's fame has increased and spread. Other editions of his work, containing later poems, only enhanced his reputation. Unlike many writers who achieve early fame only to see it fade, Burns is still widely read and appreciated.

At least part of the reason for this continuing appreciation is the fact that Burns was essentially a transitional figure between the eighteenth century neoclassicists and the Romantics who were soon to follow. Possessing some of the qualities of each school, he exhibits few of the excesses of either. He occasionally used the couplet that had been made a skillful tool by Alexander Pope and his followers, but his spirit was closer to the Romantics in his attitude toward life and his art.

Although he occasionally displayed a mild conservatism, as in the early "The Cotter's Saturday Night," he was fundamentally a rebel, and rebellion is a basic trait of the Romantics. It would have been hard for Burns to be a true neoclassicist because his background, which figures constantly in his poems, simply did not suit him for this role. He had a hard early life and a close acquaintanceship with the common people and the common circumstances of life. He was certainly not the uneducated, "natural" genius that he is sometimes pictured as—having had good instruction from his father and a tutor and having done considerable reading on his own—but he lacked the classical education that earlier poets thought necessary for the writing of true poetry.

Like the neoclassicists, however, he was skillful in taking the ideas and forms of earlier poets—in Burns's case, the Scottish poets Allan Ramsay and Robert Fergusson, as well as the anonymous composers of ballads and folk songs—and treating them in his own individual way. Thus, his verse has a wide variety of stanza forms and styles. Despite the variety of his techniques, his basic outlook in his poems is remarkably consistent. This outlook also may have a great deal to do with his popularity. Perhaps more than any other poet since Geoffrey Chaucer, Burns possessed the genial personal insight and the instinct for human feelings that can make a poem speak to everyone. Burns always saw the human aspect of things. His nature poetry, for instance, marks a departure from the intellectualizing of the eighteenth century poets; Burns's lines about nature treat it primarily as a setting in which people live.

The warmth of Burns's verse arises from this humane attitude combined with the experience he had of being in close personal contact with the people about whom he wrote. His writing never deals with subjects that he did not know intimately. Burns loved several women and claimed that they each served as great poetic inspiration. The reader may well believe this statement when he or she encounters the simple and lucidly sincere poems "Highland Mary," "Mary Morison," and the well-known song "Sweet Afton." It was this quality of sincerity that another great Scot, Thomas Carlyle, found to be Burns's greatest poetic value.

Burns was not an original thinker, but he had a few strong convictions about religion, human freedom, and morality. His condemnation of Calvinism and the hypocrisy it bred is accomplished with humor and yet with sharpness in two of his best poems, "The Holy Fair" and the posthumously published "Holy Willie's Prayer." In these and several other poems, Burns pokes occasionally none-too-gentle fun at the professional religionists of his time. Burns's intensely personal viewpoint saved him from preaching, as was the style of earlier versifiers. It is to be expected that the few poems that contain examples of his rare attempts to be lofty are unsuccessful.

Having grown up in a humble environment, Burns was especially sensitive to social relations and the value of human freedom and equality. On this subject, too, he is never didactic, but few readers have remained unmoved by the lines of probably his most famous poem in defense of the lower classes, "A Man's a Man for A' That":

> Is there, for honest poverty
> That hings his head, an' a' that?
> The coward slave, we pass him by—
> We dare be poor for a' that!
> For a' that and a' that,
> Our toil's obscure and a' that;
> The rank is but the guinea's stamp,
> The man's the gowd for a' that.
>
> . . . .
>
> Then let us pray that come it may,
> As come it will for a' that,
> That sense and worth, o'er a' the earth,
> Shall bear the gree, an' a' that.
> For a' that, an' a' that,
> It's coming yet for a' that,
> That man to man, the warld o'er,
> Shall brithers be for a' that.

It was this powerful feeling for democracy that led Burns, in his later years, to a tactless advocation of the principles of the French Revolution, a crusade that did his career as a minor government official no good. It is questionable whether Burns's heated protest against Calvinism and the strict morality it proclaimed was simply a rationalization of his own loose behavior. However many the romances he had, and however many the illegitimate children he fathered, there can be little doubt of Burns's sincere devotion, at least at the time, to the woman of his choice. In a larger sense, too, the poet's warm sympathy for his fellows is evidence of a sort of ethical pattern in his life and work that is quite laudable.

The poetic techniques in Burns's poems are unquestionably a chief reason for his popularity. Few poets have so well suited the style to the subject, and his use of earlier stanza forms and several kinds of poetic diction has a sureness and an authority that are certain to charm even the learned student of poetry.

There are three types of diction in his poetry: Scottish dialect, pure English, and a combination of the two. In "Tam O' Shanter," a later work that is perhaps his masterpiece, Burns used dialect to tell an old legend of the supernatural with great effect. The modern reader who takes the trouble to master the dialectal terminology will be highly rewarded. In this, as in most of Burns's poems, the pace and rhythm of the lines are admirably well suited to the subject.

His use of the English idiom, as in "The Vision," was seldom so successful. Usually Burns wrote in standard English when he had some lofty purpose in mind, and with the exception of "The Cotter's Saturday Night" this combination was often fatal to the poetic quality of these poems. For the general reader, probably the most enjoyable and rewarding reading consists of the poems and songs that Burns did in English, with occasional Scottish touches here and there in the lines. Most happy is this joining of language and dialect in such a poem as the famous little love lyric, "A Red, Red Rose." These three kinds of poetic diction can be found side by side in one of Burns's best poems, the highly patriotic "The Jolly Beggars," which gives as fine a picture of Scottish low life as can be found anywhere.

Naturally, Burns was most at home when he wrote in his native dialect; and, since one of the most striking characteristics of his verse is the effortless flow of conversational rhythms, it is not surprising that his better poems are those that came as natural effusions in his most familiar diction.

The total achievement of Burns is obviously great, but it should not be misunderstood. Burns lacked the precision and clarity of his predecessors in the eighteenth century, and he never was able to reach the exalted heights of poetic expression attained by Percy Bysshe Shelley and John Keats not long after him. For vigor and the little touches that breathe life into lines of poetry, however, he was unexcelled by earlier or later poets.

The claim that Burns wrote careless verse has been perhaps too much emphasized. His poems and songs are surely not carefully carved jewels, but neither are they haphazard groupings of images and rhymes. The verses seem unlabored, but Burns worked patiently at them, and with considerable effort. That they seem to have been casual utterances is only further tribute to his ability.

It may be that the highest praise of all was paid to Burns, both as man and poet, by Keats, who said that one can see in Burns's poems his whole life; and, though the life reflected was not an altogether happy one, the poet's love of freedom, of people, and of life itself appears in nearly every line.

Bibliography:

Burns, Robert. *The Complete Illustrated Poems, Songs and Ballads of Robert Burns.* Secaucus, N.J.: Chartwell Books, 1990. The complete works in original dialect, with a complete glossary. The works are arranged by category: poems, songs, ballads, fragments, and epitaphs. Illustrations add to the charm of the book.

Daiches, David. *Robert Burns.* New York: Macmillan, 1967. Biography of the poet and critical analysis of his works, with notes and explanation of terms. Index and some interesting facsimiles of handwritten poetry. Good discussion of the Kilmarnock edition and the Edinburgh years.

Ferguson, John De Lancey. *Pride and Passion: Robert Burns, 1759-1796.* New York: Russell & Russell, 1964. Complete biography of the poet's life, including the circumstances of publication of the Kilmarnock edition.

Jack, R. D. S., and Andrew Noble, eds. *The Art of Robert Burns.* Totowa, N.J.: Barnes & Noble Books, 1982. Critical analysis by several Burns scholars. Well indexed. Includes some musical transcription of Burns's songs.

McGuirk, Carol. *Robert Burns and the Sentimental Era.* Athens: University of Georgia Press, 1985. Critical look at Burns's sentimental approach to poetry, including his passion for his nation.

POETIC EDDA

Type of work: Poetry
Author: Unknown
Type of plot: Saga
Time of plot: Mythical times
Locale: Early Scandinavia and Asgard, home of the northern gods
First transcribed: Edda Sæmundar, ninth to twelfth century (English translation, 1923)

Principal characters:
ODIN, chief of the gods
FRIGG, Odin's wife
BALDER, the beloved, Odin's son
THOR, the thunder god, Odin's son
LOKI, a mischief-maker, son of a giant
FREYJA, the goddess of love, who carries off half the slain
from the battlefield

The Story:
Voluspo. Odin, chief of the gods, called an ancient wise woman to prophesy for him. She told first of the creation of the earth from the body of the giant Ymir and cataloged the dwarfs who lived beneath the earth. She then described Yggdrasil, the great ash tree that supported the universe. Its roots reached clear to the underworld, and it was guarded by the three Norns, Past, Present, and Future, who controlled the destinies of human beings. She also told briefly how Loki tricked the giant who built Asgard, the home of the gods, and how Loki himself was punished when he killed Odin's much-loved son Balder. He was bound to a rock so that the venom of a serpent dripped onto his face. The prophetess last foretold a great battle. Odin and the other gods would confront the forces of evil such as the wolf Fenrir, one of Loki's children, who was fated to kill Odin himself. In conclusion, the wise woman foretold the emergence of a new world, which would rise out of the destruction of the old one.

The Ballad of Grimnir. Odin made a wager with his wife, Frigg, over the relative virtues of two men they had saved from being lost at sea. Frigg accused Geirröth, the man Odin had saved, of miserliness and lack of hospitality. Odin went to King Geirröth disguised as Grimnir and was taken prisoner and tortured. The king's son, Agnar, befriended the prisoner, however, and was rewarded with the mythological lore that makes up most of the poem.

The Lay of Hymir. Thor sought a kettle big enough to brew ale for a feast of all the gods. He and the god Tyr went to the giant Hymir where they escaped the wrath of Hymir's nine-hundred-headed grandmother. Hymir then provided a feast for them, at which Thor ate two oxen. Finally, they joined in a fishing contest, in which Thor demonstrated his prowess by hooking Mithgarthsorm, the great serpent that surrounded the earth. Thor and Tyr stole the kettle and carried it home.

The Lay of Thrym. Loki managed to recover Thor's hammer when the giant Thrym stole it and held it hostage, demanding Freyja for his wife. Thor went to Thrym, disguised as Freyja in bridal dress, and took Loki, disguised as his serving woman, with him. After some difficulties in accounting for their huge appetites and masculine looks, Thor was given the precious hammer as a wedding gift, whereupon he slew Thrym and the two returned to Asgard.

Balder's Dream. Acting on Balder's ominous dream, Odin rode into the underworld where a wise woman told him that the blind god Hoth, guided by Loki, would throw the dart of mistletoe that would kill the otherwise impervious Balder. The murder would later be avenged by Vali, whom Odin conceived for that purpose.

Lay of Völund. Völund was a hero who once, along with his brothers, captured and lived with the swan maidens, Valkyries who lived on earth disguised as swans. When the swan maidens left them, the brothers sought them. In doing so, Völund was captured by a Swedish king, Nithuth, who accused him of stealing his treasure. While making his escape, Völund killed Nithuth's sons and sent their skulls, set in silver, to their father. He then made good his escape by flying away on wings he had made for himself.

The Lay of Helgi the Son of Hjorvarth. Helgi was befriended by a Valkyrie who sent him a sword that allowed him to do great deeds. Together with Atli, he subdued the ferocious daughter of a giant. Later, as a king in his own right, he married Svava, the Valkyrie who had aided him. He died in a duel with King Alf.

The First Lay of Helgi Hundingsbane. At an early age, Helgi, a son of Sigmund, began to do valorous deeds. Urged on by the Valkyrie Sigrun, he later engaged another king, Granmar, in a sea battle in order to release Sigrun from her obligation to marry Granmar's son Hothbrodd.

Of Sinfjotli's Death. Helgi's brother Sinfjotli was killed by his stepmother, Borghild, in revenge for his murder of her brother. She killed him by making him drink poisoned ale.

Gripir's Prophecy. Sigurth, another of Sigmund's sons, received a prophecy about his life. Gripir told him that he would avenge his father's death and fight a terrible dragon named Fafnir. Then Gripir told him how he would be sent to court Brynhild for King Gunnar, whose form he would take on. As Gunnar, he rode through a ring of fire and won Brynhild. When she learned of his deception, however, she goaded her brother-in-law to kill him.

The Ballad of Regin. Regin told Sigurth how Loki once killed Regin's brother Otr when he mistook him for an actual otter. Otr's father, Hreithmar, demanded payment in gold as recompense. When Hreithmar refused to share the "man-money" with his sons Fafnir and Regin, Fafnir killed him and took all the treasure. Once Sigurth came of age, Regin urged him to fight with Fafnir.

The Ballad of Fafnir. In Sigurth's battle with the dragon Fafnir, the hero tasted blood from the dragon's heart. Immediately, he discovered that he could understand the speech of birds. When he learned from them that Regin planned to kill him, he killed Regin as well as the dragon.

The First Lay of Guthrun. In Guthrun's lament for her dead husband, Sigurth, she told of his being killed as the result of Brynhild's fury at his deception when he courted her disguised as Gunnar. Brynhild blamed the murder on her brother Atli, who forced her to marry Gunnar.

The Short Lay of Sigurth. Brynhild described her rage at having to marry Gunnar. In the end she killed herself.

The Greenland Lay of Atli. When Guthrun's brothers visited her in Atli's court, Atli killed them. In revenge, Guthrun killed Atli's sons and fed their hearts to her husband; then she stabbed him and burned the court to the ground.

Critical Evaluation:

The two parts of the complex group of poems known as the *Poetic Edda* have rather different characteristics. The first part is composed of stories about the gods of the peoples of ancient Scandinavia. These stories deal with the creation of the earth and its peoples and with the lore that relates to the gods and their histories. Taken as a group, these poems depict a world of cold and danger in which even gods like Balder could become the victims of evil and treachery.

Some themes in these stories are familiar ones and bear close similarities with the creation stories of other peoples. There is the figure of a trickster god, here named Loki, and the journey into the underworld such as Odin's journey for information or Balder's mother's effort to recover her dead son. Other typical subjects involve riddle-telling and insult contests, the recounting of lore about the gods, giants, dwarfs, and other supernatural beings, and proverbs intended to instruct people in how to live.

Always in the background of these poems there is a sense of doom, which distinguishes them in tone from the Greek myths with which they are often contrasted. The afterlife depicted in the *Poetic Edda* is a shadowy land; only those who die heroically in battle can expect to be carried to Valhalla, where they will be feasted by the gods. Indeed, even that reward is temporary, for they wait in Valhalla for the final battle against evil, at which time they must aid the gods in their fight.

The poems of the second half of the *Poetic Edda* deal mostly with the legends of human heroes from Norse tradition. Because few of these poems are strictly narrative and many are incomplete, the stories they tell often seem fragmented, repetitious, and even contradictory. Nevertheless, they represent the main thread of a story that is retold in two other important heroic poems of early Scandinavian and Germanic literature, the *Völsunga Saga* (c. 1200-1300) and the *Nibelungenlied* (c. 1200). The latter poem was composer Richard Wagner's source for the plot of his great *Ring* cycle of operas.

In the *Poetic Edda*, as in much early northern literature, a prominent theme is the need for a family or tribe to get revenge for the death of one of its own, a social imperative in a world without law enforcement. This created endless feuding among tribal groups, as one killing led inevitably to the next. If a family failed to avenge a murder, however, either with another murder or by demanding a money payment, that family faced unbearable shame.

A common theme of this literature is a tribe's attempt to mend a feud by intermarriage, for murder of a family member, even a member by marriage, was taboo. Yet such attempts to establish peace often failed. Those are the motives behind much of the action of the story of Sigurth and Brynhild, and they are visible even in the lyric fragments that make up the *Poetic Edda*.

Ann Davison Garbett

Bibliography:
Bellows, Henry Adams, ed. and trans. *The Poetic Edda*. New York: American-Scandinavian Foundation, 1957. Although Bellows' translation is weighted by his scholarly concerns, his general introduction to the *Poetic Edda* is an excellent overview of the poems, their origins, manuscript texts, and verse forms.

Dronke, Ursula, ed. and trans. *Heroic Poems*. Vol. 1 in *The Poetic Edda*. Oxford, England: Clarendon Press, 1969. A vigorous translation of the four heroic tales that conclude the *Poetic Edda*. Also provides an exhaustive commentary on the texts.

Kellogg, Robert. "Literacy and Orality in the *Poetic Edda*." In *Vox Intexta: Orality and Textuality in the Middle Ages*, edited by A. N. Doane and Carol Braun Pasternack. Madison: University of Wisconsin Press, 1991. Discusses the *Poetic Edda* as collaboration between the oral and literate worlds. Examines evidence of the oral origins of the poems that make up the work.

MacCulloch, John A. *Eddic [Mythology]*. Vol. 2 in *The Mythology of All Races*. New York: Cooper Square, 1964. MacCulloch is interested in the mythological qualities of the Eddic tales; in retelling the stories, he analyzes and orders them by subject and compares their relationship to the mythologies of other peoples.

Tucker, John, ed. *Sagas of the Icelanders*. New York: Garland, 1989. A collection of essays that cover subjects of general interest in early Icelandic literature, including the figure of the heroine, the poets' rhetorical modes, and the figure of the poet. Also deals with individual characters from the stories, including some of the gods.

POETICAL MEDITATIONS

Type of work: Poetry
Author: Alphonse de Lamartine (1790-1869)
First published: Méditations poétiques, 1820 (English translation, 1839)

When his volume of *Poetical Meditations* appeared in 1820, Alphonse de Lamartine brought French poetry into the Romantic mode that had already become an established poetic form in England and Germany. Even in this work, however, Romanticism is slow to emerge. The number of poems in different editions of *Poetical Meditations* varies between two dozen and three dozen, but only a few poems fully exhibit the Romantic style.

Most of the poems are composed in Alexandrines, the basic verse form of French neoclassicism, and the subjects are often drawn from philosophical meditations of the previous century. Still, much is new. The detailed descriptions of external nature evoke emotions appropriate to the poems in a way the more analytical descriptions of, for example, Jean-Jacques Rousseau's *Rêveries du promeneur solitaire* (1782) do not. The autobiographical elements are also distinctly Romantic.

An analysis of the first ten poems included in the first edition of *Poetical Meditations* will define Lamartine's style, clearly Romantic but with debts to previous literary traditions. The opening poem, "L'Isolement," finds Lamartine, its first-person narrator, alone on a mountain from which he can contemplate the panorama of the landscape before him. Rousseau had exploited just such a panorama in his *Émile* (1762), in which his Savoyard vicar used the view of nature to persuade his young pupil of the existence of God. For Lamartine, the purpose of nature is evocative rather than pedagogical.

The first quatrain sets a mood of quiet melancholy: Lamartine sits sadly under an old oak tree at sunset. The references to age and the end of the day imply a basis for his emotion. The landscape, rather than Lamartine, performs the action of the poem while he remains a spectator of this "changing tableau unrolling at my feet." The active waters of the river draw his eyes to the calm lake and finally to the rising evening star. The sequence of objects, progressing ever farther from the narrator, suggests vast contemplation.

The description of nature retains neoclassical elements. Lamartine calls the rising moon "the misty chariot of the queen of shadows," a periphrasis of the very sort William Wordsworth had hoped to avoid when he advocated that Romantic poetry use "the real language of men." However, the contrast of the "somber woods" with the moon "whitening" the horizon reflects the dark/light color scheme to which the early Romantics were drawn.

The "gothic steeple" of a nearby church provides an additional Romantic motif, but then, switching to an impersonal invocation of "the traveler" who might observe this scene, Lamartine rejects the tableau because, in his mood of despair, it has no appeal to him. Finally, he turns toward death as his only hope. For the sun of the earthly landscape he will substitute the "true sun" of an idealized afterlife.

In the final quatrains, both neoclassical and Romantic images return. Lamartine hopes to be carried away on the "chariot of Dawn," a traditional personification. However, he then imagines the similar rising motion of an autumn leaf blown on the evening wind. Emotionally he cries out, "I am like the withered leaf" and appeals to the "stormy wind" to carry him away. The poet's identification of himself with the leaf and attribution of his own emotional agitation to the wind reflects the Romantic pathetic fallacy through which nature was united with human feelings.

In his second poem, "L'Homme," dedicated to George Gordon, Lord Byron, Lamartine extols the poetic vision of his Romantic predecessor. While Byron was only two years older than Lamartine, he had already published *Childe Harold* (1812) and had impressed Lamartine with the "savage harmony" of his verse. Lamartine's characterization of Byron in the opening section of "L'Homme" uses many Romantic devices. He compares the sound of Byron's poetry with lightning and wind "mixed by the storm with the voice of waterfalls," combining many of the sublime elements of nature the Romantics favored. He further portrays Byron as an eagle, dominating the landscape and deriving "voluptuous enjoyment from the cries of his prey." The important use of natural elements, the linking of the poet to nature using the image of the bird, and the savagery of the predator adding a gothic element combine to create an intensely Romantic passage.

After this preliminary description, however, Lamartine's tone changes. The balance of the rather long poem retreats from nature imagery to examine philosophically the role of the poet in relationship to the will of God. Lamartine traces the Fall of Man and his own personal evolution as a poet but never returns to the descriptive mode of his first lines.

With "Le Soir," Lamartine returns to the first-person meditation in a natural setting that he had used in "L'Isolement" with the substitution of more fluid eight-syllable lines for the Alexandrine. As in the earlier poem, however, the moon still appears as the neoclassical "chariot of the night." The principal action of the poem occurs when the rising moon casts its light upon Lamartine and causes him to ask whether the moonlight presages philosophical enlightenment. The experience inspires deep emotions. Lamartine says that the moon has "enflamed my heart" and caused "unknown emotions." The tone of the poem, however—marked as it is by a long series of questions as to the moon's intent—remains one of philosophical hesitancy.

Only after an abstract consideration of death in "L'Immortalité" does Lamartine return, in "Le Vallon," to his important use of nature imagery. The world-weary narrator seeks out the valley of his youth to await death. Such emotion coming from a poet who was not yet thirty years old reflects a Romantic despair. The poet then surrounds himself with elements of nature. At first, the "obscure valley" seems mysterious, but then two brooks "joining their waters and their murmuring" flow off into anonymity. Lamartine sees them as an emblem of his own life but notes that his soul is more troubled than their calm waters.

In "Le Vallon," Lamartine again progresses to a meditation on his life. This time, however, he never leaves the landscape. He calls on it to become for him a "place of forgetfulness" like the river Lethe, a refuge from trouble, and finally a place to hear the voice of God. Despite occasional classical allusions, the continued presence of nature and its close relationship to the speaker make this one of Lamartine's most Romantic poems.

In "Le Désespoir" and "La Providence à l'homme," general meditations on God and humankind displace the personal tone and nature imagery. However, in "Souvenir," the personal element returns as Lamartine recalls a lost love. Still seeing himself as old as an oak tree that is dropping its leaves, he remembers "your young, brilliant image/ Embellished by regret." The breeze reminds him of his beloved at their last meeting, when its "loving breath" caressed her hair. The linking of the love experience to nature gives a new meaning to this imagery.

The theme of lost love introduced in "Souvenir" was surely a reference to Julie Charles, whom Lamartine called "Elvire" in his poetry. Although Julie was married, Lamartine had fallen in love with her during the summer of 1816. He hoped to see her again the following summer but did not because she died from tuberculosis. Lamartine had already included a reference to her in the last line of "L'Immortalité," in which he called on Elvire to answer him.

In the ninth edition of *Poetical Meditations* he would also insert the poem "À Elvire" in the third position in the volume. The most important evocation of Julie Charles occurs in the tenth poem of the first edition, "Le Lac," which would become the piece for which Lamartine is best known.

Before "Le Lac" in the first edition, the Romantic elements are again restrained in "L'Enthousiasme." While enthusiasm appears as an eagle bearing inspiration to Lamartine, the dominant focus of the poem is not on the natural elements. In "Le Lac," however, nature dominates. Lamartine begins with a plea that it might be possible to stop advancing time if it leads inevitably to the death of a beloved. This appears, however, as dropping an anchor while crossing an ocean surrounded by "eternal night" that isolates us from both past and future. The image of the ocean yields to that of a lake, emblematic of a shorter period of life, near which Lamartine waits in vain for Julie.

In the first section of the poem, Lamartine addresses the lake as if it were his friend and witness to his joy with his beloved. Not only has the lake "seen" Julie sitting beside it, it has seemed to speak through the murmuring of its waters. Thus Lamartine asks the lake directly, "Do you remember?" as he recalls words Julie had spoken on its bank.

Julie's speech forms the central portion of "Le Lac," set off from the rest by a distinct verse structure. Elsewhere Lamartine varies the Alexandrine quatrains by reducing the fourth line to six syllables. As Julie speaks, the second line is also reduced, emphasizing how quickly her utterance will pass. The sense of her speech reinforces the desirability of halting time for those who are happy in the present. If a new dawn must come, however, lovers should seize the "fugitive hour" of their joy.

While Julie implores passing time to have pity on lovers, Lamartine sees it as jealous of them. In the final section of the poem, returning to his own voice and distinctive verse form, he groups together "eternity, nothingness, and past time" as "dark abysses" swallowing human life. Faced with this prospect, he finds hope for immortality only in nature. Thus he calls on the lake, rocks, and surrounding forest, a scene he had already endowed with human sensitivity, to retain the memory of his love for Julie.

The lengthy enumeration of objects in nature coupled with the intensity of emotion in this final passage exemplifies the fusion of feeling with landscape that typifies Romanticism. The contrast of "black fir trees" with the silver moon reflects the extremes of Romantic nature description, and the lyricism reinforces the meaning of the lives.

The remaining poems in *Poetical Meditations* incorporate the same varied tendencies seen in the early texts, but in "Le Lac" Lamartine has established Romantic lyricism as a component of French poetry.

Dorothy M. Betz

Bibliography:
Birkett, Mary Ellen. *Lamartine and the Poetics of Landscape*. Lexington, Ky.: French Forum, 1982. This study places Lamartine's poetry in the tradition of landscape description. Material is analyzed in terms of descriptive techniques rather than by chronological elements. There is no specific section devoted to the *Poetical Meditations*, but material from the collection is quoted extensively throughout the work.
Domvile, Lady Margaret. *Life of Lamartine*. London: Kegan, Paul, Trench, 1888. The early chapters of this biography furnish background to the *Poetical Meditations*. Chapter three, covering 1815-1821, addresses the work specifically.

George, Albert Joseph. *Lamartine and Romantic Unanimism*. New York: Columbia University Press, 1940. In this volume, Lamartine's work is analyzed in terms of his ideas concerning philosophy and his views on politics and history. An extensive index, however, directs the reader to comments on the *Poetical Meditations*.

Lamartine, Alphonse de. *The "Méditations poétiques."* Edited by David Hillery. Durham, England: University of Durham, 1993. An introduction to a selection from the poems, this volume includes brief essays on the social and political, the literary, and the technical background to the poems as well as the themes of love and death, religion, and nature.

Lombard, Charles M. *Lamartine*. New York: Twayne, 1973. This volume in the Twayne's World Authors Series presents a standard approach to Lamartine's life and work accompanied by a useful chronology of his life and a selected bibliography. Chapter 2 introduces, summarizes, and comments on the importance of *Poetical Meditations*.

POETICS

Type of work: Literary criticism
Author: Aristotle (384-322 B.C.E.)
First transcribed: c. 334-323 B.C.E. (English translation, 1705)

The significance of the *Poetics* cannot be overemphasized. In format, content, and methodology, Aristotle's analysis of the literature of Greece is the origin of Western literary criticism. His examination of the components and aims of comedy, epic, and tragedy evolved into what is probably the first, and certainly the most influential, formalist analysis of literature in the Western tradition.

At the center of Aristotle's analysis lies his explanation of the concept of mimesis, the process of representing reality in works of literature. Mimesis does not imply mimicry of the everyday world, however; Aristotle is careful to stress that the job of "the poet" (which later critics have expanded to mean the author of any form of imaginative literature) is to present portraits of humankind as a means of helping audiences learn something about themselves. Far from being lies, as Plato calls the works of poets, good poems and dramas are useful to society because readers and audiences can learn from the experiences of fictional characters without having to experience for themselves the traumas and heartbreaks they can see in tragedy or the foibles and humiliations they can experience through comedy.

Unfortunately, during the later Renaissance and neoclassical periods, the process of description employed by Aristotle in examining the drama and poetry of classical Greece became prescriptions for producing and evaluating similar works. French and English dramatists of the seventeenth and eighteenth centuries endeavored to produce plays that adhered slavishly to the unities of time, place, and action they found set down by Aristotle. Although later generations abandoned the criteria set forth in the *Poetics* for determining the value of specific genres, Aristotle's method of analysis became the basis for the method of literary analysis known as genre criticism. The idea of judging the worth of a particular poem, play, story, or novel by comparing it to designated criteria that characterize other, similar productions has become a staple of literary criticism.

Although Aristotle's reputation as one of the greatest philosophers of all time rests principally on his work in metaphysics, he nowhere shows himself more the master of illuminating analysis and style than in the *Poetics*. The conception of tragedy that Aristotle developed in this work has perpetuated the Greek ideal of drama through the ages.

Aristotle begins his essay with an exposition of the Greek idea that all poetry, or art, is representative of life. For the Greeks, the idea of poetry as imitative or representational was a natural one because a great deal of Grecian art was representational in content. By "representation" was meant not a literal copying of physical objects, although it was sometimes that, but a new use of the material presented by sense.

Aristotle's intention in the *Poetics* is to analyze the essence of poetry and to distinguish its various species. Among the arts that Aristotle mentions are epic poetry, tragedy, comedy, dithyrambic poetry, flute playing, and lyre playing. These arts, all of which a poet in Aristotle's time may have been expected to practice, are regarded as representative of life, but they are distinguished from one another by their means and their objects. The means include rhythm, language, and tune; but not all the arts involve all three, nor are these means used in the same way. For example, flute playing involves the use of rhythm and tune, but dancing involves rhythm alone.

When living persons are represented, Aristotle writes, they are represented as being better than, worse than, or the same as the average. Tragedy presents people somewhat better than average, while comedy presents people who are somewhat worse. This point alone offers strong evidence against a narrow interpretation of Aristotle's conception of art, for if people can be altered by the poet, made better or worse than in actual life, then poetry is not merely an uncreative copying of nature. A comment later in the *Poetics* indicates that the poet, in representing life, represents things as they are, as they seem to be, or as they should be. This concept certainly allows the artist a great deal more freedom than suggested by the word "imitation."

The origin of poetry is explained by Aristotle as the natural consequence of humanity's love of imitation, tune, and rhythm. People enjoy looking at accurate copies of things, he says, even when the things are themselves repulsive, such as the lowest animals and corpses. The philosopher accounts for this enjoyment by claiming that it is the result of people's love of learning; in seeing accurate copies, one learns better what things are. This view is in opposition to Plato's idea that art corrupts the mind because it presents copies of copies of reality (physical objects being considered as mere copies of the universal idea or kind). Aristotle believed that universals, or characteristics, are to be found only in things, while Plato thought that the universals had some sort of separate existence.

Comedy represents inferior persons in that they are a laughable species of the ugly. The comic character makes mistakes or is in some way ugly, but not so seriously as to awaken pity or fear.

Epic poetry differs from tragedy in that it has a single meter and is narrative in form. A further difference results from the Greek convention that a tragedy encompass events taking place within a single day, while the time span of the epic poem was unlimited.

Aristotle defines tragedy as a representation of a heroic action by means of language and spectacle so as to arouse pity and fear and thus bring about a catharsis of those emotions. The relief, or catharsis, of the emotions of pity and fear is the most characteristic feature of the Aristotelian conception of tragedy. According to Aristotle, tragedy arouses the emotions by bringing a person who is somewhat better than average into a reversal of fortune for which he or she is responsible; then, through the downfall of the hero and the resolution of the conflicts resulting from the hero's tragic flaw, the tragedy achieves a purging of the audience's emotions.

The audience feels pity in observing the tragic hero's misadventures, because the character is a vulnerable human being suffering from unrecognized faults. Fear then results from the realization of the audience that they, like the hero, can err and suffer.

Aristotle defines plot as the arrangement of the events that make up the play, character as that which determines the nature of the agents, and thought as what is expressed in the speeches of the agents. Diction is the manner of that expression.

The plot is the most important element in the tragedy (the others being character, diction, thought, spectacle, and song) because a tragedy is a representation of action. The characters exist for the sake of the action, not the action for the sake of the characters.

The two most important elements of the tragedy and of its plot are peripeteia and discovery. By "peripeteia" is meant a change of a situation into its opposite state of fortune—in tragedy, a change from a good state of affairs to the bad. A discovery is a revelation of a matter previously unknown. The most effective tragedy, according to Aristotle, results from a plot that combines peripety and discovery in a single action.

To modern readers, Aristotle's definitions of the beginning, middle, and end of a tragedy may seem either amusing or trivial, but they contain important dramatic truths. The philosopher defines the beginning as that which does not necessarily follow anything else but does necessarily give rise to further action. The end necessarily follows from what has gone before, but does not necessarily lead to further events. The middle follows the beginning and gives rise to the end.

Aristotle's definitions make sense when one realizes that the important thing about the beginning of a play is not that it is the start, but that, relative to the audience's interest and curiosity, no earlier event is needed, but further events are demanded. Similarly, for the ending, the closing events of a play should not be merely the last events presented, but they should appear necessary as a result of what has already happened, and they should not give rise to new problems that must be solved if the audience is to be satisfied.

Aristotle writes that anything that is beautiful not only must have orderly arranged parts, but also must have parts of a large enough, but not too large, size. An animal a thousand miles long or something too small to be seen cannot be beautiful. A play should be as long as possible, allowing a change of fortune in a sequence of events ordered in some apparently inevitable way, provided the play can be understood as a whole. In his conception of unity, Aristotle emphasizes a point that continues to be useful to all who compose or criticize works of art: If the presence of a part makes no difference, it has no place in the work.

A good tragedy should not show worthy persons passing from good fortune to bad, for that is neither fearful nor pitiful but shocking. Even worse is to show bad people acquiring good fortune, for such a situation causes irritation without arousing pity and fear. The tragic hero, consequently, should be one who is better than the audience, but not perfect; the hero should suffer from a flaw that shows itself in some mistaken judgment or act resulting in the hero's downfall. There has been considerable discussion about the kind of flaw Aristotle meant, but it seems clear from the examples he gives that the flaw should be such that a character who has it must inevitably be defeated in action. It is not inevitable that everyone have that flaw, but all people are liable to it. Hence, the tragic hero arouses fear in all those who see the resemblance between the hero's situation and their own. The hero arouses pity because a human being cannot be perfect like the gods; a human's end is bound to be tragic.

Aristotle concludes his *Poetics* with a careful discussion of diction and thought, and of epic poetry. Among his sensible conclusions is that what is believable although not possible is better in a play than an event that is possible but not believable.

Throughout the *Poetics*, Aristotle offers remarkably clear analyses of what Greek tragedy actually was and of what he thought it ought to be. He shows not only an adroit analytical intellect, but also an understanding of the practical problems of the art of poetry; he is sophisticated enough to realize that most questions as to the value, length, beauty, and other features of a work of art are settled relative to the kind of audience the judge prefers.

Bibliography:
Aristotle. *Poetics*. Translated by Richard Janko. Indianapolis: Hackett, 1987. Presents a first-rate translation of the *Poetics*. Thorough, extensive notes.

Else, Gerald F. *Plato and Aristotle on Poetry*. Edited by Peter Burian. Chapel Hill: University of North Carolina Press, 1986. This posthumous edition of the work of an outstanding Aristotelian scholar and translator has eleven chapters devoted to a discussion of the *Poetics*.

Grube, G. M. A., trans. *On Poetry and Style*. New York: Macmillan, 1986. Provides an excellent translation of the *Poetics*. Directly relevant to the study of language and literature. Good introduction and notes.

Halliwell, Stephen. *Aristotle's Poetics*. Chapel Hill: University of North Carolina Press, 1986.

Provides a thorough and extensive commentary on the *Poetics*. Includes Halliwell's own translation and a helpful bibliography.

Olson, Elder, ed. *Aristotle's "Poetics" and English Literature: A Collection of Critical Essays.* Chicago: University of Chicago Press, 1965. Discusses the *Poetics* and its history; also demonstrates the Aristotelian method of literary analysis. Olson's introduction is an excellent place to begin study of the *Poetics*.

POETRY OF CAMPION

Author: Thomas Campion (1567-1620)
Principal published works: Poemata, 1595; *A Booke of Ayres*, 1601; *Two Bookes of Ayres*,
  1613; *The Third and Fourthe Booke of Ayres*, 1617

Of the lyric poets of the English Renaissance, Thomas Campion is for some readers one of the most difficult to appreciate and value. He is not a "difficult" poet in the way John Donne, his more famous contemporary, is difficult, for he is not a poet, as is Donne, with whom one must struggle because of the density of his language, meaning, and imagery. Campion's language is transparent, his meaning is seldom in doubt, and his imagery is both simple and conventional. Campion comes close to being a pure lyricist whose excellence is not to be described by an appeal to intellectual complexity or to originality, in the Romantic sense of the term, but by an appeal to art, artifice, technique, and the elegant handling of tradition.

Though he wrote some fine religious lyrics and an occasional moral apostrophe, Campion's true subject is love—not the immediate and frankly sexual love of Donne's early poetry, but rather the politely erotic game of literary and aristocratic love. The poetry never pretends to be anything but an elegant and highly artificial kind of play, and the poems are full of the conventions, both thematic and stylistic, of the highly formal love poetry of the Renaissance. Amarillis, Laura, shepherds and shepherdesses, rosy cheeks, tears and sighs, Cupids, nymphs, gods and goddesses, cruel maids and faithless swains abound in Campion. The stylized voices in the poems never utter so immediate and passionate a statement as that which opens Donne's "Canonization": "For God's sake hold your tongue, and let me love." Campion's speakers utter words that evoke not an immediate situation but a set of general, literary conventions: "O Love, where are thy shafts, thy quiver, and thy bow?"

The special skills and concerns of a poet like Campion, who wrote within a set of traditional conventions—many of them now unfamiliar—must be well understood before his verse can yield its special excellence. Campion was a highly educated man who wrote for a highly sophisticated and educated society. He was trained in both law and medicine, and his schooling and his literary tastes both in reading and writing were strongly classical. His first publication was a group of greatly admired Latin poems, the *Poemata*. In many of his English poems there are verbal echoes of the great Roman poets, Horace, Martial, and, particularly, Catullus, the Roman lyricist of love *par excellence*. Not only are there specific references to the ancient poets in the poetry, but the atmosphere of many of the poems is powerfully classical, even though the poem has no definite Latin ancestor, and even though, as is usually the case, the setting and world in the poem is English and Renaissance modern (for example, "Jacke and Jone they thinke no ill," or "There is a garden in her face"). The classical influence is not merely a matter of allusion to ancient poets and mythology. Such allusions are frequent enough—for example, his imitation of Catullus' most famous poem in "My sweetest Lesbia let us live and love"—but not overwhelmingly present. More important is the stylistic influence. The sharply turned epigrammatic statements, the tightly controlled form and language, the avoidance of metaphor and other spectacular figures of speech, the bittersweet and ironic tone that characterize Campion's verse, these and other such things are largely the product of the poet's imitation in English of classical Latin poetry. The significance of all this is enhanced when it is remembered that the people for whom Campion wrote were also widely read in or at least familiar with ancient poetry. Thus a reference or turn of speech that might puzzle later readers would seem natural, elegant, and effective to Campion's original audience.

Related to these matters is Campion's advocacy of writing English poetry in classical meters. The poet, in a very controversial pamphlet, *Observations in the Art of English Poesie* (1602), argued that for English poetry to achieve the highest excellence, poets should avoid rhyme, as did the ancients, and should count poetic feet in terms of the quantitative lengths of vowel sounds rather than in the more natural to English (as opposed to Latin and Greek) method of counting strong and weak accentual stresses. Campion and others who espoused this argument had little effect, and their crusade is now thought of as a literary curiosity. As a matter of fact, Campion himself managed to write only one truly successful rhymeless poem in classical meters ("Rosecheekt Lawra, come"); all of his most admired pieces are in standard English accentual meters, and are in rhyme. Yet it is significant that Campion was involved in this controversy. It shows us how important classical practice was to him, how intense was his involvement in the literary arguments of his time, and how particular was his concern with the most technical aspects of his art.

Important as the classical aspect of Campion's art is, however, it must be made clear that much of the traditional material in the poems is drawn from the late medieval courtly love tradition as it was filtered into Renaissance English letters through the poetry of the Italian Petrarchan tradition and the sixteenth century French tradition (itself heavily influenced by the Italian accomplishment) exemplified in the poetry of Pierre de Ronsard and his followers. Nor should the native English tradition of amatory verse from Geoffrey Chaucer through Sir Thomas Wyatt and Edmund Spenser be minimized, although it, too, was heavily influenced by the Italian tradition at every stage. In this literary complex, readers were made familiar with the sighing lover, the abandoned maid, and many other such conventions. It is enough to recognize that Campion wrote within the multifaceted, cosmopolitan tradition of the Renaissance love lyric and that the classics, although not the whole of Campion's interest, were the most conscious non-English focus of his attention and taste.

Just as readers must be aware of the various literary factors that helped shape Campion's work, they must also be aware of the influence music had on the poetry. Campion, besides being a poet, was a talented composer who wrote almost all of his verse to be set to his own music. In fact, the poet did not often think of his music and his poetry separately. He composed each with an eye to the other, and his overall artistic goal, as he said, was to join his "words and notes lovingly together." In his work, song gives meaning to the poem, and poem gives meaning to the song.

Campion's success as a poet-composer had much to do with the fact that he lived in a great age of English music, the age of such composers (many of whom he knew) as William Byrd, John Wilbye, Thomas Morley, John Dowland, Thomas Weelkes, and Orlando Gibbons. The great achievements of all of these composers was in the area of vocal music, and their age thought music and poetry to be much more interdependent than did later ages. The most well-known form of English Renaissance music was the madrigal, a complex kind of song for two to seven voices (though sometimes instruments were substituted for some of the voices). Each voice sang a different melodic line, and thus the simple lyric of the madrigal tended to be dominated by the complexity of the performance. Campion did not concentrate on writing madrigals but the "ayre," a relatively simple, clear melodic line composed to be sung by one or two voices to the accompaniment of the lute. As was not true in the madrigal, in the ayre the melody and the poetry were of equal value, and neither dominated the other.

Readers of Campion's poetry should always remember that the poems alone are less than half the artistic effect Campion originally created. Both the music and, crucially, the artistry of the performer are left out. The reader should also remember that any judgment of the poems separate from the available music, no matter how sensitive, is bound to be less than adequate. An analogy might be made to the twentieth century popular song. How flat would be the experience of reading an anthology of such song poems as compared to the effect of hearing the poems and the music in performance. This analogy breaks down, for those song poems seldom claimed to be distinguished poetry, whereas Campion's lyrics (and the lyrics of many of his contemporaries, including William Shakespeare) do claim to be fine poems as well as good words to accompany good music.

As for Campion's idea of how music should be composed and how the nature of poetry was analogous to the nature of music, there is his statement from the preface to his first *Booke of Ayres*. "What Epigrams are in Poetrie, the same are Ayres in musicke, then in their chiefe perfection when they are short and well seasoned."

Even though his technical mastery and art seldom fail, Campion is better read in selection than in his entirety. His poetic world of love is narrow and can become monotonous. Among those poems of Campion most often admired are "When to Her lute Corinna Sings," "There is a Garden in Her face," "Follow Your Saint, Follow with Accents Sweet," "I Care Not for these Ladies," "Shall I Come, sweet Love, to thee?" "Never love unless You Can Beare With All the Faults of a Man," "Rose-cheekt Lawra, Come," "When Thou Must Home to Shades of Underground," and "Harke, all you ladies that do sleep." Many other poems might be named here, but these provide a fair and wide sample of the poet's excellence.

Bibliography:

Davis, Walter R. *Thomas Campion*. Boston: Twayne, 1987. An excellent beginner's source for the study of Campion's works. Covers Campion's life, song, poetry, music, masques, and reputation in a thorough but accessible fashion. Includes selected bibliography, a chronology, and an index listing individual poems.

Eldridge, Muriel T. *Thomas Campion: His Poetry and Music (1567-1620)*. New York: Vantage Press, 1971. An uncomplicated study, beginning with a brief discussion of English poetry before 1600. Also includes an examination and appreciation of Campion's poetry, music, and life. Includes a bibliography.

Kastendieck, Miles Merwin. *England's Musical Poet: Thomas Campion*. New York: Oxford University Press, 1938. One of the first studies of the poetry to consider the influences of the music as well.

Lindley, David. *Thomas Campion*. Leiden, The Netherlands: E. J. Brill, 1986. A comprehensive study of Campion's poetry, music, and court masques. Pays special attention to Campion's metrical theories and the relationships between poetry and music. Bibliography and index of first lines.

Ryding, Erik S. *In Harmony Framed: Musical Humanism, Thomas Campion, and the Two Daniels*. Kirksville, Mo.: Sixteenth Century Journal Publishers, 1993. Explores why Campion's theoretical writings favor unrhymed quantitative verse, whereas his own poetry is nearly all rhymed. Includes an interesting chapter on the lyric poetry and an extensive bibliography.

POETRY OF CARDUCCI

Author: Giosuè Carducci (1835-1907)

Principal published works: Rime, 1857; *Levia gravia,* 1868; *Odi barbare,* 1877 (*Barbarian Odes,* 1939, rev. 1950); *Nuove odi barbare,* 1882 (*New Barbarian Odes,* 1939, rev. 1950); *Terze odi barbare,* 1889 (*Third Barbarian Odes,* 1939, rev. 1950); *Rime e ritmi,* 1899 (*The Lyrics and Rhythms,* 1942); *A Selection of His Poems,* 1913.

Rarely has a poet in modern times been awarded the admiration and adulation during his lifetime that was accorded by the people of Italy to Giosuè Carducci. Regarded as a national prophet, as well as the unofficial poet laureate of Italy, he was, for many years prior to his death, something of an Italian institution. In addition to his career as poet and essayist, he was a highly successful member of the academic world. For more than forty years he served as a professor of literature at the University of Bologna. He was awarded the Nobel Prize in Literature in 1906.

As a poet, Carducci was a nonconformist in his time, a fact that accounts for much of his popularity in Italy and his importance in the history of Italian literature. When he began his career, Italian poetry was and had been for many years inferior to Italian prose. A romantic interest in the past and its glories had become a burden to poetry. Carducci pointed the way to a new style, however, by looking at contemporary events and the possibilities of the future: the greatness of Italy, its culture and its national unity. Carducci had the opinion that poetry had a part to play in the great awakening—political, religious, and literary—that seemingly was about to break in his native country.

From the beginning, Carducci reacted consciously against romanticism. As a member of the "Amici Pedanti," a circle of young Italian writers, he worked to return Italian poetry to classicism. This change, hoped Carducci, would revitalize the poetry of his native land. His verse is simple, heroic, and solemn in tone. There is none of the excessive verbiage, emotion, or metaphor typical of romantic literature. All is restrained and controlled.

Carducci also tried to revive the classical meters. This interest may be explained partly by the strong humanistic element in his education and academic environment. In his first volume of poems, *Rime,* he decries two influences on Italian culture: romanticism and Christianity. Carducci expresses through his early poems a belief that classicism in art and paganism in religion would invigorate Italian art and culture.

Another volume of poems, mainly about contemporary political events, followed. It was *Levia gravia.* Critics in Italy and abroad have felt that the political slanting of the poems in this volume weaken Carducci's oeuvre. One of Carducci's best-known and most controversial poems, *Hymn to Satan,* was published in 1865. Invoking Satan as other poets had invoked the muses, Carducci complains that Christianity is moribund and is carrying the world to death with it, that rust is gnawing at the mystical sword of the Archangel Michael. He goes on to call back paganism as a means of freeing the human mind. Satan in the poem is presented as a spirit of paganism, the spirit that evoked the sculpture, the pictures, and the literature of classical antiquity, as well as the pantheon of gods and goddesses. Carducci writes too that this was the spirit behind such great rebels against the Roman Catholic church as John Wycliffe, Hus, Girolamo Savonarola, and Martin Luther—men who unbound human thought from the fetters with which orthodoxy had, according to Carducci, bound it. Satan is in the poem not one symbol but many. He symbolizes progress, intellectuality, anticlericism, progress, and the good influence of classical thought. Satan becomes for Carducci a helper, not an adversary, of humanity.

The political aspects of Italian culture and life were never far from Carducci's mind and art. Sometimes he favored those in power and sometimes he did not. In the 1850's he was for a time the darling of the monarchists because of such poems as "La Croce di Savoia" and the "Canzone a Vittorio Emanuele," for as the years went by, Carducci tended away from his earlier republicanism and became satisfied with a monarchy for his beloved Italy.

Carducci did not, on the other hand, change his mind very much about the church. Although he became less bitter about the cultural significance of the Roman Catholic church in Italy, he could not reconcile his views of art with Christian theology, as *Hymn to Satan* shows. Carducci believed that beauty had reached its best expression in Greek and Roman art. This belief caused him to try to return to classical expression, even to the meters of classical poetry. It was in this pagan view of the world, which he tried to express, that the poet found tranquil loveliness. When Carducci wrote of his native land, he found in pagan religion and its spirit something that welcomed the reality of the land and its creatures, instead of repressing the things of this world as Christianity, with its emphasis on another, spiritual world, seemed to him to do. In Carducci's poems about the Italian countryside, there is a suggestion of the early Vergil. It is as if the poet, sometimes tired of struggling in political and cultural battles, retired to the country for peace, security, and contentment.

Carducci differs, however, from the English poets of the nineteenth century. Unlike Wordsworth, Carducci does not moralize about what he finds in nature and the rural life; unlike Keats, he shies away from the sensuous, from the emotional, and the subjective. Carducci seems merely to have looked for and found contentment of a kind. Such expression is found, for example, in "Il Bove," a poem about the mild, strong, and patient ox, whose eyes mirror for the poet the green and divine silence of the fields. It is not strange to find that the poet says in a poem to Vergil that the Roman poet's verse is to him like the sea, a line of mountains, or the breeze in tall trees. Again, in "A un Asino," Carducci used the donkey as a symbol of ancient patience and asks, at the same time, if it may not be love that moves the donkey to bray. Even "Presso una Certosa," a poem written about landscape near a monastery, is a poem on the loveliness of the countryside, a loveliness which leads the poet to think of pagan times and things, and ends with the hope that the poet may be visited by the spirit of Homer.

At times Carducci seems to feel that he could have chosen a better life by living in the countryside, instead of writing about the disturbances of his native land. His "Idyl of the Maremma" finds him writing of a vigorous countrywoman meant for bearing vigorous sons and daughters. Better to have loved and won her, to have lived with such a one in the country amid a large and healthy family, writes the poet, than to sweat in small rhymes, to write painfully of sad and miserable things, and to seek out the ambiguous answers to the riddles of the universe.

Although he was a reformer in poetry and the foe of slavish imitation of the past, Carducci revered the great poets, as his poems to Dante Alighieri, to Vergil, and to Homer testify. The poet of nineteenth century Italy did not deny the greatness of his predecessors; he simply wished to find his own vein of work, one that might be as productive for him and his age as those the great poets of the past had found for themselves and their ages. Even though he could not use the same materials as Dante, Carducci realized the greatness of *The Divine Comedy* (c. 1320) and praised Dante for it. Carducci expressed his awareness, however, that the greatness of Dante's time was gone and only the greatness of the song remained.

Few American readers know Carducci and his poetry. He was essentially a lyric poet, and much is lost when a lyric is taken from one language and remade in the words of another. In Carducci's case this is particularly true. His materials, spirit, and style remain essentially Italian, resistant to adequate translation in another language.

Bibliography:

Barricelli, Jean-Paul. "Giosuè Carducci." In *European Authors: 1000-1900: A Biographical Dictionary of European Literature*. Edited by Stanley J. Kunitz and Vineta Colby. New York: H. W. Wilson, 1967. Describes Carducci's life and works. Bibliography.

Klopp, Charles. "Giosuè Carducci (1835-1907)." In *Charles Baudelaire to the Well-Made Play*. Vol. 7 in *European Writers: The Romantic Century*, edited by Jacques Barzun and George Stade. New York: Charles Scribner's Sons, 1985. Discusses reasons for Carducci's decline in popularity after his death. Places the poet in the cultural context of his time. Bibliography.

POETRY OF CAREW

Author: Thomas Carew (1594 or 1595-1640)
Principal published works: Coelum Britannicum, 1634; *Poems,* 1640

Thomas Carew unites, with more success than any of his contemporary poets at the court of Charles I, the classical clarity of Ben Jonson with the intellectual wit of John Donne; at his best he produced work worthy of both of his masters, and almost all of his poems are polished and entertaining. Like the other best-known Cavalier poets, Sir John Suckling, Richard Lovelace, Thomas Randolph, and William Davenant, he devoted much of his attention to the song and the love lyric, complimenting real or imaginary ladies. There are few lovelier poems of this type than Carew's "Ask Me No More":

> Aske me no more where Jove bestowes,
> When June is past, the fading rose:
> For in your beauties orient deepe,
> These flowers as in their causes, sleepe.
>
> Aske me no more whether doth stray,
> The golden Atomes of the day:
> For in pure love heaven did prepare
> Those powders to inrich your haire.
>
> . . . .
> Aske me no more if East or West,
> The Phenix builds her spicy nest:
> For unto you at last shee flies,
> And in your fragrant bosome dyes.

The images of the fading rose, the golden atoms, and the phoenix are the traditional ones of Renaissance love poetry, made fresh by the purity of Carew's diction, and they combine to form a tribute which, in effect, transcends the compliment of a single lover to a particular lady and becomes a tribute to all beauty.

Like Ben Jonson, Carew builds much of his love poetry upon the imagery and the themes of the Greek and Roman lyric poets. Classical deities, especially Cupid, find their way into many of his poems, and countless of his verses are variations upon the familiar "Carpe Diem" theme of Horace, the notion expressed so well by Robert Herrick in his "Gather Ye Rosebuds While Ye May." Typical of Carew's treatment of the transience of beauty are these lines from one of his longer works, "To A. L., Persuasions to Love":

> For that lovely face will faile
> Beautie's sweet, but beautie's fraile
> 'Tis sooner past, 'tis sooner done
> Then Summers raine, or winters Sun:
> Most fleeting when it is most deare,
> 'Tis gone while wee but say 'tis here.

While the language and imagery of Carew's love poems, his skill at handling a variety of stanza forms, and the melodious quality of his verses, which were often sung, reveal his place as one of the "Sons of Ben," he adopts in many of his lyrics the cynical tone and, occasionally, the bizarre imagery of Donne's early works. He borrows the Metaphysical practice of speaking of love in terms of religion, commerce, or geography, and he uses the device skillfully; however, his language almost always seems derivative, while that of Donne impresses the reader as revelation of new and vital relationships. The song, "To my inconstant Mistress," shows Carew's use of a theological vocabulary to speak of his lady:

> When thou, poore excommunicate
> From all the joyes of love, shalt see
> The full reward, and glorious fate,
>   Which my strong faith shall purchase me,
>   Then curse thine owne inconstancie.

Carew's court poetry is witty, elegant, and amusing, but it very rarely, even at its most sensual, conveys anything of the emotional or intellectual power of Donne's work. It is in this sense typical of the writing of the Caroline poets, who were, like their French contemporaries, the *precieux*, generally concerned with form rather than with the expression of either ideas or feelings. (The presence of Charles I's queen, Henrietta Maria, sister of Louis XIII, at the English court insured some influence of contemporary French culture on English writers.) Even the highly erotic "A Rapture," a glorification of physical love, is so metaphorical in its language that it evokes little sense of real passion.

Carew was, on occasion, capable of breaking out of the conventional bonds of his generation, and he reveals an unexpected strength in his brilliant elegy on Donne, in which he follows his predecessor's techniques closely in paying tribute to him. At the very beginning of the poem, Carew imitates Donne's abrupt, terse style and his strikingly original imagery. He asks why the age has offered no epitaph for one of its great men:

> Can we not force from widdowed Poetry,
> Now thou art dead (Great Donne) one Elegie
> To crowne thy Hearse? Why yet dare we not trust
> Though with unkneaded dowe-bak't prose thy dust,
> Such as the unscisor'd Churchman from the flower
> Of fading Rhetorique, short liv'd as his houre,
> Dry as the sand that measures it, should lay
> Upon thy Ashes, on the funerall day?

Carew captures much of the spirit of Donne's achievement in his reference to "the flame/ Of thy brave Soule, that shot such heat and light,/ As burnt our earth, and made our darknesse bright." The disparate images that follow, related to the themes of gardening, the payment of debts, mining, and harvesting, are fused into a whole through the logical coherence of Carew's comments on Donne's genius and originality. Even here, however, Carew shows his allegiance to a dual tradition, concluding with a Jonsonian epitaph:

> Here lies a King, that rul'd as hee thought fit
> The universall Monarchy of wit;
> Here lie two Flamens, and both those, the best,
> Apollo's first, at last, the true Gods priest.

Carew's contrasting styles could scarcely be seen more clearly than by comparing the poem on Donne with the simple "Epitaph on the Lady Mary Villers," a lyric much like many of Jonson's elegies:

This little Vault, this narrow roome,
Of Love, and Beautie is the tombe;
The dawning beame that 'gan to cleare
Our clouded skie, lyes darkned here,
For ever set to us, by death
Sent to enflame the world beneath;
'Twas but a bud, yet did containe
More sweetnesse then shall spring againe
A budding starre that might have growne
Into a Sun, when it had blowne
This hopefull beautie, did create
New life in Loves declining state;
But now his Empire ends, and we
From fire, and wounding darts are free:
His brand, his bow, let no man feare
The flames, the arrowes, all lye here.

Carew here draws skillfully on the classical tradition for the reference to Cupid and for the brevity and conciseness of his form. His handling of the tetrameter line is, throughout his works, masterful, and he achieves an elegiac spirit almost as moving in its simplicity as Jonson's epitaph on Elizabeth, L. H.: "Under-neath this stone doth lye/ As much beautie, as could dye."

In addition to the love songs and elegies that make up the majority of Carew's poems, he wrote several long verse epistles, modeled on those of Horace and Jonson's imitations of them. These works foreshadow the long reflective poems of the neoclassic age; written in heroic couplets, they are meditative, philosophical, occasionally satirical, essentially conversations in verse. In one of these epistles, addressed "To Ben Jonson, upon Occasion of his Ode of Defiance annext to his Play of the New Inne," Carew mildly and sympathetically chides his aging master for allowing the strictures of contemporary critics to move him; though Jonson may have created all his works, like children, with equal love, onlookers "may distinguish of their sexe, and place":

Let others glut on the extorted praise
Of vulgar breath, trust thou to after dayes:
Thy labour'd workes shall live, when Time devoures
Th' abortive off-spring of their hastie houres.
Thou art not of their ranke, the quarrell lyes
Within thine own Virge, then let this suffice,
The wiser world doth greater Thee confesse
Then all men else, then Thy selfe onely lesse.

The epistle to Aurelian Townshend, a minor poet who had addressed to Carew verses requesting him to write an elegy on the recently deceased king of Sweden, Gustavus Adolphus, a powerful military commander, gives interesting insight into Carew's sense of his function as a poet. He is no chronicler of heroic deeds:

But these are subjects proper to our clyme
Tourneyes, Masques, Theaters, better become
Our Halcyon dayes; what though the German Drum
Bellow for freedome and revenge, the noyse
Concernes not us, nor should divert our joyes.

Revels and pastoral poetry are the most suitable for him and Townshend, not the chronicles of heroes; he seems to have had no sense that the "halcyon dayes" were soon to draw to a bloody close.

Carew's epistles covered a variety of subjects. As a court poet he often wrote verses welcoming courtiers who returned from abroad, congratulating members of the royal family on their birthdays or on the arrival of a new prince, or commending the plays and poems of his friends as they appeared before the public. His style varied with the subject matter, shifting from Jonsonian clarity and straightforwardness to the intricate vocabulary of the followers of Donne. The latter mode predominates in lines like the following, from the epistle "To my worthy friend Master George Sands, on his translation of the Psalmes":

> I Presse not to the Quire, nor dare I greet
> The holy place with my unhallowed feet;
> My unwasht Muse, Pollutes not things Divine,
> Nor mingles her prophaner notes with thine;
> Here, humbly at the porch she listning stayes,
> And with glad eares sucks in thy sacred layes.

Carew's most extended work is his masque, *Coelum Britannicum*, presented at Whitehall in 1634. The intellectual content of this work far surpasses that of the other Caroline masques, in which theme and dialogue were generally sacrificed to elaborate dances and complex stage effects. For the subject of the masque and for the content of most of the prose passages Carew drew upon the work of the late sixteenth century Italian philosopher Giordano Bruno. The plot concerns a revolution on Mount Olympus; the gods have been so moved by the virtue of the English monarchs that they have resolved to reform, and all the constellations, which represent the old morality, have been banished from the sky. Momus and Mercury, given the task of choosing worthy figures to replace them, listen to the claims of several bizarre figures: Wealth, Poverty, Fortune, and Pleasure. Each of these professes to be the most influential force in determining human actions. The masque ends with an elaborate pageant glorifying the virtues of King Charles and Henrietta Maria; the monarch and his courtiers, dressed as british heroes, take their places in the heavens as the new constellations.

Carew was probably the ablest of all the Cavalier poets. He shows, in flashes, an intellectual depth and a control of language that suggest his potential greatness. However, his poetic output was limited, partly by his own preference for the gay life of the court, partly by the poetic fashions of his day. He seems to have lacked that spark of genius that can transform conventions and the techniques of others into great original work.

Bibliography:
Barbour, Reid. "'Wee, of th' adult'rate mixture not complaine': Thomas Carew and Poetic Hybridity." *John Donne Journal* 7, no. 1 (1988): 92-113. Examines such characteristic qualities of Carew's poetry as doubts about the value of lyric love poems; ambivalence about investing the poet's personality in enduring matters like letters; attempts to find a form to accommodate and synthesize these ambivalencies. Shows precedents for these tendencies and traces them in several of Carew's poems.
Low, Anthony. "Thomas Carew: Patronage, Family, and New-Model Love." In *Renaissance Discourses of Desire*, edited by Claude J. Summers and Ted-Larry Pebworth. Columbia: University of Missouri Press, 1993. Discusses the unconventional absence of Petrarchism in Carew's love poetry. Traces his life circumstances and demonstrates that Carew's failure to

secure traditional patronage forced him into rebellion and a reworking of conceptions of love in economic terms.

Parker, Michael P. "Diamond's Dust: Carew, King, and the Legacy of Donne." In *The Eagle and the Dove: Reassessing John Donne*, edited by Claude J. Summers and Ted-Larry Pebworth. Columbia: University of Missouri Press, 1986. Focuses on Carew's elegy to John Donne, exploring how succeeding generations of poets reconciled the two sides of Donne's personality. Follows Carew's argument in the "Elegy," showing that Carew synthesizes Donne's biography through paradox using Donne's own poetic methods.

Sadler, Lynn. *Thomas Carew*. Boston: Twayne, 1979. A standard introduction to all aspects of Carew's life and writings. Tackles the problem of categorizing Carew and focuses on the secular nature of the poems. Includes close readings of individual poems.

Van Velzen, Antoon. "Two Versions of the Funeral Elegy: Henry King's 'The Exequy' and Thomas Carew's '. . . Elegie Upon . . . Donne.'" *Comitatus* 15 (1984): 45-57. Compares two of the best funeral elegies on John Donne. Treating the difficulty of the formal argument, he concludes that this elegy is an intricate paean to language itself, as much as it is a lament and encomium for Donne.

POETRY OF CLARE

Author: John Clare (1793-1864)
Principal published works: Poems Descriptive of Rural Life and Scenery, 1820; *The Village Minstrel and Other Poems,* 1821; *The Shepherd's Calendar,* 1827; *The Rural Muse,* 1835

Country-born and country-bred, enjoying literary success in London until the late 1820's, ending his days in a madhouse: The curve of John Clare's life is important to appreciate in any reading of his poetry. Clare's roots in the language and customs of the country, more specifically of the little village of Helpstone on the borders of the Lincolnshire Fens, are immediately evident in his earlier poems, as are his extremely delicate perceptions, the totalism of a sensibility nearly always hovering on the edge either of ecstasy or of despair. Less evident are his strong literary affiliations with the James Thomson of *The Seasons* (1726-1730), the William Wordsworth of the "Ode: Intimations of Immortality," the Byron of *Childe Harold's Pilgrimage* (1812-1818). With Robert Burns, Clare is one of the finest of the "original geniuses" of the late eighteenth and early nineteenth centuries, and he wrote in a vein more authentic and serious than was then in vogue. His own Northamptonshire version of the conserving myth of the countryside, eloquently expressed in his lament for the loss of Swordy Fell by the enclosures of the 1820's, is in the line of Thomas Gray and Wordsworth and points directly to the writings of William Barnes and Thomas Hardy later in the nineteenth century.

Clare's provincialism, his distance from the literary fashions of his early manhood, permitted him to mine his slender gift deeply. Again and again he returns to the themes, the moral and technical elements that are present in his earliest poems. The same subjects are to him always new and pressing: the importance of place, the loss of childhood innocence, the destruction of the countryside, absence in love, the poet as nature's spokesperson. There is an uncomplicated resting in nostalgic description rather than a thrusting and exploratory meditation; there is no Wordsworthian straining after the philosophical poem, and Clare's successes are therefore more limited but purer than Wordsworth's.

Clare's ordinary medium is the loosened heroic couplet, the informal ballad stanza, the simple quatrain of the later Augustans, and he is not above using the "poetic diction" that Wordsworth explicitly rejected. Clare's originality was not one of perspective or technique so much as it was the focusing of a single-minded intensity upon the problems and perceptions of people living in the country. The "ecstasy" Clare so often alludes to explains much in the tone of his poems on nature and on human love; but it is also directly related to a personal instability, the delicacy or fragility that led to the madness he himself had been anticipating.

Clare begins one of his best poems thus: "Hail, humble Helpstone. . . . Unletter'd spot! unhead in poet's song." The peculiarly Romantic celebration of the local and unique is here, but also a sense that the obscure village may be taken as standing for hundreds of others like it, places finally being encroached upon by wealth and civilization. The enclosure of common forage lands and the leveling of woodlands are concerns even as early as this poem of 1809:

> How oft I've sigh'd at alterations made,
> To see the woodman's cruel axe employ'd
> A tree beheaded, or bush destroy'd.

The resulting conviction that nature is herself somehow threatened accounts for some of the loving anxiousness in Clare's descriptions of both landscape and village life. One may take for an instance the fine stanza from "Summer Images":

To note on hedgrow baulks, in moisture spent,
The jetty snail creep from the mossy thorn,
With earnest heed and tremulous intent,
Frail brother of the morn,
That from the tiny bent's dew-misted leaves
Withdraws his timid horn,
And fearful vision weaves.

The descriptive vignette, complete in a stanza, is characteristic. Clare is a cataloger, a poet who, with an evocative title ("Morning," "Autumn") or a generalizing opening, launches a poem organized mainly into a progression of instances. "Noon" begins multiplying instances and images with the second line of the poem:

All how silent and how still;
Nothing heard but yonder mill:
While the dazzled eye surveys
All around a liquid blaze;
And amid the scorching gleams,
If we earnest look, it seems
As if crooked bits of glass
Seemed repeatedly to pass. . . .
Not a twig is seen to shake,
Nor the smallest bent to quake;

"Liquid blaze," though obviously a piece of poetic diction, is nevertheless a small triumph of authenticity. In line with this effect is Clare's inclination to relate human moods to the four seasons. One remembers his comment that the first poetry that genuinely moved him was Thomson's *The Seasons*. Perhaps the finest of his nature poems is "Autumn," written in the unrhymed stanza of William Collins' "Ode to Evening":

Soon must I view thee as a pleasant dream
Droop faintly, and so reckon for thine end,
As sad the winds sink low
In dirges for their queen;
While in the moment of their weary pause,
To cheer thy bankrupt pomp, the willing lark
Starts from his shielding clod,
Snatching sweet scraps of song.

Here as elsewhere there are comparisons made between nature and human nature. This analogy works both ways; sometimes there are such phrases as "wind-enamoured aspen" ("Summer Images"). At other times childhood and virginity find images in the blooming of trees or flowers: "Young Jenny blooming in her womanhood/ That hides from day like lilies while in bud." In the poems of Clare's madness, when he writes of the impossibility of recovering his childhood, or of repossessing the unblemished love of his first sweetheart, Mary Joyce, he unconsciously connects his loss with the moods of the natural world. He longs "for scenes, where man hath never trod," where he can

. . . sleep as I in childhood sweetly slept,
Untroubling, and untroubled where I lie,
The grass below—above the vaulted sky.

5187

In such poems as "The Village Minstrel," "To the Rural Muse," "Pastoral Poesy," and "The Progress of Rhyme," Clare sets forth the naïve poetics that informs all his lyric utterance. He engaged in a radical but fruitful confusion of the process of writing and the observation of natural phenomena: "Wordsworth I love, his books are like the fields" ("To Wordsworth"); "True poesy is not in words,/ But images that thoughts express," and observation affords "A language that is ever green. . . . As hawthorn blossoms, soon as seen,/ Give May to every heart." ("Pastoral Poesy"). It is one indication of Clare's provinciality that he meant these lines quite literally.

The most important result of this assumption about the nature and function of poetry is Clare's accuracy of image and phrase. Where the local English is most apt, he will use it, though the effect is idiosyncratic:

> —And never choose
> The little sinky foss,
> Streaking the moors whence spared
> water spews
> From pudges fringed with moss. . . .

No animal, insect, or scene is too insignificant to bear description: "I see. . . . I see" is one of Clare's most habitual phrases, and when he writes of "shower-bedimpled sandy lanes," "smoke-tanned chimney tops," or "broad old cesspools" that "glittered in the sun," he is bringing new veridical images into English poetry. In "Eternity of Nature," Clare praises the power behind nature by a marvelously convincing collection of the ways the number five recurs in the phenomena of the world:

> So trailing bindweed, with its pinky cup,
> Five leaves of paler hue go streaking up;
> And many a bird, too, keeps the rule alive,
> Laying five eggs, nor more nor less than five.

John Keats thought that Clare was too descriptive, that the images from nature tend in his poetry to remain instances rather than being integrated with sentiment and meditation. The judgment is correct as far as it goes; Clare had visual accuracy but his descriptive success must be matched against the larger enterprise of Wordsworth, who risked his poetry itself to make it a moral and teaching medium. In Wordsworth and Keats, observation leads more quickly to meditation than in Clare, a poet who does not explore the more symbolic uses of the natural image.

Clare is best known for lyric poetry that nevertheless poses serious questions about life and death and eternity. His longer works have many of the same qualities of observation to recommend them. "The Village Minstrel" and "Childe Harold" are both autobiographical, both charged with the same kind of visual acuity one finds in the shorter poems. One gets from these two poems some sense of what the "Eden" of Clare's humble childhood was like in a poor agricultural community. Clare himself never tires of emphasizing that it was in fact a genuine community; this is the burden of the excellent poem on the labors and customs of a country village presented in *The Shepherd's Calendar*. Here Clare describes the work, the sport, the violence, and the frank sexuality of provincial farm communities in the early nineteenth century. The honesty of his genre scenes, like the impetuous couplets of the poem, stand in vivid contrast to *The Shepheardes Calender* (1579) of Edmund Spenser. Clare's "Poems Written in

Madness" remain to be described, yet there is no way to describe them in terms or categories other than those used above to discuss poems written before his confinement for madness. The fact is that the superb poems from this period—"To Wordsworth," "Written in a Thunderstorm," "I've Wandered Many a Weary Mile," "I Am," "Hesperus"—represent only an unconscious focusing on the elements of despair and absence already conveyed earlier in Clare's work.

Bibliography:
Barrell, John. *The Idea of Landscape and the Sense of Place, 1730-1840: An Approach to the Poetry of John Clare.* Cambridge, England: Cambridge University Press, 1972. Convincingly places Clare in a social and cultural perspective. The study from which all further Clare criticism proceeds.
Clare, Johanne. *John Clare and the Bounds of Circumstance.* Kingston, Ontario, Canada: McGill-Queen's University Press, 1987. This study of Clare's interest in the localities around him is less sentimental about his politics than most commentaries. Also provides excellent readings of individual poems.
Haughton, Hugh, Adam Phillips, and Geoffrey Summerfield. *John Clare in Context.* Cambridge, England: Cambridge University Press, 1994. Commissioned to celebrate the bicentennial of Clare's birth. A wide-ranging collection of essays on Clare stemming from various postmodern critical perspectives. Includes essays by such critics as Seamus Heaney, John Lucas, and Nicholas Birns. Also contains an extensive annotated bibliography.
Lucas, John. *England and Englishness: Ideas of Nationhood in English Poetry, 1688-1900.* Iowa City: University of Iowa Press, 1990. Examines Clare's representation of the idea of England in comparison with those of several other poets. Also discusses Clare's depiction of nature and his inner mental state.
Sychrava, Juliet. *Schiller to Derrida: Idealism in Aesthetics.* Cambridge, England: Cambridge University Press, 1989. A convincing defense of Clare's poetic method as opposed to the dominant Romantic tradition of aesthetics represented by Wordsworth.

POETRY OF DU BELLAY

Author: Joachim Du Bellay (1522-1560)
Principal published works: L'Olive, 1549; *Vers Lyriques*, 1549; *Recueil de poésies*, 1549;
  La Musagnoeomachie, 1550; *XIII Sonnets de l'honnête amour*, 1552; *Les Antiquités de
  Rome*, 1558 (partial translation, 1591, as *Ruines of Rome*); *Les Regrets*, 1558 (*The
  Regrets*, 1984); *Poemata*, 1558; *Le Poète courtisan*, 1559

In a short life marked by illness and disappointment, the Angevin nobleman Joachim du
Bellay wrote some of the finest elegiac and satiric poetry in the French language. His earliest
verses, written before 1546, were poor imitations of Clément Marot. With a view to enriching
the French language and demonstrating its potential, Jacques Peletier du Mans, whom Du
Bellay met in 1546, turned him from these sterile efforts to composing odes and sonnets, still
in imitation, but now of Latin and Italian models.

Du Bellay, Pierre de Ronsard, and Jean-Antoine de Baïf, pupils of the Hellenist Jean Dorat,
were inspire by Peletier, who had long thought about a renewal of French poetry. Thomas
Sebillet, taking Marot and his school as guarantors of a new poetry, published his *Art Poétique*
in 1548. Though his definitions were confusing, Sebillet's thesis was essentially the same as
that of Du Bellay and Ronsard, who found themselves doubly frustrated by the theory and the
choice of model. Du Bellay had a number of sonnets and odes already written. To publish these
without commentary would have been to range himself under Sebillet's standard. In the end Du
Bellay wrote not a short preface but his weighty *The Defence and Illustration of the French
Language*, published in 1549. Apparently the manifesto of the young poets known as the
Pléiade, the work was in fact a personal text. Ronsard and the others had their say in outlining
the aims of the group, however, which included defense of a potentially great language against
the Latinizing traditions of Church, university, and humanism, itself; enrichment through the
prudent use of neologisms, archaisms, infinitives and adjectives used as nouns, antonomasia,
and other devices; and, finally, illustration (that is, ennoblement) requiring imitation and
emulation of antique literature. This last had already been undertaken if hesitatingly, by Marot.
The poet—a priest—might deliberately obscure truths, but, divinely inspired (hopefully revealed through love and through a synthesis of Christianity and Platonism), he must combine
inspiration with hard work. Mythology would enshrine such truths, the "*vestiges de rare et
antique érudition*" thus being more than ornamental. Poetry, inseparable from music, should be
"*doux*" (sweet) in intention, thrilling the soul and senses, but it might also be "*utile*" (didactic).
All these ideas, representing the thinking of the young poets at the outset of their careers, were
expressed in *The Defence and Illustration of the French Language*.

With his essay Du Bellay published *L'Olive*, a kind of "*canzoniere*" of fifty sonnets, of which
more than half were of neo-Petrarchan inspiration. Despite its literary inspiration and its frequent Petrarchan antitheses, the world of *L'Olive* is rich and sensuous in its blending of mythological references, impressions of color and sound, nature images, and intellectual subtlety.

Also published with *L'Olive* were the *Vers Lyriques*. Here the poet seems to dominate the
Horatian inspiration of his work, resulting in a more sincere expression of his thoughts than in
L'Olive. Typical themes are the rapid flight of time and the fragility of all worldly goods.

Once the program was stated, Du Bellay's activity was tireless. In 1549 he published a
Recueil de poésies, containing official, mediocre flattery, yet not as in the ode *D'écrire en sa
langue*, forgetting his art. An augmented edition of *L'Olive*, with sixty-five additional sonnets,
appeared in 1550. In the additions there is a change of tone. The poet seeks and achieves solace

for the loss of his lady in Christianity. At this moment, Petrarchism becomes diluted with a fervent Platonism, of which one may see, in the famous sonnet 113, a precise statement. The poet is liberated from the problems of time and earthly beauty by the soul's winged ascent to reexperience (*reconnaître*) the eternal Idea of Beauty, Goodness, and Truth. A striking example of Du Bellay's syncretism is to be seen in sonnet 114 of *L'Olive*, where Platonic terms are combined with a text from Saint Paul's Epistle to the Romans. There also appeared in 1550 *La Musagnoeomachie* (battle of the Muses against ignorance). François I, Henri II, great contemporary statesmen, and poets join in the struggle.

His poetry may have won the poet glory and immortality for his patrons, but the latter did not respond well. Du Bellay was by now a sick man, and his poetic vein seemed to be drying up. Yet poetry seems to have had at least a therapeutic function. Having turned to Christianity for support, Du Bellay found a new purpose: to champion Christian morality. He rejected love poetry in the earlier manner, Petrarchism being an ethical issue involving deliberate falsehood such as exaggeration of one's feelings or inordinate flattery. Love poetry in Platonic form was acceptable, however, hence the *XIII Sonnets de l'honnête amour*, a distillation of the researches of Pontus de Tyard, published in 1552, along with a translation of book 4 of Vergil's *Aeneid* and a collection of pieces including the poignant *Complainte du Désespéré*.

In 1553 a new edition of the *Recueil de poésies* appeared, containing the humorously satirical ode *A une dame*, in which postures and clichés of Petrarchan love poetry are rejected in favor of a more human, Gallic, brand of love. Du Bellay mocks too the *topoi* of neo-Platonic love poetry, but he is far from abandoning Platonism and even returns to Petrarchan conceits in some poems.

Du Bellay's satiric genius had reached maturity. His voyage to Rome as secretary to his cousin, Cardinal Jean du Bellay provided him with ample material. Spellbound by the pathetic debris of the great city, perhaps inspired by a sonnet of Baldassare Castiglione, Du Bellay began to write historical, philosophical, and gnomic meditations on time, fatality, decadence, and morality in the sonnets of the *Les Antiquités de Rome*. Both in form and in subject these poems represent a transition from the earlier works of literary inspiration to the personal manner of *The Regrets*. Sonnets in decasyllabic verse alternate with those in Alexandrines, the standard form of *The Regrets*. Often closely imitating Horace, Virgil, and Lucan, Du Bellay creates a poetry of eloquence and of striking images, the first in French literature to celebrate the melancholy beauty of ancient ruins and their significance. In one myth in particular, Du Bellay translates his vision of Rome. It is the *Gigantomachy*, a myth of origins, violent struggle, burial, and immobility.

His fascination for Rome soon turned to bitter disillusionment. In an intimate account of daily impressions, fashioned into the sonnets of *The Regrets*, Du Bellay, suffering nostalgia, pitilessly exposes the state of his heart and denounces the intrigues, vices, and nonchalant immorality of Roman society and of the Curia. This collection of 191 sonnets contains Du Bellay's greatest elegiac and satirical poetry, mature and original. Its purpose, as the poet explained in the exquisite dedicatory *Ode à Jean d'Avanson*, was to ease the sorrow of his exile and, by an act of poetic creation, achieve oblivion to misfortune.

Scorning the learned and ornamental manner of *L'Olive*, Du Bellay begins *The Regrets* with a profession of naturalness and simplicity: "I don't want to leaf through Greek texts, search out the soul of the universe"; rather, "I'll satisfy myself with writing simply." Such simplicity, such facility, is misleading, as the poet well knew when he maliciously discouraged would-be imitators of his vigorous, sinewy Alexandrines.

What is striking in *The Regrets* is Du Bellay's gift for noting the gesture, attitude, color, or detail that characterizes a person or a place. Frequent repetition of the verb "*voir*" (to see) suggests his habit of looking at things, his remarkable faculty for seeing the picturesque detail, often presented by the accumulation of precise technical terms. He often expands the theme of a sonnet in the last line, often through irony, causing the reader's imagination to yield in silence to the creative impulse it has received. Antithesis, however, is the usual instrument of Du Bellay's wit. It appears as a procedure of composition as well as a device of style. The sonnet itself is an antithetical form, and the subject matter of Du Bellay's poetry lends itself to antithetical treatment. Thus in sonnet 6 he contrasts his past life and poetic manner in the quatrains to his present in the tercets. Du Bellay's refusal to be artificial or erudite functions in fact as an artistic device, as John C. Lapp has shown in the case of mythological imagery, which, sparingly used, becomes ironic by lending relief to an idea in contrast to the "simple" language of the whole. The great myth that does dominate the poems is, of course, that of the exile: Ulysses or Jason, or both together, as in the famous sonnet 31.

In 1557, Du Bellay returned to France to flattering acclaim but also legal difficulties, which, with increasing illness, embittered his last three years. *Le Poète courtisan*, a kind of satirical last will and testament, appeared in 1559. Through his ironic advice to the would-be court poet on how to succeed—where he himself had failed—Du Bellay antithetically takes up again the arguments of *The Defence and Illustration of the French Language* that the true poet is learned and inspired, an indication that he, Ronsard, and their group had not yet achieved an uncontested victory.

Du Bellay's miserable end in 1560 must have convinced many poets that the Pléiade's early aim of seeking immortality through poetry was somewhat impractical. The judgment of posterity, however, sees Du Bellay as one of France's greatest satiric and lyric poets, second only to Ronsard in his own age and an uncontested master of the sonnet whose work helped to found modern French poetry.

Bibliography:
Clements, Robert J. *Critical Theory and Practice of the "Pleiade."* Cambridge, Mass.: Harvard University Press, 1942. Discusses the intellectual worlds of the humanists and the poets of the sixteenth century. Helpful in understanding Du Bellay's poetry.
Dickinson, Gladys. *Du Bellay in Rome*. Leiden, The Netherlands: E. J. Brill, 1960. A good presentation of the conditions in Rome in the time of Du Bellay.
Espiner-Scott, Janet. "Some Notes on Joachim Du Bellay." *Modern Language Review* 36 (January, 1941): 59-67. Contains material on Du Bellay sources and discusses significant problems presented by the works.
Keating, L. Clark. *Joachim du Bellay*. New York: Twayne, 1971. Emphasizes the importance of knowing about Du Bellay's background for appreciating the poet and his poetry. Provides an outline and analysis of Du Bellay's major works.
Lapp, John C. "Mythological Imagery in Du Bellay." *Studies in Philology* 61, no. 2, pt. 1 (April, 1964): 109-127. Shows the source of some of Du Bellay's images. An excellent, concise discussion of a very broad topic.

POETRY OF STEFAN GEORGE

Author: Stefan George (1868-1933)

Principal published works: Hymnen, 1890 (*Odes*, 1949); *Pilgerfahrten*, 1891 (*Pilgrimages*, 1949); *Algabal*, 1892 (*Algabal*, 1949); *Die Bücher der Hirten- und Preisgedichte, der Sagen und Sänge, und der hängenden Gärten*, 1895 (*The Books of Eclogues and Eulogies; of Legends and Lays, and of the Hanging Gardens*, 1949); *Das Jahr der Seele*, 1897 (*The Year of the Soul*, 1949); *Der Teppich des Lebens und die Lieder von Traum und Tod, mit einem Vorspiel*, 1899 (*Prelude, the Tapestry of Life and Songs of Dream and of Death*, 1949); *Die Fibel*, 1901 (*The Primer*, 1949); *Der siebente Ring*, 1907 (*The Seventh Ring*, 1949); *Der Stern des Bundes*, 1914 (*The Star of the Covenant*, 1949); *Das neue Reich*, 1928 (*The Kingdom Come*, 1949)

Stefan George was probably the strongest defender of the thesis "art for art's sake" ever to appear in Germany, and his sense of the aesthetic was strong enough to lead him to write his first poems in an invented language, a "lingua romana" similar to Spanish. He disregarded the German rule of grammar that calls for capitalization of all nouns. The resulting loss in reading speed was a most desired effect for the author because he wanted his readers to note that individual words were artistic instruments that may evoke as many, or more, emotions as the colors of a painter's palette. For many years he printed his books privately, and they were not offered to the public until 1899.

In 1890, George published his first series of poems. With the title of the first poem, "Initiation," he indicates how conscious he was of his radical departure from the literary mainstream and of his poetry's limited appeal to an audience used to the outpour of naturalism.

> The river calls! Defiant reeds unfurl
> Their slender banners to the languid breeze
> And check the coaxing ripples as they swirl
> To mossy shores in tender galaxies.

The author surrounded himself with a small treasured circle of devoted friends. Most of his works carry dedications; that of his next work, *Pilgrimages*, was written for the Austrian poet Hugo von Hofmannsthal, although that friendship, as the poem anticipates, never matured:

> Then I journeyed forth
> And became a stranger,
> And I sought for some one
> To share my mournfulness,
> And there was no one.

In *Hymns* and *Pilgrimages*, George illuminates the conflict between his poetic ideals and the baseness of everyday life. For his next work he used earlier historical periods and the Orient as times and places for escape from the unpleasant realities of the present. *Algabal*, written in Paris in 1892, is his personal interpretation of a Roman emperor who moves in a world of time-removed serenity and passionate feelings. George's sense of remoteness, however, never excluded his knowledge of the "mystical body of Christ" inherited from his Catholic childhood in a small town in the German Rhineland: ". . . For I, the one, comprise the multitude . . ."

The Book of Eclogues and Eulogies, of Legends and Lays, and of the Hanging Gardens indicates a turn toward tranquillity; the wanderer once in desperate search for beauty finds it in his own backyard:

> Struck with amazement, as though we were entering a region
> Frostbound when last we had seen it, yet now full of flowers,
> We, who felt old and sorrowful, gazed at each other,
> And our reflections were fused in the river below us.

The Year of the Soul, probably George's best-known book, indicates that the author no longer needed to search for remote backgrounds; an old park is sufficient for the description of images symbolizing the principles of nature and love. Beginning with autumn, the seasons of the year are portrayed, with the exception of the overworked season of spring. The poet invites an unseen friend:

> Come to the park they say is dead, and you
> Will see the glint of smiling shores beyond,
> Pure clouds with rifts of unexpected blue
> Diffuse a light on patterned path and pond.

In *The Year of the Soul* the lonely prophet speaks again: "The word of seers is not for common sharing."

In 1900, George published *Prelude, The Tapestry of Life, The Songs of Dream and of Death*; each of the main sections contains twenty-four poems, and especially in *The Tapestry of Life*, a poet's picture book, George employs the impressionistic power of words. In the prelude, the poet recollects his struggles: "When pale with zeal, I searched for hidden store. . . ." He almost regrets that his stormy period has ended:

> Give me the solemn breath that never failed,
> Give me the fire again that makes us young,
> On which the wings of childhood rose among
> The fumes our earliest offerings exhaled.

The Songs of Dream and of Death is dedicated to persons or occasions in the poet's life; the sequence ends with a forceful description of everlasting conflict:

> All this whirls, tears and pounds, flames and flies,
> Until late in the night-vaulted skies
> They are joined to a bright jewelled beam:
> Fame and glow, pain and bliss, death and dream.

By the time George published *The Seventh Ring* in 1907, a decisive influence had entered his life, the partial fulfillment of his poetic vision. This was his encounter with a young man whom he called Maximin. To George, this youth was the embodiment of a dream and temporarily—Maximin died very young—an end to loneliness. The poet described the appearance of Maximin: "softened by the mobility and vague sadness that centuries of Christian civilization have wrought in the faces of the people . . . youth in that unbroken fullness and purity that can still move mountains." When Maximin died, George considered his death in the light of a mystical, almost religious event:

The forest shivers.
In vain it clothed itself in leaves of spring,
The field your foot made consecrate is numb
And cold without the sun you bring.
The fragile blades on hilly pastures quiver,
For now you never come.

. . . .

You also were elect, so do not mourn
For all the days which unfulfillment sheathed.
Praise to your city where a god was born,
Praise to your time in which a god has breathed!

George's next work, *Star of the Covenant*, a book of a thousand verses, also deals with the significance of Maximin. Some of the poems are not rhymed, but a strong rhythmic flow is present at all times:

You took away the pain of inner schism,
You, who were fusion made incarnate, bringing
The two extremes together: light and frenzy!

The poet pleads again for a spiritual life and complains that the German people do not listen to their prophets, one being Friedrich Wilhelm Nietzsche, who, according to George, delivered his message ". . . With such insistence that his throat was cracked./ And you? The shrewd or dull, the false or true,/ You acted as if nothing had occurred." This collection ends with a chorus declaiming that the power to lead a spiritual life is available.

In 1928 George published his last volume, *The Kingdom Come*, in which he remembers the rich literary inheritance of Johann Wolfgang von Goethe and Friedrich Hölderlin. The book also contains a poetic prophecy about war, which had been written during World War I and seems to anticipate the horrors of the next world conflict.

You shall not cheer. No rise will mark the end,
But only downfalls, many and inglorious.
Monsters of lead and iron, tubes and rods
Escape their maker's hand and rage unruly.

In "Secret Germany," George expresses abhorrence for the regime and pleads that traditional German values be retained. From then on he wrote no more poetry, and after refusing to become identified with Hitler's Germany, he died in self-imposed exile in Switzerland in 1933.

During George's lifetime, his poetry appealed to only a small readership, though many were influenced by his translations of the French poets Stéphane Mallarmé, Charles Baudelaire, and Arthur Rimbaud. Those who were his admirers recognized in him a high priest of German literature, a writer who appeared at a time when the ideals of Goethe were still venerated but poetic expression was in danger of being suffocated by excessive romanticism and sentimentality. Under the poet's leadership, a George Circle was founded, which promoted the idea of transforming life to mystical heights by way of art rather than through scientific positivism. George made the German language an instrument of art and as a poet he carried Germany's classical tradition into the twentieth century. His inventiveness with the German language makes all translation efforts a most difficult undertaking, but the 1949 translations by Olga Marx and Ernst Morwitz succeed in conveying much of George's intensity of feeling into English.

Bibliography:

Antosik, Stanley J. *The Question of Elites: An Essay on the Cultural Elitism of Nietzsche, George, and Hesse*. Bern: Peter Lang, 1978. An intelligent reappraisal of a dominant aspect of early twentieth century literature.

Bennett, Edwin Keppel. *Stefan George*. New Haven, Conn.: Yale University Press, 1954. An interpretive study that appeared as part of a series on modern European literature and thought. Neither partisan nor judgmental, the appraisal is discriminating and concisely presented. Includes bibliography.

George, Stefan. *The Works of Stefan George*. Translated by Olga Marx and Ernst Morwitz. 1949. Rev. ed. Chapel Hill: University of North Carolina Press, 1974. An enlarged and newly edited version of the original English translations of George works. Offers many changes within poems, as well as additional translations intended to give a representative survey of George's earliest poems.

Goldsmith, Ulrich, K. *Stefan George*. New York: Columbia University Press, 1970. Provides a useful overview of the poet's life.

Metzger, Michael M., and Erika A. Metzger. *Stefan George*. New York: Twayne, 1972. A general introduction to the poet, presenting both a biographical sketch and an interpretation of his principal works.

Underwood, Von Edward. *A History of the Self: Essays on the Poetry of Stefan George, Hugo von Hofmannsthal, William Carlos Williams, and Wallace Stevens*. New York: Garland, 1988. A collection of comparative and interpretive essays. Includes bibliography.

POETRY OF LAFORGUE

Author: Jules Laforgue (1860-1887)
Principal published works: Les Complaintes, 1885; *L'Imitation de Notre-Dame la Lune*,
1886; *Derniers Vers*, 1890; *Le Sanglot de la Terre*, 1903 (English translation, 1956 as
Selected Writings of Jules Laforgue; 1958 as *Poems of Jules Laforgue*; 1984 as *Selected
Poems*)

Although Jules Laforgue's span of creative activity was tragically brief (about nine years),
his poetry attests a prolific and versatile innovator. His artistic evolution carried him from the
traditional Alexandrines and somewhat oratorical poems of the posthumous *Le Sanglot de la
Terre*, written between 1878 and 1882, to experimentation with the rhythm and mood of
chansons populaires in *Les Complaintes* and, finally, to culmination in *Derniers Vers*. Here
Laforgue made frequent use of free verse and of what he himself described as psychology in
dream form presented in melodic and rhythmic patterns of verse.

"Funeral March for the Death of the Earth," the most celebrated of the poems in *Le Sanglot
de la Terre*, reveals a young poet who is not afraid to indulge in an uninhibited display of his
personal views and to capitulating to a rather bleak pessimism concerning the state of the
universe. The poet's cries of despair as he bombastically depicts the horrors of civilization and
the corpse of the Earth are rarely muted, as they will be in succeeding works. Certain lines ("The
nocturnal silence of echoless calm,/ Floats, an immense and solitary wreck") are reminiscent of
Charles Baudelaire, the precursor of symbolist poetry whose spell and sphere of influence were
ubiquitous in the late nineteenth century.

One of the most distinctive qualities of Laforgue's own personal manner is effective in *Les
Complaintes:* The poet cultivates a witty and mocking detachment as an antidote to the blunt
expression of personal feelings. The theme of death recurs often in Laforgue, but it is not
personified as a sinister figure in "Complaint About Forgetting the Dead"; Laforguian irony
changes death into the "good gravedigger" who scratches at the door; if you refuse to welcome
him,

> If you can't be polite,
> He'll come (but not in spite)
> and drag you by your feet
> Into some moonlit night!

The "complaints," named for a folk-song style that the poet imitates, also reveal a flair for
inventing humorous anecdotes and dialogues couched in colloquial language; a case in point is
the "Complaint of the Outraged Husband," an amusing conversation in verse form between an
irate husband, who insists he saw his wife flirting with an officer in church, and his wife, who
maintains with injured innocence that she was piously conversing with a "life-size Christ."

A predilection for creating a cast of characters and for dramatizing experience remains a
permanent characteristic of Laforgue's style; it reappears most notably in 1886 in the form of
a verse drama called *The Faerie Council*. This work, which again demonstrates the poet's
preference for depersonalized expression of his sentiments, places on stage the Gentleman, who
bemoans the indifference of the cosmos and the tedium of existence, and the Lady, who offers
her charms as a cure for his ennui. The subject is typically Laforguian: Love is painted as
lacking in glamour, as being somewhat sordid, but it is still an acceptable escape from the

disenchanting realities of the world. The structure of this verse drama, as of many of Laforgue's poems, presents an ironical commentary on experience, since a certain frame of mind is developed in the course of the drama and then negated at the end. The earth is round "like a pot of stew," and we are mired in its banalities, but, since this is all human beings can possess, acceptance of one's lot is preferable to some sort of impassioned and futile revolt ("Why don't you see that that is truly our Earth!/ And all there is! and the rest is nothing but tax/ About which you might just as well relax!"). Gaiety and disdain are the prevailing moods of Laforgue, and he prefers these to bitterness and melancholy.

Perhaps the most startling and engaging product of Laforgue's imagination is to be found in the collection entitled *L'Imitation de Notre-Dame la Lune*. This work contains a gallery of "choirboys of the Moon," all of whom are named Pierrot. These bizarre individuals prefer lunar landscapes because the moon seems to symbolize aspiration to some absolute, whether it be savoring the love of an ideal and idealized female or giving in to the temptation of suicide and blissful nothingness. However, the thirst for self-extinction inevitably ends with an antithetical declaration of a prosaic determination to enjoy the present moment: "—Of course! the Absolute's rights are nil/ As long as the Truth consists of living."

Clowns are a favorite source of inspiration for modern painters and poets, and few are more individualized and appealing than the Pierrots of Laforgue. They are uniformly white except for a black skullcap and a scarlet mouth:

> It's, on a stiff neck emerging thus
> From similarly starchèd lace,
> A callow under cold-cream face
> Like hydrocephalic asparagus.
>
> The eyes are downed in opium
> Of universal clemency,
> The mouth of a clown bewitches
> Like a peculiar geranium.

It is worth noting that Ezra Pound was struck by the phrase "like hydrocephalic asparagus" and, in general, by Laforgue's frequent reliance upon a scientific lexicon to revivify patterns of poetic expression. In this domain, also, the French poet was an important innovator.

The Pierrots, who "feed on the absolute, and sometimes on vegetables, too," are distinguished not only by their acute awareness of death and by their refusal to seek solace and protection from their fate, but also by the inexplicable spell they cast over the opposite sex. They rhapsodize extravagantly when they talk of love, but they speak "with toneless voices." As amusing embodiments of contradictory elements, they offer another example of Laforguian irony. In addition, the portraits of these "dandies of the Moon" permit Laforgue to assume an imaginary identity and expound behind a mask a blasé and mocking view of love, life, and death.

Laforgue was one of the first poets in the nineteenth century to exploit successfully the possibilities of the free verse form. "Solo by Moonlight" in *Derniers Vers* is an excellent illustration of his talent for molding the length of the verse line to conform to the flow of thought and the association of images: Stretched out on top of a stagecoach moving rapidly through a moonlit countryside, the poet's composure, as well as his body, is jolted, for he remembers a promising love that ended in misunderstanding; the rhythm and mood are partially created by the lines of radically different length. At the same time, the poem is infused with a dreamlike atmosphere; impressions are nebulous, and the woman is only briefly glimpsed and partially understood as the poet attempts to recall the past. The theme of frustrated love is left purposely ambiguous and contributes to the evocation of psychology in dream form. A kind of paralysis engendered by boredom and a vague malaise prevented the poet from declaring himself; a simple gesture would have elicited a warm response in the woman but, "Ennui was keeping me exiled,/ Ennui which came from everything. So."

Familiar themes recur in *Derniers Vers*. "The Coming Winter" is a poem on autumn that suggests encroaching deterioration and imminent death. Startling verbal juxtapositions help avert dangers of overstatement and sentimentalism ("Rust gnaws the kilometric spleens/ Of telegraph wires on highways no one passes"), and Laforgue's sense of humor remains very much in evidence, as in "Oh! the turns in the highways,/ And without the wandering Little Red Riding Hood."

Critics have frequently noted the debt that many French writers of imposing stature owe to Laforgue's original handling of irony, versification, imagery, and colloquial language. At the same time, along with Paul Verlaine, his example has inspired composers as different as Arnold Schönberg, Darius Milhaud, and Jacques Ibert. He also influenced with profound effect the poetry of T. S. Eliot, Ezra Pound, and Hart Crane.

Bibliography:

Arkell, David. *Looking for Laforgue: An Informal Biography*. New York: Persea Books, 1979. An extremely useful, accessible biography that traces elements of Laforgue's poetry to specific events in his life. Well illustrated. Also includes translations of many of Laforgue's letters, providing insight into his personal relationships and his creative evolution.

Collie, Michael. *Jules Laforgue*. London: Athlone Press, 1977. A short, well-constructed introduction to Laforgue and his poetry. Includes sections on the poetry and its influence on later writers, a brief critical analysis by Collie, and select appraisals by other critics.

Holmes, Anne. *Jules Laforgue and Poetic Innovation*. Oxford, England: Oxford University Press, 1993. An excellent, exhaustive study, with sections on each of Laforgue's collections of poetry. The work centers on *Derniers Vers*, but there is ample information about all of the poetry, its effect on later poets, and its place within literary discourse.

Ramsey, Warren, ed. *Jules Laforgue: Essays on a Poet's Life and Work*. Carbondale: Southern Illinois University Press, 1969. A collection of twelve essays that include biographical information, analyses of the poetry, and studies of Laforgue in relation to his contemporaries and literary heirs in France and the United States.

_____. *Jules Laforgue and the Ironic Inheritance*. New York: Oxford University Press, 1953. An enduring study of Laforgue, his aesthetics, and his poetry. Includes chapters on Laforgue's influence on T. S. Eliot, Ezra Pound, and Hart Crane. Also contains an extensive bibliography and index, providing a wealth of information.

POETRY OF MACHADO

Author: Antonio Machado (1875-1939)

Principal published works: Soledades, galerías y otros poemas, 1907 (*Solitudes, Galleries and Other Poems,* 1987); *Campos de Castilla,* 1912 (*The Castilian Camp,* 1982); *Nuevas canciones,* 1924; *De un cancionero apócrifo,* 1926

The spiritual crisis brought about in Spain by the loss of its last overseas possessions in Spanish America in 1898 found expression through the works of the Spanish writers of the Generation of '98. Pessimism, analysis of the past, desire for change, and consciousness of history is reflected in productions of Spanish writers of that time.

Spain had actually been suffering a prolonged frustration in its national goals. Most of the Spanish-American colonies, discovered, explored, conquered, acculturated, and exploited by the mother country, had obtained their independence during the first quarter of the nineteenth century. A relatively small portion of the old Spanish empire remained. When Cuba and Puerto Rico gained their freedom, Spain lost all its political links with the American continent. Four centuries of Spanish rule and influence in the Americas had ended.

A strong reaction appeared among the Spanish intelligentsia. Spain was obliged to set new goals, examine its traditions, and reexamine its political life. Philosophers, fiction writers, and essayists put together their efforts to arouse the soul of their country and make it open its eyes to reality and the future. It could be thought that this generation had no place for poets, who are often unconcerned with national affairs. Antonio Machado, however, who is the best poet of the Generation of '98, fully shared the intellectual and emotional attitude of his age. The development of his themes and his poetic perspective began in the critical years following the last breath of the Spanish empire. From his first poems Machado shows the concerns of his poetry. He is, in all his books, the poet of time, of melancholy memories, of death, and of concern for his country. He would die in exile.

Perhaps no other Spanish-speaking poet has written so much about the phenomenon of time. For him, poetry is the essential method by which one may communicate with his time. Poetry is a way of bridging time and obtaining permanent, intemporal results. In other words, poetry for him is the result of inner, personal experience, in contact with his world, expressed not only by way of ideas, but mainly by way of intuition, with the intention of giving to such experiences a universal value.

Few writers have felt the burden of time as Machado did. A philosopher and poet, he went deep into the analysis of its essence both as a metaphysical entity and as a reality affecting human life. He did not theorize about it; through poetry he tried to grasp its meaning and to present its pathetic impact upon the individual.

Among his preferred ways of meeting time and interpreting his own life, Machado finds in daydreams a fit instrument. For Machado, poetry is also a daydream; life is a permanent attitude of watchful vision with open eyes. Readers can frequently discover in his poetry an ecstatic mood. Rather than recalling his memories, he used to dream of them. For him the true interior life was that of dreams and, conversely, dreams were the best way of knowing his inward being.

These dreams are not the substance of the subconscious nor are they expressed in a super-realistic manner. They are simply the manifestation of yesterday that presses upon the poet, causing him to live his life again in recollection. In this way they are made present and converted into poetic forms. Time is the span between birth and death. For Machado, who was reared in an educational environment devoid of religious training, death is only a limit, a state of absolute finiteness, rather than the last act of human life or the beginning of a different one. Since nobody can boast of having experienced death, its apprehension is only a concept, the object of belief, not of knowledge. At the same time, death is always possible. As a result of death's constant imminence, Machado experiences the anguish of death but meets it with a stoic resignation. In his poetry there is neither the cry of rebelliousness nor belief in the immortality of the soul. Sometimes death appears as something connatural with the poet—a companion. The presence of death is sometimes so sharp that Machado suddenly thinks that his end is imminent, but he is appeased by the hope of living more days until he may see the bright morning of death.

"Spain aches me," was the poignant cry of Miguel de Unamuno, one of the writers of the Generation of '98. It was an attitude shared by all his contemporaries. That generation of Spaniards took as their own the collective problems of their country. These problems were the consequence of many years of national life without collective values and endeavors. Machado devoted his pen to a poetic dissection of his country. *The Castilian Camp*, in 1912, is his contribution to the most pungent question of his generation: the past and future of Spain.

A doubled Spain appears in this book: the "official" and the "authentic" Spain. For Machado, the two Spains have been living divorced for many years. The "official" has created a Spain of tradition, laziness, individualism, and presumptions. The "authentic" is the Spain of the people, who dream and fight and think and live after their own ideals of honesty, hard work, and patriotism.

Castile is, for the writers of this generation, the heart and symbol of Spain, because it has played a special role in Spanish life for many years. Machado chooses this region and tries to find in it both the constructive and destructive forces that have molded the Spanish soul. The landscape of his vision is chiefly that of Soria, where he spent some important years of his life and where he met his wife, who died a few years later. He remembers his childhood in Seville, merry and colorful, in contrast to a less happy youth in the Castilian plateau.

The Castilian Camp abounds in strong, pessimistic poems, written mainly in the most traditional meters of Spanish poetry: the Alexandrine and the octosyllabic. Machado speaks of poor people, ancient warriors, barren fields, familiar tragedies, and the painful remembrance of his dead wife.

In "The Land of Alvargonzalez," the longest poem in the book, Machado depicts the tragedy of a rural family. The poet, in bitter, popular, and lyric *romanzas*, tells a story of envy and murder. The father is killed by his older sons; his farm, which they inherit, becomes arid; and when Miguel, the last born of the brothers, returns rich from the New World, he buys the land from his brothers. The land flourishes, and his brothers, repentant of their sin, plunge into the Black Lagoon.

The Castilian landscape is frequently associated with his wife, Leonor, dead at the age of seventeen in Soria. This only true love was born, met the poet, married him, and died in the Castilian land. Machado imagines going with her, enjoying the scenery, though the consciousness of her death makes him melancholy. Machado never gave profound expression of religious origin. His education, based on the principles of secularization of thought and the philosophy of positivism, was not concerned with the relationship between divinity and humanity. There is an agnostic attitude in most of his books. His interpellations to God are vague and made among dreams.

In Machado's poetry some preference is made toward the metaphysical treatment of love. For him, love begins as an abrupt increment of the vital energy, yet with nothing tangible that needs attention. It is like the explosion of spring, an attitude of being escorted by an impersonal and merely suggested companion. A second step in love comes later when a man encounters a real woman, but then, paradoxically, anguish and waste of life plague the lover because in spite of his efforts he cannot yield himself totally to the loved one. When she disappears from the immediate circle of the lover, oblivion comes. Finally, she becomes only a subject of reminiscence and poetry.

Time, the past, dreams, death, love, and the nation are the eternal questions of human life. Poets and philosophers have tried to find some answer to them. Antonio Machado, poet and philosopher, made an attempt to find an explanation of himself and his world in a given time and space. He did not succeed, and he did not expect to, but he left the deep, beautiful, tentative testimony of a man who thinks that he is only a traveler in this world, condemned to the yoke of time and to obtaining at best a glimpse of life's mysteries.

Bibliography:
Cobb, Carl W. *Antonio Machado*. New York: Twayne, 1971. An excellent starting point for the discussion of Machado's poetry. Contains a useful chronology of the poet's life and works, a good bibliography, and critical analyses of the major poems.
Diaz-Plaja, Guillermo. *A History of Spanish Literature*, edited and translated by Hugh A. Harter. New York: New York University Press, 1971. A necessary and interesting introduction not only to Machado's poetry, but to the famous literary and philosophical group to which he belonged, the Generation of '98. Highlights the poet's use of its themes and preoccupations.
Machado, Antonio. *Selected Poems*, edited and translated by Alan S. Trueblood. Cambridge, Mass.: Harvard University Press, 1982. A good bilingual introduction to Machado's poetry, especially for readers whose Spanish is weak or nonexistent. Contains bibliographical references for further study.
Peers, E. Allison. *Antonio Machado*. Oxford, England: Clarendon Press, 1940. Excellent critical analysis by a renowned scholar of Hispanic poetry. One of the first works to discuss Machado's transformation into a symbol of protest and liberation.
Young, Howard Thomas. *The Victorious Expression: A Study of Four Contemporary Poets*. Madison: University of Wisconsin Press, 1964. In this intricate analysis, the themes, structures, and leitmotifs of Machado's poetry are juxtaposed and contrasted to those of three of his contemporaries.

POETRY OF MÖRIKE

Author: Eduard Mörike (1804-1875)
Principal published works: Gedichte, 1838 (*Poems,* 1959); *Idylle vom Bodensee: Oder,*
Fischer Martin und die Glockendiebe, 1846

Since the Romantic period was, among other things, a revolt against the Age of Reason, it is
frequently asserted that the Romantics were sentimental eccentrics. Eduard Mörike cannot be
classified as such. He was a sensitive dreamer, a skillful poet, but above all a poet of simplicity.
A contemporary critic called him "a human being in nightgown and soft slippers." While purists
of the Romantic period will praise Friedrich Hölderlin, Mörike was able to appeal to a larger
public. Many of his poems became folklore and folksongs during his lifetime. Johannes
Brahms, Franz Schumann, and Hugo Wolf set some of his poems to music, and most of them
are still to be heard in concert halls all over the world. He was a master of classical meters, but
he abhorred strict theoretical principles in his work. D. F. Strauss, his famous theologian
contemporary, said: "Thanks to his work, nobody can sell us rhetoric for poetry." Describing
the poet's intuitive creativity, he stated that "Mörike takes a handful of earth, squeezes it ever
so little, and a little bird flies out."

Mörike made full use of the wealth of inflections that the German language offers. Some
critics, however, object to a lack of composition in his poems. Frequently past, present, and
future are interwoven without proper sequence. Mörike himself was suspicious of a purely
academic approach. In an epigram he replied to his German critics: "You can see in his poems
that he can express himself in Latin." He was a representative of the "Schwaebische Dichter-
schule" (Swabian school) which had formed around the poet Ludwig Uhland. Heinrich Heine,
who detested this lack of cosmopolitan ambitions, attacked the school with satirical comments.
Mörike always remained a native son, and some of his poems are written in Swabian dialect.
He did not leave Swabia except for a few excursions into Bavaria, Tyrol, and Switzerland, and
he disregarded the problematic speculations of his time, which caused Johann Wolfgang von
Goethe to examine all aspects of nineteenth century knowledge, and which made Hölderlin seek
refuge in the idealistic world of Greece. Goethe tried to explore the unexplorable, while Mörike
maintained a childlike vision and radiated in his poems an adoration of life without torturing
his mind with a multitude of question marks. This attitude is demonstrated in his most frequently quoted poem, "Prayer":

> Lord, send what pleaseth Thee!
> Let it be weal or woe;
> Thy hands give both, and so
> Either contenteth me.
> But, Lord, whichever
> Thou giv'st, pain or pleasure,
> O do not drench me!
> In sweet mid-measure Lieth true plenty.

A prose translation of the same poem may serve to illustrate the simple choice of words which
could not be employed in a poetical translation:

> Lord, send what you will
> Love or sorrow

I am happy
That both flows from your hand.
Do not overload me
With joy
Or with sorrow
In the middle lies Sweet contentment.

Mörike, the seventh child in a family of thirteen, was born in 1804, the son of a medical doctor. A student of theology, he entered the Lower Seminary at Urach and continued his studies at the Higher Seminary. Although he came to dislike theological study, he nevertheless became a pastor in the small Swabian village of Kleversulzbach, chiefly because his mother felt that the ministry was the proper profession for any educated man. His father had died early, and his mother came from a vicar's family. An attempt in 1828 to establish himself as writer and editor had failed. He admitted feeling "like a tethered goat" when he started his pastoral duties, and he preferred to write poetry instead of sermons. Frequently he had to borrow his Sunday sermons from a colleague. In 1838 he published his first volume under the title *Poems*. His attitude toward his parishioners is described in his poem "A Parson's Experience": "Fortunately my peasants like a 'sharp sermon.' What happens is that on Saturday evening after eleven o'clock they creep into my garden and steal my lettuce and on Sunday in the morning service they expect the vinegar for it. But I make the ending gentle: they get the oil."

After nine years, in 1843, he resigned from his position as pastor for reasons of ill health. The major reason was his desire to be free from his pastoral duties. His happiest time arrived when he obtained a position as a professor of literature in a girls' high school. A one-hour teaching assignment each week left sufficient time for writing poetry, and the girls enjoyed being lectured on poetry by a real poet. He even earned an honorary doctor's degree, and the queen attended one of his lectures. His major diversion from his literary work were his delightful drawings, which showed again his ability to create something without strenuous efforts. His drawings, issued as a separate volume, have only recently found a larger audience.

Mörike married in 1851, but his marriage resulted in separation. His close relationship with his sister Klarchen, who lived in the Mörike house, caused many conflicts. Also, in his student days he had had an unpleasant experience with the opposite sex when he fell in love with a beautiful young woman who had a doubtful reputation and who failed to remain faithful to him. Five poems with the title "Peregrina" describe his joy and sorrow. The cycle ends:

Could I forsake such beauty? The old bliss
Returns, and seems yet sweeter than before.
O come! My arms have waited long for this.
But at the look she gives my heart grows sore.
Hatred and love are mingled in her kiss.
She turns away, and will return no more.

Another love affair, which resulted in an engagement, was called off three years later. Retelling his experience, he again demonstrated his ability to evoke deep feelings with simple words:

Fare you well—you could not guess
What a pang the words imparted,
For you spoke with cheerful face,
Going on your way light-hearted.
Fare you well—time and again

Since that day these words I've spoken,
Never weary of the pain,
Though my heart as oft was broken.

In spite of unfortunate love affairs and an unhappy marriage, he never lost his serenity, which was based on a sincere belief in the goodness of his creator and his place in God's creation. In his most famous prose piece, "Mozart auf der Reise nach Prag" ("Mozart on a Voyage to Prague"), he inserted a poem, usually titled "O Soul, Remember," which indicates his sense of tranquillity while speaking about the ever-present reality of death:

A sapling springs, who knows
Where, in the forest;
A rosebush, who can say
Within what garden?
Chosen already both—
O soul, remember—
To root upon your grave
And to grow there.

Like most Romantics Mörike used nature as his major source of inspiration. When he was a curate, he was found resting in the grass of the churchyard while the honor of the Sunday sermon was given to young assistants. Restful poems like "Withdrawal" were the result of such leisure:

Let me go, world, let me go!
Come no more with gifts to woo me!
Leave this heart of mine, now, to me,
With its joy and with its woe!

In his adoration of nature he also refrained from the emotional eccentricities which can be noted in the work of his contemporaries. He described his impressions in simple rhymes, which found their way into numerous poetry collections, children's books, and school books. "September Morning" falls in this category:

The world's at rest still, sun not through,
Forest and field lie dreaming:
But soon now, when the veil drops, you
Will see the sky's unmisted blue;
Lusty with autumn and subdued,
The world in warm gold swimming.

Many love poems, free from affectations, also flowed easily from his pen. "Question and Answer" is typical:

Whence, you ask me, did the demon
Love gain entrance to my heart?
Why was not long since his venom
Wrenched out boldly with the dart?

Mörike's poems are not a product of tense creative efforts by candlelight in an attic (a setting used by most romantic painters of the era to depict poets). In all of his poems the element of spontaneity is apparent. Nothing sounds labored or contrived. One of his poems, written in bed on a morning, is "The Sisters," now a well-known Brahms duet. A popular love poem "Fair Rohtraut" was started when he saw the name in a dictionary:

> Then they rode home without a word, Rohtraut, Fair Rohtraut;
> The lad's heart sang though he made no sound:
> If you were queen and today were crowned,
> It would not grieve me!
> You thousand leaves of the forest wist
> That I Fair Rohtraut's mouth have kissed!
> —Quiet, quiet, my heart!

It is not surprising that his deep love of nature and his childlike purity of imagination made him also an outstanding teller of fairy tales and a writer of ballads. The mythical world of ghosts and elves comes alive in the "Song of the Elves" and "The Ghosts at Mummeisee."

In spite of his marriage to a Roman Catholic, he never showed an inclination to become a member of any church after he left his pastoral assignment. He was under the influence of his friend D. F. Strauss, who wrote the most unorthodox biography of Jesus of this time. That Mörike admired the ritual of the Catholic church is evident, however, in his poem "Holy Week."

Following his separation from his wife in 1873, he lived in several places and at spas, residence made possible by financial help from his friends. He died in 1875, and on his deathbed he was reconciled with his wife.

The simplicity of Mörike's poems made many of them popular during his lifetime, yet at the same time this quality prevented proper recognition of his art by many of his fellow Romantics. In spite of his unsophisticated writings no critic ever accused him of being trivial. If the test of time is considered the most valid criteria for a poet's work, Mörike easily has passed the test, and he will most probably remain a popular poet for generations to come. Gottfried Keller, a contemporary Swiss poet and novelist, said after his death: "He died like the departure of a quiet mountain spirit . . . like a beautiful day in June. If his death does not bring him closer to the people—it is only the people's fault."

Bibliography:
Adams, Jeffrey, ed. *Mörike's Muses: Critical Essays on Eduard Mörike*. Columbia, S.C.: Camden House, 1990. Ten scholarly essays provide textual and thematic analysis of Mörike's poetry; a number suggest sources for the poet's inspiration and comment on the psychological dimensions of his creative drive.
Mare, Margaret. *Eduard Mörike: The Man and the Poet*. London: Methuen, 1957. Detailed, comprehensive biography, interweaving analysis of the poetry into the life story. Quotations from the works are in German, limiting the volume's usefulness for those not familiar with the language.
Rennert, Hal H. *Eduard Mörike's Reading and the Reconstruction of his Extant Library*. New York: Peter Lang, 1985. Describes the poet's reading. Shows how other writers influenced the development of the poetry and ways the works reflect Mörike's debt to his literary masters.
Slessarev, Helga. *Eduard Mörike*. New York: Twayne, 1970. Study of the poet intended for the general reader. Sketches the life and reviews the major works, providing textual analysis and concentrated examination of poetic form in Mörike's lyrics. Also includes an assessment of Mörike's appeal to twentieth century readers.

Stern, J. P. *Idylls and Realities: Studies in Nineteenth Century German Literature.* New York: Frederick Ungar, 1971. A chapter on Mörike describes his accomplishments as a lyricist, claiming the poet "excels at showing man in contact with the natural world." Explicates a number of the poems.

POETRY OF SKELTON

Author: John Skelton (c. 1460-1529)
Principal published works: Pithy, Pleasaunt and Profitable Workes of Maister Skelton, Poet Laureate, 1568

To place John Skelton in some convenient niche in literary history is difficult, but it is even more difficult to find an appropriate artistic designation for this early Tudor poet. Nearer in time to the writing of Sir Thomas Wyatt or Henry Howard, Earl of Surrey, he is much nearer in his style to the writing of the medieval Latinists. Despite once being called a Humanist scholar, Skelton did not have much in common with the Humanists and even indulged in some feuding with them. While the Humanists (a group of scholars, associated with Desiderius Erasmus, whose intellectual focus was on the human rather than the divine) were reviving an interest in the classical Greek and Latin writers and using them for examples, Skelton continued to copy the style of fourteenth and fifteenth century writers. What he had in common with the Humanists, however, was an interest in people and the world as they are.

For example, "The Bouge of Court," is typical of the medieval tradition in several ways. It uses rhyme royal to tell a dream allegory; it relies heavily on personification and the use of court terms; and it has the usual astronomical opening and closing apology. The prologue begins with allusions to the sun, the moon, and to Mars. The narrator wishes he could write, but being warned by Ignorance not to try, he lies down and dreams of going aboard a ship, "The Bouge of Court," which is owned by Sans Peer and captained by Fortune. The narrator, who reveals that he is called Drede, is first accosted and frightened by Danger, the chief gentle-woman of Sans Peer. Before Drede can flee, he is soothed by Desire, who persuades him to stay aboard.

After this introduction comes the main body of the poem, which consists of conversation between Drede and seven of the passengers, Skelton's representations of the seven deadly sins. Drede first describes the approaching figure in unforgettable detail; then, as the figure speaks, an even sharper focus of his personality is achieved. The seven passengers are named "Favel" or Flattery, Suspect, Harvy Hafter, Disdain, Riot, Dissimulation, and Deceit.

Harvy Hafter is Skelton's most colorful creation in the poem, and he is still around:

> But as I stood musing in my mind,
> Harvy Hafter came leaping, light as lynde.
> Upon his breast he bare a versing-box,
> His throat was clear, and lustily could fayne.
> Methought his gown was all furréd with fox,
> And ever he sang, '*Sith I am nothing plain . . .*'
> To keep him from picking it was a great pain:
> He gazed on me with goatish beard;
> Whan I looked on him, my purse was half afeard.

Thus Harvy Hafter is the typical confidence man, always gay and optimistic, always ready to dispel all doubts and fears with pat answers and stale jokes.

After talking with these seven characters, Drede fears for his life and jumps overboard. The leap and hitting the water awaken him, and he seizes his pen and records his dream. In the final stanza, his apology, he states that what he has recorded is only a dream, but sometimes even dreams contain truth.

I would therewith no man were miscontent,
Beseeching you that shall it see or read
In every point to be indifferent,
Sith all in substance of slumbring cloth proceed.
I will not say it is matter indeed,
But yet oft-time such dreams be found true.
Now construe ye what is the residue!

Though this poem is typical of the medieval tradition, its importance lies in how it deviates from the tradition: Its difference is Skelton's contribution. His characters are certainly types, as in a dream allegory they must be; but they are more than the mere pictured figures of medieval writing. They are highly individualized characters, as shown by Harvy Hafter's description, and they are characterized not only by description but also by their own speech. Furthermore, Skelton's setting is more concrete than is usual in the medieval tradition.

The allegory depicts the life at court as Skelton saw it. The highest achievement of the courtier was to be recognized by the king and to maintain his favor, no matter what the means. Those who attained his favor were openly praised but privately scorned and envied by the others. Thus, if one succeeded, he failed to maintain the true friendship of his fellow courtiers, for flattery, jealousy, disdain, suspicion, and other feelings all joined forces to destroy such friendship. To Skelton, the irony of such a life was that gaining the attention of the king was accomplished purely by chance. Since this kind of court life was demeaning, in Skelton's view, he attacked it.

Another of Skelton's early poems which shows the poet still working in the medieval tradition is "Philip Sparrow." Following a medieval point of view, Skelton wrote this poem in the short-lined couplets, tercets, and quatrains now known as Skeltonic verse. This poem is Skelton's most playful and most popular work; in it readers see the poet in a mood in which he has cast dignity and restraint aside and has indulged himself in a bit of fantasy. He describes the activities of the bird, its death, its funeral, and as he describes the owner or mistress, Jane Scroop. It is a long and rather loose poem which can be broken into three distinct parts.

The first part, which takes over half of the 1,382 lines in the poem, is a dramatic monologue with Jane Scroop as narrator telling of her Philip. Through her Skelton gives the reader his appraisal of Geoffrey Chaucer, John Gower, and John Lydgate, and uses the opportunity to display his wide reading in Greek and Latin. He parodies the funeral mass by having the whole host of birds chant over the dead body of Philip Sparrow. The most delightful lines are those in which Jane talks of her pet:

It had a velvet cap,
And would sit upon my lap,
And seek after small wormes,
And sometimes white bread-crumbes;
And many times and oft
Between my breastes soft
It woulde lie and rest;
It was proper and prest.

Sometime he would gasp
When he saw a wasp;
A fly or a gnat,

> He would fly at that;
> And prettily would he pant
> When he saw an ant.
> Lord, how he would pry
> After the butterfly!

In the second part of the poem, "The Commendacione," Skelton commends and defends Jane Scroop as the composer of the first section. He also spends much time reporting "the goodly sort/ Of her features clear," and ends each section of the "Commendacione" with a refrain:

> For this most goodly floure,
> This blossom of fresh colour,
> So Jupiter me succour,
> She flourisheth new and new
> In beauty and virtue

The third part, the "Addition," was clearly added after the other two had been written. It is an answer to the critics of the poem and a protest against their criticism.

"The Tunning of Elinour Rumming," more than all the other poems together, has earned for Skelton the title of "scurrilous" or, as from Alexander Pope, "beastly." It is Skelton's most notorious work. The first part of the poem introduces the hostess, Elinour. Then follow seven sections of various scenes in the tavern. This study of Tudor lowlife is extremely realistic. To show the stench and squalor of the bar, Skelton eliminates no details, no matter how crude or coarse. Yet, there is a vitality in the realism of the scene, and the impression—no matter how unpleasant it may be to some, though to others it may be only humorous—is an unforgettable one. For example:

> Maud Ruggy thither skippéd:
> She was ugly hippéd,
> And ugly thick lippéd,
> Like an onion sided,
> Like tan leather hided.
> She had her so guided
> Between the cup and the wall
> That she was there withal
> Into a palsy fall;
> With that her head shakéd,
> And her handes quakéd,
> One's head would have achéd
> To see her nakéd.

Even Skelton decides he has gone too far in his description of the tawdry existence: "I have written too much/ Of this mad mumming/ Of Elinour Rumming."

Like many others after him, Skelton excuses himself for his descent by saying that he has written the poem to show others how to escape from such a fall. The gusto of the representation shows a familiarity with the subject that is unexpected in such a scholar and churchman.

Perhaps Skelton's most puzzling work is "Speak, Parrot." There are several reasons for the vagueness of the poem, which has been called unintelligible. In the first place, there is strong evidence to suggest that the work is a collection of many poems written at various times. Although some of the poems are even dated, the method Skelton used to date them is not conventional, so that any attempt to decipher these dates is mostly guesswork. Another reason for the vagueness is that Skelton thought that to protect himself from charges of treason he had to veil his allusions to topical incidents in allegorical language. He uses the Book of Judges for many terms of this language. Present knowledge of particular events of the day also cloud an intelligible interpretation. Finally, the device Skelton uses as framework for "Speak, Parrot" compounds the vagueness. He puts the whole narration into the mouth of a parrot that relates the poem in no particular chronological sequence, and at times the parrot speaks only gibberish.

In this poem Skelton still relies on the medieval use of allegory, and the verse form is basically rhyme royal. Except in these particulars, he is much farther from the medieval tradition in this poem than he is in, for example, "The Bouge of Court." Since Skelton went to such pains to conceal his message, his targets must have been powerful and the events well known; and members of the court probably had little trouble understanding just what Skelton was writing about. Still, by having the parrot speak, he was able to deny any treasonous charges.

With the writing of "Colin Clout" comes Skelton's complete severance from the medieval tradition. He abandons the dream structures for one narrator, personification and allegory for direct statement, and rhyme royal for Skeltonic verse. His use of Colin Clout as narrator is fortunate, for Colin simply repeats what he hears during his travels:

> Thus I, Colin Clout,
> As I go about,
> And wandering as I walk
> I hear the people talk.

Thus he cannot vouch for the truthfulness of what he hears, nor can he be blamed for his crudeness. This flexible framework also allows him to repeat in any order what he has heard, and this order, or lack of it, is sometimes frustrating.

One of Skelton's attacks in the poem is against the conflict between Church and state. He is on the Church's side, but, like Erasmus, Skelton takes a humanistic viewpoint. He argues that the Church should be independent, not parasitic on the state; that the selling of salvation leads to total disorganization of the Church; and that the clergy are ignorant, mainly because of the careless selection of priests. All of this leads the laity to distrust the clergy. As Erasmus does in his writings, Skelton calls upon the Church to cleanse itself, to carry out reform from within. He is not calling for a change in doctrine, but rather asks that the old doctrines be more closely followed. His bitterness is directed against those who are defiling the sacraments of the Church and those who allow this defiling. Thus the focus of the attack is Cardinal Wolsey, who, in Skelton's opinion, is the epitome of the sacrifice of the interests of the church to those of the state. The power of the poem lies not in the bitterness of the invective, but in the appeals for reform.

"Why Come Ye Not to Court?" is Skelton's third and most direct indictment against Wolsey. Like "Speak, Parrot" and "Colin Clout," this poem lacks any basic organization, and the lines tumble one upon another with a seeming lack of order. Furthermore, there is no chronological order to the events referred to. This loose structure might lead one to assume that the poem was composed in pieces at various times.

Skelton does not use allegorical language or biblical terms to describe Wolsey but rather speaks of him plainly as the cardinal or "red hat." The cardinal is in complete control of the kingdom, so the situation is bad, because Wolsey is concerned only with money and lavish living:

We have cast up our war,
And made a worthy truce
With, 'Cup, level suse!'
Our money madly lent,
and more madly spent:

. . . .

With crowns of gold emblazéd
They make him so amazéd
And his eyen so dazéd
That he ne see can
To know God nor man!

. . . .

Why come ye not to court?
To which court?
To the kingés court,
Or to Hampton Court?
Nay, to the kingés court.
The kingés court
Should have the excellence,
But Hampton Court
Hath the preéminence.

One of Skelton's last poems, and one of his longest, is "The Garland of Laurel." Strangely enough, it is dedicated to Wolsey; therefore, some degree of reconciliation must have taken place, for Skelton died while living in the protection of the Church. Once more the poet reverts to his medieval tradition of the dream allegory, using mostly rhyme royal to tell how the garland of laurel has come to be placed on his head. A long procession of poets, headed by Gower, Lydgate, and Chaucer come to Skelton. He agrees to carry on in the tradition and places the garland on his own head. "The Garland of Laurel" is in one respect the most remarkable poem in all literature, for no other poet has ever written sixteen hundred lines to honor himself.

Had Skelton given more time and energy to developing his lyrical poetry, he might be better known today, for he did have a definite gift for shaping verse. There are, however, only a few poems as evidence; unfortunately, Skelton did not spend much time or effort on lyrics. Some of his better ones are "Woefully arrayed," "The Manner of the World Nowadays," "Woman-hood, Wanton, ye want" and "My Darling Dear, my Daisy Flower."

Skelton is not an imitator of those who went before him, nor is he a founder of any style or school much copied by those who came after him. True, he did write in the medieval tradition, but not entirely, and he is better in those poems in which he does not follow the tradition. He had some imitators of his style in his day, but they have made no significant contribution to literature. Thus Skelton is unique. He was a poet following the medieval tradition while the other scholars were heralding England's Renaissance, yet a poet creating his own particular style; a tender poet capable of the warm humor of "Philip Sparrow"; a realistic poet capable of the crude grossness of "The Tunning of Elinour Rumming"; a religious poet, loving his church yet calling for its inner reformation; a secular poet knowledgeable in the ways of the world; and most of all, a courageous poet who spoke his mind to the powerful and pursued his individual artistic gifts.

Bibliography:
Carpenter, Nan Cooke. *John Skelton.* New York: Twayne, 1967. An excellent introductory

volume. Places Skelton in the intellectual, political, and artistic setting of his times.

Fish, Stanley Eugene. *John Skelton's Poetry*. New Haven, Conn.: Yale University Press, 1965. A closely reasoned work giving special attention to the composition and techniques of Skelton's verse. "Speak, Parrot" is extensively analyzed.

Heiserman, Arthur Ray. *Skelton and Satire*. Chicago: University of Chicago Press, 1961. Views Skelton and his poetry in terms of the traditions of medieval satire, particularly in his use of conventional rhetorical figures and allegory. Considers Skelton to be a traditional figure in the English literature of his time.

Kinney, Arthur F. *John Skelton, Priest as Poet: Seasons of Discovery*. Chapel Hill: University of North Carolina Press, 1987. Disputes William Nelson's contentions that Skelton was primarily an early Renaissance Humanist, Arthur Ray Heiserman's view that Skelton was a typically medieval satirist, and Stanley Fish's opinion that Skelton was an idiosyncratic poet. In the place of these views, Kinney advances the thesis that Skelton was foremost a priest, whose verses were concerned with moral and religious themes and ideas.

Nelson, William. *John Skelton, Laureate*. New York: Russell & Russell, 1939. Although one of the older studies of Skelton, it remains a key document. Argues that Skelton was an early Renaissance Humanist, and thus a transitional figure from the Middle Ages to the modern era.

Pollet, Maurice. *John Skelton: Poet of Tudor England*. Translated by John Warrington. Cranbury, N.J.: Bucknell University Press, 1971. Useful in placing Skelton within the political context of his times. Helpful insights as to how Skelton's poetics were shaped by his politics.

POETRY OF TRAHERNE

Author: Thomas Traherne (c. 1637-1674)
Principal published works: A Serious and Patheticall Contemplation of the Mercies of God,
1699 (better known as *Thanksgivings*); *The Poetical Works of Thomas Traherne,* 1903;
Traherne's Poems of Felicity, written c. 1655-1674, published, 1910

Thomas Traherne was one of the last seventeenth century inheritors of the Metaphysical tradition of religious poetry, developed to its height by John Donne and George Herbert, who drew of every aspect of the world around them to express their faith and their longing for closer communion with God. Much of their complexity of thought and their awareness of the essentially paradoxical nature of the Christian religion was lost on Traherne, whose concepts and style were much simpler and less compact than theirs. The greatest differences between Traherne and his predecessors undoubtedly resulted from his radically different theology. Both Donne and Herbert struggled with a strong sense of sin, a feeling of human unworthiness, and as a consequence of this realization they had an equally overwhelming perception of the miraculous, outreaching mercy of God.

Traherne, who was closer in spirit to the great Romantic poets William Blake and William Wordsworth than to his own contemporaries, wrote out of a deep conviction of innate human innocence. Original sin forms no part of his faith, though he was conscious, intellectually if not emotionally, of human corruption, which he felt was derived from the world's emphasis on materialism. Evil comes from human greed; gold, silver, and jewels are symbols not of beauty but of temptation and of that avarice that perverts youthful joy in the creation. Nature, not wealth, is for Traherne the greatest of human possessions. Those who are inheritors of the light of the stars and the fruitful soil can desire no more.

Just as Donne's complex metaphorical language reflects his equally involved theology, so Traherne's brief stanzas echo the essential simplicity of his vision. His lyrics have been compared to Blake's *Songs of Innocence* (1789), though he never achieved the sustained control of the later poet. Both his form and his devotional tone are perhaps closest to the less impassioned poems of Herbert, who may have inspired him to experiment with a wide variety of verse forms, not always successfully. Traherne's work is characterized by lines of striking loveliness in the midst of uninspired, wordy mediocrity. His limitations in his religious thought are partly responsible for those of his poetry: a narrowness of vision, a lack of awareness of many significant sides of life, and a tendency to repetitiveness. He never really mastered the poetic control of Donne, Herbert, or even of Henry Vaughan, another late Metaphysical poet with mystical tendencies, who shared Traherne's propensity for unevenness in his writing. This problem can be clearly seen in a lyric that begins with an unusual and striking vision of "new worlds beneath the water." The intensity of the opening is dissipated by the weakness of the end of the stanza:

> I saw new worlds beneath the water lie,
> New people; yea, another sky
> And sun, which seen by day
> Might things more clear display.
> Just such another
> Of late my brother
> Did in his travel see, and saw by night

A much more strange and wondrous sight;
Nor could the world exhibit such another
So great a sight, but in a brother.

Dominant themes in Traherne's poetry include the innocence of childhood, when human eyes look upon everything with delight and wonder, the glories of the natural world, and the corruptions of the commerce-directed society of the time. Perhaps the best known and most skillful treatment of these characteristic themes comes in "Wonder," a rather ecstatic statement of the poet's childhood reaction to the world around him:

How like an Angel came I down!
How Bright are all Things here!
When first among his Works I did appear
O how their GLORY me did Crown?
The World resembled his Eternitie,
In which my Soul did Walk;
And every Thing that I did see,
Did with me talk.

Like Wordsworth, Traherne suggests a kind of platonic pre-existence, when human souls were united with God. Children retain some of this divine luster until greed gradually wears it away. Though Wordsworth could not have known Traherne's poems, since they were lost until late in the nineteenth century, his "Ode: Intimations of Immortality" has surprising echoes of a poem called "News," in which Traherne ponders his early sense that there was a world of bliss beyond the one he saw. Unlike Wordsworth, however, Traherne finds the creation not a consolation for the loss of heavenly bliss, but this bliss itself:

But little did the infant dream
That all the treasures of the world were by,
And that himself was so the cream
And crown of all which round about did lie.
Yet thus it was! The gem,
The diadem,
The ring enclosing all
That stood upon this earthen ball,
The heav'nly eye,
Much wider than the sky,
Wherein they all included were,
The love, the soul, that was the king
Made to possess them, did appear
A very little thing.

In another poem, "The Apostasy," distinguished by a complex, well-handled stanza form, Traherne comments at greater length on his childish appreciation of the natural world, when he seemed to dwell in Eden before the fall:

As Eve
I did believe
Myself in Eden set,
Affecting neither gold nor ermined crowns,

> Nor aught else that I need forget;
> No mud did foul my limpid streams,
> No mist eclipsed my sun with frowns;
>   Set off with heav'nly beams,
> My joys were meadows, fields, and towns.

Temptation entered his paradise with "those little, new-invented things, fine lace and silks . . . or wordly pelf that us destroys." His own fall was gradual, but he, like all other men, was corrupted, separated, finally made "a stranger to the shining skies."

Traherne's poetry has a pervasive quality of innocence and purity; even when he speaks of corruption, he seems to be living in an incorruptible world himself, and he preserved a child's uncomplex awareness of existence. Both his language and his images reflect these characteristics. They are expanded, not compressed; a poet of mood, rather than of ideas, Traherne built much of his effect through repetition and restatement, deriving images from the preceding ones, finding new examples to express the same idea, as he does in the following stanza:

> A globe of earth is better far
> Than if it were a globe of gold; a star
>   Much brighter than a precious stone;
> The sun more glorious than a costly throne—
>   His warming beam,
>   A living stream
>   Of liquid pearl, that from a spring
> Waters the earth, is a most precious thing.

Traherne's fondness for the exclamatory tone is especially evident in a little verse appropriately entitled "The Rapture," which conveys that joy in existence that is part of so much of his poetry, especially that about childhood:

> Sweet infancy!
> O heavenly fire! O sacred light!
>   How fair and bright!
>   How great am I,
> Whom the whole world doth magnify!

The poet does have other voices. In "Insatiableness," a poem faintly reminiscent of Herbert's "The Pulley," in which God is seen withholding the gift of rest from man that "weariness" may turn him back toward the Deity, Traherne restates in three successive stanzas the impossibility of satisfying the "busy, vast, inquiring soul" of man. His conclusion differs from Herbert's; this restless spirit is, finally, proof of the existence of God: "Sure there's a God, (for else there's no delight,) One infinite."

One of the most unusual of Traherne's poems is "A Serious and Curious Night Meditation," where he deals with a theme he rarely touches on—death as a physical process, rather than as a spiritual reunion with God. Some of the images have the harsh, almost macabre realism of the true Metaphysical poets like Donne and Andrew Marvell:

> What is my Fathers House! and what am I!
> My fathers House is Earth; where I must lie:
> And I a worm, no man; that fits no room,
> Till like a worm, I crawl into my Tomb.

Even here there is a suggestion of the awareness of beauty that is characteristic of Traherne, in the lines "Whilst, at my window, pretty Birds do Ring my Knell, and with their Notes my Obit sing." The conclusion is a weaker version of Donne's triumphant affirmation in his sonnet, "Death Be Not Proud": "Sleep is Cousin-german unto Death:/ Sleep and Death differ, no more, than a Carcass/ And a skeleton." Therefore, since he sleeps peacefully in his bed, he has no reason to fear death.

Traherne's formula for "felicity," a term that recurs frequently in both his poetry and in his fine prose work, the *Centuries of Meditations* (written c. 1657-1661; published, 1908) is effectively summarized in "The Recovery." Here he presents his conviction that man's pleasure is God's reward: "Our blessedness to see/ Is even to the Deity/ A Beatific vision." Human beings see God's glory in his works and worship him through their joy:

> All gold and silver is but empty dross.
> Rubies and sapphires are but loss,
> The very sun and stars and seas
> Far less His spirit please:
> One voluntary act of love
> Far more delightful to His soul doth prove
> And is above all these as far as love.

Traherne's own joy in the works of God is perhaps the most memorable quality of his poetry; his exuberant praise of nature and the innocence of childhood is for the reader, at least, temporarily infectious. There is, however, a sameness about his work, a lack of variety in his ideas and in his vocabulary, which makes it difficult to read many of his poems at a sitting without feeling the sweetness and the smoothness rather oppressive. When even evil is described in terms of gold and silver, rubies and sapphires, words that have inevitably been associated with beauty rather than with corruption, the reader eventually begins to long for a single harsh phrase or metaphor of real ugliness. However, notwithstanding all his limitations, Traherne deserves a place of respect among the poets of his century for expressing, often very beautifully and appropriately, his own unique view of life and the way to human happiness.

Bibliography:
Clements, A. L. *The Mystical Poetry of Thomas Traherne*. Cambridge, Mass.: Harvard University Press, 1969. The most comprehensive book-length study of Traherne's poetic technique, themes, symbolism, and diction. Discusses the poems contained in the Dobell manuscript, one of the major sources of Traherne's poetry, as an interrelated sequence in the Christian contemplative tradition of writing. Includes appendices on Traherne and Renaissance poetic theory and practice, as well as on the mystical tradition.

Day, Malcolm M. *Thomas Traherne*. Boston: Twayne, 1982. A useful introduction to the Traherne canon, with a short chapter on the two most important manuscripts of Traherne's poetry, the Dobell and the Burney manuscripts. Includes a Traherne chronology and a short life history.

Leishman, James Blair. *The Metaphysical Poets: Donne, Herbert, Vaughan, Traherne*. Oxford, England: Clarendon Press, 1934. One of the best early studies of Traherne's poems placed within the context of English metaphysical poetry, though Leishman does not fully appreciate Traherne's skill as a poet and is not aware that the Dobell manuscript poems are a Metaphysical sequence.

Stewart, Stanley. *The Expanded Voice: The Art of Thomas Traherne*. San Marino, Calif.: Huntington Library, 1970. Contains two insightful, highly detailed chapters on Traherne's poetry. Believes that Traherne's poetic craftsmanship has been underappreciated, an oversight he goes a long way to rectifying.

Wallace, John Malcolm. "Thomas Traherne and the Structure of Meditation." *A Journal of English Literary History* 25, no. 2 (June, 1958): 79-89. Argues that the Dobell manuscript poems constitute a complete, five-part meditation modeled on St. Ignatius Loyola's *Spiritual Exercises* (1548).

POETRY OF VAUGHAN

Author: Henry Vaughan (1622-1695)
Principal published works: Poems, 1646; *Olor Iscanus*, 1651; *Silex Scintillans*, part 1, 1650, part 2, 1655; *Thalia Rediviva*, 1678

Henry Vaughan is best known as a religious poet, a follower of the metaphysical tradition of John Donne and George Herbert, and a precursor of William Wordsworth in his interest in the ideas of the seventeenth century Platonists, philosophers who emphasized humanity's innate good, the innocent wisdom of childhood, and the possibility of mystical union with God. Like John Donne, Vaughan turned to religious poetry relatively late in his career; he was a law student in London during the years just before the Civil War, and his first volume of verse, *Poems*, reveals his close reading of the popular court poets of the age of Charles I.

A number of his early poems are love lyrics addressed to Amoret, probably an imaginary lady. They show little originality, though they are competent, pleasant, polished works. Even at this stage in his development Vaughan was a skillful metrist, able to create many different effects through a variety of verse forms. His sentiments and images are typical of the age; his passion is strictly "platonic." It is the lady's soul he loves, though he complains that she is as heartless and unyielding as the ladies addressed by the other Cavalier poets. Cupid, the cruel god of love, plays a major part in many of Vaughan's lyrics, as he does in the works of writers like Ben Jonson and Thomas Randolph, to whom the poet acknowledges his debt.

There are, among the imitative and undistinguished lines of these poems, flashes of that gift of language that makes some of Vaughan's later lyrics rank high among the verses of his century:

> If, Amoret, that glorious Eye,
>   In the first birth of light,
>   And death of Night,
> Had with those elder fires you spy
>   Scatter'd so high
>   Received form, and sight;
> We might suspect in the vast Ring,
>   Amidst these golden glories,
>   And fierie stories;
> Whether the Sun had been the King,
>   And guide of Day,
>   Or your brighter eye should sway.

The comparison of the lady's brightness to that of the sun is commonplace, but the poet's vision of the night sky is his own.

Poems included, in addition to the typically Carolinian love lyrics, an amusing description of London night life that ended with a drinking song and a translation of Juvenal's tenth satire. Vaughan's translation reads smoothly, but it suffers greatly by comparison with Samuel Johnson's "The Vanity of Human Wishes," an adaptation of the same Latin poem. Though both English poets used iambic pentameter rhyming couplets, Vaughan's extended verse paragraphs have little of the pointed conciseness that the eighteenth century poet gave to the form. Satire was, in any case, quite foreign to Vaughan's temperament, and he wisely turned his attention to other subjects in his later works.

Most of the poems in *Olor Iscanus* were written in the mid-1640's; they also show the influence of poets of the preceding generation. Most of the poems are epistles to Vaughan's acquaintances on a variety of occasions: the publication of a volume of plays, an invitation to dinner, or the marriage of friends. The influence of Ben Jonson's poetry is clear in these works, as well as in the two elegies on Vaughan's friends who met their deaths in the Civil War. There are echoes of Jonson's famous poem on the death of Sir Henry Morison in "An Elegy on the Death of Mr. R. W. slain in the late unfortunate differences at Routon Heath, near Chester":

> Though in so short a span
> His riper thoughts had purchas'd more of man
> Than all those worthless livers, which yet quick,
> Have quite outgone their own Arithmetick.
> He seiz'd perfections, and without a dull
> And mossy gray possess'd a solid skull.

Vaughan's limitations as an elegiac poet are clear when one compares Jonson's lines on a similar subject:

> It is not growing like a tree
> In bulk doth make man better be;
> Or standing long an oak, three hundred year,
> To fall a log at last, dry, bald, and sere;
> A lily of a day
> Is Fairer far in May,
> Although it fall and die that night,
> It was the plant and flower of light.
> In small proportions we just beauties see;
> And in short measures, life may perfect be.

One of the most pleasant poems in *Olor Iscanus* is the one addressed "To the River Isca," from which the volume takes its name. This pastoral, reflective lyric, filled with the traditional images of "gentle swains," "beauteous nymphs," "bubbling springs and gliding streams," promises fame to the river through the poetry it inspired in Vaughan.

Had Vaughan's career ended with *Olor Iscanus*, he would probably have ranked with the very minor Cavalier poets. However, some event, or combination of events, perhaps the death of a beloved younger brother, brought about his religious conversion, and he found his true poetic voice in the works that appeared in the first part of *Silex Scintillans*. Vaughan's debt to George Herbert is evident in many of the poems; he followed Herbert's example in experimenting with various stanza forms and unusual patterns of syntax. Vaughan's "Sundays," like Herbert's "Prayer," consists exclusively of phrases describing the title word; neither poem contains a verb:

> Bright shadows of true Rest! some shoots of bliss,
> Heaven once a week;
> The next world's gladness prepossessed in this;
> A day to seek;
> Eternity in time; the steps by which
> We Climb above all ages; Lamps that light
> Man through his heap of dark days; and the rich,
> And full redemption of the whole weeks flight.

A number of Vaughan's themes also seem to have been drawn from Herbert's poetry, among them the ceremonies of the church, the celebration of important days in the Christian year, and the constantly emphasized relationship of human repentance and God's grace. What stands out as uniquely Vaughan's is the sense of innocence and joy that pervades much of his work. Although at some times he seems strongly aware of sin and the need for penitence, at others his Platonism seems to obliterate his consciousness of evil and he writes simple, joyous lyrics like the following:

> My Soul, there is a Country
>> Far beyond the stars,
> Where stands a winged Sentry
>> All skillful in the wars,
> There above noise, and danger
>> Sweet peace sits crown'd with smiles,
> And one born in a Manger
>> Commands the Beauteous files,
> He is thy gracious friend,
>> And (O my Soul awake!)
> Did in pure love descend
>> To die here for thy sake.

A poem often discussed in connection with Wordsworth's immortality ode is "The Retreat," in which Vaughan's Platonism is particularly evident. He refers to the glorious vision of God he preserved in his childhood and to his closeness to nature, which seemed to take him back to that heaven he inhabited before his birth:

> Happy those early dayes! when I
> Shin'd in my Angel-infancy.
> Before I understood this place
> Appointed for my second race,
> Or taught my soul to fancy ought
> But a white, Celestial thought,
> When yet I had not walked above
> A mile, or two, from my first love,
> And looking back (at that short space,)
> Could see a glimpse of his bright-face;
> When on some gilded Cloud, or flower
> My gazing soul would dwell an hour,
> And in those weaker glories spy
> Some shadows of eternity.

Some of Vaughan's other poems are far less sanguine about the human condition. "The World," whose opening lines, "I saw Eternity the other night like a great Ring of pure and endless light," are among the poet's most famous, pictures human beings as greedy and self-seeking: "the darksome statesman hung with weights and woe," "the fearful miser on a heap of rust," "the downright Epicure." The poet comments on the folly of those who reject salvation, who "prefer dark night before true light."

Another theme that seems to have fascinated Vaughan was the relationship of body and soul. Unlike the medieval poets who presented two forces pulling in opposite directions, the soul toward God and the body toward the gratification of physical desires, Vaughan sees them as harmonious, concerned chiefly about that period of separation between death and the resurrection. In "Resurrection and Immortality," the soul reassures the body, as if it were a frightened child, that all will be well:

> Like some spruce Bride,
> Shall one day rise, and cloth'd with shining light
> All pure, and bright
> Re-marry to the soul, for 'tis most plain
> Thou [the body] only fall'st to be refin'd again.

It is difficult to pinpoint characteristic images in Vaughan's poetry as a whole, for he varies his language with his theme. However, his use of light, brightness, the sun, and the stars, to reflect his sense of the glory of God, is especially memorable. There is a particularly interesting variation on this typically Platonic use of light in the poem entitled "Night":

> There is in God (some say)
> A deep, but dazzling darkness; As men here
> Say it is late and dusky, because they
>   See not all clear;
>   O for that night! where I in him
>   Might live invisible and dim.

Vaughan makes effective use of commonplace images in a number of his poems. He builds one around the analogy between the root, lying dormant in the ground before it can appear clothed in new loveliness in the spring, and the buried body, preparing in death for the resurrection. In "Man" he describes the human condition in the language of weaving:

> He knocks at all doors, strays and roams,
> Nay hath not so much wit as some stones have
> Which in the darkest nights point to their homes,
>   By some hid sense their Maker gave;
> Man is the shuttle, to whose winding quest
>   And passage through these looms
> God order'd motion, but ordain'd no rest.

Vaughan never entirely abandoned the poetic diction of some of the poems in *Olor Iscanus*, and his last volume, *Thalia Rediviva*, contains several works approaching the neoclassical manner of Edmund Waller and Sir John Denham. It should be noted, however, that many of these "late" poems were actually written many years before their publication, before Vaughan had done his best work.

Vaughan's religious poems are seldom brilliant throughout; he was a writer whose genius showed itself more fully in single fine lines than in sustained thoughts. However, his ability to convey a sense of personal feeling in his meditations, which sometimes reflect his moods of ecstasy, sometimes his melancholy view of humanity's rejection of salvation, makes his works moving in their entirety. His natural bent seems to have been more toward an exalted, visionary state than toward depression, for it is in the poems describing his joy that he is generally at his best. His sense of sin and struggle seems more often imitative of Herbert's poetry than drawn from his own feelings. Vaughan's work provides an interesting bridge between the intense struggle for personal faith that fills the poetry of Donne and Herbert and the ecstatic paeans of Richard Crashaw and Thomas Traherne.

Bibliography:
Durr, R. A. *On the Mystical Poetry of Henry Vaughan.* Cambridge, Mass.: Harvard University Press, 1962. Durr sees Vaughan's poetry as a realization and celebration of a mystical experience. He looks at major metaphors and gives a close reading to several poems. Particularly useful is a brief survey of recent studies.
Garner, Ross. *Henry Vaughan: Experience and the Tradition.* Chicago: University of Chicago Press, 1959. Focusing on Vaughan's allegorical habit of mind, Garner reads Vaughan's poetry in the light of various traditions, including Augustinianism and Hermeticism, and considers Vaughan's view of nature and of the physical universe.
Hutchinson, F. E. *Henry Vaughan: A Life and Interpretation.* Oxford, England: Clarendon Press, 1947. Uses private letters, poetry, and Vaughan's other writings to record the major events of Vaughan's life, his Welsh roots, and the intellectual development of the poet's mind.
Martz, Louis L. "Henry Vaughan: The Caves of Memory." In *The Paradise Within: Studies in Vaughan, Traherne, and Milton.* New Haven, Conn.: Yale University Press, 1964. Martz sees the influence of George Herbert in Vaughan's poetry and considers many themes and images reflective of Vaughan's spiritual and intellectual development.
Simmonds, James D. *Masques of God: Form and Theme in the Poetry of Henry Vaughan.* Pittsburgh: University of Pittsburgh Press, 1972. Seeks to correct previous misreadings of Vaughan's work. Sees in Vaughan's poetry an organic development in close touch with human experience and marked by humor, a playful spirit, and a lively awareness of the world.

POINT COUNTER POINT

Type of work: Novel
Author: Aldous Huxley (1894-1963)
Type of plot: Social realism
Time of plot: 1920's
Locale: England
First published: 1928

>
> *Principal characters:*
> PHILIP QUARLES, a novelist
> ELINOR, his wife
> SIDNEY, his father
> RACHEL, his mother
> JOHN BIDLAKE, Elinor's father
> MRS. BIDLAKE, her mother
> LITTLE PHILIP, Philip and Elinor's son
> DENIS BURLAP, the editor of *The Literary World*
> BEATRICE GILRAY, his mistress
> SPANDRELL, a cynic
> EVERARD WEBLEY, a disciple of force
> WALTER BIDLAKE, Elinor's brother
> MARJORIE CARLING, his mistress
> LUCY TANTAMOUNT, the woman with whom he is infatuated
> MARK RAMPION, an artist

The Story:

Walter Bidlake had been living with a married woman named Marjorie Carling for a year and a half, and he was growing tired of her. He felt tied to her by a moral obligation but oppressed by her attempts to possess him; she had rejected his proposal that they live together as close friends but leading independent lives. In any case, it was too late for that now, since Marjorie was pregnant. Her whining jealousy toward his latest infatuation, Lucy Tantamount, pricked Walter's conscience, and he was angry with himself for making Marjorie unhappy by going to a party at Tantamount House without her.

Elinor and Philip Quarles traveled abroad, leaving little Philip behind under the care of a governess and his grandmother, Mrs. Bidlake. Philip was a novelist, and his life consisted of jotting down in his notebook incidents and thoughts that might make material for his next novel. His mind was turned inward, introspective, and his self-centered interests gave him little time for emotional experience. Elinor wished that he could love her as much as she loved him, but she resigned herself to the unhappy dilemma of being loved as much as Philip could possibly love any woman.

Denis Burlap, editor of *The Literary World*, flattered himself with the just conceit that although his magazine was not a financial success, it at least contributed to the intellectual life of his time. Walter, one of his chief contributors, asked for more pay; Burlap hedged until Walter felt ashamed of his demands. Burlap was attracted to Beatrice Gilray, a pathetic figure who had feared the very touch of a man ever since she had been attacked by her uncle while riding in a taxicab. Burlap hoped eventually to seduce Beatrice. Meanwhile, they were living together. Also part of this social set was Spandrell, an indolent son of a doting mother who supported him, and Everard Webley, a friend of Elinor and the leader of a conservative militaristic group called the British Freemen.

Philip's father, Sidney Quarles, pretended that he was writing a long history, but he had not progressed much beyond the purchase of office equipment. His wife, Rachel, assumed the burden of managing their affairs and patiently endured Sidney's whims and mild flirtations. Now it was apparently someone in London, for Sidney made frequent trips to the British Museum to gather material for his history. The young woman appeared one day at the Quarles's country house and in loud and furious tones informed Sidney that she was pregnant. When Rachel appeared, Sidney quietly left the room. Rachel settled the affair quietly.

Marjorie continued to arouse Walter's pity and cause him to regret his association with Lucy Tantamount, particularly because Lucy was not much interested in Walter. She became tired of London and went to Paris. When Elinor and Philip returned from abroad, they found their son faring well under the care of his governess and his grandmother. John Bidlake had learned that he was dying of cancer and had returned to his wife's home. He had become a cantankerous patient and treated little Philip alternately with kindness and harshness.

Since Lucy was in Paris, Philip was able to persuade Walter to take Marjorie to the Quarles home in the country in the hope that this would lead to some sort of reconciliation. Rachel Quarles began to like Marjorie, and the pregnant woman found herself becoming more cheerful in the new environment. Shortly after she and Walter had come to the Quarles estate, Walter received a letter from Lucy in Paris, telling him that she had found a new lover who had seduced her in a shabby Parisian studio. With her newly acquired contentment, Marjorie felt sympathy for Walter, who was crestfallen at Lucy's rejection.

Everard Webley had long been in love with Elinor. Sometimes she wondered whether Philip would care if she went to another man, and she decided that it would be Philip's own fault if she turned to Everard. She felt that a breach was forming between herself and Philip, but she could not arouse his attention to make him realize what was happening. She arranged a rendezvous with Everard.

Behind the scenes of lovemaking and unfaithfulness lurked the political enmity between Spandrell and Everard. Elinor Quarles was home alone awaiting Everard's call when Spandrell and a telegram arrived simultaneously. The telegram informed Elinor that little Philip was ill and urged her to come to her father's home. Elinor asked Spandrell to wait and tell Everard that she could not keep her appointment with him. Spandrell agreed. When Everard arrived at Elinor's home, Spandrell attacked him and killed him. Spandrell lugged the dead body into a car and drove it away. Later that evening, he met Philip and told him his son was ill.

Philip arrived at the Bidlake estate the next day in time to hear the doctor say that young Philip had meningitis. Elinor stayed by the child's side for days, waiting for the crisis to pass. One night, the sick boy opened his eyes and told his parents that he was hungry. They were overjoyed at his apparent recovery; later that night, he died suddenly. As they had done in the past, Elinor and Philip escaped by going abroad.

For a long while, the Webley murder baffled the police. Despairing of ever escaping from his meaningless existence, Spandrell sent the British Freemen a note stating that Everard's murderer, armed, would be found at a certain address at a certain hour. On their arrival, the Freemen found Spandrell pointing a gun at them. They shot him.

Burlap was the only happy man among these sensualists and intellectuals. One night, he and Beatrice pretended they were children and splashed merrily while taking their bath together.

Critical Evaluation:

Aldous Huxley was one of the most intellectual writers of the twentieth century. Classically educated, he was interested in a wide range of subjects, and his novels are primarily vehicles to present his intellectual and philosophical views. In *Point Counter Point*, he describes such books as novels of ideas.

Beyond being a structurally and thematically complex novel, *Point Counter Point* is a harsh, insightful portrait of London society in the 1920's. D. H. Lawrence once praised it by saying that if the public truly understood Huxley's message, they would be banning it rather than his own *Lady Chatterley's Lover* (1928). Not only a novel of ideas, *Point Counter Point* is also a *roman à clef*, in which the characters are thinly veiled portraits, or in this case caricatures of real people. Rampion is Huxley's version of D. H. Lawrence, while Philip Quarles represents Huxley himself. Huxley reveals the novel's structure, as well as its theme, in the title. In music, counterpoint refers to notes added to the main melody, or the point, to create a second melody that combines with the first in an intended relationship. Philip Quarles, in his notebooks on writing, explains his desire to musicalize fiction. To do this, he thinks an author should "show several people falling in love or dying or praying in different ways." This describes Huxley's structure. Parallel relationships abound in the novel. Situations are introduced and later reappear with different characters. With this method, Huxley examines the central relationships in human lives: those between lovers, between parents and children, and between humans and God. The harmony sought in musical counterpoint rarely appears in this novel, however, for the society he presents lacks balance. This lack, in combination with the characters' inability to combine feelings and intellect, passion and reason, lies at the novel's core.

The very first scene sets the tone as Marjorie pleads with her lover, Walter, to stay, while at the same time she is too refined to make a scene. Clearly it would be better both for her and the relationship if she would act on her feelings, but she is unable to do so. When Walter leaves to pursue the shallow, sadistic Lucy Tantamount, he knows he is behaving badly; indeed, he has spent his entire life trying to avoid imitating his father's jolly careless sensuality but is unable to stop himself.

This first triangle is contrasted with the relationship between Philip and Elinor Quarles. She loves him, but he is too intellectual to respond to her with feeling and has instead withdrawn into a dispassionate, analytical state where Elinor is unable to reach him. While they are in India, a full moon reminds Elinor of evenings spent together in Hertfordshire when they were first in love. Although Philip understands what she means when she talks of the moon, he engages her in a debate about logic because he is unhappy about being interrupted. Discussing his feelings makes him uncomfortable and threatens his remote, frigid silence. Philip, like Walter, is fully aware of the flaws in his nature and wishes to respond differently, yet he, too, is unable to make the effort necessary to change. Elinor is driven into pursuing a relationship with Webley simply because he possesses the emotion Philip lacks. Almost all of the male-female relationships in the novel are similarly damaged.

Huxley also explores parent-child relationships and their later effect on adult behavior. While Philip and Elinor travel around the world, they entrust their young son to a nursemaid and his grandmother. Even when they return, they are not really a part of his life. When he is ill, both Philip and Elinor resent being called to his bedside. Elinor comments that nature never intended her to have children. The most painful parent-child relationship exists between Spandrell and his mother. He can pinpoint one moment in his life, when he was fifteen and watching his mother as they skied in Europe, as the dividing line between the innocent happiness of his youth and the utter cynicism and contempt he now feels. After his mother married the arrogant

General Knoyle, Spandrell deliberately starts making the worst possible choices in everything. "He was spiting her, spiting himself, spiting God." Again the lack of balance is clear.

Religion intrudes to some extent, but it is seen in most cases as promoting unnatural, rather than harmonious, behavior. Throughout their marriage, Marjorie's husband, a drunken preacher, uses religion to torment her. Huxley criticizes saints and ascetics as unnatural. Rampion contemptuously describes Saint Francis of Assisi licking the sores of lepers not to help the lepers in any way but only to degrade himself. It is Spandrell, the degenerate cynic, who most desperately searches for God yet cannot change. Rampion finds him refusing "to be a man . . . either a daemon or a dead angel."

All but two of the central characters in the novel—Rampion, the artist, and his wife, May—are missing balance. Rampion provides the counterpoint throughout the novel as the voice of balance and reason. D. H. Lawrence found his fictionalized self, "a boring gas bag." Although he illustrates balance, it is only in the early idyllic courtship scenes that Rampion does anything but pontificate. In fact, there is a good deal of satire in the presentation. However, it is clear that Huxley intends him to be the novel's central figure, since he provides a touchstone for the other characters in the story who seek his advice and approval.

"Critical Evaluation" by Mary Mahony

Bibliography:

Baker, Robert. *The Dark Historic Page: Social Satire and Historicism in the Novels of Aldous Huxley, 1921-1939.* Madison: University of Wisconsin Press, 1982. Presents four of the novel's main contrapuntal plot lines, which are centered around relationships with parents, lovers, death, and God. Argues that Spandrell is central to each of these plot lines.

Bedford, Sybille. *Aldous Huxley: A Biography.* New York: Alfred A. Knopf, 1973. Detailed biography based primarily on oral sources that traces Huxley's intellectual and moral development from early childhood on. Presents a fascinating insight into the Huxley family. Discusses the novel's theme, characterization, and critical reaction.

Bowering, Peter. *Aldous Huxley: A Study of the Major Novels.* New York: Oxford University Press, 1969. Presents Huxley as a novelist of ideas who uses minimal plot and character development so as to focus on theme and satire. Discusses Huxley's relationship with D. H. Lawrence and its influence on the themes and ideas in the novel.

Meckier, Jerome. *Aldous Huxley: Satire and Structure.* London: Chatto & Windus, 1969. An excellent introductory source that isolates major themes of *Point Counter Point* and provides the clearest overview of its structure. Includes a detailed analysis of Rampion's central role and of his ruthless assessments of other characters, as well as the use of models for many characters.

Nance, Guinevera A. *Aldous Huxley.* New York: Continuum, 1988. A clear introductory work that discusses Huxley's intellectual development and his detached, reflective presentation of a society without balance. Also analyzes the characters, parallel story lines, and recurring themes of *Point Counter Point.*

POLYEUCTE

Type of work: Drama
Author: Pierre Corneille (1606-1684)
Type of plot: Tragedy
Time of plot: 250 C.E.
Locale: Melitene, the capital of Armenia
First performed: 1642; first published, 1643 (English translation, 1655)

Principal characters:
FÉLIX, Roman governor of Armenia
PAULINE, his daughter
POLYEUCTE, his son-in-law, an Armenian nobleman
NÉARQUE, Polyeucte's friend
STRATONICE, Pauline's friend
ALBIN, Félix's friend
SÉVÈRE, a Roman warrior, in love with Pauline

The Story:

Pauline, daughter of Félix, the Roman governor in Melitene, had been married fourteen days to Polyeucte, an Armenian nobleman. Terrified by dreams which seemed to portend her husband's death, she vainly sought to delay his departure on a secret mission, the nature of which was known only to his friend Néarque. She related her fears to her friend Stratonice and told her of her earlier love for Sévère, a Roman of high birth whom her father would not allow her to marry because of Sévère's lack of fortune. When the Emperor Decie had appointed Félix governor of Armenia, she had accompanied him and dutifully married an Armenian nobleman of her father's selection. Meanwhile, they had heard that Sévère had met a hero's death while aiding the emperor in battle against the Persians. According to the report, the young Roman's body had never been found.

Pauline had dreamed that Sévère was not dead, but rather threatened her husband's life; that a band of impious Christians had thrown Polyeucte at the feet of Sévère, and that she, Pauline, crying out for aid from her father, had seen Sévère raise a dagger to pierce Polyeucte's breast. Her fears were further stirred when her father approached and said that Sévère was alive and was at that moment entering the city. It seemed that the king of Persia, struck by Sévère's gallantry, had reclaimed the body from the battlefield in order to gain the Roman an honorable burial. Miraculously, life had been restored to Sévère and the Persians had sent him to Rome in exchange for royal prisoners. Thereafter his greater deeds in war had bound him closer to the emperor, who had sent him to Armenia to proclaim the good news of his victories and to make sacrifices of thanksgiving to the gods.

His love for Pauline was what had really brought Sévère to Armenia. Sévère, informed by his servant that Pauline was wedded, decided that life was not worth living and that he would rather die in battle. First, however, he would see Pauline. When they met, she told him that if hers alone had been the choice she would, despite his poverty, have chosen him. She was married, however, and she would remain loyal to the husband whom she had learned to love. They bade each other farewell, he ready to die in battle, she to pray for him in secret.

Polyeucte returned from his mission, on which he had been secretly baptized a Christian. Ordered by a messenger from Félix to attend the sacrifices in the temple, he and Néarque planned to defy the idolatry of the worshipers there. Pauline told him of Sévère's visit but added that she had obtained his promise not to see her again. Stratonice, a witness at the temple sacrifices, hurried to Pauline with the news that Polyeucte had become a Christian, a traitor to the Roman gods. He had mocked the sacred mysteries and, with Néarque, had declared that their god alone was the almighty king of earth and heaven. This defilement, Félix declared, would cost Néarque his life, but he hoped Polyeucte might come to his senses and recant after witnessing the punishment and death of his friend.

When Albin, the friend of Félix, brought news that Néarque was dead, he added that Polyeucte had witnessed his execution undismayed. Pauline, reminding her father that Polyeucte was his choice and that in marrying him she had but fulfilled her filial duty, begged him to spare his life. Félix, fearing the thunderbolts of his gods and Sévère as well, refused to listen when Albin urged that Polyeucte's sentence be left to the emperor. Besides, he was tempted by the thought that Polyeucte's death would allow Sévère to wed his daughter and thus he would gain for himself a far more powerful protector than he now had. Meanwhile, Pauline visited Polyeucte in jail with the plea that if he must worship his chosen god he should do so silently and secretly, and thus give Félix grounds for mercy. To her importunings Polyeucte replied that he was done with mortal ties, that he loved her, but loved his God more.

Polyeucte called for Sévère and told him that even as his wedding had parted the true love of Sévère and Pauline, so now by dying he hoped to bring them happily together. He hoped also that they would die Christians. Declaring himself ready for death, he was marched off by his guards. Sévère was amazed at this example of magnanimity, but his hopes were shattered when Pauline told him she could never marry him, that it would stain her honor to wed anyone who, even innocently, had brought Polyeucte to his sad fate. She begged him, however, to try to save her husband from the death her father had ordered. He consented, if for no other reason than to prove to Pauline that he could equal her in nobility and thus be worthy of her. Félix, although he regarded this intervention on behalf of a rival as a trick to expose him to the full strength of the emperor's wrath, made one last effort to sway his son-in-law. He told Polyeucte that only on Sévère's account had he publicly taken his rigid stand and that he himself would adopt Christianity if Polyeucte would only pretend to follow the old gods until after Sévère had left the city. Polyeucte refused. Angered, Félix said he would avenge his gods and himself. When Pauline entered, Polyeucte commanded her to wed Sévère or die with him as a Christian.

Again Pauline pleaded for Polyeucte's life, and again Félix was moved to make another attempt to persuade Polyeucte to abjure his new faith, but to no avail. Bidding farewell to Pauline, Polyeucte was marched out to death by Félix's order. Pauline rushed out after him, lamenting that she too would die if he were to die. Félix ordered Albin to deter her but issued his order too late; Pauline saw her husband executed. Seeing him die, she felt that his death had unsealed her own eyes, acting as a divine visitation of grace. She declared herself a Christian, ready for death.

Sévère upbraided Félix for Polyeucte's death and threatened retaliation. Félix, suddenly yielding to a strange feeling that overcame him, declared that his son-in-law's death had made him a Christian. This sudden conversion struck Sévère as miraculous. He ordered Félix to retain his position of authority, and promised to use all his persuasion to urge Emperor Decie to revoke his cruel commands and to let all worship the gods of their choice without fear of punishment.

Critical Evaluation:

Polyeucte, although a favorite of the general public in Pierre Corneille's time, was not considered his best play. Modern criticism, however, has revised this judgment. Despite the play's somewhat improbable plot, climaxed by miraculous conversions, it holds for today's public particular religious interest, since it deals with the working of divine grace in the human soul. It is, however, the strong delineation of the main characters that has won for this work its present acclaim.

Ever since *Polyeucte*'s initial performance, critics have wondered what Pierre Corneille meant when he called the play "a Christian tragedy." Corneille was a practicing Catholic who was educated by Jesuits. He translated religious works such as *The Imitation of Christ* (1486), a work traditionally attributed to Saint Thomas à Kempis, into French. No serious critic has ever questioned the sincerity of Corneille's commitment to Christianity. For the title character in *Polyeucte* there is no conflict. Although he loves his wife, Pauline, he understands clearly that he would lose his immortal soul if he were to renounce Christianity in order to save his life. When he married Pauline, he was still a pagan, but afterward he received the gift of faith and he was converted to Christianity, a religion then persecuted throughout the Roman Empire. He respects the temporal authority of his father-in-law Félix, who is the Roman governor of Armenia, but Polyeucte realizes that he owes a higher allegiance to God than he does to the Roman Empire. Certain critics have suggested that *Polyeucte* can be viewed as a tragedy for its other three principal characters, namely Félix, Polyeucte's wife Pauline, and the Roman nobleman Sévère, but it is necessary to stress the major differences among these three characters. Until his totally unexpected conversion announced in the final scene of the fifth act, Félix acts in a petty and insensitive manner. Although he recognizes that Polyeucte and Pauline love each other and have a reasonably good marriage, he wishes that he had chosen the politically successful Sévère, who is now an influential adviser to the Roman emperor Decie rather than the Armenian Polyeucte, who has little interest in politics. Félix is from Rome, and he considers himself superior to the Armenians whom he governs. Before her marriage to Polyeucte, Pauline had been attracted to Sévère, but she willingly acceded to her father's request when he arranged her marriage to Polyeucte. Félix thought that Polyeucte would have a more promising political career than Sévère, but things turned out differently. Polyeucte never developed any interest in political intrigue, and Sévère's military valor brought him to the attention of influential people in Rome, and he quickly became a trusted confidant of Emperor Decie. Pauline loves and respects her husband who is a decent and kind man. Félix is, however, insensitive to his daughter's feelings for her husband, and he regrets bitterly that he chose the wrong husband for her. When he learns from Sévère that the Roman emperor Decie, who reigned for just two years from 249 to 251, demands that all Roman governors enforce Roman laws which required a sentence of death for people found practicing Christianity, Félix does not hesitate. He is more afraid of losing his political position than saving the life of his son-in-law. Félix also acts in a rather sadistic manner. In a vain effort to persuade Polyeucte to renounce Christianity, he forces his son-in-law to watch the execution of his friend and fellow Christian Néarque, but his martyrdom serves only to reinforce Polyeucte's commitment to Christianity. Why should he fear death? He believes that his martyrdom will guarantee his spending eternity in heaven.

For Félix and Polyeucte no tragic conflict exists, but this is not necessarily the case for Sévère and Pauline. Their passion for each other was profound, and they would have gotten married had Félix not chosen Polyeucte to marry Pauline. Pauline and Sévère are, however, responsible adults, and they both resist temptation. Neither wants to commit adultery. Although her confidante, Stratonice, and her father, Félix, tell her repeatedly that Néarque had "seduced" Polyeucte into converting to the hated religion of Christianity, Pauline still loves her husband and respects his judgment. The most emotionally charged scene in *Polyeucte* is Act IV, scene iii, which takes place in Polyeucte's prison cell. Pauline tells her husband that his desire for martyrdom means that he has rejected her after she had sacrificed everything for him. Polyeucte assures her that he still loves her so much that he wants to lead her to Christianity so that she can also be saved. She is baffled by his arguments, which she describes as a "strange blindness." Sévère is equally mystified by the behavior of Christians who willingly sacrifice their lives and even pray for those who condemn them to death. At the end of the fourth act, Sévère speaks of his intention of defending Polyeucte and other Christians who have been sentenced to death. Unfortunately, there is a tragic misunderstanding between Sévère and Félix. Félix assumes that Sévère will have him dismissed from his position if he appears weak by requesting clemency for his son-in-law or if he does not enforce Decie's cruel and unjust laws against Christians by ordering the execution of Polyeucte. Félix does not realize that Sévère believes that certain laws are so unconscionable that one's conscience requires one to resist them. Félix acts hastily and orders Polyeucte's execution before Sévère has an opportunity to reverse this unjust decision. The martyrdom of Polyeucte produces extraordinary changes in the other three major characters. Félix and Polyeucte receive the divine grace of faith and announce their conversions to Sévère, who spares them both and expresses a fervent wish that the persecution of Christians will soon end. *Polyeucte* does not truly express a tragic vision of the world, but it does illustrate Corneille's extraordinary skill in creating heroic characters whose actions are so admirable and exemplary that they provoke unexpected moral changes in others.

"Critical Evaluation" by Edmund J. Campion

Bibliography:
Abraham, Claude. *Pierre Corneille*. New York: Twayne, 1972. Contains an excellent introduction to Corneille's plays and includes an annotated bibliography of important critical studies. Discusses the meaning of divine grace and the extraordinary evolution of Pauline.
Harwood-Gordon, Sharon. *The Poetic Style of Corneille's Tragedies: An Aesthetic Interpretation*. Lewiston, N.Y.: Edwin Mellen Press, 1989. Examines the rhetorical brilliance of key speeches in *Polyeucte* and other tragedies by Corneille. Explores the emotional and religious arguments that should cause audience members not to question the sincerity of Pauline's conversion to Christianity.
Muratore, Mary Jo. *The Evolution of the Cornelian Heroine*. Potomac, Md.: Studia Humanitatis, 1982. Examines the differences between idealistic heroines such as Pauline and unsympathetic female characters, including Cleopatra and Medea. Questions the sincerity of Pauline's religious conversion after her husband's martyrdom.
Nelson, Robert J. *Corneille: His Heroes and Their Worlds*. Philadelphia: University of Pennsylvania Press, 1963. Explores the evolving nature of heroism for Corneille's male characters. Discusses the political and psychological opposition between Polyeucte and Sévère.
Pocock, Gordon. *Corneille and Racine: Problems of Tragic Form*. Cambridge, England: Cambridge University Press, 1973. Analyzes the formal structure of *Polyeucte* and explores the problematic nature of the conversion of Pauline and Félix after Polyeucte's execution. Examines the rhetorical effectiveness of key speeches in the tragedy.

POLY-OLBION

Type of work: Poetry
Author: Michael Drayton (1563-1631)
First published: part 1, 1612; part 2, 1622

The complete title of Michael Drayton's long topographical poem is *Poly-Olbion: Or, A Chorographicall Description of Tracts, Rivers, Mountaines, Forests, and other Parts of this renowned Isle of Great Britaine, With intermixture of the most Remarquable Stories, Antiquities, Wonders, Rarityes, Pleasures, and Commodities of the same, Digested in a Poem*. Quite a bit of digesting is entailed, especially when a title page note continues, "With a Table added, for direction to those occurrences of Story and Antiquitie, whereunto the Course of the Volume easily leades not." This table is Drayton's extensive index to the proper names in the poem, and it is printed separately in volume 5 of the standard edition listed in the bibliography below. The title derives from "Poly," meaning "many," and Albion, a name for England that is related to the Greek word for "happy."

Drayton's opus comprises thirty "songs," as he calls his poems, eighteen in part 1 and twelve in part 2, each preceded by a summary "Argument" of twelve to twenty lines in rhymed iambic tetrameter. Each song celebrates the natural beautifies and historic events of a particular region of Great Britain and is accompanied by an impressionistic map of that area. Although songs 22 and 24 go on for 1,638 and 1,320 lines, respectively, the songs generally run between 450 and 500 lines of rhymed alexandrines, or lines of iambic hexameter, divided frequently by caesuras and split almost evenly between end-stopped and enjambed. Allusions to British history and classical myth abound, and personification becomes a reliable narrative device, notably in the pretense that it is Drayton's muse who is speaking. The term "chorography," which is no longer used, in Drayton's time commonly specified writings about topography, and several classical models of the genre were available to Drayton. Among many influences on Drayton, the Renaissance historian and antiquary William Camden organized his *Brittania* (1596) by counties, as did Drayton. *Poly-Olbion*, part 1, is dedicated to Prince Henry, son of the reigning monarch, James I.

The frontispiece to *Poly-Olbion*, an engraving by William Hole, presents an elaborate tangle of allegorical meanings. Drayton personifies Great Britain as a woman seated within a triumphal arch. Britain holds in her right hand a scepter that signifies her power, and in her left an overflowing cornucopia symbolizing the richness of her land. The open sea behind Britain teems with ships that suggest the sea power Great Britain enjoyed under Elizabeth I, and indeed it is hard not to see the dead queen in the personified Britain. The soft folds of Britain's clothing are adorned with the peaks and valleys appropriate to a topographical poem. On the four corners of the arch appear statues of Great Britain's four conquerors: Brute, or Brutus, the legendary nephew of Aeneas; Julius Caesar; the Saxon Hengist, who conquered the land in 449; and William the Conqueror, who led the Norman triumph at Hastings in 1066, and from whom King James I traced his descent. These figures form a loose historical framework for part 1 of the poem.

Summed up broadly, Drayton's poem depicts the pre-Anglo Saxon period as the source of Great Britain's distinctive culture. The Romans and the Saxon hordes of Hengist contributed their own unique elements—for example, the Anglo Saxons brought the Christian influence—but the Normans despoiled the land by oppressing its conquered people. Significantly, considering that part 1 appeared in the middle of James I's reign (from 1603 to 1625), Drayton concludes his short poem explicating the frontispiece with these lines: "Divorst from Him [the Roman], the *Saxon sable* Horse,/ Borne by sterne *Hengist*, wins her [Britain]: but through force/ Garding the *Norman Leopards bath'd in Gules*,/ She chang'd hir Love to Him, whose Line yet rules."

Each song in part 1 is followed by "Illustrations," or several pages of dense notes expanding on the historical background and meaning of individual lines. The author of these notes was John Selden, a learned scholar and friend of Drayton, who explained his mission as illuminating "What the Verse oft, with allusion, as supposing a full knowing Reader, lets slip; or in winding steps of Personating Fictions (as some times) so infolds, that suddaine conceipt cannot abstract a Forme of the clothed Truth." The erudition of Selden's annotations can exhaust the unwary reader, especially one who ventures into the marginal glosses, speckled with Greek and Latin, that offer clarifying refinements on the illustrations themselves.

In a rather peevish address "To the General Reader" prefacing part 1, Drayton complains of a "great disadvantage" against him in "this lunatique Age." He is referring to poems that are "wholly deduc't to Chambers," "kept in Cabinets," and circulated only "by Transcription." He inveighs against so-called "coterie" poetry, the property of small elitist groups. This fashion works against a poet such as Drayton, who writes with a nationalist bias and hopes for a large public audience. He grumbles that his "unusuall tract may perhaps seeme difficult, to the female Sex; yea, and I feare, to some that think themselves not meanly learned." These cabinet poets are reviled in song 21 for "Inforcing things in Verse for Poesie unfit,/ Mere filthy stuffe, that breakes out of the sores of wit." Drayton was the first to introduce this distinction between public and private verse, now a commonplace in the literary history of the period.

In condemning coterie verse, Drayton asserted the value, going back to Aristotle's *Poetics* (c. 334–323 B.C.E.), of nemesis, or imitation, in art. He pleads in song 21 for smooth lines that flow "like swelling *Euphrates*" and states that poets are like painters in expressing things "neerest to the life." The power of the poet's art resembles that of Orpheus, who charmed the trees and rocks and led them "T' imbrace a civill life, by his inticing Layes." This theory assumes a serious civic role for the poet, a responsibility the frustrated Drayton feels has been thwarted by the cabinet poets.

Poly-Olbion has a prominent historical context and reveals some strong prejudices. For instance, Drayton had studied Welsh historians and apparently accepted their claim that the Welsh were descended from the Trojans and were the first inhabitants of Great Britain. Song 1 includes a long account of how "Noble Brutus" and his Trojan cohorts arrived in Cornwall and fought the "monstrous Giants" there. In Drayton's telling, Cornwall received its name from the Trojan Corineus, who wrestled the huge Gogmagog and threw him into the sea. This account exemplifies Drayton's fanciful blending of legend with topography.

Drayton's confidence that Great Britain had its counterparts for everything that the Greeks and Romans had leads him in song 10 to praise the historicity of the stories about Great Britain's Trojan ancestors. Throughout *Poly-Olbion*, aspects of British life are validated by their superiority to classical antecedents, as in these lines from song 7 in which the Golden Fleece is bested: "*Lug* little *Oney* first, then *Arro* in doth take [describing the confluence of three rivers],/ At *Lemster*, for her Wooll whose Staple doth excell,/ And seemes to over-match the golden *Phrygian* fell." Guy of Warwick ("The Knight through all the world renown'd for Chivalrie" in song 12) becomes a virtual Hercules through the magnificence of his accomplishments.

The legends traditionally associated with Bath, Avon, and Avalon enrich the hymns to various rivers and streams that make up song 3. The centerpiece of the song becomes the Arthurian material, such as "great Arthurs Tombe" and "holy Joseph's grave." The monastery at Glastonbury reflects "our great fathers pompe, devotion and their skill." This passage moves Selden in his illustrations to recite the story that Henry II ordered the local abbot, Henry of Blois, to dig up Arthur's body, which was duly found in a wooden coffin. It is a mark of Selden's dutifulness that he observes of the wood in this coffin, "*Girald* saith Oken, *Leland* thinks Alder."

Renaissance poets frequently pondered the mysteries of time and change, and this fondness for the mutability theme intersects in song 3 with Drayton's fascination with Stonehenge. For Drayton, the "Dull heape" stands as a memorial to some grand past now lost to time. Drayton's personified "mightie Mount" of Wansdike "doth complaine" to Stonehenge in these lines: "Ill did those mightie men to trust thee with their storie,/ That hast forgot their names, who rear'd thee for their glorie:/ For all their wondrous cost, thou that hast serv'd them so,/ What tis to trust to Tombes, by thee we easely know." Humanity can take no solace in monuments, and thus it becomes imperative for the artist—the poet, such as Drayton—to preserve the memory of a long and grand tradition.

Drayton returned to this theme in part 2, dedicated to Prince Charles, but the work begins on a bilious note. In his brief preface to part 2, "To Any That Will Read It," Drayton laments that when he began his "Herculean labour" he was hopeful of its success, "But it hath fallen out otherwise." He blames the "barbarous Ignorance" of British readers, and the greedy stationers who are eager to market their "beastly and abominable Trash." With his voice rising to a screech, Drayton curses that small number who take pride in their benightedness: "for these, since they delight in their folly, I wish it may be hereditary from them to their posteritie, that their children may bee beg'd for Fooles to the fift Generation, untill it may be beyond the memory of man to know that there was ever any other of their Families."

The bitterness in these lines anticipates the hints of pessimism in part 2. *Poly-Olbion* ends with Drayton contemplating a mysterious grouping of "Stones seventie seven" formed in a ring. He complains sadly that "The victories for which these Trophies were begun,/ From darke oblivion thou, O Time, shouldst have protected." In the final line of his work, his Herculean toil has picked up a new adjective and become "This strange *Herculean* toyle," as if perhaps even he himself cannot decide exactly what he has wrought in these 14,454 lines supplemented by the equally heroic toil of Selden in his illustrations to part 1.

Frank Day

Bibliography:

Brink, Jean R. *Michael Drayton Revisited*. Boston: Twayne, 1990. A revisionist study of Drayton influenced by the New Historicism. Attributes to Drayton more influence on literary theory than previously acknowledged. Spells out the humanist and antiquarian sources of *Poly-Olbion*. Excellent annotated bibliography.

Drayton, Michael. *Poly-Olbion*. Vols. 4 and 5 in *The Works of Michael Drayton*, edited by J. William Hebel. Oxford, England: Basil Blackwell, 1961. The standard edition, with all of the excellent editorial notes and bibliography in volume 5. The glosses and typography in the large volume 4 capture a feeling for the original text.

Elton, Oliver. *Michael Drayton: A Critical Study*. London: Constable, 1905. Praises feeling for mutability in *Poly-Olbion* and laments that the poem has become a mere museum piece. Admires Drayton's depiction of London from the river's vantage point.

Hardin, Richard Francis. *Michael Drayton and the Ovidian Tradition*. Ann Arbor, Mich.: University Microfilms, 1969. The chapter "Topographical Poetry" identifies the Ovidian elements in *Poly-Olbion* and names the predecessors in the genre, such as Boccaccio in his myth-of-locality poem *Il ninfale fiesolano* (c. 1345).

Moore, William H. "Sources of Drayton's Conception of *Poly-Olbion*." *Studies in Philology* 65, no. 5 (October, 1968): 783-803. Gives a detailed accounting of Drayton's sources for his famous topographical poem. Excellent scholarly article.

THE PONDER HEART

Type of work: Novella
Author: Eudora Welty (1909-   )
Type of plot: Regional
Time of plot: Early 1950's
Locale: Clay, a small town in Mississippi
First published: 1954

> *Principal characters:*
> MISS EDNA EARL PONDER, the proprietor of a small family hotel
> UNCLE DANIEL PONDER, her uncle, who loves to give things away
> BONNIE DEE PEACOCK PONDER, his "trial" wife

The Story:

Uncle Daniel, who was rich as Croesus and correspondingly generous, was not very bright, but he looked impressive and neat as a pin. He invariably wore spotless white suits and a red bow tie and carried a huge Stetson hat just swept off his head. Kept under his father's thumb until he was mature, he was for a long time unable to be as generous as his nature dictated. He had given Edna Earl the hotel she ran, but his father had been glad to get rid of it. The cattle and fields he gave away were easily retrieved. People liked him because he always gave something away, even if it was only small change, but he always felt alone.

After his father's death, Uncle Daniel became Edna Earl's responsibility. She felt fairly safe about his giving things away as long as he was unconcerned about money. His father had always given him an allowance of three dollars a week. She continued that practice with no objection from Uncle Daniel because he was happy to have a little change in his pocket. His desire to give things to people made a wonderful topic for Edna Earl to discuss with the traveling salesmen. Stories of Uncle Daniel involved the whole town and most of the surrounding countryside.

One day, Uncle Daniel escaped Edna Earl long enough to take a new salesgirl at the five-and-dime as his second bride. Edna Earl was rather reticent about his first wife, who had left him, though there seemed to be no rancor on either side. Since Uncle Daniel assured her that his second wife was just "on trial," Edna Earl had to sit back and see what would happen. Bonnie Dee Peacock Ponder held Uncle Daniel enthralled for five years before she disappeared. He always claimed she looked good enough to eat and that she could cut his hair better than anyone had ever done before.

Edna Earl told this story of the Ponder heart to prepare her listener, a traveling salesman guest in her hotel, for the change in Uncle Daniel since the salesman had last seen him. As she described Uncle Daniel, his married life, and his most recent experiences, Edna Earl's own situation became clear. The last respectable member of a disintegrating family, she was conscious of her dignity and jealous of the position she wished for Uncle Daniel. She felt responsible for making things run, whether it concerned Uncle Daniel's life or the rummage sale every week for the poor people in town. She wanted things to run her way, however, and did not refrain from demanding her way from the servants, the lawyers, the shopkeepers, or even the judge. Though she deplored the fact that the town was no longer on a through route, she loved it. She despised the Peacock family, but she did her duty by them because Uncle Daniel had married one of them. Edna Earl's monologue covered the hunt for Bonnie Dee, her return, her turning Uncle Daniel out of his own house, her wholesale purchase of useless things (like the washer she put on the front porch before the house was wired for electricity), her sudden death, and the trial of Uncle Daniel for her murder.

As a bribe to bring Bonnie Dee back home after she had disappeared, Edna Earl promised Uncle Daniel that Bonnie Dee would get an allowance. No one had thought to give her one during her five-year "trial" marriage. Uncle Daniel reacted slowly to the thought of money. Not until the day of the trial did he think of the wealth he had in the bank. Apparently, it was a whim that day that prompted him to go to the bank early when the only clerk there was someone who had never been warned not to give money to Uncle Daniel. He withdrew every cent he had, padded his pockets with the money, and went to the trial.

The murder trial brought together the whole town and all of Bonnie Dee's huge family from the country. Edna Earl and the lawyer she had hired did not intend to let Uncle Daniel speak in his own defense. They relied too much on his previous obedience, however, and neglected to take into account the feeling he would naturally have at being, for once, the focal point in a big situation. Uncle Daniel listened carefully to all the witnesses and then, without warning, took over the trial. Throwing bills right and left, pressing them upon all the people, he immediately convinced the jury of his innocence and even softened the hearts of Bonnie Dee's family. Afterward, however, he was more alone than ever. People still did not understand him, but now he had nothing more to give them.

Critical Evaluation:

If the origin of comedy is in the disruption of routine and logical or rational expectation, yet without resulting in genuine pain, then *The Ponder Heart* is a comic masterpiece. The world Eudora Welty creates in the small town of Clay, Mississippi, in the early 1950's is peopled by characters for whom reason and logical predictability appear to be the exception rather than the rule. The punch line, after all, is that one of the characters dies not by being smothered by her estranged husband or from a fright-induced heart attack, but from laughing.

At the center of the novel, which is narrated in a dramatic monologue to the reader—"you," a stranded guest at the Beulah Hotel three days after the famous trial—is Uncle Daniel Ponder, who has the mind of a child and is unable to deal with the world rationally. Lovable in his imbecility, Uncle Daniel spends most of his time giving things away. When, however, Grandpa Ponder attempts to commit Uncle Daniel to an asylum, the tables are turned and Grandpa ends up being detained while Uncle Daniel, then in his fifties, promptly marries Bonnie Dee Peacock, a girl of seventeen who works at the dime store.

Incongruities of all sorts show up throughout the novel, not only in how the characters behave but also in what they say. Edna Earl Ponder, who narrates the events in a torrent of clichés and colloquialisms, is master of the non sequitur. The comic centerpiece of the novel is the trial. The occasion is founded on the assumption that justice derives rationally from motivation and evidence, but in a case in which the coroner is blind and the only motive for the supposed murder appears to be love, it can be expected that justice will have little to do with reason.

As the title of the novel implies, the main theme concerns the heart, or love. The doctor has described Bonnie Dee's death as heart failure, "death by misadventure," but, as Edna Earl describes it, the prosecuting attorney, Dorris Gladney, scratching his head and pretending to think, thereupon asks the double-edged question: "'What makes the heart fail?'" The real mystery in the novel is not whether Uncle Daniel did or did not murder his childish, materialistic wife but why love fails.

Ironically, the character who seems most capable of universal and selfless love is Uncle

Daniel, but society first commits him to an asylum and then accuses him of murder. The question arises whether Uncle Daniel's benevolent and loving nature is itself the object of ridicule, for he has only the slightest grasp on reality. His "fond and loving heart" is bent on an array of women, beginning with a motorcyclist, Intrepid Elsie Fleming, at the county fair, but, as Edna Earl says, he was in his forties "before we ever dreamed that such a thing as love flittered through his mind." Welty's choice of the word "mind" here may be significant.

Grandpa Ponder arranges a marriage with the widow Miss Teacake Magee, but that lasts only two months because the noise of her heels unnerved Uncle Daniel. His love for Bonnie Dee, who stays with him for five and a half years before leaving for no apparent reason, has as much to do with her willingness to cut his hair as anything else. For her part, Bonnie Dee appears to love only "things," and her return to Uncle Daniel is obviously in response to that portion of Edna Earl's poem in the newspaper that mentions "retroactive allowance." Although Uncle Daniel does feel her loss, he is quite willing to transfer his affections to her sister, but when he gives away all his money at the climax of the trial, he has nothing to offer that she wants.

The most important character of the novel is the narrator, Edna Earl, who understands the claims of both the head and the heart and who has set aside her own craving for romantic love in order to care for her family. The last of the Ponders, and the best embodiment in the novel of Christian charity, she describes herself as "the go-between . . . between my family and the world." The closest she comes to a self-indulgent romantic love is her affection for a traveling salesman named Ovid Springer; Welty's choice of first name, an obvious reference to the Augustan poet noted for his erotic love poems, appears to be ironic, for Springer shows no romantic inclination toward Edna Earl.

Edna Earl frequently comments on love, but her observations are usually buried in such a variety of contexts that they are easily overlooked. When Grandpa Ponder tells her about his plan to "fork up a good wife" for Uncle Daniel, she informs the guest, "The heart's a remarkable thing, if you ask me." She does not, however, let on to Grandpa Ponder that she herself might wish to be married. Commenting on Uncle Daniel's inability to understand money, Edna Earl says, "The riches were all off in the clouds somewhere—like true love is, I guess, like a castle in the sky." Although she is speaking of her uncle, her own wistfulness is apparent. When she attempts to bring Bonnie Dee and her uncle together after she sets up at the Ponder place outside town and leaves Uncle Daniel at the Beulah Hotel, Edna Earl comments, "I don't know if you can measure love at all." She adds "there's a lot of it . . . Love! There's always somebody wants it."

At the end of the novel, however, there appear to be no takers for the Ponders' immense love. No longer wealthy, they have been alienated from the town, for the citizens of Clay feel guilty over having accepted Uncle Daniel's last extravagant cash giveaway. Some critics have pointed out that the future belongs to the proud but worthless Peacocks, whereas the Ponders, whose name suggests thoughtfulness and something weighty or substantial in character, are left standing alone.

"Critical Evaluation" by Ron McFarland

Bibliography:

Appel, Alfred, Jr. *A Season of Dreams: The Fiction of Eudora Welty.* Baton Rouge: Louisiana State University Press, 1965. Focuses on Edna Earl's role and comments on the illusory nature of reality in the novel. Points out that Uncle Daniel, like many of Welty's tragic characters, is left isolated by the end of the narrative.

Carson, Barbara Harrell. "In the Heart of Clay: Eudora Welty's *The Ponder Heart*." *American Literature* 59 (December, 1987): 609-625. Excellent study of Edna Earl as a "dynamic balancer of reason and feeling," both essential to human nature. Sees Uncle Daniel as an irrational man of feeling too much out of touch with reality to be capable of genuine love.

Cornell, Brenda G. "Ambiguous Necessity: A Study of *The Ponder Heart*." In *Eudora Welty: Critical Essays*, edited by Peggy Whitman Prenshaw. Jackson: University Press of Mississippi, 1979. Examines the shortcomings of the stage version of the novella, particularly with respect to the presentation of Edna Earl. Welty's use of irony and paradox help sustain the premise that life is full of mystery.

Idol, John L., Jr. "Edna Earl Ponder's Good Country People." In *The Critical Response to Eudora Welty's Fiction*, edited by Laurie Champion. Westport, Conn.: Greenwood Press, 1994. Comments on the conflict set up in the novel between town and country, with Edna Earl representing the town. Includes a review of the novel and notes differences with the 1956 Broadway stage version.

Kreyling, Michael. *Eudora Welty's Achievement of Order*. Baton Rouge: Louisiana State University Press, 1980. Includes a chapter that focuses on the "adjoining terror" that connects *The Ponder Heart* with serious comedy. Sees Edna Earl as Apollonian in her concern for knowledge and order, while Uncle Daniel is Dionysian in his spontaneity.

POOR FOLK

Type of work: Novel
Author: Fyodor Dostoevski (1821-1881)
Type of plot: Impressionistic realism
Time of plot: Nineteenth century
Locale: St. Petersburg, Russia
First published: Bednye Lyudi, 1846 (English translation, 1887)

Principal characters:
MAKAR DIEVUSHKIN, a destitute government clerk
BARBARA DOBROSELOVA, his friend
POKROVSKI, a young tutor
THE ELDER POKROVSKI, the tutor's father
BWIKOV, a wealthy landowner

The Story:

Makar Dievushkin, an impoverished government clerk, lived in an alcove in a rooming-house kitchen. Even though his accommodations were unpleasant, he consoled himself that he could see from his window the windows of Barbara Dobroselova, an unhappy young woman whom he supported in her shabby rooms across the street. Makar and Barbara corresponded; occasionally, they walked together when Barbara felt well. Makar, poor but honorable, maintained the gravest dignity in his relationship and in his correspondence with Barbara. In their poverty and loneliness, each had warm sympathy and understanding for the other.

Among the boarders was a public relations man of literary pretensions, whose style Makar greatly admired. Makar also knew a former government clerk, Goshkov, and his family of four. Goshkov had lost his job through a legal suit and was deeply in debt to the homely, shrewish landlady. Across the street, Barbara's cousin Sasha appeared for the purpose of resolving a difference that had long existed between the cousins. Sasha questioned Barbara's acceptance of Makar's charity.

Meanwhile, Makar sent gifts to Barbara and became poorer with each passing day. He pawned his uniform and, in his poverty, became the butt of jokes. Barbara, protesting somewhat weakly his sacrifices for her, sent him, in return, her life story, which she had written. Barbara was the daughter of the steward of a prince in the province of Tula. Her family moved to St. Petersburg when she was twelve years old. She did not like the city, and she detested the boarding school she attended. When Barbara was fourteen years old, her father died, debt-ridden. Her mother was consumptive. Creditors took all of their possessions, and Barbara and her mother moved to the house of a distant relative, Anna Thedorovna, whose source of income was a mystery to them. There Barbara, with her orphan cousin Sasha, was tutored by a sick young student, Pokrovski, who was intelligent but irritable. The young girls teased Pokrovski remorselessly. Barbara, however, soon regretted her behavior and vowed to redeem herself in his eyes.

Pokrovski was visited from time to time by his father, a wizened, obsequious little man who worshiped his son. The old man was inquisitive and talkative, so Pokrovski had limited the number of his visits to two a week. Old Pokrovski would do anything for his son. Barbara outgrew the tutoring, but she still had not redeemed herself with Pokrovski. Bent upon wide reading, she sneaked into his room and accidentally upset his bookshelf. Pokrovski entered, and while the pair were replacing the books, they realized that they were in love.

As Pokrovski's birthday approached, Barbara joined forces with the elder Pokrovski to buy the young tutor the works of Pushkin; they would give the set to him together. At the birthday party Barbara magnanimously let the doting old father give the books to his son. Pokrovski died soon afterward. Grief apparently weakened the old man's mind. He took his son's books and, following the funeral procession on foot, dropped a pathetic trail of books in the mud of the streets leading to the cemetery.

The friendship between Makar and Barbara continued. Barbara became concerned with Makar's indulgences in her behalf, which he could not afford; she urged him to get himself a decent uniform.

At the rooming house, Makar, utterly destitute, felt deep pity for Goshkov in his poverty. He sent Barbara a volume of the writings of the public relations man; Barbara declared the book was trash. When the possibility of her becoming a governess in a wealthy household presented itself to Barbara, Makar, despite his own poverty, proudly told her that he could continue to care for her.

Hearing that Barbara had been insulted by an importunate suitor, Makar got drunk and was brought home by the police. In desperation he borrowed money everywhere, even from Barbara. His penury seemed to affect his mind. Meanwhile, the friendship between the two had become the source of laughter to the other boarders. Makar even suspected the public relations man of maliciously gossiping in civil service circles about his having been brought home by the police. He feared for his reputation, all that he had left. Barbara invited him to live with her and her cook, Thedora; she urged him to stop borrowing and to stop copying the public relations man's style in his letters.

A lecherous old man, sent by Anna Thedorovna, called on Barbara. After Barbara and Thedora got rid of him, Barbara, in alarm, told Makar that she would have to move immediately. Lack of money, however, prevented her removal. Makar went to a rich usurer, but could offer no security, and so was refused a loan. Everything went wrong; Makar's position at the rooming house became impossible. Barbara burned her hand and could not sew for a living. She sent Makar money, which he spent on drink. Even in his abject condition, however, Makar gave coins to Goshkin that he might feed his family.

Makar made a mistake in his official work and was ordered before his superior, who was so affected at the sight of Makar's wretched person that he gave the poor clerk one hundred rubles and took his hand. These gestures saved Makar physically and morally. He regained his self-respect and faced life with a new vigor. All went well at the office and at the rooming house.

Bwikov, a wealthy landowner who had once courted Barbara and had deserted her in her misfortune, came to St. Petersburg and offered her money, which she refused. Goshkov, meanwhile, was officially absolved of guilt in a case involving misappropriation of funds and was awarded substantial damages. Moved deeply by his freedom and solvency, the man broke in mind and body and died of shock.

Bwikov returned to Barbara and offered marriage to atone for his desertion. He planned to take her to his country estate for her health. After much debate, Barbara and Makar agreed that she must marry Bwikov. Makar could not help remarking, however, that Bwikov would probably be happier married to a certain merchant's daughter in Moscow.

Barbara, preparing excitedly for a magnificent wedding, employed Makar to run countless petty errands for her. Makar planned to move into Barbara's rooms and to retain Thedora as his cook. It saddened him to think of Barbara's leaving him, of her going to the steppes to become the lady of a great estate. In a last letter, he implored her to stay but admitted that his passionate turns of phrase were to some extent only a literary exercise.

Critical Evaluation:

"Honor and glory to the young poet whose Muse loves people in garrets and basements and tells the inhabitants of gilded palaces: 'look, they are also men, they are also your brethren.'" With these words, the great critic Vissarion Belinsky hailed the arrival of Fyodor Dostoevski on the Russian literary scene. *Poor Folk*, Dostoevski's first published work, appeared serially in 1846 in a literary periodical, *Recueil de Saint Petersbourg*. In this work, Dostoevski established a theme, the miseries of Russia's downtrodden masses, from which he never wandered far during his literary career. In the epistolary novel *Poor Folk*, however, one can detect a sly humor that never appeared again in his work. Indeed, the already somewhat morbid and sick artist could hardly have seen anything but black despair in life after his sojourn in Siberia, where he was sent in 1849 for revolutionary political activities.

Poor Folk is a remarkably perceptive account of the multifarious humiliations that torment the poor. In depicting the victimized and the eccentric, Dostoevski proved himself the equal of Charles Dickens, by whom he was much influenced. His portrayal of life in "garrets and basements" is entirely devoid of sentimentality; both the dignity and the wretchedness of Makar and Barbara come to light simultaneously.

Makar's persistent generosity is what finally distinguishes him, while a poetic sensitivity to life ennobles Barbara. Both characters maintain these virtues in the face of impossible circumstances. To support Barbara, Makar must accept the chaos and stench of the three-to-a-room boardinghouse whose walls are "so greasy that your hand sticks when you lean against them." His increasing poverty turns the smallest economic reverse into disaster. The deterioration of his wardrobe is humiliating, yet it deepens his sympathy for those in similar straits. His aroused compassion for other victims induces him not only to give Goshkov twenty kopecks but also to add sugar to the poor man's tea. As her response to Pokrovski's father shows, Barbara is also capable of great generosity, but more impressive are her lyrical descriptions of her childhood and her feeling for nature. Despite Makar's literary pretensions, Barbara is by far the superior stylist, although she never boasts about her talent.

Dostoevski's main characters, however, are far from perfect human beings. Makar's love for Barbara is tainted by a desire to extract gratitude and praise from her. Barbara, in turn, reveals a shocking capacity for transforming Makar into her servant once she becomes engaged to the rich Bwikov. Both are too involved in private dreamworlds and are excessively preoccupied with their reputations. Yet these faults, suggests Dostoevski, must be seen partially as exaggerated attempts to maintain a modicum of dignity in an uncomprehending world. When one is absolutely vulnerable, certain defenses must be erected, or, as Makar explains, "Poor people are touchy—that's in the nature of things."

Bibliography:

Breger, Louis. *Dostoevsky: The Author as Psychoanalyst*. New York: New York University Press, 1989. Contains a chapter on *Poor Folk* and several chapters of biography. Discusses the symbols and associations of the novels.

Jackson, Robert Louis. *Dostoevsky's Quest for Form: A Study of His Philosophy of Art*. 2d ed. Bloomington, Ind.: Physsardt Publishers, 1978. Considers the contradiction between Dostoevski's working aesthetic and his higher aesthetic of true beauty. A mature and helpful study for the serious Dostoevski reader.

Leatherbarrow, William J. *Fedor Dostoevsky*. Boston: Twayne, 1981. Includes a biographical sketch and chronology of Dostoevski. An excellent guide for the study of Dostoevski. Commentary on *Poor Folk* and other early work.

Mackiewicz, Stanislaw. *Dostoyevsky*. Maryknoll, N.Y.: Orbis Books, 1947. Examines the women of Dostoevski's novels and the relevance of the loves of Dostoevski's life to his work. Contains biographical information as a reference to the novels.

Miller, Robin Feuer. *Critical Essays on Dostoevsky*. Boston: G. K. Hall, 1986. Contains an essay by Tolstoy and criticism and commentary on Dostoevski up to the twentieth century. A very broad spectrum of the material available on Dostoevski and how he and his novels have been perceived.

POOR WHITE

Type of work: Novel
Author: Sherwood Anderson (1876-1941)
Type of plot: Psychological realism
Time of plot: 1866-1900
Locale: Missouri and Ohio
First published: 1920

> *Principal characters:*
> HUGH MCVEY, an inventor and manufacturer
> SARAH SHEPARD, his foster mother
> STEVE HUNTER, his partner
> TOM BUTTERWORTH, his father-in-law
> CLARA BUTTERWORTH, his wife

The Story:

Born in 1866, Hugh McVey grew up in a small Missouri town as the motherless child of a drunken father. Spending his days lounging and dreaming on the banks of the Mississippi River, Hugh had no formal education, learned few manners, and became very lazy. The railroad came to town in 1880 when Hugh was fourteen, and he got a job as a factotum at the station, loading baggage and sweeping the platform. Hugh received little pay but got to live with his boss, Henry Shepard, and his wife Sarah. The childless couple treated Hugh as their own son, providing him with shelter, food, new clothes, and affection. Soon Sarah began to educate him. Sarah, who was from New England, always preserved her memory of quiet Eastern villages and large industrial cities. Determined to educate Hugh, she lavished on him the discipline and affection she would have given her own child.

The situation was difficult, at first, for both of them, but Sarah Shepard was a determined woman. She taught Hugh to read, to write, and to wonder about the world beyond the little town. She instilled within him the belief that his family had been of no account, and he grew to have a revulsion toward the poor white farmers and workers. She always held out before him the promise of the East, the progress and growth of that region. Gradually, Hugh began to win his fight against natural indolence and to adjust himself to his new way of life. When the Shepards left town, Hugh, then nineteen, was appointed station agent for the railroad.

He kept the job for a year. During that time, the dream of Eastern cities grew more and more vivid for Hugh. When his father died, Hugh gave up his job and traveled east, working wherever he could. Always lonely, always apart from people, he felt an impenetrable wall between him and the rest of the world. He kept on, through Illinois, Indiana, Ohio.

Hugh was twenty-three when he settled down in Ohio. By accident, he got the job of telegraph operator, just a mile from the town of Bidwell. There he lived alone, a familiar and puzzling figure to the people of the town. The rumor began to spread that he was an inventor working on a new device. Others suggested that he was looking over the town for a possible factory site. Hugh was doing neither as yet. Then during his walks around the farmlands, he became fascinated by the motions of the farmers planting their seeds and their crops. Slowly there grew in his mind an idea for a crop-setting machine that would save the labor of the farmers and their families.

Steve Hunter, who had just come back from school in Buffalo, was another dreamer. He dreamed of being a manufacturer, the wealthiest in Bidwell. He succeeded in convincing the town's important people that Hugh was his man, and that he was working on an invention that would make them both rich. He persuaded them to invest in a new company that would build a factory and promote Hugh's invention. Steve went to see Hugh, who had completed the blueprint for a plant-setting machine. The two young men came to an agreement.

The town idiot, who had skill in woodworking, made models of the machine, and the machine itself was finally constructed in an old building carefully guarded from the curious. When the machine failed to work, Hugh invented another, his mind more and more preoccupied with the planning of devices and machines. A factory was then built, and many workers were hired. Bidwell's industrialization began.

What was happening in Bidwell was the same growth of industrialism that was changing the entire structure of the nation. It was a period of transition. Bidwell, being a small town, felt the effects of the new development keenly. Workers became part of the community, in which there had been only farmers and merchants.

Joe Wainsworth, the harness-maker, lost his life savings to Hugh's invention. An independent man, a craftsman, he came to resent the factory, the very idea of the machine. People came into his shop less often. They were buying the machine-made harness. Joe became a broken man. His employee, Jim Gibson, a spiritual bully, really ran the business, and Joe submitted meekly.

Meanwhile, Clara Butterworth, daughter of a wealthy farmer, came back to Bidwell after three years at the university in Columbus. She, too, was lonely and unhappy. When she returned, she saw that the old Bidwell was gone and that her father, Tom Butterworth, was wealthier than before, that the growth of the town was primarily the result of the efforts of one person, Hugh McVey. A week after she met Hugh, he walked up to the farm and asked her to marry him. They eloped and were married that night. The marriage was not consummated for several days, however, because Hugh, fearing he was not good enough for Clara, could not bring himself to approach her.

For four years, they lived together in a strange, strained relationship. During those four years, Joe Wainsworth's fury against Steve Hunter, against the new age of industry that had taken his savings, increased. One day, he heard Jim Gibson brag about his stocking factory-made harnesses in the shop. That night, Joe Wainsworth killed Jim Gibson. Fleeing from the scene, he met Steve Hunter and shot him, not fatally.

Clara, Hugh, and Tom Butterworth were returning from a drive in the family's first auto-mobile when they learned what had happened. Two men had captured Joe, and when they tried to put him into the automobile to take him back to town, Joe jumped toward Hugh and sank his fingers into his neck. It was Clara who broke his grip upon her husband. Somehow the incident brought Hugh and Clara closer together.

Hugh's career as an inventor no longer satisfied him. Joe Wainsworth's attack had unnerved him and made him doubt the worth of his work. It did not matter so much if someone in Iowa had invented a machine exactly like his, and he did not intend to dispute the rights of the Iowan. Clara was bearing his child, an individual who would struggle just as he had. Clara told him of the child one night as they stood listening to the noises of the farm and the snoring of the hired hand. As they walked into the house side by side, the factory whistles blew in the night. Hugh hardly heard them. The dark Midwestern nights, men and women, the land itself—the full, deep life current would go on in spite of factories and machines.

Critical Evaluation:

In *Poor White*, Hugh McVey's life stands as an allegory for a young, war-shocked nation struggling to ride a massive wave of industrialization. Conceived at the end of the Civil War and born in 1866, McVey is at the peak of his inventing career in the late 1890's and early 1900's. Celebrations of technology were common in those years, as for example when Henry Adams philosophizes about the Gallery of Machines in "The Dynamo and the Virgin" chapter of *The Education of Henry Adams* (1907). During the late 1800's, factory smokestacks penetrated virgin skies across the Midwest as industrialism impregnated small towns. By the end of *Poor White*, Bidwell is an industrial town with factories surrounded by fields of cheap housing. New workers (strangers and recent immigrants) have flooded the town. The tide of industrialization has moved forward.

As Bidwell grows, individuals must shed their preindustrial ways of life and adapt to new roles in society. Hugh, the daydreamer, becomes an inventor, Tom Butterworth, the gentleman farmer, becomes an investor, and young farmhands from across the county become millworkers. Even mentally disabled Allie Mulberry builds models of McVey's inventions. Individuals who do not adapt cannot survive. Joe Wainsworth, the local harness maker, who refuses to sell or repair factory-made harnesses, becomes an example when his assistant Jim Gibson pushes him around, takes control of the business, and hangs eighteen manufactured harnesses on the shop wall. Joe reacts like an animal struggling to delay his extinction. Pushed to the breaking point by Jim's bragging, he slits his assistant's throat and shreds the new harnesses into a pile on the shop floor.

Growth of industry in the Midwest was not an abstract phenomenon for Sherwood Anderson, who in 1906 served as president (in title only) of United Factories Company, a mail order business in Cleveland, Ohio. He was fired after only one year when the company lost thousands of dollars in a lawsuit involving faulty incubators. The machines had been contracted for sale before the manufacturer knew whether they would work. A similar situation happens in *Poor White* when Steve Hunter and Tom Butterworth conspire to market one of Hugh's pieces of farm machinery that they suspect will never work. In 1907, Anderson moved to Elyria, Ohio, and became true president of a company that by 1911 manufactured nearly all conceivable types of roofing and painting materials. Like Steve Hunter, Anderson was a businessman, an entrepreneur who organized and profited from other people's inventions and resources. Specializing in public relations, Anderson was well acquainted with (and sometimes practiced) less-than-honest advertising tactics and business dealings. These experiences are reflected in *Poor White*.

The characters in *Poor White* come alive with intricate, often grotesque detail, such as the extended sketch of a rich lawyer's widow (Jane Orange), who is caught stealing eggs and has yolk running down her legs after a clerk hits the pocket where the eggs are hidden. Critics often discuss *Poor White* as a form of American *Bildungsroman*, and Hugh as a post-Civil War Huck Finn.

The hero of Mark Twain's *Adventures of Huckleberry Finn* (1884) tells readers at the end of the novel: "I reckon I got to light out for the Territory ahead of the rest, because Aunt Sally she's going to adopt me and sivilize me, and I can't stand it." With the closing of the American frontier, young men and women across the country began to look to science and technology as the new territory where they could stake a claim and make their mark. Getting "sivilized" is what happens to young Hugh, who has no West to run to, and who until age fourteen has spent his time lazing on the banks of the Mississippi beside his father's dilapidated shack. Sarah Shepard, like Huck's Aunt Polly, nurtures Hugh with strong New England values, and the boy resists. The momentum of industrialization drags the indolent young man forward. Although successful in manufacturing, he laments his lowly roots at the end of chapter fourteen: "By struggle and work he had conquered the dreams but could not conquer his ancestry, nor change the fact that he was at bottom poor white trash." Entrepreneurs find they must always struggle against such determinism.

The only fully developed character besides McVey is Clara Butterworth, whose sexual awakening surfaces in flirtations with farmhands and in a brief relationship with a schoolteacher. Concerned about Clara's virtue and worried that she has been associating too much with lower classes, Tom Butterworth sends his daughter away to college in Columbus to become a lady and perhaps meet a suitable husband. At college, however, Clara meets Kate Chancellor, a lesbian classmate who rejects the limitations of marriage and plans to become a doctor. Kate teaches Clara to question society's traditional expectations. Clara, rather than becoming ladylike, acts to control her life and decide with whom, if anyone, she will share it. Industrialization takes families away from the farm and allows women greater options.

As a chronicle of industrialization, *Poor White* is related to business novels such as William Dean Howells' *The Rise of Silas Lapham* (1885) and Frank Norris' *The Pit* (1903). McVey's inventions recall the numerous patents filed by Sam Hamilton in John Steinbeck's *East of Eden* (1952). With the appearance of a socialist agitator at the end of the novel, Anderson foreshadows another stage of industrial development—in the progressive era, workers renewed the fight for fair wages and safe factory conditions. Agitators appear in similar but more prominent roles in political social protest fiction such as Upton Sinclair's *The Jungle* (1906) and John Steinbeck's *In Dubious Battle* (1936). Although not the great American novel, *Poor White* is a significant literary account of America's industrial coming-of-age.

"Critical Evaluation" by Geralyn Strecker

Bibliography:
Anderson, David D. *Sherwood Anderson: An Introduction and Interpretation.* New York: Barnes & Noble Books, 1967. Discusses Hugh McVey in terms of industrialism's effect on the individual. Characterizes the struggle in Bidwell as people trying to maintain their humanity in the face of industrialism. With this novel, Sherwood Anderson shifts from seeing industry as the source of evil to accepting its potential for good.

Gelfant, Blanche Housman. *The American City Novel.* Norman: University of Oklahoma Press, 1954. Characterizes *Poor White* as "a novel of becoming," in which the changing town, growing with industrialism, plays a role parallel to that of Hugh McVey. The town and the man illustrate the process of social change.

Howe, Irving. *Sherwood Anderson.* New York: William Sloane Associates, 1951. Analyzes the book's structure.

Taylor, Welford Dunaway. *Sherwood Anderson.* New York: Frederick Ungar, 1977. Asserts that the novel's strengths outweigh its weaknesses. Characterizes the narrative as moving from "vagueness to definiteness." Tainted by stereotypes of the lower and working classes.

Townsend, Kim. *Sherwood Anderson.* Boston: Houghton Mifflin, 1987. Compares Hugh McVey and Sarah Shepard to Huck Finn and Aunt Polly in Mark Twain's *Adventures of Huckleberry Finn.* Offers a reading of Hugh's haunting of the cabbage field while inventing the planting machine.

THE POORHOUSE FAIR

Type of work: Novel
Author: John Updike (1932-   )
Type of plot: Social satire
Time of plot: 1980's
Locale: The Diamond County Home for the Aged, in New Jersey
First published: 1959

> Principal characters:
> JOHN HOOK,
> BILLY GREGG,
> GEORGE LUCAS,
> MARTHA, his wife,
> ELIZABETH HEINEMAN, and
> MRS. MORTIS, inmates in a home for the aged
> MR. CONNER, the prefect
> BUDDY, his assistant
> TED, a teenage delivery boy

The Story:

At the Diamond County Home for the Aged, in New Jersey, it was the day of the annual fair, when the elderly men and women would set up stands and sell such homemade products as quilts, candy, and peach-stone carvings to the visitors from nearby communities. This year, the great day got off to a bad start. John Hook, a ninety-four-year-old former schoolteacher, and Billy Gregg, a seventy-year-old retired electrician, discovered that the porch chairs had been given name tags so that hereafter each inmate would occupy only the chair assigned to him. This latest action by Conner, the prefect of the institution, provided an opportunity for protest.

Misunderstandings and misadventures added to Conner's burden of do-gooding humanitarianism. When Gregg introduced a diseased stray cat onto the grounds, the prefect ordered Buddy, his adoring assistant, to shoot the animal. Ted, a teenage truck driver delivering cases of Pepsi-Cola for the fair, knocked down part of a stone wall. A pet parakeet belonging to Mrs. Lucas, the wife of George Lucas, a former real-estate salesman, got loose in the infirmary. When rain threatened to ruin the fair, and the inmates took refuge in the community sitting room, Hook and Conner argued the ideals of an older America of faith and idealism against the theories of scientific determinism and social perfectibility.

Hook was a gentle, meditative man who could look back to the days of William Howard Taft, a period of greater political freedom, economic uncertainty, pride of craftsmanship, and, in times of private or public calamity, trust in God. Filled with that sense of repletion that is time's final gift to the old, he believed in the possible virtue of humanity. To Hook, this quality of virtue redeemed the human animal's capacity for folly and evil because such virtue brought humanity close to the idea of God.

In Conner's brave new world, however, there was no more place for God than there was for error. Fanatical in his belief in progress, order, hygiene, and the elimination of superstition and pain, he possessed the inhuman energy of a machine. The truth was that he did not think of the inmates under him as people; they were his charges, and it was his job to confer on them the good they often could not understand and sometimes did not want. In his view, all life should be regulated and institutionalized, as passionless as the antics of tomorrow's adolescents, who satisfy their emotional needs by undressing and then staring in curiosity but without desire at one another's nude bodies. Conner was a citizen of a planned society, and the institution was his calling.

The tensions of the day finally broke when the inmates turned on Conner and stoned him with the rubble from the damaged wall. Then the skies cleared, and the fair was held after all, but under circumstances that allowed the old people to save some remnants of their pride and self-respect. Asking only the bread of understanding, they had been offered the cold stone of charity, and they had rejected it along with a world they never made.

Critical Evaluation:

John Updike's *The Poorhouse Fair* is one of the more striking debuts by a novelist in the history of American letters. It was widely noticed but only cautiously appreciated by many prominent critics when it was published in the same year as Updike's first collection of short fiction (*The Same Door*, 1959) and one year after his earliest volume, the poetry in *The Carpentered Hen and Other Tame Creatures*. Most commentators found some element in the book to praise, emphasizing the poetic use of language, the critique of rational social engineering, or the somewhat (for its time) unconventional structure. There was a degree of consensus that Updike had not been entirely successful in connecting all of the prominent features of the novel. Within the context of his prolific work during the following decades, it is clear that Updike, in this debut novel, was presenting some of the most important themes that have informed his writing since its inception. Each element of the novel is operating in service to fundamental themes.

Updike was twenty-seven when *The Poorhouse Fair* was written, and its strongest, most passionately expressive sections are tributes to a rich cultural legacy he obtained from his neighbors in rural Pennsylvania. The central character, John Hook, is very affectionately drawn from his maternal grandfather John Hoyer. Updike's approach to Hook's characterization is a meditative exploration of the mind and soul of a man whose admirable qualities are vanishing into the emptiness of a technological wasteland. Updike recollects, in his memoir *Self-Consciousness* (1989), that "the family I grew up in was old-fashioned," with an old-fashioned notion about "trying to do the right thing," and recalls his grandfather quoting proverbs "in a clear and elocutionary voice." The Hoyers, Updike declares proudly, "had become peaceful, reasonable people who valued civilization," and Hook's generally positive outlook stems from a belief in a just American society and the conviction that God, the creator of the universe, is manifest in the world. This religious foundation, which Updike saw as a complement to, rather than a foreign element in, the life of the mind, was an integral part of his Lutheran heritage, what he called "my deepest and most fruitful self." At Oxford and at Harvard, he found himself removed from the verities of a rural Pennsylvania community and came to think of his Christianity as "battered and vestigial." The character of Stephen Conner is not just a critique of the bloodless, ultra-rational social scientists emerging in the late 1950's—he is also an expression of Updike's own doubts about the consolations of the religious tradition.

The narrative advance of *The Poorhouse Fair* is literally suspended while Hook and Conner are engaged in a debate about the existence of God. Some critics felt Conner was a target of Updike's satire, but Updike claims that once he "set Conner in motion I did the best of my ability to try to love him." Accordingly, Updike gives Conner the most powerful of modern arguments against the existence of God, and Hook is somewhat shaken by Conner's points, since he is himself a practitioner of intellectual discourse. Significantly, though, Conner is not comforted by his own assertions while Hook is able to regain his composure because he has evidence sufficiently strong to overcome the logic of Conner's ideas. The debate sets the terms of the argument: Conner's rational humanism, constructed on the creed that "prized a useful over a pleasant life" versus Hook's instinctive responses to the natural phenomena of the universe and the unruly, endlessly interesting flow of human society. For Updike, the poetry is the proof of Hook's argument.

From the beginning of his career, Updike has been dismissed as a writer whose command of language disguises his lack of anything to say. A much more discerning judgment recognizes that, as Donald Greiner puts it, Updike "lavishes so much care on his prose that its very intensity approaches poetry." In *The Poorhouse Fair*, Updike depends on the power of language to make Hook's delight in the intricate details of landscape and skyscape not only plausible but inspiring. Updike's own joy is palpable in the evocative descriptions of terrain, storm, appetite, song, and the celebratory carnival that concludes the novel. In a sense, the beauty of his writing is his own testament to God's creation. As other residents join Hook in envisioning a heavenly realm, Updike's idea of earth as a tantalizing reflection of "the giant, cosmic other" gains credence through the eloquence of their descriptions.

The community within the poorhouse, in spite of its tensions and disagreements, is another analogue of a heavenly place. Updike has remarked that "an illusion of eternal comfort reposes in clubbiness," and *the Poorhouse Fair* is designed as a fond return to the town of Shillington (which is also the setting for the *Olinger Stories: A Selection*, 1964), a location that Updike remembers with "furtive" love years later and that stood for a time in his life when the outside world had not yet intruded upon a young boy's idea of his own destiny. The visitors from the town to the fair, and the residents themselves, are patterned after the society in which Updike grew up and are all part of a picture of a way of life that even in 1959 Updike feared was being overwhelmed by the tendencies toward the controlled and mundane that Conner stands for.

The philosophical position Updike affirms is almost classically traditional, but some of the techniques he employs are conspicuously contemporary. He mentioned that he thought of *The Poorhouse Fair* as an antinovel in the mode of modernist European fiction. His shifting narrative focus, including a surreal dream-vision of a heavily medicated patient and an extended passage of unidentified voices mixed in short stretches of dialogue, confused some critics. Also daunting is the very open-ended conclusion in which Hook, the avatar of an earlier time, looks onward into an unknown future still carrying the obligations of conscience and concern that speak for the best of human intentions.

"Critical Evaluation" by Leon Lewis

Bibliography:
Detweiler, Robert. *John Updike*. Boston: G. K. Hall, 1984. A study of Updike's fiction with respect to his narrative art. The chapter on *The Poorhouse Fair* competently, if briefly, covers the setting, uses of language, character, themes, and philosophy.
Greiner, Donald J. *John Updike's Novels*. Athens: Ohio University Press, 1984. Greiner has written extensively about Updike. The chapter discussing the origins of *The Poorhouse Fair* effectively utilizes Updike's introduction to the revised edition of 1977.
Hamilton, Alice, and Kenneth Hamilton. *The Elements of John Updike*. Grand Rapids, Mich.: Wm. B. Eerdmans, 1970. A detailed discussion of the theological dimensions of *The Poorhouse Fair*, noting and explaining religious allusions and symbols.
Newman, Judie. *John Updike*. New York: St. Martin's Press, 1988. Compares *Couples* and *The*

Poorhouse Fair in a chapter that considers both books in the context of the social situation of America. Good on uses of metaphor, concluding with the idea that the novel is "diagnostic" rather than "prescriptive."

Updike, John. *Self-Consciousness: Memoirs*. New York: Alfred A. Knopf, 1989. In the essay "On Being a Self Forever," Updike discusses his religious position at length, covering many of the issues he examined in *The Poorhouse Fair*.

Vargo, Edward P. *Rainstorms and Fire: Ritual in the Novels of John Updike*. Port Washington, N.Y.: Kennikat Press, 1973. The chapter on *The Poorhouse Fair* emphasizes the use of ritual and celebration as means of expressing a religious vision.

PORGY

Type of work: Novel
Author: DuBose Heyward (1885-1940)
Type of plot: Regional
Time of plot: Early twentieth century
Locale: Charleston, South Carolina
First published: 1925

Principal characters:
PORGY, a disabled African American beggar
CROWN, a stevedore
BESS, Crown's woman

The Story:

Before the Civil War, Catfish Row had been the fine mansion of a wealthy white family. By the early 1900's, it had become home for a community of poor African American families, descendants of former slaves. Porgy, a disabled beggar, inhabited a ground-floor room. No one knew how old he was, and his large, powerful hands were in strange contrast to his frail body. Porgy's neighbor Peter transported him to and from his begging each day in his wagon.

Porgy's single vice was gambling—throwing dice with friends in the courtyard of Catfish Row. One evening in April, Robbins, the husband of Serena and father of three children, was killed by the traveling stevedore Crown, whom he had accused of cheating at dice. When police came to investigate, no one offered testimony, so the police took Peter into custody, hoping he would provide information. While Peter was in jail for ten days, the horse and wagon that he had been buying on contract were repossessed, and Porgy lost his only means of transportation.

By May, Porgy was destitute and had to find another means of getting downtown. His new emancipation came when he built a "chariot"—a goat-pulled, two-wheeled, toilet-soap crate. He no longer had to remain at one stand all day, but could roam at will and take in more money. In June, Crown's woman, Bess, came to Catfish Row. Maria, who operated a kitchen in the building, gave her food. Bess then went to live with Porgy, and became a new woman, giving up drugs and alcohol. Happier than ever, Porgy won often at gambling, so his friends became suspicious.

One day, a dandy, Sportin' Life, came to town and gave Bess cocaine. She was arrested for disorderly conduct. Porgy tried to pay her fine, but when the judge saw the beggar to whom he had often given dimes with ten dollars, he became enraged, took the money, and sentenced Bess to ten days in a filthy, overcrowded prison, where she became seriously ill with fever. With the help of Maria and other women in Catfish Row, Porgy nursed Bess back to health.

At "The Sons and Daughters of Repent Ye Saith the Lord" picnic on Kittiwar Island, Bess was accosted by Crown, who had been hiding on the island. He took her to his hut and had sex with her, but at the end of the day, he let her return to Porgy, promising that he would take her back in the fall, when cotton shipments would provide stevedoring work in Savannah.

One day in September, the "Mosquito Fleet" of fishing boats celebrated a record-breaking catch. As they prepared to go out the next morning, Catfish Row resident Clara futilely warned her husband, Jake, not to go out in his boat that day. Soon after the fleet left the pier, warning bells chimed and the hurricane flag rose over the customhouse. After an ominous calm, a hurricane struck the city. Water, driven by the shrieking wind, rose above the seawall, crossed the street, and invaded the ground floor of Catfish Row, where forty frightened residents huddled in the great second-story ballroom. During a lull in the storm, Clara saw the wreck of her husband's boat near the wharf, left her baby with Bess, and went out into the flood. A few minutes later, she was overwhelmed in the storm's sudden return. The hurricane claimed several Catfish Row fishermen. Bess and Porgy adopted Clara's baby.

In October, drays loaded with heavy bales of cotton came rumbling down the street. Catfish Row boiled with excitement, for stevedoring jobs and money would bring prosperity. The cotton, however, meant disaster to Porgy. He asked Bess whether she was his woman or Crown's. His, she answered, unless Crown seized her again as he did at the picnic. If that happened, she could not answer for herself. Porgy assured her that he would not let Crown take her away from him.

Crown returned to Catfish Row and, despite warnings from Maria, stalked Bess. When Crown broke into Porgy and Bess's room one midnight, Porgy stabbed him. The next day, the body was found in the river near Catfish Row. Again, residents gave police no information, and the community sighed in relief when the officers left without arresting anyone. A buzzard that had fed upon Crown's body lighted on the parapet above Porgy's room, forecasting doom.

Asked to identify Crown's body at the morgue, Porgy fled in his goat-cart, hotly pursued by a patrol wagon. Passersby laughed at the ridiculously one-sided race. Porgy was caught at the edge of town, but was no longer needed, because someone else had identified the body. Porgy was jailed for five days for contempt of court. Without witnesses or evidence, the police declared Crown to have come to his death at the hands of a person or persons unknown.

When Porgy returned from jail and found Serena holding Jake and Clara's orphan baby, he suspected the worst. Neighbors told him that some stevedores had gotten Bess drunk and taken her off to Savannah. Porgy knew she would never return. Serena adopted the baby. For one summer, Porgy had experienced brief glimpses of happiness, but by fall, he was left again a solitary beggar.

"The Story" updated by Geralyn Strecker

Critical Evaluation:

Perhaps the most important thing to remember when reading *Porgy* is that DuBose Heyward came from the white aristocracy of Charleston, South Carolina. Heywards came to America in the late seventeenth century, and Thomas Heyward signed the Declaration of Independence. Although Heyward had the family name, he did not share its wealth. When Heyward was two years old, his father died and his mother took in sewing to meet expenses. At the age of nine, he sold newspapers, at fourteen he worked in a hardware store, and at twenty he became a steamship checker, working among black stevedores. Venturing in insurance and real estate, at twenty-three years of age he reclaimed some black tenements in Charleston and eventually gained financial stability.

Heyward's hardships were not all economic, however. He contracted polio at the age of eighteen, typhoid at twenty, and suffered attacks of pleurisy at twenty-one and thirty-two years of age. All of these experiences influenced *Porgy*. Self-educated to a great degree, Heyward read much of James Fenimore Cooper and Charles Dickens. His first one-act play was produced in 1913. In 1920, he turned to poetry, helped found the Poetry Society of South Carolina, and became involved with writers from across the country at the MacDowell Colony in New Hampshire, where he met playwright Dorothy Hartzell Kuhns, whom he married in 1923. One of Heyward's literary goals was to disprove H. L. Mencken's charge that no good literature was produced south of the Potomac River.

Heyward wrote *Porgy*, his first novel, after reading about a handicapped man who had been pursued in his goat-cart by police. First published in 1925, *Porgy* received overwhelmingly favorable responses from critics and general readers. Dorothy and DuBose developed the plot into a play in 1927, and DuBose Heyward later collaborated with George and Ira Gershwin in creating *Porgy and Bess*, the first U.S. opera with primarily black characters, which premiered on Broadway on October 10, 1935. The novel, play, and opera share similar plots and characters, but Heyward's literary skill is best displayed in the novel, *Porgy*.

Changing fate is the novel's major theme. Catfish Row illustrates the altered fate of Charleston's white aristocracy: The once great mansion is now a tenement for poor African American families. In its courtyard, residents wager on dice, outcomes determined by fate, not skill. Characters in *Porgy* have neither good luck nor bad; instead, their luck is subject to change without notice. Early in the novel, Serena enjoys her comfortable position as a well-paid servant in a kind, wealthy family. She and her husband are well off compared to their neighbors; however, their fate changes when Robbins is killed after accusing Crown of using loaded dice. The fishermen of Catfish Row suffer a brutal twist of fate when they drown at sea during a hurricane on the day after a record catch. Fate's influence is developed extensively in Porgy's character. At the beginning of the novel, he is content, but he loses his lifeline when Peter is arrested. Nearly destitute, Porgy attempts to take fate into his own hands by creating his "second emancipation" in the form of a goat-cart. Life improves when he meets Bess, and the couple hopes to live happily ever after; however, fate, in the guises of disease and the white legal system, ensures that their happiness does not last. Even Porgy's good fortune winning at dice brings about suspicion from neighbors and contributes to his downfall.

Porgy's decay suggests another theme in the novel—that of a crumbled or crumbling Eden. The novel's action takes place between April and October, symbolizing the shift from spring to fall, birth to death, hope to despair, innocence to experience. Catfish Row's inhabitants face constant temptation, but rather than one great fall, they experience periodic falls. Bess faces serpent-like temptations in Sportin' Life, cocaine, and Crown. Just before encountering Crown on Kittiwar Island, Bess sees a snake but is not harmed—that is, until Crown tempts her to sin. Connected to the crumbling Eden theme is the deliberate contrast between barren white society (felled by the Civil War and economic devastation during Reconstruction) and the hopeful black community. Heyward makes many subtle comparisons between sterile white Christianity and the vitality of faith among Catfish Row residents. He also contrasts white medicine, which always seems to lead black patients to death and anatomy laboratories, with the black community's blend of superstition and herbal medicine. Even justice has color distinctions. The white policemen, lawyers, and judges believe wrongful deeds must be punished at any cost, even if innocents must suffer, as shown by Peter's arrest after the first murder. Catfish Row residents do not betray their neighbors to police, but deliver justice within their community, for example, Porgy's killing Crown.

Community is the key to survival in Catfish Row. The building originally housed one family, with space for individuals to isolate themselves from one another in private chambers; conversely, privacy cannot exist in the tenement, where several members of a large family often share a single room. "Family" is broadly defined in this community. When Serena cannot afford to bury Robbins, neighbors contribute to his "saucer burial"—people drop money into a saucer on the corpse's chest until the funeral expenses are met. Similarly, Bess and Porgy think nothing of adopting Clara's baby after the hurricane.

In theme and style, *Porgy* reflects several early twentieth century literary trends. It is an example of realism in its abundant use of detail, local color in its use of vernacular and local customs, naturalism in its candid details of hopeless poverty, and Southern romance in its gothic elements and melodrama. Hence, *Porgy* has been compared with William Faulkner's fiction. In genre, this novel, which includes poetry and is written in vignettes (scenes that suggest drama), can be compared to generically heterogeneous works such as Jean Toomer's *Cane* (1923). Although Heyward wrote several novels, plays, and poems, *Porgy* is considered to be his only literary success.

"Critical Evaluation" by Geralyn Strecker

Bibliography:
Alpert, Hollis. *The Life and Times of Porgy and Bess: The Story of an American Classic*. New York: Alfred A. Knopf, 1990. Traces the history of *Porgy* from Heyward's novel to the October 10, 1935, Broadway premiere of *Porgy and Bess*. Includes illustrations from several productions of the opera.

Durham, Frank. *DuBose Heyward: The Man Who Wrote Porgy*. Port Washington, N.Y.: Kennikat Press, 1965. Focuses primarily on the novel *Porgy* and its stage versions. Greatly ignores the author's other works, but offers valuable background to the story's creation and reception.

_____. "The Reputed Demises of Uncle Tom: Or, The Treatment of the Negro in Fiction by White Southern Authors in the 1920's." *Southern Literary Review* 2, no. 2 (Spring, 1970): 26-50. Discusses *Porgy* in relation to types of African Americans in literary history: from primitive portrayals in abolition literature, to the plantation myth of black man as folk figure type during Reconstruction, to the "New Negro" after World War I.

Rhodes, Chip. "Writing Up the New Negro: The Construction of Consumer Desire in the Twenties." *Journal of American Studies* 28, no. 2 (August, 1994): 191-207. Discusses desire in *Porgy* in context with other works of Southern literature. Describes Catfish Row as being in limbo between slavery and freedom.

Slavick, William H. *DuBose Heyward*. Boston: Twayne, 1981. Critical biography provides extensive discussion of the novel *Porgy*, as well as Heyward's other fiction, poetry, and drama.

PORTNOY'S COMPLAINT

Type of work: Novel
Author: Philip Roth (1933-   )
Type of plot: Bildungsroman
Time of plot: Mid-twentieth century
Locale: Newark, New Jersey
First published: 1969

> *Principal characters:*
> ALEXANDER PORTNOY, the protagonist
> SOPHIE PORTNOY, his mother
> JACK PORTNOY, his father
> MARY JANE REED, the Monkey
> KAY CAMPBELL, the Pumpkin
> SARAH ABBOTT MAULSBY, the Pilgrim
> NAOMI, an Israeli soldier

The Story:

Alexander Portnoy had a very difficult childhood and young manhood growing up in a lower-middle-class Jewish family in Newark, New Jersey. Part of his problem was his emotionally overcharged home environment; another part was the conflict between his desire to be a dutiful son and his wish to enjoy life to the utmost as a fully assimilated American. As a result he became highly neurotic and sought therapy from a psychiatrist, Dr. Spielvogel, to whom he recounts the various experiences that form the novel.

Portnoy's mother, Sophie, was an overbearing woman (a stereotypical "Jewish momma") who tormented Alex with demands he hardly knew how to fulfill. His poor, constipated father, Jack, was no help at all in containing Sophie's dictatorial control of the household. Neither was Alex's sister, Hannah, who played only a shadowy role in Alex's descriptions of the family. For example, throughout his boyhood and on into later life Portnoy could never understand what it was that he did as a little boy that made his mother lock him outside their apartment door. What crime had he committed? Try as he would to please her, at least once a month he found himself locked outside, vainly hammering on the door and pleading to be allowed back inside.

As he entered puberty, Portnoy's sex drive went into high gear. Some of the most hilarious occasions he recalled for his psychiatrist involved masturbation and an early, futile attempt to have sex with the local available teenager, Bubbles Girardi, that ended with his ejaculation into his own eye. He then had the fantasy of becoming blind and returning home with a Seeing Eye dog, which his mother would not permit in the house. In this episode Portnoy showed how the melodrama he repeatedly experienced at home influenced his rich fantasy life as well. Whether it was polio season or Alex indulging himself by eating french fries with his friend Melvin Weiner, anything and everything became an occasion for hysteria and melodrama in the Portnoy household.

Although fantasy was a large part of his life, Portnoy's "adventures" were real enough. As a college student, he took up with Kay Campbell, whom he nicknamed the Pumpkin because of her complexion and physique but who was otherwise an "exemplary" person. She represented for Portnoy the liberal, high-minded, worthy Protestant female he thought he would someday marry. When he went home with her to Iowa for Thanksgiving, he found her family to be as different from his own as could possibly be imagined. The Campbells never raised their voices, and their dinner table was a model of decorum. Portnoy was so thrilled to be their "weekend guest" that he could only reply with a polite "Thank you" to anything anyone said; he even spoke thus to inanimate objects, including a chair he accidentally bumped into.

The college romance with Kay ended when Alex casually suggested that when they got married Kay would convert to Judaism, and she indicated that she would not do so—not that Alex was a seriously observant Jew: Following his Bar Mitzvah (another farcical episode), he stubbornly refused to attend even High Holiday services, the pleas of his family notwithstanding. Alex's attraction to gentile women, shiksas, however, was a recurring part of his problems of adjustment. After the Pumpkin and college, he took up with Sarah Abbott Maulsby, the Pilgrim, so-called because of her family origins. That romance ended when Alex realized he could never marry the "beautiful and adoring girl" because their backgrounds, even the expressions they used, were so different. Moreover, Portnoy recognized that a major part of Sarah's attraction—and the attraction of others like her—was not her self but her heritage, which he was desperately and vainly trying to assimilate into his own—or to take revenge upon because he could not.

Things seemed somewhat different with Mary Jane Reed, the Monkey, a nickname she acquired from an earlier episode in which she ate a banana while another couple had intercourse. A New York model, Mary Jane was born and reared in the hills of West Virginia. Although she seemed to satisfy Portnoy's grandest sexual fantasies and encourage others, he still regarded her as essentially an uneducated hillbilly, which in important respects she was. By this time Portnoy had an important job as the Assistant Commissioner for Human Opportunity in New York, and unknown to many, his private life and his professional life were at odds with each other. As Alex tried to educate Mary Jane, she fell deeply in love with him, regarding him as her "breakthrough" to a new and different kind of life from the one she had hitherto led. She nicknamed him Breakie, and for a brief while—as when they spent a weekend in a quaint New England village inn—he fantasized that they might indeed become a couple. Afterward, however, during a trip to Europe, when they had sex together with a Roman prostitute, they quarreled bitterly, and the affair came to an abrupt halt.

Continuing his trip alone, Alex went to Israel, where he got his serious comeuppance. Trying to seduce a very attractive sabra in her army uniform, he was physically and emotionally humiliated by her. Naomi was having none of it—none of Alex's coarse sexual advances, none of his "ghetto humor" or his self-deprecating, self-mocking attitude, and especially none of the corrupt values he had developed by living in the Diaspora. To her, he was an utter schlemiel, as indeed he was without fully realizing it.

After all this, Alex finally wound up undertaking an extended series of sessions on Dr. Spielvogel's couch, from where he told his tales of self-pity and self-torture. The novel ends with the ironic (and now famous) words: "So [said the doctor]. Now vee may perhaps to begin."

Critical Evaluation:

Often grouped with two other accomplished Jewish American writers, Saul Bellow and Bernard Malamud, Philip Roth is actually as different from each of them as they are from each other. Their intellectual outlooks as well as their sense of humor are by no means similar; and if Bellow's favorite milieu is Chicago and Malamud's is New York, Roth's is Newark, New Jersey, in the 1930's and 1940's, where, like Alexander Portnoy, he grew up. Because of this association, many critics mistakenly have taken Portnoy's experiences to be Roth's—an event he fictionalizes in a later novel called *Zuckerman Unbound* (1981). The reader is warned, therefore, not to confuse fiction with biography, which Roth supplies in *The Facts: A Novelist's Autobiography* (1988).

The major conflict that Portnoy endures and that Roth suggests characterizes many young Jewish American men of his generation is described in the preliminary matter to the novel, where "Portnoy's Complaint" is given a dictionary definition. The conflict involves "strongly felt ethical and altruistic impulses" that are constantly at war with "extreme sexual longings, often of a perverse nature." Try as he may, Portnoy cannot shake off his Jewish ethical heritage for a life of unrestrained libidinous satisfaction. In Freudian terms, he is the victim of an unrelenting battle between the reality principle and the pleasure principle, the alter ego and the id, in which his poor ego emerges invariably battered and bewildered. Though much of the novel is humorous, for Portnoy what is happening to him is a very serious matter. As he cries out to Dr. Spielvogel, he is living in the middle of a Jewish joke—he is the son in a Jewish joke—but for him "*it ain't no joke.*"

In many ways, *Portnoy's Complaint* brings the confessional novel to its logical and absurd conclusion. A tour de force that has won favor with many readers and critics (like *Goodbye, Columbus*, 1959, it was made into a film), it has also been attacked by observant Jews as a travesty of Jewish life in America, and by feminists as offering demeaning, even vicious portraits of women. Roth's defense is (as it was for his earlier stories in *Goodbye, Columbus*, which won for him the National Book Award in 1960) that he is a writer who writes out of his own experience to explore the depths of human nature and human experience—not to provide palliatives or propaganda for any cause or causes. As for Portnoy's use of obscene language throughout the novel, Roth explained that he used it in the novel not so much for its realism as for a vehicle to demonstrate Portnoy's passion to be "saved"—saved from himself and from the conflict that was wearing him out. In this sense, *Portnoy's Complaint* is like Erica Jong's *Fear of Flying* (1973), often mistaken as a piece of feminist pornography instead of the serious novel about a woman's struggle to find herself that underlies all the sex and language to which many have objected.

Indeed, Roth's linguistic versatility is one of the major accomplishments of the novel, which one critic has described as "the high comedy of style," deriving from "the same contrast between innocence and experience which shapes the action, a contrast exemplified in incongruities between language and subject" (see Spacks, below). Another accomplishment is his adaptation of the stand-up comic's *spritz*, or spray of words that evokes gales of laughter from audiences by its remarkable energy and momentum. Moreover, Roth has a superb ear for the cadences and idioms of actual speech, which he deftly varies from character to character so that the novel never loses its fascination, whether Portnoy is a child bewildered by his parents or an adult trying to reason with Mary Jane Reed or an emotional cripple appealing for help from his psychiatrist Dr. Spielvogel. His use of metaphorical language rivals in its way what Southern agrarian writers have achieved in theirs. Yet the novel's lasting importance remains its tragicomic portrait of someone growing up Jewish in an urban environment in mid-twentieth century America.

Jay L. Halio

Bibliography:
Cohen, Sarah Blacher. "Philip Roth's Would-Be Patriarchs and Their *Shikses* and Shrews." *Studies in American Jewish Literature* 1 (Spring, 1975): 16-23. Reprinted in *Critical Essays on Philip Roth*, edited by Sanford Pinsker. Boston: G. K. Hall, 1982. About the women in

several of Roth's novels, including *Portnoy's Complaint*. Roth's "petulant" young men typically blame their "Yiddishe mommes" for their problems and powerlessness.

Grebstein, Sheldon. "The Comic Anatomy of *Portnoy's Complaint*." In *Comic Relief: Humor in Contemporary American Literature*, edited by Sarah Blacher Cohen. Urbana: University of Illinois Press, 1978. An excellent essay on Roth's "stand-up" humor, as developed from professional comedians such as Henny Youngman and others.

Guttmann, Allen. *The Jewish Writer in America: Assimilation and the Crisis of Identity*. New York: Oxford University Press, 1971. Contains an essay, "Philip Roth and the Rabbis," that shows Roth's sensitivity to the problems of assimilation in America.

Halio, Jay L. *Philip Roth Revisited*. New York: Twayne, 1992. The chapter "The Comedy of Excess" treats various aspects of Roth's comic mastery in *Portnoy's Complaint*. It also comments on the underlying humanity of Mary Jane Reed, the Monkey, as Portnoy, who fails to recognize her humanity, derisively nicknames her.

Spacks, Patricia Meyer. "About Portnoy." *The Yale Review* 58 (Summer, 1969): 623-635. Mainly about Roth's linguistic virtuosity in *Portnoy's Complaint*.

IL PORTO SEPOLTO

Type of work: Poetry
Author: Giuseppe Ungaretti (1888-1970)
First published: 1916 (partial translation, 1990)

Giuseppe Ungaretti's *Il porto sepolto* came out of the peculiar circumstances of World War I; Ungaretti had volunteered in May of 1915 to join the Italian military. Each of the thirty-three poems of this, Ungaretti's first volume, are tagged with the date and place of composition. Two of them were written in December, 1915, and twenty-eight were composed between April, 1916, and September, 1916. They are for the most part placed in chronological order. Thematically, the collection explores solitude and the various ways in which human beings try to bridge the spaces between one another. It shows the heights to which human aspiration can ascend, even out of the depths of trench warfare.

Il porto sepolto forms one of three parts of a larger collection, *Allegria di naufragi*, (1919, the joy of shipwrecks). The "harbor" that is "buried" is most likely the harbor off Pharos at Alexandria, the city of Ungaretti's youth. The harbor become mythic for Ungaretti. Like Atlantis, the harbor is so far below the surface, and so legendary, that it represents the unfathomable depths of the human psyche as well as the height of the most intense consciousness. It was to him, he writes, "the mirage of Italy"; it represents that part of one's early life which is submerged in the subconscious, "or in the intense heat of the mirage."

The human condition of separateness and the striving of the human mind and spirit to overcome that condition is addressed in "Pilgrimage." In it, he refers to himself as "Ungaretti/ man of pain," who gains courage from illusion. This statement is paradoxical: The first stanza shows the individual in the trenches in war, "in these bowels/ of rubble" where "hour on hour" the poet-soldier has "dragged" his "carcass/ worn away by mud/ like a sole." Ungaretti's illusion is the illusion of light beyond those pathetic, degrading, and dehumanizing because disconnecting conditions. He writes, "Beyond/ a searchlight/ sets a sea/ into the fog," showing his illusion to be the possibility of order, of light, of form rather than chaos, of purification (the sea) instead of putrefaction ("bowels of rubble"). Toward the close of the poem, the faculty of the imagination is shown to lift the human spirit above the physical and psychological depths of the trenches: From the trenches, he perceives the essential similarity and the ultimate connectedness of things and seeks to communicate that vision in his poetry. The title "Pilgrimage" indicates more than a mere journey. It is a religious journey from the physicality of despair into the open air of spiritual aspiration.

Ungaretti was rooted in more than one literary and philosophical tradition, and he derives imagery from Italian and other Western cultures, from Asian literary traditions, and from the modern world. His images and symbols evoke thereby a curious admixture of resonances, often concerned with the search for identity. Such a theme is explored in "In Memoriam," written on September 30, 1916, at Locvizza. This funereal and contemplative poem concerns a friend, who was named Mohammad Sheab, from his days at a French school in Alexandria. Sheab was an Arab, with whom Ungaretti later attended school in Paris. Ungaretti perceived Sheab and himself as individuals estranged from their roots, and on this estrangement Ungaretti blames the suicide of Sheab, "Descendent/ of emirs of nomads," who changes his name from Mohammad to Marcel, who cannot remember how to live with Arab culture, and who takes his own life at 5 Rue des Carmes, to be buried in Ivry. In contrast, Ungaretti, the soldier-poet, finds his connection to Italy and to the Italian people.

The fact that Ungaretti was a man of both Asian and Western cultures, that he was fluent in at least three languages, and was a writer in three literary traditions becomes apparent again in "Phase," in which he describes the depths of love as being in the "eye/ of thousandth-and-one night," clearly an allusion to the famous collection of tales. He mixes the Asian image of the "deserted garden" with the western myth of the dove descending. In "June," he writes of the end of an evening of lovemaking, comparing the way in which "the sky is shut" to the concurrent movement of "the jasmine" "in my African land."

"Rivers," written at Cotici, August 16, 1916, opens with the poet holding onto a "crippled tree," which is alone in a ravine and which has as a quality "the laziness of a circus/ before or after the performance." If this were the traditional symbol of a tree of life, it would come to represent a life "crippled," "*mutilato*"—a life made dysfunctional through having been made the object of harm. The tree seems to be emblematic of human anguish. While on the one hand the "circus" might appear to be lazy specifically when the performance is not on, it may also represent social instability and disorder. The poet-soldier, in repose, then watches the clouds pass in front of the moon, and the following morning he rests "like a relic." In writing of the rivers, he establishes a stark setting and places himself first in Bedouin culture as "a pliant fiber/ of the universe." He writes of the Serchio, to which his ancestry is connected, of the Nile, which witnessed the growth of the young man, and of the Seine, where his identity was "remingled and remade" and where he gained self-knowledge. After separating things in order to examine them in the harsh glare of desert light, he resolves and modulates through a visual paradox: Night falls, and he writes, "now my life seems to me/ a corolla/ of shadows."

In the middle of the series, the poem "Leavetaking" expresses Ungaretti's poetics. In eight lines which run in fluid movement, he writes of poetry as "the world humanity/ one's own life/ flowering from the word"—and the reader envisions the most abstract expression, "the world humanity," quickly transformed into concreteness through a special kind of metaphor: Flowers come out of words, and the flowers, and the words, and the action of the flowers coming from the words, all express life. Each word has the power to so impress one that, as he describes it, "it is dug into my life/ like an abyss." He tells readers to read every word, and to let every word pour out its full complex of meanings. It is with this advice from the poet that the reader can approach the poetry. Ungaretti's verse cannot be read quickly, but rather it must be allowed to unfold itself word by word; the reader must allow the poet to re-create in him or her the poet's experience or perception. He does not relate experience, but rather he re-creates it, and to enter into that re-creation is the reader's challenge. Everything in Ungaretti's poetry depends not upon the narrative line, but upon each word.

Il porto sepolto marks such a dramatic break from the Italian poetry of the nineteenth century that Ungaretti has been seen as the first modern Italian poet. In "Morning," written at Santa Maria La Longa, he writes a poem of two lines: "Immensity/ illumines me," which typifies the intensity and the sparseness of diction that characterize Ungaretti's work.

Ungaretti himself described the intent of *Il porto sepolto:* Although clearly written by a soldier, it does not praise war and heroic glory. Rather, it is a cry for human connection, for brotherhood in the face of suffering. Participating in the waging of war paradoxically heightened Ungaretti's vision of the essential integrity of all things in the cosmos and affirmed for him the possibility that the virtue of brotherly love could sustain a very fragile humanity in the face of cataclysm. He expresses the tenuousness of life during war in "Soldiers," and of human communication in "Brothers," by comparing both to leaves on the verge of falling from trees. He closes "Brothers" with the image of "man facing his fragility," although facing it along with, and sustained by, his "Brothers." "Watch" displays Ungaretti's paradox that through contemplating loss and death so often, he is actually engaging in a poetry of life. As he holds his dead, "massacred comrade," he is moved by the image of death to speak; not even in love letters has he himself "held/ so/ fast to life" as in physically holding his dead friend.

The dominant contrast in Ungaretti is physical place: the desert, through which one roams alone, with only the memory of the promised land. It is the calling of poetry, according to Ungaretti, to redeem humanity, to make real the promised land. It is the possibility of poetry to help humanity become pure and to attain its own perfection, to overcome its own anguish, to be in harmony with the universe.

The setting of Ungaretti's poetry is often stark, elemental, although peopled with the subjects of the poems. He plays with the senses, often accomplishing difficult things with great agility, such as the verbal re-creation of sound. For example, in "Pleasure," he compares the feeling of remorse after a day's pleasure to the haunting sound of "a dog's bark/ lost in the/ desert." Similarly, in "Solitude," he writes that the sound of his own voice in anguish can "wound/ like lightning bolts/ the faint bell/ of the sky."

Ungaretti faced the challenge of an Italian poet of his time, either to write in or not write in literary Italian. He chose to pare down his language so far that he thought he might reach the essence of each word and each line, and, in fact, he put much work into revision for poetic compression and for the concentration of perception. It was Ungaretti's belief that to break through into a new era of poetry in Italian, one would have to be intensely introspective, able to perceive one's existence as part of a greater whole, and unequivocally able to express the consciousness of one's own conscience. This, Ungaretti accomplished.

Donna Berliner

Bibliography:

Auster, Paul. "Man of Pain." *The New York Review of Books*, April 29, 1976, 35-37. A general introduction to Ungaretti.

Brose, Margaret. "Metaphor and Simile in Giuseppe Ungaretti's *L'Allegria*." *Lingua E Stile* (March, 1976): 43-73. Discusses Ungaretti's adaptations of Symbolist techniques as well as of other aesthetic and stylistic devices.

Cary, Joseph. *Three Modern Italian Poets: Saba, Ungaretti, Montale*. New York: New York University Press, 1969. Introductory chapter provides accessible background information. The chapter on Ungaretti traces his career from his early days through his later poetry of anguish.

Creagh, Patrick. Introduction to *Selected Poems: Giuseppe Ungaretti*. Edited and translated by Patrick Creagh. Harmondsworth, Middlesex, England: Penguin, 1971. Discusses Ungaretti's poetics.

Jones, Frederic J. *Giuseppe Ungaretti: Poet and Critic*. Edinburgh: Edinburgh University Press, 1977. First third of the book is a cultural biography. Describes Ungaretti's perspective and examines his work in terms of his connections to Alexandria, Paris, and Italy.

O'Neill, Tom. "Ungaretti and Foscolo: A Question of Taste." *Italian Quarterly* 12, no. 45 (Summer, 1968): 73-89. Traces thematic and aesthetic development with awareness of the prose works and of the biography.

Ungaretti, Giuseppe. *The Buried Harbour: Selected Poems of Giuseppe Ungaretti*. Canberra, Australia: Leros Press, 1990. A good recent translation of selections from *Il porto sepolto*.

THE PORTRAIT OF A LADY

Type of work: Novel
Author: Henry James (1843-1916)
Type of plot: Psychological realism
Time of plot: c. 1875
Locale: England, France, and Italy
First published: serial, 1880-1881; book, 1881

Principal characters:
ISABEL ARCHER, an American heiress
GILBERT OSMOND, her husband
RALPH TOUCHETT, her cousin
MADAME MERLE, her friend and Osmond's former mistress
PANSY OSMOND, Osmond's daughter
LORD WARBURTON, Isabel's English suitor
CASPAR GOODWOOD, Isabel's American suitor
HENRIETTA STACKPOLE, an American newspaper correspondent
and Isabel's friend

The Story:

Upon the death of her father, Isabel Archer had been visited by her aunt, Mrs. Touchett, who considered her so attractive that she decided to give her the advantage of more cosmopolitan experience. Isabel was quickly carried off to Europe so she might see something of the world of culture and fashion. On the day the two women arrived at the Touchett home in England, Isabel's sickly young cousin, Ralph Touchett, and his father were taking tea in the garden with their friend Lord Warburton. The young nobleman, who had just been confessing his boredom with life, was much taken with the American girl's grace and lively manner.

Isabel had barely settled at Gardencourt, her aunt's home, when she received a letter from an American friend, Henrietta Stackpole, a newspaperwoman who was writing a series of articles on the sights of Europe. At Ralph's invitation, Henrietta came to Gardencourt to visit Isabel and obtain material for her writing. Soon after Henrietta's arrival, Isabel heard from another American friend and a would-be suitor, Caspar Goodwood, who had followed her abroad and learned her whereabouts from Henrietta. Isabel, irritated by his aggressiveness, decided not to answer his letter.

On the day she received the letter from Goodwood, Lord Warburton proposed to her. Not wishing to seem indifferent to the honor of his proposal, she asked for time to consider it, but she decided finally that she would not be able to marry the young Englishman because she wished to see considerably more of the world before she married. She was also afraid that marriage to Warburton, although he was a model of kindness and thoughtfulness, might prove stifling.

Because Isabel had not seen London on her journey with Mrs. Touchett and since it was on Henrietta Stackpole's itinerary, the two young women, accompanied by Ralph Touchett, went to the capital. Henrietta soon made the acquaintance of a Mr. Bantling, who began to squire her around. When Caspar Goodwood visited Isabel at her hotel, she again refused him, though when he persisted, she agreed that he could ask for her hand again in two years.

While the party was in London, a telegram came from Gardencourt, informing them that old

Mr. Touchett was seriously ill of gout and his wife much alarmed. Isabel and Ralph left on the afternoon train. Henrietta remained under the escort of her new friend.

During the time Mr. Touchett lay dying and his family was preoccupied, Isabel spent a great deal of time with Madame Merle, an old friend of Mrs. Touchett, who had come to Gardencourt to spend a few days. She and Isabel were thrown together a great deal and exchanged many confidences. Isabel admired the older woman for her ability to amuse herself, for her skill at needlework, painting, and the piano, and for her ability to accommodate herself to any social situation. For her part, Madame Merle spoke enviously of Isabel's youth and intelligence and lamented the life that had left her, at middle age, a widow with no children and no visible success in life.

When her uncle died, he left Isabel, at his son's instigation, half of his fortune. Ralph, impressed with his young cousin's brilliance, had persuaded his father that she should be given the opportunity to fly as far and as high as she might. He knew he could not live long because of his pulmonary illness, and his legacy was enough to let him live in comfort.

As quickly as she could, Mrs. Touchett sold her London house and took Isabel to Paris with her. Ralph went south for the winter to preserve what was left of his health. In Paris, the new heiress was introduced to many of her aunt's friends among American expatriates, but she was not impressed. She thought their indolent lives worthy only of contempt. Meanwhile, Henrietta and Mr. Bantling had arrived in Paris, and Isabel spent much time with them and Edward Rosier, another dilettante living on the income from his inheritance. She had known Rosier when they were children and she had been traveling abroad with her father. Rosier explained to Isabel that he could not return to his own country because there was no occupation there worthy of a gentleman.

In February, Mrs. Touchett and her niece went to the Palazzo Crescentini, the Touchett house in Florence. They stopped on the way to see Ralph, who was staying in San Remo. In Florence they were joined once more by Madame Merle. Unknown to Isabel or her aunt, Madame Merle also visited her friend Gilbert Osmond, another American who lived in voluntary exile outside Florence with his art collection and his young convent-bred daughter, Pansy. Madame Merle told Osmond of Isabel's arrival in Florence, saying that as the heir to a fortune, Isabel would be a valuable addition to Osmond's collection.

The heiress who had already rejected two worthy suitors did not refuse the third. She had been quickly captivated by the charm of the sheltered life Gilbert Osmond had created for himself. Her friends were against the match. Henrietta Stackpole was inclined to favor Caspar Goodwood and convinced that Osmond was interested only in Isabel's money, as was Isabel's aunt. Mrs. Touchett had requested Madame Merle, the good friend of both parties, to discover the state of their affections; she was convinced that Madame Merle could have prevented the match. Ralph Touchett was disappointed that his cousin should have fallen from her flight so quickly. Caspar Goodwood, learning of Isabel's intended marriage when he revisited her after the passage of the two years agreed upon, could not persuade her to reconsider her step. Isabel was indignant when he commented on the fact that she did not even know her intended husband's antecedents.

After they were married, Isabel and Gilbert Osmond established their home in Rome, in a setting completely expressive of Osmond's tastes. Before three years had passed, Isabel began to realize that her friends had not been completely wrong in their objections to her marriage. Osmond's exquisite taste had made their home one of the most popular in Rome, but his ceaseless effort to press his wife into a mold, to make her a reflection of his own ideas, had not made their marriage one of the happiest.

Osmond had succeeded in destroying a romance between Pansy and Edward Rosier, who had visited the girl's stepmother and found the daughter attractive. Osmond had not succeeded, however, in contracting the match he desired between Pansy and Lord Warburton. Warburton had found Pansy as pleasing as Isabel had once been, but he had dropped his suit when he saw that the girl's affections lay with Rosier.

Ralph Touchett, his health growing steadily worse, gave up his wanderings on the Continent and returned to Gardencourt to die. When Isabel received a telegram from his mother telling her that Ralph would like to see her before his death, she felt it her duty to go to Gardencourt at once. Osmond reacted to her wish as if it were a personal insult. He expected that his wife would want to remain at his side and that she would not disobey any wish of his. He also made it plain that he disliked Ralph.

In a state of turmoil after that conversation with her husband, Isabel met the Countess Gemini, Osmond's sister. The countess, who was visiting the Osmonds, had seen how matters lay between her brother and Isabel. An honest soul, she had felt more sympathy for her sister-in-law than for her brother. To comfort Isabel, she told her the story of Gilbert's past. After his first wife had died, he and Madame Merle had had an affair for six or seven years. During that time, Madame Merle, who was then a widow, had borne him a child, Pansy. Changing his residence, Osmond had been able to pretend to his new circle of friends that the original Mrs. Osmond had died in giving birth to the child.

With this news fresh in her mind and still determined to go to England, Isabel stopped to say good-bye to Pansy, who was staying in a convent where her father had sent her to get over her affair with Rosier. There she also met Madame Merle, who with her keen intuition immediately perceived that Isabel knew her secret. When she remarked that Isabel need never to see her again, that she would go to America, Isabel was certain Madame Merle would also find in America much to her own advantage.

Isabel arrived in England in time to see her cousin before his death. She stayed on briefly at Gardencourt after the funeral, long enough to bid good-bye to Lord Warburton, who had come to offer condolences to her aunt and to reject a third offer from Caspar Goodwood, who knew of her marital problems. When she left to start her journey back to Italy, Isabel knew that her first duty was not toward herself but to put her house in order.

Critical Evaluation:

The Portrait of a Lady, usually regarded as the major achievement of Henry James's early period of fiction writing, is also recognized to be one of literature's great novels. In it, James shows that he has learned well from two European masters of the novel. Ivan Turgenev taught him how to use a single character who shapes the work and is seen throughout in relationship to the other characters, and from George Eliot he had learned the importance of a tight structure and a form that develops logically out of the given materials. He advances in *The Portrait of a Lady* beyond George Eliot in minimizing his own authorial comments and analysis and permitting his heroine to be seen through her own tardily awakening self-realization, as well as through the consciousness of the men and women who are closest to her. Thus his "portrait" of a lady is one that grows slowly, stroke by stroke, with each new touch bringing out highlights and shadows until at the end of the novel Isabel Archer stands revealed as a woman whose experiences of excitement, joy, pain, and knowledge, have given her an enduring beauty and dignity.

Isabel is one of James's finest creations and one of the most memorable women in the history of the novel. A number of sources have been suggested for her. She may have been partly drawn from James's cousin Mary "Minny" Temple, whom he was later to immortalize as Milly Theale in *The Wings of the Dove* (1902). Isabel has also been compared to two of George Eliot's heroines, Dorothea Brooke in *Middlemarch* (1871-1872) and Gwendolen Harleth in *Daniel Deronda* (1876); to Diana Belfield in an early romantic tale by James entitled "Longstaff's Marriage"; to Bathsheba Everdene in Thomas Hardy's *Far from the Madding Crowd* (1874); and even to Henry James himself, some of whose early experiences closely parallel those of Isabel. Yet while James may have drawn from both real and fictional people in portraying Isabel Archer, she possesses her own identity, having grown, as James later wrote in his preface to the novel, from his "conception of a certain young woman affronting her destiny." He visualized her as "an intelligent but presumptuous girl" who was nevertheless "complex" and who would be offered a series of opportunities for free choice in confronting that destiny. Because of her presumption in believing that she knew more about herself and the world than she actually did, Isabel made mistakes, including the tragic error of misjudging Gilbert Osmond's nature. Her intelligence, however, though insufficient to save her from suffering, enabled her to achieve a moral triumph in the end.

Of the four men in Isabel's life, three love her and one uses her innocence to gain for himself what he would not otherwise have had. She refuses to marry Lord Warburton because, though he offers her a great fortune, a title, an entry into English society, and an agreeable and entertaining personality, she believes she can do better. She turns down the equally wealthy Caspar Goodwood because she finds him stiff and is frightened by his aggressiveness. Her cousin, Ralph Touchett, does not propose because he does not wish her to be tied to a man who daily faces death. She does not even suspect the extent of his love and adoration until she learns of it just as death takes him from her, which almost overwhelms her. She accepts Gilbert Osmond because she is deceived by his calculated charm and because she believes that he deserves what she can offer him: a fortune that will make it possible for him to live in idleness but surrounded by the objects of the culture she believes he represents, and a mother's love and care for his supposedly motherless daughter. Half of the novel is given over to Isabel's living with, adjusting to, and finally triumphing over that disastrous choice.

In his preface, James uses an architectural figure to describe *The Portrait of a Lady*. He says the "large building" of the novel "came to be a square and spacious house." Much of what occurs in the novel occurs in or near a series of houses, each of which relates significantly to Isabel or to other characters. The action begins at Gardencourt, the tudor English country house of Daniel Touchett that Isabel finds more beautiful than anything she has ever seen. The charm of the house is enhanced by its age and natural setting beside the Thames above London. It contrasts greatly with the "old house at Albany, a large, square, double house" belonging to her grandmother, which Isabel in her childhood had found romantic and in which she had indulged in dreams stimulated by her reading. Mrs. Touchett's taking Isabel from the Albany house to Gardencourt is a first step in her plan to "introduce her to the world." When Isabel visits Lockleigh, Lord Warburton's home, she sees it from the gardens as resembling "a castle in a legend," though inside it has been modernized. She does not view it as a home for herself, or its titled owner as her husband, despite the many advantages of both. The front of Gilbert Osmond's house in Florence is "imposing" but of "a somewhat uncommunicative character," a "mask." It symbolizes Osmond, behind whose mask Isabel does not see until after she is married to him. The last of the houses in *The Portrait of a Lady* is the Palazzo Roccanera, the Roman home of the Osmonds, which James first describes as "a kind of domestic fortress . . . which smelt of historic deeds, of crime and craft and violence." When Isabel later broods over it during her night-long meditation in chapter 42, it is "the house of darkness, the house of dumbness, the house of suffocation."

Isabel is first seen at Gardencourt on her visit with Mrs. Touchett, and it is here that she turns down the first of three proposals of marriage. It is fitting that she should be last seen here with each of the three men who have loved her. Asserting the independence on which she has so long prided herself, she has defied her imperious husband by going to England to see the dying Ralph, whose last words tell her that if she is now hated by Osmond, she has been adored by her cousin. In a brief conversation with Lord Warburton after Ralph's death, Isabel turns down an invitation to visit him and his sisters at Lockleigh. Shortly afterward, a scene from six years earlier is reversed: Then she had sat on a rustic bench at Gardencourt and looked up from reading Caspar Goodwood's letter (in which he writes that he will come to England and propose to her) to see and hear Warburton preparing to propose. Now Caspar surprises her by appearing just after she has dismissed Warburton. There follows the one sexually passionate scene in the novel. In it Isabel has "an immense desire to appear to resist" the force of Caspar's argument that she should leave Osmond and turn to him. She pleads with streaming tears, "As you love me, as you pity me, leave me alone!" Defying her plea, Caspar kisses her, but he possesses her for a moment only. Immediately after she flees into the house and then to Rome, as Caspar learns in the brief scene in London with Henrietta Stackpole that closes the novel. James leaves the reader to conclude that Isabel's love for Pansy Osmond has principally determined her decision to continue enduring a marriage that she had freely—though so ignorantly and foolishly—chosen.

"Critical Evaluation" by Henderson Kincheloe

Bibliography:

Grover, Philip. *Henry James and the French Novel: A Study in Inspiration*. New York: Barnes & Noble Books, 1973. Analyzes all of James's works up to and including *The Portrait of a Lady*. Tries to show the ways in which James was influenced by Honoré de Balzac, Gustave Flaubert, and the French *l'art pour l'art* movement. Compares the themes and subjects of French writers with those of James.

Kelley, Cornelia Pulsifer. *The Early Development of Henry James*. Rev. ed. Urbana: University of Illinois Press, 1965. Traces the development of the Jamesian novel from *Roderick Hudson* (1876) through *The Portrait of a Lady*. Examines French influences on James but also claims that the two novelists who influenced James most significantly were Turgenev and George Eliot, whose influence can be seen best in *The Portrait of a Lady*.

Kirschke, James J. *Henry James and Impressionism*. Troy, N.Y.: Whitston Press, 1981. Traces impressionist influences on James and claims that impressionism is the key to comprehending the modernist movement in literature and the pictorial arts.

Matthiessen, F. O. *Henry James: The Major Phase*. New York: Oxford University Press, 1944. Written by one of the foremost critics of American literature, this study examines James's expatriatism and the paradox that although James had cut himself off from America, his novels deeply searched the American consciousness.

Poirier, Richard. *The Comic Sense of Henry James: A Study of the Early Novels*. New York: Oxford University Press, 1967. Claims that all James's novels prior to *The Portrait of a Lady* are an apprenticeship for the writing of that work. Traces all the themes and characters of *The Portrait of a Lady* to earlier works.

PORTRAIT OF THE ARTIST AS A YOUNG DOG

Type of work: Short fiction
Author: Dylan Thomas (1914-1953)
First published: 1940

Posthumous biographical studies of Dylan Thomas record a change in appreciation that was long overdue. During his lifetime, Thomas was regarded in the United States as a great English poet and reciter, but only after his death did his work—which includes poetry, fiction, dramas, essays, and impressionistic sketches—come to be regarded as a multifaceted whole. Representative of this reassessment was the growing respect accorded his first collection of short stories, which is also a mock-autobiography, that Thomas mockingly titled in imitation of James Joyce's *A Portrait of the Artist as a Young Man* (1916).

If his critics are right in concluding that most of Thomas' best poetry was written in Swansea before he left Wales for London at the age of twenty, it may also be suggested that this collection of short stories set in Swansea and environs laid the foundations for much of the work that was to follow. "One Warm Saturday," the final story in the collection, seems to anticipate the events of Thomas' next book of prose, the unfinished novel, *Adventures in the Skin Trade* (1955), which uses the same surrealistic style. In both the story and the novel, the ever-pursued eludes capture by the hero as reality dissolves around him. In fact, this may well be the underlying theme of the entire collection *Portrait of the Artist as a Young Dog*.

The relationship of these stories to the Thomas canon, however, is not entirely straightforward. *Adventures in the Skin Trade* was the first prose work; Thomas called it his "Welsh book." It was commissioned by a London publisher, and the first chapter appeared in the periodical *Wales* in 1937. The previous year, Richard Church had suggested that Thomas write some autobiographical prose tales. After his marriage in July, 1937, Thomas took up this project but set to work in a very different style. He first produced "A Visit to Grandpa's," in which the surrealism is muted and the lyrical tone sustained by the young narrator; this story, standing second in *Portrait of the Artist as a Young Dog*, became Thomas' favorite broadcast and reading material. The most interesting feature of the new style of story is the rapid succession of apparently logical but often haphazardly related events, the whole ending in a diminuendo that seems anticlimactic. The intention of the play of event on the diminutive observer is to record, by means of an episode that largely concerns or happens to others, a stage in the observer's growth, that is, in his development as a "young dog."

The development of the Dylan Thomas found in the collection into the "young dog" of the final tales is related to the development of the real Thomas as a writer. This is seen principally in his use of autobiographical material for prose, poetry, and drama. Thomas delivered the typescript of *Portrait of the Artist as a Young Dog* to his publisher, in lieu of the "Welsh book," in December, 1939. Nine days later, talking to Richard Hughes, he remarked that the people of Laugharne, where he was then living, needed a play of their own. This remark is usually recognized as the origin of *Under Milk Wood*, which was first broadcast as a radio drama in 1954. Some years earlier, Thomas had toyed with the notion of doing another imitation of Joyce, a sort of Welsh *Ulysses* that would cover twenty-four hours in the life of a Welsh village. The notion of imitating Joyce and the suggestions of Church and Hughes coalesced with his development of a distinct prose style (instead of a prose extension of his verse, as in *Adventures in the Skin Trade*) and resulted in his best-known prose and drama. Certainly the autobiographical base is common to both works and to his poetry.

Fern Hill and Ann Jones stood model to Gorsehill and Auntie Ann of the first story, "The Peaches," and also to the poems "Fern Hill" and "Ann Jones." The fourth story, "The Fight," is a version of Thomas' first meeting with Daniel Jones, the Welsh composer, when they were boys in Swansea. Trevor Hughes, his first genuine admirer, became the central character of the eighth story, "Who Do You Wish Was with Us?" and some of Thomas' experiences on the *South Wales Daily Post* are recorded in four of the stories, especially the last two.

Although composed of short stories, the book is given a sense of direction by careful ordering of the sequence and by repeated and cumulative details inside the stories. The ten stories fall into three periods of life: childhood, boyhood, and young manhood. The central character is called Dylan Thomas, and although this fact is not stressed in every story, it is obliquely indicated in most. Some characters reappear in more than one tale, including his cousin Gwilym Jones and his older colleagues in journalism. The chief cohesive factor in the collection, however, is not the central character so much as the fact that each story celebrates a visit or an excursion either within the provincial town or just beyond it. The town and its environs become a character in the book, elaborated in the names of its houses, its shops and pubs, and its weather, which ranges from the warmth of summer evenings on the beach to wet wintry nights. The locales of the stories, like the seasons of the year, change from story to story and help create the image of the region as a setting for the gallery of minor characters who dominate each story. The hero remains, as he says in "Just Like Little Dogs," a lonely and late-night observer of the odd doings of the townsfolk. The landmarks of the locale become associated with the stories of chance or temporary acquaintances met on his excursions. As is certainly true of *Under Milk Wood* (1953), these stories too generally imply that everyone has a skeleton in the kitchen cupboard.

That skeleton is generally a private vice that is not too vicious and may be both comic and pathetic. From the first three stories, "The Peaches," "A Visit to Grandpa's," and "Patricia, Edith and Arnold," readers learn that Dylan's Uncle Jim is drinking his pigs away; Cousin Gwilym has his own makeshift chapel and rehearses his coming ministry there; Grandfather Dan dreams he is driving a team of demon horses and has delusions about being buried; the Thomases' maid, Patricia, is involved with the sweetheart of the maid next door. In the next pair of stories, "The Fight" and "Extraordinary Little Cough," the pains and pleasures of boyhood begin to affect the hero, chiefly in finding a soul mate, a fellow artist. He also encounters the horror of viciousness in his companions. The remainder of the stories deal with young manhood and are varied in subject and treatment—from the recital of a tale told to the narrator to the final story in which the narrator for the first time becomes the protagonist, although an ineffectual one. Most of the stories include an episode set at night, and it seems a pity that the best of Thomas' night stories, the ghostly "The Followers," could not have been included in the collection.

The stories are arranged in roughly chronological order, culminating in "One Warm Saturday" and "Old Garbo," which show Thomas' inner way of escape from his hometown as reality disappears in a wash of beer and a montage of what-might-have-been. In real life, Thomas took to London and to drink as a way to get out of Swansea; by the time he arrived in London, he had already discovered how to blur the concrete outlines of provincial life and make its values jump. He was to do this best in *Under Milk Wood*. There is another possible explanation for his ability to see events under the conditions of dream, and that is his Welshness; there is a hint of that in the story "Where Tawe Flows," titled after the "Great Welsh Novel" that a character named Mr. Thomas and three older friends are writing in weekly installments. Mr. Thomas is about to leave for London and a career as a freelance journalist. The novel is supposed to be a study of provincial life, but the collaborators are only at the second chapter. Readers do not hear

Mr. Thomas' contribution because he has spent the week writing the story of a dead governess who turned into a vampire when a cat jumped over her at the moment of her death. One of the foursome offers, instead, the biography of a character named Mary, an account supposed to be realistic but as fantastic as anything the real Thomas ever wrote.

Portrait of the Artist as a Young Dog collects the tensions of provincial life to the breaking point, as does Joyce's *A Portrait of the Artist as a Young Man*. At the end of both books, the hero breaks from home and the style becomes distinctly broken. The increasingly nonrealistic style at the end of both books, a formal expression of the protagonists' whirling thoughts, could be somehow symptomatic of the breaking of ties with Dublin and Swansea. In both books, but more obviously in Joyce, the break is long prepared in the tensions as they mount from a highly imaginative childhood through the pains of adolescence to the frustrations of university study or journalism on a provincial daily. The tensions are so strong that they expel their subjects far from their place of origin. If readers want to know why Joyce died in Zurich or Thomas in New York, the answer is in their own autobiographies of provincial life.

Bibliography:

Greenway, William. "The Gospel According to Dylan Thomas." *Notes on Contemporary Literature* 20, no. 1 (January, 1990): 2-4. Does not assert that Thomas is a religious writer but that he achieved a biblical tone in much that he wrote.

Korg, Jacob. *Dylan Thomas*. Rev. ed. New York: Twayne, 1992. Argues that although the tone of the stories is generally comic, the personal futility and inadequacy of the characters produces irony. Individuals come to recognize a shared sense of loss.

Peach, Linden. *The Prose Writing of Dylan Thomas*. New York: Barnes & Noble Books, 1988. Shows Thomas shedding his fears of the darker side of sexuality, not so much condemning people for their idiosyncrasies as recording those characteristics with fascination.

Pratt, Annis. "Dylan Thomas's Prose." In *Dylan Thomas: A Collection of Critical Essays*, edited by C. B. Cox. Englewood Cliffs, N.J.: Prentice-Hall, 1966. Shows that Thomas turned away from the tumultuous psychic drama of his early prose and moved from those inward concerns to a confrontation with the events of the social world. Asserts that in *Portrait of the Artist as a Young Dog* and subsequent work he speaks through a mask.

Seib, Kenneth. "*Portrait of the Artist as a Young Dog:* Dylan's *Dubliners*." In *Critical Essays on Dylan Thomas*, edited by Georg Gaston. Boston: G. K. Hall, 1989. Concludes that Thomas sought to do for Welshmen what Joyce did for the Irish: write a chapter of their moral history and allow them to view themselves through his eyes. The stories are linked by repetitive theme and metaphor.

A PORTRAIT OF THE ARTIST AS A YOUNG MAN

Type of work: Novel
Author: James Joyce (1882-1941)
Type of plot: Bildungsroman
Time of plot: 1882-1903
Locale: Ireland
First published: serial, 1914-1915; book, 1916

> *Principal characters:*
> STEPHEN DEDALUS, an Irish student
> SIMON DEDALUS, his father
> EMMA, his friend

The Story:

When Stephen Dedalus went to school for the first time, his last name soon got him into trouble. It sounded too Latin, and the boys teased him about it. The other boys saw that he was sensitive and shy, and they began to bully him. School was filled with unfortunate incidents for Stephen. He was happy when he became sick and was put in the infirmary away from the other boys. Once, when he was there just before the Christmas holidays, he worried about dying and death. As he lay on the bed thinking, he heard the news of Charles Stewart Parnell's death. The death of the great Irish leader was the first date he remembered—October 6, 1891.

At home during the vacation, he learned more of Parnell. His father, Simon Dedalus, worshiped the dead man's memory and defended him on every count. Stephen's aunt, Dante Riordan, despised Parnell as a heretic and a rabble-rouser. The fierce arguments that they got into every day burned themselves into Stephen's memory. He worshiped his father, and his father said that Parnell had tried to free Ireland, to rid it of the priests who were ruining the country. Dante insisted that the opposite was true. A violent defender of the priests, she leveled every kind of abuse against Simon and his ideas. The disagreement between them became a problem which, in due time, Stephen would have to solve for himself.

Returning to school after the holidays, Stephen got in trouble with Father Dolan, one of the administrators of the church school he attended. Stephen had broken his glasses, and he could not study until a new pair arrived. Father Dolan saw that Stephen was not working, and thinking that his excuse about the glasses was false, he beat the boy's hands. For once, the rest of the boys were on Stephen's side, and they urged him to complain to the head of the school. With fear and trembling, Stephen went to the head and presented his case. The head understood and promised to speak to Father Dolan about the matter. When Stephen told the boys about his conversation, they hoisted him in their arms like a victorious fighter and called him a hero.

Afterward, life was much easier for Stephen. Only one unfortunate incident marked the term. In the spirit of fun, one of his professors announced in class that Stephen had expressed heresy in one of his essays. Stephen quickly changed the offending phrase and hoped that the mistake would be forgotten. After class, however, several of the boys accused him not only of being a heretic but also of liking Lord Byron, whom they considered an immoral man and therefore no good as a poet. In replying to their charges, Stephen had his first real encounter with the problems of art and morality. They were to follow him throughout his life.

On a trip to Cork with his father, Stephen was forced to listen to the often-told tales of his father's youth. They visited the places his father had loved as a boy. Each night, Stephen was forced to cover up his father's drunkenness and sentimental outbursts. The trip was an education in everything Stephen disliked. At the end of the school year, Stephen won several prizes. He bought presents for everyone, started to redo his room, and began an ill-fated loan service. As long as the money lasted, life was wonderful. Then one night when his money was almost gone, he was enticed into a house by a woman wearing a long pink gown. He learned what love was at age sixteen.

Not until the school held a retreat in honor of Saint Francis Xavier did Stephen realize how deeply conscious he was of the sins he had committed with women. The sermons of the priests about heaven and hell, especially about hell, ate into his mind. At night, his dreams were of nothing but the eternal torture that he felt he must endure after death. He could not bear to make confession in school. At last, he went into the city to a church where he was unknown. There he opened his unhappy mind and heart to an understanding and wise old priest, who advised him and comforted his soul. After the confession, Stephen promised to sin no more, and he felt sure that he would keep his promise. For a time, Stephen's life followed a model course. He studied Aquinas and Aristotle and won acclaim from his teachers. One day, the director of the school called Stephen into his office; after a long conversation, he asked him if he had ever thought of joining the order of the Jesuits. Stephen was deeply flattered. Priesthood became his life's goal.

When Stephen entered the university, however, a change came over his thinking. He began to doubt, and the longer be studied, the more confused and doubtful he became. His problems drew him closer to two of his fellow students, Davin and Lynch, and farther away from Emma, a girl for whom he had felt affection since childhood. He discussed his ideas about beauty and the working of the mind with Davin and Lynch. Stephen would not sign a petition for world peace, winning the enmity of many of the fellows. They called him antisocial and egotistic. Finally, neither the peace movement, the Irish Revival, nor the church itself could claim his support.

Davin was the first to question Stephen about his ideas. When he suggested to Stephen that Ireland should come first in everything, Stephen answered that to him Ireland was an old sow that ate her offspring.

One day, Stephen met Emma at a carnival, and she asked him why he had stopped coming to see her. He answered that he had been born to be a monk. When Emma said that she thought him a heretic instead of a monk, his last link with Ireland seemed to be broken. At least he was not afraid to be alone. If he wanted to find and to understand beauty, he had to leave Ireland, where there was nothing in which he believed. His friend's prayers, asking that he return to the faith, went unanswered. Stephen got together his belongings, packed, and left Ireland, intending never to return. He did intend to write a book someday that would make clear his views on Ireland and the Irish.

Critical Evaluation:

A Portrait of the Artist as a Young Man by James Joyce is possibly the greatest example in the English language of the *Bildungsroman*, a novel tracing the physical, mental, and spiritual growth and education of a young person. Other examples of this genre range from Flaubert's *A Sentimental Education* (1869) to D. H. Lawrence's *Sons and Lovers* (1913). Published in 1916, the work stands stylistically between the fusion of highly condensed Naturalism and Symbolism found in *Dubliners* (1914) and the elaborate mythological structure, interior monologues, and stream-of-consciousness style of *Ulysses* (1922). There is a consistent concern for entrapment, isolation, and rebellion from home, church, and nation in all three of these works.

The novel is autobiographical, but in the final analysis, the variants from, rather than the parallels with, Joyce's own life are of the greater artistic significance. The events of Stephen Dedalus' life are taken from the lives of Joyce, his brother Stanislaus, and his friend Byrne, covering the period between 1885 and 1902. The book begins with the earliest memories of his childhood, recounted in childlike language, and ends when Stephen is twenty-two years old with his decision to leave his native Dublin in search of artistic development to forge the conscience of his race. In the intervening years, like Joyce, Stephen attends the Jesuit Clongowes Wood School, which he must leave because of family financial difficulties, attends a day school in Dublin, has his first sexual experience, has his first religious crisis, and finally attends University College, where he decides on his vocation as a writer. The dedication to pure art involves for Stephen, and Joyce, a rejection of the claims on him of duty to family, to the Catholic church, and to Irish Nationalism, either of the political type or of the literary type espoused by the writers of the Irish Renaissance. In his characterization of Stephen, however, Joyce eliminates much of himself: his sense of humor; his love of sport; his own graduation from the university before leaving Dublin; his desire to attend medical school in France; his deep concern for his mother's health; his affection for his father; and the lifelong liaison he established with Nora Barnacle, who left Ireland with Joyce in 1904. The effect of these omissions is to make a narrower, more isolated character of Stephen than Joyce himself.

On one level, *A Portrait of the Artist as a Young Man* is an initiation story in which an innocent, idealistic youth with a sense of trust in his elders is brought slowly to the recognition that this is a flawed, imperfect world, characterized by injustice and disharmony. Stephen finds this fact at home, at school, at church, in relationships with women and friends, and in the past and present history of his nation. His pride, however, prevents him from seeing any shortcomings in himself. In the second portion of the novel, he becomes involved in the excesses of carnal lust; in the third portion, in the excesses of penitent piety, which also eventually disgust him. In the fourth section, in which he assumes Lucifer's motto, I Will Not Serve, although he sees himself as a pagan worshiper of beauty, he becomes involved in excessive intellectual pride. In the final portion of the novel, Stephen develops his aesthetic theory of the epiphany—the sudden revelation of truth and beauty—through the artistic goals of "wholeness, harmony, and radiance." Therefore, his final flight from his actual home—family, church, nation—is still part of an almost adolescent rejection of the imperfections of this world and an attempt to replace it with the perfection of form, justice, and harmony of artistic creation.

Stephen Dedalus' very name is chosen to underline his character. His first name links him to Saint Stephen, the first martyr to Christianity; Stephen Dedalus sees himself as a martyr, willing to give up all to the services of art. His last name, Dedalus, is famous from classical antiquity. It was Daedalus, the Athenian exile, who designed the great caste for King Minos of Crete and later designed the famous labyrinth in which the monstrous Minotaur was kept captive. Later, longing to return to his own land but imprisoned in his labyrinth, Daedalus invented wings for himself and his son, Icarus, to fly from the labyrinth. Stephen, the artist, sees Dublin as the labyrinth from which he must fly in order to become the great artificer Daedalus was. It is important to remember, however, that Daedalus' son, Icarus, ignored his father's instructions on how to use the wings; because of pride and the desire to exceed, he flew too close to the sun, and his wings melted. He plunged into the ocean and drowned. It is only later, in *Ulysses*, that Stephen recognizes himself as "lap-winged Icarus" rather than as Daedalus.

Joyce's technical skill is obvious in the series of interwoven recurrent symbols of the novel. The rose, for example, which is associated with women, chivalric love, and creativity, appears throughout the novel. In addition, water is found in almost every chapter of the novel: It can be the water that drowns and brings death; it can also be the water that gives life, symbolic of renewal as in baptism and the final choice of escape by sea.

The central themes of *A Portrait of the Artist as a Young Man*—alienation, isolation, rejection, betrayal, the Fall, the search for the father—are developed with amazing virtuosity. This development is the second, following *Dubliners*, of the four major parts in Joyce's cyclical treatment of the life of man that moves, as the great medieval cyclical plays, from Fall to Redemption, from isolation and alienation to acceptance. Joyce's analysis of the human condition and of the relationship of art to life is later developed in *Ulysses* and *Finnegans Wake*. Joyce has emphasized the importance of the word "young" in the title of this work, and his conclusion, in the form of Stephen's diary which illustrates Stephen's own perceptions, words, and style, forces the reader to become more objective and detached in his judgment of Stephen. The reader realizes that all of Stephen's previous epiphanies have failed and recognizes in these final pages the human complexity of Stephen's important triumph in escaping from the nets of Ireland; the reader, however, also realizes that Stephen's triumph is complicated by important losses and sacrifices.

"Critical Evaluation" by Ann E. Reynolds

Bibliography:

Booth, Wayne. "The Problem of Distance in *A Portrait*." In *The Rhetoric of Fiction*. Chicago: University of Chicago Press, 1961. Booth goes beyond the negative appraisal of Hugh Kenner (see below) and suggests that it is impossible to judge whether the portrayal of Stephen is ironical or not because of a failure in the narrative authority.

Brown, Richard. *James Joyce and Sexuality*. Cambridge, England: Cambridge University Press, 1985. An analysis of the political implications in Joyce's works, especially in marriage and other intimate relationships.

Kenner, Hugh. *Dublin's Joyce*. Bloomington: Indiana University Press, 1956. Kenner was the first to suggest that the portrayal of Stephen Dedalus was not directly autobiographical but deeply ironic. He continues to maintain this negative view of Stephen in his recent criticism.

McCabe, Colin. *James Joyce and the Revolution of the Word*. New York: Barnes & Noble Books, 1979. A poststructuralist interpretation of the novel that points out the difficulties of establishing any secure critical reading of the book.

Scholes, Robert, and Richard M. Kain, eds. *The Workshop of Dedalus: James Joyce and the Raw Materials for "A Portrait of the Artist as a Young Man."* Evanston, Ill.: Northwestern University Press, 1965. The best source study available on the novel. Includes notebooks, fragments of the manuscript, and biographical information to help readers understand the contexts in which the novel was created.

Staley, Thomas F., and Bernard Benstock, eds. *Approaches to Joyce's "Portrait": Ten Essays*. Pittsburgh: University of Pittsburgh Press, 1976. A collection of some important essays that demonstrate various ways of reading Joyce's *A Portrait of the Artist as a Young Man*.

Tindall, William York. *A Reader's Guide to James Joyce*. New York: Noonday Press, 1959. A close reading of Joyce's works that discovers symbol and image patterns within *A Portrait of the Artist as a Young Man*.

THE POSSESSED

Type of work: Novel
Author: Fyodor Dostoevski (1821-1881)
Type of plot: Psychological realism
Time of plot: Mid-nineteenth century
Locale: Russia
First published: Besy, 1871-1872 (English translation, 1913)

>Principal characters:
>STEPAN VERHOVENSKY, a provincial patriot and mild progressive
>PYOTR, his nihilist son
>VARVARA STAVROGIN, a provincial lady and Stepan's employer
>NIKOLAY, her son and a victim of materialism
>MARYA, Nikolay's wife
>SHATOV, the independent son of one of Varvara's serfs
>ALEXEI KIRILLOV, a construction engineer

The Story:

Stepan Verhovensky, a self-styled progressive patriot and erstwhile university lecturer, was at loose ends in a provincial Russian town until Varvara Stavrogin hired him to tutor her only son, Nikolay. Stepan's radicalism, which was largely a pose, shocked Varvara, but the two became friends. When Varvara's husband died, Stepan looked forward to marrying the widow. They went together to St. Petersburg, where they moved in daringly radical circles. After attempting without success to start a literary journal, they left St. Petersburg, Varvara returning to the province and Stepan, in an attempt to assert his independence, going to Berlin. After four months in Germany, Stepan, realizing that he was in Varvara's thrall emotionally and financially, returned to the province to be near her.

Stepan became the leader of a small group that met to discuss progressive ideas. The group included Shatov, the independent son of one of Varvara's serfs, a liberal named Virginsky, and Liputin, a man who made everyone's business his business. Nikolay Stavrogin, whom Stepan had introduced to progressivism, had gone on to school in St. Petersburg and from there into the army as an officer. He had resigned his commission, however, returned to St. Petersburg, and gone to live in the slums. When he returned home, at Varvara's request, he proceeded to insult the members of Stepan's group. He bit the ear of the provincial governor during an interview with that dignitary. Everyone concluded that he was mentally unbalanced, and Nikolay was committed to bed. Three months later, apparently recovered, he apologized for his actions and again left the province.

Some months after that, Varvara was invited to visit a childhood friend in Switzerland, where Nikolay was paying court to her friend's daughter, Lizaveta. Before the party returned to Russia, Lizaveta and Nikolay broke their engagement because Nikolay was interested in Dasha, Varvara's servant woman. In Switzerland, Nikolay and Stepan's son, Pyotr, met and found themselves in sympathy on political matters.

A new governor, von Lembke, came to the provinces. Stepan was lost without Varvara and visibly deteriorated during her absence. Varvara arranged for Dasha, who was the sister of Shatov and twenty years old, to marry Stepan, who was fifty-three. Dasha submitted passively

5275

to her mistress' wishes, and Stepan reluctantly consented to the marriage, but he balked when he discovered from a member of his group that he was being used to cover up Nikolay's relations with the girl.

New arrivals in the province were Captain Lebyadkin and his idiot, crippled sister, Marya. One day, Marya attracted the attention of Varvara in front of the cathedral, whereupon Varvara took the cripple home with her. She learned that Nikolay had known the Lebyadkins in St. Petersburg. Pyotr assured Varvara, who was suspicious, that Nikolay and Marya Lebyadkin were not married.

Using his personal charm and representing himself as a mysterious revolutionary agent returned from exile, Pyotr began to dominate Stepan's liberal friends and became, for his own scheming purposes, the protégé of Yulia, the governor's wife. Nikolay at first followed Pyotr in his political activities but then turned against the revolutionary movement and warned Shatov that Pyotr's group was plotting to kill Shatov because of information he possessed. Nikolay confessed to Shatov that on a bet he had married Marya Lebyadkin in St. Petersburg.

As a result of a duel between Nikolay and a local aristocrat who hated him, a duel in which Nikolay emerged victorious without killing his opponent, Nikolay became a local hero. He continued to be intimate with Dasha, and Lizaveta had meanwhile announced her engagement to another man. Pyotr sowed seeds of dissension among all classes in the town. He disclosed von Lembke's possession of a collection of radical manifestos; he caused a break between Stepan and Varvara; and he secretly incited the working people to rebel against their masters.

Yulia led the leaders of the town in preparations for a grand fête. Pyotr, seeing in the fête the opportunity to bring chaos into the orderly community, brought about friction between von Lembke, who was an inept governor, and Yulia, who actually governed the province through her salon. At a meeting of the revolutionary group, despair and confusion prevailed until Pyotr welded it together with mysterious talk of orders from higher revolutionary leaders. He talked of many other such groups engaged in similar activities. Shatov, who attended the meeting, denounced Pyotr as a spy and a scoundrel and walked out. Pyotr disclosed to Nikolay his nihilistic beliefs and proposed that Nikolay be brought forward as the Pretender when the revolution had been accomplished.

Blum, von Lembke's secretary, raided Stepan's quarters and confiscated all of Stepan's private papers, among them some political manifestos. Stepan went to the governor to demand his rights under the law and witnessed in front of the governor's mansion how dissident workers who had been quietly demonstrating for redress of their grievances were lashed into turmoil. Von Lembke appeased Stepan by saying that the raid on his room was a mistake.

The fête was doomed from the start. Many agitators without tickets were admitted. Liputin read a comic and seditious poem. Karmazinov, a great novelist, made a fool of himself by recalling the follies of his youth. Stepan insulted the agitators by championing the higher culture. When an unidentified agitator rose to speak, the afternoon session became a bedlam, so that it was doubtful whether the ball would be able to take place that night. Abetted by Pyotr, Nikolay and Lizaveta eloped in the afternoon to the country house of Varvara.

The ball was not canceled, but few of the landowners of the town or countryside appeared. Drunkenness and brawling soon reduced the ball to a rout, and the evening came to a sorry end when fire was discovered raging through some houses along the river. Captain Lebyadkin, Marya, and their servant were discovered murdered in their house, which remained unburned in the path of the fire. When Pyotr informed Nikolay of the murders, Nikolay confessed that he had known of the possibility that violence would take place but that he had done nothing to prevent it. Horrified, Lizaveta went to see the murdered pair; she was beaten to death by the enraged townspeople because of her connections with Nikolay. Nikolay left town quickly and quietly.

When the revolutionary group met again, they all mistrusted one another. Pyotr explained to them that Fedka, a former convict, had murdered the Lebyadkins for robbery, but he failed to mention that Nikolay had all but paid Fedka to commit the crime. He warned the group against Shatov and said that a fanatic named Kirillov had agreed to cover up the proposed murder of Shatov. After Fedka denounced Pyotr as an atheistic scoundrel, Fedka was found dead on a road outside the town.

Marie, Shatov's wife, returned to the town. The couple had been separated for three years; Marie was ill and pregnant. When she began her labor, Shatov procured Virginsky's wife as midwife. The couple were reconciled after Marie gave birth to a baby boy, for the child served to make Shatov happy once more. He left his wife and baby alone to keep an appointment with the revolutionary group made for the purpose of separating himself from the plotters. Pyotr attacked and shot him, then weighted his body with stones and threw it into a pond. After the murder, Pyotr went to Kirillov to get his promised confession for the murder of Shatov. Kirillov, who was Shatov's neighbor and who had seen Shatov's happiness at the return of his wife, at first refused to sign, but Pyotr finally prevailed on him to put his name to the false confession. Then, morally bound to end his life, Kirillov shot himself. Pyotr left the province.

Stepan, meanwhile, left the town to seek a new life. He wandered for a time among peasants and at last became dangerously ill. Varvara went to him, and the two friends were reconciled before the old scholar died. Varvara disowned her son. Marie and the baby died of exposure and neglect when Shatov failed to return home. One of the radical group broke down and confessed to the violence that had been committed in the town at the instigation of Pyotr. Liputin escaped to St. Petersburg, where he was apprehended in a drunken stupor in a brothel.

Nikolay wrote to Dasha, the servant, suggesting that the two of them go to Switzerland and begin a new life. Before Dasha could pack her things, however, Nikolay returned home secretly and hanged himself in his room.

Critical Evaluation:

Fyodor Dostoevski was nearly fifty years old when the final version of *The Possessed* (also translated as *The Devils*) appeared. Because of his poverty, he had been forced to write the book first in serial form for a Moscow literary review. Many readers thought the novel raged so wildly against liberalism and so-called atheistic socialism that they concluded the once progressive author must have become a reactionary. Dostoevski himself lent credibility to this notion by his public statements. In a famous letter to Alexander III, Dostoevski characterized *The Possessed* as a historical study of the perverse radicalism that results when the intelligentsia detaches itself from the Russian people. In another letter, he proclaimed, "He who loses his people and his nationality loses his faith in his country and in God. This is the theme of my novel."

Given the nature of Dostoevski's personal history, a movement toward conservatism would not have been illogical. An aristocrat by birth, Dostoevski had involved himself deeply in the Petrashevski Circle, a St. Petersburg discussion group interested in utopian socialism. Part of this group formed a clandestine revolutionary cadre, and Dostoevski was arrested for his participation in the conspiracy. There followed a mock execution, four years of imprisonment, and another four years of enforced service as a private in the Siberian army. Although he was freed in 1858, Dostoevski remained under surveillance and his right to publish was always in jeopardy. He thus had every inducement to prove to government censors his fidelity to the regime and its principles.

In fact, *The Possessed* is not a reactionary novel, nor does Dostoevski in the book defend the institutions of monarchy, aristocracy, or censorship. He upholds Russian orthodoxy in a way that suggests a theocratic challenge to the status quo. His exaltation of the peasantry constitutes no defense of capitalism or imperialism. While appearing to embrace Russian nationalism, he presents an image of small-town culture that is anything but approving. His portrait of the ruling class is as devastating as any essay on the subject by Karl Marx or Friedrich Engels.

Dostoevski's critique of radical political ideas proceeds from a basis other than that of extremist conservatism. The key to that basis is partially revealed in Shatov's statement that half-truth is uniquely despotic. *The Possessed* is at once a criticism of a variety of political and philosophical half-truths and a searching toward a principle of wholeness, a truth that has the capacity to reunite and compose the fragmented human psyche, the divided social and political order, and the shattered relationship with God. Dostoevski does not describe that truth, believing the truth too mysterious and grand to be expressed in human language. Rather, he points to it by showing the defects and incompleteness in positions that pretend to be the truth.

It is through the enigmatic character of Nikolay Stavrogin that Dostoevski most fully carries out his quest for wholeness, for Stavrogin has embraced and discarded all the philosophies that Dostoevski deems inadequate. As a result, Stavrogin is the embodiment of pure negativity and pure emptiness. He is also pure evil, more evil still than Pyotr, who at least has his absolute devotion to Stavrogin as the ruling principle in his life. From Stepan Verhovensky, Stavrogin learned skepticism and the tolerant principles of "higher liberalism." In St. Petersburg, he advances to utopian socialism and a more passionate faith in the possibility of salvation through science. The elitism and shallow rationalism of this faith cause Stavrogin to take up messianic Russian populism. After he is led beyond this stage to an investigation of orthodox theology, he finds himself unable to commit to the Christian faith and perpetrates the hideous crime he later confesses to Father Tihon.

At each step in his development, Stavrogin trains disciples who propagate his teachings and carry them to their logical extremes. Pyotr belongs partly to Nikolay's "socialist period," while Shatov embraces the populist creed and Kirillov elaborates the themes of the theological phase. In Pyotr, socialist criticism of traditional society has produced a monomaniacal fascination with the revolutionary destruction and violence by which a new order is to emerge. Modeling this character after the infamous Russian terrorist Sergey Nechayev, Dostoevski suggests that Pyotr is the natural outcome of socialism's faith in the power of reason to establish absolute values. Shigolov's rational defense of a socialist tyranny shows how thoroughly rational structures rely on nonrational premises. For Pyotr, the absence of rational certainties means that all behavior is permissible and all social orders are equally valid. He chooses to fight for a society based on the hunger of human beings for submission, their fear of death, their longing for a messiah. Like Niccolò Machiavelli, Pyotr decides that only by founding society on the most wretched aspects of human nature can anything really lasting and dependable be built. As his messiah, Pyotr has chosen Stavrogin, whose awe-inspiring and arbitrary will could be the source of order in a new society.

Kirillov elevates Pyotr Verhovensky's fascination with strength of will into a theological principle. Kirillov is not content with the limited transcendence of the determinisms of nature. He aspires to the total freedom of God. Paradoxically, this freedom can be achieved only through suicide, that act that overcomes the natural fear of death by which God keeps human beings in thrall. Not until all people are prepared at every moment to commit suicide can humanity take full responsibility for its own destiny. The great drawback in Kirillov's view is that it causes him to suppress his feelings of love and relatedness to his fellow human beings.

Shatov's nationalistic theology is an attempt to do justice to these feelings. Rebelling against Kirillov's isolated quest for godhood, Shatov wishes to achieve the same goal by submerging himself in the life of a "God-bearing people." Yet Shatov's creed remains abstract and sentimental until Marya returns and provides him with a real person to love.

The birth of Marya's child, together with Stepan Verhovensky's "discovery" of the Russian people, are the symbols by which Dostoevski reveals his own answer to Nikolay Stavrogin. The child is for Shatov an unimaginable act of grace. Significantly, Kirillov experiences a sudden serenity and a confirmation of his mystical insight that "everything is good." For Dostoevski, the source of this grace is God, who brings exquisite order to the most corrupted human situations. Shatov's rapturous love stands in utter contradiction to Stavrogin's empty indifference. Because the child's real father is Stavrogin, Shatov's love is all the more wondrous. Stavrogin's final inability to respond to Lizaveta's love is the logical result of his long struggle to free himself of the dependency on his family, his people, and his church. He boasts that he does not need anyone; from that claim comes spiritual and moral death. All that Stavrogin has touched, including Shatov, is dead in the end.

The magnificence of Dostoevski's artistry is nowhere more apparent than in the conclusion to *The Possessed*, for he does not embody his great theme—human wholeness through human dependence—in a titanic character like Stavrogin or Kirillov but in the all-too-human Stepan. This quixotic buffoon, who is both laughable and pitiable, ultimately attains the dignity he seeks. He himself is surprised by it all, for it comes in a way he least expected it: through an encounter with his people, reunion with Varvara, and the administration of the sacrament.

"Critical Evaluation" by Leslie E. Gerber

Bibliography:

Frank, Joseph. *Dostoevsky: The Miraculous Years, 1865-1871*. Princeton, N.J.: Princeton University Press, 1955. A comprehensive critical biography. Frank outlines the sociocultural context in which *The Possessed* was written and evaluates the novel's response to the corrosive doctrines of Russian nihilism.

Holquist, Michael. *Dostoevsky and the Novel*. Princeton, N.J.: Princeton University Press, 1977. An examination of Dostoevsky's works as studies in the problem of self-identification. Holquist's discussion of *The Possessed* highlights Stavrogin's struggle to resist group pressures and to assert himself.

Ivanov, Viacheslav. *Freedom and the Tragic Life: A Study in Dostoevsky*. New York: Noonday Press, 1971. An investigation into the religious and mythical foundations of Dostoevsky's artistic work. Ivanov argues that *The Possessed* depicts in symbolic forms the relationship between the powers of evil and the daring human spirit.

Mochul'skii, Konstantin. *Dostoevsky: His Life and Work*. Translated by Michael A. Minihan. Princeton, N.J.: Princeton University Press, 1967. A detailed analytical discussion of the evolution of Dostoevsky's art. Examines the ways in which *The Possessed* emerged from two different preliminary projects and describes the central ideological and spiritual themes of the work.

Peace, Richard. *Dostoyevsky: An Examination of the Major Novels*. Cambridge, England: Cambridge University Press, 1971. Includes two chapters on *The Possessed*, in which Peace discusses the historical background for the novel and analyzes the significant interrelationships among the main characters. Concludes that the secondary figures serve to highlight the tragic situation of the central protagonist.

THE POSTMAN ALWAYS RINGS TWICE

Type of work: Novel
Author: James M. Cain (1892-1977)
Type of plot: Psychological realism
Time of plot: 1933
Locale: Southern California
First published: 1934

>   *Principal characters:*
>   FRANK CHAMBERS, a young drifter
>   NICK PAPADAKIS, the proprietor of the Twin Oaks Tavern
>   CORA PAPADAKIS, Nick's young wife
>   MR. SACKETT, the district attorney
>   MR. KATZ, a lawyer
>   MADGE ALLEN, the keeper of an animal farm

The Story:

For years, Frank Chambers had been in trouble with the law as he drifted back and forth across California, always looking for a con or a dollar. When he came to Nick Papadakis' restaurant, he saw the same old dreams invested in a tiny hash house just like all the restaurants down the road. The one difference was that this hash house contained Cora, a svelte, beautiful, sensuous woman who had married her Greek husband to get out of an even worse life as a waitress in Los Angeles. She had won a beauty contest in the Midwest and taken a bus to California. There, when she found her prospects to be nonexistent, she married a man who at least had the advantage of owning property.

The attraction between Cora and Frank was almost instantaneous, and before Frank had been there a week, he had slept with Cora. She was the one who first proposed getting rid of her husband so they could run away. Frank planned to have Cora bludgeon her husband while he was in the bath. Then Frank would climb a ladder into the bathroom and remove the body. From the beginning things went wrong. A passing motorcycle patrolman stopped to chat with Frank and probably saw the ladder. Then, just when Cora hit her husband, all the lights went out, which was seen by the patrolman as he left. Frank rushed in to find Cora standing in the bathroom and her husband splashing around in the water. Quickly they patched him up and called an ambulance. They had no idea what had happened to the lights. Eventually Nick was taken to a hospital room, where Frank, Cora, and several policemen watched him, no one sure what he would say. When he awoke, he said something about slipping in the shower. The motorcycle patrolman was suspicious and accompanied Frank and Cora back to the restaurant to see what had happened to the fuse box. They found a dead cat there that had obviously been electrocuted.

Frank and Cora enjoyed themselves while Nick was in the hospital, but when he returned one week later he told Cora that he wanted a son. She was appalled by the prospect and turned to Frank again. She tried to tempt him by promising that they could take over the restaurant once her husband was dead, but Frank was impatient to be on the road.

The second time Cora and Frank tried to kill Nick was very complex. Nick had acquired tickets to a Santa Barbara street fair, to which he invited Frank and Cora. They stayed in a hotel for the weekend and then headed back. Cora drove because her husband was drunk and Frank was pretending to be drunk. On the way to Ventura, Nick passed out. They stopped the car and Cora got out, after which Frank got into the car and sent it over an embankment. He tried to get out in time but was not successful. After the car crashed, Nick died and Frank had a broken leg. In spite of that, he and Cora were both charged with murder. A jail guard furnished Frank with the name of a good lawyer after the police persuaded Frank to sign a document saying that Cora had killed the Greek and had been planning to kill him as well. That turned them against each other, but Katz, the attorney, had devised a scenario in which Cora was guilty of the murder. Katz had read the details of a life and accident policy that Nick had taken out right after his "accident" in the bathtub. Because Frank had been a "guest" in the car, Katz argued that he had the right to collect the full $10,000 of the policy. Katz figured that the jury would be sympathetic toward Cora and that the manslaughter with which she was charged would be treated as a technicality. As a result, Frank was acquitted and Cora was given six months in jail, with three months suspended. Katz charged them $5,000 for his services.

Cora went briefly to jail and Frank went to Mexico, where he met another woman with whom he stayed. Cora learned of this when she got home, and she presented Frank with proof of his infidelity. Cora wanted to improve the restaurant and make it a success. Frank wanted nothing to do with it.

In an attempt at reconciliation (by this time Frank knew that Cora was pregnant), Frank and Cora went to the beach, where Cora succumbed to a cramp. Frank carried her to shore and put her into the car. On the way to the hospital, Frank tried to pass a truck and collided with an abutment. Turned around in his seat, Frank could hear the dripping of Cora's blood on the hood of the car. She had been thrown through the windshield and died instantly.

A jury quickly convicted Frank of murder for the purpose of collecting on Cora's life insurance and the restaurant and property. Nothing Katz could say this time made any difference. Frank wrote the story from death row.

"The Story" by John Jacob

Critical Evaluation:

Three related genres that developed in the United States during the 1930's were the hard-boiled private detective novel, which departed from the genteel English novel of detection; the proletarian novel, which derived from European naturalism and American realism; and the tough-guy novel, which derived from both of those strands. Dashiell Hammett's *The Maltese Falcon* (1929) and Raymond Chandler's *The Big Sleep* (1939) are perhaps the best-known examples of the private detective novel. B. Traven's *The Death Ship* (1934) is a good example of the proletarian novel, and Horace McCoy's *They Shoot Horses, Don't They?* (1935) belongs to the minor classics of tough-guy novels. These and novels like them expressed the mood of American society during the Depression, and they influenced motion pictures, affected the tone and attitude of more serious writers, and inspired some European novelists during the 1940's. The quintessence of these genres is represented by James M. Cain's *The Postman Always Rings Twice.*

Although Frank Chambers, the twenty-four-year-old narrator of Cain's novel, belongs to that legion of unemployed who became tramps of the road, hoboes of the rails, and migrant workers, Cain is not deliberately interested in depicting the social ills of his time; if there is an attack on conditions that produced a man like Frank, it is only implicit. Frank is an easygoing fellow, remarkably free of bitterness, even when given cause; although he commits murder and pistol-whips a blackmailer, he is not willfully vicious. A spontaneous creature of action whose psychological nature readily accommodates ambivalent attitudes, he can be fond of Nick Papadakis and weep at his funeral after having seduced his young wife Cora and twice attempted to kill him.

Although this novel is concerned, as are many of Cain's, with murder and other forms of violence, it cannot be classified as a detective tale. Cain, like the readers he has in mind, is fascinated by the intricacies of civil and insurance law, but he is primarily interested in presenting an inside view of the criminal act. Yet Frank is no gangster and Cora no moll; they are not far removed in status or aspiration from the average person who reads the book.

Frank and Cora lie down in the great American dreambed of the 1920's, only to wake up in the 1930's in a living nightmare. Only a lurid decade could have produced such a lurid relationship and such a lurid tale. When they meet at Nick's Twin Oaks Tavern on a highway outside Los Angeles, Frank has just been thrown off a truck, having sneaked into the back for a ride up from Tijuana, and Cora is washing dishes in the restaurant. To demonstrate the animal impact of their encounter, Cain has them meet on page 5, make love on page 15, and decide to murder the obese, middle-aged Greek on page 23. Sharing the dream of getting drunk and making love without hiding, they go on what Cain calls "the Love-Rack." He regards the concept of "the wish that comes true" as a terrifying thing. This terror becomes palpable as soon as Frank and Cora believe they have gotten away with murder and have acquired money, property, and freedom.

In the background, however, each has another dream, which mocks the shared realization of the immediate wish. Cora came to Hollywood from a small town in Iowa bemused by the dream most girls of the 1930's cherished: to become a film star. She failed, and Nick rescued her from a hash house. Basically her values are middle-class, and above all she wants respectability, even if murder is the prerequisite. An anachronism in the age of technology, though he has a certain skill as a garage mechanic, Frank desires to be always on the move, compelled by something of the spirit of the open road that Walt Whitman celebrated. For a moment, but only for a moment, he shares this romantic, idyllic vision with Cora. After the failure of their first attempt to murder Nick, they set out together for a life of wandering. In the criminal affair of these lovers, these deliberate outsiders, two central dreams of the American experience—unrestrained mobility and respectable sedentariness—and two views of the American landscape—the open road and the mortgaged house—collide. As the dreams finally betray them, they begin to turn on each other, for basically what Frank wants is Cora, the sexual dynamo, and what Cora wants is an instrument to be used to gain her ends—money and respectability.

Although the novel's larger thematic dimensions exist in the background, as a kind of fable of the American experience, giving it a lasting value in literature, Cain is more immediately concerned with the lovers and with the action that results from their wish. This action keeps in motion certain elements that almost guarantee the reader's interest: illicit love; murder; the smell of tainted money; sexual violence that verges on the abnormal; and the strong characterizations of such men as Sackett, the district attorney, Katz, the eccentric lawyer, and Madge, the pickup who takes Frank to South America to capture jaguars. Cain plays on the universal wishes of the average American male.

What fascinates serious readers of literature is Cain's technique for manipulating reader response. Not only does he almost automatically achieve certain thematic ironies inherent in his raw material, but the ironies of action are stunningly executed. Frank cons Nick out of a free meal, for example, but the con backfires when Nick cons Frank into staying on to operate the service station, a situation that eventually leaves three people dead.

Cain's structural techniques are impressive. Each development, each scene, is controlled, and inherent in each episode is the inevitability of the next. Everything is kept strictly to the essentials; the characters exist only for the immediate action; there is almost no exposition as such. Cain is the acknowledged master of pace. Violence and sexual passion are thrust forward at a rate that is itself part of the reader's vicarious experience. Contributing to this sense of pace is the swift rhythm of the dialogue, which also manages to keep certain undercurrents flowing. Frank's character justifies the economy of style, the nerve-end adherence to the spine of the action. Albert Camus modeled the style of *The Stranger* (1942) on Cain's novel and cut his character Meursault to the pattern of Frank Chambers. Cain has written what has been called a pure novel, for his deliberate intentions go no further than the immediate experience, brief as a motion picture is, as unified in its impression as a poem usually is. Though Frank writes his story on the eve of his execution, Cain does not even suggest the simplest moral, that crime does not pay. An intense experience, which a man tells in such a way as to make it, briefly, the reader's experience, it is its own reason for being.

Bibliography:
Ahnebrink, Lars. *Beginnings of Naturalism in American Fiction*. New York: Russell & Russell, 1961. Provides useful introductory criticism.
Cain, James M. *The Complete Novels*. New York: Wings Books, 1994. Contains critical commentary and a comparison of *The Postman Always Rings Twice* and Cain's other novels.
Hoopes, Roy. *Cain*. New York: Holt, Rinehart and Winston, 1982. The definitive biography of Cain. Includes a filmography and publications lists.
Madden, David. *James M. Cain*. New York: Twayne, 1970. A critical approach to Cain's writing and influences.
Wolfe, Tom. Introduction to *Cain X 3*. New York: Alfred A. Knopf, 1969. A useful collection because of Wolfe's "new realism" approach to Cain's novels.

THE POT OF GOLD

Type of work: Drama
Author: Plautus (c. 254-184 B.C.E.)
Type of plot: Comedy
Time of plot: Second century B.C.E.
Locale: Athens
First performed: Aulularia, 200-191 B.C.E. (English translation, 1767)

Principal characters:
EUCLIO, a miser
PHAEDRIA, his daughter
MEGADORUS, Euclio's rich neighbor, who wished to marry Phaedria
EUNOMIA, Megadorus' sister
LYCONIDES, Eunomia's son, in love with Phaedria
STAPHYLA, a slave belonging to Euclio

The Story:

The grandfather of Euclio, an Athenian miser, had entrusted a pot of gold to his household deity after burying the pot in the hearth. The god, angered in turn at the grandfather, the father, and Euclio himself, had kept the secret of the treasure from all, until finally the daughter of Euclio, Phaedria, had endeared herself to the god. In an effort to help the young woman, the deity showed Euclio where the gold was hidden, so that the miser, by using the money as a dowry, might marry his daughter to Lyconides, the young man who had seduced her.

Euclio, miserly and distrustful by nature, was thrown into a feverish excitement by the discovery of the gold. He feared that someone would learn of its existence and either steal or gull it from him. After carefully hiding the gold in his house once more, he was afraid that even his old female slave, Staphyla, might learn of its whereabouts. Staphyla was worried by her master's strange behavior and by the fact that her young mistress was pregnant.

Meanwhile Megadorus, a wealthy neighbor and uncle of Lyconides, planned to marry Euclio's daughter himself, and he enlisted the aid of his sister Eunomia in his suit. Megadorus declared that he was so pleased with Phaedria's character that he would marry her, contrary to the Athenian custom, without a dowry.

Seeing Euclio in the street, Megadorus went out to ask the old miser for his daughter's hand. Euclio, distrustful because of his new-found gold, thought Megadorus was in reality plotting to take the gold from him, but Megadorus assured him that all he wanted was to marry Phaedria, with or without a dowry; he even offered to pay the expenses of the wedding. Upon these terms Euclio agreed to marry his daughter to Megadorus. After Megadorus left, however, Euclio could not convince himself that the prospective bridegroom was not after the pot of gold.

Euclio informed Staphyla of the proposed marriage, which was to take place the same day. Staphyla knew that when Phaedria was married she would no longer be able to conceal her pregnancy, but she had little time to worry. Soon a caterer, bringing cooks, entertainers, and food, arrived at Euclio's house to prepare the wedding feast. Megadorus had hired the caterer as he had promised.

Returning from the marketplace with incense and flowers to place on the altar of his household god, Euclio was horrified to see all the strangers bustling about his house, for he immediately suspected they were seeking his pot of gold. In a fury of apprehension, Euclio first drove all the caterer's people from the house and then removed his pot of gold from its hiding place. Only after he had removed it from the house did he tell them to return to their work.

Euclio decided to take the gold and hide it in the nearby temple of Faith. On the way he met Megadorus, who asked Euclio to join him in drinking a bottle or two of wine. Euclio refused, suspecting that Megadorus wanted to get him drunk and then steal the pot of gold. Going on to the temple of Faith, Euclio hid the money. Although he did not know it, a slave belonging to Lyconides, the young man who had violated Euclio's daughter, observed where the money was placed. The slave was just taking the money from its hiding place when Euclio, rushing back to see if it was still safe, prevented the theft.

In an effort to find a safe hiding place for his gold, Euclio took it to the grove of Silvanus. The slave, anxious to please his master and repay Euclio for a beating, watched where Euclio hid the gold in the grove.

In the meantime, Lyconides, having learned of Megadorus' plans to marry Phaedria, went to Eunomia, his mother, and told her that he himself wanted to marry her. Pressed by Eunomia for his reasons, Lyconides revealed that he had violated the young woman while he was drunk and that he wished to make amends by marrying her. Even as they spoke, the excitement in Euclio's house among the women told Eunomia and Lyconides that Phaedria's baby had been born. Eunomia agreed to help her son.

Lyconides went to Euclio to tell of his guilt in violating the miser's daughter. He found Euclio greatly upset, for the miser had just discovered the theft of his gold from Silvanus' grove. Lyconides believed that Euclio was angry with him because he had fathered the daughter's child. Euclio, on the other hand, thought that the crime to which Lyconides was confessing was the theft of the gold. Finally the young man convinced Euclio that he had not stolen the miser's gold. He then told Euclio about having violated Phaedria and of the birth of the child. Megadorus had, in the meantime, renounced his claim to Phaedria. Euclio, who had looked forward to the marriage of his daughter and the rich Megadorus, felt that he had been utterly betrayed by the world.

After Euclio and Lyconides parted, the slave appeared and told Lyconides about the pot of gold he had stolen. Lyconides insisted that the slave bring the gold to him. After a lengthy argument the slave reluctantly obeyed; he hated to think that the gold would be returned to the miserly Euclio.

When the slave brought the gold to Lyconides, the young man went to the house of Euclio and returned the treasure. The miser was so happy to have the pot of gold once more in his hands that he readily agreed to a marriage between his daughter and Lyconides, in spite of the fact that Lyconides had violated Phaedria and caused her to bear a child out of wedlock. Strangely enough, after the wedding Euclio had a change of heart and gave the entire pot of gold to the newly wedded couple.

Critical Evaluation:

The Pot of Gold is an example of Plautus' dramaturgy at its best. The plot has two strands of action: Euclio's frantic attempts to keep his pot of gold safe from thieves, and Phaedria's offers of marriage on the very day she gives birth to Lyconides' illegitimate baby. Both lines of action are skillfully interwoven, the dramatic pace is swift and purposeful, and one scene arises from another with no digressions. This farce also exhibits Plautus' verbal exuberance to good effect—his punning, his comic alliteration, his idiomatic language, his metrical variety, and his keen sense of timing. Few playwrights knew how to handle a joke with such deftness, though merely reading them can be tiresome, especially in translation. It is necessary to visualize the action taking place on a stage to get some idea of Plautus' ability.

Plautine drama was quite similar to nineteenth and twentieth century musical comedy. It used song and dance as part of the action, required considerable theatrical experience, and was based on adapted works. Plautus borrowed heavily from the Greek writers of the New Comedy, and it is often conjectured that *The Pot of Gold* was taken from a play by Menander, although it is impossible to determine which one. The miser has been a stock figure of farce almost from its inception.

The text of *The Pot of Gold* is no longer complete, as the conclusion is missing. On the basis of the two Arguments summarizing the plot—verses that preface the play and that were added by later Roman editors—the ending can, however, be reconstructed.

The main interest of this play lies in the character of Euclio. Three generations of poverty, hard toil, and thrift have had their effect on his personality. Euclio is so stingy that the neighbor's servants make jokes about it, and when he uncovers a pot of gold in his house, his only thought is to keep it from being stolen. The gold acts as a curse for him. It makes him suspicious of every kind word, every good deed, and every person entering or leaving his house. He even suspects that the cooks are using a rooster to locate his gold. He acts like a madman in his apprehension, distractedly dashing in and out of his home. The gold is a burden that has cut him off from everyone. He does not realize that his daughter is pregnant, and learns of it only after she has given birth. Such a person invites the very thing that is feared. Ironically, in trying to find the safest hiding place of all, he unwittingly gives himself away and the gold is stolen. Yet that only increases his frenzy. In the best scene in the play, where Lyconides tries to tell him that he drunkenly made love to Phaedria, Euclio is so preoccupied with the theft that he thinks Lyconides is confessing to having taken the gold. Even when he learns of Phaedria's pregnancy and birthing, it is a minor concern to him. Clearly, something dramatic must have taken place to induce the change of heart in him that causes him to realize that his daughter could use the gold as a dowry. What happened to transform Euclio is part of the missing conclusion.

The subplot by which Phaedria is at last married off to a man who loves her seems perfunctory, but it ties in nicely with Euclio's obsession. Megadorus is elderly, rich, innocent of Phaedria's condition, and willing to take her without a dowry. He sends his cooks to prepare the wedding feast at Euclio's house, which prompts Euclio to remove the gold. After it is stolen, Lyconides becomes the instrument by which it is returned, which establishes him as the successful suitor. Presumably Megadorus withdrew on learning that Phaedria was not a virgin. From the beginning of the play we know that Megadorus is simply the means of getting Lyconides to propose.

Like most Plautine comedies, this play had considerable influence on European drama. Seventeenth century versions of Plautus' play include works by Ben Jonson, Molière, and Thomas Shadwell. Henry Fielding's *The Miser* (1733) was also based in part on the Plautine comedy. Yet certainly the finest re-creation of Euclio was Molière's Harpagon in *The Miser* (1672).

"Critical Evaluation" by James Weigel, Jr.

Bibliography:
Anderson, William S. *Barbarian Play: Plautus' Roman Comedy.* Toronto: University of Toronto Press, 1993. An important critical study. In a section entitled "The Pregnant Virgin: *Aulularia*," Anderson focuses on plotting techniques, and the chapter "Comic Language,

Metre, and Staging" explains why Euclio, who is often called Plautus' best comic villain, dominates the stage. Useful checklist of criticism.

Arnott, W. Geoffrey. *Menander, Plautus, Terence*. Oxford, England: Clarendon Press, 1975. Disagrees with the prevailing interpretations of the character of Euclio, which according to Arnott ignore the climate of the age in which the play was written. Plautus' genius is evident in the subtle techniques he uses to bring Euclio to life.

Duckworth, George E., ed. *The Complete Roman Drama*. New York: Random House, 1942. 2 vols. The general introduction to this standard work is a good starting point for the study of Roman comedy. The essay prefacing *The Pot of Gold* includes a concise plot summary and analysis, historical information, and an indication of the play's later influence.

Hunter, R. L. *The New Comedy of Greece and Rome*. Cambridge, England: Cambridge University Press, 1985. A well-organized work that ranges from matters of form to thematic and didactic considerations. In the final chapter, Hunter shows how Plautus alters his sources to make Euclio a more complex character.

Segal, Erich. *Roman Laughter: The Comedy of Plautus*. Cambridge, Mass.: Harvard University Press, 1968. Euclio is discussed at length in the chapter "Puritans, Principles, Pleasures" and more briefly elsewhere. An index of passages is a useful guide to specific comments on the play. Extensive notes.

POWER

Type of work: Novel
Author: Lion Feuchtwanger (1884-1958)
Type of plot: Historical
Time of plot: Mid-eighteenth century
Locale: Germany
First published: Jud Süss, 1925 (English translation, 1926)

Principal characters:
JOSEF SÜSS OPPENHEIMER, a court favorite
RABBI GABRIEL, his uncle
NAEMI, his daughter
KARL ALEXANDER, the duke
MARIE AUGUSTE, the duchess
WEISSENSEE, a politician
MAGDALEN SIBYLLE, his daughter

The Story:

All of Prussia rejoiced, and European courts lost their best topic of scandal when Duke Eberhard Ludwig broke with the countess who had been his mistress and returned to his wife to beget another heir to the throne. The countess had been his mistress for thirty years, bleeding the country with her extravagant demands for wealth and jewels. Ludwig was too vain, however, to remain her lover when she grew fat and middle-aged.

The countess sent for Isaac Landauer, the wealthy international banker who was her financial agent. Unable to advise her as to the means by which she could keep her hold on the duke, he offered to liquidate her possessions and send them to another province. The countess, who had a strong belief in black magic, nevertheless insisted that Landauer must bring to her the Wandering Jew to help cast a spell on Ludwig.

Landauer went to his young friend, Joseph Süss Oppenheimer and offered half of what his dealings with the countess would bring him if the young man would aid Landauer in the countess' scheme. The so-called Wandering Jew was an uncle of Süss, Rabbi Gabriel, whose melancholy demeanor and mystic ways had caused people to think that he was the legendary Wandering Jew. Süss considered the offer. It was tempting, but for some unknown reason the young man was half afraid of his uncle, whose presence always instilled in his nephew a feeling of inferiority. Furthermore, Rabbi Gabriel was rearing motherless, fourteen-year-old Naemi, the daughter whom Süss wished to conceal from the rest of the world. At last, however, he sent for Rabbi Gabriel.

Penniless Prince Karl Alexander came to Wildbad in hopes of gaining the grant of a substantial income from the duke. Süss, discovering the poverty of the prince, made himself the financial adviser of that destitute nobleman. Although Landauer warned him that Karl Alexander was a poor risk, Süss continued his association with the prince merely because he hoped to ingratiate himself with the nobility. Half in gratitude, half in jest, the prince granted Süss admission to his levees.

On his arrival in Wildbad, Rabbi Gabriel told Süss that he intended to bring Naemi to his nephew. Landauer, however, no longer needed Gabriel to help carry out the countess' scheme, and the rabbi returned to his home. The countess had been banished from the duchy, taking with her the money procured by Landauer.

Süss became the favorite of Prince Karl Alexander. To Wildbad also came Prince Anselm Franz of Thurn and Taxis and his daughter, Princess Marie Auguste. Their mission was to urge Prince Karl Alexander to marry the princess and turn Catholic. Angry because the duke had refused to give him a pension, the prince consented.

Duke Eberhard Ludwig died suddenly, and Karl Alexander, now a Catholic, inherited the duchy. Süss became a court favorite, appointed by the new duchess to be keeper of her privy purse. Although Jews were forbidden to live in the duchy, the people had to acknowledge that the duke should be allowed his private court Jew.

Rabbi Gabriel had bought a little white house where he lived with Naemi and a servant. For three days, while the uncle was away, Süss went to Hirsau to visit his daughter. Then he returned to his duke. Since Karl Alexander's succession, Süss had slyly directed him in measures which were resulting in a complete control of Swabia by the duke himself. The Constitution and the Parliament were powerless. Great noblemen had been ruined. Although his income was enormous, Süss refrained from holding any office. Süss had picked one former cabinet member, Weissensee, as President of the Ecclesiastical Council. One night he gave a party to which Weissensee brought his daughter, Magdalen Sibylle. Süss, noting the duke's attentiveness toward Weissensee's daughter, enticed her into his bedroom, where the duke followed. After that evening, the duke sent gifts to Magdalen Sibylle, his declared mistress, and Weissensee was promoted to a high office. Weissensee hated Süss and secretly hoped to bring the favorite into disfavor at court. Learning that Süss had a daughter, he planned to place the Jew in the same position that Süss had placed him on the night Karl Alexander had taken Magdalen Sibylle.

The murder of a child revived the old legend that Jews sacrificed a Christian child at the Passover feast, and a Jew, Reb Jecheskel Seligmann, was arrested for the crime. Pressure was put on Süss to use his power to save the innocent man, but he refused because of the danger to his position at court. Then Rabbi Gabriel sent word to Süss that Naemi had heard rumors of his wickedness. At last Süss decided that he would help the arrested man. In rescuing Seligmann, he felt anew his power as the court Jew. Soon afterward, at the request of Rabbi Gabriel, he went to visit his mother. He learned from her that his real father had been a great Christian marshal in the German army. Confused, Süss finally decided that he was a Jew and would remain so.

Convinced at last that Süss was a swindler, the duke threatened to dismiss and dishonor him, but when Süss offered his own fortune in exchange for proof of any financial trickery, the duke changed his mind and roared his anger at the enemies of Süss. Realizing that the favorite now had more power than ever, Weissensee continued to plot his revenge. Arranging for the duke to spend some time at his home in Hirsau while Rabbi Gabriel was not at home, Weissensee took the duke to Süss's daughter. With visions of a heavenly rescue, the quiet, lonely child climbed to the roof of the house to escape from her attacker. She fell from the roof to her death.

Outwardly Süss professed forgiveness toward the duke, but he pocketed more and more funds from the ducal treasury. His personality altered. Instead of ingratiating himself at court, he criticized and ridiculed his acquaintances. Filling the duke's head with dreams of conquest, Süss inveigled him into leading a new military coup. At the same time he planned the duke's destruction. While Karl Alexander lay dying at the scene of his defeat, Süss rained over his head a torrent of pent-up abuse. His enemies ordered his arrest.

For many months, the case against Süss dragged on. Finally, he was put into a stinking, rat-infested hole, where every day the authorities plied him for a confession, but he remained stubbornly alive and sane. Sentenced to hang, he assailed the court with icy, cutting words. He could have freed himself by declaring his Christian birth, but he kept silent. On the day of the hanging Süss died with the name "Adonai," the Hebrew name for God, on his lips, and the word was echoed by all the Jews who had gathered to watch him die.

Critical Evaluation:

The theme of *Power* is anti-Semitism. The central thought that Lion Feuchtwanger wished to communicate is that no Jew can ever be safe, whether or not he trusts the political and social system, and whether or not he achieves power in that system. In the end, Feuchtwanger says, the Jew will be murdered—and there will only be other Jews to mourn his passing. Feuchtwanger was an important literary figure in pre-World War II Germany who was forced to flee the Nazis. He was a friend of playwright Bertolt Brecht and was at the center of much of the significant literary activity of the Weimar Republic. The flavor of the cultural life of Weimar is evident in *Power*. The density of the prose, the brutality, the sensuality and perversion, the breakdown of values, minds, and political institutions, have all been taken by Feuchtwanger and transposed to eighteenth century Germany, where they become the perfect medium for tracing the development of anti-Semitism.

In the 1920's, when *Power* was first published, anti-Semitism had not yet reached genocidal proportions. There were a few groups, right-wing nationalists for the most part, who denounced the Jews as the cause of Germany's defeat; but at the same time, there were still Jews in positions of prominence in German social, cultural, and political life. It is to Feuchtwanger's special credit that he had the historical and dramatic insight to understand the embryonic stirrings of homicidal racism in Europe and especially in Germany and to develop this theme in a novel. Additionally, the use of a minority group as a scapegoat, and the casual indifference (or outright collaboration) of officialdom in the violence committed against it, are phenomena which retain their significance for the contemporary reader. *Power* is incredibly and horribly prophetic.

Bibliography:

Kahn, Lothar. *Insight and Action: The Life and Work of Lion Feuchtwanger.* Madison, N.J.: Fairleigh Dickinson University Press, 1975. A definitive and thorough biography. Many insights into the milieu in which Feuchtwanger worked. Much discussion of *Power*.

Laqueur, Walter. "Central European Writers as a Social Force." *Partisan Review* 59, no. 4 (1992): 639-665. Describes Feuchtwanger's trip to the Soviet Union in 1936. Feuchtwanger regarded the Soviet Union as a bulwark against fascism.

Small, William. "In Buddha's Footsteps: Feuchtwanger's *Jud Süss*, Walther Rathenau, and the Path to the Soul." *German Studies Review* 12, no. 3 (1989): 469-485. Describes the parallels between *Power* and the life of Walther Rathenau. Sees a division between spiritual and material values in the novel.

THE POWER AND THE GLORY

Type of work: Novel
Author: Graham Greene (1904-1991)
Type of plot: Psychological realism
Time of plot: 1930's
Locale: Mexico
First published: 1940

Principal characters:
THE PRIEST, a fugitive priest
MARCÍA, the mother of his child
FATHER JOSÉ, a renegade priest
A LIEUTENANT OF POLICE
A POOR MESTIZO

The Story:

In a state in Mexico, the church had been outlawed and the priests driven underground on threat of being shot. After several months, word went out from the governor's office that there was still one priest who was moving from village to village carrying on the work of the church by administering the sacraments and saying Mass. A young lieutenant of police, an ardent revolutionist and an anticlerical, persuaded his chief to let him search for the priest, who, as the authorities saw it, was guilty of treason.

Two photographs were pasted up together in the police station. One was the picture of a fugitive American bank robber who had killed several police officers in Texas; the other was that of the priest. No one noticed the irony, least of all the young lieutenant, who was far more interested in arresting the clergyman. At the same time that the officer was receiving permission to make a search for the priest, the priest was in the village; he had come there in order to get aboard a boat that would take him to the city of Vera Cruz and safety.

Before the priest could board the boat, word came to him that an Indian woman was dying several miles inland. True to his calling, the priest mounted a mule and set out to administer the last rites to the dying woman, although he realized that he might not find another ship to carry him to safety. There was one other priest in the vicinity, Father José. Father José, however, had been cowardly enough to renounce the church, even to the point of taking a wife, a shrewish old woman. The authorities paid no attention to him at all, for they thought, in Father José's case correctly, that a priest who had renounced his vows was a detriment and a shame to the church.

After completing his mission, the priest came back to the coast, where he spent the night in a banana warehouse. The English manager on the plantation allowed him to hide there. The following day, he set out on muleback for the interior, hoping to find refuge from the police and from the revolutionary party of Red Shirts. As he traveled, he thought of his own past and of himself as a poor example of the priesthood. The priest was a whiskey priest, a cleric who would do almost anything for a drink of spirits. In addition, he had in a moment of weakness fathered a child by a woman in an inland village. Although he considered himself a weak man and a poor priest, he was still determined to carry on the work of the church as long as he could, not because he wanted to be a martyr but because he knew nothing else to do.

After twelve hours of travel, he reached the village where his onetime mistress and his child lived. The woman took him in overnight, and the following morning he said a Mass for the villagers. Before he could escape, the police entered the village. Marcía claimed him as her husband, and his child, a girl of seven years, named him as her father. In that manner, because of his earlier sins, he escaped. Meanwhile, the police had decided on a new tactic in uncovering the fugitive. As they passed through each village, they took a hostage. When a certain length of time had passed without the apprehension of the priest, a hostage was shot. In this way, the lieutenant of police in charge of the hunt hoped to persuade the people to betray their priest. After the police had left the village without discovering him, the priest mounted his mule and went on his way. He traveled northward in an effort to escape the police and, if possible, to make his way temporarily into another state.

Some hours after leaving the village, the priest met with a mestizo who joined him. Before long, the mestizo discovered that the priest was the one for whom the police were searching. He promised that, as a good Catholic, he would not betray the secret, but the priest was afraid that the promised reward of seven hundred pesos would be too much of a temptation for the poor man.

When they reached a town, however, it was the priest's own weakness that put him into the hands of the police. He had to have some liquor, the sale of which was against the law. He managed to buy some illegally, but his possession of the contraband was discovered by one of the revolutionary Red Shirts, who came after him. The priest was tracked down by a posse, caught, and placed in jail. Fortunately, he was not recognized by the police, but since he had no money, he was kept in jail to work out the fine.

The lieutenant of police, who was searching feverishly for him, unknowingly did the priest a good turn. Seeing the ragged old man working about the jail, the lieutenant stopped to talk with him. The priest claimed to be a vagrant who had no home of his own. The lieutenant felt sorry for the old fellow, released him, and gave him a present of five pesos. The priest left town and started out across the country to find a place of temporary safety. After traveling for some time, he met an Indian woman who could speak only a few words of Spanish. She managed to make him understand that something was wrong with her child. He went with her and found that the baby had been shot; his immediate guess was that the American bandit had done the deed.

After performing rites over the child, the priest continued his flight. He eventually made his way into the next state, where he was given sanctuary by a German plantation owner. After resting a few days, he planned to go to a city and present his problems to his bishop. Before he could leave, however, he was found by the mestizo, who said that the American bandit, a Catholic, was dying and needed the priest. The priest answered the call, although he was sure he was being led into a trap. The bandit was really dying, but he lay in the state from which the priest had just escaped. A party of police was with him, waiting for the priest's appearance in order to arrest him.

Immediately after the bandit's death, the police closed in and the priest was captured. Taken back to the capital of the state and tried for treason, he was found guilty and sentenced to be shot. The lieutenant of police, who felt somewhat sorry for the old priest, tried to persuade the renegade Father José to hear the priest's last confession, but Father José, who feared the authorities, refused. The priest was led out and shot without the benefit of the church's grace. Nevertheless, the lieutenant of police had not succeeded in removing the church's influence; on the evening of the day on which the priest died, another priest secretly made his way into the town where the execution had taken place.

Critical Evaluation:

The Power and the Glory is one of the most powerful of Graham Greene's novels, and many critics consider it his finest. The story arose from Greene's journey through Tabasco and Chiapas in 1938. President Plutarco Elías Calles, in the name of revolution, had closed the churches and exiled and murdered priests and practicing Catholics. In Greene's journalistic account of his visit, *The Lawless Roads* (1938), he describes characters and settings that reappear and form the basis of his novel.

The theme of the hunted man establishes an exciting and nightmarish atmosphere to this novel and makes it a thriller. Greene has, moreover, created characters who are at once human and symbolic. The priest and the lieutenant embody the extreme dualism in the human spirit: godliness versus godlessness, love versus hatred, spirituality versus materialism, concern for the individual versus concern for the state. After the lieutenant captures the priest, Greene provides an extended dialogue between these two figures that forms a disputation that lies at the heart of his parable of good and evil.

The lieutenant is the antithesis of the priest, but ironically his obsession with the hunt and with the task of eradicating all traces of Catholicism from his country leads him to live a life that is ironically priestlike. His simple lodgings, for example, are described as "comfortless as a prison or a monastic cell." Like the priest, he has an abiding concern for the children and the suffering poor.

The priest, who has endured pain, anxiety, and guilt for years, recognizes in his suffering the purposeful presence of God's love: "It might even look like—hate. It would be enough to scare us—God's love." This philosophic insight is hard won. The priest is keenly aware of his weakness and failure as a man and as a priest. An alcoholic, a scandalous priest with an illegitimate child, a man terrified of pain and death, he harbors no illusions about himself. It is, in fact, his self-knowledge that raises him to the level of the heroic.

When he is in prison for possessing brandy, he tells one of the pious inmates who thinks he is a martyr, "My children, you must never think the holy martyrs are like me. . . . I am a whisky priest." Unlike Father José, however, who has married and accepted the life of a grotesque buffoon, mocked by the children, the whisky priest is redeemed by his keen sense of responsibility for his sins and for the suffering he has brought upon others. His purgatory is in Mexico, in his years of flight, and especially in the torment of his own conscience.

He accepts his loss of peace in the belief that the only reason God denies him rest is so "that he could still be of use in saving a soul, his or another's." After he sees his daughter, Brigida, his love and sense of responsibility for this child and her blighted innocence overwhelm him. A bastard with the hunted alcoholic priest as the father, she appears to have lost her innocence prematurely and has little hope for joy in the world. Through her—and, ironically, through the sin out of which she was conceived—he finds his salvation. He knows that the love he feels for his daughter should encompass every soul in the world, but "all the fear and the wish to save [are] concentrated unjustly on the one child." His final recognition that sainthood is the Christian's most important destiny suggests that he has achieved a form of saintly martyrdom himself.

The lieutenant, on the other hand, is a diminished figure at the end of the novel. For one thing, once the obsession with the hunt has been satisfied, "He felt without a purpose, as if life had drained out of the world." The child Luis, who earlier had admired him, now hates him, suggesting the lieutenant's and the state's failure to win the sympathy of the youth through violent social revolution.

In the providential plan of the novel, the lieutenant's hunt for and persecution of the priest turns the priest into a martyr in the eyes of the people. The lieutenant hates the rich and loves the poor, he says, but he cannot understand or tolerate pain. He wants to let his heart speak "at the end of a gun," if necessary, to bring about a social utopia.

To be sure, the whisky priest is a Greene saint, not a Saint Francis or a Saint Anthony whose life shines in the legends of selfless, charitable actions. Greene undercuts any sentimentality in his hero. The daughter he prays and dies for is doomed: "The world was in her heart already, like the small spot of decay in a fruit." His final prayer is spoken with brandy on his lips. It is the priest's humanity, however, that Greene celebrates, in contrast with the abstract compulsion of the lieutenant "who cared only for things like the state, the republic."

The novel concludes with a mysterious stranger knocking at the door of Luis' home. The stranger identifies himself as a priest, and Luis "put his lips to his hand before the other could give himself a name." The fugitive church, the reader is thus assured, continues to be a vital presence in Mexico and will survive the oppression. Greene's fable of the conflict between spirituality and materialism, between the individual and the state, between love and hatred, comes full circle. Like the phoenix, the Catholic church rises out of the ashes of its martyrs to challenge desperate measures of a godless state.

"Critical Evaluation" by Richard Kelly

Bibliography:

Allott, Kenneth, and Miriam Farris. *The Art of Graham Greene.* London: Hamish Hamilton, 1951. An invaluable study of Greene as an author whose obsessions shape the themes and characters of his fiction. Such obsessive themes as betrayal, the fear of failure, and the hunted man illuminate their reading of *The Power and the Glory.*

Atkins, John. *Graham Greene.* London: Calder & Boyars, 1966. One of the most engaging studies of Greene, this book relates some of Greene's earlier, less-known works to his major novels.

DeVitis, A. A. *Graham Greene.* Boston: Twayne, 1986. A fine introductory study of Greene's major novels with a sensitive reading of Greene's Catholicism and how it influences his fiction. More than a dozen pages dedicated to *The Power and the Glory.*

Kelly, Richard. *Graham Greene.* New York: Frederick Ungar, 1984. Provides a brief biography of the author, followed by analyses of his novels, thrillers, short fiction, and plays. Extends Allott's argument that Greene's creativity was obsessional, examining Greene's later writings.

Zabel, Morton Dauwen. "Graham Greene: The Best and the Worst." In *Craft and Character in Modern Fiction.* New York: Viking Press, 1957. Despite the many volumes of critical material on Greene, this piece still ranks at the very top for its perceptive critical insights into Greene's fictional world.

THE POWER OF DARKNESS

Type of work: Drama
Author: Leo Tolstoy (1828-1910)
Type of plot: Domestic tragedy
Time of plot: Nineteenth century
Locale: Russia
First published: Vlast tmy: Ili, "Kogotok uvyaz, vsey ptichke propast," 1887 (English
translation, 1890); first performed, 1888

Principal characters:
NIKITA AKIMITCH TCHILIKIN, a laborer
ANISYA, his mistress
PETER IGNÁTITCH, Anisya's husband, a well-to-do peasant
MATRYONA, Nikita's mother
AKIM, Nikita's father
AKOULINA, Peter's daughter by his first marriage
MARINA, an orphan girl

The Story:

Peter Ignátitch, a well-to-do peasant, was forty-two years old and sickly. His second wife, Anisya, was only thirty-two. Still feeling young, she had started an affair with Nikita, their hired man. Peter considered Nikita a loafer and had thought of dismissing him. As he was explaining his intention to his wife, they learned that Nikita was talking about getting married and leaving their farm. Anisya complained to Peter that Nikita's departure would leave her with more work than she could handle.

When Anisya and Nikita were alone, he told her that in spite of his marriage plans he would always come back to her. Anisya threatened to do violence to herself if Nikita went away, adding that when her husband died Nikita could marry her and become master of the farm. Nikita declared, however, that he was satisfied with his lot. Matryona, Nikita's mother, came in and said that Nikita's marriage was his father's plan, not her own, and that he need not worry about it. She then asked Nikita to leave the room.

Left alone with Matryona, Anisya confessed her love for Nikita. Matryona, who said that she had known of their affair all along, gave Anisya some poison and advised her to bury her husband before spring; she suggested also that Nikita would make a good master on the farm. Concerning the marriage, she explained that Nikita had had an affair with Marina, an orphan girl, and that when Akim, his father, learned about it he had insisted that Nikita marry her. Matryona had suggested that they talk the matter over with Peter, who was Nikita's master. Having explained the situation, Matryona again urged Anisya to use the poison on Peter, who was near death anyway.

At that point Peter and Akim came in, discussing Nikita's proposed marriage. Peter seemed to approve of the match until Matryona told him that Marina was promiscuous and so had no claim on Nikita. To determine the truth of this charge, Peter sent for Nikita, who falsely swore that there had been nothing between him and Marina. As a result, the marriage was called off. Marina visited Nikita and pleaded her love, saying that she had always been faithful to him, but Nikita sent her away, saying that he was no longer interested in her.

Six months later, Anisya and Matryona were worried because Peter was about to die but had not told anyone where his money pouch was hidden. Anisya told Matryona that she had put the poison into Peter's tea. As they stood talking in the courtyard, Peter appeared on the porch of his house, saw Nikita, who was happening by, and asked his forgiveness, a formal request made by the dying. Nikita was temporarily struck with remorse. Matryona, who then helped Peter back into the house, discovered that the money pouch was hanging by a cord around the sick man's neck. Anisya went into the house and came out again with the money pouch, which she gave to Nikita. She then returned to the house, only to reappear a short time later, wailing a formal lament for Peter, who had just died.

Nine months after Peter's death, Nikita, who had married Anisya and become the master of the farm, grew tired of his wife and began an affair with Akoulina, Peter's daughter by his first marriage. Anisya was afraid to say anything for fear that her murder of Peter would be discovered.

In the following autumn, Matryona arranged a marriage for Akoulina, who had become pregnant by Nikita. Matryona told the father of the suitor that Akoulina herself could not be seen because she was sickly; at that moment, in fact, Akoulina was delivering her child in the barn. Nikita could not decide what to do about the child, but Anisya gave him a spade and told him to dig a hole in the cellar. Nikita balked at the suggestion, feeling that he was not to blame for all his troubles. Anisya, happy that she could force Nikita into sharing her own guilt, told him that he was already guilty because he knew that she had poisoned Peter and because he had accepted Peter's money pouch. At last Nikita went to the cellar and dug the hole.

When Anisya brought the baby to him, covered with rags, Nikita was horrified to discover that the infant was still alive. Anisya and Matryona pushed Nikita into the cellar, where he murdered the baby. After he had completed the deed he reappeared in a frenzy, threatening to kill his mother and claiming that he could still hear the baby whimpering. He then went off to forget his troubles in drink.

Some time after that Akoulina's wedding feast was held at Nikita's farm. Nikita saw Marina, who had been able to marry respectably and who was now a wedding guest. Alone and troubled, he told Marina that his only happiness had been with her. Distraught, Marina left Nikita to himself. Then Matryona and Anisya came to tell him that the bridal pair awaited his formal blessing. Feeling that it would be impossible to give his blessing, Nikita thought of committing suicide until Mitritch, a drunken ex-soldier, appeared and began to talk of his experiences, concluding with the thought that a person should never be afraid of anyone. With this thought in mind, Nikita decided to join the wedding feast.

When Nikita appeared before the guests, he was holding Akim by the hand. Suddenly, instead of blessing the bridal pair, he fell on his knees before his father. Proclaiming that he was guilty and wished to make his confession, he begged forgiveness of Marina, whom he had misused, and of Akoulina, saying that he had poisoned Peter. Although Akoulina said that she knew who had poisoned her father, a police officer, who happened to be a guest at the wedding, wanted to arrest Nikita immediately. Akim prevented him by saying that his son must attend to God's business first. Nikita then confessed that he had seduced Akoulina and murdered her child. Finally, turning again to his father, Nikita asked for his forgiveness. Akim told him that God would forgive him and show him mercy. Nikita was then bound and led away.

Critical Evaluation:

Leo Tolstoy came to playwriting relatively late in his career, after he had completed his prose masterpieces *War and Peace* (1865-1869) and *Anna Karenina* (1877) and at a time when his religious conversion prompted him to view his writing in moralistic, rather than artistic, terms. Hence, the works of this period are heavily didactic and lack much of the balance, scope, and humanity of this previous efforts. Nevertheless, *The Power of Darkness* is a potent realistic play, one of the most intense and moving dramas of the period, and perhaps the outstanding realistic play of the pre-Chekhovian Russian theater.

Although there was no direct influence, *The Power of Darkness* resembles the powerful naturalistic dramas that were, at that time, rejuvenating Western theater. As in a typical naturalistic play, *The Power of Darkness* shows a group of weak, ordinary people who, after committing petty crimes out of greed, sexual jealousy, and self-deception, find themselves caught up by forces they cannot understand or control, driven to further, greater crimes, and ultimately destroyed by the momentum of the evil they had so thoughtlessly unloosed. Small sins automatically lead to bigger ones; lesser crimes require more extreme deeds to maintain concealment; casual observers or passive accomplices are drawn into active conspiracy. Each evil deed, the participants believe, will be the last one and the one to lead them, finally, to happiness. Instead, the opposite is the case; they bind themselves tighter and tighter in a suffocating net of their own making.

Tolstoy's chronicling of this disintegration is fascinating in its realistic accuracy. Even in the midst of their depravity, the characters retain a certain sympathy; they are trapped and drawn to their destruction almost unconsciously. The catalyst is Nikita's mother, Matryona, the one character who seems consciously and deliberately evil, and she is one of the most fascinating creations of the modern stage. She plays on the others and seems to enjoy intrigue for its own sake. She is the consummate hypocrite, acting the role of pious matron, while engineering diabolical schemes. As Peter dies, for example, from the poison she had supplied, Matryona offers him religious consolation.

However, if in the process of disintegration and self-destruction described in *The Power of Darkness* it resembles naturalistic plays, its resolution is quite different. To the naturalists, human beings were the helpless victims of biological and economic circumstances. Naturalistic plays and novels were intended to illustrate that hopeless situation in the face of an impersonal scientific universe. Tolstoy's vision was quite the opposite. To him, the power of darkness was more than balanced by the power of light, and his play is, above all, not a story of damnation but of redemption.

The focus of redemption is on Nikita. From the beginning of the play his sin is clearly the product of arrogance and sensuality, rather than any positive inclination to evil. When circumstances force him to the most vicious of the crimes, the murder of the baby, he is too weak to withstand the pressure of his mother, and he commits the act in a half-conscious frenzy. Immediately he is overwhelmed by guilt and remorse. He hears the breaking bones, the cries of the dying child, and seems on the edge of madness—but he is not granted that escape. He prepares to commit suicide, but that, too, is denied him.

Nikita's insight comes when, in the midst of his suicide attempt, he is accosted by the drunken laborer Mitritch, who tells him a parable about the devil's power, concluding with the statement that, "when you begin to be afraid of people, then the devil, with his cloven hoof, will snatch you up right away and stick you wherever he wants to."

Nikita thus realizes that his descent into evil has been the result of his fear of the opinion of men and his own foolish desire for transient material pleasures. Shorn of that fear he gains his resolve and goes to the wedding party to confess. He accepts all of the blame for the crimes, which is, in a spiritual sense, true, even though the other conspirators are responsible for the crimes as well. Yet despite the magnitude of his guilt, he is redeemed.

Bibliography:

Christian, R. F. *Tolstoy: A Critical Introduction*. Cambridge, England: Cambridge University Press, 1969. A starting place for critical research.

De Courcel, Martine. *Tolstoy: The Ultimate Reconciliation*. Translated by Peter Levi. New York: Charles Scribner's Sons, 1988. A long and thorough discussion of Tolstoy, public and critical reception of *The Power of Darkness*, and the events of Tolstoy's life that surrounded the play and the time immediately following it.

Noyes, George Rapall. *Tolstoy*. Mineola, N.Y.: Dover, 1968. Connects the many works of Tolstoy and refers to biographical information pertinent to the understanding of his writings. Composed greatly of Tolstoy's published writings, diaries, and letters. Explains the theme of conversion in *The Power of Darkness* and the dramatic differences between this play and Tolstoy's novels.

Simmons, Ernest J. *Introduction to Tolstoy's Writings*. Chicago: University of Chicago Press, 1968. Discusses all the works of Tolstoy that have proved to have enduring significance. Devotes a chapter to Tolstoy's dramatic writings. Also discusses the literary devices and theatrical production of *The Power of Darkness*.

Troyat, Henri. *Tolstoy*. Translated by Nancy Amphoux. Garden City, N.Y.: Doubleday, 1967. Gives biographical information concerning the time of writing *The Power of Darkness* and Tolstoy's intentions for it. Includes many illustrations.

PRAGMATISM
A New Name for Some Old Ways of Thinking

Type of work: Philosophy
Author: William James (1842-1910)
First published: 1907

No more illuminating or entertaining account of pragmatism has ever been written than William James's *Pragmatism: A New Name for Some Old Ways of Thinking*. It is, however, more than a popular exposition prepared for the academic audiences of Lowell Institute and Columbia University during the winter of 1906-1907. It is historic philosophy in the making. Although James was profoundly influenced by Charles Sanders Peirce, who invented the basic statement and name of pragmatism, he was an independent thinker with a distinctive creative direction of his own.

Peirce's essay "How to Make Our Ideas Clear" introduced the pragmatic notion that ideas are clarified by considering what would be expected in the way of experience if certain actions were to be carried out. The concept of the "sensible effects" of an object is the extent of the human conception of the objects, according to Peirce. His clear, radical, entertaining essay appeared in *The Popular Science Monthly* in January, 1878, but professional philosophers were not interested in theory advanced by a mathematician, particularly when the theory went against the prevailing idealism of American philosophers. It was not until James revived the idea in 1898 with a talk on "Philosophical Conceptions and Practical Results" that pragmatic philosophy began to stir up controversy. With his lectures on meaning and truth that were published under the titles *Pragmatism* and *The Meaning of Truth*, the former in 1907 and the latter in 1909, James brought pragmatism into the forefront of American thought.

In his first lecture on "The Present Dilemma in Philosophy," James distinguished between the temperamentally "tender-minded" and "tough-minded." The former inclines toward a philosophy that is rational, religious, dogmatic, idealistic, and optimistic, the latter toward a philosophy that is empirical, irreligious, skeptical, materialistic, and pessimistic. James went on to state his conviction that philosophy can satisfy both temperaments by becoming pragmatic.

His lecture on the pragmatic method begins with one of the most entertaining anecdotes in philosophical discourse. James describes a discussion by a group of philosophers on the question: Does a man go around a squirrel that is on a tree trunk if the squirrel keeps moving on the tree to keep the trunk always between himself and the man? Some of the philosophers claimed that the man did not go around the squirrel, while others claimed that he did. James settled the matter by saying, "Which party is right depends on what you practically mean by 'going round' the squirrel." It could be said that the man goes around the squirrel since he passes from the north of the squirrel to the east, south, and west of the squirrel. On the other hand, the man could be said not to go around the squirrel since he is never able to get on the various sides of the squirrel itself. "Make the distinction," James said, "and there is no occasion for any further dispute."

James then applied the method to a number of perennial philosophical problems, but only after a careful exposition of the meaning of pragmatism. He described the pragmatic method as a way of interpreting ideas by discovering their practical consequences, that is, the difference the truth of the idea would make in our experience. He asks, "What difference would it practically make to anyone if this notion rather than that notion were true?" and he replies, "If no practical difference whatever can be traced, then the alternatives mean practically the same thing, and all dispute is idle."

In his lecture, James argued that the pragmatic method was not new: Socrates, Aristotle, John Locke, George Berkeley, and David Hume had used it. What was new was the explicit formulation of the method and a new faith in its power. Pragmatism is to be understood, however, not as a set of grand theories but as a method that turns attention away from first principles and absolutes toward facts, consequences, and results in the human experience.

A bare declaration would hardly have been enough to make pragmatism famous. James devoted a considerable part of his lectures to brief examples of the application of the pragmatic method. He cited with approval Berkeley's analysis of matter as being made up of sensations. Sensations, he said, "are the cash-value of the term. The difference matter makes to us by truly being is that we then get such sensations." Similarly, James claimed, Locke applied the pragmatic method when he discovered that unless "spirit" is defined as consciousness, the term means nothing.

Is materialism or theism true? Is the universe simply matter acting and interacting, or is God involved? James considers this problem pragmatically and reaches a curious result. As far as the past is concerned, he says, it makes no difference. If rival theories are meant to explain what is the case and if it makes no difference which theory is true, then the theories do not differ in meaning. If one considers the difference now and in the future, however, the case is different: "Materialism means simply the denial that the moral order is eternal. . . . Spiritualism means the affirmation of an eternal moral order and the letting loose of hope."

To this kind of analysis some critics have answered with the charge that James is one of the "tender-minded" philosophers he chastised in his earlier lectures. Yet throughout the course of this series of lectures and in subsequent books, James continued to use pragmatism as a way of combining the tough and tender temperaments. He extended the use of the term "difference" so that the meaning of an idea or term was no longer to be understood merely in terms of sense experiences, as Peirce had urged, but also in terms of passionate differences, of effects upon human hopes and fears. The essays in *Pragmatism* show this liberalizing tendency hard at work.

The temperate tone of James's suggestions concerning the religious hypothesis is clear in one of his later lectures in the book, "Pragmatism and Religion," in which he writes that "Pragmatism has to postpone dogmatic answer, for we do not yet know certainly which type of religion is going to work best in the long run." He states again that the tough-minded can be satisfied with "the hurly-burly of the sensible facts of nature," and that the tender-minded can take up a monistic form of religion; but those who mix temperaments, as James does, prefer a religious synthesis that is moralistic and pluralistic and allows for human development and creativity in various directions.

Pragmatism is important not only as a clear statement of the pragmatic method and as an illustration of its application to certain central problems, but also as an introductory exposition of James's pragmatic theory of truth. His ideas were developed more fully two years later in *The Meaning of Truth*.

Beginning with the common notion that truth is a property of ideas that agree with reality, James proceeded to ask what was meant by the term "agreement." He decided that the conception of truth as a static relation between an idea and reality was in error, that pragmatic analysis shows that true ideas are those that can eventually be verified, and that an idea is said to be verified when it leads usefully to an anticipated conclusion. Since verification is a process, it becomes appropriate to say that truth "happens to" an idea, and that an idea "becomes true, is made true by events." A revealing summary statement is this: "'The true,' to put it very briefly, is only the expedient in the way of our thinking, just as 'the right' is only the expedient in the way of our behaving."

The ambiguity of James's account, an ambiguity he did not succeed in removing, allows extremes of interpretation. On the one hand, a reader might take the tender-minded route, something in the manner of James himself, and argue that all kinds of beliefs about God, freedom, and immortality are true insofar as they lead people usefully in the course of their lives. Tough-minded readers, on the other hand, might be inclined to agree with James that an idea is true if the expectations in terms of which the idea makes sense are expectations that would be met, if one acted—but they might reject James's suggestions that this means that a great many ideas that would ordinarily be regarded as doubtful "become true" when they satisfy the emotional needs of a believer.

One difficulty with which James was forced to deal resulted, it might be argued, not from his idea of truth as the "workableness" of an idea but from his inadequate analyses of the meanings of certain terms such as "God," "freedom," and "design." James maintained that, pragmatically speaking, these terms all meant the same thing, that is, the presence of "promise" in the world. If this were so, then it would be plausible to suppose that the idea that the world is promising would be true if it were shown to have worked out. If, however, James's analysis is mistaken, if "God" means more than the possibility of things working out for the better, then James's claim that beliefs about God are true if they work loses its plausibility. Whatever its philosophic faults, *Pragmatism* offers readers the rare experience of confronting first-rate ideas by way of a clear and entertaining, even informal, style.

Bibliography:

Barzun, Jacques. *A Stroll with William James*. New York: Harper & Row, 1983. Instructively discusses important subtleties surrounding the terms "pragmatism" and "pragmatic" in this readable introduction to James's intellectual world.

Moore, Edward C. *William James*. New York: Washington Square Press, 1965. An accessible overview, written by a philosopher, which includes a useful outline of the central arguments in *Pragmatism* (pp. 70-114).

Olin, Doris, ed. *William James: "Pragmatism," in Focus*. London: Routledge & Kegan Paul, 1992. Essentially a casebook, the complete text of *Pragmatism* is presented together with Olin's succinct introduction and six discussions, including sophisticated philosophical commentaries by G. E. Moore and Bertrand Russell.

Perry, Ralph Barton. *The Thought and Character of William James, as Revealed in Unpublished Correspondence and Notes, Together with His Published Writings*. 2 vols. Boston: Little, Brown, 1935. In volume 2, Perry devotes chapters 77-79 to providing a wealth of valuable primary sources (principally letters to and from James) that explicate the origins of *Pragmatism*, the book's critical reception, and James's responses to points made by his critics. Includes James's self-estimate of *Pragmatism* and a related *New York Times* interview with him.

Skrupskelis, Ignas K. *William James: A Reference Guide*. Boston: G. K. Hall, 1977. Provides annotated references to reviews, articles, and doctoral dissertations on *Pragmatism* and James's other works.

THE PRAIRIE
A Tale

Type of work: Novel
Author: James Fenimore Cooper (1789-1851)
Type of plot: Adventure
Time of plot: 1804
Locale: Western plains of the United States
First published: 1827

> *Principal characters:*
> NATTY BUMPPO, an old frontiersman
> ISHMAEL BUSH, a desperado
> ESTHER BUSH, his wife
> ELLEN WADE, Esther's niece
> ABIRAM WHITE, Esther's brother
> DR. BATTIUS, a naturalist
> PAUL HOVER, Ellen's lover
> CAPTAIN MIDDLETON, a soldier in the United States Army
> INEZ, his wife
> HARD-HEART, a Pawnee chief

The Story:

Shortly after the time of the Louisiana Purchase, the family of Ishmael Bush traveled westward from the Mississippi River. Ishmael was accompanied by his wife, Esther, and their sons and daughters. Also in the caravan were Esther's niece, Ellen Wade; Esther's brother Abiram White; and Dr. Battius, a physician and naturalist. As this company searched for a camping place one evening, they met an aged trapper, Natty Bumppo, and his dog. The trapper directed them to a nearby stream.

After night had fallen, Bumppo discovered Ellen in a secret meeting with her lover, Paul Hover, a wandering bee hunter. The three were captured by a band of Sioux. While the Indian raiders stole all the horses and cattle from Ishmael's party, the captives escaped. Unable to proceed across the prairie, the emigrant family occupied a naturally fortified hilltop that Bumppo showed them.

A week later, Paul, Bumppo, and Dr. Battius were gathered around Bumppo's campsite. They were soon joined by a stranger, who introduced himself as Captain Middleton of the United States Army. Bumppo was delighted to find that Middleton was the grandson of an old friend whom he had known in the days of the French and Indian wars. The young officer had come to find his wife, Inez, who had been kidnapped by Abiram White shortly after her marriage. She was now a captive in Ishmael's camp. Paul, Bumppo, and Dr. Battius agreed to help Middleton rescue her.

On the same day, Ishmael and his sons left their camp to hunt buffalo. That evening, they returned with meat, but Asa, the oldest son, did not return with the other hunters. In the morning, the entire family set out to search for him and found his dead body in a thicket; he had been shot in the back with one of Bumppo's bullets. His family buried him and returned to camp, only to find that both Ellen and Inez were gone.

The young women, who had been rescued by Middleton and his friends, were making their escape across the prairie when their progress was interrupted by a meeting with the Pawnee warrior Hard-Heart. After the warrior had galloped away on his horse, the travelers found themselves in the path of a stampeding herd of buffalo. The group was saved from being trampled to death at the last moment by the braying of Dr. Battius' donkey, for at the strange sound the herd turned aside. However, Middleton's party was soon captured by a band of Sioux pursuing the buffalo herd. They were the same Indians who had earlier captured Bumppo, Paul, and Ellen. At the same time, Ishmael and his sons approached on foot, searching for the two girls. The Indians remounted and gave horses to their captives so that all could ride to Ishmael's camp while he and his sons were away. During the Indian raid on the camp, Bumppo helped his friends escape on horseback.

They rode as far as possible before making camp for the night; yet in the morning, they found that the Sioux had followed them and had set fire to the prairie in order to drive them into the open. Bumppo rescued the party by burning off the nearby prairie before the larger fire reached it. As they started off, they met the Hard-Heart again. From him, they learned that the Sioux and Ishmael's family had joined forces in order to search for them. Since Hard-Heart and the little band had a common enemy in the Sioux, he agreed to take them to his Pawnee village for protection.

The fugitives crossed a nearby river. As they reached the far bank, the Sioux appeared on the opposite shore. That night, the fugitives remained free, but snow fell and made it impossible for them to escape without being tracked. They were captured and taken to the Sioux village. Hard-Heart, Paul, and Middleton were bound by their savage captors. Out of respect for his age, Bumppo was allowed to roam freely, but he declined to leave his friends. The women were placed in the lodge of the Sioux chief.

Using Bumppo as an interpreter, the Sioux chief asked Inez to be his wife. Ishmael asked the chief to give him Inez, Ellen, and Bumppo, as had been previously agreed. When the chief refused, Ishmael departed angrily. The Indians gathered in council to decide the fate of Hard-Heart. Many wished to torture him to death. An old warrior stepped forward and declared that he wished to make the Pawnee his adopted son, but Hard-Heart refused to become a member of the Sioux tribe. The Sioux began to torture their captives, but Hard-Heart escaped and joined a war party of his own Pawnees, who arrived on the scene.

Leaving their women to guard the prisoners, the Sioux prepared to fight. The braves of the two tribes gathered on the opposite banks of a river, neither side daring to make the first move. Then Hard-Heart challenged the Sioux chief to single combat. Meanwhile, Bumppo helped the rest of the captives to escape. Shortly afterward, they fell once more into the hands of Ishmael. Hard-Heart was victorious over the Sioux chief, and his warriors put the remaining Sioux warriors to flight in the battle that followed.

The next morning, Ishmael held a court of justice to deal with his captives. He realized his mistake in carrying Inez away from her husband and allowed the couple their freedom. He gave Ellen her choice of remaining with his family or going with Paul. She chose to go with her lover. Ishmael allowed Dr. Battius his freedom because he did not think that the scientist was worth the bother. Then Bumppo came up for judgment.

Ishmael still believed that Bumppo had shot his son, Asa, but Bumppo revealed that it was really Abiram who had done the cowardly deed. Abiram confessed his crime and then fainted. Ishmael was reluctant to pronounce judgment on his brother-in-law, but he felt it his duty to do so. That evening, he gave Abiram the choice of starving to death or hanging himself. Late that night, Ishmael and Esther returned to find that Abiram had hanged himself. They buried him and continued on their way back to the frontier settlements.

Middleton, Paul, and the young women invited Bumppo to return to the settlements with them, where they would see to him in his last days. He refused, choosing to remain in the Pawnee village with Hard-Heart.

A year later, when Middleton's duties as an army officer brought him near the Pawnee village, he visited Bumppo. He found the old trapper near death, but Bumppo revived sufficiently to greet his old friend. At sundown, however, he seemed to be breathing his last. As the sun sank beneath the horizon, he made one last tremendous effort. He rose to his feet and, as if answering a roll call, he uttered a loud and firm "Here"—then fell back dead into the arms of his friends.

Critical Evaluation:

The Prairie is the third title published in James Fenimore Cooper's Leatherstocking tales, but in the series of five tales published together in 1850, *The Prairie* concluded the saga of Natty Bumppo. This book picks up on two important themes from the two Leatherstocking tales that preceded it in publication, *The Pioneers* (1823) and *The Last of the Mohicans* (1826): the wasting of America's natural resources and the vanishing of the American Indian as a race. Leatherstocking in *The Pioneers* had condemned the wasteful cutting and burning of trees, the greater slaughter of passenger pigeons, and the seining of fish that were left to rot on the lakeshore. In *The Prairie*, the old trapper complains: "What the world of America is coming to, and where the machinations and inventions of its people are to have an end, the Lord, He only knows. . . . How much has the beauty of the wilderness been deformed." The theme of the "vanishing American" was touched on in *The Pioneers* with the death of Chingachgook. It became a leading theme in *The Last of the Mohicans* and returns in *The Prairie* with the war between the Pawnees and the Sioux (resembling the war between the Delawares and the Mingoes in the earlier tale), which makes it easier for such white settlers as Ishmael Bush and his large family to take over what had been the Indians' ancient homeland.

Certain resemblances between characters and character relationships in *The Last of the Mohicans* and *The Prairie* can also be seen. The genteel Captain Duncan Uncas Middleton is a grandson of Duncan Heyward and Alice Munro, who represented gentility in *The Last of the Mohicans*. The old trapper's love for his adopted son, Hard-Heart, parallels the feeling that Hawkeye had earlier had for young Uncas. The enmity of Hard-Heart and Mahtoree is as fierce as that of Uncas and Magua, though the two feuds end differently. Finally, in comic absurdity the pedantic wordiness of Dr. Obed Battius resembles—indeed, it even surpasses—the talk and the psalm singing of David Gamut.

There are many improbabilities of plot in *The Prairie*, and the narrative is obstructed by the old trapper's long-windedness and Dr. Battius' ridiculous vocabulary and views. Ishmael Bush is, however, one of Cooper's best-drawn characters, and the old trapper is both pathetic and noble as he approaches his death. The death scene itself so impressed the English novelist William Makepeace Thackeray that he imitated it in drawing the death scene of Colonel Newcome in *The Newcomes* (1853-1855).

Bibliography:

Brotherston, Gordon. "*The Prairie* and Cooper's Invention of the West." In *James Fenimore Cooper: New Critical Essays*, edited by Robert Clark. London: Vision Press, 1985. Defines *The Prairie* as "the most distinctive if not the best written" of Cooper's novels about Native Americans. Explores the lasting historical and cultural images Cooper helped create.

Dekker, George. *James Fenimore Cooper: The American Scott*. New York: Barnes & Noble

Books, 1967. Argues persuasively that Cooper deserves more respect from scholars and students, although his weaknesses are real and serious. Devotes three chapters to *The Prairie*, concluding that many ideas in this work were handled better in the other Leatherstocking tales.

Fields, Wayne. "Beyond Definition: A Reading of *The Prairie*." In *James Fenimore Cooper: A Collection of Critical Essays*, edited by Wayne Fields. Englewood Cliffs, N.J.: Prentice-Hall, 1979. Compares the prairie and the forest as representational landscapes. Ishmael Bush's experiences demonstrate that human beings need laws and limits to survive.

Överland, Orm. *The Making and Meaning of an American Classic: James Fenimore Cooper's "The Prairie."* New York: Humanities Press, 1973. Discusses biographical and historical contexts, sources and method of composition, and a reading with early critical reception. Accessible for students, and interesting for its Scandinavian approach to American history and culture.

Rans, Geoffrey. *Cooper's Leather-Stocking Novels: A Secular Reading*. Chapel Hill: University of North Carolina Press, 1991. The chapter "The Uses of Memory" uses *The Prairie* to show how a nation uses selective memory of its past, particularly of its past injustices, to move forward.

THE PRAISE OF FOLLY

Type of work: Satire
Author: Desiderius Erasmus (1466?-1536)
First published: Moriæ Encomium, 1511 (English translation, 1549)

Considered by many to be the father of modern letters, Desiderius Erasmus spent a lifetime producing some of the most important scholarly works of the early Renaissance. Ironically, *The Praise of Folly,* written as an amusement, became the most enduring of his contributions to Western literature. Erasmus himself never thought highly of this work, yet it is the one for which he is best remembered. He wrote it in approximately seven days in 1509, while he was recovering from an illness at the home of his English friend, Sir Thomas More. It was not until two years after its writing that he had the book secretly printed in France. More than forty editions of *The Praise of Folly* appeared in the author's lifetime. The work caused Erasmus considerable trouble; his portraits of the clergy did little to endear him to the hierarchy of the Roman Catholic church, and for years the volume was banned as anti-Catholic. Nevertheless, the treatise has passed into the canon of Western literature, ranking as one of the premier examples of satiric writing in European letters.

The Praise of Folly makes use of one of the oldest forms of rhetorical discourse: the encomium. In a mock encomium, Erasmus makes use of the satirical devices of one of the world's most influential satirists, Lucian, to poke gentle fun at the tradition of praising great people and great ideas. Putting words of wisdom in the mouth of Folly, Erasmus highlights the paradoxical relationship between conventional wisdom and the religious dimensions of human life. Like all great satirists, Erasmus focuses on specific targets (especially the clergy of his own day), but his general aim is to tell his readers something about universal human nature. Beneath his carefully constructed argument, Erasmus echoes the biblical lesson that, in the eyes of the world, it is truly folly to adopt the Christian lifestyle; in that folly, however, lies real wisdom.

Although written five centuries ago, *The Praise of Folly* is still an effective analytic examination of humankind's abilities and vanities. It not only gives the modern reader an idea of the struggle of the Humanists in their effort to rid the world of the conventions and forms of the Middle Ages, but also provides insight into continuing problems of life. As the result of this work and several others, Erasmus became one of the most popular men of letters of his time, and, consequently, one of the most influential. He was of prime importance in the spread of Humanism throughout the northern part of Europe and was instrumental in many aspects of both the Reformation and the later phase of the Renaissance. Everything he did was to aid humankind in tearing away the veils of foolish traditions and customs, in order that people could find the road back to the true God and their true selves.

The form itself is an immediate indication of the type of work that the book is to be. Written as a parody of a classical oration, the essay sets Folly as the orator. Her subject is society, and she quickly becomes a many-sided symbol that stands for all that is natural in people, all of their misdirected efforts, and all of their attempts to get the wrong things out of life. She discusses the problem of wisdom and tells how it can be united with action to gain success in a world of folly; she is concerned with the way in which reason and simple Christian advice can be presented to humankind; she wonders what Christian Humanists can do for themselves and the world. Parody, irony, and satire are used throughout the essay to show people what they do and what they should do. No one is spared. Neither king nor prince, pope nor priest, aristocrat nor worker escapes the indignation that Erasmus feels toward society.

At the beginning of her oration, Folly declares that she is giving a eulogy for herself, and she justifies the impertinence by saying that she knows herself better than anyone else and that no one else will do it for her. Her father, she says, is Plutus, the real father of all people and gods, and she was born out of his passion for Youth. Significantly, her birth took place in the Fortunate Isles, and she lists among her followers Drunkenness, Ignorance, Self-love, Flattery, Forgetfulness, Laziness, Pleasure, Madness, Sensuality, Intemperance, and Sound Sleep—all of whom help her to gain control of all things.

It is Folly, for instance, who leads people to marriage and the conception of life, thus prolonging this life that is so foolish. It is Pleasure, one of her followers, who makes life bearable at all. It is Forgetfulness who makes youth such a carefree time, and who restores this same characteristic to old age, thereby bringing about a second childhood. By throwing off care and avoiding wisdom, one can achieve perpetual youth.

Folly goes on to say that she is the source of all that is pleasurable in life. People will never be completely divorced from Folly, because they are ruled more by passion than by reason, and the two most ruling passions are anger and lust. One of the chief sources of men's pleasure, of course, is women, who are even more subject to folly than are men. Men's coarser looks are a result of the infection of wisdom.

Friendship also derives from Folly, because it makes people ignore the faults and defects of others. Marriage itself is held together with compromise, infatuation, and duplicity. Without Folly, people could not get along with each other; they would soon begin to hate themselves and everything would seem sordid and loathsome.

Folly praises herself under the guise of Prudence, because she allows humans to have first-hand experience with the world. She frees people from the shame and fear that cloud their minds and inhibit their actions, thus preventing real experience. Thanks to Prudence, people go along with the crowd, which is Folly. It is Folly who has caused all the great achievements of humanity; wisdom and learning are no great help. Everything that a person does is motivated by self-love, vainglory, flattery, or other followers of Folly.

To lead such a life of folly, error, and ignorance is to be human; it is to express one's true nature. All other forms of life are content with limitations, but humans are vainly ambitious. Those who are most ignorant are the happiest; those who are most deluded are those who delight in telling lies. For an example, one might consider the priests—those who propose to gain happiness by relying on magic charms and prayers, saints and particular rites. There is no happiness without Folly, because all emotions belong to Folly, and happiness depends on expressing one's human nature, which is full of folly.

Among the most foolish people, therefore, are those who try to deny their true nature and find happiness through the Christian religion. Folly proves that this religion has more to do with her nature than with wisdom by showing that children, women, old people, and fools take more delight in it than do others. It is they who are always nearest the altars. In the way that Christianity is most often taught and practiced, humans must deny their true nature by disdaining life and preferring death. One must overlook injuries, avoid pleasure, and feast on hunger, vigils, tears, and labors. One must give up and scorn all physical pleasures, or at least take them more lightly than spiritual pleasures.

Folly is at her most serious when she says that this is the most foolish way, and the only sure way, to true happiness. Only by forgetting the body and everything physical can a person approach this goal. People must give themselves up completely to the spiritual aspects of life in order to achieve it. Few are able to accomplish this task completely enough while in this world to approach an experience that, she says, is close to madness. This madness, in turn, is similar to the heavenly joys that one will experience after death when the spirit has completely left the body.

Bibliography:

Halkin, Léon-E. *Erasmus: A Critical Biography.* Translated by John Tonkin. New York: Blackwell, 1993. Analyzes many different levels of meaning in *The Praise of Folly* and describes Erasmus' contrast between worldly wisdom and Christian folly. Contains an excellent biographical guide for research on Erasmus.

Kaiser, Walter. *Praisers of Folly: Erasmus, Rabelais, and Shakespeare.* Cambridge, Mass.: Harvard University Press, 1963. Examines *The Praise of Folly* within the Renaissance tradition of the mock encomium. Also contains solid comments on representations of folly by William Shakespeare and François Rabelais.

Phillips, Margaret Mann. *Erasmus and the Northern Renaissance.* Rev. ed. Woodbridge, England: Boydell and Brewer, 1981. Clear introduction to the life and career of Erasmus by an Erasmus scholar. Contains an excellent analysis of the religious dimension of *The Praise of Folly.*

Screech, Michael A. *Ecstasy and the Praise of Folly.* London: Duckworth, 1980. Contains a very clearly presented explanation of religious ecstasy and the paradoxically positive concept of Christian folly. Describes the profound influence of St. Paul on Erasmus' understanding of Christian folly.

Williams, Kathleen, ed. *Twentieth-Century Interpretations of "The Praise of Folly."* Englewood Cliffs, N.J.: Prentice-Hall, 1969. Contains an annotated bibliography of important English-language studies and several essays by major Erasmus scholars who explore various aspects of the paradoxical nature of *The Praise of Folly.*

PREFACE TO SHAKESPEARE

Type of work: Literary criticism
Author: Samuel Johnson (1709-1784)
First published: 1765

Samuel Johnson's preface to *The Plays of William Shakespeare* has long been considered a classic document of English literary criticism. In it Johnson sets forth his editorial principles and gives an appreciative analysis of the "excellences" and "defects" of the work of the great Elizabethan dramatist. Many of his points have become fundamental tenets of modern criticism; others give greater insight into Johnson's prejudice than into Shakespeare's genius. The resonant prose of the preface adds authority to the views of its author.

Perhaps no other document exhibits the character of eighteenth century literary criticism better than what is commonly known as Johnson's *Preface to Shakespeare*. Written after Johnson had spent nine years laboring to produce an edition of the plays, the *Preface to Shakespeare* is characterized by sweeping generalizations about the dramatist's work and by stunning pronouncements about his merits, judgments that elevated Shakespeare to the top spot among European writers of any century. At times, Johnson displays the tendencies of his contemporaries to fault Shakespeare for his propensities for wordplay and for ignoring the demands for poetic justice in his plays; readers of subsequent generations have found these criticisms more a reflection on the inadequacies of the critic than of the dramatist. What sets Johnson's work apart from that of his contemporaries, however, is the immense learning that lies beneath so many of his judgments; he consistently displays his familiarity with the texts, and his generalizations are rooted in specific passages from the dramas. Further, Johnson is the first among the great Shakespeare critics to stress the writer's sound understanding of human nature. Johnson's focus on character analysis initiated a critical trend that would predominate Shakespeare criticism (in fact, all of dramatic criticism) for more than a century, and lead to the great work of critics such as Samuel Taylor Coleridge, Charles Lamb, and A. C. Bradley.

The significance of the *Preface to Shakespeare*, however, goes beyond its contributions to Shakespeare scholarship. First, it is the most significant practical application of a critical principle that Johnson espoused consistently and that has become a staple of the practice since: comparison. His systematic attempt to measure Shakespeare against others both classical and contemporary became the model. Second, the *Preface to Shakespeare* exemplifies Johnson's belief that good criticism can only be produced after good scholarship has been practiced. The critic who wishes to judge an author's originality or an author's contributions to the tradition must first practice sound literary reading and research, in order to understand what has been borrowed and what invented.

Characteristically, Johnson makes his Shakespearian criticism the foundation for general statements about people, nature, and literature. He is a true classicist in his concern with the universal rather than with the particular; the highest praise he can bestow upon Shakespeare is to say that his plays are "just representations of general nature." The dramatist has relied upon his knowledge of human nature, rather than on bizarre effects, for his success. "The pleasures of sudden wonder are soon exhausted, and the mind can only repose on the stability of truth," Johnson concludes. It is for this reason that Shakespeare has outlived his century and reached the point at which his works can be judged solely on their own merits, without the interference of personal interests and prejudices that make criticism of one's contemporaries difficult.

Johnson feels that the readers of his time can often understand the universality of Shakespeare's vision better than the audiences of Elizabethan England could, for the intervening centuries have freed the plays of their topicality. The characters in the plays are not limited by time or nationality; they are rather "the genuine progeny of common humanity, such as the world will always supply, and observation will always find."

Implicitly criticizing earlier editors of Shakespeare, who had dotted their pages with asterisks marking particularly fine passages, Johnson contends that the greatness of the plays lies primarily in their total effect, in the naturalness of the action, the dialogue, and the characterization. Again and again Johnson stresses the same point: "This, therefore, is the praise of Shakespeare, that his drama is the mirror of life." His personages are drawn from the world familiar to everyone: "Shakespeare has no heroes; his scenes are occupied only by men, who act and speak as the reader thinks that he should himself have spoken or acted on the same occasion."

That Shakespeare wrote "contrary to the rules of criticism" was, for Johnson, not a problem. Aside from the fact that Aristotle's rules were not widely known during Shakespeare's time, Johnson notes: "There is always an appeal open from criticism to nature." Life itself justifies the mingling of comedy and tragedy on the stage; together they exhibit "the real state of sublunary nature, which partakes of good and evil, joy and sorrow, mingled with endless variety of proportion and innumerable modes of combination."

While Johnson is aware of Shakespeare's skills in both comedy and tragedy, he suggests that his natural forte was the former: "In tragedy he is always struggling after some occasion to be comick; but in comedy he seems to repose, or to luxuriate, as in a mode of thinking congenial to his nature." Johnson later criticizes some of the tragic speeches as bombast, forced, unnatural emotion, and he complains that all too often scenes of pathos are marred by "idle conceits," and those inspiring terror and pity by "sudden frigidity." Yet the critic later confesses that in spite of these flaws one finds one's mind seized more strongly by Shakespeare's tragedies than by those of any other writer.

Johnson praises Shakespeare's language as that of the "common intercourse of life," used among those who speak only to be understood, without ambition or elegance. One of Johnson's most stringent objections to Shakespeare's work arises from Johnson's strong conviction that literature is, or should be, essentially didactic. He is disturbed by Shakespeare's disregard of poetic justice. Johnson was convinced that the writer should show the virtuous rewarded and the evil punished, and he finds that Shakespeare, by ignoring this premise, "sacrifices virtue to convenience." The fact that in life evil often triumphs over good is no excuse in Johnson's eyes: "It is always a writer's duty to make the world better."

Shakespeare's careless plotting and his "disregard for distinctions of time and place" are also noted as flaws; "we need not wonder to find Hector quoting Aristotle, when we see the loves of Theseus and Hippolyta combined with the Gothick mythology of fairies." Although Johnson dislikes Shakespeare's bawdry, he is willing to concede that that fault, at least, might have rested with the indelicacy of the ladies and gentlemen at the courts of Elizabeth I and James I, rather than with the playwright. These minor "errors" are far less irritating to Johnson than Shakespeare's use of puns: "A quibble was to him the fatal Cleopatra for which he lost the world, and was content to lose it." Puns, being language's form of disorderly conduct, disturbed Johnson's neoclassical understanding.

Johnson's contemporaries often condemned Shakespeare for his lack of attention to the Aristotelian unities of time, place, and action, which were assiduously observed by the French classical dramatists and their English imitators. Johnson notes that Shakespeare observed unity of action, in giving his plays a beginning, a middle, and an end, and in developing his plot by cause and effect. Moreover, he sees no harm in Shakespeare's failure in most cases to limit his action to one place and one day. Most strict neoclassical critics maintained that such limitations of time and space were necessary for dramatic credibility. Johnson finds this assertion ridiculous, for every member of the audience knows that all drama is illusion: "He that can take the stage at one time for the palace of the Ptolemies, may take it in half an hour for the promontory of Actium. Delusion, if delusion be admitted, has no certain limitation." Real dramatic credibility comes from the validity of the emotions presented: "The reflection that strikes the heart is not, that the evils before us are real evils, but that they are evils to which we ourselves may be exposed."

Anticipating the historical critics of the nineteenth and twentieth centuries, Johnson assesses some of the aspects of Elizabethan England that probably influenced Shakespeare. He stresses the fact that the dramatist was in many ways a pioneer, for he had few truly outstanding English works of drama or poetry to build on. Shakespeare's complicated plots can be traced to the popularity of the elaborate pastoral romances read by his audiences and occasionally used as sources for the plays.

Johnson does not emphasize Shakespeare's learning, noting that he could have read in translation the classical works he mentions. The playwright's greatest knowledge came not from books, but from life: "Mankind was not then to be studied in the closet; he that would know the world, was under the necessity of gleaning his own remarks, by mingling as he could in its business and amusements."

Concluding his general commentary, Johnson summarizes Shakespeare's gifts to English literature: "The form, the characters, the language, and the shows of the English drama are his. . . . To him we must ascribe the praise, unless Spenser may divide it with him, of having first discovered to how much smoothness and harmony the English language could be softened."

In the remainder of the Preface Johnson delineates his editorial standards, rejecting the temptation to follow the practices of his predecessors, who had emended, essentially rewritten, the plays where they could not understand or did not like what they found in the earliest texts of Shakespeare's works. Johnson followed Pope in basing his edition on the original quarto versions of the plays and on the first folio, and he attempted, he says, to leave them as nearly as possible as he found them. His explanatory notes are to contain not only his own ideas, but also the views of earlier critics. He quotes others more often to refute them than to praise them, believing that "the first care of the builder of a new system, is to demolish the fabricks which are standing."

In a final exhortation to the reader Johnson places his efforts in perspective; notes are often necessary, but they are necessary evils. The reader who has not yet experienced Shakespeare's genius must first ignore the editor's aids and simply read for "the highest pleasure that the drama can give." Johnson's modesty is in itself a tribute to Shakespeare; his whole task as editor and critic was to make the great plays more accessible to the public, and his criticism still gives valuable insights to the modern lover of Shakespeare.

Bibliography:
Hagstrum, Jean H. *Samuel Johnson's Literary Criticism.* Chicago: The University of Chicago Press, 1968. This study is useful in placing the *Preface to Shakespeare* in the general context of Johnson's critical principles. Dividing Johnson's literary criticism into such topics as nature, pleasure, and wit, Hagstrum argues that Johnson's critical thought originated from actual experience.

Sherbo, Arthur. *Samuel Johnson, Editor of Shakespeare: With an Essay on "The Adventurer."* Champaign: The University of Illinois Press, 1956. A chapter analyzes Johnson's *Preface to Shakespeare* in detail and places it in the context of eighteenth century criticism.

Smallwood, P. J., ed. *Johnson's "Preface to Shakespeare": A Facsimile of the 1778 Edition with Introduction and Commentary by P. J. Smallwood.* Bristol: Bristol Classical Press, 1985. An especially helpful companion volume; most of this book consists of extensive commentary aimed at elucidating every detail of the *Preface to Shakespeare.*

Stock, R. D. *Samuel Johnson and Neoclassical Dramatic Theory: The Intellectual Context of the "Preface to Shakespeare."* Lincoln: University of Nebraska Press, 1973. A lengthy, detailed review of the critical context that Johnson inherited, concluding with a close look at the *Preface to Shakespeare.* Bibliography.

Tomarken, Edward. *A History of the Commentary on Selected Writings of Samuel Johnson.* Columbia, S.C.: Camden House, 1994. Especially useful as a survey of what critics have said of Johnson's Shakespeare criticism. Argues that Johnson's work is a model of criticism that continues to offer valuable instruction.

PREJUDICES

Type of work: Essays
Author: H. L. Mencken (1880-1956)
First published: 1919-1927: first series, 1919; second series, 1920; third series, 1922; fourth series, 1924; fifth series, 1926; sixth series, 1927

During the fantastic decade of the 1920's, few literary events were so eagerly awaited in the United States as the appearance of a new volume of H. L. Mencken's *Prejudices*. A wide range of people enjoyed the spectacle of the Sage of Baltimore, as he was called, pulling yet another popular idol down from its pedestal. Mencken's iconoclasm was accomplished with so much gusto and with such vigorous and picturesque language as to enchant a whole generation grown weary of the solemnity of much American writing. Indeed, the decade badly needed an iconoclast, for what later became almost exclusively thought of as "the jazz age" was also the era of the Ku Klux Klan and the Anti-Saloon League, of Babbittry and boosterism.

Mencken's essays in these volumes can be divided into two categories: literary criticism and criticism of the contemporary American scene. Literary criticism Mencken defined as a "catalytic process" in which the critic served as the catalyst. As a critic, however, Mencken derived mainly from James Huneker, whom he admired enormously and had known personally. Huneker had been familiar with Continental writers, then not too well known in America, and his criticism was essentially impressionistic, often couched in breezy, epigrammatic language. Mencken carried certain of these characteristics much further; indeed, his verbal acrobatics became his hallmark. His was a racy, pungent style very effective for the "debunking" then so popular and deliberately calculated to drive conservative readers into frenzies. Mencken's chief target, of which he never tired, was the Puritan tradition in American literature with its consequent timidity, stuffiness, and narrow-mindedness. As he saw it, the Puritan was afraid of esthetic emotion and thus could neither create nor enjoy art. This fear had inhibited American literature, he claimed, and had made American criticism timid and conventional. Further, criticism had fallen into the hands of the professors, and there was nothing—not even a prohibition agent—that Mencken detested so much as the average American university professor. Hence he heaped scorn on such men as Paul Elmer More, Irving Babbitt, Stuart P. Sherman, and William Lyon Phelps for years.

It is ironic that the critical writings of some of these men have withstood the passage of time more successfully than have those of Mencken. For though less a geographical provincial than they, he was more provincial in time and was interested mainly in the contemporary. Of the older native writers, he really admired only Edgar Allan Poe, Mark Twain, and Walt Whitman—the nonconformists. Even among the progressives of his age his preferences were curiously limited. He had great regard for Joseph Conrad and Theodore Dreiser, but he overlooked much of the talent that was budding during the 1920's. That he should have overpraised some of his contemporaries, James Branch Cabell, for example, or Dreiser, should not be held against him; few critics are sufficiently detached to escape this fault. Dreiser was an important writer but not the "colossal phenomenon" that Mencken called him.

Mencken's greatest failure as a critic was his blindness to poetry. In the third series of *Prejudices* he included an essay, "The Poet and His Art," a study so full of false assumptions, logical fallacies, and plain misstatements of fact as to be an embarrassing legacy for a critic to have left behind him. Because Dante Alighieri's theology was unacceptable to Mencken, he therefore judged that Dante could not really have believed what he wrote; according to

Mencken, *The Divine Comedy* (c. 1320) was a satire on the Christian doctrine of heaven and hell.

The essays dealing with the national scene were written in the same slashing manner and naturally infuriated far more readers, since Mencken here attacked men, institutions, and ideas familiar to everyone. Many of these pieces retained little significance in later times, for they dealt with situations reserved for that particular decade. Yet some of them are valid still: "The Sahara of the Bozart" (second series) is in some ways almost as true of the South today as it was in 1920; his comments on the farmer ("The Husbandman," fourth series) are even more appropriate, and his dissections of such eminent figures as Theodore Roosevelt and Thorstein Veblen are still funny.

Of Americans in general, Mencken had a low opinion, considering them a mongrel people incapable of high spiritual aspiration. His opinion of democracy was equally low. It was, he felt, merely a scheme to con the have-nots in their unending battle with the haves. The inferiority of Americans Mencken attributed to the lack of a genuine aristocracy and to Puritanism. Without an aristocracy, there could be no real leadership in America, and the vacuum would inevitably be filled by politicians, whom he detested. Nor did he have any faith in reform or reformers.

As for Puritanism, Mencken believed that it had always been the dominant force in American history and had left Americans the narrow-minded victims of religious bigotry. The predominance during the 1920's of the more extreme forms of religious fundamentalism gave some support to his argument. In his attacks on religion, however, he made the mistake of throwing the baby out with the bathwater. Because he himself was a complete skeptic, he could not believe that there could be intelligent and yet sincere Christians.

Mencken's enemies were always urging him, in anguished tones, to leave this country if he found it so distasteful. His reply was that nowhere else could so much entertainment be had so cheaply. According to his calculations, it cost him personally only eighty cents a year to maintain Warren Harding in the White House. Where could a better show be found for the money? In spite of his exaggerations, crudities, and often bad taste, Mencken performed a valuable service as a national gadfly, and his cynical wit provided the sting at just the right historic moment.

Bibliography:

Fitzpatrick, Vincent. *H. L. Mencken.* New York: Continuum, 1989. Assesses Mencken's influence on American life and letters through the presentation of significant relationships and battles. Notes Mencken's intent in *Prejudices* to attack cherished beliefs and stir up his fellow Americans.

Geismar, Maxwell. *The Last of the Provincials: The American Novel, 1915-1925.* Boston: Houghton Mifflin, 1949. Views Mencken as the dominant literary voice of the 1920's, supporting the conquest of American values of older rural life. Concludes that *Prejudices* reflects his efforts to champion the new economic order of industrialization over Puritan conscience and the reaches of the American hinterland.

Kazin, Alfred. *On Native Ground: An Interpretation of Modern American Prose Literature.* New York: Reynal & Hitchcock, 1942. Classic treatment of the emergence of modern American literature. Considers Mencken's capacity for imposing his skepticism on the new generation. Believes Mencken is the perfect illustration of America's passage into the second half of the twentieth century.

Lippman, Walter. "H. L. Mencken." *Saturday Review of Literature* (December 11, 1926): 413-415. One of the earliest and most astute assessments of Mencken's ideas. Insists that

Mencken's effectiveness lies in his ability to alter prejudices. Sees Mencken as a personal force overwhelmingly preoccupied with popular culture working for the liberty of an ideal democracy.

Williams, W. H. A. *H. L. Mencken*. Boston: Twayne, 1977. A chronological study of Mencken's life, focusing on the development of his ideas and the way he draws on them throughout his criticism. Evaluates Mencken's social criticism in the 1920's and concludes that his involvement with the struggle between the countryside and the city, as shown in *Prejudices*, was his major theme of the decade.

THE PRELUDE
Or, The Growth of a Poet's Mind

Type of work: Poetry
Author: William Wordsworth (1771-1850)
First published: 1850

The Prelude: Or, The Growth of a Poet's Mind, which was not published until shortly after William Wordsworth's death in 1850, was planned as the introductory section of a long autobiographical and philosophical poem that was never finished, entitled *The Recluse.* In that ambitious work, Wordsworth intended to trace in blank verse the development of his views on humanity, society, and nature. Of the projected three parts, only the second, *The Excursion* (1814), written between 1799 and 1805, was completed and published. The important "Friend" to whom the poem is addressed is Samuel Taylor Coleridge.

Wordsworth strongly advocated the use of poetry for the expression of individual emotions and insights. *The Prelude* contains many fine passages that illustrate the clarity and force of his use of language to provide both a precise description of nature and a grasp of its meaning. Although the poem contains long prosaic stretches, it also conveys a sense of the calm beauty and power of nature that distinguishes Wordsworth's verse.

The work begins with an account of the poet's childhood in the English Lake Country. With many digressions addressed to nature and its power, wisdom, and infusing spirit, the poet describes the influence of nature on his solitary childhood. Some of the sense of awe and pleasure that he found in nature, as well as some of his clearest and most penetrating use of diction, is evident in the passage in which he describes having found a boat in a cave, unchaining the boat, and rowing out into the center of a lake:

> . . . lustily
> I dipped my oars into the silent lake,
> And, as I rose upon the stroke, my boat
> Went heaving through the water like a swan;
> When, from behind that craggy steep till then
> The horizon's bound, a huge peak, black and huge,
> As if with voluntary power instinct
> Upreared its head. I struck and struck again,
> And growing still in stature the grim shape
> Towered up between me and the stars, and still,
> For so it seemed, with purpose of its own
> And measured motion like a living thing,
> Strode after me.

The image of the peak is invested with such simplicity and power that it is transformed into a force conveying both terror and beauty to the guilty boy who has stolen a ride in a boat.

The poet speaks of his youthful love of freedom and liberty, which he enjoyed in rambles through the woods and on mountain paths where he did not feel fettered by the claims of society and schoolwork. He makes sure to reassure the reader, however, that he was outwardly docile and obedient, keeping his rebellion and sense of freedom in the realm of the spirit. This combination of outward calm and inward rebellion helps explain Wordsworth's ability to control highly individualistic thought in calm, dignified, unostentatious verse forms and diction. Wordsworth does not use the speech of common man; indeed, his speech is often abstract, speculative, and pervaded with a sense of the mystery and meaning of nature. Yet at its best Wordsworth's diction has a dignity and calm control, a lack of pretense, through which the force of his inner meaning gently radiates.

Wordsworth describes his journey through Cambridge, telling of experiences there and discussing the fact that he neither was nor cared to be a scholar. Despite his studies, he continues to concentrate inwardly on the spirit of things, the power of nature, and the impetus nature gives to his feelings. At this point, Wordsworth begins to speculate on the differences between reason and emotion or passion, to equate reason with scholars and emotion with his own apprehension of the world of nature:

> But all the meditations of mankind,
> Yea, all the adamantine holds of truth
> By reason built, or passion, which itself
> Is highest reason in a soul sublime;

Throughout the poem, Wordsworth makes the distinction between reason and passion, and he attributes an ultimate sterility to the quality of reason while glorifying the element of passion or imagination.

Wordsworth tells of traveling to the Alps after leaving Cambridge. The mountains there reminded him of the mountains familiar to him from his childhood, and he felt again and even more keenly that the majesty and awe of the scenery found reflection in his spirit. He begins, more strongly, to feel his kinship with nature and juxtaposes that with a description of his life among the crowds and industries of London after his return from Europe. Dissatisfied with life in London, he describes going to France during the early stages of the French Revolution. In this section he expresses his feeling that he had not cared for human beings sufficiently and that, in his devotion to nature, he has neglected his feeling for his fellow creatures. Recalling his early love for freedom and liberty and adding his new conviction of the importance of political liberty, Wordsworth became strongly attracted to the cause of the French Revolution, feeling, as he says in *The Prelude*, that he was tied emotionally and spiritually to the popular struggle against the monarchy. The bloodiness of the revolution, however, and popular ingratitude and refusal to acknowledge the heroes who championed its cause with greatest fervor and sincerity, disillusioned Wordsworth. He began to feel that blood had poisoned the cause of liberty and returned to England.

Disillusioned and alone, he sought to bring meaning back into his life. The penultimate section of *The Prelude* is titled "Imagination and Taste, How Impaired and Restored." At that period of his life he turned back to nature, finding there not solace alone but a sense of law and order lacking in human society. He began to realize the difference in scale between nature and people and the range and effect of nature in comparison to the tiny ineffectuality of human beings. Sections of resolution in the poem frequently include passages such as the following interpolation in the midst of a narrative section:

> O Soul of Nature! that, by laws divine
> Sustained and governed, still dost overflow
> With an impassioned life, what feeble ones
> Walk on this earth!

In his view, nature provides not only awe and spiritual impetus for human beings but also order, rules of conduct, and the means of molding human behavior. In the final sections of the poem,

Wordsworth uses nature as the authority for his new morality and assumes a much more overtly moral tone. He didactically advocates the importance of faith and obedience and of not relying on unaided human reason. What was, in the earlier sections, the praise of emotion and freedom in opposition to rational restraint here becomes the praise of the restraint of faith and spirit in opposition to rational license. This change is illustrative of a change in Wordsworth's career from the poet advocating the simple joy and freedom of nature to the sage defending abstract and conventional truths. His attitude becomes clear in the following passage from the conclusion of the poem:

> . . . but, the dawn beginning now
> To re-appear, 'twas proved that not in vain
> I had been taught to reverence a Power
> That is the visible quality and shape
> And image of right reason; that matures
> Her processes by steadfast laws; gives birth
> To no impatient or fallacious hopes,
> No heat of passion or excessive zeal,
> No vain conceits; provokes to no quick turns
> Of self-applauding intellect; but trains
> To meekness, and exalts by humble faith.

The Prelude documents Wordsworth's changing attitudes toward nature and human beings while at the same time reflecting the different characteristics of his diction and poetic power. No other single poem expresses his reverence for nature with such power and simplicity. *The Prelude* is truly a monument to Wordsworth's career, evolving ideas, and transforming use of poetry.

Bibliography:
Bloom, Harold, ed. *William Wordsworth's "The Prelude."* New York: Chelsea House, 1986. Contains an introductory essay with a comprehensive overview of *The Prelude* as well as nine essays on the poem. Includes a chronology and a bibliography.
Drabble, Margaret. *Wordsworth.* New York: Arco, 1969. A short introductory study of Wordsworth's life and works for the general reader. Chapter 4, in which Drabble discusses *The Prelude*, notes that the various texts of the poem cover a long period in Wordsworth's life, during which his style and opinions changed considerably.
Lindenberger, Herbert. *On Wordsworth's "Prelude."* Princeton, N.J.: Princeton University Press, 1963. Asserts that much of the success of *The Prelude* is due to the manner in which Wordsworth was able to find a mode of language and organization to encompass his poem's personal history and prophetic utterance.
Noyes, Russell. *William Wordsworth.* Updated by John O. Hayden. Boston: Twayne, 1991. Provides an overview of Wordsworth's life and works. Chapter 4 deals with *The Prelude* and notes that the poem is an idealization, not a factual rendering, of the poet's life.
Wordsworth, William. *"The Prelude," 1799, 1805, 1850.* Edited by Jonathan Wordsworth, M. H. Abrams, and Stephen Gill. New York: W. W. Norton, 1979. Contains excerpts from sixteen sources of contemporary reaction to Wordsworth's poem as well as seven modern critical essays. Also includes a selected bibliography and chronology of Wordsworth's life.

PRELUDES FOR MEMNON

Type of work: Poetry
Author: Conrad Aiken (1889-1973)
First published: 1931

Conrad Aiken produced a remarkable variety of works, encompassing many different literary genres, among them short stories, novels, literary criticism, and a fascinating stream-of-conscious autobiographical essay. Any one of these works would mark him an important literary figure in the twentieth century. His greatest literary accomplishment, however, emerges in his poetry.

For many reasons, Aiken has been largely neglected by the academic and critical establishments. A quite individual and extremely personal writer, he never fit conveniently into any particular poetic movement. Unlike such poets of his time as e. e. cummings, he was not interested in challenging poetic form and line; he did not use poetry as a means of social comment as W. H. Auden and Stephen Spender did, nor was he a Symbolist in the tradition of T. S. Eliot and William Butler Yeats. Aiken is a more traditional poet; in many ways, in fact, he is a descendant of the Romantic movement. He built on the traditional form, using elements from a variety of styles to form his personal poetic search for meaning.

Aiken's poetry challenges the imagination by presenting complex images and ideas that are not always readily accessible to the reader. Although his language is elegant and expressive, he seldom uses sustained descriptions to illustrate a theme. For the most part, his poetry is reflective rather than dramatic. Metaphors appear, are dropped, and reappear almost at random. This is particularly true in *Preludes for Memnon,* which has as an alternative title, *Preludes to Attitude.* This series of sixty-three poems, taken together with its companion work, *Time in the Rock* (1936), also called *Preludes to Definition*, forms the core of Aiken's most mature work and contains the central themes and ideas in his writing. It is a series of meditations, images to greet the day. None of the individual poems is given an individual title, and there is no theme that builds from one poem to another. Instead, each poem deals with a separate song or search for attitude. Each explores a new theme or presents a different reflection on an old theme.

The title figure, Memnon, is the son of Tithonus, a mortal, grandson of the king of Troy and Eos, the goddess of the dawn. After the death of Hector, Troy's greatest warrior, Memnon attempted to avenge him but was slain by Achilles. Eos' grief at the loss of her son was so great that Zeus, moved to pity, made Memnon immortal. The name Memnon was also connected with a seventy-foot column in Alexandria dedicated to Amenhotep III. In 27 B.C.E., the column was partly destroyed by an earthquake; it remained standing, but the earthquake had produced an unusual phenomenon in the column: When the sun's rays first touched it each dawn, musical sounds resembling harp strings could be heard. These were interpreted as Memnon greeting his mother, the dawn.

Aiken's concern is with the individual's search for identity. In a preface, written in 1965, to the joint publication of *Preludes for Memnon* and *Time in the Rock*, Aiken states the dilemma that inspired the poems. At a time when Sigmund Freud, Albert Einstein, Charles Darwin, and Friedrich Nietzsche had redefined the world and the old religions, philosophy, ethics, language, and poetry were no longer able to answer the questions raised by science and mathematics, Aiken wanted to explore ways in which human beings could search for belief. For Aiken, it was vital that people search both inside the self and outside, in the world. The first prelude begins with a discussion of winter, the reality in nature, and the symbolic meaning of winter in the soul:

Winter is there, outside, is here in me:
Drapes the planets with snow, deepens the ice on the moon,
Darkens the darkness that was already darkness.
The mind too has its snows, its slippery paths,
Walls bayoneted with ice, leaves ice-encased.

As the poem continues, Aiken introduces other motifs, which recur repeatedly at random places throughout the collection: the void; chaos; memory, which here appears as a juggler balancing the colored balls of inconsequential human action and thoughts; the distorting mirror; silence. Aiken ends by describing the angelic and demoniac wings that conjure the echo of the abyss, of death. With the poem's final line, Aiken reminds his reader: "And this is you."

This prelude provides no simple picture; it is, rather, part of Aiken's attempt to define the complex and shifting realities in human identity. Because Aiken believed that identity lies within human consciousness, his poetry explores that world. It is a place of ever-changing focuses, new ideas, contradictory thoughts. Paradox is central to many of the preludes. Aiken presents the contrasts between growth and dying, birth and death, winter and summer, silence and sound. Understanding these contrasts provides the only way to establish identity or, indeed, to protect the soul in a changing, impermanent universe.

Critics often turn to Aiken's own life to explain his fascination with identity and paradox. In *Ushant* (1952), his autobiographical essay, Aiken recalls the tragic event that shaped his life and psyche forever. When he was eleven, his father had killed his mother and then shot himself; having heard the shot, Aiken had gone to their room and discovered them. With this tragedy, he wrote later, he lost his parents physically but found himself tied to them forever. After their death, his brothers were sent to live together with family in Georgia, while he was sent alone to be raised by relatives in New England.

Aiken became interested in Freud and his theories, feeling he must continually search for self-understanding, balance, and harmony. He always remained aware of the dark side of existence, both in nature and in human beings; yet he also saw hope, and his poems examine these differing aspects of human nature, together and separately.

A major theme, symbol, and controlling device in Aiken's poetry is music. The idea of a prelude or introduction provides a key to the poems as individual examinations of meaning that resemble Memnon's morning greetings to his mother. Music imposes order on sound, and Aiken uses the imagery of music in many ways. Prelude 4 begins with the image of music springing out of silence to bring delight. Such joy does not always last, and prelude 5 describes symbols of despair, things broken and spilled while "the string snaps, and the music stops." Prelude 9 equates beauty and music, and prelude 21 compares human lives to a series of notes: Daily, people rise to the first simple note and by evening the chord breaks and is silent.

Time is the subject of many preludes. Prelude 28, for example, begins with the clock announcing that time has come, and it continues to remind of the passage of time, of days coming and going; in conclusion, the heart ticks like the clock. Prelude 19 is a reminder that, if one were to watch long enough, the cycle of existence could be seen to repeat itself over and over again.

Many poems face directly the paradox in human beings and nature. Prelude 13 introduces a question Aiken poses several times: How is it possible to find a beginning or an ending, when no such thing exists in nature? In the continuum of time, what enables an individual to point to a moment and say with certainty, yes, this is where something started or ended. Prelude 27 provides another study in the contrast and flux that exists in the world. Nothing remains; even love turns to other emotions. Yet Aiken presents the reverse as well; out of decay, a daffodil will grow. Aiken frequently reverses ideas to express paradox, as in prelude 50:

> The world is intricate, and we are nothing.
> The world is nothing: we are intricate.
> Alas, how simple to invert the world
> Inverting phrases.

The poem goes on to explore the ambiguous nature of human beings, capable of believing two disparate ideas, feeling two contradictory emotions at the same time. Prelude 49 reinforces the conflicts in human nature: People kill both what they hate and what they love; what distinguishes the two is that they kill what they love slowly and with far more subtlety.

In many poems, language, even poetry itself, is the subject. Aiken, whose choice of words is thoughtful and precise, laments the failure of language. Prelude 5 discusses symbol and its imperfect ability to convey thought. For him, each symbol is both more and less than it appears on the page. A symbol, he declares, is as transient as the ghost of a thought. Prelude 28 reinforces the imprecision of words that seem precise, requesting the reader to take someone else's words and change the meaning that person intended the words to have. This poem centers on the effect of inherited words. When people accept foreign definitions, they become slaves to meanings from other people's consciousness. Parents and ancestors hand down words that reflect their identity, which may be quite different from the reality that their descendants have experienced.

Ultimately, Aiken's poetry deals with the human need to deal with the contradictions and despair of the world. Individuals must use their own words, find an identity, discover balance. This is an ongoing task, a cycle without end; human beings must, as prelude 42 states, be forever vigilant, exploring their consciousness, redefining themselves, renewing their identity.

> Then say: I was a part of nature's plan:
> Knew her cold heart, for I was consciousness:
> Came first to hate her, and at last to bless;
> Believed in her; doubted; believed again.

Mary Mahony

Bibliography:

Aiken, Conrad. *Ushant.* New York: Duell, Sloan and Pearce, 1952. A thinly veiled autobiographical essay that provides enormous insight into Aiken's attitudes toward writing and life. An important introductory source to help readers understand the complex imagery in Aiken's poetry.

Denney, Reuel. *Conrad Aiken.* Minneapolis: University of Minnesota Press, 1964. An excellent introductory source, which provides brief biographical details with a detailed analysis of Aiken's central themes, stressing five major characteristics of his poetry. Clear analysis of the language, style, and themes in *Preludes to Memnon.*

Marten, Harry. *The Art of Knowing: The Poetry and Prose of Conrad Aiken.* Columbia: University of Missouri Press, 1988. Discusses the organization of the *Preludes to Memnon,* including Aiken's views on consciousness, identity, and the change and flow in the life cycle. Analyzes poetic line and style.

Martin, Jay. *Conrad Aiken: A Life of His Art.* Princeton, N.J.: Princeton University Press, 1962.

Traces Aiken's critical reputation and his development as a poet. Provides clear analysis of Aiken's style and themes, finding the *Preludes to Memnon* the central defining work of Aiken's career.

Spivey, Ted, and Arthur Waterman, eds. *Conrad Aiken: A Priest of Consciousness*. New York: AMS Press, 1989. An excellent collection of essays that provides clear insights into Aiken's work. Individual essays deal with Aiken's views on consciousness and language; essays on the *Preludes to Memnon* discuss metapoetics and provide a contextual reading of several poems.

THE PRETENDERS

Type of work: Drama
Author: Ludovico Ariosto (1474-1533)
Type of plot: Farce
Time of plot: c. 1500
Locale: Ferrara, Italy
First performed: 1509; first published, as *I suppositi*, 1509 (English translation, 1566)

> *Principal characters:*
> DULIPPO, posing as a servant, actually Erostrato
> EROSTRATO, posing as a student, actually Dulippo
> POLINESTA, a young lady of Ferrara
> DAMON, a wealthy merchant, her father
> CLEANDRO, an ancient doctor of law, her suitor
> A SIENESE, posing as Erostrato's father
> FILOGONO, a wealthy Sicilian merchant, father of Erostrato
> PASIFILO, a meddlesome parasite
> BALIA, Polinesta's nurse

The Story:

Balia, nurse to beautiful young Polinesta, was concerned over her mistress' practice of sleeping with her father's servant, Dulippo. Polinesta reproved Balia, reminding her that it was she who had first given Dulippo access to Polinesta's bedroom. Polinesta also reassured Balia by explaining that Dulippo was, in reality, not a servant, but Erostrato, the son of a wealthy Sicilian merchant. Having come to Ferrara to pursue his studies, he had fallen in love with Polinesta upon his arrival. Consequently, he had taken the name of his servant Dulippo and secured employment in the house of his beloved's father. Meanwhile, the true Dulippo had assumed the identity of Erostrato and occupied the house next door.

This affair had been going on for two years, but now it was being complicated by the fact that the doddering old doctor of law, Cleandro, had become a suitor for Polinesta's hand, tempting her father with an offer of two thousand ducats. The real Erostrato was attempting to forestall him by having the false Erostrato ask for her, too, and by having him meet Cleandro's offer.

The old doctor arrived in the company of his ever-hungry parasite, Pasifilo, and the two ladies retired. Cleandro's eyesight was so bad that he could not tell who they were. Under Pasifilo's prodding, Cleandro boasted that he would go to any price to secure Polinesta. He had, he claimed, amassed a fortune of ten thousand ducats during the time he had lived in Ferrara, and he boasted that this was the second fortune he had made. The first he had lost at the fall of Otranto twenty years before. That loss, he recalled sadly, was nothing to the loss of his five-year-old son, captured by the Turks during the battle.

After Cleandro had gone, the false Dulippo appeared to invite Pasifilo to dinner. The false Erostrato confronted the false Dulippo with bad news: Damon, Polinesta's father, doubted Erostrato's ability to match Cleandro's offer for his daughter. The two connivers agreed that they must devise some ruse to convince the grasping merchant of their ability to pay.

The false Dulippo, to alienate Cleandro and Pasifilo, told the old doctor that Pasifilo had insulted Cleandro, illustrating the insults in an extremely comic way. After Cleandro left enraged, the false Erostrato arrived, this time with good news. He had met a foolish Sienese gentleman whom he had frightened with the claim that all visitors from Siena would be persecuted in Ferrara. The Sienese had sought protection by agreeing to pose as Erostrato's father. He would meet any sum that Cleandro could offer.

The trick was never played. Damon had overheard Balia quarreling with a servant over the propriety of Polinesta's conduct and had learned of his daughter's two-year-old affair. Dulippo and Balia were thrown into Damon's private dungeon. Damon, aware of the extralegal nature of this procedure, swore the servant to secrecy, but, unknown to him, Pasifilo, who had been sleeping off an attack of indigestion in the stables nearby, had awakened in time to overhear everything.

Meanwhile, to complicate matters further, Filogono, Erostrato's true father, had arrived from Sicily. He had written asking Erostrato to return home but his pleas had been ignored, and he had decided to come in person for his son. He was conducted to Erostrato's house by a local innkeeper. The false Erostrato saw him in time, however, and attempted to hide.

A hilarious bit of byplay followed in which the Sienese, aided by Erostrato's servants, on the one hand, and Filogono, assisted by his servants, on the other, both claimed to be Erostrato's father. Finally Filogono espied the false Erostrato, whom he knew as his servant Dulippo, and called on him to substantiate his claim. He was confounded when the real Dulippo declared that he was Erostrato, that the Sienese was Filogono of Sicily, and that the old man was an impostor or mad. Certain that Dulippo had done away with his son, Filogono went off to seek aid from the authorities.

Pasifilo arrived to cadge a dinner from Erostrato. Concerned over the affair with Filogono, for he really loved the old man who had been a father to him, the false Erostrato asked Pasifilo if he had seen Dulippo, and Pasifilo told him the whole story of the discovery and imprisonment. Afraid that the ruse had gone too far, the servant rushed off to confess all to Filogono, leaving Pasifilo, to the latter's delight, in charge of the dinner.

Filogono returned with the lawyer he had retained—old Cleandro. He explained how his trusted servant whom he had saved from the Turks twenty years before had betrayed him. On hearing his story, Cleandro closely questioned Filogono about the boy. To Cleandro's delight, the real Dulippo turned out to be the old man's long-lost son.

Next came Damon. Polinesta had revealed the whole truth of her affair, and he had rushed out to check up on her claim that his servant was actually the wealthy and highborn Erostrato.

Finally the false Erostrato returned to make his confession, and all the entanglements were straightened out. The true Erostrato was released and united with his mistress, whom his father promised to procure as his bride—thereby pacifying Damon. Cleandro renounced his claim on Polinesta; he had wanted a wife only to produce an heir and now he had one in the true Dulippo. Even Cleandro and Pasifilo were reconciled, and Pasifilo was given a permanent invitation to dine at Cleandro's house.

Critical Evaluation:

Ludovico Ariosto, best known for his epic masterpiece *Orlando furioso* (1516, 1532), wrote many other works. His four comedies include *The Pretenders*. There are two basic versions of *The Pretenders*: The first was a prose edition, produced in Ferrara in 1509 and enacted in the ducal palace, and the second was reworked in verse and performed ten years later in Rome for Pope Leo X. The story and action of both versions are the same, but the second, versified one is more developed. The dialogue is more intricate at times, and central figures have more depth. Comedy emerged in the late fifteenth and early sixteenth centuries as a major form of dramatic literature in Italy, and Ariosto was a crucial element in its popularity and in its influence on literature in other European countries. *The Pretenders* was written and debuted not only in a thriving, leading center of Italian theater, but also at the theater's zenith.

Ariosto was a poet and humanist employed in the service of several members of the politically dominant Este family in Ferrara during the early sixteenth century. Besides his administrative duties, he found time for study and composition. The works that resulted were written for his courtly audience, and, because of his ties with the court, his works were performed publicly. His minor works include his comedies, and he quickly earned a reputation as a skilled composer who was able not only to provide entertainment but also to incorporate into his plays his acquaintance with Renaissance humanistic studies of classical (ancient) literature.

Ariosto's reflection of classical Roman literature is known as erudite comedy; it is a style based upon the poet's familiarity with and a conscious imitation of ancient works. *The Pretenders* mirrors the story of the ancient Roman playwright, Titus Plautus, and his *Menaechmi* (late third or early second century B.C.E.). The basis of both plays is mistaken identities and humorous situations, and, eventually, all players become aware of the true identities of one another—which results in a happy resolution of the confused situation. Ariosto also drew upon Plautus' other plays and the works of another Roman author, Terence, for formation of some of the characters and incidents in *The Pretenders*.

Italian critics have tended to dismiss erudite comedy as an artificial, unimaginative imitation of Roman comedies with no true appeal of its own as literature; however, the Renaissance Italian comics did not seek to create a new, innovative form of drama. Ariosto and other Renaissance litterateurs drew upon their humanistic studies of antiquity. The audience recognized the works of ancient authors. *The Pretenders*, as other contemporary Italian comedies, however, also accomplished other aims. *The Pretenders* furthered the evolution of Italian as a literary language and reflects Ariosto's historical situation. The comedy is set in his own city, in his own time, and with stereotypical characters that the audience would have readily recognized. Above all, it was designed as earthy, ribald, pleasing entertainment.

In contrast with earlier humanistic playwrights who adopted classical figures or settings for their plays (Poliziano's *Orfeo*, 1480, for example), Ariosto and other erudite comic writers adhere to the structure of classical plays while setting them in contemporary situations. The plays of Plautus and Terence follow a pattern of five acts; this pattern was considered a rule to be followed absolutely. Ariosto followed this rule, but some of the individual scenes do not advance the action; these scenes have been inserted for their own sake. Ancient authors and commentators hold to a tripartite development—three basic stages—for the unfolding of a play, and Ariosto follows that strategy. First, acts I and II present the general predicament of the central figures. The audience learns that Erostrato and Dulippo have exchanged identities and the audience learns why they have done so. Second, acts III and IV introduce complications, incidents that arise from the characters' intentional confusion of identities—but the complications were not anticipated by the characters. The intensified efforts of Cleandro as a suitor for Polinesta and the arrival of the true Filogono are examples of these complications. Third, act V resolves the situation, but it does so in a way that surpasses the original contrivances; for example, the revelation of Dulippo as Cleandro's lost son provides an extra twist to the circumstances. Everyone is left happy.

The audience would have expected that the mistaken identities of the play's characters would lead to farcical situations. There are also other typical elements of erudite comedy in *The Pretenders*. There are servants who outwit nobles; parasites who do duty for patrons and thereby advance the action; figures who talk in asides to the playgoers; the unexpected arrival of persons who could unravel the scheme; and persons lost long ago, whose identities, in the play's denouement, are revealed. The audience would have enjoyed the amusement of distinct moments caused by all these features, but they would also have eagerly awaited the incidents which contained complications; the audience would have especially awaited the twist in the resolution. The forms of the comedy would have been unpredictable; therefore, although the essential style of Renaissance comedies, and *The Pretenders* in particular, would have been fundamentally formulaic, there would have been substantial opportunity for Ariosto to manipulate the specific situation to the enjoyment of his audience.

Contemporary life has a crucial role in the play. Regardless of the ancient Roman inspiration for the plot, the setting is entirely Italian. There are references to specific geographic and political features of the society of Ferrara. The invasion of the Italian peninsula by the Turks decades earlier not only reinforces the contemporary setting but also provides a key incident crucial to the successful resolution of the plot. Dulippo had become lost in the course of the Turkish incursion. Ariosto also reflects Italy's heritage of vernacular literature. The story of Erostrato, a rich noble youth, disguising himself as a servant in order to enjoy being with his desired love, comes from Giovanni Boccaccio's *Decameron* (1353), which helped to establish the Italian language as a vehicle for serious literature in the fourteenth century.

"Critical Evaluation" by Alan Cottrell

Bibliography:
Ariosto, Ludovico. *The Comedies of Ariosto*. Translated by Edmond M. Beame and Leonard G. Sbrocchi. Chicago: University of Chicago Press, 1975. Translations of Ludovico Ariosto's four comedies, including *The Pretenders*. Rendered into very enjoyable English with accompanying notes. Introduction situates Ariosto in his literary heritage and the historical circumstances of Renaissance Ferrara and discusses various themes and rhetorical devices that Ariosto employed in his comedies. Each play is briefly analyzed.
Griffin, Robert. *Ludovico Ariosto*. New York: Twayne, 1974. Critical study of Ariosto. Chapter 2 is devoted to consideration of his minor works, including *The Pretenders* and other satires and lyrics.
Orr, David. *Italian Renaissance Drama in England Before 1625: The Influence of "Erudita" Tragedy, Comedy, and Pastoral on Elizabethan and Jacobean Drama*. University of North Carolina Studies in Comparative Literature 49. Chapel Hill: University of North Carolina Press, 1970. Discussion of the general influence of Italian drama on English drama during the Renaissance. Includes evaluation of a 1566 translation of *The Pretenders*.
Radcliff-Umstead, Douglas. *The Birth of Modern Comedy in Renaissance Italy*. Chicago: University of Chicago Press, 1969. Explains the importance of interpreting Italian Renaissance comedy according to its historical setting.

PRIDE AND PREJUDICE

Type of work: Novel
Author: Jane Austen (1775-1817)
Type of plot: Domestic realism
Time of plot: Early nineteenth century
Locale: Rural England
First published: 1813

Principal characters:
MR. BENNET, the father of five daughters
MRS. BENNET, his wife
JANE BENNET, the oldest daughter and the family beauty
ELIZABETH BENNET, her father's favorite
MARY,
CATHERINE (KITTY), and
LYDIA BENNET, the younger sisters
MR. BINGLEY, an eligible bachelor
CAROLINE BINGLEY, his sister
MR. DARCY, Bingley's friend
MR. COLLINS, a vicar
LADY CATHERINE DE BOURGH, Darcy's aunt and Collins' patroness

The Story:

The chief business of Mrs. Bennet's life was to find suitable husbands for her five daughters. Consequently, she was elated when she heard that nearby Netherfield Park had been let to a Mr. Bingley, a gentleman from the north of England. Gossip reported him to be a rich and eligible young bachelor. Mr. Bingley's first public appearance in the neighborhood was at a ball. With him were his two sisters, the husband of the older, and Mr. Darcy, Bingley's friend. Bingley was an immediate success in local society, and he and Jane, the oldest Bennet daughter, a pretty girl of sweet and gentle disposition, were attracted to each other at once. His friend, Darcy, however, seemed cold and extremely proud and created a bad impression. In particular, he insulted Elizabeth Bennet, a girl of spirit and intelligence and her father's favorite, by refusing to dance with her when she was sitting down for lack of a partner; he said in her hearing that he was in no mood to prefer young ladies slighted by other men. On later occasions, however, he began to admire Elizabeth in spite of himself, and at one party she had the satisfaction of refusing him a dance.

Jane's romance with Bingley flourished quietly, aided by family calls, dinners, and balls. His sisters pretended great fondness for Jane, who believed them completely sincere. Elizabeth was more critical and discerning; she suspected them of hypocrisy, and quite rightly, for they made great fun of Jane's relations, especially her vulgar, garrulous mother and her two ill-bred officer-mad younger sisters. Miss Caroline Bingley, who was eager to marry Darcy and shrewdly aware of his growing admiration for Elizabeth, was especially loud in her ridicule of the Bennet family. Elizabeth herself became Caroline's particular target when she walked three miles through muddy pastures to visit Jane when she fell ill at Netherfield Park. Until Jane was able to be moved home, Elizabeth stayed to nurse her. During her visit, Elizabeth received enough attention from Darcy to make Caroline Bingley long sincerely for Jane's recovery. Her fears were not ill-founded. Darcy admitted to himself that he would be in some danger from the charm of Elizabeth, if it were not for her inferior family connections.

Elizabeth acquired a new admirer in Mr. Collins, a ridiculously pompous clergyman and a distant cousin of the Bennets, who would someday inherit Mr. Bennet's property because that gentleman had no male heir. Mr. Collins' patroness, Lady Catherine de Bourgh, had urged him to marry, and he, always obsequiously obedient to her wishes, hastened to comply. Thinking to alleviate the hardship caused the Bennet sisters by the entail that gave their father's property to him, Mr. Collins proposed to Elizabeth. Much to her mother's displeasure and her father's relief, she firmly and promptly rejected him. He almost immediately transferred his affections to Elizabeth's best friend, Charlotte Lucas, who, being twenty-seven years old and somewhat homely, accepted at once.

During Mr. Collins' visit and on one of their many walks to Meryton, the younger Bennet sisters, Kitty and Lydia, met a delightful young officer, Mr. Wickham, who was stationed with the regiment there. Outwardly charming, he became a favorite among all the ladies, including Elizabeth. She was willing to believe the story that he had been cheated out of an inheritance left to him by Darcy's father, who had been his godfather. Her belief in Darcy's arrogant and grasping nature deepened when Wickham did not come to a ball given by the Bingleys, a dance at which Darcy was present.

Soon after the ball, the entire Bingley party suddenly left Netherfield Park. They departed with no intention of returning, as Caroline wrote Jane in a short farewell note, in which she hinted that Bingley might soon become engaged to Darcy's sister. Jane believed that her friend Caroline was trying gently to tell her that her brother loved elsewhere and that she must cease to hope. Elizabeth, however, was sure of a plot by Darcy and Caroline to separate Bingley and Jane. She persuaded Jane that Bingley did love her and that he would return to Hertfordshire before the winter was over. Jane almost believed her, until she received a letter from Caroline assuring her that they were all settled in London for the winter. Even after Jane told her this news, Elizabeth remained convinced of Bingley's affection for her sister and deplored the lack of resolution that made him putty in the hands of his scheming friend.

About that time, Mrs. Bennet's sister, Mrs. Gardiner, an amiable and intelligent woman with a great deal of affection for her two oldest nieces, arrived for a Christmas visit. She suggested to the Bennets that Jane return to London with her for a rest and change of scene and—so it was understood between Mrs. Gardiner and Elizabeth—to renew her acquaintance with Bingley. Elizabeth was not hopeful for the success of the plan and pointed out that proud Darcy would never let his friend call on Jane in the unfashionable London street on which the Gardiners lived. Jane accepted the invitation, however, and she and Mrs. Gardiner set out for London.

The time drew near for the wedding of Elizabeth's friend Charlotte Lucas, who asked Elizabeth to visit her in Kent. Despite feeling that there could be little pleasure in such a visit, Elizabeth promised to do so. She did not approve of Charlotte's marrying simply for the sake of an establishment, and since she did not sympathize with her friend's decision, she thought their days of real intimacy were over. As March approached, however, she found herself eager to see her friend, and she set out with pleasure on the journey with Charlotte's father and sister. On their way, the party stopped in London to see the Gardiners and Jane. Elizabeth found her sister well and outwardly serene; she had not seen Bingley and his sisters had paid only one call. Elizabeth was sure Bingley had not been told of Jane's presence in London and blamed Darcy for keeping it from him.

Soon after arriving at the Collins' home, the whole party was honored, as Mr. Collins repeatedly assured them, by a dinner invitation from Lady Catherine de Bourgh. Elizabeth found her to be a haughty, ill-mannered woman and her daughter thin, sickly, and shy. Lady Catherine was extremely fond of inquiring into the affairs of others and giving them unsolicited advice. Elizabeth turned off her meddling questions with cool indirectness and saw from the effect that she was probably the first who had ever dared do so.

Soon after Elizabeth's arrival, Darcy came to visit his aunt and cousin. He called frequently at the parsonage, and he and Elizabeth resumed their conversational fencing matches, which culminated in a sudden and unexpected proposal of marriage; he couched his proposal, however, in such proud, even unwilling, terms that Elizabeth not only refused him but was able to do so indignantly. When he requested her reason for her emphatic rejection, she mentioned his part in separating Bingley and Jane, as well as his mistreatment of Wickham, whereupon he left abruptly. The next day, he brought a long letter in which he answered her charges. He did not deny his part in separating Jane and Bingley but gave as his reasons the improprieties of Mrs. Bennet and her younger daughters and also his sincere belief that Jane did not love Bingley. As for his alleged mistreatment of Wickham, he wrote that he had in reality acted most generously toward Wickham, who was an unprincipled liar and had repaid his kindness by attempting to elope with Darcy's young sister. At first incensed at the tone of the letter, Elizabeth was gradually forced to acknowledge the justice of some of what he wrote; she regretted having judged him so harshly but was relieved not to see him again before returning home.

There, she found her younger sisters clamoring to go to Brighton, where the regiment formerly stationed at Meryton had been ordered. When an invitation came to Lydia from a young officer's wife, Lydia was allowed to accept it over Elizabeth's protests. Elizabeth was asked by the Gardiners to go with them on a tour that would take them into Derbyshire, Darcy's home county. She accepted, reasoning that she was not very likely to meet Darcy merely by going into his county. While they were there, however, Mrs. Gardiner decided they should visit Pemberley, Darcy's home. Elizabeth made several excuses, but her aunt insisted. Only when she learned that the Darcy family was not in residence did Elizabeth consent to go along.

At Pemberley, an unexpected and embarrassing meeting took place between Elizabeth and Darcy. He was more polite than Elizabeth had ever known him to be, and he asked permission for his sister to call upon her. The call was duly paid and returned, but the pleasant intercourse between the Darcys and Elizabeth's party was suddenly cut short when a letter from Jane informed Elizabeth that Lydia had run away with Wickham. Elizabeth told Darcy what had happened, and she and the Gardiners left for home at once. After several days, the runaway couple was located and a marriage arranged between them. When Lydia came home as heedless as ever, she told Elizabeth that Darcy had attended her wedding. Suspecting the truth, Elizabeth learned from Mrs. Gardiner that it was indeed Darcy who brought about the marriage by giving Wickham money.

Soon after Lydia and Wickham left, Bingley came back to Netherfield Park, accompanied by Darcy. Elizabeth, now much more favorably inclined toward him, hoped his coming meant that he still loved her, but he gave no sign. Bingley and Jane, on the other hand, were still obviously in love with each other, and they soon became engaged, to the great satisfaction of Mrs. Bennet. Soon afterward, Lady Catherine paid the Bennets an unexpected call. She had heard it rumored that Darcy was engaged to Elizabeth. Hoping to marry her own daughter to Darcy, she had come to order Elizabeth not to accept the proposal. The spirited girl was not to be intimidated by the bullying Lady Catherine and coolly refused to promise not to marry Darcy, even though she was regretfully far from certain that she would have the opportunity to do so again. However, she did not have long to wonder. Lady Catherine, unluckily for her own purpose, repeated to Darcy the substance of her conversation with Elizabeth, and he knew

Elizabeth well enough to surmise that her feelings toward him must have greatly changed. He immediately returned to Netherfield Park, and he and Elizabeth became engaged. Pride had been humbled and prejudice dissolved.

Critical Evaluation:

In 1813, her thirty-eighth year, Jane Austen published her second novel *Pride and Prejudice*. She had begun this work in 1796, when she was twenty-one, calling it *First Impressions*. It had so delighted her family that her father had tried, without success, to have it published. Eventually Austen put it aside, probably not to return to it until her first published novel, *Sense and Sensibility*, appeared in 1811. The version entitled *First Impressions* is no longer extant, but it was presumably radically rewritten, since *Pride and Prejudice* is in no way an apprenticeship novel but a completely mature work. *Pride and Prejudice* continues to be the author's most popular novel, perhaps because readers share Darcy's admiration for the "liveliness" of Elizabeth Bennet's mind.

The original title, *First Impressions*, focuses on the initial errors of judgment out of which the story develops, whereas the title *Pride and Prejudice*, besides suggesting the kind of antithetical topic that delighted rationalistic eighteenth century readers, indicates the central conflicts that characterized the relationships between Elizabeth Bennet and Darcy, and between Jane Bennet and Bingley.

As in all of Austen's novels, individual conflicts are defined and resolved within a rigidly delimited social context, in which relationships are determined by wealth and rank. The oft-quoted opening sentence establishes the societal values that underlie the main conflict: "It is a truth universally acknowledged, that a single man in possession of a good fortune, must be in want of a wife." Mr. and Mrs. Bennet's opening dialogue concerning the eligible Bingley explores this truth. Devoid of individuality, Mrs. Bennet is nevertheless well attuned to society's edicts. Mr. Bennet, an individualist to the point of eccentricity, represents neither personal conviction nor social conviction, and he views with equal indifference Bingley's right to his own reason for settling there and society's right to see him primarily as a potential husband. Having repudiated society, Mr. Bennet cannot take seriously either the claims of the individual or the social order.

As the central character, Elizabeth, her father's favorite and her mother's least favorite child, must come to terms with the conflicting values implicit in her parents' antithetical characters. She is like her father in her scorn of society's conventional judgments, but she champions the concept of individual merit independent of money and rank. She is, indeed, prejudiced against the prejudices of society. From this premise, she attacks Darcy's pride, assuming that it derives from the causes that Charlotte Lucas identifies: "with family, fortune, everything in his favour . . . he has a right to be proud."

Flaunting her contempt for money, Elizabeth indignantly spurns Charlotte's advice that Jane ought to make a calculated play for Bingley's affections. She loftily argues, while under the spell of Wickham's charm, that young people who are truly in love should be unconcerned about financial standing. As a champion of the individual, Elizabeth prides herself on her discriminating judgment and boasts that she is a student of character. Significantly, it is Darcy who warns her against prejudiced conclusions, reminding her that her experience is quite limited. Darcy is not simply the representative of a society that primarily values wealth and consequence—as Elizabeth initially views him—but also a citizen of a larger society than the village to which Elizabeth has been confined by circumstance. Consequently, it is only when she begins to move into Darcy's world that she can judge with true discrimination both individual merit and the dictates of the society that she has rejected. Fundamentally honest, she revises her conclusions as new experiences warrant, and in the case of Darcy and Wickham she ends up radically altering her opinion.

More significant than the obviously ironic reversals, however, is the growing revelation of Elizabeth's unconscious commitment to society. Her original condemnation of Darcy's pride coincides with the verdict of Meryton society. Moreover, she shares society's regard for wealth. Even while denying the importance of Wickham's poverty, she countenances his pursuit of the ugly Miss King's fortune, discerning her own inconsistency only after she learns of his bad character. Most revealing, when Lydia Bennet runs off with Wickham, Elizabeth instinctively understands the judgment of society when she laments that Wickham would never marry a woman without money.

Almost unconsciously, Elizabeth acknowledges a connection between wealth and human values at the crucial moment when she first looks upon Pemberley, the Darcy estate. She is not entirely joking when she tells Jane that her love for Darcy began when she first saw his beautiful estate. Elizabeth's experiences, especially her discoveries of the well-ordered Pemberley and Darcy's tactful generosity to Lydia and Wickham, lead her to differentiate between Charlotte's theory that family and fortune bestow a "*right* to be proud" and Darcy's position that the intelligent person does not indulge in false pride. Darcy's pride is real, but it is regulated by responsibility. Unlike his aunt, Lady Catherine de Bourgh, who relishes the distinction of rank, he disapproves less of the Bennets' undistinguished family and fortune than of the lack of propriety displayed by most of the family. Therefore, Elizabeth scarcely overstates her case when, at the end, she assures her father that Darcy has no improper pride.

Elizabeth begins by rejecting the values and restraints of society as they are represented by such people as her mother, the Lucases, Miss Bingley, and Lady Catherine. Instead, she initially upholds the claims of the individual, which are elsewhere represented only by her whimsical father. By the end of the novel, the heart of her conflict appears in the contrast between her father and Darcy. She loves her father and has tried to overlook his lack of decorum in conjugal matters, but she has been forced to see that his freedom is really irresponsibility, the essential cause of Jane's misery as well as Lydia's amorality. The implicit comparison between Mr. Bennet's and Darcy's approach to matrimony illustrates their different methods of dealing with society's restraints. Unrestrained by society, having been captivated by the inferior Mrs. Bennet's youth and beauty, Mr. Bennet consulted only his personal desires and made a disastrous marriage. Darcy, in contrast, defies society only when he has made certain that Elizabeth is a woman worthy of his love and lifetime devotion.

When Elizabeth confronts Lady Catherine, her words are declarative not of absolute defiance of society but of the selective freedom that is her compromise and very similar to Darcy's: "I am only resolved to act in that manner, which will, in my own opinion, constitute my happiness, without reference to you, or to any person so wholly unconnected with me." Austen does not falsify the compromise. If Elizabeth dares with impunity to defy the society of Rosings, Longbourne, and Meryton, she does so only because Darcy is exactly the man for her and, further, because she can anticipate "with delight . . . the time when they should be removed from society so little pleasing to either, to all the comfort and elegance . . . at Pemberley." In a sense, her marriage to Darcy is a triumph of the individual over society; but, paradoxically, Elizabeth achieves her most genuine conquest of pride and prejudice only after she has accepted the full social value of her judgment that "to be mistress of Pemberley might be something!"

Granting the full force of the snobbery, the exploitation, the inhumanity of all the evils that diminish the human spirit and are inherent in a materialistic society, the novel clearly confirms the cynical "truth" of the opening sentence. At the same time, without evading the degree of Elizabeth's capitulation to society, it affirms the vitality and the independent life that is possible, at least to an Elizabeth Bennet. *Pride and Prejudice*, like its title, offers deceptively simple antitheses that yield up the complexity of life itself.

"Critical Evaluation" by Catherine E. Moore

Bibliography:
Bloom, Harold, ed. *Modern Critical Interpretations: Jane Austen's "Pride and Prejudice."* New York: Chelsea House, 1987. Contains nine essays treating such topics as manners and propriety, love, intelligence, and society. Includes a chronology and bibliography.
Brown, Julia Prewitt. *Jane Austen's Novels: Social Change and Literary Form*. Cambridge, Mass.: Harvard University Press, 1979. A response to critics who claim that Austen does not write about important issues because she writes about domestic life. Choosing a spouse points to life's complexity, which intelligent characters know; the foolish choose badly, dooming themselves and future generations.
Honan, Park. *Jane Austen: Her Life*. New York: St. Martin's Press, 1987. A detailed biography that depicts Austen's life and work and provides a portrait of England and the age. The chapter on *Pride and Prejudice* focuses on the novel's reflection of a changing society in which economics, social class, and character all affect individual happiness.
Mansell, Darrel. *The Novels of Jane Austen: An Interpretation*. New York: Barnes & Noble Books, 1973. An interesting interpretation that insists Austen is less interested in imitating reality than in depicting the psychological progress of Elizabeth and Darcy. The chapter on *Pride and Prejudice* provides an excellent analysis of Austen's use of irony.
Moler, Kenneth L. *"Pride and Prejudice": A Study in Artistic Economy*. Boston: Twayne, 1989. Intended as a student's companion to the novel, a useful book for the first-time reader of Jane Austen. Includes a historical context and critical reception of the novel. Also examines the themes of moral blindness and self-knowledge, art, and nature, as well as Austen's use of symbolism, language, and literary allusion.

THE PRINCE

Type of work: Politics
Author: Niccolò Machiavelli (1469-1527)
First published: Il principe, 1532 (English translation, 1640)

This is the book that gives meaning to the adjective "Machiavellian." It is an ingenious and fascinating study of the art of practical politics, composed by a man who never rose higher than the position of secretary to the Second Chancery in Florence. The success of his book can be attributed partly to his wit and partly to his having known some of the most clever and powerful rogues of the Renaissance. His model for the "prince" was Cesare Borgia, a man who used all means of conquest, including murder, to achieve and hold political power.

Niccolò Machiavelli never pretended that his book was a guide to the virtuous. On the other hand, he did not set out to prescribe the way to wickedness. He meant his account to be a practical guide to political power, and, through a combination of experience, logic, and imagination, he constructed one of the most intriguing handbooks of Western civilization: a primer for princes.

In beginning a discussion concerned with the manners and attitudes of a prince—that is, a ruler of a state—Machiavelli writes:

> Since . . . it has been my intention to write something which may be of use to the understanding reader, it has seemed wiser to me to follow the real truth of the matter rather than what we imagine it to be. For imagination has created many principalities and republics that have never been seen or known to have any real existence, for how we live is so different from how we ought to live that he who studies what ought to be done rather than what is done will learn the way to his downfall rather than to his preservation.

This passage makes it clear that Machiavelli intends to explain how successful politicians really work rather than how they ought to work.

The Prince begins with a one-paragraph chapter that illustrates Machiavelli's logical approach to the problem of advising prospective princes. He claims that all states are either republics or monarchies. Monarchies are either hereditary or new. New monarchies are either entirely new or acquired. Acquired states have either been dominated by a prince or been free; they are acquired either by a prince's own arms or by those of others; and they fall to him either by fortune or because of his own character and ability.

Having outlined this inclusive logical bifurcation, Machiavelli first discusses the problems connected with governing a hereditary monarchy, then discusses mixed monarchies.

In each case, as he develops his argument, Machiavelli considers what the logical alternatives are, and what should be done in each case if the prince is to acquire and hold power. In writing of mixed monarchies, for example, he points out that acquired states are either culturally similar to the conquering state or not, and then considers each possibility. If the acquired state is culturally similar, it is no problem to keep it; but if the acquired state is different in its customs, laws, or language, then there is a problem to be solved. One solution might be to have the ruler go to the acquired territory and live there. As an example, Machiavelli refers to the presence of the Turkish ruler in Greece.

Another possible solution to the problems resulting when an acquired territory differs culturally from the conquering state is the establishment of colonies. Colonies are inexpensive to acquire and maintain, he argues, because the land is acquired from a few landowners of the conquered territory and they are the only ones who complain. Such a plan is preferable to maintaining soldiers, for policing a new state not only is expensive but also offends the citizens being policed.

Thus, by the device of considering logical alternatives, Machiavelli uses his limited experience to build a guide to power. What he says, although refreshing in its direct approach to the hard facts of practical politics, is not entirely fanciful or naïve. Not only did Machiavelli, through his diplomatic missions, come to know intimately such leaders as Louis XII, Julius II, the Emperor Maximilian, and Cesare Borgia, but he also used his time to advantage, noting political tricks that actually worked and building up his store of psychological truths.

It is doubtful that any ruler or rebel ever succeeded simply because he followed Machiavelli to the letter, but it may well be that some political coups have been the result of inspiration from *The Prince*. (Shortly after Fidel Castro's overthrow of the Batista government in Cuba in 1959, a newspaper account reported that among the books on Castro's revolutionary reading list was *The Prince*.)

What is inspiring for the politically ambitious in *The Prince* is not the substance but the attitude, not the prescription but the unabashed, calculating, and aggressive air with which the author analyzes the means to power. For the reader without political ambition, *The Prince* is a sometimes amusing and sometimes frightening reminder of the realities of political fortune. For example, Machiavelli writes that one who helps a prince to power is bound to fall himself, because he has contributed to the success either by his cleverness or by his power, and no prince can tolerate the existence of either in another person close to him.

Machiavelli considers this question: Why did the kingdom of Darius, occupied by Alexander the Great, not rebel after Alexander's death? The answer is that monarchies are governed either by a prince and his staff, or by a prince and a number of barons. A monarchy controlled by the prince through his representatives is difficult to conquer, because the entire staff owes its existence to the prince and is, consequently, loyal. Once such a monarchy is captured, however, power is easily maintained. So it was in Alexander's case. On the other hand, a nation like the France of Machiavelli's day is ruled by a king and barons. The barons are princes of a sort over their portions of the state, and they maintain control over their subjects. It is easier to conquer such a state, because there are always unhappy barons willing to join a movement to overthrow the king. Once conquered, however, such a state is difficult to hold because the barons may regroup and overthrow the new prince.

Sometimes power is acquired through crime, Machiavelli admits, and he cites a violent example: the murder of Giovanni Fogliani of Fermo by his nephew Oliverotto. Machiavelli advises that the cruelty necessary to attain power be kept to a minimum and not be continued, for the purely practical reason that the prince will lose power otherwise. The best thing to do, Machiavelli says, is to commit one's acts of cruelty all at once, not over an extended period.

This cold practicality is echoed in such injunctions as those to the effect that if one cannot afford to be generous, then one must accept with indifference the name of miser; it is safer to be feared than to be loved, if one must choose; a prince need not have a morally worthwhile character, but he must appear to have it; if a prince's military support is good, he will always have good friends; to keep power one must be careful not to be hated by the people; it is always wiser for a prince to be a true friend or a true enemy than to be neutral; a prince should never listen to advice unless he asks for it; and it is better to be bold than cautious.

Machiavelli's prime examples are Francesco Sforza and Cesare Borgia, particularly the latter. The author writes that he is always able to find examples for his points by referring to the deeds of Borgia. Considering the value of using auxiliary arms, the military force of another state, Machiavelli refers to Borgia's unfortunate experience with auxiliaries in the capture of Romagna. Finding the auxiliaries untrustworthy, Borgia turned to mercenaries, but they were no better, so he finally used only his own troops. Machiavelli's conclusion in regard to auxiliary troops is that "If any one . . . wants to make sure of not winning he will avail himself of troops such as these."

After reviewing Cesare Borgia's rise to power (with the remark that "I could not suggest better precepts to a new prince than the examples of Cesare's actions"), Machiavelli concludes that "I can find nothing with which to reproach him, rather it seems that I ought to point him out as an example . . . to all those who have risen to power by fortune or by the arms of others." This praise follows a description of such acts as Borgia's killing of as many of the hapless lords he had despoiled "as he could lay hands on."

Machiavelli praises the actions of other leaders, such as Francesco Sforza and popes Alexander VI and Julius II, but only Cesare Borgia wins unqualified praise. Sforza, for example, is recognized as having become duke of Milan "by the proper means and through his own ability," but later on he is criticized because of a castle he built when he should have been trying to win the goodwill of the people.

The Prince concludes with a plea to the Medici family to free Italy from the "barbarians" who ruled the republic of Florence and kept Italy in bondage. Machiavelli makes a plea for liberation, expresses his disappointment that Borgia is not available because of a turn of fortune, and closes with the capitalized cry that "THIS BARBARIAN OCCUPATION STINKS IN THE NOSTRILS OF ALL OF US."

Unfortunately for the author, his plea to the Medici family did him no good, and he died with the Republic still in power. Perhaps he himself was not bold enough; perhaps he was not cruel enough. In any case, he left behind a work to be used by any leader who is willing to be both.

Bibliography:
Burnham, James. *The Machiavellians: Defenders of Freedom.* New York: John Day, 1943. Presents the theories of power advocated by Machiavelli in *The Prince.* Gives a positive critique of those theories. Summarizes the principles of all Machiavellian writers and their effect on succeeding centuries.

Garver, Eugene. "*The Prince*: A Neglected Rhetorical Classic." In *Machiavelli and the History of Prudence.* Madison: University of Wisconsin Press, 1987. Asserts that *The Prince* should be studied as a work of rhetoric as well as from nonliterary standpoints. Reveals rhetorical principles found in *The Prince* and shows how they contribute to Renaissance rhetoric.

Gilbert, Felix. *Machiavelli and Guicciardini: Politics and History in Sixteenth-Century Florence.* Princeton, N.J.: Princeton University Press, 1965. Presents Machiavelli as a victim of late fifteenth century Florentine politics and shows the relationship between those events and the writing of *The Prince.* Good bibliographic essay on Machiavelli.

Parel, Anthony. "*The Prince.*" In *The Machiavellian Cosmos.* New Haven, Conn.: Yale University Press, 1992. Emphasizes Machiavelli's combination of virtue and fortune in relationship to principalities. Discusses how *The Prince* used that relationship to explain past and present principalities with logical consequences of power and glory.

Rudowski, Victor. *The Prince: A Historical Critique.* New York: Twayne, 1992. Puts *The Prince* in historical context. Defines terms and identifies individuals in *The Prince.* Presents the impact of the book on European monarchs for several centuries. Includes the initial critical reception of Machiavelli's masterpiece.

THE PRINCE AND THE PAUPER

Type of work: Novel
Author: Mark Twain (Samuel Langhorne Clemens, 1835-1910)
Type of plot: Social satire
Time of plot: Sixteenth century
Locale: England
First published: 1881

> *Principal characters:*
> Tom Canty, a London street beggar
> John Canty, his father
> Edward, the Prince of Wales
> Miles Hendon, a disinherited knight
> Hugh Hendon, his brother
> Hugo, a thief

The Story:

Tom Canty and the Prince of Wales were born in London on the same day, the first unwanted and the second long awaited. While the prince, Edward Tudor, lay robed in silks, Tom Canty grew up in the filth of Offal Court. When he was still a small child, Tom's father forced him to beg during the day, and he beat the boy at night. Gathering a ragtag court of street urchins around him, Tom often pretended that he was a prince. One day, hoping to see Prince Edward of England, he invaded the royal precincts, but when he tried to approach the prince he was cuffed by a guard and ordered away. Edward, who had witnessed the incident, protected Tom and took the young beggar into the palace. There, in the privacy of Edward's chamber, Tom confessed his longing to be a prince. When the two boys exchanged garments, they discovered that they were identical in appearance. Before they could switch clothes again, Edward was mistaken for the beggar boy and thrown out of the palace. He wandered helplessly in the streets, mocked by people whom he approached with pleas that they pay homage to him as their rightful prince.

In the palace, it was thought that the prince had gone mad because he could recall none of the royal matters that he was supposed to know. King Henry issued an edict that no one should discuss the royal lapse of memory, and the princesses Mary and Elizabeth kindly tried to aid their supposed brother, who by that time was too frightened to confess that he was Tom Canty, a beggar dressed in the prince's clothing.

While he was ill, King Henry VIII had given the great seal of the kingdom to Prince Edward for safekeeping. When Henry demanded the return of his seal, Tom reported that he did not know where it was.

The Prince of Wales was still wandering the streets as a homeless waif when King Henry died. Edward was found by John Canty, Tom's father, and brought to Offal Court, but during the wild celebration of the ascension to the throne of the Prince of Wales, Edward escaped from his supposed father. Again tormented by crowds who laughed at his protests that he was now the king of England, Edward was rescued by Miles Hendon, the disinherited son of a baronet. Thinking Edward was mad, Miles pitied the little boy and pretended to pay him the homage due to a monarch.

Miles had loved a girl named Edith, who was coveted by Miles's brother Hugh. Hugh had gained his father's confidence by trickery, and Miles had been turned from home. Edward declared that Miles had suffered unjustly and promised the adventurer any boon he might ask. Recalling the story of De Courcy, who, given a similar opportunity by King John, requested that he and all of his descendants might be permitted to wear hats in the presence of the king of England, Miles wisely asked that he be permitted to sit in Edward's presence, for the young king had been ordering Miles about like a personal servant.

Having had the role of king of England thrust upon him, Tom was slowly learning to conduct himself royally. Because his attendants thought him mad, he was able to be honest about his lack of training and his failure to recall events that would have been familiar to Edward. At the same time, his gradual improvement offered hope that his derangement was only temporary.

John Canty lured Edward away from Miles's protection and took the boy to Southwark to join a pack of thieves there. Still vainly declaring himself king, Edward again became the center of ridicule. One of the thieves, Hugo, undertook to teach Edward the tricks of his trade. Making his escape, Edward wandered to a farmhouse where a kind woman, pitying the poor, insane beggar boy who declared himself king of England, fed him. Edward wandered on to the hut of a hermit who naïvely accepted Edward's claim to royalty. In turn, the hermit, who really was mad, revealed to Edward that he was an archangel. While Edward slept, the hermit brooded over the wrongs done him by King Henry. Believing Edward to be the king, as he had claimed, the hermit planned to murder him. He managed to tie up the boy while he slept. John Canty and Hugo, following the trail of the escaped waif, rescued him and forced him to rejoin the band of rogues. Again he was compelled to aid Hugo in his dishonest trade. At last, Miles found the boy and saved him.

Miles was on his way back to Hendon Hall to claim his heritage and Edith for a wife. When they arrived at their destination, they found that Miles's father was dead and that Hugh, married to Edith, was now master of Hendon Hall. Only five of the old servants were still living, and all of them, in addition to Hugh and Edith, pretended not to recognize Miles. Denounced as a pretender, Miles was sentenced to the stocks, where the abuse showered on him by the mob so enraged Edward that he protested loudly. When the guards decided to whip the boy, Miles offered to bear the flogging instead. Grateful to his friend, Edward dubbed Miles an earl, which only made the imprisoned man sorrow for the boy's relapse into insanity. Upon Miles's release from the stocks, the two set out for London, where they arrived on the day before the coronation of King Edward VI.

In regal splendor, enjoying the adulation of his subjects, Tom Canty rode through the streets of London toward Westminster Abbey. There, just as the crown was about to be set on his head, a voice rang out demanding that the ceremony cease, and the real king, clothed in rags, stepped forth. As the guards moved to seize the troublemaker, Tom, recognizing Edward, ordered them to halt. The Lord Protector cut through the confusion by asking the ragged king to locate the great seal that had been lost since King Henry's death. Edward, after much dramatic hesitation, managed to remember the exact location of the seal. Tom admitted that he had innocently used it to crack nuts.

Miles, when brought before the rightful King Edward, exercised his privilege of sitting in the king's presence. At first, he had doubted that the waif was really the king, but when Edward ordered his outraged guards to permit that disrespectful act, Miles knew that his young friend had not been insane after all. Edward confirmed Miles's title of earl and stripped Hugh of his titles and land. After Hugh died, Miles married Edith, who had refused to acknowledge his identity because Hugh had threatened to kill Miles.

Tom returned to Offal Court with Edward's promise that he and his family would be honored for the rest of their lives. Edward righted many wrongs he had encountered during his adventures. John Canty, whom he wanted to hang, was never heard from again.

Critical Evaluation:

The Prince and the Pauper was Mark Twain's earliest attempt to join his fascination for Europe's romantic past with his natural bent for satirizing the injustices and social conventions of his own age. He was to do the same later, to far better effect, in *A Connecticut Yankee in King Arthur's Court* (1889) and, again with less success, in *Personal Recollections of Joan of Arc* (1896). *The Prince and the Pauper* is an ideal story for children, though it must also be granted that it is a children's story very rewarding for adults.

In the novel, Mark Twain employs many themes and devices he learned so expertly as a teller of tall tales, including tongue-in-cheek irony, ridiculous understatement, exaggeration, coincidence, and exchange of identities. He also used the occasion to underscore some of the social follies and injustices of his own age without actually having to attack them directly. He did this by treating the social and legal conventions of Tudor England satirically, trusting that his readers would recognize the parallels with their own times. Religious intolerance is the target of "In Prison," a chapter in which two women who have befriended Edward and Miles are burned at the stake because they are Baptists. Tom Canty, as king, labors to change laws that are unduly harsh or blatantly unjust, and Edward learns of the unnecessary cruelty of prisons at first hand, as well as the nature of poverty.

Mark Twain's major criticism of society both in Tudor times and in his own is that people mistake outward appearance as the gauge of true worth. The novel suggests that anyone could be a king, just as Tom Canty, given the opportunity to be a king, learns to be a good one. Tom and Edward are equally intelligent and virtuous young boys, though born to different kinds of "court." Chance and circumstances alone determine much of an individual's outward behavior and appearance.

Bibliography:

Baetzhold, Howard G. *Mark Twain and John Bull.* Bloomington: Indiana University Press, 1970. Includes a twenty-page chapter that documents Mark Twain's British sources for historical details in the novel.

Cummings, Sherwood. *Mark Twain and Science: Adventures of a Mind.* Baton Rouge: Louisiana State University Press, 1988. Cummings examines the often overlooked influence of Mark Twain's reading of French history on many details in the novel. Summarizes the novel's flaws, but notes that an important theme in the work is the power of training.

Rasmussen, R. Kent. *Mark Twain A to Z.* New York: Facts On File, 1995. An indispensable reference on Mark Twain's life and works. Contains a detailed analytical plot synopsis, background and publishing history, essays on major characters and places, and other topics, including dramatic adaptations of *The Prince and the Pauper.*

Stahl, John Daniel. "American Myth in European Disguise: Fathers and Sons in *The Prince and the Pauper.*" *American Literature* 58, no. 2 (May, 1986): 203-216. Analyzes symbolic father-son relationships in the novel. Notes similarities to other orphaned sons in Twain's works.

Twain, Mark. *The Prince and the Pauper.* Edited by Victor Fischer and Lin Salamo. Berkeley: University of California Press, 1979. The most authoritative edition available. Corrected text restores the book as Mark Twain intended it to be published. Includes a twenty-five-page historical introduction, the author's extensive working notes, a chapter that was removed from the first edition, and all 192 original illustrations.

THE PRINCE OF HOMBURG

Type of work: Drama
Author: Heinrich von Kleist (1777-1811)
Type of plot: Historical
Time of plot: 1675
Locale: Prussia
First published: Prinz Friedrich von Homburg, 1821 (English translation, 1875);
   first performed, 1821

> *Principal characters:*
> FREDERICK WILLIAM, the elector of Brandenburg
> THE ELECTRESS
> PRINCESS NATALIE OF ORANGE, the niece of the elector
> FIELD MARSHAL DORFLING
> PRINCE FREDERICK ARTHUR OF HOMBURG
> COLONEL KOTTWITZ, a member of the regiment of the princess of Orange
> COUNT HOHENZOLLERN, a member of the elector's suite

The Story:

   After three days of heading a cavalry charge in pursuit of the Swedes, Prince Frederick Arthur of Homburg had returned to Fehrbellin. Exhausted and battle-weary, the prince fell into a dreamlike sleep, weaving a laurel wreath as he half dozed. The elector of Brandenburg, Frederick William, was informed by Count Hohenzollern of the prince's strange condition, and the elector, the electress, and their niece, Princess Natalie, went to the garden where he slept. The elector took the wreath from the prince, entwined it in his neck-chain and gave it to Natalie. They backed away as the somnambulistic prince followed, murmuring incoherently, and as they retreated inside, the prince snatched a glove from Natalie's hand. When the prince awoke, he told Count Hohenzollern about the occurrence, which he thought had been a dream. Hohenzollern reproved him for his romantic fantasies and urged him to make ready for the coming battle with the Swedes.

   The field marshal of Brandenburg was dictating the orders of battle to his officers; but the prince, who was to play an important role in the battle, was absorbed with his thoughts. Hoping to remember from whom he had obtained the glove, he wore it in his collar. The electress and Natalie were present, and plans were being formed to send them to a place of safety. As the field marshal reached the section of the orders that pertained to the prince, Natalie, preparing to depart, suddenly realized that she had but one glove. The prince, who loved Natalie, quickly became aware that he held the missing glove. In order to be sure it was hers, he dropped it on the floor in front of him. Natalie claimed it, and the prince, in a fit of ecstasy, did not hear his battle orders clearly, though his mission was to be a key one.

   The battlefield of Fehrbellin resounded with cannon, and the elector's forces were sure of victory. As the rout of the Swedes became apparent, the prince precipitately gave orders to advance. His colleagues made an effort to dissuade him from this impetuous action, and they insisted that he hear the order of battle again, for he was supposed to remain in his position until a given signal. However, when the prince rebuked Kottwitz, an elderly colonel, for lack of fervency, Kottwitz, rather than appear unpatriotic, joined the prince in the advance.

   The electress and Natalie had paused during their journey to safety at a house in a nearby village, where news reached them that the elector had died in battle; both he and his great white horse were reported to have been killed during the bombardment. The prince sought out the women and took the opportunity to tell the distraught Natalie of his love for her and to offer her his protection. The elector had been her only relative, and now that he was dead she was alone in the world.

The elector was not dead, however. He had changed horses with one of his officers, and that officer, astride the white horse, had been mistakenly identified as the elector. The same messenger who brought word that the elector was still alive had further news for rejoicing. The war was over for the time being, and the elector had returned to Berlin.

It was apparent to the elector that Prince Frederick had ignored the battle order, and although terms for peace with the Swedes were being discussed, the strong military spirit of the elector prompted him to punish the prince for failing to follow orders. The prince was sentenced to die and placed in prison to await the day of his execution. He was, however, given permission to visit the electress and begged clemency through her. She was touched by his plea, as was Natalie, who threw herself at the feet of the elector to beg for the prince's life. In addition to Natalie's plea, the officers of the elector's army circulated a petition asking that the prince's life be spared. At last the elector agreed to pardon him.

Natalie took the letter of pardon from the elector to the prince's cell. In the letter, the elector specified that the prince's sword would be returned if the young man thought the elector had been unjust in his sentence. The prince thereupon refused the pardon, for his military training and nationalistic spirit prompted him to realize that the sentence was just.

The officers of the army visited the elector to plead on the prince's behalf. Count Hohenzollern made the strongest case. Had the elector not deceived the young prince by snatching the laurel wreath and entwining it with his neck-chain, the prince would not have felt an uncontrollable destiny forcing him into battle. Therefore, it was the elector's own fault that the prince's mind had been clouded by what he thought was a vision foretelling valorous deeds. The elector countered by blaming Count Hohenzollern himself for the whole affair, for he was the one who had led the elector to the sleeping prince.

When the prince appeared before the assembled officers and the elector, he was ready to die; nevertheless, he made such a strong plea to the elector that he was able to save himself. In the meantime, peace with Gustaf Karl of Sweden had been effected by promising Natalie's hand to a Swedish nobleman. The prince begged the elector to revoke the agreement and to attack the Swedes instead. The elector, ordering his troops to resume battle, tore up the death warrant. Prince Frederick Arthur was hailed as the hero of the field of Fehrbellin.

Critical Evaluation:

Heinrich von Kleist's last play *The Prince of Homburg* is a play of contrast, between the heart, feelings, and spontaneous, intuitive action on the one hand and the head, reflection, and rational thinking on the other. Dream and reality operate simultaneously. In thus incorporating the tension of opposites, this play reflects the Kleistian mind. In his personal life, Kleist was constantly tortured by such demands of the bourgeois life as having a career, earning a livelihood, and creating a name for himself. His quest for knowledge or absolute truth did not permit him to accept the trodden path. Even the notion of absolute truth failed to provide him comfort, for he saw flaws there, too. Alienated from the world and disenchanted with the existing order of religion, politics, and literature, he often contemplated ending his life, and at the age of thirty-four he did so.

The two main protagonists in *The Prince of Homburg* are by nature utterly different. The prince is a young man incapable of reflection, and he lets his heart rule his mind. The elector of Brandenburg, the sovereign, is a mature man who considers the autonomy of rules to be just. For him, the state needs the submission of its citizens: All sacrifices in its name are justified. Conversely, individuality for the elector is synonymous with anarchy. The prince is an individual led by his feelings. When he impetuously advances, thus failing to follow the elector's orders, it becomes clear that he does not posses the necessary calm and mature judgment of a military commander. Some critics have analyzed the play's opposition between the individual and the state and concluded that the resolution is synonymous with the victory of one over the other. Others have interpreted the elector's softening toward the prince and the prince's acceptance of his death sentence, as a compromise.

The elector, in his Prussian belief in obedience to authority, cannot tolerate disobedience. It takes the prince a while to realize that he must lose his life for leading his country to victory against the Swedish army at Fehrbellin. At the thought of his impending death the prince loses all sense of dignity. In portraying the weak prince groveling at the feet of the electress and begging his beloved Natalie to approach the elector for his pardon, Kleist brilliantly captures the humanness in the prince. He thereby also mocks the sublime portrayals of death in the dramas of antiquity, for in reality death is invariably accompanied by fear. Kleist does not present the prince as the embodiment of valor who can sacrifice himself for the sake of the state. He even forsakes his love for Natalie, assuming, though wrongly so, that the elector may take a more severe view of his situation once he knows that the prince is the hindrance to the plan to marry Natalie to the king of Sweden.

Instead of emphasizing the feminine characteristics of the two women in the play, Kleist focuses more on their ability to take control of the situation. In Act I, scene i, when Hohenzollern leads the elector, his wife, and Natalie to the garden where the prince of Homburg sits bareheaded with his shirt open at the throat in a somnambulistic state weaving a laurel wreath, the electress is the only one to sympathize with his condition. She interrupts Hohenzollern and her husband and recommends that they try to help him instead of making fun of him. Later, when the prince has sunk into the depths of despair, Natalie makes a compelling argument for the prince. She cleverly conveys to the elector that he has the power to grant the prince mercy, and that if he refused to do so it would be inhuman. She appeals to his emotions when she says that he will not be able to enjoy Prussia's victory if it is gained at the cost of a friend's life. By the last scene of the play, when Natalie crowns him with a laurel wreath and announces his pardon, the prince has lost his composure and dignity so thoroughly that he faints. Natalie, with compassion and understanding, exclaims, "Heavens—killed with joy!"

Upon recovering, the prince cannot believe that his crowning and pardon are really taking place. As in the first scene, where his somnambulistic state was responsible for his confused state of mind, in the resolution of the play too it seems as if he cannot distinguish between reality and dream. To his question: "No, it's a dream! Do say—is it a dream?" the mature veteran of war Colonel Kottwitz answers, "A dream, what else?" The prince has felt the proximity of death and knows now that life is transitory. Only one thing is certain, and that is death. In the midst of the joyful occasion, he asks the seemingly naïve but in fact profound question about the dreamlike quality of life. Colonel Kottwitz displays his understanding of the hidden meaning in his question when he agrees that life is a mere dream. Kleist thus ends his play with a reference to life's being a preparation toward death. When military officers shout about war while preparing for battle, they are at the same time preparing for their end.

"Critical Evaluation" by Vibha Bakshi Gokhale

Bibliography:
Doctorow, E. L. Foreword to *Plays,* by Heinrich von Kleist, edited by Walter Hinderer. New York: Continuum Publishing, 1982. Refers to the paradoxical nature of Kleist's plays. In the discussion of *The Prince of Homburg,* suggests that the main theme of the play is not the victory of state over individual but the existential angst of the individual.

Greenberg, Martin. Introduction to *Five Plays,* by Heinrich von Kleist. New Haven, Conn.: Yale University Press, 1988. A brilliant discussion of the duality inherent in *The Prince of Homburg.*

Maass, Joachim. *Kleist: A Biography.* Translated by Ralph Manheim. New York: Farrar, Straus & Giroux, 1983. Written in an anecdotal style with a sense of humor, it makes for a light reading. The chapter on *The Prince of Homburg* sees the influence of Kleist's own emotional and psychological makeup on the characters he creates.

McGlathery, James M. *Desire's Sway: The Plays and Stories of Heinrich von Kleist.* Detroit: Wayne State University Press, 1983. Regards the emotional outbursts of Kleist's characters as manifestations of their erotic desires. Analyzes the prince in *The Prince of Homburg* as a lovesick man wishing to be united with his beloved.

Reeve, William C. *Kleist on Stage, 1804-1987.* Montreal: McGill-Queen's University Press, 1993. An excellent source for a history of production of Kleist's various plays. The chapter on *The Prince of Homburg* describes its reception when first staged in 1821 and through the 1980's, including the enthusiasm it generated during the Nazi era.

THE PRINCESS
A Medley

Type of work: Poetry
Author: Alfred, Lord Tennyson (1809-1892)
First published: 1847

> *Principal characters:*
> WALTER VIVIAN, the heir to Vivianplace, an English estate
> THE POET
> LILIA, Walter Vivian's sister
> FIVE COLLEGE STUDENTS, friends of Walter and the Poet
> THE PRINCE
> THE KING, his father
> CYRIL and
> FLORIAN, two friends of the Prince
> PRINCESS IDA, ruler of a women's college
> KING GAMA, her father
> ARAC, her brother
> PSYCHE and
> BLANCHE, her tutors
> AGLAIA, the daughter of Psyche, and
> MELISSA, the daughter of Blanche, characters in a story told by
> Walter Vivian and his friends

The Story:

Prologue. The poet and five college companions joined their friend Walter Vivian on his father's estate, where they viewed the exhibition of a neighboring institute, of which Walter's father was patron. A book of family history relating the courage of a female ancestor inspired Lilia, Walter's sister, to speak out for women's rights, particularly that of education. Walter mentioned how at college the seven friends had told chain stories to pass away the time; Lilia suggested that they tell such a story now. Walter agreed and decided that Lilia would be the heroine, "grand, epic, homicidal," and the poet, who would begin the story, the hero. Each of the seven friends was to narrate a part of the story, and between each part the women sang one of the six songs.

Part 1. The young prince, whose family suffered from a curse laid down by a sorcerer, learned that the princess to whom he was once betrothed as a child now rejected him and wished to "live alone/ Among her women." He begged the king, his father, to be allowed to investigate this puzzle, but the warlike king replied that they would settle the dispute by war. Driven by an inner conviction, the prince rode off to the southern kingdom of the princess, accompanied by his two friends Cyril and Florian. At a town near the palace where the young women had established their women's college, the prince obtained women's clothes for Cyril, Florian, and himself, and they entered the college disguised, bearing a letter of introduction from King Gama, the princess' father.

Part 2. The college portress led the disguised males to Princess Ida, who greeted them as new students and explained the rules to them: For three years they must not correspond with home, leave the boundaries of the college grounds, or converse with men. Ida told them they must give up convention and work for the freedom of women. She seemed surprised when the newcomers extravagantly praised the prince, her former suitor. The men next encountered Florian's sister Psyche and Ida's favorite tutor. They admired Aglaia, Psyche's daughter, while Psyche lectured them on the history of feminine slavery. When Psyche recognized her brother beneath his disguise, she nearly betrayed them, but her natural affection overcame her duty to Ida. Melissa, the daughter of Ida's other tutor Blanche, also learned their identity but refused to reveal their secret.

Part 3. Ida invited the newcomers to travel with her, but before their departure the prince had his first seizure, the curse-inflicted malady of his family. Recovering, he acted as his own mock-ambassador in trying to acquaint Ida with his passion for her and with her unnatural attitude toward men; he alluded to her missing "what every woman counts her due,/ 'Love, children, happiness.'" Ida reiterated her dedication to her ideals, claiming that while children may die, "great deeds" cannot.

Part 4. A maid sings "Tears, Idle Tears," but Ida remained unmoved by the expressed sentiment of love. The prince replied with his song, "O Swallow," a love song, but Ida spurned his "mere love poem," saying she admires only art addressed to great ends. At this point, Cyril sang a bawdy song that disclosed their true identity. The women fled in panic, and Ida in her haste fell into the river. The prince rescued her but was captured by her retinue and experienced his second seizure.

Part 5. The prince and his companions, whom the princess had released out of gratitude, stumbled into the camp of the prince's father. Gama, the prince, and the king argued about how to win Ida's hand; the king was in favor of attacking, but Gama and the prince suggested peaceful means. Taunted as a coward, the prince agreed to a tournament where he would face Ida's brother Arac, who championed women's rights. Again the prince fell into a trance, in which he was unable to distinguish shadow and substance. Awakening, he found the tournament ready to begin; he fought Arac, was wounded, and fell into a deep coma.

Part 6. The prince was in a mystic trance. Ida in her triumph sang "Our enemies have fallen," then opened the palace as a hospital for the wounded. Her insistence on ascetic withdrawal and her unnatural contempt for men remained evident; after gazing on the wounded prince, however, she begged the king to allow her to care for him. She embraced Psyche, whom she had dismissed as a traitor, and disbanded the college over Blanche's objections.

Part 7. The palace became a hospital where the young women nursed the sick. Ida was heartsick because her ideals had been frustrated, but she found peace in aiding the wounded men. As she tended the prince as he lay in his delirious state, she began to love him and, casting off her falser self, kissed him. That roused him from his coma, and he fell into a blissful sleep. That night, he awakened to find her reading to him the poems "Now Sleeps the Crimson Petal" and "Come Down, O Maid." In the second poem, love is described as being of the valley, not of the mountain heights where Ida's idealism had carried her.

Ida admitted her lack of humility and her desire to achieve power rather than truth, yet she continued to regret the collapse of her idealistic plans to help women achieve status. The prince, who respected her idealism, replied that they would work together for her goal. He told her that women were not "undevelopt" men and that they should join with man in love; from this union, the man gains "sweetness" and "moral height," the woman "mental breadth" without losing "the childlike in the larger mind." Either sex alone is "half itself," and together in marriage each "fulfils/ Defect in each." The prince attributed his rebirth into a better life to Ida.

Conclusion. The poet explained the feud that had arisen between the mockers (the men) and the realists (the women). To satisfy both, he proposed what he called his "strange diagonal."

Critical Evaluation:

After the success of *Poems* (1842), Alfred, Lord Tennyson's friends and reviewers encouraged him to tackle a theme of modern life. Tennyson settled on what might be called the woman question—that is, the role of education for women, and their place in society—and wrote *The Princess*. As early as 1839, Tennyson had been interested in women's education, which provided the theme and core of the poem. Using the high Victorian notion of women's proper rights and duties, Tennyson attempted to enlarge on the social theme. Other issues he explored in *The Princess* were the false ambition and delusive ideals that can lead a woman to a path of sexual and intellectual solitude that is unnatural. Yet for all its intellectual ideas and the seriousness with which Tennyson treated them, *The Princess* reveals the poet's inability to dramatize a poem whose social themes deeply touch him. To this end, the poet reverts to a mock archaic style that is at once evasive in its playfulness and deprecatory in its whimsicality.

Both *The Princess*' prologue and conclusion are unpretentious in their naïve idyllic tone. The message is clear: universal harmony between classes of humankind, between the sexes, between humankind and science and nature, and between all creation and "the Heaven of Heavens." The poem is more properly a showcase for the six intercalated songs, however, which were added in 1850. These songs, among them "Tears, Idle Tears" and "Now Sleeps the Crimson Petal," give more credence to the poem's subtitle, *A Medley*, than the poem's title. *The Princess*, with its prologue and conclusion, serves merely as a frame for the six songs, the poem's narrative veering away from what Tennyson had set out to write.

Sexuality is the subject of *The Princess*. The concern is with the principal characters discovering and accepting their own sexual natures. The issue of women's rights and the romantic love story both climax in the prince's long conciliatory speech to Princess Ida in part 7: "The woman's cause is man's; they rise or sink/ Together . . ./ For woman is not undevelopt man,/ But diverse. Could we make her as the man,/ Sweet Love was slain; his dearest bond is this,/ Not like to like, but like in difference." The question of feminism here is being carried beyond the social sphere into psychosexual terms. The story might be characterized as tracing the complementary movements of the princess toward true femininity and of the prince toward true masculinity.

In part 1, the prince is described as being "like a girl." He and his friends, Cyril and Florian, are arrayed in female garb. To the prince's taunting foes, it is a case of "like to like." To the prince's father, it is simply a matter of effeminacy. These views oversimplify the prince. He reveals to the princess that he is not a homosexual nor a "scorner of [her] sex/ But venerator." Such veneration has led him to attempt to win Princess Ida by disguising rather than asserting his sexuality. The prince's devotion to women is not generalized; he notes that he was devoted to one—his mother. As in Carl G. Jung, this female image, the anima, is subsequently identified with other women, in this case Princess Ida, to whom he had been "proxy wedded" in childhood. Women, to the prince, are unassailable paragons.

The barrier to love is in Ida. She denies her femininity as much as he conceals his masculinity. Jung contends that the anima produces moods (the prince's seizures) and the animus—the masculine element in women—produces opinions, to which the princess clings. Against this opinionated female mind, instinct prevails. After the prince is wounded in a fight, Princess Ida moves into her own element and begins to accept a part of her own nature that she had repressed, thus approaching selfhood. She tells her followers to lift up their natures. Eventually, she is kissed by the prince. After this taste of passion, Ida loses her contempt for conventionalized love poems; her reading the erotic "Now Sleeps the Crimson Petal" demonstrates her acceptance of and response to a different sort of love poetry.

The prince's move toward selfhood requires that he cast off the brute self embodied in his father—the manly man his father wishes his son to become. As he reveals his full nature, he seems inclined to grant woman hers. He reminds his father that women have as many differences as men do, acknowledging in woman a wholeness lacking in "the piebald miscellany, man." The prince's tribute to distinctive womanhood in part 7 shows his progress from veneration of women to genuine appreciation.

The poem is a series of oppositions wherein the prince and the princess, in taking possession of each other and their selfhoods, represent a unity and wholeness. The prince tells Ida that "either sex alone/ Is half itself." They look to a time when "The man [will] be more of woman, she of man." This ideal is the reward of accepting sexuality instead of rejecting it. In *The Princess*, Tennyson takes a positive view toward sex. When viewed falsely, it separates man and woman. The prince expects that his marriage to Ida will "accomplish thou my manhood and thyself," affirming their relationship as neither degrading idol worship nor a jealousy-ridden contest but as a mutual enterprise for self-knowledge and fulfillment.

The Princess is a poem with serious ideas underlying its charming execution. At the time of its publication, it was labeled trivial, incongruous, and in poor taste. Later readings of the poem, however, show that Tennyson anticipated Jungian analysis and the coming of a day when women would be the social equals of men.

"Critical Evaluation" by Thomas D. Petitjean, Jr.

Bibliography:

Bailey, Albert Edward. *Notes on the Literary Aspects of Tennyson's "Princess."* 1897. Reprint. Folcroft, Pa.: Folcroft Library Editions, 1973. A book-length study of the literary aspects of Tennyson's *The Princess*, written at a time when the values of the Victorians were being harshly assessed and revamped. Useful in comparing the sentimentality of the Victorians with the author's more secular age.

Bloom, Harold, ed. *Alfred Lord Tennyson.* Modern Critical Views. Edgemont, Pa.: Chelsea House, 1985. A collection of modern essays that demonstrate how Tennyson voiced the doubts, beliefs, and clouded hopes of a generation of men and women faced with secularism, political turmoil, industrialization, and "the woman question."

Hall, Donald E. "The Anti-Feminist Ideology of Tennyson's *The Princess*." *Modern Language Studies* 21 (Fall, 1991): 49-62. Argues that Tennyson's poem, while purporting to be a solution to "the woman question," is essentially antifeminist in its approach to this topic.

Killham, John. *Tennyson and "The Princess": Reflections of an Age.* London: Athlone Press, 1958. Historical, book-length, critical study of *The Princess*. Captures the mood of the times during which the poem was written, offering a prefeminist reading.

Sedgwick, Eve Kosofsky. "Tennyson's *Princess*: One Bride for Seven Brothers." In *Critical Essays on Alfred Lord Tennyson*, edited by Herbert F. Tucker. New York: Maxwell Macmillan International, 1993. A reading of *The Princess* based on Sedgwick's specialized gender- and feminist-based critical approach.

THE PRINCESS CASAMASSIMA

Type of work: Novel
Author: Henry James (1843-1916)
Type of plot: Social realism
Time of plot: Late nineteenth century
Locale: London
First published: serial, 1885-1886; book, 1886

Principal characters:

HYACINTH ROBINSON, an orphan, apprenticed bookbinder, and
    revolutionary
MISS AMANDA PYNSENT, the dressmaker who raised Hyacinth
PRINCESS CASAMASSIMA, an Italian princess with "modern" ideas
ANASTASIUS VETCH, a musician and a friend of Miss Pynsent
PAUL MUNIMENT, the chemist who leads Hyacinth into revolutionary
    work
LADY AURORA LANGRISH, a noblewoman who works for the good of the
    poor
MILLICENT HENNING, Hyacinth's childhood playmate

The Story:

Florentine Vivier, a French dressmaker, gave birth to an illegitimate son and accused an Englishman, Lord Frederick Purvis, of being the boy's father. When Lord Frederick and his family refused to recognize the baby, Florentine Vivier stabbed Lord Frederick to death, a crime for which she received the maximum prison sentence; she entrusted her son, whom she called Hyacinth Robinson, to Miss Amanda Pynsent, a poor dressmaker, who raised the boy without telling him the unfortunate circumstances surrounding his birth.

Years later, Mrs. Bowerbank, a prison matron, visited Miss Pynsent to tell her that Florentine Vivier was dying in the prison hospital and had asked to see her son, now ten years of age. Miss Pynsent consulted Mr. Vetch, a violinist in a Bloomsbury theater, who was her closest friend. On his advice, she took Hyacinth to the prison but did not tell him that the woman was his mother. The grim prison frightened him, and at first his mother spoke only in French, saying that she feared he was ashamed of her. She embraced him pitifully before the matron bustled the visitors away.

During the following years, the rowdy family of Millicent Henning, Hyacinth's childhood friend, was ejected from their quarters next to Miss Pynsent's shop in Lomax Place. When Mr. Vetch had a copy of Lord Bacon's *Essays* bound as a gift for Hyacinth, he met the master bookbinder Eustache Poupin, who had been exiled from France after the Commune of 1871. Mr. Vetch learned that he and Poupin had a common bond of hate for the existing social and political fabric. Poupin secured an apprenticeship for Hyacinth with Crookenden's bookbindery and taught him French and socialism.

Millicent Henning, grown to a bold, handsome young woman, unexpectedly appeared in Lomax Place to renew her friendship with Hyacinth. Poupin introduced Hyacinth to a chemist and revolutionary named Paul Muniment, who took him to visit his crippled sister, Rose Muniment. There they met Lady Aurora Langrish, who devoted her time to caring for the poor and who admired Paul a great deal. She was a spinster much neglected by her large and wealthy family. Paul led Hyacinth more deeply into revolutionary activity. Hyacinth had meanwhile looked up the newspaper reports of his mother's trial, and he considered himself the aggrieved son of Lord Frederick Purvis.

Mr. Vetch got tickets for Hyacinth to take Millicent to see the play, *The Pearl of Paraguay*. Captain Godfrey Sholto, whom Hyacinth had met at a revolutionists' discussion group at "The Sun and Moon" public house, came from his box at the theater to invite Hyacinth to meet the Princess Casamassima and her old companion, Madame Grandoni.

Prince Casamassima tried to see the princess to beg her to return to him, but she refused to see him. As the prince left her house, he saw Hyacinth ushered in, at the princess' invitation, to tea. Later, Hyacinth bound a copy of Tennyson poems as a gift for the princess, but when he tried to deliver his gift, he learned that she had left London for a series of visits in the country. Hyacinth encountered Captain Sholto in a bar and, as Sholto hurried him strangely along, they encountered Millicent. Hyacinth suspected that Millicent had arranged to meet Sholto.

Paul Muniment announced at a meeting at The Sun and Moon that the revolutionary organizer Hoffendahl, who had spent twelve years in Prussian prisons, was in London. When Hyacinth declared his readiness to give his life for the cause, Paul took him to see Hoffendahl. There he swore an oath to perform an act of violence whenever Hoffendahl should send the order. Meanwhile, the princess had invited Hyacinth to stay at her country house, Medley. The princess was extremely pleasant, and Hyacinth stayed on in the country. One day, Captain Sholto rode up to Hyacinth as he was walking on the estate and asked Hyacinth to obtain an invitation to dinner for him. Clearly, Hyacinth had replaced Sholto as the princess' favorite.

He returned from Medley to find Miss Pynsent dying. In her will, she left a small sum of money to him. Mr. Vetch added to this sum and advised Hyacinth to travel on the Continent. On his return, he heard that the princess had sold all her beautiful furnishings, had moved to a tawdry, lower-middle-class house in Madeira Crescent, and had become friendly with Paul Muniment, who was now deeply involved in revolutionary activities. In the meantime, Hyacinth's own contact with wealth and leisure had made life seem more valuable and the society that produces and appreciates art more tolerable.

After the prince followed the princess and observed her going out with Paul Muniment, he demanded that Madame Grandoni tell him what she was doing. As the prince left Madame Grandoni, he met Hyacinth. While they were walking away from the house, they saw Paul and the princess return and enter together. Madame Grandoni abandoned the princess, and the prince wrote to Paul saying that he would send no more money to his wife.

At Poupin's, Hyacinth found the German worker Schinkel with sealed orders for him. He was to go to a grand party and there assassinate a duke. Mr. Vetch tried to keep Hyacinth from doing some desperate action. Hyacinth went to the store where Millicent worked, only to find her talking to Captain Sholto. The princess, going to Hyacinth's room, found Schinkel waiting. She demanded that he break in. Inside, they found that Hyacinth had shot himself in the heart.

Critical Evaluation:

The Princess Casamassima represents an attempt by Henry James, who had made his reputation as a novelist of the upper classes, to capture the full spectrum of modern urban life. He continued to depict the life of the idle rich in the figure of the prince, but his characters the princess and Lady Aurora agree that the rich have a responsibility to use their wealth toward some useful end. In this novel, James made a significant addition to his previous spectrum of characters with a gallery of striving working-class figures: the sublime figure of Millicent Henning, who claws her way out of Lomax Place to the relative affluence of the West End shops; Anastasius Vetch, who makes the grand gesture of forgiving a debt of about seventeen pounds; and the hero of the book, Hyacinth Robinson, a journeyman bookbinder with a commitment to revolutionary socialism. James also examined the sick and the dispossessed in the figure of the invalid, Rose Muniment, whose greatest treasure is a bed jacket given her by Lady Aurora. Finally, James depicted the shadowy figures of the revolutionary anarchists, whose goal, or so they claim, is nothing less than the total destruction of all these social classes.

The all-pervading irony of James's novel, however, is that none of these figures is quite what each claims. The princess plays at revolution because she is bored with her empty upper-class life, and her only real commitment is a monetary one. Yet her money buys her neither worthwhile deeds nor true involvement in the making of policy. Hyacinth begins his career caring deeply about society and committed to the need for revolution, but once he has been exposed to the princess' wealth and the beauty of fine material objects, he no longer wants to destroy the rich but merely to reallocate their wealth. As he comes to realize, there is "nothing more terrible than to find yourself face to face with your obligation and to feel at the same time the spirit originally prompting it dead within you."

Even the minor figures are false to themselves and their stated ideals. Lady Aurora continues to minister to Rose Muniment mainly because she is devotedly in love with the invalid's brother, Paul; Paul Muniment, in his turn, uses the revolutionary cause to pad his own pockets and further his personal ambitions. The only character who remains true to herself is Millicent Henning, and she does so out of shallowness, not nobility; she entrusts her fate to capitalist society, never looking ahead to the day when her beauty will fade and her modeling talents will no longer be in demand.

James could write *The Princess Casamassima* because he himself, as an American and a writer, was an outsider gazing in at the riches of the upper classes. As James says in his 1904 preface to the novel, "I had only to conceive his watching the same public show I had watched myself." Yet where Hyacinth never becomes more than a spectator of the princess' wealth and freedom, James succeeded in penetrating the great mansions and in becoming a figure in demand; between October, 1878, and June, 1879, he was invited out to dinner more than one hundred times. Hyacinth, on the other hand, binds books in beautifully tooled leather, but he cannot write, publish, or market them. Similarly, when the princess gives up her beautiful West End mansion and moves to the dreary reaches of Madeira Crescent, the reader is asked to admire the noble sacrifice she has made of all her beautiful possessions; nevertheless, James notes, she still uses only the finest tea.

As usual in a novel by James, the battle lines are ultimately drawn not according to social class or geographic background but according to psychological type. It may be impossible to declare that Hyacinth is a successful individual, but it is clear that he is a caring and loyal one. Neither Hyacinth nor the narrator ever decides whether the princess' revolutionary ardor is "superficial or profound," but her attachment to Hyacinth justifies our sympathy for her. Conversely, Paul Muniment seems attached to no one but himself; his cold ambition makes him the villain in the reader's eyes, even though he never commits any crime. Morality is always tied to personal honor for James.

James's greatest accomplishment is his creation of a shadowy underground world of incipient violence, hidden by fog, darkness, and obscurity from the everyday perceptions of the middle and upper classes. Although James lacked any direct knowledge of the revolutionary movement, he blended contemporary newspaper accounts, recent fiction, and his own experience as an outsider in creating a world of idealistic yet deeply disaffected individuals in search of a dramatic event that could change their lives and the world in which they live. In the late

Victorian period, when accuracy was a major criterion in art, James was criticized for his lack of concrete detail in describing his socialists and anarchists, but this position eroded with time. As conditions change, some works of art that are firmly rooted in their time and place become irrelevant to later times. Works such as *The Princess Casamassima*, however, remain vital and relevant far beyond the time of their creation. This novel's vitality is largely the result of James's contrast between a public world of cabs, public bars, West End shops, and country estates and an immense underworld that carries on "in silence, in darkness" and along "invisible, impalpable wires." James's vision of reality is closely attuned to the complex world of later times, as people continued to feel abused, even manipulated, by faceless forces beyond their control.

"Critical Evaluation" by Hartley S. Spatt

Bibliography:
Bell, Millicent. *Meaning in Henry James.* Cambridge, Mass.: Harvard University Press, 1991. Bell focuses on James's belief that a novel is "about nothing so much as its own coming-into-being." Chapter 4 discusses the conflict in *The Princess Casamassima* between naturalism and impressionism.
Johnson, Warren. "*Hyacinth Robinson* or *The Princess Casamassima?*" *Texas Studies in Literature and Language* 28, no. 3 (Fall, 1986): 296-323. Both Hyacinth and the princess are masks for the author, who investigates their fates in order to test his own freedom; the novel is named after the princess because we "prefer her knowledge to Hyacinth's example."
Jolly, Roslyn. *Henry James: History, Narrative, Fiction.* Oxford, England: Clarendon Press, 1993. Jolly discusses *The Princess Casamassima* as a novel in which James tries to unite history and fiction; the main conflict for Hyacinth and the princess alike is fought between their personal visions of the future and the social constraints on those visions.
Seltzer, Mark. *Henry James and the Art of Power.* Ithaca, N.Y.: Cornell University Press, 1984. Seltzer applies the ideas of Michel Foucault on power and subterfuge to James's work. In chapter 1, he uses *The Princess Casamassima* to link naturalism with the novelist's will to power.
Tilley, Wesley H. *The Background of "The Princess Casamassima."* Gainesville: University of Florida Press, 1961. Tilley traces the sources of James's knowledge of anarchism to articles in *The Times* of London and finds models for Millicent, for Muniment, and for Hoffendahl in actual subjects of news reports during the 1870's and 1880's.

THE PRINCESS OF CLÈVES

Type of work: Novel
Author: Madame Marie de La Fayette (Marie-Madeleine Pioche de la Vergne, 1634-1693)
Type of plot: Love
Time of plot: Sixteenth century
Locale: France
First published: La Princesse de Clèves, 1678 (English translation, 1679)

> *Principal characters:*
> THE PRINCESS DE CLÈVES, née Chartres, a beautiful young noblewoman
> THE PRINCE DE CLÈVES, her husband
> MADAME DE CHARTRES, her mother
> THE DUKE DE NEMOURS, in love with the princess
> THE VIDAME DE CHARTRES, the uncle of the princess
> THE QUEEN DAUPHINE, Mary, Queen of Scots, and a friend of the princess

The Story:

The court of Henri II of France was filled with many intrigues, as much of the heart as of anything else. The court itself was divided into several groups. One group was partial to the queen, who was at odds with Henri II because he chose to be guided in his personal life and in his government by Diane de Poitiers, the Duchess de Valentinois, who had been his father's mistress and was now a grandmother in her own right. A second group was that which surrounded the Duchess de Valentinois. A third group was that which had as its center Princess Mary, wife of the dauphin, the beautiful and brilliant young woman who was also queen of Scotland.

Into this scene of rivalry came Madame de Chartres, with her very beautiful daughter, to be married to a nobleman with a rank as high as possible; Madame de Chartres hoped even for a prince of royal blood. Unfortunately for the mother's hopes, the intrigues of the court kept her from arranging a match so brilliant or advantageous. A marriage with either Monsieur de Monpensier, the Chevalier de Guise, or the Prince de Clèves seemed the best that could be made, and there were obstacles to a marriage with either of those, as Madame de Chartres discovered. Each of the groups at the court was afraid that such a marriage would upset the status of the powers as they stood.

Finally the arrangements were made for a marriage to the Prince de Clèves. The gentleman, however, was perturbed by the attitude of his bride. He loved her greatly, and she seemed to love him dutifully but without the abandon for which he wished. He tried to be satisfied when she told him that she would do her best to love him, but that she felt no real passion for him or any man. The marriage was celebrated in grand style, and a fine dinner party, attended by the king and queen, was given at the Louvre.

For many months no one at the court, where extramarital attachments were the rule rather than the exception, dared to say anything about the young wife. Thanks to her mother's solicitude and her own lack of passion where men were concerned, the Princess de Clèves kept a spotless reputation. Her mother, who soon was on her deathbed, knew from various conferences the princess had had with her—unusual conferences for a married woman to have with her mother, for in reality they were confessions—that the princess had no inclinations to stray from her marital vows.

5351

One evening, however, there was a court ball given in honor of one of the king's daughters, whose marriage was impending. A late arrival at the ball was the Duke de Nemours, the most handsome and gallant courtier in France. At his entrance, the Princess de Clèves, who had never seen the duke before, was ordered by the king to dance with him.

In spite of the fact that Queen Elizabeth of England had taken an interest in the Duke de Nemours and had expressed the wish that the young man would visit her court, he remained where he could be near the Princess de Clèves. Even the repeated requests of the French king, who saw in de Nemours a possible consort for Queen Elizabeth, could not remove the duke from her side. Meanwhile, the Princess de Clèves did everything she could to conceal her love for the duke from everyone, even from her lover himself. She was determined to remain a faithful and dutiful wife.

One day, while the princess and the duke were in the apartments of the Queen Dauphine, the princess saw de Nemours steal a miniature portrait of herself. Although she had ample opportunity, the princess said nothing to stop him from taking her picture. Sometime later, the duke was injured by a horse in a tournament, and several people noted the look of distress on the face of the Princess de Clèves. The court was beginning to realize that love was blossoming between the two.

As soon as she realized what was happening in her heart, the Princess de Clèves went to her husband and asked him to take her away from Paris for a time. They went to an estate in the country. While they were there, the princess confessed to her husband that she was falling in love with someone. Admiring her candor, he promised to help her overcome the passion. Although she refused to name the man she loved, the Prince de Clèves guessed that it was one of three men, a trio which included the Duke de Nemours, but he had no proof. Although neither knew it, while the princess was confessing her love, the Duke de Nemours was hiding so close to them that he could overhear what was said.

Months went by, and gradually, despite her efforts to keep away from him, the princess indicated to her husband that the Duke de Nemours was the man she loved. The prince was torn by jealousy, but his wife's confession and her obvious efforts to curb her love prevented him from taking any action in the matter. His only recourse was to accuse her at intervals of not being fair to him in loving another.

The strain became too much for the Princess de Clèves, and she asked her husband's permission to retire to a country estate near Paris. He yielded graciously but sent one of his own retainers to make sure of her conduct while she was away. The retainer returned to report that twice, at night, the Duke de Nemours had entered the garden where the princess was; the retainer did not know and so could not report that his mistress had refused to see the man who loved her.

After the retainer had made his report, the prince fell ill of a fever. When the princess returned, she was unable to convince him that she had not been unfaithful, even though he wanted to believe her. Rather than stand in the way of her happiness, he languished and died.

Some months after her husband's death, the Duke de Nemours prevailed upon the princess' uncle, the vidame de Chartres, to intercede for him with the princess. The uncle agreed and arranged for an interview between the two. At that time the princess told the duke that, in spite of her love for him, she could never marry him. Soon afterward, she retired to her estate in the Pyrenees. She fell gravely ill there and, during her recuperation, experienced a religious conversion. She spent six months of each year praying in a convent and the remaining six months doing charitable work in her parish. Several years later she died, although she was still quite young.

Critical Evaluation:

Although critics have disagreed sharply concerning the ending of this novel, the mother-daughter relationship in this novel, the contrasts between appearance and reality, and the meaning of the various representations of love, almost all scholars agree that *The Princess of Clèves* was the first profound psychological novel written in France. The many different narrative techniques employed by Madame de La Fayette and the changing perspectives cause readers to reach wildly diverse interpretations each time they reread the work.

Madame de La Fayette included in this novel several stories told by various characters. These stories illustrate in a subtle manner the feelings of her central characters. In the second of the four parts of *The Princess of Clèves*, Marie Stuart, who was married to King Francis II of France and later became Queen of the Scots, spoke about the tragic death of Anne Boleyn, the mother of Queen Elizabeth I, whom the Duke de Nemours had considered marrying. Marie Stuart attributed the beheading of Anne Boleyn to the irrational jealousy of her husband Henry VIII who had falsely suspected her of marital infidelity. Marie Stuart suggests that, in addition to being excessively violent, Henry VIII was a hypocrite because it was he and not Anne Boleyn who had committed adultery. Soon after her execution at the Tower of London, he married Jane Seymour. His adulterous affair must have begun before Anne Boleyn's death on the alleged charge of adultery. At first glance, this story seems to have little to do with the plot of *The Princess of Clèves*, but when one rereads this novel, one comes to see a similarity between this and the Prince de Clèves's unjustified jealousy directed against his wife. Moreover, Henry VIII's obvious infidelity and hypocrisy lead one to believe that the Prince de Clèves and the Duke de Nemours probably both had mistresses, although they demanded absolute fidelity from the princess, who had, in fact, remained faithful to her marriage vows. These and other stories in this novel subtly but effectively help one to understand that the Prince de Clèves and the Duke de Nemours may not necessarily be as sympathetic as the courtiers believe them to be. Appearance and reality are often quite different in *The Princess of Clèves*. Although these inserted stories serve to illustrate the moral weakness and the bad faith of the two leading male characters in this novel, many critics have tended to downplay the importance of these stories because these stories are incompatible with the traditional view of the Prince de Clèves and the Duke de Nemours as basically sympathetic characters and not as victimizers of the Princess de Clèves.

Another technique which Madame de La Fayette used very well in this novel was to describe the same scene from the point of view of several different characters. Excellent examples of this narrative technique can be found in the descriptions of the courtship and wedding of the princess and her decision to retire permanently from the royal court near the end of this novel. Each character reveals part of what actually happened, and readers must decide on their own what each scene means for them and the fictional characters. The preparations for the wedding of Mademoiselle de Chartres to the Prince de Clèves illustrate nicely Madame de La Fayette's skill in presenting several different perspectives on the same scene. The Prince de Clèves and Madame de Chartres are eagerly making plans for an elaborate palace wedding reception. For them, this was to be a glorious social event, but Mademoiselle de Chartres approaches this wedding with a complete lack of enthusiasm. She feels betrayed by her mother, who wants to force her to marry a man for whom the sixteen-year-old princess "felt no particular attraction." She tells the prince that she will agree to marry him if both Madame de Chartres and he insist, but she points out to him that she could never love him, although she intends to remain faithful to her marriage vows out of respect for herself and because of her desire not to risk her immortal soul by committing the mortal sin of adultery. Readers admire her honesty, but they suspect that the wedding reception was not an especially joyous experience for the new couple. The Princess de Clèves views this arranged marriage as yet another example of the exploitation of women by insensitive men such as her husband.

Another example of Madame de La Fayette's skill in using this narrative technique can be found at the end of this novel when the Princess de Clèves, whose husband has just died, decides to leave the royal court in order to seek inner peace on her country estate in the Pyrenees. Once the Duke de Nemours realizes that she would probably never return to Paris, he asks numerous influential people at the royal court, including the queen herself and the princess' uncle the Vidame de Chartres, to write to her in an effort to persuade her of the foolishness of her decision to abandon courtly pleasures for what he and many literary critics considered a boring existence in a small and remote country village. While she was staying at her country estate, the young widow falls gravely ill and the narrator suggests that this close brush with death has caused the princess to "see the things of this life differently from the way they appear when one is in good health." Madame de La Fayette seems to be suggesting that the princess is preparing herself spiritually for the next life, whereas those still at the royal court are indifferent to such thoughts. Her behavior is incomprehensible to superficial characters such as the Duke de Nemours, but it makes perfect sense if one concludes that the young widow experienced a spiritual conversion shortly before her death. Madame de La Fayette ends this psychological novel with this comment on the title character: "Her life, which was quite short, left inimitable examples of virtue." This is a very sensible interpretation for readers who agree with the narrator, but it seems utter madness to readers who share the Duke de Nemours' belief that no intelligent person would ever want to leave the apparent splendor of a royal court. Ever since its first publication in 1678, *The Princess of Clèves* has remained a marvelously ambiguous novel whose meaning for readers depends on those characters with whom they identify.

"Critical Evaluation" by Edmund J. Campion

Bibliography:

Haig, Stirling. *Madame de La Fayette*. New York: Twayne, 1970. Contains a very thoughtful overview of Madame de La Fayette's career as a novelist. Haig describes very well her place in the development of the historical novel as a genre in seventeenth century France.

Henry, Patrick, ed. *An Inimitable Example: The Case for "La Princesse de Clèves."* Washington, D.C.: Catholic University of America Press, 1992. Includes twelve excellent essays which illustrate feminist, sociocritical, psychological, and religious interpretations of this novel. Contains a thorough bibliography of critical studies on *The Princess of Clèves*.

Kaps, Helen Karen. *Moral Perspective in "La Princesse de Clèves."* Eugene: University of Oregon Press, 1968. Contains a thoughtful analysis of the moral dimensions of the major and secondary characters in this novel. Kaps explains Madame de La Fayette's subtle and effective use of many different narrative techniques in this novel.

Raitt, Janet. *Madame de La Fayette and "La Princesse de Clèves."* London: Harrap, 1971. Contains a very clear introduction to this novel. Raitt describes very well the true originality of *The Princess of Clèves*.

Tiefenbrun, Susan W. *A Structural Analysis of "La Princesse de Clèves."* The Hague, The Netherlands: Mouton, 1976. Contains an excellent study of the formal structure of this novel. Tiefenbrun clearly explains the complicated relationships among the princess, her husband, and the Duke de Nemours.

PRINCIPLES OF POLITICAL ECONOMY

Type of work: Economics
Author: John Stuart Mill (1806-1873)
First published: 1848

John Stuart Mill's central concern in *Principles of Political Economy* is the production and distribution of wealth, which he defines as everything that serves human desires that is not provided gratuitously by nature. The most important elements in wealth are goods currently produced.

Production requires labor and appropriate natural objects. The labor devoted to a product is rewarded out of its sale proceeds, but before these are realized, advances to workers are required, which come from capital. Productive labor is what yields an increase in material wealth.

Capital consists of wealth used for productive activity. Capital provides the tools and materials needed to carry on production, as well as subsistence for the laborers while the production process is going on. The quantity of a nation's industry is limited by its stock of capital. Increased capital means increased ability to hire workers, and thus increased output and employment. The accumulation of capital results from saving. It is not from demand for commodities, but from capital, that demand for labor arises, although the demand for commodities determines in what productive activities workers can find employment.

Differences in the productivity of nations may arise from geographic factors such as climate and fertility of soil. There are also important differences in labor quality: in physical vigor; in ability to persevere in pursuit of distant objectives; in skill, knowledge, and trustworthiness. Productivity is enhanced by legal and social institutions favoring security of person and property, and by effective cooperation as manifested in division of labor. As a result of greater specialization of workers and equipment, large-scale productive establishments are often more efficient than small ones.

The rate at which production grows depends on the rate of growth of labor, capital, and land, and on improvements in productive technique. Increases in population tend to raise the total quantity of production by increasing the labor supply but may, by increasing the number of consumers, keep down the living standards of the working class. Unless birth rates are limited, increases in population and labor supply must continually tend to force wages to low levels.

The rate at which capital increases reflects the flow of saving, which depends on the level of income and the desire to accumulate rather than to consume. Willingness to save is encouraged when the expected profits of investment are high and when uncertainty and insecurity are at a minimum. Whether a society is progressive or backward depends in large degree on the level of saving it achieves.

The real limits to production growth arise from the limited quantity and limited productiveness of land. Cultivation of land is subject to diminishing returns—that is, increased application of labor and capital by any given proportion will increase total output only in some lesser proportion. Tendencies toward diminishing return can be counteracted by improvements in methods of production, but these are more likely to produce decreasing costs in industry than in agriculture. The pressure of population growth against diminishing returns is the principal cause of widespread poverty.

Although the laws of production are essentially physical, the principles of distribution are social; once the goods are produced, they can be distributed as people wish. An important determinant of income distribution is the nature and distribution of private property. Some critics find much fault with the institution of private property and propose socialist systems involving democratic management of productive operations and equal division of the product. Such schemes cannot be dismissed as impracticable. Some people might shirk their responsibilities to work, but this is also a serious defect of other property and wage arrangements. A communitarian society would have to guard against an excessive birthrate and might encounter problems in determining who should perform which tasks. Practices relating to private property have not conformed to the ideal of assuring to each person the fruits of his or her labor or abstinence. The best system will be one that is consistent with the greatest amount of human liberty and spontaneity.

The produce of society is divided among the three classes who provide productive agents: labor, capital, and land. Wages are determined by the proportion between population (supply) and capital (demand); thus high birthrates tend to inhibit increases in wage rates. Limitation of births by the working class would be promoted by the extension of education and by any sudden, rapid improvement in their condition.

The profits of the capitalist are the reward for abstinence, for risk-taking, and for the effort of superintendence. Profits arise from the fact that labor produces more than is required for its subsistence; workers depend on the relationship between the productivity of labor and the wage rate. The rent of land is determined by the demand for it (and its produce), the supply of land being fixed. Differences in rent reflect differences in productivity on lands of different quality. Growth of population and capital tends to increase rents as demand for food increases.

As economic systems expand through growth of labor and capital, the rate of profit tends to decline because higher food prices force up wage costs. The declining rate of profit may halt the increase of capital and produce a stationary state. This state of affairs would not necessarily be bad, provided no one were poor, and provided the unseemly struggle for wealth and power were replaced by more elevated pursuits. Social improvement would also result from improvement of the relationship between employer and worker, perhaps through profit sharing or through cooperatives of producers or consumers.

The value of any article comes from the amounts of other things for which it can be exchanged in the market. To possess value, an article must possess utility (be desired) and be subject to some difficulty of attainment. Value tends to that level at which the quantity that buyers will take (demand) is equal to the quantity that sellers will offer (supply). Since cost of production is a chief determinant of supply, value tends to equal cost (plus a normal profit for capital), unless monopoly conditions prevail. Although labor is the chief element of cost, capital must also be rewarded or it will not be forthcoming. The longer the waiting period between the application of labor and the emergence of the finished product, the greater the capital cost.

Money provides a common measure of value and facilitates specialization and exchange. Variations in the general price level tend to be proportional to changes in the quantity of money, or in its rapidity of circulation, assuming the quantity of goods remains unchanged. Since credit may serve as a substitute for actual money, it can also influence the level of prices. Expansion or contraction of credit, in such forms as promissory notes or bank deposits, are principal elements accounting for periodic commercial crises. A paper currency not convertible into precious metal is liable to depreciate through excessive issue.

Although the supply of any individual commodity may exceed the demand for it, it is not possible for the supply of all commodities to be excessive. Each person's willingness to work and produce reflects his or her desire to acquire goods for consumption or investment. In international exchanges, value depends not on the absolute levels of labor and capital required to produce an item, but on the comparative costs. A country may be able to import cloth more cheaply than to produce it, by paying for it with exports of another product in which its labor and capital are highly efficient, even though it could produce cloth with less labor and capital than the country from which it imports. Both participants in such trade tend to benefit from it, and total world output may be increased by the more efficient use of resources through specialization.

Should a country's imports be excessive in relation to its exports, it will tend to export gold and silver to pay the difference. The outflow of money will tend to reduce the price level in that country, and raise it elsewhere, until the trade imbalance is rectified. The proper functions of government extend, at the very least, to defining and determining the rights of property and contract, the rules of partnerships and corporations, the regulation of insolvency, the monetary system, and weights and measures. In addition, government activity may be necessary where the consumer cannot judge or achieve his or her own interest (for example, the education of children), or in cases where each person's desire can be effectuated only if all conform (for example, limiting work hours). Government may undertake activities beneficial to the public, from which no private person could realize a profit (for example, providing lighthouses, or financing scientific research). Charity will be offered by private persons in any case, so it may be better to have it provided by the government so as to minimize possible harmful effects. Government should avoid activities based on fallacious doctrines: policies of tariff protection, price-fixing, restricting entry into a business or occupation, or prohibiting trade union activity.

Limitation of government activity is desirable to avoid undue enhancement of central power or the use of coercive authority in ways that infringe on important individual freedoms. Enlargement of government may also impair the efficiency of its operations.

Taxation should be imposed so as to exact equal sacrifice from each person. This result could be achieved by an income tax that takes a fixed proportion of income beyond a minimum exemption. Taxation of inheritance and of unearned increases in land rent is highly desirable, but current saving should be excluded in calculating taxable income. There is a presumption in favor of laissez-faire; that is, the burden of proof is on those who favor extension of the role of government.

Although no longer a blueprint for specific economic reforms, Mill's *Principles of Political Economy* remains one of the most provocative, systematic statements of liberal political and economic thought in Western literature. Applying the principles of Utilitarian philosophy to a study of the economic system in England, Mill explains why, in democratic societies, it is imperative for labor and management to share in decision making and participate as equals in determining the future of business. Mill is convinced that only such collective brainpower will guarantee that people receive fair treatment and that business will prosper.

Mill's stance is not pure socialism, however. He advocates a laissez-faire approach by government, so that the private sector bears chief responsibility for managing its own affairs. He insists, however, that individuals with superior education and insight—a cadre of "intellectual elite"—take responsibility for managing business affairs in such a way that the poor will benefit. As he does in all his writings, Mill emphasizes the necessity that corporations operate for the benefit of those employed by them as well as those who have invested in them or who manage business operations.

Throughout the *Principles of Political Economy*, Mill insists on recognition of the rights of individuals and the importance of allowing individuals certain liberties that permit them to achieve dignity and happiness. His approach may have been radical to contemporaries, most of whom believed that the right to make decisions in any business rested solely with those who invested in it and who stood to gain or lose financially from its success or failure. Nevertheless, Mill's farsighted analysis of the symbiotic relationship between workers and supervisors has become the model for enlightened labor-management practices in modern Western-style businesses in the twentieth century.

Bibliography:

Borchard, Ruth. *John Stuart Mill the Man*. London: C. A. Watts, 1957. *Principles of Political Economy* is placed in the context of Mill's life. Discusses the work's ideas, reception, and relation to Mill's socialism.

Schwartz, Pedro. *The New Political Economy of J. S. Mill*. Durham, N.C.: Duke University Press, 1972. A comprehensive study of Mill's political economy, offering a detailed analysis of Mill's theory of economic and social policy. Lengthy bibliography provides an excellent guide for further study.

Spiegel, Henry William. *The Growth of Economic Thought*. 3d. ed. Durham, N.C.: Duke University Press, 1991. Mill's ideas on political economy are seen in the broad context of economic thought from biblical times to the 1980's. Mill's ideas are reviewed in a separate chapter. Each chapter has a substantial, annotated bibliography.

Thomas, William. *Mill*. New York: Oxford University Press, 1985. One chapter analyzes and interprets Mill's theory of political economy. Brief, helpful section on further reading.

Woods, Thomas. *Poetry and Philosophy: A Study in the Thought of John Stuart Mill*. London: Hutchinson, 1961. Mill's ideas on economics are examined in the larger context of his thought and the influence of Auguste Comte and other social philosophers. Discusses the influence of poetry in general, and William Wordsworth in particular, on Mill's thinking.

THE PRISONER OF ZENDA

Type of work: Novel
Author: Anthony Hope (Sir Anthony Hope Hawkins, 1863-1933)
Type of plot: Adventure
Time of plot: 1880's
Locale: The fictional kingdom of Ruritania
First published: 1894

Principal characters:

RUDOLF RASSENDYLL, an English gentleman
LADY ROSE BURLESDON, his sister-in-law
RUDOLF, king of Ruritania
MICHAEL, DUKE OF STRELSAU, King Rudolf's half brother
ANTOINETTE DE MAUBAN, Michael's beloved
PRINCESS FLAVIA, a woman betrothed to King Rudolf
FRITZ VON TARLENHEIM, a loyal subject to the king
COLONEL SAPT, another loyal subject

The Story:

To his sister-in-law, Lady Rose Burlesdon, Rudolf Rassendyll was a great disappointment. In the first place, he was twenty-nine years old and had no useful occupation. Second, he bore such a striking resemblance to the Elphbergs, the ruling house of Ruritania, that Rose thought him a constant reminder of an old scandal in which her husband's family had been involved. More than a hundred years before, a prince of the country of Ruritania had visited England and had become involved with the wife of one of the Rassendyll men. A child was born, who had the red hair and the large straight nose of the Elphbergs. Since that unfortunate event, five or six descendants of the English lady and the Ruritanian prince had the characteristic nose and red hair of their royal ancestor. Rose thought Rudolf's red hair and large nose a disgrace for that reason.

Rassendyll himself, however, had no concern over his resemblance to the Ruritanian royal family. A new king was to be crowned in that country within a few weeks, and he decided to travel to Ruritania for the coronation in order to get a close view of his unclaimed relatives. Realizing that his brother and sister-in-law would try to prevent his journey, he told them that he was going to take a tour of the Tyrol. After he left England, his first stop was Paris, where he learned something more about affairs in the country he was to visit. The new king, also called Rudolf, had a half brother, Michael, duke of Strelsau. Michael would have liked to become king, and it was hinted that he would try to prevent the coronation of Rudolf. Rassendyll also learned that there was a beautiful lady, Antoinette de Mauban, who loved Michael and had his favor. She, too, was traveling to Ruritania for the coronation.

When he reached Ruritania and found the capital city crowded, Rassendyll took lodging in Zenda, a small town approximately fifty miles from the capital, and prepared to go by train for the coronation. Zenda was part of Michael's domain; his hunting lodge was only a few miles from the inn where Rassendyll stopped. Rassendyll also learned that King Rudolf was a guest at his half brother's hunting lodge while waiting for the coronation. There were more rumors of a plot against the king and talk that Black Michael, as he was called, planned to seize the throne.

Every day, Rassendyll walked through the woods near the hunting lodge. One day he heard two men discussing his close resemblance to the king. The men introduced themselves as Fritz von Tarlenheim and Colonel Sapt, faithful friends of King Rudolf. While they talked, the king himself appeared. The king had shaved his beard, but otherwise he and Rassendyll were identical. The king was pleased to meet his distant cousin and invited Rassendyll to the lodge. There the king drank so much that Fritz and Sapt could not wake him the next morning.

This was the day of the coronation, and, as the king slept in his stupor, Fritz and Sapt proposed a daring plan to Rassendyll. They knew that if the king did not appear for the coronation, Black Michael would seize the throne. Their plan was to shave Rassendyll's beard, dress him in the king's clothes, and have him crowned in the king's place. By the time the ceremonies were over, the king would have recovered, would take his rightful place, and no one would be the wiser. It was a dangerous gamble, for exposure would mean death, but Rassendyll agreed to the plot.

Fritz and Sapt locked the king in the wine cellar and left a servant to tell him of the plan when he awoke. Rassendyll, with Fritz and Sapt, proceeded to the palace. With the two men to help him, he carried off the deception; he even convinced the Princess Flavia that he was the real king. His role with Flavia was the most difficult for Rassendyll, for he had to be gracious and yet not commit the king too far.

The success of the conspirators did not last long. When they returned that night to the lodge, they found the servant murdered and the real king gone. Black Michael's men had worked well. Black Michael knew that the supposed king was an imposter, and Rassendyll, Fritz, and Sapt knew that Black Michael had the real king. Neither group, however, dared call the other's hand. Rassendyll's only chance was to rescue the rightful king. Black Michael's hope was to kill both Rassendyll and the king and thus seize the throne and Princess Flavia for himself. Rassendyll was attacked and almost killed many times. Once he was saved by a warning from Antoinette de Mauban, for, although she loved Michael, she would not be a party to murder. Also, she did not want Michael to be successful, for his coup would mean his marriage to Flavia. Michael learned of her aid to Rassendyll and held her a semiprisoner in the hunting lodge where he had hidden the king.

Playing the part of the king, Rassendyll was forced to spend much time with Flavia. He wanted to tell her his real identity, but Fritz and Sapt appealed to his honor and persuaded him that all would be ruined if Flavia learned that he was not the true king.

When they learned that King Rudolf was dying, Rassendyll, Fritz, and Sapt knew that they must take a daring chance to rescue him. They and part of the king's army attacked the lodge. Those not aware of the deception were told that Black Michael had imprisoned a friend of the king. There was a bloody battle both outside and inside the lodge. Black Michael was killed and King Rudolf wounded before the rescue was completed. When he knew that the king would live, Rassendyll realized that his part in the deception was over. The king sent for him and thanked him for his brave work in saving the throne. Princess Flavia also sent for him. She had been told the whole story, but her only concern was to learn whether Rassendyll had spoken for himself or the king when he had given her his love. He told her that he would always love only her and begged her to go away with him. She, however, was too honorable to leave her people and her king, and she remained in Ruritania, later to marry the king and rule with him.

Rassendyll left Ruritania and spent a few weeks in the Tyrol before returning to England. His sister-in-law, still trying to get him to lead a more useful life, arranged through a friend to get him a diplomatic post. When he learned the post would be in Ruritania, he declined it. Rassendyll resumed his former idle life, with one break in his monotonous routine. Each year,

Fritz and Rassendyll met in Dresden, and Fritz always brought with him a box containing a rose, a token from Flavia.

Critical Evaluation:

Despite its severe brevity and occasional plot weaknesses, *The Prisoner of Zenda* is among the most enduring of adventures. In part, the reasons for this are predictable. Mystery, intrigue, suspense, and love are integrated neatly in the tale. There is plenty of adventure, much of it framed as a conflict between evident good and evil, and there is a strong central character— Rudolf Rassendyll—to hold the book together. It is, therefore, a highly formulaic and popular story, yet it is also much more than that. In its touches of ethical ambiguity and its clever use of disguise (both thematic and dramatic), *The Prisoner of Zenda* takes up the complex matter of defining, then judging, humanity's moral nature.

Early branded a wastrel by his sister-in-law, Rassendyll in time proves his sincerity and honor. What he learns, simply, is value—a theme that Anthony Hope explores not only in his major character but also socially in his excoriations of kings and gentry. What the reader learns, as the sister-in-law does not, is the difference between real and apparent nobility. Readers come to judge Rassendyll not by his complexion or his attitude of indifference but by his courageous, constant actions. In the same way, his "kingliness" is evidenced not in borrowed robes and crowns but in a quality of spirit that cannot be counterfeited.

Nevertheless, Rassendyll's character is also qualified throughout the novel. He is genuinely tempted by the throne and by Flavia's attendant charms. Too often he ignores the morality of his actions: once when he backstabs a guard and again when, madly vengeful, he destroys two of Black Michael's hirelings. With bold strokes, Hope defines Rassendyll's identity through two character foils—the dissipated real king (significantly, a namesake and distant relative), and the brash knave, Rupert Hentzau. The former reinforces Rassendyll's worst qualities even as he illustrates, by contrast, the best. On the other hand, Hentzau appears at a glance to be thoroughly different from Rassendyll, yet Rudolf's fascination with Rupert's attractive evil clearly suggests an affinity between them. When Rassendyll spares his enemy, then later tries desperately to slay him, the psychological overtones are plain. Regretfully, he has let the evil in himself escape.

The themes of moral ambiguity ("if it were a sin may it be forgiven me," says Rudolf at one point) and political chicanery in the novel fit well with the idea of individual honor. What is to be gained by acting honorably in a world without principle? This is a penetrating question, especially toward the end of the adventure when Rudolf and Flavia must elect honorable self-sacrifice or selfish love. Their choice of the former, it seems, points out the novel's answer. The world becomes a measure better, and an individual a measure greater, only as there are those ready to prefer honor over happiness.

Bibliography:

Mallet, Sir Charles Edward. *Anthony Hope and His Books: Being the Authorized Life of Sir Anthony Hope Hawkins.* Port Washington, N.Y.: Kennikat Press, 1968. Examines the influence of Anthony Hope's life on *The Prisoner of Zenda.* Chronicles the instantaneous success of the book and its warm reception by authors such as Robert Louis Stevenson, Sir Arthur Quiller-Couch, and Andrew Lang. Examines the book's sequel, *Rupert of Hentzau* (1898), and the adaptation of *The Prisoner of Zenda* for stage. Examines Anthony Hope's style of writing.

Putt, S. Gorley. "*The Prisoner of Zenda*: Anthony Hope and the Novel of Society." *Essays in Criticism* 6 (January, 1956): 38-59. Places *The Prisoner of Zenda* in its proper late Victorian milieu. Unlike the aesthetic writers of the 1890's, Anthony Hope celebrates traditional values such as honor, virtue, and sacrifice.

Wallace, Raymond P. "Cardboard Kingdoms." *San Jose Studies* 13, no. 2 (Spring, 1987): 23-34. Compares *The Prisoner of Zenda* to George Barr McCutcheon's Graustark series and George Meredith's *Adventures of Harry Richmond* (1871). Considers the appeal of imaginary kingdoms and royalty to late Victorian readers, and finds the attractions of imaginary realms more appealing than realistic elements of the 1890's.

THE PRIVATE LIFE OF THE MASTER RACE

Type of work: Drama
Author: Bertolt Brecht (1898-1956)
Type of plot: Epic theater
Time of plot: 1933-1938
Locale: Germany
First performed: selected scenes (in French), 1938; complete version (in English), 1945; (first published (in English), 1944; original version, 1945, as *Furcht und Elend des dritten Reiches*

Principal characters:
VARIOUS CITIZENS OF THE THIRD REICH

The Story:

During the first years of the Nazi regime, techniques for suppressing opposition were rapidly perfected. One object of suppression was any radio capable of receiving broadcasts from Russia. The Nazis relied on the German distrust of communism to aid in harsh enforcement of the law. Soon neighbors were betraying neighbors. Sets were confiscated and the owners beaten.

In Berlin, in 1933, a storm trooper came to visit his sweetheart, who was a maid in a wealthy home. While she was feeding him in the kitchen, the cook's brother came in with a tube to repair the family radio. Since the brother, a common worker, did not give the Heil Hitler greeting plainly enough, the trooper put on a demonstration to show the Nazi power. He pretended to explain the current methods of exposure by staging a scene at the welfare office. He was the more anxious to scare the worker because he had drunk the Nazi's beer.

The trooper, ostensibly in mufti, pretended that he was in a welfare line discussing the things wrong in Germany. The worker answered him by imitating the common complaints heard from non-Nazis. Simulating camaraderie, the trooper clapped the worker on the shoulder. On arriving at the office, the man would be closely interrogated, for there was a chalk cross on his shoulder. The trooper had drawn the cross on his hand and transferred it to the worker's shoulder with a friendly pat. After that bit of dramatizing the worker left abruptly.

In the concentration camps the Socialists, the Communists, and the non-political liberals realized too late that they should have united before Adolf Hitler came to power. Now they were impotent. In the factories there were broadcasts by happy workers who had been carefully coached in what they were to say. In private homes a member of the family would be returned in a zinc box; the official explanation was always that death had come from natural causes.

By 1935, even the scientists were afraid. Spied on by their Nazi employees, they were often handicapped in their laboratories by the prohibition against correspondence with foreign scientists. It was forbidden even to mention the name of Albert Einstein, for he was a Jew. In Frankfurt a Jewish wife was packing. Her husband was a prominent physician and an Aryan. She had stood her racial stigma as long as she dared, but now their friends were beginning to cut them socially. Carefully tending to her wifely duties, she telephoned to friends, asking them to look after things in her absence. After she had finished calling, she prudently burned the notebook containing the telephone numbers. Then she began rehearsing the speech she would make to her husband.

She would be brave. She would go to Amsterdam for a few weeks until the persecution died down. Really, the only reason she was leaving was to relieve her husband from embarrassment.

As she went through the carefully thought-out speech, her husband came in. At once she broke down. The husband pretended to believe that she would be gone only a short while, and when things were better he would come to Amsterdam for her. He would like a few days outside of Germany himself. Surely the Nazis could not for long shackle the intellectuals.

Even the judges were confused. They had come to the point where they gave decisions the way the party wanted them, but sometimes it was difficult to know just what the party desired. In Augsburg three storm troopers broke into a store run by a Jew and took some valuable jewelry after wounding the Jew. To the judge the case looked like a simple one; the Jew had offered great provocation, the storm troopers had acted rightly in defending the honor of the party. After talking with the prosecutor, however, the judge was not sure how he should decide.

There was race pollution mixed in the case. The Jewish store manager had a nineteen-year-old daughter about whom there had been rumors. The father also had an Aryan partner who had access to party headquarters. The owner of the building had changed his testimony. Perhaps the case was clear-cut; the judge would decide against the storm troopers, for German justice was honorable even for Jews.

The inspector in the case confused the judge again. He said the prosecutor was inducing the judge to give the wrong decision because he wanted the judge's post for himself. The harassed judge asked an older colleague for advice, but the other man could give him little help. With a heavy heart the judge prepared to go into his courtroom, where ribald storm troopers occupied every seat.

Perhaps one of the most effective devices of the regime was to teach the children in the youth organizations to inform on their parents. In 1936 a man who had been released from a concentration camp came to call on a man and a wife with whom he had worked in the resistance movement. The couple were afraid to take him into their confidence again. The meeting was an embarrassing one. The couple tried not to notice the released man's shrunken hand with the missing fingers, and he in turn pretended not to notice their lack of confidence in him.

As food became scarcer in the stores, the waiting lines were longer in the mornings. Butter was sacrificed to cannons and prices rose beyond the ability of the people to pay. The store owners themselves led a precarious existence, for they never knew when they would be arrested for infractions of rules. A butcher, who had been a Nazi before 1933, forced his son to join the storm troopers, but his loyalty did him little good. When he refused to put cardboard hams in his window, the Nazis began to persecute him. In despair the butcher hanged himself in his shop window over a card that announced to the world that he had voted for Hitler.

There were faint signs of resistance to the all-powerful regime. Farmers were supposed to hand over their grain to the government and buy feed at a fixed price. Here and there, however, a farmer would take the precaution of having his wife and children stand guard. While they watched he would feed grain to his hungry pigs.

In Lubeck, in 1937, a fisherman lay dying. He had argued long hours with his storm trooper son over Hitler's evident determination to start a war. Now as the dying man talked with his pastor he dared to mention the life to come. The son left his father's bedside without speaking. The pastor had referred to the Sermon on the Mount; no good Nazi could be taken in by Jewish superstition.

In Hamburg, in 1938, just after the union with Austria, a small group discussed ways and means of getting out an opposition leaflet. Such a project was almost impossible. A woman in the group read a letter from an executed father to his small son, a letter in which the father declared that his hard fate would not have been in vain if his son remained true to the common people.

Critical Evaluation:

The Private Life of the Master Race is composed of seventeen scenes or one-act plays that were taken from a longer work about the Third Reich. The scenes form a pageant of the first five years of Adolf Hitler's reign. In the usual sense these scenes do not make a play, for there are no characters who appear in more than one scene; the unity of the work is maintained only by the historical sequence and by a fragmentary narration.

The play is an example of epic theater, of which Bertolt Brecht is the most famous practitioner, although he did not originate it. Brecht outlines his ideas regarding epic theater in his notes to *Rise and Fall of the City of Mahagonny* (1929). Epic theater is intended as a direct contrast to theater as it is normally understood, which in the West means theater as described by Aristotle. Such theater may be called dramatic theater. Dramatic theater aims at creating the illusion of life, at creating suspense, and at affecting the emotions. Epic theater aims at avoiding any illusion that what is happening onstage is real, at deflating suspense, and at engaging the intellect. Dramatic theater aims at showing what is eternal in human life; the implicit message of dramatic theater is therefore conservative. Epic theater aims at showing what changes in human life; the explicit, radical message of epic theater is that change is possible.

In the 1920's Germans by the millions had been rendered destitute by World War I and by peacetime inflation, and they turned either to the Communists or to the Fascists in search of a solution. Brecht was among those who looked for a Marxist answer. His art, however, was never simplistic. He owed much to the Russian Formalists, an association of writers and thinkers who flourished between the Russian Revolution and the years of Stalinist suppression. His chief aesthetic technique stemmed from an idea of the Russian Formalists. Brecht's technique, *Verfremdung* (alienation), means to make strange, to find technical means to defamiliarize and make distant, in the belief that truth once rendered strange and seen from afar, is easier to grasp. Habits of attention must be broken, so goes the argument, in order for one to grasp what is really taking place. Brecht was willing to speak openly about his own times.

Brecht argued that the desperate times, as well as the coming Marxist society, called for an entirely different art, one that would help people to see through capitalist society and not just into it.

In 1933, when Hitler became the de facto ruler of Germany, Brecht's Marxism made him a marked man, and he went to live in Denmark. Later he moved to other places, not returning home until after World War II. This explains the unusual publication history of the play. *The Private Life of the Master Race* is a didactic play by an exile, and seeks to trace in its scenes the ways in which the Nazis consolidated their power. The play intends to show the world how such catastrophes can occur, and to bear witness against the atrocities of Hitler. Brecht employs a number of quite different techniques in the play, perhaps to keep the audience constantly defamiliarized. The play lacks dramatic unity. It consists in a series of interruptions. The interrupting of the action is one of the chief techniques in epic theater. Brecht often uses songs to do this. The illusion of theater is constantly being exposed. Some scenes make their point almost altogether through action: The scene titled "Physicists" is filled with unsettling motion; doors abruptly pop open, characters speak softly or shout. Epic theater was intentionally hybrid, and this play is a mixture of naturalism, satire, expressionism, and other techniques, less or more familiar. There is a unity of theme: Each scene reveals how the Nazis subjected all human relations to the rule of the lie.

"Critical Evaluation" by David Bromige

Bibliography:

Benjamin, Walter. *Understanding Brecht*. Translated by Anna Bostock with an introduction by Stanley Mitchell. London: NLB, 1973. Acutely insightful commentary by one of Brecht's contemporaries and fellow Germans, who in 1940 killed himself rather than fall into the hands of the Gestapo.

Bentley, Eric. *The Brecht Commentaries, 1943-1980*. New York: Grove Press, 1981. Reviews and articles by Brecht's principal American translator and champion. Includes essay on *The Private Life of the Master Race*.

Fuegi, John. *Brecht and Company: Sex, Politics, and the Making of the Modern Drama*. New York: Grove Press, 1994. Examines Brecht's output from many angles, with much biographical detail.

Hayman, Ronald. *Brecht: A Biography*. New York: Oxford University Press, 1983. More than a dozen references to *The Private Life of the Master Race* dot this large and detailed survey.

Witt, Hubert, ed. *Brecht as They Knew Him*. Translated by John Peet. London: Lawrence & Wishart, 1975. Interesting compilation from the writings of more than thirty associates or commentators.

PRIVATE LIVES

Type of work: Drama
Author: Noël Coward (1899-1973)
Type of plot: Comedy of manners
Time of plot: 1930
Locale: France
First performed: 1930; first published, 1930

> *Principal characters:*
> SIBYL CHASE, a bride
> ELYOT CHASE, her husband
> AMANDA PRYNNE, Elyot's first wife
> VICTOR PRYNNE, her husband

The Story:

Sibyl Chase loved being married. She was as much in love with the idea of being a bride as she was with her husband Elyot, perhaps more so. On the first night of their honeymoon, Sibyl went into raptures over Elyot, but she did not forget, or let him forget, that she knew he had loved his first wife Amanda madly. She was certain that the breakup of that marriage had been Amanda's fault and that she had been a mean-tempered and probably a wanton woman. When Sibyl told him that she knew how to handle a husband, how to make him happy, Elyot feared that she meant she knew how to manage a husband. He was a trifle disturbed.

Unknown at first to the Chases, Amanda was honeymooning at the same hotel with her new husband, Victor Prynne. Victor had much the same ideas about marriage as Sibyl had. He intended to take care of Amanda, to make her forget that dreadful brute to whom she had been married. The fact that Amanda never asked to be taken care of was unimportant. Victor would teach her to be a suitable wife.

When Amanda and Elyot saw each other again, each wanted to move out of the hotel before their respective mates knew about the presence of the other couple. Sibyl and Victor, however, who were not accustomed to making abrupt changes without reason, refused to leave. Amanda and Elyot thereupon decided that they were not culpable when they talked together again and recalled their happy times together. Both tried for a time to avoid the issue uppermost in their hearts and minds, but at last Elyot broke off the polite conversation to say that he still loved Amanda. They fell into each other's arms.

Amanda tried for a time to make them consider Sibyl and Victor, but Elyot easily convinced her that those two would suffer more if they all lived a lie. After making plans to go to Paris, Amanda and Elyot left without a word of explanation.

Because they had fought so violently and so often in their married days, Amanda made Elyot promise that whenever they started to bicker they would use a password and each keep quiet for two minutes. In Amanda's flat in Paris, they were often forced into quick use of the magic password, for they were torn equally between love and hate. Amanda's conscience bothered her a little, but Elyot could easily soothe that nagging little voice with love, logic, or a flippant remark. Sorry that they had wasted five years of separation after their divorce, they agreed to marry each other again as soon as Sibyl and Victor would divorce them. Elyot was annoyed when he learned that Amanda had spent those five years in having little affairs with various men, but he saw no reason for her being annoyed at his own transgressions.

Their quarrels occurred over nonsensical things for the most part. At the root was often Amanda's concern for the moral questions involved in their past and present relationship. When Elyot brushed these aside with worldly and flippant comments, Amanda came back to him more passionately than before.

The last explosion occurred when Amanda mentioned a man of whom Elyot had always been jealous. Without knowing quite how the quarrel got out of hand, they found themselves throwing things at each other and slapping each other viciously. The magic password failed to work. As each slammed into a different bedroom, neither was aware that Sibyl and Victor had come into the room at the height of the rumpus and settled themselves quietly on the sofa.

The next morning, Sibyl and Victor had a very sensible discussion concerning the situation they had found the night before. Sibyl wept copiously, not so much from sorrow as from custom; it was the right thing for an injured wife to do. Each blamed the other's mate for the sordid scene in Amanda's apartment. When Amanda and Elyot joined them, they were very polite with each other and with Sibyl and Victor. At first the situation was like a morning call for coffee. When Amanda and Elyot admitted that they were sorry, that it was all a mess and a mistake, Sibyl and Victor agreed that the culprits were not contrite enough. Elyot, in particular, seemed crass about the whole thing, particularly to Victor, who wanted to thrash him. Elyot could see no use in heroics; he honestly admitted that his flippancy was only an attempt to cover real embarrassment.

Initially, Amanda and Elyot had refused to speak to each other, but as Sibyl and Victor continued to be proper and to mouth little platitudes about morals and the sanctity of marriage, Elyot winked at Amanda. While the injured spouses made and reversed plans for divorces, the sinners paid less and less attention. At last Sibyl and Victor began to quarrel, each accusing the other of weakness in still loving such a wicked and worldly person as Amanda or Elyot. When Sibyl gave Victor a resounding slap, he in turn shook her soundly. In the midst of the quarrel, Amanda and Elyot picked up their suitcases and tiptoed out the door together.

Critical Evaluation:

In the centuries since William Shakespeare wrote, probably the best British dramatists have been those who wrote comedies of manners, from the Restoration period, to Oscar Wilde at the end of the nineteenth century, to Noël Coward in the twentieth century. To paraphrase one critic, Coward actually wrote comedies of *bad* manners; when society's rules prove too stringent for his characters, they sulk, throw tantrums, become regressive, or go into denial. This may sound unpleasant, but Coward renders these reactions hilariously funny. A professional actor by the age of twelve, Coward brought a sure sense of theater to his dramas, an informed ability to decide what lines, moves, and situations would prove most telling. He often acted in his own plays, and it was while playing the lead in *The Vortex* (written by Coward, and first produced in Hampstead, London, in 1924) that he won fame as both actor and writer. Later in life, he was successful as an actor both in motion pictures and in television shows.

Private Lives is vintage Coward. The situation is at once unlikely and provocative: Two newlywed couples honeymooning at the same hotel turn out to have a prior connection—one of the husbands used to be married to one of the wives. Elyot Chase and Amanda Prynne find the moonlight and their chance propinquity irresistible. All their romantic feelings for each other come flooding back, causing them to abandon their new mates. Such behavior is inexcusable by any measure of decency, but Coward wins some sympathy for the erring couple. To begin with, he makes their mates slightly unsympathetic—a bit doltish, a trifle too eager to please. By contrast, the dialogue only starts to crackle when Elyot and Amanda are alone together, and their witty duels are entertaining. The audience is encouraged to believe what Elyot and Amanda are inclined to believe, that they belong together and made a mistake in divorcing each other.

That said, it must be admitted that there are severe limitations to this play. Witty though they are, the characters are shallow people, with neither work nor aspirations to give them personality. The fact that they lead pampered lives in the shadow of World War I and the Great Depression without once referring to either of these giant catastrophes calls their creator's humanity into question. Elyot and Amanda are particularly selfish, self-indulgent, spoiled, and infantile, but Coward's heart appears to be with them. They cannot live without each other, but they cannot live with each other. Moreover, they cannot face these or any other facts for more than a few seconds without a drink, a cigarette, a quarrel, or a change of subject. They appear to have no parents to care for, neither do they have (or speak of having) children. So bleak are their lives, that some authorities have proclaimed Coward as a forerunner of Samuel Beckett and Harold Pinter. *Private Lives* is a far cry from Pinter's *The Dumb Waiter* (1959) or Beckett's *Waiting for Godot* (1952). Its characters are not waiting for anything—they are far too impatient.

Even so, they show us a truth of being human. Their attempts to make light of their lot point out their profound vulnerability. With nothing to count on except each other, there is nothing of which they can be sure. Although they long to be swept off their feet—for in the grip of an impulse, one can, however briefly, feel confident—at the same time, they do all they can to avoid losing their heads. Perhaps the best passages in *Private Lives* are those where the characters walk a tightrope between sentimentality and cynicism, as in Act II, when Elyot and Amanda discuss their heartbreak and their longing for each other. Although the audience can be sure that this mood will not last long, it is just as certain that it will recur. Noël Coward and his leading lady, Gertrude Lawrence, for whom these roles were created, were brilliant at skirting such issues, turning the English gift for understatement into a highly stylized comedic mode. To hear their recorded performance is to grasp how this delicate work could best be presented. There is a sense of the private that will not be violated, even in the casual and rather promiscuous world of *Private Lives*. What is admirable about these four characters has to do with their inviolability, which, try as they might, they cannot shed.

"Critical Evaluation" by David Bromige

Bibliography:
Coward, Noël. *Future Indefinite*. New York: Doubleday, Doran, 1954. A continuation of his autobiography. Charmingly written, witty, gossipy, and with much of biographical interest.
_____. *Present Indicative*. New York: Doubleday, Doran, 1937. Detailed autobiography, in which Coward says of *Private Lives*: "As a complete play, it leaves a lot to be desired. . . . (T)he secondary characters [Sybil and Victor] . . . are little better than ninepins, lightly wooden, and only there to be repeatedly knocked down and stood up again." Declares that he wrote the play as a vehicle for himself and Gertrude Lawrence in the principal roles.
Lahr, John. *Coward the Playwright*. New York: Methuen, 1982. Chronological study, with extended excerpts from individual plays. Notes that *Private Lives* is the first play Coward wrote after the advent of the Great Depression following the stock market crash of October, 1929, and that the play catches the mood of dissolution: "a plotless play for purposeless people."
Lesley, Cole. *The Life of Noël Coward*. London: Penguin Books, 1978. Thorough account of

one of the most charismatic entertainment careers of the twentieth century. Replete with quotations from Coward's peers, both friends and enemies.

Levin, Milton. *Noël Coward*. New York: Twayne, 1968. Survey of Coward's body of work that neither idolizes nor condemns him. Sound comments on the structure and impact of *Private Lives*.

Mander, Raymond, and Joe Mitchenson. *Theatrical Companion to Coward*. London: Rockcliff, 1957. Full information on casts, productions, biographical background, and critical reception. Excellent introduction by Terence Rattigan.

Tynan, Kenneth. *The Sound of Two Hands Clapping*. London: Jonathan Cape, 1975. Witty book by one of Britain's foremost drama critics. The passages on Coward sum up much that the post-World War II generation found objectionable in his work.

PROFANE HYMNS

Type of work: Poetry
Author: Rubén Darío (Félix Rubén García Sarmiento, 1867-1916)
First published: Prosas profanas, 1896 (English translation, 1922)

The poems in *Profane Hymns* are linked through the feelings and emotions the various lyrics evoke, rather than the ideas they present. It seems to have been Rubén Darío's purpose to re-create in his readers an appreciation of the awakening to a sense of pleasure, including sensual, even erotic pleasure, which the poet himself encountered in his own life. The poems attempt to recapture those emotions through the use of allusive, symbolic language and setting. While there is certainly an acknowledgment that such pleasure is fleeting, there is also the insistence that pleasure is no less real for being transitory.

"It was a gentle air" is a representative poem expressing this sensibility. Set in a kingly court, perhaps "in the reign of Louis, King of France," perhaps a completely imaginary setting that never existed in reality, the poem tells in a dreamlike fashion of a time when courtiers and courtesans assumed various guises—sometimes of classical deities and at other times of simple shepherds and their lovers, yet all are equally artificial while remaining, in some paradoxical fashion, real. Throughout the poem there is a constant sense of the erotic, never quite openly stated, but expressed in a subtle, hinted fashion. The power of the verse—and perhaps its true meaning—comes in its use of the sound and resonance of the words and their rhythms, and their references to lost golden ages. The French court before the Revolution, the mythical Arcadia are evoked as representative of times and places where beauty and pleasure were accorded their true and therefore dominant place in human life. Time and modern life has left this land behind, the poems remember and, in a sense, re-create beauty and pleasure for the reader. In this fashion, lost beauty is revived, even if only in the mind of the reader.

"Sonatina" continues the theme through the metaphor of the fairy tale. The sad princess sits in her tower, waiting for her prince to come and rescue her. She is like a butterfly, imprisoned in its cocoon and ready to awake. Already, in the distance, "the joyous knight who adores you unseen" is on his way. The poem is about the princess in the beautiful, tragic moment before her deliverance.

The poems "Blazon" and "The Swan" use the swan, that most typically poetic of birds, in subtly different fashions. In "Blazon," the "snow-white Olympic swan" is praised as the symbol and the inspiration of true poetry. The swan is, in a sense, both the poem and the poet who makes art and who makes his or her life into a work of art: "the regal bird who, dying, rhymes the soul in his song." This power is heightened in "The Swan," where through the romantic power of art, the song of the swan that was once heard only at its death now never ceases, and instead of marking an end signals "a new dawning and a new life."

"Symphony in Gray Major" is one of the key poems in *Profane Hymns*. In an impressionistic fashion the poem presents a seaside scene where the sun, the waves, and the old sailor dozing and dreaming on the wharf merge into memories of other places and other times ("that distant land of mists") which return to blend into the present. "Symphony in Gray Major" is notable not for what it reveals, but for what it suggests.

Although Latin American literature has a long and honorable history, it was not until the end of the nineteenth century that it began to produce writers, especially poets, whose innovative techniques and technical mastery brought them worldwide recognition as significant and influential artists. Among this group, one of the first, and certainly one of the most important, was Rubén Darío, whose *Profane Hymns* is among the most innovative and enduring works of Latin American verse. As a key part of Darío's complete writings—which are considerable, given the brief span of his life—*Profane Hymns* is indicative of the scope, breadth, and power of his poetic achievements.

Born in Metapa, Nicaragua, and christened Félix Rubén García Sarmiento, the poet began a lifetime of wandering at the age of fourteen that was not to cease until his early death. By the age of nineteen Darío was living and studying in Chile, where he spent several years that were critical to his development as a writer, absorbing the latest productions of authors both of Central and South America and Europe. He later lived in Argentina, Spain, and France, where he edited an influential and innovative literary journal, *Mundial*, in Paris.

With the outbreak of World War I, Darío returned to Latin America. To relieve his considerable financial difficulties he embarked upon a strenuous lecturing tour, which took him as far north as New York City in the United States, where he fell seriously ill. He came home to Nicaragua, where he died on February 6, 1916.

At an early time during his travels, he had shortened his name to Rubén Darío. The writer Octavio Paz, among others, has seen in this choice of names a deliberate attempt by the poet to link himself to the great literary and artistic traditions of the Middle East, uniting both the Jewish (Ruben) and non-Jewish (Darius, king of Persia) heritages. Whatever the ultimate source or reason, the choice in name clearly indicates that Rubén Darío considered himself to be, like his poetry, original, but he also tacitly acknowledged his debt to the great creations and creators of the past.

Latin America had always maintained close cultural ties with Europe and prided itself on its transatlantic culture. This was especially true in artistic matters, including literary influences. After the middle of the nineteenth century, these European influences exerted a profound pressure on Latin American writers. The literary models of modernism and Symbolism, largely inspired by French examples, were especially important, and Darío shows a considerable influence by both in *Profane Hymns*.

Modernism helped writers such as Darío break free of the conventions of older poetry. Modernism encouraged new and innovative uses of language, including the incorporation and adaptation of peasant or folk forms and the creation of new and individual poetic structures. In the hands of a writer such as Darío, modernism and the use of rhythm were more than poetic forms or devices. Modernism and rhythm became for him a way of looking at the world and seeing that everything in the world was mysteriously yet intimately connected. It was the poet alone who could express these connections through the power of his art. For the modernist such as Darío, analogy was an exalted expression of the imagination.

Darío was also deeply influenced by the writings of authors such as Edgar Allan Poe and Walt Whitman, but his natural preference, reinforced by his readings of the French poets such as Charles Baudelaire, was for the aristocratic refinements and symbolic mannerism of Poe, rather than the democratic vistas and demotic cadences of Whitman. Darío's careful choice of words, his preference for sensuous and emotionally laden rhythmic patterns, and his refined and often rarefied subject matter all reveal his debt to Poe and to Poe's French admirers. Throughout *Profane Hymns* the scenes and settings are of far-off and long-ago places, often aristocratic and courtly, with an emphasis on the artificial and the self-consciously theatrical.

The influence of modernism and Symbolism is especially notable in *Profane Hymns*, which relies primarily on sensations and feelings rather than on ideas or logical progression. It displays this most clearly in the way that its various poems present the reader with a succession of different facets of human emotion. Darío, using his masterful command of language, symbolism, and analogy, moves smoothly from the frivolous tone, to the hedonistic, to the erotic, and ends, finally, in a wistful, almost elegiac reflective fashion, affirming the presence and importance of beauty in human life while accepting beauty's momentary and perhaps illusory nature.

Profane Hymns occupies a central position in Rubén Darío's works. It reveals an artist who is capable of exploring to the utmost the limits of language and imagery and who does so with wit, imagination, and a natural affection for the positive rhythms of human existence.

Michael Witkoski

Bibliography:

Foster, David William, and Virginia Ramos Foster, eds. *Modern Latin American Literature.* New York: Frederick Ungar, 1975. A collection of brief but penetrating observations regarding Darío written by critics, scholars, and fellow writers. Extremely helpful in following the course of Darío's reputation over the years.

Gonzales-Gerth, Michael, and George D. Schade, eds. *Rubén Darío Centennial Studies.* Austin: University of Texas Press, 1970. Considers various aspects of Darío's work and is especially helpful in revealing the extent of his knowledge and mastery of other poets and their contributions.

Imbert, Enrique Anderson. "Rubén Darío." In *Latin American Writers.* Edited by Carlos A. Sole. New York: Charles Scribner's Sons, 1989. Assesses Darío's work both as an independent body and as an influence on Latin American literature in general. Argues convincingly that Darío's writings divide Latin American literature into "before" and "after" periods and that therefore Darío is a major transitional figure.

Moreno, Cesar Fernandez, ed. *Latin America in Its Literature.* Translated by Mary G. Berg, English edition edited by Ivan A. Schulman. New York: Holmes & Meier, 1980. A thematic study of the continent's writers. Addresses Darío's contributions in a number of areas. Significant essays touching on Darío include "Ruptures of Tradition," "The Language of Literature," and "Social Functions of Literature." Excellent for placing Darío within the social, political, and cultural context.

Paz, Octavio. Introduction to *Selected Poems*, by Rubén Darío. Translated by Lysander Kemp. Austin: University of Texas Press, 1965. An insightful and rewarding study of Darío by one of the premier Latin American writers, placing him within the context of both Hispanic literature in particular and world literature in general.

_____. "The Siren and the Seashell." In *The Siren and the Seashell, and Other Essays on Poets and Poetry.* Translated by Lysander Kemp. Austin: University of Texas Press, 1976. A revised version of the introduction to the *Selected Poems.* Sets Darío amid the cultural and artistic temper of his times.

THE PROFESSOR'S HOUSE

Type of work: Novel
Author: Willa Cather (1873-1947)
Type of plot: Psychological realism
Time of plot: A few years after World War I
Locale: Hamilton, a Midwestern university town near Lake Michigan
First published: 1925

Principal characters:
GODFREY ST. PETER, a middle-aged teacher and historian
LILLIAN ST. PETER, his wife
ROSAMOND and
KATHLEEN, their daughters
LOUIE MARCELLUS, Rosamond's husband
SCOTT MCGREGOR, Kathleen's husband
TOM OUTLAND, a former student at Hamilton
AUGUSTA, a seamstress

The Story:

The Oxford prize for history brought Professor Godfrey St. Peter not only a certain international reputation but also the sum of five thousand pounds. The five thousand pounds, in turn, built the St. Peter family a new house, into which the professor had been frankly reluctant to move.

For half a lifetime, the attic of the old house had been his favorite spot—it was there that he had done his best writing, with his daughters' dress forms for his only company—and it was in this workroom that Augusta, the family sewing woman, found him when she came to transfer the dress forms to the new house. To her astonishment, the professor declared quizzically that she could not have them; he intended to retain the old house in order to preserve his workroom intact, and everything must be left as it was.

Nevertheless, the new house made its own claims. That same evening found the professor host at a small dinner party for a visiting Englishman. The professor's daughters and their husbands were present, and during dinner, the conversation turned to the new country house being built by Rosamond and Louie. Louie explained to the visitor why the name Outland had been selected for the estate. Tom Outland had been a brilliant scientific student at Hamilton, as well as the professor's protégé. Before being killed in the war, he had been engaged to Rosamond. His will had left everything to her, including control of his revolutionary invention, the Outland vacuum. Later, Louie Marcellus himself had married Rosamond and successfully marketed Tom's invention. The new house, Louie concluded, would serve in some measure as a memorial to Outland.

Louie's lack of reserve visibly irritated the McGregors, and the professor himself maintained a cool silence. The next morning, his wife took him to task for it. Lillian had been fiercely jealous of her husband's interest in Tom Outland. The professor found himself reflecting that people who fall in love, and who go on being in love, always meet with something that suddenly or gradually makes a difference. Oddly enough, in the case of Lillian and her husband, it had seemed to be his pupil, Tom Outland.

5374

More and more, the professor sought the refuge of his study in the old house, where he could insulate himself against increasing family strain. Even there, however, interruptions came. Once it was Rosamond, self-conscious about accepting all the benefits of the Outland invention. Her father refused to share her good fortune but suggested that she aid cancer-ridden Professor Crane, who had collaborated with Tom in his experiments. Rosamond stiffened immediately, for outside the family, she recognized no obligations.

Soon there was more evidence that the family was drifting apart. Kathleen confessed to her father her violent reaction to Rosamond's arrogance. It became known that Louie, attempting to join the Arts and Letters Club, had been blackballed by his brother-in-law. The professor was distressed by the rift between his daughters, both of whom he loved, although he had a special affection for Kathleen.

Louie Marcellus' real fondness for the St. Peters was demonstrated when the time came for the professor to fill a lecture date in Chicago. Louie and Rosamond, paying all bills, took them to Chicago, installed them in a luxurious hotel suite, and tempted them with diversions. During a performance of Mignon, Lillian, softened by memories aroused by the opera, confirmed the Professor's impression that her resentment of Tom Outland had affected their marriage.

Louie's next plan was even more elaborate: He and Rosamond would take the professor and Lillian to France for the summer. The professor loved France, but he recognized the futility of trying to compromise his and Louie's ideas of a European vacation. He begged off, pleading the pressure of work, and eventually the others departed without him.

The professor moved back into the old house and luxuriated in independence. He decided to edit for publication Tom Outland's youthful diary, and constantly he turned over in his mind the events in Tom's dramatic history. Years before, Tom had appeared on the professor's doorstep as a sunburned young man who was obviously unaccustomed to the ways of society. Tom wanted to go to college, although his only previous instruction had come from a priest in New Mexico. Interested and curious, the professor saw to it that Tom had a chance to make up his deficiencies and enter the university. The St. Peter house became the boy's second home, and the little girls were endlessly fascinated by his tales of the Southwest. To them, he confided that his parents had died during their wagon journey westward and that he had been adopted by a kindly worker on the Santa Fe Railroad.

Tom's diary was chiefly concerned with his strangest boyhood adventure. To regain his strength after an attack of pneumonia, he became a herd rider on the summer range. With him went his closest friend, Roddie Blake. On the range, Tom and Roddie were challenged by the nearness of the mysterious Blue Mesa, hitherto unclimbed and unexplored. They saved their wages and made plans; when their job was finished, they set out to conquer Blue Mesa.

They made a striking discovery. In the remote canyons of the mesa were Indian rock villages, undisturbed for three hundred years and in a miraculous state of preservation. This gift of history stirred Tom to a strong decision. His find should be presented to his country; the relics must not be exploited for profit. With Roddie's consent, he took six hundred dollars, boarded a train, and left for Washington. Weeks later he returned, worn out by red tape and indifference, only to learn that Roddie had finally weakened and sold the Indian treasures to a foreign scientist. In a climax of bitterness, he quarreled with Roddie. A year later, he walked into the professor's garden.

Recalling Tom Outland had always brought the professor a kind of second youth. Tom was the type of person the professor had started out to be—vigorous, unspoiled, and ambitious. Marrying Lillian had brought happiness, nonetheless real for having now faded; but it had chained him, he felt, and diverted the true course of his life. Now, reviewing the past, the professor suddenly felt tired and old. At the news that the travelers would soon return, he thought he could not again assume a family role that had become meaningless.

When Augusta came for the keys to reopen the new house, she found the professor lying unconscious on the floor of his den. Its one window had blown shut and the unvented gas stove had done the rest. Augusta sent for the doctor, and the professor was revived. He found that his temporary release from consciousness had cleared his mind. He was not only ready to face his family, but he was also ready to face himself and a problem that came too late for him to flee.

Critical Evaluation:

During her lifetime, Willa Cather was known primarily for her novels, notably *One of Ours* (1922), which won the Pulitzer Prize, and such classics of Midwestern and Western life as *O Pioneers!* (1913), *My Ántonia* (1918), and *Death Comes for the Archbishop* (1927). However, later studies of her life and works have led critics to conclude that Cather deserves an even higher place in the annals of American literature than she has generally been given. They point not only to her influence on other writers, especially the help she gave those who were new and unknown during her years as an editor of *McClure's*, but also to the craftsmanship she displayed in hundreds of articles, reviews, and essays, as well as in her short stories, many of which appeared in national magazines noted for the high quality of their fiction.

Cather is no longer called a local color writer or a women's writer. Instead, critics are finding themselves ever more impressed with the depth of Cather's knowledge, as revealed in her subtle and effective allusions; with her technical virtuosity, anticipating the methods of modernism; and with her profound vision, which enabled her to identify the most troublesome issues of her time.

Although it is not among Cather's most famous novels, *The Professor's House* is one of her most interesting. The work is dominated by the character of the protagonist. Godfrey St. Peter is a rather unlikely hero, in that he is a middle-aged professor established in his profession but not famous outside of his discipline, a married man without any plans for an extramarital affair, and a father whose daughters are safely married off and out of the house. His immediate problem, the move to a new house, would seem to be a purely domestic matter.

However, Cather soon makes it clear that there is much more at issue than a change of environment. The professor is a man caught between three worlds, and ill at ease in all of them. His movements among the worlds, in search of a home, constitute the real plot of the novel.

The world where the professor is happiest is the house where he spent the early days of his marriage. When everyone else moves out, the professor's first reaction to the change might be called denial. Arguing that he cannot work anywhere except in his little attic, the professor leases the house for an extended period. Thus, at least during working hours, he can pretend that nothing has changed. He can even pretend that the unseen empty rooms are inhabited by a loving wife and two young, innocent children. To the professor, the old house is the past, and as long as he remains in it, the past still exists.

The world that contains everything the professor loathes and fears is represented by the new house. It was purchased with his money, but the place has been taken over by Lillian. In the new house, Lillian is no longer the person the professor married; instead, she is as coldly materialistic as the era in which she is living. Lillian seems quite at ease with her daughters, especially the wealthy Rosamond, and enchanted with her sons-in-law, who remind her of her youth. However, whenever he enters this world, the professor finds himself plunged into despair. It is no wonder that as soon as Lillian leaves for Europe, he moves back into the old house.

The professor is also aware of the existence of a third world, Tom Outland's Blue Mesa. Though he has never actually been there, the professor still feels the call of the unspoiled villages that Outland described so vividly. Like Outland, the professor saw Blue Mesa as symbolizing nature and a life in harmony with nature, and with Outland, he grieved when it was pillaged. Since Outland's death, however, Blue Mesa has taken on some added meanings for the professor. Not only does it represent a past that was lived and lost by his alter ego, Outland, but it also symbolizes all that he himself has lost.

This interpretation of *The Professor's House* makes it clear why Cather constructed her novel as she did. The first long section establishes the nature of the two worlds between which the professor is expected to choose. Cather then brings Tom back to life, so that he can put the case for the third world, Blue Mesa. In the final section, however, the professor has to face the fact that two of his options are no longer available. The old house will not enable him to return to his "first" youth, nor can his memories of Outland and Blue Mesa take him back to his "second," lost youth. The possibilities before him are either escape into death or acceptance of the house and the corrupt, materialistic world.

By sending Augusta to save the professor, it may be argued that Cather has begged her own question. Her professor never does decide whether death is worse than a joyless life. In later novels, however, such as *Death Comes for the Archbishop*, Cather would be more optimistic. While she still saw greed as a major force in the modern world, she also believed that dedicated human beings could triumph over it. If there had been a sequel to *The Professor's House*, the professor might well have won.

"Critical Evaluation" by Rosemary M. Canfield Reisman

Bibliography:
Bloom, Harold, ed. *Willa Cather*. New York: Chelsea House, 1985. A collection of studies of Cather. Two important and very different interpretations of *The Professor's House* appear in essays by David Daiches and E. K. Brown. The place to start.
Leddy, Michael. "*The Professor's House*: The Sense of an Ending." *Studies in the Novel* 23 (Winter, 1991): 443-451. Believes the ending makes a valid point although appearing vague. The fact that the professor is able to rediscover his boyhood home in Kansas points to a renewal or rebirth at the end.
Love, Glen A. "*The Professor's House:* Cather, Hemingway, and the Chastening of American Prose Style." *Western American Literature* 24 (February, 1990): 295-311. Says Cather's writing style is closer to the modern style because of her economy and lack of emotion. Uses *The Professor's House* as an example of that prose style.
O'Brien, Sharon. *Willa Cather: The Emerging Voice*. New York: Oxford University Press, 1987. Says the professor is the alter ego of Cather.
Stout, Janis P. "Autobiography as Journey in *The Professor's House*." *Studies in American Fiction* 19 (Autumn, 1991): 203-215. Examines the writing of autobiography and the boundaries between literature and life. Specifically looks at Cather's travels and how these affect her inspirations and writing of *The Professor's House*.
Yongue, Patricia Lee. "Willa Cather's *The Professor's House* and Dutch Genre Painting." *Renascence* 31 (Spring, 1979): 155-167. Equates a pictorial, psychological, and structural significance with "Tom Outland's Story." The professor's house was made to look like a Dutch painting. Places emphasis on visualizing the description as if it were a picture.

PROMETHEUS BOUND

Type of work: Drama
Author: Aeschylus (525/524-456/455 B.C.E.)
Type of plot: Tragedy
Time of plot: Antiquity
Locale: A barren cliff in Scythia
First performed: Prometheus desmōtes, date unknown (English translation, 1777)

> *Principal characters:*
> PROMETHEUS, a Titan
> HEPHAESTUS, his kinsman and the god of fire
> KRATOS, Might
> BIA, Force
> OCEANUS, the god of the sea
> Io, the daughter of the river god Inachus
> HERMES, the winged messenger of the gods

The Story:

Condemned by Zeus for giving fire to mortals, the Titan Prometheus was brought to a barren cliff in Scythia by Hephaestus, the god of fire, and two guards named Kratos and Bia. There he was to be bound to the jagged cliffs with bonds as strong as adamant. Kratos and Bia were willing to obey Zeus's commands, but Hephaestus experienced pangs of sorrow and was reluctant to bind his kinsman to the storm-beaten cliff in that desolate region where no one ever came and where Prometheus would never again hear the voice or see the form of a human being. He grieved that the Titan was doomed forever to be guardian of the desolate cliff, but he was powerless against the commands of Zeus. At last, he chained Prometheus to the cliff. He riveted his arms beyond release, thrust a wedge of adamant straight through his heart, and put iron girths on both his sides with shackles around his legs. After Hephaestus and Bia departed, Kratos remained to hurl one last taunt at Prometheus, asking him what aid he expected humankind to offer their benefactor. The gods who gave Prometheus his name, which meant Forethinker, had been foolish, Kratos pointed out, for Prometheus required a higher intelligence to do his thinking for him.

Alone and chained, Prometheus called upon the winds, the waters, mother earth, and the sun to look on him and see how the gods tortured a god. He admitted that he would have to bear his lot as best he could because the power of fate was invincible, but he remained defiant. He had committed no crime, he insisted; he had merely loved humankind. He remembered how the gods first conceived the plan to revolt against the rule of Kronos and seat Zeus on the throne. At first Prometheus did his best to bring about a reasonable peace between the ancient Titans and the gods. When he failed, and to avoid further violence, he had ranged himself on the side of Zeus, who through the counsel of Prometheus overthrew Kronos. Once on the throne, Zeus parceled out to the lesser gods their share of power, but he ignored mortals. His ultimate plan was to destroy them completely and create another race that would cringe and be servile to Zeus's every word. Among all the gods, only Prometheus objected to this heartless proposal, and it was Prometheus' courage, his act alone, which had saved human beings from burial in the deepest black of Hades. It was he who had taught blind hopes to spring within the hearts of mortals, and he had given them the gift of fire. He had understood the significance of these deeds, had sinned willingly.

Oceanus, Prometheus' brother, came to offer aid out of love and kinship, but he first offered Prometheus advice and preached humility in the face of Zeus's wrath. Prometheus remained proud, defiant, and refused his offer of help on the grounds that Oceanus himself would be punished were it discovered that he sympathized with a rebel. Convinced by Prometheus' argument, Oceanus took sorrowful leave of his brother.

Once more Prometheus recalled that human beings were creatures without language who had been ignorant of everything before Prometheus came and told them of the rising and setting of stars, of numbers, of letters, of the function of beasts of burden, of the utility of ships, of curing diseases, of happiness and lurking evil, and of methods to bring wealth in iron, silver, copper, and gold out of the earth. In spite of his torment, he rejoiced that he had taught the arts to humankind.

Io, daughter of the river god Inachus, came to the place where Prometheus was chained. Because she was beloved by Zeus, his wife, Hera, had out of jealousy turned Io into a cow and set Argus, the hundred-eyed monster, to watch her. When Zeus had Argus put to death, Hera sent a gadfly to sting Io and drive her all over the earth. Prometheus prophesied her future wanderings to the end of the earth and that the day would come when Zeus would restore her to human form and together they would conceive a son named Epaphus. Before Io left, Prometheus also named his own rescuer, Hercules, who with his bow and arrow would kill the eagle devouring his vital parts.

Hermes, Zeus's messenger, came to see Prometheus and threatened him with more awful terrors at the hands of angry Zeus. Prometheus, still defiant, belittled Hermes' position among the gods and called him a mere menial. Suddenly there was a turbulent rumbling of the earth, accompanied by lightning, thunder, and blasts of wind. Zeus shattered the rock with a thunderbolt and hurled Prometheus into an abysmal dungeon within the earth. Such was the terrible fate of the Fire-Bearer who defied the gods.

Critical Evaluation:

In several ways *Prometheus Bound* is something of a puzzle. The date of its first production is unknown, though it can probably be assumed to have come rather late in Aeschylus' career, possibly between 466 B.C.E. and 456 B.C.E., the year of his death. Because this is the only surviving play of the Aeschylean trilogy on Prometheus, it is also not known whether it was intended to be the first or second in the trilogy, though it is known that it was to be followed by *Prometheus Unbound. Prometheus Bound* is the one extant play by Aeschylus to deal directly with a metaphysical problem by means of supernatural characters. Yet even the questions raised in the work remain unresolved. It is a mystery centering on a mystery.

The situation of the play is static: Prometheus is fastened to a Scythian crag for having enabled humankind to live when Zeus was intending to destroy this ephemeral creature. Once Hephaestus wedges and binds him down, Prometheus is immobile. Thereafter the theatrical movement lies in his visitors—the chorus of nymphs, Oceanus, Io, and Hermes. Essentially this is a drama of ideas, and those ideas probe the nature of the cosmos. It is irrelevant that the characters are extinct Greek gods, for the issues that Aeschylus raises are eternal ones.

The Greeks loved a contest, and *Prometheus Bound* is about a contest of wills. On the one side is Zeus, who is omnipotent in this world, while on the other is Prometheus, who has divine intelligence. Neither will give an inch, for each feels he is perfectly justified. Zeus rules by right of conquest, and Prometheus resists by right of moral superiority. On Zeus's side are Might and Force, the powers of compulsion and tyranny, but Prometheus has knowledge and prescience.

Zeus, inscrutable and majestic as he is, does not appear except through his agents who enforce his will. The drama begins and ends with the exercise of his power, which is used here simply to make Prometheus suffer. This power first binds Prometheus to a crag and finally envelops him in a cataclysm. Zeus has a fearsome capacity to inflict pain, not merely on Prometheus but on Io as well, and in both instances it was motivated by what he perceived as their disobedience. Prometheus opposed Zeus by giving human beings the fire and skills needed to survive; Io resisted Zeus's love. Prometheus, being a Titan, had shown rebellion on the divine plane, while Io rebels on the human level. The price of their rebellion is written in their flesh, and both regard Zeus as their persecutor.

Aeschylus certainly disliked political tyranny, but it is a mistake to read this play merely as a parable of human inhumanity. The issues go far deeper, for Prometheus has omniscience and therefore knew what would come of his revolt. He made a great personal sacrifice when he supported humankind out of compassion. He is a savior and a tremendous hero, but his knowledge does not keep him from suffering like a mortal, nor does it make him accept his pain calmly. He knows why he suffers but defies his fate nevertheless, for he is convinced that he is right and Zeus wrong. Moreover, he claims that Zeus is not the ultimate power, indeed, that Zeus must submit to the Fates and the Furies.

Prometheus holds the winning hand in this play, for he possesses a secret that Zeus needs to retain his power. This knowledge is his only consolation in his torment. Every counsel to moderation or humility is vain, for Prometheus has no intention of giving up the joy of seeing Zeus humbled just to alleviate his own agony. This motivation comes through clearly in the bitter dialogue with Hermes.

Prometheus is not only self-righteous and vengeful, but also full of arrogant pride. He chooses his pain; perhaps he even deserves it. No one justifies Zeus, for he is beyond any notion of justice, but Prometheus exults in justifying himself to any divinity who will listen. Yet because of his services to humankind, the audience must feel compassion for him. He is an authentic tragic hero, arousing both pity and fear.

As a dramatic character, Io represents the human condition. The daughter of a god, she is shut out of her home by Zeus's command, given a bestial body, and made to run over the face of the earth in pain, stung by the ghost of many-eyed Argus (conscience). Only in the distant future will she and Zeus be reconciled.

The resolution of the Zeus-Prometheus conflict in Aeschylus' *Prometheus Unbound* can only be surmised. It is possible that Zeus gained in maturity after centuries of rule and decided to release the Titan, after which Prometheus may have given him the secret. Just as human beings evolved through the gifts of Prometheus into civilized creatures, Zeus may have changed and made his reign one of wisdom and force. It is hard to believe that Prometheus would alter unless such a change did come about in Zeus, but this is pure speculation. The debate between Prometheus and Zeus remains open. Aeschylus never solves this dilemma in the play, he merely shows it in the strongest dramatic terms. Tautly written, *Prometheus Bound* is profound precisely because it remains an enigma.

"Critical Evaluation" by James Weigel, Jr.

Bibliography:
Grene, David. "Introduction to *Prometheus Bound*." In *Aeschylus: The Complete Greek Trage-dies*, edited by David Grene and Richmond Lattimore. Vol. 1. Chicago: University of Chicago Press, 1969. Reviews eighteenth century criticism of *Prometheus Bound* and

compares it to Aristotle's *Poetics* (c. 334/323 B.C.E.). Discusses problems with the play, including an episodic plot, the improbable and extravagant characters, and the uncouth diction.

Kitto, H. D. F. *Greek Tragedy: A Literary Study*. London: Methuen, 1970. Dates *Prometheus Bound* in the category of Old Tragedy. One chapter offers a detailed examination of the play.

_____. *Poiesis: Structure and Thought*. Berkeley: University of California Press, 1966. Discusses what is known as Farnall's Dilemma: that Aeschylus was writing about Zeus in a derogatory sense and that the playwright should have been prosecuted for blasphemy. Because he was not, he could not have written *Prometheus Bound*.

Podlecki, Anthony J. *The Political Background of Aeschylean Tragedy*. Ann Arbor: University of Michigan Press, 1966. Discusses similarities between *Prometheus Bound* and the *Oresteia* (458 B.C.E.).

Stanford, William Bedell. *Aeschylus in His Style: A Study in Language and Personality*. Dublin: Dublin University Press, 1942. Claims that Aeschylus borrowed language in *Prometheus Bound* from two types of source, one literary and the other colloquial. Designed to help students better understand the language of Aeschylus.

Thomson, George. *Aeschylus and Athens: A Study in the Social Origins of Drama*. New York: Grosset & Dunlap, 1968. Presents history and interpretations of the myth of Prometheus; explains how this myth fits into *Prometheus Bound*.

PROMETHEUS UNBOUND
A Lyrical Drama in Four Acts

Type of work: Poetry
Author: Percy Bysshe Shelley (1792-1822)
Type of plot: Allegory
Time of plot: Antiquity
Locale: Asia
First published: 1820

Principal characters:
PROMETHEUS, a Titan
EARTH, his mother
ASIA, Prometheus' wife
JUPITER, king of the gods
DEMOGORGON, supreme power, ruling the gods
MERCURY, messenger of the gods
HERAKLES, hero of virtue and strength
PANTHEA and
IONE, the Oceanides

The Story:

Prometheus, the benefactor of humankind, was bound to a rocky cliff by order of Jupiter, who was jealous of the Titan's power. Three thousand years of torture Prometheus suffered there, while heat and cold and many torments afflicted him. An eagle continually ate at his heart. Prometheus nevertheless continued to defy the power of Jupiter. At last Prometheus asked Panthea and Ione, the two Oceanides, to repeat to him the curse he had pronounced upon Jupiter when Jupiter had first begun to torture him. Neither his mother Earth nor the Oceanides would answer him. At last the Phantasm of Jupiter appeared and repeated the curse. When Prometheus heard the words, he repudiated them. Now that he had suffered tortures and found that his spirit remained unconquered, he wished pain to no living thing. Earth and the Oceanides mourned that the curse had been withdrawn, for they thought Jupiter had at last conquered Prometheus' spirit.

Then Mercury approached with the Furies. Mercury told the captive that he would suffer even greater tortures if he did not reveal the secret that Prometheus alone knew—the future fate of Jupiter. Jupiter, afraid, wished to avert catastrophe by learning the secret, and Mercury promised that Prometheus would be released if he revealed it. Prometheus, however, refused. He admitted only that he knew Jupiter's reign would come to an end, that he would not be king of the gods for all eternity. Prometheus said that he was willing to suffer torture until Jupiter's reign ended. Although the Furies tried to frighten him by describing the pains they could inflict, they knew they had no power over his soul.

The Furies mocked Prometheus and humankind, showing him visions of blood and despair on earth; they showed the Passion of Christ and humanity's disregard for his message of love. Fear and hypocrisy ruled; tyrants took the thrones of the world. A group of spirits appeared and prophesied that Love would cure the ills of humankind. They prophesied also that Prometheus would be able to bring Love to earth and halt the reign of evil and grief. When the spirits had gone, Prometheus acknowledged the power of Love, for his love for Asia, his wife, had enabled him to suffer pain without surrendering.

While Asia mourned alone in a lovely valley for her lost husband, Panthea appeared to tell of two dreams she had had. In one, she saw Prometheus released from bondage and all the world filled with sweetness. In the other dream she had received only a command to follow. Just then the echoes in the valley broke their silence. They called Asia and Panthea to follow them. The listeners obeyed. Asia and Panthea followed the echoes to the realm of Demogorgon, the supreme power ruling the gods. They stopped on a pinnacle of rock, but spirits beckoned them down into Demogorgon's cave. There he told them that he would answer any question they put to him. When they asked who had made the living world, he replied that God had created it. Then they asked who had made pain and evil. Prometheus had given knowledge to humankind, but humankind had not eradicated evil with all the gifts of science. They asked whether Jupiter was the source of these ills, the evil master over humanity.

Demogorgon answered that nothing that served evil could be master, for only eternal Love ruled all. Asia asked when Prometheus would gain his freedom and bring Love into the world to conquer Jupiter. Demogorgon then showed his guests the passage of the Hours. A dreadful Hour passed, marking Jupiter's fall; the next hour was beautiful, marking Prometheus' release. Asia and Panthea accompanied this spirit of the Hour in her chariot and passed by Age, Manhood, Youth, Infancy, and Death into a new paradise.

Meanwhile, Jupiter, who had just married Thetis, celebrated his omnipotence over all but the human soul. Then Demogorgon appeared and pronounced judgment on Jupiter. Jupiter cried for mercy, but his power was gone. He sank downward through darkness and ruin. At the same time Herakles approached Prometheus. In the presence of Asia, Panthea, the Spirit of the Hour, and Earth, the captive was set free. Joyfully, Prometheus told Asia how they would spend the rest of their days together with Love. Then he sent the Spirit of the Hour to announce his release to all humankind. He kissed Earth, and Love infused all of her animal, vegetable, and mineral parts.

The Spirit of Earth came to the cave where Asia and Prometheus lived and told them of the transformation that had come over humankind. Anger, pride, insincerity, and all the other ills of humanity had passed away. The Spirit of the Hour reported other wonders that took place. Thrones were empty, and all ruled over themselves, free from guilt or pain. People were, however, still subject to chance, death, and mutability, without which they would oversoar their destined place in the world.

Later in a vision Panthea and Ione saw how all the evil things of the world lay dead and decayed. Earth's happiness was boundless, and even the moon felt the beams of Love from Earth as snow melted on its bleak lunar mountains. Earth rejoiced that hate, fear, and pain had left humankind forever. Humanity was now master of its fate and of all the secrets of Earth.

Critical Evaluation:

Prometheus Unbound glorifies the rebellious impulse toward freedom in the human spirit. The poem dramatizes and explains Percy Bysshe Shelley's philosophical and religious under-standing, which was individual. *Prometheus Unbound* is Shelley's credo; the impulse to freedom and to rebel against authoritarian orthodoxy is one he valued highly. Shelley's beliefs typify Romanticism. As did such Romantic poets as William Blake, Lord Byron, and Samuel Taylor Coleridge, Shelley wrote of the freedom of the individual and of the primacy of the imagination. Institutions, social structures, and established belief were, in these poets' view, suspect. For them, evil lay in limitation imposed on the human spirit, which, when free, was good.

Shelley and other Romantic poets also at times did more than write about their beliefs. They were activists in the causes of liberty and reform of their times. Shelley, for example, favored vegetarianism, freedom for Ireland and for slaves, the abolition of monarchy and marriage, the overthrow of established religion, extension of the franchise, empowerment of the working class, and equality for women. He advocated these ideas in his writing, which in his time was a provocative and courageous act. While a student at Oxford he collaborated on a pamphlet titled *The Necessity of Atheism* (1811) and sent copies to all the college authorities and every bishop in the Church of England. He was expelled as a result.

Prometheus Unbound is a play in verse in which the poetry takes precedence over the drama. This work could not easily be brought to the stage; the reader may best realize the drama of the conflicts of gods and allegorical figures with the imagination. From Prometheus' opening oration to the paean-like ending, the reader is carried along with the delicacy, vivacity, thunder, or choric effect of the lines. The spacelessness of the work is its virtue, and its muted, ethereal effect is lyrically matchless. This work illustrates how well Shelley fashions not only his own invented lyric patterns but also the Pindaric ode, the fourteen-syllable line, the Spenserian stanza, couplets, and infinite variations of the Greek choral effects. Every conceivable meter can be detected; the inversions, the intricately developed rhythm patterns are numerous. A "lyrical flowering" seems an appropriate phrase for the entire work, perhaps Shelley's greatest.

Although Shelley wrote poetry that was intended to generate controversy, and that did, his poetry is unmatched in its civilized, urbane, and elegant spirit. His work is still capable of offending those whose political or religious convictions are conservative. Perhaps for this reason, his verse is sometimes wrongly described as being strident or self-centered.

Prometheus Unbound uses the well-known Greek myth as a vehicle for Shelley's themes. The playwright Aeschylus' tragedy, *Prometheus Bound* (fifth century B.C.E.), was known to Shelley, who could read Greek. In Aeschylus' version of the myth, Prometheus made humanity out of clay. Zeus, envious, retaliated by oppressing humanity and depriving it of fire. Prometheus stole fire from heaven for humanity and taught people many arts. Zeus then caused Prometheus to be chained to a rock and refused to free him until Prometheus agreed to reveal a secret prophecy with which he had been entrusted.

In the preface to *Prometheus Unbound*, Shelley points out that writers in ancient Greece felt free to revise myths as needed for their themes. Shelley states that it is not his purpose to restore the lost play, *Prometheus Unbound*, that Aeschylus was supposed to have written after *Prometheus Bound*. Rather, Shelley intends in his play to create a new myth appropriate to Shelley's times. Shelley compares Prometheus with Satan, who, in Christian myth and in John Milton's *Paradise Lost* (1667), rebels (for many Romantics, heroically) against God. "Prometheus," Shelley argues, "is . . . the type of the highest perfection of moral and intellectual nature, impelled by the purest and the truest motives to the best and noblest ends."

"Critical Evaluation" by Dennis R. Dean

Bibliography:
Baker, Carlos. *Shelley's Major Poetry: The Fabric of a Vision*. Princeton, N.J.: Princeton University Press, 1948. An introductory survey of Shelley's most important writings in verse, this standard work includes a chapter and an appendix on the poem.
Cameron, Kenneth Neill. *Shelley: The Golden Years*. Cambridge, Mass.: Harvard University Press, 1974. In part a biography, this survey of Shelley's work from 1814 to 1822 analyzes all of his important poetry and culminates with a two-chapter discussion of the poem.

King-Hele, Desmond. *Shelley: The Man and the Poet.* New York: Yoseloff, 1960. Shelley's evident interest in science is explored.

Shelley, Percy Bysshe. *Prometheus Unbound: A Variorum Edition.* Edited by John Lawrence Zillman. Seattle: University of Washington Press, 1959. Offers a full text of the poem and line-by-line commentary on it. There are also eight appendices, including "The Prometheus Story Before Shelley."

Wasserman, Earl R. *Shelley's "Prometheus Unbound": A Critical Reading.* Baltimore: The Johns Hopkins University Press, 1965. An example of close reading and profound thought, Wasserman's philosophical interpretation of *Prometheus Unbound* defends the poem's fundamental unity.

THE PROMISED LAND

Type of work: Novel
Author: Henrik Pontoppidan (1857-1943)
Type of plot: Social criticism
Time of plot: Late nineteenth century
Locale: Denmark
First published: Det forjættede land, 1891-1895 (English translation, 1896)

Principal characters:

EMANUEL HANSTED, a clergyman and a reformer
HANSINE, his wife
MISS TONNESEN, his former fiancée
DR. HASSING, a physician

The Story:

Emanuel Hansted, the minister son of a wealthy Copenhagen couple, had left his hometown years before to take over a pastorate in the country. Somewhat of a reformer, he had become enthusiastic about the socialism rife in Europe in the second half of the nineteenth century, and to prove his fellowship with the peasants whom he served, he had married a peasant girl and had undertaken to farm the land on which the rectory was situated.

As the years passed Hansted's wife, Hansine, presented him with three children; his land, however, repaid him only with debts. Although he tried experiment after experiment, Emanuel's fields did not produce enough to support his family. Stubbornly, Emanuel refused to acknowledge that he was no farmer; he even continued to refuse any payment from his parishioners and gave away the money he received for the benefit of the poor.

Despite his sacrifices, despite his never-flagging efforts to share their lives, and his ties with them through marriage, the peasants did not accept him as one of themselves. The fact that he had come among them as an outlander was too strong for them to forget, even in the times of stress that came when the newly formed People's Party of Denmark, representing chiefly the peasantry, was trying to control the government in order to provide for the education of the masses and to improve the lot of the common people generally.

To the casual eye, Emanuel might have seemed a peasant, for he had nothing to do with the few gentry who lived in the vicinity. He even distrusted the doctor, whom he had to call in occasionally to treat a member of his family. Indeed, Emanuel summoned Dr. Hassing only when an emergency existed. As for his family, Emanuel had put his father and his sister entirely out of his mind; only his wife and children, who tied him to the peasantry, were acknowledged as kin.

One summer, all of nature and humankind seemed determined to show that Emanuel was a misfit in the rural area he had adopted. His crops were even poorer than usual. He had borrowed the seed he put into the ground, and, after it was planted, nature refused to send the weather he needed to produce successful yields in the fields. In Copenhagen the Conservative Party gained in strength and defeated the People's Party—first in small items, then in large. As the peasants lost their political power, the people of Emanuel's parish began to look upon him as one who belonged on the other side.

As if that were not enough, Emanuel's oldest child, a son, began to suffer from an ear inflammation that had gone untended for two years. At last, upon Hansine's insistence, Emanuel sent for Dr. Hassing. The physician could not believe that Emanuel had permitted the child's health to fall into such a dangerous state; Emanuel, on his part, could not understand that the child was really ill. Failing to follow the doctor's advice, he treated his son as if he were well and healthy. The boy died as a result of his father's failure to face reality,

Before long, Emanuel and Hansine began to drift apart, for their son's death had erected a barrier between them that had been years in the making. Hansine felt that her husband was unhappy, and she believed that he actually wanted to escape from the dismal, unappreciative rural parish.

Quite by chance, while out walking alone to prepare his Sunday sermon, Emanuel came upon Dr. Hassing and a small party of picnickers. Prevailed upon to join the group, he found among them Miss Tonnesen, his former fiancée from Copenhagen. Emanuel walked back to Dr. Hassing's home with the picnickers and, because it was growing dark, remained for supper. The genteel conversation, the quiet wealth of the home, the very food on the table, the music after supper—all of these things reminded Emanuel of what he had lost when he had refused Miss Tonnesen's love, rejected the family warmth of his parents' home, and turned instead toward the simple, rude life of the peasants. In the days following he ridiculed the people with whom he had spent a few hours, but Hansine saw that he was merely trying to convince himself that he had chosen the right path in his life's work.

A few weeks later Miss Tonnesen, who had gone out into the rural area to prove to herself that her former suitor had sunk beneath her, visited the rectory. Her father had been the former rector of the parish; under his care the rectory had been a place of beauty, both within and without. His daughter, seeing it for the first time in many years, was amazed to see how Emanuel had let it fall into disrepair. Only a few of the rooms, equipped with the barest of essentials, were in use. The gardens and lawns were overgrown; even the outbuildings and fields had been years without proper care. Miss Tonnesen could scarcely believe that the man she had loved could have permitted the grounds in his charge, and himself as well, to slip into the state in which she found them.

Miss Tonnesen's visit bothered Hansine. She saw in the other woman all that her husband had given up when he had married her instead of a woman from his own social class. Even Hansine's children asked if they could go to Copenhagen to visit the beautiful lady. Emanuel himself realized that Miss Tonnesen represented something he had lost but could still regain. He became dissatisfied with the peasantry, and they quickly sensed his unrest. His farmworkers left him when, angry because the rains ruined any chance he had of harvesting a crop of rye, he abused them for their laziness.

The climax came when the director of the district high school, a man who as head of the institution had done much for the peasants, died. Everyone in the region went to the funeral. After it was over, a political meeting formed of its own accord. Emanuel, when asked to address the meeting, spoke out against the sloth and narrow prejudices of the peasants. As he spoke, murmuring arose; he finally had to stop speaking when the crowd began to shout insults and ridicule. As he slowly left the meeting, he could hear a new speaker declaring that the pastor should return to his own people.

He met Hansine at the edge of the crowd; slowly they started home. On the way back Hansine told Emanuel that he ought to return to Copenhagen and she to her former life. He sadly agreed. The children, it was decided, would go with their father. To Emanuel's delight, his father and sister wrote him to return as soon as possible. As a result, one morning he and his remaining two children climbed into a carriage and drove away, while Hansine turned to walk to her parents' cottage.

Critical Evaluation:

Nobel Prize winner Henrik Pontoppidan attempted in *The Promised Land* to illustrate the conflicts that overtake a human being who attempts to submerge his instincts to his intellectual beliefs. Emanuel Hansted is a complicated, tormented individual, divided between theory and instinct, duty and passion. He is not entirely sympathetic, but he is understandable and pitiable. A dreamer, he tries unsuccessfully to gain the confidence of the peasants but, despite his efforts to make himself one with the soil and the peasant life, his urban background ultimately betrays his ambitions.

Pontoppidan's novel reflects the class distinctions and the division between town and country folk in nineteenth century Denmark, at a time when the peasants were struggling for a greater voice in the affairs of that country. As in the case of so many European novels dealing with social problems, the characterization, the plot, and the happenings are secondary to the social meaning and the tone of the work. As a result, the characters are types rather than individuals, and in a plot subordinate to theme the happenings are not skillfully tied together. Quite obviously these items were relatively unimportant to the author; he was intent upon giving a picture of the struggle between the People's Party and the Conservatives, and the effects of that struggle on individuals. Sympathetic to the less favored group, Pontoppidan, like so many problem novelists, told only one side of the story; one result is that his upper-class characters, like those of the American novelist Theodore Dreiser, are often overdrawn.

Pontoppidan writes with a deceptively aloof, almost cold, style, but his characters are warm-blooded, many-faceted human beings. Hansine, Emanuel's wife, speaks little, but it is clear that she feels deeply. He married her because she was a peasant, because he felt that she would help him to forget his past, but gradually she comes to realize that they are wrong for each other. With great artistry, the author subtly suggests her feelings, implying much with few words. Her sacrifice at the end of the book is both inevitable and touching.

Emanuel's past in Copenhagen is only revealed in pieces, through allusions in conversation. His former relationship with the attractive, sophisticated Ragnhild Tonnesen is disclosed bit by bit; the reader discovers the realities behind the appearances slowly. This technique requires great control on the part of the author, but it builds with relentless inevitability to the emotional crisis at the heart of the book. Politics and religion play an important part in the novel, but primarily it is a story of human beings.

Emanuel saw everything evil in the sophistication of his past life in the city and made the mistake of seeing only good in the crude life of the peasants. He craved truth and justice and saw a moral earnestness in the peasant faces which touched him deeply. So completely did he reject the city and its ways, including science and progress, that he refused to let a doctor see his son until it was too late to save the boy's life. There was a dormant power in the people, he believed, and he wanted to be the one to raise it. As one of the other characters comments, however, he only sacrificed himself—and his family—to his opinions. Niels, on the other hand, is his exact opposite, a young upwardly mobile peasant, writing for the local newspapers in his spare time, ambitious, hopeful for the future. Everywhere, signs of change are in the air, but Emanuel cannot understand where they are leading. His vague dreams and misplaced ideals only lead him astray. His doubts and struggles are vividly portrayed by the author in this important novel of the birth of the modern age in Denmark.

Bibliography:

Gray, Charlotte Schiander. "From Opposition to Identification: The Social and Psychological Structure Behind Henrik Pontoppidan's Literary Development." *Scandinavian Studies* 51

(Summer, 1979): 273-284. Explicitly influenced by Freudian psychological theory. Sees Emmanuel Hansted as a kind of negative parallel to the author. Pontoppidan swerves away from Hansted's excessive idealism in his own authorial perspective.

Jones, W. Glyn. "Henrik Pontoppidan (1857-1943)." *Modern Language Review* 52, no. 3 (July, 1957): 576-583. Emphasizes Pontoppidan's interest in Danish history and politics, especially his relationship to the Estrup regime. Sees the novel as the author's moral judgment upon the Danish nation.

Madsen, Borge. "The Promised Land." In *Scandinavian Studies*, edited by Carl F. Bayerschmidt and Erik J. Friis. Seattle: University of Washington Press, 1965. Emphasizes the inner psychology of Emmanuel Hansted, exploring the motivations behind his impracticality and the novel's ambivalent perspective toward the fantastic.

Mitchell, P. M. *Henrik Pontoppidan*. Boston: Twayne, 1979. The only book-length study of Pontoppidan in English. Emphasizes the novel's skepticism toward traditional Danish state and church structures. Discusses the novel within the wider context of Pontopiddan's career in which it was not the final word. An excellent beginning for further study.

Robertson, John George. "Henrik Pontoppidan." In *Essays and Addresses on Literature, 1935.* Reprint. Freeport, N.Y.: Books for Libraries Press, 1968. Explores the novel as a manual for the disillusioned. Sees Pontopiddan's work as heavily influenced by Henrik Ibsen.

THE PROPHET

Type of work: Poetry
Author: Kahlil Gibran (Gibran Kahlil Gibran, 1883-1931)
Type of plot: Philosophical
Time of plot: Ielool, the month of reaping
Locale: The city of Orphalese
First published: 1923

> *Principal characters:*
> ALMUSTAFA, a mystic and prophet
> ALMITRA, a seer

Kahlil Gibran's *The Prophet* belongs to that group of unique publishing events that includes Edward FitzGerald's *The Rubáiyát of Omar Khayyám* (1859) and certain of the works of William Blake, to whom Gibran was compared. FitzGerald's translation appeals especially to the impressionable young adult, and a generation ago the poem was sometimes bound in leather in a miniature edition and used as a prom favor at college dances. Similarly, *The Prophet* owes much of its popularity to the young, who find in Gibran's poetry the elusive quality of sincerity. Word of mouth recommendations rather than the publisher's promotions have pushed hard-cover sales of this thin volume to truly remarkable numbers, considering that it is a book of poetry.

In order to understand the power of Gibran's poetry it is necessary to know something of his life, of the agonies of remorse that burned within him, of the loneliness of spirit that heightened his senses. Gibran Kahlil Gibran was born in Bechari (Basharri), Lebanon, the son of a poor shepherd family. When he was twelve, his mother took the family to Boston, hoping, like many immigrants of the day, to gain wealth quickly and then return to the homeland, where Gibran's easygoing father had remained to care for the family's small holdings. Soon the opportunities in the new world were apparent and the mother decided that the sensitive Kahlil must be educated so that he could become a great man. The older son and the two daughters joined the mother at unskilled labor in order to earn the money with which Kahlil might gain an education. Within a few years the family had been decimated by tuberculosis and only Kahlil and his sister Mariana remained. Kahlil never completely recovered from his grief and his sense of guilt over the fact that his family had, in a sense, died for him.

Bolstered by the loyalty and industry of Mariana, Kahlil Gibran began to write and draw, illustrating his own writings, as had William Blake. Financial success was elusive, but Gibran gained a patron who prevailed upon him to go abroad for study. He spent two years in Paris, then returned to the United States and soon set up a studio in Greenwich Village, where he worked for the remainder of his life. He began to publish in 1918 with *The Madman*, and in 1923 appeared his masterpiece, *The Prophet*, which has been translated into more than a dozen languages.

The illustrations that accompany most of the poetry Gibran produced are often as striking as his words, and his works now hang in some of America's finest art museums. Always frail, he was driven beyond endurance by an inner force that would not let him rest, and death overtook him in 1931 in the full flower of his productivity. His body was returned to Lebanon and buried with great honors in the village of his birth.

The Prophet comprises twenty-six poetic essays on various aspects of life, preceded by an introduction and followed by a farewell, wherein the Prophet promises to return to his people, borne by another woman after a momentary rest upon the wind. Thus, the continuity of life is implied, the circle of birth and death and rebirth.

The introduction, called "The Coming of the Ship," tells how the Prophet is about to board the ship that has arrived to take him back to his native land after twelve years among the people of the city of Orphalese. During these twelve years the people of the city have come to love and revere the Prophet for his wisdom and gentle spirit, and they gather in the great square before the temple and beseech him not to leave but to remain forever in their midst. As the multitude weeps and pleads, Almitra, the seer who had first befriended the Prophet on his arrival in the city, comes out of the sanctuary and asks him to speak to them of life before he departs.

She asks first that he speak of love, whereupon the Prophet admonishes the hushed audience to follow love when he beckons even though he may wound as he caresses, even though he may destroy dreams as he entices. For love demands complete commitment, a testing in the sacred fires, if one is to see into one's own heart and have knowledge of life's heart. The cowardly should cover themselves and flee from love, and those who can never be possessed by love can never know fulfillment.

The Prophet is then asked in turn to speak of marriage, children, giving, eating and drinking, work, joy and sorrow, houses, clothes, buying and selling, and, by a judge of the city, crime and punishment. In response to the latter request the Prophet speaks at length, pointing out that whereas the most righteous cannot rise above the highest which is in all people, so the weak and wicked cannot fall below the lowest in all people; therefore, people must condemn lightly, for they, the whole, are not entirely blameless for the evil done by one of their parts.

Then a lawyer in the crowd asks for comment on laws, an orator on freedom, and a woman priest on reason and passion, whereupon the Prophet compares reason to a ship's rudder and passion to its sails. Without both, the ship is useless. Without the rudder it will toss aimlessly; without the sails it will lie becalmed like a wingless bird.

The Prophet then speaks of pain, self-knowledge—wherein he likens the self to a limitless, an immeasurable, sea—teaching, friendship, talking, time, good and evil, prayer, pleasure, beauty—which he finds too elusive for definition—religion, and death. Of the last he urges mature acceptance, for, like the brook and the lake, life and death are one.

By the time the Prophet has finished speaking twilight has fallen, and he goes straightway to his ship, there to bid a final farewell to his followers. As the ship lifts anchor the sorrowful crowd disperses until only Almitra remains upon the seawall, watching his ship recede into the dusk and remembering his promise to return in another way at another time.

Gibran's insistent subjectivity, shrouded in a religious-like mysticism, swirls the reader toward the center of a vortex where evil has been flung aside and the human soul stands revealed in all its nobility and goodness.

Bibliography:
Gibran, Jean. *Kahlil Gibran: His Life and World.* Boston: New York Graphic Society, 1974. General overview of Gibran's life and the influences that shaped his writings. General references to *The Prophet* are found throughout.
Nassar, Eugene Paul. "Cultural Discontinuity in the Works of Kahlil Gibran." *MELUS* 7, no. 2 (Summer, 1980): 21-36. Looks at Gibran's experiences of cultural alienation and how these became the theme of loneliness that recurs throughout his writings, including *The Prophet.* Compares this poem to writings of William Blake, Walt Whitman, and others.

Nu'aymah, Mikha'il. *Kahlil Gibran: A Biography*. New York: Philosophical Library, 1973. A view of Gibran's life, times, and the influences that shaped his writings. Discusses Gibran's style and the form used in this poem; compares them to *Thus Spoke Zarathustra* (1883-1892) by Friedrich Nietzsche.

Young, Barbara. *This Man from Lebanon: A Study of Kahlil Gibran*. New York: Alfred A. Knopf, 1945. As a long-time secretary and confidant to Gibran, Young provides an intimate, behind-the scenes picture of Gibran's life and times. *The Prophet* is discussed as it relates to influential events and people in Gibran's life.

PROSERPINE AND CERES

Type of work: Short fiction
Author: Unknown
Type of plot: Myth
Time of plot: Antiquity
Locale: Mediterranean
First published: Unknown

> *Principal characters:*
> CERES, the goddess of fertility
> PROSERPINE, her daughter
> HADES, the king of the underworld
> VENUS, the goddess of love
> CUPID, her son
> TRIPTOLEMUS, the builder of a temple to Ceres
> ARETHUSA, a fountain nymph
> ALPHEUS, a river god
> DIANA, the goddess of the hunt
> JUPITER, the king of the gods
> MERCURY, a messenger of the gods

The Story:

One of the Titans, Typhoeus, long imprisoned for his part in the rebellion against Jupiter, lay in agony beneath Mount Aetna on the island of Sicily in the Mediterranean Sea. When Typhoeus groaned and stirred, he shook the sea and the island of Sicily so much that the god of the underworld, Hades, became frightened lest his kingdom be revealed to the light of day.

Rising to the upper world to make entrance to his kingdom, Hades was discovered by Venus, who ordered her son Cupid to aim one of his love darts into the breast of Hades and so cause him to fall in love with Proserpine, daughter of Ceres, goddess of fertility.

Proserpine had gone with her companions to gather flowers by the banks of a stream in the beautiful vale of Enna. There Hades, stricken by Cupid's dart, saw Proserpine, seized her, and lashed his fiery horses to greater speed as he carried her away. In her fright the girl dropped her apron, full of flowers she had gathered. At the River Cyane, Hades struck the earth with his scepter, causing a passageway to appear through which he drove his chariot and took his captive to the underworld.

Ceres searched for her daughter everywhere. At last, sad and tired, she sat down to rest. A peasant and his daughter found her in her disguise as an old woman; they took pity on her and urged her to go with them to their rude home. When the three arrived at the house, they found that the peasant's only son, Triptolemus, was dying. Ceres first gathered some poppies. Then, kissing the child, she restored him to health. The happy family bade her to join them in their simple meal of honey, cream, apples, and curds. Ceres put some of the poppy juice in the boy's milk. That night when he was sleeping, she placed the child in the fire. The mother, awakening, seized her child from the flames. Ceres assumed her proper form and told the parents that it had been her plan to make the boy immortal. Since the mother had hindered that plan, she would instead teach him the use of the plow.

Then the goddess mother continued her search for Proserpine until she returned to Sicily.

5393

There, at the very spot Hades had entered the underworld, she asked the river nymph if she had seen anything of her daughter. Fearful of punishment, the river nymph refused to tell what she had seen but gave to Ceres the belt of Proserpine, which the girl had lost in her struggles.

Ceres decided to take revenge upon the land, to deny it further gift of her favors so that herbage and grain would not grow. In an effort to save the land which Ceres was intent upon cursing, the fountain Arethusa told the following story to Ceres. Arethusa had been hunting in the forest, where she was formerly a woodland nymph. Finding a stream, she decided to bathe. As she sported in the water, the river god Alpheus began to call her. Frightened, the nymph ran, the god pursuing.

The goddess Diana, seeing her plight, changed Arethusa into a fountain that ran through the underworld and emerged in Sicily. While passing through the underworld, Arethusa saw Proserpine, now queen of the dead, sad at the separation from her mother but at the same time bearing the dignity and power of the bride of Hades. Ceres immediately demanded help from Jupiter, ruler of the gods. The king of the gods said that Proserpine should be allowed to return to the valley of Enna from which she had been abducted only if in the underworld she had taken no food.

Mercury was sent to demand Proserpine for her mother. Proserpine, however, had eaten of a pomegranate. She had eaten only part of the fruit, however, so a compromise was made. Half of the time she was to pass with her mother and the rest with Hades. Ceres, happy over the return of Proserpine during one half of each year, caused the earth to be fertile again during the time Proserpine lived with her.   .

Ceres remembered her promise to the peasant boy, Triptolemus. She taught him to plow and to plant seed, and he gathered with her all the valuable seeds of the earth. In gratitude the peasant's son built a temple to Ceres in Eleusis where priests administered rites called the Eleusinian mysteries. Those rites surpassed all other Greek religious celebrations. The mysteries involved, as does the story of Proserpine and Ceres, the cycle of death and growth.

Critical Evaluation:

This fertility myth seems to have Mycenaean (pre-Homeric) origins, but the earliest and in many ways the best version that survives is from the late seventh century B.C.E. in the Homeric hymn to Demeter, or Ceres. Demeter (either "earth mother" or "grain mother") and her daughter Persephone (corrupted by the Romans into Proserpina) were originally two aspects of one mythic personality: The mother was associated with the harvest, the daughter with the sprouting grain. The Greeks, fearfully avoiding mention of the daughter's name, called her simply Kore, that is, "grain" maiden. This practice of avoiding the actual name was usual with the powerful and mysterious chthonian (underworld) deities whom the Greeks wished not to risk offending.

The literary history of the myth is extensive, including two appearances in Ovid (*Metamorphoses*, c. 8 C.E., and *Fasti*, before 8 C.E.), but there are only minor variations, such as where the rape occurred, who Triptolemus was, how many pomegranate seeds Proserpine ate, and how much of the year she remains with Hades. The above synopsis, which is a conflation of Ovid's accounts, differs from the Homeric hymn in the Triptolemus episode. In the hymn, Ceres' hosts, Celeus and Metanira, are not peasants but the rulers of Eleusis, near Athens. In her old age, Metanira bears a child, Demopho(o)n, whom she gives to Ceres, disguised as Doso, to suckle. Triptolemus was one of Eleusis' youthful nobility and was among the first to participate in Ceres' mysteries, or secret rites, in the temple built by Celeus. The hymn also has Proserpine spend one-third of the year with her husband below the earth; this reflects a tripartite seasonal year of spring, summer, winter. Despite mention in the hymn that Proserpine emerges to the upperworld in the spring, reputable scholars argue that her four months' absence is associated with the summer-long storage of harvested grain in June. (The grain was put in jars in the cool earth till planting in the winter.) The traditional interpretation is that the fresh seed grain is planted in the winter and the maiden shoots emerge in the early spring.

The so-called Eleusinian mysteries most closely resembled what one might call a universal religion. Its objective was preparation for eternal peace through understanding the mystery of cyclic growth. Although great numbers of Greek-speaking persons were initiated into the mysteries, little authoritative information about them survives. Clement of Alexandria, a convert to Christianity, reveals that votaries dramatized the myth of Ceres and Proserpine, fasted, handled sacred objects, and partook of the sacramental porridge of water, flour, and mint that Ceres was offered at Eleusis. The so-called Lesser Mysteries were celebrated in Athens in the early spring; they consisted of prayers, purifications, and the like. The Great Mysteries were performed in September/October; nine days of grand procession from Athens to Eleusis and back featured numerous rituals, at the height of which priests and priestesses were consecrated. Certainly the mysteries relied heavily on symbolic ritual and mythic reenactment. The nine days of the Greater Mysteries correspond to the nine days of Ceres' fasting as she searched for her daughter; the pomegranate with its many "bloody" seeds symbolizes fertility; Proserpine's marriage to Hades metaphorically explains the mystery of fertilization and growth within the earth. It is even theorized that the secret dramas included ritualistic sexuality, imitating the *hieros gamos* ("sacred union") of the underworld deities that brings fertility to the fields. Such a ritual was common to a number of cults, and within the myth of Ceres herself is her union with her brother Jupiter, the sky god, which produced Proserpine.

The basic structure of the myth is simple: peaceful innocence, sudden violence, misguided revenge, and finally reconciliation; within this dramatic structure, the mythmakers have woven origins of the Eleusinian cult. Ovid's insertion of the Arethusa myth is forced, since it is merely preparation for its lengthier telling immediately following in the *Metamorphoses*. There are also some excellent descriptive sequences: the gathering of flowers by Proserpine, the sudden dark violence of Hades, the awesome burning of Metanira's child in the fire. Finally, the characterizations of both in Ovid's versions and in the hymn are classic: Proserpine as the innocent virgin, carefully protected; Demeter, the doting mother; Hades, the lustful villain who creates trouble when he makes an unprecedented appearance in the upperworld; Jupiter, the supreme administrator and magistrate, who must act to prevent the extinction, through starvation, of humanity (the gods' sacrificers) and who must strike a compromise between forces of equal power. The resolution is no doubt necessary to explain why in other myths Proserpine seems quite at ease in her role as queen of the dead. It is likely that her character is a confusion of the witch goddess, Hecate, and a primitive earth goddess. In the underworld, she rules with authority. There she appears to the various heroes who descend to Hades, including Orpheus, Aeneas, and others; she is also the object of an attempted rape by Theseus and Pirithous. The most significant twentieth century adaptation of the myth is the musical drama *Persephone* (1934) by Igor Stravinsky and André Gide, in which the heroine willingly sacrifices herself to bring joy and youth to the gloomy realm below.

"Critical Evaluation" by E. N. Genovese

Bibliography:
Campbell, Joseph. *The Masks of God: Occidental Mythology*. New York: Viking Press, 1964. Discusses images and symbolism of Proserpine and her mother Ceres.

Donovan, Josephine. *After the Fall: The Demeter-Persephone Myth in Wharton, Cather, and Glasgow*. University Park: Pennsylvania State University Press, 1989. Analyzes fictional symbols of Proserpine and Ceres in American women writers. Examines the image of the daughter and mother relationship as it is revealed in modern treatments.

Frazer, James. *The Golden Bough: A Study in Magic and Religion*. New York: Macmillan, 1922. Analyzes the Eleusinian mysteries associated with Ceres and Proserpine. Shows their similarities to the Egyptian goddesses Isis and Osiris, the Syrian Ishtar, and so on. Traces the movement of the beliefs to Northern Europe. Some mention of human sacrifice associated with Proserpine's death.

Gimbutas, Marija. *The Language of the Goddess*. San Francisco: Harper & Row, 1989. Puts Proserpine and Ceres in the context of their symbolic meaning: life giving and fertility. Ceres is seen as the earth mother and appears as a pregnant woman in pottery and burial sites.

Graves, Robert. *The Greek Myths*. New York: Penguin Books, 1960. A thorough retelling of the story of Ceres and Proserpine as corn goddesses. Proserpine is also connected with images of Aphrodite and Adonis. Claims Proserpine is involved with the Eleusinian mysteries.

PSEUDOLUS

Type of work: Drama
Author: Plautus (c. 254-184 B.C.E.)
Type of plot: Comedy
Time of plot: Late third century B.C.E.
Locale: Athens
First performed: 191 B.C.E. (English translation, 1774)

Principal characters:
SIMO, an old Athenian gentleman
CALIDORUS, his son
PSEUDOLUS, Simo's servant
BALLIO, a procurer, owner of Phoenicium
HARPAX, a messenger
SIMIA, a servant of one of Calidorus' friends
PHOENICIUM, a slave girl loved by Calidorus

The Story:

Pseudolus, a servant of the Athenian Simo, observed one day that his master's son Calidorus was deeply despondent about something. Questioning him on the matter, Pseudolus was given a letter from Phoenicium, a slave girl with whom Calidorus was in love. She had written that Ballio, her master, had sold her to a Macedonian military officer for the sum of twenty minae. However, the transaction was not yet complete; the officer had given Ballio fifteen minae to seal the bargain and had arranged that Phoenicium was to be delivered to a servant of his who would bring the remaining five minae and a letter bearing a seal to match the one the officer had made with his ring and left in Ballio's keeping. This servant was to arrive on the festival of Bacchus, now being celebrated. Calidorus was thoroughly upset by this news, for he had no money with which to buy Phoenicium and no prospect of acquiring any. At loose ends, he appealed to the wily Pseudolus for help. With great self-confidence, the servant promised to trick Calidorus' father, Simo, out of the money.

Before any plan could be formulated, Ballio appeared, cursing and beating some of his slaves. Calidorus and Pseudolus approached him and begged him to reconsider his bargain, pointing out that Phoenicium had been promised to Calidorus as soon as the young man could find the money to pay for her. The unscrupulous Ballio remained unmoved and even taunted Calidorus with his poverty and his inability to get money from his father. Before they parted, however, he craftily pointed out that today was the day on which the officer had agreed to send his final installment of the payment for Phoenicium and that if the promised money were not received, Ballio would be free to sell her to another bidder.

As Pseudolus was revolving various plans in his mind, he overheard Simo talking to a friend and learned that the old man had already heard of Calidorus' plight and had steeled himself in advance against any plea for money that his son might make. Finding his task thus complicated, Pseudolus stepped forward and brazenly admitted his commission, telling Simo that he intended to get the twenty minae from him and that Simo should consequently be on his guard. The slave also told his master that he intended to trick Ballio out of the slave girl. Simo was skeptical, but Pseudolus finally goaded him into promising to pay for the girl if Pseudolus was successful in getting her away from the procurer.

Soon afterward Pseudolus was fortunate enough to overhear a newcomer identify himself as Harpax, the Macedonian captain's messenger, come to conclude the dealings for Phoenicium. Accosting the messenger, Pseudolus identified himself as one of Ballio's servants and persuaded Harpax to allow him to deliver the sealed letter that was to identify the rightful purchaser. Then he induced Harpax to go to an inn to rest from his journey until Pseudolus came to get him. When the messenger had gone, Calidorus appeared in the company of a friend, and in the conversation that followed, the latter agreed to lend five minae for the execution of Pseudolus' plot. He agreed, moreover, to allow his servant Simia to be used in the enterprise.

Once these arrangements were made, the three left to conclude their preparations. Ballio appeared in the company of a cook, and it became clear that it was the procurer's birthday and that he was preparing a feast for his customers. Before Ballio went into his house, he disclosed that Simo had met him in the marketplace and had warned him to be on his guard against Pseudolus' plot.

Immediately after Ballio went in, Pseudolus appeared with Simia. During their conversation, Simia revealed himself to be shrewd and wily, and in the ensuing confrontation with Ballio he proved as apt a dissembler as Pseudolus himself. For when Ballio came out of his house, Simia approached and asked directions to find the procurer. Ballio identified himself, but, suspicious, he asked Simia the name of the man who had sent him. For a moment, the eavesdropping Pseudolus was afraid that his plot had collapsed, for Simia had not been told the name of the Macedonian captain. Simia adroitly evaded the trap, however, by pretending suspicion on his part and refusing to give Ballio the sealed letter until the procurer had himself identified Phoenicium's purchaser. Ballio did so, received the letter and the money and released Phoenicium into Simia's custody.

After Simia and Phoenicium had gone, Ballio, congratulating himself on having outwitted Pseudolus, chuckled at the prospect of the servant making his tardy effort to obtain the girl. When Simo appeared, the procurer expressed his certainty that Pseudolus had been foiled and declared that he would give Simo twenty minae and relinquish his right to the girl as well if Pseudolus were successful in his plot.

At that moment Harpax entered, grumbling that Pseudolus had not come to get him as he had promised to do. Confronting Ballio, he learned the procurer's identity and set about to close the bargain his master had made. Ballio, convinced that Harpax was in the employ of Pseudolus, did his best to humiliate the messenger, until Harpax mentioned having given the sealed letter to a "servant" of Ballio. From the description, Ballio realized with chagrin that he had been thoroughly duped. Simo held him to his word regarding the twenty minae and the relinquishing of his rights to Phoenicium, and Harpax, learning that the girl was no longer available, insisted that Ballio return the fifteen minae the captain had already deposited.

Meanwhile, Pseudolus, Calidorus, and Phoenicium were celebrating their victory with wine. Pseudolus later met Simo and demanded the twenty minae which the old man owed him for having successfully tricked Ballio. As the money was not coming out of his own pocket, Simo turned it over with good grace. Pseudolus returned half the sum and took his master off to drink to their good fortune.

Critical Evaluation:

Between the death of Aristophanes, the first Greek master of comedy, and the Roman Plautus, who has been described as the most successful comic poet in the ancient world, the Greek Menander created the New Comedy. Only one complete play by Menander is now extant, but most Roman comedies are known, from fragments and various accounts, to be imitations of Greek models. Only twenty of the approximately one hundred plays written by Plautus—who is also the first known professional playwright—remain.

Plautus was the first Latin author whose work has survived; he was very popular in Rome. His plays greatly influenced the comedies of William Shakespeare and Molière, and, as recently as 1962, a combination of three of his plays, including *Pseudolus* (which literally means "the trickster"), achieved considerable success on Broadway and later as a motion picture entitled *A Funny Thing Happened on the Way to the Forum* (1966).

Whereas some of Shakespeare's comedies have been described as being serious, dark, or even problem plays, the comedies of Plautus are almost always festive and playful. Performed at planting or harvest festivals, the plays offered Roman audiences an opportunity to free themselves temporarily from the confines of their society, which demanded strict adherence to law, filial obedience—fathers could legally execute their children—and pursuit of financial gain. Roman morality has been described as puritanical, and the institution of slavery was vital to Roman civilization. What the comedian offers was an inversion of these cultural values: The slave becomes master over his master, the son over his father, youth over age. In the comic world of Plautus, money and morality merely get in the way, and those who are committed to either are usually the villains.

Actually, the term villain is a bit severe for a play like *Pseudolus*. The pimp (in Latin, *leno*) Ballio is more of a rascal than a villain. He is a blocking character, that is, he prevents the good characters, the slave Pseudolus and his master's son, Calidorus, from having a good time. "Having a good time" in this case means arranging for Calidorus to gain possession of his girlfriend, Phoenicium, before Ballio can sell her to a Macedonian officer with the nearly unpronounceable name of Polymachaeroplagides. (Roman audiences would probably have laughed over such awkward Greek names; this one roughly translates as "many swords at the side.") The officer himself never appears on stage, but his orderly, Harpax (the name means "snatcher" or "thief"), is there to be outwitted, along with nearly everyone else, by the clever Pseudolus.

To turn the world familiar to his Roman audience upside down, Plautus sets the play in Athens, although perhaps any city in Greece would have sufficed, given the Roman prejudice against Greeks. Far from being the homeland of rational thinking or of Platonic idealism, the stage in Athens is a place of frivolity and license. The fact that Greek slaves often served as tutors and that knowledge of Greek was prized among Roman aristocrats did not prevent their being the objects of ridicule. Whereas, however, Calidorus performs as a typically inept adolescent in love and out of money, and Ballio is greedy, irascible, and heartless, Pseudolus is presented as being clever, witty, and loyal. Perhaps in this characterization Plautus is paying some tribute to the Greek mind.

The plot is simple and conventional, which is what the audience would have expected. Sincere romantic love would have been out of place, and it is appropriate that Calidorus' boyish passion for Phoenicium is conventionally erotic. His role as a spendthrift and, therefore, penniless son, and his father Simo's role as a well-to-do and unsympathetic parent are conventional, as is Ballio, the unlikable pimp who first appears on stage lashing his slaves. Similarly, the clever Pseudolus is conventionally likable. What makes the play work is the way Pseudolus outwits Ballio and at the same time manages to trick Simo into funding their adventure. Through a friend of Calidorus, Ballio acquires the services of Simia (the name means "monkey"), who masquerades as Harpax and proves equally clever when it comes to duping Ballio. Plautus also sets up a subplot involving a cook hired by Ballio for his birthday banquet; Plautus does not develop that plot, but the cook has some good moments in the play.

The range of comic characters and the thematic triumphs of slave over master, youth over age, and love (of a sort) over profit account for much of the appeal of this comedy. Some of the clever wordplay also translates well, as in an early scene when Calidorus and Pseudolus call Ballio such names as "scoundrel" and "slime," only to hear him placidly agree with them. Throughout the play, Pseudolus likes to refer to his schemes in military terms because he sees himself leading his legions against Ballio and taking on Simo. Above all, the satisfaction granted to the audience in this play is that of watching an unpleasant person get outsmarted.

Pseudolus appears toward the end of the play highly intoxicated and in a mood to celebrate, and it is in keeping with the tone of the play that Simo cannot resist being proud of his slave's wily triumph, even though he himself has been shown up. Part of Pseudolus' victory lies in the fact that he is so brazen as to tell Simo from the first to be on the watch for him. Plautus thus asserts a kind of comic justice. In the spirit of inverted values and of distorted historical probabilities, Pseudolus insists that Simo join him in his drunken carouse. He then turns to those in the audience and invites them to the next performance.

"Critical Evaluation" by Ron McFarland

Bibliography:
Garton, Charles. "How Roscius Acted Ballio." *Personal Aspects of the Roman Theatre.* Toronto: Hakkert, 1972. The most renowned actor of his day, Roscius played Ballio, instead of the lead role of Pseudolus. Refers to comments of Cicero and examines the role and how the actor appeared on stage.
Plautus, Titus Maccius. *Pseudolus/Plautus.* Edited by M. M. Wilcock. Bristol, England: Bristol Classical Press, 1987. Latin text with valuable introduction and commentary. Includes close plot analysis.
Segal, Erich. *Roman Laughter: The Comedy of Plautus.* Cambridge, Mass.: Harvard University Press, 1968. Valuable study of Plautus' work, setting social and cultural contexts for the plays and commenting on their appeal to Roman audiences.
Slater, Niall. *Plautus in Performance: The Theatre of the Mind.* Princeton, N.J.: Princeton University Press, 1985. Chapter on *Pseudolus* follows the evolution of Pseudolus' scheme, which he concocts as he goes. Emphasizes the power of language through which Pseudolus, speaking for Plautus, constructs a metadrama (a play about making a play) by using theatrical metaphor and direct address to the audience.
Wright, John. "The Transformation of Pseudolus." *Transactions of the American Philological Association* 104 (1974): 403-416. Reflects on problems with the play, including inconsistency over Calidorus' awareness of the fact that his mistress has been sold by Ballio and the apparent weakness of Pseudolus as a fully developed character. Argues that Pseudolus is transformed by metaphoric language, being associated with such various roles as cook, teacher, and poet (playwright).

PURGATORY

Type of work: Drama
Author: William Butler Yeats (1865-1939)
Type of plot: Fantasy
Time of plot: Early twentieth century
Locale: Ireland
First performed: 1938; first published, 1939

Principal characters:
AN OLD MAN
A BOY, the Old Man's sixteen-year-old son

The Story:

An Old Man and his adolescent son stood before a ruined old house, behind which stood only one bare tree. The boy complained of long wandering carrying a heavy pack while having to listen to his father's talk. Ignoring the complaints, the Old Man instructed the boy to study the house, which once was the scene of camaraderie, storytelling, and jokes. He was now the only living person with such memories. Although the boy scoffed at these reminiscences as pointless, the Old Man continued with his moonlit reverie about the cloud-shadowed house. He had visited the site one year earlier when the tree was as bare as it was that night. Fifty years earlier, before lightning had struck it, he had seen the tree at the height of its beauty, ennobled with luxuriantly green leaves just as the house had been luxurious with intellectual life.

At the Old Man's direction, the boy set down his pack and stood in the ruined doorway, squinting to see the person the Old Man said was still inside. He saw no one. The floors, windows, and roof were gone; the only recognizable object was an eggshell that a jackdaw had dropped. Unbelievable to the boy was the Old Man's insistence that souls in Purgatory returned regularly to reenact their still troubling former transgressions. Since they were dead, insisted the Old Man, the souls could understand the consequences of their failings. Those who had been made to suffer from the soul's earthly actions might eventually offer forgiveness, but those whose transgressions were self-inflicted must render their own forgiveness or rely on God's mercy.

Disgusted, the boy told the man to tell his fantastic story to the jackdaws if he must but to leave him alone. Forcefully, the father commanded his angry son to sit on a stone; the house belonged to the boy's grandmother and was where the Old Man was born. Caught by this revelation, the boy sat and listened to the Old Man's tale.

The Old Man's mother owned more than the house; her property extended as far as one could see. Kennels and stables had housed prize animals; one of her horses raced at Curragh, a nearby racetrack. There, she had met and quickly married a lowly groom; after this, her mother had never spoken to her again. The Old Man shared his grandmother's condemnation of his mother's impulsive passion. The boy disagreed, for the groom, his grandfather had won both the woman and wealth. Seeming not to hear the boy, the Old Man repeated his description of his mother's hasty mistake, that she had merely looked at the groom, then married him, but that she had never known her bridegroom's true character, for she died soon after in giving birth to her son, the Old Man. Thereafter, her husband had squandered all her wealth.

Exciting memories of the great house animated the Old Man: Military officers, members of parliament, governors of foreign lands, Irish patriotic heroes had lived or visited there, loving the ancient trees and profuse flowers. Then the husband had lain the land waste, felled the trees, and ruined the house. "To kill a house," the Old Man cursed, "I here declare a capital offense."

Ignoring the Old Man's bitterness, the boy envisioned his father's grand childhood with its horses and fine clothes. Ignoring his son's covetousness, the Old Man sneered at his father's ignorance. The Old Man had been forbidden to attend school, so he had learned to read from a gamekeeper's wife and learned Latin from a priest. In the great library, fine old books had been plentiful. What of that education had the Old Man passed on to him, the boy asked. Since the boy was a only bastard conceived in a ditch with a peddler's daughter, he received only what was due his station, replied the Old Man. When the Old Man was sixteen, his drunken father had burned down the great house, destroying all the treasures in it. The boy suddenly realized that he, too, was sixteen. Tentatively, he asked if the rumor were true that the Old Man had killed his dissolute father in the burning house. The Old Man confessed that he had, but that because the body was charred he was never convicted. Threatened by his dead father's friends, however, he had disguised himself and fled, to return to his father's low station by becoming a wandering peddlar. He boasted that he still used the murder weapon to cut his dinner meat.

Suddenly, the Old Man heard hoofbeats and remembered that this was the anniversary of his mother's wedding night. Although the boy could not see anything, the Old Man saw and described a vision of a ghostly young woman, the Old Man's mother, inside the ruined house awaiting her husband's late return from a drinking spree. The spectral husband stabled the horse, and the woman led him to her bedroom. Entering the dream scene, the Old Man shouted in vain to his mother not to let his father touch her to beget him. Then he realized that the scene must be repeated because his mother's remorse for her marriage was the cause of the reenactment.

While the Old Man is fantasizing, the boy tried to steal his inheritance from his bundle of money. Halting the boy, the Old Man justified his stinginess by asserting that the boy was like his dissolute grandfather and would have squandered everything on drink. As they struggled for the bundle, the dream lit up a vision of the ghostly grandfather pouring whiskey. The boy threatened to continue the family murders by killing the Old Man, then paused, horrified, when he too saw the Old Man's vision of the man and woman, his grandparents. Quickly, the Old Man repeatedly stabbed the boy, then sang a lullaby to the young corpse.

The vision faded and was replaced by moonlight on the bare tree. The Old Man assured his dead mother that his murderous act would finish the cycle of repeated scenes and that his killing his son would stop the family's generational pollution. He would wander in distant lands, far from the nightmare. Then he heard approaching hoofbeats again and realized that the nightmare was about to begin anew. Dejected, the Old Man pleaded with God to rescue his mother from her cycle of remorse.

Critical Evaluation:

Written in 1938, the year before he died, *Purgatory* demonstrates William Butler Yeats' lifelong fascination with the connections between the present world and the past and future. In fact, in his last public appearance in August, 1938, on the occasion of the play's opening, the aged Irish poet-dramatist told the audience that the drama expressed his beliefs about this world and the next. *Purgatory*, asserted Yeats, was symbolic, not allegorical. The plot does not represent a story in a real-world context.

To Yeats, geometric symbols of circles and conical gyres expressed the repetitious pattern of time, which incorporates past and present into future cycles. In *Purgatory*, the Old Man believes that souls in purgatory bring the past into the present by re-living past transgressions. The repeated hoofbeats of his father's ghost approaching at the play's end indicate that the cycle will continue into the future also and that the Old Man's prayer for God to release his mother's soul from its recurrent dream clearly will not be granted.

Purgatory, like other Yeats plays—*Calvary* (1921), *The Resurrection* (1927), and *The Words upon the Windowpane* (1930)—explores possibilities of life after death, especially ritualistic death. Killing his father in the inferno the father had created resembles a ritual of punishment; killing his son, whom he identifies with the hated father, after watching his own begetting repeats the murder ritual. Many Yeats plays center on father/son relationships, especially those about the Irish mythic hero Cuchulain, who kills a young man before remorsefully learning that the victim was his own son.

The thought of his mother's life after death is agonizing for the Old Man. While he prays to relieve his mother's dream, he is evidently interested in his own relief as well. His anguish in watching sexual relations between his father and mother has obvious Oedipal ramifications. In the Greek tale, Oedipus vengefully kills his father, marries his mother, and fathers children. In this drama, too, the son appears to be jealous of his father's privilege; he cannot tear himself from the scene. He loathes the sight in the vision of his mother's lust and calls out to her not to let her husband touch her using the argument that they will beget the husband's murderer. He is fascinated with his ghost-mother's ability to experience sexual pleasure even while bringing on her own remorse. Pleasure leading to destruction, and the interweaving of sex and death, is a familiar theme in Yeats' drama. Here, sexual culmination in the vision is directly followed by the boy's murder. Irony is evident when the boy is only able to see the Old Man's vision during the moment before he is killed, when he tries to stop the vision from repeating. Another common Yeats theme is the impossibility of lasting love, which resonates in the story of the mother's haste leading to betrayal and isolation from her bridegroom.

As in other Yeats plots with simple plots involving violence, the narrative drive of *Purgatory* concentrates on an intensely dramatic moment, here the torturing vision. Stage directions are rare, as is characteristic of Yeats' verse plays; the reader must infer from the dialogue what action would actually be seen on stage. For example, the reader finds out about the boy's location and his subsequent attempt to steal solely from the dialogue itself, when the Old Man commands the boy to sit on the rock, and later to "Come back!/ And so you thought to slip away,/ My bag of money between your fingers." The play's quick resolution is also typical of Yeats' dramas, as is his combining art and religion in some of the symbolism. Yeats believed that the supernatural world met the natural through dreams, both pleasant and unpleasant.

The play has been variously interpreted. Among those who have studied it, some contend that underlying the play is Yeats' anger against a domineering, overly talkative, and emotionally undemonstrative father. In *Purgatory*, the Old Man never addresses the boy as his son; only once does the boy address him as "Father," and that is when the Old Man is about to confess to having murdered his father. The boy challenges his father, just as the Old Man challenged his father; each ignores the other's concerns.

Some critics have attempted to interpret the play's symbols. The Old Man's knife can be thought to have Freudian implications; the eggshell might represent broken femaleness or cycles of birth and death. The bare tree, which inhabits many Yeats plays and often symbolizes seasonal rebirth, here might be thought to represent the mother's stripped wealth. Birds are ever-present in Yeats poetry and drama, often representing spiritual soaring; in *Purgatory*, a jackdaw has discarded from a nest, a site for births, the only sign of life in the ruined house, an eggshell. The nightmare cycles of *Purgatory* could be interpreted as symbolizing the political violence in Irish history, which Yeats often deplored in such works as the poem "September

1913." Certainly the ruined great house bears an unmistakable resemblance to Coole, Lady Gregory's ruined home where Yeats often lived during his most productive years. He often lamented the fall of the Irish aristocracy in his poetry.

The play never gained widespread popularity, perhaps because the symbols are not sufficiently defined. Undoubtedly, *Purgatory* is a disturbing work for its treatment of such human taboos as filicide, parricide, and a son's observation of sexual relations between his parents. Yet beyond that, the play offers rich poetic imagery, impassioned characters, and intense dramatic climaxes, and it is permeated by themes that permeate Yeats' entire oeuvre.

Nancy A. Macky

Bibliography:

Bradley, Anthony. *William Butler Yeats*. New York: Frederick Ungar, 1979. A clearly written overview of Yeats's life, with a discussion of his accomplishments as dramatist in the Irish context. Includes photographs of productions, including those of *Purgatory*.

Jeffares, A. Norman, ed. *W. B. Yeats: The Critical Heritage*. Boston: Routledge & Kegan Paul, 1977. An excellent collection of contemporary critical comment on several Yeats plays, including a chapter on *Purgatory* and its relationship to Yeats's other works.

Moore, John Rees. *Masks of Love and Death: Yeats as Dramatist*. Ithaca, N.Y.: Cornell University Press, 1971. Chapter 14 focuses on *Purgatory* as a dark view of fate taking vengeance on mean-spirited materialism.

Nathan, Leonard. *The Tragic Drama of William Butler Yeats*. New York: Columbia University Press, 1965. Discusses *Purgatory* as an objective tragedy with supernatural elements.

Ure, Peter. *Yeats the Playwright*. New York: Barnes & Noble Books, 1963. A thorough investigation of all Yeats's major plays, showing relationship of structure, theme, and character. Chapter 5, "From Grave to Cradle," includes a discussion of *Purgatory*.

PURPLE DUST

Type of work: Drama
Author: Sean O'Casey (John Casey, 1880-1964)
Type of plot: Satire
Time of plot: 1940's
Locale: Clune na Geera, Ireland
First published: 1940; first performed, 1944

> *Principal characters:*
> CYRIL POGES, a pompous English businessman
> JACK O'KILLIGAIN, a foreman stonemason
> BASIL STOKE, Poges's colleague
> SOUHAUN, Poges's mistress
> AVRIL, Stoke's mistress
> THREE IRISH WORKMEN

The Story:

Three workmen were standing languidly in a large, gloomy room that once had been the living room of a ruined Elizabethan mansion. The three pondered the wisdom of two English gentlemen, Cyril Poges and Basil Stoke, in coming to live in such a decaying old house. Although the fresh paint had brightened things up a bit, it covered, for the most part, rotting wood. The sudden appearance of the sixty-five-year-old Poges and the thirtyish, serious Basil, followed by their mistresses, Souhaun and Avril, confirmed the workmen's suspicions that the owners were slightly awry in their thinking. The group danced in, boisterously singing of the joys of country living. The handsome foreman, Jack O'Killigain, explained to the workmen that these were people who saw historical loveliness in decaying ruins, and who took foolish delight in any locale with a story behind it. With the reappearance of the pretty Avril, O'Killigain exerted his poetic Irish charm to entice her into a rendezvous later that night.

Poges, Basil, and Souhaun returned from a walk in the fields. Poges and Basil talked excitedly about the glories of past history and its better times, much to the disgust of O'Killigain, who firmly believed that life in its present state was far more worth living. His philosophy was lost on the other two, who went about their comic business of hanging pictures and discovering aspects of country living—new business for them, but common enjoyment for the hardy Irish workmen.

Although Poges wanted to forget the outside world and its ways, his reverie was constantly interrupted by prosaic occurrences: arguments with Basil and the women, altercations with his butler over men outside who wished to know if he desired roosters and hens, and interruptions by one of the workmen, who informed him of an excellent buy in a cow. Poges raged that he would get in touch with the Department of Agriculture. At Poges's displeasure over the disconnected telephone, another workman lost his temper. Poges heard himself scorned as a man who thought that the glory of the world could be stuffed into a purse, a man who was patronizing toward the Irish, a mighty race a thousand years older than his own. Basil and Avril left for a horseback ride, in spite of warnings that Irish horses were true horses, instead of English animals. The predictions were accurate; a battered Basil appeared shortly afterward and announced that his horse indeed had become wild and ungovernable, and that, when last seen, Avril was riding away quite naked with O'Killigain.

The next day brought a cold dawn. Though Poges and Basil had spent the night fully clothed, they had almost frozen to death in the old house, along with the rest of the household. Poges still tried to rationalize; the cold air would revitalize them and exhilarate them. Barney, the butler, and Cloyne, the maid, were disgusted with the whole situation; they thought the place an unlighted dungeon. As Barney struggled to light a damp fire, Cloyne rushed back into the room to scream that there was a wild bull in the entrance hall. This announcement caused a great panic among the transplanted city dwellers. Basil reentered with a gun, then ran for his life as Poges roared for help and Cloyne fainted. A workman saved them all by shooing out a harmless cow that had innocently wandered into the hallway.

Later, Poges thought he had found a friend in the workman, who reminisced with him over glorious days in the past. Once again Poges expressed his philosophy that all the greats had gone with their glory, their finery turned to purple dust, and that today's man was shallow by comparison. O'Killigain and another workman later transfixed Poges, however, with their poetic tellings of the glorious Irish past and the fight for independence (an event not blurred in the mists of distant time). Although Poges was momentarily surprised to find that these country workers had such depth, his spirit of English nationalism quickly asserted itself.

Poges's calamities continued. His next misadventure was with an oversized, heavy garden roller. Though his friends warned him, Poges persisted in his efforts to operate the machine. The result was a wrecked wall, as Poges let the roller get away from him to roll into and through the side of the house. Following closely on this incident, a terrified Basil shot and killed the indolent cow that had earlier invaded the hallway.

An interview with the local canon lifted Poges's spirits when the churchman praised Poges for restoring a portion of the past to slow down the reckless speed of the present. As the workmen continued to bring in furniture, Souhaun almost succumbed to one of the workmen and his poetic charm. The moving into the room of a gilded desk-bureau proved to be another disaster. The top was first scarred by a workman's boot; then the bureau and the entrance were both damaged as the piece of furniture was pushed and pried through the door.

The wind was rising and storm clouds were brewing ominously, so the workmen were sent away, but not before O'Killigain and the workman had entreated Avril and Souhaun to accompany them. The beautiful picture of Irish life conjured quickly by the men left the women quite unsettled, but Poges and Basil made great fun of the workmen's poetic proposals. As the day grew darker and the rain fell, Poges found still other troubles; the postmaster arrived to complain about Poges's midnight phone calls to him. Suddenly the sound of a galloping horse was heard over the howl of the wind.

Warned that the river was rising, the terrified group in the darkened room made plans to climb to the roof before the house was flooded. Souhaun was nowhere to be found; she was with the workman on the galloping horse. O'Killigain, who had said that he would come for Avril when the river rose, appeared as he had promised. Avril left, renouncing Basil as a gilded monkey. Basil ran for the roof and a defeated Poges followed slowly, longing for dear England.

Critical Evaluation:

In *Purple Dust*, Sean O'Casey returned to certain stylistic aspects of his earlier plays, including the mixture of moving poetry with extravagant comedy. Although the occasional poetic passages of the Irish workmen concerning their noble past are indeed beautiful, the emphasis of the play is on the profoundly comic situation of two stuffy Englishmen trying to adjust to the rigors of the bucolic life. O'Casey, as usual, is extolling the hardy Irish, and disapproves of those who cling to the past without partly looking to the future. When people venerate the past without a true sense of understanding and appreciation, as do Poges and Stoke, the result is especially disastrous.

Purple Dust may be O'Casey's funniest play. He begins with a potentially hilarious situation, the attempt by two stuffy Englishmen to restore an ancient, ramshackle Tudor mansion in the Irish countryside in the face of opposition from the local citizenry. To this beginning he adds a cast of broad, colorful, and sometimes poetic types, and, utilizing a thin but completely functional plot line, presents a sequence of zany scenes that would have fit nicely into a Marx brothers film.

Purple Dust has, however, some serious content. Eschewing the kind of abstract symbolism and forced rhetoric that damaged such earlier "idea" plays as *Within the Gates* (1933), *The Star Turns Red* (1940), and *Oak Leaves and Lavender: Or, A World on Wallpaper* (1946), O'Casey mixes comedy with message so adroitly in *Purple Dust* that he is able to present some strident satire and provocative ideas without losing any humor or theatrical effectiveness.

Cyril Poges and Basil Stoke are two brilliant comedic and satiric creations. Poges is the self-made man, the blustery pragmatic tycoon who has bullied his way to the top and believes he can impose his will on anyone and anything. At the same time, he senses his lack of depth and tries to compensate by consuming large amounts of culture; he fancies himself an instant expert on art, history, poetry, and literature because he has bought great quantities of it. Stoke, on the other hand, represents inherited wealth, position, and formal education. He considers himself a thinker and speaks in long, abstract, convoluted sentences that turn the simplest thing into a complex metaphysical problem. Their hilarious debate over the nature of a primrose is an example of the hilarious lunacy that O'Casey is able to inject into his satire.

Regardless of their differences, both men are embodiments of the British capitalist. Their various pretensions and blind spots set them up as perfect dupes for the canny rural Irish workmen. The chief symbol of the play is, of course, the absurd Tudor house that the two Englishmen mean to refurbish as a way of making a connection with the historical "grandeur" of the past (Tudor England restored in rural Ireland) as well as finding pastoral simplicity in the present. They add any object to the house that seems vaguely historical, regardless of its authenticity or its appropriateness—a "Jacobean" table, "Cambodian" bowl (from Woolworth's), a set of medieval armor, a "quattrocento" bureau—while at the same time denying themselves such "luxuries" as modern indoor plumbing and electricity on the grounds that they are historically inauthentic.

Their so-called culture soon turns to disaster—the bowls are smashed, the bureau is broken to pieces, and finally the house itself is submerged. Their dream of bucolic simplicity likewise turns into a nightmare; the animals keep them awake at night, a cow wanders into the house and they flee in terror from the "wild beast," and the gentle autumn rain grows into a flood that inundates them all.

O'Casey is not attacking tradition as such—only a false, pretentious, and ignorant use of it. Opposed to the old English capitalists are the young Irish workers, and two of them, Jack O'Killigain and Philip O'Dempsey, articulate O'Casey's positive vision of humanity, tradition, and Ireland. Poges's ignorance of history is contrasted with O'Dempsey's profound grasp of his heroic historical and cultural background. He divorces himself from most of his contemporaries and aligns himself with the Irish heroes of the past. These visions are put into action when, as the flood waters start pouring in on Poges and Stoke, O'Killigain and O'Dempsey spirit the women, Avril and Souhaun, off to a mountain sanctuary. The survivors of the new flood will be the young, the passionate, and the Irish.

Bibliography:

Benstock, Bernard. *Paycocks and Others: Sean O'Casey's World*. Dublin: Gill and Macmillan, 1976. A comprehensive thematic survey of all of O'Casey's works. Establishes the place of *Purple Dust* in O'Casey's development and connects it to the rest of the playwright's output. Discusses the play's contributions to O'Casey's concept of the hero.

Kosok, Heinz. *O'Casey the Dramatist*. Translated by Heinz Kosok and Joseph T. Swann. New York: Barnes & Noble Books, 1985. The chapter on *Purple Dust* opens with a succinct treatment of the play's different texts. There are also notes on various productions. Concentrates on the interplay of satire, farce, and other comic elements in *Purple Dust*.

Krause, David. *Sean O'Casey: The Man and His Work*. New York: Macmillan, 1960. A comprehensive treatment of O'Casey from a biographical and critical point of view. *Purple Dust* is said to inaugurate the tone of O'Casey's later plays.

O'Casey, Sean. "Purple Dust in Their Eyes." In *Under a Colored Cap*. New York: Macmillan, 1963. A critical response to reviews of the 1962 London production of *Purple Dust*. The essay considers the play's political aspects and argues for their relevance to the playwright's vision.

O'Riordan, John. *A Guide to O'Casey's Plays*. New York: Macmillan, 1984. An exhaustive treatment of O'Casey's plays, covering all twenty-three of the playwright's major and minor works, with notes on production histories. Literary sources for *Purple Dust* are assessed, and its intellectual underpinnings considered.

PYGMALION

Type of work: Drama
Author: George Bernard Shaw (1856-1950)
Type of plot: Comedy
Time of plot: c. 1900
Locale: London
First published: 1912; first performed, 1913 (in German), 1914 (in English)

> *Principal characters:*
> HENRY HIGGINS, a phonetician
> ELIZA DOOLITTLE, a flower girl
> ALFRED DOOLITTLE, her father, a dustman
> COLONEL PICKERING, another phonetician
> MRS. PEARCE, Higgins' housekeeper
> FREDDY EYNSFORD HILL, a poor young gentleman

The Story:

Late one evening in the Covent Garden theater district of London, playgoers were attempting to summon cab drivers in the rain when a crowd gathered around an unkempt young woman selling flowers. The flower girl had been speaking in a very strong Cockney dialect and a distinguished gentleman had been transcribing her speech into a notebook. The gentleman, Henry Higgins, was a professional phonetician, who earned a handsome income teaching people how to change their accents and pass as members of the upper class. Higgins amazed the crowd by using his analysis of their accents to locate where individuals lived. Appalled by the flower girl's lower-class dialect, Higgins boasted that in a matter of months he could teach her how to speak properly and pass as a duchess at an ambassador's garden party.

The next morning, in the drawing room and laboratory of Higgins' Wimpole Street residence, Higgins was showing Pickering his elaborate equipment for recording speech when the house-keeper, Mrs. Pearce, announced the arrival of the flower girl, Eliza Doolittle. Eliza wanted to take lessons form Higgins so she could improve her speech and get a place as a clerk in a proper flower shop. Higgins was impressed by the percentage of her wealth that Eliza was willing to pay and accepted her as a student, making a wager with Pickering that in six months he could pass Eliza off as a duchess. Mrs. Pearce asked what was to become of Eliza when Higgins had finished his teaching, but Higgins dismissed the question as trivial. After Mrs. Pearce took Eliza away to bathe, Pickering asked Higgins if his intentions toward Eliza were honorable and Higgins assured Pickering that he was a confirmed bachelor, determined not to let women into his life.

After putting Eliza in her bath, Mrs. Pearce reentered the drawing room to set down rules for Higgins' behavior while Eliza was in the house—proper dress and table manners and no swearing. Eliza's father, Alfred Doolittle, a dustman, or trash collector, arrived and attempted to extort money from Higgins. When Higgins insisted that Doolittle take his daughter back immediately, he drove down Doolittle's price to a five-pound note. Higgins offered Doolittle ten pounds, but Doolittle refused the extra five because he did not want to be tempted to save the money. On his way out, Doolittle did not immediately recognize his daughter Eliza, who looked clean and well dressed.

After a few months, Eliza's training had gone so well that Higgins decided to test her by bringing Eliza to his mother's flat for a formal visit. Henry arrived first to prepare his mother, informing her that Eliza only had two topics she could converse on—the weather and everyone's health. Unfortunately, as Henry was explaining the situation, three unexpected visitors were announced—Mrs. Eynsford Hill, her daughter Clara, and her son Freddy. Initially, Henry was upset with the intrusion of the Hills, but then he welcomed them as a greater challenge for Eliza's performance. When Eliza arrived she was exquisitely dressed and produced an impression of remarkable distinction and beauty. She began conversing quite adeptly, but as she got more engaged in the conversation she slipped back into some of her lower-class speech patterns. However, Higgins was able to convince the Hills that her speech was a new and fashionable way of speaking, the "new small talk," and when Eliza left the Hills were convinced that she was a lady of high society, and Freddy had obviously fallen in love with Eliza. After the Hills left, Henry was exultant, but his mother asked what was to be done with Eliza after the lessons were completed.

When the time came for Eliza's performance at the ambassador's garden party, she succeeded splendidly. Afterward, Higgins and Pickering celebrated their triumph, talking of how glad they were that their work was over and complaining that they had ultimately gotten bored by the whole affair. Eliza, on the other hand, was brooding and silent. Higgins wondered out loud where his slippers were, and Eliza left the room and fetched them for him. Higgins and Pickering talked of the evening as if Eliza were not there, and as they were leaving for bed, Eliza threw Higgins' slippers after him, calling him a selfish brute. Now Eliza asked the question, "What's to become of me?"

That evening, Eliza left Higgins' flat to walk the streets of London, and by morning she had gone to stay with Henry's mother. Later that morning, Higgins and Pickering, bewildered and worried about Eliza's disappearance, came to see Henry's mother. They were shortly followed by Eliza's father, who entered dressed like a gentleman, complaining that his life had been ruined because of Higgins. Henry's joking letter to an American millionaire had led to Alfred's inheriting a huge sum of money, and now everyone was begging money from him. His life was no longer impoverished, free, and simple.

Henry's mother revealed that Eliza was upstairs and angered by the insensitivity and indifference Higgins had shown her. Mrs. Higgins asked Doolittle to step outside so as not to shock Eliza. When Eliza came downstairs, she met Higgins and Pickering as a refined lady, the transformation complete. Eliza explained that she had learned her nice manners from Pickering and that the real difference between a lady and a flower girl was not how she behaved but how she was treated.

When Eliza's father reentered the room, Eliza was shocked by his appearance. Doolittle reported that he was now a victim of middle-class morality and on his way to his wedding. Alfred invited every one to come to the wedding, and Pickering and Mrs. Higgins left to get ready, leaving Eliza and Henry behind. Pickering had urged Eliza to return to live with him and Higgins, but in her last conversation with Henry, Eliza had decided to leave Higgins forever. She claimed that she was only looking for a little kindness and that she would marry Freddy Eynsford Hill. She would earn her living as a teacher of phonetics, teaching others as she had been taught. Higgins was incensed but impressed with Eliza's spirit and finally saw her as more of an equal. As Eliza left, vowing never to see Higgins again, Henry asserted confidently that she would return.

"The Story" by Terry Nienhuis

Critical Evaluation:

Throughout his career George Bernard Shaw agitated for the reform of the vagaries of English spelling and pronunciation, but his assertion that *Pygmalion* was written to impress upon the public the importance of phoneticians is immaterial. *Pygmalion*, like all of Shaw's best plays, transcends its author's didactic intent. The play is performed and read not for Shaw's pet theories but for the laughter its plot and characters provoke.

The play is a modern adaptation of the Pygmalion myth (though some have claimed that it is a plagiarism of Tobias Smollett's *The Adventures of Peregrine Pickle*, 1751), in which the sculptor-king Pygmalion falls in love with Galatea, a creature of his own making, a statue that the goddess, Aphrodite, pitying him, brings to life. The Pygmalion of Shaw's play turns up as Henry Higgins, a teacher of English speech; his Galatea, Eliza Doolittle, a Cockney flower girl whom Higgins transforms into a seeming English lady by teaching her to speak cultivated English. In the process of transforming a poor, uneducated girl into a lady, Higgins irrevocably changes a human life. By lifting Eliza above her own class and providing her with no more than the appurtenances of another, Higgins makes her unfit for both. On this change and Higgins' stubborn refusal to accept its reality and its consequences, Shaw builds his play.

From the beginning, when Higgins first observes her dialectal monstrosities, Eliza is characterized as a proud, stubborn girl, though educated only by the circumstances of her poverty and gutter environment. She has the courage to ask Higgins to make good his boast that he can pass her off as a duchess within three months, and she calls on him and offers to pay him for elocution lessons that will enable her to work as a saleswoman in a flower shop. Like all the proud, she is also sensitive, and she tries to break off the interview when Higgins persists in treating her as his social inferior. Higgins can best be understood in contrast to Colonel Pickering, his foil, who finances the transformation. As a fellow phonetician, Pickering approves of the project as a scientific experiment, but as a gentleman and a sensitive human being, he sympathizes with Eliza. It is Higgins' uproariously tragic flaw that he, like all of Shaw's heroes, is not a gentleman. He is brilliant and cultured, but he lacks manners and refuses to learn or even affect any, believing himself to be superior to the conventions and civilities of polite society and preferring to treat everyone with bluntness and candor. He is, or so he thinks until Eliza leaves him, a self-sufficient man. When he discovers that she has made herself an indispensable part of his life, he goes to her and in one of the most remarkable courtship scenes in the history of the theater, pleads with her to live with Pickering and himself as three dedicated bachelors. At the end of the play, he is confident that she will accept his unorthodox proposition, even when she bids him good-bye forever.

As a matter of fact, Shaw himself was never able to convince anyone that Eliza and Higgins did not marry and live happily ever after. The first producer of the play, Sir Herbert Beerbohm Tree, insisted on leaving the impression that the two were reconciled in the end as lovers, and this tradition has persisted. Enraged as always by any liberties taken with his work, Shaw wrote an essay that he attached to the play as a sequel, in which he denounced sentimental interpretations of *Pygmalion*.

He concedes that *Pygmalion* is a romance in that its heroine undergoes an almost miraculous change, but he argues that the logic of the characterization does not permit a conventional happy ending. Higgins is, after all, a god and Eliza only his creation; an abyss separates them. Furthermore, Shaw contends, their personalities, backgrounds, and philosophies are irreconcilable. Higgins is an inveterate bachelor and likely to remain so because he will never find a woman who can meet the standards he has set for ideal womanhood—those set by his mother. Eliza, on the other hand, being young and pretty, can always find a husband whose demands on a woman would not be impossible to meet. Therefore, Shaw insists, Eliza marries Freddy Eynsford Hill, a penniless but devoted young man who played only an insignificant role in the play. Stubbornly, Shaw would not even permit them the luxury of living happily ever after: They have financial problems that are gradually solved by opening a flower shop subsidized by Colonel Pickering. Shaw's Pygmalion is too awe-inspiring that his Galatea should ever presume to love him.

Even with the addition of this unconventional ending to the play, *Pygmalion* would be highly atypical of Shavian drama were it not for the presence of Alfred Doolittle, Eliza's father. Through Doolittle, Shaw is able to indulge in economic and social moralizing, an ingredient with which Shaw could not dispense. Like Eliza, Doolittle undergoes a transformation as a result of Higgins' meddling, a transformation that in his case is, however, unpremeditated. Early in the play, Doolittle fascinates Higgins and Pickering by his successful attempt to capitalize on Eliza's good fortune. He literally charms Higgins out of five pounds by declaring himself an implacable foe of middle-class morality and insisting that he will use the money for a drunken spree. Delighted with the old scoundrel, Higgins mentions him in jest to a crackpot American millionaire who subsequently bequeaths Doolittle a yearly allowance of three thousand pounds if he will lecture on morality. Thus this dustman becomes transformed into a lion of London society, and the reprobate becomes a victim of bourgeois morality. Although he appears only twice in the play, Doolittle is so vigorous and funny that he is almost as memorable a comic character as Higgins.

The play itself is memorable because of its vigor and fun, notwithstanding Shaw's protestations about its message. As a matter of fact, Shaw probably insisted so strenuously on the serious intent of the play because he too realized that *Pygmalion* was his least serious, least didactic, play.

Bibliography:

Berst, Charles A. *"Pygmalion": Shaw's Spin on Myth and Cinderella.* New York: Twayne, 1995. An excellent source for students that examines the literary and historical contexts of the play and provides an intelligent and thorough interpretation tracing Eliza's transformation into a woman and lady. Focuses on Shaw's use of the Pygmalion myth and the Cinderella fairy tale.

Bloom, Harold, ed. *George Bernard Shaw's "Pygmalion."* New York: Chelsea House, 1988. A judicious selection of eight critical essays that represent major interpretations of the play. In his introduction, Bloom argues that *Pygmalion* is Shaw's masterpiece. Excellent for students.

Hornby, Richard. "Beyond the Verbal in *Pygmalion.*" In *Shaw's Plays in Performance*, edited by Daniel Leary. University Park: Pennsylvania State University Press, 1983. Examines Shaw's stagecraft and the performance qualities inherent in the play as a script. Goes beyond "the purely verbal or literary" qualities of the play to show how the visual and aural elements convey meaning.

Huggett, Richard. *The Truth About "Pygmalion."* New York: Random House, 1969. A fascinating narrative account of the original 1914 London production, in which "three of the most monstrous egoists the theatre ever produced" participated: actress Mrs. Patrick Campbell, who played Eliza; actor Sir Herbert Beerbohm Tree, who played Higgins; and Shaw himself.

Silver, Arnold. *Bernard Shaw: The Darker Side.* Stanford, Calif.: Stanford University Press, 1982. A major part of this challenging and unconventional book on Shaw is a very thorough and complex psychological interpretation of *Pygmalion* that shows Shaw working out intense personal conflicts. Fascinating materials for more advanced students.

QUENTIN DURWARD

Type of work: Novel
Author: Sir Walter Scott (1771-1832)
Type of plot: Historical
Time of plot: 1468
Locale: France and Flanders
First published: 1823

> Principal characters:
> QUENTIN DURWARD, a Scottish cadet
> LUDOVIC LESLY or LE BALAFRÉ, his maternal uncle
> ISABELLE, the countess of Croye, a servant, disguised as Jacqueline
> LADY HAMELINE, her aunt
> KING LOUIS XI
> COUNT PHILIP DE CRÈVECŒUR, of Burgundy
> CHARLES, the duke of Burgundy
> WILLIAM DE LA MARCK, a Flemish outlaw
> HAYRADDIN MAUGRABIN, a Bohemian

The Story:

When Quentin Durward, a young Scottish gentleman, approached the ford of a small river near the castle of Plessisles-Tours, in France, he found the river in flood. Two people watched him from the opposite bank. They were King Louis XI in his common disguise of Maître Pierre, a merchant, and Tristan l'Hermite, marshal of France. Quentin entered the flood and nearly drowned. Arriving on the other side and mistaking the king and his companion for a burgher and a butcher, he threatened the two with a drubbing because they had not warned him of the deep ford. Amused by Quentin's spirit and daring, Maître Pierre took him to breakfast at a nearby inn to make amends. At the inn, Quentin met a beautiful young peasant, Jacqueline, who actually was Isabelle, the countess of Croye. Quentin tried to learn why the merchant, Maître Pierre, acted so much like a noble. He saw many other things that aroused his curiosity, but for which he found no explanation.

Shortly afterward, Quentin met Ludovic Lesly, known as Le Balafré, his maternal uncle, who was a member of King Louis' Scottish Archers. Le Balafré was exceedingly surprised to learn that Quentin could read and write, something which neither a Durward nor a Lesly had heretofore been able to do. Quentin discovered the body of a man hanging from a tree. When he cut the man down, he was seized by two officers of Tristan l'Hermite. They were about to hang Quentin for his deed, when he asked if there were a good Christian in the crowd who would inform Le Balafré of what was taking place. A Scottish archer heard him and cut his bonds. While they prepared to defend themselves from the mob, Le Balafré rode up with some of his men and took command of the situation, haughtily insisting that Quentin was a member of the Scottish Archers and beyond the reach of the marshal's men. Quentin had not joined the guards as yet, but the lie saved his life. Le Balafré took Quentin to see Lord Crawford, the commander of the guards, to enroll him. When the Scottish Archers were summoned to the royal presence, Quentin was amazed to see that Maître Pierre was King Louis.

Count Philip de Crèvecœur arrived at the castle to demand audience with the king in the name of his master, the duke of Burgundy. When the king admitted Crèvecœur, the messenger presented a list of wrongs and oppressions, committed on the frontier, for which the duke of Burgundy demanded redress. The duke also requested that Louis cease his secret and underhanded dealings in the towns of Ghent, Liège, and Malines, and, further, that the king send back to Burgundy, under safeguard, the person of Isabelle, the countess of Croye, the duke's ward, whom he accused the king of harboring in secret. Dissatisfied with the king's replies to these demands, Crèvecœur threw his gauntlet to the floor of the hall. Several of the king's attendants rushed to pick it up and to accept the challenge, but the king ordered the Bishop of Auxerre to lift the gauntlet and to remonstrate with Crèvecœur for thus declaring war between Burgundy and France. The king and his courtiers then left to hunt wild boars.

During the chase, Quentin Durward saved the king's life by spearing a wild boar when Louis slipped and fell before the infuriated beast. The king decided to reward Quentin with a special mission. He was ordered to stand guard in the room where the king entertained Crèvecœur and others; at a sign from the king, Quentin was to shoot the Burgundian. The king, however, changed his mind; the signal was not given. Then the king made Quentin the personal bodyguard of Isabelle and her aunt, Lady Hameline, on their way to seek the protection of the Bishop of Liège.

En route to Liège, the party was assaulted by the Count de Dunois and the duke of Orleans. Quentin defended himself with great courage and received timely help from Lord Crawford, who arrived with a body of Scottish Archers. Lord Crawford made both men prisoners. The party's guide on the second half of the journey was Hayraddin Maugrabin, a Bohemian; his brother had been the man whom Quentin had cut down earlier. Nothing untoward occurred until the small party reached Flanders. There Quentin discovered, by following Hayraddin, that a plot had been hatched to attack his party and carry off the women to William de la Marck, the Wild Boar of Ardennes. Quentin frustrated these plans by going up the left bank of the Maes instead of the right. He proceeded safely to Liège, where he gave over the women into the protection of the bishop at his castle of Schonwaldt. Four days later, William de la Marck attacked the castle and captured it during the night. Lady Hameline escaped. In the bishop's throne room in the castle, William de la Marck murdered the churchman in front of his own episcopal throne. Aroused by the brutality of William, Quentin stepped to the side of Carl Eberson, William's son, and placed his dagger at the boy's throat; he threatened to kill the lad if William did not cease his butchery. In the confusion, Quentin found Isabelle and took her safely from the castle in the disguise of the daughter of the Syndic of Liège. They were pursued by William's men but were rescued by a party under Count de Crèvecœur, who conducted them safely to the court of the duke of Burgundy at Peroune.

The king came to the castle of the duke of Burgundy, asserting the royal prerogative of visiting any of his vassals. Disregarding the laws of hospitality, the duke imprisoned Louis and then held a council to debate the difficulties between France and Burgundy. Hayraddin appeared as a herald from William de la Marck, who had married the Lady Hameline. Toison d'Or, the duke's herald, however, unmasked Hayraddin because he knew nothing of the science of heraldry. The duke released Hayraddin and set his fierce boar hounds upon him, but ordered the dogs called off before they tore Hayraddin to shreds. Then he ordered that Hayraddin be hanged with the proper ceremony.

The king and the duke also debated the disposal of Isabelle's hand and fortune, but she had fallen in love with Quentin and said that she preferred the cloister to any of the suggested alliances. The duke solved the problem, at least to his satisfaction, by declaring that Isabelle's hand would be given to the man who brought him the head of William de la Marck.

The king and the duke joined forces to assault Liège. Their combined forces gallantly besieged the city but were forced to go into bivouac at nightfall. That night, William made a foray but was driven back into the city. The next day, the forces of the king and the duke attacked once more, made breaches in the wall, and poured into the city. Quentin came face-to-face with William de la Marck, who rushed at him with all the fury of the wild boar for which he was named. Le Balafré stood by and roared out for fair play, indicating that this should be a duel of champions. At that moment, Quentin saw a woman being forcibly dragged along by a French soldier. When he turned to rescue her, Le Balafré attacked de la Marck and killed him.

Le Balafré was announced as the man who had killed de la Marck, but he gave most of the credit to Quentin's valiant behavior and deferred to his nephew. While it was agreed that Quentin was responsible for de la Marck's death, there was still the problem of his lineage, which the duke questioned. Lord Crawford was indignant, and he recited the pedigree of Quentin and thereby proved his gentility. Without more ado, Quentin and Countess Isabelle were betrothed.

Critical Evaluation:

Quentin Durward appeared when Sir Walter Scott's career as a novelist was nearly a decade old. Although Scott was still signing his novels "By the Author of Waverley," his authorship was by no means unknown. The "Wizard of the North" touched the familiar formulas of his fiction with an undeniable magic. With *Waverley* (1814), Scott had invented the historical novel, a new genre. This fictional treatment of the last of the Stuart uprisings in 1745, manifesting genuine insight into events "Sixty Years Since," had been solidly founded upon his knowledge of Scotland, its history, and its people. The author had perceived in the Jacobite-Hanoverian conflict the clash of two cultures at the very moment when the former was passing away forever and the other was just coming into being. He had made figures from history a part of his fiction, through them creating the tensions in which his fictitious characters were caught. This first novel established the pattern and theme for the serious historical novel, not only Scott's "Waverley Novels" but also those of later writers such as James Fenimore Cooper.

Abounding in wealth and fame, his energies given also to public service, business, an estate in Scotland, an active social life, and other kinds of writing, Scott worked too hard and wrote too fast—one novel a year, sometimes two. With his tenth novel, *Ivanhoe* (1820), he sagaciously determined that his English reading public, after so many Scottish novels, would welcome a foray into English history. *Ivanhoe* became the talk of London, and his career gained new impetus. By 1823, however, his publisher, conscious of Scott's waning popularity, advised him to turn to other kinds of writing. The author, however, boldly moved into the foreign territory of fifteenth century France and once again created a literary sensation—the reception of his new novel in Paris rivaled that of *Ivanhoe* in London. After *Quentin Durward*, Scott was recognized as a great writer, both at home and abroad.

Quentin Durward stands as a milestone in Scott's career rather than as a significant novel. His own remarks on the work contain casual apologies for his license with historical facts; some critics charge him with the worse fault of allowing superficial knowledge to make of *Quentin Durward* a mere costume romance rather than a serious historical novel. Others rate it simply as a good tale of adventure.

Nevertheless, *Quentin Durward* provides a good example of the conflict at the heart of Scott's best historical novels—the thematic clash between the old order and the new. The order that is passing away is the age of chivalry with its feudal system and its chivalric code. The age that is coming into being takes its traits from the leader who, rather than the titular hero, is the central character of the novel—King Louis XI of France. Louis is the antithesis of the chivalric ideal. Honor is but a word to him; he studies the craft of dissimulation. His unceremonious manners express contempt rather than knightly humility. He exercises the virtues of generosity and courtesy only with ulterior motives. Crafty and false, committed to his own self-interest, he is a complete Machiavellian.

If Louis is the chief representative of the new age, no one is a genuine survivor of the old, despite noblemen who cling to a narrow concept of honor or imitate medieval splendor. Although Louis' principal rival, Charles of Burgundy, is his direct opposite, he is an inadequate symbol of chivalry. When Quentin says that he can win more honor under Charles's banner than under those of the king, Le Balafré counters with a description more accurate: "The Duke of Burgundy is a hot-brained, impetuous, pudding-headed, iron-ribbed dare-all." The decay of chivalry is epitomized in the hopelessness of Quentin's search for a leader who would keep his honor bright and is confirmed by his ultimate conclusion that none of these great leaders is any better than the other. During the dramatic episode at Charles's court, when the king, ironically, is prisoner of his own vassal, the court historian, Des Comines, reminds Louis—who knows better than anyone else—that strict interpretation of the feudal law is becoming outdated, while opportunity and power drive men to compromise and alter the old codes of chivalry.

Quentin Durward is the standard-bearer of the old order. Desiring to follow a man who will never avoid a battle and will keep a generous state, with tournaments and feasting and dancing with ladies, he lives upon ideas of brave deeds and advancement.

Quentin's ideals, however, are impossible from the start. His rootlessness is symptomatic of the dying culture he reveres. His only real ties are with the mercenary band of Scottish Archers. Their weatherbeaten leader, Lord Crawford, one of the last leaders of a brave band of Scottish lords and knights, as well as Quentin's kinsman, the hideously scarred, almost bestial Le Balafré, serve as evidence that the glorious past is irrevocably past.

Although Quentin is introduced as a simple and naïve youth, he is not a rare example of perfect chivalry. Equipped only with a rude mountain chivalry, he has his fair share of shrewdness and cunning. Far more politic than his experienced kinsman Le Balafré, this simple youth counsels Isabelle on the ways of telling half-truths with a skill that would credit Louis himself. Although it offends his dignity as a gentleman to accept money from a rich plebeian— ironically, King Louis disguised—he immediately discerns that the simple maid of the little turret is far more attractive after she is revealed as Isabelle, the countess of Croye, a highborn heiress. Presented by the king with an unpleasant crisis—an order to be prepared to kill the noble Crèvecœur from ambush—in which it would be "destruction in refusing, while his honor told him there would be disgrace in complying," Quentin chooses compliance.

As an emblem of the future, Quentin is neither as contemptible as his wily king nor as foolish as his older comrades deem him. The venerable Lord Crawford defends him well when he argues: "Quentin Durward is as much a gentleman as the king, only as the Spaniard says, not so rich. He is as noble as myself, and I am chief of my name." The youthful squire successfully endures the perilous journey, the chivalric testing of a man, bravely and skillfully evading the snares of the wicked, from the literal traps in and around Louis' castle to the treacherous ambush planned by the king and the more horrible fate threatening him during the sack of Schonwaldt. Therefore, only partially valid is Crèvecœur's ironic description of Quentin's trials as a pleasant journey full of heroic adventure and high hope. Crèvecœur's capitulation at the end is more just: "But why should I grudge this youth his preferment? Since, after all, it is sense, firmness, and gallantry which have put him in possession of Wealth, Rank, and Beauty!"

In the characterization of both Quentin and Louis, Scott dramatizes the ambiguities that afflict a time of transition. Although Louis lacks any real sense of moral obligations, he nevertheless understands the interests of France and faithfully pursues them. Detested as too cautious and crafty, he nevertheless exhibits a coolness before the wrath of Charles that far outshines the brave deeds of arms that Quentin values. If Quentin too passively drifts into the service of Louis, he can summon courage enough to defy the king and principle enough to support the king in adversity—even at the cost of telling a little falsehood and the risk of sacrificing his life.

In this novel, as in others, Scott vividly depicts the various ways in which men cope with a world of changing values, where as Crèvecœur's speech jocularly implies, sense and firmness have replaced gallantry, and wealth and rank have toppled beauty in the scale of things. It is this view of reality that seems most characteristic of the author: He is, like Quentin, most certainly a Romantic, idealizing the glories of a legendary time; but he understands the practical demands of a present reality and the value of a Louis or of a shrewd and brave youth such as Quentin Durward.

"Critical Evaluation" by Catherine E. Moore

Bibliography:

Hart, Francis. *Scott's Novels: The Plotting of Historic Survival.* Charlottesville: University Press of Virginia, 1966. Excellent discussion of historical background, providing insight into the characters of Charles of Burgundy and Louis XI. Analyzes the theme, the importance of power in politics, and raises questions about the difficult moral issues raised by political allegiance.

Johnson, Edgar. *Sir Walter Scott: The Great Unknown.* 2 vols. New York: Macmillan, 1970. Extensively researched biography exploring Scott, both as a man and as a writer. Provides clear summary of action and good analysis of character, theme, and setting, showing a society in which basic values have broken down, forcing the protagonist to fit into this corrupt world without losing his soul. An excellent introductory source.

Shaw, Harry E. *The Forms of Historical Fiction: Sir Walter Scott and His Successors.* Ithaca, N.Y.: Cornell University Press, 1983. Compares *Quentin Durward* to the other Waverley novels, discussing plot structure and noting that Scott described Louis XI as the novel's central character.

Sutherland, John. *The Life of Walter Scott: A Critical Biography.* Oxford, England: Basil Blackwell, 1995. Describes Scott's research for a new setting, studying maps of France. Compares details in the plot to incidents occurring in Scott's private life.

Wagenknecht, Edward. *Sir Walter Scott.* New York: Continuum, 1991. Clear, detailed discussion of the political background, theme, and characterization. Asserts that Quentin Durward is a realistic hero, while the characterization of James I is the finest in the novel.

THE QUEST FOR CERTAINTY

Type of work: Philosophy
Author: John Dewey (1859-1952)
First published: 1929

John Dewey remains one of America's most influential philosophers, social reformers, and educators. His system of thought is part of an American school of pragmatism that began with Charles Sanders Pierce (1838-1914), grew with William James (1842-1910), and blossomed with John Dewey (1859-1952). Pragmatism continues to influence American educators, philosophers, and social scientists. Dewey's *A Quest for Certainty* is a collection of lectures, the Gifford Lectures, that Dewey delivered in 1929 at the University of Edinburgh, Scotland. William James was one of the first Americans invited to deliver the Gifford Lectures, and he noted that American writers and philosophers had long listened to European scholars, but that this monologue became a dialogue when American pragmatists, such as James and Dewey, were invited to deliver the Gifford Lectures. Having just retired from full-time teaching at Columbia University, Dewey was seventy years old when he presented these eleven lectures. They represent Dewey's mature philosophy, his theory of knowledge.

Devoting the first three lectures to the failure of modern philosophy, Dewey demonstrates a need for pragmatism, a philosophy that can heal the schism created by modern thinkers between practice and theory. Dewey associates practice with experience, and experience is the realm of science, of the senses, and of common sense. Theory he associates with religion and philosophy, disciplines that dismiss experience and embrace abstraction. The separation of these two realms in modern times causes people to give prestige to the rational, religious, and philosophical as permanent, unsoiled, and absolute and to denigrate the practical as unreliable, physical, manual, and changing.

In his first lecture, "Escape from Peril," Dewey blames the present philosophical crisis on a long tradition of Western thinking going back to the Greeks. The Greeks began the quest for certainty, for permanent absolute answers to the ultimate questions in life. At first these answers were provided by religions, by references to gods as the ultimate cause and meaning of earthly experiences. Greek philosophers shifted this search for certainty from a religious quest to a rational quest, attempting to use reason to reach answers to questions such as: What is truth? What exists? and What is justice? Dewey argues that so long as philosophers and theologians remain in the realm of pure, abstract thought, in a realm where they hope to find absolute, unchanging answers, they will fail to connect their theories to practical experience.

Dewey attacks this separation of theory and practice, arguing that philosophers were looking for absolutes that do not exist. Dewey develops a method of inquiry that replaces the "quest of absolute certainty by cognitive means" with the "search for security by practical means." He notes that the denigration of the practical realm, of sense experience, was easy in a society or culture in which religious beliefs were preeminent, but in modern societies the rise of science has challenged religion and philosophy, a challenge that philosophers have attempted to reconcile in numerous, flawed ways. When philosophers could no longer dismiss the findings of science, their preoccupation was the reconciliation of theory and practice, of religion and science, of essence and experience. To this end modern philosophers struggled to unify a world divided into the realm of the body and the realm of the spirit.

In his third lecture, "Conflict of Authorities," Dewey analyzes several modern attempts to reconcile these differences, arguing that each attempt ultimately privileges the abstract realm at the expense of human experience. Taking the philosophy of Baruch Spinoza as exemplifying idealism, Dewey explores how Spinoza's monism posits the physical realm as a means to the spiritual or ideal. Dewey then examines Immanuel Kant's influential solution of a division of pure reason and practical reason into two separate spheres, the one a realm of certainty, the other a realm of human activity and doubt. Dewey discusses Kant's solution as the most prevalent in modern times. Dewey attacks Kant's solution as the theory that most clearly and destructively separates practice from experience. Finally, Dewey explores the dialectic idealism of Georg Wilhelm Friedrich Hegel, admiring Hegel's concern with the practical, the imperfect realm, but questioning Hegel's tendency toward seeking an ideal state of certainty. For Dewey, the danger in all modern philosophy is that method and content have been divided.

In lecture four, "The Art of Acceptance and the Art of Control," Dewey begins to outline his theory of inquiry, a method that will replace these failed modern ones, a theory of inquiry that he bases on the scientific method. Dewey asserts that this method is so common, so pervasive, and so obvious, that philosophers have not recognized it or created a theory of knowledge around it. This theory of knowledge is based on scientific method. Dewey also asserts, as a caveat, that modern science too often views data as unrelated particulars divorced from human experience. To gain knowledge, however, people must advance a method that explains how they learn from experience. Experience is the only source of knowledge—for Dewey, experiences are what exist.

To prove that reason cannot operate independent of experience and that knowledge of the physical realm cannot exist independent of reason, Dewey considers the interconnection of mathematical principles and the world of experience, arguing that mathematical principles— ideas that come close to pure abstraction—only exist in the physical realm: "Mathematical space is not a kind of space distinct from so-called physical and empirical space, but is a name given to operations ideally or formally possible with respect to a thing having spacious qualities." To illustrate his method further, Dewey analyzes the analogy of a good doctor diagnosing a patient's illness, a technique that Dewey posits as exemplifying his epistemology.

Doctors have ideas and theories that they learned in school and from books, but this abstract knowledge is not enough—a good doctor must also have experience. When doctors see patients, they form hypotheses concerning the patients' illnesses, but the doctors must then perform experiments to confirm or reject these hypotheses. With each case and with each experience, the good doctor gains knowledge. Thus, experienced doctors form better hypotheses. Essential to this method is "the appreciation and use . . . of direct experience." At the core of Dewey's philosophy is his epistemology, his theory of how people know what they know. This theory has been labeled instrumental logic, but it is really a commonsense theory of scientific method. Dewey's theory relies on reflective experimentation.

In his ninth lecture, Dewey returns to the question of certainty and the method that should be employed in situations in which one is uncertain. Dewey states that uncertainty arises in new situations and that humans wish to quell the fear or doubt that arises in such situations. One may alleviate uncertainty quickly by retreating to an abstract realm. An example of this would be a person who, when in trouble, prays, hoping that the prayer will solve the problem. Humans want to eliminate uncertainty or fear quickly. Dewey argues against such methods. The intelligent person has a delayed reaction to uncertainty, a reaction that allows uncertainty to linger. People should experiment in an uncertain situation, and this is done by means of manipulation. By experimenting, people change their relationship to the situation that is creating fear, and, perhaps, create a new situation from which they can learn.

In his tenth lecture, "The Construction of Good," Dewey extends his epistemology into an ethics by arguing that values are not absolutes that exist prior to and separate from a particular circumstance. The good arises from what one experiences in a specific situation, and this will change as conditions change. Again, method is essential to determine the good. People cannot separate the means from the end—this would be the same as separating practice from theory. People must know how and why something is good, and this consideration returns them to a particular situation, a particular problem. Dewey's epistemology draws on a commonsense means of knowing, and his ethics draws on a practical means of valuing. Dewey believes that philosophers have spent too much time searching for the good in a permanent, transcendent realm, while most people find value in particular experiences.

Dewey ends *The Quest for Certainty* with the lecture, "The Copernican Revolution." Nicolaus Copernicus, relying on scientific experimentation, asserted that the sun, not the earth, was at the center of the solar system. Thus, he displaced the Ptolemaic notion that dominated the Middle Ages. Kant compared himself to Copernicus, saying that he created a revolution in philosophy as Copernicus created one in science, but Dewey maintains that Kant's philosophy in maintaining a realm of pure reason is Ptolemaic in that it places human beings and their quest of certainty at the center of the system. Dewey, on the other hand, sees himself and other American pragmatists performing a Copernican revolution by basing philosophy, education, and social theory on experience, and by privileging a method of inquiry that does not ignore human experience.

The Quest for Certainty is a significant work in that it presents the mature theory and method of an influential American philosopher. The lectures delineate his objection to previous philosophy, his own theory of inquiry, and his ethics. These lectures do not explore his authoritative theories of aesthetics, education, and politics. Dewey, in other works, extends his method of experimental inquiry into education, advocating experimentation as the way to knowledge. Dewey also argued that the active exchange of ideas that should occur in school could model the democratic process. A society based on his theories of education and democracy would form a community of free inquirers who test their ideas in a public forum, not an abstract or isolated realm.

Roark Mulligan

Bibliography:
Burke, Tom. *Dewey's New Logic: A Reply to Russell*. Chicago: University of Chicago Press, 1994. Contrasts Dewey's instrumental logic with Bertrand Russell's more abstract theory of symbolic logic. In so doing, Burke elaborates on ideas raised in *The Quest for Certainty*.
Dewey, John. *The Middle Works, 1899-1924*. Edited by Jo Ann Boydston. Carbondale: Southern Illinois University Press, 1976. This collection of John Dewey's works includes a bibliography and an index.
Hook, Sidney. *John Dewey: An Intellectual Portrait*. New York: John Day, 1939. Still valuable. Offers a sympathetic and thoughtful analysis of John Dewey as a person and philosopher.
Kulp, Christopher B. *The End of Epistemology: Dewey and His Current Allies on the Spectator Theory of Knowledge*. Westport, Conn.: Greenwood Press, 1992. Explores Dewey's theory of knowledge, the same theory that is developed in *The Quest for Certainty*. Analyzes the relationship of Dewey's theory to that of more recent philosophers.
Thomas, M. Halsey. *John Dewey: A Centennial Bibliography*. Chicago: University of Chicago Press, 1962. An extensive bibliography of John Dewey's writing and of secondary sources on Dewey.

THE QUEST OF THE HOLY GRAIL

Type of work: Fiction
Author: Unknown
Type of plot: Arthurian romance
Time of plot: Early eighth century
Locale: England, France, and Wales
First published: c. 1300

> *Principal characters:*
> JOSEPH OF ARAMATHEA, a disciple of Christ
> MERLIN THE MAGICIAN, a wizard
> KING ARTHUR, king of the Britons
> PERCEVAL, son of Alein and seeker of the Grail
> GAUVAIN or GAWAIN and
> HURGAINS, knights of the Round Table
> THE FISHER KING

The Story:

Joseph of Aramathea was a disciple of Christ who, along with his colleague, Nicodemus, attended the tomb of Christ. While washing the body of Christ, Joseph accidently opened a wound. To prevent Christ's blood from spilling, Joseph took the goblet from which Christ drank during the Last Supper and collected the blood therein. He then hid the Grail in his house. The Jews, incensed upon hearing that he had taken the cup, imprisoned Joseph in a dark cell, but Nicodemus escaped. In the cell, Christ appeared to Joseph with the vessel Joseph thought he had hidden. Christ gave Joseph the vessel, with strict orders that only three persons would ever gain possession of it. Joseph was not, however, told who they were to be.

Hundreds of years later, Merlin, after choosing Arthur to become king of the Britons, came to the court of Britain and revealed the story of the Holy Grail. He explained the story of the three tables: one made by the Lord for the Last Supper, one by Joseph of Arimathea, and the last by his own hands. He told them that the Grail was passed by Joseph to the rich Fisher King, an old, frail man whose mission was to await the coming of the purest knight in the world. To this knight he would he pass the Grail and tell of its mighty power and secrets. Only then would the Fisher King's ailments and age be lifted. After his revelations, Merlin vanished to faraway lands to await the reign of Arthur. Meanwhile, Alein le Gros was dying and was visited by the Holy Ghost, who told him that his own father, Brons, lived in the islands of Ireland and possessed the Holy Grail. Alein was told that he would not be allowed to die until his son, Perceval, found Brons and was taught the secrets of the Grail. First, however, Perceval had to go to the Court of King Arthur and be taught the ways of chivalry and honor. He went willingly and joyously.

One Easter, King Arthur decided to hold a tournament to honor the Round Table. Perceval, learning the ways of knighthood, wanted no part of the tournament, but for the love of a woman, Aleine, niece of Sir Gawain, he agreed to fight. She sent him a suit of red armor, and he entered the contest as an unknown, anonymous knight. He defeated all opponents and claimed his right to sit at the Round Table. Arthur protested, but with some urging gave in to the new knight. Before long, Perceval vowed never to lie, to be pure, and to seek the Grail. Sir Gawain, Sagremors, Beduers, Hurgains, and Erec took the same vow, and all set forth on their quests.

Two days after beginning the quest for the Holy Grail, Perceval found the body of the knight Hurganet, with a damsel weeping over it. Hurganet, she said, had saved her from a giant and had ridden with her into a tent. They were warned to run and not await the tent's master, who would surely kill them.

The lord of the tent, Orgoillow Delandes, soon appeared, wearing red armor, and slew Hurganet. Upon hearing this story, Sir Perceval vowed revenge for Hurganet's death and rode forth to the tent, where he also was warned of its master. Soon he was face to face with the knight of the tent. He overcame him and sent him to Arthur's court with the damsel.

Continuing his quest, Perceval came to a fine castle. He entered, but found the castle uninhabited. Only a chess board decorated the castle. He played chess, and the pieces began to play against him. Three times he was checkmated. Angry at his defeat, he attempted to toss the pieces into the castle moat but was stopped by the entrance of a beautiful damsel. Overcome by her beauty, Perceval asked for her love. She agreed to love him if he would capture the white stag of the wood. To this end, she lent him one hound and warned him to take care of the beast. He agreed, chased and captured the stag, cut off its head, and started back to the castle. An old hag had made off with the hound and vowed not to return it to him until he went to a certain grave and said "Felon, he that put you there." After Perceval heeded the old lady's words, a knight in black armor appeared upon a black horse, and challenged Perceval. Perceval soon overcame the black knight, but while he was fighting, a second man took both the stag's head and the hound. Perceval followed, but could not catch him.

Many feats followed. Perceval came to his home and, with his niece, rode to the home of his uncle, a hermit, who told him of the table, the Grail, and his destiny. He continued to wander for seven years, sending more than a hundred knights prisoner to Arthur. Finally, Perceval found the Fisher King, was told the secrets of the Holy Grail, and all was well in Britain.

Critical Evaluation:

Among prose and poetry dedicated to the Grail, three distinct explanations for the Grail are provided: One work indicates that the Grail was the cup from which Christ drank at the Last Supper, one proposes that it was only used by Joseph of Arimathea to gather Jesus' blood, and the third is a combination of the two. Furthermore, the means by which the Grail is transferred from hand to hand, ultimately to Perceval, changes from account to account. This may well be a result of the antiquity of the stories, but the fact that the Holy Grail only occurs in the most recent of Arthurian texts indicates yet another addition to the Christianization of King Arthur. The first historical references to King Arthur can be dated as far back as 548, the anonymously written *Quest of the Holy Grail* dates only as far back as c. 1300, long after the Christianization of Britain by Augustine. By this time, the great institutions of learning, primarily Cambridge, Oxford, and the University of Paris, were well established. This allowed scholars and writers better access to libraries and to their predecessors, such as Robert de Boron. Boron's poems were the primary sources for the anonymous poet of *Quest of the Holy Grail.*

There is an exaggerated and nostalgic concept of chivalry in the poem. The late Middle Ages, during which the *Quest of the Holy Grail* was written, saw little chivalry, few knights in armor, and even fewer heros. Thus the writers of the day looked to the past for a great hero. To these people, only Jesus himself, or a saint, could be a truly pure man. King Arthur had already been elevated to immortality over the centuries, so by logical extension his knights, among them Sir Perceval, himself added to the story by the French, became immortal heroes. According to this version, however, Perceval does not begin his quest as a holy or pure man. He deceives his way into Arthur's favor, and, were it not for his father's purity, would have been cast into hell for taking his seat at the Round Table. It takes some time before he vows to be chaste and never to kill again.

The fact that the story spends a great deal of time explaining the origin of the Holy Grail and its place in the ultimate plan of God indicates several possibilities regarding the background and intent of the author. First, it can be established that the author was Christian. By 1300, virtually all of Europe was ruled by the Roman Catholic church, either directly or indirectly. England, however, was one of the most tolerant nations toward non-Christians. The *Quest of the Holy Grail* indicates that the author believed the Grail stories propagated by Robert de Boron, and that although the real King Arthur would most certainly have been a pagan, he is referred to as a Christian who ruled his people by the grace of God. The concept of predestination is also reinforced throughout the story, as each character is led to his destiny by the Holy Ghost.

The Christian origin is obvious, but there is one possible pagan explanation for the Grail. Celtic folklore tells that a chalice, or grail, can be a symbol of sustenance, a vessel of life providing food, water, and even wine (which brings one closer to God). Thus it is the life-giver, and is feminine. It is what Carl Jung called an archetypal symbol, part of the universal consciousness, understood by all persons of all cultures. Thus, although there are many possibilities to explain the author's passion for the Grail stories, the influences of the time in which it was written seem to have had the most effect on the author, and his understanding of the Joseph of Arimathea poem by Robert de Boron indicate an educated man with a good knowledge of French. The anonymous author may have been a priest or monk. Whether the author was a priest, monk, or scholar, there is no denying the importance of the *Quest of the Holy Grail* as a literary work. Like all other Arthurian romances, it provided the British with a sense of history and national pride. It could even be said that these tales were not mere stories and poems, but propaganda by either the throne or the Church regarding the Christianizing of Britain. After all, once the Grail and its secrets had been retrieved by Perceval, all curses and plagues placed upon pagan Britain were lifted for all time.

"Critical Evaluation" by Gordon Robert Maddison

Bibliography:

Nutt, Alfred. *Studies on the Legend of the Holy Grail.* New York: Cooper Square, 1965. Focuses on the Celtic origins of the tale. A good starting text for the serious student.

Waite, Arthur Edward. *The Holy Grail: The Galahad Quest in the Arthurian Literature.* New York: University Books, 1961. Approaches the mystical side of the tale, providing new insight.

Weston, Jessie L. *The Quest of the Holy Grail.* New York: Barnes & Noble Books, 1964. This classic on the subject of the Grail was first published in 1913, but remains one of the clearest descriptions of the Grail cycle.

Wilhelm, James J., ed. *The Romance of Arthur: An Anthology of Medieval Texts in Translation.* New York: Garland, 1994. Critical edition of some of the best translations of early Arthurian literature.

QUICKSAND

Type of work: Novel
Author: Nella Larsen (1891-1964)
Type of plot: Psychological realism
Time of plot: Late 1920's
Locale: The southern and northern United States; Copenhagen, Denmark
First published: 1928

> *Principal characters:*
> HELGA CRANE, a mulatto teacher
> JAMES VAYLE, her fiancé
> DR. ROBERT ANDERSON, a teacher at Naxos, an elite institute for black
>   youth
> PETER NILSSEN, Helga's benevolent uncle
> KATRINA and
> POUL DAHL, her aunt and uncle in Copenhagen
> MRS. JEANETTE HAYES-RORE, a lecturer on race relations
> ANNE GREY, Mrs. Hayes-Rore's elegant niece
> AXEL OLSEN, a Danish portrait painter
> THE REVEREND MR. PLEASANT GREEN, an Alabama preacher

The Story:

Abandoned by her black father, held at bay by her white immigrant mother, Helga was no stranger to the loneliness of an "unloved, unloving, and unhappy" childhood. Now her young adulthood had become just as troubled. Helga wanted to flee the snobbery, drabness, and rigidity of Naxos, the school for black youth where she had taught for two listless years. She therefore broke her engagement to the well-heeled black Atlantan James Vayle (much to the delight of his family, who had viewed her as their social inferior) and gave notice of her resignation to her principal, Dr. Anderson. This gentle young man was one of the few at that dour institution who could make Helga laugh and feel completely at ease. Yet when he complemented her ladylike behavior, she assumed he was simply another social snob and departed at once.

In her new destination of Chicago, harsh reality withered Helga's excitement. What was meant to be a reunion with her Uncle Peter, who had financed her studies, turned out to be a tense confrontation. He had remarried, and his new wife did not want to associate with Helga because of Helga's black parentage. Jobs, too, proved difficult to obtain unless the work was menial. At last, Helga secured temporary employment as a traveling companion for the civil rights activist and orator Mrs. Hayes-Rore.

Although the older woman's sobriety, plumpness, and haphazard grooming were the antitheses of Helga's enthusiasm, slimness, and impeccable style, the two became fast friends. Mrs. Hayes-Rore became a confidante to the young woman. In fact, she arranged for Helga to achieve another dream: to live and work in Harlem, the sophisticated black capital of America.

Helga lodged in New York with Anne Grey, Mrs. Hayes-Rore's wealthy, widowed niece. Anne initiated Helga into her Harlem socialite's lifestyle of exclusive parties, expensive clothes, daring interracial romances, theater and gallery openings, servants, leisure, and excess. Working as a secretary by day, attending social and cultural events by night, Helga almost accomplished the perfectly balanced, stimulating life that she had always craved. Yet, the allure of Harlem days and nights became clouded by the hypocrisy that belied Anne's pleasant demeanor. Anne spurned racial prejudice and social inequality; yet, she despised the music, dances, clothes, speech, and mannerisms associated with her own African American community. Helga's disillusionment with Anne was compounded by a replay of the old smothering restlessness and unhappiness, and a new wave of love for Dr. Anderson confused her.

Helga fled America to visit relatives in Copenhagen. Overseas, people saw her as an exotic curiosity. Her relatives, the Dahls, paraded her around in outrageous outfits, elephantine jewelry, and peacock colors that reflected their own stereotypical assumptions about being *sorte*, the Danish word for "black." Soon, the dormant dissatisfaction flared; her aunt and uncle insisted on making life decisions for her, and all the Danes were somewhat detached and cold because of her mulatto identity.

Axel Olsen, a portrait painter, symbolized all the behaviors that began to frustrate Helga. He humiliated her by bombarding her with gifts of expensive clothes that caricatured her as either an African savage or an Arab concubine. He insulted her by courting her formally through her relatives. He infuriated her with his attitude that mingled desire and contempt for her ethnicity.

When Axel "insinuated marriage" to her, Helga learned that her friend Anne had been betrothed to Dr. Anderson. Heartsick and lonely for black companions again, Helga refused Olsen's proposal and returned to New York.

In Harlem, Helga swept away heartbreak in an undertow of parties and socializing. Vayle resurfaced at one summer party and again proposed to Helga. She laughed him aside. When she went upstairs to repair a hem, Dr. Anderson belatedly confirmed the love between them by giving her a kiss in secret. He later downplayed the moment, however, leaving Helga devastated.

She soothed her mangled pride and unrequited passions in the church. Having married the Reverend Mr. Pleasant Green, she moved to Alabama and immersed herself in an exhausting routine of charity work, Bible instruction, homemaking, and childbearing. This did not stave off the familiar restiveness and loneliness, however, which returned now accompanied by despair. As Helga nursed the temptation to abandon her marriage and children, she became pregnant with her fifth child.

Critical Evaluation:

Larsen aligns herself with one of the agendas of the Harlem Renaissance: to expose the divergences and varieties among black artists' themes, styles, imaginative references, and politics. In her novels *Quicksand* and *Passing* (1929), the characters are distinctive. Instead of depicting the folksy, rural Southerners or the urban Northern wits who populated the works of African American writers Zora Neale Hurston, Langston Hughes, and Claude McKay, Larsen represents the black bourgeoisie in general and the female among this class in particular. Modernism's influence is apparent in her characters' interior reflections and in her technique, which combines abrupt, jagged sentences, condensed visual images, a potpourri of cultural references, and sketches of decadent, anonymous city life.

The title, *Quicksand*, alludes to the novel's theme of the gender- and race-specific pitfalls that have historically affected all African American women, regardless of skin complexion, social class, marital status, sexual orientation, regional affiliation, or education. Helga's quest for romantic love, her beauty, and her sexual freedom reject the extreme stereotyping of all black women as either hypersexed prostitutes or undesirable laboring machines. Yet, both whites and blacks pigeonhole her in one of these two categories. As she searches Chicago for employment, men of both races assume she is a whore and solicit her services. Because shops and schools discriminate against her race, it is easy to be hired as a domestic, reinforcing the stereotype of all black women as mammies.

Helga is characterized from the novel's beginning by detailed descriptions of her striking facial features, alluring skin, and impeccably tasteful attire, which includes shoes, blouses, dresses, scarves, hats, jewelry, handkerchiefs, purses, hair ornaments, and corsages. More than mirroring her moods, her attentive grooming and sophisticated, often inappropriate, fashions show Helga's determination to resist uniform definitions of womanhood. In the cities of Chicago, New York, and Copenhagen, she resists social pressures to suppress her unconventionality, spontaneity, imagination, and passion.

After her retreat from life into numb piety, the descriptions change. Once fashion dominated her thoughts. Now Helga focuses constantly on the ills of her body as it rebels against domestic labor, pastoral service, and unmitigated childbearing. The only description of Helga's garments refers to an old, unappealing nightgown, a remnant of her fashionable days. Larsen delineates Helga's body by nothing but brief comments about her starving, endlessly aching limbs. Helga's hair, always arranged in the past in glorious styles and decorated with flowers and combs, is now always in disarray, scattering on pillows or flying at angles. This artistic technique conveys the psychological death that ensues for women like Helga who are bound too tightly by domestic duties and social expectations.

Quicksand vocalizes the precautionary outcry among Harlem Renaissance artists and intellectuals, including Larsen, that the historical underpinnings of stereotypes came from deep within society and that black people's attitudes toward themselves had been globally and adversely affected by racist perspectives. Wherever Helga goes, her ethnicity is scrutinized and distorted. Ironically, Danish society appreciates variety and difference—in food, art, conversation, and languages. Yet, even the Danes are oblivious to varieties and differences among African Americans, as Helga learns when one contends that all "Negroes were black and had woolly hair."

By the turn of the century, black churches and civic and benevolent organizations had launched an organized assault on "the race problem." This movement of self-help predicated that black people's advancement and full citizenship in American society depended upon education, labor, morality, discipline, thrift, respectability, and entrepreneurship. *Quicksand* thematically accuses this movement of having traded its visionary and innovative origins for elitism, self-hate, and orthodoxy. For instance, Naxos, where Helga is first employed, is but an anagram of "Saxon." It owes its existence, ironically, not to black entrepreneurs but to white philanthropists. It exemplifies, ironically, not the individualism and enterprise of Horatio Alger and Poor Richard but only frigid sameness and kneejerk obedience.

Naxos' black students conform to the "formal calm" of European models of gender and behavior. The women wear muted pastels instead of bolder colors and prints. Both men and women attend sermons by paternalistic whites who exhort them to remain in a subordinate social position. Even among the faculty, the highest aspirations are to marry into the race's "good stock" and "first families," which also happen to constitute the race's fairest-skinned people.

Larsen's characterization of progressive blacks or race representatives extends this critique of the self-help movement. Unoriginal leaders such as Mrs. Hayes-Rore rehash clichéd solutions. She virtually plagiarizes her speeches from the published works of foregone black leaders. Nor does she, a "lemon-colored woman," publicly address the taboos of adultery and rape that undergird national anxieties about mulattoes and race-mixing. Love itself is deadened by self-help when Vayle argues for marriage to Helga on the theory that the "better class" must bear children in order to advance the race.

Since enslavement, black politics and black religion have been intertwined. Such nineteenth century orators as David Walker, Maria Stewart, Frederick Douglass, and Sojourner Truth have argued for emancipation and enfranchisement by employing scriptural rationales. Evoking literal quicksand, Larsen relegates this combination of political and religious activism to bygone days. She uses images of unconsciousness, drowning, choking, and burial to present the sterility and passivity of black Christianity.

Christians are like zombies, drugged by impassioned worship and zealous calls to duty into abandoning individual will and personal responsibility. Their pastors' ulterior motives are ease and authority, and black women enable the bulk of this by abusing their bodies, limiting their social contacts, and neglecting their dreams. The Reverend Green resembles Mrs. Hayes-Rore. With her, he shares hypocrisy and opportunism, especially as he flirts with the female membership right under the nose of his new wife.

In *Quicksand*, religion is thus a sibling to self-help and its perils. Both reflect what Larsen sees as a self-enslavement of African Americans. Both retard the very progress that the artists of the Harlem Renaissance espouse.

Barbara McCaskill

Bibliography:
Carby, Hazel V. *Reconstructing Womanhood: The Emergence of the Afro-American Woman Novelist.* New York: Oxford University Press, 1987. Discusses Helga's denial of sexuality in light of historical representations of black female identity.
Davis, Thadious M. *Nella Larsen, Novelist of the Harlem Renaissance: A Woman's Life Unveiled.* Baton Rouge: Louisiana State University Press, 1994. The definitive literary biography of Larsen. Considers the author's mixed motives for writing *Quicksand* and argues that Helga enacts unresolved anger toward her disempowered and remote mother.
Larson, Charles R. *Invisible Darkness: Jean Toomer and Nella Larsen.* Iowa City: University of Iowa Press, 1993. Discusses the autobiographical underpinnings of Larsen's writing: her childhood, marriage, and self-exile from the literary world. Appends bibliography of primary works, reviews, and criticism.
McDowell, Deborah E. " 'That Nameless . . . Shameful Impulse': Sexuality in Nella Larsen's *Quicksand* and *Passing.*" In *Black Feminist Criticism and Theory,* edited by Joe Weixlmann and Houston A. Baker, Jr. Greenwood, Fla.: Penkeville, 1988. Describes Larsen's attempt to portray black women as both sexual and respectable.
Wall, Cheryl A. "Passing for What? Aspects of Identity in Nella Larsen's Novels." In *Black American Literature Forum* 20, nos. 1/2 (1986): 97-111. Asserts that Helga deviates from conventional depictions of tragic mulattoes who pass for white. Instead, she assumes and discards inauthentic identities.

THE QUIET AMERICAN

Type of work: Novel
Author: Graham Greene (1904-1991)
Type of plot: Tragedy
Time of plot: Early 1950's
Locale: Vietnam
First published: 1955

>   *Principal characters:*
>   THOMAS FOWLER, an English newspaper correspondent and the novel's
>   narrator
>   ALDEN PYLE, the quiet American, and an undercover agent in Vietnam
>   PHUONG, at first Fowler's mistress and then Pyle's
>   VIGOT, the French police chief investigating Pyle's murder

The Story:

Alden Pyle, an American undercover agent, was found murdered in French Saigon. In the early 1950's, the French still controlled Vietnam as a colony, but they were losing control of the country to the Communist revolutionaries. Pyle had come to investigate conditions and had befriended an English newspaper correspondent, Thomas Fowler. Vigot, the French police chief, ordered Fowler and his former mistress, Phuong, to his office for questioning. Fowler was under suspicion because he was one of the last people to have seen Pyle alive, and Pyle took Phuong away from Fowler.

Vigot interrogated Fowler, who proclaimed not only his innocence but also his ignorance of what happened to Pyle. Phuong, who did not understand English, said nothing. After the interrogation, Fowler told her that Pyle had been murdered. Her reaction was surprisingly mild, and she revealed almost nothing about her feelings. Fowler then went over the sequence of events that led to Pyle's murder and Vigot's summons to police headquarters.

Pyle had befriended Fowler during his first days in Saigon. Fowler was a reluctant companion. He disliked Americans, especially ones like Pyle who seemed on a mission to save the world. Pyle never admitted to Fowler that he was a CIA agent—indeed no reference is made to the Central Intelligence Agency in the novel, except for Fowler's suggestion that Pyle might work for the Office of Strategic Services (OSS). Established in World War II, the OSS was the precursor of the postwar CIA. To Fowler, Pyle was an innocent who read books on Vietnam but did not understand the reality of people's lives. Fowler believed that the Vietnamese should be left alone. He did not believe that their lives could be improved by Westerners. He considered himself a reporter without political commitments or opinions. He was an older man (not saying how much older) who disdained Pyle's idealism. Pyle wanted to save Vietnam from communism. Fowler found this attitude ridiculous and dangerous because it meant Pyle would involve himself with the local Vietnamese anticommunist military, who seemed to Fowler no more than gangsters. If the French were to lose Vietnam, it could not be saved by Americans looking for a "third force" (some group other than the Communists or the French).

The "third force" was a theory Pyle had adopted from a book on Vietnam by York Harding. To Fowler, both Harding and Pyle ignored reality to pursue theory. Pyle even condoned the terrorist acts of General Thé, an anticommunist thug. General Thé blew up a café, maiming men, women, and children. To Pyle, this atrocity was a mistake. He planned to straighten it out with the general. To Fowler, the atrocity proved that Pyle was doing great harm in spite of his good intentions.

On the personal level, Pyle took Fowler's mistress away from him because Pyle believed that Phuong had to be saved. Pyle earnestly wanted to know if Fowler loved Phuong and meant to marry her. When Fowler admitted he used Phuong for his selfish pleasure, Pyle offered her marriage and a home in America, which she accepted.

In spite of their political and personal conflicts, Fowler found it hard to reject Pyle. On a mission to observe the war in action, Fowler was injured and Pyle risked his own life to save him. Fowler knew that Pyle meant well, and Pyle complicated Fowler's feelings about him by constantly saying he knew that Fowler was not nearly as cynical and selfish as he said he was.

Pyle's dangerous innocence and idealism so outraged Fowler that he decided he must thwart Pyle's plans to coordinate another terrorist act with General Thé. Fowler informed a Communist agent of Pyle's plot. Thus it was Fowler's own intervention in politics that led to Pyle's death. Exactly how Pyle died and exactly who was responsible were never made clear. Fowler realized, however, that Pyle's death was his doing, even though he had only wanted Pyle stopped, not murdered.

Phuong returned to Fowler after Pyle's death. Fowler also got a cable from his wife announcing that she would give him a divorce. A happy Phuong went to tell her sister that she is to be the "second Mrs. Fowlaire." Meanwhile, Fowler brooded on Pyle's story. His last words revealed his guilt and his sense of responsibility for Pyle's murder: "Everything had gone right with me since he had died, but how I wished there existed someone to whom I could say that I was sorry."

Critical Evaluation:

The Quiet American is considered one of Graham Greene's major achievements. The story is told with great economy, superb characterization, and sophisticated irony. The plot resembles that of a mystery story. A crime has been committed. Who is the murderer? As in most mystery stories, as much needs to be learned about the victim as about the villain. Yet what is learned takes on political, moral, and religious significance. The story ends in mystery as well. Who exactly killed Pyle is not revealed, but the burden of the crime, like the burden of telling the story, is Fowler's.

Fowler is a fascinating character and narrator because he simultaneously reveals and conceals so much about himself and his involvement in the story. On the one hand, he is openly contemptuous of Pyle. Like other Americans, Pyle is so obsessed with his mission to save the world that he does not register the reality around him. It is ludicrous for him to think that Phuong is an innocent he must rescue. She has stayed with Fowler because he offers her security. She leaves Fowler for Pyle because he offers her even more wealth and protection. Pyle is shocked because Fowler says he is merely using Phuong for his own pleasure and because of his need to have a woman beside him to stave off loneliness. It never occurs to Pyle that Phuong has acted just as selfishly or that Pyle himself is using people.

On the other hand, Fowler is not entirely honest with himself. He claims to be disengaged, not only from politics but also from the sentiments of love Pyle professes. Yet Fowler's vehement rejection of Pyle's worldview and his passionate defence of the Vietnamese (who, he believes, should be allowed to worked out their own destiny, free of the French, the Americans, and any other intruding power) surely reveal anything but cynicism. In this respect, Pyle is right to see good in a man who claims to be without scruples.

Indeed, Pyle loses his life because of Fowler's moral outrage. Fowler is so revolted by the bombing atrocity at the café that he determines to put a stop to Pyle's activities. Fowler's passion is hardly consistent with his affectation of aloofness. Actually, he cares deeply about Phuong and about the Vietnamese. He believes in self-determination, which ironically is the ideology that Americans claim to support. Americans think they are supporting freedom by allying themselves with the anticommunists.

Thus, there are multiple ironies in *The Quiet American*. Fowler says he is a cynic, but he acts like a wounded idealist. Pyle says he is an idealist, but his trafficking with anticommunist thugs involves him in cynical and brutal plots. Phuong looks like a delicate, manipulable, and passive victim, and yet like many other Vietnamese she is a survivor who plays one side against the other and bends with the political winds. Fowler declares to Vigot that he is not guilty, retells the story of his involvement with Fowler to absolve himself, yet concludes by realizing that he is guilty.

The novel's title is also ironic. In one sense, Pyle is quiet—even unassuming. He is not aggressive. He patiently questions Fowler about his tie to Phuong and even declares his love for her to Fowler before he courts her. Pyle is the opposite of loud, vulgar Americans such as his boss Joe, or the noisy American journalist Granger. In another sense, however, Pyle is anything but quiet. He stirs up Saigon with explosions; he turns Fowler's life into turmoil.

An even greater irony is that for all their differences, Fowler and Pyle are alike in their moral earnestness. Fowler is the sophisticated European who has learned not to wear his heart on his sleeve. He denies any form of selfless behavior. Pyle is naïve American who is openhearted and believes he acts for the good of others. Yet both men cause great damage because they care about others. They are implicated in the evil that Fowler thinks he can elude and that Pyle thinks he can eliminate.

The political and moral divide between Fowler and Pyle is not as great as Fowler has supposed. His narrative ironically binds him to Pyle—a fate Fowler has consistently tried to avoid. The novel dramatizes Fowler's fate in the scene where he refuses to call Pyle by his first name. He also refuses to let Pyle call him Tom and insists on being called Thomas. No formalities can really separate the two men, however; Fowler's own narrative shows them to be twinned souls.

The religious basis of Greene's fiction has often been noted by his critics. He is a Catholic novelist who believes in the universality of human nature, that human beings cannot separate themselves from one another, and that all souls are alike in their propensity to sin. Although Fowler refers to himself several times as an atheist, Pyle refuses to believe him, saying the world does not make sense without a concept of God. Fowler retorts that the world does not make sense with a concept of God. At the end of his narrative, however, Fowler is clearly seeking the solace of a higher power. He does not refer to God, but he mentions his good luck since Pyle has died. Phuong has returned to him; his wife has agreed to divorce him after initially indicating she would not. Everything seems to have fallen in place for a man worried about growing old and desiring the companionship of a younger woman. Yet Fowler is nevertheless disturbed. He tells Phuong he is sorry. She does not understand. To her, the telegram from Fowler's wife means that she will be happy. She does not know that Fowler needs to unburden himself. His story is part of his unburdening, but his last words reveal that he needs "someone else to whom I could say I was sorry." He has made a kind of confession; he has been unable to absolve himself of sin. His is a religious sentiment, a craving for a being to whom he wants himself to be accountable. He is on the verge of admitting his need for God.

Carl Rollyson

Bibliography:
DeVitis, A. A. *Graham Greene*. Rev. ed. Boston: Twayne, 1986. Treats the novel as a transitional work, telling of Greene's experience in Indochina, his use of an unreliable narrator, and the novel's existentialism. Discusses the novel's links to Greene's religious fiction.

Gaston, Georg M. A. *The Pursuit of Salvation: A Critical Guide to the Novels of Graham Greene*. Troy, N.Y.: Whitston, 1984. Calls *The Quiet American* the most flawless novel Greene ever wrote but also one of his most controversial and misunderstood. Argues that critics have simplified the book's politics and that the book's real issue is personal salvation.

McEwan, Neil. *Graham Greene*. New York: St. Martin's Press, 1988. Concentrates on Fowler's development as narrator and on Greene's Catholicism. Compares the novel to Henry James's of meetings between Europeans and Americans and suggests that Greene's anti-American bias weakens his satire.

O'Prey, Paul. *A Reader's Guide to Graham Greene*. New York: Thames and Hudson, 1988. Discusses the novel in terms of Greene's traveling. Compares *The Quiet American* to Greene's other political novels.

Sharrock, Roger. *Saints, Sinners, and Comedians: The Novels of Graham Greene*. Notre Dame, Ind.: University of Notre Dame Press, 1984. Compares the novel to Greene's preceding fiction, compares the novelist's treatments of real places with that of other great novelists, analyzes Greene's political opinions, relates them to Fowler's, and concludes that *The Quiet American* is Greene's most carefully constructed novel.

QUO VADIS
A Narrative of the Time of Nero

Type of work: Novel
Author: Henryk Sienkiewicz (1846-1916)
Type of plot: Historical
Time of plot: c. 64 C.E.
Locale: Rome
First published: Quo vadis, 1896 (English translation, 1896)

> *Principal characters:*
> VINICIUS, a young Roman patrician
> LYGIA, a foreign princess whom Vinicius loves
> PETRONIUS, Vinicius' uncle and an intimate friend of Nero
> NERO, the Roman emperor
> CHILO, a Greek sycophant
> PETER, a leader of the Christians
> TIGELLINUS, Petronius' enemy and Nero's friend

The Story:

When Vinicius returned to Rome, after duty in the colonies, he called on his uncle, Petronius, who was one of the most influential men in Rome. A friend of Emperor Nero, Petronius owned a beautiful home, choice slaves, and numerous objects of art. Petronius had no delusions about the emperor. He knew quite well that Nero was coarse, conceited, brutal, and thoroughly evil. Petronius was happy to see his handsome young nephew. Vinicius had fallen in love with Lygia, daughter of a foreign king, now living with Aulus, Plautius, and Pomponia. He asked his uncle to help him get Lygia as his concubine. Petronius spoke to Nero, and Lygia was ordered to be brought to the palace. The giant Ursus was sent as Lygia's devoted servant by her foster parents.

At a wild orgy in the palace, Vinicius attempted to make love to Lygia. Through the watchfulness of Acte, who was a Christian and a former concubine of Nero, he did not succeed. Lygia herself was a Christian, and she feared both the lust of Vinicius and that of the emperor himself. Then Acte received information that Lygia would be handed over to Vinicius. At the same time, the daughter of Empress Augusta died. The empress and her circle believed that Lygia had bewitched the child. Alarmed at the dangers threatening Lygia, Acte and Ursus planned Lygia's escape.

That night the servants of Vinicius came and led Lygia away from the palace. Meanwhile Vinicius waited at his house, where a great feast was to take place in honor of his success in securing Lygia. Lygia, however, never arrived, for on the way to his house a group of Christians had suddenly attacked the servants of Vinicius and rescued their fellow Christian. Her rescuers took Lygia outside the city walls to live in a Christian colony.

Vinicius was furious. Petronius sent some of his own men to watch the gates of the city. Day after day Vinicius grew more and more upset. Finally, Chilo, a Greek who passed as a philosopher, offered for a sufficient reward to find Lygia. By pretending to be a convert, he learned where the Christians secretly met. He and Vinicius, together with a giant named Croton, went there and then followed Lygia to the house where she was staying. When they attempted to seize her, Ursus killed Croton. Vinicius was injured in the scuffle. For a few days he stayed with the Christians, who took care of him. Lygia nursed him until she became aware of her love for the pagan patrician. Afterward, rather than succumb to temptation, she left him to the attentions of others.

Vinicius had heard the Christians speaking at their meeting. While recuperating, he was amazed at their goodness, at their forgiveness, at their whole religious philosophy. He heard their leader, Peter, talk of Christ and of Christ's miracles, and his mind became filled with odd and disturbing thoughts. He realized that he must either hate the God who kept Lygia from him, or love him. Strangely enough, Vinicius became convinced that he no longer had the desire to take Lygia by force. He maintained his contacts with the Christians. At last, after he had accepted their faith, Lygia agreed to marry him.

In the meantime Nero had gone to Antium. There the noble Tigellinus planted in his mind the idea that he should burn Rome in order to write and sing a poem about the tremendous catastrophe. Accordingly, Nero set fire to Rome, and almost all the city was destroyed. Vinicius rushed from Antium to save Lygia. Luckily, she had left the city before the fire gained headway. The populace was angry and violent about the fire. Rebellion was in the air. The empress and the Jews at court persuaded Nero to blame the Christians for the fire. Chilo, who had been befriended by the Christians and whose abominable crimes had been wiped away by Christian forgiveness, turned traitor. He gave the emperor all the information he had about the Christians and led the guards to the hiding places of the sect. Cruel persecutions began.

Petronius tried desperately to stop Nero and save Vinicius. Failing in his attempt, he knew that his own days were numbered. The Christians were crammed first into prisons and then brought into the arena for the entertainment of the populace. Virgins were raped by the gladiators and then fed to starving lions. Christians were crucified and burned alive. After Lygia had been seized and imprisoned, Vinicius failed in an attempt to rescue her.

Her turn at last came to be led into the arena to amuse the brutal populace. She was stripped, and tied to the back of a raging bull. When the bull was sent running into the arena, Ursus rushed forward and locked his strong arms around the animal. To the astonishment of all, the bull yielded and died. Then the people demanded that Lygia and Ursus be set free, and the emperor had to obey the public clamor. Petronius advised Vinicius that they should all leave the city, for Nero had ways of removing people who had offended him.

The persecutions continued, and the spectacles in the arena grew more and more ghastly. At last the people sickened of the bestial tortures. One of the dying Christians looked straight at Nero and accused him of all of his infamous crimes. While Glaucus, a martyr, was being burned alive, he looked at Chilo, the Greek who had betrayed them. Glaucus, who had been left for dead by Chilo, forgave the Greek who had caused the Christian's wife and children to be sold into slavery. Moved by the dying man's mercy, Chilo cried out in a loud voice that the Christians were innocent of the burning of Rome and that the guilty man was Nero. Despairing of his own fate, Chilo was on the point of complete collapse, but Paul of Tarsus took him aside and assured him that Christ was merciful to even the worst of sinners. Then he baptized the Greek. When Chilo went back home, he was seized by the emperor's guards and led away to his death in the arena.

Vinicius and Lygia escaped to Sicily. When Petronius heard that the emperor had ordered his own death, he invited some of the patricians to his house at Cumae, where he had gone with Nero and the court. There at a great feast he read an attack against Nero and astounded everyone by his foolhardiness. Then he and Eunice, a slave who loved him, stretched out their arms to a physician. While the party continued and the astonished guests looked on, Petronius and Eunice bled to death in each other's arms.

Nero returned to Rome. His subjects hated him more than ever. A rebellion broke out at last, and he was informed that his death had been decreed. He fled. With some of his slaves around him, he attempted to plunge a knife into his throat, but he was too timid to complete the deed. As some soldiers approached to arrest him, a slave thrust the fatal knife into his emperor's throat.

Critical Evaluation:

Since it has become commonplace in the twentieth century to assume that serious fiction cannot appeal to a wide readership, the enduring popularity of a novel with the general public can obscure its literary merits. Such has been the case with *Quo Vadis*, a work acclaimed by an early reviewer as "one of the great books of our day," subsequently translated into dozens of languages, and still in print more than a century after its initial publication. The deft handling of the central characters and the focus on external action, coupled with the author's championing of traditional Christian values, has been both a strength and a liability.

While some have seen Sienkiewicz as a kind of prophet revealing in his novel a way out of the moral morass that characterizes the modern era, others have dismissed *Quo Vadis* as propaganda that does little more than pander to popular sentiment by offering simplistic solutions to complex moral and social dilemmas.

To appreciate the literary merits of the novel, it may be helpful to understand the source of the novelist's inspiration for the work. During the nineteenth century, there emerged among the populace throughout Europe and America an interest in the civilizations of Greece and Rome, and writers found in the annals of classical societies fertile material for a number of popular works. Readers throughout the western hemisphere were treated to historical tales such as Edward Bulwer-Lytton's *The Last Days of Pompeii* (1834), John Henry Newman's *Callista* (1856), and Nicholas Wiseman's *Fabiola* (1854) in England (translated into Polish and widely read in Sienkiewicz's native land), and a number of Polish novels such as Józef Ignancy Kraszewski's many historical works. Sienkiewicz found a parallel between the moral chaos of his time and the history of Rome. The success of novels set in classical Rome convinced Sienkiewicz that the time was right for employing the history of Rome as a means of making a commentary on his own age and on timeless issues about human values.

Like all serious historical novelists, Sienkiewicz chooses his materials carefully so that the period he depicts is one in which a momentous historical crisis is imminent. The Rome of Nero is particularly decadent, and the growing popularity of Christianity as an antidote to the excesses of paganism is a matter of record. The novelist is careful to provide accurate historical details in his work, displaying his wide reading in the literature by classical figures and about life in ancient Rome. Like all good historical novelists, however, he is interested primarily in character and action rather than in setting. *Quo Vadis* is no mere period piece, but rather is intended to demonstrate the conflict of values represented by the two great ideologies which dominated the western world in the early centuries after the birth of Christ: Christianity and Paganism as represented by the worship of the Romans, whose rule extended over much of what is now Europe and the Middle East.

Sienkiewicz reveals the conflict between these two opposing worldviews through a number of his central characters, both fictional and historical. The love story of Vinicius and Lygia provides the novelist an opportunity to dramatize the transforming power of Christianity, as readers see Vinicius move from lust for the attractive servant to a mature acceptance not only of his beloved but of her faith as well. The conflict of values is presented to readers most fully through the story of Petronius. This noble pagan is disgusted with the excesses he sees at Nero's court, and he is ready to see changes take place in Roman society. Nevertheless, he is not willing to give up easily what he finds good in his heritage. Possessing the Stoic virtues that characterize the best of the Romans, he never fully accepts the message of Christ; even at the end of the novel he retains enough of his pagan beliefs to commit suicide as a final gesture of defiance toward the emperor he has come to despise.

Petronius' story reveals that, far from being a simple propagandist for Christianity, Sienkiewicz remains faithful enough to the character he has created to allow him to die in a manner befitting a noble Roman. He is far more than that, however, as numerous critics have observed. The protagonist has been described as the embodiment of nineteenth century values. This should not be surprising, since the aim of the novel is to point out the universality of Petronius' struggle against the forces of savagery, political despotism, and moral degeneracy. Like the distinguished gentlemen of Western Europe, he values moderation and personal dignity over political preferment. Additionally, Sienkiewicz complements his portrait of Petronius with depictions of several other admirable Romans, balancing the sadism of Nero and the excesses of those close to the emperor with scenes of men and women who lead dignified lives even though they have not yet been touched by Christianity. Sienkiewicz's message seems to be that the potential exists for people of good will in any age to withstand the evils of even the most corrupt society and maintain personal dignity, although often at great cost. Written at a time of great political chaos in his own country, and on the eve of a century when political and moral upheavals would become commonplace, *Quo Vadis* retains its didactic value for individuals looking for guidance in times of crisis.

"Critical Evaluation" by Laurence W. Mazzeno

Bibliography:
Giergielewicz, Mieczyslaw. *Henryk Sienkiewicz*. New York: Twayne, 1968. General survey of Sienkiewicz's achievements. A chapter on *Quo Vadis* discusses the novelist's adaptation of classical sources, his development of the idea of the fated dominance of Christianity, and his handling of plot and structure.
Kridl, Manfred. *A Survey of Polish Literature and Culture*. Translated by Olga Sherer-Virski. New York: Columbia University Press, 1956. Discusses the novelist's techniques, which he repeats in many of his works, including *Quo Vadis*. Describes Sienkiewicz's use of history in this novel of ancient Rome.
Krżyanowski, Julian. *A History of Polish Literature*. Translated by Doris Ronowicz. Warsaw: PWN-Polish Scientific Publishers, 1978. Stresses the importance Sienkiewicz places on the accuracy of historical detail in his novels. Notes how he uses this approach successfully in *Quo Vadis*.
Lednicki, Waclaw. *Henryk Sienkiewicz: A Retrospective Synthesis*. The Hague: Mouton, 1960. Assessment of the novelist's career; gives readers a sense of the relative value of *Quo Vadis* to other works by the writer.
Miłosz, Czesław. *The History of Polish Literature*. New York: Macmillan, 1969. Comments on the uneven quality of Sienkiewicz's fiction. Believes the novelist presents a simplistic portrait of the classical period in *Quo Vadis*.

RABBIT ANGSTROM NOVELS

Type of work: Novels
Author: John Updike (1932-   )
Type of plot: Domestic realism
Time of plot: 1950's-1980's
Locale: Mt. Judge and Brewer, Pennsylvania, and Florida
First published: Rabbit, Run, 1960; *Rabbit Redux,* 1971; *Rabbit Is Rich,* 1981; *Rabbit at Rest,* 1990

Principal characters:

HARRY "RABBIT" ANGSTROM, the main character, a former high-school basketball player
JANICE SPRINGER ANGSTROM, his wife, whose family owned a car dealership
NELSON ANGSTROM, son of Rabbit and Janice
REBECCA ANGSTROM, daughter of Rabbit and Janice, drowned in infancy
PRU ANGSTROM, Nelson's wife
CHARLIE STAVROS, a salesman for Springer Motors, Janice's lover
RUTH LEONARD, a prostitute, Harry's mistress
SKEETER, a black militant
JILL PENDLETON, a runaway flower child who was killed in a fire

The Story:

Rabbit, Run. Harry Angstrom, nicknamed "Rabbit," was a high-school basketball star in Brewer, Pennsylvania. Rabbit did not go to college. Following a stint in the army, he married Janice Springer, who was pregnant with his child. One day, Rabbit stopped on his way home from work to play basketball with a group of young boys, remembering his days as a basketball star. After the excitement of the game, he returned to the reality of his dirty, cluttered apartment and a wife who had been drinking too much. On a sudden impulse, Rabbit, feeling trapped by family responsibilities, got in his car and headed south in an attempt to flee from the pressures that crowded his life. He got as far as West Virginia and then turned back to Brewer. Still unwilling to return to his family, he sought out his old coach, Marty Tothero, and through Tothero met Ruth Leonard, a prostitute. Rabbit left his wife, who was pregnant with their second child, to move in with Ruth.

After Janice had the baby, Rebecca, Rabbit returned home, and they tried to resume their life together. During a quarrel, Rabbit walked out on Janice and went to Ruth's apartment. Janice got drunk and while she was bathing Rebecca, she accidentally let the baby drown. At the graveside, Rabbit shocked everyone by blaming Janice for the baby's death, saying, "You all keep acting as if I did it. I wasn't anywhere near. She's the one." After the funeral, he went to Ruth's apartment and discovered that she was pregnant with his child. Again Rabbit ran.

Rabbit Redux. Rabbit, now thirty-six years of age, was no longer trying to run away from his problems. He worked hard as a linotypist in a local print shop, a job that tied him to events that took place in the summer of 1969: the Apollo moon shot, the race riots in York and Reading, and Ted Kennedy's problems following the Chappaquiddick drowning of Mary Jo Kopechne. Janice was working in her father's Toyota agency and having an affair with Charlie Stavros, one of the salesmen. Rabbit was laid off, and Janice moved in with Charlie. She left Rabbit to take care of Nelson.

Rabbit met Jill, a rich, eighteen-year-old flower child who was running away from her family. She moved in with Rabbit, later bringing in Skeeter, a black Vietnam veteran who had jumped bail on a drug-dealing charge. Skeeter tried to educate Rabbit on black history and radical politics as they smoked marijuana and argued about the morality of the Vietnam War. A fire destroyed the house and, in spite of Nelson's heroic attempt to save her, Jill died in the fire. Janice left Charlie, and she and Rabbit reconciled.

Rabbit Is Rich. Rabbit, at forty-six years of age, was moderately wealthy, running the Springer family's Toyota dealership. He and Janice had moved into a new home and joined the country club. Golf replaced basketball, and Rabbit gained weight. When Rabbit and Janice engaged in wife-swapping on a vacation in the Caribbean, Rabbit was disappointed that he did not win Cindy, the woman who most attracted him. In the exchange, he drew Thelma, the wife of Ronnie Harrison, an old teammate of Rabbit's. Rabbit continued the affair with Thelma when they all returned to Brewer.

Rabbit took a personal interest in the news, viewing oil prices and the decline of the dollar as they affected his Toyota business. An avid reader of *Consumer Reports*, Rabbit seemed obsessed with financial news and investment advice. He invested in gold Krugerrands and spread them over Janice's body, reveling in the sight and feel of the gold coins. Material wealth was at the center of Rabbit's life.

Although he was comfortable with his own lifestyle, Rabbit was disappointed in his son. Uncoordinated and lacking in athletic talent, Nelson possessed none of his father's grace. He was irresponsible, wrecking his father's car and failing to graduate from Kent State. Nelson returned to Brewer with Pru, his pregnant girlfriend, and the two were married. With the birth of Judy, Rabbit became a grandfather and reaffirmed his belief in life.

Rabbit at Rest. Rabbit focused on his heart trouble, Nelson's drug addiction, and Janice's new career. While Nelson, Pru, and their children, Judy and Roy, were visiting Rabbit and Janice in their Florida condo, Rabbit and Judy went sailing. When their sailboat capsized, Rabbit struggled to get Judy safely to shore. In contrast to the tragedy of the drowning death of his daughter, Rabbit was able to save the child. The physical effort, however, put added stress on Rabbit's heart. Rabbit and Janice returned to Brewer, where Rabbit underwent angioplasty. Janice enrolled in a real estate course, determined to have a career as a realtor. Nelson brought the family to the brink of financial disaster by stealing from the business to support his drug habit.

In Nelson's absence, Rabbit and Pru had a sexual encounter. When Nelson returned from the drug rehabilitation program, Pru confessed the transgression. Rather than face Janice and Nelson, Rabbit again took flight, this time to the condo in Florida, where Janice stubbornly refused to join him. In an attempt to live in a more healthy way, Rabbit began walking. On one of his trips, he joined a group of young black men in a game of basketball. Exhilarated by the challenge, he returned to the neighborhood and played a game of one-on-one with a young man. During the game, Rabbit dropped to the ground with a massive heart attack. Janice and Nelson rushed to the hospital in Florida, where Janice learned that Rabbit had no chance to live. Rabbit's last words were spoken to Nelson: He told him that dying was not so bad.

Critical Evaluation:

A major contemporary American author, John Updike was awarded the Pulitzer Prize, the National Book Critics Circle Award, and the American Book Award for *Rabbit Is Rich*. Updike was graduated from Harvard in 1954 and worked on the staff of *The New Yorker*. He published poems, short stories, essays, and book reviews, in addition to several novels. The domestic life of the American middle class provides the major subject for those novels, as his characters struggle to find meaning and a sense of values in a changing world. *Rabbit, Run*, his second novel, begins the series of four novels that traces the life of Harry Angstrom, the former basketball star who searches for meaning beyond the confines of an unhappy marriage and the ordinary struggles of daily life. Each of the novels chronicles the history and culture of the decade before it was published, as it shows Rabbit's journey through middle age, prosperity, retirement, and death.

The image of the basketball court provides the frame for the series. In the first novel, the neighborhood basketball game reminds Rabbit of how much he misses the excitement of his high-school years. This longing for something more in his life drives him to flee from his responsibilities. A similar game on a basketball court in Florida is the scene of the massive heart attack that leads to Rabbit's death.

The rabbit image is central to the novel. On the first page, Updike describes Harry's rabbitlike appearance with his broad white face, pale blue eyes, and "nervous flutter under his brief nose." Nervous blinks and quick movements on the basketball court add to the image of a rabbit. His desire to flee in the midst of trouble resembles a rabbit's instinct to run and hide. The first novel ends with more rabbit imagery as "he feels the wind on his ears" and with "a kind of sweet panic growing lighter and quicker and quieter, he runs." On his last trip in *Rabbit at Rest*, Rabbit, again running away from conflict, refers to the inside of his car as a cave.

Updike employs a number of devices to show the history of each decade and its effect on the main character. Rabbit's job as a typesetter for the Brewer newspaper links him to news events and provides him with an opportunity to comment on the events of the time. His arguments with Skeeter focus on the Vietnam War and race relations. In *Rabbit at Rest*, Rabbit, retired and lacking a purpose, spends hours watching television news and reading the newspaper, keeping up with current events. On his final trip from Brewer to Florida, Rabbit tours his old neighborhood, remembering stages of his life. On the road, as Rabbit listens to a golden oldies station on the radio, song lyrics remind him of the women and events in his life. News reports periodically interrupt the music, bringing news of Jim and Tammy Bakker, a bombing in Colombia, and the score of a Miami Dolphins-Philadelphia Eagles game.

The song lyrics show how Rabbit was seduced by the American dream. As Tony Bennett croons "Be My Love," Gogi Grant sings "The Wayward Wind," or Nat "King" Cole sings "Ramblin' Rose," Rabbit concentrates on the lyrics. He never liked Frank Sinatra's "foghorn" voice, preferring Elvis singing "Love Me Tender," or Ray Charles "dreaming of yesterdays." As Johnny Ray cries, "If your sweetheart sends a letter of good-bye," Rabbit remembers the "Dear John" letter that his first love, Mary Ann, sent him when he was in the army. Rabbit is the American dreamer, believing in the lyrics of the songs, always longing for something more. At the end of his life, Rabbit feels betrayed by the promise of the music that led him "down the garden path," a path that ends in disillusionment. Rabbit searches for meaning in his life until the end, and when death finally comes, he accepts it with grace.

Judith Barton Williamson

Bibliography:
Detweiler, Robert. *John Updike*. Boston: Twayne, 1984. Asserts the central theme of *Rabbit, Run* is an ironic search for the nonexistent Grail, and classifies *Rabbit Redux* as a quest novel. Calls *Rabbit Is Rich* a novel of lost opportunities and second chances, of ghosts and new life.

Doner, Dean. "Rabbit Angstrom's Unseen World." In *John Updike: A Collection of Critical Essays*, edited by David Thorburn and Howard Eiland. Englewood Cliffs, N.J.: Prentice-Hall, 1979. Compares *Rabbit, Run* to Updike's short story, "Ace in the Hole" (1959), whose protagonist was also a former high-school basketball star. Focuses on Rabbit's religious nature, observing that of all the people gathered at the baby's graveside, Rabbit is the only one who believes in God.

Greiner, Donald J. *John Updike's Novels*. Athens: Ohio University Press, 1984. Points out that Updike used three Rabbit novels to record the tone of a decade: religious speculation in *Rabbit, Run*, political concerns in *Rabbit Redux*, and economic practicalities in *Rabbit Is Rich*.

Newman, Judie. *John Updike*. New York: St. Martin's Press, 1988. One chapter, "The World of Work," deals with the major themes of the first three novels: work, technology, and sex.

Uphaus, Suzanne Henning. *John Updike*. New York: Frederick Ungar, 1980. Discusses the religious images Updike used in *Rabbit, Run* to show the contradictions of Rabbit's character and the confusion and uncertainty of contemporary society. Argues that although the characters are portrayed realistically and convincingly, the historical emphasis of *Rabbit Redux* causes them to become agents of history.

RABBIT BOSS

Type of work: Novel
Author: Thomas Sanchez (1944-   )
Type of plot: Historical realism
Time of plot: 1846-1950's
Locale: Nevada and California
First published: 1973

> Principal characters:
> RABBIT BOSS, chief of the Washo
> GAYABUC, his son, later Rabbit Boss
> PAINTED STICK, Gayabuc's wife
> CAPTAIN REX, their son, latter Rabbit Boss
> AYAS, Captain Rex's son, later Rabbit Boss
> JOE BIRDSONG, the last Rabbit Boss

The Story:

In 1846, Gayabuc, the son of the powerful Rabbit Chief or Rabbit Boss of the Washo Indians, set out on a hunting expedition in the midst of winter to obtain meat for his first-born son's birth celebration. He encountered the Donner party, a group of whites who were forced by starvation into cannibalism. Gayabuc returned to his family empty-handed and warned them about the white people who eat themselves. Gayabuc's father refused to believe Gayabuc's account and asserted that Gayabuc dreamed it. Painted Stick, Gayabuc's wife, believed that he came back without meat because he was forced to hunt in winter when game was scarce. Their son was born in winter because their first sexual union had occurred in spring, just before Painted Stick's first menstruation. Gayabuc and Painted Stick violated Washo tradition by engaging in sexual relations before Painted Stick underwent the puberty ritual of the Dance of the Woman. The repercussions of their transgression culminated in Gayabuc's unlucky encounter at Donner Lake.

The cannibalism of the whites at Donner Lake continued to influence Gayabuc during the ensuing spring. Spring was the time that the Washos hunted the rabbits that provided their food and clothing. Gayabuc's father, the Rabbit Chief, was the leader of the hunt. Gayabuc believed that investigating the white invasion should take precedence over engaging in the hunt, but his father strongly disagreed. The men of the tribe voted and sided with Gayabuc. The women and children conducted the hunt while the men explored the deserted white encampment. There they found animal traps that they had never seen before. One of them contained a rabbit that was mangled by the trap, foreshadowing the eventual oppression of the Washos by the whites.

Gayabuc succeeded his father as Rabbit Chief. Gayabuc realized that his shamanic role as chief hunter was vital to the survival of his people and to their way of life. During the spring hunt, Gayabuc dreamed about the location of the prey. He realized that in his role as Rabbit Chief, his spiritual and moral power was essential to the preservation of the tribe. Gayabuc noted, "All this I have dreamed. If I were dead, all this would not have been dreamed. . . . If I were dead, there would be no other to tell you this."

The disrupting influence of the whites became evident in the life of Captain Rex, the son of Gayabuc and Painted Stick. Captain Rex followed the old ways at first and inherited the position of Rabbit Chief. As the railroad encroached on Washo land, however, the quality of life declined for the Washo. There were few rabbits to hunt, and the office of Rabbit Chief became obsolete. Captain Rex learned English from a white woman. As a result of his being bilingual, the white railroad workers employed him as a translator. Although the whites depended upon his bilingual capability, the Washo people mistrusted him. As a result of his cultural confusion, he became a drunkard, a petty thief, and a gambler.

Captain Rex's penchant for drink and gambling led to a confrontation with the whites. Accused of stealing whiskey and horses, Captain Rex found himself facing a lynch mob. John C. Luther, the Bummer, saved Rex from the mob because he falsely believed that Rex knew where to mine for gold. Luther organized an expedition to search for the gold, with Captain Rex serving as a guide. Molly Moose, Luther's Washo mistress, accompanied them. When the group camped, the men entertained themselves by raping Molly. They tied Rex to a tree to keep him from interfering. Most of the men eventually left the camp to find the gold. The men realized that Rex had given them misinformation, and they returned to camp seeking vengeance. Molly cut Rex's bonds, rescued him, and they fled. Molly became Captain Rex's wife and bore him Ayas. In old age, Captain Rex, along with many of his tribe, contracted tuberculosis. He died when the whites burned the Indian encampment to rid the area of the disease.

Ayas was raised by his grandmother, Painted Stick, for the first six years of his life. When she died, he was taken in by the Dora family, who employed him as a farm worker. When they no longer needed him, they gave him to Abe Fixa, an elderly, blind dairyman. He became the boy's surrogate father and named him Bob. After Abe's death, Bob was placed in a government school for Indian children. There an elderly Washo revealed to him his true name and heritage. Bob was subsequently kidnapped by a remnant of his tribe and taken to live with them in the mountains. He lived a traditional Washo life, but eventually left the camp because all the people were either dead or dying.

Bob traveled east and worked in the stockyards of Omaha, Nebraska. There he experienced the beginnings of a conversion to Christianity. He subsequently escaped the stockyards and joined two men on the road selling homemade whiskey. He became a medicine show pitchman, selling the concoction to various Indian tribes. Bob made his way back to California and was employed on the Dixel ranch as a ranchhand and Rabbit Boss. By the 1920's, the Rabbit Boss was regarded more as an exterminator than a powerful shaman.

During his tenure at the Dixel ranch, Bob was converted to Christianity. His fervor led to his being known as Hallelujah Bob. He preached the gospel to the Washo, although later in his life he followed the Ghost Dance religion. The Washo believed that it was not good for a man to live alone, and Medicine Maggie volunteered to live in his house. She became the mother of Sarah Dick and Joe Birdsong.

Joe Birdsong was the last of the Rabbit Bosses. Although Dixel viewed the job of Rabbit Boss in a pragmatic way, Joe still held a reverence for the tradition underlying what had once been an exalted office. Joe also felt a deep attachment to the land that he inherited from his father. White developers tried to force him to sell, and he refused. To get him to turn the property over to them, the developers told Joe that his title to the property was not binding because his father had not been a citizen when he gave the land to Joe. Dixel informed Joe that he would no longer need a Rabbit Boss to conduct the spring extermination, because he had bought a machine to kill the rabbits. In defiance of Dixel, Joe and Sarah Dick conducted the hunt. When Joe returned to his cabin after the hunt, Dixel's wife was there to warn him that her husband had been murdered and that the sheriff believed that Joe committed the crime. Joe escaped into the mountains and lived off the land for almost a year. During that time, he was accidentally shot in the leg by a group of deer hunters. The leg became infected, and the infection gradually spread throughout his body. During the spring thaw, he reached the shores of Donner Lake and died from starvation and infection.

Critical Evaluation:

Rabbit Boss is Thomas Sanchez's first novel. Although Sanchez is not an American Indian, he was greatly influenced by his contact with American Indians when he attended a boys' boarding school for disadvantaged children. Sanchez chose to write about the Washo because he wished to demonstrate the cultural arrogance of the European Americans and the effect that their attitude of superiority had on Native American society.

The theme of cultural dichotomy is reinforced by characterization and language. For example, Gayabuc and Painted Stick are portrayed as Adam- and Eve-like figures. They had premarital intercourse, so they believe they have sinned against the ways of their people. Gayabuc's first encounter with the whites is somehow linked to this initial transgression, bringing further bad luck to the tribe. Their ensuing contact with the whites causes their expulsion from their land, which, in turn, adversely affects their traditions and ceremonies. Captain Rex is probably the most tragic figure in the novel. He is caught between two cultures and is an outcast in both. At one point in the story, his clothing signifies his position. He appears wearing a pair of pants given to him by the white woman who taught him English, with a tattered rabbit blanket around his shoulders. The pants represent the "civilizing" influence of white culture; the worn blanket signifies the fading dignity and power of the Rabbit Chief.

Language is especially important in understanding the interrelations between whites and Indians and their cultural differences. The oral tradition in American Indian society is central in maintaining their cultural existence and identity. The importance of the oral tradition is underscored when Proud Dog first reveals to Bob his Indian identity. After Proud Dog dies, Bob and the children share stories from their different tribes. It is a way of affirming their identity as Indians and regaining a sense of pride that the whites had stripped from them.

Although language is a way for the Indians to affirm their cultural identity among themselves, it is also a means to differentiate themselves from the whites. After Gayabuc first witnesses the cannibalism of the Donner party, his father asks him what he saw and he answers, "Them." The Indians continually refer to the whites in the terms of "they," "their," and "them." The whites are the "other." They "eat of themselves," which is repulsive to the Washo and certainly uncivilized. The European Americans are referred to as White Ghosts or "the white burden." This latter phrase is also used to describe the snow of winter, which links the harshness of the season to the oppressiveness of the white society.

The portrayal of whites as cannibals in the first scene of the novel recurs throughout the book. To the Washo, cannibalism is abhorrent, because to eat a member of one's own species or one's totemic animal means a loss of power or "musege." The cannibalism of the Donner party foreshadows the environmental and social cannibalism that the whites perpetrate on the land and on the Washo. From a Washo point of view, it is ironic that even though the white people destroy the land and mistreat the Washo, their power only continues to grow as the Washo are reduced to a remnant of what they once were.

Pegge Bochynski

Bibliography:
Bonetti, Kay. "An Interview with Thomas Sanchez." *The Missouri Review* 14, no. 2 (1991):

77-95. An informative interview with Sanchez, in which he discusses the biographical and historical background that informs the plot of the novel, particularly the influence of his family, his education, and the Vietnam War.

Gueder, P. A. "Language and Ethnic Interaction in *Rabbit Boss*: A Novel by Thomas Sanchez." In *Language and Ethnic Relations*, edited by Howard Giles and Bernard Saint-Jacques. Elmsford, N.Y.: Pergamon Press, 1979. Methodic discussion of the way language is used in the novel to reveal the disturbing interethnic relationship between the Washo and the whites.

Marovitz, Sanford E. "The Entropic World of the Washo: Fatality and Self-Deception in *Rabbit Boss*." *Western American Literature* 19 (November, 1984): 219-230. Detailed analysis of the structure, themes, and characters, focusing on the desire of the Washo to integrate their way of life into the dominant culture and how that desire precipitates their decline.

Sanchez, Thomas. "The Visionary Imagination." *Melus* 3, no. 2 (1976): 2-5. Sanchez reveals his reasons for writing the novel, the influence of American Indian thought on the structure of the novel, character motivation, and the contemporaneous political events that influenced the plot.

THE RAINBOW

Type of work: Novel
Author: D. H. Lawrence (1885-1930)
Type of plot: Psychological realism
Time of plot: Nineteenth and early twentieth centuries
Locale: England
First published: 1915

> *Principal characters:*
> TOM BRANGWEN, a farmer
> LYDIA LENSKY, his wife
> ANNA LENSKY, Lydia's child by her first husband
> WILL BRANGWEN, Anna's husband
> URSULA BRANGWEN, Anna and Will's daughter
> ANTON SKREBENSKY, Ursula's lover

The Story:

Tom Brangwen was descended from a long line of small landholders who had owned Marsh Farm in Nottinghamshire for many generations. Tom was a man of the soil, and he lived alone on his farm with only an old woman for his company and housekeeper. Then a Polish widow, Lydia Lensky, became the housekeeper of the vicar of the local church. She brought her small daughter, Anna, with her. One evening a few months later, Tom Brangwen found the courage to present the widow with a bouquet of daffodils in the vicar's kitchen and to ask her to be his wife.

Judged by the standards of the world, their marriage was a satisfactory one. They had two sons, and Tom was kind to his stepdaughter. Knowing his stepdaughter, however, was easier for him than knowing Lydia. The fact that they were of different nationalities, cultures, and even languages kept them from ever becoming intellectually intimate with each other. There were times when one or both felt that their marriage was not what it should be and that they were not fulfilling the obligations imposed upon them by their mating. On one occasion, Lydia even suggested to her husband that he needed another woman.

Little Anna was a haughty young girl who spent many hours imagining herself a great lady or even a queen. In her eighteenth year, a nephew of Tom Brangwen came to work in the lace factory in the nearby village of Ilkeston. He was only twenty years old, and the Brangwens at Marsh Farm looked after him and made him welcome in their home.

Anna Lensky and young Will Brangwen fell in love, with a naïve, touching affection for each other. When they soon announced to Tom and Lydia that they wished to be married, Tom leased a home for them in the village and gave them a present of twenty-five hundred pounds so they would not want because of Will's small salary.

The wedding was celebrated with rural pomp and hilarity. After the ceremony, the newly married couple spent two weeks alone in their cottage, ignoring the world and existing only for themselves. Anna was the first to come back to the world of reality. Her decision to give a tea party both bewildered and angered her husband, who had not yet realized that they could not continue to live only for and by themselves. It took him almost a lifetime to come to that realization.

Shortly after the marriage, Anna became pregnant, and the arrival of the child brought to Will the added shock that his wife was more a mother than she was a married lover. Each year, a new baby came between Will and Anna. The oldest was Ursula, who remained her father's favorite. The love that Will wished to give his wife was given to Ursula, for Anna refused to have anything to do with him when she was expecting another child, and she was not happy unless she was pregnant.

In the second year of his marriage, Will Brangwen tried to rebel. He met a young woman at the theater and afterward took her out for supper and a walk. After that incident, the intimate life of Will and Anna gained in passion, enough to carry Will through the daytime when he was not needed in the house until the night when he could rule his wife. Gradually, he became free in his own mind from Anna's domination.

Since Ursula was her father's favorite child, she was sent to high school, a rare privilege for a girl of her circumstances in the last decade of the nineteenth century. She drank up knowledge in her study of Latin, French, and algebra. Before she had finished, however, her interest in her studies was divided by her interest in a young man, the son of a Polish friend of her grandmother. Young, blond Anton Skrebensky, a lieutenant in the British Army, was introduced in the Brangwen home, and during a month's leave, he fell in love with Ursula, who was already in love with him. On his next leave, however, he became afraid of her because her love was too possessive.

After finishing high school, Ursula took an examination to enter the university. Even though she passed the examination, she decided to teach school for a time, for she wanted to accumulate money to carry her through her education without being a burden to her parents. Anna and Will were furious when she broached the subject of leaving home. They compromised with her, however, by securing for her a position in a school in Ilkeston. Ursula spent two friendless, ill-paid, and thankless years teaching at the village elementary school. At the end of that time, she was more than ready to continue her education. She decided to become a botanist, for in botany she felt she was doing and learning for herself things that had an absolute truth.

One day, after the end of the Boer War, Ursula received a letter from Anton Skrebensky, who wrote that he wished to see her again while he was in England on leave. Within a week, he arrived in Nottingham to visit her at school. Their love for each other was rekindled with greater intensity than they had known six years earlier. During the Easter holidays, they went away for a weekend at a hotel, where they passed as husband and wife. They went to the Continent as soon as Ursula had finished classes for the summer. Skrebensky increasingly pressed for marriage, wanting Ursula to leave England with him when he returned to service in India, but she wanted to return to college to take her degree.

Ursula so neglected her studies during this time that she failed the final examinations for her degree. She studied all summer before taking them again, but failed again. Skrebensky thereupon urged her to marry him immediately. In India, he insisted, her degree would mean nothing anyway. One evening, at a house party, they realized that there was something wrong in their mating and that they could not agree enough to make a successful marriage. They left the party separately. A few weeks later, Skrebensky left for India as the husband of his regimental commander's daughter.

After he had gone, Ursula learned that she was pregnant. Not knowing that he was already married, she wrote to Skrebensky and promised to be a good wife if he still wished to marry her. Before his answer came from India, Ursula contracted pneumonia and lost the child. One day, as she was convalescing, she observed a rainbow in the sky. She hoped that it was the promise of better times to come.

Critical Evaluation:

Even while composing *The Rainbow*, D. H. Lawrence realized that neither the critics nor the general readers would accept his novel. He wrote to Amy Lowell about the critical reception of a book of his short stories, telling her, "The critics really hate me. So they ought." It is a curious remark from any writer, but especially from one who was so intent on working a moral change in his readers. Lawrence knew, however, not only that his was fiction "shocking" in its treatment of sexuality, particularly that of women—and it was to become more shocking yet—but that he also created character and experience that challenged the way the critics viewed the world. In his fiction, and this became fully apparent in *The Rainbow*, he dramatized experience as dynamic, shifting, and elusive. For him, the world was neither stable, nor certain, nor finally rationally explicable; his vision undercut all the preconceptions of the Edwardian critics. Their "hatred" of Lawrence's fiction was actually self-defense. When *The Rainbow* appeared during the first years of World War I, it seemed to validate Lawrence's argument against those who saw civilization as stable, knowable, and controllable.

One central question preoccupies Lawrence in *The Rainbow*: Is the self capable of expansion, of becoming an entity, of achieving freedom, especially in an age where the traditional supports of community, family, and religion have been weakened or eliminated? In Will and Anna Brangwen's generation, the first to enter the industrial world, the self does survive, though only minimally. If, unlike Tom and Lydia Brangwen, Will and Anna fail to create the "Rainbow," an image of the fully realized self in passionate community, and if their love degenerates to lust, they at least endure. True freedom, however, is denied them.

For Ursula, their daughter and the novel's heroine, the question of freedom hardly pertains, at least at the beginning. It is simply a matter of her survival. Her vision of the "Rainbow" at the end must be taken as a promise of freedom—and for many readers an unconvincing one—rather than as fulfillment. Nevertheless, it is a perception she earns by surviving both the inner and the outer terrors of her world.

The Rainbow is primarily a psychological novel, in which Lawrence is primarily concerned with states of feeling and being that exist below the level of history. Nevertheless, the social and political backgrounds are of utmost importance; indeed they are of central significance to an understanding of the question of self-realization. For if Lawrence explores the dialectic of the psyche, he does so in an understanding of the determining impact that history has on that psychological drama.

A novel of three generations, *The Rainbow*'s time span runs from 1840 to 1905. In the background, yet ever-present, are the major cultural changes of the age: the rapid expansion of industry; the diminution of arable land; the transformation of society from one based on the hamlet and town to a truly urban one; the breakdown of the nuclear family; and the spread of education. In short, Lawrence dramatizes the English revolution from a feudal to a democratic, capitalistic society. In the foreground of these radical changes are the relationships between Tom and Lydia, Will and Anna, and Ursula and Anton. As the novel moves in time from the middle of the nineteenth to the beginning of the twentieth century and in space from Ilkeston, Beldover, and Nottingham to London and Paris, what becomes increasingly apparent is that both relationships and the sanctity of the self are harder to sustain.

In the first generation, Tom Brangwen and Lydia are firmly rooted in the earth. After an early crisis, their marriage flowers into a relationship of deep and lasting love, under whose influence their daughter, Anna, also grows. Nevertheless, though their life moves according to the rhythms of nature, it is limited by its pure physicality; it is fated, moreover, to be overwhelmed by other rhythms, those created by the motion of the piston. In fact, Tom himself is drowned when a canal bursts and floods his farm. The symbolic significance of his death—the rural life killed off by the industrial—is emphasized by its appearance at the structural midpoint of the novel.

The second generation, Anna and Will, move from the farm at Ilkeston first to the town of Beldover and finally to a major industrial city, Nottingham. Their escape from the limiting existence on the farm to the greater individual liberty of the town, however, exacts a great cost: Their love and marriage, although bountiful, fail to fulfill them. Because of their insistence on the self, they cannot make the deep connection that Tom and Lydia achieved. They are sustained by the rich fecundity of their marriage but are left without unity.

It is left to Ursula to carry out the quest that her parents abandoned: that search for the completely free self in unity. The forces confronting her, however, are even greater than those her parents faced. Not only is the new society, characterized by the machine, hostile to the individual, but it has successfully destroyed the community. Cut off as she is from the life of feeling and freed from the restraints imposed by the older society, Ursula wanders through London and Paris preyed on by all, especially by Anton Skrebensky, who would swallow her if she allowed him. Nevertheless, she survives as an independent self, aided by the strength she has inherited. Yet Ursula has not discovered the necessary relationship to the whole spectrum of human life. That she can only imagine in her final vision of the "Rainbow." It was precisely her vision, which was also Lawrence's, of human beings fully free, connected, and equal that challenged so effectively the worldview of the Edwardians and led to their uneasiness. Lawrence showed his critics that there was no hope for society based on what they themselves were.

"Critical Evaluation" by David L. Kubal

Bibliography:
Bloom, Harold, ed. *D. H. Lawrence's "The Rainbow."* New York: Chelsea House, 1988. A collection of sophisticated critical essays, ranging from 1966 to 1984, covering Lawrence's Romanticism and the theological and psychological dimensions of *The Rainbow*. Also includes an introduction, chronology, bibliography, and index.
Clarke, Colin, comp. *D. H. Lawrence: "The Rainbow" and "Women in Love," a Casebook.* London: Macmillan, 1969. Extracts from a number of critical essays, among them those by Roger Sale, S. L. Goldberg, and Julia Moynahan. A short bibliography and index.
Kinkead-Weekes, Mark, ed. *Twentieth Century Interpretations of "The Rainbow": A Collection of Critical Essays.* Englewood Cliffs, N.J.: Prentice-Hall, 1971. A collection of essays in four parts, one of which is on the interpretation of the three generations. Essays by Marvin Mudrick, Keith Sagar, and Laurence Lerner, among others. The concluding essay by Kinkead-Weekes discusses the making of the novel. Includes a chronology.
Sagar, Keith. *D. H. Lawrence: Life into Art.* New York: Viking, 1985. Concentrates on the process of Lawrence's writing as a creative artist. In a chapter on *The Rainbow*, entitled "New Heavens and Earth," Sagar focuses on the novel's genesis, as well as its critical reception and banning. Index.
Smith, Frank Glover. *D. H. Lawrence: "The Rainbow."* London: Edward Arnold, 1971. A short introduction to *The Rainbow*.

RAINTREE COUNTY

Type of work: Novel
Author: Ross Lockridge, Jr. (1914-1948)
Type of plot: Historical realism
Time of plot: Late nineteenth century
Locale: Indiana, Tennessee, Georgia, Washington, D.C., and New York
First published: 1948

Principal characters:

> JOHN WICKLIFF SHAWNESSY, teacher, Civil War veteran, and longtime
> resident of Raintree County, Indiana
> NELL GAITHER, a woman with whom he is in love
> SUSANNA DRAKE, a visitor from the South who becomes John's first wife
> ESTHER ROOT, John's student and later his second wife
> GARWOOD B. JONES, John's boyhood friend and later a United States
> senator
> JERUSALEM WEBSTER STILES, John's teacher and later his friend
> FLASH PERKINS, fastest runner in Raintree County and later John's
> companion in the Civil War

The Story:

There was a big celebration in Raintree County, Indiana, on July 4, 1892. The birthday of the nation was noted with the usual parades and fireworks, and everyone was excited that Indiana Senator Garwood Jones was returning to his hometown to make a speech. Among those who greeted the senator was his old friend and rival, John Wickliff Shawnessy, who had once opposed Jones for political office and lost.

As Shawnessy experienced the events of the day, his mind wandered back to other times. Shawnessy had grown up in Raintree County, the son of T. D. Shawnessy, a physician and preacher, and Ellen Shawnessy, a wise and gentle woman. John's early life was haunted by the legend of the raintree, a magic tree with yellow flowers that was rumored to grow somewhere in the county. Most of the county was easy to travel over, so the most likely place for the fabulous raintree to be hidden was deep in a swamp at the end of a lake in the middle of the county. John vowed that he would find the raintree some day. He also had another dream of writing a great epic that would encapsulate and explain not only Raintree County but also the American republic.

John's adolescence was affected by three people. Jerusalem Webster Stiles, known as the Perfessor, established an academy that young Johnny Shawnessy attended, along with his friends Garwood Jones and Nell Gaither. The Perfessor was only a few years older than his students. He had a cynical, worldly-wise attitude that frequently put him in conflict with his fellow citizens and that occasioned a debate with the more optimistic Shawnessy that lasted a lifetime. Garwood was a smoother self-promoter than the Perfessor; he knew how to manipulate people, telling them what they wanted to hear. Even as a youth he was well on his way to a successful career in politics.

Nell Gaither was a spirited blonde beauty with whom John was deeply in love. She loved him too, but both were too shy to approach each other. They communicated only through vague hints and inscriptions in books they gave each other. John's love for Nell was made permanent when he saw her naked, rising from the lake. Nell later revealed that she had known that he was there. Graduation day for the Perfessor's academy was packed with excitement. When John had his graduation picture taken, he met in the photographer's studio a beautiful visitor from the South, Susanna Drake. After the graduation ceremony, everyone went to the lake, and John and Nell (who was apart for once from her usual escort, Garwood) were about to consummate their love for each other when they were interrupted by cries from their companions—a posse was hunting for the Perfessor, who had run off with a minister's wife. In fact, the couple had missed their train and the minister's wife was back home. Johnny found the Perfessor and helped him to escape.

That same year, the Fourth of July celebration was enlivened by a race between Johnny and Flash Perkins, a runner who had never been beaten. Johnny's friends planned to fix the race by getting Flash drunk, but this scheme backfired when Johnny got drunk instead. He won the race anyway, and once again everyone went to the lake to picnic. His inhibitions loosened by drink, Johnny made love for the first time—with Susanna Drake.

Later Susanna told Johnny that she was pregnant, and he did the honorable thing and married her. They made a trip to New Orleans, where Johnny learned of Susanna's tragic past. Her mother had gone insane, and her father was rumored to have had an intimate relationship with a slave. All of these people had died in a fire that destroyed the plantation house; only Susanna survived. Susanna was horrified that she might be her father's child by the slave, and she was also worried that she might go mad like her mother.

After they returned to Raintree County, Susanna gave birth to a son, but soon her madness began to assert itself, and Susanna burned down her and John's house, killing their child. Hopelessly insane, she was sent back to the South.

Meanwhile, the Civil War had begun; John had not yet served in the Union Army because he had a family. Once Susanna was sent away, however, he became a soldier, meeting once again Flash Perkins and the Perfessor, who was a war correspondent. John and Flash were in the battle of Chickamauga; Flash was killed and John wounded during General William T. Sherman's march through Georgia.

John recovered from his wounds in Washington, D.C., where he and the Perfessor witnessed the assassination of Abraham Lincoln. Back home, people got the false report of John's death. After spending two years in New York with the Perfessor, John went back to Raintree County after his mother's death. He discovered that Nell Gaither had married Garwood Jones and had died in childbirth. John opposed Garwood for Congress, but the county was not ready to hear John's message of reconciliation with the South. John settled down to become the local schoolteacher, and after Susanna ran away from her keepers and was declared dead, he took for his second wife one of his students, Esther Root. Esther's father disapproved of the marriage and refused to accept his daughter, even though John and Esther prospered and raised a family.

One event almost ruined John. A local preacher tried to attack John, saying that John had an illicit relationship with a local widow, but the Perfessor, in town for the celebration of July 4, 1892, showed that it was actually the preacher who was guilty of adultery with one of the local women. The Perfessor, who had once been run out of town by an angry minister, had the pleasure of revealing a minister as a hypocrite. As John returned from the celebration, he thought of all of his life and the lives of his friends and country as a great quest like the one he started for the raintree long before.

Critical Evaluation:

Raintree County is a long and complex novel with an appeal to many audiences. It is at once a historical novel, a gothic romance, and a love story. Its technique, through which the events of the day of July 4, 1892, are interrupted by flashbacks and those flashbacks by further digressions, is that of the modern novel, with its insistence on the importance of psychological rather than chronological time. The overlay of Christian and pagan myths links the book to the great tradition of western literature and philosophy. The forty years covered by the novel were a period of great strife leading to industrialization and territorial growth. The issue of slavery and the dual culture of the pre-Civil War United States led to that struggle that freed the slaves and settled the issue of the permanence of the Union. John Shawnessy is involved in this conflict on political and personal levels. He participates in a political race and in Sherman's march to the sea, and is a witness to Lincoln's assassination. The battle scenes are among the book's most vivid and memorable.

The question of slavery also touches John's personal life. His first wife, Susanna, was bedeviled by the fear that she might be half black. In the racist society of the antebellum South, being half black was a worse fate than being insane. Susanna is not the child of her crazed legal mother but of her father's black mistress, but the realization that she is black drives her insane anyway. John's relationship with Susanna and the creepy situations they encounter when they visit the South comprise the part of the novel that resembles a grim gothic tragedy.

The three women in John's life also make the novel a love story, one that does not end, as most such stories do, in marriage or rejection. Instead, the love story lasts through all the years of John's life. John's most intense love is for blonde Nell Gaither, but both are cut off from each other precisely because of this intensity and perhaps because of their familiarity with each other since childhood. When the brunette Susanna Drake arrives, the novelty of her beauty and behavior sweeps John off his feet. Susanna also uses trickery to capture John, playing on his sense of honor, something Nell would be too principled to do. John and Nell love each other in part because of their shared sense of honor, but that very feature of their lives also makes them unable to connect as lovers. After the tumult of his early emotional life, John is at last able to find peace with his third love, Esther.

The use of the flashback technique, which blends all of John's experiences into recollections on July 4, 1892, is reminiscent of James Joyce's *Ulysses* (1922). Joyce packed all of his character's lives, through memory and daydream, into one day, demonstrating that the past is not over but rather continues to be relived in the present. The last sentence of each chapter of *Raintree County* leads into the first sentence of the next chapter, even though the two sections may describe scenes that occurred forty years apart, also suggesting the continuity of time. The flashback technique also allows Lockridge to maintain interest by generating suspense as he withholds several key events until the last hundred pages of the novel. The reader does not learn of Nell's death or how the Fourth of July race was won, for example, until late in the novel.

The mythic overlay gives the novel a universal quality that relates it to the heroic stories of literature. Many of the key scenes of *Raintree County* take place by the river that runs through Raintree County or in the dense swamp at the end of Paradise Lake. John strips to go swimming and sees Nell also naked there. Drunk, and stunned by Susanna's beauty, he makes love for the first time there. There also he obtains glimpses of the legendary raintree. The tree, the swamp, the forest around it, and the river all suggest the garden of Eden. The mysterious raintree, with its golden blossoms, is something that John sets out to find like a hero on a quest. To find the raintree would be to possess a power that no one else has; John wishes that he possessed the power to write the great epic that would explain his life and that of the nation. The raintree does not symbolize the tree of knowledge in the Bible, the eating of which brought on sin and awareness of good and evil. It symbolizes the tree that is never mentioned in the biblical account, the tree of life. At the end of *Raintree County*, it seems that John has neither found the raintree nor written his great work, but he has found what the tree symbolizes. The novel's great story is John's own life and the lives of others whom he knew.

"Critical Evaluation" by Jim Baird

Bibliography:
Blotner, Joseph L. *"Raintree County* Revisited." *Western Humanities Review* 10 (Winter, 1956): 57-64. Reassesses the novel favorably and places it in both Western and American literary traditions.
Erisman, Fred. *"Raintree County* and the Power of Place." *Markham Review* 8 (Winter, 1979): 36-40. Argues that much of the power of *Raintree County* derives from the tension between its contrasting urban and rural settings.
Greiner, Donald J. "Ross Lockridge and the Tragedy of *Raintree County." Critique* 20, no. 3 (April, 1979): 51-63. Identifies the author of the novel with the hero of the book and notes that both were on a quest. Shawnessy survived his failure to write a great epic, and Lockridge, who killed himself shortly after the book was published, could not accept that his epic was over.
Lockridge, Larry. *Shade of the Raintree: The Life and Death of Ross Lockridge, Jr., Author of "Raintree County."* New York: Viking Press, 1994. The definitive biography of the book's author, written by his son.
White, Ray Lewis. *"Raintree County* and the Critics of '48." *MidAmerica* 11 (1984): 149-170. Assesses the first critical reception of the novel.

A RAISIN IN THE SUN

Type of work: Drama
Author: Lorraine Hansberry (1930-1965)
Type of plot: Family
Time of plot: 1950's
Locale: Chicago, Illinois
First performed: 1959; first published, 1959

Principal characters:
    LENA YOUNGER, a retired domestic, matriarch of an extended African
        American family
    WALTER, her son
    RUTH, Walter's wife
    BENEATHA, Walter's sister
    TRAVIS, Walter and Ruth's son
    JOSEPH ASAGAI, a Nigerian student, Beneatha's suitor
    GEORGE MURCHISON, a student, Beneatha's suitor
    BOBO, Walter's friend
    KARL LINDER, a representative of a suburban homeowner's association

The Story:

Walter Younger, Sr. ("Big Walter") died, leaving his widow, Lena, with a life insurance policy worth $10,000. Lena wanted to use the money as a down payment on a house in the suburbs so that her family could leave its crowded, shabby, Chicago apartment. Lena's son, Walter, disgusted with his job as a rich white man's chauffeur, wanted to invest the insurance money in a liquor store with two partners, Willy and Bobo. Beneatha, Walter's younger sister, a college student, wanted to use part of the money to pay for medical school.

In the play's opening scenes, the family argued over how to spend the insurance money. Walter told his sister to forget about medical school and become a nurse or get married like other women. He appealed to his mother to give him the money so that he could pursue his dream of entrepreneurship and thereby improve the family's circumstances, but Lena was skeptical about investing in the liquor business. Beneatha and her mother also argued about religion. Lena maintained that Beneatha needed God's help to become a doctor, and Beneatha asserted that God had little to do with her educational achievements.

As Act I ended, Lena informed Walter that his wife, Ruth, was pregnant and was considering ending her pregnancy by abortion because she did not wish to add another family member to their crowded household. Lena encouraged Walter to confront his wife and express his desire to have another child, but Walter stormed out of the apartment in anger. As he left, Lena called him a disgrace to his father's memory.

During the first two acts, Beneatha was visited by two suitors, Joseph Asagai and George Murchison. Asagai, who had recently returned from his native Nigeria, brought Beneatha a traditional African gown and headdress and encouraged her not to become an assimilationist Negro by forgetting her African heritage. George, the son of a well-to-do African American family, urged Beneatha to divorce herself from her heritage and not to take her studies too seriously.

In Act II, Lena announced to her family that she had made a down payment on a single-family home in Clybourne Park, an all-white neighborhood. When he heard the news, Walter was outraged and accused his mother of destroying his dream of owning his own business. Walter became deeply depressed, missing three days of work, spending his time at a local tavern, and drinking heavily. Having seen her son's depression, Lena had a change of heart. She informed Walter that she put only $3,500 down on the house, and she gave him the rest, commanding him to deposit $3,000 in a bank account earmarked for Beneatha's medical school tuition and allowing him to invest the remainder as he saw fit.

Walter's mood changed dramatically when his mother gave him the money. He made peace with his wife, and he excitedly told his son, Travis, that he would make a business transaction that would make the family wealthy.

As the Younger family packed for its move to its new suburban home, Karl Linder, a representative of the Clybourne Park Improvement Association, visited and offered to buy the Youngers' new home at a profit in an effort to keep a black family from integrating an all-white neighborhood. Walter boldly expelled Linder.

Immediately after Linder's departure, Walter's friend, Bobo, arrived, announcing the grim news that their business partner, Willy, had taken Bobo and Walter's money and left town instead of using it to purchase the liquor store. Walter sadly informed his family that all $6,500 was lost, including the money that Walter was supposed to set aside for Beneatha's schooling. Lena beat her son for his irresponsible behavior.

At the opening of Act III, as the family unpacked, Walter called Linder, informing him that he was ready to make a deal with him. Walter explained to his family that he intended to humble himself before Linder and agree to sell the family's new home for a profit. Hearing Walter's decision, Beneatha called her brother a toothless rat.

When Linder arrived, however, Walter underwent a profound change. Standing behind his son, he informed Linder that his family had decided to move into its new home in Clybourne Park. Walter spoke eloquently of his father's hard work and his family's pride. He proudly introduced Beneatha as a future doctor, and he introduced his son, Travis, as the sixth generation of Youngers in America. Linder left disappointed, and the Youngers began packing again.

In the final scene, Lena commanded the moving men, and the Youngers began carrying boxes out of the apartment. Beneatha announced that Asagai had proposed marriage, and Lena proudly told Ruth that Walter had finally come into his manhood that day. The play ended with Lena leaving her family's shabby apartment for the final time.

Critical Evaluation:

A Raisin in the Sun was the first play by an African American woman to be produced on Broadway. It enjoyed a successful run and won the New York Drama Critics Circle Award. It has been reproduced often at regional and university theaters since its first production in 1959. Two film versions have appeared. The 1961 version starred Sidney Poitier as Walter, and an American Playhouse television production in 1989 featured Danny Glover in that role.

Lorraine Hansberry's play confronts crucial issues that have faced African Americans: the fragmentation of the family, the black male's quest for manhood, and the problems of integration. Like Tennessee Williams' *The Glass Menagerie* (1944), Arthur Miller's *Death of a Salesman* (1949), Eugene O'Neill's *Long Day's Journey into Night* (1956), and other classic American plays, *A Raisin in the Sun* is fundamentally a family drama. Lena, the family matriarch, is attempting to keep her family together in difficult circumstances. She is the family's moral center, urging her children to end their quarreling, accept their responsibilities, and love and support one another. That the Youngers pull together in the closing scenes is more a credit to Lena than to her spirited but sometimes inconsiderate children, Walter and Beneatha. By allowing Lena to play this central role in the Younger family, Hansberry asserts the importance of the mother figure in the African American family.

An equally absorbing development in Hansberry's drama is Walter's quest for manhood. As the play opens, his father—"Big Walter"—has recently died, and Walter wants more than anything else to take his father's place as head of the family. Walter's job as a white man's chauffeur gives him a feeling of inferiority, and his wish to purchase a liquor store is an assertion of economic independence, a desire to provide for his family and live out his version of the American Dream. Walter's selfishness and irresponsibility, however, prevent him from becoming the legitimate head of the family, and only in the end, when he vanquishes Linder and asserts his family's pride, is Walter able to achieve his manhood.

The play also confronts the problems of racial integration that African Americans faced throughout the twentieth century. As the play opens, the Youngers are trapped in their Chicago tenement, unable to break an invisible barrier that keeps them from the white suburban neighborhood. Linder's attempt to bribe the Youngers into observing the unwritten rules of northern segregation vividly illustrates the problems that even upwardly mobile black families had when they attempted to leave the inner city and move into the mainly white suburbs. Walter's decision not to sell out to Linder and the white neighbors whom he represents is an act of heroism and an act of protest. As the play ends, the Youngers assert their rights as American citizens by choosing to live where they please.

Hansberry's play is realistic in setting, characterization, and dialogue. In addition to confronting universal African American issues, it reflects the circumstances of African Americans in the 1950's—the beginning of the Civil Rights movement. The doors of opportunity, if not wide open, are at least unlocked for black Americans. Jackie Robinson had integrated major league baseball, and the United States Supreme Court had outlawed school segregation. Hence, Beneatha's dream of becoming a doctor is a realistic one, as is Walter's dream of becoming an entrepreneur.

These opportunities, however, create tensions and competition in the Younger family, dramatized by Walter's verbal battles with his mother and sister and Beneatha's arguments with her mother. Moreover, the elusiveness of these dreams creates frustration that leads to bitterness. The play's title comes from a line in a Langston Hughes poem: "What happens to a dream deferred?/ Does it dry up/ Like a raisin in the sun?" Although the play ends on a euphoric note, with the Youngers fulfilling the traditional American Dream of owning a home in the suburbs, there is no guarantee that their future will be trouble free.

The play also captures the spirit of the budding feminist movement. Hansberry was the contemporary of feminist writers such as Adrienne Rich and Gloria Steinem, and the playwright reflects their dissatisfaction with traditional feminine roles in the post-World War II years. Beneatha's desire to become a physician, an occupation held by few women in the 1950's, and her rejection of the conventional life she would lead as the wife of George Murchison, suggest her rebellion against the conventions that kept women in the home or restricted to traditionally female occupations such as nursing and teaching. Beneatha's fascination with Asagai and his African heritage forecast the celebration of black Americans' African roots that would occur in the 1960's.

The success of *A Raisin in the Sun* opened theater doors to other African American dramatists such as James Baldwin, Amiri Baraka, Ed Bullins, and Ntozake Shange. Unfortunately, the promise suggested by Hansberry in *A Raisin in the Sun* was never completely fulfilled. A handful of plays written after *A Raisin in the Sun* did not receive equal critical attention, and Hansberry died of cancer before her thirty-fifth birthday.

James Tackach

Bibliography:

Bigsby, C. W. E., ed. *Poetry and Drama.* Vol. 2 in *The Black American Writer.* Deland, Fla.: Everett/Edwards, 1969. Provides a historical development of African American drama, with a full chapter devoted to Hansberry's plays.

Carter, Steven R. *Hansberry's Drama: Commitment amid Complexity.* Urbana: University of Illinois Press, 1991. A detailed study of Hansberry's entire canon. Chapter 2 focuses on the stage version of *A Raisin in the Sun,* and the following chapter discusses the two film versions as well as the hit musical, titled *Raisin,* that appeared in 1973.

Cheney, Anne. *Lorraine Hansberry.* Boston: Twayne, 1984. An excellent introduction to Hansberry and her works. Treats *A Raisin in the Sun* as a celebration of the African American family.

Keyssar, Helene. *The Curtain and the Veil: Strategies in Black Drama.* New York: Burt Franklin, 1981. A critical study of African American drama focusing on the ambivalence of black playwrights, with a full chapter devoted to *A Raisin in the Sun.*

Schlueter, June, ed. *Modern American Drama: The Female Canon.* Cranbury, N.J.: Associated University Presses, 1990. A collection of twenty-two essays on female American playwrights, with a full chapter devoted to Hansberry.

RALPH ROISTER DOISTER

Type of work: Drama
Author: Nicholas Udall (1505?-1556)
Type of plot: Farce
Time of plot: Sixteenth century
Locale: England
First performed: c. 1552; first published, 1566?

Principal characters:
RALPH ROISTER DOISTER, a well-to-do, cowardly braggart
MATTHEW MERRYGREEK, Roister Doister's hanger-on
DAME CHRISTIAN CUSTANCE, a well-to-do widow
GAWIN GOODLUCK, Dame Custance's fiancé
SYM SURESBY, Gawin Goodluck's friend

The Story:

Matthew Merrygreek, a gay young rascal who likened himself to the grasshopper of the fable, had often had fun and money at the expense of Ralph Roister Doister, a well-to-do, doltish young man who bragged long and loud of his bravery but failed to act anything but the coward when called to action. In addition, Ralph Roister Doister imagined himself in love with every woman he met, and he swore each time he fell in love that he could not live without the woman who had most lately caught his eye. One day, meeting Merrygreek on the street, he asserted that he was now madly in love with Dame Christian Custance, a widow reported to be wealthy. She had captivated Roister Doister when he saw her at supper. Merrygreek, anxious to please the man he constantly gulled, agreed to help Roister Doister pursue his suit. He assured the foolish braggart that the widow was certain to accept him and that Roister Doister ought really to try to marry someone of higher station and greater fortune.

Merrygreek went for musicians to serenade Dame Custance, while Roister Doister waited in front of the widow's home. As he waited, three of the widow's servant women came from the house and talked and sang. When they noticed Roister Doister, he came up, talked to them, and tried to kiss them. After talking with them for a time, Roister Doister gave them a love letter to deliver to their mistress. He boasted that he had written it himself.

Given the letter by her serving-woman, Dame Custance was furious. She reminded her servants that she was an honorable woman, affianced to Gawin Goodluck, who had been for some months on a sea voyage. Dame Custance refused to break the seal of the letter, much less read it. Meanwhile, to further his suit, Roister Doister sent his servant to the widow's house with some love gifts, a ring and a token in a cloth. The young servant, after some trouble, convinced the widow's serving-women to take the gifts to their mistress, even though she had been angry at receiving the letter.

Handed the gifts, the widow became even angrier, lectured her servants on their conduct, and finally sent a boy to find the man who had delivered the gifts to her house. Merrygreek, after many a laugh over what happened during Roister Doister's suit, finally went to Dame Custance and revealed his scheme for gulling Roister Doister. The widow said she would never marry such a doltish man, but agreed to join in the fun at the braggart's expense. She went so far as to read the letter he had written to her and said she would make a reply.

Rejoining Roister Doister, Merrygreek listened to the suitor's woeful tale and then told him in outrageous terms that the widow had refused his suit, called him vile names, and accused him of cowardice. Roister Doister immediately vowed that he would assault the widow's house with intent to kill her in combat, along with all her servants. Over Merrygreek's protests, Roister Doister set out to get his men together. Merrygreek laughed and waited, knowing that the cowardly braggart would never carry out his vow.

When they arrived at the widow's house, Merrygreek offered Roister Doister an excuse for not leading the assault. Instead, the braggart began once more to woo the widow with music and song. He sent Merrygreek to call the widow from her house. Dame Custance went out to Roister Doister and repeated her refusal of his foolish proposal. Then she read his letter aloud, and by rephrasing it and repunctuating it she made the letter as insulting as Roister Doister had meant it to be loving. The result thoroughly confused the suitor, who vowed it was not the letter he had sent to her. After she left, Roister Doister sent for the scrivener who had actually written the letter for him. The scrivener took the letter, read it correctly, and convinced Roister Doister that someone had tricked him.

In the meantime Sym Suresby, friend of the widow's fiancé, arrived to tell Dame Custance that her affianced suitor, Gawin Goodluck, had returned from his voyage and would be with her shortly. Suresby saw and heard enough of the conversation between the widow and Roister Doister to think that the widow was unfaithful to Goodluck. He went off, leaving the widow furious at the tomfoolery of Roister Doister. When she chased Roister Doister off, he again vowed to have revenge on the widow and her servants. Gathering his men, he approached her house a second time.

The widow, meanwhile, had gone to a trusted friend to enlist his support in getting rid of the troublesome Roister Doister, who threatened to ruin her approaching marriage to Goodluck. The friend consented to aid her. They also enlisted Merrygreek, who agreed to help them and at the same time pull more tricks at the expense of Roister Doister.

The foolish suitor and his men were routed by the widow with household utensils used as weapons. Having proved himself a coward as well as a fool, Roister Doister renounced his suit for the widow's hand. When Goodluck appeared soon afterward, Dame Custance was able to assure him that the reports he had had from Sym Suresby were muddled and that she had never broken her vows to him. She did, however, berate Suresby for not making certain of the truth before repeating what he had heard.

Merrygreek returned on behalf of Roister Doister and asked forgiveness of the widow and Goodluck. When he promised them that they should have much fun at Roister Doister's expense if they would but agree, they assented heartily and invited Merrygreek and Roister Doister to have dinner with them that very day.

Critical Evaluation:

Ralph Roister Doister presents no problems of interpretation, but knowing its historical and literary contexts helps in imagining how it appeared to audiences in its own time. For example, it was written for performance by schoolboys, which explains why its language is clearer than that of *Gammer Gurton's Needle* (1566), another play written at about the same time. The author, Nicholas Udall, was a canon of St. George's Chapel, Windsor Castle, and *Ralph Roister Doister*, with its psalmody and mock requiem, was perhaps performed at Windsor Chapel as early as September, 1552, in front of an audience including the young King Edward VI.

Udall was a distinguished classical scholar, who studied at Corpus Christi College, Oxford, well known for its Humanistic studies. Udall, in fact, by the time he wrote *Ralph Roister Doister*, had translated the *Apophthegmes* and Latin commentaries on the New Testament by the Dutch scholar and Humanist Desiderius Erasmus. Udall's efforts as a classicist, as a scholar of Humanism, and as a teacher inform the theme, structure, and intent of his *Ralph Roister Doister*. The classical influence on *Ralph Roister Doister* comes largely from the Roman dramatist Terence, whose comedies were a feature of the medieval school curriculum. Terence's plays were praised for their comparative wholesomeness and for the excellence of their Latin. Udall's devotion to Terence appears in his *Floures for Latin Spekynge* (1534), which became a standard school textbook. The fourth century B.C.E. grammarian Donatus studied Terence and found in his plays certain principles that became fixed in the scholarship that Udall would have known. The five-act structure which Udall uses in *Ralph Roister Doister*, for example, may have originated with Terence. The general familiarity of the educated of the time with Roman comedy may help explain why Renaissance comedies preceded tragedies.

The biggest debts in *Ralph Roister Doister* are to Plautus' *Miles Gloriosus* (c. 206 B.C.E.) and Terence's *Eunuchus* (pr. 161 B.C.E.). The *miles gloriosus* is the braggart soldier, the huffing, puffing windbag who is a parody of real military virtue. William Shakespeare's Falstaff is an example of this character type. Roister Doister appears as a parody of a parody. He is not by nature robust enough to look for women as a real roisterer would. Without the mischievous Matthew Merrygreek to puff him up and urge him on, Ralph would hardly attempt as much as he does. He is silly and full of himself, however, and when he meets Dame Christian Custance he falls in love with her as quickly as he does with all others. He is something of a fool for love.

Ralph derives clearly from Plautus' braggart soldier, but the scheme that Merrygreek involves him in comes straight out of Terence's *Eunuchus*. The subplot of that ancient comedy features a braggart, Thraso, who is egged on by the parasitical Gnatho (the inspiration for Matthew Merrygreek) to court a faithful woman, who stays true to her absent lover. Thraso assaults the woman's house just as his descendant Ralph vows to assault the house of Dame Custance. In each case the blusterers collapse.

In *Ralph Roister Doister* it is not Terence's young Roman woman who is wooed, but a redoubtable Christian widow whose name reveals her resistance to bold suitors. Dame Custance is capable of the kind of broad humor sometimes found in the morality plays, and recalls Geoffrey Chaucer's Wife of Bath somewhat, but she hardly indulges in shocking coarseness. When Gawin Goodluck's friend, Sym Suresby, mistakenly suspects Dame Custance of betraying Goodluck, she compares herself to two famous heroines, the biblical Esther and Susanna of the Apocryphal story.

Matthew Merrygreek owes something to the parasite Gnatho but also owes much to the figure of Vice from medieval morality plays. Vice would have been a familiar villain to Udall's audience. This stock character personified human deviltry. He represents the world's corruption that has to be overcome, but it is impossible to ignore his genius for bawdiness and amusing shenanigans. Falstaff and Ben Jonson's Volpone are in this tradition; a truly evil villain such as Iago, however, is beyond the limits of such a character. A true monster is more likely to be found in a tragedy. Matthew's ultimate harmlessness is implicit in the Prologue's assurance that "all scurrility we utterly refuse."

Writing for a cast of students, Udall would have been careful to write a work that was properly instructive. Delight comes to sweeten the instruction in the broad slapstick nonsense, such as the rout of Ralph and his followers by the widow armed with pots and pans, and instruction comes in the good-natured depiction of a virtuous woman complemented by a good man. Moreover, Roman themes and character types are well meshed with English materials. Such irreproachable citizens as Sym Suresby and Tristram Trusty speak well of the morals of London's middle-class citizenry.

The meter of the play is a rhymed hexameter, but it does not scan well. In Udall's time, stress scansion was not yet fixed in practice, and the blank verse of Christopher Marlowe and Shakespeare was not to be used first until Thomas Sackville and Thomas Norton wrote *Gordoduc* (c. 1561). *Ralph Roister Doister* may seem primitive to today's readers, but it offers much to appreciate.

"Critical Evaluation" by Frank Day

Bibliography:
Bevington, David M. *From "Mankind" to Marlowe: Growth of Structure in the Popular Drama of Tudor England.* Cambridge, Mass.: Harvard University Press, 1962. Discusses *Ralph Roister Doister* in one chapter, commenting on the casting, Matthew Merrygreek's debt to the old Vice character, and the play's frequent allusions.
Downer, Alan S. *British Drama: A Handbook and Brief Chronicle.* East Norwalk, Conn.: Appleton-Century-Crofts, 1950. Explains the Roman influences on *Ralph Roister Doister*, discussing how Ralph represents the *miles gloriosus*, or braggart soldier. Stresses the moral intention of the author, assumed to be Nicholas Udall.
Eaton, Walter Prichard. *The Drama in English.* New York: Charles Scribner's Sons, 1930. Begins with English drama's origins in the church and follows its progress into the market square. Chapters on the miracle plays, the moralities, and the interludes are followed by one titled "The First English Comedy—*Ralph Roister Doister.*"
Udall, Nicholas. *Nicholas Udall's Roister Doister.* Edited with an introduction by G. Scheur-weghs. Louvain, Belgium: Librairie Universitaire, C. Uystpruyst, 1939. The scholarly apparatus treats Udall's life and the play's sources. Copious notes elucidate vocabulary and other textual matters.
Whitworth, Charles Walters, ed. *Three Sixteenth-Century Comedies.* New York: W. W. Norton, 1984. An accessible modern paperback edition containing *Ralph Roister Doister.* A long introduction sets these works in historical context, and footnotes facilitate reading.

THE RAMAYANA

Type of work: Poetry
Author: Valmiki (fl. fourth century B.C.E.)
Type of plot: Epic
Time of plot: Antiquity
Locale: India
First transcribed: Rāmāyana, c. 350 B.C.E. (English translation, 1870-1874)

Principal characters:
RAMA, a prince and incarnation of Vishnu
SITA, his wife
LAKSHMAN, his brother and loyal follower
DASA-RATHA, his father, the king of the Kosalas
RAVAN, Demon-king of Lanka (Sri Lanka)
KAIKEYI, one of King Dasa-ratha's wives and enemy of Rama

The Story:

King Dasa-ratha of the Kosalas, who kept his court at Ayodhya, had four sons, though not all by the same mother. According to legend, the god Vishnu, in answer to King Dasa-ratha's supplications, had given a divine liquor to each of the king's wives, so that they might bring forth sons, each of whom was partly an incarnation of Vishnu. Of the sons born, Rama was the handsomest and strongest of all, his mother having drunk more of the magic beverage than Dasa-ratha's other wives.

When Rama grew to manhood he heard of Sita, beautiful, talented, and virtuous daughter of King Janak and the Earth-mother. King Janak was the possessor of a wondrous bow, a mighty weapon that had belonged to the gods, and King Janak resolved that whoever could bend the bow should have Sita for his wife. The king knew that no ordinary mortal could possibly accomplish the feat.

Rama and his brothers traveled to the court of King Janak and were granted permission to try drawing the mighty bow. With ease Rama bent the bow, with such strength that the weapon snapped in two. King Janak promised that Sita should be Rama's bride and that each of his half brothers, too, should have a noble bride from the people of Videha.

So Sita became the wife of Rama; her sister Urmila became the bride of Lakshman, Rama's favorite brother; Mandavi and Sruta-kriti, cousins of Sita, became the wives of Bharat and Satrughna, the other half brothers of Rama. When all returned to Ayodhya, Dasa-ratha, fearing that rivalry between his children might create unhappiness and tragedy in his house, sent Bharat and Satrughna to live with their mothers' people.

Years passed, and King Dasa-ratha grew old. Wishing to have the time and opportunity to prepare himself for the next life, he proposed that Rama, his favorite son, should become regent. The king's council and the populace rejoiced in the proposal, and plans were made to invest Rama with the regency and place him on the Kosala throne. Before the preparations had been completed, however, Manthara, a maid to Queen Kaikeyi, one of King Dasa-ratha's wives, advised the queen that Rama's succession to the throne should be prevented and that Bharat, Queen Kaikeyi's son, should become regent. The ill advice was heard, and Queen Kaikeyi remembered that she had been promised two boons by her husband. So when King Dasa-ratha came to her, she asked that Bharat should be made regent and that Rama should go into exile for fourteen years. King Dasa-ratha was sad, but he had given his word and he had to fulfill his promises. Like a dutiful son, Rama heard his father's decision and prepared to go into exile. He expected to go alone, but his wife Sita and his brother Lakshman prepared to go with him to share his lonely and uncomfortable exile in the dismal Dandak forest. The Kosala people mourned his departure and accompanied him on the first day of his journey away from Ayodhya.

Leaving his native country, Rama journeyed south. He and his companions crossed the Ganges River and came to the hermitage of Bharad-vaja, a holy man. After visiting with him they went on to the hill of Chitrakuta, where stood the hermitage of Valmiki, a learned and holy man. There they learned that King Dasa-ratha had died the day after Rama's departure from Ayodhya, remembering in his hour of death a curse laid on him by a hermit whose son he had accidentally killed. Rama stayed with Valmiki for a time. Bharat returned to Ayodhya to become regent, as his mother had planned. However, he recognized Rama's claim and set out on a journey to find Rama and to ask him to become king of the Kosalas. Rama, however, having given his word, remained in exile as he had vowed to do. Bharat returned to Avodhya to place Rama's sandals on the throne as a symbol of Rama's right to the kingship.

In order that his kinsmen might not find him again, Rama left Valmiki's hermitage, and after a long journey he established his own hermitage near the dwelling of Agastya, a holy and learned man. There Rama, Sita, and Lakshman lived in peace until they were disturbed by a demon-maiden, enamored of Rama, who had been repulsed in her addresses by both Rama and Lakshman. Spurned and seeking revenge, she went to her brother, Ravan, demon-king of Lanka, and asked his help. Ravan was a powerful being who through asceticism had achieved power even over the gods. His domination, according to legend, could be broken only by an alliance of humans and the monkey people. Ravan sent a demon in the disguise of a deer to lead Rama astray while on the hunt. When Rama failed to return, Sita insisted that Lakshman go look for him. In the absence of the brothers, Ravan came and abducted Sita.

Rama, having learned what had happened, allied himself with the monkey people in order to make war upon the demons and win back his beloved wife. Hanuman, one of the monkey people's leaders, found Sita at Ravan's palace and led Rama and the forces of the monkey people to Ceylon. There Ravan's city was besieged and many battles were fought, with combat between the great leaders of both sides and pitched battles between the forces of good and evil. Finally Ravan and his demon forces were defeated, Ravan was killed, and Sita was rescued and restored to her husband. Sita, who had remained faithful to Rama throughout her captivity, proved in an ordeal by fire that she was still virtuous and worthy to be Rama's wife.

Rama, Sita, and Lakshman returned in triumph to Ayodhya, where Rama was welcomed and became king of the Kosala people. Rumors were spread, however, that Sita had not been faithful to her husband, until at last Rama sent his wife away, and she went to live at the hermitage of Valmiki. Shortly after her arrival at the hermitage she gave birth to Rama's sons.

More years passed and the two sons grew up, tutored in their youth by the wise Valmiki, who took his charges eventually to Ayodhya. There Rama, recognizing them as his sons, sent for Sita and had her conducted to his court. Since her virtue had been in doubt, she was asked for a token that she had been true to her marriage vows. The earth opened to a great chasm, and the Earth-mother herself rose up on her throne to speak on behalf of Sita and to take her to the land of the gods. Thus Sita was taken away from the husband and the people who had doubted her.

Critical Evaluation:

The story of Rama is one of the most popular tales among the people of India, where the story holds great religious significance. In India, where the tale has been recounted for generations, there are several versions of the story, but the main outlines remain the same, with Rama and Sita as the idealized versions of man and woman. To the Western reader the characters may appear to be human beings with supernatural powers, roughly equivalent to certain figures in Greek legend and myth, but to Hindus the characters of the *Ramayana* (the fortunes of Rama) are more than this; they are gods. Scholars disagree on the various versions of the *Ramayana*, and the problem of the original story and additions by later generations of storytellers will perhaps never be solved. The best approach for a general reader is probably to accept the story as it is told.

The *Ramayana* is one of two Hindu epics, the other being the earlier *Mahabharata*. Whereas the *Mahabharata* is a heroic (or folk) epic deriving from an oral tradition, the *Ramayana* is more nearly a literary epic, written in conscious imitation of the heroic tradition. Whatever the original may have been, the *Ramayana* has been altered many times by subsequent rewriting and recension. In its extant versions, the *Ramayana* contains about 24,000 couplets (less than one-fourth the length of the *Mahabharata*) and is divided into seven books. The *Mahabharata* is eighteen books. Of the seven books of the *Ramayana*, the central story covers books 2 through 6. Book 1 is introductory. Book 7 appears to be a species of appendix. It provides both epilogue to and critique of the preceding six books. It also provides instruction for the recital of the *Ramayana* by minstrels in much the same way that medieval texts coach jongleurs in their repertoire and their performance. The *Ramayana*, like most Western epics and unlike the *Mahabharata*, has unity, which stems from concentration on one main story.

One of the major themes in the central narrative is the relationship between destiny and volition, with the consequent consideration of personal responsibility or the lack of it. The key questions ultimately revolve around the power of the gods, for the keeping of human promises hinges upon belief in divine retribution. Hence, King Dasa-ratha rescinds his proposal that Rama should succeed him as regent in order to honor his prior promise to Queen Kaikeyi. So, too, Rama dutifully accepts Bharat as regent and goes into exile, in deference to the king's expressed wishes (really, the gods' demands). Just as Rama accepts his fate, so also his brother Lakshman and his wife Sita accept theirs. Lakshman simply does his duty and perseveres, but Sita is subjected to the most stringent of tests. After being kidnapped by Ravan, she is called upon to prove her virtue. The trial being so debilitating, Sita is finally rescued by her Earth-mother. All of these claims upon human endurance require intervention by the gods. The message of the *Ramayana* thus seems to be that human volition is subservient to divine will. The corollary also appears to establish the social order as subject to the divine order.

Closely allied to the theme of free will versus fate is the theme of duty. One aspect of this theme of duty is Rama's behavior, often cited as a model for emulation. Rama's submission to his father's decision, his acceptance of exile, and his fidelity to his promise to remain in exile all bespeak Rama's filial piety and deference to duty. This view of duty follows the pattern traditional for warriors, princes, and kings; as such, it is compatible with ideals presented in the *Mahabharata* as well as with Western ethical assumptions. The other, and more important, aspect of the theme of duty is less conventional in an epic, for this aspect concerns not wars and the affairs of state, the usual epic grist, but human love and domestic matters. This aspect of duty, then, deals with Sita's story, which, all things considered, comprises the main plot line in the epic. Sita, like Rama, is held up as an exemplar of ideal behavior—for women. Her behavior is characterized by sweetness, tenderness, obedience, patient suffering, and, above all, faithfulness; her piety and self-sacrifice ultimately qualify her for relief from mortal travail by being reabsorbed into her Earth-mother. She endures all without complaint and thus became the model for the perfect woman, wife, and mother, her image of duty unalloyed.

The *Ramayana* also deals with typical Hindu motifs. There is, for example, the Brahman's curse which King Dasa-ratha remembers on his deathbed. Also, there is the asceticism, as exemplified in Valmiki's hermitage and in Rama's own abstemious life after leaving Valmiki's hermitage. In addition, this asceticism reflects another Hindu value: the emphasis on social order, which is manifested in the caste system. The orderly functioning of society, with all people acknowledging their proper places in it, is a high priority in the Hindu ethos. Furthermore, the concepts of truth and duty provide the definitive guidelines for action. Truth and duty go hand in hand to create twin obligations for Dasa-ratha and Bharat as well as Rama and Sita and every devout Hindu. The didactic elements of the *Ramayana* reinforce these typical Hindu motifs. Most explicitly, the teachings of Valmiki convey the precepts. Yet the implicit message of the plot and of the human interaction conveys the ethical and moral substance even more clearly. Thus the Hindu ideals of faith and conduct are both taught and demonstrated in the *Ramayana*.

In addition to the Hindu motifs, as well as the themes of duty and free will versus fate, the *Ramayana* also presents an interesting juxtaposition of the natural and the supernatural. The central narrative begins with the natural or "real-world" events: the political machinations at the court of King Dasa-ratha; the banishment of Rama, Sita, and Lakshman; and the death of King Dasa-ratha and the subsequent dilemma of Bharat when Rama refuses the throne. The next half of the narrative deals with the supernatural: the intrusion of the demon-maiden; the intervention of Ravan; the alliance with the monkey people; the real and allegorical battle between the forces of good and the forces of evil; and the Earth-mother's absorption of Sita. This combination of natural and supernatural worlds synthesizes the ethical and spiritual concerns of Hinduism, incorporating the concepts of fatalism and duty. Through this synthesis, the *Ramayana* goes beyond the confines of a national cultural epic to become part of the sacred literature of Hinduism. This religious perspective has made the *Ramayana* one of the best known and best loved works in India.

"Critical Evaluation" by Joanne G. Kashdan

Bibliography:
Narayan, R. K. *The Ramayana.* New York: Viking Press, 1972. Narayan has based his *Ramayana* on the Tamil poet Kamban's version of the original. The easy-flowing prose of Narayan's *Ramayana* makes for an enjoyable reading of the great epic for all age groups. His succinct epilogue refers to differences in the original Sanskrit version and the Tamil version.

Shaw, J. C. *The Ramayana Through Western Eyes.* Bangkok, Thailand: Distributed by D. K. Today, 1988. Shortened Thai version of the *Ramayana* with beautiful colored plates. The warfare and magic that appears in the original version has been excluded. Each chapter is introduced by excerpts from English poems.

Smith, H. Daniel, ed. *The Picturebook Ramayana: An Illustrated Version of Valmiki's Story.* Syracuse: Maxwell School of Citizenship and Public Affairs, Syracuse University, 1981. The basic plot of Rama's story is explained in the summary preceding the illustrations, which are accompanied by verses from the *Ramayana.* Appropriate for college level as well as junior and senior high school students.

Venkatesananda, Swami. *The Concise Ramayana of Valmiki.* Albany: State University of New York Press, 1988. This condensed version of the epic is divided into seven chapters that describe Rama's life from his birth until his death. The simple narrative style of the book and appropriate chapter intervals make it very readable.

Vyas, Shantikumar Nanooram. *India in the Ramayana Age*. New Delhi: Atma Ram & Sons, 1967. Analyzes social and cultural conditions in ancient India as portrayed in Valmiki's *Ramayana*. Includes a chapter on the position of women during this time.

RAMEAU'S NEPHEW

Type of work: Novel
Author: Denis Diderot (1713-1784)
Type of plot: Philosophical
Time of plot: 1761
Locale: Paris
First published: German translation, 1805; French original, 1821 as *Le Neveu de Rameau*
  (English translation, 1897)

Principal characters:
  JEAN-FRANÇOIS RAMEAU, the nephew of the composer Jean-Philippe
    Rameau, also HE
  DENIS DIDEROT, the author, also MYSELF

The Story:

Myself and He first discussed geniuses. Myself stressed their benefit to the larger society and future generations, but He berated them for personal flaws with which they harm themselves and those around them—they would be better off, He averred, amassing a fortune in business so they could live splendidly and pay buffoons like him to make them laugh and procure girls for them. He conceded that He was vexed at lacking genius himself and declared that He would like to be someone else, on the chance of being one. He also remarked that He loved to hear discreditable things about geniuses—it let him bear his mediocrity more easily.

At this point, He began singing famous songs He wished that He had composed, and He detailed the good life that fame and fortune would have afforded him—a fine house, good food and wine, pretty women, a gaggle of flatterers, falling asleep with the gentle hum of praise in his ears. This alluring vision soon gave way to austere reality, however, for He had been banished by his former patron. Rameau acknowledged that he himself was a foolish, lazy, impudent, greedy ne'er-do-well, but he added that those with whom he had lived had liked him precisely because of those qualities. He was their buffoon, their great greedy boob. In their mediocrity, they needed someone to despise.

Myself advised Rameau either to apologize to his patron or to be courageous enough to be poor. That latter idea did not appeal to Rameau because there were so many wealthy fools to exploit. He admitted self-contempt, but only for not making more lucrative use of his God-given talent for flattery, bootlicking, and seducing bourgeois daughters for his master.

Myself, distressed by these frank avowals of turpitude and perverted feelings, sought to change the subject. Talk shifted to music (with mime of violin and keyboard) and education, but He disclosed scams of the music tutoring trade and went on to assert that such "idioms" are common to all professions and are the means by which restitution is achieved. Should He gain wealth, he would be happy to disperse it by gorging, gambling, wenching, and maintaining a whole troop of flatterers.

"You would certainly be doing honor to human nature," Myself dryly remarked. "Openly or no, most think as I do," He retorted. He dismissed patriotism (there are no countries, only tyrants and slaves), aiding friends (gratitude is a burden), even the devotion to the education of one's children. Myself, while admitting delight in sensual pleasures, said that even more he liked solving problems, reading good books, instructing his children, doing his duty. While he would give all to have written a great work, better still would be to rehabilitate the Huguenot

Calas (Voltaire's great legal victory over Church and monarchy).

Rameau wanted none of Myself's kind of happiness, finding it strange and rare (and adding that the virtuous are ill-humored). It was easier to follow one's natural vices, so congenial to French people and their little needs. Myself again suggested that He hurry back to his former patron, but He revealed a new motive: pride. He was quite willing to be abject, but at his pleasure, not under duress. He also told more of the grim situation in "our house," which included a grouchy master (the financier Bertin) and a mistress who was a stupid, second-rate actress growing fat, as well as fallen poets and despised musicians who formed a mob of shameful toadies eager to tear down all that succeeds. He also detailed the faux pas—a brash quip about the hierarchy of freeloaders at Bertin's table—which had led to his expulsion. The passage betrays that He wanted both the benefits of being a parasite and the pleasure of feeling superior to his benefactors. Asked if he spread malicious gossip about them, He replied that they should expect as much—would you blame a tiger that bites off a hand thrust into its cage? Asked why He was so open about his vices, He revealed that He wanted admiration for sublimity in wickedness, and He described in admiring detail a man who had cleverly robbed and betrayed a Jew.

Again horrified, Myself shifted the subject to a lengthy discussion of French versus Italian new music, which elicited Rameau's most elaborate singing pantomime, a jumble of airs, emotions, and orchestral instruments. Startled chess players and passersby watched the spectacle of a man possessed. Myself wondered why a person so sensitive to refinements in music was so insensible to virtue, and he asked what Rameau wanted for his own son. Rameau, a fatalistic and passive parent, hoped that the boy would learn the "golden art" of averting disgrace, shame, and the penalties of the law, but he seemed unconcerned about giving his son direction. Myself observed that should the boy grow up uniting infant reasoning with adult passion, he might well strangle his father and sleep with his mother.

Asked why, for all his understanding of music, he had never created a great work, Rameau blamed his star, the low-grade people around him, and need, which forced him to take positions vis-à-vis his superiors. As He said, the needy man does not walk like the rest; he skips, twists, cringes, and crawls. While He contended that all must take positions, Myself declared that a philosopher like Diogenes, who had mastered his desires, did not. Rameau replied that he wanted good food, bed, clothes, rest, and much else that he would rather owe to kindness than toil. Myself insisted that He had overlooked the cost. Undeterred and uninstructed, He declared cheerfully that he who laughs last laughs best.

"The Story" by R. Craig Philips

Critical Evaluation:

Rameau's Nephew submits to no simple classification. Although the narrative is fictional, the characters were actual persons and the ideas they expound in the book probably closely resemble the opinions they actually held. There is the problem of deciding how much of Denis Diderot can be found in the character Rameau, and how much of Rameau in that of Diderot. In general, however, the Diderot in the book is a mild champion of traditional values whereas Rameau is a vivacious apologist for roguery. The brilliant turns of this satirical dialogue raise the suspicion that the author Diderot is delighted with the convention-defying attitudes of his friend Rameau; perhaps Diderot believes Rameau more than Rameau believes himself.

The dialogue is a satirical critique of manners and morals. It makes specific reference to prominent writers, musicians, politicians, critics, and other leading figures of eighteenth century France. Many of the comments are unkind, and some are painfully so—or would have been had the work been published at the time of its composition. Diderot saw to it, however, that his lively satire remained unpublished, not only because of its references to living persons but also because of a reluctance to stir up the censor and all those to whom Rameau's carefree morality might have proved unacceptable.

The character Rameau is marvelously wrought to suit Diderot's intention. Although Rameau is a fully drawn individual and convincing, as witty rogues in literature usually are, he is not simply one thing or another. On the contrary, Diderot states that Rameau is simultaneously his own opposite. Sometimes Rameau is thin, sometimes fat; sometimes he is filthy, sometimes powdered and curled. His physical vacillation is matched by vacillations of mood. Sometimes he is cheerful, sometimes depressed; sometimes he is courageous, sometimes timid to the point of being fearful. Rameau is a sensualist and a lover of wine and women, but his passionate defense of an egoistic hedonism is a sign of his need to apologize for his manner: His morality is a device to prop up his manner. Underneath Rameau's abandon can be perceived a poignant longing for depth and respectability.

Having created a character whose contrary traits reveal the human being in self-conflict—thus providing the motive for a discussion of morality—Diderot provides Rameau with a gentlemanly antagonist, the man of ideas, Diderot himself. Diderot's mild responses, ostensibly intended to counter Rameau's philosophy, actually, with the acuity of a Socrates, incite Rameau to a passionate defense of the sense-gratifying life of a social parasite.

Rameau, who contradicts himself within himself, and Diderot, who contradicts Rameau, together bring out the difficulty of all moral problems and of morality itself. Human beings are neither merely intellectual nor merely sensual; their desire to understand is often in conflict with their desires, and their desires in conflict with one another. Consequently, no one moral rule or set of principles will do. To be a good person, one must have a kind of moral genius. For such a person, rules are instruments to be used only with ingenuity, and sometimes they need to be discarded altogether. People who are at war with themselves, or with another, as Rameau is with himself and with Diderot, may not be able to attain a just victory. Sometimes there is no such thing as the proper answer. For a good person, life is a creative struggle that must be judged as works of art are judged, without dogmatism and with respect for the impossible goals the human spirit sets for itself. Perhaps the theme of the dialogue is best understood dialectically: Without the restraint of reason and human consideration, the human being becomes something worse than a fool, but without attention to the fact of human appetites the moralist becomes something less than a human being.

Rameau is the fool and Diderot the moralist, but Rameau fancies himself as something of the classic fool, the darling of the courts, the discerning jester who makes the bitter truth palatable. In reality, he comes close to being a compromising sponger, a guest who is tolerated in great houses only because he is sometimes an amusing conversationalist. Although he comes close to being merely parasitical, he is saved by his own need for apology. A man who must speak to Diderot is already more than a professional guest.

The dialogue is presented against a background of chess. The narrator takes shelter in the Regency Café, where the finest chess players of Paris compete. When Rameau enters and engages Diderot in conversation, he begins a kind of verbal chess game that shows him to be a brilliant and erratic player pitted against a slower but cannier Diderot. Rameau's attitude is revealed at once when, in response to Diderot's expression of interest in the games, he speaks scornfully of the players—although they are the best in Paris. When Diderot remarks that Rameau forgives nothing but supreme genius, Rameau retorts that he has no use for mediocrity.

The dialogue must be read carefully for, to continue the chess metaphor, the moves are deceptive. Like Fyodor Dostoevski, Diderot appreciated the exceptional individual who stepped beyond the bounds of conventional morality; unlike Friedrich Nietzsche, he did not deify the immoralist. *Rameau's Nephew* is a skillful and satirical attempt to do justice to both the moralist and the animal in human beings.

Bibliography:
Crocker, Lester. *The Embattled Philosopher: A Biography of Denis Diderot.* East Lansing: Michigan State University Press, 1954. A lively, very readable, and solid study. Evokes the antithetical tendencies in Diderot's personality, treats with balance Diderot's famous feud with Rousseau, and includes a lengthy, perceptive analysis of *Rameau's Nephew.*
Doolittle, James. *Rameau's Nephew: A Study of Diderot's "Second Satire."* Geneva: Librairie E. Droz, 1960. A reflective study of Diderot's most famous creative work. Insightful. Relies heavily on the text itself—and is free of the critical jargon and interpretive excesses of some more recent works.
Fellows, Otis. *Diderot.* Boston: Twayne, 1977. A sympathetic, clear introduction to Diderot's life and work. Relying heavily on earlier scholarship, Fellows reports varied interpretive views of Diderot's major writings.
Furbank, Philip Nicholas. *Diderot: A Critical Biography.* London: Martin Secker & Warburg, 1992. Emphasizes Diderot's literary works, particularly his fiction, and cites lengthy passages from his correspondence to clarify the issues that absorbed the philosopher. Furbank's interpretations make use of contemporary literary theory.
Wilson, Arthur. *Diderot.* New York: Oxford University Press, 1972. A comprehensive study of Diderot, richly detailed and absorbing. Treats the man and his social world with assurance and subtle judgment. Describes Diderot's courage in going ahead with his *Encyclopédie* (1751-1772) even after others deserted the project.

THE RAPE OF LUCRECE

Type of work: Poetry
Author: William Shakespeare (1564-1616)
Type of plot: Tragedy
Time of plot: 500 B.C.E.
Locale: Rome
First published: 1594

> *Principal characters:*
> COLLATINE, a Roman general
> LUCRECE, his wife
> TARQUIN, Collatine's friend and son of the Roman king

The Story:

At Ardea, where the Romans were fighting, two Roman leaders, Tarquin and Collatine, spoke together one evening. Collatine described his beautiful young wife, Lucrece, in such glowing terms that Tarquin's passions were aroused. The next morning, Tarquin left the Roman host and journeyed to Collatium, where the unsuspecting Lucrece welcomed him as one of her husband's friends. As Tarquin told her many tales of Collatine's prowess on the battlefield, he looked admiringly at Lucrece and decided that she was the most beautiful woman in Rome.

In the night, while the others of the household were asleep, Tarquin lay restless. Caught between desire for Lucrece and dread of being discovered, to the consequent loss of his honor, he wandered aimlessly about his chamber. On the one hand, there was his position as a military man who should not be the slave of his emotions; on the other hand was his overwhelming desire. He feared the dreadful consequences that might be the result of his lustful deed. His disgrace would never be forgotten. Perhaps his own face would show the mark of his crimes and the advertisement linger on even after death. He thought for a moment that he might try to woo Lucrece but decided that such a course would be to no avail. She was already married and was not mistress of her own desires. Again he considered the possible consequences of his deed.

At last, emotion conquered reason. As Tarquin made his way to Lucrece's chamber, many petty annoyances deterred him. The locks on the doors had to be forced; the threshold beneath the door grated under his footstep; the wind threatened to blow out his torch; he pricked his finger on a needle. Tarquin ignored these omens of disaster. In fact, he misconstrued them as forms of trial that only made his prize more worth winning.

When he reached the chamber door, Tarquin began to pray for success. Realizing, however, that heaven would not countenance his sin, he declared that Love and Fortune would henceforth be his gods. Entering the room, he gazed at Lucrece in sleep. When he reached forward to touch her breast, she awoke with a cry of fear. He told her that her beauty had captured his heart and that she must submit to his will. First he threatened Lucrece with force, telling her that if she refused to submit to him, he would not only kill her but also dishonor her name. His intention was to murder one of her slaves, place him in her arms, and then swear that he killed them because he had seen Lucrece embracing the man. If she yielded, however, he promised he would keep the whole affair secret. Lucrece began to weep and plead with Tarquin. For the sake of her hospitality, her husband's friendship, Tarquin's position as a warrior, he must pity her and refrain from this deed. Her tears serving only to increase his lust, Tarquin smothered her cries with the bed linen while he raped her.

Shame-ridden, he stole away, leaving Lucrece desolate. She, horrified and revolted, tore her nails and hoped the dawn would never come. In a desperate fury, she railed against the night; its darkness and secrecy had ruined her. She was afraid of the day, for surely her sin would be revealed. Still worse, through her fall, Collatine would be forever shamed. It was Opportunity that was at fault, she claimed, working for the wicked and against the innocent. Time, the handmaiden of ugly Night, was hand-in-hand with Opportunity, but Time could work for Lucrece now. She implored Time to bring misery and pain to Tarquin. Exhausted from her emotional tirade, Lucrece fell back on her pillow. She longed for a suicide weapon; death alone could save her soul.

As the dawn broke, she began to consider her death. Not until she had told Collatine the complete details of her fall would she take the step, however, for Collatine must revenge her on Tarquin. Lucrece called her maid and asked for pen and paper. Writing to Collatine, she asked him to return immediately. When she gave the messenger the letter, she imagined that he knew of her sin, for he gave her a sly, side glance. Surely everyone must know by now, she thought. Her grief took new channels. Studying a picture of the fall of Troy, she tried to find the face showing greatest grief. Hecuba, who gazed mournfully at Priam in his dying moments, seemed the saddest. Lucrece grieved for those who died in the Trojan War, all because one man could not control his lust. Enraged, she tore the painting with her nails.

Collatine, returning home, found Lucrece robed in black. With weeping and lamentations, she told him of her shame, but without naming her violator. After she had finished, Collatine, driven half-mad by rage and grief, demanded the name of the traitor. Before revealing it, Lucrece drew promises from the assembled soldiers that the loss of her honor would be avenged. Then, naming Tarquin, she drew a knife from her bosom and stabbed herself.

Heartbroken, Collatine cried that he would kill himself as well, but Brutus, his friend, stepped forward and argued that woe was no cure for woe; it was better to revenge Lucrece. The soldiers left the palace to carry the bleeding body of Lucrece through Rome. The indignant citizens banished Tarquin and all his family.

Critical Evaluation:

The story of Tarquin's violation of Lucrece is an ancient Roman legend that has been presented in many versions other than in this poem by William Shakespeare. The Elizabethans were especially fond of this legend, so Shakespeare had numerous sources upon which to draw. Compared with his other writings, this poem is far more conventionally Elizabethan, yet its passages of great emotion and its consistently beautiful poetry rank it above other interpretations of the story known in his day.

The Rape of Lucrece was entered at the Stationers' Register on May 9, 1594. Like *Venus and Adonis*, which had been published the previous year, it was finely printed by Richard Field and dedicated to the Earl of Southampton. Both of these narrative poems had been written while the theaters were closed because of the plague, but these companion pieces are not the idle products of a dramatist during a period of forced inactivity. Rather, as the dedications and the care in publication indicate, they are efforts at what, in Shakespeare's day, was a more serious, more respectable type of composition than writing plays.

Longer and graver in tone than *Venus and Adonis*, *The Rape of Lucrece* was extremely popular, going through many editions, and was quoted frequently by contemporaries. The stern Gabriel Harvey, a Cambridge fellow and friend of Edmund Spenser, enthusiastically approved of the poem and paired it with *Hamlet* (1600-1601) for seriousness of intent. The poem may be the "graver labor" that Shakespeare promises Southampton in the dedication to *Venus and*

Adonis. Whether or not Shakespeare intended to pair the poems, *The Rape of Lucrece* does provide a moralistic contrast to the view of love and sexuality expressed in the earlier poem.

The genre of *The Rape of Lucrece* is complaint, a form popular in the later Middle Ages and the Renaissance, and particularly in vogue in the late 1590's. Strictly speaking, the complaint is a monologue in which the speaker bewails his or her fate or the sad state of the world. Shakespeare, however, following the example of many contemporaries, took advantage of the possibilities for variety afforded by dialogue. The poem includes the long set speeches and significant digressions that had become associated with the complaint. The poetic style is the highly ornamented sort approved by sophisticated Elizabethan audiences.

The rhyme royal stanza may have been suggested by its traditional use in serious narrative or, more immediately, by Samuel Daniel's use of it in his popular *Complaint of Rosamond* (1592). Certainly *The Rape of Lucrece* shares with Daniel's poem the Elizabethan literary fascination with the distress of noble ladies. Despite the subject matter, the poem is not sensual, except in the lushness of its imagery. Even the passion of the rape scene is attenuated by a grotesquely extended description of Lucrece's breasts. The long, idealized description of the heroine is a rhetorical tour de force, not sexual stimulation. The theme of heroic chastity is always paramount, and readers are never distracted by action. Indeed, the prose "argument" that precedes the poem describes a story with enormous possibilities for action and adventure, but Shakespeare, consistent with his higher purpose, chooses to focus, reflectively and analytically, on the moral and psychological issues. Although the result is sometimes boring, there are occasional signs of Shakespeare's dramatic ability, especially in the exchanges before the rape.

The characters are static and stylized, but the revelation of the characters is skillfully done. As Tarquin's lust wrestles with his conscience, he is portrayed in an agony of indecision. The main medium of his internal conflict is the conventional theme of the antagonism of passion and reason. This section is a compendium of reflections on and rationalizations for the destructive power of lust. Tarquin thinks in terms of conventional images, but the contrasts and antitheses, as he is tossed back and forth between commonplaces, effectively represent his inner struggle. When he gives in, it is more a tribute to the potency of lust than a delineation or indictment of his character. When Lucrece appeals to the very concerns that have bedeviled Tarquin, there is a dramatic poignancy that most of the rest of the poem lacks. After the rape, the change in Tarquin's thoughts from lust to guilt and shame is striking.

Lucrece's complaint is also wholly conventional in substance, but contrast and antithesis again give a vitality to her grief as she rationalizes her suicide as not the destruction of her soul but the only way to restore her honor. The imagistic alternations from day to night, clear to cloudy, reflect her anguish and the difficulty of her decision.

The poem's structure suggests that the exploration and decoration of conventional themes concerning lust and honor are the main intent. *The Rape of Lucrece* centers on the mental states and moral attitudes of the characters immediately before and after the crucial action. The rape is a premise for the reflections, the suicide a logical result. The set speeches are reinforced by free authorial moralizing. Significant digressions, like the long physical description of Lucrece and her extended apostrophe to Opportunity, further elaborate the main themes. The longest and most effective digression is Lucrece's contemplation of the Troy painting. The opportunities for finding correlatives are fully exploited. The city of Troy is apt, because it has been brought to destruction by a rape, and Paris is the perfect example of the selfishness of lust. Sinon, whose honest exterior belies his treachery, reminds Lucrece of the contrast between appearance and reality, nobility and baseness, that she had noted in Tarquin. The whole digression, which repeats by means of allusion, is ornamental rather than explanatory.

The severe paring of the plot further reveals Shakespeare's main concern. Collatine, the offended husband, appears only briefly, suffers silently, and does not even personally initiate the revenge; he does not intrude on the crucial issues. The bloodthirstiness of Lucrece's plea for revenge is another sign that elucidation of character is unimportant compared to the beautiful expression of moral imperatives. The revenge itself is, mysteriously, instigated by Brutus (an action that makes more sense in other versions of the tale) and is carried out perfunctorily in a few closing lines, because it is secondary to the themes of the poem.

Regardless of its moral earnestness and occasional tedium, *The Rape of Lucrece* is gorgeously ornamented with figures of speech, especially alliteration and assonance, and with figures of thought that please more for their brilliance of execution than their depth of conception. *The Rape of Lucrece* is, like *Venus and Adonis*, a rhetorical showpiece.

"Critical Evaluation" by Edward E. Foster

Bibliography:
Bullough, Geoffrey. *Narrative and Dramatic Sources of Shakespeare*. Vol. 1. New York: Columbia University Press, 1957. Reprints the sources and analogues Shakespeare used, or may have used, in creating the poem; provides an intelligent introduction to how those sources pertain.
Donaldson, Ian. *The Rapes of Lucretia*. Oxford, England: Clarendon Press, 1982. Thorough study of the Lucretia story in Western art and literature. Describes how Shakespeare's version of the story redirects the meaning of the myth to apply to late sixteenth century English culture.
Kuhl, E. P. "Shakespeare's *Rape of Lucrece*." *Philological Quarterly* 20, no. 3 (July, 1941): 352-360. A seminal article interpreting the poem as a political narrative to warn Shakespeare's patron, the Earl of Southampton, of the dangers of abusing power.
Prince, F. T., ed. Introduction to *The Poems*, by William Shakespeare. New York: Methuen, 1960. Classic introduction to the poem and its background, sources, and text. Although sometimes uncritical by contemporary standards, it remains a good starting point for study of the poem, especially for Prince's appreciation of the poem as poetry.
Stimpson, Catharine. "Shakespeare and the Soil of Rape." In *The Woman's Part: Feminist Criticism of Shakespeare*, edited by Carolyn Ruth Swift-Lenz, Gayle Greene, and Carol Thomas Nealy. Champaign: University of Illinois Press, 1980. Excellent introduction to feminist responses to the poem. Examines Lucrece's position in the patriarchy.

THE RAPE OF THE LOCK

Type of work: Poetry
Author: Alexander Pope (1688-1744)
Type of plot: Mock-heroic
Time of plot: Early eighteenth century
Locale: London
First published: 1712

> *Principal characters:*
> BELINDA, Miss Arabella Fermor
> LORD PETRE, Belinda's suitor
> THALESTRIS, Belinda's friend
> ARIEL, a sprite
> UMBRIEL, a gnome

The Story:

At noon, when the sun was accustomed to awaken both lap dogs and lovers, Belinda was still asleep. She dreamed that Ariel appeared to whisper praises of her beauty in her ear. He said that he had been sent to protect her because something dreadful—what, he did not know—was about to befall her. He also warned her to beware of jealousy, pride, and, above all, men.

After Ariel had vanished, Shock, Belinda's lap dog, thought that his mistress had slept long enough, and he awakened her by lappings of his tongue. Rousing herself, Belinda spied a letter on her bed. After she had read it, she promptly forgot everything that Ariel had told her, including the warning to beware of men.

Belinda, aided by her maid, Betty, began to make her toilet. Preening before her mirror, she was guilty of the pride against which Ariel had cautioned her.

The sun, journeying across the sky, witnessed its brilliant rival, Belinda, boating on the Thames with her friends and suitors. All eyes were upon her, and like the true coquette she smiled at her swains but favored no one more than another. Lord Petre, one of Belinda's suitors, admired a lock of her hair and vowed that he would have it by fair means or foul. So set was he on getting the lock that, before the sun rose that morning, he had built an altar to Love and had thrown on it all the trophies received from former sweethearts, meanwhile asking Love to give him soon the prize he wanted and to let him keep it for a long time. Love, however, granted him only half his prayer.

Everyone except Ariel seemed happy during the cruise on the Thames. That sprite summoned his aides, and reminded them that their duty was to watch over the fair Belinda, one sylph to guard her fan, another her watch, a third her favorite lock. Ariel himself was to guard Belinda's lap dog, Shock. Fifty sylphs were dispatched to watch over the maiden's petticoat, in order to protect her chastity. Any negligent sylphs, warned Ariel, would be punished severely.

After her cruise on the Thames, Belinda, accompanied by Lord Petre and the rest of the party, visited one of the palaces near London. There Belinda decided to play ombre, a Spanish card game, with two of her suitors, including Lord Petre. As she played, invisible sylphs sat on her important cards to protect them.

Coffee was served after the game. Sylphs guarded Belinda's dress to keep it from becoming spotted. The fumes from the coffee sharpened Lord Petre's wits to the point where he thought of new stratagems for stealing Belinda's lock. One of his cronies handed him a pair of scissors. The sylphs, aware of Belinda's danger, attempted to warn her before Lord Petre could act, but as the maid bent her head over her coffee cup he clipped the lock. Even Ariel was unable to warn Belinda in time.

At the rape of her lock, Belinda shrieked in horror. Lord Petre cried out in triumph. He praised the steel used in the scissors, comparing it with the metal of Greek swords that overcame the Trojans. Belinda's fury was as tempestuous as the rage of scornful virgins who have lost their charms. Ariel wept bitterly and flew away.

Umbriel, a melancholy gnome, took advantage of the human confusion and despair to fly down to the center of the earth to find the gloomy cave of Spleen, the queen of all bad tempers and the source of every detestable quality in human beings, including ill-nature and affectation. Umbriel asked the queen to touch Belinda with chagrin, for he knew that, if she were gloomy, melancholy and bad temper would spread to half the world. Spleen granted Umbriel's request and collected in a bag horrible noises such as those uttered by female lungs and tongues. In a vial she put tears, sorrows, and griefs. She gave both containers to Umbriel.

When the gnome returned to Belinda's world, he found the girl disheveled and dejected. Pouring the contents of the magic bag over her, Umbriel caused Belinda's wrath to be magnified many times. One of her friends, Thalestris, fanned the flames of the maiden's anger by telling her that her honor was at stake and that behind her back her friends were talking about the rape of her lock. Thalestris then went to her brother, Sir Plume, and demanded that he confront Lord Petre and secure the return of the precious lock. Sir Plume considered the whole episode much magnified from little, but he went to demand Belinda's lock. Lord Petre refused to give up his prize.

Next Umbriel broke the vial containing human sorrows, and Belinda was almost drowned in tears. She regretted the day that she ever entered society and also the day she learned to play ombre. She longed for simple country life. Suddenly she remembered, too late, that Ariel had warned her of impending evil.

In spite of Thalestris' pleas, Lord Petre was still adamant. Clarissa, another of Belinda's circle, wondered at the vanity of women and at the foolishness of men who fawn before them. Clarissa felt that both men and women need good sense, but in making her feelings known she exposed the tricks and deceits of women and caused Belinda to frown. Calling Clarissa a prude, Thalestris gathered her forces to battle with Belinda's enemies, including Clarissa and Lord Petre. Umbriel was delighted by this Homeric struggle of the teacups. Belinda pounced upon Lord Petre, who was subdued when a pinch of snuff caused him to sneeze violently. She demanded the lock, but it could not be found. Some thought that it had gone to the moon, where also go love letters and other tokens of tender passions. The muse of poetry saw it ascend to heaven and become a star.

Critical Evaluation:

The Rape of the Lock, generally considered the most popular of Alexander Pope's writings as well as the finest satirical poem in the English language, was written at the suggestion of John Caryll, Pope's friend, ostensibly to heal a family row which resulted when an acquaintance of Pope, Lord Petre, playfully clipped a lock of hair from the head of Miss Arabella Fermor. Pope's larger purpose in writing the poem, however, was to ridicule the social vanity of his day and the importance that was attached to trifles.

When Robert Lord Petre cut off a lock of Arabella Fermor's hair one fateful day early in the eighteenth century, he did not know that the deed would gain fame, attracting attention over several centuries. Nor did he perhaps foresee the ill feeling his act would create between the Petre and Fermor families. The story would probably have been soon lost among the trivia of family histories, had not John Caryll asked his good friend the poet Alexander Pope to write a little poem about the episode, one which would show the comic element of the family quarrel and thus help heal it.

What began as a trivial event in history, turns, under the masterly guidance of Pope's literary hand, into one of the most famous poems in the English language, and perhaps the most perfect example of burlesque in English. *The Rape of the Lock* was begun at Caryll's behest ("This verse, to Caryll, Muse! is due") in 1711; Pope spent about two weeks on it and produced a much shorter version than the one he wrote two years later; adding more additions in 1717, he then developed the final draft of the poem as it now stands.

The poem uses the essentially trivial story of the stolen lock of hair as a vehicle for making some thoroughly mature and sophisticated comments on society and on women and men. Pope draws on his own classical background—he had translated the *Iliad* (c. 800 B.C.E.) and the *Odyssey* (c. 800 B.C.E.)—to combine epic literary conventions with his own keen, ironic sense of the values and societal structures shaping his age. The entire poem, divided into five cantos, is written in heroic couplets (pairs of rhymed iambic pentameter lines). Pope makes the most of this popular eighteenth century verse form, filling each line with balance, antithesis, bathos, allusions to serious epic poetry, and puns.

The literary genre of burlesque typically takes trivial subjects and elevates them to seemingly great importance; the effect is comic, and Pope manages an unbroken sense of amusement as he relates "What dire offense from amorous causes springs,/ What mighty contests rise from trivial things."

From the opening lines of the poem, suggestions of the epic tradition are clear. Pope knew well not only the *Iliad* and the *Odyssey*, but also John Milton's *Paradise Lost* (1667). The narrator of *The Rape of the Lock* speaks like Homer, raising the epic question early in the poem: "Say what strange motive, goddess! could compel/ A well-bred lord t' assault a gentle belle?" Pope's elaborate description of Belinda's toilet in canto 1 furthers comparison with the epic; it parodies the traditional epic passage describing warrior shields. Belinda's make-up routine is compared to the putting on of armor: "From each she nicely culls with curious toil,/ And decks the goddess with the glittering spoil."

The effect of using epic conventions is humorous, but it also helps establish a double set of values in the poem, making the world of Belinda and Sir Plume at the same time trivial and significant. The poem rewards a reading that focuses on the seriousness of Belinda's activities and experience. The truth is, for a woman of her place and time, the rape of the lock was a serious matter. Epic conventions contribute to this double sense in each canto. The first canto is the epic dedication and invocation. The second is the conference of protective gods. The third details the games and the banquet. The fourth tells of the descent into the underworld. The fifth tells of heroic encounters and apotheosis. The overall result is that, although readers are presented with a basically silly situation, they have characters such as Clarissa who utter the always sensible virtues of the eighteenth century:

> Oh! if to dance all night, and dress all day,
> Charmed the smallpox, or chased old age away;
> Who would not scorn what housewife's cares produce,
> Or who would learn one earthly thing of use? . . .
> But since, alas, frail beauty must decay. . . .
> And she who scorns a man, must die a maid;
> What then remains but well our power to use,
> And keep good humor still what'er we lose?

Clarissa, in these lines from canto 5, expresses the norm of Pope's satire: the intelligent use of reason to control one's temperamental passions.

The heroic couplet merges perfectly with the epic devices in the poem, for as a verse form the heroic couplet naturally seems to express larger-than-life situations. It is, therefore, profoundly to Pope's credit that he successfully applies such a verse form to a subject which is anything but larger than life.

Pope, perhaps more than anyone else writing poetry in the eighteenth century, demonstrates the flexibility of the heroic couplet. Shaped by his pen, it contains pithy aphorisms, social commentary, challenging puns, and delightful bathos. (The last of these juxtaposes the serious with the small, as in the line, "wrapped in a gown for sickness and for show"). The key, if there is a key, to the classic popularity of *The Rape of the Lock* is the use of the heroic couplet to include—sometimes in great cataloged lists—those little, precise, and most revealing details about the age and the characters that peopled it. The opening lines of canto 3 illustrate Pope's expert use of detail. The passage describes court life at Hampton Court, outside London, and is a shrewd comment on the superficiality of the people there:

> Hither the heroes and the nymphs resort,
> To taste awhile the pleasures of a court;
> In various talks th' instructive hours they passed,
> Who gave the ball, or paid the visit last;
> One speaks the glory of the British queen,
> And one describes a charming Indian screen;
> A third interprets motions, looks, and eyes;
> At every word a reputation dies.
> Snuff, or the fan, supply each pause of chat,
> With singing, laughing, ogling, and all that.

The poet's criticism of such life is clear by the swift juxtaposition of Hampton Court life with a less pretty reality in the following lines:

> Meanwhile, declining from the noon of day,
> The sun obliquely shoots his burning ray;
> The hungry judges soon the sentence sign,
> And wretches hang that jurymen may dine.

Though always its critic, Pope held a keen interest in the life of London's aristocracy. A Catholic by birth, he was not always in favor with the Crown, but before the queen's death in 1714, he enjoyed meeting with a group of influential Tories. Sir Richard Steele and Joseph Addison, England's first newspaper editors, courted him on behalf of the Whig party, but he refused to become its advocate.

Forbidden by law from living within several miles of London, he lived much of his adult life at Twickenham, a village on the Thames not too far from London but far enough. He transformed his dwelling there into an eighteenth century symbol, with gardening and landscaping; he included vineyards, and the house had a temple and an obelisk to his mother's memory. During the 1720's he built his grotto, an underpass connecting his property under a dividing road; it was a conversation piece, with, according to one contemporary, bits of mirror on the walls which reflected "all objects of the river, hills, woods, and boats, forming a moving picture in their visible radiations." For Pope, four feet, six inches tall and sick all his life, it was a symbol of the philosophic life and mind. Although he never married, his biographers tell us he felt a warm, if not always happy, affection for Martha and Teresa Blount, neighbors during his youth. Pope enjoyed great literary fame even during his lifetime, and near the end of his life, when he entered a room, whispers of "Mr. Pope, Mr. Pope," would buzz among the occupants.

"Critical Evaluation" by Jean G. Marlowe

Bibliography:
Bloom, Harold, ed. *Alexander Pope's "The Rape of the Lock."* Edgemont, Pa.: Chelsea House, 1988. Contains eight articles that examine such topics as the poem's satirical intent, its social context, Pope's miniaturist tendencies, and the game of ombre. Includes a selected bibliography.

Clark, Donald B. *Alexander Pope.* New York: Twayne, 1967. Provides in-depth studies of several individual poems, including *The Rape of the Lock.* Includes pertinent historical, biographical, and philosophical information.

Grove, Robin. "Uniting Airy Substances: *The Rape of the Lock* 1712-1736." In *The Art of Alexander Pope,* edited by Howard Erskine-Hill and Anne Smith. New York: Barnes & Noble Books, 1979. Focuses on Pope's revisions of "The Rape of the Lock." Provides many useful observations pertaining to Pope's aesthetic values.

Pollak, Ellen. "Rereading *The Rape of the Lock:* Pope and the Paradox of Female Power." *Studies in Eighteenth-Century Culture* 10 (1981): 429-444. Reads the poem from a feminist perspective. Argues convincingly that the poem is an allegory of the social and sexual initiation of a woman.

Wimsatt, William K., Jr. "The Game of Ombre in *The Rape of the Lock.*" *Review of English Studies,* new series 1 (1950): 136-143. Discusses in great detail the poem's most dominant image. Wimsatt also concludes that Pope manipulated the rules of ombre to suit his purposes.

RASSELAS

Type of work: Novel
Author: Samuel Johnson (1709-1784)
Type of plot: Philosophical
Time of plot: Eighteenth century
Locale: Abyssinia and Cairo
First published: The Prince of Abissinia: A Tale, 1759

> *Principal characters:*
> RASSELAS, Prince of Abyssinia
> NEKAYAH, his sister
> PEKUAH, her maid
> IMLAC, a poet

The Story:

It was the custom in Abyssinia for the sons and daughters of the emperor to be confined in a remote place until the order of succession to the throne was established. The spot in which Rasselas and his brothers and sisters were confined was a beautiful and fertile valley situated between high mountains. Everything needed for a luxurious life was present in the valley. Entertainers were brought in from the outside world to help the royal children pass the time pleasantly. These entertainers were never allowed to leave, for the outside world was not to know how the royal children lived before they were called on to rule.

It was this perfection that caused Rasselas, in the twenty-sixth year of his life, to become melancholy and discontented. He was unhappy because he had everything to make him happy; he wanted more than anything else to desire something that could not be made available to him. When he talked of his longing with an old philosopher, he was told that he was foolish. The old man told him of the misery and suffering of the people outside the valley and cautioned him to be glad of his present situation. Rasselas, however, knew that he could not be content until he had seen the suffering of the world.

For many months, Rasselas pondered on his desire to escape from the valley. He took no action, however, for the valley was carefully guarded and there was no chance for anyone to leave. Once he met an inventor who promised to make some wings for him so that he could fly over the mountains, but the experiment was a failure. In his search for a way to escape, his labor was more mental than physical.

In the palace, there was a poet, Imlac, whose lines pleased Rasselas by their intelligence. Imlac also was tired of the perfect life in the valley, for in the past he had traveled over much of the world. He had observed the evil ways of humankind and had learned that most wickedness stemmed from envy and jealousy. He had noticed that people envy others with more worldly goods and oppress those who are weak. As he talked, Rasselas longed more than ever to see the world and its misery. Imlac tried to discourage him, for he believed that Rasselas would long for his present state if he ever saw the violence and treachery that abounded in the lands beyond the mountains.

When Imlac realized he could not deter the prince, he agreed to join him in his attempt to leave the perfect state. Together the two men contrived to hew a path through the side of a mountain. When they were almost ready to leave, Rasselas saw his sister Nekayah watching them. She begged to accompany the travelers, for she also was bored with the valley and longed to see the rest of the world. She was Rasselas' favorite sister, so he gladly allowed her and her maid, Pekuah, to join them.

The four made their way safely through the path in the mountainside. They took enough jewels with them to supply them with money when they reached a city of trade. They were simply dressed, and no one recognized them as royalty. In Cairo, they sold some of their jewels and rented a magnificent dwelling. They entertained great people and began to learn the customs of people different from themselves. Their objective was to observe all possible manners and customs so that they could make their own choices about the kind of life each wanted to pursue; but they found many drawbacks to every form of living.

Rasselas and Nekayah believed that it was only necessary to find the right pursuit to know perfect happiness and contentment. Imlac knew that few people lived by choice, but rather by chance and the whims of fortune. Rasselas and Nekayah, however, believed that their chance birth had at least given them the advantage of being able to study all forms of living and thus to choose the one most suitable for them to pursue. So it was that the royal pair visited with persons of every station. They went into the courts and the fields. They visited sages of great fame and hermits who had isolated themselves to meditate. Nowhere did they find a person completely happy and satisfied; everyone desired what another had, and all thought their neighbors were more fortunate than they were.

Only once did Rasselas find a happy man: a philosopher who preached the doctrine of reason. He stated that by reason, a person can conquer passions and disappointments and thus find true happiness. When Rasselas called on the sage the following day, however, he found the old man in a fit of despair. His daughter had died in the night, and the reason that he had urged others to use failed completely on the occasion of the philosopher's own grief.

Imlac and Nekayah spent long hours discussing the advantages of one kind of life over another. They questioned the state of marriage as compared with celibacy, and life at court as compared with pastoral pleasures, but at no time could they find satisfactory solutions for their questions. Nowhere could they find people living in happiness. Imlac suggested a visit to the pyramids so that they might learn of people of the past. While they were in a tomb, Pekuah was stolen by Arabs, and it was many months before she was returned to Nekayah. Pekuah told her mistress that she had spent some time in a monastery while she waited for her ransom, and she believed that the nuns had found the one truly happy way of life.

Their search continued for a long period. Often they thought they had found a happy person, but always they found much sorrow in the life they thought so serene. After a visit to the catacombs and a discourse on the soul, Nekayah decided that she would cease looking for happiness on earth and live so that she might find happiness in eternity.

The Nile flooded the valley and confined them to their home for a time. The four friends discussed the ways of life that promised each the greatest happiness. Pekuah wished to retire to a convent; Nekayah desired knowledge more than anything and wanted to found a woman's college where she could both teach and learn; Rasselas thought he wanted a small kingdom where he could rule justly and wisely; Imlac said he would be content to drift through life, with no particular goal. All knew their desires would never be fulfilled, and they began to look forward to their return to the Abyssinian valley where everyone seemed happy and there was nothing to desire.

Critical Evaluation:

According to his own statement, Samuel Johnson wrote *Rasselas* in the evenings of one week in 1759 to defray the expenses of his mother's funeral. Nevertheless, one should not assume either that the tale was completely spontaneous or that its mood was entirely determined by his mother's illness and death. Johnson had very likely been considering the subject for some time. His translation of Father Lobo's *A Voyage to Abyssinia* in 1735, Johnson's use of an Asian setting in his early play *Irene* (1737), and his employment of the device of the Asian apologue in several *Rambler* papers (which he edited from 1750-1752) all pointed the way. Furthermore, *Rambler* papers numbers 204 and 205 suggested part of the theme of *Rasselas* in telling how Seged, Lord of Ethiopia, decided to be happy for ten days by an act of will, and how this quest for pleasure was in vain. Even closer in theme is Johnson's finest poem, *The Vanity of Human Wishes* (1749).

The mood of *Rasselas* may seem to be predominantly gloomy, involving, if not cynicism, at least a tragic view of life. Still, it is possible to see in it some of the qualities of an ironic satire. The manuscript title of the book, *The Choice of Life*, is a key both to its plan and to its philosophy. Human nature being what it is, Johnson indicates, happiness can be only illusory, accidental, and ephemeral, existing more in hope than in reality, and, in the end, always being nothing when compared with life's miseries. Those who seek for happiness through a choice of life are destined to end in failure. This reading of the story may seem simply pessimistic, but there is another aspect of it that recognizes the multifariousness of life, which resists and defeats facile theories about existence such as those of the young travelers in the novel. In this aspect there is opportunity for some comedy.

Johnson skillfully begins with the conventional conceit of a perfect bliss that exists in some earthly paradise. Rasselas, an Abyssinian prince, his sister, and two companions escape from what they have come to regard as the boredom of the perfect life in the Happy Valley to set out on a search for true happiness in the outside world. They try all kinds of life: pleasure-loving society, solitude, the pastoral life, life of high and middle estates, public and private life. Although Rasselas holds that happiness is surely to be found, they find it nowhere. The simple life of the country dweller so praised by Jean-Jacques Rousseau and his followers is full of discontent. People with wealth and power cannot be happy, because they fear the loss of both. The hermit, unable to answer the question about the advantages of solitude, returns to civilization. The philosopher who preaches the philosophic systems of happiness succumbs to grief over the death of his daughter. A philosopher who thinks one can achieve happiness by "living according to nature" cannot explain what this phrase means. The abduction of the maid Pekuah enables Rasselas' sister, Nekayah, to learn that one "who has no one to love or to trust has little to hope." Pekuah reports on her return that the female "happy valley" of the harem is boring, because the women talk of nothing but the tediousness of life.

In the final chapter, all the travelers decide on an ideal vocation. Nevertheless, says the narrator, "they well knew that none could be obtained." So they resolve to return to Abyssinia. Such a return is not necessarily a defeat. All have achieved a valuable education and have lost their insularity. As one contemporary critic has suggested, instead of ending in rationalistic despair, the four have learned to ask important questions: What activity is most appropriate to humankind? What can best satisfy each person and fulfill his or her destiny?

Voltaire's *Candide* and Johnson's *Rasselas* were published within two months of each other. Both attacked the fashionable optimism of their day. Candide begins in the best of all possible castles; Rasselas, in the Happy Valley. Each has a philosopher friend—Pangloss and Imlac. Each sets out to explore the world, although for different reasons. Each is disillusioned. In contrast, Voltaire's wit is brilliant, slashing, and iconoclastic, and is exerted on a tangible and vivid world. Johnson's is deliberate and speculative, balanced, measured, and conservative. His world is fanciful. If, like Sir Thomas More in his *Utopia* (1516), Johnson chose to set his story in a non-Christian part of the world, he did so because he wished to deal with humanity on a purely naturalistic level and discuss basic issues without involving religious considerations that were too specific to his time. Johnson does not allow his deeply religious nature, however, so unlike Voltaire's skepticism, to go entirely unperceived. One does not forget, for example, that after Imlac's discussion of the nature of the soul, Princess Nekayah is moved to insist that the choice of life is no longer so important as the choice of eternity.

To many readers, *Rasselas* has long seemed to be chiefly a series of essays, narrative and digressive, like those in the *Rambler*, loosely strung together with a narrative thread that could be described more nearly as plan than plot. Chapters such as "A Dissertation on the Art of Flying," "A Dissertation on Poetry," "A Disquisition upon Greatness," and "The Dangerous Prevalence of Imagination" can be lifted out of their context and almost stand independently as separate literary works. The characters are two-dimensional, and the dialogue is far from lifelike. In places, the style is so rhythmic and sonorous as to suggest poetry rather than prose. For these and other reasons, the right of the narrative to be called a novel has frequently been questioned.

More recent critics have suggested illuminating patterns in the structure of *Rasselas*. One useful suggestion is to regard the novel as having three sections or movements of sixteen chapters each, ending with a kind of coda. The first concerns the Happy Valley and the theme of the choice of life, centered on the restless prince and his determination to find happiness outside. The second section, in which the travelers make their comprehensive survey of humanity, is focused on Rasselas' experiments upon life and the discovery that no one fits his theory and possesses happiness. The section ends with Imlac's famous apostrophe to the pyramids. In the third section, the travelers, now no longer mere observers, find themselves actually involved in life as the victims of others. The chief incidents here are Pekuah's abduction and return, the encounter with the astronomer, the brief meeting with the disillusioned old man, the final visit to the catacombs, and the abandonment of the quest. To some critics, the coda, "A Conclusion in Which Nothing Is Concluded," is an aesthetic defect. In all fairness, however, it can probably be regarded as such only by those who would require Johnson to append more of a moral tag than he thought wise. The travelers' discoveries concerning life and the fallacy of their quest can be considered to have positive, rather than only negative, value and can be regarded as conclusion enough.

"Critical Evaluation" by Lodwick Hartley

Bibliography:

Burke, John J., Jr., and Donald Kay, eds. *The Unknown Samuel Johnson.* Madison: University of Wisconsin Press, 1983. Offers new interpretations of *Rasselas'* theme and meaning in light of Johnson's private life.

Curley, Thomas. "The Spiritual Journey Moralized in *Rasselas.*" *Anglia* 91 (1973): 35-55. Generally positive review, focusing on the moral overtones of Johnson's choice-of-life ideology as it relates to the circumstances and actions of the travelers in *Rasselas.*

Ehrenpreis, Irvin. "*Rasselas* and Some Meanings of 'Structure' in Literary Criticism." *Novel* 14, no. 2 (Winter, 1981): 101-117. A rather disparaging view of Johnson's artistic abilities, noting the shallowness of his characters and the inconsistencies within the structure of *Rasselas.*

Nath, Prem, ed. *Fresh Reflections on Samuel Johnson: Essays in Criticism.* Troy, N.Y.: Whitston, 1987. Contains a broad range of critical essays dealing with Johnson's writings, with particular emphasis on its artistic nature. Useful for its opposing interpretations of theme and meaning in *Rasselas*.

Wahba, Magdi, comp. *Bicentenary Essays on "Rasselas."* Cairo: Société Orientale de Publicité Press, 1959. Focuses on *Rasselas* as a positive message of hope and call from despair, offering a counterargument to the pessimistic interpretation in force since its publication in the eighteenth century.

THE RAZOR'S EDGE

Type of work: Novel
Author: W. Somerset Maugham (1874-1965)
Type of plot: Psychological realism
Time of plot: Early twentieth century
Locale: Chicago, Paris, and India
First published: 1944

> *Principal characters:*
> LARRY DARREL, restless former aviator
> ISABEL BRADLEY, his fiancée
> GRAY MATURIN, the man Isabel marries
> ELLIOTT TEMPLETON, snobbish expatriate
> SOPHIE MACDONALD, tragic victim of circumstances
> SOMERSET MAUGHAM, narrator of the story

The Story:

Larry Darrel, a World War I aviator who saw his best friend killed, did his best to adjust to postwar life as a businessman in Chicago, but just could not handle it. Everything seemed too superficial and materialistic to this young man, whose encounters with the horrors of war had awakened in him a deep desire to probe the mysteries of life. Determined to discover meaning in life and in himself, he dropped out of the Chicago business world of the 1920's and went to India, where he spent five years in meditation and study. Eventually, he felt pulled back to the world he had known previously, but instead of returning to the United States, he went to Europe. There he worked as a common laborer, sometimes on a farm, sometimes in a mine, all the while getting closer to discovering the deeper meaning of life.

In the meantime, his former fiancée, Isabel Bradley, tired of waiting for him and impatient with behavior she could not comprehend, married Gray Maturin, an outgoing fellow and successful Chicago businessman. When the stockmarket crashed in 1929, Gray lost everything, and he and Isabel fled to Paris, where they were able to live more frugally on a modest inheritance. Isabel had never stopped loving Larry, and when the two crossed paths in Paris, Isabel tried hard to get Larry to tell her just what had gone wrong. When he tried to explain his spiritual quest, she again did not understand and lost patience with him.

Two influential gentlemen figured importantly in the lives of Larry and Isabel. One was Elliott Templeton, a wealthy American who divided his time between Chicago and Paris, with regular visits to the French Riviera. Elliott was everything that Larry had come to disdain— selfish, snobbish, superficial. The other gentleman was the narrator, Somerset Maugham himself, a successful and widely-traveled author who was a close friend of all concerned. For example, he was present when Sophie MacDonald, the debutante turned tramp, showed up at a café where he was dining one evening with Larry, Isabel, and Gray.

Sophie had been happily married and the mother of two when her husband and children were killed in a car crash that only she survived. Unable to cope with the loss and the grief, Sophie had drifted to Paris, where she had become an alcoholic and a prostitute. Larry was terribly upset by her condition, and decided to do something about it. He got her to stop drinking and even proposed marriage to her. When Isabel heard this, she was jealous and planned to stop it. One day she invited Sophie to stop by her apartment. Sophie arrived to encounter a scene of domestic bliss—a bitter reminder of everything she had lost. Isabel excused herself to run the children to the dentist, promising to return shortly. She had left a bottle of what had once been Sophie's favorite liqueur in a conspicuous spot. The longer Sophie waited, the more agitated and depressed she became until finally she had one drink. It was not long before the bottle was empty, and when Isabel returned, Sophie was gone—for good. Eventually, her body was found washed ashore in Toulon, where she had returned to a life of alcohol, drugs, and sex.

Elliott Templeton died as he had lived, a snob. On his deathbed he fretted over not having received an invitation to a ball being given by a wealthy American "princess." When Maugham learned that Templeton was not on the guest list, he wangled an invitation and had it delivered. Templeton was delighted and relieved, and although he could not attend, he took great pleasure in sending his regrets, giving as his reason "a previous engagement with his Blessed Lord."

In Paris, Maugham had a long conversation with Isabel, during which she gave him a carefully edited version of the events of that fateful afternoon when Sophie had drunk the liqueur. Maugham accused her of lying, and when she became angered, he insisted that she had been responsible for Sophie's death. She then admitted the whole scheme, but remained unrepentant, claiming that at least she had spared Larry a miserable marriage. Maugham then took delight in telling her that Larry planned to return to the United States and work as a common laborer, whereupon Isabel burst into tears, crying, "Now I really have lost him."

In the end, Larry did return to the United States, vowing to take a job in a garage or become a taxi driver. He had no desire for fame and was without ambition, an attitude Maugham said he respected but could not entirely share.

Critical Evaluation:

Somerset Maugham took the title for this novel from a line in the *Katha-Upanishad* (c. 1000-c. 600 B.C.E.), an ancient book of Hindu wisdom: "The sharp edge of a razor is difficult to pass over: thus the wise say the path to Salvation is hard." In the late 1930's, Maugham traveled throughout India and spent considerable time in the presence of a renowned Indian sage and holy man called Bhagavan. One of Bhagavan's disciples, and the probable source for Larry Darrel, was an American sailor who was on a quest for spiritual enlightenment. Maugham frankly admitted that he himself was unable to find complete satisfaction in the life of the spirit. He so respected the attempt on the part of others to abjure materialism in favor of inner peace, however, that he wrote *The Razor's Edge* in an attempt to articulate to himself the essence of his ambition.

Maugham starts the novel with the disclaimer that he has serious misgivings about in what direction the novel will go or if, in fact, it will even turn out to be a novel. By the end he has produced a novel; it was always Maugham's chief virtue as a writer that he could not help turning experience into first-class fiction. Fortunately, by adhering to the traditional novel form, Maugham is able to preserve the distance necessary to allow the characters to reveal themselves fully and to permit readers the freedom to make up their own minds. A comparison of two central characters, Larry Darrel and Elliott Templeton, will serve to illustrate this point. Although these two men are worlds apart in character, they are presented with equal sympathy and objectivity. As a result, these opposites help unlock the mystery of each other's character. Templeton is vain and worldly, a hedonist and a snob who can only function in the right society and among expensive things. Darrel is selfless and otherworldly, a compassionate man who cares little for his own comfort or for the company of others, and he places no value on material things beyond necessity and function.

Maugham places himself somewhere between these two men and tries to remain impartial. On the one hand he finds Templeton's affectations charming and harmless and he appreciates

Templeton's sophisticated tastes. On the other hand, he has an abiding respect for Darrel's pursuit of satisfying answers to ultimate questions. He knows that Templeton is shallow because he has never felt the need to look below the surface of life. Darrel has had shattering wartime experiences that will not let him rest until he can penetrate their meaning and understand what life is about. In the end Maugham is quite frank about his own shortcomings on the spiritual side, for he admits that he is a product of Templeton's world and generation, not Darrel's.

The Razor's Edge was ahead of its time. It spoke more to the generation of the sixties than it did to that of the forties, when it was written, or to that of the twenties and thirties, when it takes place. Much of its success is owing to Maugham's "detached involvement." Maugham is a character and a participant in his own book, much in the style of the "new journalism" so popular in the 1960's. When Maugham wangles the invitation for Elliott Templeton, he is simply stepping in where he has to in order to give the reader the clearest example possible of Templeton's pretentiousness. Similarly, when he confronts Isabel about Sophie and the bottle of liqueur, he is clearly interfering in his own story, but only he can get away with calling her a liar and forcing her to confess because he is an outsider who has nothing to lose. Finally, when he identifies Sophie's body, he is the only one who is able to salvage any dignity from such a sordid tragedy. Maugham's participation in the story gives it the authenticity of a factual account.

Somerset Maugham is probably the most underrated author of the twentieth century. It is commonly admitted, even by those who admire him, that Maugham's main problem—other than the fact that he was too popular—was that he wrote too clearly. He is a born storyteller and a gentleman; he believes he owes the reader the best story he can tell in a manner most likely to please. A hundred pages into *The Razor's Edge*, Maugham begins a digression with the statement that in order to give the reader a moment's rest, he is starting upon a new section, but that he is only doing it for the reader's convenience. The preceding section had been a transcription of a conversation in which Larry had recounted his travels and revealed some of his most profound reflections. Realizing that the reader might need a respite from the weighty philosophizing, Maugham graciously interrupts the transcription at a point where he says a natural interruption occurred.

Maugham is one of the most frequently filmed writers, another strike against him in some quarters. *The Razor's Edge* was made into a highly successful film in 1946 and remade in 1984. Like all good novels, it can be read on several levels, ranging from a comedy of manners, to a social drama, to an intense search for religious revelation.

Thomas Whissen

Bibliography:
Brunauer, Dalma. "The Road Not Taken: Fragmentation as a Device for Self-Concealment in *The Razor's Edge*." *Journal of Evolutionary Psychology* 8, nos. 1-2 (March, 1987): 24-33. An original and penetrating insight into the psychology of spirituality in the novel.
Connolly, Cyril. "The Art of Being Good." In *The Condemned Playground—Essays: 1927-1944*. London: Routledge & Kegan Paul, 1945. Maugham is praised for his handling of major characters, especially his sensitive portrayal of Larry Darrel, and for his determination to use his narrative talents in the service of truth.
Cordell, Richard A. *Somerset Maugham: A Biographical and Critical Study*. Bloomington: Indiana University Press, 1969. Includes a judicious commentary on *The Razor's Edge* as a novel worthy of the interest of a discriminating reader.

Hawkinson, Kenneth Steven. *Three Novels by W. Somerset Maugham: An Analysis Based on the Rhetoric of Wayne C. Booth*. Dissertation Abstracts International 47, no. 7 (January, 1987): 2370A. Provocative analysis of *The Razor's Edge* according to Booth's critical theories as outlined in his highly regarded *Rhetoric of Fiction*.

Morgan, Ted. *Maugham: A Biography*. New York: Simon & Schuster, 1980. A good, gossipy biography with illuminating details about the background of *The Razor's Edge*.

Weeks, Edward. "The Atlantic Bookshelf." *Atlantic Monthly* 173 (May, 1944): 123-129. One of the few contemporary reviews to see *The Razor's Edge* as ahead of its time. Discusses the tension between "the urgent quest of youth and the cynical retreat of age."

THE REAL LIFE OF SEBASTIAN KNIGHT

Type of work: Novel
Author: Vladimir Nabokov (1899-1977)
Type of plot: Parody
Time of plot: Early twentieth century
Locale: Russia, England, and France
First published: 1941

> *Principal characters:*
> V., the narrator of the story and biographer of Sebastian Knight
> SEBASTIAN KNIGHT, V.'s half brother

The Story:

V. wanted to write a biography of his deceased half brother, Sebastian Knight. Writing the book was V.'s act of homage, or commemoration, for whom he believed to be an unjustly forgotten novelist. V. had a rival, a Mr. Goodman, who had previously written a biography of Sebastian Knight. V. objected to Mr. Goodman's book on the grounds that it was false, insensitive, and full of clichés in its portrayal of Sebastian and his unique genius. The true reason for V.'s disgust with Goodman's biography, however, slowly emerged: jealousy. Goodman had written a book before V. wrote his book, and Goodman had experienced what V. never had: four years of close contact with Sebastian. Goodman's book was commercially successful, and some of Sebastian's manuscripts had been left with him—which resulted in a lawsuit.

When V.'s attempts to gather information from several of Sebastian's friends and acquaintances proved unsuccessful, he, like Goodman, turned to Sebastian's novels for information. In his first novel, as a protest against the conventionality of second-rate authors, Sebastian had written a parody of a detective novel titled *The Prismatic Bezel*. The secret of Sebastian's success with this novel was his use of formal innovation, and V. assimilated some of his half brother's techniques in his own biography of Sebastian. The heroes of Sebastian's detective novel were called "methods of composition" because Sebastian sought to convey a way of seeing a personality rather than the essence of a personality.

In his examination of Sebastian's next book, *Success*, V. noted that Sebastian elevated chance and coincidence into mystical, significant forces. The most significant element in *Success*, however, was the conjuror, who figured prominently in the work. This character made an appearance in V.'s life in the form of a man called Mr. Silbermann, whom V. met on a train. In V.'s search for a mysterious woman whom Sebastian had pursued just before he died, V. needed to obtain a list of the women who had stayed at the resort hotel that Sebastian had visited the summer he met the woman. Silbermann expressed his sorrow for Sebastian's death, and he agreed to help V.; he produced the list, but he advised V. that the pursuit of the woman was pointless.

The rest of Vladimir Nabokov's novel consisted of a series of hints and guesses about various identities and suggestions about various possibilities that the reader might entertain; one possibility, for example, might be that V. would successfully find his way through the maze of clues that obscured the identity of the woman Sebastian loved; another possibility might be that Sebastian's spirit would assist his half brother by easing V. into the evanescent world of a novelist's imaginings; and yet another possibility might be that V.'s obsession with his half brother would lead him into a nightmare world in which his goal receded even as he seemed to be drawing nearer. Another possibility was that the whole book might be a fictitious biography invented by Sebastian himself and populated by characters from all of his novels.

The main point of this exercise in the attempted re-creation of another's life later became clear. At the point at which Sebastian's last novel ended, V. said that he felt as if he and his half brother were on the brink of some absolute truth—that Sebastian knew the "real truth" about death, and he was going to reveal it. The conclusion of Sebastian's novel anticipated the conclusion of V.'s biography; Sebastian announced that he had been granted a great truth. He had discovered the arbitrariness of the personality, and he had conceived the book as the means by which this arbitrariness could best be conveyed. In Nabokov's novel, this moment of revelation was anticipated by a mock death scene in which V. rushed to the bedside of his dying half brother and listened from an adjoining room to the rhythm of Sebastian's breathing. The truth his brother was about to impart suddenly vanished, and all that remained was the simpler truth, the human emotion of the love V. felt for him.

This profound rush of emotion turned out to be a ploy designed to trick those who, like V., were prone to sentimentality. When he left the room, V. learned that he had in fact, been visiting someone else and that Sebastian had died the night before. Life had played another joke on him.

V. then announced that he was Sebastian Knight, and Nabokov's novel concluded with a vision of all the characters from Sebastian's life around him on a lighted stage. He was impersonating his half brother, and his act of sympathetic identification reached a type of completion. These were not the closing remarks of the real Sebastian, who had all the while been pretending to be a nonexistent person. What V. did in the process of researching his biography was to shape his own understanding of his subject; he located that understanding on the edge of the ineffable. Unable to discover the contiguous, linear, horizontal narrative he sought, he told the story of his frustration, and in doing so created the circular, vertical account that ended, not by announcing a truth, but by imparting an imaginative one.

Critical Evaluation:

In his works, Vladimir Nabokov explores the origins of creativity, the relationship of the artist to his work, and the nature of invented reality. A brilliant and controversial prose stylist, Nabokov entertains, inspires, and shocks his readers with his love of intellectual and verbal games. His technical genius, as well as the exuberance of his creative imagination, mark him as a major twentieth century author.

The Real Life of Sebastian Knight is about the complications that ensue when V. tries to sort out the details of the life of a person he hardly knew. The book reveals the complexities involved in any attempt to present a self in language—Nabokov's chief subject in the novel. By focusing on the conflation of life and art, by designing the reader's quest to mimic the narrator's, Nabokov foregrounds the issues involved in making fiction.

Sebastian Knight's "real life" is elusive; that is, the conventional means of reconstructing his life and writing his biography—interviewing friends and acquaintances, tracking down differ-ent accounts of relationships, and examining letters and documents—only lead to a series of comic dead ends in Nabokov's novel. Not only do fictional characters pop into existence out of nowhere, thereby disorienting the reader, but Nabokov further confuses readers by forcing them to ask continually, "Who is speaking?"

A major theme of Nabokov's novel is the theoretical and practical possibility of biography. V.'s warning to the reader to remember that what is told is shaped by the teller, reshaped by the listener, and concealed from both by the dead man of the tale, suggests that Nabokov's conception of the relationship between a life and a biography is complex.

Nabokov's novel is a detective story and a quest for self knowledge. The title itself points in both these directions, and the clues that accumulate as the novel progresses lead the reader toward the identity of a man who has been re-created through the process of observing himself reflected in a mirror. This mirror is actually many mirrors, since the narrator gets many glimpses of the identity of Sebastian Knight, and of himself, from a variety of sources. In this respect, the characters of Nabokov's novel are similar to the characters in one of Sebastian's novels, *The Prismatic Bezel*. In *The Real Life of Sebastian Knight*, what the characters compose is Sebastian Knight's real life; the reader's and the narrator's sense of that life depends in part on the accumulation of scattered bits of information and impressions which the characters impart. Sebastian's life is, quite literally, composed, just as a painting or a musical composition is composed.

The image created, then, is not the person but, instead, others' idea of him, and that idea is always misleading because it is, of necessity, incomplete and external. Nabokov makes this a fundamental idea on which he bases the structure of his novel. Sebastian Knight has no real life apart from the people who compose him, and to pay attention to the conceptions other people have of him is, in the end, to pay attention to Sebastian himself. In short, Nabokov seems to turn the fragmentary nature of perception into the very source of self-knowledge.

The source of the real life of Sebastian Knight is his work, yet this work is a mask he wears over his own face. Anyone who tries to reconstruct the real life of this man, therefore, is doomed from the beginning to reconstruct the life of his mask, his imaginative life. Both men who attempt to accomplish this biographical reconstruction wear masks; what they write down will also be the life of a veil over reality, rather than reality itself. What the reader perceives, then, at the end of Nabokov's novel is a composition that is at least twice removed from the facts; there is Sebastian; there is Sebastian with his mask on; and there is Sebastian's biographer with a mask on.

Readers are obliged to interpret Nabokov's novel on various levels simultaneously. At no time can they be certain which dimension has the familiar and comfortable solidarity of what is considered factual reality. The game consists chiefly in keeping alert enough to follow the shifting perceptions that characterize this kind of fiction; the danger is believing that one has found the "reality" promised by the narrator.

Like Sebastian himself, Nabokov uses the novel as a game, as a springboard to higher regions of intellectual activity. His purpose is to jar readers out of habitual modes of response to the world and lead them back into it with a fresh vision. Nabokov's primary concern is the reality of the imagination—that is, that reality cannot be conceived of as existing apart from the imagination. The act of perception involves both perceiver and perceived, and the knowledge gained from perception is a combination of the "facts"—the thing perceived—and the imagination, the frame of the mind of the perceiver. It is impossible to know anything as it is in itself; what people know is the idea of the thing itself. In this respect, everything wears a mask, and the very act of knowing is the act of being deceived. The narrator of Nabokov's novel says that he is Sebastian Knight, and yet this is to admit that he is a man whom he cannot know, except as he projects imaginative ideas of the individual. Self-knowledge is a curse when it is viewed in this way, and it is a kind of death. The narrative calls into question the nature of reality. Only illusion—only what one creates out of one's own imagination—seems to be real. Nabokov's novel, *The Real Life of Sebastian Knight*, ends with the sentence: "I am Sebastian, or Sebastian is I, or perhaps we both are someone whom neither of us knows."

Genevieve Slomski

Bibliography:

Alexandrov, Vladimir E. *Nabokov's Otherworld*. Princeton, N.J.: Princeton University Press, 1991. Dismantles the widespread critical view that Nabokov is first and foremost a metaliterary writer. Suggests, instead, that an aesthetic rooted in his intuition of a transcendent realm is the basis of his art.

Hyde, G. M. *Vladimir Nabokov: America's Russian Novelist*. London: Marion Boyars, 1977. Discusses Nabokov's novels as parodies of realism and parodies of themselves. The novels reveal the author's continuity with classic Russian literature, and they reevaluate that tradition.

Maddox, Lucy. *Nabokov's Novels in English*. Athens: University of Georgia Press, 1983. Thorough investigation of narrative structure, characterization, and theme in Nabokov's novels.

Rampton, David. *Vladimir Nabokov*. New York: St. Martin's Press, 1993. Insightful analysis of Nabokov's fiction. Discusses formal innovation, as well as theme and characterization. Includes bibliography of primary and secondary works.

Roth, Phyllis, comp. *Critical Essays on Vladimir Nabokov*. Boston: G. K. Hall, 1984. Excellent collection of essays on the play of language in Nabokov's works. Discusses the relationship between the life and art of Nabokov. Includes annotated bibliography.

REBECCA

Type of work: Novel
Author: Daphne du Maurier (1907-1989)
Type of plot: Gothic
Time of plot: 1930's
Locale: England
First published: 1938

> *Principal characters:*
> MAXIM DE WINTER, the owner of Manderley
> MRS. DE WINTER, Maxim's wife and the narrator
> MRS. DANVERS, the housekeeper at Manderley
> FRANK CRAWLEY, the estate manager of Manderley
> JACK FAVELL, Rebecca's cousin
> COLONEL JULYAN, a magistrate

The Story:

Manderley was gone. Since the fire had destroyed their home, Mr. and Mrs. de Winter had lived in a secluded hotel away from England. Occasionally, Mrs. de Winter recalled the circumstances that had brought Manderley and Maxim de Winter into her life.

A shy, sensitive orphan, she had been traveling about the Continent as companion to an overbearing American social climber, Mrs. Van Hopper. At Monte Carlo, Mrs. Van Hopper forced herself upon Maxim de Winter, owner of Manderley, one of the most famous estates in England. Before approaching him, Mrs. Van Hopper had informed her companion that Mr. de Winter was recovering from the shock of the tragic death of his wife, Rebecca, a few months previously.

During the following days, the young woman and Mr. de Winter became well acquainted; when Mrs. Van Hopper decided to return to America, Maxim de Winter unexpectedly proposed to her companion. Already deeply in love with him, the young woman accepted, and they were married shortly afterward.

After a long honeymoon in Italy and southern France, Mr. and Mrs. de Winter returned to Manderley. Mrs. de Winter was extremely nervous, fearing that she would not fit into the life of a great estate like Manderley. The entire staff had gathered to meet the new mistress. Mrs. Danvers, the housekeeper, had been devoted to her former mistress and immediately began to show her resentment toward the new Mrs. de Winter.

Gradually, Mrs. de Winter pieced together the story of Rebecca. She learned that Rebecca had been a beautiful, vivacious woman and a charming hostess. As Mrs. de Winter became acquainted with the relatives and friends of her husband, she became convinced that they found her lacking in those qualities that had made Rebecca so attractive and gracious. One day, she went secretly to the closed rooms Rebecca had occupied. Everything was as Rebecca had left it before her fatal sail in her boat. Mrs. Danvers suddenly appeared and forced her to view Rebecca's lovely clothes and other personal possessions.

When the bishop's wife suggested that the traditional Manderley fancy dress ball be revived, Mr. de Winter gave his consent. Mrs. de Winter announced her intention of surprising them all with her costume. At Mrs. Danvers' suggestion, she planned to dress as an ancestress whose portrait hung in the hall at Manderley; but as Mrs. de Winter descended the stairs that night, a silence fell over the guests, and her husband turned angrily away without speaking. Realizing that something was wrong, Mrs. de Winter returned to her room. Beatrice, Mr. de Winter's sister, went to her immediately and explained that Rebecca had worn the identical costume to her last fancy dress ball. Again, Mrs. Danvers had humiliated her new mistress. Although Mrs. de Winter reappeared at the ball in a simple dress, her husband did not speak to her all evening. Her belief that he had never ceased to love Rebecca became firmly established in her mind. The next day, a steamer ran aground in the bay near Manderley. A diver was sent down to inspect the damaged steamer and discovered Rebecca's boat and in its cabin the remains of a human body. Mr. de Winter had previously identified the body of a woman found in the river as that of Rebecca.

Unable to keep silent any longer, Mr. de Winter told his wife the whole story of Rebecca and her death. The world had believed their marriage a happy one, but Rebecca had been an immoral woman, incapable of love. To avoid the scandal of a divorce, they made a bargain: Rebecca was to be outwardly the fitting mistress of Manderley, but she would be allowed to go to London periodically to visit her dissolute friends. All went well until she began to be careless, inviting her friends to Manderley and receiving them in the boathouse. Then she began to plague Frank Crawley, the estate manager of Manderley, and Giles, Mr. de Winter's brother-in-law. After Frank and others had seen Rebecca's cousin, Jack Favell, at the boathouse with her, there had been gossip. One evening, Mr. de Winter had followed her to the boathouse to tell her that their marriage was at an end. Rebecca taunted him; she suggested how difficult it would be to prove his case against her and asserted that should she have a child it would bear his name and inherit Manderley. She assured him with a smile that she would be the perfect mother as she had been the perfect wife. She was still smiling when he shot her. Then he put her in the boat and sailed out on the river. There he opened the seacocks, drilled holes with a pike, and leaving the boat to sink, rowed back in the dinghy.

Mrs. de Winter was horrified, but at the same time, she felt a happiness she had not known before. Her husband loved her; he had never loved Rebecca. With that discovery, her personality changed. She assured her husband that she would guard his secret.

A coroner's inquest was held, for the body in the boat was that of Rebecca. At the inquest, it was established that a storm could not have sunk the boat; evidence of a bolted door, the holes, and the open seacocks pointed to the verdict of suicide which the coroner's jury returned.

That night Jack Favell, drunk, appeared at Manderley. Wildly expressing his love for Rebecca and revealing their intimate life, he tried to blackmail Mr. de Winter by threatening to prove that de Winter had killed his wife. Mr. de Winter called the magistrate, Colonel Julyan, to hear his case. Favell's theory was that Rebecca had asked her husband to free her so that she could marry Jack, and that de Winter infuriated, had killed her.

From Rebecca's engagement book, it was learned that she had visited a Doctor Baker in London on the last day of her life. Colonel Julyan and Mr. and Mrs. de Winter, with Jack Favell following in his car, drove to London to see Doctor Baker. On checking his records, the doctor found that he had examined a Mrs. Danvers on the day in question. They realized that Rebecca had assumed the housekeeper's name. Doctor Baker explained that he had diagnosed Rebecca's ailment as cancer in an advanced stage. Colonel Julyan suggested that the matter be closed since the motive for suicide had been established.

Driving back to Manderley after leaving Colonel Julyan at his sister's home, Mr. de Winter told his wife that he believed that Colonel Julyan had guessed the truth. He also realized that Rebecca had intimated that she was pregnant because she had been sure that her husband would kill her; her last evil deed would be to ruin him and Manderley. Mr. de Winter telephoned Frank from the inn where they stopped for dinner, and the estate manager reported that Mrs. Danvers had disappeared. His news seemed to upset Mr. de Winter. At two o'clock in the morning, they approached Manderley. Mrs. de Winter had been sleeping. Awaking, she thought by the blaze of light that it was dawn. A moment later, she realized that she was looking at Manderley, going up in flames.

Critical Evaluation:

For nearly four decades, Daphne du Maurier excited and terrified readers with some of the best suspense novels of the twentieth century. She was one of a small group of writers who, by their artistic ingenuity, had insight into character and situation, had technical virtuosity, and elevated popular formula fiction into serious literature. There is no better example of her skill and power than her early suspense masterpiece, *Rebecca*.

The basic structure of *Rebecca* is that of what may be called the modern gothic romance, but du Maurier utilized and transformed the rigid formula of this popular genre to create a very original and personal fiction. The unnamed narrator, at least for the first two-thirds of the novel, is the typical heroine of a gothic romance. Although her character is not deep, her qualities and desires are carefully chosen to provoke maximum interest and sympathy. Two narrative questions animate the rather leisurely early chapters of the novel: Can the heroine, an orphan with little training or worldly experience, adjust to the unfamiliar, demanding social role as mistress of Manderley? Can she win and keep the love of her passionately desired, but enigmatic, even sinister husband, Maxim de Winter? These two elements—Manderley, the isolated, beautiful, but ultimately threatening setting, and de Winter, the charming, handsome, rich, but moody and mysterious male love object—are essential in the genre.

After the de Winters set up residence at Manderley, these two questions lead to the dominating, almost spectral presence of Maxim's first wife, Rebecca. Her presence is made more threatening by Mrs. Danvers, the efficient, sinister, intimidating housekeeper, who still serves her original mistress, and by Jack Favell, Rebecca's crudely handsome, lascivious cousin. They, along with the gradual revelation that Rebecca's death was not accidental, give the novel that sense of growing menace that is so important to the gothic romance.

Approximately two-thirds of the way through the book, however, du Maurier adds a special twist to the story that takes it out of the gothic romance category and establishes the book as a unique suspense thriller. Maxim finally breaks down and confesses to the heroine that Rebecca was "vicious, damnable, rotten through and through," and that he murdered her when she tormented him about a "son and heir" that was not his. Thereafter, the focus shifts from the heroine's mysterious danger to her husband's legal fate. Instead of fearing for the physical safety of the narrator, the reader is placed in the ironic position of rooting for the criminal to escape detection and punishment. Furthermore, the "villains"—Mrs. Danvers and Jack Favell—become petty, pitiable creatures rather than seriously dangerous conspirators.

Most important, the heroine is freed by this knowledge from Rebecca's onerous legacy. Knowing that Maxim loves and needs her and faced with a threat that is real and specific, rather than undefined and pervasive, she can deal with her situation in a direct, forceful way as an emotionally whole, self-confident woman. The heroine thus grows from a pretty household decoration to the mistress of Manderley, from a girl to a woman, and from a child bride to a mature wife. It is, finally, du Maurier's skill and sensitivity in describing her heroine's maturity in a manner that is psychologically believable and emotionally satisfying that qualifies *Rebecca* as a unique and serious work of art.

Bibliography:

Beauman, Sally. "Rereading *Rebecca.*" *The New Yorker*, November 8, 1993, 127-138. Provides a modern analysis of the novel. A revealing comparison of du Maurier's life and the plot of the novel.

Du Maurier, Daphne. *The Rebecca Notebook and Other Memories*. Garden City, N.Y.: Doubleday, 1980. Examines the birth and adolescence of a novel. Contains all textual notes and personal commentary by the author. A comparison of this source and the final text is fascinating. Also included are family anecdotes.

Hollinger, Karen. "The Female Oedipal Drama of *Rebecca* from Novel to Film." *Quarterly Review of Film and Video* 14, no. 4 (1993): 17-30. A feminist view of the translation of a Gothic novel into the film media.

Kelly, Richard. *Daphne du Maurier*. Boston: Twayne, 1987. Discusses the notebook for *Rebecca* as well as subsequent film and television versions. Includes commentary from periodicals and a list of all works in chronological order.

Shallcross, Martyn. *The Private World of Daphne du Maurier*. New York: St. Martin's Press, 1992. An insightful, sympathetic overview of the author by a close family friend. Includes many pictures and a chronological bibliography of the du Maurier canon.

THE RECRUITING OFFICER

Type of work: Drama
Author: George Farquhar (1678?-1707)
Type of plot: Comedy
Time of plot: Early eighteenth century
Locale: Shrewsbury, England
First performed: 1706; first published, 1706

Principal characters:
CAPTAIN PLUME, the recruiting officer, a gay blade
SYLVIA BALANCE, Captain Plume's fiancée
MR. WORTHY, Captain Plume's friend
MELINDA, Mr. Worthy's fiancée and cousin of Sylvia Balance
JUSTICE BALANCE, Sylvia's father
ROSE, the pretty young daughter of a farmer
SERGEANT KITE, Captain Plume's aide

The Story:

Captain Plume, commander of a company of grenadiers, and his aide, Sergeant Kite, went to Shrewsbury to enlist a number of recruits for Captain Plume's command. They went to Shrewsbury because of success in gaining recruits in that city some months before, and because of Captain Plume's amorous successes at the same time. Upon the arrival of the pair they were greeted with the news that a young woman who had just given birth to a child had named Captain Plume as the father. At the captain's request, Sergeant Kite married the woman and went on record as the father of the child. This was not the first time he had done as much for the captain; he had accumulated a list of six wives in the same manner.

Captain Plume also found his good friend, Mr. Worthy, at Shrewsbury. Mr. Worthy had been a happy-go-lucky chap, much like Captain Plume, until his fiancée had inherited a fortune. The girl, Melinda, had taken on airs after becoming a rich woman, and she proceeded to make life miserable for Worthy. His latest grievance was that another officer on recruiting duty, one Captain Brazen, had apparently become a successful rival for Melinda's hand and fortune. Captain Plume asked Worthy about Sylvia Balance, whom the captain loved but could not marry because his life was too uncertain and he had too little money. Worthy told Captain Plume that Sylvia Balance still thought very well of him.

While Worthy and Captain Plume talked, Melinda and Sylvia were having a conversation of their own, in which Sylvia told her cousin that she was determined that the captain should not leave Shrewsbury alone. The two women quarreled, and after Sylvia's departure Melinda wrote a letter to Sylvia's father telling him that Captain Plume intended to dishonor Sylvia. That evening Captain Plume had dinner with Sylvia and her father, Justice Balance, who considered the captain a fine match for his daughter. During the evening, news came from Germany by mail that Justice Balance's son and heir had died. Immediately the attitude of Justice Balance toward Captain Plume changed, for he did not like to think of the captain as the husband of his daughter if she were to have all his fortune. Calling Sylvia into private conference, he told her of the change in his attitude. Although the girl was very much in love with the captain, she promised that she would not marry without her father's consent. Captain Plume left the house without learning what had happened. A short time after his departure Melinda's spiteful letter to Sylvia's father arrived. In order to get her away from the captain, Justice Balance immediately sent Sylvia by coach to one of his country estates.

Worthy and Captain Plume interpreted Sylvia's departure erroneously. They thought that she believed herself too good for the captain after she had inherited a fortune of two thousand pounds a year. The captain, claiming that he would get along as well without her, proceeded to go about his business of recruiting. While doing so he met a farmer's pretty young daughter, named Rose. Rose and he immediately fancied one another, and the captain went so far as to give his half-promise that he would make the girl his wife. In return, she helped him to add almost a dozen more recruits to his company. These included her own brother and her former sweetheart.

One day Sylvia, disguised in some of her brother's clothes, returned to Shrewsbury, where she met the two recruiting officers, Captain Plume and Captain Brazen, in the company of Melinda. When she told them that she was Mr. Willful, a young man of good family who wished to enlist, they both bid for the new recruit, who finally agreed to join Captain Plume's company. The captain was so pleased with young Mr. Willful that he proffered his friendship, even though the recruit was to be an enlisted man in the company.

Saying that he would be censured for entering the army voluntarily, the recruit asked Captain Plume to have him impressed into service by the provisions of the acts of Parliament. The captain agreed to do so. To help her deception, and also to test the direction of Captain Plume's affections, Sylvia in her disguise pretended to be in love with Rose.

The fiancée of Worthy, meanwhile, had been to see a fortune-teller who was really Sergeant Kite in disguise. The fortune-teller told Melinda that she would die unmarried if she let a man who was to call on her at ten o'clock the following morning leave the country. He had also managed to secure a copy of her handwriting, which he showed her in an attempt to make her think the devil was his helper. Melinda was so impressed that she promised herself to follow the fortune-teller's advice.

Justice Balance decided that the best way to keep his daughter's honor and fortune from falling into the hands of Captain Plume was to provide the officer with the soldiers he needed and to draft them according to the provision made by Parliament. In order to do so, the justice opened his court and had the bailiff bring in a number of men who were eligible for the draft. Among the men was Sylvia in her disguise as Mr. Willful. She had been accused, as a man, of having taken Rose as a common-law wife. In the courtroom Mr. Willful behaved impudently, and the justice decided to punish the brash young man by sending him off as a private in Captain Plume's company. Thus Sylvia tricked her father into sending her away with the captain. In fact, the justice ordered Captain Plume not to discharge Mr. Willful for any reason.

After the hearing Justice Balance went to his home, where he learned that his daughter, dressed in her deceased brother's clothes, had disappeared from his country estate. The justice immediately realized that he had been tricked, that the Mr. Willful whom he had sent off with Captain Plume was really Sylvia. He also thought that Captain Plume had been a party to the deception. When the captain called at the justice's home a short time later, it was soon apparent that he knew nothing of the scheme, for he agreed to discharge the new soldier at Justice Balance's request.

Mr. Willful was called in and unmasked as Sylvia. Then the father, realizing how much his daughter loved the captain, gave them permission to marry. Immediately thereafter Worthy and Melinda arrived to say that they had also reached an agreement and were to be married shortly. Melinda also apologized for the spiteful letter she had sent to Justice Balance. Captain Plume, pleased over the prospect of a handsome fortune coming to him with his wife, announced that he was retiring from the army. He turned over all the recruits he had enlisted to Captain Brazen, who had been unsuccessful in finding any men for his company.

Critical Evaluation:

The Recruiting Officer is classified as a Restoration comedy, something of a misnomer for several reasons. Restoration literature is usually taken to mean British literature written between 1660 (the time of the ascent to the British throne by Charles II, which had been vacant since the execution of his father, Charles I in 1649) and 1700. It is convenient to classify works written in the last forty years of the seventeenth century with the word "Restoration," but additionally there is something distinctly different about much of the work of that period, particularly in drama. The recognizable characteristics of Restoration literature tend to slip over into the literature of the early eighteenth century. George Farquhar wrote *The Recruiting Officer* in 1705. He had, however, written plays as early as 1698, so there is some justification in calling him a Restoration playwright.

The play is best understood in comparison with more perfectly exemplary Restoration comedy. A Restoration comedy has a happy ending, and usually a happy ending in which young men and women come together in matrimony or a sincere pledge of marriage. It begins with males and females meeting, circling warily, engaging in the pleasures and pains of courtship (often harassed by concerned parents or social conventions), falling into short-lived quarrels, and finally coming together in mutual love. The Restoration comedy is, in short, something like life. Restoration comedy also has its own conventions. These conventions arose from the expectations of the Restoration audience. That audience included the court of Charles II, who had lived in France, developing a taste for the sophisticated, risqué comedies of that country. He and his courtiers were the first patrons, financial supporters, and audience for the revived theater. They liked characters dressed as they were dressed, living in London, and living idealized, happy, upper-class lives. Actors and, in a great development in English theater, actresses were expected to talk much in the manner of the court and with smart-set arrogance and high wit. Restoration audiences not only wanted the best-looking man to win the prettiest woman, but also expected him to be the cleverest man on the stage, since intelligence and wittiness were the most admired qualities in the high society of the time. The contest between the leading man and contenders for that role was often played out in terms of intelligence. Intelligence, in turn, is often measured by one's ability to deceive others and to use one's sophistication to achieve one's social goals, such as marriage and other moneymaking connections. Brazen, for instance, is a man who thinks he is witty but is really a dupe for both Plume and Worthy.

This play is a second-stage comedy, in the sense that the couples (often two couples work toward matrimony) have already gone through some initial phases of their relationships before the play begins. They are now in difficulty but still in love, and they must work their way through misunderstandings to achieve a resolution. Plume is the smartest man on the stage. Worthy is also intelligent, and both of them are witty. The leading ladies in Restoration comedies are often quite as witty as their suitors and not reluctant to go after their men. Restoration comic conventions run throughout the play. Sylvia's use of disguise is a common feature of Restoration comedy, for example. It also is an excuse to show off her figure. Fashion of the time allowed women to display their bosoms, but their voluminous dresses hid the rest of their bodies. Her disguise, therefore, was a bit risqué for the play's times. The play's mockery of old men is also a commonplace of Restoration comedy, and country folk in such plays are always fools. The play's placement in a province is uncommon, since London is the usual locale for these dramas.

This play, however, differs tonally from much Restoration comedy. The wit is brilliant, but it is less cruel, and the innocent ignorance of country folk is not jeered at quite as rudely as might be considered usual in a Restoration play. Advantage is taken of them, and there is a blind eye turned on the conduct of Plume and Kite by the local magistrates, but it would not have seemed harsh to audiences aware of the difficulty of recruiting for the War of Spanish Succession, which had been going on for several years.

Plume, like most Restoration heroes (not to mention Charles II), has a questionable past, but he takes some care of his former conquests. He begins with an attempt to seduce Sylvia, but learns to love her. Genuine feeling throughout the play culminates in engagements. Justice Balance, who approves of Plume initially, turns against him when Silvia becomes his sole heir, but he is not so much punished as brought to his senses. A Restoration play might have given him, at least, a physical beating. All in all, the play is gentler than a typical Restoration comedy, and less dismissive of flawed characters. In this way, it connects with the plays of the early eighteenth century, which were on their way to the sentimentality of late eighteenth century drama.

Some characters are outside the romantic structure. Brazen is a marvelous grotesque. He is an example of sheer stupidity as a comic force. Sergeant Kite is a comic whirlwind. His fortune-teller is one of the finest pieces in the comic repertoire, and his comments upon the way of the world are examples of how these plays, seemingly trivial, are full of wisdom about human folly.

"Critical Evaluation" by Charles Pullen

Bibliography:

Burns, Edward. *Restoration Comedy: Crises of Desire and Identity*. London: Macmillan, 1987. A general study of Restoration comedy, with emphasis upon disguise.

Cunningham, John E. *Restoration Drama*. London: Evans Brothers, 1966. Discusses Farquhar in conjunction with the other Restoration masters of comedy.

Miner, Earl. *Restoration Dramatists: A Collection of Essays*. Englewood Cliffs, N.J.: Prentice-Hall, 1966. A volume of the best essays on the genre by some of the best critics. Gives several different views of the period that are helpful in understanding how Farquhar is different from the writers of the earlier period.

Palmer, John. *The Comedy of Manners*. New York: Russell & Russell, 1962. Considers Restoration comic writers as part of the longer tradition of the comedy of manners. There is a chapter on Farquhar.

Schneider, Ben Ross. *The Ethos of Restoration Comedy*. Champaign: University of Illinois Press, 1971. The morality of these comedies has been a source of discussion since the 1690's. This book attempts to put the problem in historical perspective.

THE RED AND THE BLACK

Type of work: Novel
Author: Stendhal (Marie-Henri Beyle, 1783-1842)
Type of plot: Psychological realism
Time of plot: Early nineteenth century
Locale: France
First published: Le Rouge et le noir, 1830 (English translation, 1898)

> *Principal characters:*
> JULIEN SOREL, an opportunist
> MONSIEUR DE RÊNAL, the mayor of Verrières
> MADAME DE RÊNAL, his wife
> MATHILDE DE LA MOLE, Julien's mistress
> FOUQUÉ, Julien's friend

The Story:

Julien Sorel was the son of a carpenter in the little town of Verrières, France. After Napoleon was defeated, Julien came to believe that the church rather than the army was the way to power. Because of his assumed piety and his intelligence, Julien was appointed as tutor to the children of Monsieur de Rênal, the mayor of the village.

Madame de Rênal had done her duty all of her life. Although she was a good wife and a good mother, she had never been in love with her husband, who was a coarse man and hardly likely to inspire love in any woman. Madame de Rênal was immediately attracted to the pale young tutor and gradually fell in love with him. Julien, thinking it a duty he owed himself, made love to her to gain power over her. He discovered after a time that he had actually fallen in love with Madame de Rênal.

Julien went on a holiday to visit his friend Fouqué, who tried to persuade Julien to go into the lumber business with him. Julien declined, for he enjoyed his new life too much. His love affair with Madame de Rênal was, however, revealed to Monsieur de Rênal by an anonymous letter written by Monsieur Valenod, the local official in charge of the poorhouse. Valenod, who had become rich on graft, was jealous because Monsieur de Rênal had hired Julien as a tutor and because he himself had at one time made unsuccessful advances to Madame de Rênal.

Monsieur de Rênal agreed to send Julien to the seminary at Besançon, principally to keep him from becoming tutor at Monsieur Valenod's house. After Julien had departed, Madame de Rênal was filled with remorse for her adultery and she became extremely religious.

Julien did not get on well at the seminary, for he found it full of hypocrites. The students did not like him and feared his sharp intelligence. His only friend was the Abbé Pirard, a highly moral man. One day Julien went to help decorate the cathedral and by chance saw Madame de Rênal there. She fainted, but he could not help her because of his liturgical duties. The experience left him weak and shaken.

The Abbé Pirard lost his position at the seminary because he had supported the Marquis de La Mole, who was engaged in a lawsuit against Monsieur de Frilair, the vicar general of Besançon. When the Abbé Pirard left the seminary, the marquis obtained a living for him in Paris and hired Julien as his secretary.

Julien was thankful for his chance to leave the seminary. On his way to Paris he called secretly on Madame de Rênal. At first, conscious of her previous sin, she repulsed his advances but then yielded once again to his pleadings. Monsieur de Rênal became suspicious, and when he decided to search his wife's room, Julien had to jump out the window to escape discovery, barely escaping with his life.

Finding Julien a good worker, the marquis entrusted him with many of the details of his business. Julien was also allowed to dine with the family and to mingle with the guests afterward. He found the Marquise de La Mole to be extremely proud of her nobility. The daughter, Mathilde, seemed to be of the same type, a reserved girl with beautiful eyes. The son, the Comte de La Mole, was an extremely polite and pleasant young man. Julien found Parisian high society boring, however. No one was interested in discussing ideas.

Julien enjoyed stealing volumes of Voltaire from the marquis' library and reading them in his room. He was astonished when he discovered that Mathilde was doing the same thing. Before long, they were spending much of their time together, although Julien was always conscious of his position as servant and sensitive to slights. Despite her pride, Mathilde fell in love with him because he was so different from the young men of her own class.

After Julien spent two nights with her, Mathilde decided that it was degrading to be in love with a secretary. Her pride was an insult to Julien. Smarting, he planned to gain power over her and, consequently, over the household.

Meanwhile the marquis had entrusted Julien with a diplomatic mission on behalf of the nobility and clergy who wanted the monarchy reestablished. On this mission, Julien met an old friend who advised him how to win Mathilde back, and upon his return he put the plan into effect by beginning to pay court to a virtuous lady who was often a visitor in the de La Mole home. He began a correspondence with her, all the while ignoring Mathilde, who thereupon realized how much she loved him. She threw herself at his feet. Julien had won, but this time he did not let her gain the upper hand. As he continued to treat Mathilde coldly, her passion increased. In this way he maintained his power.

When Mathilde became pregnant, she was joyful, for she thought Julien would now realize how much she cared for him. She had made the supreme sacrifice and would now have to marry Julien and give up her place in society. Julien, however, was not so happy about her condition, for he feared the results when Mathilde told her father.

At first, the marquis was furious. Eventually, he decided that the only way out of the difficulty was to make Julien rich and respectable. He gave Julien a fortune, a title, and a commission in the army. Overwhelmed with his new wealth and power, Julien scarcely gave a thought to Mathilde. Then the Marquis received a letter from Madame de Rênal, whom Julien had suggested to the marquis for a character recommendation. Madame de Rênal was again filled with religious fervor; she revealed to the marquis the whole story of her relationship with Julien. The marquis thereupon retracted his permission to let Julien marry his daughter.

Julien's plans for glory and power were ruined. In a fit of rage, he rode to Verrières, where he found Madame de Rênal at church. He fired two shots at her before he was arrested and taken off to prison. There he promptly admitted his guilt, for he was ready to die. He had had his revenge. Mathilde, who was still madly in love with Julien, arrived in Verrières and tried to bribe the jury, and Fouqué came and begged Julien to try to escape, but Julien ignored the efforts of his friends to help.

He was tried, found guilty, and given the death sentence, even though his bullets had not killed Madame de Rênal. In fact, his action had only rekindled her passion for him. She visited him and begged him to appeal his sentence. The two were as much in love as they had ever been. When Monsieur de Rênal ordered his wife to come home, Julien was left to his dreams of his one great love, Madame de Rênal. Mathilde only bored and angered him with her continued solicitude.

The Red and the Black / STENDHAL

On the appointed day, Julien went calmly to his death. The faithful Fouqué obtained the body so as to bury it in a cave in the mountains where Julien had once been fond of going to indulge in his daydreams of power. A famous ancestor of Mathilde had once been loved with an extreme passion. When that ancestor was executed, the woman had taken his severed head and buried it. Mathilde had always admired this family legend. After the funeral ceremony at the cave, she now did the same for Julien, burying his head with her own hands. Later, she had the cave decorated with Italian marble. Madame de Rênal did not go to the funeral, but three days after Julien's death, she died in the act of embracing her children.

Critical Evaluation:

Criticism of *The Red and the Black* might well begin with the novel's subtitle, *A Chronicle of 1830*. The thirty years of the nineteenth century that had elapsed at the time Stendhal wrote his novel divide rather neatly into two periods: the Napoleonic era, which ended with the Congress of Vienna in 1815, and the Bourbon Restoration, the restoration of the French monarchy, which extended from 1815 to 1830.

The first of these periods, dominated by Napoleon, is often associated with the "red" of Stendhal's title, red signifying, among other possibilities, military distinction (the means by which Napoleon began his rise to eminence) or revolution (the means by which the liberal bourgeoisie undertook to secure a measure of power). The second period, probably signified by Stendhal's "black," is associated with the clergy, who recaptured some of their former influence after 1815 and thus became a means to personal advancement, or reaction, political and social retrenchment by which the aristocracy undertook to recover their former dominance.

Julien Sorel, possessed of both ability and ambition, admires Napoleon in private, but he also knows that the man who was once emperor is anathema to those who now hold power. His only escape from the coarse and limited world that seems to suit his father and brothers is through the exercise of learning. He has achieved a mastery of Latin, particularly of the New Testament, which he has practically memorized. When he becomes tutor to the Rênal children, he takes his first step toward the life he desires, but that step also requires him to assume a role similar to one played by minor clergy. Julien knows that there will be no further steps unless he is willing to practice a hypocrisy that, while not pervasive among all clergy, almost always characterizes those who hope to get on in life.

His clerical advancement begins, ironically enough, in his illicit affair with Madame de Rênal. This affair, which Julien starts not out of passion but rather as a self-test of his resolve, becomes something serious and creates the necessity for sending the young man away to a seminary, where he further cultivates the hypocrisy necessary to achieve his goals. Though Julien recognizes and even honors the sincerity he occasionally discovers in a clergyman, his own goals have little to do with spiritual life. As he sees more of the world, he comes to realize that his ambition is larger than most of what the church can offer. What he finds attractive is not the liberal bourgeoisie, which might fit with his admiration of Napoleon, but the reactionary aristocracy, who may be shallow in their thinking but represent both the power and style to which he aspires.

Although Julien begins with attitudes that might be identified with Napoleonic liberalism, his belief in his own self-worth and in his right to a place among the aristocracy impels him toward the very structures of power and authority that had attempted to quell liberalism. One of the ironies of liberalism, in Stendhal's time and now, is that it tends to promote a democratization of style with which the Julien Sorels of the world have little sympathy. If the aristocracy resists free thought as something threatening to their privilege, they may nonetheless exercise their power in the protection of a style that continues to exert appeal.

All of this becomes clear to Julien after he leaves the seminary to assume duties as secretary to the Marquis de La Mole. He finds himself in the world he has coveted. When he discovers that he is not alone in reading Voltaire in secret, that Mathilde, the marquis' beautiful daughter reads Voltaire also, it seems that he may be able to live among the rich and powerful while cultivating a freedom of thought that the rich and powerful consider seditious. When he begins a love affair with Mathilde, it seems that he may get everything he wants, especially after Mathilde becomes pregnant and the Marquis de La Mole decides to legitimize Julien by providing him with a title and a commission in the army. That commission would mean a final escape from black clerical clothing into a uniform which, if not red, is nevertheless still a military uniform worn by the privileged orders.

The Red and the Black may be read as a tragic novel. The collapse and subsequent end of Julien Sorel's life results, after all, from the very thing that was critical to his ascent, namely his success in passionate love, first with Madame de Rênal, then with Mathilde de La Mole. Though Julien is handsome in a pale, refined sort of way, he seems less driven by passion than many young men and makes use of his success in love only as a tool in the service of his ambition. The women who love him are sincere, however, and when he is exposed for his earlier affair by its object, Madame de Rênal, his response is to attempt to kill her. Stendhal, who was himself strongly attracted to women and had many love affairs, seems to indicate that passionate love must be fit into life's equations, especially among those who wish to live completely and despite the sometimes tragic results. The tragic moment in *The Red and the Black* comes with the hero's self-knowledge, when Julien realizes late in the story that he truly loves Madame de Rênal. *The Red and the Black* is a major novel of early nineteenth century France. Beyond being a chronicle of its own time, it is penetrating in its analysis of love and ambition and of the schemes, open or concealed, by which they are served.

"Critical Evaluation" by John Higby

Bibliography:

Adams, Robert M. *Stendhal: Notes on a Novelist.* New York: Funk and Wagnalls, 1959. Does not include a thorough discussion of *The Red and the Black* but provides a readable, intelligent, and frequently amusing introduction to Stendhal.

Auerbach, Erich. "In the Hotel de La Mole." In *Mimesis: The Representation of Reality in Western Literature,* translated by Willard Trask. Princeton, N.J.: Princeton University Press, 1953. One of the most important twentieth century studies of literary realism. The chapter on Stendhal is excellent.

Pearson, Roger. *Stendhal's Violin: A Novelist and His Reader.* Oxford, England: Clarendon Press, 1988. A long chapter entitled "Time and Imagination in *Le Rouge et le noir*" is divided into subchapters that are partly self-contained and partly sequential.

Talbot, Emile J. *Stendhal Revisited.* New York: Twayne, 1993. The chapter on *The Red and the Black,* subtitled "The Play of the Text," discusses playfulness in literature.

Tillett, Margaret. *Stendhal: The Background to the Novels.* London: Oxford University Press, 1971. References to *The Red and the Black* are scattered throughout the book. A generally useful source.

THE RED BADGE OF COURAGE
An Episode of the American Civil War

Type of work: Novel
Author: Stephen Crane (1871-1900)
Type of plot: Psychological realism
Time of plot: 1861-1865
Locale: A Civil War battlefield
First published: 1895

Principal characters:
    HENRY FLEMING, a young recruit
    JIM CONKLIN, a veteran
    WILSON, another veteran

The Story:

The tall soldier, Jim Conklin, and the loud soldier, Wilson, argued bitterly over the rumor that the troops were about to move. Henry Fleming was impatient to experience his first battle, and as he listened to the quarreling of the seasoned soldiers, he wondered if he would become frightened and run away under gunfire. He questioned Wilson and Conklin, and each man stated that he would stand and fight no matter what happened.

Henry had come from a farm, where he had dreamed of battles and longed for army life. His mother had held him back at first. When she saw that her son was bored with the farm, she packed his woolen clothing and, with a warning that he must not associate with the wicked kind of men who were in the military camps, sent him off to join the Yankee troops. One gray morning, Henry awoke to find that the regiment was about to move. With a hazy feeling that death would be a relief from dull and meaningless marching, Henry was again disappointed. The troops made only another march. He began to suspect that the generals were stupid fools, but the other men in his raw regiment scoffed at his idea and told him to shut up.

When the fighting suddenly began, there was very little action in it for Henry. He lay on the ground with the other men and watched for signs of the enemy. Some of the men around him were wounded. He could not see what was going on or what the battle was about. Then an attack came. Immediately Henry forgot all of his former confused thoughts, and he could only fire his rifle over and over; around him, men behaved in their own strange individual manners as they were wounded. Henry felt a close comradeship with the men at his side—men who were firing at the enemy with him.

Suddenly the attack ended. To Henry, it seemed strange that the sky above should still be blue after the guns had stopped firing. While the men were recovering from the attack, binding wounds, and gathering equipment, another surprise attack was launched from the enemy line. Unprepared and tired from the first fighting, the men retreated in panic. Henry, sharing their sudden terror, ran too.

When the fearful retreat had ended, the fleeing men learned that the enemy had lost the battle. Now Henry felt a surge of guilt. Dreading to rejoin his companions, he fled into the forest. There he saw a squirrel run away from him in fright. The fleeing animal seemed to vindicate in Henry's mind his own cowardly flight; he had acted according to nature, whose creatures ran from danger. Then, seeing a dead man lying in a clearing, Henry hurried back into the retreating column of wounded men. Most were staggering along in helpless bewilderment, and some were being carried on stretchers. Henry realized that he had no wound and that he did not belong in that group of staggering men. There was one pitiful-looking man, covered with dirt and blood, wandering about dazed and alone. Everyone was staring at him and avoiding him. When Henry approached him, the young boy saw that the soldier was Jim Conklin. He was horrified at the sight of the tall soldier. He tried to help Jim, but with a wild motion of despair, Jim fell to the ground dead. Once more Henry fled.

His conscience was paining him. He wanted to return to his regiment to finish the fight, but he thought that his fellow soldiers would point to him as a deserter. He envied the dead men who were lying all about him. They were already heroes; he was a coward. Ahead he could hear the rumbling of artillery. As he neared the lines of his regiment, a retreating line of men broke from the trees ahead of him. The men ran fiercely, ignoring him or waving frantically at him as they shouted something he could not comprehend. He stood among the flying men, not knowing what to do. One man hit him on the head with the butt of a rifle.

Henry went on carefully, the wound in his head paining him a great deal. He walked for a long while until he met another soldier, who led Henry back to his regiment. The first familiar man Henry met was Wilson. Wilson, who had been a terrible braggart before the first battle, had given Henry a packet of letters to keep for him in case he was killed. Now Henry felt superior to Wilson. If the man asked him where he had been, Henry would remind him of the letters. Lost was Henry's feeling of guilt; he felt superior now, his deeds of cowardice almost forgotten. No one knew that he had run off in terror. Wilson had changed. He no longer was the swaggering, boastful man who had annoyed Henry in the beginning. The men in the regiment washed Henry's wound and told him to get some sleep.

The next morning, Wilson casually asked Henry for the letters. Half sorry that he had to yield them with no taunting remark, Henry returned the letters to his comrade. He felt sorry for Wilson's embarrassment. He felt himself a virtuous and heroic man. Another battle started. This time Henry held his position doggedly and kept firing his rifle without thinking. Once he fell down, and for a panicky moment he thought that he had been shot, but he continued to fire his rifle blindly, loading and firing without even seeing the enemy. Finally someone shouted to him that he must stop shooting, that the battle was over. Then Henry looked up for the first time and saw that there were no enemy troops before him. Now he was a hero. Everyone stared at him when the lieutenant of the regiment complimented his fierce fighting. Henry realized that he had behaved like a demon.

Wilson and Henry, off in the woods looking for water, overheard two officers discussing the coming battle. They said that Henry's regiment fought like mule drivers, but that they would have to be used anyway. Then one officer said that probably not many of the regiment would live through the day's fighting. Soon after the attack started, the color-bearer was killed, and Henry took up the flag, with Wilson at his side. Although the regiment fought bravely, one of the commanding officers of the army said that the men had not gained the ground that they were expected to take. The same officer had complimented Henry for his courageous fighting. He began to feel that he knew the measure of his own courage and endurance. His outfit fought one more engagement with the enemy. Henry was by that time a veteran, and the fighting held less meaning for him than had the earlier battles. When it was over, he and Wilson marched away with their victorious regiment.

Critical Evaluation:

The Red Badge of Courage, Stephen Crane's second novel (*Maggie: A Girl of the Streets* had appeared under a pseudonym in 1893) and his most famous work, has often been considered the first truly modern war novel. The war is the American Civil War, and the battle is presumed to be the one fought at Chancellorsville, though neither the war nor the battle is named in the novel. Further, there is no mention of Abraham Lincoln or the principal battle generals, Joseph Hooker (Union) and Robert E. Lee and "Stonewall" Jackson (Confederate). This is by design, since Crane was writing a different kind of war novel. He was not concerned with the causes of the war, the political and social implications of the prolonged and bloody conflict, the strategy and tactics of the commanding officers, or even the real outcome of the battle in which historically the combined losses were nearly thirty thousand men (including "Stonewall" Jackson, mistakenly shot in darkness by one of his own men).

From beginning to end, the short novel focuses upon one Union Army volunteer. Though other characters enter the story and reappear intermittently, they are distinctly minor, and they are present primarily to show the relationship of Henry Fleming (usually called only "the youth") to one person, to a small group of soldiers, or to the complex war of which he is such an insignificant part. Much of the story takes the reader into Henry's consciousness. Readers share his boyish dreams of glory, his excitement in anticipating battle action, his fear of showing fear, his cowardice and flight, his inner justification of what he has done, his wish for a wound to symbolize a courage he has not shown, the ironic gaining of his false "red badge," his secret knowledge of the badge's origin, his "earning" the badge as he later fights fiercely and instinctively, his joy in musing on his own bravery and valiant actions, his anger at an officer who fails to appreciate his soldiery, and his final feeling that "the great death" is, after all, not a thing to be feared so much. Now, he tells himself, he is a man. In centering the story within the consciousness of an inexperienced youth caught in a war situation whose meaning and complexities he cannot understand, Crane anticipates Ford Madox Ford, Ernest Hemingway, and other later novelists.

Crane has been called a realist, a naturalist, an impressionist, and a Symbolist. He is all of these in *The Red Badge of Courage*. Though Crane had never seen a battle when he wrote the novel, he had read about them; he had talked with veterans and had studied history under a Civil War general; and he had imagined what it would be like to be a frightened young man facing violent death amid the confusion, noise, and turmoil of a conflict that had no clear meaning to him. Intuitively, he wrote so realistically that several early reviewers concluded that only an experienced soldier could have written the book. After Crane had later seen the Greeks and Turks fighting in 1897 (he was a journalist reporting the war), he told Joseph Conrad, "My picture of war was all right! I have found it as I imagined it."

Although naturalistic passages appear in the novel, Crane portrays in Henry Fleming not a helpless chip floating on the indifferent ocean of life but a youth sometimes impelled into action by society or by instinct yet also capable of consciously willed acts. Before the first skirmish, Henry wishes he could escape from his regiment and consider his plight: " . . . there were iron laws of tradition and law on four sides. He was in a moving box." In the second skirmish, he runs "like a rabbit." When a squirrel in the forest flees after Henry throws a pine cone at him, Henry justifies his own flight: "There was the law, he said. Nature had given him a sign." He is not, however, content to look upon himself as on the squirrel's level. He feels guilt over his cowardice. When he carries the flag in the later skirmishes, he is not a terrified chicken or rabbit or squirrel but a young man motivated by pride, by a sense of belonging to a group, and by a determination to show his courage to an officer who had scornfully called the soldiers in his group a lot of "mule drivers."

From the beginning, critics have both admired and complained about Crane's impressionistic writing and his use of imagery and symbols in *The Red Badge of Courage*. Edward Garnett in

1898 called Crane "the chief impressionist of our day" and praised his "wonderful fervour and freshness of style." Joseph Conrad (himself an impressionist) was struck by Crane's "genuine verbal felicity, welding analysis and description in a continuous fascination of individual style," and Conrad saw Henry as "the symbol of all untried men." By contrast, one American critic in 1898 described the novel as "a mere riot of words" and condemned "the violent straining after effect" and the "absurd similes." Though H. G. Wells liked the book as a whole, he commented on "those chromatic splashes that at times deafen and confuse . . . those images that astonish rather than enlighten."

Yet judging by the continuing popularity of *The Red Badge of Courage*, most readers are not repelled by Crane's repeated use of color—"blue demonstration," "red eyes," "red animal—war," "red sun"—or by his use of images—"dark shadows that moved like monsters," "the dragons were coming," guns that "belched and howled like brass devils guarding a gate." Only in a few passages does Crane indulge in "arty" writing—"the guns squatted in a row like savage chiefs. They argued with abrupt violence"—or drop into the pathetic fallacy—"The flag suddenly sank down as if dying. Its motion as it fell was a gesture of despair." Usually the impressionistic phrasing is appropriate to the scene or to the emotional state of Henry Fleming at a particular moment, as when, after he has fought, he feels heroically, the sun shines "now bright and gay in the blue, enameled sky."

A brilliant work of the imagination, *The Red Badge of Courage* will endure as what Crane afterward wrote a friend he had intended it to be, "a psychological portrayal of fear."

"Critical Evaluation" by Henderson Kincheloe

Bibliography:
Bloom, Harold, ed. *Stephen Crane's "The Red Badge of Courage."* New York: Chelsea House, 1987. Examines style, technique, narrative method, and psychological aspects of Crane's novel. Places the novel in the epic tradition.
Cazemajou, Jean. "*The Red Badge of Courage*: The 'Religion of Peace' and the War Archetype." In *Stephen Crane in Transition: Centenary Essays*, edited by Joseph Katz. Dekalb: Northern Illinois University Press, 1972. Finds a balance in the novel between a metaphoric view of war as chaos and confusion, and a view of a world at peace. War and peace function more as archetypes than as realities in the novel.
LaFrance, Marston. *A Reading of Stephen Crane.* Oxford, England: Clarendon Press, 1971. Identifies Crane's genius not in creating literary naturalism, but rather in his psychological portrayal of Henry Fleming. Praises Crane's use of third-person limited point of view.
Mitchell, Lee Clark, ed. *New Essays on 'The Red Badge of Courage.'* New York: Cambridge University Press, 1986. Traces the novel's evolution; concludes that the original draft served as an outline to be expanded into the 1895 version. Identifies Crane's abstraction of the Civil War from its historical context as a distinctive contribution to American literature.
Solomon, Eric. *Stephen Crane: From Parody to Realism.* Cambridge, Mass.: Harvard University Press, 1966. Credits Crane with countering a tradition of dashing heroes in war fiction by using parody and with giving the war novel a new form that afterward became the model. Maintains that Crane selects his war stories for their value as fiction, creating rather than reliving war experiences.

REDBURN
His First Voyage

Type of work: Novel
Author: Herman Melville (1819-1891)
Type of plot: Bildungsroman
Time of plot: Mid-nineteenth century
Locale: New York, the Atlantic Ocean, and England
First published: 1849

> *Principal characters:*
> WELLINGBOROUGH REDBURN, a young lad on his first voyage
> CAPTAIN RIGA, the master of the *Highlander*
> HARRY BOLTON, a young English prodigal

The Story:

Wellingborough Redburn's father had died, leaving the mother and children poorly provided for, although the father had been a highly successful merchant and at one time a wealthy man. When Redburn was in his middle teens, he decided to take some of the burden off his mother by going to sea. Given an old gun and a hunting jacket by an older brother, Redburn left his home by the Hudson River and went to New York to seek a berth on a ship.

A college friend of his older brother aided Redburn in finding a berth on a ship bound for Liverpool. Unfortunately, the friend had emphasized the fact that Redburn came from a good family and had wealthy relatives; consequently, Captain Riga, master of the *Highlander*, was able to hire the young lad for three dollars a month. Having spent all his money and unable to get an advance on his wages, Redburn had to pawn his gun for a shirt and cap to wear aboard ship.

During his first few days out of port, Redburn thought that he had made a dreadful mistake in going to sea. His fellow sailors jeered at him as a greenhorn. He made many silly mistakes; he became violently seasick; and he discovered that he did not even have a spoon with which to take his portion of the food from the pots and pans in which it was sent to the forecastle. His coat proved inappropriate for life at sea; it shrunk after getting wet. His fellow crewmen found the odd coat amusing and gave Redburn the nickname "Buttons" in derisive reference to its many buttons. Most horrifying of all was the suicide of a sailor who dived over the side of the ship in a fit of delirium tremens.

As the thirty-day cruise to Liverpool from New York wore on, Redburn learned how to make himself useful and comfortable aboard the ship. When he went aloft alone to release the topmost sails, he earned a little respect from his fellow seamen, although they never did, throughout the voyage, let him forget that he was still inexperienced and had signed on as a "boy." Redburn found the sea fascinating in many ways; he also found it terrifying, as when the *Highlander* passed a derelict schooner on which three corpses were still bound to the railing.

For Redburn, one of the liveliest incidents of the voyage was the discovery of a little stowaway on board the *Highlander*. The small boy had been on board the vessel some months before, when the father had been a sailor signed on for a trip from Liverpool to New York. The father had since died, and the boy had stowed himself away in an effort to return to England. Everyone on the ship, including the usually irascible Captain Riga, took a liking to the homesick stowaway and made much of him.

Redburn had little in common with his fellow crew members, most of whom were rough fellows many years older than he. Through them, however, he received an education quite different from that which he had been given in school. At first he tried to talk about church and good books to them, but he soon discovered that such conversation only irritated them into more than their usual profanity and obscenity. Redburn thought that they were not really very bad men but that they had never had the chance to be good men. Most of all, he disliked them because they looked upon anyone who could not follow the seaman's trade as a fool.

A long, low skyline in the distance was Redburn's first glimpse of Ireland. He met his first European when an Irish fisherman hailed the *Highlander* and asked for a line. When he had hauled fifteen or so fathoms of the line into his boat, the Irishman cut the line, laughed, and sailed away. Even though the rope was not Redburn's, he, boylike, felt that the man had played a scurvy trick.

When the *Highlander* arrived at Liverpool, Redburn decided that the English city was not a great deal different from New York. Sailors and ships, he found, were the same in one place as in another, with a few notable exceptions. His trips into the city, away from the waterfront, and excursions into the Lancashire countryside convinced him that he, as an alien, was not welcome. People distrusted him because of his ragged clothing, and he had no money to purchase a new outfit, even though Captain Riga had advanced him three dollars, one month's pay, upon the ship's arrival in port.

Redburn's greatest disappointment came when he tried to use for his excursions an old guidebook he had brought from his father's library. The guidebook, almost half a century old, was no longer reliable, for streets and structures it mentioned were no longer in existence. Redburn felt that the whole world must have changed since his father's time; he saw in the unreliable guidebook a hint that as the years passed the habits and ideals of youth had to be charted anew. Each generation, he learned, had to make its own guidebook through the world.

While in Liverpool, Redburn met Harry Bolton, a young Englishman of good family but a prodigal son. Bolton said that he had shipped on two voyages to the East Indies; now he wanted to emigrate to America. With Redburn's help, Harry Bolton was enrolled as a "boy" on the *Highlander* for its return trip to New York. The two boys, traveling on Bolton's money, made a quick excursion to London before the ship sailed, but they were back in Liverpool within forty-eight hours. Redburn saw little of England beyond the port where he had arrived.

On the return trip to America, the ship carried a load of Irish emigrants. Redburn quickly felt sorry for them but, at the same time, superior to the miserable wretches crowded between the decks. The steerage passengers suffered a great deal during the voyage. Their quarters were cramped at best, and during heavy weather, they could not remain on deck. For cooking they had a stove placed on one of the hatches, one stove for five hundred people. Worst of all, an epidemic of fever broke out, killing many of the emigrants and one of the sailors.

Bolton had a miserable trip, and Redburn was sorry for him, too. The English boy had lied in saying he had been at sea before. Bolton could not bear to go aloft in the rigging, and he, in place of Redburn, became the butt of all the jokes and horseplay that the crew devised.

After the ship reached America, however, the voyage seemed to both Redburn and Bolton to have been a good one. They discovered that they really hated to leave the vessel which had been home to them for several weeks. Their nostalgia for the vessel, however, was soon dissipated by Captain Riga. The Captain dismissed Redburn without any pay because the lad had left his duties for one day while the ship was at Liverpool. The Captain even told Redburn that he owed the ship money for tools he had dropped into the sea. Bolton was given a dollar and a half for his work; the pittance made him so angry that he threw it back on the Captain's desk. The two boys then left the ship, glad to be back on land once more.

Critical Evaluation:

Like most of Herman Melville's work, *Redburn* does not follow a conventional plot structure of complication, climax, and resolution, nor does the novel have characters who gradually develop and interact within a framework of interrelated events and circumstances. *Redburn* is a *Bildungsroman*, a novel that deals with the development of a young protagonist moving from adolescence to maturity. Redburn is told by a first-person narrator who, in the course of his commentary, moves from innocence to experience. At the outset, young Wellingborough Redburn's existence is protected, safe from the iniquities of the world outside village life. His enthusiasm to go to sea is the natural desire of postadolescence to move from the innocent state of childhood into the real world, to challenge that which adults have simultaneously idealized and, for as long as they could, withheld from children. The real world, however, proves to be a darker and more forbidding place than the naïve Redburn is prepared to enter. The rules of fair play and benevolence that have governed his childhood are greatly diminished, and in their place, Redburn finds little kindness and understanding; instead, he finds more than enough selfish indifference and pointless malevolence.

Melville places great emphasis on symbols to convey complex ideas. The glass ship, the moleskin shooting jacket, and the Liverpool guidebook all invite a variety of critical interpretations. As a child growing up in his father's house, Redburn is fascinated by a glass ship kept in a glass case. It is the basis of his great passion to go to sea, for he has grown up studying the minute detail of its glass spars and rigging and its glass figurine sailors earnestly plying their trade. The glass ship, although a strong stimulant for the imagination of an impressionable youth, suggests a fragile, tentative reality, like the imagined notion of a world one has not directly experienced. Having lived a sheltered life in his mother's home in the Hudson River valley, Redburn is as ill-prepared to undertake a genuine voyage upon the high seas as is the glass ship. Melville seems to suggest that people are more resilient than glass, and with the aid of luck and good fortune, people can withstand suffering and the mystery of what often seems a pointless universe.

The reality of the actual voyage is a harsh and brutal experience, one for which Redburn lacks both the psychological and practical necessities. On his departure, his older brother gives him two items: a fowling piece (a gun for hunting birds) and a cumbersome shooting jacket with large horn buttons, many pockets, and long skirts. Redburn has little money, however, and he has no idea of the basic necessities for his new undertaking. The gun is pawned at the first opportunity, perhaps suggesting that such a weapon is useless for the kinds of battles Redburn must now face. The jacket, however, has deeper symbolic implications, much like a similar article of clothing in *White-Jacket* (1850), the novel generally viewed as Melville's sequel and companion piece to *Redburn*. The shooting jacket makes Redburn the object of derision by his fellow-seafarers. The jacket earns him the nickname Buttons. As Redburn performs his seaman's tasks, he is repeatedly drenched by rain and seawater. Day by day the shooting jacket shrinks; the seams begin to widen to the point of splitting; and moving and working with the jacket on become increasingly difficult. The jacket has become the symbol of the world Redburn has left behind. One critic has called the jacket an "obsessive emblem" of his lost gentility and social humiliation.

The concept of advancing to a new identity and breaking with the past is further enhanced by the incident of the Liverpool guidebook. Redburn has brought with him the guidebook that his father had used on a visit to that same city fifty years previously. The book on which Redburn—as a friendless stranger in a foreign city—had hoped to rely on, however, proves to be worthless. Following the map, he attempts to find Riddough's Hotel, the place where his father had stayed, but the hotel is a thing of the past, having been torn down decades earlier. New buildings now stand in its place, and its name is unknown to passersby. His father's Liverpool no longer exists in what Redburn now sadly realizes is a world marked by change, rather than constancy. Having hoped to follow in the comforting security of his father's footsteps, he knows now that he must chart his own course, as generations that follow him must do.

Melville surrounds Redburn with a collection of curious characters, few of them fully developed. For the most part, they seem close to caricature, primarily serving as foils for Redburn to offer observations regarding their moral shortcomings. The most compelling, however, is Jackson, the prototype of the tortured individual who would in various guises appear in Melville's later works. Jackson is the forerunner of Claggart in *Billy Budd, Foretop-man* (1924), Babo in *Benito Cereno* (1856), and Ahab in *Moby Dick* (1851). Like them, he is a formidable leader of men—but he is also a tortured soul consumed by nihilism, believing in nothing and hating everything. For all his enmity, however, there is a curious paradox about Jackson; he is the Cain figure, the proud and forbidding outcast in whom, in spite of his wickedness, there is something pitiable and touching. *Redburn* is the first of Melville's novels to use the symbolic import of the sea as a backdrop for this kind of paradox and for the related, compelling subjects that troubled Melville most: the loss of innocence, the confrontation with evil, and the shifting ambiguities that connect innocence and evil.

"Critical Evaluation" by Richard Keenan

Bibliography:
Branch, Watson G., ed. *Melville: The Critical Heritage*. London: Routledge & Kegan Paul, 1974. Contemporary reviews of *Redburn* in British and American periodicals. Interesting for comparison with later Melville scholarship. The novel was widely praised at its publication, but praised for its qualities as an adventure story rather than as serious fiction.
Bredahl, Carl A., Jr. *Melville's Angles of Vision*. Gainesville: University of Florida Press, 1972. Emphasizes Melville's concern with characters in their environment. Discusses Redburn as first-person narrator adjusting to the psychological implications of life at sea.
Hillway, Tyrus. *Herman Melville*. Boston: Twayne, 1963. Excellent analysis of Melville's characterization, particularly in the degree to which it improved since the publication of his earlier novels. Particular attention given in this regard to the tragic contradictions in the character of Harry Bolton.
Kirby, David. *Herman Melville*. New York: Continuum, 1993. Treats the relationship between Melville's creative imagination and his life. Offers an engaging contrast between the fanciful *Mardi* and *Redburn*, which reveals Melville's personal experience.
Rosenberry, Edward H. *Melville*. London: Routledge & Kegan Paul, 1979. Places particular emphasis on *Redburn* as an initiation novel in which personal experience is paramount in the development of the character of the mature adult. Rosenberry makes an interesting distinction between lust for life and a talent for living in *Redburn*.

REFLECTIONS IN A GOLDEN EYE

Type of work: Novel
Author: Carson McCullers (1917-1967)
Type of plot: Psychological realism
Time of plot: 1930's
Locale: A Southern military base, probably Fort Bragg, North Carolina
First published: 1941

Principal characters:
> PRIVATE ELLGEE WILLIAMS, a soldier
> CAPTAIN WELDON PENDERTON, an ambitious officer
> LEONORA PENDERTON, his wife
> FIREBIRD, her horse
> MAJOR MORRIS LANGDON, Leonora's lover
> ALISON LANGDON, his sick wife
> ANACLETO, her Filipino servant

The Story:

Seven characters were involved in a murder on a Southern army post: "two officers, a soldier, two women, a Filipino, and a horse." The soldier was Private Ellgee Williams, a clean-living man who had neither friends nor enemies and was assigned to the stables because he was good with horses. One of the officers was Captain Weldon Penderton, who was married to Leonora Penderton. He knew that his wife had lovers, and he often became enamored of them. He asked for a soldier to be sent to clear some woods behind his house. The soldier was Private Williams, whom Penderton already disliked because the young man had once spilled coffee on a new and expensive suit. Williams cleared the woods thoroughly, cutting back a tree that Penderton did not want cut.

That evening, the Pendertons were expecting dinner guests, Major Morris Langdon and his wife Alison. Major Langdon was Leonora Penderton's latest lover, and Captain Penderton was also interested in him. As they prepared for the guests, Penderton criticized his wife for not wearing shoes, and she stripped naked in front of him, making him furious. As she stripped, Private Williams passed by the window and saw her.

Williams had never before seen a naked woman. His father, a Holiness preacher, had reared him to believe that women carried deadly diseases. Therefore, Williams had avoided women. In fact, he had no real attachments to anyone. After he saw the scene between the Pendertons, he stayed and watched their dinner party through the window. The next day, Private Williams was different. He thought of other times he had behaved spontaneously. There was the time he had bought a cow that his family did not need. There was the time he felt moved by the spirit at a revival, and the time he committed a crime. His enlistment in the army had also been a spontaneous act. He knew he was about to do something unpredictable again.

For two weeks he observed the Captain's house and its patterns. Then he went to the windows and looked in, observing a blackjack game between Leonora Penderton and Major Langdon. Leonora could not add the cards; she had to be told whether she had won or lost. Langdon asked his wife, who also was there, if she had seen her friend Lieutenant Weincheck that day. She replied that she had, and she and Leonora discussed the Lieutenant's interest in art and music, an interest that Alison, but none of the rest of them, shared.

Alison Langdon was ill, both physically and emotionally. She had a weak heart. Her husband's infidelity left her depressed and ailing. The death of their baby, Catherine, three years previously, had weakened her immensely. A few months before, she had snipped off her nipples with a pair of gardening shears. She sat knitting, near tears, at the Pendertons' house as her husband played cards with his lover. When she went home, her husband stayed to play another hand.

Major Langdon felt like an outsider in his own house. His baby, born three years previously, had had a small deformity that made her repulsive to him. His wife and her houseboy, Anacleto, had taken care of the sick child for eleven months. The baby's death had been a relief to the Major but torture to his wife.

When the Major returned home, Anacleto was dancing around preparing a tray for Alison. Langdon was quite annoyed, and when Anacleto fell at the bottom of the stairs, the Major mouthed to him, "I-wish-you-had-bro-ken-your-neck." Alison remembered discovering that her husband was having an affair with Leonora Penderton. She and Anacleto had driven up to the Langdons' house and realized that Leonora and Major Langdon were there alone together in the dark.

Captain Penderton wanted to hate Alison Langdon, but he could not. She had once been witness to his stealing a silver spoon at a dinner party, one of only two times he had given in to a constant desire to be a thief.

Private Williams began coming to the Pendertons' house at night and squatting by Leonora Penderton's bed to watch her sleep. After he touched a strand of her hair, he no longer feared that touching a woman could give him a fatal disease. One day Captain Penderton went to the stables and asked for his wife's horse, Firebird, which Williams saddled for him. Penderton, a mediocre horseman, had trouble handling Firebird. The horse reacted negatively to him and eventually threw him. Penderton took a switch and beat the horse. He then realized that a naked Williams had seen him. The private took the horse back to the stables, and Penderton went home on foot, arriving two hours late for a large dinner party he and his wife were hosting.

From that time forward, Penderton went out of his way to see Williams. His feelings toward the private were almost obsessive, but they were also ambivalent, encompassing both love and hate.

The night of the party, Alison Langdon could not sleep. Anacleto came to her room and painted with water colors while they talked. He stared into the fire and described a peacock with one golden eye in which was reflected something he called "tiny and. . . . " Mrs. Langdon finished the description: "Grotesque."

Williams continued to visit Mrs. Penderton's room. He did not think much about his past, even about the time he stabbed an African American man in an argument over manure and hid the body in a quarry. He did, however, come to realize that Captain Penderton was following him.

One night Alison Langdon saw Williams sneak into the Pendertons' house and went there to tell her friends about the intruder. Captain Penderton did not believe her, and word got around that she had completely lost her mind. She then decided that she must leave her husband, so she and Anacleto packed and prepared to go. Major Langdon took this as proof of her insanity and had her sent to an institution in Virginia, where, two days later, she died of a heart attack. Anacleto left and was not heard from again. Morris Langdon mourned his wife's death and spent even more time at the Pendertons'.

Williams went to the Pendertons' for the seventh time. This time the Captain saw him coming. He went into his wife's bedroom and shot to death the man with whom he was obsessed.

Critical Evaluation:

Reflections in a Golden Eye was published one year after Carson McCullers' brilliant and well-received first novel, *The Heart Is a Lonely Hunter* (1940). The second work was often harshly criticized for dealing with morbid and depressing subjects, as well as for its grotesque characters. Detractors pointed to such incidents as Alison Langdon's cutting off her nipples with gardening shears and Weldon Penderton's putting a purring kitten into a frozen mailbox as evidence that McCullers was interested only in the darkest side of human nature.

Southern playwright Tennessee Williams, McCullers' friend, came to her defense. In an introduction to a later edition of the work, he explained that the world itself is full of morbidity and grotesqueness and that McCullers' novel encapsulates those qualities in a tiny space, thereby intensifying their effects.

Admirers of *Reflections in a Golden Eye* have also praised its economy. In 110 pages, McCullers paints thorough portraits of three characters: Captain Penderton, Private Williams, and Alison Langdon. Even characters who are less thoroughly drawn pique the reader's interest. This is especially true of the Filipino houseboy, Anacleto, who adores and emulates his mistress, even straining with her during labor. His dedication to her is both admirable and perverse.

Reflections in a Golden Eye explores the problems inherent in denying one's true nature and attempting too much to conform. Private Williams and Captain Penderton both try to deny their sexuality, resulting in one man's killing the other. The novel also shows what happens when a person fails to live up to his or her obligations to another. Major Langdon cannot be a true husband to Alison or a true father to his child; as a result, his wife becomes increasingly ill. Captain Penderton's inability to have a real relationship with his wife drives her to other men, again often causing pain to innocent people.

Setting the novel on an army base intensifies the work's effect. Where people are expected to conform, nonconformity seems even more grotesque. As McCullers says, on the post most men are expected to do no more than "follow the heels ahead of [them]." The people in this novel, however, are all out of step.

Reflections in a Golden Eye further illuminates one of McCullers' strongest themes: the effect of love on the lover. Major Langdon and Leonora Penderton have an affair; their love is requited, and they are the least interesting of the main characters. Langdon becomes sympathetic only after the death of his wife, when he wishes even that Anacleto were there so that he would have some daily reminder of Alison.

Captain Penderton, Alison Langdon, and Private Williams all love someone who cannot or will not love them in return. Penderton loves Williams; Williams loves Penderton's wife; and Mrs. Langdon loves her dead child. All are ultimately destroyed by their love.

A related theme, also common with McCullers, is isolation. Almost everyone in the novel is in some way alone. Although the characters try to make connections, these attempts often result in further separation.

Respect for *Reflections in a Golden Eye* has increased with time. The short novel is now considered one of McCullers' masterpieces, although its grotesque characters, violent events, and unconventional sexuality continue to disturb readers.

M. Katherine Grimes

Bibliography:
Carr, Virginia Spencer. *The Lonely Hunter: A Biography of Carson McCullers*. Garden City, N.J.: Anchor Press, 1975. This definitive biography of Carson McCullers has numerous

photographs and a good index. Discusses the circumstances surrounding the writing and publication of *Reflections in a Golden Eye*.

_____. *Understanding Carson McCullers*. Columbia: University of South Carolina Press, 1990. Argues that the characters in *Reflections in a Golden Eye* are grotesque. Describes characters and plot, giving a brief overview of contemporary reviews of the book.

Cook, Richard M. *Carson McCullers*. New York: Frederick Ungar, 1975. Cook analyzes the main characters in the novel and discusses the theme of isolation.

Graver, Lawrence. *Carson McCullers*. Minneapolis: University of Minnesota Press, 1969. Noteworthy for its vituperative attack on *Reflections in a Golden Eye*, which Graver criticizes for "luridness of subject" and "lack of artistry."

McDowell, Margaret B. *Carson McCullers*. Boston: Twayne, 1980. Describes the book's plot, then discusses its comic effects, the use of the gothic, its "fragmented vision of human existence," the motif of isolation, and its horror.

REFLECTIONS ON THE REVOLUTION IN FRANCE

Type of work: Politics
Author: Edmund Burke (1729-1797)
First published: 1790

Edmund Burke was deeply involved in English public life as a Whig politician who served 1765-1794 as a member of Parliament. This experience convinced him that governments must respond to the practical needs of the peoples they governed and that political crises did not all yield to the same measures. When he saw what was unfolding in France in 1789 and 1790, he became alarmed that the revolutionaries were ignoring the wisdom achieved by long experience and that they were acting on assumptions that were contrary to human nature. *Reflections on the Revolution in France* was intended to warn the people of England against being caught up by the same enthusiasm for destructive change that Burke saw infecting the citizens of France.

The Reign of Terror had not yet begun when Burke took up his pen in 1790 (some would say it is foreseen in Burke's castigation of the revolutionaries), but in July, 1789, the Bastille had been taken and the Comitù des Recherches had been formed and given numerous repressive police powers. In August, the National Assembly promulgated a *Declaration of the Rights of Man and Citizen.* Two months later, the king's family was transferred from Versailles to Paris. In November, the National Assembly appropriated the church's property, which soon became the basis of a new paper currency known as *assignats.* The religious orders, excepting those concerned with charity or education, were shut down in February, 1790, and finally, in July, the hereditary nobility were stripped of their titles and perquisites. These were the drastic changes taking place in France as Burke wrote the *Reflections.*

In late 1789, a young French friend of Burke, Charles-Jean-François Depont, asked Burke for his thoughts on the recent events in France. After a first, short letter of response, Burke began again in earnest with the words "Dear Sir" and did not stop until he had written the entire book, 250 pages in the Penguin paperback edition. He explains that he will "throw out" his thoughts and express his feelings "just as they arise in my mind, with very little attention to formal method." There are no chapter divisions or subheads but only long, dense paragraphs packed with balanced statements and striking turns of phrase. Burke seizes a subject and wrings it dry, his tone frequently modulating between contempt and solemnity.

If his improvised style holds the reader with its rhetorical inventiveness, the substance of his account is often not to be trusted. His silly story of the mob's takeover of Versailles on October 6, 1789, which features the queen's servant being "cut down" by a "band of cruel ruffians and assassins," is a lurid fiction. This passage in particular was immediately ridiculed and hurt Burke's credibility. The *Reflections on the Revolution in France* should not be read as history, however, but as a work of political theory that expresses a coherent point of view.

On November 4, 1789, Dr. Richard Price, a dissenting minister, preached in an area of London known as the Old Jewry a fiery sermon praising the upheaval going on in France. Burke identifies (not quite verbatim) three fundamental rights that Price insisted the English people had acquired: "to choose our own governors"; "to cashier them for misconduct"; and "to frame a government for ourselves." Burke rejects this talk of "rights" and cites the Declaration of Right (the bill of rights written under William and Mary) as "the cornerstone of the constitution" and as the embodiment of the true principles of the Revolution of 1688.

The "Glorious Revolution" did not, Burke says, give people the lasting right to elect their own rulers but only the opportunity to resolve a crisis at that specific time. The British people were free to fill the throne only "upon the same grounds on which they might have wholly abolished their monarchy, and every other part of their constitution." In other words, the people had hardly any grounds, for a hereditary monarchy is rooted in British history. "An irregular, convulsive movement may be necessary to throw off an irregular, convulsive disease. But the course of succession is the healthy habit of the British constitution."

As for the second claim of the Revolution Society, the "right of cashiering their governors for *misconduct*," Burke focuses on the vagueness of the word misconduct. No general principle of fundamental importance can be based on language so ill-defined. The "virtual abdication" of King James II that resulted in the succession crisis was forced by specific charges of "nothing less than a design, confirmed by a multitude of illegal overt acts, to *subvert the Protestant church and state*" and of "having broken the *original contract* between king and people."

The third right that Burke accuses Price and his followers of advocating is the "right to form a government for ourselves." Burke dismisses this claim by appealing to a "uniform policy" stretching from the Magna Carta of 1215 to the Declaration of Right, a policy that reveals an "*entailed inheritance* derived to us from our forefathers . . . without any reference whatever to any other more general or prior right." Burke's discussion relies heavily on the bedrock assumption underlying his entire political theory, a conviction that the British system of law and government evolved from basic principles in nature itself. Indeed, *Reflections on the Revolution in France* can perhaps be understood as a long gloss on one magnificent, swelling sentence: "Our political system is placed in a just correspondence and symmetry with the order of the world, and with the mode of existence decreed to a permanent body composed of transitory parts; wherein, by the dispensation of a stupendous wisdom, moulding together the great mysterious incorporation of the human race, the whole, at one time, is never old, or middle-aged, or young, but in a condition of unchangeable constancy, moves on through the varied tenour of perpetual decay, fall, renovation, and progression." That sentence encapsulates both Burke's political philosophy and his theology.

Burke's faith in a natural order of things approaches the conviction that whatever is, is right, simply because it is. If every human institution were not the best of its kind, then the institution would have evolved otherwise. This vision reflects an innate pragmatism that trusts no a priori judgments and leaves all arrangements to be forged in experience. He sneered at the French rationalists and especially at Jean-Jacques Rousseau. In a "Letter to a Member of the National Assembly" (1791) in which he responded to questions about *Reflections on the Revolution in France*, Burke blisters Rousseau as "the great professor and founder of *the philosophy of vanity* in England" and "the insane *Socrates* of the National Assembly." These philosophes and their rabble-rousing followers in England, Burke claims, inflame weak minds with their prating about "natural" rights that are mere abstractions too often born of greed and envy. They intend to abolish religion and to replace it with an education "founded in a knowledge of the physical wants of men; progressively carried to an enlightened self-interest, which, when well understood, they tell us will identify with an interest more enlarged and public."

Dr. Price and the other dissenting clergy represented in the Revolution Society applauded the National Assembly when it seized the property of the Catholic church. As a defender of the sacredness of private property rights, Burke was horrified by the seizure, and he argues at length in *Reflections on the Revolution in France* that the corporate holdings of the church should enjoy the same status as an individual's property. The dissidents who attack the church forget its "duty to make a sure provision for the consolation of the feeble and the instruction of the ignorant" and seem to regard religion, "the great ruling principle of the moral and natural world, as a mere invention to keep the vulgar in obedience."

A third group whose perceived corruption Burke assails is the "stockjobbers," as he calls them, those individuals who put their own private economic interests above the nation's and seek to further them by exploiting the possibilities opened up by a dismantled church economy. Among these, Burke targets speculators who fear for their investments because of the accumulating national debt, and many British readers must have been sensitive to that danger.

Prominent among the many enemies of the church and the monarchy cited by Burke is a certain alienated personality that he describes as "discontented men of quality" who evince no love of country or of humankind. They fail "to love the little platoon we belong to in society" and "generally despise their own order," and they exhibit "a selfish and mischievous ambition" and "distempered passions." Had Burke lived to read Fyodor Dostoevski's *The Possessed* (1913), he would have found in that novel's cankered nihilists precisely the sensibility to which he objected. His allegiance to the established church extends to a sympathy for those church members deprived of their rank and fortune. Speaking always of what is ideal, and well aware that many clergy betray that ideal, Burke defends the privileges accorded ecclesiastics, who, with the nobility, provide models for the humble to aspire to. As he says, "[S]ome part of the wealth of the country is as usefully employed as it can be, in fomenting the luxury of individuals. It is the publick ornament. It is the publick consolation. It nourishes the publick hope."

Admitting to but a slight knowledge of the character of the French nobility, Burke argues that his lifetime study of "human nature" compensates for that deficiency. He ascribes to the French nobles a "high spirit" and "a delicate sense of honour." Their behavior toward the "inferior classes" appears good-natured and "more nearly approaching to familiarity" than the practice of their British counterparts. The fact that commoners who had achieved wealth did not enjoy adequate esteem in society Burke judges to be "one principal cause of the old nobility." Yet he considers the nobility and the established church as the embodiment of the sacred principle of private property. "Nobility is a graceful ornament to the civil order. It is the Corinthian capital of polished society." The leveling instinct is therefore false to human nature. Holding these beliefs, then, it was natural for Burke to interpret the events in France as a threat to the foundations of a civil society in Britain.

Frank Day

Bibliography:
Blakemore, Steven, ed. *Burke and the French Revolution.* Athens: University of Georgia Press, 1992. Six essays written for the bicentennial.

Chapman, Gerald. *Edmund Burke: The Practical Imagination.* Cambridge, Mass.: Harvard University Press, 1967. This sophisticated analysis argues that Burke's absurd account of the events at Versailles led to a distortion of his position.

Lock, F. P. *Burke's Reflections on the Revolution in France.* London: Allen & Unwin, 1985. Besides offering authoritative commentary, Lock carefully explains the sequence of events that led up to Burke's response.

Mitchell, L. G. "Introduction to *Reflections on the Revolution in France*, by Edmund Burke. Oxford and New York: Oxford University Press, 1993. A concise and informative introduction to one of the most readily available paperback editions of the *Reflections on the Revolution in France.*

Paine, Thomas. *Rights of Man.* 1791. Reprint. Edited by Henry Collins. Harmondsworth, England: Penguin, 1969. The famous response to Burke by the pamphleteer whose *Crisis* papers helped win the American Revolution.

THE REIVERS
A Reminiscence

Type of work: Novel
Author: William Faulkner (1897-1962)
Type of plot: Psychological realism
Time of plot: May, 1905
Locale: Yoknapatawpha County, Mississippi, and Memphis and Parsham, Tennessee
First published: 1962

Principal characters:

LUCIUS PRIEST, the eleven-year-old narrator

BOON HOGGANBECK, a part-Chickasaw Indian and the poorest shot in the county

NED WILLIAM MCCASLIN, the Priests' coachman and a black member of the McCaslin and Priest families

LUCIUS QUINTUS PRIEST (BOSS), young Lucius' grandfather, a Jefferson banker, and owner of the stolen Winton Flyer

MISS SARAH, his wife

MAURY PRIEST, his son and Lucius' father

MISS ALISON, Maury Priest's wife

MISS REBA RIVERS, the proprietress of a Memphis brothel

EVERBE (MISS CORRIE) CORINTHIA, one of Miss Reba's girls and the beloved of Boon Hogganbeck

MR. BINFORD, Miss Reba's landlord and protector

MINNIE, Miss Reba's maid

OTIS, Miss Corrie's delinquent nephew from Arkansas

SAM CALDWELL, a railroad brakeman and Boon's rival

UNCLE PARSHAM HOOD, a dignified old black man who befriends young Lucius Priest

LYCURGUS BRIGGINS, his grandson

BUTCH LOVEMAIDEN, a brutal deputy sheriff

MCWILLIE, Acheron's rider

COLONEL LINSCOMB, Acheron's owner

MR. VAN TOSCH, the owner of Coppermine, the stolen racehorse renamed Lightning

BOBO BEAUCHAMP, Mr. van Tosch's stableboy and Ned William McCaslin's cousin

DELPHINE, Ned's wife and the Priests' cook

The Story:

In 1905, eleven-year-old Lucius Priest was on his way to Memphis with Boon Hogganbeck, a tough, faithful, but completely unpredictable and unreliable part-Chickasaw Indian who was mad about machinery, and freeloading Ned William McCaslin, the Priests' black coachman and handyman. They were driving the Winton Flyer owned by young Lucius' grandfather and "borrowed" for the excursion without his permission or knowledge. Lucius' grandfather, the president of a Jefferson bank and the owner of the second automobile ever to be seen in the county, had gone to Louisiana to attend a funeral. Boon Hogganbeck had tempted the boy with the proposal that they drive the Winton Flyer to Memphis, and Lucius had finally succumbed to the temptation. After considerable conniving, they had set out, only to discover shortly afterward that Ned William McCaslin had hidden under a tarpaulin on the backseat.

Because of the condition of the roads, the truants were forced to make an overnight stop at Miss Ballenbaugh's, a small country store with a loft above it that held mattresses for the convenience of fishermen and fox or coon hunters. The next morning, after one of the breakfasts for which Miss Ballenbaugh was famous, they started out early and soon reached Hell Creek bottom, the deepest mud hole in all Mississippi. There was no way around it. If they had gone around it in one direction, they would have ended up in Alabama, in the other, they would have fallen into the Mississippi. The automobile became mired and remained stuck in spite of their labors with shovel, barbed wire, block and tackle, and piled branches. On the gallery of a paintless cabin nearby, his two mules already harnessed in plow gear, a barefooted redneck watched and waited. When the three gave up in exasperation, this backwoods opportunist appeared and pulled the car out of the slough, remarking that mud was one of the best crops in the region. Some stiff bargaining followed. Boon claimed that six dollars was too much for the job, all the more because one of his passengers was a boy and the other a black. The man answered that his mules were color blind.

Having passed Hell Creek Bottom, they arrived in Memphis, but instead of going to the Gayoso Hotel, as Lucius expected (the McCaslins and Priests always stayed at the Gayoso because a distant member of the family had in Civil War times galloped into the lobby in an effort to capture a Yankee general), Boon drove his passengers to Miss Reba's house on Catalpa Street, so that he could see Miss Corrie, one of Miss Reba's girls. That night, Ned, a reckless gambling man, traded the stolen automobile for a stolen racehorse never known to run any better than second. Before the three could return to Jefferson, it was necessary for young Lucius to turn jockey and win a race against a better horse, Colonel Linscomb's Acheron. He also fought with Otis, the vicious nephew who slurred Miss Corrie, and with this chivalric gesture he restored her self-respect. Boon and Ned became involved in difficulties with the law, represented by a corrupt deputy sheriff named Butch Lovemaiden. It was discovered that Otis has stolen the gold tooth prized by Miss Reba's maid, Minnie. Boon found that he had rivals for Miss Corrie's charms, and he had to fight them. As a result of these delays, Lucius was forced to assume a gentleman's responsibilities of courage and conduct. He lost the innocence of childhood and was at times close to despair, but he realized that to turn back would not be homesickness but shame.

Lucius survived his ordeal, but at considerable cost to his conscience and peace of mind. Grandfather Priest, who arrived to straighten everything out, had the final word on his escapade. When the boy asked how he could forget his folly and guilt, he told him that he would not be able to because nothing in life is ever forgotten or lost. When Lucius wanted to know what he could do, his grandfather said that he must live with it. To the weeping boy's protests, he replied that a gentleman can live through anything because he must always accept the responsibility of his actions and the weight of their consequences. Grandfather Priest concluded by telling Lucius to go wash his face: A gentleman may cry, but he washes his face afterward.

Critical Evaluation:

Subtitled *A Reminiscence*, *The Reivers*, which was posthumously awarded the 1963 Pulitzer Prize in fiction, begins on a note of action recalled in memory. About a fourth of the way through the novel, one of William Faulkner's most engaging yarns finally begins, a tall story whose idiom and spirit is reminiscent of a Huck Finn escapade brought forward in time. Its presence in *The Reivers* is not so much a matter of imitation as of a common source, for there is a sense in which Faulkner stands at the end of a literary tradition rather than, as many of his admirers claim, at the beginning of a new one. Through all of his writing runs a strain of broad folk humor and comic invention going back through Mark Twain to Augustus Baldwin Longstreet's *Georgia Scenes* (1835) and George Washington Harris' *Sut Lovingood's Yarns* (1867), and beyond them to the Davy Crockett almanacs and the anonymous masters of oral anecdote who flourished in the old Southwest. The early American was by nature a storyteller. The realities of frontier life and his own hard comic sense created a literature of tall men and tall deeds repeated in the trading post, the groggery, the rafters' camp, and wherever men met on the edge of the wilderness. These stories, shaped by a common experience and imagination, had a geography, a mythology, and a lingo of their own. Some were streaked with ballad sentiment, others with bawdy humor, but mostly these tales were comic elaborations of character, of fantastic misadventures in which the frontiersman dramatized himself with shrewd appraisal and salty enjoyment. Through them goes a raggle-taggle procession of hunters, peddlers, horse traders, horse thieves, eagle orators, prophets, backwoods swains, land speculators, and settlers, which creates a picture of the country and the times.

Faulkner's Yoknapatawpha County lies, after all, in the same geographical belt with the Mississippi River and the Natchez Trace, and these are regions of history, folklore, and fantasy revealed in tall-story humor. This humor came into Faulkner's fiction as early as *Mosquitoes* (1927), in the account of Old Hickory's descendant who tried raising sheep in the Louisiana swamps and came to feel so much at home in the water that he turned into a shark. It contributes to effects of grotesque outrage and exaggeration in *As I Lay Dying* (1930), gives *Light in August* (1932) a warming pastoral glow, adds three episodes of pure comedy to *The Hamlet* (1940) and provides illuminating comment on the rise and fall of Flem Snopes. Faulkner's habit in the past, however, was to subordinate his racier effects to the more serious concerns of human mortality and the disorder of the moral universe. Not until he wrote *The Reivers* did he give free play to his talent for comedy of character and situation and, like Mark Twain in *Adventures of Huckleberry Finn* (1884), make it the master bias of structure and theme.

There are other parallels with Twain's novel. One is the unmistakable flavor of a style derived from the drawled tones of reminiscence. In *Adventures of Huckleberry Finn*, this style was shaped to reveal habits of thought and feeling in art, a truly colloquial style marvelously tuned in pulse and improvisation and with including the incorrectness of folk speech in its idiom. In *The Reivers*, this style is made to support both a burden of feeling within a boy's range of response and an old man's accumulation of a lifetime's reflections. It is a style that can record sensory impressions with poetic finality.

Like *Adventures of Huckleberry Finn*, *The Reivers*, too, is a story of initiation, of innocence corrupted and evil exorcised. Both novels show the world through the eyes of childhood, an effective device that freshens experience and corrects judgment. Between the two novels there is this important difference: Huck is protected by the earthy nonchalance of his own native shrewdness and resourcefulness from the contamination of the shore. Young Lucius Priest lives by the code of his class, the code of a gentleman, and he brings its values to the bordello and to the racetrack. The true test is not innocence itself but what lies behind the mask of innocence. Grandfather Priest claims that when adults speak of childish innocence, they really mean ignorance. Actually, children are neither, in his opinion, for an eleven-year-old can envision any crime. If he possesses innocence, it is probably lack of appetite, just as his ignorance may be a lack of opportunity or ability.

Under its surface of fantastic invention and tall-story humor, *The Reivers* is a moral fable in the Faulknerian manner. Yet its effect is different from that of the earlier, darker studies of manners and morals. In tragedy—and Faulkner was a great tragic artist—the human soul stands naked before a god who is not mocked. In comedy, it is not what is possible in humans that is revealed, but what is probable in conduct or belief. Thus, in comedy, people are viewed in relation to some aspect of their society. In *The Reivers*—the title means plunderers or freebooters—a master of comedy was at work to show the testing of young Lucius Priest's code of gentlemanly behavior in a world of evasion and deceit where it would have been easier to run from the responsibilities than to stand up and face them.

The triumph of *The Reivers* is in the manner of its telling. The novel presents the story of a boy, but the story is told by a man grown old and wise enough through the years of accumulated experience to look back on his adventure, relish it in all its qualities, and, at the same time, pass judgment on it. This judgment is never harsh. Lucius Priest, telling the story to his grandson, is revealed as a person of tolerance and understanding of much that is deeply and irrevocably ingrained in the eternal condition of humankind, and his point of view gives the novel added depth and dimension.

The Reivers is a minor Faulkner work. Nevertheless, it is a good yarn in the tall-story tradition, skillfully told, comic in effect, and shrewd in its observations on manners, morals, politics, and human nature. More to the point, the novel broadens the reader's knowledge of Faulkner's legendary Mississippi county.

Bibliography:
Bell, Haney H., Jr. "The Relative Maturity of Lucius Priest and Ike McCaslin." *Aegis* 2 (1973): 15-21. Examines the heroic effort and coming of age. Ultimately finds the story "The Bear" to be a greater struggle toward maturity than that depicted in *The Reivers*.
Brooks, Cleanth. *William Faulkner: The Yoknapatawpha Country*. New Haven, Conn.: Yale University Press, 1963. Contains separate chapters on the most important Faulkner novels, including *The Reivers*, and provides description of plot and comparisons between the characters and subtexts of the works. One of the most helpful and accessible books on *The Reivers*.
Vickery, Olga W. *The Novels of William Faulkner*. Rev. ed. Baton Rouge: Louisiana State University Press, 1964. A thorough examination of all of Faulkner's novels, summarizing Faulkner's technique, style, themes, and the encompassing philosophy that unifies his works.
Williams, David. *Faulkner's Women: The Myth and the Muse*. Montreal: McGill-Queen's University Press, 1977. Considers the women in Faulkner's novels from the aspect of psychoanalysis and Jungian archetypes. Includes a discussion of male and female characters in *The Reivers*.
Wittenberg, Judith B. *Faulkner: The Transfiguration of Biography*. Lincoln: University of Nebraska Press, 1979. Essentially a Faulkner biography, but one that draws on scenes from Faulkner's novels to find his views on artists, family, and human responsibility. Lucius Priest of *The Reivers* is found to be exemplary in his heroic conduct.

REMEMBRANCE OF THINGS PAST

Type of work: Novel
Author: Marcel Proust (1871-1922)
Type of plot: Psychological realism
Time of plot: Late nineteenth and early twentieth centuries
Locale: France
First published: À la recherche du temps perdu, 1913-1927 (English translation, 1922-1931, 1981): *Du côté de chez Swann*, 1913 (*Swann's Way*, 1922); *À l'ombre des jeunes filles en fleurs*, 1919 (*Within a Budding Grove*, 1924); *Le Côté de Guermantes*, 1920-1921 (*The Guermantes Way*, 1925); *Sodome et Gomorrhe*, 1922 (*Cities of the Plain*, 1927); *La Prisonnière*, 1925 (*The Captive*, 1929); *Albertine disparue*, 1925 (*The Sweet Cheat Gone*, 1930); *Le Temps retrouvé*, 1927 (*Time Regained*, 1931)

> *Principal characters:*
> MARCEL, the narrator
> MARCEL'S GRANDMOTHER, a kind and wise old woman
> MONSIEUR SWANN, a wealthy broker and aesthete
> MADAME SWANN, formerly a cocotte, Odette de Crecy
> GILBERTE, their daughter and later Madame de Saint-Loup
> MADAME DE VILLEPARISIS, friend of Marcel's grandmother
> ROBERT DE SAINT-LOUP, her nephew and Marcel's friend
> BARON DE CHARLUS, another nephew and a Gomorrite
> MADAME VERDURIN, a vulgar social climber
> PRINCE and PRINCESS DE GUERMANTES and
> DUKE and DUCHESS DE GUERMANTES, members of the old aristocracy

The Story:

All of his life Marcel found it difficult to go to sleep at night. After he had blown out the light, he would lie quietly in the darkness and think of the book he had been reading, of an event in history, of some memory from the past. Sometimes he would think of all the places in which he had slept—as a child in his great-aunt's house in the provincial town of Combray, in Balbec on a holiday with his grandmother, in the military town where his friend, Robert de Saint-Loup, had been stationed, in Paris, in Venice during a visit there with his mother.

He remembered always a night at Combray when he was a child. Monsieur Swann, a family friend, had come to dinner. Marcel had been sent to bed early, where he lay for hours nervous and unhappy until at last he heard Monsieur Swann leave. Then his mother had come upstairs to comfort him. For a long time, the memory of that night was his chief recollection of Combray, where his family took him to spend a part of every summer with his grandparents and aunts. Years later, while drinking tea with his mother, the taste of a small sweet cake suddenly brought back all the impressions of his old days at Combray.

He remembered the two roads. One was Swann's way, a path that ran beside Monsieur Swann's park, where lilacs and hawthorns bloomed. The other was the Guermantes way, along the river and past the château of the Duke and Duchess de Guermantes, the great family of Combray. He remembered the people he saw on his walks. There were familiar figures like the doctor and the priest. There was Monsieur Vinteuil, an old composer who died brokenhearted and shamed because of his daughter's friendship with a woman of bad reputation. There were the neighbors and friends of his grandparents. Most of all, he remembered Monsieur Swann, whose story he pieced together slowly from family conversations and village gossip.

Monsieur Swann was a wealthy Jew, accepted in rich and fashionable society. His wife was not received, however, for she was his former mistress, Odette de Crecy, a prostitute with the fair, haunting beauty of a Botticelli painting. It was Odette who had first introduced Swann to the Verdurins, a vulgar family that pretended to despise the polite world of the Guermantes. At an evening party given by Madame Verdurin, Swann heard played a movement of Vinteuil's sonata and identified his hopeless passion for Odette with that lovely music. Swann's love was an unhappy affair. Tortured by jealousy, aware of the vulgarity and pettiness of the Verdurins, determined to forget his unfaithful mistress, he went to Madame de Saint-Euverte's reception. There he heard Vinteuil's music again. Under its influence he decided, at whatever price, to marry Odette.

After their marriage, Swann drifted more and more into the bourgeois circle of the Verdurins. When he went to see his old friends in Combray and in the fashionable Faubourg Saint-Germain, he went alone. Many people thought him both ridiculous and tragic.

On his walks Marcel sometimes saw Madame Swann and her daughter, Gilberte, in the park at Combray. Later, in Paris, he met the little girl and became her playmate. That friendship, as they grew older, became an innocent love affair. Filled also with a schoolboyish passion for Madame Swann, Marcel went to Swann's house as much to be in her company as in Gilberte's, but after a time, his pampered habits and brooding, neurasthenic nature began to bore Gilberte. His pride hurt, he refused to see her for many years.

Marcel's family began to treat him as an invalid. With his grandmother, he went to Balbec, a seaside resort. There he met Albertine, a girl to whom he was immediately attracted. He also met Madame de Villeparisis, an old friend of his grandmother and a connection of the Guermantes family. Madame de Villeparisis introduced him to her two nephews, Robert de Saint-Loup and Baron de Charlus. Saint-Loup and Marcel became close friends. While visiting Saint-Loup in a nearby garrison town, Marcel met his friend's mistress, a young Jewish actress named Rachel. Marcel was both fascinated and repelled by Baron de Charlus; he was not to understand until later the baron's corrupt and depraved nature.

Through his friendship with Madame de Villeparisis and Saint-Loup, Marcel was introduced into the smart world of the Guermantes when he returned to Paris.

One day, while he was walking with his grandmother, she suffered a stroke. The illness and death of that good and unselfish old woman made him realize for the first time the empty worldliness of his smart and wealthy friends. For comfort he turned to Albertine, who came to stay with him in Paris while his family was away. Nevertheless, his desire to be humored and indulged in all of his whims, his suspicions of Albertine, and his petty jealousy finally forced her to leave him and go back to Balbec. With her, he had been unhappy; without her, he was wretched. Then he learned that she had been accidentally killed in a fall from her horse. Later he received a letter, written before her death, in which she promised to return to him.

More miserable than ever, Marcel tried to find diversion among his old friends. They were changing with the times. Swann was ill and soon to die. Gilberte had married Robert de Saint-Loup. Madame Verdurin, who had inherited a fortune, now entertained the old nobility. At one of her parties Marcel heard a Vinteuil composition played by a musician named Morel, the nephew of a former servant and now a protégé of the notorious Baron de Charlus.

His health breaking down at last, Marcel spent the war years in a sanatorium. When he returned to Paris, he found still greater changes. Robert de Saint-Loup had been killed in the war. Rachel, Saint-Loup's mistress, had become a famous actress. Swann was also dead, and his widow had remarried and was now a fashionable hostess who received the Duchess de Guermantes. Prince de Guermantes, his fortune lost and his first wife dead, had married Madame Verdurin for her money. Baron de Charlus had grown senile.

Marcel went to one last reception at the Princess de Guermantes' lavish house. There he met the daughter of Gilberte de Saint-Loup; he realized how time had passed, how old he had grown. In the Guermantes library, he happened to take down the novel by George Sand that his mother had read to him that remembered night in Combray, years before. Suddenly, in memory, he heard again the ringing of the bell that announced Monsieur Swann's departure and knew that it would echo in his mind forever. He saw then that everything in his own futile, wasted life dated from that long ago night in his childhood, and in that moment of self-revelation he saw also the ravages of time among all the people he had ever known.

Critical Evaluation:
Remembrance of Things Past is not a novel of traditional form. Symphonic in design, it unfolds without plot or crisis as the writer reveals in retrospect the motifs of his experience, holds them for thematic effect, and drops them, only to return to them once more in the processes of recurrence and change. This varied pattern of experience brings together a series of involved relationships through the imagination and observation of a narrator engaged in tracing with painstaking detail his perceptions of people and places as he himself grows from childhood to disillusioned middle age. From the waking reverie in which he recalls the themes and characters of his novel to that closing paragraph with its slow, repeated echoes of the word time, Marcel Proust's novel is great art distilled from memory itself, the structure determined entirely by moods and sensations evoked by the illusion of time passing, or seeming to pass, recurring, or seeming to recur.

In *Remembrance of Things Past*, Proust, together with Leo Tolstoy (*War and Peace*, 1865-1869), Fyodor Dostoevski (*The Brothers Karamazov*, 1879-1880), Thomas Mann (*Joseph and His Brothers*, 1933-1943), and James Joyce (*Ulysses*, 1922), transformed the novel from a linear account of events into a multidimensional art. The breakthrough was not into Freudian psychology, or existentialism, or scientific determinism, but into a realization that all things are, or may be, interwoven, bound by time, yet freed from time, open to every associational context.

What is reality? Certainly there is the reality of the sensory experience; yet any moment of sensory experience may have numerous successive or even simultaneous realities as it is relived in memory in different contexts, and perhaps the most significant reality—or realities—of a given act or moment may come long after the moment when the event first took place in time. Percy Shelley, in *A Defence of Poetry* (1840), said, "All things exist as they are perceived: at least in relation to the percipient." Things which may have seemed inconsequential at the moment of their occurrence may take on richly multifaceted meanings in relation to other events, other memories, other moments. The initial act is not as significant, not as real, as the perceptions of it which may come in new contexts. Reality, thus, is a context, made up of moods, of recollections joined by chance or design, sets of associations that have grown over the years. This concept of the notion of reality, one that had been taking shape with increased momentum since the Romantic movement, opened the way to "those mysteries . . . the presentiment of which is the quality in life and art which moves us most deeply."

The elusive yet pervasively important nature of reality applies not only to events, such as the taste of the madeleine (or small cake), but also to the absence of events, for the failure of Marcel's mother to give him his accustomed good-night kiss proved to be an occasion which memory would recall again and again in a variety of relationships. Thus reality can and inevitably for all people does sometimes include, if not indeed center on, the nonbeing of an event. That nonexistence can be placed in time and in successive times as surely as events that did happen; moreover "it"—that nothing where something might or should have been—may become a significant part of the contexts which, both in time and freed from time, constitute reality.

Such thematic variations and turns of thought have led some to identify Proust as a dilettante. Perhaps, in its literal sense, the term is justified, for his mind must have delighted in what, to the reader, may be unexpected turns of thought. In this he is most closely to be associated with Thomas Mann, whose consideration of time in the first volume of *Joseph and His Brothers* leads the reader into labyrinthine but essential paths; or whose speculations about the God-man relationship in volume 2, in the section headed "Abraham Discovers God," lead the reader down a dizzying path of whimsical yet serious thought. The fact remains, however, that Mann and Proust have opened doors of contemplation that modern readers cannot afford to ignore if they would increase their understanding of themselves, the world in which they live, and the tenuous nature of reality and of time.

What Proust does with time and reality he also does with character. Although he is a contemporary of Freud, and although Freudian interpretation could be applied to some of his characters in part, his concept of character is much too complex for reduction to the superego, the ego, the id, and the subconscious. Character, like reality, is a changing total context, not static and not a thing in itself to be held off and examined at arm's length. Baron de Charlus is at once a study of character in disintegration and a caricature, reduced in the end to a pitiable specimen, scarcely human. It is Marcel, however, the persona of the story, who is seen in most depth and frequently in tortured self-analysis. His character is seen in direct statements, in his comments about others and about situations, in what others say to him or the way they say it, even in descriptive passages which would at first glance not seem to relate to character at all. "Only the exhaustive can be truly interesting," Mann said in the preface to *The Magic Mountain* (1924). Proust surely agreed. His detail is not of the catalog variety, however; it works cumulatively, developmentally, with the thematic progression of symphonic music.

Finally the totality of the work is "the remembrance of things past," or as the title of the seventh and final volume has it, the past recaptured. To understand it in its full richness, one must become and remain conscious of the author, isolated in his study, drawing upon his recollections, associating and reassociating moments, events, personalities (his own always central), both to recapture the past as it happened and to discover in it the transcendent reality which supersedes the time-bound moment of the initial occurrence. The total work is a story, a succession of stories, and a study of the life process, which, as one comes to understand it, must greatly enrich one's own sense of self and of the life one lives.

"Critical Evaluation" by Kenneth Oliver

Bibliography:
Deleuze, Gilles. *Proust and Signs*. Translated by Richard Howard. New York: George Braziller, 1972. Deleuze's landmark reading of Proust depicts the work as a search in which the disillusioned narrator learns to decode and discard the signs of worldliness and the signs of love, concluding that only the signs of art offer a kind of fulfillment that can withstand the corrosive force of time.
De Man, Paul. *Allegories of Reading*. New Haven, Conn.: Yale University Press, 1979. Uses Proust to manifest the uncertainty of meaning by documenting the disjunction between grammar and rhetoric in the work.

Genette, Gérard. "Proust Palimpsest" and "Proust and Indirect Language." In *Figures in Literary Discourse*, translated by Alan Sheridan. Oxford, England: Basil Blackwell, 1982. A classic analysis of Proust's use of figurative devices in general and of metaphor in particular.

Hill, Leslie. "Proust and the Art of Reading." *Comparative Criticism* 2 (1980): 167-185. Uses Proust's text to test the reader response theories of Roland Barthes, who posits a new kind of reader in the aftermath of the death of the author. Hill's work is the definitive article on reader response theory and Proust.

Kristeva, Julia. *Proust and the Sense of Time*. Translated by Stephen Bann. New York: Columbia University Press, 1993. Kristeva's insightful reading is grounded in an investigation of the genesis of meaning. She traces the successive stages of subjectivity through which Proust's narrator passes.

THE RENAISSANCE
Studies in Art and Poetry

Type of work: Essays
Author: Walter Pater (1839-1894)
First published: 1873 as *Studies in the History of the Renaissance*; revised as *The Renaissance: Studies in Art and Poetry*, 1877, 1888, 1893

In the preface to *The Renaissance*, Walter Pater writes, "The subjects of the following studies . . . touch what I think the chief points in that complex, many-sided movement." The subjects themselves are the French, Italian, and German writers, painters, and sculptors, ranging from the thirteenth to the eighteenth century, in whose lives and in whose works Pater finds represented the many sides, the divergent attitudes and aims, of the Renaissance.

Pater's method is impressionistic. The task of the aesthetic critic, he says, is first to realize distinctly the exact impression that a work of art makes upon him, then to determine the source and conditions—the "virtue"—of that impression, and finally to express that virtue so that the impression it has made on him may be shared by others. *The Renaissance* is the record of the impressions induced in the refined sensibilities of Walter Pater by the art he studied.

The Renaissance, for Pater, was "not merely the revival of classical antiquity which took place in the fifteenth century . . . but a whole complex movement, of which that revival of classical antiquity was but one element or symptom." Accordingly, in the first chapter, he finds the roots of the movement in twelfth and thirteenth century France, illustrated in two prose romances of that time *Amis and Amile* and *Aucassin and Nicolette*. It is in their "spirit of rebellion and revolt against the moral and religious ideas of the time" that these tales prefigure that later "outbreak of the reason and the imagination," the high Renaissance of fifteenth century Italy.

One important part of that later Renaissance, according to Pater, was the effort made by fifteenth century Italian scholars "to reconcile Christianity with the religion of ancient Greece." Pico della Mirandola typified that effort, both in his writings and in his life; he was "reconciled indeed to the new religion, but still [had] a tenderness for the earlier life." Lacking the historic sense, Pico and his contemporaries sought in vain, as Pater saw it, a reconciliation based on allegorical interpretations of religious belief; "the Renaissance of the fifteenth century was . . . great, rather by what it designed . . . than by what it actually achieved."

In discussing Botticelli, Pater acknowledges that he is a painter of secondary rank, not great as Michelangelo and Leonardo da Vinci are great. Nevertheless his work has a distinct quality, "the result of a blending in him of a sympathy for humanity in its uncertain condition . . . with his consciousness of the shadow upon it of the great things from which it shrinks." He is a forcible realist as well as a visionary painter. Part of his appeal to Pater is simply because "he has the freshness, the uncertain and diffident promise which belong to the earlier Renaissance"— that age that Pater called "perhaps the most interesting period in the history of the mind."

The chapter titled "Luca della Robbia" is as much about sculpture in general as it is about Luca. The limitation of sculpture, says Pater, is that it tends toward "a hard realism, a one-sided presentment of mere form." The Greeks countered this tendency by depicting the type rather than the individual, by purging the accidental until "their works came to be like some subtle extract or essence, or almost like pure thoughts or ideas." This sacrificed expression, however. Michelangelo, "with a genius spiritualized by the reverie of the middle age," offset the tendency of sculpture toward realism by "leaving nearly all his sculpture in a puzzling sort of incompleteness, which suggests rather than realizes actual form." Luca della Robbia and other fifteenth century Tuscan sculptors achieved "a profound expressiveness" by working in low relief earthenware, the subtle delineation of line serving as the means of overcoming the special limitation of sculpture.

In "The Poetry of Michelangelo" Pater discusses not so much the poetry itself as his impressions of it. No one, says Pater, need be reminded of the strength of Michelangelo's work. There is, however, another and equally important quality of his work, and that Pater refers to variously as "charm," "sweetness," and "a lovely strangeness." It is in a "brooding spirit of life," achieved only through an idealization of life's "vehement sentiments," that this quality of sweetness resides. There were, says Pater, two traditions of the ideal that Michelangelo might have followed: that of Dante, who idealized the material world, and that of Platonism. It was the Platonic tradition that molded Michelangelo's verse; "Michelangelo is always pressing forward from the outward beauty . . . to apprehend the unseen beauty . . . that abstract form of beauty, about which the Platonists reason." Yet the influence of Dante is there too, in the sentiment of imaginative love. To Pater, Michelangelo was "the last . . . of those on whom the peculiar sentiment of the Florence of Dante and Giotto descended: he is the consummate representative of the form that sentiment took in the fifteenth century." In this sentiment is another source of his "grave and temperate sweetness."

The fifteenth century witnessed two movements: the return to antiquity represented, says Pater, by Raphael and the return to nature represented by Leonardo da Vinci. In Leonardo the return to nature took on a special coloring, for his genius was composed not only of a desire for beauty but also of a curiosity that gave to his paintings "a type of subtle and curious grace." His landscapes, as in the background of his masterpiece, *La Gioconda*, partake of the "*bizarre* of *recherché*." One of the most famous passages in the book is Pater's description of *La Gioconda*. Pater sees in her the image of archetypal woman: "All the thoughts and experience of the world have etched and moulded" her features.

In "The School of Giorgione" (which did not appear in the first edition of *The Renaissance*), Pater propounds his famous dictum that "All art constantly aspires towards the condition of music." The "condition of music" is a complete fusing, an interpenetration, of matter and form. The other arts achieve perfection in the degree that they approach or approximate this condition. Giorgione and others of the Venetian school are representative of the aspiration toward perfect identification of matter and form in their realization that "painting must be before all things decorative." Their subjects are from life, but "mere subject" is subordinated to "pictorial design," so that matter is interpenetrated by form.

In the chapter on Joachim du Bellay, Pater turns from Italy to France, to the theories and the elegant verse of the *Pléiad*. Du Bellay wrote a tract in which he sought "to adjust the existing French culture to the rediscovered classical culture." In this tract, says Pater, the Renaissance became aware of itself as a systematic movement. The ambition of the *Pleiad* was to combine the "music of the measured, scanned verse of Latin and Greek poetry" with "the music of the rhymed, unscanned verse of Villon and the old French poets."

The longest chapter of *The Renaissance* is devoted to Johann Joachim Winckelmann, the German scholar of antiquity. His importance, for Pater, is chiefly that he influenced Johann Wolfgang von Goethe, who "illustrates a union of the Romantic spirit . . . with Hellenism . . . that marriage . . . of which the art of the nineteenth century is the child." The Hellenic element, characterized by "breadth, centrality, with blitheness and repose," was made known to Goethe by Winckelmann, who consequently stands as a link between antiquity (and the Renaissance) and the post-Enlightenment world.

The most celebrated part of *The Renaissance*—and indeed of the author's entire body of writing—is the conclusion. Here Pater utters the famous, and frequently misinterpreted, dicta: "Not the fruit of experience, but experience itself, is the end" and "To burn always with this hard, gemlike flame, to maintain this ecstasy, is success in life." These statements must be seen in the context of Pater's conception of the nature of human existence.

For Pater reality is human experience. It consists not in the objective, material world but in the impressions of color, odor, and texture which that world produces in the observer's mind. Each impression endures for but a single moment and then is gone. Life is made up of the succession of these momentary impressions, and life itself is brief.

Not to make the most of these moments, not to experience them fully, is to waste a lifetime. "What we have to do," says Pater, "is to be for ever curiously testing new opinions and courting new impressions." Given the brevity of human life and given as well the brevity of the very impressions that constitute human lives, "we shall hardly have time to make theories about the things we see and touch." Hence, "not the fruit of experience, but experience itself, is the end."

This emphasis on experience also leads Pater to distinguish among kinds of experience. The highest kind, he says, is the great passions (themselves a kind of wisdom) we gain from art. "For art comes to you proposing frankly to give nothing but the highest quality to your moments as they pass."

Pater omitted the conclusion from the second edition of the book, fearing "it might possibly mislead some of those young men into whose hands it might fall." Having explained his beliefs more fully in *Marius the Epicurean* (1885) and having altered the conclusion slightly, he restored it to later editions of *The Renaissance*.

In what may seem a curious irony, Pater stands with Matthew Arnold and John Ruskin as one of the great aesthetic critics of the nineteenth century. The seemingly radical differences between them—Pater pronouncing the primacy of art for art's sake, Ruskin and Arnold insisting on its moral value—tend to obscure some important similarities that offer insight into the ways the Victorians viewed the production and appreciation of art, poetry, and music. All are intent on close scrutiny of the work under examination; all emphasize the seriousness of purpose that great artists bring to their works, and all are convinced that the impact of art on humanity is profound.

Pater, however, stands on its head the famous Arnoldian dictum that the purpose of the viewer or reader is "to see the object as in itself it really is"; Pater insists instead that the principal task of anyone who really wishes to appreciate art is "to know one's own impression of the object of art as it really is." The focus in *The Renaissance*, and in other writings by Pater, is on the significance of the individual impression made by art on the viewer or reader. For him, great art is not dependent on social or political context, and it does not exist principally to deliver a message or emphasize some moral dictum. Instead, art is essentially intended to stir the senses of those who partake in the aesthetic experience (reading a poem or novel, observing a painting or sculpture, listening to a musical composition).

Many of Pater's contemporaries found his approach disconcerting, especially his decoupling of art from the historical and political milieu in which it is produced. Nevertheless, Pater's influence can be seen distinctly in the late nineteenth century movement that is frequently, and unfortunately, labeled as "decadence," in which artists consciously attempted to divorce their works from the more mundane aspects of life. Oscar Wilde, Arthur Symons, and W. B. Yeats are the best among many of the generation whom Pater influenced. His insistence on looking closely at the art object to isolate and appreciate its beauty, rather than simply using it as a means for political or moral commentary, lies at the heart of one of the great critical movements of the twentieth century, New Criticism, whose proponents insist that great art is intrinsically worthwhile and that standards of judgment must rest on aesthetic rather than moral or political principles.

Bibliography:

Buckler, William E., ed. Introduction to *Walter Pater: Three Major Texts*. New York: New York University Press, 1986. Examines *The Renaissance* and two other major works by Pater in an effort to define and elucidate the writer's critical method.

Bullen, J. B. "The Historiography of Studies in the History of the Renaissance." In *Pater in the 1990's*, edited by Laurel Brake and Ian Small. Greensboro, N.C.: ELT Press, 1991. Analyzes Pater's method of writing *The Renaissance*, seeing the work ultimately as a revelation of Pater's vision of himself.

Crinkley, Richmond. *Walter Pater: Humanist*. Lexington: The University Press of Kentucky, 1970. The first chapter discusses *The Renaissance* in relation to Pater's whole achievement. Also examines a number of Pater's major ideas about the relationship between life and art.

Hill, Donald L., ed. *The Renaissance: Studies in Art and Poetry, The 1893 Text*. Berkeley: University of California Press, 1980. Pater's text is presented with scholarly thoroughness and care. More than two hundred and fifty pages of textual and explanatory notes.

Seiler, R. M., ed. *Walter Pater: The Critical Heritage*. London: Routledge & Kegan Paul, 1980. Surveys the reception of *The Renaissance* by Pater's contemporaries and reviews Pater's critical reputation from 1895 to the 1970's. Included are seventeen reviews of *The Renaissance* that were published in the years immediately following its appearance.

RENÉE MAUPERIN

Type of work: Novel
Authors: Edmond de Goncourt (1822-1896) and Jules de Goncourt (1830-1870)
Type of plot: Naturalism
Time of plot: Nineteenth century
Locale: France
First published: 1864 (English translation, 1888)

> *Principal characters:*
> RENÉE MAUPERIN, a sensitive, talented girl in her late teens
> HENRI MAUPERIN, her brother
> MADAME DAVARANDE, her sister
> MONSIEUR MAUPERIN, Renée's father
> MADAME MAUPERIN, his wife
> NAOMI BOURJOT, Renée's friend and the fiancée of Henri Mauperin
> MADAME BOURJOT, her mother and the lover of Henri Mauperin
> MONSIEUR DENOISEL, a family friend of the Mauperins
> DE VILLACOURT, the shabby heir of an old French family

The Story:

Renée Mauperin's father had served under the first Napoleon and battled for the liberal forces until he became a husband and father, when his new responsibilities forced him to return home. After acquiring a family he had ceased being a scholar and political figure in order to pursue the more financially reliable career of sugar refiner. His wife was a very proper woman, one who wished to see her children married well and respectably.

The two oldest children of the Mauperins were model children, so well disciplined and quiet that they failed to excite their father's interest. Renée, however, the third child, born late in his life, was a lively youngster from the beginning. She loved horses and action, was demonstrative in her affection, and had an artistic but spirited personality. While these qualities endeared her to her father, they made her the bane of her mother's existence. The oldest daughter had dutifully married and become the respectable Madame Davarande, but Renée had already summarily dismissed a dozen suitors of good family and fortune and showed no inclination to accept any who came seeking her hand.

Almost as great a worry to Madame Mauperin was her son, on whom she doted. Henri Mauperin was a political economist and a lawyer; he was also a cold and calculating fellow, though his mother, in her excessive love for him, failed to realize just how selfish he was. She thought that he had never given a thought to marriage and chided him for his lack of interest. She felt that at the age of thirty he should have settled down.

Not knowing his plans, Madame Mauperin arranged to have him often in the company of Naomi Bourjot, the only daughter of a very rich family known to the Mauperins for many years. The only difficulty lay in convincing Naomi's father that Henri, who had no title, was a suitable match for his daughter. Henri himself, having realized that this was the greatest difficulty, had undertaken to gain the aid of Madame Bourjot in his suit for her daughter. His method of securing the mother's aid was to become her lover.

On the occasion of an amateur theatrical, Naomi, Renée, and Henri came into one another's company, although Naomi had to be forced into the venture by her mother. Madame Bourjot had known that Henri wanted to marry her daughter, but she had no idea that he was really in love with the girl. It was only Henri's portrayal of Naomi's lover on stage that revealed the true state of his affections. Rather than lose him altogether, Madame Bourjot, as Henri had anticipated, resolved to help him win her daughter and the family fortune, although tearful and bitter scenes preceded that decision. Urged on by Madame Bourjot, Naomi's father reluctantly consented to the marriage on the condition that Henri Mauperin acquire the government's permission to add "de Villacourt" to his name.

Naomi had meanwhile discovered that Henri and her mother had been lovers. Although she loved Henri, she was dismayed by this discovery. Nevertheless, she had to go through with the marriage. Naomi's only consolation was to tell what she knew to Renée, who was horrified to learn of her brother's actions. When she confronted him with the story, he curtly and angrily told her that the affair was none of her business.

A short time later, when the antagonism between Renée and her brother had been superficially smoothed over, she accompanied him to the government offices where he received permission to make the desired addition to his name. While waiting for him, she overheard two clerks saying that the real de Villacourt family had not really died out and that one member, a man, was still alive; the clerks even mentioned the address. Her knowledge gave Renée an opportunity for revenge, although she had no idea what might happen if she put her plan into action. What she did was to take a copy of the newspaper announcing that the title "de Villacourt" was to be given to Henri Mauperin and send it to the real de Villacourt, a villainous lout who immediately planned to kill the upstart who had dared to appropriate his title.

The real de Villacourt journeyed to Paris and learned that, penniless as he was, he had no legal means to regain his title. Then he went to the apartment of Henri Mauperin and attempted to beat the young man. Henri, however, was no coward and challenged the man to a duel. The arrangements were made by Monsieur Denoisel, a friend of the Mauperin family for many years. He also served as Henri's second in the affair. Henri shot de Villacourt and thought the duel was over, but the man was not fatally wounded. Calling Henri back, he shot and killed him. Denoisel was given the unhappy duty of reporting Henri's untimely death. The one who seemed to take the news hardest was Renée. No one expected her to make so much of her brother's death, since they had never been close.

One day, in a conversation, Denoisel remarked that someone had sent the newspaper clipping to de Villacourt. Renée, fearful that she had been discovered as the author of her brother's death, had a heart attack. For many months, she lay ill, apparently with no desire to live. Even after many weeks, the realization that she had not revealed her guilt prevented her recovery. Her father called in the best specialists he could find, but they only remarked that her condition had been caused by some terrible shock. When told that she had recently lost a brother, they said that his death was probably not the real cause of her illness.

Despite all efforts on her behalf, Renée Mauperin wasted away and finally died. The tragedy of the Mauperins did not end there. They lost their third child, Madame Davarande, a few months afterward, when she died in childbirth. Childless and alone, the elder Mauperins traveled abroad, seeking thereby to ease their grief and loneliness.

Critical Evaluation:

Above all, Edmond and Jules de Goncourt valued truth in literature; in all of their novels, they attempted to find the truth of the subject they chose. In this they were in the vanguard of a literary trend in the late nineteenth century known as naturalism, which reached its zenith in the works of Émile Zola. In *Renée Mauperin*, they analyzed with shrewdness and precision a particular segment of Parisian society. Viewing this world through the eyes of an intelligent and sensitive young woman, they depicted the shallowness and pettiness of many of the self-satisfied people who dominated society and tried to dominate her.

The book also describes the various conditions of women in mid-nineteenth century France. There is the impetuous young Renée, who as a child cuts Denoisel's hair and smokes her father's cigarette and who later struggles against the conventions imposed on young Parisian women in 1864. There is Madame Mauperin, with her passion for "symmetry" and her fairly ordinary habit of overvaluing her son and undervaluing her daughter. Two other typical types of the period are Madame Davarande, the society matron who is religious only because she believes that God is chic, and Madame Bourjot, an intelligent woman married to a shallow and petty fool. In that society, the authors seem to suggest, only a shallow person seems able to find contentment, and this seems particularly to be the case for women.

Many of the other characters, notably Renée's doting and scholarly father and the sophisticated and subtle Abbé Blampoix, are well drawn. The Goncourt brothers were not known for character analysis, but their characterization in this novel surpassed that in many of their other books. Renée's sudden admission of having inadvertently caused her brother's death is skillfully and devastatingly handled; the moment reveals complexities of Renée's character that up to that point had been only suggested. The novel is filled with witty conversations that bring the era to life. The authors knew the value and interest of precise details and integrated them into the book through conversations and descriptions, often using them to delineate character. Frequently, the conversations are used to suggest a comment on society, as when a room full of talking people is described as "voices . . . all mingled together in the Babel: it was like the chirping of so many birds in a cage." It is this cage that Renée wants to escape, but ultimately this is only possible through her death.

The novelistic strength of the Goncourts lay in pure observation. Perhaps they were less broad in their accomplishments than the greatest nineteenth century novelists, but in their best books, such as *Renée Mauperin*, they combined a precise and vivid picture of the society they knew so well with a sympathetic and touching story and shrewd observations on human nature.

Bibliography:
Baldick, Robert. *The Goncourts*. London: Bowes and Bowes, 1960. A very brief but excellent survey of the Goncourts' novels. Concentrates on biographical background to the novels, but also provides some exploration of major themes in the works and aspects of literary style. Emphasizes the Goncourts' scorn of the bourgeoisie's lack of aesthetic sensibility.

Billy, André. *The Goncourt Brothers*. Translated by Margaret Shaw. London: A. Deutsch, 1960. The standard biography of the Goncourts focuses on events in the lives of the brothers from which the novels emerged. Also provides examples of contemporary reaction to their novels.

Grant, Richard B. *The Goncourt Brothers*. New York: Twayne, 1972. A solid survey of the life and works of Jules and Edmond de Goncourt. Integrates the lives of the authors with detailed stylistic and thematic analysis of their novels. The chapter on *Renée Mauperin* elaborates the brothers' political views and traces their derogatory commentary on bourgeois taste.

Nelson, Brian, ed. *Naturalism in the European Novel: New Critical Perspectives*. New York: Berg, 1992. An assortment of essays by prominent scholars. Includes several important discussions of the Goncourts' role in the development of social documentary as a literary genre.

Silverman, Debora. *Art Nouveau in Fin-de-Siècle France: Politics, Psychology, and Style*. Berkeley: University of California Press, 1989. Although Silverman's book primarily concerns itself with the collecting habits and art criticism of the brothers Goncourt, it provides some valuable insight into their fictional works from a feminist perspective.

REPRESENTATIVE MEN
Seven Lectures

Type of work: Essays
Author: Ralph Waldo Emerson (1803-1882)
First published: 1850

Emerson's *Representative Men: Seven Lectures* was first presented as a course of lectures in Boston in the winter of 1845-1846 and later during his visit to England in 1847. The volume opens with a discussion of the uses of great men and follows with six chapters on men who represent humanity in six aspects: Plato as philosopher, Emanuel Swedenborg as mystic, Michel Eyquem de Montaigne as skeptic, William Shakespeare as poet, Napoleon Bonaparte as man of the world, and Johann Wolfgang von Goethe as writer.

The book has often been mentioned in connection with Thomas Carlyle's *Heroes and Hero-Worship*, which was published in 1841, but whereas Carlyle saw the hero as a divinely gifted individual above and apart from the common man, Emerson conceived of the great man as a lens through which men may see themselves. For Emerson the great man is one who through superior endowments "inhabits a higher sphere of thought, into which other men rise with labor and difficulty." Such men may give direct material or metaphysical aid, but more frequently they serve indirectly by the inspiration of their accomplishment of things and by their introduction of ideas. The great man does stirring deeds; he reveals knowledge and wisdom; he shows depths of emotion—and others resolve to emulate him. He accomplishes intellectual feats of memory, of abstract thought, of imaginative flights, and dull minds are brightened by his light. The true genius does not tyrannize; he liberates those who know him. For Emerson, all men are infinitely receptive in capacity; they need only the wise man to rouse them, to clear their eyes and make them see, to feed and refresh them. Yet even the great man has limits of availability. People get from one what they can and pass on to another who can nourish mind or spirit or inform a dulled palate. As people are infinitely receptive, so are they eternally hungry; and as people find sustenance, through them the spirit of the world's great men diffuses itself. Thus, through the ages the cumulative effect of great men is that they prepare the way for greater men.

Emerson views the representative philosopher Plato as an exhausting generalizer, a symbol of philosophy itself, a thinker whom people of all nations in all times recognize as kin to themselves. He absorbed the learning of his times, but Emerson sees in him a modern style and spirit identifying him with later ages as well. Plato honors the ideal, or laws of the mind, and fate, or the order of nature. Plato defines. He sees Unity, or Identity, on the one hand and Variety on the other. In him is found the idea (not original, it is true) of one deity in whom all things are absorbed. A balanced soul, Plato sees both the real and the ideal. He propounds the principle of absolute good, but he illustrates from the world around him. In this ability lies his power and charm. He is a great average man in whom other men see their own dreams and thoughts. He acknowledges the Ineffable and yet asserts that things are knowable; a lover of limits, he yet loves the illimitable. For Plato, virtue cannot be taught; it is divinely inspired. It is through Socrates that we learn much of Plato's philosophy, and to Emerson the older philosopher is a man of Franklin-like wisdom, a plain old uncle with great ears, an immense talker, a hard-headed humorist, an Aesop of the mob to whom the robed scholar Plato owed a great debt.

For Emerson the two principal defects of Plato as a philosopher are, first, that he is intellectual and therefore always literary, and second, that he has no system. He sees so much that he argues first on one side and then on another. Finally, says Emerson, the way to know

Plato is to compare him, not with nature (an enigma now, as it was to Plato), but with other men and to see that through the ages none has approached him.

Emerson would have preferred to discuss Jesus as the representative mystic, but to do so would have meant sailing into dangerous waters: The orthodox believers of the time would probably have objected to the inclusion of Jesus as a representative man. Emerson chose Swedenborg instead, but in reading this chapter of the book one gets the notion that Emerson was forcing himself to praise this eighteenth century mystic. Emerson remarks that this colossal soul, as he calls him, requires a long focal distance to be seen. Looking more closely, he finds in Swedenborg a style "lustrous with points and shooting spiculae of thought, and resembling one of those winter mornings when the air sparkles with crystals." He summarizes some of Swedenborg's leading ideas: "the universality of each law in nature; the Platonic doctrine of the scale or degrees; the version or conversion of each into other, and so the correspondence of all the parts; the fine secret that little explains large, and large, little; the centrality of man in nature, and the connection that subsists throughout all things." He quotes a passage of Swedenborg's theology that must have appealed to the Unitarian Emerson: "Man is a kind of very minute heaven, corresponding to the world of spirits and to heaven. Every particular idea of man, and every affection, yea, every smallest part of his affection, is an image and effigy of him. A spirit may be known from only a single thought. God is the grand old man." Yet when Emerson comes to the Swedenborgian mystical view that each natural object has a definite symbolic value—as, a horse signifies carnal understanding; a tree, perception; the moon, faith—he rebels at its narrowness. As for Swedenborg's theological writings in general, Emerson complains of their immense and sandy diffuseness and their delirious incongruities. Emerson warns that such books as Swedenborg's treatise on love should be used with caution, and he suggests that a contemplative young man might read these mysteries of love and conscience once, and then throw them aside forever. As Emerson continues his examination, he finds Swedenborg's heavens and hells dull, he objects to the theological determination of Swedenborg's mind and to the failure of Swedenborg in attaching himself "to the Christian symbol, instead of to the moral sentiment, which carries innumerable christianities, humanities, divinities, in its bosom." When Emerson imagines the impatient reader complaining, "What have I to do with jasper and sardonyx, beryl and chalcedony," and so on, Emerson's own writing awakes as from a semislumber, and one is reminded of his warning in "Self-Reliance" that when a man "claims to know and speak of God and carries you backward to the phraseology of some old moldered nation in another country, in another world, believe him not."

As Emerson perhaps felt relieved after having completed his lecture on Swedenborg, he surely must have anticipated with great pleasure his next on the skeptic Montaigne. He confesses to having had a love for the *Essays* (1588) since he was a young man. "It seemed to me," he says, "as if I had written the book, in some former life, so sincerely it spoke to my thought and experience." He is not repelled by Montaigne's grossness—his frank intimacy about himself—because the Frenchman is scrupulously honest in his confessions. As Emerson had found Swedenborg disagreeably wise and therefore repellent, he is in contrast drawn to Montaigne, whose motto, *Que scais je?* was a constant reminder to the essayist to stick to the things he did know, such as his farm, his family, himself, and his likes and dislikes in food and friends. Emerson is charmed by Montaigne's conversational style, his calm balance, and his stout solidity. The skeptic is not the impassioned patriot, the dogmatic adherent of creed or party. He is wary of an excess of belief, but he turns also from an excess of unbelief. He is content to say there are doubts. Yet for Emerson, when he turns from Montaigne the man to the skeptic in general whom he represents, the doubter is at base a man of belief. He believes in the moral design of the universe and that "it exists hospitably for the weal of souls." Thus, concludes Emerson, skepticism is finally dissolved in the moral sentiment which remains forever supreme. The skepticism is on the surface only; it questions specifics, but the skeptic can serenely view man's high ambitions defeated and the unequal distribution of power in the world because he believes that deity and moral law control the universe. Emerson himself was at bottom such a believer, though he had passed through his skeptical stage in life to arrive at his belief.

The discussion of Shakespeare as the representative poet begins with the comment: "Great men are more distinguished by range and extent than by originality." Shakespeare, like his fellow dramatists, used a mass of old plays to experiment with. Building upon popular traditions, he was free to use his wide-ranging fancy and his imagination. Borrowing in all directions, he used what he borrowed with such art that it became his.

Emerson touches upon the mystery of Shakespeare's biography, mentioning the paucity of clear facts (only a few more have become known since the time when Emerson wrote), and then concluding, as have many of Shakespeare's readers, that his plays and his poetry give all the information that is really needed. In the sonnets readers find the lore of friendship and of love. Through the characters of his plays people know the man because there is something of him in all of the characters.

The dramatic skill of Shakespeare is to Emerson less important than his poetry and philosophy and the broad expanse of his book of life, which pictured the men and women of his day and prefigured those of later ages. Shakespeare was inconceivably wise and made his characters as real as if they had lived in his home. His power to convert truth into music and verse makes him the exemplary poet. His music charms the ear and his sentence takes the mind. In his lines experience has been transformed into verse without a trace of egotism. One more royal trait of the poet Emerson finds in Shakespeare: His name suggests joy and emancipation to people's hearts. To Emerson, Shakespeare was master of the revels to humankind. It is this fact that Emerson regrets: The world's greatest poet used his genius for public amusement. As the poet was half-man in his role as entertainer, so the priests of old and of later days were half-men who took the joy and beauty out of life while they moralized and warned of the doom to come. Only in some future time, says Emerson, will there arise a poet-priest who may see, speak, and act with equal inspiration.

A frequently quoted remark of Emerson is that he liked people who could do things. His expansive praise of Napoleon in the opening pages of his portrayal of the Corsican as the representative man of the world is based upon his belief that Napoleon could and did do what masses of other men merely wanted to. Napoleon was idolized by common men because he was an uncommonly gifted common man. He succeeded through the virtues of punctuality, personal attention, courage, and thoroughness, qualities that others possess in lesser degrees. Emerson writes of Napoleon's reliance on his own sense and of his scorn of others' sense. To him Napoleon is the agent or attorney of the middle class, with both the virtues and the vices of the people he represented. He was dishonest, stagy, unscrupulous, selfish, perfidious, and coarse. He was a cheat, a gossip, and when divested of his power and splendor he is seen to be an impostor and a rogue.

Emerson finds Napoleon the supreme democrat who illustrates in his career the three stages of the party: the democrat in youth, the conservative in later life, and the aristocrat at the end—a democrat ripe and gone to seed. Napoleon conducted an experiment in the use of the intellect without conscience. The experiment failed, however, because the French saw that they could not enjoy what Napoleon had gained for them. His colossal egotism drove him to more attempts at conquest, and so his followers deserted him. Yet Emerson asserts that it was not Napoleon's fault. He was defeated by the eternal law of man and of the world. Here, as before, Emerson sees the moral order in the universe. "Every experiment," he says, "by multitudes or by individuals, that has a selfish aim, will fail. . . . Only that good profits which we can taste with all doors open, and which serves all men."

Having considered Napoleon as a man of action who failed after having achieved enormous successes, Emerson turns to Goethe as the representative scholar or writer, a man whose intellect moved in many directions and whose writings brought him fame as the greatest of German authors. Emerson calls him the soul of his century, one who clothed modern existence with poetry. Emerson, a lover of nature himself, remarks that Goethe said the best things about nature that ever were said.

Realizing the impossibility of analyzing the full range of Goethe's writings, Emerson chooses *Wilhelm Meister's Apprenticeship* (1795-1796) for rather brief comment. He describes it as provoking but also unsatisfactory, but though he has considerable praise for this novel in which a democrat becomes an aristocrat, readers do not really learn much about it. In fact, one feels that Emerson was struggling with a difficult subject in dealing with Goethe. One comment is worthy of noting, however, since it seems a reference to Emerson himself when he says that Goethe is "fragmentary; a writer of occasional poems and of an encyclopedia of sentences."

Among Emerson's works, *Representative Men* has received modest praise, and such chapters as those on Montaigne and Shakespeare have occasionally been reprinted. One of the aptest statements ever made about Emerson's book is that of Oliver Wendell Holmes, who wrote: "[Emerson] shows his own affinities and repulsions, and writes his own biography, no matter about whom or what he is talking."

Bibliography:
Allen, Gay Wilson. *Waldo Emerson: A Biography*. New York: Viking, 1981. An excellent research tool. Addresses *Representative Men: Seven Lectures* in a thorough, accessible style. Pertinent and lucid discussion focuses on Emerson's thought as it is expressed in his choices of representative men. Makes reference to Emerson's journals and their value for understanding Emerson's texts.
Berry, Edmund G. *Emerson's Plutarch*. Cambridge, Mass.: Harvard University Press, 1961. Pages 86-245 make nineteen valuable references to Emerson's work in *Representative Men: Seven Lectures*. Assesses the influence of Plutarch upon Emerson's thought.
Cameron, Kenneth Walter, ed. *Literary Comment in American Renaissance Newspapers: Fresh Discoveries Concerning Emerson, Thoreau, Alcott and Transcendentalism*. Hartford, Conn.: Transcendental Books, 1977. Includes an evaluation of *Representative Men: Seven Lectures* published in *New York Weekly Tribune* in 1850. Offers interesting insight into the work's strengths and weaknesses.
Carpenter, Frederic Ives. *Emerson Handbook*. New York: Hendricks House, 1967. Primary information for background understanding of the ideas behind Emerson's essays. Addresses shaping influences of Emerson's thought. Bibliographies.
Emerson, Ralph Waldo. *1820-24*. Vol. 1 in *Journals of Ralph Waldo Emerson*. Edited by Ralph Waldo Emerson and Waldo Emerson Forbes. Boston: Houghton Mifflin, 1990. Some journal entries go back to Emerson's youth. In this volume, the young Emerson presents ideas that find their way into his adult work, *Representative Men: Seven Lectures*. Brief readings include "Martyrdom" (136), "Habit" (136-137), "Men of God" (230-231), and "Aristocracy" (311-312). Instills a deeper appreciation of Emerson's insights.

THE REPUBLIC

Type of work: Philosophy
Author: Plato (c. 427-347 B.C.E.)
Time of plot: Fifth century B.C.E.
Locale: The Piraeus, Greece
First transcribed: Politeia, 388-366 B.C.E. (English translation, 1701)

Principal personages:
SOCRATES, the Athenian philosopher
CEPHALUS, an old man
POLEMARCHUS, his son
THRASYMACHUS, a Sophist
GLAUCON and
ADEIMANTUS, Plato's brothers

The Republic is the first in a long line of works that are generally classified as Utopian literature. Although Plato is primarily interested in political issues, he is less concerned with mapping out a practical strategy for revamping current practices in the Greek city-states than he is in explaining the optimal ways people should be governed. Subscribing to what some commentators have described as an unashamedly elitist viewpoint, Plato makes it clear that some people are destined to rule, others to be ruled. Essentially antidemocratic, he concentrates on describing ways those who have the capacity to lead should be educated for their positions of great responsibility. Such an attitude no doubt seems alien and even threatening to modern readers, especially those in Western societies, where democracy in some form or other has been in favor for more than two hundred years. *The Republic* may grate on the nerves of some who dislike Plato's concepts of social engineering and his distaste for artists. Others may feel his disdain for the masses links him with that most maligned of all political philosophers, Niccolò Machiavelli, whose advice is based on the notion that retaining power is the primary duty of those who rule.

One must remember, however, that Plato is at heart a philosopher. In *The Republic* he is interested in identifying the qualities of justice that should determine the governance of society. Undeterred by any popular sentiments for or against any particular political practice—Athens was a democracy during the years when Plato was writing his dialogues and teaching—the philosopher focuses on the ethical dimensions of leadership. He asks crucial questions: How ought one to govern, and how ought one be educated to serve in this significant social role? He is the first of the great political philosophers of the West.

The Republic presents a fascinating defense of the author's conception of the ideal state and gives the most sustained and convincing portrait of Socrates as a critical and creative philosopher. Other dialogues featuring Socrates may be superior as studies of the personality and character of Socrates, but *The Republic* is unexcelled as an exhibition of the famed Socratic method being brought to bear on such questions as "What is justice?" and "What kind of state would be most just?"

Although the constructive arguments of this dialogue come from the mouth of Socrates, it is safe to assume that much of the philosophy is Plato's. As a rough reading rule, one may say that the method is Socratic, but the content is provided by Plato himself. Among the ideas which are presented and defended in *The Republic* are the Platonic theory of ideas (the formal prototypes of all things, objective or intellectual), the Platonic conception of the nature and obligations of the philosopher, and the Platonic theory and criticism of poetry. The central concern of the author is with the idea of justice in the state.

The dialogue is a discussion between Socrates and various friends while they are in the Piraeus for a festival. The discussion of justice is provoked by a remark made by an old man, Cephalus, to the effect that the principal advantage of being wealthy is that a man near death is able to repay what he owes to the gods and to people, and is thereby able to be just in the hope of achieving a happy afterlife. Socrates objects to this conception of justice, maintaining that whether a person should return what he has received depends on the circumstances. For example, a man who has received dangerous weapons from his friend while sane should not, if he is just, return those weapons if his friend, while mad, demands them.

Polemarchus amends the idea and declares that it is just to help one's friends and return to them what they are due, provided they are good and worthy of receiving the good. Enemies, on the other hand, should have harm done to them for, as bad, that is what they are due. Socrates compels Polemarchus to admit that injuring anyone, even a wicked man, makes him worse; and since no just man would ever sanction making men worse, justice must be something other than giving good to the good and bad to the bad.

Thrasymachus then proposes the theory that justice is whatever is to the interest of the stronger party. His idea is that justice is relative to the law, and the law is made by the stronger party according to his interests. In rebuttal, Socrates maneuvers Thrasymachus into saying that sometimes rulers make mistakes. If this is so, then sometimes the law is against their interests; when the law is against the interests of the stronger party, it is right to do what is not to the interest of the stronger party.

The secret of the Socratic method is evident from analysis of this argument. The term "interest" or "to the interest of" is ambiguous, sometimes meaning what one is interested in, what one wants, and at other times what one could want if one were not in error. Examples in everyday life of such ambiguity are found in such statements as: "Although you want it, it is not really to your interest to have it." Socrates adroitly shifts from one sense of the expression to the other so that Thrasymachus apparently contradicts himself. In this indirect way Socrates makes it clear both to the "victim" and to the onlookers that the proponent of the claim—in this case, Thrasymachus—has not cleared it of all possibility of misinterpretation.

Socrates then goes on to say that justice must be relative to the needs of those who are served, not to the desires of those who serve them. The physician, for example, as physician, must make the health of the patient the primary concern if the physician is to be just. Socrates suggests that their understanding of justice would be clarified if they were to consider a concrete case, say the state: If by discussion they could come to understand what a state must be in order to be just, it might be possible to generalize and to arrive at an idea of justice itself.

Beginning with an account of what a state would have to be in order to fulfill its functions as a state, Socrates then proceeds to develop the notion of an ideal state by asking what the relations of the various groups of citizens to each other should be.

Every state needs three classes of citizens: the Guardians, who rule and advise the rest; the Auxiliaries, who provide military protection for the state; and the Workers, the providers of food, clothing, and such useful materials. In a just state these three classes of citizens function together, each doing its own proper business without interfering with the tasks of the other classes.

Applying this idea to the individual, Socrates decides that just people are those who give to each of their individual functions its proper task, relating them to one another in a harmonious way. Just as the state has three distinct elements, the governing, the defending, and the producing bodies, so the individual person has three corresponding elements, the rational, the spirited, and the appetitive. By the spirited element Plato means the passionate aspect of one's nature, one's propensity to anger or other irrational emotions. He so uses the term anger that he allows for what might be called righteous indignation, the passionate defense of reason against desire. The rational element is the discerning and calculating side of one's nature, and it is what enables one to be wise and judicious. The appetitive side of a person is the inclination to desire some things in preference to others.

A just person, then, is one who keeps each of the three elements of one's nature doing its proper work, with the rational element in command. A person is brave, says Socrates in the dialogue, if the spirited element remains always in the service of reason. One is wise if one is governed by reason, for reason takes into account the welfare of the entire person; and one is temperate if the spirit and appetite work harmoniously under the guidance of reason.

In order to discover those citizens best suited to be Guardians, Socrates proposes that the ideal state educate all its citizens in music and gymnastics, continually observing them to decide upon the sort of occupation for which they would best be fitted. He also argues that the Guardians and Auxiliaries should have no private property, and that they each should share a community of wives and children.

These communal features of the ideal state have led many critics to dismiss Plato's construction as unacceptable. It is well to remember that in the dialogue Socrates tells his listeners that he is not concerned about the practicality of his state; the conception of the state is constructed merely to bring out the nature of justice. In considering the education of the Guardians, Socrates builds the conception of the philosopher as the true aristocrat or rational thinker, the ideal ruler for the ideal state. The philosopher is a lover of wisdom, and the philosopher alone manages to keep appetite and spirit in harmony with reason. Consequently, the Guardians of the state should be educated as philosophers, supplementing their training in arithmetic, geometry, astronomy, and music with training in the philosophic skills of dialectic. The prospective Guardians should not be allowed to undertake philosophic education until they are old enough to take it seriously, not as mere amusement. After his philosophic training the prospective Guardian should take part in the active life of his times, so that at fifty he can assume political power with some knowledge of the actual matters with which he shall be concerned.

In connection with his discussion of the philosopher, Socrates introduces his famous story of the cave. People are like prisoners in a cave, facing away from the light. Unable to see themselves or anyone else because they are shackled, people observe only the shadows of things on the wall in front of them, not realizing that the reality is something quite different from the shadows. The philosopher is like one who leaves the cave, comes to know things as they really are, and returns reluctantly to help the shackled ones, who think that shadows make up the true world.

The philosopher comes to know reality through a study of the ideas or forms of particular things. The world of experience is like the world of shadows, but the world of ideas is the true reality. For every class of objects, such as beds (Socrates' example), there is an idea-bed, a form shared by all particular beds. One who studies only the individual beds made by carpenters, or only the pictures of beds made by artists, knows only copies of reality (and, in the case of the imitative artist, only copies of copies); but the philosopher, making the effort to learn the idea itself, comes closer to reality.

Socrates objects to poetry and to art whenever they are imitative, which they usually are. Although he admits that some poetry can be inspiring in the patriotic training of the Guardians, he stresses the point that imitative art is corrupting because it is misleading. It represents physical things, which in turn are merely copies of the forms or ideas. Works of art are copies of physical things; hence, works of art are at least two steps removed from reality. Furthermore, the artist paints only a single aspect of a thing; hence, strictly speaking, art is three steps removed from reality. It is on this account, as well as because of the immoral effect of the poetic style of all but the most noble poets, that Socrates recommends that imitative poets be banned from the state.

The Republic closes with Socrates' reaffirmation of his conviction that only the just person is truly happy, for only one who is just harmonizes reason, appetite, and spirit by loving wisdom and the form of the good. The soul is immortal, he argues, because the soul's illness is injustice, and injustice does not destroy a soul. Since the soul cannot be destroyed by any illness other than its own, and its own cannot destroy it, it must be immortal. Socrates concludes by using a myth about life after death to show that the just and wise ones will prosper in this life and "during the journey of a thousand years."

Bibliography:

Hall, Robert W. *Plato*. London: Allen & Unwin, 1981. An excellent discussion of Plato's political thought, most of it devoted to *The Republic*. Two chapters in particular—"Athenian Democracy" and "Plato's Political Heritage" help place Plato and his work within wider historical, cultural, and political contexts.

Howland, Jacob. *"The Republic": The Odyssey of Philosophy*. New York: Twayne, 1993. The ideal starting point for the study of *The Republic*. Provides a chapter discussing literary and historical contexts, a chronology of Plato's life and works, extensive notes, and a bibliography.

Lycos, Kimon. *Plato on Justice and Power: Reading Book I of Plato's "Republic."* Albany: State University of New York Press, 1987. A useful, if somewhat advanced introduction to *The Republic*, focusing on book 1, which, Lycos argues, shows "how inadequacies of traditional Greek views about justice are to be overcome."

Plato. *Republic*. Translated by Robin Waterfield. New York: Oxford University Press, 1994. This fine translation of *The Republic* contains an introduction, a bibliography, and notes.

White, Nicholas P. *A Companion to Plato's "Republic."* Indianapolis, Ind.: Hackett, 1979. A tremendously learned and cogent commentary, based on a book-by-book summary of *The Republic*. The introductory chapters before the summary are especially helpful, as is the bibliography.

REQUIEM

Type of work: Poetry
Author: Anna Akhmatova (Anna Andreyevna Gorenko, 1889-1966)
First published: Rekviem, 1963 (English translation, 1964)

Anna Akhmatova was a prominent voice in Russian poetry of the twentieth century for more than fifty years. When she died in 1966, she was hailed as one of the eminent poets of her country, ranked with Aleksandr Blok, Boris Pasternak, and Osip Mandelstam. Her several collections attest the high quality of her craft. She drew attention to her poetry at the very start of her career, participating in a short-lived but eclectic group of poets called the Acmeists in the second decade of the twentieth century. She then struck her own path, and, although she was frequently regarded with suspicion by the Soviet authorities, she managed to retain the aura of brilliance and integrity until her last days.

It is generally agreed that her highest achievements were two cyclical poems, *Poem Without a Hero* (1960) and *Requiem.* Both are Akhmatova's poetic answers to the vicissitudes of life in Russia under Communism, and, because of that, their publication was delayed; in fact, *Requiem* first appeared abroad and was not published in Russia itself until many years later.

Requiem was written between 1935 and 1943, with a brief prose foreword added in 1957. Since its publication in Germany in 1963, it has been symbolic of both the suffering and silent defiance of the Russian people during the reign of terror perpetrated by Joseph Stalin and his henchmen. The poem is more than a protest against tyranny; it reflects the poet's personal tragedy. Her only son, Lev Gumilev, a prominent young Orientalist, was arrested on trumped-up charges and exiled to hard labor. Released during World War II, he was arrested again and released only in 1956. During his imprisonment, Akhmatova stood waiting in lines in front of the prison off and on for seventeen months, trying to learn the fate of her son and secure his release. Although *Requiem* is basically autobiographical, it should not be read purely as such, but primarily as any mother's grief. The poem itself is not as much a direct accusation of the inhumane treatment of the Soviet citizen, but a deeply felt outcry against the injustice done to all the children of Russia. Through her outcry, Akhmatova expresses a great love of and loyalty to Russia, and it is in this manner that one mother's grief and tragedy become a symbol of all of Russia, expressed in a perfect fusion of content and form.

Requiem opens with the brief prose introduction written in 1957, which places the poem in the fearful years of the secret police terror. She relates that, as she stood in line before the prison walls, an unknown woman asked, "Can you describe this?" "Yes, I can," Akhmatova replied. The first lines of the motto explain why she chose not to become an émigré.

> No, not under a foreign heavenly dome,
> Not under the shield of foreign wings—
> I was with my people in those hours,
> There where, unhappily, my people were.

These four lines are the best example of the style that follows—direct, precise, brief, and simple. They represent the full power of emotion that characterizes the entire poem.

In the opening poem, Akhmatova dedicates *Requiem* to all who suffered during the purges of the 1930's, those who waited before prison gates, wept upon hearing the sentences, and lived in the relentless fear of the powerless. Although the wind is still refreshing and the sunset beautiful, that beauty is lost on those in the vigil. The poet combines brief, contrasting sketches of the prison and Leningrad with the mood of the frightened, yet still hopeful, participants of the vigils. Recalling her friends from the two-year ordeal in 1940, she sends them her greetings, wherever they may be.

The spirit of the dedication is preserved in the introduction to the entire poem. Here she weeps for the "ranks of the condemned" and for the "innocent Rus'" (a poetic, endearing term for Russia) that "contorts under bloody boots and the tires of Black Marias" (black-painted prison vans). In these first two poems, Akhmatova is able to surmount personal grief and becomes a speaker for all who suffered with her, indeed for all victims of the country and perhaps all of humankind. In the following poems, she concentrates on her own grief as she observes the "stars of death" shining over her. In poem 1 (1935) she recalls how her son was taken away at dawn, the cold of icons on his lips and deadly sweat on his forehead. She likens herself to the wives who followed their husbands, army officers exiled to Siberia in the previous centuries. She deftly evokes the images of the Russian past, thus universalizing her personal misfortune.

In the next two poems, she feels the heavy burden of her situation, speaking in tones of self-pity. She evokes the stillness of the "quiet Don," an apparent sarcastic allusion to the novel *And Quiet Flows the Don* (1928) by Mikhail Sholokhov, a staunch supporter of the Communist rule. She is ill and alone, with a husband (Nikolay Gumilev, who was killed by the Bolsheviks during the revolution) in his grave and their only son in prison. She pleads with them to pray for her, instead of the other way around. In poem 3, she even utters a denial of her plight, wishing that the nightmare would go away and the dark curtains cover the windows of her lightless room.

In poem 4, Akhmatova juxtaposes the past and the present. Addressing her own merry past, when she was loved and admired by her many friends, she sees herself now as only one of the three hundred standing in the vigil, her bitter tears hot enough to melt the winter ice, and under the crosses—a symbolic reference to their tragedy—while innocent lives are being snuffed out behind the prison walls.

The pervasive uncertainty of the times carries over into the next poem. The mother does not know what is to become of her son, or "who is a man and who is a beast," or how long the agony will last. In a funereal image of flowers and incense, there is again an allusion to death. In the dedication poem, it was first associated with stars, while now "a huge star/ threatens an impending death," a reference to the Communist emblem as well as to any natural phenomenon, for Akhmatova uses nature in conjunction with the certainty of death throughout the cycle. From poem 5 on, death becomes the most frequent image. Again there is a natural reference to white nights that speak of physical death in alluding to Akhmatova's son. More important and more moving is the depiction of mental death or madness and the need to kill memory ("One should again learn how to live"). Even in the midst of a bright summer day, the poet declares that she had foreboded a deserted house.

Poem 6, "To Death" (1939), expresses the poet's resignation to the inevitable and her death wish. She awaits death with indifference, not knowing only in what form it will come. There is a certain sense of deliverance: "I dimmed the light and open the door/ To you, so simple and beautiful." For the first time, she refers forebodingly to her son's exile to Siberia and to the horrible parting without saying good-bye:

> The Yenisei is swirling,
> The Pole Star glittering. And the blue eyes
> I love are closing in the final horror.

The grief brings the mother close to madness in poem 9 (1940). In a reference to death, the "black valley" beckons, bereft of any memories of her son and allowing no consolation. Juxtaposing the images of nature with those of her son, she admits that the oncoming madness will not allow her to experience anything any more,

> Not the dear coolness of his hands;
> Nor the waving shadows of lime-trees,
> Nor the distant whispering sound
> Of his parting words of consolation.

Perhaps the most dramatic poem of the cycle is "Crucifixion" (1940-1943). Written during the war years, it underscores tersely the tragedy of Russia. By quoting Christ's biblical words to his mother, "Do not weep for Me, who am in the grave," the poet seems to liken her own grief, and by transference that of all Russian mothers, to that of the Mother of God. It is as if she searches for some meaning in her son's sacrifice, something such as the redemption of humankind, as in Christ's case. If so, the poem expresses some hope. There is also an afterthought of doubt that the sacrifice of her son would have any lasting meaning, hinted at in the closing lines: "And there where Mother stood silently/ no one even dared to look at her."

A two-part epilogue echoes the prose foreword in poetic form. Its main message is contained in a plea not to forget the ordeals she and her people have endured. As if sensing that she, too, may be guilty of this sin, she asks that, should a monument ever be erected to her, it should be there where she stood three hundred hours and where no door was opened for her. She sees herself as "the tortured mouth through which hundred million people cry." She reiterates that it was out of love and loyalty that she chose not to emigrate but rather to commemorate in some way these years and her people:

> And I am praying not only for myself,
> But for all those who stood there with me
> In bitter cold, and in July heat,
> Under that blinding-red prison wall.

The contents of *Requiem* command most of our attention, yet the poem displays stylistic excellence as well. In its combination of conventional and innovative verses, it is typical of the author's poetic craft. Brief personal sketches are spelled by contemplative verses, with skillful transitions from words of emotion to words of description, from the soul to nature, from feeling to fact. Through such mixture of facts and feeling, *Requiem* adds a human touch to history, serving as a steady reminder that a painful past should never be forgotten.

When Akhmatova was asked in an interview taken shortly before her death whether *Requiem* would ever be published in the Soviet Union, she replied: "What does it matter? Hundreds of thousands of people, most of whom had never even heard of me, have read it in transcript or handwritten copies." The events in Russia in the late 1980's and early 1990's proved Akhmatova right.

Vasa D. Mihailovich

Bibliography:
Haight, Amanda. *Anna Akhmatova: A Poetic Pilgrimage*. London: Oxford University Press, 1976. An excellent study of Akhmatova's poems by one of the best authorities on her works.

Hayward, Max. "Anna Akhmatova." In *Writers in Russia 1917-1978*. San Diego: Harcourt Brace Jovanovich, 1983. A fine biographical sketch of Akhmatova and discussion of the conditions under which she wrote her poems, including *Requiem*.

Leiter, Sharon. "The Terror and the War." In *Akhmatova's Petersburg*. Philadelphia: University of Pennsylvania Press, 1983. A review of Akhmatova's life in her beloved St. Petersburg and of political circumstances that provided the material for and led to the writing of *Requiem*.

Mihailovich, Vasa D. "The Critical Reception of Anna Akhmatova." *Papers on Language and Literature* 5 (1969): 95-112. A thorough survey of critical works through 1968, in Russian and other languages, about Akhmatova's works, including *Requiem*.

Reeder, Roberta. *Anna Akhmatova: Poet and Prophet*. New York: St. Martin's Press, 1994. The most extensive book in English on Akhmatova. Scholarly discussion of all facets of her life and works. Discusses *Requiem* in detail (pp. 211-222), focusing on its artistic quality and the fascinating genesis of the poem created in the midst of the terror under which Akhmatova lived. Long, useful bibliography.

Thomas, D. M. Introduction to *Anna Akhmatova: "Requiem" and "Poem Without a Hero."* Translated by D. M. Thomas. London: Paul Elek, 1976. A brief but useful introduction to Akhmatova and to the poems by the translator. Includes a cursory comparison with other translations of *Requiem*.

REQUIEM FOR A NUN

Type of work: Novel
Author: William Faulkner (1897-1962)
Type of plot: Psychological realism
Time of plot: 1930's
Locale: Mississippi
First published: 1951

Principal characters:
> MRS. GOWAN STEVENS née Temple Drake, the mother of a murdered child
> GOWAN STEVENS, her husband
> GAVIN STEVENS, a lawyer and Gowan's uncle
> NANCY MANNIGOE, a confessed murderer
> GOVERNOR OF MISSISSIPPI
> MR. TUBBS, the jailer of Jefferson

The Story:

Act I. The early settlers of what later became Yoknapatawpha County had founded the town of Jefferson, thereby escaping the "terrible freedom" of the wilderness. The courthouse evolved from a wooden lean-to built on the old log jail to the antebellum, colonial Georgian courthouse designed by Colonel Sutpen's imported French architect. The town had grown around the courthouse, was burned to the ground by the invading Union troops during the Civil War, and was rebuilt during Reconstruction with the help of carpetbaggers who remained afterwards to prosper and eventually become part of the local community.

In the 1930's, Nancy Mannigoe was sentenced at the courthouse for the murder of the youngest child of Mr. and Mrs. Gowan Stevens. Nancy's defense lawyer and great-uncle to the slain girl, Gavin Stevens, followed both Gowan and his wife Temple back to their home and tried to get Temple to tell the truth about what really happened on the day of the murder.

Act II. In the governor's mansion late on the night before Nancy's execution, Gavin has persuaded Temple to tell the governor the true story of her past and of its effects on the murder of her daughter. Temple was preparing to run away with Pete, who was blackmailing her with incriminating letters she had written to his brother, Alabama Red, her former lover from Memphis who had been killed by Popeye Vitelli. Temple also recounted the main events of her abduction and incarceration in a Memphis brothel. There is a flashback to the Stevenses' living room back in Jefferson, where Temple had recounted the events of the evening when she was preparing to escape with Pete. Nancy had tried to stop Temple's flight.

Back in the governor's office, Temple talked about the trial. When Gowan came in, they both discussed the past eight years of their marriage and the pain of attempting to live down Temple's notorious past and of trying to expiate Gowan's guilt for having abandoned her to Popeye's clutches. Temple, Gowan, and Gavin returned to Jefferson without having convinced the governor that he should postpone Nancy's execution.

Act III. Gavin and Temple visited Nancy in the county jail just before her execution. They discussed human suffering and the need to believe even in the face of that suffering. Gowan came to take his wife home, and, in leaving, Temple declared that they were all doomed.

Critical Evaluation:

William Faulkner began work on the historical narrative of *Requiem for a Nun* immediately after the publication of *Sanctuary* (1931), with which it is obviously connected. He soon became absorbed in work on another novel, *Absalom, Absalom!* (1936), and it took a decade and a half for him to return to the saga of Temple Drake. The book is unorthodox in structure. In the 1950's, Faulkner published a form of the work as a play without the connective prose text. Originally, however, he conceived of the work as an experimental novel, not as a play with prose introductions. This was to be the last major experiment with structure for this writer, who had spent his career creating innovative prose.

The novel is divided into three parts or acts, each with a prose introduction that traces a portion of the history of Faulkner's mythic Mississippi landscape. The introductory section to Act I, "The Courthouse," describes the way Yoknapatawpha County was carved out of the wilderness and the founding of the town of Jefferson. "The Golden Dome," the introduction to Act II, gives a thumbnail sketch of the history of the capitol of Mississippi at Jackson, of how the capitol got its name, and of how it grew into a thriving railhead with a population of more than two hundred thousand. Act III opens with a history of Jefferson during and after the Civil War: The courthouse was gutted when the Yankees burned the town, and it was rebuilt during Reconstruction exactly as it had been before. After that, the country seat prospered into the twentieth century, but the lingering memories of the war and of the past shaped the town and its inhabitants. In between these historical narratives, the novel tells the story of the circumstances surrounding the trial and conviction of Nancy Mannigoe, an African American, for the murder of Mr. and Mrs. Gowan Stevens' child.

For students of Faulkner's work, the introductory prose sections provide the most comprehensive exposition of the history of Yoknapatawpha County and the founding of Jefferson, its county seat. In these sections, Faulkner not only filled in much of the information missing from his other prose works about the history of the county but also explored his ideas on the place and function of memory in the shaping of communal consciousness and in the formation of a sense of place and belonging.

These prose essays are also considered to contain some of the finest writing Faulkner ever produced. He used these brief sections to play with various strategies of narration, prose structure, and expository forms. The prose sections and the dramatic narratives complement one another: The historical sections are objective and collective in nature, whereas the dramatic sections are individual and personal in tone; the former provide the context within which the latter operate.

Requiem for a Nun is the continuation more than twenty years later of Faulkner's earlier novel *Sanctuary*, in which Temple Drake, then a college co-ed, was abducted and held hostage in a Memphis bordello by the odd criminal Popeye Vitelli. The experiences of the first novel do more than merely provide the background for *Requiem for a Nun*, however, for they also establish the parameters within which Temple, now Mrs. Gowan Stevens, must work out her moral and emotional redemption. Even the use of her two names, which establishes the conflicts being worked out in Act II, is symbolic of her divided nature: Temple Drake is the dark, sexual side of her personality, and Mrs. Gowan Stevens is the more conventional social side. The integration of the two sides establishes the dramatic tension of the fiction and gives it its narrative direction.

The psychological division within Temple also deepens the novel's emotional resonance and moral ambiguity and enriches the plot by implicating the past in the murder. Temple must confront her complicity in the death of her own child. She must confess that she hired Nancy not out of compassion for her fallen state but rather so that she could relive the dark side of her own nature with someone who had had a similar fate. Temple does not talk through her past to expiate it but to bring it into the present. She needs to resurrect the degradation to cope with the obligation she feels toward Gowan, who married her out of an obligation motivated by his own fear of failure and guilt.

In spite of outward appearances, Temple needs to recover a part of herself that was hidden in the marriage that had redeemed her socially in the eyes of the community but that had been purchased at a great personal cost. It is her struggle to become a whole, integrated individual that provides the connection between the historical prose narratives, which deal with the greater community, and the personal, dramatic narratives. The most famous line in the novel is probably her comment that not only is the past "never dead," it is not "even past."

The most significant element that raises this issue is the presence of the letters Temple had written to Alabama Red, her lover from Memphis, in which she had detailed their sexual liaison. When Alabama's brother, Pete, uses the letters to blackmail Temple, he sets events in motion that eventually lead to Nancy's tragic act of smothering Temple's infant daughter. The letters remind Temple not only of her degradation but also of the pleasure she experienced in it, a pleasure she has for eight years sublimated in her marriage and in bearing her two children. Faulkner's description of this perverse yet liberating sexuality plays off against the conventionally tamed and sanctioned carnality within the institution of marriage to Gowan. Even that sexuality has its perverse side, since it is a reminder of Gowan's having abandoned Temple to Popeye. Temple and Gowan are, as she states at the conclusion of the novel, "doomed" to a life of recriminations and guilt, everlasting and ever-circling. Only through Nancy's acceptance of death and grace will Temple finally be able to discover a kind of peace in her own soul.

Charles L. P. Silet

Bibliography:
Blotner, Joseph. *Faulkner: A Biography.* 2 vols. New York: Random House, 1974. A comprehensive biography of Faulkner, which includes a historical discussion of his ancestors, his development as a writer, and the genesis of his work. An excellent beginning source.
Izard, Barbara, and Clara Hieronymous. *"Requiem for a Nun": Onstage and Off.* Nashville, Tenn.: Aurora, 1970. Traces the evolution of the text, its sources and the French adaptation by Albert Camus, and the performances of the dramatic portion of the novel in Germany, Greece, and Great Britain.
Polk, Noel. *Faulkner's "Requiem for a Nun": A Critical Study.* Bloomington: Indiana University Press, 1981. An exhaustive analysis of the novel that draws on the academic scholarship generated by the work and by Faulkner's career.
_____, ed. *Requiem for a Nun: A Concordance to the Novel.* West Point, N.Y.: Faulkner Concordance Advisory Board, 1979. Establishes a critical tool of immense value to those who wish to examine the novel in depth and detail.
Ruppersburg, Hugh M. *Voice and Eye in Faulkner's Fiction.* Athens: University of Georgia Press, 1983. A fine, detailed, but easily accessible overall introduction to the study of the novel.
Watson, Jay. *Forensic Fictions: The Lawyer Figure in Faulkner.* Athens: University of Georgia Press, 1993. In chapter 5, "Maieutic Forensics: Or, *Requiem for a Nun* and the Talking Cure," the author focuses on the role of Gavin Stevens, Faulkner's quintessential lawyer.

RESURRECTION

Type of work: Novel
Author: Leo Tolstoy (1828-1910)
Type of plot: Social realism
Time of plot: Late nineteenth century
Locale: Russia
First published: Voskreseniye, 1899 (English translation, 1899)

Principal characters:
PRINCE DMITRI IVANOVITCH NEKHLUDOFF, a gentleman
KATERINA MIKHAELOVNA MASLOVA (KATUSHA), a prostitute
VALDEMAR SIMONSON and
VERA DOUKHOVA, political prisoners

The Story:
Katerina Maslova, better known as Katusha, was being led out of prison to attend her trial for murder. Of illegitimate birth, she had been taken in by Sophia and Mary Ivanovna, well-to-do sisters who had cared for her and begun to educate her. When she was sixteen years old, Katusha was seduced by her guardians' nephew, Prince Dmitri Ivanovitch Nekhludoff. Learning that she was to become a mother, Katusha went to stay with a village midwife until her child was born. The baby was taken to the foundling hospital, where it soon died, and Katusha, after a series of tribulations, became a prostitute. When she was twenty-six years old, she was accused of complicity in the murder of a Siberian merchant.

While Katusha was being led into court, Nekhludoff, her seducer, lay in bed considering his position. He had recently been having an affair with a married woman, even though he was almost engaged to marry Princess Mary Korchagin. He also thought of having given away some of his lands to the peasants. Having arisen, Nekhludoff was reminded that he had to serve that day as a juror in the criminal court.

In court, Nekhludoff was astonished to see that the defendant was Katusha and that she was accused of having helped rob and poison the merchant from Siberia. The trial was disgusting because the officials were vain, stupid, and more concerned with formalities and their own self-interest than with a fair trial for the accused.

When Nekhludoff was a student at the university, he had spent his summers with his aunts, and it was there that he had first come to know and to like Katusha. He had given her books to read and had eventually fallen in love with her. When he next returned, three years later, military life had made him depraved and selfish, and he seduced her. On the following day, he had given her money and left for his regiment. When he returned after the war, he had learned that she had become pregnant and had gone away. Somewhat relieved, he had tried to forget her.

Now, at the trial, the sight of Katusha filled Nekhludoff with a mixture of loathing and pity. At first, he was afraid that his relation to her would be discovered, but Katusha did not recognize him, and gradually he began to feel remorse for the life to which he had driven her. Because of a careless legalistic oversight by the jury, Katusha, though innocent, was sentenced to four years of hard labor in Siberia. Driven by his uneasy conscience, Nekhludoff went to a lawyer to discuss the possibility of an appeal.

Later, when he was with the Korchagins, he realized that their life was empty and degenerate. He felt the need to cleanse his soul and decided that he would marry Katusha and give up his land.

When Nekhludoff went to the prison and revealed himself to Katusha, the girl treated him coldly. She seemed proud of her occupation as a prostitute, because it alone gave some meaning to her otherwise empty life. The next time he visited her, she behaved coarsely to him, and when he said that he wanted to marry her, she became angry with him and returned to her cell.

On his next visit to the prison, Nekhludoff was told that Katusha could not be seen because she had become drunk on vodka bought with money he had given her. Nekhludoff then went to see Vera Doukhova, a revolutionist acquaintance who had sent him a note from the prison. He was surprised at the inordinate pride Vera took in the sacrifices she had made for the revolutionary cause. Vera told him that if he obtained a position for Katusha in the prison hospital, her situation would improve. Nekhludoff arranged to have Katusha transferred.

By this time, Nekhludoff was no longer enamored with the prospect of marrying Katusha. He was still determined to go through with his plan, however, and started out on a journey to settle his estates in anticipation of his departure for Siberia. At Panovo, he saw the miserable conditions of the people. He saw Matrona Kharina, Katusha's aunt, and learned about the death of his child at the foundling hospital. He gave up his title to the land at Panovo and arranged for the peasants to have communal holdings in it, an act that brought him great joy.

Nekhludoff then went to St. Petersburg. His chief reason was to appeal Katusha's case to the senate and to try to secure the release of Lydia Shoustova, an innocent prisoner who was Vera Doukhova's friend. In St. Petersburg, he came within the aristocratic circle of his aunt, Katerina Ivanovna Tcharsky, who claimed to be interested in evangelism but who had no pity for the unfortunate of the world. Nekhludoff went to see various prominent people. The next day he learned that Lydia Shoustova had been released.

Katusha's case was put before the senate. Because one of the senators considered himself to be a Darwinian and thought that Nekhludoff's morality in the case was disgusting, the girl's sentence was upheld. On the same day, Nekhludoff met an old friend, Selenin, who was now a public prosecutor. He was an intelligent, honest man, but he had had been drawn into the tangled web of "correct" society and its standards. Nekhludoff began to see the same principle at work in all official circles: to condemn some who might be innocent in order to be assured of catching the truly guilty.

Back in Moscow, Nekhludoff visited Katusha to persuade her to sign a petition to the emperor. During his visit, he felt love taking hold of him once more. Katusha also loved Nekhludoff, but she felt that marriage to a woman like herself would be bad for him. While Nekhludoff was preparing for his journey to Siberia with Katusha, he began to study and to think about the nature of criminal law. Although he began to read much on the subject, he could not find the answer to his desire to know by what right some people punish others. He also began to feel that the only reasonable kinds of punishment were corporal and capital, which were both unfortunate and effective, whereas imprisonment was simply unfortunate.

On the long march to Siberia, Nekhludoff followed the prisoners and saw Katusha whenever possible. He also saw the horrible conditions of the exiles. Nekhludoff began to feel a new love for Katusha composed of tenderness and pity. He also learned to understand the point of view of the revolutionists, for Katusha had been allowed to travel with the political prisoners. One of these, Valdemar Simonson, fell in love with Katusha. He told Nekhludoff that he wished to marry the girl but that she wanted Nekhludoff to decide for her. Nekhludoff said that he would be pleased to know that Katusha was well cared for. When she learned of his answer, Katusha would not speak to Nekhludoff.

At a remote town in Eastern Siberia, Nekhludoff collected his mail and learned that Katusha's sentence to hard labor had been commuted to exile in a less remote region of Siberia.

When he went to tell Katusha the news, he realized how much he wanted to have a family. Katusha said that she preferred to stay with Simonson; however, she refused to say that she loved him. She told Nekhludoff that he would have to live his own life.

Nekhludoff felt that he was not needed any longer and that his affair with Katusha was ended. He saw that evil existed because those who tried to correct it were themselves evil and that society had persevered, not because of systems of punishments, but because of human pity and love. Because he realized that the Sermon on the Mount could indeed be a practical law, that night Nekhludoff's new life began.

Critical Evaluation:

Resurrection is characteristic of Leo Tolstoy, one of Russia's foremost novelists, because of its rich visual record of people and settings and its deftness in presenting the vices of petty officialdom, the humor of small people who want to seem great, and the hollowness of ritualistic orthodoxy. Tolstoy was convinced that evil begins when people cease to listen to their conscience and become self-centered. The public theme of the novel revolves around the shortcomings of social organizations. The personal theme, which involves the need for forgiveness, takes a form characteristic of Tolstoy: human failure revealed by a sin committed in semi-ignorance, followed by a long and soul-strengthening atonement.

The greatest strength of *Resurrection* is in its penetrating exposure of an unjust social order. A secondary focus is on the personal level in the effect of Nekhludoff's philosophical and political conversion, specifically in his relationship with Katusha, without whom Nekhludoff's reawakening and self-sacrifice could not have occurred.

In his student days, Nekhludoff's social convictions were idealistic. He believed in perfectibility and rejected the principle of ownership of land by the elite. His idealism dimmed, however, after he entered military life, and he quickly abandoned all thoughts of perfection. He sacrificed both his relationship with Katusha and his own values to establish a public image that mirrored the standards of the aristocracy. It was not until his conscience was aroused at Katusha's trial ten years later that he questioned his life and, upon Katusha's conviction, dedicated himself to her rescue and to his spiritual atonement.

Nekhludoff thus came to view human nature as dualistic—animal and spiritual—and he struggled to negate the animal instincts that had led him to sin. He realized that he could deceive others, but not himself and, guided by an inner sense of righteousness, set about, to correct the wrong he had caused.

When Nekhludoff entered the world of prisoners and peasants, he began to realize the extent of the injustice of society. Innocent people who had been incarcerated by error, political prisoners whose only crime was in holding differing opinions, and a crew of stonemasons imprisoned because of outdated visas were among those who flocked to Nekhludoff for help.

It soon became evident to Nekhludoff that social circumstance created criminals rather than the obverse: He rejected the concept of natural depravity based on individual or class characteristics. He further understood that the conditions that created powerlessness, poverty, hunger, sickness, and crime among the peasant classes were supported by the powerful in order to maintain the wealth of the privileged. Both government and science professed a desire to ameliorate these conditions but actually refused to consider the root of the problem. The only means of righting the situation, he found, was by returning the land to the people who worked it. Yet when Nekhludoff gave his land to the peasants, his wealthy friends and family grew concerned about his mental health, and the peasants eyed his offer with hostile suspicion. Nekhludoff's exploration of the causes of injustice led him to ask the haunting question of whether truth is at work in the process of law. It was obvious to him that the law did not contain truth by decree or by the process of the courts, although such a notion was popularly accepted. The fact was, Nekhludoff concluded, that the purpose of the law was to uphold class interests and that those who carried out the law and those to whom the law catered were equally criminal with those upon whom the judgment of the law fell. The basic fallacy of the legal system was the belief that people have the power to judge one another. Evildoers cannot judge evildoers, Nekhludoff contended. The processes of judgment and punishment were not only harmful, cruel, and immoral but also ineffective. Justice, he decided, was not served by social systems. That society and order exist at all, despite the acts of both lawful and lawless criminals, is simply because people still pity and love one another.

In the course of the novel, Nekhludoff's resurrection is paralleled by Katusha's spiritual reawakening. At her first reunion with Nekhludoff after her conviction, she repressed her memories of youth and the pain of Nekhludoff's betrayal to the point of oblivion, for she had hardened herself to the necessities of survival as a prostitute. Nekhludoff realized that his sin against her was even greater than he had known, that Katusha had died and that another person called Maslova had taken her place. Although Nekhludoff assumed responsibility not only for Katusha's freedom but also for her spiritual renewal, his influence was only one of the factors that went into the emergence of the new Katusha. Katusha realized that Nekhludoff was again using her, but as he persisted in following her, old feelings for him reawakened. Ultimately, she sacrificed her love in order to save him from degradation, thus shouldering Nekhludoff's burden for the third time. First she had suffered from his betrayal and from bearing his illegitimate child, then in allowing him to sacrifice himself for her, and finally in denying her love for him, by which means she released him from his pledge to marry her. Clearly, the novel's primary concern is Nekhludoff's resurrection.

The process of Nekhludoff's social reversal and spiritual regeneration is least convincing in his personal relationships. He shifts from victimizing Katusha to rescuing her, first taking advantage of her for his physical gratification and then using her to achieve his spiritual atonement. He remains the overlord whose decision precludes dialogue. He professes to see himself, like Jesus, not as the master but as the servant, but he is indeed a masterful servant. He imposes on Katusha the heavy burden of his self-sacrifice—his offer to marry her—without speaking a word of care or love. Nekhludoff's primary concern, it seems, is for the gratification resulting from humbling himself. Nekhludoff proclaims that he is dedicated to following God's will in his own conscience as far as he is able to do so and that in fulfilling such a commitment he will find peace and security.

The final, or perhaps first, genuine step in Nekhludoff's resurrection is the revelation of the truth in the gospel of Christianity. Accordingly, Nekhludoff recognizes that human beings' only duty is to fulfill these laws, but that they must do so without the guidance of the state church, which Nekhludoff judges to be as corrupt as the other institutions in society. Priests, for example, swear in witnesses at court proceedings with an air of self-importance but do not question whether justice is done. Ironically, prisoners corralled into prison chapels chant prayers for the powers that oppress them. Cynical, heretical priests lead their people farther into the darkness of superstition by telling them that "it is good for them." Nekhludoff's disgust for such hypocritical religion is as great as his disdain for his former life and all it represented, but it is his personal religious stance that propels him into a deep and revolutionary understanding of society and justice—an understanding that reflected Tolstoy's beliefs.

"Critical Evaluation" by Mary Peace Finley

Bibliography:

De Courcel, Martine. *Tolstoy: The Ultimate Reconciliation.* Translated by Peter Levi. New York: Scribner's Sons, 1988. A thorough discussion of Tolstoy, touching on all his important works. Describes the people and events in Tolstoy's life during the long and arduous writing of *Resurrection* and includes an analysis of that novel.

Noyes, George Rapall. *Tolstoy.* New York: Dover Publications, 1968. Connects the many works of Tolstoy with reference to biographical information that is pertinent to the understanding of his writings. Includes many of Tolstoy's published writings, diaries, and letters. Concludes that *Resurrection* is a novel of accessories, where the importance lies in gestures, mannerisms, and analysis of its characters' thoughts.

Rowe, William W. *Leo Tolstoy.* Boston: Twayne, 1986. Indicates the historical facts from which Tolstoy contrived *Resurrection.* Suggests the possible meanings and images of the novel. Includes biographical information as well as discussions of several novels and stories. An excellent source.

Simmons, Ernest J. *Tolstoy.* London: Routledge & Kegan Paul, 1973. Focuses on Tolstoy as a major thinker of his time and a religious, social, and political reformer. Describes Tolstoy's childhood and life as a writer, and explains Tolstoy's motivation to write *Resurrection* and the structure and intent of the novel.

Troyat, Henri. *Tolstoy.* Translated by Nancy Amphoux. Garden City, N.Y.: Doubleday, 1967. A thorough treatment of the author, with many illustrations. Gives a long explanation of the conditions surrounding the writing of *Resurrection* and some explanation of the text.

THE RETURN

Type of work: Novel
Author: Walter de la Mare (1873-1956)
Type of plot: Ghost
Time of plot: Nineteenth century
Locale: England
First published: 1910

> *Principal characters:*
> ARTHUR LAWFORD, a middle-aged Englishman
> SHEILA, his wife
> ALICE, their teenage daughter
> THE REVEREND BETHANY, a rector
> HERBERT HERBERT, a bookish recluse
> GRISEL HERBERT, his sister

The Story:

Late one September evening, Arthur Lawford, who was recovering from an attack of influenza, was walking in an ancient churchyard. There he found the grave of a man named Nicholas Sabathier, who had killed himself in 1739. Suddenly tired, Lawford stopped to rest and fell asleep. When he awoke, he felt very strange and quite recovered from his illness. He felt so well that he practically ran home.

Going up to his room to dress for dinner, Lawford lit a candle and prepared to shave. He stopped in horror when he saw that his whole physical being had changed; he was now lean-faced and dark, an entirely different person. The only thing that could have happened, he thought, was that his nap in the churchyard had changed him into someone else, perhaps the occupant of the grave, Sabathier. Still thankful that he retained his own mind, Lawford tried to think what to do. As he stood undecided, his wife came to call him to dinner. When she came into the room, she was horrified and refused at first to believe that the person she saw was her husband.

The Lawfords called in the rector, the Reverend Bethany, who was also horrified. He was willing to believe, however, that something had happened to Lawford, and that the person he saw was not an impostor. The three decided to wait until a week had passed before doing anything drastic. Sheila Lawford refused to stay with her husband at night; he seemed too much a stranger to her in his new shape. She tried to get him to remain in his room, but he found it necessary to go out in the evening. On one of his rambles at dusk, he met an old woman who had been a school friend of his mother's. She failed to recognize him in his new shape, even though he prompted her by telling her where she had known his mother. She did say he looked somewhat like the late Mrs. Lawford.

On another of his rambles, this time back to the same churchyard, Lawford met a strange man named Herbert Herbert. They talked over the grave of Nicholas Sabathier, and Lawford hinted at his own history. Herbert seemed interested and asked Lawford to come to tea the following day. When they shook hands to part, light fell on Lawford's face for the first time. As it did, Herbert gave an obvious start.

When Lawford went to tea the next day, Herbert told him that his was the face of Nicholas Sabathier, whose picture was in a book Herbert owned. The book also contained an autobiography of Sabathier, which revealed him as a man very fond of women. Tea was served by Grisel Herbert, the host's sister. Seeing the look of fear on Lawford's face when he left, she ran after him with the book her brother had mentioned. The two went for a walk, during which Lawford felt that he wrestled with an alien spirit and won out over it.

Alice, Arthur's daughter, returned home from school. When she accidentally met her father, the shock caused her to faint. Her mother tried to make her believe it was someone else, a doctor. Alice went to her father in secret and told him that she knew him and hoped all would turn out well in the end. After several arguments with her changed husband, Sheila finally decided to go away for a few days, leaving Lawford alone in the big house to wrestle with his problem. Although he hoped to throw off the spirit that had taken possession of him, he feared that it might conquer him entirely.

Lonely after his wife had gone, Lawford turned to the Herberts, of whom neither the rector nor anyone else had previously heard. He spent several days and nights with his new friends. Lawford felt that he was getting better, that he was conquering whatever had taken hold of him. Grisel seemed especially helpful.

One night, Lawford went back to his house alone. There he had fearful dreams and once again had a spiritual battle with something he could not name. The following day, he went to see the Herberts, who took him on a picnic. They walked many miles until, as they came over a hill, Lawford saw a village. The village awakened strange, horrible memories in him. He turned to Grisel and told her that she knew what memories they were; she made no denial.

The next day, Grisel and Lawford went out together for a long walk, during which they revealed their mutual feeling that they had come to love each other in another life. It seemed as if Nicholas Sabathier and a woman he loved were talking to each other through them. At last, Grisel told Lawford that he was pursuing a dream that could never reach reality. They returned to the Herberts' house, where Grisel told her brother, who seemed not in the least surprised, that Nicholas Sabathier had come to say good-bye for a while. They made their farewells. Lawford, somewhat returning to himself, remarked that he had never appreciated life before his strange adventure.

Lawford went back to his own house. It was locked. He went in quietly and listened to a conversation between his wife and some friends she had entrusted with the secret of his change. The friends refused to believe what had happened, in spite of what Sheila had seen, which one of them had also seen, plus the picture and account of Sabathier, which Sheila had found in the house. They advised her to have him placed in an asylum as mad, or else put into prison as an impostor. Lawford was standing in the hall and overheard the whole conversation. When they left, he remained, still silent, in the house.

That evening was the eve of St. Michael and All Angels, the same night on which Nicholas Sabathier had killed himself in 1739. As he sat in the quiet house, Lawford felt himself returning to his original condition. Unexpectedly, he was visited by the old lady whom he had met on his walk, the woman who had known his mother at school. She had come to see him in order to assure herself that the man she had met was not Lawford. This evening she immediately recognized him as her school friend's son, with almost no resemblance to the stranger who had accosted her. When she left, she made some ambiguous remarks that left Lawford wondering if she had not, in some fashion, learned more than she revealed. Nevertheless, he decided that he was sufficiently himself once more to write to his wife and let her know of the change. He sat down to write, but because of what he had overheard earlier in the evening, he was unable to put into words what he wanted to say. Fatigued, he fell asleep over the table.

As Lawford slept, the rector came into the room, recognized him as his own parishioner again, and sat down to watch over the sleeping man. Before long, the rector was also sound asleep.

Critical Evaluation:

The Return was among the earliest of Walter de la Mare's "ghost stories," and it contains many of the features that were to become intrinsic to his work in that vein—not least, of course, the ambiguity that requires the addition of quotation marks to the description. Although *The Return* uses an author-omniscient viewpoint rather than employing a possibly unreliable narrator (as many of de la Mare's later tales of this genre do) the question of what has happened to Arthur Lawford remains stubbornly unresolved, and defiantly unresolvable.

The ending of the story is particularly revealing in this respect; countless tales of surreal experience written in the previous century had been resolved by a final awakening, but de la Mare's ends with both the protagonist and his observer falling asleep. Climactic awakenings implicitly condemn not only the particular supernatural intrusions of individual stories to the world of dreams, but all supernatural intrusion into people's everyday life. De la Mare's reversal of the formula is no mere refusal of a cliché; it amounts to a claim that people's conscious lives are perpetually and inescapably shadowed by the supernatural, metaphorically, if not literally. Sleep can offer no release from this shadowing; at the beginning of the story, it is Lawford's lapse into sleep that facilitates the change that overtakes him. The text tells us nothing about the condition he will be in when—or if—he awakes from the slumber that overtakes him as he tries to explain to his absent wife that he has decided to "blunder on" within their unsatisfactory relationship.

It is difficult to say with certainty what actually happens in the course of the plot of *The Return*. Perhaps the soul of Nicholas Sabathier really does emerge from the suicide's grave to bid for possession of Lawford's body, only to fail on the anniversary of its previous retreat into oblivion. In that case, Lawford's spiritual battles really are the elements of a war of self-preservation. The main support for this thesis, however, is provided by the Herberts, whose own real existence seems to be a matter of some doubt; nor is the Herberts' support for a frankly supernatural explanation free from its own intrinsic ambiguities. Whether or not the Herberts inhabit the same world as Lawford's wife and her determinedly mundane friends, they are certainly not of that world. They represent a whole new world of possibilities, into which he might escape if only he had the will to do so, but it is a world that has problematic aspects of its own.

The alternative interpretation of Lawford's experience is that contemplation of the wrack and ruin of his life has combined with the symbol of Sabathier's gravestone to release something that has always been locked up within him: the man that he might have been. Support for this view is provided by the fact that his convalescence has given him the sense that "behind all these past years, hidden as it were from his daily life, lay something not quite reckoned with." He reflects, morosely, that people all keep their crazy sides to themselves; this licenses the theory that what happens to him might be a brief liberation of his "crazy side," forcing a long-overdue reckoning on which he is, in the end, incompetent to evaluate or follow through.

If this is so, the story becomes a bleak meditation on the subject of impotence. Unlike Doctor Jekyll, who found his other self so monstrous in appetite, inclination, and strength as to be uncontrollable once unleashed, poor Lawford surrenders his commitment to the "lawful," only to find his hidden self beset by uncertainties and confusions of its own. In the end, his metamorphosis is so tentative that there seems no prospect of his reaping the perverse rewards of reckless self-indulgence.

In *The Return*, Herbert calls attention to the significance of Sabathier's name, linking it to the hypothetical gatherings that witch-hunters called "sabbats" but suggesting that it might better be construed as a verb meaning "to bemuse or estrange with otherness." This is an appropriate description of what Lawford's possessor has done to him, and Lawford adopts it, speaking lightly to Grisel of the time "before I was Sabathiered."

In Lawford's conversations with Grisel, the notion of returning is incessantly invoked, but in several different ways. One return is that of "Nicholas Sabathier," whether that is an actual spirit from the historical past or merely a potential self that Arthur Lawford has put away and stifled. The more important return is that which Lawford decides to make in spite of the temptations that Grisel lays before him: the return that takes him back to his own house to overhear what he is, and will remain, in the estimation of the others. Herbert cannot understand why Lawford makes this choice, but Grisel can; she knows that love alone is not enough to sustain a relationship, and that the demands of an unsatisfactory wife are always likely to prevail if there is a child to be considered.

When he wrote *The Return*, Walter de la Mare's life had recently undergone a considerable change. For nearly twenty years he had worked as a clerk for an oil company, but, at the age of thirty-six, he had been granted a Civil List pension that allowed him to retire to the country and devote himself entirely to writing. It is not unnatural, in such circumstances, that a man might find abundant time to contemplate what he had been, what he had become, and what he might henceforth make of himself. Nor is it surprising that he might conclude that whatever he might once have made of himself, he was by now irrevocably confirmed in his own identity. However pusillanimous the last paragraph of the novel may seem, when Bethany's response to the imagined "roar of Time's Winged Chariot hurrying near" is simply to go to sleep, it is certainly realistic. If the ambiguity of his subsequent work is any guide, de la Mere never quite made up his mind as to whether that kind of realism ought to be seen as an appalling kind of cowardice, or as the quiet but triumphant heroism of common sense.

"Critical Evaluation" by Brian Stableford

Bibliography:
Briggs, Julia. "On the Edge: Walter de la Mare." In *Night Visitors: The Rise and Fall of the English Ghost Story*. Winchester, Mass.: Faber & Faber, 1977. Offers a reverent account of de la Mare's ghost stories, drawing various comparisons between *The Return* and his short fiction.
Clute, John. "Walter de la Mare." In *Supernatural Fiction Writers: Fantasy and Horror*, edited by Everett F. Bleiler. New York: Charles Scribner's Sons, 1985. A sensitive discussion of de la Mare's ambiguous use of the supernatural. Gives more attention to *The Return* than most such essays, which often concentrate entirely on his short fiction.
McCrosson, Doris Ross. *Walter de la Mare*. New York: Twayne, 1966. A compact but thorough account of de la Mare and his work. Chapter 8 is devoted to *The Return*.
Reid, Forrest. *Walter de la Mare: A Critical Study*. Winchester, Mass.: Faber & Faber, 1929. An early study of de la Mare's work, written when his reputation was at its height. Chapter 8 is a detailed critique of *The Return*, relatively uncolored by comparisons with the later ghost stories.
Whistler, Theresa. *Imagination of the Heart: The Life of Walter de la Mare*. London: Duckworth, 1993. A recent biography of de la Mare, much more detailed than earlier ones. *The Return* is set in its biographical context in chapter 8, which deals with the author's relationship with the poet Henry Newbolt, who was the prime mover in procuring de la Mare's Civil List pension.

THE RETURN OF THE KING

Type of work: Novel
Author: J. R. R. Tolkien (1892-1973)
Type of plot: Epic
Time of plot: The Third Age in a remote legendary past
Locale: Middle Earth, chiefly Gondor, Mordor, and the Shire
First published: 1955

Principal characters:

FRODO BAGGINS, the Ring-bearer
SAMWISE GAMGEE (SAM), his loyal servant and the temporary
  Ring-bearer
MERIADOC BRANDYBUCK (MERRY) and
PEREGRIN TOOK (PIPPIN), Frodo's cousins and the chief scourers of
  the Shire
GANDALF (MITHRANDIR), a wizard and the White Rider
ARAGORN (ELESSAR), the returned king
ÉOMER, the nephew of King Théoden and his successor as king of Rohan
EOWYN, Éomer's sister and a beautiful shield-maiden
DENETHOR, the steward of Gondor and the father of Boromir and
  Faramir
FARAMIR, the hope of Gondor after Boromir's death
GOLLUM, a corrupted hobbit and once the owner of the Ring
SARUMAN (SHARKEY), a traitor wizard and the corrupter of the Shire
SAURON, the Dark Lord of Mordor

The Story:

Gandalf and Pippin rode on Shadowfax to the Realm of Gondor and were admitted to the presence of Denethor, Steward of Gondor. Pippin told of the heroic death of Boromir, Denethor's son, and swore allegiance to the kingly old man. Gandalf did not hinder this, although Pippin sensed tension between the two. Beregond of the Guard gave the hobbit the passwords and told him how Gondor, closest of free lands to Mordor, bore the brunt of the Dark Lord's wrath.

After the departure of Gandalf, Théoden and his Riders, with Aragorn, Merry, Legolas, and Gimli, rode back to Dunharrow. They were joined by Rangers, Aragorn's kindred. Aragorn, sorely troubled, said haste demanded that he travel the Paths of the Dead. He had wrestled with the will of Sauron in his seeing stone, hoping to distract Sauron so that Frodo and Sam might fulfill their mission of destroying Sauron's Ring. Théoden's niece Eowyn begged Aragorn not to take the Paths of the Dead, from which none had returned, or to take her with him. He refused. Leading his company underground, he summoned the ghosts of oathbreakers who had failed to fight Sauron and who could have no peace until they kept the oath sworn to Aragorn's ancestor. They followed him, and wherever they passed, they spread terror.

Théoden and his nephew Éomer summoned the Riders of Rohan to answer Gondor's call for aid. Eowyn and Merry were denied a place among the combatants. When the Riders left, a young warrior, Dernhelm, smuggled Merry under a cloak. The darkness that Sauron sent out to dismay his enemies concealed the movements of Rohan's Riders.

When Faramir, the younger son of Denethor, came back from his outpost and reported his meeting with Frodo, Denethor was coldly furious that he had not taken the Ring by force. Boromir, he said, would have brought it to his father. Gandalf replied that if Boromir had taken it, he would have fallen and replaced the Dark Lord only by becoming another Dark Lord, whom even his father would not have known.

Sauron's army, led by the chief of the Ringwraiths, attacked Gondor. Faramir returned to battle but was wounded by Ringwraiths. Despair seized Denethor, who decided to burn himself and the unconscious but still living Faramir. Pippin sought Gandalf to prevent this mad act. The hosts of Mordor battered down the gate, and the chief Ringwraith entered, confronted only by Gandalf. Horn blasts announced the arrival of Rohan, and the Ringwraith vanished to return on his reptilian flying mount. Théoden's horse went mad with fright and fell on his master. Sick with fear, Merry crawled behind the monster, but Dernhelm faced the Ringwraith. According to an old prophecy, no living man could destroy the Ringwraith; but Dernhelm was discovered to be Eowyn, not a man. She decapitated his monstrous steed. Merry thrust from behind with his blade of Westernesse, and Eowyn struck at the Ringwraith's head. Both were stunned, but the Ringwraith's empty cloak and armor collapsed on the ground, and a shrill wail ran down the wind. Aragorn arrived in ships with reinforcements. The battle was won, but the cost was great. Denethor, thwarted by Beregond and Gandalf in his attempt to burn Faramir, burned himself, clutching his seeing stone, through which the will of Sauron had entered Gondor. At Théoden's death, Éomer became King of Rohan. In the Houses of Healing, Aragorn treated Faramir, Eowyn, and Merry. Gandalf, Aragorn, and others marched to the Black Gate of Mordor to distract Sauron yet again and keep his Eye from Frodo. At the Gate, Mordor's hordes attacked them.

Meanwhile, Sam had made his way into Mordor to try to rescue Frodo. The orcs had fought over Frodo's mithril coat, and most of them were dead. Sam killed the lone guard and disguised Frodo and himself with orc armor. Nightmare days followed as they struggled across the ashen land toward Mount Doom, often escaping capture by seeming miracles, once being taken for orcs and forced to join them until they escaped by a fortunate accident. As Sam carried the exhausted Frodo on his back, struggling toward Mount Doom and its restless fires, Gollum, who had been trailing them, leaped from a high rock, knocking Sam down; Gollum grappled with Frodo for the Ring. Frodo flung him off and announced that if Gollum ever touched him again, he would be cast into the fire. Frodo moved on. Sam raised Sting, his dagger, to kill Gollum but could not strike the wretched, repulsive creature. Gollum fled. Sam followed Frodo into the fissure in the side of Mount Doom. There, beside the Crack of Doom with its fearful flames, Frodo put on the Ring, and Sauron became aware of him. The Dark Lord called his Ringwraiths from the battle. Gollum dashed past Sam and struggled with Frodo for the Ring, which he captured by biting off Frodo's finger. Dancing with joy, Gollum lost his balance and fell into the fire. The volcano erupted; the towers of Mordor disintegrated; and the Ringwraiths flew into the flames and were destroyed. The hosts of Mordor scattered like dust. The Captains of the West saw a pall of smoke rise above Mordor, lean threateningly toward them, and then blow away. Gandalf and three great Eagles picked up Frodo and Sam, who lay on an island of stone slowly being covered by molten lava, and brought them back for Aragorn's healing.

They were present at the crowning of Aragorn as King Elessar. Frodo took the crown from Faramir, the steward of Gondor, and bore it to Gandalf, who crowned the king. Celeborn and Galadriel came, and Elrond with his two sons brought his daughter Arwen Evenstar to marry Aragorn and become queen. King Éomer of Rohan then took Théoden's body back to his country. He gave the hand of his sister Eowyn to Faramir, whom she had grown to love in the

Houses of Healing. The guests scattered—Legolas and Gimli to visit Fangorn, Celeborn and Galadriel to Lothlorien, Gandalf and the hobbits to Rivendell to visit Bilbo. Gandalf sent the four hobbits to the Shire after telling them they would find evil, which they could now remedy without help from him. Lotho Sackville-Baggins had set up a dictatorship; backing him was the mysterious Sharkey. Merry and Pippin took charge of scouring the Shire with the help of other hobbits who had needed only a leader. They killed or drove away the Boss's ruffians and learned that Sharkey was Saruman, whom Treebeard had released after Sauron's overthrow. Saruman tried to stab Frodo, but the mithril coat saved him again. Saruman and his henchman Wormtongue, who had murdered Lotho, were banished. Wormtongue hated Saruman and cut his throat. The wizard's body shriveled with rapid decay. Hobbits killed the fleeing Wormtongue.

Sam brought beauty back to the Shire, sprinkling over it the dust given him in Lothlorien by Galadriel. He married Rosie Cotton, and they lived in Bag End, looking after Frodo. Every year, Frodo's wounds troubled his body and his spirit until he joined Gandalf, Bilbo, Galadriel, and Elrond and sailed away to the overseas haven of the elves. Thus ended the Third Age.

Critical Evaluation:

The Return of the King is the final volume of *The Lord of the Rings* (1955), J. R. R. Tolkien's epic fantasy of war between good and evil. Divided into two sections, *The Return of the King* carries the disparate narrative threads of *The Two Towers* (1954) to their conclusions, drawing the War of the Ring to an ending that is at once happy and sad.

As in *The Two Towers*, the first portion (book 5) of *The Return of the King* is a sweeping view of a world at war. This section weaves together the experiences of several different heroes, large and small, each of whom must play a part to defeat the armies of the Dark Lord. By contrast, much of book 6 concentrates again on only three characters, the presence of each of whom is necessary for the destruction of the ruling Ring. The narrow focus of the ringbearer and his companions is united with the vast panorama of the world outside only after the Ring is gone. By employing this dual narrative style, Tolkien is able to address widely divergent questions regarding the ability of good to defeat evil.

The great battle of the War of the Ring takes place before the gates of Minas Tirith, chief city of Gondor. Throughout the story, Gondor has been portrayed as the essential fortress of the West, the most powerful defense against the triumph of evil. Although waning in strength, Gondor has remained true to the high vision of its founders, refusing to compromise with evil even as the days grow dark. It is, however, not enough. Sauron has marshaled armies so powerful that Lord Denethor, certain of the defeat of his city, goes mad.

Yet the day is saved. The gate of Minas Tirith is broken, and its armies quail in fear, but rescue comes from several sources. From the north, the Riders of Rohan attack with the dawn, dismaying the human allies of the Dark Lord. The Captain of Mordor is slain by a woman of Rohan and a hobbit of the Shire. Ships arrive from the south bearing Aragorn and his fellow Rangers of Westernesse. From the city ride the knights of Dol Amroth, leading the army of Gondor with renewed hope. The great wizard Gandalf does what he can to bring order to these events, but a power far stronger than even his subtle mind is at work. Together, this array of forces is just enough to defeat Sauron's first attack. Good has triumphed not because of the will or strength of any one warrior, but because of the cooperation of all in a just cause. Each army suffers grievously, but the sufferings stand for nought in the face of defeating the great evil.

As the Captains of the West stand together to push the enemy to his last throw, the focus of the story shifts to Mordor, where three indomitable spirits make their way to Orodruin, the mountain of fire. Here is the same story etched in fine detail: Good triumphs not because of the heroic exploits of any one of them, but because of the necessary contributions of all three.

Who is the hero of *The Lord of the Rings*? Frodo is the sacrificial martyr, dragging his body through the desert of Mordor while the Ring eats away at his mind. He must carry the Ring to the fire, because no one else has the strength of will. Yet Frodo would never have made it without Sam at his side, thinking of food and water, pointing the way, finally carrying his master up the side of the mountain. Only Frodo could take the Ring, but without Sam he would have lain down in Mordor and died.

When they reach the fire, Frodo's will fails him at last. The Ring takes possession of his mind, spinning illusions of greatness and fending off its own destruction. Sam is helpless at this turn of events. He has brought his master to the mountain, but his master cannot fulfill the quest. Gollum has a last part to play. Seizing the Ring in a last act of treachery and deceit, the maddened hobbit oversteps himself and falls into the fire with the Ring. Good comes of this last evil act, for the Ring is destroyed at last.

In both the War of Gondor and the final destruction of the Ring, good may be perceived as a force more powerful than any one individual, more powerful even than the actions of all the characters combined. The triumph of Gondor is achieved through the coordinated actions of many, a series of carefully timed events that no one person orchestrates. The Ring is destroyed because three vastly dissimilar hobbits are drawn to the fire, each with an essential part in the drama. Goodness is more than a quality within each individual. It is an active force guiding the actions of those who walk the earth, at times in spite of themselves.

In a lecture delivered in 1939, J. R. R. Tolkien argued that one of the essential ingredients of a successful fairy story is a happy ending. Whether *The Lord of the Rings* is successful in that regard is an open question. Certainly the forces representing good win a complete victory; Sauron and his minions are vanquished, the free peoples flourish, and Aragorn gains his crown. Yet there is an underlying element of change and loss. Their work finished, Elrond, Galadriel, and Gandalf must leave Middle Earth. Frodo and Bilbo, wounded by possession of the Ring, depart also. The younger hobbits become the recognized heroes of the Shire, while Sam Gamgee inherits all that might have come to Frodo. It is a bittersweet ending at best.

"Critical Evaluation" by Robert Kuhn McGregor

Bibliography:
Carter, Lin. *Tolkien: A Look Behind "The Lord of the Rings."* New York: Ballantine Books, 1969. Basic introduction to the trilogy. Contains a summary of *The Return of the King* and includes chapters on allegory, fairy stories, elements of classical epic and fantasy in the trilogy, and the sources Tolkien used.

Ellwood, Gracia Fay. *Good News from Tolkien's Middle Earth.* Grand Rapids, Mich.: William B. Eerdmans, 1970. In his introduction, Ellwood asserts the "aliveness" of all things in Middle Earth, as in the human unconscious. Traces the blend of sacred and secular in the work and interprets Gandalf, Frodo, and Aragorn as complementary heroes. The chapter on Aragorn and *The Return of the King* emphasizes the human need for a king.

Giddings, Robert, ed. *J. R. R. Tolkien: This Far Land.* Totowa, N.J.: Barnes & Noble Books, 1983. Essays on varied topics, including narrative structure, which show how each episode in *The Return of the King* is described through a major character. Other essays address Tolkien's relevance, humor, and female characters.

Isaacs, Neil D., and Rose A. Zimbardo, eds. *Tolkien: New Critical Perspectives.* Lexington: University Press of Kentucky, 1981. An introduction to earlier Tolkien criticism. Includes a chapter on Frodo as the old hero and Aragorn as the new, as well as a discussion of the combination of mythic and Christian elements in *The Return of the King*.

Petty, Anne C. *One Ring to Bind Them All: Tolkien's Mythology*. Tuscaloosa: University of Alabama Press, 1979. Good introduction to Tolkien and mythology. Includes a chapter entitled "Trial, Death, and Transfiguration" and a structuralist interpretation of the trilogy.

THE RETURN OF THE NATIVE

Type of work: Novel
Author: Thomas Hardy (1840-1928)
Type of plot: Tragedy
Time of plot: Mid-nineteenth century
Locale: Egdon Heath, in southern England
First published: 1878

> *Principal characters:*
> DIGGORY VENN, a reddleman
> DAMON WILDEVE, the proprietor of the Quiet Woman Inn
> THOMASIN YEOBRIGHT, Wildeve's fiancée
> MRS. YEOBRIGHT, Thomasin's guardian
> CLYM YEOBRIGHT, Mrs. Yeobright's son
> EUSTACIA VYE, a young woman who wants to escape the heath

The Story:

Egdon Heath was a gloomy wasteland in southern England. Against this majestic but solemn, brooding background a small group of people were to work out their tragic drama in the impersonal presence of nature.

Guy Fawkes Day bonfires were glowing in the twilight as Diggory Venn, the reddleman, drove his van across the heath. Tired and ill, Thomasin Yeobright, the young girl whom Diggory loved, lay in the rear of his van. She had rejected his marriage proposal in order to marry Damon Wildeve, proprietor of the Quiet Woman Inn. Now, Diggory was carrying the girl to her home at Blooms-End. She had gone to marry Wildeve in a nearby town, but the ceremony had not taken place because of an irregularity in the license. Shocked and shamed, Thomasin had asked her old sweetheart, Diggory, to take her home.

Mrs. Yeobright, Thomasin's aunt and guardian, heard the story from the reddleman. Concerned for the girl's welfare, she decided that the wedding should take place as soon as possible. Mrs. Yeobright had good cause to worry, for Wildeve's intentions were not wholly honorable. Later in the evening, after Wildeve had assured the Yeobrights, rather casually, that he intended to go through with his promise, his attention was turned to a bonfire blazing on Mistover Knap. There old Captain Vye lived with his beautiful granddaughter Eustacia. At dusk, Eustacia had started a fire on the Heath as a signal to her lover, Wildeve, to come to her. Although he had intended to break with Eustacia, he decided to obey her summons.

Meanwhile, Eustacia was waiting for Wildeve in the company of young Johnny Nunsuch. When Wildeve threw a pebble in the pond to announce his arrival, Eustacia told Johnny to go home. The meeting between Wildeve and Eustacia was unsatisfactory for both. He complained that she gave him no peace. She, in turn, resented his desertion. Meanwhile, Johnny Nunsuch, frightened by strange lights he saw on the heath, went back to Mistover Knap to ask Eustacia to let her servant accompany him home but kept silent when he came upon Eustacia and Wildeve. Retracing his steps, he stumbled into a sand pit where the reddleman's van stood. Diggory learned from the boy of the meeting between Eustacia and Wildeve. Later, he overheard Eustacia declare her hatred of the heath to Wildeve, who asked her to run away with him to America. Her reply was vague, but the reddleman decided to see Eustacia without delay to beg her to let Thomasin have Wildeve.

Diggory's visit to Eustacia was fruitless. He then approached Mrs. Yeobright, declared again his love for her niece and offered to marry Thomasin. Mrs. Yeobright refused the reddleman's offer because she felt that the girl should marry Wildeve. She confronted the innkeeper with vague references to another suitor, with the result that Wildeve's interest in Thomasin awakened once more.

Shortly afterward, Mrs. Yeobright's son, Clym, returned from Paris, and a party to welcome him gave Eustacia the chance to view this stranger about whom she had heard so much. Uninvited, she went to the party disguised as one of the mummers. Clym was fascinated by this interesting and mysterious young woman disguised as a man. Eustacia dreamed of marrying Clym and going with him to Paris. She even broke off with Wildeve, who, stung by her rejection, promptly married Thomasin to spite Eustacia.

Clym Yeobright decided not to go back to France. Instead, he planned to open a school. Mrs. Yeobright strongly opposed her son's decision. When Clym learned that Eustacia had been stabbed in church by a woman who thought that Eustacia was bewitching her children, his decision to educate the people of the heath was strengthened. Much against his mother's wishes, Clym visited Eustacia's home to ask her to teach in his school. Eustacia refused because she hated the heath and the country peasants; as the result of his visit, however, Clym fell completely in love with the beautiful but heartless Eustacia.

Mrs. Yeobright blamed Eustacia for Clym's wish to stay on the heath. When bitter feeling grew between mother and son, he decided to leave home. His marriage to Eustacia made the break complete. Later, Mrs. Yeobright relented somewhat and gave a neighbor, Christian Cantle, a sum of money to be delivered in equal portions to Clym and Thomasin. Christian foolishly lost the money to Wildeve in a game of dice. Fortunately, Diggory won the money from Wildeve, but, thinking that all of it belonged to Thomasin, he gave it to her. Mrs. Yeobright knew that Wildeve had duped Christian. She did not know that the reddleman had won the money away from the innkeeper, and she mistakenly supposed that Wildeve had given the money to Eustacia. She met Eustacia and asked the girl if she had received any money from Wildeve. Eustacia was enraged by the question; in the course of her reply to Mrs. Yeobright's charge, she said that she would never have condescended to marry Clym had she known that she would have to remain on the heath. The two women parted angrily.

Eustacia's unhappiness was increased by Clym's near-blindness, a condition brought on by too much reading, for she feared that this meant she would never get to Paris. When Clym became a woodcutter, Eustacia's feeling of degradation was complete. Bored with her life, she went by herself one evening to a gypsy dance. There she accidentally met Wildeve and again felt an attraction to him. The reddleman saw Eustacia and Wildeve together, told Mrs. Yeobright of the meeting, and begged her to make peace with Eustacia for Clym's sake. She agreed to try.

Mrs. Yeobright's walk at noon across the hot, dry heath to see her son and daughter-in-law proved fatal. When she arrived in sight of Clym's house, she saw her son from a distance as he entered the front door. Then, while she rested on a knoll near the house, she saw another man entering, but she was too far away to recognize Wildeve. After resting for twenty minutes, Mrs. Yeobright went on to Clym's cottage and knocked. No one came to the door. Heartbroken by what she considered a rebuff by her own son, Mrs. Yeobright started home across the heath. Overcome by exhaustion and grief, she sat down to rest, and a poisonous adder bit her. She died without knowing that inside her son's house Clym had been asleep, worn out by his morning's work. Eustacia did not go to the door because, as she later explained to her husband, she had thought he would answer the knock. The real reason for Eustacia's failure to go to the door was fear of the consequences if Mrs. Yeobright found her with Wildeve.

Clym awoke with the decision to visit his mother. Starting out across the heath toward her house, he stumbled over her body. His grief was tempered by bewilderment over the reason for her being on the heath at that time. When Clym discovered that Eustacia had failed to let his mother enter the house and that Wildeve had been in the cottage, he ordered Eustacia out of his house. She went quietly because she felt in part responsible for Mrs. Yeobright's death.

Eustacia took refuge in her grandfather's house, where a faithful servant thwarted her in an attempt to commit suicide. In utter despair over her own wretched life and over the misery she had caused others, Eustacia turned to Wildeve, who had unexpectedly inherited eleven thousand pounds and who still wanted her to run away with him. One night, she left her grandfather's house in order to keep a prearranged meeting with the innkeeper; but in her departure, she failed to receive a letter of reconciliation which Thomasin had persuaded Clym to send to her. On her way to keep her rendezvous with Wildeve, she lost her way in the inky blackness of the heath and either fell accidentally or jumped into a small lake and was drowned. Wildeve, who happened to be near the lake when she fell in, jumped in to save her and also drowned.

Originally, *The Return of the Native* ended with the death of Eustacia and of Wildeve, but, in order to satisfy his romantic readers, Hardy made additions to the story in a later edition. The faithful Diggory married Thomasin. Clym, unable to abolish ignorance and superstition on the heath by teaching, became an itinerant preacher.

Critical Evaluation:

Thomas Hardy was born in Dorset, England, on June 2, 1840. Although he attended several grammar schools and studied French at King's College, Hardy had little formal education. Later, however, he read extensively in the Bible, the classics, and recent scientific publications. He was an architect's apprentice from 1856 to 1874 and later an ecclesiastical architect. During this time, he wrote poetry, which was not published until after he was a well-known novelist. His first novel, *Desperate Remedies*, was published in 1871. In 1872, he married Emma Gifford; after her death in 1912, he married Florence Dugdale. When storms of protest arose over the pessimism and the violation of strict Victorian sexual mores in *Tess of the D'Urbervilles* (1891) and *Jude the Obscure* (1895), Hardy gave up the novel but continued to write poetry. He died on January 11, 1928, and his ashes were placed in the Poets' Corner at Westminster Abbey. Among his best works are *Far from the Madding Crowd* (1874) and *The Return of the Native*.

In *The Return of the Native*, there is a strong conflict between nature or fate, represented by Egdon Heath, and human nature, represented by the characters in the novel, especially Eustacia. The title of the first chapter, "A Face on Which Time Makes but Little Impression," establishes the heath's role as much more significant than merely a setting for the action. The word "face" suggests that the heath assumes anthropomorphic proportions and becomes, in essence, a major character in the novel; somber and dark, "The storm was its lover, and the wind its friend." While the characters struggle and become tired and disillusioned—or die—the heath remains indifferent and unchanged. The heath is a formidable foe; in fact, those who struggle against it—Eustacia, Wildeve, and Mrs. Yeobright—eventually die.

The heath, then, becomes a symbol of permanence. Other aspects of the setting become symbolic, and they also intensify the somber tone of the novel. Light and dark imagery is significant in that the dominance of dark imagery adds to the novel's pessimism. The bonfires on the heath provide small areas of light in the blackness of the night, yet the furze burns quickly and is soon extinguished, like the momentary happiness of Eustacia and Clym and the wild passion of Eustacia and Wildeve. The moon's eclipse on the night Clym proposes to Eustacia foreshadows the eclipse of their love. On the night of Eustacia's death, the violent storm echoes her violent emotions as she cries out against her fate.

Like his character Eustacia, Hardy often seems to blame fate for many of the catastrophes of life. Many critics believe that, in this novel, fate is completely dominant and that the characters are helpless victims of its malevolence. Such a view, however, seems inadequate. Admittedly, fate does play a significant role; for example, Eustacia accidentally meets Wildeve at the gypsy dance. Mrs. Yeobright just happens to choose an extremely hot day to visit Clym, just happens to arrive when Wildeve is there, and just happens to be bitten by the adder when she collapses from fatigue. Eustacia does not receive Clym's letter because her grandfather believes she is asleep. Much of the novel's tragedy, however, can be traced to the characters' motivations, decisions, and actions.

Mrs. Yeobright may seem victimized by Eustacia's failure to open the door to her, but one must remember that Mrs. Yeobright never accepts Eustacia and attempts to turn Clym against her. She feels socially superior to Eustacia, distrusts her because she is a free spirit, calls her lazy and irresponsible, hints that she is behaving indiscreetly with Wildeve, and, in general, is jealous of her because she wants to keep Clym to herself. She refuses to attend Clym's wedding and treats Eustacia in a condescending manner as they speak together near the pool. She then harbors her grudge and keeps away from her son and his wife long enough for the gulf between them to widen greatly.

Clym, too, brings much of his trouble upon himself. He is flattered by Eustacia's attention and passion for him but never really sees her as an individual totally different from himself. Without regard for her hatred of the heath and her longing for the excitement of Paris, he assumes that she will be a vital part of his teaching mission. After their marriage, he ignores her and devotes his time to his studies, which, perhaps, helps to bring about the physical blindness that becomes symbolic of his blindness to reality. Martyring himself as a furze cutter, he intensifies Eustacia's hatred for the heath and fails to see that his physical fatigue and his degrading work deal a crushing blow to his marriage. Even his desire to teach is selfish and unrealistic; he tries to escape from life's conflicts into an abstraction of truth, and he desires to impose his views on others. The view of Clym at the end of the novel is ironic; as an itinerant preacher "less than thirty-three," he may suggest a Christ figure; yet in his self-righteousness, he fails to find the meaning of love.

Eustacia, who blames fate for her tragedy, is the novel's most ambiguous character; even the author seems to have ambivalent feelings toward her. She is an exciting, passionate "queen of the night" whose romanticism makes her long to be "loved to madness" by a man great enough to embody her dreams. Allowing her imagination to convince her that Clym can master this role, she marries him, hoping to manipulate him, as she had manipulated Wildeve, and thus get to Paris. After her marriage, however, her liaison with Wildeve is at first innocent; only after Clym banishes her from his house does she agree to accept Wildeve's offer to help her leave the heath. Despite her desperation, Eustacia refuses to be humbled. Realizing that a lack of money will cause her to lose her honor for a man who is "not great enough" to meet her desires, she drowns herself to avoid humiliation. It is more believable that she dies willingly rather than accidentally, because only in death does she seem to find peace.

Although Eustacia has lost in her battle with the heath, her struggle proves that she is a strong, defiant character who is defeated partly by forces beyond her control and partly by her own refusal to give up her dream. Despite her selfishness and hauteur, her lively spirit gives life to the novel and makes her, in the end, its tragic but unforgettable heroine.

"Critical Evaluation" by Janet Wester

Bibliography:

Bloom, Harold, ed. *Thomas Hardy's "The Return of the Native."* New York: Chelsea House, 1987. Introduction addresses the relation of Arthur Schopenhauer and Percy Bysshe Shelley to Hardy, then discusses the "transformation" of Eustacia. Contains essays Brooks calls the "best modern interpretations" written by Lawrence, Howe, Brooks, Eggenschwiler, Meisel, Gregor, Fleishman, and Johnson.

Gindin, James, ed. *Thomas Hardy: "The Return of the Native."* New York: W. W. Norton, 1969. Contains the novel, twelve of Hardy's poems and the portion of his autobiography related to the novel, five contemporary criticisms, and fourteen later critiques on the characters, themes, and techniques of the novel. Ends with a selected bibliography.

Jewell, John. "Hardy's *The Return of the Native*." *The Explicator* 49, no. 3 (Spring, 1991): 159-162. Focuses on Hardy's symbolic use of red through his use of the reddle. Concludes that, because of the red dye's location on the ewe, the "reddle functions as a kind of scarlet letter." Explores the character of Diggory Venn as a symbol of evil.

Lawrence, D. H. "Study of Thomas Hardy." In *Selected Literary Criticism*, edited by Anthony Beal. New York: Viking Press, 1956. Published after Lawrence's death. Provides an early psychological study of Hardy's characters, focusing on what Clym and Eustacia desire. Explains why *The Return of the Native* is the "first tragic and important novel." Probes into the tragic effects of the heath on its inhabitants.

Tighe, Mary Ann. "*The Return of the Native:* Self-Improvement Leads to Literary Judgment." *English Journal* 70, no. 5 (September, 1981): 30-32. A teacher describes her success with having her students role-play three predicaments, later studying Hardy's portrayal of the same conflicts, the theme of fate, and Greek tragedy traditions.

THE REVENGE OF BUSSY D'AMBOIS

Type of work: Drama
Author: George Chapman (c. 1559-1634)
Type of plot: Tragedy
Time of plot: Sixteenth century
Locale: Paris
First performed: c. 1610; first published, 1613

Principal characters:
CLERMONT D'AMBOIS, the brother of Bussy d'Ambois, a soldier of
fortune recently murdered
BALIGNY, Clermont's brother-in-law
CHARLOTTE, Clermont's sister
MONTSURRY, Bussy's murderer
TAMYRA, his wife
DUC DE GUISE
HENRY III, the king of France
MAILLARD, Baligny's lieutenant

The Story:

Clermont d'Ambois had vowed to avenge the murder of his brother, Bussy. Although he doubted the virtue of repaying violence with violence, he had made a solemn promise to Bussy's ghost. His sister Charlotte, unambiguous in her feelings, was impatient for immediate revenge, and her marriage to Baligny had been made under the stipulation that he, too, pledge himself to effect the death of Montsurry, Bussy's murderer. Tamyra, the wife of Montsurry and former mistress of Bussy, had returned to her husband, but she made no secret of her hatred of him and her desire for his death. The design of these people was obstructed by the cowardly Montsurry, who had barricaded himself in his home.

Clermont, who insisted on a fair duel and who would allow no one else to discharge his duty, had instructed Baligny to deliver his challenge. Baligny's entrance to Montsurry's home was accomplished with the help of a decadent nobleman, the Marquess Renel. Renel, visiting Montsurry on business, bribed the guards to admit Baligny. When Baligny entered, Montsurry was terrified and refused to accept the proffered challenge. Baligny left the challenge with Tamyra, who promised to make her husband read it.

This plot was not the only one in which Baligny was involved. A treacherous man, he based his actions on the belief that troubles for others meant blessings for himself. Wearing a different mask for every acquaintance, he was able to gain people's confidence and thus discover their dissatisfactions and sow the seeds of further discontent. In dealing with King Henry III, he expounded the doctrine that any evil done out of loyalty to a king was justified. Such a philosophy being agreeable to King Henry, Baligny had become his trusted agent. In talking to the Duc de Guise, on the other hand, he expressed the belief that conspiracy was sometimes defensible.

The principal object of jealousy in the court at this time was the Guise faction. King Henry was fearful and jealous of the increasing influence of the Duc de Guise, and Baligny strove to increase his distrust. Guise's closest friend was Clermont d'Ambois, whom Guise not only admired but endeavored to emulate. He saw in Clermont a valor equal to Bussy's and, more important, a profound knowledge of life. Clermont's principles of restraint, unworldliness, and stoic acceptance guided the actions of the powerful duke. Because of the close relationship between the two men, jealousy of Guise was often extended to include Clermont. Thus Baligny was able to convince King Henry of the advantage of getting rid of Clermont. He suggested that Clermont be invited to visit Cambrai and there, away from his friends at court, be arrested.

Baligny induced Clermont to go to Cambrai on the pretext of reviewing a muster of the king's troops. In his conversation with Clermont, Baligny attempted to weaken Clermont's tie with Guise by criticizing the latter for his part in the St. Bartholomew's Day Massacre. The schemer's efforts were wasted on Clermont, who was convinced of Guise's virtue.

While Clermont was being entertained by his sister in Cambrai, he received an anonymous letter informing him of the betrayal and of Baligny's complicity in it. Refusing to think evil of his sister's husband, he dismissed the letter as false. Charlotte, who could think of little but avenging Bussy's death, regarded the message as an effort further to enfeeble Clermont's weak will in carrying out his duty.

Maillard, Baligny's lieutenant, had been instructed by the king to apprehend Clermont. When Maillard came to Charlotte's house, ostensibly for the purpose of accompanying Clermont on a tour, the latter asked him if he were charged to arrest him. Maillard's obvious signs of guilt convinced Clermont that his earlier suspicions about the journey had been justified. Clermont offered to let Maillard take him peacefully, but Maillard denied that any intrigue was afoot. Although quite certain of the consequences, Clermont, with characteristic acceptance of fate, followed Maillard.

The plan was to take Clermont while he was reviewing the troops. Two soldiers disguised as lackeys were to lead him into an ambush, where several men would seize him. Clermont's strength exceeded even the estimate of his attackers, however. The disguised soldiers succeeded only in unhorsing him. Afoot, he easily beat them off and drove straight through the ambush. He ran until, exhausted, he fell to the earth and was captured.

Believing that outer circumstances had no power to touch the inner man without his will, he accepted his capture with little concern. His only worry was that he would be unable to keep an appointment with his mistress, the Countess of Cambrai, and his one request was that a message be sent to her. Other people, however, did not accept his internment with so much complacency. Upon receiving his message, the countess sent him jewels that she hoped would effect his release and vowed that she would cry until her eyes poured out. When the Duc de Guise heard the news, he rushed to King Henry and spoke so passionately and eloquently of Clermont's virtues that the weak-willed king, unable to answer Guise, ordered that Clermont be released.

After his release, Clermont went to the house of the Duc de Guise. There he again met Bussy's ghost, who chided him for not having exacted the revenge. Guise, who had been implicated in Bussy's murder, felt that the ghost should thunder threats against him, but Clermont asserted that the duke had fully compensated for his error. Guise was also worried about a plot against him; he believed that his efforts at propagating the Catholic cause were endangered. Clermont wanted him to retire from his plans, but Guise regarded withdrawal as an abandonment of France.

A plot was indeed threatening the Duc de Guise; King Henry, with Baligny's encouragement, had ordered his murder. The king, in addition to his longstanding jealousy of Guise, had been angered at having his hand forced over Clermont. As the duke was on his way to visit the king, Henry's men stepped from behind a wall hanging and killed him.

With the assistance of Tamyra, Clermont gained access to Montsurry's house. There he found Charlotte, disguised as a man. She had planned to kill Montsurry herself but had been stopped by the ghost. When Clermont drew his sword, Montsurry at first refused to defend himself and did so only after Clermont offered to let Tamyra stab him. Although Montsurry at last gained sufficient courage to conduct himself courageously in the duel, Clermont succeeded in killing him. Soon after Clermont had fulfilled his duty to his brother, he received the news that the Duc de Guise had been killed by the king's men. The death of his friend and patron was a severe blow to Clermont, whose life had been centered on his relationship with the powerful duke. Believing that his purpose in this world was destroyed, he took his own life.

Critical Evaluation:

The Revenge of Bussy d'Ambois is a portrait of George Chapman's ideal tragic hero. All other elements of the play are subordinated to the revelation of the character and philosophy of Clermont d'Ambois. Clermont, with his stoic idealism, is an interesting and compelling figure. The title of Chapman's sequel to his tragedy *Bussy d'Ambois* (1604) might suggest that the play is but another of the many revenge tragedies or tragedies of blood that were popular in the last decades of Queen Elizabeth I's reign and the first years of her successor, James I. *The Revenge of Bussy d'Ambois* does contain elements of the traditional revenge tragedy: A good man has been murdered; his kinsman is sworn to avenge the murder; a scheming villain is guilty of the crime; a ghost appears to encourage the revenge. Here, however, similarities end. Chapman has changed some key elements of the typical revenge tragedy: The delay in carrying out the act of revenge is not motivated by uncertainty, since the guilt of the villain is known by all; the stage remains remarkably free of bloodshed; and—most significant—the protagonist who must be the "scourge" to avenge the wrongful death of his brother seems too philosophic to take on the task. As a result, *The Revenge of Bussy d'Ambois* has often been compared unfavorably with such revenge tragedies as William Shakespeare's *Hamlet* (1600-1601) or Thomas Kyd's *The Spanish Tragedy* (c. 1587), or with the more sensational tragedies of blood such as John Ford's *'Tis Pity She's a Whore* (1633), plays that contain virtually all elements of their respective genres and bring the action to a final climax in which much blood is shed on stage, as villain and hero meet their deaths.

Unquestionably, the play has structural and dramaturgical shortcomings. Most noticeable is Chapman's focus on rhetoric rather than action. Much of the dialogue of *The Revenge of Bussy d'Ambois* is little more than extended soliloquizing about the nature of humankind and the need for stoic acceptance of one's fate. The general knowledge that Montsurry has murdered Bussy lends little suspense to the drama; there is none of the tension created by Shakespeare in *Hamlet* over the guilt of the king and the complicity of the queen in the murder of the prince's father. Further, Montsurry's overt cowardice makes him an unworthy villain and cheapens the revenge Clermont seeks to gain by killing him. Many critics have chastised the playwright for simply pandering to popular sympathies for such dramas while remaining reticent to portray on stage the consequences of crime and punishment.

Such a reading does a disservice to Chapman. While *The Revenge of Bussy d'Ambois* makes use of some conventions of the genre, the play is a revenge tragedy only in a negative sense. That is, Chapman uses the elements of the genre as an ironic commentary on the inadequacy of the moral stance taken by those who celebrate revenge. Steeped as he was in the classical tradition, Chapman grafts onto the revenge drama the form of the classical tragedy, creating a portrait of the noble hero forced by circumstances to serve as a pawn of fate in carrying out an action that is reprehensible, yet necessary in a society in which moral and political authority have become separated.

Central to Chapman's concept for this drama is the portrait he creates of his ideal hero,

Clermont. Unlike other characters who carry out acts of violence to revenge the murders of those they love, Clermont is an ideal gentleman. He is a pillar of virtue, reluctant to act even though he knows his brother's murder should not go unpunished. His delay in carrying out his revenge comes not from calculation or from concern about the justice of his cause; in fact, he is hopeful that justice can be meted out through other means than the murder he is being encouraged to commit. Only when he is convinced that justice will not be served by those in power does he bring himself to act. Stoic by nature, he is willing to accept his fate; he does not rail against the forces of nature or against God, as other revengers tend to do. Like the true Stoic, he takes his own life when he determines there is no further purpose to be served by living.

A good portion of the drama is given over to characters who scheme to eliminate Clermont, seen by them as a cancer in the realm of the French king. Led by Clermont's brother-in-law, Baligny, and abetted by courtiers allied against Clermont's patron, the Duc de Guise, this faction manipulates the king against the protagonist, making it impossible for Bussy's murder to be avenged by lawful means. Clermont is able to act with dignity even when these forces overpower him and have him imprisoned; like the true Stoic, he is able to achieve inner peace by relying on the knowledge that he is blameless in any plots against the sovereign.

In many ways, Chapman's Clermont is closer to the tragic heroes of Greek and Roman dramas than he is to his Renaissance counterparts. The play itself is reminiscent of classical rather than Elizabethan drama in other ways as well. Although much violence is talked about, little is seen on stage; instead, declamation and argumentation replace action as the principal staples of Chapman's dramatic art. In plotting and in characterization, he follows the lead of a much admired contemporary, Ben Jonson, whose adoption of classical principles is seen most clearly in *Sejanus* (1603), a play Chapman admired. Hence, in *The Revenge of Bussy d'Ambois* and in his other dramatic productions, Chapman furthers the integration of classical principles on the English stage.

"Critical Evaluation" by Laurence W. Mazzeno

Bibliography:
Bowers, Fredson. "The School of Kyd." *Elizabethan Revenge Tragedy 1587-1642*. Princeton, N.J.: Princeton University Press, 1940. Claims Chapman reverses the traditional pattern of the revenge tragedy in his sequel to *Bussy d'Ambois*. Explains how he introduces the concept of virtue into the character of the revenger, and makes him a respectable gentleman.

MacLure, Millar. *George Chapman: A Critical Study*. Toronto: University of Toronto Press, 1966. Briefly notes historical sources for the drama. Focuses on Chapman's development of his tragic hero and discusses the playwright's abilities as a dramaturge.

Rees, Ennis. *The Tragedies of George Chapman: Renaissance Ethics in Action*. Cambridge, Mass.: Harvard University Press, 1954. Concentrates on the political and ethical dimensions of the drama. Highlights Chapman's careful depiction of contrasting qualities between Bussy and Clermont.

Spivack, Charlotte. *George Chapman*. New York: Twayne, 1967. Relates *The Revenge of Bussy d'Ambois* to revenge tragedies popular during the period. Comments on Chapman's handling of language and dramatic conventions.

Wieler, John William. *George Chapman: The Effect of Stoicism on His Tragedies*. New York: King's Crown Press, 1949. Explains how the drama reveals Chapman's interest in Stoicism; sees that interest causing the playwright to change his attitude toward the character of Clermont, whom he eventually repudiates.

THE REVENGER'S TRAGEDY

Type of work: Drama
Author: Cyril Tourneur (c. 1575-1626)
Type of plot: Tragedy
Time of plot: Renaissance
Locale: A city in Italy
First performed: 1606-1607; first published, 1607

Principal characters:
VENDICE, the revenger, disguised as Piato
HIPPOLITO, his brother, also called Carlo
CASTIZA, their sister, object of Lussurioso's lust
GRATIANA, their mother, a widow
THE DUKE, the ruler of the principality
LUSSURIOSO, his legitimate son
SPURIO, his illegitimate son
THE DUCHESS, his recent bride
AMBITIOSO,
SUPERVACUO, and the
UNNAMED THIRD SON, the Duchess' sons by a previous marriage
ANTONIO, the Duke's final successor

The Story:

Vendice held a skull in his hand. It belonged to his betrothed, who had been poisoned by the Duke when she resisted his lecherous advances. Vendice watched as the Duke, accompanied by his new wife and his two sons, passed through the city. Combined with the hate provoked by this horrible murder was outrage over the death of Vendice's father, caused by the same corrupt ruler. Vendice's brother also reported that he had been asked by Lussurioso, the Duke's heir and a man as depraved as his father, to locate a pander. Vendice disguised himself as Piato, a pander, and was hired by Lussurioso, thereby gaining access to the ducal household.

The sons of the Duchess were as corrupt as the Duke's. The third son had recently raped the wife of Antonio, who subsequently killed herself. When the third son was brought to trial and sentenced, the Duke put off the son's execution and ordered that he be kept in prison. His two older brothers promised to help him escape. Their mother, the Duchess, revealed her love for Spurio, the Duke's illegitimate son, who hated his father. Spurio accepted the Duchess' advances because adultery with his stepmother would avenge him on his father.

As Lussurioso's pander, Vendice was commissioned to set up an assignation with his own sister, Castiza. Vendice was delighted when Castiza emphatically rejected Lussurioso's suit but horrified when their mother tried to persuade her daughter to yield.

Having returned to the ducal palace, Vendice learned from Hippolito that the Duchess and Spurio had been seen together and had an appointment for that very night. Vendice used this information to deflect Lussurioso from his pursuit of Castiza. Ostensibly to protect his father's honor but actually to get rid of Spurio, his hated half-brother, Lussurioso rushed to the Duke's bedchamber and attacked the man in bed with the Duchess. This man was not Spurio, but the Duke, who, not seriously injured, ordered Lussurioso taken to prison under sentence of death.

The Duchess' sons, eager to eliminate their stepbrothers, attempted to trick the Duke by seeming to ask for mercy for Lussurioso while depicting the heinousness of killing a ruler. The crafty Duke surprised them by granting their request. What they did not know was that Lussurioso had already been released through a prior order of the Duke's. When they informed the jailer that it was the Duke's command that "their brother" was to die, the jailer, with only the Duchess' third son in custody, executed their younger brother.

Meanwhile, Vendice continued plotting. The Duke had commanded him, still disguised as Piato, to bring him a woman in some secluded spot. Knowing that the Duchess and Spurio were to meet in a particular lodge, Vendice selected this place and brought the skull of his betrothed, decked out in rich attire. On the mouth of the skull, he smeared the same poison that the Duke had used to kill her. The Duke kissed the poisoned skull, while Vendice and Hippolito, who had been waiting, compelled him to spend his dying moments watching his wife embrace his bastard son. Nine years after Gloriana's death, Vendice was avenged on the Duke for killing his beloved.

Before the meeting arranged by Vendice, the Duke had stated that he was taking an undisclosed journey; hence no one knew where he was nor made attempts to find him. Lussurioso, however, had resolved to dismiss Piato, whose information had led to his imprisonment, and he ordered Hippolito, whom he knew to have a brother unknown to the court, to bribe that brother to kill Piato. Thus, Vendice was in the strange position of being hired to murder himself. Vendice and Hippolito decided to dress the still undiscovered body of the Duke in the clothes discarded by Piato, believing that Piato would be assumed to have fled in the Duke's clothes. The brothers also decided to punish their mother because she had urged their sister to yield to Lussurioso. They were, however, so moved by her repentance that they spared her life and returned to the ducal palace to complete their plot.

The Duke's corpse, now dressed in the old clothes of Piato, was still lying in the lodge. The brothers planned to show it to Lussurioso, tell him the manner of his father's death, and then kill him. However, Lussurioso did not come alone. Vendice and Hippolito had only opportunity to point out the form of the supposed Piato lying on a couch, say he was drunk, and then stab him on Lussurioso's command. Discovering the true identity of the corpse, Lussurioso, pleased that the death made him the new duke, gave three orders: to search for Piato, the suspected murderer; to hold revels in honor of his succession to the title; and to banish the Duchess.

The Duchess' two remaining sons resolved to murder the new duke. As the new duke and his nobles sat and argued over the ominous portent of a comet blazing in the sky, Vendice, Hippolito, and two other lords, in the fantastic costumes of masquers, entered and performed their dance. At its conclusion, they drew their swords and killed Lussurioso and his three companions.

Ambitioso, Supervacuo, Spurio, and a fourth noble came into the hall, dressed in similar costumes and bent on the same bloody errand. Finding Lussurioso and his companions already dead, the would-be murderers fell out among themselves. Ambitioso killed Supervacuo and Spurio killed Ambitioso only to be stabbed by the fourth noble. When Antonio and the guards rushed in, they assumed that the masquers whom they found there had been the only murderers. The surviving fourth noble convinced them otherwise. Lussurioso was not quite dead, but had to undergo the final agony of having the returning Vendice whisper in his ear the full account of his revenge.

The ducal line having been wiped out, Antonio was proclaimed ruler. Vendice could not resist telling the new duke that he and his brother had been the avengers. Antonio ordered them to be executed, asserting that the men who had murdered the old Duke and his family might well murder him. Vendice accepted his sentence calmly, saying it was time for him to die.

Critical Evaluation:

The Revenger's Tragedy appeared after the two most popular revenge plays in English Renaissance drama. Thomas Kyd's *The Spanish Tragedy* (c. 1587) was the first. The second was William Shakespeare's *Hamlet, Prince of Denmark* (c. 1600-1601), the most written-about play there is. Both of these plays would have been familiar to audiences and to playwrights, such as Cyril Tourneur, of the time. *The Revenger's Tragedy* might be called the perfect revenge play, but some exploration of why Vendice does not seem as real as Hieronimo or Hamlet is needed.

In *The Spanish Tragedy*, Hieronimo vows not to bury the body of his murdered son until he discovers who the murderers are. He tries to be just and not to act rashly. For this, Hieronimo is rebuked for his delay by Bel-Imperia, whose lover was killed by the same men. Hieronimo and Bel-Imperia kill the two murderers at a masque, and Bel-Imperia kills herself. Hieronimo is somewhat unsatisfying as a revenger: He is neither unfeeling nor violent by nature. Sometimes he seems mad. As a killer, he lacks verve.

Hamlet is also an inept revenger. Hamlet spends a good part of the play attempting to verify the ghost's story. He too can be frustrating for an audience expecting a more exuberant killer.

There is no indication that Vendice experiences any kind of self-doubt. Rather, he presents himself as a most able revenger whose resolve never wavers. His brother, Hippolito, acts in unison and shares Vendice's conviction that the Duke and his family are too corrupt to be saved. Presumably, Antonio, whose wife was raped by the Duchess' third son, would agree. Hippolito claims (Act V, scene ii) there are five hundred men who would assist in fighting this Duke. Vendice is consequently much less isolated than either Hieronimo or Hamlet.

Vendice initially appears as a bright young courtier, able even to argue his mother into persuading his sister to submit to Lussurioso's proposition. He blames his mother for succumbing to his words and blames all women for tempting men. Vendice's sense of his own righteousness never wavers. As is clear from Vendice's assertion in Act III, scene v that a tragedy may be measured by the blood that flows and from his claim in Act V, scene iii that the death of the lustful is always good and that thunder indicates that heaven is pleased, he perceives himself as an agent of justice. Moreover, Vendice is didactic. Vendice forces the Duke to listen to a catalog of the Duke's sins as he is dying. Vendice also reveals himself, for learning's sake, to Lussurioso as he is dying.

The Revenger's Tragedy is not a simple presentation of good versus evil. With the exception of Castiza, there is little evidence of good. There is little evidence of any character's having the capacity to celebrate beauty for its own sake or to experience the complexities of love for another. Vendice's hatred of vice includes no comparable love of any virtue other than sexual abstinence. Rather, Tourneur presents blatant evil and an avenger whose identity rests solely on his extirpation of the evildoers.

In his last speech, Vendice asserts that "'Tis time to die when we are ourselves our foes," but he remains pleased that he and his brother have murdered a rotten "nest of dukes." He is also smug in his awareness that he and Hippolito could have escaped unknown if they had wished. As he is taken out to be executed, Vendice's attitude is essentially self-congratulatory.

There is much irony in this play. Vendice clearly has reason for revenge, but from Act III, scene v onward, his unflinching devotion to bloodshed renders him less and less sympathetic as it becomes increasingly clear that he believes he is divinely authorized. Few details are known about either Gloriana or Vendice's father, so Vendice's own personal history remains amorphous. Unlike Hamlet, he does not care about having his story told after his death. In fact, whether he has a story of his own is in question.

Vendice is ultimately a type. His unflagging hatred reduces him to the impersonal. With the righteousness of youth or of those obsessed, unburdened by self-doubt, Vendice is absolutely intent on eliminating every corrupt member of the royal household. Vendice and his success as a revenger may satisfy an audience initially, but not its sense of ultimate justice.

Carol Bishop

Bibliography:

Brucher, Richard T. "Fantasies of Violence: *Hamlet* and *The Revenger's Tragedy.*" *Studies in English Literature, 1500-1900* 211 (Spring, 1981): 257-270. Argues that as revenge tragedies, *The Revenger's Tragedy* and *Hamlet* are exactly opposite. Likens Vendice to Marlowe's Barabas or to Harry Callahan of the Dirty Harry films.

Coddon, Karin S. "'For Show or Useless Property': Necrophilia and *The Revenger's Tragedy.*" *English Literary History* 61 (Spring, 1994): 71-88. Offers historical information on attitudes toward and practices involving the dead. Argues that the skull of Gloriana functions as a symbol of female perfection and sinful female sexuality.

Finke, Laurie A. "Painting Women: Images of Femininity in Jacobean Tragedy." *Theatre Journal* 36 (October, 1984): 357-370. Argues that men idealize women's beauty to avoid the reality of death. Discusses how the painted woman is viewed with hostility in Tourneur's play, in John Webster's *The Duchess of Malfi* (c. 1613), and in John Ford's *'Tis Pity She's a Whore* (1633).

McMillin, Scott. "Acting and Violence: *The Revenger's Tragedy* and Its Departures from *Hamlet.*" *Studies in English Literature, 1500-1900* 24 (Spring, 1984): 275-291. Argues that Tourneur's play is about the theater and that the play abounds with double identities.

Ornstein, Robert. *The Moral Vision of Jacobean Tragedy.* Madison: University of Wisconsin Press, 1965. The chapter on Tourneur is basic critical reading. Argues that Vendice cannot save himself from his own cynicism.

THE REVOLT OF THE MASSES

Type of work: Essay
Author: José Ortega y Gasset (1883-1955)
First published: La rebelión de las masas, 1929 (English translation, 1932)

Among the few Spanish authors of the modern era known beyond his national boundaries is José Ortega y Gasset, professor of metaphysics, literary critic and journalist, and a representative of the school that believes in the rule of an intellectual aristocracy or small group of superior men, not the privileged caste of the old feudal nobility. Born in Madrid, Ortega y Gasset sought in Málaga the thorough training of a Jesuit college, then took his doctorate in philosophy at the Central University of Madrid in 1904. Further study in Germany preceded his teaching career in Madrid. When Primo de Rivera y Orbaneja became dictator, overthrowing the monarchy, Ortega y Gasset, a critic of the monarchy, stopped teaching and began to write for the influential *El Sol.* In 1923, he founded the *Revista de Occidente,* the leading Spanish intellectual publication until 1936. The ascendancy of another dictator, Francisco Franco, led to Ortega y Gasset's leaving Spain. Ortega y Gasset traveled widely, lecturing in Buenos Aires, Paris, and the United States. Returning to Spain in 1945, he died in Madrid in 1955.

The Revolt of the Masses had its seeds in an earlier book, *España invertebrada* (1922; invertebrate Spain), in an article titled "Masas" (1926), and several lectures delivered in Argentina in 1928. As he wrote in a footnote to the title of the first chapter: "My purpose now is to collect and complete what I have already said, and so to produce an organic document concerning the most important fact of our time."

Repetition and interpolated material weaken the structural unity of the book, and the colloquial style may grate on the reader before the final pages are reached. Nevertheless, the work is seminal and provocative. Ortega y Gasset advocates a European confederation with judicial and political unity, an "integration, not a lamination," of nations, ultranational rather than international, where a new liberalism and a totalitarian form will each correct the excesses of the other. The resulting equilibrium, he promises, would produce a new faith.

In his final paragraph, Ortega y Gasset acknowledges that his contemporary situation results from basic defects in European culture, but he postpones any consideration of that problem, and so the work is incomplete. However, for the Buenos Aires edition of 1938, Ortega y Gasset added a prologue for French readers and an epilogue for English readers, in which he denied the accusation that his theme was the decadence of Spain since 1580. He is no pessimist. While he does look back on the good old days, he insists that a return to the past is impossible. Stressing the advances and improvements of today, he asserts that if anything superior is eventually evolved, it will be based on technical knowledge and liberal democracy.

Ortega y Gasset's main thesis is that among human beings there are two types of individuals: the excellent or superior man, who makes demands on himself, and the common man, who is content with what he is. The development and activities of these types are shown against the perspective of Western history.

Greece and Rome evolved from rural communities and became cities. The ancients, concerned with their past, were unconscious of a future. Gradually the state came into existence, built in the Middle Ages by the feudal nobles. The state was relatively small. Ortega y Gasset quotes the economist Werner Sombart for the statement that Europe, from 700 to 1800, never had a population of more than 180,000,000. Each state was directed by its superior individuals, without whom humanity would cease to preserve its essentials. The mass man accepted higher authority and in general followed the orders of a select minority.

The first divergence came when the bourgeoisie adopted gunpowder, which the nobles never thought of using, and with it won battles against the nobility. Eventually a middle class took over the state and made it so powerful that "state intervention" has become a symbol of danger. What were once privileges became rights, even though the masses attack the institutions by which these rights are sanctioned.

During the nineteenth century the population of Europe rose to 460,000,000, and part of it overflowed to settle in the Americas. In Ortega y Gasset's view, however, those who look with astonishment at the rapid growth of the New World should turn their eyes to Europe, where the population increase has been even more spectacular. Friedrich Nietzsche foresaw a "flood tide of Nihilism rising." Actually, the world as it was organized during the nineteenth century automatically created a new type of person, provided with formidable appetites and powerful means of satisfying them. The nineteenth century left these new people to their own devices. Believing in direct action, they intervened violently in everything. Having been previously guided by others, these "barbarian products of modern civilization" determined to govern the world for and by themselves, and in their self-satisfaction, according to Ortega y Gasset, they now threatened the degeneration of human culture.

In tracing the development of the mass man, Ortega y Gasset repeats his assertion that the civilization of the nineteenth century can be summed up under two headings: liberal democracy and technology. Modern technical advance represents the cooperation of capitalism and experimental science. The scientist is likely to become a mass man, a primitive, since he confines his knowledge to so small an area. There was a time, the author asserts, when people could be divided into the learned and the ignorant, but currently even those learned in science are frequently ignorant of the inner philosophy of the science they cultivate.

Ortega y Gasset discusses historians, or "philologists," as he calls them, who turn their attention to sources instead of the future. The author does not believe in the absolute determinism of history, because in his view the past does not tell people what to do, but what to avoid. Life has become greater in scope than ever before, presenting a greater array of choices. Circumstances offer a dilemma for the mass man to decide, but he has no concept of the future. In the Mediterranean countries, where the triumph of the masses has made its greatest advance, the mass man lives for the moment, with no consideration for future existence.

Life has become worldwide in character, but time and space cannot be easily obliterated. The "purchasing power of life" has been broadened. People believe themselves capable of creation without knowing what to create. Power has brought insecurity. Liberal democracy based on technical knowledge is the highest type of public life yet known. The perfect organization of the nineteenth century gave the impression that it represented natural things, and therefore should belong to everybody; but all that it represents had earlier beginnings.

According to Ortega y Gasset, bolshevism and fascism are examples of retrogression in politics, because they handle rational elements in an antihistorical, even archaic, way. Consequently, the political hope of Europe lies in those who abhor archaic and primitive attitudes. Ortega y Gasset does not believe in the "decadence of Europe," a legend begun by intellectuals who felt themselves stifled by their nationality and who longed to borrow from other literatures, or by politicians similarly motivated. If there should be a decadence among European nations, the result, he argues, would be the creation of a United States of Europe. There is no one else to "rule," by which Ortega y Gasset means "to control public opinion." New York and Moscow represent two sections of European order. Writing in 1929, Ortega y Gasset believed that Russia would need centuries before it could aspire to rule, but that it would never succeed if there was in Europe a political union with a new Western moral code and a new inspirational program of life.

In one important sense, the title of this work is misleading, in the light of recent history. The author is not referring to either actual revolt—*rebelión* is the Spanish word he uses—or to the Marxian proletarian revolution. What he had in mind was the mass man whose claim to the right to act is, in effect, a rebellion against his own destiny. Since that is what he, according to Ortega y Gasset, is doing at the present time, Ortega y Gasset considered his efforts to be a revolt of the masses.

Bibliography:

Dobson, Andrew. *An Introduction to the Politics and Philosophy of José Ortega y Gasset.* Cambridge, England: Cambridge University Press, 1989. An erudite, readable overview of Ortega y Gasset's political and philosophical background. Chapter 5, "*Nacionalización* and Decentralisation," and chapter 6, "Fascism?," are of particular interest to readers of *The Revolt of the Masses.*

Gray, Rockwell. *The Imperative of Modernity: An Intellectual Biography of José Ortega y Gasset.* Berkeley: University of California Press, 1989. A study of the evolution of Ortega y Gasset as an intellectual. Chapter 5, "The Level of the Times: 1929-1930," includes a discussion of the ideas in *The Revolt of the Masses,* arguing that the ideas are typical of European intellectuals during the period between the two world wars.

Lee, Donald C. "Ortega's Revolting Masses: A Reinterpretation." In *Ortega y Gasset Centennial.* Madrid: Ediciones, José Porrúa Turanzas, 1985. Reevaluates Ortega's work more than fifty years after its initial publication and applies its propositions to the late twentieth century. Expands upon Ortega's propositions for a united Europe.

Ouimette, Victor. *José Ortega y Gasset.* Boston: Twayne, 1982. Gives a succinct biography of Ortega y Gasset, including a synopsis of the social and political background of late nineteenth and early twentieth century Spain. Chapter 4, "Ratiovitalism," includes a subsection devoted to *The Revolt of the Masses.*

Raley, Harold C. *José Ortega y Gasset: Philosopher of European Unity.* Tuscaloosa: University of Alabama Press, 1971. A study of Ortega y Gasset's concept of European unity. The author considers this idea, an important one in *The Revolt of the Masses,* as integral to the development of the philosopher's body of works.

REYNARD THE FOX

Type of work: Short fiction
Author: Unknown
Type of plot: Satire
Time of plot: Middle Ages
Locale: Europe
First transcribed, c. 1175-1250 (English translation, 1481)

> *Principal characters:*
> REYNARD, the fox
> NOBLE, the lion, king of beasts
> ISENGRIM, the wolf
> TIBERT, the cat
> BRUIN, the bear
> OTHER ANIMALS AND BIRDS

The Story:

When Noble, the great Lion-king, held court during the Feast of the Pentecost, all the animals told the king of their grievances against Reynard the fox. The list of sins and crimes was almost as long as the list of animals present. First to complain was Isengrim the wolf, whose children had been made blind by the crafty fox. Panther told how Reynard had promised the hare that he would teach him his prayers, but when the hare had stood in front of Reynard as he was instructed, Reynard had grabbed him by the throat and tried to kill him. To Chanticleer the cock Reynard had gone disguised as a monk, saying that he would never eat flesh again, but when Chanticleer relaxed his vigilance over his flock and believed the villain, Reynard had grabbed his children and eaten them.

So the complaints went on, with only Tibert the cat and Grimbard the brock (badger) speaking in Reynard's defense. These two reminded the king of the crimes committed by the complainers, but the king was stern; Reynard must be brought to court to answer for his sins. Bruin the bear was sent to bring the culprit in. Bruin was strong and brave, and he promised the king that he would not be fooled by Reynard's knavery or flattering tongue.

When Bruin arrived at Reynard's castle and delivered the king's message, Reynard welcomed the bear and promised to accompany him back to court. In fact, Reynard said that he wished they were already at court, for he had abstained from meat and eaten so much of a new food, called honeycombs, that his stomach was swollen and uncomfortable. Bruin fell into the trap and begged to be taken to the store of honey. Reynard pretended to be reluctant to delay their trip to court, but at last he agreed to show Bruin the honey. The wily fox led Bruin into a trap in some tree trunks, where the poor bear was set upon by humans and beaten unmercifully. He escaped with his life and sadly made his way back to court, mocked by the taunts of his betrayer.

Enraged at the insult to his personal messenger, the king sent Tibert the cat to tell Reynard to surrender himself at once, under penalty of death. Tibert, however, fared no better. He was tricked into jumping into a net trap by the promise of a feast on mice and rats. He, too, escaped and returned to the court, no longer a defender of the traitorous Reynard. The next time the king sent Grimbard the brock to bring the fox in. He was also warmly received by Reynard's promise

5579

to accompany him to court. This time the evil fox actually kept his promise, confessing all of his sins to the brock as they journeyed.

At court, Reynard was confronted by all of his accusers. One by one they told of his horrible crimes against them. Reynard defended himself against them all, saying that he was a loyal and true subject of the king and the object of many lies and deceits. The king was unmoved and sentenced Reynard to death. On the gallows, the fox confessed his sins, saying that he was the more guilty because he did not steal from want, since money and jewels he had in great plenty. Hearing Reynard speak of his treasure, the greedy king wanted it for himself, and he asked Reynard where the jewels were hidden. The fox said that he would gladly tell him the hiding place, for the treasure had been stolen in order to save the king's life. Crafty Reynard told a story about a treasure that the other animals were going to use to depose the king and make Bruin the ruler in his place. In order to save the life of his sovereign, Reynard had stolen the treasure from the traitors and now had it in his possession. The foolish king, believing the smooth liar, ordered Reynard released from the gallows and made a favorite at court. Bruin the bear and Isengrim the wolf were arrested for high treason.

Reynard said that he himself could not show the king the treasure because he had to make a pilgrimage to Rome to ask the pope to remove a curse from him. For his journey he was given the skin of the bear and the shoes of the wolf, leaving those two fellows in terrible pain. The king then put his mail around Reynard's neck and a staff in his hand and sent him on his way. Kyward the hare and Bellin the ram accompanied Reynard on the pilgrimage. They stopped at the fox's castle to bid his wife good-bye, and there Reynard tricked the hare, killed him, and ate all but the head. That he sent back to the king by the ram, that stupid animal thinking he was carrying a letter for the monarch. The king was so furious that he gave the ram and all of his lineage to the wolf and the bear to atone for the king's misjudgment of them.

Complaints against the fox again poured into the king's ear. At last he determined to lay siege to Reynard's castle until the culprit was captured. This time there would be no mercy. Grimbard the brock, however, hurried to the castle and warned Reynard of the plot. The crafty fellow went immediately to the court to plead his case before the king.

On the way he again confessed to the brock that he was guilty of many sins, but he made them seem mild in comparison with those of the animals now accusing him. To the king also he confessed that he had sinned, but he denied the worst of the crimes laid to his doing. His plea was that he would not have surrendered voluntarily had he been so guilty. His words were so moving that most of his accusers kept silent, fearing that the king would again believe Reynard and punish those who would condemn him. Only the wolf and the bear held fast to their accusations. With the help of his aunt, the ape, Reynard once more excused himself in the king's eyes and made the monarch believe that it was the injured who were the guilty. Again Reynard talked of lost jewels of great value, jewels that he would search for and present to the king.

Only Isengrim the wolf would not accept Reynard's lies. He challenged the fox to a fight. Reynard would have been hard put to fight with the wolf except that Isengrim's feet were still sore from Reynard's taking of his shoes sometime before. Furthermore, the ape shaved off Reynard's fur and covered him with oil so that the wolf could not get hold of him. Even so, Isengrim would have defeated him had he not listened to Reynard's oily promises of all the rewards Isengrim would receive were he to let Reynard go. At last the king stopped the fight and ordered all the animals to a great feast. There he forgave Reynard for all of his sins after taking the scamp's promise that he would commit no more crimes against his fellow animals. The king made Reynard high bailiff of the country, thus setting him above all the others. From that time on the mighty of the forest would bow to the cunning of the weak.

Critical Evaluation:

Reynard the Fox is a beast fable, generally a satirical genre in which human follies are portrayed as belonging to animals. The underlying framework of this popular medieval literary form is a series of stories linked by common characters. In *Reynard the Fox*, the character of Reynard provides the connective thread. Most versions of *Reynard the Fox* are long, and the episodes are only vaguely related. In addition, the point of such beast fables is satire of the contemporary social and political scenes. *Reynard the Fox* satirizes the medieval court, judicial system, and much else.

The origin of the form, however, is still subject to scholarly debate. Since *Reynard the Fox* is one of the most important examples of this genre, the debate, in this case, is quite significant. Some scholars maintain that the beast fable derives from the oral folk tradition of storytelling, later being formalized in writing by medieval monastic scribes. Other scholars find precedents among classical Latin authors to explain the origin of the beast fable. Both schools of thought have defensible positions, and both take their stand on the same set of facts, since many versions of the *Reynard the Fox* stories are extant.

Some basic information emerges from the dispute. First, Ovid's *Metamorphoses* (c. 8 C.E.) contains stories similar to those in the *Reynard the Fox* series. Second, Aesop's Fables (fourth century B.C.E.) includes specific Reynard episodes. Limited medieval access to such classical precedents, however, renders the influence of these models moot. The earliest manifestations of *Reynard the Fox* are stories about the animosity between Reynard and his enemy, Isengrim the wolf. These stories may be derived from popular French, English, Dutch, Low German, and Latin folktales. They seem to have initiated in the Low Countries, northern France, and northeastern Germany, although precedence cannot be definitely assigned. The earliest versions were in verse, although later versions appeared in prose.

A rather short poetic rendering of *Reynard the Fox* stories was done in medieval Latin by an eighth century cleric, Paulus Diaconus (Paul the Deacon), from Charlemagne's court. The basic Isengrim story—*Ysengrimus*—is attributed to Master Nivardus of Ghent, who wrote it in Latin at about 1148.

The evolution of vernacular versions is still open to question; some scholars claim priority for France, and others insist upon Germanic primacy. The issue has not been resolved, but there is no question that twelfth and thirteenth century Flanders, West Germany, and northern France were fertile grounds for this literary form, especially for Reynard stories.

At approximately the same time that *Ysengrimus* was produced, there appeared in France a compilation called *Le Roman de Renart*, from the hands of several authors (many, according to medieval custom, anonymous). This vernacular compilation deals mostly but not exclusively with stories of the protagonist Reynard facing his antagonist Isengrim the wolf. The stories are usually arranged in chronological rather than in topical order; unfortunately, this arrangement tends to undermine the ideological impact of the stories. The didactic element is much stronger in the almost simultaneous (c. 1180) vernacular redaction of Heinrich der Glîchesaere.

Reynard the Fox appeared in Latin, French, German, Flemish, Dutch, and English versions—testimony to its popularity. It is evident, however, that questions about origins and the chronological order of various versions cannot be unequivocally answered with the information at hand. As is the case with much medieval history and literature, final answers must wait upon the discovery of further evidence, most likely from a presently unknown cache of medieval manuscripts—if such a cache exists.

In the meantime, it is still possible to evaluate the extant material on its own terms, because *Reynard the Fox* evolved as the archetype of the beast fable. The central focus of the series concentrates on a single significant episode—Reynard's healing of the sick lion, in most versions—and other stories are spin-offs from this episode, all involving moralistic messages. The cast of animals varies from story to story and from version to version: Fox, lion, and wolf are constants; badger, bear, stag, rooster, cat, hare, camel, bear, ant, and others appear occasionally. The didactic factor is another constant, and for the temper of the times, it is a remarkably pragmatic one.

Indeed, the Reynard series is a lesson in ethics and morality. None of the animals is a paragon of virtue. All are vulnerable or corruptible or both; not even King Lion is exempt. They live in a world that recognizes no moral codes and where survival depends upon wit and exploitation of others. Isengrim the wolf is doomed because he carries to extremes his penchant for besting everything and everybody. His compulsion is to surpass, and this compulsion blinds him to the necessary cooperation required for survival. By contrast, Reynard is pliable, adaptable, and fundamentally amoral. He survives because he is flexible. Yet, in the process, he becomes venal, power-hungry, and oblivious to humane values. Significantly, Geoffrey Chaucer's "Nun's Priest's Tale" (in *The Canterbury Tales*; 1387-1400) relates a Reynard story—the fox's attempt and failure to abduct the rooster Chanticleer—to demonstrate the weakness and the power of flattery. Reynard's tactics thus become an object lesson in compromised integrity. Reynard is the ultimate opportunist, knowing no scruple. To be sure, Reynard is neither explicitly praised nor explicitly condemned in the context of medieval ethics or morality. Rather, he is held forth as an implicit example of what not to do. In this sense, the best didactic functions of the beast fable are upheld. For it is the didactic element in such works that constitutes their intended benefit. Although scholarly disputes continue about the origins and the development of the beast fable, in the last analysis the more crucial point is the moral import of such stories. In this respect, *Reynard the Fox* succeeds.

"Critical Evaluation" by Joanne G. Kashdan

Bibliography:

Bellon, Roger. "Trickery as an Element of the Character of Renart." *Forum for Modern Language Studies* 22, no. 1 (January, 1986): 34-52. Examines *Reynard the Fox* in terms of its use of archetypal elements of the medieval fable. Provides insight into the social significance of the trickster character.

Blake, N. F. "Reflections on William Caxton's Reynard the Fox." *Canadian Journal of Netherlandic Studies* 4, no. 1 (May, 1983): 69-76. Provides a thorough exploration of William Caxton's translation of the medieval classic. Blake's treatment provides a general consideration of *Reynard*'s place in the Germanic literary tradition, folk narrative, and European fable.

Owen, D. D. R., trans., ed. *The Romance of Reynard the Fox*. Oxford, England: Oxford University Press, 1994. Notes and introduction offer a comprehensive overview of the fable, its history, its place in medieval art, and its revelations about medieval society.

Varty, Kenneth. "Animal Fable and Fabulous Animal." *Bestia: Yearbook of the Beast Fable Society* 3, no. 1 (May, 1991): 5-14. Discussion of European beast fables considers *Reynard the Fox* within its historical, aesthetic, and ideological context. Also considered is the evolution of the animal in European folklore.

_____. *Reynard the Fox: A Study of the Fox in Medieval English Art*. Leicester, England: Leicester University Press, 1967. Considers Reynard the Fox's impact on the visual art and literature of the medieval period. Presentation includes color plates and textual excerpts.

RHADAMISTUS AND ZENOBIA

Type of work: Drama
Author: Prosper Jolyot de Crébillon (1674-1762)
Type of plot: Tragedy
Time of plot: About 60 C.E.
Locale: Artanissa, capital of Iberia
First published: Rhadmiste et Zénobie, 1711 (English translation, 1768); first performed, 1711

> *Principal characters:*
> RHADAMISTUS, the king of Armenia
> ZENOBIA or ISMENIA, his wife
> PHARASMANES, the king of Iberia, Rhadamistus' father
> ARSAMES, Rhadamistus' brother
> HIERO, Armenian ambassador, Rhadamistus' confidant
> MITHRANES, captain of the guards of Pharasmanes
> HYDASPES, Pharasmanes' confidant
> PHENICE, Zenobia's confidante

The Story:

Zenobia, wife of Rhadamistus, was the prisoner of Pharasmanes, the king of Iberia. When Phenice, her companion, attempted to persuade her that she should accept the love Pharasmanes was offering her in the hope that she would become his queen, Zenobia, who had been using the name Ismenia, revealed that she could not accept Pharasmanes because the king was her uncle and the father of Rhadamistus. Zenobia explained that her father, Mithridates, had reared Rhadamistus as if the boy were his own son; but when Pharasmanes invaded the Armenian kingdom of Mithridates, Mithridates turned against Rhadamistus and refused to allow him to marry Zenobia as Rhadamistus had expected. Rhadamistus had then attacked the kingdom of Mithridates and had driven the king into exile. Zenobia, to protect her father, had offered to wed Rhadamistus; only after the wedding had she learned that Rhadamistus had murdered her father. In rage, Rhadamistus had then attacked his bride and thrown her into the Araxes. Believing her dead, he had no knowledge of her rescue. Zenobia ended her account by telling Phenice that Rhadamistus had been killed by his own father, who had been jealous of his son's rise to power. The most compelling reason against marrying Pharasmanes, Zenobia told Phenice, was that she was in love with Rhadamistus' brother and Pharasmanes' son, Arsames.

When Arsames came to Zenobia from a campaign in Albania, he asked her whether she intended to marry Pharasmanes that day, as he had heard. He declared his love for her and his jealousy of his father. Zenobia assured him that she would not marry Pharasmanes, but she also declared that she could never consider marriage with Arsames. Arsames, knowing Zenobia only as Ismenia, was forced to accept her decision.

Pharasmanes appeared and criticized Arsames for returning to Iberia without permission. When Arsames declared that he came in support of his father to meet the invasion planned by Corbulo on behalf of Rome and Syria, Pharasmanes dismissed the excuse and forbade his son to profess love for Ismenia or ever to see her again. Pharasmanes, having dismissed Arsames, warned Ismenia that he would not tolerate refusal. In desperation, Zenobia appealed to Phenice to tell the Roman ambassador of her plight.

Rhadamistus, however, still lived. Tortured by repentance, knowing himself to be the murderer of Zenobia's father, and believing himself to be the murderer of his wife, he arrived in Iberia as the representative of Rome and the Roman choice for king of Armenia. Rhadamistus told his companion Hiero how he had been wounded by Pharasmanes' soldiers and how Corbulo had rescued him. Rhadamistus, vowing revenge on his father, had joined forces with Corbulo and been appointed Roman ambassador. Hiero told Rhadamistus that the Armenians, fearing Pharasmanes, hoped to persuade Arsames to become their king.

When Pharasmanes entered, Rhadamistus told him that Nero did not choose to have Pharasmanes become king of Armenia. Pharasmanes answered that Rome had better get its legions together, for he was determined to invade Armenia. He then supported his claim to the throne by referring to his brother, Mithridates, and to his son, Rhadamistus. Rhadamistus, who had managed to keep his identity hidden from his father, then angered Pharasmanes by declaring that the king should not expect to be heir to those he had murdered. Only Rhadamistus' status as ambassador kept Pharasmanes from ordering him seized.

Arsames, not recognizing Rhadamistus, refused to join with him in a revolt against Pharasmanes; but he urged the ambassador to take Ismenia from Iberia. Arsames also told Rhadamistus of his love for Ismenia, which for some hidden reason she could not return. Rhadamistus, who had no way of knowing that Ismenia and Zenobia were the same, agreed to help Ismenia.

When Zenobia came to Rhadamistus he recognized her immediately, but only his outcry made her realize that the ambassador was the husband who had tried to murder her. Rhadamistus, throwing himself at her feet, blamed himself for all his deeds, and Zenobia, partly from duty and partly from pity, forgave him his crimes.

Zenobia, who thought herself guilty because of her love for Arsames, could not wholly condemn Rhadamistus. When Arsames again told her of his love, she revealed that Rhadamistus was alive and that he was her husband. Rhadamistus interrupted the conversation and gave way to angry jealousy when he learned that Zenobia had revealed his identity. Zenobia remonstrated with him, pointing out that she would never have admitted her love for Arsames had not Rhadamistus' anger prompted her. Rhadamistus, ashamed of his outburst, begged their forgiveness.

Pharasmanes, fearing that Arsames was in league with the Romans, for he had seen his son talking to the Roman ambassador, arrested Arsames and sent his soldiers to capture the envoy. His anger was further aroused when he observed that the ambassador had taken Ismenia with him. He pursued Rhadamistus and wounded him with his sword. Arsames' grief stirred Pharasmanes strangely; he felt that somehow he had done a terrible act. Rhadamistus, dying, appeared before Pharasmanes and by a reference to Mithridates made his identity known to his father. Pharasmanes, realizing at last the fatal consequences of his jealousy and his lust for power, directed Arsames to take the Armenian throne. Sacrificing his own love for Zenobia as punishment for having killed his son, Pharasmanes relinquished Zenobia to Arsames and told them to flee from him lest his jealousy once again lead him to slay one of his own offspring.

Critical Evaluation:

Rhadamistus and Zenobia, for all its static presentation of background material in the first act, is successful at creating the tragic sense, the realization of the self-defeating character of human passion. Few members of a contemporary audience would tolerate Crébillon's play on the stage; the lengthy expository passages, the unmotivated antipathies, the awkward and precipitous close—all are weaknesses. For the reader, the play still offers passages of quiet force and power, and within the whole there are parts to be remembered.

Eighteenth century French tragedy became weighted down with philosophical speculations and undramatic, polemical material. Some dramas were nearly unactable, despite attempts to pour life into them with melodramatic horrors. Crébillon, in his attempts to startle and in his efforts to fill his plays with stately speeches, fits this pattern. Crébillon's tragedies were modeled after those of the Roman tragic writer Seneca, and like them specialize in horror; however, Seneca's tragedies were meant only to be read, while Crébillon's plays, such as *Rhadamistus and Zenobia*, were intended for the stage. Crébillon said that he aimed to move his audience to pity through terror, but his tragedies are at times merely sensational, depending less upon psychological analysis than upon violent and unnatural crimes.

Rhadamistus and Zenobia is considered Crébillon's finest play, although the plot is so complicated as to be almost incomprehensible. When it was first produced, it was greeted with tremendous respect and popularity. It was one of the most acted eighteenth century tragedies at the Comedie Francaise, and Zenobia was considered one of the choice tragic roles for eighteenth century French actresses. This play and a few of Crébillon's other most successful works are considered to possess a vigor and passion unsurpassed in French classical drama, but even his admirers admit to a want of culture and a lack of care in his style and verse, although isolated passages are well done.

The subject of *Rhadamistus and Zenobia* has close analogies with Jean Racine's *Mithridates* (1673). The heroine (disguised) is loved by a whole family, who have been chiefly occupied with murdering her own family. There are swelling speeches and occasional inspiration, but the drama is melodramatic. In *Rhadamistus and Zenobia*, Crébillon keeps within the conventional form of tragedy, but his plot is a chaotic swirl of mistaken identity, recognitions, and tangled family relations. The audiences of his day thrilled, however, to the suspenseful story and the violence and terror it portrays. In *Rhadamistus and Zenobia*, readers can see how much Crébillon resembled Pierre Corneille, both in his defects and virtues as a dramatic poet. In Crébillon's attempt to make his diction energetic, he gives way to excesses. He never possesses, even in this play, the polish of his enemy, Voltaire, although he achieves a rugged power beyond Voltaire. Crébillon does not fathom the heart of the human soul in this or any other of his plays, but he keeps alive the classical tradition, and his genius for inventing tense and tragic situations stimulated other writers. Voltaire himself used four of Crébillon's plots. The importance of *Rhadamistus and Zenobia* in the development of French drama cannot be denied.

Bibliography:
Badir, Magdy Gabriel, and David J. Langdon. *Eighteenth-Century French Theatre: Aspects and Contexts.* Calgary, Alberta: University of Alberta Press, 1986. Although this collection of essays does not deal directly with *Rhadamisthus and Zenobia*, the essays in this volume by Patrick Brady and David Trott describe the transformation of French tragedy after the death of Racine in 1699.
Jourdain, Eleanor F. *Dramatic Theory and Practice in France: 1690-1808.* New York: Benjamin Blom, 1968. Analyzes Crébillon's use of sentimentality and violence to move his spectators. Includes an analysis of Crébillon career.
Lancaster, Henry C. *Sunset: A History of Parisian Drama in the Last Years of Louis XIV: 1701-1715.* Baltimore: The Johns Hopkins University Press, 1945. Historical study of French theater during the last years of Louis XIV's reign. Lancaster analyzes Crébillon's skills as a tragic playwright in *Rhadamistus and Zenobia* and the psychological differences between the murderer Rhadamisthus and the dignified Zenobia.
Tilley, Arthur. *The Decline of the Age of Louis XIV: 1687-1715.* New York: Barnes & Noble

Books, 1968. Describes the evolution of French theater during the last part of Louis XIV's reign and explains clearly the historical importance of many neglected playwrights, including Crébillon.

Yarrow, P. J. *The Seventeenth-Century: 1600-1715*. In *A Literary History of France*. New York: Barnes & Noble Books, 1967. Contains a clear historical overview of neoclassical French theater and literature from 1600 to 1715.

RHINOCEROS

Type of work: Drama
Author: Eugène Ionesco (1912-1994)
Type of plot: Absurdist
Time of plot: Indeterminate
Locale: A small provincial town in France
First performed: 1959, in German; 1960, in French; first published, 1959 as *Rhinocéros*
(English translation, 1959)

Principal characters:
BERENGER, the unheroic hero, unkempt and apathetic
JEAN, his friend, fastidious and self-confident
DAISY, Berenger's girlfriend, a secretary at the office where he works
THE WAITRESS
THE GROCER
THE GROCER'S WIFE
THE OLD GENTLEMAN
THE LOGICIAN
THE HOUSEWIFE
THE CAFÉ PROPRIETOR
MR. PAPILLON, Berenger's boss
DUDARD and
BOTARD, fellow employees of Berenger
MRS. BOEUF, the wife of another employee
A FIREMAN
THE LITTLE OLD MAN
THE LITTLE OLD MAN'S WIFE

The Story:
In a square in a small provincial town, a large number of comic types passed by chatting. Jean and Berenger conversed across a table at a sidewalk café. Jean berated his unshaven friend for drinking too much. Berenger complained that his life was still unsettled. Jean, who proceeded to lecture Berenger about duty, told him that he must get used to life as it is. Everything was interrupted by a rhinoceros, which thundered by immediately offstage. The townspeople were astounded and alarmed. Before long another rhinoceros galloped by, or perhaps it was the same one returning. The civic alarm was noticeably less acute the second time.

To the townspeople came a startling revelation: The rhinoceroses were townspeople who had undergone a strange metamorphosis. By the next day, the number of rhinoceroses was increasing. Berenger visited Jean, who turned into a rhinoceros. His voice became progressively hoarser and eventually unintelligible. His manner became aggressive and hostile toward humans. He made periodic checks with the bathroom mirror, each time noting that his skin had become greener and a bump on his head had grown larger. During his last visit to the bathroom Jean's transformation was completed, and Berenger barely escaped being trampled. As Berenger fled the building, rhinoceros heads popped into view in doorways and windows; the lethargic Berenger was precipitated into a state of panic.

Everyone in the town, except Berenger, changed into a rhinoceros. Berenger sought refuge in his room. For a time, before he was deserted by his last friend, Dudard, and by his fiancée, Daisy, Berenger tried to think of some way to combat a trend that he could see only as ominous. He decided to write to the newspapers, write a manifesto, or go to see the mayor or his assistant if the mayor should be occupied at the time. Berenger's plans, ineffectual to begin with, were forgotten when, at the end, he was alone.

Berenger expressed his firm intention to remain a human being, to hold out no matter what. He began to feel the terrible stress of utter isolation. He saw that he was in an intolerable, absurd position. He was not sure what language he was speaking. He became ashamed of his appearance and of his normal voice. He tried to become a rhinoceros, but he did not know how to effect the change. Then, either because he failed or perhaps because his courage reasserted itself, he declared that he would make a stand against the creatures. He was the last man left and he planned to remain a man; he would not give in.

Critical Evaluation:

Although Eugène Ionesco's style seemed quite startling to theatergoers when they first experienced his curious one-act plays in the early 1950's, by the time *Rhinoceros* opened in 1959 he had been recognized as one of France's preeminent dramatists. Early plays such as *The Bald Soprano* (1950), *The Lesson* (1951), and *The Chairs* (1952) had surprised critics and public alike. As the public became more familiar with Ionesco's dramas, they found that his unconventional use of theater conventions was at least consistent.

Gradually, in France and elsewhere, he and a number of other playwrights (including Samuel Beckett, Jean Genet, and Arthur Adamov) were identified as writing what eventually was called the Theater of the Absurd. Absurdist plays are characterized by a number of features. Their plots seem slight and their action appears to be almost arbitrary. Characters are usually one-dimensional, sketched out rather than fully drawn, and are often called by only a first or a last name or by their profession. Dialogue is frequently nonsensical, maintaining the form of actual language but lacking the communicative capacity usually associated with speech or writing. Absurdist playwrights emphasize the ways in which life becomes irrational and depict how easily ordinary existence can appear to be unintelligible. Isolated in a world that seems overwhelmingly chaotic and ridiculous, the protagonist in an absurdist play typically fights a losing battle in a minefield of strange, and occasionally hilarious, paradoxes.

A major difference between *Rhinoceros* and Ionesco's previous works is that this play is written for a large stage. It utilizes a good-sized cast and requires some stunning visual effects. The plays that came before were intended for smaller, more intimate theaters and tend to rely more upon the actors' performances. *Rhinoceros* received its French premiere at one of France's most prestigious playhouses, the Odéon in Paris, under the guidance of Jean-Louis Barrault, the great postwar actor-director. Moreover, the play went on to highly successful runs in London and New York. *Rhinoceros*, not surprisingly therefore, is Ionesco's best-known play, and its production was the high point in his career. In France, Ionesco remains a highly regarded and often-produced dramatist, but his international reputation has diminished since the 1970's. His early work—those plays up to and including *Rhinoceros*—is what remains widely known.

Ionesco wrote and spoke about some of what had inspired him to write this play. Born in Romania, he had left for France in 1938, around the time that many of his friends began to follow the Iron Guard movement—a Romanian fascist political organization, which during World War II allied itself with the Nazis. He began to notice how his friends, whom he had known for many years, seemed to have been as if infected by the movement's right-wing ideology, and he noticed how people with whose views he had once sympathized suddenly became monstrous to him. From his comments, one can easily connect his experience with the action of the play: the seeming invasion of the town by rhinos and the sudden change through which human beings are converted into beasts.

The play's implications extend beyond the playwright's own life, however. People in many different countries have been able to relate to the play. When, for example, *Rhinoceros* was first performed in Düsseldorf, Germany, the audiences immediately recognized the story because they had lived through the period when the German people had succumbed to the Nazi Party and only a few had resisted. In a more immediate way, however, this play, written in French and intended for postwar French audiences, comments on how, after France had been defeated by Germany in 1940 and then occupied by the German Army until 1944, many French people had been lured into sympathizing with the Nazis. Even though this play was not produced in France until 1960, the shame many French people felt about how some of their own citizens had collaborated with the Germans remained very strong.

Rhinoceros has much to say about how people are often willing to follow the prevailing political scheme blindly. In conforming to the rhinos' ideology, the townspeople become themselves savage creatures. They lose their humanity, their individuality, their sense of self. Their identities, completely reshaped by their adherence to rhino values, are transformed by their desire to go along with the herd, to be just like everyone else, and to play it safe. The extent to which all the characters in the play, with the notable exception of Berenger, collaborate with the rhinoceroses makes them, in the end, no better than the thick-skinned beasts. In fact, the people become rhinos.

Ionesco goes beyond this political parable to explore the way through which the external affects the soul. The only person to emerge from the play as a fully developed character is Berenger, Ionesco's Everyman, who appears in several other of his plays. In Berenger's long final monologue, the playwright offers the audience a glimpse of how difficult it is for one person to stand alone against the political tide. Attracted to the notion of being one of the crowd and frightened by his lonely position as the very last human being on Earth, Berenger goes through a series of ambivalent reversals as he vows to fight to the end. He starts to feel doubt about how important it is to be a human being even as he valiantly tries to remain human.

Clearly, his decision to continue to resist seems sadly doomed. Perhaps what Ionesco wishes the audience to appreciate is the admirable effort of withstanding the forces of evil and the absurd struggle from which Berenger can never emerge as victor. This peculiarly contradictory pairing of victory and defeat makes Berenger an existential hero, whose courage derives not from any ultimate triumph but from his stoic acceptance of failure.

"Critical Evaluation" by Kenneth Krauss

Bibliography:
Danner, G. Richard. "Bérenger's Defense of Humanity in *Rhinocéros.*" *French Review: Journal of the American Association of the Teachers of French* 53, no. 2 (December, 1979): 207-214. An illuminating article that explores the beliefs of the main character of *Rhinoceros.* The author finds a number of complexities in Berenger's struggle to maintain his own humanity and to justify that of others.
Esslin, Martin. *The Theatre of the Absurd.* 3d rev. ed. New York: Penguin, 1980. A good place to begin any research on Ionesco's plays. Examines how *Rhinoceros* connects with Ionesco's

earlier works and suggests that this work, which on one level seems quite comprehensive, is in fact highly ambiguous.

Jacquart, Emmanuel. "Ionesco's Political Itinerary." In *The Dream and the Play: Ionesco's Theatrical Quest*, edited by Moshe Lazar. Malibu, Calif.: Undena, 1982. Ionesco's Everyman, Berenger appears in several plays that characterize government and society as oppressive. This article offers an interesting look at the political implications of *Rhinoceros*. Helpful to an understanding of the playwright's political views.

Lane, Nancy. *Understanding Eugène Ionesco*. Columbia: University of South Carolina Press, 1994. Although many have come to regard Ionesco's work as dated and limited, Lane sees his work as continuing to be both significant and relevant to the modern stage. Her discussion of *Rhinoceros* is guided by her belief that it is one of Ionesco's major plays.

Rigg, Patricia. "Ionesco's Berenger: Existential Philosopher or Philosophical Ironist?" *Modern Drama* 35, no. 4 (December, 1992): 538-551. A lucid examination of *Rhinoceros* and its main character. In trying to determine whether Berenger is an existential hero or an embodiment of paradox, Rigg manages to illuminate much of the philosophical background of the play.

THE RHYMES

Type of work: Poetry
Author: Gustavo Adolfo Bécquer (1836-1870)
First published: Rimas, 1871 (English translation, 1891)

Appraised by many critics to be among the greatest love poets, Gustavo Adolfo Bécquer had not published any books before his death at age thirty-four. Although Bécquer had little money for his education because of the death of his parents when he was nine years old, he read voraciously and was writing odes by the time he was twelve. Bécquer obtained literary recognition when he was twenty-four with the publication of *Cartas literarias a una mujer* (literary letters to a woman) in 1860 in the periodical *El Contemporáneo.* After Bécquer's death, his friends collected the poet's poems that had been printed in periodicals and published them in a book. *The Rhymes* are the poet's major work.

Bécquer's poetry reflects a tendency toward Romanticism, a literary tendency advocated by the liberals upon their return to Spain in 1833 after the death of Fernando VII, who had exiled them. The desire of the Spanish people to depose this oppressive Bourbon monarch corresponded with their desire to free themselves from French classicism which, as Spanish artists saw it, represented the point of view of the cultured elite of another country, and that restricted one's freedom to compose works in one's own style. Romanticism directly opposes such classical restraints as using plots or subjects taken strictly from ancient sources and using formal language in a highly stylized format. Bécquer's poetry treats one of the themes characteristic of Romanticism: love. He shows the multiple facets of love: a longing for the ideal woman, disillusionment, and intense despair. Bécquer's poems expose the states of his soul as they waver into light or into darkness. His poems do not necessarily relate to real love affairs; Bécquer even indicates that he has mixed fact with fiction in his memory. Bécquer is so focused on love that he considers it an enigmatic power enlivening nature and permeating the universe.

The structure of *The Rhymes* reflects Bécquer's inner life. His work can be divided into sections that represent different spiritual states. Bécquer's work begins with his supreme attraction toward art in poems 1 through 8, in which he hopes to attain glory through the immortality of his creation. Rhyme 2 compares his spiritual state with a flickering light whose final spark may guide his footsteps to glory, and rhyme 7 refers to his underdeveloped talents; he, like Lazarus, is waiting for a voice to call him.

The next section, consisting of poems 9 to 12, reveals the vague foreshadowing of the proximity of love. Rhyme 9 portrays the image of the kisses that nature gives to her surroundings such as the radiant clouds becoming purple and gold from the sun's kiss. Rhyme 11 is presented in dialogue form with two women each relating her attributes in the first person singular and the poet's response. Bécquer rejects the passionate brunette full of desires that transcend shame and the tender blonde longing to make his dreams come true. He chooses the woman who is a fleeting phantom of light and mist. This phantasmic woman with whom Bécquer is enamored represents the feminine ideal of Romanticism, for she is not physical being but a spiritual projection: a shadow, a phantom, or a dream. Bécquer has thus embarked upon an impossible quest for an inaccessible woman.

The next division presented in rhymes 12 through 15 shows the poet's undefined feeling of love in the process of forming. In rhyme 12 Bécquer describes the physical features of the woman that so attracts him. Her eyes are as green as the sea, her cheeks are rose colored, and her mouth is like rubies. Rhyme 15 emphasizes the powerful image of the woman's unavoidable eyes, which penetrate his soul.

The poet is then ready to declare his love in rhymes 16 through 24. His beloved appears like an image of a red flower asleep in the heart of the beloved; but upon inclining her head in times of sadness, she seems to him like a broken white lily. Bécquer links his concepts of love, flower, and sadness through his use of rhyme: *amor, flor,* and *dolor.* In rhyme 21 Bécquer defines the "you" of the poems, the woman, as poetry.

Rhymes 25 through 29 continue to express the poet's idealized love; at last he arrives at the perfect union of his soul with that of his beloved. Rhyme 24 completes this union through its image of the two red tongues of fire growing close together and upon kissing, forming a single flame. The exaltation of their love is continued in Rhymes 25 through 29.

The idealized love begins to rupture in rhyme 30. This rupture, produced by pride and tears, results in the separation of the poet from his beloved, each taking separate paths. Rhymes 31 through 36 show the effect of the broken love upon the poet; he is dismayed. His sadness leaves a permanent mark on his heart, producing a profound discouragement within his soul. He reveals his bitterness through his confusion of tears with laughter and pride with dignity. These distressing sentiments lead the poet to consider death for the first time; he fills his mind with melancholy memories of the past and in rhyme 41 laments both his beloved's betrayal and her ingratitude. Rhyme 42 accentuates the poet's complaint, indicating that in his imagination he has not seen an abyss as deep as the heart of the woman who has betrayed him. Since the poet, reacting to his melancholy in frenzy, cannot silence the memory within his soul, he decides to let himself be carried away into the distant places that rhyme 52 suggests. After this delirious declaration, Bécquer becomes calm and delivers his best known poem, "Volverán las oscuras golondrinas" (the dark swallows will return). The poet is saved by faith in his own love. Although the external manifestation of love (the faithful swallows, who return every year to the same nest) disappears, Bécquer will not be overcome with complete despair, because his love is unchangeable. In the form of a symmetric ballad, the poem shows the future alternating with the past (the future year's return of the swallows recalls their past return and the poet's past love) and at the same time shows how the future cannot be the same as the past.

After the relatively optimistic poem "Volverán las oscuras golondrinas," rhymes 54 through 55 disclose that Bécquer is inspired by memory and tears of repentance; rhymes 56 through 57 reveal the resurgence of the poet's loss of faith in love. The poet's skepticism is more ironic in rhymes 58 through 59, culminating in rhyme 60, in which evil deflowers the flowers of which Bécquer is fond. The next few poems demonstrate the poet's skeptical sentiments until his concentration on sadness and tears causes him to ponder death, and the final poems relate the yearning for the soul's infinite qualities, linking death with awakening.

The Rhymes reflect Romantic qualities of melancholy, passion, and yearnings, but they also contain the element of ambiguity, signaling a new concept of poetry that was developing during the decade of the 1860's, when Bécquer was composing his poetry. Bécquer believed that poetry, like love, permeates every aspect of life and that the poet needs to suggest this idea to the reader. Hence, Bécquer's beloved in *The Rhymes* does not represent a person of flesh and blood; she appears as a symbol of the states of his soul. The poet's attempt to transmit to the reader the subtle nuances of his sentiments is reflected by his copious use of metaphors. Since precise terms for the fleeting impressions that the poet wishes to discuss do not exist, he opts for the tools of poetry. Bécquer chooses his words and imagery for their imprecise emotional implication in order to suggest those feelings that cannot be directly designated.

Bécquer is one of those poets on whom the mantle of envisioning an innovative concept of poetry fell. Although he died with promise of obscurity, his poems have been widely read, imitated, and heralded as a high point of the Romantic era. Admiration for his innovation and sympathy for his lamentable life give the reader reasons to appreciate his melodious, impassioned verses.

Linda Prewett Davis

Bibliography:
Bell, Aubrey F. G. *Contemporary Spanish Literature*. New York: Russell & Russell, 1966. Briefly discusses Bécquer's poetic techniques. Shows how his poetry marks a transition from Romanticism to the modernist innovations of the twentieth century.

Brenan, Gerald. *The Literature of the Spanish People*. 2d ed. Cambridge, England: Cambridge University Press, 1970. Describes the characteristics of the poetry of the nineteenth century. Appraises the poetry of Bécquer and examines his place in literary history.

Bynum, B. Brant. *The Romantic Imagination in the Works of Gustavo Adolfo Bécquer*. Chapel Hill: University of North Carolina Press, 1993. Aptly explains how Bécquer utilizes romantic techniques in *The Rhymes*. Contains an excellent list of consulted works.

Pattison, Walter T., and Donald W. Blezniek. *Representative Spanish Authors*. Vol. 2. New York: Oxford University Press, 1963. Concisely relates the brief history of the nineteenth century and the tenets of Romanticism. Gives an excellent introduction to *The Rhymes*.

Turnbull, Eleanor L. *Ten Centuries of Spanish Poetry: An Anthology in English Verse with Original Texts*. Baltimore: The Johns Hopkins University Press, 1955. Presents the Spanish and English texts of the best-known poems of Bécquer. Contains a brief but informative introduction to Bécquer's poetry by the renowned scholar Pedro Salinas.

RHYMES

Type of work: Poetry
Author: Petrarch (Francesco Petrarca, 1304-1374)
First published: Rerum vulgarium fragmenta, 1470 (English translation, 1879)

Of the 366 poems included in the collection that Petrarch made of his poetry, 317 are sonnets, twenty-nine canzoni, nine sestine, seven ballate, and four madrigals. In giving the work the title *Rerum vulgarium fragmenta,* Petrarch called attention to the fact that the brief poems were written not in Latin but in the vernacular. The work also became known as *Rime (Rhymes)* or *Canzoniere.*

In considering the sonnets and songs of Petrarch, the poet is invariably compared with Dante Alighieri, who also wrote in the vernacular Italian instead of Latin. Both these giants of Italian literature centered their poetry around a gracious lady suddenly discovered, idealized, and then praised throughout a lifetime. Dante wrote his *The New Life* (c. 1292) about Beatrice Portinari, whom he met when he was nine and she eight years old; he never stopped worshiping her as the ideal woman, and he continued to celebrate her in his poetry even after her death in 1290. Petrarch's ideal woman was Laura, possibly Laura de Noves, whom he first met on April 6, 1327, when he was in his twenty-second year. Laura died on the same day in 1348 from the plague.

Like Dante, Petrarch kept his passion at a distance—one might say at a poetic distance—from the woman who charmed him. In the works of both Dante and Petrarch, however, it is difficult to believe that the love was merely an excuse for the poetry; something of human passion, not just creative passion, burns in the poetry with a warmth that survives the centuries. It may be that this enduring emotion can be attributed to those distant ladies who set the poets to writing immortal poetry, but it is more reasonable to suppose that poetic genius worked in both cases to turn a sudden fancy into a lifelong poetic enterprise.

Critics have never ceased wondering who Laura may have been, or whether she was. Even Petrarch's contemporaries were not certain, and some of them contended that the Laura of the poems was an invention, an ideal based on no model whatsoever. Petrarch denied the charge, pointing out that it would be madness to spend years writing hundreds of poems about an entirely imaginary woman. More significantly, the poems too deny the charge by the force of their feeling and imagery.

For both Dante and Petrarch the idealization process took them beyond earth to heaven. That is, the poetic figures of Beatrice and Laura are not merely ideal mortal, physical women but also spiritually significant, by their person and manner representing beings who symbolize the highest values the human soul can hope to attain. Dante made Beatrice an inspiration even in Paradise and used her as the central guiding figure of the second half of *The Divine Comedy* (c. 1320). In writing of the painter Simon, Petrarch comments in poem 77:

> But certainly Simon saw paradise
> Wherein this gentle lady had her place;
> There he saw her and portrayed in such guise
> That is the witness here of her fair face.

Later, writing more explicitly of Laura after her death, Petrarch speaks of "Seeing her now on such intimate term/ With Him who in her life had her heart's right," and, in the same sonnet 345, he concludes:

> For fairer than before, my inner eye
> Sees her soar up and with the angels fly
> At the feet of our own eternal Lord.

It has been traditional to divide the sonnets and songs into two major parts, the one including poems written while Laura was living, and the other those written after her death. Poem 3 of the collection tells of the first meeting:

> It was the day when the sun's rays turned white
> Out of the pity it felt for its sire,
> When I was caught and taken by desire,
> For your fair eyes, my lady, held me quite.

In poem 5, Petrarch works the syllables of the name "Laura" into his verse in order to describe what happens when his sighs call her with the name that Love wrote on his heart: "Thus to LAUd and REvere teaches and vows/ The voice itself . . ." ("Così LAUdare e REverire insegna/ La voce stessa . . .").

In poem 6 appears one of Petrarch's many puns on Laura's name, when he writes of Love as holding the bridle of his desire and thus being directed "Only to reach the laurel and its sour fruit . . ." ("Sol per venir al lauro . . ."). Again, in the following poem, he speaks of the "love of laurel." It was in part because of such puns that Petrarch was accused of inventing the character "Laura."

These plays with words were the least of Petrarch's accomplishments in the sonnet form. He was so adept at using the fourteen lines to express a complete idea or image with all its emotional correlate that poets have taken him as a model ever since. A full appreciation of the poet comes only from reading his poetry and sensing the beauty that results from his sensitive use of the sound and sense of language within the sonnet form. Although translation does not always succeed in reproducing the finely wrought rhythms of Petrarch's verse, the best has the great virtue of coming close to the form, sound, and even syntax of the original. Even those who do not understand Italian can gain an appreciation of the original.

One of the advantages of Petrarch's having chosen to write in the tradition of love poetry is that he writes of his beloved from a poignant distance. In making Laura unobtainable, he secured her forever in his poetry. In poem 16, for example, he reminds his readers that he was never able to possess his Laura:

> A rain of bitter tears falls from my face
> And a tormenting wind blows with my sighs
> Whenever toward you I turn my eyes,
> Whose absence cuts me from the human race.

Much of Petrarch's poetry is concerned with the shortness of life, the inevitableness of death, and the end of all that is fair and young on earth, all matters that are related to Laura. Thus the poetry before her death has a great deal in common with the poetry written afterward. The greatest difference in the later works is that regret and speculation have now taken the place of fear for her loss. Before her death Petrarch amused himself with poetically metaphysical imagery by which he claimed that Laura would outshine stars and draw the angels to her, but after her death the poetic amusement is either absent or tempered by a sober recognition of the fact of death. If Laura is shown reverent respect by anyone in heaven, it is because of her spirit. In the following image from sonnet 127, later readers were reminded of John Donne:

> To count the constellations one by one
> And to pour in a goblet all the seas
> Was perhaps my intention when I took
> This small sheet to relate such mysteries.

Not all the poems are about Laura. Petrarch writes of Italy at war, of nature, of God and the love of God, of life and death, and of other matters of universal concern. Yet even these poems have a human dimension because they are fixed in the context of the Laura poetry. Perhaps it is because Petrarch had the heart and wit to be a love poet that he compels respect for his thoughts about universal matters as well.

After Laura's death, Petrarch wrote a sonnet of lament (poem 267), which begins, "Alas! the lovely face, the eyes that save/ Alas! the charming countenance and proud!" In the poem that followed, he asks, "What shall I do? What do you counsel, Love?/ It is now time to die./ And I have waited longer that I would./ My lady died and did my heart remove." The long lament ends:

> Flee the clearness, the green,
> Do not go near where there is song and laughter,
> Canzone, follow after
> Weeping: you are not fit for merry folk,
> A widow, without comfort, in black cloak.

Petrarch's lamentations gradually change character toward the end of the collection. Grief gives way to reflection, and reflection turns his thoughts to spiritual love—thus to the love of God. Laura becomes the symbol of what human beings should strive for, even though in life she was physically desirable as a woman. Because "Death quelled the sun wonted to over-whelm" him and "Dust is the one who was my chill and spark," Petrarch is able to write in sonnet 363, "From this I see my good" and "I find freedom at last, bitter and sweet/ And to the Lord whom I adore and greet,/ Who with his nod governs the holy things,/ I return, tired of life, and with life sated."

Bibliography:

Bernardo, Aldo S. *Petrarch, Laura, and the "Triumphs."* Albany: State University of New York Press, 1974. Analyzes the poetic image of Laura from various perspectives. Devotes the first half of the book to Laura and the poems in *Rhymes.*

Jones, Frederic J. *The Structure of Petrarch's "Canzoniere": A Chronological, Psychological, and Stylistic Analysis.* Cambridge, England: D. S. Brewer, 1995. Examines the first and early part of the *Rhymes.* A study of the psychological evolution of Petrarch's work that attempts to systematize the emotional ebb and flow of his relationship with Laura.

Mazzotta, Giuseppe. "The *Canzoniere* and the Language of the Self." In *Petrarch: Modern Critical Views,* edited by Harold Bloom. New York: Chelsea House, 1989. Emphasizes the importance of the poet's image of himself being central to the *Rhymes.*

Petrarch. *For Love of Laura: Poetry of Petrarch.* Translated by Marion Shore. Fayetteville: University of Arkansas Press, 1987. An excellent translation of selected poems of the *Rhymes.* The selection captures the spirit of the collection's two major sections, which are rendered into the form of the English sonnet.

_____. *Petrarch's Lyric Poems: The Rime Sparse and Other Lyrics.* Translated and edited by R. M. Durling. Cambridge, Mass.: Harvard University Press, 1976. Provides a poetic English translation of Petrarch's *Rhymes.*

Sturm-Maddox, Sara. *Petrarch's Laurels*. University Park: Pennsylvania State University Press, 1992. Considers the fundamental issue of relating the laurel branch, symbol of poetic genius, and Petrarch's ideal love, Laura. Shows how the poet connected the two in several of his works, but especially in the *Rhymes*, and how he thereby created the image of Laura.

RICEYMAN STEPS

Type of work: Novel
Author: Arnold Bennett (1867-1931)
Type of plot: Social realism
Time of plot: 1919
Locale: Riceyman Steps, a suburb of London
First published: 1923

> *Principal characters:*
> HENRY EARLFORWARD, a bookseller
> MRS. VIOLET ARB, the owner of a nearby shop
> ELSIE, the maid for both Earlforward and Mrs. Arb
> JOE, Elsie's friend
> DR. RASTE, a physician

The Story:

Henry Earlforward owned a bookstore left to him by his uncle, T. T. Riceyman. It was cluttered, dusty, and badly lighted. Earlforward lived in a back room of the shop; the upstairs of the building was filled with old books. Elsie, his cleaning girl, came into the shop one night. She told Henry that she also worked for Mrs. Arb, who owned the confectioner's shop next door, and that Mrs. Arb had sent her for a cookbook. Henry found one containing recipes for making substantial meals out of practically no food at all. A little later, Elsie returned and said that Mrs. Arb thanked him, but the book was too expensive.

His curiosity became aroused, and he went to Mrs. Arb's shop. Even though he marked down the price of the book, Mrs. Arb still refused to buy it. Henry became more interested, for it was clear that Mrs. Arb was no spendthrift. The following Sunday they went for a walk, and from then on, they became close friends. At last, Violet Arb sold her shop and agreed to marry Henry. When Violet asked him about a wedding ring, he seemed surprised, for he had supposed the one she already owned would do. He got a file, sawed off the ring, sold it, and bought another, all without really spending a penny. They were married one morning and for a honeymoon spent the day in London.

They visited Madame Tussaud's Waxworks and the Chamber of Horrors. Henry, who had thought the wedding breakfast expensive enough, was distressed at being forced to spend more money. He wondered if he had been deceived, if Violet were not a spendthrift after all. He began to complain about his lame foot. Violet was dismayed; she had wanted to see a motion picture. Henry could not be persuaded to change his mind. He did not, he said, want a painful leg on his wedding day.

When they passed by the shop that night, Henry thought the place was on fire. It was glowing with light, and men were working inside. Violet explained that the men had been engaged to clean the dirty, cluttered shop. She had planned the work as her wedding gift to him, but he had spoiled the surprise by coming home before the men had finished their task. Henry showed Violet a safe that he had bought to safeguard her valuables and her money.

Violet soon discovered that miserly Henry would not light a fire, would have no electric light, and would eat practically nothing. On their first morning together, she cooked an egg for him, but he refused to eat it. Later, Elsie ate it in secret. At another time, Violet had Elsie cook steaks, but Henry would not touch them. There was an argument in which Violet called him a miser who was starving her to death. He left the room and his steak. That night, Elsie ate it.

When Violet discovered that Elsie had eaten the steak, there was another row; but Elsie began to eat more and more when nobody was there to observe her. The girl was half-starved in the miserly household. To stop Elsie's thefts of food, Henry went to bed, called Elsie to his room, announced he was seriously ill, and asked if she thought it right to steal food while he lay dying. Elsie was glum and frightened.

A short time later, Henry actually became ill. In defiance of the Earlforwards, Elsie managed to get Dr. Raste to examine Henry. The doctor said that the sick man would have to go to the hospital. Then the doctor discovered that Violet was also ill. At first, Henry refused to go to the hospital, but Violet finally persuaded him to go. When the doctor called the next morning, it was Violet, however, who went to the hospital. Henry stayed at home in the care of Elsie.

In the meantime, Elsie had been hoping for the return of Joe, her sweetheart. He had been employed by Dr. Raste, had been ill, and had wandered off. Elsie was sure he would return some day.

One night, Elsie wanted to send a boy to the hospital to inquire about Violet. When she asked Henry for sixpence for the messenger, he said she could go herself. Not wanting to leave him, she picked up his keys, went downstairs, and opened the safe. Amazed to find so much money there, she borrowed sixpence and put an I.O.U. in its place. Then she dashed out to find a boy to carry her note. When she came back, she found Joe waiting for her. He was shabbily dressed and sick.

Elsie quietly carried Joe up to her room and took care of him, taking pains so that Henry would not suspect his presence in the house. When Joe began to improve, he told her he had been in jail. Elsie did not care. She continued to take care of Henry and promised him that she would never desert him. The hospital informed them that Violet was to have an operation. That night, Elsie went next door to the confectioner's shop. Mrs. Belrose, the wife of the new proprietor, telephoned the hospital and was told that Violet had died because her strength had been sapped through malnutrition.

Henry seemed to take the news calmly enough, but he grew steadily worse. Dr. Raste came again and said that he must go to a hospital, but Henry refused. Without Elsie's knowledge, he got up and went downstairs, where he discovered with dismay Elsie's appropriation of the sixpence. He sat down at his desk and began to read his correspondence.

Elsie was in her room taking care of Joe. To the neighbors, the house seemed quite dark. Accordingly, Mrs. Belrose insisted that her husband go over to inquire about the sick man. He discovered Henry's body lying in the shop. A relative came from London and sold the shop to Mr. Belrose. Joe recovered and went back to work for Dr. Raste. Elsie intended to marry Joe, so she also went to work for Dr. Raste.

Critical Evaluation:

The word "Riceyman" rings throughout *Riceyman Steps*. The name is intimately associated with the family of Henry Earlforward, whose uncle, T. T. Riceyman, bequeathed the bookshop to Henry. The Riceyman Steps—that is, the steps that lead from the hurly-burly of King's Cross Road up to Riceyman Square—sit directly over the Underground Railway, which throbs with the passage of trains. These steps make Riceyman square into something of a stage setting, situated in the middle of Clerkenwell, a shabby neighborhood much loved by old T. T. Riceyman, who never tired of reciting how the original tunnel near Clerkenwell Green collapsed, in the spring of 1862. The three opening chapters that sketch this history set the stage for the drama that ensues.

Riceyman Steps tells two love stories, one dry and unsatisfying but a love story nevertheless, and the other tender and gratifying. Henry's marriage to Mrs. Violet Arb soon becomes little more than a struggle between two opposed sensibilities, with Violet yearning for something of the world's rich experiences as Henry suffocates her with his pathological acquisitiveness. Something clearly human and sexual, however, drives Henry to visit Violet's shop the first time. Her smile uplifts him, and he becomes "a little bit flurried." He admires her "fine movement" and his male vanity moves him to conceal his limp.

Things thus begin conventionally, although they do not exactly follow the usual account of a man's way with a maid (or widow, for that matter). The eccentric wooing that brings two lonely people together is presented with warmth. The two offer much to solace each other throughout life. The abbreviated honeymoon outing foretells what will go wrong. The story is an ancient one: Once the male has preened and courted and won, he drops the pose of the lover and shows his true colors—and Henry's colors are extremely gray and drab. Violet's dream of marital happiness dissolves into a waking nightmare. Violet is an attractive character, lively, intelligent, and outgoing, and given half a chance she would make much of her life. She turns instead into the victim of fate, in the tradition of naturalism.

Various symbols help propel the narrative, among them light and fire, the wedding cake, and the safe. Henry cannot abide electric lights burning in his establishment, nor can he allow anyone to burn a candle. Fires consume fuel, and fuel costs money. So Henry, Violet, and Elsie live worse than primitive cave dwellers, burrowing away in the cold darkness, the two women yearning for light and warmth in their lives. Compared to the bookshop, the Belroses' establishment next door, taken over from Violet, positively blazes with a mad exuberance of electric lights. The brightness of the Belrose shop is an external sign of the human generosity and benign vision of life that reign within.

Food also means extravagance, and, when Violet prepares the steak for Henry, his turning away from it indicates not only his stomach ailment but also his rejection of anything juicy and self-indulgent in life. The piece of wedding cake that the newlyweds eat seems to lead directly to Henry's illness, not literally but as a sign that anything so rich and foreign to his nature will poison him at some deep level. As their illnesses progress, Henry and Violet think back on the cake as a turning point in their lives.

Henry Earlforward's safe looms up as a tangible, gross, heavy object embodying all of his parsimony. That he would leave his keys where Elsie could get them to unlock the safe is ironic. She does not steal from Henry, but his discovery that she had borrowed sixpence from the safe—to use in his service—bespeaks to him a monstrous betrayal. He dies, overcome by this last, bitter realization of fortune's power, and when the light burns on into the night over Henry's dead body, Mr. Belrose hurries across Riceyman Square to find an explanation.

The physical diseases that kill Henry and Violet complement the disorders that dominate their lives. A stomach cancer consumes Henry, destroying the body of a man described on the first page as "in the prime of life." It is not so much his stinginess that the cancer signifies, for he had been just as stingy before the cancer gripped him. Instead it is his stinginess with human feeling that drags him down. He abuses Violet and Elsie with his niggardliness and his cruel oversight of their very ordinary behavior. In Violet's case, fibroid tumors strike her reproductive organs. Her life, already blighted by death and a constant hunger for something besides emotional and material penury, closes with an illness that mocks the barrenness of her existence. There is something spiteful about Arnold Bennett's choice of these fatal diseases, almost as if he as their creator was telling Henry and Violet that they must be punished appropriately for their failures in life.

Elsie and her Joe are the lovers whose story is tender and gratifying. Elsie, "a strongly-built wench," emerges as a kind of proletarian Earth Mother, gifted with practical competencies and a good heart that combine to see her through tough spots. Readers know it is a chancy thing, but with a little luck Elsie and Joe will make the most of their position with Dr. Raste.

Riceyman Steps succeeds because of its deft characterization of the miser. Henry Earlforward is part of a literary tradition, the humors figure, someone dominated so completely by a single trait that he becomes an emblem of it. The narrative relentlessly tracks Henry's decay amid the gloom of his dingy shop, cluttered systematically by a merchant who knows his customers. Violet is the victim of Henry's meanness, and Elsie goes about caring and trying to do in the manner of a heroine left over from a Dickens novel. The miser of Riceyman Steps achieves long literary life in dying miserably.

"Critical Evaluation" by Frank Day

Bibliography:

Broomfield, Olga R. R. *Arnold Bennett*. Boston: Twayne, 1984. A good overview of the life and works, a reliable bibliography of Bennett's publications, and a judicious selection and annotation of secondary sources. An excellent starting place.

Drabble, Margaret. *Arnold Bennett*. New York: Alfred A. Knopf, 1974. Admires Bennett's work in general and praises *Riceyman Steps* for its use of London setting. Identifies F. Sommer Merryweather's *Lives and Anecdotes of Misers* (1850) as an important source for *Riceyman Steps*.

Hepburn, James G. *The Art of Arnold Bennett*. Bloomington: Indiana University Press, 1963. Close analysis of Bennett's technique, symbols, images, and allegories. Praises *Riceyman Steps* as a "complex study of love and death."

Lucas, John. *Arnold Bennett: A Study of His Fiction*. New York: Methuen, 1974. Admires Bennett's development of character in *Riceyman Steps* and his symbolism. Speculates on the possible psychosomatic origins of Henry Earlforward's cancer. One of the best analyses of the novel.

Woolf, Virginia. *Mr. Bennett and Mrs. Brown*. London: The Hogarth Press, 1924. A notorious attack on Bennett and his style by the most famous of the Bloomsbury group. Argues that Bennett relies too much on external facts and physical descriptions in trying to create characters.

RICHARD II

Type of work: Drama
Author: William Shakespeare (1564-1616)
Type of plot: Historical
Time of plot: Fourteenth century
Locale: England
First performed: c. 1595-1596; first published, 1600

Principal characters:
RICHARD II, the king of England
JOHN OF GAUNT, the duke of Lancaster, Richard's uncle
EDMUND OF LANGLEY, the duke of York, another uncle of Richard
HENRY BOLINGBROKE, the duke of Hereford and the son of John of Gaunt
DUKE OF AUMERLE, son of the duke of York
THOMAS MOWBRAY, the duke of Norfolk
EARL OF NORTHUMBERLAND, a supporter of Bolingbroke

The Story:

During the reign of Richard II, the two young dukes Henry Bolingbroke and Thomas Mowbray quarreled bitterly, and the king finally summoned them into his presence to settle their differences publicly. Although Bolingbroke was the oldest son of John of Gaunt, the duke of Lancaster, and therefore a cousin of the king, Richard was perfectly fair in his interview with the two men and showed neither any favoritism.

Bolingbroke accused Mowbray, the duke of Norfolk, of mismanaging military funds and of helping to plot the murder of the dead duke of Gloucester, another of the king's uncles. These charges Mowbray forcefully denied. Richard decided that to settle the dispute the men should have a trial by combat at Coventry, and the court adjourned there to witness the tournament.

Richard, ever nervous and suspicious, grew uneasy as the contest began. Suddenly, just after the beginning trumpet sounded, the king forbade that the combat take place. Instead, he banished the two men from the country. Bolingbroke was to be exiled for six years and Mowbray for the rest of his life. At the same time Richard exacted their promise that they would never plot against him. Persisting in his accusations, Bolingbroke tried to persuade Mowbray to plead guilty to the charges before he left England. Mowbray, refusing to do so, warned Richard against Bolingbroke's cleverness.

Not long after his son had been banished, John of Gaunt, duke of Lancaster, became ill and sent for Richard to give him advice. Although the duke of York pointed out that giving advice to Richard was too often a waste of time, John of Gaunt felt that perhaps a dying man would be heeded where a living one was not. From his deathbed he criticized Richard of extravagance and of mishandling the public funds and impoverishing the nation. John of Gaunt warned Richard also that the kingdom would suffer for his selfishness.

Richard paid no attention to his uncle's advice, and after John of Gaunt had died, the king seized his lands and wealth to back his Irish wars. The aged duke of York, another of Richard's uncles, attempted to dissuade the king from his course, pointing out that Bolingbroke had influence among the people. York's fears were soon confirmed. Bolingbroke, hearing that his father's lands had been seized by the king's officers, used the information as an excuse to terminate his banishment. Gathering together troops and supplies, he landed in the north of

England, where he was joined by other dissatisfied lords, including Lord Ross, Lord Willoughby, the earl of Northumberland, and the earl's son, Henry Percy, known as Hotspur.

Richard, heedless of all warnings, had set off for Ireland to pursue his war, leaving his tottering kingdom in the hands of the weak duke of York, who was no match for the wily Bolingbroke. When the exiled traitor reached Gloucestershire, the duke of York visited him at his camp. Caught between loyalty to Richard and despair over the bankrupt state of the country, York finally yielded his troops to Bolingbroke. Richard, returning to England and expecting to find an army of Welshmen under his command, learned that after hearing false reports of his death they had gone over to Bolingbroke. Moreover, the strong men of his court—men like the earl of Wiltshire, Bushy, and Green—had all been executed.

Destitute of friends and without an army, Richard took refuge in Flint Castle. Bolingbroke, using his usurped titles and estates as his excuse, took Richard prisoner and carried him to London. There Richard broke down. He showed little interest in anything and spent his time philosophizing on his downfall. When he was brought before Bolingbroke and the cruel and unfeeling earl of Northumberland, Richard was forced to abdicate his throne and sign papers confessing his political crimes. Bolingbroke, assuming royal authority, ordered Richard imprisoned in the Tower of London.

During a quarrel among the young dukes of the court, the bishop of Carlisle announced that Mowbray had made a name for himself while fighting in the Holy Land and had then retired to Venice and died there. When Bolingbroke affected grief over the news, the bishop turned on him and denounced him for his part in ousting Richard. Bolingbroke, armed with the legal documents he had collected to prove his rights, prepared to assume the throne as Henry IV. Richard predicted to the earl of Northumberland that Bolingbroke would soon come to distrust his old aide for his part in unseating a king. Soon after that, Richard was sent to the dungeons at Pomfret Castle and his queen was banished to France.

At the duke of York's palace, the aging duke sorrowfully related to his duchess the details of the coronation procession of Henry IV. When the duke discovered that his son Aumerle and other loyal followers of Richard were planning to assassinate Henry IV at Oxford, York immediately started for the palace to warn the new monarch. The duchess, frantic at the thought of her son's danger, advised Aumerle to reach the palace ahead of his father, reveal his treachery to the king, and ask the royal pardon. She herself pleaded for her son before the king and won Aumerle's release.

Having punished the conspirators, Henry IV grew uneasy at the prospect of other treasonable activities, for while Richard lived there was always danger that he might be restored to power. Henry IV suggested casually to his faithful servant Sir Pierce Exton that he murder Richard at Pomfret.

Exton's plan worked. In his dungeon, Richard was provoked to quarrel with his guard and in the struggle that ensued the knight drew his sword and struck down his unhappy prisoner. He then placed Richard's body in a coffin, carried it to Windsor Castle, and there presented it to Henry IV. Distressed over the news of mounting insurrection in the country, King Henry pretended horror at the murder of Richard and vowed to make a pilgrimage to the Holy Land to atone for the death of his fallen cousin.

Critical Evaluation:

Part of William Shakespeare's second tetralogy of historical plays (with *Henry IV*, Parts I and II, and *Henry V*), *Richard II* is also his second experiment in the *de casibus* genre of tragedy, dealing with the fall of an incompetent but not unsympathetic king. It is also part of the lyrical group of plays written between 1593 and 1596, in which Shakespeare's gradual transformation from poet to playwright can be traced. The sources of the play include the 1587 second edition of Raphael Holinshed's *Chronicles* (1577); the chronicles of Jean Froissart and Edward Hall; George Ferrers and William Baldwin's *A Mirror for Magistrates* (1555); Samuel Daniel's verse epic on the War of the Roses, *The Civil Wars* (1595-1609); and a play by an unknown author, entitled *Thomas of Woodstock*.

The themes of the play are associated, in one way or another, with the question of sovereignty. Bolingbroke's challenge to Richard focuses on the divine right of kings and its historical basis and social implications. Connected with this is the matter of a subject's duty of passive obedience, especially as seen in the characters of Gaunt and York. Richard's arbitrariness in the opening scenes suggests the dangers of irresponsible despotism; throughout the play, Shakespeare follows his thoughts and strange behavior and contrasts that with the caginess and certainty of Bolingbroke, whose thoughts are only shown translated into action; Richard thus becomes a study of the complex qualities of the ideal ruler. In this respect, the play reflects the Renaissance fascination with optimal behavior in various social roles, as seen, for example, in Niccolò Machiavelli's *The Prince* (1513), Roger Ascham's *The Schoolmaster* (1570), and Sir Thomas Elyot's *The Boke Named the Governour* (1531). Yet Shakespeare's psychological realism does not reach a falsely definitive conclusion, creating rather a tragic aura of uncertainty around Richard, which makes him a most attractive character. In many ways, the play is not so much a contest for power as a struggle within Richard himself to adjust to his situation.

This is the first of Shakespeare's plays with a central figure who is an introspective, imaginative, and eloquent man. It is, therefore, not surprising that the work includes some of his finest lyrical passages. *Richard II* is in fact the only play Shakespeare wrote entirely in verse, a verse supported by a regal formality of design and manner, and a profuse and delicate metaphorical base. Intricately interwoven throughout the play are image-patterns centered around the eagle, the lion, the rose, the sun (which begins with Richard but moves to Bolingbroke), the state as theater, the earth as a neglected or well-tended garden, and the rise and fall of fortune's buckets. The complicated imagery illustrates the subconscious workings of Shakespeare's imagination that will enrich the great tragedies to follow. As Henry Morley said, the play is "full of passages that have floated out of their place in the drama to live in the minds of the people." These passages include Gaunt's great apostrophe to England in Act II, scene i, York's description of "our two cousins coming into London," Richard's prison soliloquy in Act V, scene iv, and his monologues on divine right and on the irony of kingship.

So poetic is Richard II, that critics speculate Shakespeare may have written the part for himself. Richard, the lover of music, spectacle, domestic courtesy, and dignified luxury, would be the ideal host to Castiglione's courtier. His whimsical personality is balanced to great dramatic effect by his self-awareness. He seems fascinated with the contradictory flow of his own emotions; and this very fascination is a large part of his tragic flaw. Similarly, Richard's sensitivity is combined with a flair for self-dramatization that reveals only too clearly his ineptitude as a strong ruler. He plays to the wrong audience, seeking the approval of his court rather than that of the common people; he seems to shun the "vulgar crowd" in preference to the refined taste of a court that can appreciate his delicate character. The last three acts, in which Richard's charm as a man are emphasized, are obviously more central to the play's aesthetic than the first two, which reveal his weakness as a king. His sentimental vanity in the abdication scene is so effective that it was censored during Elizabeth's lifetime. The alternation of courage and despair in Richard's mind determines the rhythm of the play; Samuel Taylor Coleridge observes that "the play throughout is a history of the human mind."

When Richard speaks of "the unstooping firmness of my upright soul" we understand that he is compensating verbally for his inability to act. He insists on the sacramental nature of kingship, depending for his support on the formal, legal rituals associated with the throne; he is all ceremony and pathetically fatal pomp. Yet, from the outset, Richard contradicts even the logic of sovereign ceremony when he arbitrarily changes his decision, and banishes the two opponents in the joust. Bolingbroke is quick to note the king's weakness and steps into the power vacuum it creates. For Bolingbroke is the consummate actor who can be all things to all men by seeming so. He is impressed by the kingly power Richard wields: "Four lagging winters and four wanton springs/ End in a word: such is the breath of kings." He likes what he sees and, in deciding to imitate it, surpasses Richard. Even when Bolingbroke is ceremonious, as when he bows his knee to Richard before the abdication, he is acting. The difference is that he knows the most effective audience. Richard laments that he has seen Bolingbroke's courtship of the common people: "How he did seem to dive into their hearts." He recognizes the actor in Bolingbroke, and fears its power. It is not coincidental that York compares the commoners to the fickle theater audience. As in so many plays of Shakespeare, the theater itself becomes a central image; Richard's monologues are a stark contrast to Bolingbroke's speeches not only because they reveal internal states but also because they are narcissistically oriented. They reach inward, toward secrecy and communicative impotency; Bolingbroke speaks actively, reaching outward toward the audience he wishes to influence. His role can be compared usefully to that of Antony in *Julius Caesar* (1599-1600), Richard's to that of Brutus. The tension between the two styles of speaking, moreover, no doubt reflects the transformation in Shakespeare himself that will make the plays to follow more strikingly dramatic than sheerly poetic. The Bolingbroke of *Henry IV*, Parts I and II (1597-1598) is born in *Richard II*, his realistic, calculating, efficient, politically astute performance directly antithetical to Richard's impractical, mercurial, meditative, and inept behavior. Bolingbroke is an opportunist, favored by fortune. A man of action and of few words, Bolingbroke presents a clear alternative to Richard when the two men appear together. If Richard is the actor as prima donna, Bolingbroke is the actor as director.

"Critical Evaluation" by Kenneth John Atchity

Bibliography:
Evans, Gareth Lloyd. *The Upstart Crow: An Introduction to Shakespeare's Plays.* London: J. M. Dent and Sons, 1982. A comprehensive discussion of the dramatic works of William Shakespeare. While the major emphasis is on critical reviews of the plays, there are also discussions of sources and information on the circumstances surrounding the writing of the plays.

Holderness, Graham, ed. *Shakespeare's History Plays: "Richard II" to "Henry V."* New York: St. Martin's Press, 1992. An anthology of critical works on Shakespeare's history plays. James L. Calderwood's "Richard II: Metadrama and the Fall of Speech" discusses the language used in the play and the power of that language as used by King Richard and his rival, Bolingbroke.

Leggatt, Alexander. *Shakespeare's Political Drama: The History Plays and the Roman Plays.* New York: Routledge, 1988. A discussion of the Shakespeare plays dealing with English history from the reign of King Henry II to that of Henry VIII, and with the three plays dealing with Roman history.

Pierce, Robert B. *Shakespeare's History Plays: The Family and the State.* Columbus: University of Ohio Press, 1971. A general discussion of Shakespeare's history plays. Pierce considers

Richard II to be a direct forerunner of the plays on Henry IV and V.

Ribner, Irving. *The English History Play in the Age of Shakespeare*. 1957. Rev. ed. London: Methuen, 1965. A discussion of history plays in the Elizabethan era of English drama and Shakespeare's contributions in the field. Considers the development of the form and the sources.

RICHARD III

Type of work: Drama
Author: William Shakespeare (1564-1616)
Type of plot: Historical
Time of plot: Fifteenth century
Locale: England
First performed: c. 1592-1593; first published, 1597; revised, 1623

Principal characters:
EDWARD IV, the king of England
RICHARD, his brother, the duke of Gloucester
GEORGE, his brother the duke of Clarence
QUEEN ELIZABETH, wife of Edward IV
LADY ANNE, the widow of the son of Henry VI and later the wife
　　of Richard III
QUEEN MARGARET, the widow of Henry VI
EDWARD, the Prince of Wales and son of Edward IV
RICHARD, the duke of York, another son of Edward IV
THE DUKE OF BUCKINGHAM, an accomplice of the duke of Gloucester
LORD HASTINGS, a supporter of Prince Edward
LORD STANLEY, the earl of Derby
SIR WILLIAM CATESBY, a court toady
HENRY TUDOR, the earl of Richmond and later King Henry VII

The Story:
　　After the conclusion of the wars between the houses of York and Lancaster, Edward IV was firmly restored to the throne. Before long, however, his treacherous brother Richard, the hunchbacked duke of Gloucester, resumed his plans for gaining the throne. Craftily he removed one obstacle in his path when he turned the king against the third brother, the duke of Clarence (whose given name was George) by telling the king of an ancient prophecy that his issue would be disinherited by one of the royal line whose name began with the letter G. Clarence was immediately arrested and taken to the Tower. Richard went to him, pretending sympathy, and advised him that the jealousy and hatred of Queen Elizabeth were responsible for his imprisonment. After promising to help his brother secure his freedom, Richard, as false in word as he was cruel in deed, gave orders that Clarence be stabbed in his cell and his body placed in a barrel of malmsey wine.
　　Hoping to make his position even stronger, Richard then made plans to marry Lady Anne, the widow of Prince Edward, the former Prince of Wales whose father was the murdered Henry VI. Edward had been slain by Richard and his brothers after the battles had ended, and Lady Anne and Henry's widow, Queen Margaret, were the only remaining members of the once powerful House of Lancaster still living in England. Intercepting Lady Anne at the funeral procession of Henry VI, Richard attempted to woo her. Although she hated and feared her husband's murderer, she was persuaded to accept an engagement ring when Richard insisted that it was for love of her that he had murdered her husband.
　　Richard went to the court, where Edward IV lay ill. There, he affected great sorrow and indignation over the news of the death of Clarence, thereby endearing himself to Lord Hastings and the duke of Buckingham, who were friends of Clarence. He insinuated that Queen Elizabeth

and her followers had turned the wrath of the king against Clarence, which brought about his death. Richard managed to convince everyone except Queen Margaret, who knew well what had really happened. Openly accusing him, she attempted to warn Buckingham and the others against Richard, but they ignored her.

Edward IV, ailing and depressed, tried to make peace among the factions in his realm, but he died before he could accomplish this end. His son, Prince Edward, was sent for from Ludlow to take his father's place. At the same time, Richard imprisoned Lord Grey, Lord Rivers, and Lord Vaughan, who were followers and relatives of the queen, and had them executed.

Terrified, Queen Elizabeth sought refuge for herself and her second son, the young duke of York, with the archbishop of Canterbury. When Richard heard of the queen's action, he pretended much concern over the welfare of his brother's children and set himself up as their guardian. He managed to remove young York from the care of his mother and had him placed in the Tower along with Prince Edward. He announced that they were under his protection and that they would remain there only until Prince Edward had been crowned.

Learning from Sir William Catesby, a court toady, that Lord Hastings was a loyal adherent of the young prince, Richard contrived to remove that influential nobleman from the court by summoning him to a meeting ostensibly called to discuss plans for the coronation of the new king. Although Lord Stanley warned Hastings that ill luck awaited him if he went to the meeting, the trusting nobleman kept his appointment with Richard in the Tower. There, on the basis of trumped-up evidence, Richard accused Hastings of treason and ordered his immediate execution. Richard and Buckingham then dressed themselves in rusty old armor and pretended to the lord mayor that Hastings had been plotting against them; the lord mayor was convinced by their false protestations that the execution was justified.

Richard plotted to seize the throne for himself. Buckingham, supporting him, spoke in the Guildhall of the great immorality of the late King Edward and hinted that both the king and his children were illegitimate. Shocked, a citizens' committee headed by the lord mayor approached Richard and begged him to accept the crown. They found him in the company of two priests, with a prayer book in his hand. So impressed were they with his seeming piety, that they repeated their offer after he had hypocritically refused it. Pretending great reluctance, Richard finally accepted, after being urged by Buckingham, the lord mayor, and Catesby. Plans for an immediate coronation were made.

Lady Anne was interrupted during a visit to the Tower with Queen Elizabeth and the old duchess of York and ordered to Westminster to be crowned Richard's queen. The three women heard with horror that Richard had ascended the throne; they were all the more suspicious of him because they had been prevented from seeing the young princes. Fearing the worst, they sorrowed among themselves and foresaw doom for the nation.

Soon after his coronation, Richard suggested to Buckingham that the two princes must be killed. When Buckingham balked at the order, Richard refused to consider his request to be elevated to the earldom of Hereford. Proceeding alone to secure the safety of his position, he hired Sir James Tyrrel, a discontented nobleman, to smother the children in their sleep. To make his position still more secure, Richard planned to marry Elizabeth of York, his own niece and daughter of the deceased Edward IV. Spreading the news that Queen Anne was mortally ill, he had her secretly murdered. He removed any threat from Clarence's heirs by imprisoning his son and by arranging a marriage for the daughter that considerably lowered her social status.

None of these precautions, however, could stem the tide of threats that were beginning to endanger Richard. In Brittany, Henry Tudor, the earl of Richmond, gathered an army and invaded the country. When news of Richmond's landing at Milford reached London, Buckingham fled from Richard, whose cruelty and guilt were becoming apparent to even his closest friends and associates. Buckingham joined Richmond's forces, but shortly afterward Richard captured and executed him.

In a tremendous final battle, the armies of Richmond and Richard met on Bosworth Field. There, on the night before the encounter, all the ghosts of Richard's victims appeared to him in his sleep and prophesied his defeat. They also foretold the earl of Richmond's victory and success. The predictions held true. The next day, Richard, fighting desperately, was slain in battle by Richmond, after crying out the offer of his ill-gotten kingdom for a horse, his own having been killed under him. The earl mounted the throne and married Elizabeth of York, thus uniting the houses of York and Lancaster and ending the feud.

Critical Evaluation:

Richard III is the last of a series of four plays that began with the three parts of *Henry VI.* These plays, though not strictly speaking a tetralogy, trace the bloody conflicts between the houses of Lancaster and York and interpret the events leading up to the establishment of the Tudor dynasty. Despite Richard's painful experiences, the drama remains a history rather than a tragedy. Richard does not have the moral stature to be a tragic hero, who may murder, but only in violation of his own nature. Richard, by contrast, is a natural intriguer and murderer. Even as bloody a character as Macbeth contains within him an earlier, nobler, Macbeth. Richard is too intelligent and self-aware, and too much in control of himself and those around him, to raise any of the moral ambiguities or dilemmas that are necessary to tragedy. Nor does Richard achieve any transcendent understanding of his actions.

Richard is, nevertheless, the dominating figure in the play and a fascinating one. All the other characters pale before him. The play is primarily a series of encounters between him and the opponents who surround him. Because Richard is physically small and has a humpback, many commentators have suggested that his behavior is a compensation for his physical deformity. Yet Richard is not a paranoid; everyone really does hate him. The deformity, a gross exaggeration of the historical reality, is more likely a physical representation of the grotesque shape of Richard's soul in a Renaissance world that took such correspondences seriously. In any case, Shakespeare created good theater by representing Richard as deformed, by which means his plots seem all the more grotesque.

Richard is also the master rhetorician in a play in which Shakespeare for the first time shows the full power of his language. Richard's speeches and the staccato exchanges among characters present the nervous energy that informs the more ambitious later plays. From his opening soliloquy, Richard fascinates not only with his language but also with his intelligence and candor. Until the very end, he is the stage manager of all that occurs. As a villain, he is unique in his total control and in the virtuosity of his performance. Even Iago pales before him, for Richard, in soliloquies and asides, explains to the audience exactly what he is going to do and then carries it off.

In his opening speech, it is immediately clear that Richard will preside if not eventually prevail. He reveals not only his self-confident awareness of his own physical limitations and intellectual superiority but also a disarming perception of his own evil and isolation. His honest villainy is more total than Iago's both in the way that he is able to convince every character that he is his only friend and in the full step-by-step disclosure of his intentions to the audience. Since everyone is against him, he almost generates involuntary sympathy.

Shakespeare's plot is the relentless working out of Richard's schemes as they lead to his final destruction. His first confrontation, with Anne, is a model of Richard's abilities: The exchange begins with Anne's heaping abuse on her husband's murderer and ends with Richard extracting from her a promise of marriage. Anne is overwhelmed more by the brilliance and audacity of Richard's rhetorical wit than by the logic of his arguments. Yet the audience sees what an improbably brief time Richard needs to be successful. It is part of the definition of this villain that he could succeed in such a wildly improbable adventure. Richard is frequently shown using those who hate him for his own benefit, in a perverse gratification of his ostensible desire for power and his submerged desire to be loved. Only his mother is able to see through to the total corruption of his heart.

Richard sees the path to kingship as being simply a matter of ingratiating himself with the right people and of murdering all those who stand in his way. He contracts the murder of Clarence in the tower amid a good bit of gallows humor, which sets the appropriately grim tone. Like a good Machiavel, he builds on past success and takes advantage of any fortuitous circumstances. He uses the death of Clarence to cast suspicion on Elizabeth and her party and to get the support of Buckingham, and he seizes on the death of Edward IV to have the influential nobles imprisoned and killed. Most events happen at Richard's instigation, and others he deftly turns to his own advantage. He efficiently removes all near claims to the throne by lies, innuendoes, and direct, vigorous action.

So appealing is his virtuosity and so faithful is he in informing the audience of his plans, that Shakespeare is even able to arouse sympathy for him when the tide of opposition to him swells under the leadership of Richmond. Shakespeare neatly figures the balance of power by setting up the opposing camps on opposite sides of the stage. The ominous appearances of the ghosts, to Richmond as well as Richard, portend that retribution is at hand. Although he is unnerved for the first time, Richard behaves with martial valor and struggles determinedly to the last. This last show of courage is the final complication of a consummate villain.

"Critical Evaluation" by Edward E. Foster

Bibliography:
Farrell, Kirby. "Prophetic Behavior in Shakespeare's Histories." *Shakespeare Studies* 19 (1987): 17-40. Refers to historical prophecies in examining various kinds of prophecy in the play, both conscious and unconscious.

Hamel, Guy. "Time in Richard III." *Shakespeare Survey* 40 (1988): 41-49. Examines how time is used in the play and how Shakespeare constructs relationships between various references to time.

Hassel, R. Chris, Jr. *Songs of Death: Performance, Interpretation, and the Text of "Richard III."* Lincoln: University of Nebraska Press, 1987. Examines the play from various angles, including the theatrical and acting history of the play, the role of Providence, and the characters and their motives.

Miner, Madonne M. "'Neither Mother, Wife, nor England's Queen': The Roles of Women in *Richard III.*" In *William Shakespeare's "Richard III,"* edited by Harold Bloom. New York: Chelsea House, 1988. The three sections of the essay examine the depth of characterization given to the women and their interactions. Also discusses the imagery of femaleness in the play.

Neill, Michael. "Shakespeare's Halle of Mirrors: Play, Politics, and Psychology in *Richard III.*" In *William Shakespeare's "Richard III,"* edited by Harold Bloom. New York: Chelsea House, 1988. Examines the idea of theatricality in the play. Neill argues that Richard, like Hamlet, is an actor in the dramatic events that surround him.